CH90921549

The Philosophy of Religion Reader

Philosophy of religion today is a fascinating and flourishing field. This new Reader brings together a collection of classical and contemporary key writings, offering students a comprehensive and completely up to date overview of the field. Global in perspective, it includes selections from non-theistic sources, as well as those from the Western theistic traditions of philosophy of religion and philosophical theology. Ten thematic sections, chosen to reflect current trends and research interests in the field, include debates that will be of interest to students and scholars alike:

- Religious diversity
- The nature and attributes of God/Ultimate Reality
- Arguments for and against the existence of God
- Faith, reason, and evidence
- Science, religion, and miracles
- The self and the human condition
- Religious experience
- The problem of evil
- Death and the afterlife
- Recent trends

To aid student learning, editorial introductions begin each thematic section, and each selection is supported with a contextual introduction, essay questions for discussion and a list of annotated further readings. There are also extensive bibliographies.

Chad Meister is Director of Philosophy at Bethel College, USA. He has written and edited a number of books on philosophy of religion including *The Routledge Companion to the Philosophy of Religion*, co-edited with Paul Copan (2007).

The Philosophy

of Religion

Reader

Edited by

Chad Meister

Routledge
Taylor & Francis Group

LONDON AND NEW YORK

First published 2008
by Routledge
2 Park Square, Milton Park, Abingdon, Oxon OX14 4RN

Simultaneously published in the USA and Canada
by Routledge
711 Third Avenue, New York, NY 10017

Routledge is an imprint of the Taylor & Francis Group, an informa business

Typeset in Perpetua and Bell Gothic by The Running Head Limited, Cambridge

British Library Cataloguing in Publication Data
A catalogue record for this book is available from the British Library

Library of Congress Cataloging in Publication Data

The philosophy of religion reader / edited by Chad Meister.
    p.   cm.
  Includes bibliographical references and index.
  1. Religion—Philosophy. I. Meister, Chad V., 1965–
  BL51.P453 2007
  210—dc22

                          2007014437

ISBN10 0-415-40890-3 (hbk)
ISBN10 0-415-40891-1 (pbk)
ISBN13 978-0-415-40890-5 (hbk)
ISBN13 978-0-415-40891-2 (pbk)

CONTENTS

ACKNOWLEDGMENTS

I would like to thank the following contributors for their helpful reviews and comments: Marilyn McCord Adams, Pamela Sue Anderson, Michael Behe, Robin Collins, Paul Copan, William Lane Craig, Stephen Davis, Daniel Dennett, Douglas Geivett, Roger Gottlieb, William Hasker, John Hick, David Kalupahana, Sallie King, Robin Le Poidevin, J. P. Moreland, Tom Morris, Paul Moser, Graham Oppy, Alvin Plantinga, Nicholas Rescher, William Rowe, Joseph Runzo, Quentin Smith, Richard Swinburne, Charles Taliaferro, and Keith Ward. Their kind assistance has made this work a much better volume than it would have been otherwise.

I am grateful to a number of friends and colleagues, especially Harold Netland, James Stump, Timothy Erdel, and David Reed, for their insightful suggestions and advice. I am also thankful for the efforts of David Wright, Adam Cramer, and Joel Dendiu for their excellent editorial help. In addition, I am indebted to my wife, Tammi, for her extraordinary assistance, her eye for detail, and especially her encouragement during my writing and editing fury in recent days.

Special thanks are due to Lesley Riddle and Gemma Dunn at Routledge for their superb editorial support and to Julene Knox for her efforts in obtaining permissions.

PERMISSIONS

John Hick: from *An Interpretation of Religion*, 2nd ed., New Haven: Yale University Press, 2004, 233–51. Reproduced with permission.

Keith Ward: "Truth and the Diversity of Religions," *Religious Studies* 26, 1, pp. 1–18, March, 1990, © Cambridge University Press, reprinted with permission.

Alvin Plantinga: "Pluralism: A Defense of Religious Exclusivism" from *The Rationality of Belief and the Plurality of Faith*, edited by Thomas D. Senor. Copyright © 1995 by Cornell University. Used by permission of the publisher, Cornell University Press.

Joseph Runzo: "God, Commitment, and Other Faiths: Pluralism Versus Relativism," *Faith and Philosophy*, 5, October, 1988, 343–64. Reproduced by kind permission of the author.

The Dalai Lama: *Ancient Wisdom, Modern World: Ethics for the New Millennium*, London: Abacus Books, 2001, 219–31. Copyright © Tenzin Gyatso, the Fourteenth Dalai Lama of Tibet, 1999. Reproduced with permission.

"The Role of Religion in Modern Society," from *Ethics for the New Millennium* by the Dalai Lama and Alexander Norman, copyright © 1999 by His Holiness the Dalai Lama. Used by permissions of Riverhead Books, an imprint of Penguin Group USA Inc.

Avicenna: "On The Nature of God" *Avicenna on Theology*, translated by Arthur J. Arberry, London: John Murray, 1951, 25–35. Reproduced by kind permission of the estate of A. J. Arberry.

Moses Maimonides: "Divine Simplicity, Negative Theology, and God-Talk" from *The Divine Attributes*, Joshua Hoffman and Gary S. Rosenkrantz, Oxford: Blackwell, 2002, 166–78. Reproduced by permission of Blackwell Publishing. Boethius: from *The Consolations of Philosophy*, 2002, Mineola, NY: Dover Publications.

Ramanuja: as quoted in John Braisted Carman, *The Theology of Ramanuja: An Essay in Interreligious Understanding*, London: Yale University Press, 1974, 67–70, 73–6. Reproduced with permission.

Thomas V. Morris: from *Our Idea of God: An Introduction to Philosophical Theology*, 159–84. Copyright © Thomas V. Morris. Reproduced by permission of the author and Regent College Publishing.

Gaunilo of Marmoutier: *In Behalf of the Fool* in *St. Anselm: Basic Writings*, translated by S. N. Deane. Second edition Copyright © 1962 by Open Court Publishing Company. Reprinted by permission of Open Court Publishing Company, a division of Carus Publishing Company, Peru, IL.

Immanuel Kant: from *Critique of Pure Reason*, translated by Norman Kemp Smith, New York: St. Martin's Press, 1965, 500–7. Reproduced by permission of Palgrave Macmillan.

Charles Hartshorne: from *The Logic of Perfection*. Copyright © 1977 by Open Court Publishing Company. Reprinted by permission of Open Court Publishing Company, a division of Carus Publishing Company, Peru, IL.

Paul Copan: "The Moral Argument" in *The Rationality of Theism*, edited by Paul Copan and Paul K. Moser, New York: Routledge, 2003, 149–74. Reproduced by permission of Taylor & Francis Books, UK.

From: J. P. Moreland: "The Argument from Mind" in *The Routledge Companion to Philosophy of Religion*, edited by Chad Meister and Paul Copan, Copyright © 2007 Routledge. Reproduced by permission of Taylor & Francis Books, UK.

William James: from *Essays in Pragmatism*, edited by Alburey Castell. Copyright 1948 by Hafner Publishing Company. Reprinted with permission of The Free Press, a Division of Simon & Schuster Adult Publishing Group.

Alvin Plantinga: "Is Belief in God Properly Basic?" in *Nous XV*, 1981, 41–51. Reproduced by permission of Blackwell Publishing.

Blaise Pascal: from *Pensées*, revised edition translated by A. J. Krailsheimer, New York: Penguin Books, 1995, 121–7. Copyright © 1966, 1995 A. J. Krailsheimer. Reproduced by permission of the Penguin Group (UK) Inc.

David Hume: "Of Miracles" in *An Enquiry Concerning Human Understanding* (first published under the title *Philosophical Essays Concerning Human Understanding*), edited by Eric Steinberg, Indianapolis, Indiana: Hackett Publishing, 1977, 72–90. Copyright © 1977 by David Hume. Reprinted by permission of Hackett Publishing Company, Inc. All rights reserved.

Richard Swinburne: from *Is There a God?*, Oxford: Oxford University Press, 1996, 114–23. By permission of Oxford University Press, Inc.

Alvin Plantinga: from *God and Other Minds: A Study of the Rational Justification of Belief in God*. Copyright © 1967 by Cornell University. Used by permission of the publisher, Cornell University Press.

Daniel C. Dennett: from *Breaking the Spell: Religion as a Natural Phenomenon*, New York: Viking, 2006, 24–44. Copyright © 2006 by Daniel C. Dennett. Used by permission of Viking Penguin, a division of Penguin Group (USA) Inc.

Augustine: from *Confessions*, translated by Henry Chadwick, New York: Oxford University Press, 1991, Book II.iv(9)–x(18), 28–34. By permission of Oxford University Press, Inc.

Friedrich Nietzsche: from *Beyond Good and Evil*, translated by Walter Kaufmann, copyright © 1966 by Random House, Inc. Used by permission of Random House, Inc.

Soren Kierkegaard: from *Fear and Trembling*. © 1941 Princeton University Press, 1969 renewed. Reprinted by permission of Princeton University Press.

Nagarjuna: from *Mulamadhyamakakarika*, in *The Fundamental Wisdom of the Middle Way: Nagarjuna's Mulamadhyamakakarika*, translated by Jay L. Garfield, New York: Oxford University Press, 1995, 48–9. By permission of Oxford University Press, Inc.

D. T. Suzuki: from *Essays in Zen Buddhism by D T Suzuki*, 79–83, edited by Christmas Humphreys, published by Rider. Reprinted by permission of The Random House Group Ltd.

William James: from "Mysticism" in *The Varieties of Religious Experience: A Study in Human Nature*, Routledge 2002. Reproduced by permission of Taylor & Francis Books, UK.

Julian of Norwich: from *Revelations of Divine Love*, translated by Elizabeth Spearing, London: Penguin Books, 1998, 42–50. Translation copyright © 1998 by Elizabeth Spearing.

Sigmund Freud: from *The Future of an Illusion*, translated by James Strachey. Copyright © 1961 by James Strachey, renewed 1989 by Alix Strachey. Used by permission of W. W. Norton & Company, Inc. Reprinted by permission of The Random House Group Ltd.

D. T. Suzuki: "Satori, or Enlightenment" in *Zen Buddhism: Selected Writings of D. T. Suzuki*, edited by William Barrett, Garden City, New York: Doubleday Anchor Books, 1956, 83–108. Reprinted by permission of The Random House Group Ltd.

R. Douglas Geivett: "The Evidential Value of Religious Experience" in *The Rationality of Theism*, edited by Paul Copan and Paul K. Moser, New York: Routledge, 2003, 175–203. Reproduced by permission of Taylor & Francis Books, UK.

William Rowe: "The Problem of Evil and Some Varieties of Atheism," *American Philosophical Quarterly* 16 (1979), 335–41. Reproduced by permission of the editor of *American Philosophical Quarterly*.

John Hick: "An Irenaean Theodicy" from *Encountering Evil*, © 1981 Stephen T. Davis. Used by permission of Westminster John Knox Press.

Alvin C. Plantinga: "The Free Will Defense" in *God, Freedom, and Evil* © 1974 Wm Eerdmans Publishing Company, Grand Rapids, Michigan. Reprinted by permission of the publisher, all rights reserved.

Marilyn McCord Adams: "Horrendous Evils and the Goodness of God" in *The Problem of Evil*, edited by Marilyn McCord Adams and Robert Merrihew Adams, New York: Oxford University Press, 1990, 209–21 Reprinted by courtesy of the Editor of the Aristotelian Society: © 1990.

David J. Kalupahana: from *The Principles of Buddhist Psychology*, Albany, New York: State University of New York Press, 1987, 79–87. Copyright © 1987 State University of New York. All rights reserved.

Plato: *Phaedo* in *Five Dialogues*, translated by G. M. A. Grube, Indianapolis, Indiana: Hackett Publishing Company, 1981, 100–5; 118–20. Translation © 1981 by G. M. A. Grube. Reprinted by permission of Hackett Publishing Company, Inc. All rights reserved.

Stephen T. Davis: *Risen Indeed: Making Sense of the Resurrection*, © 1993 Wm Eerdmans Publishing Company, Grand Rapids, Michigan. Reprinted by permission of the publisher, all rights reserved.

Charles Taliaferro: "Why We Need Immortality," in *Modern Theology*, 6:4, 1990, 367–77. Reproduced by permission of Blackwell Publishing.

Robin Le Poidevin: from *Arguing for Atheism: An Introduction to the Philosophy of Religion*, Copyright © 1996 Routledge, pp. 135–46. Reproduced by permission of Taylor & Francis Books, UK.

Pamela Sue Anderson: "Feminism in Philosophy of Religion," in Deane-Peter Baker and Patrick Maxwell, eds., *Explorations in Contemporary Continental Philosophy of Reli-*

Chad Meister

GENERAL INTRODUCTION

Philosophy and religion

Aristotle, one of the most significant philosophers of all time, observed that human beings by nature desire to know. We are, indeed, a curious lot—ever attempting to figure out our world and our place in it. In fact, in certain ways, we are all philosophers. The word "philosophy" comes from two ancient Greek terms: *philos* (love) and *sophia* (wisdom). Historically, "philosophy" has usually meant the love of wisdom and the desire to find truth and understanding in fundamental matters of inquiry. I doubt that many individuals have desired to be as foolish, or to believe as many falsehoods, as possible. To the contrary, I suspect that in one way or another, most human beings throughout history have been seekers of wisdom and truth. I presume that you are such a person; whether you have realized it or not, you are a philosopher.

The development of philosophy as a specific discipline of study has had a long and interesting evolution, and over the past several decades it has blossomed into a variety of sub-disciplines. Today, there is philosophy of history, philosophy of science, philosophy of mind, even philosophy of sport, to name a few. Our concern in this volume, however, is with philosophy of religion.

Philosophy of religion is simply philosophical reflection on religious ideas. By the phrase "philosophical reflection," I mean the thoughtful analyses of ideas, terms, arguments, and evidences used to support claims of various sorts. The phrase "religious ideas," however, is a bit more difficult to define. While our world is filled with a rich variety of religions, attempting to offer a definition of the term "religion" is notoriously difficult given the broad variety of the different traditions. Central to some religions is a personal God and other spiritual entities; for other religions, no God or spirits are posited at all. Some religions view the continued, personal existence of the individual in an afterlife as paramount to understanding reality—much more important than earthly activities. Others see what we do in *this* life as fundamental, with little if any consideration of the hereafter. Other differences loom. Nevertheless, the following seems to capture the essence of the concept of religion, at least as it relates to the major world religions: *a religion involves a system of beliefs and practices primarily centered around a transcendent Reality, either personal or impersonal, which provides ultimate meaning and purpose to life.* Religious ideas include the central issues that have been discussed and debated within the religious traditions throughout the centuries—issues such as the existence and nature of God/Ultimate Reality, the role of faith and evidence in religious belief, and what happens to a person after death. This volume consists of philosophical reflections on religious ideas, and, as such, it includes many of these central issues.

The structure and scope of this book

Philosophy of religion today is a fascinating and flourishing field, and this book contains a fairly comprehensive collection of over sixty classical and contemporary essays by philosophers reflecting on religious ideas. There are multiple anthologies currently in print on philosophy of religion, so one might wonder why yet another volume on the topic is needed. Until recently, philosophy of religion in the West has primarily focused on the Western theistic traditions. As a result, the diversity of religious thought expressed by those in other traditions has been widely ignored. However, as the presence, awareness, and practice of these other religions grow in the West, it is increasingly important to philosophically engage with them. I have attempted to provide that opportunity in this volume. So while this collection includes many of the important traditional topics from the West—both classical essays as well as cutting-edge contemporary pieces—it is multicultural in perspective and includes significant global components.

This book also incorporates a number of pedagogical features to enrich your learning experience. For example, I have offered introductions to the various sections and to each individual essay to contextualize the material. For the more philosophically complex selections, I have provided longer explanatory introductions and definitions of technical terms. At the end of each essay, I have added provocative reflection questions to clarify important points and reinforce your understanding as well as an annotated bibliography to encourage your continued study of the topic. At the end of the volume, I have included a glossary of terms and an index. My intention in providing all these aids is to make this work as beneficial and helpful as possible.

The book consists of ten sections which focus on what I take to be the most important issues in philosophy of religion given the space restraints of such a work (other important topics could, no doubt, be included).

1 Religious diversity
2 The nature and attributes of God/Ultimate Reality
3 Arguments for and against the existence of God
4 Faith, reason, and evidence
5 Science, religion, and miracles
6 The self and the human condition
7 Religious experience
8 The problem of evil
9 Death and the afterlife
10 Recent trends

This anthology is designed to be a stand-alone work for courses in religious studies and philosophy of religion. However, it would be an excellent companion to my forthcoming textbook entitled *Introducing Philosophy of Religion*—a text which I have intentionally designed to work in conjunction with this volume. These two works taken together provide an ideal exploration of the philosophy of religion.

My hope is that through your engagement with the material in this volume, you will find yourself reflecting deeply on important religious issues which have inspired great minds throughout history.

PART ONE

Religious diversity

In Part One we begin with the issue of religious diversity—perhaps the central topic among recent discussions in philosophy of religion. It is not surprising that this is a major issue given the great influx of religious traditions and the growing awareness of religious beliefs beyond one's own. There are many relevant questions that arise in the religiously diverse milieu in which we typically find ourselves today, and in this section I have honed in on a few that I consider to be most significant.

To begin, the issue of salvation, or liberation, or fulfillment (nirvana, moksha, etc.) in religion is paramount. Wherever we look in world history, we find people attempting to answer a central question of humanity: "What is wrong with us, and how can we solve the problem?" It is widely agreed that things are not as they should be. As a global community we are constantly at war, frequently judging others, ever hoping for a future time in which there will be no more tears and terror. As individuals we are regularly missing our own mark—not living up to our own standards of morality, justice, and accomplishment. We are hoping for a time when things will be better, and we are always wanting more—more than we are, more than we have, and more than we can get.

Huston Smith, one of the most eloquent authorities on the history of religions, summarizes this longing:

> The world's offerings are not bad. By and large they are good. Some of them are good enough to command our enthusiasm for many lifetimes. Eventually, however, every human being comes to realize with Simone Weil that "there is no true good here below, that everything that appears to be good in this world is finite, limited, wears out, and once worn out, leaves necessity exposed in all its nakedness." When this point is reached, one finds oneself asking even of the best this world can offer, "Is this all?"[1]

Philosopher of religion John Hick makes a similar point with respect to the adherents of the major religions: "They all recognize that there is something deeply and tragically defective in our ordinary human situation, both individually and collectively."[2] The essence of religion involves an attempt to solve this very real human predicament. Every religion, then, offers hope — salvific hope — as it responds in unique ways to this yearning for salvation, liberation, and fulfillment.

But what are we to make of the inimitable and seemingly contradictory responses provided by the religious traditions? Various solutions have been offered. On one end of the spectrum is religious pluralism — the idea that all the world's religions are correct in that they each provide valid responses to God (or Ultimate Reality) even though they are culturally conditioned forms of response. At the other end of the spectrum is religious exclusivism — the idea that only one religion is correct, and while other religions may have "truths" within them, only one offers salvation to humankind.

In the first essay, John Hick defends a version of religious pluralism. His "pluralistic hypothesis" is probably the leading position today on the topic of religious pluralism and is worth a careful read. To date, over a hundred and thirty journal articles and over a hundred critical discussions in books have been offered in response to Hick's seminal work on religious pluralism. In the second selection, Keith Ward provides one of these responses and notes positive aspects of the hypothesis as well as significant deficiencies in it.

At the opposite end of the spectrum from pluralism is exclusivism, and in the third selection Alvin Plantinga provides an ardent defense of it. He responds to two major objections to exclusivism: one moral and the other epistemological.

Another kind of response to the problem of conflicting truth claims is offered in the fourth selection by Joseph Runzo. After first explicating six different possible responses, he defends a position which, he maintains, better reflects the actual beliefs of religious adherents than does either pluralism or the other options he has presented. He calls this view "religious relativism" — the view that the correctness of a particular religion is relative to the worldview within which it falls. Relativism is similar to pluralism in that more than one religion can be correct (depending on its plausibility within the worldview of its adherents), but it differs from pluralism in that it supports the uniqueness of one's own tradition and accepts the conflicting truth claims in the various religions as appropriate expressions of divine/human engagement.

It is no doubt true that conflict in the name of religion is widespread. In the final selection of this section, Tenzin Gyatso — the current Dalai Lama — notes that this conflict comes primarily from two different arenas: (1) religious diversity, including doctrinal, cultural, and practical differences, and (2) non-religious factors, including political, economic, and institutional issues. His proposed solution to the conflict raised by religious diversity is inter-religious harmony — a harmony that appreciates the value of other faith traditions beyond one's own without conceding to the view that they are all ultimately the same. In developing such harmony, he suggests that the key involves developing an understanding of other faith traditions through dialogue at all levels — from scholarly debate to the sharing of religious experiences. Once such religious harmony is established, he believes that religion has an incredible opportunity to speak to significant moral issues such as peace and disarmament, social justice, the environment, and a host of other matters relevant to humanity and the world.

Notes

1   Huston Smith, *The World's Religions: Our Great Wisdom Traditions* (New York: HarperSan-Francisco, 1991), 20.
2   John Hick, "The Next Step Beyond Dialogue," in Paul F. Knitter, ed., *The Myth of Religious Superiority* (New York: Orbis, 2005), 3.

Chapter 1

John Hick

RELIGIOUS PLURALISM AND THE PLURALISTIC HYPOTHESIS

John Hick is Danforth Professor of the Philosophy of Religion, Emeritus, at Claremont Graduate University. He is one of the leading contemporary philosophers of religion and the most prominent advocate of religious pluralism. In this essay, taken from his monumental work, *An Interpretation of Religion*, 2nd edn (2004), he argues for the pluralistic hypothesis: "that the great world faiths embody different perceptions and conceptions of, and correspondingly different responses to, the Real [Ultimate Reality] from within the major variant ways of being human; and that within each of them the transformation of human existence from self-centredness to Reality-centredness is taking place."

Utilizing Immanuel Kant's concepts of the *noumena* (the world as it is in itself, of which we can have no pure experience) and the *phenomena* (the world as we experience it), Hick maintains that the world's religions are culturally conditioned forms of religious response to our ambiguous universe. Yet they can offer a valid response, for religious experiences are analogous to our (phenomenal) experiences of the world.

> The lamps are different, but the Light is the same.
>
> Jalalu'l-Din Rumi [13th century])[1]

1. The need for such an hypothesis

I have argued that it is rational on the part of those who experience religiously to believe and to live on this basis. And I have further argued that, in so believing, they are making an affirmation about the nature of reality which will, if it is substantially true, be developed, corrected and enlarged in the course of future experience. They are thus making genuine assertions and are making them on appropriate and acceptable grounds. If there were only one religious tradition, so that all religious experience and belief had the same intentional object, an epistemology of religion could come to rest at this point. But in fact there are a number of different such traditions and families of traditions witnessing to many different personal deities and non-personal ultimates.

To recall the theistic range first, the history of religions sets before us innumerable gods, differently named and often with different characteristics. A collection of names of Mesopotamian gods made by A. Deinel in 1914 contains 3,300 entries (Romer 1969, 117–18). In Hesiod's time there were said to be 30,000 deities (Hume [1757] 1956, 28, n. 1). And if one could list all the past and present gods and goddesses of India, such as Agni, Vayu, Surya, Aryaman, Aditi, Mitra, Indra, Varuna, Brahma, Vishnu, Lakshmi, Shiva, Kali, Ganesh . . . and of the Near East, such as Osiris, Isis, Horus, Re, Yahweh, Baal, Moloch, An, Enlil, Ea, Tiamat, Enki, Marduk . . . and of southern Europe such as Zeus, Kronos, Hera, Apollo, Dionysus, Hephaestus, Poseidon, Aphrodite, Hermes, Mars, Athena, Pan . . . and of northern Europe, such as Odin, Thor, Balder, Vali, Freyr, Frigg, Woden, Rheda, Erce, Donar, Fosite . . . and of Africa, such as Nabongo, Luhanga, Ngai, Nyama, Amaomee, Lesa, Ruhanga, Kolo, Naymbe, Imana, Kimbumba, Molimo, Ohe . . . and also of the Americas, Australasia, northern Asia and the rest of the world they would probably form a list as bulky as the telephone directory of a large city. What are we to say, from a religious point of view, about all these gods? Do we say that they exist? And what would it be for a named god, say Balder, with his distinctive characteristics, to exist? In any straightforward sense it would at least seem to involve there being a consciousness, answering to this name, in addition to all the millions of human consciousnesses. Are we then to say that for each name in our directory of gods there is an additional consciousness, with the further attributes specified in the description of that particular deity? In most cases this would be theoretically possible since in most cases the gods are explicitly or implicitly finite beings whose powers and spheres of operation are at least approximately known; and many of them could coexist without contradiction. On the other hand the gods of the monotheistic faiths are thought of in each case as the one and only God, so that it is impossible for there to be more than one instantiation of this concept. It is thus not feasible to say that all the named gods, and particularly not all the most important ones, exist—at any rate not in any simple and straightforward sense.

Further, in addition to the witness of theistic religion to this multiplicity of personal deities there are yet other major forms of thought and experience which point to non-personal ultimates: Brahman, the Dharmakaya, Nirvana, Sunyata, the Tao . . . But if the ultimate Reality is the blissful, universal consciousness of Brahman, which at the core of our own being we all are, how can it also be the emptiness, non-being, void of Sunyata? And again, how could it also be the Tao, as the principle of cosmic order, and again, the Dharmakaya or the eternal Buddha-nature? And if it is any of these, how can it be a personal deity? Surely these reported ultimates, personal and non-personal, are mutually exclusive. Must not any final reality either be personal, with the non-personal aspect of divinity being secondary, or be impersonal, with the worship of personal deities representing a lower level of religious consciousness, destined to be left behind in the state of final enlightenment?

The naturalistic response is to see all these systems of belief as factually false although perhaps as expressing the archetypal daydreams of the human mind whereby it has distracted itself from the harsh problems of life. From this point of view the luxuriant variety and the mutual incompatibility of these conceptions of the ultimate, and of the modes of experience which they inform, demonstrates that they are 'such stuff as dreams are made on'. However I have already argued in Chapter 13* that it is entirely reasonable for the religious person, experiencing life in relation to the transcendent— whether encountered beyond oneself or in the depths of one's own being—, to believe in the reality of that which is thus apparently experienced. Having reached that conclusion one cannot dismiss the realm of religious experience and belief as illusory, even though its internal plurality and diversity must preclude any simple and straightforward account of it.

Nor can we reasonably claim that our own form of religious experience, together with that of the tradition of which we are a part, is veridical whilst the others are not. We can of course claim this; and indeed virtually every religious tradition has done so, regarding alternative forms of religion either as false or as confused and inferior versions of itself. But the kind of rational justification set forth in Chapter 13 for treating one's own form of religious experience as a cognitive response—though always a complexly conditioned one—to a divine reality must (as we have already noted) apply equally to the religious experience of others. In acknowledging this we are obeying the intellectual Golden Rule of granting to others a premise on which we rely ourselves. Persons living within other traditions, then, are equally justified in trusting their own distinctive religious experience and in forming their beliefs on the basis of it. For the only reason for treating one's tradition differently from others is the very human, but not very cogent, reason that it is one's own! Later (in Part 5) we shall be considering criteria by which one might judge and even seek to grade the religious traditions. The conclusions to be drawn there do not support the picture of a single 'true' religion in the midst of a number of 'false' ones. But in the meantime let us avoid the implausibly arbitrary dogma that religious experience is all delusory with the single exception of the particular form enjoyed by the one who is speaking.

Having, then, rejected (in Chapter 7) the sceptical view that religious experience is *in toto* delusory, and the dogmatic view that it is all delusory except that of one's own tradition, I propose to explore the third possibility that the great post-axial faiths constitute different ways of experiencing, conceiving and living in relation to an ultimate divine Reality which transcends all our varied visions of it.

2. The real in itself and as humanly experienced

In discussing (in Chapter 1) problems of terminology I opted—partly as a matter of personal linguistic taste—for 'the Real' (in preference to 'the Ultimate', 'Ultimate Reality', 'the One' or whatever) as a term by which to refer to the postulated ground of the different forms of religious experience. We now have to distinguish between the Real *an sich* and the Real as variously experienced-and-thought by different human communities. In each of the great traditions a distinction has been drawn, though with varying degrees of emphasis, between the Real (thought of as God, Brahman, the Dharmakaya . . .) in itself and the Real as manifested within the intellectual and experiential purview of that tradition. Thus Hindu thought distinguishes between *nirguna* Brahman, Brahman without attributes, exceeding the grasp of human language, and *saguna* Brahman, Brahman with attributes, known within human religious experience as Ishvara, the personal creator and governor of the universe. In Mahayana Buddhism there is the distinction between, on the one hand, the ultimate Dharmakaya and, on the other hand, this diversified into the heavenly Buddhas constituting the Sambhogakaya and, again, these incarnate in the Nirmanakaya. There is also the related distinction, first enunciated by T'an-luan and taken up by Shinran into the Pure Land tradition, between the *dharmata dharmakāya*, the Dharmakaya *an sich*, and the *upaya dhamakāya*, or Dharma characterised, known as the personal Amida, the Buddha of infinite compassion. In a passage quoted by Shinran, T'an-luan said:

> Among Buddhas and bodhisattvas there are two aspects of dharmakaya: dharmakaya-as-suchness and dharmakaya-as-compassion. Dharmakaya-as-compassion arises out of dharmakaya-as-suchness, and dharmakaya-as-suchness emerges into [human consciousness through] dharmakaya-as-compassion. These two aspects of dharmakaya differ but are not separate; they are one but not identical. (Shinran [1250] 1979, 5)

As a commentator says, 'the ultimate formless and nameless dharmakaya-as-suchness (nirvana) manifests itself in the world as Amida Buddha, dharmakaya-as-compassion, emerging in this samsaric ocean to make itself comprehensible to men' (Shinran [1250] 1979, 6).

Again, the Taoist scripture, the *Tao Te Ching*, begins by affirming that 'The Tao that can be expressed is not the eternal Tao'.[2] In the West the Jewish thinker Maimonides distinguished between the essence and the manifestations of God (*Guide to the Perplexed*, bk I, ch. 54); and the Kabbalist mystics distinguished between En Soph, the absolute divine reality beyond human description, and the God of the Bible. In Islam it is proclaimed that Allah transcends human experience and yet is manifested to human awareness: in a haunting Qur'anic phrase, 'The eyes attain Him not, but He attains the eyes' (6:103). And among the Sufis, Al Haq, the Real, is the abyss of Godhead underlying the self-revealed Allah. The Christian mystic Meister Eckhart distinguished between the Godhead (*Gottheit/deitas*) and God (*Gott/deus*). Again, Paul Tillich has spoken of 'the God above the God of theism' (1952, 189). And Gordon Kaufman has recently distinguished between the 'real God' and the 'available God', the former being an 'utterly unknowable X' and the latter 'essentially a mental or imaginative construction' (Kaufmann 1972, 85–6; compare 1981). Again, Ninian Smart speaks of 'the noumenal Focus of religion which so to say lies beyond the phenomenal Foci of religious experience and practice' (Smart 1984, 24; compare 1981, ch. 6). A more traditional Christian form of the distinction is that between God *a se* in God's infinite self-existent being, beyond the grasp of the human mind, and God *pro nobis*, revealed in relation to humankind as creator and redeemer.[3] The infinite divine reality must pass out into sheer mystery beyond the reach of our knowledge and comprehension and is in this limitless transcendence *nirguna*, the ultimate Godhead, the God above the God of theism, the Real *an sich*.

In one form or another such a distinction is required by the thought that God, Brahman, the Dharmakaya, is unlimited and therefore may not be equated without remainder with anything that can be humanly experienced and defined. Unlimitedness, or infinity, is a negative concept, the denial of limitation. That this denial must be made of the Ultimate is a basic assumption of all the great traditions. It is a natural and reasonable assumption: for an ultimate that is limited in some mode would be limited by something other than itself; and this would entail its non-ultimacy. And with the assumption of the unlimitedness of God, Brahman, the Dharmakaya, goes the equally natural and reasonable assumption that the Ultimate, in its unlimitedness, exceeds all positive characterisations in human thought and language. Thus Gregory of Nyssa:

> The simplicity of the True Faith assumes God to be that which He is, namely, incapable of being grasped by any term, or any idea, or any other device of our apprehension, remaining beyond the reach not only of the human but of the angelic and all supramundane intelligence, unthinkable, unutterable, above all expression in words, having but one name that can represent His proper nature, the single name being 'Above Every Name'. (*Against Euno-mius*, I:42—Schaff and Wace [1892] 1956, V:99)

Augustine, continuing this tradition, declared that 'God transcends even the mind' (*De Vera Religione*, 36:67—Burleigh 1953, 259). St Thomas Aquinas reiterated that 'by its immensity, the divine substance surpasses every form that our intellect reaches' (*S. c. G.*, I:14:3—Pegis 1955, 96–7);[4] and 'The first cause surpasses human understanding and speech. He knows God best who acknowledges that whatever he thinks and says falls short of what God really is' (*In librum De Causis*, 6—Copleston 1955, 131–2). Eckhart said that 'God is without name, for no one can comprehend anything about him' (Eliade 1985, 200). St John of the Cross said that God 'is incomprehensible and transcends all things' ([16th century] 1958, 310). The theme, indeed, runs through the history of Christian thought.[5]

In Islam the notion of *subhānahu* likewise means that God is above all that we say of him. God is 'beyond what they describe' (Qur'an 23:91; 37:180; 6:101). Within the Hindu tradition the Upanishads say of Brahman, 'There the eye goes not, speech goes not, nor the mind' (*Kena* Up., 1:3—Radhakrishnan 1969, 582) and speak of 'unthinkable form' (*Mundaka* Up., III:1:7—Radhakrishnan 1968, 688); and affirm that Brahman is that 'before which words recoil, and to which no understanding has ever attained' (*Taittiriya* Up., II.4.1 and II.9.1—Radhakrishnan, 1968, 545 and 552). And with this sense of the divine infinity there often comes the awareness that 'To say that God is Infinite is to say that He may be apprehended and described in an infinity of ways' (Underhill 1955, 238).

The traditional doctrine of divine ineffability, which I want to apply to the Real *an sich*, has however been challenged.[6] In considering the challenge we need to distinguish two issues: (1) Does it make sense to say of X that our concepts do not apply to it? and (2) If this does (though in a qualified formulation) make sense, what reason could we have to affirm it? A response to the second question will be postponed until we come to consider the relationship between the postulated Real *an sich* and its experienced *personae* and *impersonae*. But in response to the first issue: it would indeed not make sense to say of X that *none* of our concepts apply to it. (Keith Yandell (1975, 172) calls this no-concepts interpretation 'strong ineffability'.) For it is obviously impossible to refer to something that does not even have the property of 'being able to be, referred to'.[7] Further, the property of 'being such that our concepts do not apply to it' cannot, without self-contradiction, include itself.[8] But these are logical pedantries which need not have worried those classical thinkers who have affirmed the ultimate ineffability of the divine nature.

Such points might however usefully have prompted them to distinguish between what we might call substantial properties, such as 'being good', 'being powerful', 'having knowledge', and purely formal and logically generated properties such as 'being a referent of a term' and 'being such that our substantial concepts do not apply'. What they wanted to affirm was that the substantial characterisations do not apply to God in God's self-existent being, beyond the range of human experience. They often expressed this by saying that we can only make negative statements about the Ultimate. It is *neti, neti*, not this, not this (*Brhadāranyaka* Up., IV:5:15—Radhakrishnan 1969, 286). 'We are unable to apprehend [the divine substance] by knowing what it is. Yet we are able to have some knowledge of it by knowing what it is not' (Aquinas, *S. c. G.*, I:14:2—Pegis 1955, 96).[9] This *via negativa* (or *via remotionis*) consists in applying negative concepts to the Ultimate—the concept of not being finite, and so on—as a way of saying that it lies beyond the range of all our positive substantial characterisations. It is in this qualified sense that it makes perfectly good sense to say that our substantial concepts do not apply to the Ultimate. The further question, why we should affirm that there is an Ultimate to which our substantial concepts do not apply, will be taken up in section 4.

Using this distinction between the Real *an sich* and the Real as humanly thought-and-experienced, I want to explore the pluralistic hypothesis that the great world faiths embody different perceptions and conceptions of, and correspondingly different responses to, the Real from within the major variant ways of being human; and that within each of them the transformation of human existence from self-centredness to Reality-centredness is taking place. These traditions are accordingly to be regarded as alternative soteriological 'spaces' within which, or 'ways' along which, men and women can find salvation/liberation/ultimate fulfilment.

3. Kant's epistemological model

In developing this thesis our chief philosophical resource will be one of Kant's most basic epistemological insights, namely that the mind actively interprets sensory information in terms of concepts, so that the environment as we consciously perceive and inhabit it is our familiar three-dimensional world of objects interacting in space. This is a highly generalised version of Kant's complex theory of the forms and categories of perception which he found to be inherent in the structure of any unitary finite consciousness. There is continuing debate about the precise character and implications of Kant's arguments in the *Critique of Pure Reason* as well as of the relation between this and his earlier and later works. For the first *Critique* contains several different strands of thought whose mutual consistency can be questioned and whose relative importance has been variously estimated. I do not however propose to enter into questions of Kantian exegesis: for to do so could only divert attention from the application of the basic Kantian insight to an area to which he himself did not apply it, namely the epistemology of religion.[10] For Kant's broad theme, recognising the mind's own positive contribution to the character of its perceived environment, has been massively confirmed as an empirical thesis by modern work in cognitive and social psychology[11] and in the sociology of knowledge.[12] In applying it to the epistemology of religion we are therefore employing a well consolidated development of contemporary understanding.

The basic principle that I am adapting from Kant's philosophy had in fact already been succinctly stated long before by St Thomas Aquinas, although without any thought of the kind of application being proposed here, when he wrote that 'Things known are in the knower according to the mode of the knower' (*S. T.*, II/II, Q. 1, art. 2). He applied this basic epistemological principle to faith considered as propositional belief, concluding that although God *a se* is simple and undifferentiated, God can only be known by human beings through complex propositions. I want to apply the same principle to faith understood (as in Chapter 10.2) in a very different way, as the interpretive element within all awareness of our environment; and to argue that in relation to the divine the 'mode of the knower' differs within different religio-cultural systems so that the Real is thought-and-experienced in a wide variety of ways. A near contemporary of St. Thomas, the Muslim thinker al Junaid, drew precisely this conclusion in a metaphor which he applied to the plurality of forms of awareness of God: 'The colour of the water is the same as that of its container' (Nicholson [1914] 1963, 88).

But whilst the Thomist maxim, that things known are in the knower according to the mode of the knower, says in principle all that is needed as the starting point for a pluralistic epistemology of religion, Kant's later much more detailed development of the theme is particularly helpful because he went on to distinguish explicitly between an entity as it is in itself and as it appears in perception. For the realisation that the world, as we consciously perceive it, is partly our own construction leads directly to a differentiation between the world *an sich*, unperceived by anyone, and the world as it appears to, that is as it is perceived by, us.[13] The distinction plays a major part in Kant's thought. He points out that since the properties of something as experienced 'depend upon the mode of intuition of the subject, this object as appearance is to be distinguished from itself as object in itself' (*Crit. Pure Reason*, B69—1958, 88). And so Kant distinguished between noumenon and phenomenon, or between a *Ding an sich* and that thing as it appears to human consciousness. As he explains, he is not here using the term 'noumenon' in the positive sense of that which is knowable by some faculty of non-sensible intuition (for we have no such faculty), but in the negative sense of 'a thing in so far as it is not an object of our sensible intuition' (B307—1958, 268). In this strand of Kant's thought—not the only strand, but the one which I am seeking to press into service in the epistemology of religion—the noumenal world exists independently of our perception of it and the phenomenal world is that same world as it appears to our human consciousness. The world as it appears is thus entirely real: in being a 'transcendental idealist' Kant is, as he says, 'an empirical realist' (A370—1958, 346). Analogously, I want to say that the noumenal Real is experienced and thought by different human mentalities, forming and formed by different religious traditions, as the range of gods and absolutes which the phenomenology of religion reports. And these divine, *personae* and metaphysical *impersonae*, as I shall call them, are not illusory but are empirically, that is experientially, real as authentic manifestations of the Real.

Kant's own reason for distinguishing between noumenon and phenomenon was peculiar to his complex philosophical architectonic. He came to it through a critical discussion of space and time which, he argued, cannot be objective realities but must instead be forms which the mind imposes on the sensory manifold. From this it follows that the world *an sich* differs from the world of human experience in not being temporally and spatially ordered. But we do not need to follow Kant at this point in order to arrive at the distinction between things as they are in themselves and those same things as humanly perceived. For it arises out of elementary reflection upon our experience.

We quickly realise that the same thing appears in either slightly or considerably differ-ent ways to different people owing both to their varying spatial locations in relation to it and to differences in their sensory and mental equipment and interpretive habits. Again, physics tells us that the surface of the table, which looks and feels to us as a continuous smooth, hard, brown expanse is a whirling universe of minute discharging quanta of energy in largely empty space, and that these quanta are neither continuous nor smooth nor hard nor brown. And so we differentiate between the physicist's inferred table-as-it-is-in-itself and that same entity as it is perceived, identified, labelled, understood and used by us in ordinary life. The basic distinction seems unavoidable and indisputable, though Kant is the philosopher who has grappled most radically and most thought-provokingly with it.

However Kant himself (in his three *Critiques*) would not have sanctioned the idea that we in any way experience God, even as divine phenomenon in distinction from divine noumenon. God was not for him a reality encountered in religious experience but an object postulated by reason on the basis of its own practical functioning in moral agency. According to him the categorical character of moral obligation presupposes the reality of God as making possible the *summum bonum* in which perfect goodness and perfect happiness will coincide. God must accordingly be postulated as 'a cause of the whole of nature, itself distinct from nature, which contains the ground of the exact coincidence of happiness with morality' (*Crit. Pract. Reason*, II:2:5—1956, 129). The idea of God, thus indirectly established, then functions as a regulative idea whereby we 'regard all order in the world as if it had originated in the purpose of supreme reason' (*Crit. Pure Reason*, B714—1958, 559–60).

But for Kant God is postulated, not experienced. In partial agreement but also par-tial disagreement with him, I want to say that the Real *an sich* is postulated by us as a presupposition, not of the moral life, but of religious experience and the religious life, whilst the gods, as also the mystically known Brahman, Sunyata and so on, are phe-nomenal manifestations of the Real occurring within the realm of religious experience. Conflating these two theses one can say that the Real is experienced by human beings, but experienced in a manner analogous to that in which, according to Kant, we experi-ence the world: namely by informational input from external reality being interpreted by the mind in terms of its own categorial scheme and thus coming to consciousness as meaningful phenomenal experience. All that we are entitled to say about the nou-menal source of this information is that it is the reality whose influence produces, in collaboration with the human mind, the phenomenal world of our experience. This takes place through the medium of certain concepts which Kant calls the categories of the understanding. In Kant's system of thought these are *a priori* and hence univer-sal and invariable modes of human perception. The pure categories or pure concepts of the understanding (for example, substance) are schematised in terms of temporality to produce the more concrete categories which are exhibited in our actual experience of the world. (Thus, for example, the pure concept of substance is schematised as the more concrete idea of an object enduring through time.) The impact of our environ-ment upon our sensory equipment then comes to consciousness in forms prescribed by these schematised categories.

The situation is basically the same, I suggest, in the case of our awareness of the Real—though within the similarity there are also major differences. Some of these have been discussed by William Forgie, who characterises the kind of view I am presenting as

'Hyper-Kantianism' (Forgie 1985a). The main difference is that the categories (Forgie prefers to call them 'category-analogues') of religious experience are not universal and invariable but are on the contrary culture-relative. It is possible to live without employing them; and when they are employed they tend to change and develop through time as different historical influences affect the development of human consciousness. Forgie is however mistaken, in my opinion, in regarding such a theory of religious categories as a 'rival view' (208) to Kant's. For Kant was solely concerned, in his discussion of the categories, with the construction of the physical world in sense perception. One who is concerned with the construction of the divine within religious experience has the option of accepting or rejecting Kant's view of sense perception. One theory neither requires nor is incompatible with the other. We have already noted that Kant's own epistemology of religion was quite unrelated to his understanding of sense perception. But this fact does not bar others, inspired by his basic insights, from seeing religious and sense experience as continuous in kind, thereby extending Kant's analysis of the one, in an appropriately adapted form, to the other.

In the religious case there are two fundamental circumstances: first, the postulated presence of the Real to the human life of which it is the ground; and second, the cognitive structure of our consciousness, with its capacity to respond to the meaning or character of our environment, including its religious meaning or character. In terms of information theory, we are speaking of the transmission of information from a transcendent source to the human mind/brain and its transformation by the mind/brain into conscious experience.[14] The transference of information from a source to a receiver, and its transformability from one mode to another, are among the ultimately mysterious facts of which we have to take account. Information is conveyed not only by such physical means as electro-magnetic radiations but also by forms of mind-to-mind and matter-to-mind causation such as are observed in ESP phenomena.[15] These do not depend upon physical contiguity but perhaps upon a universal cognitivity of mental life which is restricted in individual organisms by the limited and selective processing capacity of the brain.[16] The 'presence' of the Real consists in the availability, from a transcendent source, of information that the human mind/brain is capable of transforming into what we call religious experience. And, as in the case of our awareness of the physical world, the environing divine reality is brought to consciousness in terms of certain basic concepts or categories. These are, first, the concept of God, or of the Real as personal, which presides over the various theistic forms of religious experience; and second, the concept of the Absolute, or of the Real as non-personal, which presides over its various non-theistic forms.[17]

The relation between these two very different ways of conceiving and experiencing the Real, as personal and as non-personal, is perhaps a complementarity analogous (as has been suggested by Ian Barbour[18]) to that between the two ways of conceiving and registering light, namely as waves and as particles. That is to say, the purely physical structure of light is not directly observable; but under different sets of experimental conditions it is found to have wave-like and particle-like properties respectively. If we act upon it in one way it appears to behave like a shower of particles, and if in another way, like a succession of waves. The reality itself is such that it is able to be validly conceived and observed in both of these ways. Analogously the divine Reality is not directly known *an sich*. But when human beings relate themselves to it in the mode of I-Thou encounter they experience it as personal. Indeed in the context of that relationship it *is* personal, not It but He or She. When human beings relate themselves to the Real in the mode of non-personal awareness they experience it as non-personal, and in the context of this relationship it *is* non-personal.

Each of these two basic categories, God and the Absolute, is schematised or made concrete within actual religious experience as a range of particular gods or absolutes. These are, respectively, the *personae* and the *impersonae* in terms of which the Real is humanly known. And the particularising factor (corresponding, in its function, to time in the schematisation of the Kantian categories) is the range of human cultures, actualising different though overlapping aspects of our immensely complex human potentiality for awareness of the transcendent. It is in relation to different ways of being human, developed within the civilisations and cultures of the earth, that the Real, apprehended through the concept of God, is experienced specifically as the God of Israel, or as the Holy Trinity, or as Shiva, or as Allah, or as Vishnu . . . And it is in relation to yet other forms of life that the Real, apprehended through the concept of the Absolute, is experienced as Brahman, or as Nirvana, or as Being, or as Sunyata . . .

On this view our various religious languages—Buddhist, Christian, Muslim, Hindu . . . —each refer to a divine phenomenon or configuration of divine phenomena. When we speak of a personal God, with moral attributes and purposes, or when we speak of the non-personal Absolute, Brahman, or of the Dharmakaya, we are speaking of the Real as humanly experienced: that is, as phenomenon.

4. The relation between the real *an sich* and its *personae* and *impersonae*

It follows from this distinction between the Real as it is in itself and as it is thought and experienced through our religious concepts that we cannot apply to the Real *an sich* the characteristics encountered in its *personae* and *impersonae*. Thus it cannot be said to be one or many, person or thing, substance or process, good or evil, purposive or non-purposive. None of the concrete descriptions that apply within the realm of human experience can apply literally to the unexperiencable ground of that realm. For whereas the phenomenal world is structured by our own conceptual frameworks, its noumenal ground is not. We cannot even speak of this as a thing or an entity. (We shall see later—in Chapter 16.4—that the Buddhist concept of *śūnyatā* in one of its developments, namely as an anti-concept excluding all concepts, provides a good symbol for the Real *an sich*.) However we can make certain purely formal statements about the postulated Real in itself. The most famous instance in western religious discourse of such a formal statement is Anselm's definition of God as that than which no greater can be conceived. This formula refers to the ultimate divine reality without attributing to it any concrete characteristics. And in this purely formal mode we can say of the postulated Real *an sich* that it is the noumenal ground of the encountered gods and experienced absolutes witnessed to by the religious traditions.

There are at least two thought-models in terms of which we can conceive of the relationship between the Real *an sich* and its *personae* and *impersonae*. One is that of noumenon and phenomena, which enables us to say that the noumenal Real is such as to be authentically experienced as a range of both theistic and non-theistic phenomena. On this basis we cannot, as we have seen, say that the Real *an sich* has the characteristics displayed by its manifestations, such as (in the case of the heavenly Father) love and justice or (in the case of Brahman) consciousness and bliss. But it is nevertheless the noumenal ground of these characteristics. In so far as the heavenly Father and Brahman are two authentic manifestations of the Real, the love and justice of the one and the consciousness and bliss of the other are aspects of the Real as manifested within human experience. As the noumenal ground of these and other modes of experience, and yet transcending all of them, the Real is so rich in content that it can only be finitely experienced in the various partial and inadequate ways which the history of religions describes.

The other model is the more familiar one in western thought of analogical predication, classically expounded by Aquinas. According to him we can say that God is, for example, good—not in the sense in which we say of a human being that he or she is good, nor on the other hand in a totally unrelated sense, but in the sense that there is in the divine nature a quality that is limitlessly superior and yet at the same time analogous to human goodness. But Aquinas was emphatic that we cannot know what the divine super-analogue of goodness is like: 'we cannot grasp what God is, but only what He is not and how other things are related to Him' (*S. c. G.*, I:30:4—Pegis 1955, 141). Further, the divine attributes which are distinguished in human thought and given such names as love, justice, knowledge, power, are identical in God. For 'God . . . as considered in Himself, is altogether one and simple, yet our intellect knows Him according to diverse conceptions because it cannot see Him as He is in Himself.'[19] When we take these two doctrines together and apply them to the Real we see that, whilst there is a noumenal ground for the phenomenal divine attributes, this does not enable us to trace each attribute separately upwards into the Godhead or the Real. They represent the Real as both reflected and refracted within human thought and experience. But nevertheless the Real is the ultimate ground or source of those qualities which characterize each divine *persona* and *impersona* insofar as these are authentic phenomenal manifestations of the Real.

This relationship between the ultimate noumenon and its multiple phenomenal appearances, or between the limitless transcendent reality and our many partial human images of it, makes possible mythological speech about the Real. I define a myth as a story or statement which is not literally true but which tends to evoke an appropriate dispositional attitude to its subject-matter. Thus the truth of a myth is a practical truthfulness: a true myth is one which rightly relates us to a reality about which we cannot speak in non-mythological terms.[20] For we exist inescapably in relation to the Real, and in all that we do and undergo we are inevitably having to do with it in and through our neighbours and our world. Our attitudes and actions are accordingly appropriate or inappropriate not only in relation to our physical and social environments but also in relation to our ultimate environment. And true religious myths are accordingly those that evoke in us attitudes and modes of behaviour which are appropriate to our situation in relation to the Real.

But what is it for human attitudes, behaviours, patterns of life to be appropriate or inappropriate within this ultimate situation? It is for the *persona* or *impersona* in relation to which we live to be an authentic manifestation of the Real and for our practical response to be appropriate to that manifestation. To the extent that a *persona* or *impersona* is in soteriological alignment with the Real, an appropriate response to that deity or absolute is an appropriate response to the Real. It need not however be the only such

response: for other phenomenal manifestations of the Real within other human traditions evoke other responses which may be equally appropriate.

Why however use the term 'Real' in the singular? Why should there not be a number
of ultimate realities? There is of course no reason, *a priori*, why the closest approximation
that there is to a truly ultimate reality may not consist in either an orderly federation or
a feuding multitude or an unrelated plurality. But if from a religious point of view we
are trying to think, not merely of what is logically possible (namely, anything that is
conceivable), but of the simplest hypothesis to account for the plurality of forms of religious experience and thought, we are, I believe, led to postulate 'the Real'. For each of
the great traditions is oriented to what it regards as the Ultimate as the sole creator or
source of the universe, or as that than which no greater can be conceived, or as the final
ground or nature of everything. Further, the 'truthfulness' of each tradition is shown
by its soteriological effectiveness. But what the traditions severally regard as ultimates
are different and therefore cannot all be truly ultimate. They can however be different
manifestations of the truly Ultimate within different streams of human thought-and-
experience—hence the postulation of the Real *an sich* as the simplest way of accounting
for the data. But we then find that if we are going to speak of the Real at all, the exigen-
cies of our language compel us to refer to it in either the singular or the plural. Since
there cannot be a plurality of ultimates, we affirm the true ultimacy of the Real by
referring to it in the singular. Indian thought meets this problem with the phrase 'The
One without a second'.[21] The Real, then, is the ultimate Reality, not one among others;
and yet it cannot literally be numbered: it is the unique One without a second.

But if the Real in itself is not and cannot be humanly experienced, why postulate
such an unknown and unknowable *Ding an sich*? The answer is that the divine noumenon
is a necessary postulate of the pluralistic religious life of humanity. For within each tradition we regard as real the object of our worship or contemplation. If, as I have already
argued, it is also proper to regard as real the objects of worship or contemplation within
the other traditions, we are led to postulate the Real *an sich* as the presupposition of
the veridical character of this range of forms of religious experience.[22] Without this
postulate we should be left with a plurality of *personae* and *impersonae* each of which is
claimed to be the Ultimate, but no one of which alone can be. We should have either to
regard all the reported experiences as illusory or else return to the confessional position in which we affirm the authenticity of our own stream of religious experience
whilst dismissing as illusory those occurring within other traditions. But for those to
whom neither of these options seems realistic the pluralistic affirmation becomes inevitable, and with it the postulation of the Real *an sich*, which is variously experienced and
thought as the range of divine phenomena described by the history of religion. This is
accordingly the hypothesis that is now to be developed.

Notes

*   [All references to Chapter and Part numbers refer to the original source, *An Interpretation
    of Religion: Human Responses to the Transcendent*, 2nd edn. (New Haven, CT: Yale University
    Press, 2004).]

1. R. A. Nicholson [1950] 1978, 166.
2. *Tao Te Ching* 1982, 17. There has been considerable discussion of the enigmatic first chapter of the *Tao Te Ching* and its different interpretations (see e.g. David Loy 1985); but the translation which I have quoted seems to reflect the nearest there is to a current consensus.
3. Thus Calvin taught that we do not know God's essence but only God as revealed to us ([1559] 1962, I:xiii:21).
4. Cf. *Summa Theologica*, part I, Q. 12, art. 7. On this aspect of Aquinas' thought see further Wilfred Cantwell Smith 1979, ch. 5.
5. For example, Lactantius, *On the Wrath of God* (quoted by Otto [1917] 1936, 99); Dionysius the Areopagite, *On the Divine Names*, ch. 1; Augustine, *On Christian Doctrine*, 1:6; John Scotus Erigena, *On the Division of Nature*, bk I; *Theologia Germanica*, ch. 1.
6. See e.g. William Alston 1956; Keith E. Yandell 1975 and 1979; Peter C. Appleby 1980; Alvin Plantinga 1980.
7. Thus Augustine goes too far when he says that 'God is not even to be called ineffable because to say that is to make an assertion about him' (*On Christian Doctrine*, 1:6).
8. Cf. Plantinga 1980, 23 and 25.
9. Cf. bk I, ch. 30, para. 4, and *Summa Theologica*, part I, Q. 12, art. 7. See also W. A. Wolfson 1957.
10. The best-known use of the Kantian epistemology in the philosophy of religion is Rudolf Otto's view of the concept of the holy or the numinous as an *a priori* category of the human mind. He held that this religious *a priori* is non-rational but is schematised by the operations of rationality. Thus 'The *tremendum*, the daunting and repelling moment of the numinous, is schematized by means of the rational ideas of justice, moral will, and the exclusion of what is opposed to morality; and schematized thus, it becomes the holy "Wrath of God" . . . The *fascinans*, the attracting and alluring moment of the numinous, is schematized by means of the ideas of goodness, mercy, love, and, so schematized, becomes all that we mean by Grace . . .' (Otto [1917] 1936, 144–5). For a more recent use, with much more in common with the thesis being developed here, see Robert Oakes 1973.
11. See e.g. Barry F. Anderson 1975; William N. Dember 1960; S. T. Fiske 1984; Harvey, Hunt and Schroder 1961.
12. See e.g. Berger and Luckmann 1967; Burkart Holzner 1968; Arbib and Hesse 1986.
13. And also as it may appear to creatures with different cognitive equipment from our own. Kant was conscious that he was investigating the specifically *human* forms and categories of perception (*Crit. Pure Reason*, B59).
14. For an important discussion of information theory in relation to the epistemology of religion see John Bowker 1978.
15. For indications that information is conveyed extra-sensorily in a non-linguistic mode, see Ian Gratton-Guinness 1985.
16. Cf. Naranjo and Ornstein 1971, 170–2.
17. The term 'Absolute' seems to be the best that we have, even though it is not ideal for the purpose, being more naturally applied to some non-personal manifestations of the Real than to others. It is more naturally applicable, e.g., to Brahman than to Nirvana—although Edward Conze found it proper to say that 'The ultimate reality, also called Dharma by the Buddhists, or Nirvana, is . . . very much akin to the philosophical notion of the "Absolute" . . .' (Edward Conze 1975; Masao Abe also identifies *Mu*, Nothingness, with the absolute—Abe 1985a, 20).
18. Ian Barbour 1974, ch. 5. Cf. Conrad Hyers 1983.
19. *Summa Theologica*, part I, Q. 13, art. 12 – Regis 1945, I:133. Or, more succinctly, 'All divine perfections are in reality identical', *Compendium theologiae*, 22, cited by F. C. Copleston 1955, 135.

20. This concept of myth is developed more fully in Chapter 19.2–4.
21. *Chāndogya* Up., VI:2:4 (Radhakrishnan 1969, 449). Cf. Shankara [7th–8th century] 1978, 54. Maimonides grappled with the same problem: 'It would be extremely difficult for us to find, in any language whatsoever, words adequate to this subject, and we can only employ inadequate language. In our endeavour to show that God does not include a plurality, we can only say "He is one", although "one" and "many" are both terms which serve to distinguish quantity. We therefore make the subject clearer, and show to the understanding the way of truth by saying He is one but does not possess the attribute of unity' ([12th century] 1904, 81).
22. 'If we do not postulate the ultimate Focus, the subject, the inaccessible X lying beyond the contents of belief and experience, we might consider the real Focus as it enters into lives itself to be a projection' (Ninian Smart 1981, 187).

Reference bibliography

Abe, Masao
    1985a: *Zen and Western Thought* (London: Macmillan, and Honolulu: University of Hawaii Press).
Alston, William
    1956: 'Ineffability', in *Philosophical Review*, vol. 65, no. 4.
Anderson, Barry F.
    1975: *Cognitive Psychology: The Study of Knowing, Learning and Thinking* (New York and London: Academic Press).
Appleby, Peter C.
    1980: 'Mysticism and Ineffability', in *International Journal for Philosophy of Religion*, vol. II, no. 3.
Aquinas, Thomas
    1945: *Basic Writings of Saint Thomas Aquinas*, English Dominican Trans., ed. Anton Pegis, vol. 2 (New York: Random House).
Arbib, Michael A., and Mary B. Hesse
    1986: *The Construction of Reality* (London and New York: Cambridge University Press).
Augustine
    1953: *Augustine's Early Writings*, trans. J. H. S. Burleigh (London: SCM Press, and Philadelphia: Westminster Press).
Barbour, Ian
    1974: *Myths, Models and Paradigms* (New York: Harper & Row).
Berger, Peter, and Thomas Luckmann
    1967: *The Social Construction of Reality* (New York: Doubleday Anchor).
Bowker, John
    1978: *The Religious Imagination and the Sense of God* (Oxford: Clarendon Press).
Calvin, Jean
    1962: *Institutes of the Christian Religion*, 2 vols [1559], Library of Christian Classics vols 20–1, trans. Ford Lewis Battles, ed. John T. McNeill (Philadelphia: Westminster Press).
Conze, Edward
    1975: *Buddhism: Its Essence and Development* [1951] (New York: Harper & Row).
Copleston, F. C.
    1955: *Aquinas* (Harmondsworth, Middlesex: Penguin Books).
Dember, William N.
    1960: *The Psychology of Perception* (New York: Henry Holt).

Dionysius the Areopagite
  1977: *On the Divine Names and the Mystical Theology* [1920], trans. C. E. Rolt (London: SPCK).
Eckhart, Meister
  1941: *Meister Eckhart: A Modern Translation*, trans. Raymond Blakney (New York and London: Harper Torchbooks).
Eliade, Mircea
  1985: *A History of Religious Ideas*, vol. III [1983].
Fiske, S. T.
  1984: *Social Cognition* (Reading, MD: Addison-Wesley).
Forgie, J. William
  1985a: 'Hyper-Kantianism in Recent Discussions of Mystical Experience', in *Religious Studies*, vol. 21, no. 2.
Gratton-Guinness, Ian
  1985: 'Is Psi Intrinsically Non-Linguistic?', in *Journal of the Society for Psychical Research*, vol. 53, no. 799.
Gregory of Nyssa
  1956: *Against Eunomius*, in Schaff and Wace 1956, vol. 5. Grand Rapids, Michigan: Eerdmans.
Holzner, Burkart
  1968: *Reality Construction in Society* (Cambridge, MA: Schenkman).
Hume, David
  1956: *Natural History of Religion* [1757], ed. H. E. Root (London: Adam & Charles Black).
Hyers, Conrad
  1983: 'The Unity and Ambiguity of Religion: Rethinking the Doctrine of Double-Truth', in *World Faiths Insight*, New Series (Summer).
John of the Cross, St
  1958: *Ascent of Mount Cannel* [16th century], trans. E. Allison Peers (Garden City, NY: Image Books).
Kant, Immanuel
  1958: *Critique of Pure Reason*, trans. Norman Kemp Smith [1929] (London: Macmillan, and New York: St. Martin's Press).
Kaufman, Gordon D.
  1972: *God the Problem* (Cambridge, MA: Harvard University Press).
  1981: *The Theological Imagination* (Philadelphia: Westminster Press).
  1985: *Theology for a Nuclear Age* (Manchester: Manchester University Press, and Philadelphia: Westminster Press).
Loy, David
  1985: 'Chapter One of the *Tao Te Ching:* A "New" Interpretation', in *Religious Studies*, vol. 21, no. 3.
Maimonides, Moses
  1904: *Guide for the Perplexed* [12th century], trans. M. Friedlander, 2nd edition (London: Routledge & Kegan Paul).
Naranjo, Claudio, and Robert Ornstein
  1971: *On the Psychology of Meditation* (London and New York: Penguin Books).
Nicholson, R. A.
  1963: *The Mystics of Islam* [1914] (London and Boston: Routledge & Kegan Paul).
  1978: *Rumi: Poet and Mystic* [1950] (London: George Allen & Unwin).
Oakes, Robert
  1973: 'Noumena, Phenomena, and God', in *International Journal for Philosophy of Religion*, vol. 14, no. 1.

Otto, Rudolf
  1936: *The Idea of the Holy* [1917], trans. John H. Harvey (London and New York: Oxford
    University Press).
Pegis, Anton C., (trans.)
  1955: *On the Truth of the Catholic Faith: Summa contra Gentiles*, vol. 1 (Garden City, NY: Image
    Books).
Plantinga, Alvin
  1995: 'Pluralism: A Defense of Religious Exclusivism', in Thomas D. Senor (ed.), *The
    Rationality of Belief and the Plurality of Faith*. Ithaca: Cornell University Press.
  2000: *Warranted Christian Belief* (New York and Oxford: Oxford University Press).
Qur' an
  1977: trans. A. Yusuf Ali, 2nd edition (New York: American Trust Publications).
Radhakrishnan, S., (trans.)
  1968: *The Principal Upanishads* (London: George Allen & Unwin and New York: Humanities
    Press).
Romer, W. H. Ph.
  1969: 'The Religion of Ancient Mesopotamia', in C. Jouco Bleeker and Geo Widengren
    (eds.), *Historia Religionum: Handbook for the History of Religions, Vol. I Religions of the Past*.
    Leiden: Brill, 1969
Shankara
  1978: *Crest Jewel of Discrimination* [7th–8th century] 3rd edition, trans. Swami Prabha-
    vananda and Christopher Isherwood (Hollywood, CA: Vedanta Press).
Shinran
  1979: *Notes on 'Essentials of Faith Alone,' a Translation of Shinran's Yuishinsho-mon'i* [1250]
    (Kyoto: Hongwanji International Centre).
Smart, Ninian H.
  1981: *Beyond Ideology: Religion and the Future of Western Civilization* (San Francisco: Harper &
    Row).
  1984: 'Our Experience of the Ultimate', in *Religious Studies*, vol. 20, no. 1.
  1986: *Concept and Empathy*, ed. Donald Wiebe (London: Macmillan, and New York: New
    York University Press).
Smith, Wilfred Cantwell
  1979: *Faith and Belief* (Princeton, NJ: Princeton University Press).
Tao Te Ching
  1982: trans. Ch'u Ta-Kao (London and Boston: Mandala Books).
Theologia Germanica [1516]
  1937: trans. Susanna Winkworth (London: Macmillan).
Tillich, Paul
  1952: *The Courage to Be* (New Haven: Yale University Press).
Underhill, Evelyn
  1955: *Mysticism* [1911], 12th edition (New York: New American Library).
Wolfson, W. A.
  1957: 'Negative Attributes in the Church Fathers', in *Harvard Theological Review*, vol. 50.
Yandell, Keith E.
  1975: 'Some Varieties of Ineffability', in *International Journal for Philosophy of Religion*, vol. 6,
    no. 3.
  1979: 'The Ineffability Theme', in *International Journal for Philosophy of Religion*, vol. 10,
    no. 4.

Questions for reflection

1 Professor Hick begins the essay by noting that throughout history there have been innumerable gods with different names and characteristics. He then goes on to explain and defend his "pluralistic hypothesis." What do you make of the fact that there are and have been so many different views of God and the gods? Is there a better answer than Hick's pluralistic hypothesis? If so, what is it?

2 How does Hick utilize Kant's concepts of the noumenal world and phenomenal world to account for the various understandings of the Real as expressed in the different religions?

3 Describe the difference between the Real in itself and the Real as humanly experienced. Do you agree with Hick's analysis? Explain.

4 There is an ancient allegory about several blind men and an elephant. According to the allegory, each of the blind men runs his hands over the animal. One of them feels the trunk and believes it is a snake; another feels the leg and believes it is a tree; another feels the tail and believes it is a rope; and so on. Does this allegory provide a helpful image of Hick's religious pluralism? Why or why not? Can you think of any objections to the allegory in terms of the way religion is actually held and experienced?

Further reading

Gavin D'Costa, ed. (1990) *Christian Uniqueness Reconsidered*. New York: Orbis. (Essays by Rowan Williams, John Cobb, Wolfhart Pannenberg, Lesslie Newbigin, Jürgen Moltmann, Paul Griffiths, and others criticizing the pluralist position.)

John Hick (1985) *Problems of Religious Pluralism*. London: Macmillan, and New York: St. Martin's Press. (Articles on various aspects of religious pluralism.)

John Hick (2004) *An Interpretation of Religion*. 2nd edn. New Haven, CT: Yale University Press. (The classic work on religious pluralism from which the above essay was taken.)

Paul Knitter, ed. (2005) *The Myth of Religious Superiority: A Multifaith Exploration*. New York: Orbis. (Essays by Christian, Jewish, Muslim, Hindu, and Buddhist pluralists.)

Chapter 2

Keith Ward

TRUTH AND THE DIVERSITY OF RELIGIONS

Keith Ward is former Regius Professor of Divinity at the University of Oxford and a Fellow
of the British Academy. In this essay, Professor Ward interacts with John Hick's pluralistic hypothesis and claims that, while the hypothesis is an "elegant and morally attractive
solution of the problem of error in religion" ("error" in that different religious claims conflict with one another), it is also "riddled with difficulties." In his analysis, Professor Ward
makes an insightful distinction between different senses of the pluralistic hypothesis, most
notably between *hard pluralism* (the view that many religious traditions "do not contain
mutually exclusive beliefs, but are equally valid paths of salvation and of authentic experience of the Real," or Ultimate Reality), and *soft pluralism* (the view that the Real can
manifest in different religious traditions and human beings can respond appropriately to
It). He has sympathies with the latter and agrees with important aspects which follow from
it; namely, that no tradition has the complete truth about God, that they probably all (or at
least the "great" traditions) contain some truths and some falsities, and thus we should look
to other traditions to help inform our own. Regarding hard pluralism, however, he argues
that it is incoherent since if the Real is wholly unknowable, then one cannot claim the following: (1) to know that all experiences of the Real are equally authentic, and (2) that all
paths to the Real are equally valid.

I will be concerned with only one problem about truth which is raised by the diversity
of religions which exist in the world. The problem is this: many religions claim to state
truths about the nature of the universe and human destiny which are important or even
necessary for human salvation and ultimate well-being. Many of these truths seem to
be incompatible; yet there is no agreed method for deciding which are to be accepted;
and equally intelligent, informed, virtuous and holy people belong to different faiths. It
seems, therefore, that a believing member of any one tradition is compelled to regard
all other traditions as holding false beliefs and therefore as not leading to salvation.

Since each faith forms a minority of the world's population, all religious believers thus seem committed to saying that most intelligent, virtuous and spiritually devoted people cannot know the truth or attain salvation. This is a problem, because it is in tension with the belief, held by many traditions, that the supremely real being is concerned for the salvation of all rational creatures. How can this be so if, through no fault of their own, most creatures cannot come to know the truth and thereby attain salvation?

Among those who have seen this as a problem and have proposed a philosophical defence of one solution to it, John Hick must take a foremost place. His book, *An Interpretation of Religion* (London, 1989), is a statement of the position which has come to be known as religious pluralism. This major work, filled with illuminating discussions of the phenomena of religious belief and with fresh and lucid insights, is meant to be, not the end of the debate, but an opening up of discussion which might clarify the problem and its solutions further, and might establish a coherent framework for developing inter-faith dialogue and for a credible religious faith held in full awareness of and with full respect for the beliefs of others. My aim is to contribute to this discussion; and I shall do it by using the time-honoured philosophical technique of niggling and irritating criticism of various theses Hick presents. My argument will be that Hick's position is philosophically unacceptable as it stands, though it would be unwise simply to reject it wholesale; and I hope that my attack, such as it is, will be taken as a tribute to the force of the issues Hick places before us.

Hick's pluralistic hypothesis

The pluralistic hypothesis is that religions provide different valid but culturally conditioned responses to a transcendent reality, and offer ways of transcending self and achieving a limitlessly better state centred on that reality. Thus no one tradition possesses a set of absolute and exclusive truths, while all others are delusory and ineffective for salvation. All will, or at least can be, saved by adhering to their own traditions, which purvey differing, but authentic, responses to the ultimately real. All can know the truth and attain salvation in their own traditions; so believers no longer have to condemn all others as mistaken, and no longer have to wonder why their God leaves the majority of creatures in mortal error. Here is an elegant and morally attractive solution of the problem of error in religion; and it is one that has great appeal for those who are reluctant to say that they alone are right and everyone else is wrong.

Nevertheless the hypothesis is riddled with difficulties; and the most obvious one can be put very forthrightly. To believe a proposition is to think that it is true. To think that it is true is to affirm that reality is as it is described by that proposition. Insofar as our affirmations are fallible, it is always possible that reality is not as some proposition asserts it to be. Thus an affirmation by its nature excludes some possible state of affairs; namely, one which would render the proposition false. If an assertion excludes nothing, it affirms nothing. In that sense, all truth-claims are necessarily exclusive.

It immediately follows that, where any truth-claim is made, it is logically possible to make another truth-claim which the first claim excludes. It is logically impossible for all possible truth-claims to be compatible. So it is possible for religious traditions to contain incompatible truth-claims, claims which exclude one another. Since this is a matter of logical possibility, it is a necessary truth that not all possible religious traditions can be equally true, authentic or valid. One can easily construct traditions which are strictly incompatible and of them, at least, pluralism must be false. That is, they will not consist of equally valid concepts of ultimate reality. One does not even need to invent such traditions, since, for example, Satanism and Christianity are fundamentally opposed both morally and factually.

But if this version of pluralism, which we might call "extreme pluralism," is incoherent, it might nevertheless be the case that many religious traditions, and maybe all the major ones that exist on our planet, do not contain mutually exclusive beliefs, but are equally valid paths of salvation and of authentic experience of the Real. This is "hard pluralism"; and it is a contingent hypothesis; whether or not it is true will be a matter for careful investigation. But it certainly looks as though many claims exclude one another. The Buddhist assertion that there is no creator god excludes the Christian assertion that there is one all-perfect creator. The Muslim assertion that Allah has no son excludes the Christian assertion that God has an only-begotten Son. What is the pluralist to do about these *prima facie* incompatible claims?

Hick's strategy is to retreat from discussing particular religious beliefs and to talk instead of "religion"; to retreat from discussing specific truth-claims and to talk instead of "religious traditions." This may seem innocuous, but it can be, and turns out to be, very misleading. It is well-known that definitions of religion are hard to find; and Hick proposes that we regard "religion" as a family-resemblance concept, so that there is no essential core definition. Yet he is concerned with only one sort of religion or one feature of religious beliefs. He characterizes the central strand of religion with which he is chiefly concerned as "awareness of and response to a reality that transcends ourselves and our world."* Fairly rapidly, he nominalizes the verb "transcends," and speaks of "belief in the transcendent," saying that "most forms of religion have affirmed a salvific reality that transcends human beings and the world" (6). What he is doing is to pick out one class of religious beliefs, or one set of religious phenomena which can be defined in terms of belief in a transcendent salvific reality. There is nothing wrong with that; but it should be noted that it picks out one area of agreement in truth-claims by definition. Faiths which lack that central belief are not going to be counted; conversely, faiths which are counted are assured of a minimal degree of agreement to begin with. They will all agree on something, so they will not be incompatible in all respects. But, so far, this is not really pluralism (the acceptance of very different beliefs as equally valid); it is exclusivism at a relatively abstract and general level (those are excluded who do not believe in one transcendent salvific reality). It is also an acceptance of some truth-claim—the claim that there is such a reality which can bring creatures to a limitlessly good state—as "absolute," or true for everyone, regardless of their point of view or cultural situation.

Even when this area of agreement has been defined, however, there remain many incompatible truth-claims, which notoriously divide religions from each other. Hick's strategy now is to direct our focus of attention away from such particular truth-claims, which he regards as unsettlable and therefore (we shall have to look again at this "therefore") not necessary for salvation; and to look instead at the "religious traditions" as totalities "which mediate the Real" and within which the "salvific process occurs" (370). The point about a "religious tradition" is that it is not just a collection of truth-claims. . . . Anthropologists and sociologists can provide illuminating accounts of religion and reasons for religious belief without ever raising the issue of truth. Moreover, identical religious assertions can be interpreted in many ways, as conversation with any two

Anglican priests soon shows. Thus if one asks the question, "Can people find resources to help them love others and find meaning in life more or less equally in many traditions?," the answer is obviously going to be affirmative.

Viewed as social phenomena, religious traditions are forms of life which are culturally and ethnically differentiated. Since they contain many possibilities of diverse interpretation, and many dimensions of significance, it becomes apparent that a person will usually belong to such a tradition by birth, and can find within it many resources of meaning and moral teaching. As it seems absurd to say that one culture is "true" and all others "false," so the use of the expression "religious tradition" subtly leads one to say that one cannot compare such traditions for truth; and that therefore one is not to be preferred to the others, except as an expression of cultural imperialism.

It is indeed odd to speak of a whole religious tradition as being true or false, especially when one remembers that people as diverse as Quakers and Tridentine Catholics presumably exist within "the Christian tradition." Yet in the end the traditions that exist in the world today go back to particular individuals, known or unknown, who did propound particular beliefs. The "great traditions" are Scriptural traditions; and the scriptures contain, among many other things, teachings about the nature of reality and the way to salvation. There are particular truth-claims; and even though they can be interpreted variously, one can isolate a particular interpretation and ask of it whether it is true or false. Though the ascension of Jesus into heaven can be interpreted variously, one can ask whether it is true that he physically rose in the air; and there is a correct and precise answer to the question, however hard it is for us to know that answer.

Having isolated traditions which might plausibly be said to believe in one transcendent salvific reality, the hard pluralist then stresses the cultural totality and complexity of such traditions, and suggests that "we always perceive the transcendent through the lens of a particular religious culture" (8). Since whole cultures cannot reasonably be compared for truth and falsity, recognition of this fact should lead each tradition to "de-emphasise its own absolute and exclusive claim" (3), and accept that it is one among many ways to knowledge of and union with the transcendent. The correct response to this claim is to refrain from speaking of religio-cultural traditions, with all the problems of boundary-definition that brings with it, and to insist on focusing on particular truth-claims, and on particular interpretations of them, which can be properly assessed for truth and falsity. Then the question is not whether all traditions constitute different responses to the transcendent, which covers so many possibilities that it is almost bound to be true in some sense, but whether all specific truth-claims are equally warranted by the facts. When the question is put like that, it is obvious that they are not.

The hard pluralist response must now be to accept that disputes about truth, both of historical fact and about human origins and destiny, do exist, both within and between specific parts of diverse religions; but to assert that this is irrelevant both to knowledge of the Real itself and to the completion of the salvific process of moving from selfish egoism to the limitlessly better state of "Reality-centredness." There are two parts to this claim, one to do with knowledge of the Real and one to do with the nature and possibility of salvation. I shall consider each in turn, beginning with the claim that, though disputes about events in the past and future of the world are real enough, when it comes to speaking of the ultimately Real, different beliefs "constitute different ways in which the same ultimate Reality has impinged upon human life" (373). Moreover, these different ways of impinging are equally veridical for different observers.

Knowledge of the real

Many religious beliefs do speak of a transcendent reality; and they do say that this reality is ineffable, or beyond the grasp of human thought. If this is so, it may seem that no
humanly formulated truth-claim can apply to it as it really is; so that all claims must be
inadequate finite attempts to characterize an infinite reality, and none will be markedly
better than any others. But three major difficulties at once arise: if the Real is ineffable,
how can one know that it exists? If no truth-claim can apply to it, how can one be entitled
to say anything of it? And if this reality is unknowable, how can we know that all claims
about it are equally valid, except in the sense that all are completely mistaken? Hick
quotes a number of authoritative sources from a range of religions to show that ineffability is a common characteristic of the ultimately Real. "The Tao that can be expressed
is not the eternal Tao" (*Tao Te Ching*); God is "incapable of being grasped by any term"
(Gregory of Nyssa); Nirguna Brahman is such that all words fall back from attaining
it (Sankara). Inexpressibility by any human concepts is certainly a feature of the ultimate object of devotion or striving in many religious traditions. And it may seem a short
move from saying that two ideas are of an ineffable reality to saying that they are of the
same reality; for what could distinguish two ineffables?

It can easily be seen that this argument is invalid, however. If X is indescribable by
me, and Y is indescribable by me, it does not follow that X is identical with Y. On the
contrary, there is no way in which X could be identified with Y, since there are no criteria of identity to apply. It is rather like saying, "I do not know what X is; and I do not
know what Y is; therefore X must be the same as Y." If I do not know what either is, I *ipso
facto* do not know whether they are the same or different. To assert identity is thus to
commit the quantifier-shift fallacy, of moving from "Many religions believe in an ineffable Real" to "There is an ineffable Real in which many religions believe."

The principle of economy may be appealed to; to identify X and Y, and so have one
unknown, is simpler than to keep them distinct. But how do I know that ultimate reality is simple and not complex? The blunt truth is that I am not entitled to assert identity
or difference of ineffable objects. Hick says, "It (the Real *an sich*) cannot be said to be
one or many, person or thing, substance or process, good or evil, purposive or non-
purposive" (246). But if it cannot be said to be one or many, one is not even entitled to
use the singular term "it." There may be many unknowns beyond the universe. Hick
uses the singular because, he says, "there cannot be a plurality of ultimates"; but he says
in the same paragraph, that there is "no reason *a priori* why the closest approximation
that there is to a truly ultimate reality" may not consist in "an unrelated plurality." So
I think we must either remain truly agnostic, or confess that the Real can be said to be
one; and that is a piece of real and definite knowledge, opposed to all forms of simple
polytheism. It is also opposed to at least some forms of Buddhism; as Paul Williams
writes of Tibetan Buddhism, which he espouses, "There is no Being, no Absolute at
all." Many Christians, too, of course, explicitly reject the apophatic doctrine that God
is ultimately unknowable, supposing that he is truly known in Christ. So there does not
seem to be much hope of uniting all traditions around even the rather short creed of one
ineffable reality. They may say there is no such reality; or that there is more than one;
or that it is not ineffable.

Suppose, however, one considers those strands of thought which do speak of one
transcendent ineffable reality. It is not at all clear that different religions think of that

which they say to be ineffable as the same in each case. It is unlikely in the extreme that they simply mean to say, "As well as everything I have said, there are some things I do not know about, which exist beyond the universe." This very statement would be self-contradictory, in asserting, "I know X exists," which entails, "I know at least one thing about X (that it exists beyond the universe)," at the same time as, "I know nothing about X." But ineffability cannot in any case be sensibly interpreted to mean, "Lack of knowledge." What I know absolutely nothing about must be, one feels, hardly worth mentioning. One finds a much more positive characterization in, for instance, Aquinas' notion of Divine simplicity, in many ways the key concept for his interpretation of the Divine. Simplicity is an ontological, not an epistemic, property, for Aquinas. That is, it is not that I do not know what God is; I *do* know that the being of God is such that it contains no distinctions, no parts, no complexity which human concepts could grasp. The Divine being is unlimited, and therefore beyond human comprehension. It is not just unknowable by us—in which case, it might well be internally complex for all we know. On the contrary, we know—thinks Aquinas—that the Divine being is utterly simple; and we know this by an argument from the nature of the world to its ultimately self-sufficient cause. . . .

Seeking to defend his view that the Real is radically unknowable, Hick dismisses as "logical pedantry" the logical point that the Real must at least have the property of "being able to be referred to" (239). But there is more meat to the point than he admits. For if X has the property of being able to be referred to, this reference must be accomplished either by ostentation or description. Ostentation is ruled out by definition, for an object which transcends the universe. So any reference must be made by description; X must be identified as "the X which. . . ." Further, if an identifying reference is to have any hope of succeeding, one must be able to pick out X as some sort of substance, process or stuff. It is not enough to say, "the X which exists beyond the universe," if there may be many such things. One will need to say, "X is the one and only thing which satisfies the properties. . . ." Hick gives the game away by using the term "the Real." For him, X is the one and only thing which is real in the fullest sense (i.e., independent, self-existent, unchanging in its essential nature, unlimited by anything else. . .). This is a description which could only apply to one thing, if it could apply at all. The object is identified descriptively by constructing a notion of a unique sort of reality upon which all others depend. Whether such a reference could ever succeed is another question; but for it even to have meaning, it is apparent that quite a lot of our concepts do need to apply to X.

But these, says Hick, are "purely formal and logically generated properties"; they are not "substantial properties," like being good, powerful or wise. Now, he says, the claim to ineffability is that substantial properties do not apply to the being of God beyond the range of human experience. Does this distinction between formal and substantial properties hold? The distinction between form and substance might most naturally be taken as a distinction between what is said and the form in which it is said. Thus the substance, or content, of "The cat sat on the mat" is whatever is asserted by the utterance of those words. The form is the syntax or grammatical structure of English; noun, verb and predicate; a structure which enables me to say anything at all. Study of the structure will give me no particular content; it is like doing Logic with nothing but ps and qs; I can go on for pages without knowing what I am talking about (perhaps that is not well put; I can set out possible argument forms without actually uttering an argument).

Now if I say, "*X* is to be used as a noun" that could be called a formal property of *X*; it tells me what sort of term *X* is, without telling me what real thing *X* might be. But if I say, "*X* is the referent of some noun," I am talking about some actual object, not a term. And I am saying what sort of thing it is; a thing which could be referred to by description, by someone with human conceptual equipment. I am saying, "This object is such that it can be identified by some human language user." That may not tell me much about it, but it does have content; it is a synthetic proposition, though it is obvious, in the sense that I would hardly be speaking of the object if it could not be identified, at least in thought. And of course it invites further questions about how it can be identified. We must conclude that the statement "*X* is an identifiable object" attributes a substantial property to *X*, the property of being identifiable; and the more one spells out the manner of identifying it, the more one will say about *X*. In fact, Hick includes as a formal property the property of being that than which nothing greater can be conceived (246). Far from being purely formal, that property entails (in the concept of "greatness") the idea of value, of the rationally desirable, and thus of goodness, which he admits to being a substantial property, in at least one clear sense.

Moreover, this is an absolute truth about God. For if it is true from our viewpoint that God is maximally great, then it is true of God that, from our viewpoint, he is maximally great. The distinction which is often made between absolute truths and relative truths is insupportable. An absolute truth is supposed to be one which states what is the case independent of any particular person believing it. A relative truth states what is the case, from the point of view of a particular person; that is, it states what truly appears to be the case to some observer. But if *A* will truly appear as *B* to *P*, then it is true of *A* that it will appear as *B* to *P*. And this truth is absolute; it does not depend upon anybody knowing or believing it, since it may be true even though *P* never exists. So we know many true things about God, but we also know that much of God transcends our thoughts.

I propose that Hick has seized upon some very difficult and disputed statements of major religious intellectuals and has taken the doctrine of the *via negativa* out of relation to its complementary doctrine of the *via eminentia*, to produce a new doctrine that the Real *an sich* is wholly unknowable. Then he argues that, since one unknowable is indistinguishable from another, they are all the same. Since all human concepts are bound to be inadequate to the Real, if it is unknowable, and since we have no way of choosing between different descriptions, we must say that all the "great world faiths embody different perceptions and conceptions of, and correspondingly different responses to, the Real" (240).

When Kant foisted the doctrine of the noumenal realm upon the philosophical world, it was in the form of an undigested remnant of his pre-Critical view that the noumenal, or intelligible world, was the real world, and was knowable by pure intellect, whereas the senses give a confused appearance of this realm of rational spirits. In his Critical doctrine, he confined the intellect strictly to the realm of the senses, and justified the categories as necessary and universal preconditions of the possibility of scientific knowledge. The noumenal lost its theoretical role entirely. It has often been pointed out that a residual inconsistency vitiates Kant's idea of the noumenal, since to say that it exists as the cause of the phenomenal applies the categories beyond the permissible range of cognitive meaning. When this inconsistency is cleared away, Kant can be interpreted as proposing that Reason necessarily constructs an Ideal of a perfect value and reality, to be used as a regulative idea in our practical conduct of life. It has no theoretical validity, and is to be judged by its efficacy in enabling us to live a moral life, or to conceive of the rationality of such a life.

The nature of the possibility of salvation

Hick makes a similar move, revealing that the real focus of his concern is not with theoretical truth, but with the "salvific efficacy" of religions. When he comes to state criteria of assessing religious phenomena, he says that "the basic criterion is soteriological" (14); that is, efficacy in leading humans from self-centredness to Reality-centredness, most readily observable by growth in love or compassion. Yet, like Kant, he is unable to renounce theoretical claims entirely. This is hardly surprising, since even to say that a limitlessly better state is possible for all is a factual statement about the future, which is presumably experientially accessible in principle. Thus the theistic picture of the universe sees it as "a creative process leading to a limitlessly good end state in conscious communion with God" (179). This picture can be confirmed beyond rational doubt by conscious experience of that end state. Now there are certainly views which would refute this picture. Any atheistic view or any non-realist religious view would deny the existence of such an end state; so there is no question that some religious views deny precisely what traditional theism asserts. As Hick says, non-realism in religion offers "a radically different vision" (208) of things, which leaves no place for ultimate cosmic optimism. Samkhya Yogins, Advaitic Vedantins and many Buddhists, both Theravadin and Mahayana, would also deny that the universe is a creative process leading to an end state; they see the world as an illusory cycle of ills, without beginning or end. And even if the individual can achieve a limitlessly good end state, it will not be one of conscious communion with a perfect creator; it will be entry into the quiescent state of desirelessness, far beyond personhood as we understand it. Assertions made about the nature of the universe and about ultimate human destiny are very different. Is it not obvious that at most one set of such views can be true? And if Hick does not hesitate to exclude non-realist religious views and atheistic views of the world, why should he hesitate to exclude views which take a different view of human destiny, even though they might agree on the existence of a perfect supreme reality?

I think that he has increasingly come to feel, and argues at length in *An Interpretation of Religion*, that we cannot reasonably claim "that our own form of religious experience. . . is veridical whilst the others are not" (235). He allows that virtually every religious tradition has done so, but then proposes the following argument:

(1)   By something akin to Swinburne's Principle of Credulity, *A* is justified in thinking that what seems to be the case probably is the case, in the absence of strong countervailing reasons. So if *A* seems to apprehend God's presence, she is justified in thinking that God is in fact present, and therefore that God exists.
(2)   By the principle of universalizability, however, B is similarly justified in believing that reality is non-dual, on the basis of her experiences of *samadi* or enlightenment.
(3)   Since the fact that "*A* is me" is not a relevant reason for giving *A*'s views greater force than *B*'s, it seems that *A* and *B* are equally justified in believing contradictory things.

(4)   Therefore, it is implausible to believe that all religious experience is delusory except one's own.
(5)   This suggests the Pluralistic Hypothesis, that different types of religious experience are veridical but partial responses to a reality which cannot be adequately described by any set of beliefs alone.

This argument is plainly invalid. The trouble lies with step (4). A sharp distinction is to be made between justification and truth. I can be justified in believing something false (e.g., that the earth is flat) due to imperfect knowledge. In complex situations, given rather different initial information, people may be justified in believing contradictory things. But contradictory beliefs cannot both be true; so all that follows is that at least one person is justified in believing something false. Hick has already argued that both atheists and theists can be rationally justified in adopting the views of the world they do adopt, given the ambiguous nature of that world. But it does not follow that each must accept the other's view as equally true. The very reverse is the case. If I am rationally justified in believing X, and you are rationally justified in believing not-X, then we are both justified in believing the other to be deluded, or in some other way mistaken.

Now something *does* follow from this about the character of such beliefs. I must admit other believers may have reasons which seem just as strong to them to accept their views as I have to accept mine. Therefore, I cannot claim that they are obviously or detectably mistaken. And I cannot seriously claim that my view is obviously or clearly true. So I must admit the equal right of others to exist and hold the views they do. And I must admit the fallibility and theoretical uncertainty of my view. To accept this might in itself be a great advance in religion, but it does not constitute a reason for accepting hard pluralism. It could be a reason for denying any right to believe any view in this area. However, one can argue, as Hick does, that the matter is so important that I am justified in making some choice. It may even be that I *must* believe something in this area, though it is hard to say how detailed my beliefs must be. In fact Hick vacillates, sometimes saying that, because conflicting views have so little to choose between them, it is not important to hold such views, and one should concentrate simply on the practical matter of salvation. But at other times (e.g., as between realist and non-realist religious views) he says that it is important to choose a realist and cosmically optimistic view, because only that offers good news to all.

Whichever he says, it *is* reasonable to claim that our own experiences are veridical whilst all others are not. It is unreasonable to claim anything else. But the situation does not have to have this all-or-nothing character. Surely we do not wish to say that centuries of prayer, meditation, sanctity and devotion in other traditions are founded on illusion? Surely they must be putting people in touch with the real spiritual reality, whatever it is? Hick himself gives the answer: "There seems to me to be no difficulty in principle in the thought that a person may be correctly experiencing some aspects of reality whilst falsely experiencing others" (220). That is, there may well be something veridical in what great religious traditions experience, but also (very often) something false. He even tells us how to discriminate: we accept some belief as veridical "because it evokes a confirming echo within our own experience" (220). We reject others because they clash with our experience. There are many echoes of our experience in the religious experiences of others; and we may take these to be veridical. By parity of reasoning, we may think that our own tradition, even our own present experience within that tradition, is liable to contain many mistakes, though we will not know what they are. Humility is certainly in order; it does sound arrogant to say "my religious experience is perfectly correct; all others are totally false." But we can say: "My religious experience is correct in important respects, though it may contain many errors. The experiences of others may contain many veridical elements; but there are important misinterpretations, too." The veridical elements will be those which seem to echo my own; the errors those which clash with my own; nor will I be able to identify the errors in my own. I can be on the lookout for such errors, and look to other traditions to help me identify them. And I can look for elements other traditions have which may complement, rather than contradict, my own. Thus my beliefs are always revisable; and others may always be capable of disclosing new insights. Yet those beliefs which lie near the core of my belief-system must be given preference over competing beliefs.

Hick does precisely this, of course. He identifies many errors in the Christian tradition—belief in Hell and literal belief in incarnation are just two which he takes to be morally undesirable and rationally insupportable. His core-beliefs are that one should turn from selfish egoism to attain a limitlessly good end-state by some sort of relation to a reality of supreme value; and he is only prepared to accept beliefs which are compatible with these. The suggestion is that any set of beliefs which result in such an end-state is likely to be true; others are not. The trouble is that this criterion is quite unusable, as Hick's discussion makes very clear. Some of the most obviously deluded, restrictive and exclusive belief-systems produce astonishing commitment, assurance, love and self-sacrifice. On the other hand, as Hick points out, the great Scriptural traditions have histories replete with hatred, intolerance and violence; so that none of them emerges as much better than any others, in the long sad history of human fanaticism. It seems, then, that either the suggested criteria of adequacy do not enable us to choose between many different beliefs, or that they are in tension with the criterion of consistency with other well-established knowledge. In this situation, might it not be better to abandon the Kantian *noumenon*, say that we do know something about the Real—namely, that it is an ultimate unity of reality and value—and thus that criteria of adequacy, at this abstract level, are metaphysical criteria of providing the most intelligible account of the genesis of the universe from an ultimately real and perfect source? Hick tends to dismiss metaphysical speculations, together with particular historical claims, as unsettlable and unnecessary to salvation. But of course his whole book is a metaphysical exploration of what can be intelligibly said about the object of religious faith; and the fact that his version of pluralistic religious realism is unsettlable and highly disputable does not stop him from asserting both its truth and its importance for a correct (non-exclusive) understanding of salvation.

This brings us back to the question, which I deferred earlier, of whether unsettlable beliefs can be necessary for salvation. Hick finds this "implausible" (369), but it is rendered immediately more plausible by the consideration that the very concept of what salvation is involves beliefs which are theoretically unsettlable in practice. If one asks what is necessary for salvation, one might be asking whether any beliefs are requisite for the final attainment of wholly fulfilled human life. Atheists, of course, will deny that there is any such final attainment, or even any such possible notion as that of a wholly fulfilled life; "do your own thing" might better be their motto. So the mere acceptance of the concept of a wholly fulfilled life presupposes the very contestable belief that there is a proper goal of human activity. If there is such a consciously attained goal, then one cannot achieve it without having the correct belief about what it is, and how one has come to achieve it. In this sense the possession of some particular beliefs is necessary to salvation. People without those beliefs will not attain salvation, for the simple reason that salvation consists in attaining a state which entails possessing such beliefs; i.e., it entails that one knows what salvation is and that one has attained it. At such a point, of course, one may suppose that religious disputes will finally be settled. As Hick says, "To participate knowingly in fulfilment would confirm the reality of God beyond the possibility of rational doubt" (179). In other words, at least some important metaphysical claims about the existence and nature of God are settlable by experience in principle.

But one might also ask whether any beliefs are requisite *now* if one is to have a reasonable hope of attaining salvation later, or if one is to be on the right path towards salvation. Different views exist on this question, but Hick seems to me correct in thinking that if there is a God of universal love, he will not make our loss of eternal life dependent merely upon making an honest mistake. So one might suppose that a positive response to whatever seems to be good and true, by a conscience as informed as one can reasonably expect, and a commitment to seek truth and realize goodness, is sufficient to dispose one rightly to salvation. Some beliefs are requisite, but they will depend on particular circumstances, since what one is justified in believing at one time may well be different from what one is justified in believing at another. Nevertheless, if one believes in such a God of love, one will also think that he will eventually bring rational creatures to know what he truly is, so that the search for truth will issue in a specific set of true beliefs sometime. Thus it is misleading, though in one sense true, to say that no metaphysical beliefs are essential to salvation. It may not be essential to your eventual salvation that you hold them now, but it is essential to your actual salvation that you come to hold them. Metaphysics, however difficult and disputable, is important to faith (I don't mean anything very grand by this, just beliefs about the nature of what is ultimately real).

In a recent paper, Hick refers to the "novel," "astonishing," and "bizarre" doctrine that "the salvific power of the dharma taught five hundred years earlier by the Buddha is a consequence of the death of Jesus." But one need not deny that the dharma is an effective way of overcoming egoism and attaining inner peace and compassion, when one asserts that it does not bring one into a conscious loving relationship with a personal God. Nor is it bizarre to hold that one can be brought into such a relationship only by the saving activity of God uniting human nature to himself in the life and death of Jesus, and subsequently in those who come to accept Jesus as Lord and Saviour. It is not that Buddhists attain salvation by the Middle Way, though somehow the efficacy of this way depends on something that had not yet happened. Buddhists do not attain Christian salvation, since their Way does not lead to that personal relationship with God which is salvation. They attain a high degree of compassion and inner peace, and their unselfish devotion to the truth as they see it will surely fit them to receive salvation from a personal God when his saving activity becomes clear to them. There is a salutary reminder here that metaphysics is not what saves us; for Christians, the act of God, establishing creatures in knowledge and love of him, does that. But metaphysics is needed to set out the coherence of the concept of a God who can so act in a world like this.

Hard, soft, and revisionist pluralism

It may help at this point if we distinguish what we may call soft pluralism from hard pluralism. Soft pluralism is the view that the Real can manifest in many traditions, and humans can respond to it appropriately in them. I think this view is defensible and important, and it is certainly different from the view, held by many, that there is only one God, who only reveals himself in one tradition and only saves those who belong to that tradition—the restrictive interpretation of the decree of the Council of Florence, "Outside the Church there is no salvation." It is coherent to hold that there is a God who is infinite and beyond human comprehension in his essential nature, who discloses something of that nature, as it stands in relation to us, in many religious traditions. It is coherent to hold that in many (though not all) religious traditions, believers aim to overcome selfish desire in relation to a supreme objective value which promises bliss, knowledge and freedom, and that this does constitute a positive and appropriate response to God, as disclosed to them. It is also coherent to hold that no tradition has the completeness of truth about God, that all contain many revisable and corrigible beliefs, and that we should look to other traditions to complement, correct or reshape our own. This is certainly part of Hick's thesis.

But another form of the thesis is also at work, a thesis both more intolerant of virtually all actual religious traditions and sliding at times into incoherence. The intolerance surfaces in many stringent remarks about the bizarre, primitive and astonishing beliefs held by orthodox believers. The incoherence appears in the claim of hard pluralism that all (or at least all "great") traditions are equally valid paths to salvation and equally authentic modes of experience of a Real which is a completely unknowable postulate of the religious life. It is the stress on equal validity, equal authenticity and complete unknowability which is incoherent. These three claims constitute an inconsistent triad of propositions, since one cannot assert all of: (1) There is something wholly unknowable; (2) all experiences of it are equally authentic; and (3) all paths to fuller experience of it are equally valid. If (1) is true, (2) and (3) cannot be asserted. Not only is there no way of knowing if they are true; they cannot be true, if they entail (as they do) experiential knowledge of the wholly unknowable. If there are any criteria of authenticity at all, it must be possible to distinguish more and less authentic experiences. But this can only be done by means of some concept of the Real which can be described more or less adequately. Once one has such a concept, there may indeed be experiences which give equally authentic knowledge of it, but that can only be so if those experiences are complementary, not contradictory. That means (as is the case with the often quoted wave-particle duality of light) that competent observers must agree that both of two descriptions of an object can be true, in different conditions of observation. Unfortunately, most Buddhists will not agree that it is true that there is an omnipotent personal agent who brings about changes in history; and most Christians will not agree that the idea of God is an imaginative projection which needs to be overcome in the recognition of one non-dual reality. Hard pluralism is as strongly falsified as any contingent hypothesis is ever likely to be.

Yet it might be insisted that this situation must be changed. There is another version of pluralism, which might be termed "revisionist pluralism," which asserts that all the Scriptural traditions need to be radically revised, in consequence of the rise of the natural sciences, of Biblical scholarship and of post-Enlightenment critical thinking in general. The idea of an infallible Scriptural revelation will need to be discarded, and many particular beliefs revised in the light of new knowledge of the world and of human psychology. Now if this is done in all the great Scriptural traditions, one will be much less clear about which beliefs are essential or even central to each tradition; and the revised beliefs may well turn out to be compatible with similarly revised beliefs in other traditions.

If a Buddhist is prepared to regard belief in reincarnation as a myth, a Christian thinks of the Incarnation as a mistaken fourth-century doctrine, and a Muslim agrees that the Koran is a fallible and morally imperfect document, they might well be able to agree much more than they used to. One can see the Scriptural faiths, defined by their acceptance of infallible revelation (and even the Buddhist scriptures are regarded in that way by many orthodox believers), as belonging to past history just as surely as their tribal predecessors do. Religion can move to a more universal phase, in which insights are selected from many traditions, while most of their differences are relegated to the museum of dead beliefs. I suspect that Hick wishes to commend revisionist pluralism, too. There is much to be said for it, but it cannot be said that it sees all existing traditions as equally valid perceptions of truth. On the contrary, most existing traditions have to be radically purged of error, in the light of the more adequate views of a post-Critical age. It is ironic that this view, which sees the great traditions as "earlier stages in an evolution of which it is the culmination" is precisely of the type which Hick earlier characterises as unacceptably arrogant (2). Revisionist pluralism makes its own absolute and exclusive claim—it is just true that there is one Reality of supreme value which will bring all creatures to good; and anything which denies this or tries to restrict the ways in which this may happen is false.

Revisionist pluralism is incompatible with hard pluralism, since it denies that unrevised traditions are equally adequate forms of religious truth. It is compatible with soft pluralism, but not entailed by it, since it is possible that one existing tradition characterizes the Real most adequately; that is, that its central truth-claims are more adequately descriptive of the Real than competing alternatives. To the extent that the Real is a personal and active self-disclosing agent, one might think that an existing tradition which claims to have witnessed the self-disclosing acts of this agent is more likely to be adequate than the conclusions of a highly abstract and speculative philosophical hypothesis. But that is a question of the acceptability and coherence of particular conceptions of ultimate reality, which needs to be argued out in detail. One thing is certain, that revisionist pluralism is not in a position to assert moral superiority, greater tolerance or greater impartiality over any particular tradition as such, when traditions are taken as not excluding ultimate salvation for others, since the claims each must make for itself are logically on a par.

Religious believers do not have to suppose that the majority of the human race are excluded from salvation, as long as they have a view which allows for a development of knowledge after death. They are, however, committed to thinking that most people are mistaken in their beliefs about the ultimate nature of reality. That is, after all, not a very surprising thought, though it is a sad one. It should lead to a keen sense of one's own fallibility, a deeper appreciation of the attempts of others to understand human nature and destiny, and a firm stress on the primacy of moral and spiritual practice in religion. These are the leading themes of John Hick's recent work, which he formulates in the pluralist hypothesis. I have suggested that in at least one sense (soft pluralism) his case is persuasive. There are other senses, however, which, if I am right, are not sustainable. On this, at least, truth is exclusive, and one of us must be wrong.

Note

*   [John Hick, *An Interpretation of Religion: Human Responses to the Transcendent* (New Haven and London: Yale University Press, 1989), p. 3. Page references to this work will be made parenthetically throughout this chapter.]

Questions for reflection

1   Describe one of the central criticisms of the pluralistic hypothesis offered by Professor Ward. Do you agree with him? Why or why not?
2   Do you hold to hard pluralism? Soft pluralism? Revisionist pluralism? Explain your own position regarding these different viewpoints and why you hold it.
3   Do you agree with Professor Ward's assessment that hard pluralism is incoherent? Explain.
4   How would you define religious truth?

Further reading

Gavin D'Costa (1986) *Theology and Religious Pluralism*. Oxford: Blackwell. (A critique of Hick.)
John Hick (2004) *An Interpretation of Religion*. 2nd edn. New Haven, CT: Yale University Press. (Hick's definition of "pluralism" is offered in chapter 8.)
Harold Netland (1991) *Dissonant Voices*. Grand Rapids, MI: Eerdmans. (An evangelical response.)
Alan Race (1983) *Christians and Religious Pluralism*. London: SCMP. (Where the trichotomy exclusivist, inclusivist, and pluralist first appears.)
Keith Ward (2004) *The Case for Religion*. Oxford: Oneworld. (An alternative reading of pluralism to Hick's.)

Chapter 3

Alvin Plantinga

A DEFENSE OF RELIGIOUS EXCLUSIVISM

Alvin Plantinga is John A. O'Brien Professor of Philosophy at the University of Notre Dame. In this selection he responds to two types of objections to religious exclusivism—the view that at least some of the tenets of one religion are true and that propositions which are incompatible with those tenets are false. The first type of objection is a moral one in which it is claimed that the exclusivist is arrogant, dishonest, oppressive, or the like. The second type of objection is an intellectual or epistemic one, and he focuses on three varieties: (1) a *justification* objection in which it is claimed that the exclusivist holds unjustified beliefs; (2) an *irrationality* objection in which it is claimed that it is not rational to affirm exclusivism; and (3) a *warrant* objection in which it is claimed that the exclusivist has no, or at least not much, warrant for his exclusivist position. These objections, argues Plantinga, are either unsatisfactory or worse, self-defeating. However, he concludes by noting that the realities of religious pluralism—the wide variety of human religious response—could reduce one's degree of belief in her exclusivist views. On the other hand, it could also have just the opposite effect; it could bring about a deepened understanding of and appreciation for her exclusivist views.

When I was a graduate student at Yale, the philosophy department prided itself on diversity: and it was indeed diverse. There were idealists, pragmatists, phenomenologists, existentialists, Whiteheadians, historians of philosophy, a token positivist, and what could only be described as observers of the passing intellectual scene. In some ways, this was indeed something to take pride in; a student could behold and encounter real live representatives of many of the main traditions in philosophy. It also had an unintended and unhappy side effect, however. If anyone raised a philosophical question inside, but particularly outside, class, the typical response would be a catalog of some of the various different answers the world has seen: there is the Aristotelian answer, the existentialist answer, the Cartesian answer, Heidegger's answer, perhaps the Buddhist answer, and so on. But the question "what is the truth about this matter?" was often greeted with disdain as unduly naive. There are all these different answers, all endorsed by people of great intellectual power and great dedication to philosophy; for every argument *for* one of these positions, there is another *against* it; would it not be excessively naive, or perhaps arbitrary, to suppose that one of these is in fact *true*, the others being false? Or, if there really is a truth of the matter, so that one of them is true and conflicting ones false, wouldn't it be merely arbitrary, in the face of this embarrassment of riches, to *endorse* one of them as the truth, consigning the others to falsehood? How could you possibly know which was true?

Some urge a similar attitude with respect to the impressive variety of religions the world displays. There are theistic religions but also at least some nontheistic religions (or perhaps nontheistic strands of religion) among the enormous variety of religions going under the names "Hinduism" and "Buddhism"; among the theistic religions, there are strands of Hinduism and Buddhism and American Indian religion as well as Islam, Judaism, and Christianity; and all these differ significantly from one another. Isn't it somehow arbitrary, or irrational, or unjustified, or unwarranted, or even oppressive and imperialistic to endorse one of these as opposed to all the others? According to Jean Bodin, "each is refuted by all"[1]; must we not agree? It is in this neighborhood that the so-called problem of pluralism arises. Of course, many concerns and problems can come under this rubric; the specific problem I mean to discuss can be thought of as follows. To put it in an internal and personal way, I find myself with religious beliefs, and religious beliefs that I realize aren't shared by nearly everyone else. For example, I believe both

> (1) The world was created by God, an almighty, all-knowing, and perfectly good personal being (one that holds beliefs; has aims, plans, and intentions; and can act to accomplish these aims)

and

> (2) Human beings require salvation, and God has provided a unique way of salvation through the incarnation, life, sacrificial death, and resurrection of his divine son.

Now there are many who do not believe these things. First, there are those who agree with me on (1) but not (2): there are non-Christian theistic religions. Second, there are those who don't accept either (1) or (2) but nonetheless do believe that there is something beyond the natural world, a something such that human well-being and salvation depend upon standing in a right relation to it. And third, in the West and since the Enlightenment, anyway, there are people—*naturalists*, we may call them—who don't believe any of these three things. And my problem is this: when I become really aware of these other ways of looking at the world, these other ways of responding religiously to the world, what must or should I do? What is the right sort of attitude to take? What sort of impact should this awareness have on the beliefs I hold and the strength with which I hold them? My question is this: how should I think about the great religious diversity the world in fact displays? Can I sensibly remain an adherent of just one of these religions, rejecting the others? And here I am thinking specifically of *beliefs*. Of course, there is a great deal more to any religion or religious practice than just belief, and I don't for a moment mean to deny it. But belief is a crucially important part of most religions; it is a crucially important part of *my* religion; and the question I mean to ask here is what the awareness of religious diversity means or should mean for my religious beliefs.

Some speak here of a *new* awareness of religious diversity, and speak of this new awareness as constituting (for us in the West) a crisis, a revolution, an intellectual development of the same magnitude as the Copernican revolution of the sixteenth century and the alleged discovery of evolution and our animal origins in the nineteenth.[2] No doubt there is at least some truth to this. Of course, the fact is all along many Western Christians and Jews have known that there are other religions and that not nearly everyone shares *their* religion.[3] The ancient Israelites—some of the prophets, say—were clearly aware of Canaanitish religion; and the apostle Paul said that he preached "Christ crucified, a stumbling block to Jews and folly to the Greeks" (I Cor. 1:23). Other early Christians, the Christian martyrs, say, must have suspected that not everyone believed as they did. The church fathers, in offering defenses of Christianity, were certainly apprised of this fact; Origen, indeed, wrote an eight-volume reply to Celsus, who urged an argument similar to those put forward by contemporary pluralists. Aquinas, again, was clearly aware of those to whom he addressed the *Summa contra gentiles*, and the fact that there are non-Christian religions would have come as no surprise to the Jesuit missionaries of the sixteenth and seventeenth centuries or to the Methodist missionaries of the nineteenth. In more recent times, when I was a child, *The Banner*, the official publication of the Christian Reformed Church, contained a small column for children; it was written by "Uncle Dick," who exhorted us to save our nickels and send them to our Indian cousins at the Navaho mission in New Mexico. Both we and our elders knew that the Navahos had or had had a religion different from Christianity, and part of the point of sending the nickels was to try to rectify that situation.

Still, in recent years probably more of us Western Christians have become aware of the world's religious diversity; we have probably learned more about people of other religious persuasions, and we have come to see more clearly that they display what looks like real piety, devoutness, and spirituality. What is new, perhaps, is a more widespread sympathy for other religions, a tendency to see them as more valuable, as containing more by way of truth, and a new feeling of solidarity with their practitioners.

There are several possible reactions to awareness of religious diversity. One is to continue to believe what you have all along believed; you learn about this diversity but continue to believe, that is, take to be true, such propositions as (1) and (2) above, consequently taking to be false any beliefs, religious or otherwise, that are incompatible with (1) and (2). Following current practice, I call this *exclusivism*; the exclusivist holds that the tenets or some of the tenets of *one* religion—Christianity, let's say—are in fact true; he adds, naturally enough, that any propositions, including other religious beliefs, that are incompatible with those tenets are false. Now there is a fairly widespread belief that there is something seriously wrong with exclusivism. It is irrational, or egotistical and unjustified,[4] or intellectually arrogant,[5] or elitist,[6] or a manifestation of harmful pride,[7] or even oppressive and imperialistic.[8] The claim is that exclusivism as such is or involves a vice of some sort: it is wrong or deplorable; and it is this claim I want to examine. I propose to argue that exclusivism need not involve either epistemic or moral failure and that furthermore something like it is wholly unavoidable, given our human condition.

These objections are not to the *truth* of (1) or (2) or any other proposition some-one might accept in this exclusivist way (although, of course, objections of that sort are also put forward); they are instead directed to the *propriety* or *rightness* of exclusivism. And there are initially two different kinds of indictments of exclusivism: broadly moral or ethical indictments and broadly intellectual or epistemic indictments. These over-lap in interesting ways, as we shall see below. But initially, anyway, we can take some of the complaints about exclusivism as *intellectual* criticisms: it is *irrational* or *unjustified* to think in an exclusivistic way. And the other large body of complaint is moral: there is something *morally* suspect about exclusivism: it is arbitrary, or intellectually arro-gant, or imperialistic. As Joseph Runzo suggests, exclusivism is "neither tolerable nor any longer intellectually honest in the context of our contemporary knowledge of other faiths."[9] I want to consider both kinds of claims or criticisms; I propose to argue that the exclusivist is not as such necessarily guilty of any of these charges.

Moral objections to exclusivism

I first turn to the moral complaints: that the exclusivist is intellectually arrogant, or ego-tistical, or self-servingly arbitrary, or dishonest, or imperialistic, or oppressive. But first three qualifications. An exclusivist, like anyone else, will probably be guilty of some or all of these things to at least some degree, perhaps particularly the first two; the question is, however, whether she is guilty of these things just by virtue of being an exclusivist. Second, I shall use the term "exclusivism" in such a way that you don't count as an exclusivist unless you are rather fully aware of other faiths, have had their existence and their claims called to your attention with some force and perhaps fairly frequently, and have to some degree reflected on the problem of pluralism, asking yourself such questions as whether it is or could be really true that the Lord has revealed himself and his programs to us Christians, say, in a way in which he hasn't revealed himself to those of other faiths. Thus my grandmother, for example, would not have counted as an exclusivist. She had, of course, *heard* of the heathen, as she called them, but the idea that perhaps Christians could learn from them, and learn from them with respect to reli-gious matters, had not so much as entered her head; and the fact that it *hadn't* entered her head, I take it, was not a matter of moral dereliction on her part. The same would go for a Buddhist or Hindu peasant. These people are not, I think, plausibly charged with arrogance or other moral flaws in believing as they do.

Third, suppose I am an exclusivist with respect to (1), for example, but nonculpably believe, like Thomas Aquinas, say, that I have a knock-down, drag-out argument, a demonstration or conclusive proof of the proposition that there is such a person as God; and suppose I think further (and nonculpably) that if those who don't believe (1) were to be apprised of this argument (and had the ability and training necessary to grasp it, and were to think about the argument fairly and reflectively), they too would come to believe (1). Then I could hardly be charged with these moral faults. My condition would be like that of Gödel, let's say, upon having recognized that he had a proof for the incompleteness of arithmetic. True, many of his colleagues and peers didn't believe that arithmetic was incomplete, and some believed that it *was* complete; but presumably Gödel wasn't arbitrary or egotistical in believing that arithmetic is in fact incomplete. Furthermore, he would not have been at fault had he nonculpably but *mistakenly* believed that he had found such a proof. Accordingly, I shall use the term "exclusivist" in such a way that you don't count as an exclusivist if you nonculpably think you know of a demonstration or conclusive argument for the beliefs with respect to which you are an exclusivist, or even if you nonculpably think you know of an argument that would convince all or most intelligent and honest people of the truth of that proposition. So an exclusivist, as I use the term, not only believes something like (1) or (2) and thinks false any proposition incompatible with it; she also meets a further condition C that is hard to state precisely and in detail (and in fact any attempt to do so would involve a long and at present irrelevant discussion of ceteris paribus clauses). Suffice it to say that C includes (1) being rather fully aware of other religions, (2) knowing that there is much that at the least looks like genuine piety and devoutness in them, and (3) believing that you know of no arguments that would necessarily convince all or most honest and intelligent dissenters of your own religious allegiances.

Given these qualifications, then, why should we think that an exclusivist is properly charged with these moral faults? I shall deal first and most briefly with charges of oppression and imperialism: I think we must say that they are on the face of it wholly implausible. I daresay there are some among you who reject some of the things I believe; I do not believe that you are thereby oppressing me, even if you do not believe you have an argument that would convince me. It is conceivable that exclusivism might in some way *contribute to* oppression, but it isn't in itself oppressive.

The important moral charge is that there is a sort of self-serving arbitrariness, an arrogance or egotism, in accepting such propositions as (1) or (2) under condition C; exclusivism is guilty of some serious moral fault or flaw. According to Wilfred Cantwell Smith, "except at the cost of insensitivity or delinquency, it is morally not possible actually to go out into the world and say to devout, intelligent, fellow human beings: '. . . we believe that we know God and we are right; you believe that you know God, and you are totally wrong.'"[10]

So what can the exclusivist have to say for herself? Well, it must be conceded immediately that if she believes (1) or (2), then she must also believe that those who believe something incompatible with them are mistaken and believe what is false. That's no more than simple logic. Furthermore, she must also believe that those who do not believe as she does—those who believe neither (1) nor (2), whether or not they believe their negations—*fail* to believe something that is true, deep, and important, and that she *does* believe. She must therefore see herself as *privileged* with respect to those others—those others of both kinds. There is something of great value, she must think, that *she* has and *they* lack. They are ignorant of something—something of great importance—of which she has knowledge. But does this make her properly subject to the above censure?

I think the answer must be no. Or if the answer is yes, then I think we have here a genuine moral dilemma; for in our earthly life here below, as my Sunday School teacher used to say, there is no real alternative; there is no reflective attitude that is not open to the same strictures. These charges of arrogance are a philosophical tar baby: get close enough to them to use them against the exclusivist, and you are likely to find them stuck fast to yourself. How so? Well, as an exclusivist, I realize I can't convince others that they should believe as I do, but I nonetheless continue to believe as I do: and the charge is that I am as a result arrogant or egotistical, arbitrarily preferring my way of doing things to other ways.[11] But what are my alternatives with respect to a proposition like (1)? There seem to be three choices.[12] I can continue to hold it; I can withhold it, in Roderick Chisholm's sense, believing neither it nor its denial; and I can accept its denial. Consider the third way, a way taken by those pluralists who, like John Hick, hold that such propositions as (1) and (2) and their colleagues from other faiths are literally false although in some way still valid responses to the Real. This seems to me to be no advance at all with respect to the arrogance or egotism problem; this is not a way out. For if I do this, I will then be in the very same condition as I am now: I will believe many propositions others don't believe and will be in condition C with respect to those propositions. For I will then believe the denials of (1) and (2) (as well as the denials of many other propositions explicitly accepted by those of other faiths). Many others, of course, do not believe the denials of (1) and (2), and in fact believe (1) and (2). Further, I will not know of any arguments that can be counted on to persuade those who do believe (1) and (2) (or propositions accepted by the adherents of other religions). I am therefore in the condition of believing propositions that many others do not believe and furthermore am in condition C. If, in the case of those who believe (1) and (2), that is sufficient for intellectual arrogance or egotism, the same goes for those who believe their denials.

So consider the second option: I can instead *withhold* the proposition in question. I can say to myself: "the right course here, given that I can't or couldn't convince these others of what *I* believe, is to believe neither these propositions nor their denials." The pluralist objector to exclusivism can say that the right course under condition C is to *abstain* from believing the offending proposition and also abstain from believing its denial; call him, therefore, "the abstemious pluralist." But does he thus really avoid the condition that, on the part of the exclusivist, leads to the charges of egotism and arrogance? Think, for a moment, about disagreement. Disagreement, fundamentally, is a matter of adopting conflicting propositional attitudes with respect to a given proposition. In the simplest and most familiar case, I disagree with you if there is some proposition p such that I believe p and you believe $-p$. But that's just the simplest case: there are also others. The one that is at present of interest is this: I believe p and you withhold it, fail to believe it. Call the first kind of disagreement "contradicting"; call the second "dissenting."

My claim is that if contradicting others (under the condition C spelled out above) is arrogant and egotistical, so is dissenting (under that same condition). For suppose you believe some proposition p but I don't: perhaps you believe it is wrong to discriminate against people simply on the grounds of race, but I, recognizing that there are many people who disagree with you, do not believe this proposition. I don't disbelieve it either, of course, but in the circumstances I think the right thing to do is to abstain from belief. Then am I not implicitly condemning your attitude, your *believing* the proposition, as somehow improper—naive, perhaps, or unjustified, or in some other way less than optimal? I am implicitly saying that my attitude is the superior one; I think my course of action here is the right one and yours somehow wrong, inadequate, improper, in the circumstances at best second-rate. Also, I realize that there is no question, here, of *showing* you that your attitude is wrong or improper or naive; so am I not guilty of intellectual arrogance? Of a sort of egotism, thinking I know better than you, arrogating to myself a privileged status with respect to you? The problem for the exclusivist was that she was obliged to think she possessed a truth missed by many others; the problem for the abstemious pluralist is that he is obliged to think he possesses a virtue others don't, or acts rightly where others don't. If, in condition C, one is arrogant by way of believing a proposition others don't, isn't one equally, under those reflective conditions, arrogant by way of withholding a proposition others don't?

Perhaps you will respond by saying that the abstemious pluralist gets into trouble, falls into arrogance, by way of implicitly saying or believing that his way of proceeding is *better* or *wiser* than other ways pursued by other people, and perhaps he can escape by abstaining from *that* view as well. Can't he escape the problem by refraining from believing that racial bigotry is wrong, and also refraining from holding the view that it is *better*, under the conditions that obtain, to withhold that proposition than to assert and believe it? Well, yes, he can; then he has no *reason* for his abstention; he doesn't believe that abstention is better or more appropriate; he simply does abstain. Does this get him off the egotistical hook? Perhaps. But then, of course, he can't, in consistency, also hold that there is something wrong with *not* abstaining, with coming right out and *believing* that bigotry is wrong; he loses his objection to the exclusivist. Accordingly, this way out is not available for the abstemious pluralist who accuses the exclusivist of arrogance and egotism.

Indeed, I think we can show that the abstemious pluralist who brings charges of intellectual arrogance against exclusivism is hoist with his own petard, holds a position that in a certain way is self-referentially inconsistent in the circumstances. For he believes

(3) If S knows that others don't believe *p* and that he is in condition C with respect to *p*, then S should not believe *p*;

this or something like it is the ground of the charges he brings against the exclusivist. But, the abstemious pluralist realizes that many do not accept (3); and I suppose he also realizes that it is unlikely that he can find arguments for (3) that will convince them; hence he knows that he is in condition C. Given his acceptance of (3), therefore, the right course for him is to abstain from believing (3). Under the conditions that do in fact obtain—namely, his knowledge that others don't accept it and that condition C obtains—he can't properly accept it.

I am therefore inclined to think that one can't, in the circumstances, properly hold (3) or any other proposition that will do the job. One can't find here some principle on the basis of which to hold that the exclusivist is doing the wrong thing, suffers from some moral fault—that is, one can't find such a principle that doesn't, as we might put it, fall victim to itself.

So the abstemious pluralist is hoist with his own petard; but even apart from this dialectical argument (which in any event some will think unduly cute), aren't the charges unconvincing and implausible? I must concede that there are a variety of ways in which I can be and have been intellectually arrogant and egotistic; I have certainly fallen into this vice in the past and no doubt am not free of it now. But am I really arrogant and egotistic just by virtue of believing what I know others don't believe, where I can't show them that I am right? Suppose I think the matter over, consider the objections as carefully as I can, realize that I am finite and furthermore a sinner, certainly no better than those with whom I disagree, and indeed inferior both morally and intellectually to many who do not believe what I do; but suppose it *still* seems clear to me that the proposition in question is true: can I really be behaving immorally in continuing to believe it? I am dead sure that it is wrong to try to advance my career by telling lies about my colleagues; I realize there are those who disagree; I also realize that in all likelihood there is no way I can find to show them that they are wrong; nonetheless, I think they *are* wrong. If I think this after careful reflection—if I consider the claims of those who disagree as sympathetically as I can, if I try my level best to ascertain the truth here—and it *still* seems to me sleazy, wrong, and despicable to lie about my colleagues to advance my career, could I really be doing something immoral in continuing to believe as before? I can't see how. If, after careful reflection and thought, you find yourself convinced that the right propositional attitude to take to (1) and (2) in the face of the facts of religious pluralism is abstention from belief, how could you properly be taxed with egotism, either for so believing or for so abstaining? Even if you knew others did not agree with you? So I can't see how the moral charge against exclusivism can be sustained.

Epistemic objections to exclusivism

I turn now to *epistemic* objections to exclusivism. There are many different specifically epistemic virtues, and a corresponding plethora of epistemic vices; the ones with which the exclusivist is most frequently charged, however, are *irrationality* and *lack of justification* in holding his exclusivist beliefs. The claim is that as an exclusivist, he holds unjustified beliefs and/or irrational beliefs. Better, *he* is unjustified or irrational in holding these beliefs. I shall therefore consider those two claims, and I shall argue that the exclusivistic views need not be either unjustified or irrational. I shall then turn to the question whether his beliefs could have *warrant*: that property, whatever precisely it is, that distinguishes knowledge from mere true belief, and whether they could have enough warrant for knowledge.

Justification

The pluralist objector sometimes claims that to hold exclusivist views, in condition C, is *unjustified—epistemically* unjustified. Is this true? And what does he mean when he makes this claim? As even a brief glance at the contemporary epistemological literature shows, justification is a protean and multifarious notion.[13] There are, I think, substantially two possibilities as to what he means. The central core of the notion, its beating heart, the paradigmatic center to which most of the myriad contemporary variations are related by way of analogical extension and family resemblance, is the notion of *being within one's intellectual rights*, having violated no intellectual or cognitive duties or obligations in the formation and sustenance of the belief in question. This is the palimpsest, going back to Descartes and especially Locke, that underlies the multitudinous battery of contemporary inscriptions. There is no space to argue that point here; but chances are when the pluralist objector to exclusivism claims that the latter is unjustified, it is some notion lying in this neighborhood that he has in mind. (And, here we should note the very close connection between the moral objections to exclusivism and the objection that exclusivism is epistemically unjustified.)

 The duties involved, naturally enough, would be specifically *epistemic* duties: perhaps a duty to proportion degree of belief to (propositional) evidence from what is *certain*, that is, self-evident or incorrigible, as with Locke, or perhaps to try one's best to get into and stay in the right relation to the truth, as with Roderick Chisholm,[14] the leading contemporary champion of the justificationist tradition with respect to knowledge.

But at present there is widespread (and, as I see it, correct) agreement that there is no duty of the Lockean kind. Perhaps there is one of the Chisholmian kind,[15] but isn't the exclusivist conforming to that duty if, after the sort of careful, indeed prayerful, consideration I mentioned in the response to the moral objection, it still seems to him strongly that (1), say, is true and he accordingly still believes it? It is therefore hard to see that the exclusivist is necessarily unjustified in this way.

The second possibility for understanding the charge—the charge that exclusivism is epistemically unjustified—has to do with the oft-repeated claim that exclusivism is intellectually arbitrary. Perhaps the idea is that there is an intellectual duty to treat similar cases similarly; the exclusivist violates this duty by arbitrarily choosing to believe (for the moment going along with the fiction that we choose beliefs of this sort) (1) and (2) in the face of the plurality of conflicting religious beliefs the world presents. But suppose there is such a duty. Clearly, you do not violate it if you nonculpably think the beliefs in question are not on a par. And, as an exclusivist, I do think (nonculpably, I hope) that they are not on a par: I think (1) and (2) true and those incompatible with either of them false.

The rejoinder, of course, will be that it is not alethic parity (their having the same truth value) that is at issue: it is epistemic parity that counts. What kind of epistemic parity? What would be relevant here, I should think, would be internal or internalist epistemic parity: parity with respect to what is internally available to the believer. What is internally available to the believer includes, for example, detectable relationships between the belief in question and other beliefs you hold; so internal parity would include parity of propositional evidence. What is internally available to the believer also includes the phenomenology that goes with the beliefs in question: the sensuous phenomenology, but also the nonsensuous phenomenology involved, for example, in the belief's just having the feel of being right. But once more, then, (1) and (2) are not on an internal par, for the exclusivist, with beliefs that are incompatible with them. (1) and (2), after all, seem to me to be true; they have for me the phenomenology that accompanies that seeming. The same cannot be said for propositions incompatible with them. If, furthermore, John Calvin is right in thinking that there is such a thing as the Sensus Divinitatis and the Internal Testimony of the Holy Spirit, then perhaps (1) and (2) are produced in me by those belief-producing processes, and have for me the phenomenology that goes with them; the same is not true for propositions incompatible with them.

But then the next rejoinder: isn't it probably true that those who reject (1) and (2) in favor of other beliefs have propositional evidence for their beliefs that is on a par with mine for my beliefs; and isn't it also probably true that the same or similar phenomenology accompanies their beliefs as accompanies mine? So that those beliefs really are epistemically and internally on a par with (1) and (2), and the exclusivist is still treating like cases differently? I don't think so: I think there really are arguments available for (1), at least, that are not available for its competitors. And as for similar phenomenology, this is not easy to say; it is not easy to look into the breast of another; the secrets of the human heart are hard to fathom; it is hard indeed to discover this sort of thing even with respect to someone you know really well. But I am prepared to stipulate both sorts of parity. Let's agree for purposes of argument that these beliefs are on an epistemic par in the sense that those of a different religious tradition have the same sort of internally available markers—evidence, phenomenology, and the like—for their beliefs as I have for (1) and (2). What follows?

Return to the case of moral belief. King David took Bathsheba, made her pregnant, and then, after the failure of various stratagems to get her husband Uriah to think the baby was his, arranged for Uriah to be killed. The prophet Nathan came to David and told him a story about a rich man and a poor man. The rich man had many flocks and herds; the poor man had only a single ewe lamb, which grew up with his children, "ate at his table, drank from his cup, lay in his bosom, and was like a daughter to him." The rich man had unexpected guests. Instead of slaughtering one of his own sheep, he took the poor man's single ewe lamb, slaughtered it, and served it to his guests. David exploded in anger: "The man who did this deserves to die!" Then, in one of the most riveting passages in all the Bible, Nathan turns to David, stretches out his arm and points to him, and declares, "You are that man!" And David sees what he has done.

My interest here is in David's reaction to the story. I agree with David: such injustice is utterly and despicably wrong; there are really no words for it. I believe that such an action is wrong, and I believe that the proposition that it isn't wrong—either because really nothing is wrong, or because even if some things are wrong, this isn't—is false. As a matter of fact, there isn't a lot I believe more strongly. I recognize, however, that there are those who disagree with me; and once more, I doubt that I could find an argument to show them that I am right and they wrong. Further, for all I know, their conflicting beliefs have for them the same internally available epistemic markers, the same phenomenology, as mine have for me. Am I then being arbitrary, treating similar cases differently in continuing to hold, as I do, that in fact that kind of behavior is dreadfully wrong? I don't think so. Am I wrong in thinking racial bigotry despicable, even though I know there are others who disagree, and even if I think they have the same internal markers for their beliefs as I have for mine? I don't think so. I believe in Serious Actualism, the view that no objects have properties in worlds in which they do not exist, not even nonexistence. Others do not believe this, and perhaps the internal markers of their dissenting views have for them the same quality as my views have for me. Am I being arbitrary in continuing to think as I do? I can't see how.

And the reason here is this: in each of these cases, the believer in question doesn't really think the beliefs in question are on a relevant epistemic par. She may agree that she and those who dissent are equally convinced of the truth of their belief, and even that they are internally on a par, that the internally available markers are similar, or relevantly similar. But she must still think that there is an important epistemic difference: she thinks that somehow the other person has made a mistake, or has a blind spot, or hasn't been wholly attentive, or hasn't received some grace she has, or is in some way epistemically less fortunate. And, of course, the pluralist critic is in no better case. He thinks the thing to do when there is internal epistemic parity is to withhold judgment; he knows there are others who don't think so, and for all he knows, that belief has internal parity with his; if he continues in that belief, therefore, he will be in the same condition as the exclusivist; and if he doesn't continue in this belief, he no longer has an objection to the exclusivist.

But couldn't I be wrong? Of course I could! But I don't avoid that risk by withholding all religious (or philosophical or moral) beliefs; I can go wrong that way as well as any other, treating all religions, or all philosophical thoughts, or all moral views, as on a par. Again, there is no safe haven here, no way to avoid risk. In particular, you won't reach safe haven by trying to take the same attitude toward all the historically available patterns of belief and withholding: for in so doing, you adopt a particular pattern of belief and withholding, one incompatible with some adopted by others. You pays your money and you takes your choice, realizing that you, like anyone else, can be desperately wrong. But what else can you do? You don't really have an alternative. And how can you do better than believe and withhold according to what, after serious and responsible consideration, seems to you to be the right pattern of belief and withholding?

Irrationality

I therefore can't see how it can be sensibly maintained that the exclusivist is unjustified in his exclusivistic views; but perhaps, as is sometimes claimed, he or his view is irrational. Irrationality, however, is many things to many people; so there is a prior question: what is it to be irrational? More exactly: precisely what quality is it that the objector is attributing to the exclusivist (in condition C) when the former says the latter's exclusivist beliefs are irrational? Since the charge is never developed at all fully, it isn't easy to say. So suppose we simply consider the main varieties of irrationality (or, if you prefer, the main senses of "irrational") and ask whether any of them attach to the exclusivist just by virtue of being an exclusivist. I believe there are substantially five varieties of rationality, five distinct but analogically[16] connected senses of the term "rational"; fortunately, not all of them require detailed consideration.

1   *Aristotelian Rationality.* This is the sense in which man is a rational animal, one that has *ratio*, one that can look before and after, can hold beliefs, make inferences, and is capable of knowledge. This is perhaps the basic sense, the one of which the others are analogical extensions. It is also, presumably, irrelevant in the present context; at any rate, I hope the objector does not mean to hold that an exclusivist will by that token no longer be a rational animal.

2   *The Deliverances of Reason.* To be rational in the Aristotelian sense is to possess reason: the power of thinking, believing, inferring, reasoning, knowing. Aristotelian rationality is thus *generic*. But there is an important more specific sense lurking in the neighborhood; this is the sense that goes with reason taken more narrowly, as the source of a priori knowledge and belief.[17] An important use of "rational" analogically connected with the first has to do with reason taken in this more narrow way. It is by reason thus construed that we know *self-evident* beliefs—beliefs so obvious that you can't so much as grasp them without seeing that they couldn't be false. These are among the *deliverances of reason*. Of course, there are other beliefs—$38 \times 39 = 1482$, for example—that are not self-evident but are a consequence of self-evident beliefs by way of arguments that are self-evidently valid; these too are among the deliverances of reason. So say that the deliverances of reason are the set of those propositions that are self-evident for us human beings, closed under self-evident consequence. This yields another sense of rationality: a belief is *rational* if it is among the deliverances of reason and *irrational* if it is contrary to the deliverances of reason. (A belief can therefore be neither rational nor irrational, in this sense.) This sense of "rational" is an analogical extension of the fundamental sense, but it is itself extended by analogy to still other senses. Thus we can broaden the category of reason to include memory,

experience, induction, probability, and whatever else goes into science; this is the sense of the term when reason is sometimes contrasted with faith. And we can also soften the requirement for self-evidence, recognizing both that self-evidence or a priori warrant is a matter of degree, and that there are many propositions that have a priori warrant but are not such that no one who understands them can fail to believe them.[18]

Is the exclusivist irrational in *these* senses? I think not; or at any rate the question whether he is isn't the question at issue. For his exclusivist beliefs are irrational in these senses only if there is a good argument from the deliverances of reason (taken broadly) to the denials of what he believes. I myself do not believe there are any such arguments. Presumably, the same goes for the pluralist objector; at any rate his objection is not that (1) and (2) are demonstrably false or even that there are good arguments against them from the deliverances of reason; his objection is instead that there is something wrong or subpar with believing them in condition C. This sense too, then, is irrelevant to our present concerns.

3   *The Deontological Sense.* This sense of the term has to do with intellectual *require-ment*, or *duty*, or *obligation*: a person's belief is irrational in this sense if in forming or holding it she violates such a duty. This is the sense of "irrational" in which, according to many contemporary evidentialist objectors to theistic belief, those who believe in God without propositional evidence are irrational.[19] Irrationality in this sense is a matter of failing to conform to intellectual or epistemic duties; and the analogical connection with the first, Aristotelian sense is that these duties are thought to be among the deliverances of reason (and hence among the deliverances of the power by virtue of which human beings are rational in the Aristotelian sense). But we have already considered whether the exclusivist is flouting duties; we need say no more about the matter here. As we saw, the exclusivist is not nec-essarily irrational in this sense either.

4   *Zweckrationalität.* A common and very important notion of rationality is *means-end* rationality—what our Continental cousins, following Max Weber, sometimes call *Zweckrationalität*, the sort of rationality displayed by your actions if they are well cal-culated to achieve your goals. (Again, the analogical connection with the first sense is clear: the calculation in question requires the power by virtue of which we are rational in Aristotle's sense.) Clearly, there is a whole constellation of notions lurk-ing in the nearby bushes: what would *in fact* contribute to your goals, what you *take* it would contribute to your goals, what you *would* take it would contribute to your goals if you were sufficiently acute, or knew enough, or weren't distracted by lust, greed, pride, ambition, and the like, what you would take it would contribute to your goals if you weren't thus distracted and were also to reflect sufficiently, and so on. This notion of rationality has assumed enormous impor-tance in the last one hundred fifty years or so. (Among its laurels, for example, is the complete domination of the development of the discipline of economics.) Rationality thus construed is a matter of knowing how to get what you want; it is the cunning of reason. Is the exclusivist properly charged with irrationality in this sense? Does his believing in the way he does interfere with his attaining some of his goals, or is it a markedly inferior way of attaining those goals?

An initial caveat: it isn't clear that this notion of rationality applies to belief at all. It isn't clear that in *believing* something, I am acting to achieve some goal. If believing is an action at all, it is very far from being the paradigmatic kind of action taken to achieve some end; we don't have a choice as to whether to have beliefs, and we don't have a lot of choice with respect to which beliefs we have. But suppose we set this caveat aside and stipulate for purposes of argument that we have sufficient control over our beliefs for them to qualify as actions: would the exclusivist's beliefs then be irrational in this sense? Well, that depends upon what his goals *are*; if among his goals for religious belief is, for example, not believing anything not believed by someone else, then indeed it would be. But, of course, he needn't have *that* goal. If I do have an end or goal in holding such beliefs as (1) and (2), it would presumably be that of believing the truth on this exceedingly important matter, or perhaps that of trying to get in touch as adequately as possible with God, or more broadly with the deepest reality. And if (1) and (2) are *true*, believing them will be a way of doing exactly that. It is only if they are *not* true, then, that believing them could sensibly be thought to be irrational in this means-ends sense. Since the objector does not propose to take as a premise the proposition that (1) and (2) are false—he holds only that there is some flaw involved in *believing* them—this also is presumably not what he means.

5   *Rationality as Sanity and Proper Function.* One in the grip of pathological confusion, or flight of ideas, or certain kinds of agnosia, or the manic phase of manic-depressive psychosis will often be said to be irrational; the episode may pass, after which he regains rationality. Here "rationality" means absence of dysfunction, disorder, impairment, pathology with respect to rational faculties. So this variety of rationality is again analogically related to Aristotelian rationality; a person is rational in this sense when no malfunction obstructs her use of the faculties by virtue of the possession of which she is rational in the Aristotelian sense. Rationality as sanity does not require possession of particularly exalted rational faculties; it requires only normality (in the nonstatistical sense), or health, or proper function. This use of the term, naturally enough, is prominent in psychiatric discussions—Oliver Sacks's man who mistook his wife for a hat,[20] for example, was thus irrational.[21] This fifth and final sense of rationality is itself a family of analogically related senses. The fundamental sense here is that of sanity and proper function, but there are other closely related senses. Thus we may say that a belief (in certain circumstances) is irrational not because no sane person would hold it, but because no person who was sane and had also undergone a certain course of education would hold it, or because no person who was sane and furthermore was as intelligent as we and our friends would hold it; alternatively and more briefly, the idea is not merely that no one who was functioning properly in those circumstances would hold it but rather no one who was functioning *optimally*, as well or nearly as well as human beings ordinarily do (leaving aside the occasional great genius), would hold it. And this sense of rationality leads directly to the notion of *warrant*; I turn now to that notion; in treating it we also treat *ambulando* this fifth kind of irrationality.

Warrant

So the third version of the epistemic objection: that at any rate the exclusivist doesn't have warrant, or anyway *much* warrant (enough warrant for knowledge), for his exclusivistic views. Many pluralists—for example, Hick, Runzo, and Wilfred Cantwell Smith—unite in declaring that at any rate the exclusivist certainly can't *know* that his exclusivistic views are true.[22] But is this really true? I shall argue briefly that it is not. At any rate from the perspective of each of the major contemporary accounts of knowledge, it may very well be that the exclusivist knows (1) or (2) or both. First, consider the two main internalistic accounts of knowledge: the justified true belief account(s) and the coherentist account(s). As I have already argued, it seems clear that a theist, a believer in (1), could certainly be *justified* (in the primary sense) in believing as she does: she could be flouting no intellectual or cognitive duties or obligations. But then on the most straightforward justified true belief account of knowledge, she can also *know* that it is true—if, that is, it *can* be true. More exactly, what must be possible is that both the exclusivist is justified in believing (1) and/or (2) and they be true. Presumably, the pluralist does not mean to dispute this possibility.

For concreteness, consider the account of justification given by the classical Chisholm.[23] On this view, a belief has warrant for me to the extent that accepting it is apt for the fulfillment of my epistemic duty, which (roughly speaking) is that of trying to get and remain in the right relation to the truth. But if after the most careful, thorough, thoughtful, open, and prayerful consideration, it still seems to me—perhaps more strongly than ever—that (1) and (2) are true, then clearly accepting them has great aptness for the fulfillment of that duty.[24]

A similarly brief argument can be given with respect to coherentism, the view that what constitutes warrant is coherence with some body of belief. We must distinguish two varieties of coherentism. On the one hand, it might be held that what is required is coherence with some or all of the other beliefs I actually hold; on the other, that what is required is coherence with my *verific* noetic structure (Keith Lehrer's term): the set of beliefs that remains when all the false ones are deleted or replaced by their contradictories. But surely a coherent set of beliefs could include both (1) and (2) together with the beliefs involved in being in condition C; what would be required, perhaps, would be that the set of beliefs contain some explanation of why it is that others do not believe as I do. And if (1) and (2) *are* true, then surely (and a fortiori) there can be coherent verific noetic structures that include them. Hence neither of these versions of coherentism rules out the possibility that the exclusivist in condition C could know (1) and/or (2).

And now consider the main externalist accounts. The most popular externalist account at present would be one or another version of *reliabilism*. And there is an oft-repeated pluralistic argument (an argument that goes back at least to John Stuart Mill's *On Liberty* and possibly all the way back to the third century) that seems to be designed to appeal to reliabilist intuitions. The conclusion of this argument is not always clear, but here is its premise, in John Hick's words:

> For it is evident that in some ninety-nine percent of cases the religion which an individual professes and to which he or she adheres depends upon the accidents of birth. Someone born to Buddhist parents in Thailand is very

likely to be a Buddhist, someone born to Muslim parents in Saudi Arabia to be a Muslim, someone born to Christian parents in Mexico to be a Christian, and so on.[25]

As a matter of sociological fact, this may be right. Furthermore, it can certainly produce a sense of intellectual vertigo. But what is one to do with this fact, if fact it is, and what follows from it? Does it follow, for example, that I ought not to accept the religious views that I have been brought up to accept, or the ones that I find myself inclined to accept, or the ones that seem to me to be true? Or that the belief-producing processes that have produced those beliefs in me are unreliable? Surely not. Furthermore, self-referential problems once more loom; this argument is another philosophical tar baby.

For suppose we concede that if I had been born in Madagascar rather than Michigan, my beliefs would have been quite different.[26] (For one thing, I probably wouldn't believe that I was born in Michigan.) But, of course, the same goes for the pluralist. Pluralism isn't and hasn't been widely popular in the world at large; if the pluralist had been born in Madagascar, or medieval France, he probably wouldn't have been a pluralist. Does it follow that he shouldn't be a pluralist or that his pluralistic beliefs are produced in him by an unreliable belief-producing process? I doubt it. Suppose I hold

(4) If S's religious or philosophical beliefs are such that if S had been born elsewhere and elsewhen, she wouldn't have held them, then those beliefs are produced by unreliable belief-producing mechanisms and hence have no warrant;

or something similar: then once more I will be hoist with my own petard. For in all probability, someone born in Mexico to Christian parents wouldn't believe (4) itself. No matter what philosophical and religious beliefs we hold and withhold (so it seems), there are places and times such that if we had been born there and then, then we would not have displayed the pattern of holding and withholding of religious and philosophical beliefs we *do* display. As I said, this can indeed be vertiginous; but what can we make of it? What can we infer from it about what has warrant and how we should conduct our intellectual lives? That's not easy to say. Can we infer *anything at all* about what has warrant or how we should conduct our intellectual lives? Not obviously.

To return to reliabilism, then: for simplicity, let's take the version of reliabilism according to which S knows *p* iff the belief that *p* is produced in S by a reliable belief-producing mechanism or process. I don't have the space, here, to go into this matter in sufficient detail: but it seems pretty clear that if (1) and (2) are true, then it *could be* that the beliefs that (1) and (2) be produced in me by a reliable belief-producing process. For either we are thinking of *concrete* belief-producing processes, like your memory or John's powers of a priori reasoning (*tokens* as opposed to *types*), or else we are thinking of *types* of belief-producing processes (type reliabilism). The problem with the latter is that there are an enormous number of *different* types of belief-producing processes for any given belief, some of which are reliable and some of which are not; the problem (and a horrifying problem it is[27]) is to say which of these is the type the reliability of which determines whether the belief in question has warrant. So the first (token reliabilism) is the better way of stating reliabilism. But then, clearly enough, if (1) or (2) is true, it could be produced in me by a reliable belief-producing process. Calvin's Sensus

Divinitatis, for example, could be working in the exclusivist in such a way as reliably to produce the belief that (1); Calvin's Internal Testimony of the Holy Spirit could do the same for (2). If (1) and (2) are true, therefore, then from a reliabilist perspective there is no reason whatever to think that the exclusivist might not know that they are true.

There is another brand of externalism that seems to me to be closer to the truth than reliabilism: call it (faute de mieux) "proper functionalism." This view can be stated to a first approximation as follows: S knows *p* iff (1) the belief that *p* is produced in S by cognitive faculties that are functioning properly (working as they ought to work, suffering from no dysfunction), (2) the cognitive environment in which *p* is produced is appropriate for those faculties, (3) the purpose of the module of the epistemic faculties producing the belief in question is to produce true beliefs (alternatively: the module of the design plan governing the production of *p* is aimed at the production of true beliefs), and (4) the objective probability of a belief's being true, given that it is produced under those conditions, is high.[28] All this needs explanation, of course; for present purposes, perhaps, we can collapse the account into the first condition. But then clearly it *could* be, if (1) and (2) are true, that they are produced in me by cognitive faculties functioning properly under condition C. For suppose (1) is true. Then it is surely possible that God has created us human beings with something like Calvin's Sensus Divinitatis, a belief-producing process that in a wide variety of circumstances functions properly to produce (1) or some very similar belief. Furthermore, it is also possible that in response to the human condition of sin and misery, God has provided for us human beings a means of salvation, which he has revealed in the Bible. Still further, perhaps he has arranged for us to come to believe what he means to teach there by way of the operation of something like the Internal Testimony of the Holy Spirit of which Calvin speaks. So on this view, too, if (1) and (2) are true, it is certainly possible that the exclusivist *know* that they are. We can be sure that the exclusivist's views lack warrant and are irrational in this sense, then, only if they are false; but the pluralist objector does not mean to claim that they *are* false; this version of the objection, therefore, also fails. The exclusivist isn't necessarily irrational, and indeed might *know* that (1) and (2) are true, if indeed they *are* true.

All this seems right. But don't the realities of religious pluralism count for anything at all? Is there nothing at all to the claims of the pluralists?[29] Could that really be right? Of course not. For many or most exclusivists, I think, an awareness of the enormous variety of human religious response serves as a *defeater* for such beliefs as (1) and (2)—an *undercutting* defeater, as opposed to a *rebutting* defeater. It calls into question, to some degree or other, the sources of one's belief in (1) or (2). It doesn't or needn't do so by way of an *argument*; and indeed, there isn't a very powerful argument from the proposition that many apparently devout people around the world dissent from (1) and (2) to the conclusion that (1) and (2) are false. Instead, it works more directly; it directly reduces the level of confidence or degree of belief in the proposition in question. From a Christian perspective, this situation of religious pluralism and our awareness of it is itself a manifestation of our miserable human condition; and it may deprive us of some of the comfort and peace the Lord has promised his followers. It can also deprive the exclusivist of the *knowledge* that (1) and (2) are true, even if they *are* true and he *believes* that they are. Since degree of warrant depends in part on degree of belief, it is possible, though not necessary, that knowledge of the facts of religious pluralism should reduce an exclusivist's degree of belief and hence of warrant for (1) and (2) in such a way as to deprive him of knowledge of (1) and (2). He might be such that if he *hadn't* known the facts of pluralism, then he would have known (1) and (2), but now that he *does* know those facts, he doesn't know (1) and (2). In this way he may come to know less by knowing more.

Things *could* go this way with the exclusivist. On the other hand, they *needn't* go this way. Consider once more the moral parallel. Perhaps you have always believed it deeply wrong for a counselor to use his position of trust to seduce a client. Perhaps you discover that others disagree; they think it more like a minor peccadillo, like running a red light when there's no traffic; and you realize that possibly these people have the same internal markers for their beliefs that you have for yours. You think the matter over more fully, imaginatively recreate and rehearse such situations, become more aware of just what is involved in such a situation (the breach of trust, the breaking of implied promises, the injustice and unfairness, the nasty irony of a situation in which someone comes to a counselor seeking help but receives only hurt) and come to believe even more firmly the belief that such an action is wrong—which belief, indeed, can in this way acquire more warrant for you. But something similar can happen in the case of religious beliefs. A fresh or heightened awareness of the facts of religious pluralism could bring about a reappraisal of one's religious life, a reawakening, a new or renewed and deepened grasp and apprehension of (1) and (2). From Calvin's perspective, it could serve as an occasion for a renewed and more powerful working of the belief-producing processes by which we come to apprehend (1) and (2). In that way knowledge of the facts of pluralism could initially serve as a defeater, but in the long run have precisely the opposite effect.

Notes

1   *Colloquium Heptaplomeres de rerum sublimium arcanis abditis,* written by 1593 but first published in 1857. English translation by Marion Kuntz (Princeton: Princeton University Press, 1975). The quotation is for the Kuntz translation, p. 256.

2   Thus Joseph Runzo: "Today, the impressive piety and evident rationality of the belief systems of other religious traditions inescapably confronts Christians with a crisis—and a potential revolution." "God, Commitment, and Other Faiths: Pluralism vs. Relativism," *Faith and Philosophy* 5 (1988), 343.

3   As explained in detail in Robert Wilken, "Religious Pluralism and Early Christian Thought," *Pro Ecclesia* 1 (1992), 89–103. Wilken focuses on the third century; he explores Origen's response to Celsus and concludes that there are striking parallels between Origen's historical situation and ours. What is different today, I suspect, is not that Christianity has to confront other religions but that we now call this situation "religious pluralism."

4   Thus Gary Gutting: "Applying these considerations to religious belief, we seem led to the conclusion that, because believers have many epistemic peers who do not share their belief in God . . . , they have no right to maintain their belief without a justification. If they do so, they are guilty of epistemic egoism." *Religious Belief and Religious Skepticism* (Notre Dame: University of Notre Dame Press, 1982), p. 90 (but see the following pages for an important qualification).

5   "Here my submission is that on this front the traditional doctrinal position of the church has in fact militated against its traditional moral position, and has in fact encouraged Christians to approach other men immorally. Christ has taught us humility, but we have approached

them with arrogance. . . . This charge of arrogance is a serious one." Wilfred Cantwell Smith, *Religious Diversity* (New York: Harper and Row, 1976), p. 13.

6   Runzo, "Ethically, Religious Exclusivism has the morally repugnant result of making those who have privileged knowledge, or who are intellectually astute, a religious elite, while penalizing those who happen to have no access to the putatively correct religious view, or who are incapable of advanced understanding." "God, Commitment, and Other Faiths," p. 348.

7   "But natural pride, despite its positive contribution to human life, becomes harmful when it is elevated to the level of dogma and is built into the belief system of a religious community. This happens when its sense of its own validity and worth is expressed in doctrines implying an exclusive or a decisively superior access to the truth or the power to save." John Hick, "Religious Pluralism and Absolute Claims," in Leroy Rouner, ed., *Religious Pluralism* (Notre Dame: University of Notre Dame Press, 1984), p. 197.

8   Thus John Cobb: "I agree with the liberal theists that even in Pannenberg's case, the quest for an absolute as a basis for understanding reflects the long tradition of Christian imperialism and triumphalism rather than the pluralistic spirit." "The Meaning of Pluralism for Christian Self-Understanding," in Rouner, *Religious Pluralism*, p. 171.

9   "God, Commitment, and Other Faiths," p. 357.

10   Smith, *Religious Diversity*, p. 14. A similar statement: "Nor can we reasonably claim that our own form of religious experience, together with that of the tradition of which we are a part, is veridical whilst others are not. We can of course claim this; and indeed virtually every religious tradition has done so, regarding alternative forms of religion either as false or as confused and inferior versions of itself. . . . Persons living within other traditions, then, are equally justified in trusting their own distinctive religious experience and in forming their beliefs on the basis of it. . . . let us avoid the implausibly arbitrary dogma that religious experience is all delusory with the single exception of the particular form enjoyed by the one who is speaking." John Hick, *An Interpretation of Religion* (New Haven: Yale University Press, 1989), p. 235.

11   "The only reason for treating one's tradition differently from others is the very human but not very cogent reason that it is one's own!" Hick, *An Interpretation of Religion*, p. 235.

12   To speak of a choice here suggests that I can simply choose which of these three attitudes to adopt; but is that at all realistic? Are my beliefs to that degree within my control? Here I shall set aside the question whether and to what degree my beliefs are subject to my control and within my power. Perhaps we have very little control over them; then the moral critic of exclusivism can't properly accuse the exclusivist of dereliction of moral duty, but he could still argue that the exclusivist's stance is unhappy, bad, a miserable state of affairs. Even if I can't help it that I am overbearing and conceited, my being that way is a bad state of affairs.

13   See my "Justification in the Twentieth Century," *Philosophy and Phenomenological Research* 50, supplement (Fall 1990), 45 ff., and see Chapter 1 of my *Warrant: The Current Debate* (New York: Oxford University Press, 1993).

14   See the three editions of *Theory of Knowledge* referred to in Note 23.

15   Some people think there is, and also think that withholding belief, abstaining from belief, is always and automatically the safe course to take with respect to this duty, whenever any question arises as to what to believe and withhold. But that isn't so. One can go wrong by withholding as well as believing: there is no safe haven here, not even abstention. If there is a duty of the Chisholmian kind, and if I, out of epistemic pride and excessive scrupulosity, succeed in training myself not to accept ordinary perceptual judgments in ordinary perceptual circumstances, I am not performing works of epistemic supererogation; I am epistemically culpable.

16   In Aquinas's sense, so that the analogy may include causality, proportionality, resemblance, and the like.

17   But then (because of the Russell paradoxes) we can no longer take it that the deliverances of reason are closed under self-evident consequence. See my *Warrant and Proper Function* (New York: Oxford University Press, 1993), Chapter 6.

18   See my *Warrant and Proper Function*, Chapter 6. Still another analogical extension: a *person* can be said to be irrational if he won't listen to or pay attention to the deliverances of reason. He may be blinded by lust, or inflamed by passion, or deceived by pride: he might then act contrary to reason—*act* irrationally but also *believe* irrationally. Thus Locke: "Let never so much probability land on one side of a covetous man's reasoning, and money on the other, it is easy to foresee which will outweigh. Tell a man, passionately in love, that he is jilted; bring a score of witnesses of the falsehood of his mistress, 'tis ten to one but three kind words of hers shall invalidate all their testimonies . . . and though men cannot always openly gain-say, or resist the force of manifest probabilities, that make against them; yet yield they not to the argument." *An Essay Concerning Human Understanding,* ed. A. D. Woozley (New York: World Publishing Co., 1963), bk. IV, sec. xx, p. 439.

19   Among those who offer this objection to theistic belief are Brand Blanshard, *Reason and Belief* (London: Allen and Unwin, 1974), pp. 400ff.; Antony Flew, *The Presumption of Atheism* (London: Pemburton, 1976), pp. 22ff.; and Michael Scriven, *Primary Philosophy* (New York: McGraw-Hill, 1966), pp. 102 ff. See my "Reason and Belief in God," in Alvin Plantinga and Nicholas Wolterstorff, eds., *Faith and Rationality* (Notre Dame: University of Notre Dame Press, 1983), pp. 17ff.

20   Oliver Sacks, *The Man Who Mistook His Wife for a Hat* (New York: Harper and Row, 1987).

21   In this sense of the term, what is properly called an "irrational impulse" may be perfectly rational; an irrational impulse is really one that goes contrary to the deliverances of reason; but undergoing such impulses need not be in any way dysfunctional or a result of impairment of cognitive faculties. To go back to some of William James's examples, that I will survive my serious illness might be unlikely, given the statistics I know and my evidence generally; perhaps we are so constructed, however, that when our faculties function properly in extreme situations, we are more optimistic than the evidence warrants. This belief, then, is irrational in the sense that it goes contrary to the deliverances of reason; it is rational in the sense that it doesn't involve dysfunction.

22   Hick, *An Interpretation of Religion*, p. 234; Runzo, "God, Commitment, and Other Faiths," p. 348; Smith, *Religious Diversity*, p. 16.

23   See his *Perceiving: A Philosophical Study* (Ithaca: Cornell University Press, 1957), the three editions of *Theory of Knowledge* (New Jersey: Prentice Hall, 1st ed., 1966; 2nd ed., 1977; 3rd ed., 1989), and *The Foundations of Knowing* (Minneapolis: University of Minnesota Press, 1982); and see my "Chisholmian Internalism," in David Austin, ed., *Philosophical Analysis: A Defense by Example* (Dordrecht: D. Reidel, 1988), and Chapter 2 of *Warrant: The Current Debate.*

24   Of course, there are many variations on this internalist theme. Consider briefly the postclassical Chisholm (see his "The Place of Epistemic Justification," in Roberta Klein, ed., *Philosophical Topics* 14, no. 1 (1986), 85, and the intellectual autobiography in *Roderick M. Chisholm,* ed., Radu Bogdan [Dordrecht: D. Reidel, 1986], pp. 52ff.), who bears a startling resemblance to Brentano. According to this view, justification is not *deontological* but *axiological.* To put it another way, warrant is not really a matter of justification, of fulfilling duty and obligation; it is instead a question whether a certain relation of fittingness holds between one's evidential base (very roughly, the totality of one's present experiences and other beliefs) and the belief in question. (This relationship's holding, of course, is a valuable state of affairs; hence the axiology.) Can the exclusivist have warrant from this perspective? Well, without more knowledge about what this relation is, it isn't easy to tell. But here at the least the postclassical Chisholmian pluralist would owe us an explanation why he thinks the exclusivist's beliefs could not stand in this relation to his evidence base.

25   *An Interpretation of Religion*, p. 2.

26   Actually, this conditional as it stands is probably not true; the point must be stated with more care. Given my parents and their proclivities, if I had been born in Madagascar, it would probably have been because my parents were (Christian) missionaries there.

27   See Richard Feldman, "Reliability and Justification," *The Monist* 68 (1986), 159–74, and Chapter 9 of my *Warrant and Proper Function*.

28   See Chapter 10 of my *Warrant:The Current Debate* and the first two chapters of my *Warrant and Proper Function* for exposition and defense of this way of thinking about warrant.

29   See William P. Alston, "Religious Diversity and Perceptual Knowledge of God," *Faith and Philosophy* 5 (1988), 433 ff.

Questions for reflection

1   Do you agree with Professor Plantinga's response to the moral objection to religious exclusivism? Why or why not?

2   Which of the three epistemic objections do you find most persuasive? Why? Are you persuaded by Plantinga's response to it?

3   Is it reasonable to hold to exclusivism without having evidence for one's religious beliefs? Explain.

4   Should one look for evidence for one's religious beliefs? If so, what would such evidence look like? If not, why not?

5   What does the awareness of religious diversity mean for your religious (or nonreligious) beliefs?

Further reading

David Basinger (2002) *Religious Diversity: A Philosophical Assessment.* Aldershot: Ashgate. (Offers a study of the major epistemic issues concerning religious diversity.)

Paul J. Griffiths (2001) *Problems of Religious Diversity.* Oxford: Blackwell. (Analyzes a number of philosophical questions raised by religious diversity.)

Robert McKim (2001) *Religious Ambiguity and Religious Diversity.* Oxford: Oxford University Press. (Focuses on themes related to divine hiddenness and religious diversity and their implications for religious belief.)

Harold Netland (2001) *Encountering Religious Pluralism: The Challenge to Christian Faith and Mission.* Downers Grove, IL: InterVarsity Press. (Provides a defense of Christian exclusivism while interacting extensively with John Hick's religious pluralism.)

Philip L. Quinn and Kevin Meeker, eds. (2000) *The Philosophical Challenge of Religious Diversity.* New York: Oxford University Press. (A philosophical engagement in a variety of issues relevant to religious diversity; contains the selection above.)

Chapter 4

Joseph Runzo

RELIGIOUS RELATIVISM

Joseph Runzo is Professor of Philosophy, Religious Studies, and Honors at Chapman University and a Life Fellow at Clare Hall, Cambridge University. In this selection he distinguishes six different responses to religious diversity and defends the one he dubs "religious relativism," a position which minimally includes the epistemic view of conceptual relativism whereby "first-order truth-claims about reality—e.g., that persons or subatomic particles or that God exists—are relative to the world-view of a particular society." He also argues that religious relativism has several advantages over John Hick's religious pluralism: (1) it offers a better account for the actual cognitive beliefs held by the adherents of the great world religions, (2) it maintains the dignity of the various religions by accepting their differences as real and significant, and (3) it does not reduce the sense of the reality of God to a mere "image" as pluralism unintentionally does, but rather keeps God as the real direct object of religious faith.

Crises in religion historically precipitate revolutions in religious thought. Today, the impressive piety and evident rationality of the belief systems of *other* religious traditions, inescapably confronts Christians with a crisis—and a potential revolution. How should Christians respond responsibly to the conflicting claims of other faiths? More pointedly, should Christians abjure traditional claims to the one truth and the one way to salvation? As even Descartes (rather quaintly) observes in his *Discourse on Method*,

> . . . I further recognised in the course of my travels that all those whose sentiments are very contrary to ours are yet not necessarily barbarians or savages, but may be possessed of reason in as great or even a greater degree than ourselves. I also considered how very different the self-same man, identical in mind and spirit, may become, according as he is brought up from childhood amongst the French or Germans, or has passed his whole life amongst Chinese or cannibals.[1]

Religious beliefs, like many philosophical orientations, seem largely an accident of birth. If you are born in India, you are likely to be a Hindu; if born in France, you are likely to be a Christian. Moreover, on their own grounds, Buddhists and Muslims and adherents of other great religious faiths, seem rationally justified in their beliefs. This raises the *problem of religious pluralism*: the mutually conflicting systems of truth-claims of the world's religions, if taken separately, appear rationally justified—but are they *correct*? Is only one system of religious truth-claims correct, is more than one system correct, or are all religious systems mistaken?

Descartes, concluding from the diversity of opinion which he observed that "it is much more custom and example that persuade us than any certain knowledge," attempts to arrive at a method for attaining certainty, despite the fact that "there is nothing imaginable so strange or so little credible that it has not been maintained by one philosopher or other."[2] Likewise, is there one correct religious system, and can we know what it is? Or is the search for universal or certain truth in religious matters as overambitious as Descartes was philosophically overly ambitious?

A major problem with the desire for a comforting certainty in religious matters is identified in Tillich's observation that the church has become all too insular: "theologians have become careless in safeguarding their idea of a personal God from slipping into 'henotheistic' mythology (the belief in *one* god who, however, remains particular and bound to a particular group)."[3] But if henotheism poses a danger on one side, a too ready acceptance of pluralism in religion poses a danger on the other side. For an uncritical pluralism undermines the strength of commitment of faith. How then can we both remain fully committed to our most basic truth-claims about God, and at the same time take full account of religious pluralism? Christians today must be responsive to other faiths, but responsive *within* the Christian vision expressed in the Vatican II Declaration *Nostra Aetate*: ". . . all peoples comprise a single community, and have a single origin . . . God . . . One also is their final goal: God."[4]

After explaining why the problem of religious pluralism is a problem of conflicting *truth*-claims, I will set out six possible responses, religious and non-religious, to the conflicting truth-claims of the world's religions. Then I will assess each response in turn from an external, religious (but not necessarily Christian) point of view, ultimately focusing on the Pluralist and Relativist responses. I will end by defending the Relativist response from an internal, Christian perspective, and explain how it incorporates strengths, without some of the salient weaknesses, of other possible responses to the conflicting truth-claims of the world religions.

I

In the *Dynamics of Faith*, Tillich suggests that "The conflict between religions is not a conflict between forms of belief, but it is a conflict between expressions of our ultimate concern. . . . All decisions of faith are existential, not theoretical, decisions."[5] It *would* be a gross distortion of faith to reduce it to merely theoretical concerns or to questions of belief. But in avoiding this intellectualist distortion of faith Tillich is mistaken to suggest that the conflict between religions is not a conflict between truth-claims. True, a religious way of life importantly involves such elements as ritual and symbols, and a moral ordering of one's life. But our beliefs, or more comprehensively, our world-views—i.e., the total cognitive web of our interrelated concepts, beliefs, and processes of rational thought—determine the very nature of our ultimate concern. For all experience, understanding, and praxis—whether it concerns the mundane or the *mysterium tremendum*—is structured by our world-views. Consequently, conflicts between religious traditions fundamentally stem from conflicts of belief, conflicts over specific claims about how meaning and value are to be achieved, and what is the desired telos for humankind.

In assessing the conflict of truth-claims among world religions it must be kept in mind that a religion is not itself true or false any more than any other human institution such as art, government, or law, is in and of itself true or false. A total institution—aesthetic, political, legal, or religious—is only more or less expedient, only more or less effective in meeting its intended goals. What is true or false, and what is most fundamentally in conflict between such systems, are the underlying, specific truth-claims within the systems. Now, in the conflict of religious truth-claims, all of the world's major religions agree that the divine, or the Absolute, or the Real, is One, transcends the natural order, and is ultimately inexpressible. As *Ecclesiastes* puts it, God "has put eternity into man's mind, yet so that he cannot find out what God has done from the beginning to the end." (Eccles. 3:11, RSV) But though they have this general point of agreement, and though each religious tradition includes truth-claims and even scriptural material which is expendable, there is a fundamental or "vital core" of beliefs in each religion which is definitive of that very tradition.[6] And it is particular elements of this "vital core" of beliefs that are incompatible among world religions.

For instance, there is no intractable conflict between claims in the Muslim tradition that Mahdis will periodically appear to revive faith in God, and orthodox Christian claims that Jesus represents the final prophetic revelation of God. For Christians could come to accept, and Sunnis could come to reject, further prophetic revelations from God *via* Mahdis, without impugning the respective orthodox status of Jesus or Mohammed.[7] But traditionally it *is* essential to monotheistic traditions, like Christianity, Islam, Judaism and Ramanujan Hinduism, that the correct human perception of the divine is the perception of a personal deity. In contrast, on a Hinayana (Theravada) Buddhist view, God does not exist, and in much of the Hindu tradition, the notion of a personal deity is talk about an illusory state of affairs bound to this life. Or, to take another trenchant conflict among religious truth-claims, consider some of the diverse notions of the relation of humanity to Ultimate Reality. In Hinayana Buddhism there is no real question of one's relation to Ultimate Reality, for the goal of liberation is the complete extinction of the ego; in Islam the basic human relation to God is one of slave to master; in orthodox Judaism the central relation is one of a servant to his or her God.

Thus, because they make essentially different truth-claims, different religious traditions are structured by *essentially* different world-views, offering *essentially* different paths to what is perceived as Ultimate Reality. Since a person's world-view, then, is inherently constitutive of their religious way of life, the question is whether the differences in *truth-claims* among the world religions, and the consequent differences in the (putative) paths to Ultimate Reality, are significant or ultimately irrelevant.

We can also see that the conflict among the world religions is fundamentally a conflict of *truth-claims* if we consider the meaning of "faith" and of "religion." Faith is the more encompassing notion. Faith can be either religious or non-religious: we speak of faith in the progress of science or in the inevitableness of dialectical materialism, as much as of Christian or Muslim faith. Therefore, I will use the term "faith" to refer to a person's fundamental commitment to any world-view, a commitment which is a total dispositional state of the person involving affective, conative, and cognitive elements.

Religion, on the other hand, involves a particular form of faith, focused within a specific religious tradition. To distinguish religious from non-religious faith, I will define a religion or religious tradition as a set of symbols and rituals, myths and stories, concepts and truth-claims, which a community believes gives ultimate meaning to life, *via* its connection to a transcendent God or Ultimate Reality *beyond* the natural order. Thus religion is a *human* construct (or institution) which fundamentally involves beliefs at two levels: (I) it involves the meta-belief that the religion in question does indeed refer to a transcendent reality which gives meaning to life, and (II) it involves specific beliefs—including vital core beliefs—about the nature of that ultimate reality and the way in which it gives meaning to life. The first sort of belief, (I), is shared by the world religions. The second sort of belief, (II), is the point of conflict among the world religions.

II

There are six possible responses, religious and non-religious, to the conflicting truth-claims of vital core beliefs among the world religions:[8]

1. *Atheism*: all religions are mistaken.
2. *Religious Exclusivism*: only one world religion is correct, and all others are mistaken.
3. *Religious Inclusivism*: only one world religion is fully correct, but other world religions participate in or partially reveal some of the truth of the one correct religion.
4. *Religious Subjectivism*: each world religion is correct, and each is correct insofar as it is best for the individual who adheres to it.
5. *Religious Pluralism*: ultimately all world religions are correct, each offering a different, salvific path and partial perspective *vis-a-vis* the one Ultimate Reality.
6. *Religious Relativism*: at least one, and probably more than one, world religion is correct, and the correctness of a religion is relative to the worldview(s) of its community of adherents.

One obvious response to the conflicting truth-claims of the world's religions is the Atheist response, (1). Is it not most plausible, given the enormity of the conflict among truth-claims, that all religious traditions are simply false in different ways, rather than that one is correct, or that several are correct in different ways? In the absence of a generally acceptable deductive proof or inductive proof with a high probability, for the existence of God or the Absolute, there is no incontrovertible reply to this query. Indeed, there are important sociological and psychological arguments, like those of Feuerbach and Freud, which lend support to the Atheist response.

At stake here is the basic religious presupposition that only reference to a transcendent divine or ultimate reality gives ultimate meaning to human life. This meta-belief (I) is supported in the various religious traditions by appeals to religious experience, purported transformations of people's lives, the claimed necessity of a "leap of faith," and so on. These are internal considerations which will not, of course, prove that the Atheist response (1) must be mistaken. But in this discussion we can set aside the Atheist response if we take the basic religious metabelief (I) as a presupposition.

Turning to the second response, Exclusivism in its strongest form is exemplified by the traditional Roman Catholic dogma, *Extra ecclesiam nulla salus*. Exclusivism is the view that salvation can only be found either (as in the dogma just cited) inside a particular *institutional* structure, or on the basis of a specified tradition of religious beliefs, symbols, and rituals—e.g., as Karl Barth says of Christianity, "the Christian religion is true, because it has pleased God, who alone can be the judge in this matter, to affirm it to be the true religion."[9] But such unqualified Exclusivism seems untenable in the face of the problem of religious pluralism. In Ernst Troeltsch's words, regarding Christianity,

> a study of the non-Christian religions convinced me more and more that their naive claims to absolute validity are also genuinely such. I found Buddhism and Brahminism especially to be really humane and spiritual religions, capable of appealing in precisely the same way to the inner certitude and devotion of their followers as Christianity,[10]

Principal considerations against Exclusivism within *any* religious tradition include the following: Historically, it is largely a matter of geographical accident whether one grows up as a Hindu or Buddhist, Christian or Muslim, etc. Theologically, a strict reading of Exclusivism condemns the vast majority of humanity to perdition, which certainly appears contrary to the notion of a loving God, as well as seeming to contradict the idea of an Absolute which is the telos of all humankind. Ethically, Religious Exclusivism has the morally repugnant result of making those who have privileged knowledge, or who are intellectually astute, a religious elite, while penalizing those who happen to have no access to the putatively correct religious views, or who are incapable of advanced understanding. Sociologically, Exclusivism is a concomitant of sectarianism, serving as a rationale for enforcing discipline and communal cohesion.[11] Epistemologically, one could not *know* with certainty that there is only one correct set of religious truth-claims or only one institutional structure providing a path to salvation—a consideration exacerbated by the fact that all religions at some point make Exclusivist claims. And religiously, Exclusivism is highly presumptuous, ignoring the fact that religious truth-claims are human constructs, human attempts to know Ultimate Reality, subject to the limitations and fallibility of the human mind.

It is of course possible that the Exclusivism of some particular religious tradition is correct. But given these weighty considerations against Exclusivism, we must turn to responses (3)–(6), responses that hold that in some form each of the great world religions is at least in part correctly directed toward the divine or Absolute. The problem is how to avoid the serious moral, theological, empirical, and epistemological deficiencies of Exclusivism without dissipating the very cohesiveness and vitality of one's own religious tradition which Exclusivism properly seeks to protect.

III

A natural alternative to take to meet these concerns is Inclusivism. This has become an especially prominent view in Roman Catholic theology since Vatican II. Religious Inclusivists jointly hold two theses: That other religions convey part of the truth about Ultimate Reality and the relation of humanity to Ultimate Reality, but that only one's own tradition most fully provides an understanding of Ultimate Reality, and most adequately provides a path to salvation. Thus, *Nostra Aetate* states both that "The Catholic Church rejects nothing which is true and holy in [other] religions," and that the cross of Christ "is the sign of God's all-embracing love" and "the fountain from which every grace flows."[12]

From these foundations, Christian Inclusivism has been developed in considerable detail by Karl Rahner, who suggests that those in the non-Christian traditions can be "anonymous" Christians. Since, Rahner suggests, "we have to keep in mind . . . the necessity of Christian faith *and* the universal salvific will of God's love and omnipotence,"

> we can only reconcile them by saying that somehow all men must be capable of being members of the Church; and this capacity must not be understood merely in the sense of an abstract and purely logical possibility, but as a real and historically concrete one.[13]

In the same vein, R. C. Zaehner offers an historical argument for Inclusivism:

> The drive towards the integration of . . . the personal and the collective, has been characteristic of the most original thinkers in [all religions] during the first two-thirds of the twentieth century . . . . This unity in diversity is the birthright of the Catholic Church . . . all the other religions, in their historical development, grow into 'other Catholic Churches' . . . [For while one God] is the inspiration of all religions and peculiar to none . . . . The only religion that has from the beginning been both communal and individual is Christianity.[14]

Inclusivism is typically based on the notion that one's own religion most fully possesses a particular element which is most essential to religion. Zaehner looks to the integration of the personal and collective; Kant holds that true religiosity is identical to the moral life; Schleiermacher proposes that underlying genuine religion is "the feeling of absolute dependence"; Rudolph Otto emphasizes a numinous sense of the holy, a sense of the *mysterium tremendum*; *Nostra Aetate* declares that "from ancient times down to the present, there has existed among diverse peoples a certain perception of that hidden power which hovers over the course of things and over the events of human life"; and John Baillie suggests that all humans have a knowledge of God through a felt presence of the divine such that all people "already believe in him."[15]

That other religious traditions, in accordance with the religious meta-belief (I), might provide some apprehension of Ultimate Reality, is not at issue here. Rather, Inclusivism supposes that a *particular* sort of apprehension and understanding of Ultimate Reality is elemental to all religion. However, in the first place we could not *know* that all humans have the same sort of elemental apprehension of Ultimate Reality. Second, the empirical evidence supports precisely the opposite supposition. Even in the broadest terms, the notion of an elemental apprehension of Ultimate Reality is understood in *personal* terms in the monotheistic traditions, while it is *non-personal* in Confucianism and in Hindu and Buddhist traditions. And third, each religion tends to see itself as the culmination of *the* elemental apprehension of Ultimate Reality: "other religions can have their own fulfillment theology. Sri Aurobindo sees the world religious process converging on Mother India rather than the Cosmic Christ, and Sir Muhammad Iqbal sees it converging upon a kind of ideal Islam."[16]

So when Rahner, for example, says that the Christian has, "other things being equal, a still greater chance of salvation than someone who is merely an anonymous Christian,"[17] this can only be a statement of faith, not one of certain knowledge. Yet the strength of Inclusivism *is* this unequivocal faith—*within* an acceptance of other traditions—that one's own religion is salvific. Inclusivism expresses an appropriate religious disposition. But Inclusivism ultimately fails as a warranted epistemological thesis. This failure leads us to the pluralistic types of responses to the problem of religious pluralism.

IV

Subjectivism, Pluralism, and Relativism are all pluralistic responses to the conflicting truth-claims of world religions. All three views share a basic *idealist epistemology*: i.e., they share the basic assumption that the world we experience and understand is not the world independent of our perceiving but a world at least in part structured by our minds. Thus these pluralistic views share the epistemic view expressed in the Kantian dictum that "[sensible] intuitions without concepts are blind,"[18] a view sometimes expressed in the contemporary notion that all experiencing is experiencing-*as*. But further, they share the assumption that there is more than one set of human concepts—more than one world-view—which is valid for understanding the world. Thus they share the sort of *pluralist* epistemology expressed by William James in *The Varieties of Religious Experience*: "why in the name of common sense need we assume that only one . . . system of ideas can be true? The obvious outcome of our total experience is that the world can be handled according to many systems of ideas, . . ."[19] The three pluralistic religious responses all hold that one's perception of religious truth is in some sense relative to one's world-view. Typically this view is supported on the grounds of the ineluctable enculturation or the historicity of all thought and experience, or, as in the Whorf hypothesis, by suggesting a necessary connection between language, which varies from community to community, and truth, which consequently varies.

The most radical of the pluralistic responses to the conflicting truth-claims of the world religions is Subjectivism, where religious truth and salvation are literally as varied as individuals are diverse. As a general view in epistemology, subjectivism is a form of relativism about truth. It is the extreme epistemological position that truth is relative to each individual's idiosyncratic world-view. Thus, on a Religious Subjectivist's view, religion is a radically private affair, often understood as purely a matter of one's individual relation to the divine or Absolute. But subjectivism, and therefore Religious Subjectivism, is conceptually incoherent. Truth-bearers are statements or propositions. Statements or propositions are comprised of concepts. And precisely what Wittgenstein's "private-language" argument demonstrates is that concepts are social constructions and cannot be purely private, individual understandings.[20] Thus, since statements and propositions are comprised of concepts, and concepts are social constructs, truth cannot be idiosyncratically individualistic. Religious Subjectivism, then, must be rejected.

The two remaining pluralistic views, Religious Pluralism and Religious Relativism, are often conflated. John Hick offers a concise description of Pluralism as the view that

"There is not merely one way but a plurality of ways of salvation or liberation . . . taking place in different ways within the contexts of all the great religious traditions."[21] Pluralism holds that there is only one Ultimate Reality, but that Ultimate Reality is properly, though only partially, understood in different ways. Following a metaphor which Hick employs, just as the historian does not have direct access to figures of history, and consequently different historians develop different perspectives on historical figures like Genghis Khan or Sun Yat-Sen because of historians' different methods of inquiry, cultural backgrounds, etc., so too, different religious traditions or different theologies, not having direct access to the divine, offer different enculturated "images" of the one Ultimate Reality.[22] On the Pluralist account, there is no ultimate conflict between these different perspectives, since there still remains one set of truths, even if those truths are imperfectly and only partially understood within each perspective. Religious Pluralism, then, focuses on the viability of different religious *perspectives* on Ultimate Reality.

Religious Relativism, in contrast, is directly a thesis about differences of religious *truth-claims*. The Religious Relativist minimally holds the general epistemic view, which I shall designate as "conceptual relativism," that first-order truth-claims about reality— e.g., that persons or that subatomic particles or that God exists—are relative to the world-view of a particular society.[23] More precisely, a conceptual relativist definitively holds that, corresponding to differences of world-view, there are mutually incompatible, yet individually adequate, sets of conceptual-schema-relative truths.[24] Thus for the Religious Relativist, unlike the Pluralist, truth itself is relative and plural.

However, Religious Pluralism and Religious Relativism do share two underlying Kantian theses. They share the Kantian metaphysical division (though the Kantian terminology may not be employed) between noumena and phenomena, distinguishing between God in Himself or the Absolute in itself, and God or the Absolute as humanly experienced. And as we have seen, they share the Kantian epistemic notion that all experience, and so all religious experience, is structured by the (culturally and historically conditioned) world-view of the percipient. Thus, Religious Pluralism and Religious Relativism hold that differences of religious perception cannot just be treated as a matter of some people simply being wrong about the nature of the divine Reality, but rather that such differences of perception are inherent to religious perception and conception. Given these points of fundamental agreement, which position, Pluralism or Relativism, better accounts for the conflicting truth-claims of the world religions?

V

An important exponent of Religious Pluralism is Wilfred Cantwell Smith. Cantwell Smith argues that the notions of "religion" and of "a religion" are obsolete.[25] He holds that only God and humanity are "givens"—global universals—and that the centrality given to religion is misguided and the conception of a religion as a belief system mistaken. Rather than starting from a particular religious tradition and then considering God and humanity, one should start from God and humanity and consider particular religious traditions from this global perspective. Smith reaches the Pluralist conclusion that the one truth about the religious life of humankind is conveyed in the various Buddhist, Christian, Islamic, and so on, forms.[26]

Quite correctly, I think, Smith is attempting to circumvent the obstacles which *religion* often places between humans and their response to the divine. But there are several problems with his approach. First, he suggests replacing the world-view(s) of particular religious traditions with another world-view on which it is presupposed that God and humanity are givens in the experience of all humans. This is neither a neutral world-view, nor one which will be shared by all religious persons. Many adherents of particular religious world-views would reject the generalized approach to the divine Cantwell Smith proposes as so amorphous that it fails to capture *their* religious beliefs. Second, Smith's position rests on the dubious thesis, which we have already addressed, that there *is* a universal, innate experience or conception of the divine. Smith himself effectively argues against *Christian* Exclusivism by asking: "how could one possibly know?" that only the Christian faith is correct.[27] But the same argument is equally applicable to Smith's own position: how could one possibly *know* that there is a global, innate apprehension or "givenness" of God and humanity? If anything, the evidence most strongly supports the conclusion that all humankind does not share the same innate concept or primal experience of Ultimate Reality, much less of the nature of God, or even of humanity, *per se*.

John Hick has developed another, rather impressive and comprehensive, Pluralist approach, in part by following out a key aspect of Cantwell Smith's work, *viz.* the rejection of the idea that a religion is fundamentally a set of beliefs. Proposing instead that religion definitively concerns "the transformation of human existence from self-centredness to Reality-centredness,"[28] Hick essentially argues that the apparently conflicting truth-claims of the world's religions are, in the final analysis, irrelevant, and that the world religions can be reconciled, and the integrity of each preserved, through this more fundamental shared goal of moving from self- to Reality-centeredness.

Hick explicitly employs the two Kantian theses underlying both Pluralism and Relativism. He employs the Kantian thesis that all experience is structured by the mind by suggesting that specific forms of religious awareness "are formed by the presence of the divine Reality, . . . coming to consciousness in terms of the different sets of religious concepts and structures of religious meaning that operate within the different religious traditions":[29] i.e., *as* divine *personae* (e.g., Yahweh, Allah, etc.) for theists and *as* divine *impersonae* (e.g., Brahman, the Dharma, the Tao, etc.) for non-theists.[30] Regarding the phenomenal/noumenal distinction, he supports the distinction between personal and non-personal divine phenomena and the Eternal noumenon, on the basis of what he takes to be strong inductive evidence from religious experience.[31] And indeed we do find consistent differentiation in the world religions between Ultimate Reality as we experience it and as it is in itself. There is the Hindu distinction between *saguna* Brahman and *nirguna* Brahman; the Jewish Cabalistic distinction between the God of the Bible and En Soph; and in the Christian tradition, Eckhart's distinction between God *qua* Trinity and the Godhead itself, and more recently, Tillich's notion of "the God above the God of theism," and so on.

Hick does allow for the logical possibility that only one religion might be correct, but he thinks that the overwhelming facts of religious diversity make Religious Pluralism the most plausible response to the conflicting truth-claims of world religions.[32] A comprehensive Religious Pluralism like Hick's fully confronts the diversity of religious truth-claims. As such, it is an admirable and helpful response to the challenge which these conflicting claims presents. But even so, Religious Pluralism has significant shortcomings.

VI

Religious Pluralism fails to adequately account for the necessary, central role of cognition in religious faith. Hick suggests that differences of belief among the world religions are

> of great philosophical importance as elements within our respective theories
> about the universe; but they are not of great *religious*, i.e. soteriological,
> importance. For different groups can hold incompatible sets of theories all
> of which constitute intellectual frameworks within which the process of sal-
> vation/liberation can proceed.[33]

Of course, even incompatible theories can serve as guides to the same religious goal. But from this it neither follows that systems of belief and theory are irrelevant to guiding one to that goal, nor that it is unimportant which *particular* belief system one holds for reaching that end. Rather, the cognitive content of religious faith is essential for providing a coherent and sufficiently comprehensive view of reality as a basis for purposive action and an effective, directive guide to "salvation/liberation." Further, the *specific* cognitive content of one's faith is of paramount importance since it is precisely what delimits one's *specific* path to salvation/liberation. And the specific path to salvation/liberation is not just a means to an end but is itself an integral part of the goal of salvation/liberation. This is expressed in the New Testament in the idea that the Kingdom of God is not future but begins in the lives of those who enter the new covenant now: "asked by the Pharisees when the kingdom was coming, he [Jesus] answered them, 'The kingdom of God is not coming with signs to be observed; . . . the kingdom of God is in the midst of you.'" (Luke 17:20–21, RSV) Consequently since the specific path to salvation/liberation is itself part of that very salvation/liberation, a specific religious world-view is importantly constitutive of what makes a way of life a (particular) *religious* way of life.

Indeed, it would seem that specific religious cognitive content is essential to making it meaningful even to be committed at all to a religious way of life. True, de-emphasizing specific doctrines—such as the idea that the Christ-event is the definitive self-revelation of the divine—makes it easier to reconcile apparently conflicting religious truth-claims, especially the notion of a personal God with the notion of a non-personal Absolute. But the more such specific doctrines are set aside, the more questionable it becomes whether a *religious*, as opposed to a non-religious, commitment is what gives life ultimate significance. Insofar as the specificity of religious doctrines is de-emphasized, the basic religious meta-belief (I) that religion does indeed refer to a transcendent Reality which gives meaning to life becomes less plausible. The plausibility of (I) rests in large part on the evidence of religious experience. But as any hypothesis about the nature of reality is made more indefinite, the available inductive evidence to support that hypothesis is not increased, as for example Hick's defense of Religious Pluralism seems to suggest, but decreased. For, evidence for an indefinite hypothesis is correspondingly indefinite or ambiguous.

Another difficulty with Religious Pluralism is this. Exactly what a recognition of pluralism in general seems to acknowledge is that humans, and human conceptions, fundamentally differ. But then, to the extent that the differences of human conception embedded in the world religions are regarded as inconsequential, the dignity of the individual and the value of each distinct community of faith is lessened.

To see how this applies to Christianity, consider Maurice Wiles' observation that, "there are two fundamental characteristics of the conception of God . . . it must be a profoundly personal concept, . . . And secondly it is God in relation to us with which we have to do."[34] The Christian understanding that the universe is under the providence of a God who has revealed Himself as a personal being—One who understands and loves humanity—is and must be a conception of God as He manifests Himself *to us*. Yet this conception of an essentially *personal* God is not incidental but central to both corporate and individual Christian faith. Hick attempts to account for this by suggesting that among the world religions the Real is experienced as *either* personal or non-personal.[35] While this Religious Pluralist view properly acknowledges that theistic understanding is an understanding of Ultimate Reality not *an sich* but *as* it confronts us in history, it obviates the significance of the Christian understanding of a personal God as *somehow* correctly revealing the nature of Ultimate Reality in itself. A personal reality might have nonpersonal aspects, but it could not be identical to something which is non-personal. Hence, this Pluralist account entails that the monotheist's experience of a *personal* divine reality *cannot*, to that extent, correctly represent the nature of the Real in itself.

Finally, Religious Pluralism is deficient insofar as it unintentionally undermines the sense of the reality of God. It is part of the fundamental meta-belief (I) of religion that the God or the Absolute of which humans speak is real and not a metaphysical illusion or psychological delusion. But if the God of which monotheists speak is only an "image," only a perspective on an unknowable, noumenal reality, than the God of history will not be a real God. I will address this last point more fully below.

These deficiencies must be met if a pluralistic resolution to the conflicting truth-claims of the world religions is to be successful. Yet despite these shortcomings, Religious Pluralism has an obvious strength which must be retained for any successful pluralistic resolution. Religious Pluralism offers a reconciliation of the disparate world religious traditions which avoids the theologically unacceptable and epistemically unsupportable religious imperialism which we find in Exclusivism, and even in Inclusivism.

VII

If, then, we reject the religious imperialism of the Exclusivist and Inclusivist views that one's own tradition must be either the sole or at least the fullest arbiter of truth about the divine, we have two choices about how to deal with the irreducible plurality of religious conception and experience. We can either take the approach of Pluralism, treat the incompatible beliefs among differing religious world-views as ultimately inessential, and conclude that the great world religions simply offer different perspectives on Ultimate Reality. Or we can accept the doctrines which adherents of different world religions so ardently profess and passionately follow as *essential* to their faith. I have suggested that the former approach runs the danger of undermining the basic religious meta-belief (I), and reducing the substance of religious world-views to vacuity, obviating just those differences in the path to salvation/liberation which give significance to each individual religious tradition. If I am right about this, we are led to conclude that different religions have different constitutive sets of truth-claims, and that—while these sets of core truth-claims are mutually incompatible—each set of truth-claims is probably adequate in itself.

This is the Religious Relativist response to the problem of religious pluralism.[36] Granted, the different religious world-views among the world's great religious traditions are complementary insofar as they have a commonality in the religious experiences and perceptions of humankind. But different religious world-views are, ultimately, irreducibly plural, with features that are incompatible if not contradictory vis-a-vis other religious world-views. Further, corresponding to each distinct religious world-view, there is a different set of possible religious *experiences*. For what can be experienced depends on what *can be* real or unreal, and what can be real—i.e., what is possible—is determined by the percipient's world-view.[37] This means that each distinct religious world-view delineates a distinct possible divine reality[38]—though just to the extent that religious world-views "overlap," characteristics of these distinct possible divine realities will overlap.

For instance, monotheistic truth-claims will be most directly about God *as* humans experience Him, for they are most directly about divine reality *relative to* a particular theistic world-view. But then each theology, as a product of human constructive reasoning, will delimit only one *possible* divine reality. There will be other *contrasting*—though not totally mutually exclusive—valid theologies, held by other sincere women and men of faith, delimiting other possible divine phenomenal realities.

Importantly, on this Religious Relativist account, "The" God of history, delimited by the strictures of a particular theology is *not*, if He exists,[39] somehow unreal *vis-a-vis* the noumenal. God *qua* noumenal lies "behind," so to speak, the possible plurality of real phenomenal divine realities, delimited by different monotheistic world-views. But noumenal and phenomenal reality are two different categories of reality. And just as there is nothing unreal about nuclear weapons or pains or piano concertos because they are part of phenomenal reality, "The" God of history, "The" God one confronts, is not less real, if He exists, just because He is not in the category of the noumenal. What could be *more* real than that which we do experience? And to try to transcend our experience for something putatively "untainted" by human thought is not only the worst sort of degenerate Platonism, it is to turn away from the means we *do* have in experience for understanding the divine and our own humanity in relation to the divine.

Among the possible responses to the problem of religious pluralism, this Religious Relativist account of a possible plurality of phenomenal divine realities seems to offer the best explanation of the differing experiences and incompatible conceptions of the great religious traditions. The Atheist response to the problem of religious pluralism is ruled out if we presuppose the religious meta-belief (I). Religious Exclusivism is neither tolerable nor any longer intellectually honest in the context of our contemporary knowledge of other faiths. Religious Subjectivism is conceptually incoherent. Religious Inclusivism does not go far enough toward solving the problem of religious pluralism. And Religious Pluralism has serious deficiencies which Religious Relativism avoids.

First, Religious Relativism reasserts the central role which cognition has in a religious life. The path to salvation is itself part of the salvific process. And one's religious world-view, as a guide for attitudes and actions, is inseparable from that path. Moreover, if all experience is conceptualized, then one will quite literally not be able to have any experience of the divine without a world-view which, e.g., enables one to experience the world *as* under the providence of God, or *as* an environment for working out one's *Karma*, etc. But then, as Religious Relativism asserts, *specific* truth-claims are essential to a religious tradition and way of life, and the conflict among the claims of the world religions cannot be resolved by de-emphasizing those conflicting claims.

Second, it follows from this that Religious Relativism treats adherents of each religious tradition with fullest dignity. Regarding Christianity, we could say, as the Pluralist must, that the doctrine of the Incarnation cannot be taken literally and cannot mean for *any* Christian that Jesus uniquely manifests the presence of God.[40] Or, we can allow that on *some* world-views this would be a perfectly rational view, delineating a world where Jesus *is* the definitive self-manifestation of God. Ironically, we fall back into a certain measure of the old absolutism that undergirds Exclusivism if we take the inflexible, even though Pluralist, first course. In contrast, Relativism not only allows with Pluralism that the world's great religions could have the same telos, it allows for the likelihood that more than one of the conflicting sets of *specific* truth-claims, which adherents of the differing world religions themselves regard as vital to their faith, is correct.

Third, that it is essential for the direct object of theological conception to be a *real* God seems to leave a Pluralist view like Hick's caught between two problematic options. As in his earlier work, the God of theology can be characterized as an "image" of God. But then the God of theology does not have the ontological status of an existent entity with causal properties in the phenomenal world. This will unintentionally reduce the sense of the reality of God, for what theology would then be most directly referring to would not be *God*, but a human *idea* of the noumenal. So to speak about *God*, would be to speak about something noumenal about which we can only know that we do not know its true character. In contrast, on Religious Relativism the God of theology can be a *real* God, not just a conception of or perspective on the divine. God *qua* phenomenal is not just, in Tillich's phrase, "a symbol for God."

On the other hand, the Pluralist might hold, as Hick does in his more recent work,[41] that the divine phenomena just *are* the divine noumenon *as* experienced by humans via their particular religio-cultural perspectives. While this does indicate a more substantive ontological status for divine personae and impersonae, it threatens to collapse the phenomena/noumena distinction and runs counter to the basic idealist epistemology which underlies both Pluralism and Relativism. First, this suggests that the divine noumenon is itself experienced. One can postulate an unexperienced divine noumenon, and one can talk about divine phenomena which are (putatively) experienced. But this cannot amount to talk about the same thing—even if in different ways—for that would effectively be to eliminate the divine noumenon. And given an idealist epistemology, one cannot claim that the divine noumenon *is* experienced insofar as it appears to us in various ways, *even though* we cannot characterize the noumenal. For the conceptualization of all experience implies that what we experience can, in principle, be characterized.

Second, that a particular divine phenomenon somehow manifests the divine noumenon is a matter of faith. And while it could be a matter of reasonable faith for an individual to claim that the divine phenomenon which *they* experience somehow manifests Ultimate Reality in itself, it would not make sense to say that it was a matter of one's *faith* that the various divine phenomena, which adherents of all the great world religions feel that they experience, all *do* manifest Ultimate Reality. Rather this would amount to a hypothesis or theory about the world religions. And I do not see how we could know that this hypothesis is true; how could we know that the divine phenomena of all the great world religions *are* (or most probably are) the divine noumenon *as* experienced by humans? One's faith warrants one's own religious commitment; it cannot warrant the mutually conflicting commitments of others.

In contrast, on a Religious Relativist account, what is putatively experienced is not the noumenal Ultimate Reality, but e.g., the *real* God of history. Now, I do think that it is a mistake to suppose that one can *know* that specific claims which we make about phenomenal divine reality are also true of the divine noumenon, since this would obviate the very point of the noumena/phenomena distinction. But I think it is perfectly sensible to make the bare claim that there *is* a noumenal—*whatever* its character—which, so to speak, "lies behind" the phenomenal reality which we experience. Presumably there is no one-to-one correspondence between phenomena and noumena and hence no *direct* check from our successes and failures to the nature of the noumenal. But the greater the correspondence between our conception of the phenomenal and the character of the noumenal (whatever it is), the more our purposive activity, carried out within phenomenal reality as *we* understand it, will be successful and the closer—in principle—our understanding of the phenomenal will correspond to the noumenal.[42] For the monotheist it is a matter of faith that, in this manner, one's *own* experience of the presence of "The" God of history does increase, on the whole, one's understanding of God in Himself.

VIII

One obvious point of resistance to this Religious Relativist account is the notion that there may be more than one phenomenal reality, and more than one phenomenal divine reality. But this notion initially seems strange only because we are used to thinking in terms of that one possible world which *we* regard as *the* (unique) actual world. Commonly, we treat any other conception of the actual world as simply false or mistaken. But if one accepts the idea that phenomenal reality is relative to a world-view, and that therefore there is a plurality of actual worlds corresponding to the plurality of distinct world-views, that does not undermine or alter what *we* call the actual world—i.e., the world delimited by *our* schemas.

Recognizing that others might be responding to a different phenomenal God is like recognizing that others might rationally claim to discern a cyclical recurrence of events in history where you discern none. One can accept that there *could* be states of affairs which others but not you experience, without thereby committing yourself to the existence of any *particular* such state of affairs.[43] To have faith in only one real (phenomenal) God is to say that for *oneself* there is only one real God who lives and moves and has His being; for others there may be other real entities which are "The" God of *their* history. But just as any actual event or state of affairs is by definition an event or state of affairs in *your* actual world, any actual event which you acknowledge as an act of God is an act of the real God who confronts *you* within (your) history.

IX

Frank Whaling raises another possible objection to both Pluralism and Relativism. Whaling argues that these views avoid "the necessity of theological ordering of any sort," and that they have "the appearance of being a somewhat abstract exercise in the theology of religion, rather than a summing-up of where the Christian community around the world actually is."[44] The second, descriptive point, that Christians do not currently tend to be Religious Pluralists or Relativists, misses the question of whether Christians *ought* to move toward Pluralism or Relativism in the face of the challenge of the conflicting truth-claims of the world religions. But with respect to the first point, it *would* be a serious defect of any pluralistic response to the world religions if diverse religious truth-claims cannot be compared and assessed. Here Pluralism and Relativism offer two quite different approaches.

Pluralists most naturally approach the apparently conflicting truth-claims of world religions from the perspective of a "global theology."[45] That is, the Pluralist fundamentally attempts to look at religious traditions from an external, or inclusive point of view.[46] But the unavoidable historicity and the inherent enculturation of our thought obviate the very possibility of being able to assume this purported global perspective. There can be no such thing as a "neutral" or "objective" perspective in either religious or non-religious matters. Hence, any attempt to assess other faiths from a genuinely global perspective is inherently impossible.

Religious Relativism, on the other hand, avoids this difficulty by suggesting an internal approach to assessing other faiths. Relativism, more fundamentally than Pluralism, recognizes the inextricably socio-historical conditioning of one's perspective, and hence fundamentally recognizes that judgments about *other* faiths will necessarily be made from the point of view of one's *own* faith. This is simply to acknowledge an inherent condition of the human mind, and does not entail falling back into the religious imperialism we found in Exclusivism and Inclusivism. For there are general meta-criteria that can be applied across world-views to assess the acceptability of a world-view. These criteria include the internal coherence of a world-view, its comprehensiveness, thoroughness of explanation (e.g., that it does not depend on ad hoc hypotheses), the efficaciousness of the world-view in producing its intended end, considerations of parsimony, and so on. Thus Relativism, while not attempting to assume the stance of an impossible "neutral" global theology, can employ these meta-criteria to assess other faiths and so meet Whaling's objection. Further, this gives Relativism a strength that we observed in Religious Inclusivism. Religious Relativism, while recognizing that salvation *could* come to others in other traditions, supports the strength of commitment to one's own tradition.

X

While the Pluralist attempts to solve the problem of religious pluralism by setting aside conflicting truth-claims and emphasizing a universality and unity to all religions, the Religious Relativist can resolve the problem of religious pluralism by accepting these conflicting truth-claims as an appropriate manifestation of divine/human interaction. In the spirit of the Leibnizian notion that not just the quantity of good, but the *vari-*

ety of good things makes this "the best of all possible worlds"—the world that a good God would create—we *should* expect correct religious beliefs and veridical religious experiences to be as richly varied as human needs and human individuality. Contrary to the Pluralist conception, an ultimate uniformity of the central elements of all religious traditions is not an ultimate value. Where Pluralism tends to homogenize religion, if one believes that God indeed has providence over the world, then precisely what the evidence of the world we find ourselves in indicates is that a diversity of religious truth-claims is intrinsically valuable, and divinely valued. Rather than a problem to be solved, the conflicting truth-claims of the great religious traditions, and even conflicting systems *within* traditions, can be accepted as a profound indication of God's manifest love and delight in the diverse worlds of His creatures.

That our religious beliefs have a correlation to the transcendent divine reality is a matter of faith. Since our perception and understanding are ineluctably limited to our world-view, even if what we believe is true about God *qua* phenomenal turns out to be true also of God *qua* noumenal, we could never *know* that that was so. We cannot *know* that we possess the requisite conceptual resources to apply to God in Himself, or *know* that we have formed ideas which are true of God *qua* noumenal, or *know* that our ideas do properly refer to the noumenal God. But just because we cannot know these things to be true *vis-a-vis* the noumenal God, this clearly does not entail that they are not the case. I do not see how it could be shown that it is *impossible* that our concepts or beliefs do in fact correctly refer to the noumenal. Quite the contrary, it is a matter of reasonable faith that Christian religious experience and theological conception *do* provide the basis for proper reference and proper talk about God in Himself. Yet to acknowledge that we cannot transcend our world-views, and that they in turn are inescapably structured by our limiting socio-historical perspective, is to recognize the fundamental fallibility and finitude of even our noblest conceptions and highest values. There is thus a religiously appropriate humbleness which Religious Relativism brings to our claims to religious truth.

Faced with the inescapable challenge of the claims of other faiths, it may now be time for Christians to move toward a Christian Relativism. A Christian Relativism would combine the strengths of Exclusivism and Inclusivism, and of Pluralism, without their respective disadvantages. A Christian Relativism would enable us to say, on the one hand, that salvation through Christ is definitive, without committing us, on the other hand, to the unsupportable view that salvation is exclusively Christian. A Christian Relativism would sustain Christian commitment and support Christian claims to truth, without claiming to be the only truth.[47]

Notes

1   René Descartes, *Discourse on the Method of Rightly Conducting the Reason*, in *The Philosophical Works of Descartes*, trans. Elizabeth S. Haldane & G. R. T. Ross (Cambridge: Cambridge University Press, 1969), vol. 1, p. 90.
2   Descartes, *Discourse on Method*, pp. 91 and 90.
3   Paul Tillich, *Christianity and the Encounter of the World Religions* (New York: Columbia University Press, 1963), p. 91.
4   *Nostra Aetate* ("Declaration on the Relationship of the Church to Non-Christian Religions"), in *The Documents of Vatican II* (America Press, 1966), pp. 660–61.

5   Paul Tillich, *Dynamics of Faith* (New York: Harper and Row, Harper Torchbooks, 1958), p. 66.

6   On this point see R. C. Zaehner, "Religious Truth," in *Truth and Dialogue in World Religions: Conflicting Truth-Claims*, ed. John Hick (Philadelphia: Westminster Press, 1974), p. 3.

7   Just as Muslims could accept or reject Mohammed Ahmad—of Khartoum fame during his theocratic state of 1882–1898—as a genuine Mahdi, without impugning the central role of Mohammed.

8   Raimundo Panikkar offers a similar list of possible responses in "Religious Pluralism: The Metaphysical Challenge," (in *Religious Pluralism*, ed. Leroy S. Rouner [Notre Dame, Indiana: University of Notre Dame Press, 1984], p. 98), but he does not clearly distinguish and analyze Pluralism vs. Relativism.

9   Karl Barth, *Church Dogmatics* (Edinburgh: T. & T. Clark, 1956), I/2, p. 350.

10 Ernst Troeltsch, "The Place of Christianity Among the World Religions," in *Christian Thought: Its History and Applications*, ed. Baron R. Hugel (New York: Meridian Books, Living Age Books, 1957), p. 52.

11 For an excellent of analysis of the role of Exclusivism within Christianity to achieve and preserve unity within an emerging sect, see Jean Runzo, *Communal Discipline in the Early Anabaptist Communities of Switzerland, South and Central Germany, Austria, and Moravia 1525–1550* (Ann Arbor, Michigan and London, England: University Microfilms International, 1978).

12 *Nostra Aetate*, in *Documents of Vatican II*, pp. 662 and 667.

13 Karl Rahner, *Theological Investigations*, vols. 1–20 (London: Darton, Longman & Todd; New York: Seabury Press, 1961–84), vol. 6, p. 391.

14 Zaehner, "Religious Truth," pp. 18 and 17.

15 John Baillie, *Our Knowledge of God* (New York: Charles Scribner's Sons, 1959), p. 255.

16 Frank Whaling, *Christian Theology and World Religions: A Global Approach* (Basingstoke: Marshall Pickering, 1986), p. 87.

17 Rahner, *Investigations*, vol. 5, p. 132.

18 Kant, *Critique of Pure Reason*, trans. Norman Kemp Smith (London: Macmillan, 1933), p. 93.

19 William James, *The Varieties of Religious Experience* (New York: Random House, The Modern Library, 1902), p. 120.

20 Ludwig Wittgenstein, *Philosophical Investigations*, 3rd edition, trans. G. E. M. Anscombe (New York: Macmillan Co., 1953), I. 268 b.

21 John Hick, *Problems of Religious Pluralism* (New York: St. Martin's Press, 1985), p. 34.

22 John Hick, *God Has Many Names* (Philadelphia: Westminster Press, 1982), p. 96.

23 Another form of relativism, epistemological relativism, holds that *second-order* meta-logical or meta-linguistic claims about what sorts of statements could be true or meaningful are only relative truths. This form of relativism seems to engender the paradoxical if not self-stultifying view that *all* truth is relative. Conceptual relativism about first-order truth does not in itself lead to this problem. I discuss this in *Reason, Relativism and God* (London: Macmillan, and New York: St. Martin's Press, 1986), pp. 38–41 and 45–48.

24 For an extended analysis of conceptual relativism see *Reason, Relativism and God*, ch. 2, especially pages 35–50. In contrast to subjectivism, on conceptual relativism world-views are largely societal constructs, and so different individuals can share the same world-view, or possess overlapping world-views.

25 See Wilfred Cantwell Smith, *The Meaning and End of Religion* (New York: Harper and Row, 1978).

26 See Wilfred Cantwell Smith, "A History of Religion in the Singular," in *Towards a World Theology* (Philadelphia: Westminster Press, 1981), pp. 3–20.

27 Wilfred Cantwell Smith, *Religious Diversity* (New York: Harper and Row, 1976), p. 16.

28   John Hick, *Problems of Religious Pluralism*, p. 29.

29   Hick, *Problems of Religious Pluralism*, p. 41.

30   Hick, *Problems of Religious Pluralism*, pp. 42–43. See also *God Has Many* Names, p. 59.

31   See Hick, *God Has Many Names*, p. 91.

32   Hick, *Problems of Religious Pluralism*, p. 99.

33   Hick, *Problems of Religious Pluralism*, pp. 93–94.

34   Maurice Wiles, *Faith and the Mystery of* God (Philadelphia: Fortress Press, 1982), p. 120. Other examples suggested by Raimundo Panikkar of religion-specific truth-claims which are essential to a religion and make the world religions irreducibly plural are the sense of historical consciousness in Christianity and the notion of *Karma* in various Asian religions. See "Religious Pluralism: The Metaphysical Challenge."

35   Hick, *Problems of Religious Pluralism*, pp. 39–44.

36   Though he refers to his own position as "pluralism," I take Panikkar's view to be a form of Religious Relativism when he says that "If we take religious pluralism seriously we cannot avoid asserting that truth itself is pluralistic" and that "being itself is pluralistic." ("Religious Pluralism: The Metaphysical Challenge," pp. 111–12.)

37   On the relativity of reality to world-views, see e.g., W. V. O. Quine, "Ontological Relativity" and "On What There Is," in , respectively, *Ontological Relativity and Other Essays* (New York: Columbia University Press, 1969) and *From a Logical Point of View* (New York: Harper and Row, Harper Torchbooks, 1953.) On the relativity of thinghood, see Nicholas Rescher, *Conceptual Idealism* (Oxford: Basil Blackwell, 1973), p. 108.

38   On this view of the relativity of reality to world-views and the consequent notion that there is more than one divine reality corresponding to the plurality of distinct religious world-views see *Reason, Relativism and God*, pp. 59–62 and pp. 238–42. For related views on the idea that reality is relative and that there is more than one actual world, see Nelson Goodman, *Ways of Worldmaking* (Indianapolis: Hackett, 1978), e.g., pp. 20–21, and for an analysis of this notion as it applies to the sciences, see Thomas Kuhn, *The Structure of Scientific Revolutions* (Chicago: University of Chicago Press, 2nd ed., 1970), e.g., pp. 109 and 116.

39   A world-view only delimits what is possible; it does not determine what is the case. A monotheist's world-view only delimits what God qua phenomenal could be. Whether that God actually exists, and what His nature actually is within what it could be, are further matters, independent of the world-view.

40   See Hick, *God Has Many Names*, p. 58 and *Problems of Religious Pluralism*, pp. 34–35.

41   See e.g., Hick, *Problems of Religious Pluralism*, p. 98.

42   Three conditions must be met for reference to God *qua* noumenal to be possible: (1) One must possess the requisite conceptual resources (whatever they are) to have concepts which *are* applicable to the noumenal, (2) one (subsequently) must actually form ideas which *are* literally true of the noumenal, and (3) there must be an appropriate causal connection between one's ideas and the noumenal, so that one's truth-claims *in fact* refer to the intended noumenal entity. In *Reason, Relativism and God* I argue that condition (3) can be met if the term used to designate the noumenal—in this case "God"—is used as a rigid designator (see pp. 246–53).

43   Also notice, to acknowledge that there may be other realities which are incompatible with your actual world does not mean that you are accepting incompatibilities *within* your world.

44   Whaling, *Christian Theology and World Religions*, pp. 95 and 98.

45   "While there cannot be a world religion, there can be approaches to a world theology. . . . a global theology would consist of theories or hypotheses designed to interpret the religious experience of mankind as it occurs not only within Christianity but also within the other great streams of religious life, . . ." (John Hick, *God Has Many Names*, p. 21.)

46   For example, this is explicit in Hick's essay, "On Grading Religions," *Religious Studies*, vol. XVII (1982), reprinted in *Problems of Religious Pluralism*.

47   I am grateful to William Alston and John Hick for helpful comments which made this a better paper, and to the National Endowment for the Humanities for a Summer Stipend Fellowship which supported my work on this topic.

Questions for reflection

1   What is Religious Relativism? How does it differ from Religious Pluralism?
2   What are some objections to Hick's pluralism raised by Runzo? Do you agree with the objections? Explain.
3   What are some reasons Professor Runzo does not accept Religious Exclusivism and Inclusivism? Do you agree with these reasons? Why or why not?
4   Of the six responses to the conflicting truth-claims of the core beliefs among the world religions, which one best captures what you believe? What are your reasons for holding this position (if you don't hold to any of them, which one do you find most plausible, and why)?

Further reading

Peter Byrne (1995) *Prolegomena to Religious Pluralism: Reference and Realism in Religion.* New York: St. Martin's Press. (A clear analysis of philosophical consequences of religious pluralism.)

Nicholas Rescher (1993) *Pluralism: Against the Demand for Consensus.* Oxford: Oxford University Press. (A defense of philosophical pluralism and a rejection of the need for rationalistic consensus.)

Joseph Runzo (2001) *Global Philosophy of Religion: A Short Introduction.* Oxford: Oneworld. (An exceptionally clear and insightful textbook on global philosophy of religion; chapter two includes Professor Runzo's further reflection on religious relativism and pluralism.)

Keith Ward (1994) *Religion and Revelation.* New York: Oxford University Press. (This is Volume II in Ward's important tetralogy which sets out a pluralistic, systematic philosophical theology.)

Chapter 5

Tenzin Gyatso, the Dalai Lama

INTERRELIGIOUS HARMONY

Tenzin Gyatso—the fourteenth Dalai Lama—is the spiritual leader of the Tibetan people. He has received international recognition, including the Nobel Peace Prize, for his assiduous efforts for human rights and world peace. In this essay, he maintains that while religion has historically been a major source of conflict, nonetheless, if understood and practiced appropriately, religion can play a leading role in encouraging understanding and respect toward all people. In order to establish this attitude, he maintains that interreligious harmony is necessary—a harmony that appreciates the value of other faith traditions outside of one's own without acquiescing to syncretism.

It is a sad fact of human history that religion has often been a major source of conflict. Even today, individuals are killed, their communities destroyed and societies destabilized as a result of religious bigotry and hatred. It is no wonder that many question the place of religion in human society. Yet when we think carefully, we find that conflict in the name of religion arises from two principal sources. There is that which arises simply as a result of religious diversity—the doctrinal, cultural and practical differences between one religion and another. Then there is the conflict that arises in the context of political, economic and other factors, mainly at the institutional level. Interreligious harmony is the key to overcoming conflict of the first sort. In the case of the second, some other solution must be found. Secularization and in particular the separation of the religious hierarchy from the institutions of the state may go some way to reducing such institutional problems. Our concern in this chapter is with interreligious harmony, however.

This is an important aspect of what I have called universal responsibility. But before examining the matter in detail, it is perhaps worth considering the question of whether religion is really relevant in the modern world. Many people argue that it is not. Now I have observed that religious belief is not a precondition either of ethical conduct or of happiness itself. I have also suggested that whether a person practises religion or not, the spiritual qualities of love and compassion, patience, tolerance, forgiveness, humility and so on are indispensable. At the same time, I should make it clear that I believe that these are most easily and effectively developed within the context of religious practice. I also believe that when an individual sincerely practises religion, that individual will benefit enormously. People who have developed firm faith, grounded in understanding and rooted in daily practice, are in general much better at coping with adversity than those who have not. I am convinced, therefore, that religion has enormous potential to benefit humanity. Properly employed, it is an extremely effective instrument for establishing human happiness. In particular, it can play a leading role in encouraging people to develop a sense of responsibility towards others and of the need to be ethically disciplined.

On these grounds, therefore, I believe that religion is still relevant today. But consider this too: some years ago, the body of a Stone Age man was recovered from the ice of the European Alps. Despite being more than five thousand years old, it was perfectly preserved. Even its clothes were largely intact. I remember thinking at the time that were it possible to bring this individual back to life for a day, we would find that we have much in common with him. No doubt we would find that he too was concerned for his family and loved ones, for his health and so on. Differences of culture and expression notwithstanding, we would still be able to identify with one another on a basic human level. And there could be no reason to suppose any less concern with finding happiness and avoiding suffering on his part than on ours. If religion, with its emphasis on overcoming suffering through the practice of ethical discipline and cultivation of love and compassion, can be conceived of as relevant in his time, it is hard to see why it should not be equally so today. Granted that in the past the value of religion may have been more obvious in that human suffering was more explicit due to the lack of modern facilities. But because we humans still suffer, albeit that today this is experienced more internally as mental and emotional affliction, and because religion in addition to its salvific truth claims is concerned to help us overcome suffering, surely it must still be relevant.

How then might we bring about the harmony that is necessary to overcome interreligious conflict? As in the case of individuals engaged in the discipline of restraining their response to negative thoughts and emotions and cultivating spiritual qualities, the key lies in developing understanding. We must first identify the factors that obstruct it. Then we must find ways to overcome them.

Perhaps the most significant obstruction to interreligious harmony is lack of appreciation of the value of others' faith traditions. Until comparatively recently, communication between different cultures, even different communities, was slow or nonexistent. For this reason, sympathy for other faith traditions was not necessarily very important— except of course where members of different religions lived side by side. But this attitude is no longer viable. In today's increasingly complex and interdependent world, we are compelled to acknowledge the existence of other cultures, different ethnic groups, and, of course, other religious faiths. Whether we like it or not, most of us now experience this diversity on a daily basis.

I believe that the best way to overcome ignorance and bring about understanding is through dialogue with members of other faith traditions. This I see occurring in a number of different ways. Discussions among scholars in which the convergence and, perhaps more importantly, the divergence between different faith traditions is explored and appreciated are very valuable. On another level, it is helpful when there are encounters between ordinary but practising followers of different religions in which each shares their experiences. This is perhaps the most effective way of appreciating others' teachings. In my own case, for example, my meetings with the late Thomas Merton, a Catholic monk of the Cistercian order, were deeply inspiring. They helped me develop a profound admiration for the teachings of Christianity. I also feel that occasional meetings between religious leaders joining together to pray for a common cause are extremely useful. The gathering at Assisi in Italy in 1986, when representatives of the world's major religions gathered to pray for peace, was, I believe, tremendously beneficial to many religious believers insofar as it symbolized the solidarity and commitment to peace of all those taking part.

Finally, I feel that the practice of members of different faith traditions going on joint pilgrimages together can be very helpful. It was in this spirit that in 1993 I went to Lourdes, and then to Jerusalem—a site holy to three of the world's great religions. I have also paid visits to various Hindu, Islamic, Jain and Sikh shrines both in India and abroad. More recently, following a seminar devoted to discussing and practising meditation in the Christian and Buddhist traditions, I joined an historic pilgrimage of practitioners of both traditions in a programme of prayers, meditation, and dialogue under the Bodhi tree at Bodh Gaya in India. This is one of Buddhism's most important shrines.

When exchanges like these occur, followers of one tradition will find that, just as in the case of their own, the teachings of others' faiths are a source both of spiritual inspiration and of ethical guidance to their followers. It will also become clear that irrespective of doctrinal and other differences, all the major world religions are concerned with helping individuals to become good human beings. All emphasize love and compassion, patience, tolerance, forgiveness, humility and so on, and all are capable of helping individuals to develop these. Moreover, the example given by the founders of each major religion clearly demonstrates a concern for helping others find happiness through developing these qualities. So far as their own lives were concerned, each conducted themselves with great simplicity. Ethical discipline and love for all others was the hallmark of their lives. They did not live luxuriously like emperors and kings. Instead, they voluntarily accepted suffering—without consideration of the hardships involved—in order to benefit humanity as a whole. In their teachings, all placed special emphasis on developing love and compassion and renouncing selfish desires. And each of them called on us to transform our hearts and minds. Indeed, whether we have faith or not, all are worthy of our profound admiration.

At the same time as engaging in dialogue with followers of other religions, we must, of course, implement in our daily life the teachings of our own religion. Once we have experienced the benefit of love and compassion, and of ethical discipline, we will easily recognize the value of others' teachings. But for this, it is essential to realize that religious practice entails a lot more than merely saying, 'I believe' or, as in Buddhism, 'I take refuge.' There is also more to it than just visiting temples, or shrines or churches. And taking religious teachings is of little benefit if they do not enter the heart but remain at the level of intellect alone. Simply relying on faith without understanding and without implementation is of limited value. I often tell Tibetans that carrying a *mala* (something like a rosary) does not make a person a genuine religious practitioner. The efforts we make sincerely to transform ourselves spiritually are what make us a genuine religious practitioner.

We come to see the overriding importance of genuine practice when we recognize that, along with ignorance, individuals' unhealthy relationships with their beliefs is the other major factor in religious disharmony. Far from applying the teachings of our religion in our personal lives, we have a tendency to use them to reinforce our self-centred attitudes. We relate to our religion as to something we own or as a label that separates us from others. Surely this is misguided? Instead of using the nectar of religion to purify the poisonous elements of our hearts and minds, there is a danger when we think like this of using these negative elements to poison the nectar of religion.

Yet we must acknowledge that this reflects another problem, one which is implicit in all religions. I refer to the claims each has of being the one 'true' religion. How are we to resolve this difficulty? It is true that from the point of view of the individual practitioner, it is essential to have a single-pointed commitment to our own faith. It is also true that this depends on the deep conviction that one's own path is the sole mediator of truth. But at the same time, we have to find some means of reconciling this belief with the reality of a multiplicity of similar claims. In practical terms, this involves individual practitioners finding a way at least to accept the validity of the teachings of other religions while maintaining a whole-hearted commitment to their own. As far as the validity of the metaphysical truth claims of a given religion is concerned, that is of course the internal business of that particular tradition.

In my own case, I am convinced that Buddhism provides me with the most effective framework within which to situate my efforts to develop spiritually through cultivating love and compassion. At the same time, I must acknowledge that while Buddhism represents the best path for me—that is, it suits my character, my temperament, my inclinations and my cultural background—the same will be true of, for example, Christianity for Christians. For them, Christianity is the best way. On the basis of my conviction, I cannot therefore say that Buddhism is best for everyone.

I often think of religion in terms of medicine for the human spirit. Independent of its usage and suitability to a particular individual in a particular condition, we cannot really judge a medicine's efficacy. We are not justified in saying this medicine is very good because of such and such ingredients. If you take the patient and its effect on that person out of the equation, it hardly makes sense. What is relevant is to say that in the case of this particular patient with his or her particular illness, this medicine is the most effective. Similarly with different religious traditions, we can say that this one is most effective for this particular individual. But it is unhelpful to try to argue on the basis of philosophy or metaphysics that one religion is better than another. The important thing is surely its effectiveness in individual cases.

My way to resolve the seeming contradiction between each religion's claim to 'one truth and one religion' and the reality of the multiplicity of faiths is thus to understand that in the case of a single individual, there can indeed be only one truth, one religion. However, from the perspective of human society at large, we must accept the concept of 'many truths, many religions.' To continue with our medical analogy, in the case of one particular patient, the suitable medicine is in fact the only medicine. But clearly that does not mean that there may not be other medicines suitable to other patients.

To my way of thinking, the diversity that exists amongst the various religious traditions is enormously enriching. There is thus no need to try to find ways of saying that ultimately all religions are the same. They are similar in that they all emphasize the indispensability of love and compassion in the context of ethical discipline. But to say this is not to say that they are all essentially one. The contradictory understanding of creation and beginninglessness articulated by Buddhism, Christianity and Hinduism, for example, means that in the end we have to part company when it comes to metaphysical claims, in spite of the many practical similarities that undoubtedly exist. These philosophical contradictions may not be very important in the beginning stages of religious practice. But as we advance along the path of one tradition or another, we are compelled at some point to acknowledge fundamental differences. For example, the concept of rebirth in Buddhism and various other ancient Indian traditions may turn out to be incompatible with the Christian idea of salvation. This need not be a cause for dismay, however. Even within Buddhism itself, in the realm of metaphysics there are diametrically opposing views. At the very least, such diversity means that we have different frameworks within which to locate ethical discipline and the development of spiritual values. That is why I do not advocate a 'super' or a new 'world' religion. It would mean that we would lose the unique characteristics of the different faith traditions.

Some people, it is true, hold that the Buddhist concept of *shunyata*, or emptiness, is ultimately the same as certain approaches to understanding the concept of God. Nevertheless, there remain difficulties with this. The first is that while of course we can interpret these concepts, to what extent can we be faithful to the original teachings? There are compelling similarities between the Mahayana Buddhist concept of *dharmakaya*, *sambogakaya* and *nirmanakaya* and the Christian trinity of God as Father, Son and Holy Spirit. But to say, on the basis of this, that Buddhism and Christianity are ultimately the same is to go a bit too far, I think! As an old Tibetan saying goes, we must beware of trying to put a yak's head on a sheep's body—or vice versa.

What is required instead is that we develop a genuine sense of religious pluralism, in spite of the different claims of different faith traditions. This is especially true if we are serious in our respect for human rights as a universal principle. In this regard, I find the concept of a world parliament of religions very appealing. To begin with, the word 'parliament' conveys a sense of democracy, while the plural 'religions' underlines the importance of the principle of a multiplicity of faith traditions. The truly pluralist perspective on religion which the idea of such a parliament suggests could, I believe, be of great help. It could help avoid the extremes of religious bigotry on the one hand, and the urge toward unnecessary syncretism on the other.

Connected with this issue of interreligious harmony, I should perhaps say something about religious conversion. This is a question which must be taken extremely seriously. It is essential to realize that the mere fact of conversion alone will not make an individual a better person—that is to say, a more disciplined, a more compassionate, a more warm-hearted person. In general, it is better for the individual to concentrate on transforming themselves spiritually through the practice of restraint, virtue and compassion than through conversion to another faith. To the extent that the insights or practices of other religions are useful or relevant to our own faith, it is valuable to learn from others. In some cases, it may even be helpful to adopt certain of them. Yet when this is done wisely, we can remain firmly committed to our own faith. This way is best because it carries with it no danger of confusion, especially with respect to the different ways of life that tend to go with different faith traditions.

Given the diversity to be found among individual human beings, it is of course bound to be the case that out of many millions of practitioners of a particular religion, a handful will find that another religion's approach to ethics and spiritual development is more satisfactory. For some, the concept of rebirth and *karma* will seem highly effective in inspiring the aspiration to develop love and compassion within the context of responsibility. For others, the concept of a transcendent, loving creator will come to seem more so. In such circumstances, it is crucial for those individuals to question themselves again and again. They must ask, 'Am I attracted to this other religion for the right reasons? Is it merely the cultural and ritual aspects that are appealing? Or is it the essential teachings? Do I suppose that if I convert to this new religion it will be less demanding than my present one?' I say this because it has often struck me that when people do convert to a religion outside their own heritage, quite often they adopt certain superficial aspects of the culture to which their new faith belongs. But their practice may not go very much deeper than that.

In the case of a person who decides after a process of long and mature reflection to adopt a different religion, it is very important that they remember the positive contribution to humanity of each religious tradition. The danger is that the individual may, in seeking to justify their decision to others, criticize their previous faith. It is essential to avoid this. Just because that tradition is no longer effective in the case of one individual does not mean it is no longer of benefit to humanity. On the contrary, we can be certain that it has been an inspiration to millions of people in the past, that it inspires millions today, and that it will inspire millions in the path of love and compassion in the future.

The important point to keep in mind is that ultimately the whole purpose of religion is to facilitate love and compassion, patience, tolerance, humility, forgiveness and so on. If we neglect these, changing our religion will be of no help. In the same way, even if we are fervent believers in our own faith, it will avail us nothing if we neglect to implement these qualities in our daily lives. Such a believer is no better off than a patient with some fatal illness who merely reads a medical treatise but fails to undertake the treatment prescribed.

Moreover, if we who are practitioners of religion are not compassionate and disciplined, how can we expect it of others? If we can establish genuine harmony derived from mutual respect and understanding, religion has enormous potential to speak with authority on such vital moral questions as peace and disarmament, social and political justice, the natural environment and many other matters affecting all humanity. But until we put our own spiritual teachings into practice, we will never be taken seriously. And this means, among other things, setting a good example through developing good relations with other faith traditions.

Questions for reflection

1   What does it mean to have interreligious harmony? Is it possible to have interreligious harmony while affirming that one's own religious tradition is true? Why or why not?

2   The Dalai Lama asserts that "the whole purpose of religion is to facilitate love and compassion, patience, tolerance, humility, forgiveness, and so on." Do you agree with this statement? If not, what is the whole purpose of religion?

3   Do you agree with the Dalai Lama that while religion has historically been a major

source of conflict, nonetheless, if understood and practiced appropriately, it can play a leading role in encouraging understanding and respect toward all people? Explain your answer.

Further reading

Tenzin Gyatso, the Dalai Lama (1998) *Freedom in Exile: The Autobiography of the Dalai Lama of Tibet*, new edn, London: Abacus. (The autobiography of a significant man of peace.)

Robert McKim (2005) *Religious Ambiguity and Religious Diversity.* Oxford: Oxford University Press. (Carefully examines two central issues—the religious ambiguity of the world and the diversity of religious faiths.)

Perez Zagorin (2005) *How the Idea of Religious Toleration Came to the West.* Princeton, NJ: Princeton University Press. (A scholarly but readable and engaging presentation of the origins of religious toleration in the West since the Enlightenment.)

PART TWO

The nature and attributes of God/Ultimate Reality

Throughout recorded history, people from all varieties of cultures and persuasions have wondered about the existence of God. As it turns out, a large majority of human beings have affirmed some sort of belief in a divine reality. Certainly not everyone has had such a belief, especially those in the more industrialized and educated cultures of the previous and present centuries. We will soon look at some of the most thoughtful work, both pro and con, on this very issue. Before we get there, however, it will be helpful to reflect on what the term "God," or "Ultimate Reality," actually connotes. What do we mean when we use these terms? What have the great thinkers meant when they referred to God or Ultimate Reality? What is the nature of Ultimate Reality? These are the kinds of questions on which we will focus in this section.

There are, of course, both theistic and non-theistic understandings of God, or Ultimate Reality. We begin this section with the writings of monotheistic thinkers. Monotheism, or what is sometimes referred to as "Ethical Monotheism," is the view that God exists as a perfect being and that his nature can be at least partly described through the use of various "omnis": omniscient (all-knowing), omnipotent (all-powerful), omnibenevolent (morally perfect), and so forth. This is the view of God traditionally held by adherents of the three monotheistic religions of Judaism, Christianity, and Islam. There is also a longstanding tradition within Hinduism that affirms various monotheistic attributes, such as God's being infinite, personal, and good.

In chapters six through ten, a variety of these traditional attributes of God are examined in the works of classical monotheistic thinkers. First, Avicenna, a Muslim philosopher from the Medieval period, argues that God is a Necessary Being, that God is one, that God is uncaused, and that God is omniscient. Moses Maimonides, a Medieval Jewish rabbi and philosopher, argues in the following chapter that God is a simple being; that is, God is not divisible, either physically or metaphysically. He also examines the way we refer to God and maintains that only negative ascriptions should be utilized when referring to God.

The Medieval Christian philosopher/theologian Boethius replies to an objection commonly raised against theism: that divine providence contradicts human free will. According to Boethius, God can have certain knowledge of past, present, and future events, and yet human beings can still have a robust freedom of the will. Following Boethius is Thomas Aquinas, the leading Christian philosopher/theologian of the Middle Ages. While admitting that understanding God's power is difficult, Aquinas nevertheless explicates and defends the notion of divine omnipotence. The next reading is by a classical Vedantan Hindu philosopher, Ramanuja. He expounds on the Vedas—the sacred Hindu texts—and maintains that, contrary to some Hindu teachings, Brahman is in fact personal, infinite, and good and is separate from his creation.

For Ramanuja, as for each of the other monotheistic thinkers included here, God is a personal being. But what does it mean to affirm personhood of God? Recent discussions about the personal nature of God in philosophical theology have focused on the Trinity and the nature of Christ (who is held by Christians to be God incarnate). Thomas Morris offers a philosophical examination of these two central Christian doctrines. They are both admittedly difficult doctrines to grasp, and they are sometimes taken to be paradoxes or mysteries that the human mind simply cannot understand. Morris, however, takes a stab at them—one that stays within the bounds of Christian orthodoxy.

Another major topic of discussion in philosophical theology has to do with a seeming contradiction between one of God's attributes—namely, omniscience—and human free will. Consider this: if God has exhaustive knowledge of all future events, including human actions, how could we freely choose to do those actions? For example, if God already knows today what you will have for lunch tomorrow, then it appears that you could not freely choose something else for lunch tomorrow. For if you do choose something else, God would be wrong and thus not omniscient. William Hasker defends a view of God's knowledge which, unlike the traditional concepts such as the one defended by Boethius, posits a future that is open and uncertain. This view, he maintains, allows for human freedom without denying God's omniscience and avoids the contradictions which arise from the traditional view of God's knowledge.

This challenge of the traditional view of God is taken even further by Christian and Jewish scholars who hold to a position known as "process theology." Nicholas Rescher provides a helpful synopsis of the process notion of divine reality in the next reading. He maintains that God is not a substance in the classical sense of the term. Rather, God is involved within the spatiotemporal world as an active participant; God is "a *process* that is at work in and beyond the world." On this view of God, he maintains, many of the difficulties which have arisen regarding the traditional notion of God simply evaporate.

As noted above, there are also non-theistic ways of understanding Ultimate Reality. The next three selections, fourteen through sixteen, are just such perspectives: one from Hinduism, the next from Taoism, and the last from Buddhism. First, then, I include a work by one of the most significant Hindu philosophers through the centuries. Shankara is perhaps historically the most prominent proponent of Advaita Vedanta (non-dual) Hinduism. On this view, Ultimate Reality is understood monistically—Brahman, the divine Reality, is one, and is everything.

In the next chapter, excerpts are taken from a classic Taoist text, the *Tao Te Ching*—believed to be the work of Lao Tzu. Scholars disagree on its meaning, and it has been interpreted in numerous ways, but one thing seems fairly evident: central to Taoism and the *Tao Te Ching* is the Tao, the ineffable, fundamental reality and ground of being. In this selection I have included sections of the classic work which focus primarily on the Tao.

Finally, in chapter sixteen, Buddhist philosopher K. N. Jayatellike puts forth a view of

Ultimate Reality that makes no reference to divinity whatsoever. For him, nirvana is the highest good, a state of perfection. It is a kind of extinction, an extinction of all desires — like the blowing out of a candle — and a realization that there are no substantial entities to experience desires. This is the emancipated state of becoming; this is Ultimate Reality; this is nirvana.

Theistic perspectives of Ultimate Reality

Chapter 6

Avicenna

GOD'S NATURE AND KNOWLEDGE

Avicenna (also known as Ibn Sina—980–1037 CE) was a Muslim physician, scientist and one of the central philosophers in the Medieval Islamic tradition. A prolific author, he wrote hundreds of books on a wide range of topics, including medicine, astronomy, geometry, arithmetic, music, philosophy, and theology. As a Muslim, Avicenna believed that God (or Allah) is Ultimate Reality, and everything else comes from Him. Also as a Muslim, he believed that the Qur'an is a divinely inspired book given by God to the prophet Muhammad. It contains divine truth, and one of its central truths is that God is ultimate and one. But what this truth means was debated among Islamic philosophers and theologians of the Medieval period. Avicenna, being well-studied in both theology and philosophy, attempted to understand the nature of God while being faithful both to the Qur'an and to reason. In this selection, Avicenna first argues that there must exist a *Necessary Being* (that is, a Being that cannot not exist; a *contingent being*, on the other hand, such as a human being, does not exist necessarily), and that this being must be one. He uses language with which many contemporary readers may not be familiar. For example, the term "Quiddity" is frequently mentioned. It is derived from the Latin word "quidditas" and means the "whatness" of a thing (that is, roughly, a thing's nature or essence). Through an analysis of different kinds of causes, along with an examination of how God's essence is identical with His being, or existence, Avicenna attempts to demonstrate how God has no cause whatsoever. His argument for God's being a Necessary Being, along with the essence/being identity claim, affects a number of further theological issues, including what God knows, which he expounds upon here as well.

That there is a Necessary Being

Whatever has being must either have a reason for its being, or have no reason for it. If it has a reason, then it is contingent, equally before it comes into being (if we make this mental hypothesis) and when it is in the state of being—for in the case of a thing whose being is contingent the mere fact of its entering upon being does not remove from it the contingent nature of its being. If on the other hand it has no reason for its being in any way whatsoever, then it is necessary in its being. This rule having been confirmed, I shall now proceed to prove that there is in being a being which has no reason for its being.

Such a being is either contingent or necessary. If it is necessary, then the point we sought to prove is established. If on the other hand it is contingent, that which is contingent cannot enter upon being except for some reason which sways the scales in favour of its being and against its not-being. If the reason is also contingent, there is then a chain of contingents linked one to the other, and there is no being at all; for this being which is the subject of our hypothesis cannot enter into being so long as it is not preceded by an infinite succession of beings, which is absurd. Therefore contingent beings end in a Necessary Being.

Of the unicity of God

It is not possible in any way that the Necessary Being should be two. Demonstration: Let us suppose that there is another necessary being: one must be distinguishable from the other, so that the terms "this" and "that" may be used with reference to them. This distinction must be either essential or accidental. If the distinction between them is accidental, this accidental element cannot but be present in each of them, or in one and not the other. If each of them has an accidental element by which it is distinguished from the other, both of them must be caused; for an accident is what is adjoined to a thing after its essence is realized. If the accidental element is regarded as adhering to its being, and is present in one of the two and not in the other, then the one which has no accidental element is a necessary being and the other is not a necessary being. If, however, the distinction is essential, the element of essentiality is that whereby the essence as such subsists; and if this element of essentiality is different in each and the two are distinguishable by virtue of it, then each of the two must be a compound; and compounds are caused; so that neither of them will be a necessary being. If the element of essentiality belongs to one only, and the other is one in every respect and there is no compounding of any kind in it, then the one which has no element of essentiality is a necessary being, and the other is not a necessary being. Since it is thus established that the Necessary Being cannot be two, but is All Truth, then by virtue of His Essential Reality, in respect of which He is a Truth, He is United and One, and no other shares with Him in that Unity: however the All-Truth attains existence, it is through Himself.

That God is without cause

A necessary being has no cause whatsoever. Causes are of four kinds: that from which a thing has being, or the active cause; that on account of which a thing has being, or the final and completive cause; that in which a thing has being, or the material cause; and that through which a thing has being, or the formal cause.

The justification for limiting causes to these four varieties is that the reason for a thing is either internal in its subsistence, or a part of its being, or external to it. If it is internal, then it is either that part in which the thing is, potentially and not actually, that is to say its matter; or it is that part in which the thing becomes actually, that is to say its form. If it is external, then it can only be either that from which the thing has being, that is to say the agent, or that on account of which the thing has being, that is to say its purpose and end.

Since it is established that these are the roots and principles of this matter, let us rest on them and clarify the problems which are constructed upon them.

Demonstration that He has no active cause: This is self-evident: for if He had any reason for being, this would be adventitious and that would be a necessary being. Since it is established that He has no active cause, it follows on this line of reasoning that His Quiddity [His essence or nature] is not other than His Identity, that is to say, other than His Being; neither will He be a subsistence or an accident. There cannot be two, each of which derives its being from the other; nor can He be a necessary being in one respect, and a contingent being in another respect.

Proof that His Quiddity is not other than His Identity, but rather that His Being is unified in His Reality: If His Being were not the same as His Reality, then His Being would be other than His Reality. Every accident is caused, and every thing caused requires a reason. Now this reason is either external to His Quiddity, or is itself His Quiddity: if it is external, then He is not a necessary being, and is not exempt from an active cause; while if the reason is itself the Quiddity, then the reason must necessarily be itself a complete being in order that the being of another may result from it. Quiddity before being has no being; and if it had being before this, it would not require a second being. The question therefore returns to the problem of being. If the Being of the Quiddity is accidental, whence did this Being supervene and adhere? It is therefore established that the Identity of the Necessary Being is His Quiddity, and that He has no active cause; the necessary nature of His Being is like the quiddity of all other things. From this it is evident that the Necessary Being does not resemble any other thing in any respect whatsoever; for with all other things their being is other than their quiddity.

Proof that He is not an accident: An accident is a being in a locus. The locus is precedent to it, and its being is not possible without the locus. But we have stated that a being which is necessary has no reason for its being.

Proof that there cannot be two necessary beings, each deriving its being from the other: Each of them, in as much as it derives its being from the other, would be subsequent to the other, while at the same time by virtue of supplying being to the other, each would be precedent to the other: but one and the same thing cannot be both precedent and subsequent in relation to its being. Moreover, if we assume for the sake of argument that the other is non-existent: would the first then be a necessary being, or not? If it were a necessary being, it would have no connexion with the other: if it were not a necessary being, it would be a contingent being and would require another necessary being. Since the Necessary Being is One, and does not derive Its being from anyone, it follows that He is a Necessary Being in every respect; while anything else derives its being from another.

Proof that He cannot be a Necessary Being in one respect and a contingent being in another respect: Such a being, in as much as it is a contingent being, would be connected in being with something else, and so it has a reason; but in as much as it is a necessary being, it would have no connexions with anything else. In that case it would both have being and not have being; and that is absurd.

Demonstration that He has no material and receptive cause: The receptive cause is the cause for the provision of the place in which a thing is received; that is to say, the place prepared for the reception of being, or the perfection of being. Now the Necessary Being is a perfection in pure actuality, and is not impaired by any deficiency; every perfection belongs to Him, derives from Him, and is preceded by His Essence, while every deficiency, even if it be metaphorical, is negated to Him. All perfection and all beauty are of His Being; indeed, these are the vestiges of the perfection of His Being; how then should He derive perfection from any other? Since it is thus established that He has no receptive cause, it follows that He does not possess anything potentially, and that He has no attribute yet to be awaited; on the contrary, His Perfection has been realized in actuality; and He has no material cause. We say "realized in actuality", using this as a common term of expression, meaning that every perfection belonging to any other is non-existent and yet to be awaited, whereas all perfection belonging to Him has being and is present. His Perfect Essence, preceding all relations, is One. From this it is manifest that His Attributes are not an augmentation of His Essence; for if they were an augmentation of His Essence, the Attributes would be potential with reference to the Essence and the Essence would be the reason for the Attributes. In that case the Attributes would be subsequent to a precedent, so that they would be in one respect active and in another receptive; their being active would be other than the aspect of their being receptive; and in consequence they would possess two mutually exclusive aspects. Now this is impossible in the case of anything whatsoever; when a body is in motion, the motivation is from one quarter and the movement from another.

If it were to be stated that His Attributes are not an augmentation of His Essence, but that they entered into the constitution of the Essence, and that the Essence cannot be conceived of as existing without these Attributes, then the Essence would be compound, and the Oneness would be destroyed. It is also evident, as a result of denying the existence of a receptive cause, that it is impossible for Him to change; for the meaning of change is the passing away of one attribute and the establishment of another; and if He were susceptible to change, He would possess potentially an element of passing-away and an element of establishment; and that is absurd. It is clear from this that He has no opposite and no contrary; for opposites are essences which succeed each other in the occupation of a single locus, there being between them the extreme of contrariety. But He is not receptive to accidents, much less to opposites. And if the term "opposite" is used to denote one who disputes with Him in His Rulership, it is clear too on this count that He has no opposite. It is further clear that it is impossible for Him not to be; for since it is established that His Being is necessary, it follows that it is impossible for Him not to be; because everything which exists potentially cannot exist actually, otherwise it would have two aspects. Anything which is receptive to a thing does not cease to be receptive when reception has actually taken place; if this were not so, it would result in the removal of both being and not-being, and that is untenable. This rule applies to every essence and every unified reality, such as angels and human spirits; they are not susceptible to not-being at all, since they are free from corporeal adjunctions.

Demonstration that He has no formal cause: A formal, corporeal cause only exists and is confirmed when a thing is possessed of matter: the matter has a share in the being of the form, in the same way that the form has a part in the disposition of the matter in being in actuality; such a thing is therefore caused. It is further evident as a result of denying this cause to Him, that He is also to be denied all corporeal attributes, such as time, space, direction, and being in one place to the exclusion of all other; in short, whatever is possible in relation to corporeal things is impossible in relation to Him.

Proof that He has no final cause: The final cause is that on account of which a thing has being; and the First Truth has not being for the sake of anything, rather does everything exist on account of the perfection of His Essence, being consequent to His Being and derived from His Being. Moreover the final cause, even if it be posterior in respect of being to all other causes, yet it is mentally prior to them all. It is the final cause which makes the active cause become a cause in actuality, that is to say in respect of its being a final cause.

Since it is established that He is exalted above this last kind of cause too, it is clear that there is no cause to His Attributes. It is also evident that He is Pure Benevolence and True Perfection; the meaning of His Self-Sufficiency likewise becomes manifest, namely that He approves of nothing and disapproves of nothing. For if He approved of anything, that thing would come into being and would continue to be; while if He disapproved of anything, that thing would be converted into not-being and would be annulled. The very divergency of these beings proves the nullity of such a proposition; for a thing which is one in every respect cannot approve of a thing and of its opposite. It is also not necessary for Him to observe the rule of greater expediency or of expediency, as certain Qualitarians have idly pretended; for if His acts of expediency were obligatory to Him, He would not merit gratitude and praise for such acts, since He would merely be fulfilling that which it is His obligation to perform, and He would be to all intents and purposes as one paying a debt; He would therefore deserve nothing at all for such benevolence. In fact His acts proceed on the contrary from Him and for Him, as we shall demonstrate later.

His attributes as interpreted according to the foregoing principles

Since it is established that God is a Necessary Being, that He is One in every respect, that He is exalted above all causes, and that He has no reason of any kind for His Being; since it is further established that His Attributes do not augment His Essence, and that He is qualified by the Attributes of Praise and Perfection; it follows necessarily that we must state that He is Knowing, Living, Willing, Omnipotent, Speaking, Seeing, Hearing, and Possessed of all the other Loveliest Attributes. It is also necessary to recognize that His Attributes are to be classified as negative, positive, and a compound of the two: since His Attributes are of this order, it follows that their multiplicity does not destroy His Unity or contradict the necessary nature of His Being. Pre-eternity for instance is essentially the negation of not-being in the first place, and the denial of causality and of primality in the second place; similarly the term One means that He is indivisible in every respect, both verbally and actually. When it is stated that He is a Necessary Being, this means that He is a Being without a cause, and that He is the Cause of other than Himself: this is a combination of the negative and the positive. Examples of the positive Attributes are His being Creator, Originator, Shaper, and the entire Attributes of Action. As for the compound of both, this kind is illustrated by His being Willing and Omnipotent, for these Attributes are a compound of Knowledge with the addition of Creativeness.

God's knowledge

God has knowledge of His Essence: His Knowledge, His Being Known and His Knowing are one and the same thing. He knows other than Himself, and all objects of knowledge. He knows all things by virtue of one knowledge, and in a single manner. His Knowledge does not change according to whether the thing known has being or not-being.

Proof that God has knowledge of His Essence: We have stated that God is One, and that He is exalted above all causes. The meaning of knowledge is the supervention of an idea divested of all corporeal coverings. Since it is established that He is One, and that He is divested of body, and His Attributes also; and as this idea as just described supervenes upon Him; and since whoever has an abstract idea supervening upon him is possessed of knowledge, and it is immaterial whether it is his essence or other than himself; and as further His Essence is not absent from Himself; it follows from all this that He knows Himself.

Proof that He is Knowledge, Knowing and Known: Knowledge is another term for an abstract idea. Since this idea is abstract, it follows that He is Knowledge; since this abstract idea belongs to Him, is present with Him, and is not veiled from Him, it follows that He is Knowing; and since this abstract idea does not supervene save through Him, it follows that He is Known. The terms employed in each case are different; otherwise it might be said that Knowledge, Knowing and Known are, in relation to His Essence, one. Take your own experience as a parallel. If you know yourself, the object of your knowledge is either yourself or something else; if the object of your knowledge is something other than yourself, then you do not know yourself. But if the object of your knowledge is yourself, then both the one knowing and the thing known are your self. If the image of your self is impressed upon your self, then it is your self which is the knowledge. Now if you look back upon yourself reflectively, you will not find any impression of the idea and quiddity of your self in yourself a second time, so as to give rise within you to a sense that your self is more than one. Therefore since it is established that He has intelligence of His Essence, and since His Intelligence is His Essence and does not augment His Essence, it follows that He is Knowing, Knowledge and Known without any multiplicity attaching to Him through these Attributes; and there is no difference between "one who has knowledge" and "one who has intelligence", since both are terms for describing the negation of matter absolutely.

Proof that He has knowledge of other than Himself: Whoever knows himself, if thereafter he does not know other than himself this is due to some impediment. If the impediment is essential, this implies necessarily that he does not know himself either; while if the impediment is of an external nature, that which is external can be removed. Therefore it is possible—nay, necessary—that He should have knowledge of other than Himself, as you shall learn from this chapter.

Proof that He has knowledge of all objects of knowledge: Since it is established that He is a Necessary Being, that He is One, and that the universe is brought into being from Him and has resulted out of His Being; since it is established further that He has knowledge of His Own Essence, His Knowledge of His Essence being what it is, namely that He is the Origin of all realities and of all things that have being; it follows that nothing in heaven or earth is remote from His Knowledge—on the contrary, all that comes into being does so by reason of Him: He is the causer of all reasons, and He knows that of which He is the Reason, the Giver of being and the Originator.

Proof that He knows all things by virtue of one knowledge, in a manner which changes not according to the change in the thing known: It has been established that His Knowledge does not augment His Essence, and that He is the Origin of all things that have being, while being exalted above accident and changes; it therefore follows that He knows things in a manner unchanging. The objects of knowledge are a consequence of His Knowledge; His Knowledge is not a consequence of the things known, that it should change as they change; for His Knowledge of things is the reason for their having being. Hence it is manifest that Knowledge is itself Omnipotence. He knows all contingent things, even as He knows all things that have being, even though we know them not; for the contingent, in relation to us, is a thing whose being is possible and whose not-being is also possible; but in relation to Him one of the two alternatives is actually known. Therefore His Knowledge of genera, species, things with being, contingent things, manifest and secret things—this Knowledge is a single knowledge.

Questions for reflection

1   Avicenna offers an argument for the existence of a Necessary Being in the first section of this essay. Is it a plausible argument? Explain.

2   In the second section, Avicenna argues for the unicity (oneness) of the Necessary Being. Does this argument count against the Trinitarian view of the Christian God? If so, how so? If not, why not?

3   Are you familiar with the four kinds of causes Avicenna utilizes? If not, do some research on them (note Aristotle's work, the *Physics*). Which of the four causes do we still hold to today? Is it reasonable to believe in final causes?

4   If it can be established that God is a Necessary Being, that He is one, that He is uncaused, and that His essence is identical with His being, does it follow that He is Knowing, Living, Willing, Omnipotent, etc.? On what basis does Avicenna make this claim?

5   Avicenna argues that God has knowledge of all things, and that His knowledge is unchanging. If this is true, does it eliminate His free will? Does it eliminate human free will?

Further reading

Arthur J. Arberry (1951) *Avicenna on Theology*. London: John Murray. (A short but fine collection of theological essays from which this selection was taken. For a pdf link of this work, go to http://umcc.ais.org/~maftab/ip/pdf/bktxt/arb-sin-2.pdf.)

Cicero ([45 BCE] 1933) *De natura deorum*. [*On the Nature of the Gods*]. Trans. H. Rackham. London: Heinemann. (A helpful resource of Graeco-Roman philosophical theology.)

Lenn E. Goodman (2005) *Avicenna*. London: Routledge. (A helpful introduction to Avicenna's philosophical theories.)

Thomas V. Morris (1991) *Our Idea of God*. Notre Dame, IN: University of Notre Dame Press. (A good introduction to issues in philosophical theology.)

Richard Swinburne (1993) *The Coherence of Theism*. Rev. edn. Oxford: Clarendon Press. (A careful examination of the nature and attributes of God, as well as a defense of the coherence of theism, from a prominent Christian philosopher.)

Chapter 7

Moses Maimonides

DIVINE SIMPLICITY, NEGATIVE THEOLOGY, AND GOD-TALK

Moses Maimonides, also known as Rambam (1135–1204 CE), was a Jewish rabbi, well-studied in the Hebrew Scriptures and writings, and a philosopher in Spain and Egypt in the Middle Ages. He is widely recognized to be one of the greatest philosophers in Jewish history. His concern was, among other things, the way language is used in reference to God. Since God is a simple Being—that is to say, since God is unlike creatures in that he has no complexity or composition (i.e., no spatial and temporal parts, no existence/essence composition, no ultimate distinctions between his attributes)—reference to God cannot be like reference to non-simple beings such as humans and animals. But how, then, can we make reference to God? In order to deal with this problem, as well as to respond to the Islamic literalists who had seemingly anthropomorphized God, Maimonides developed a negative theology (sometimes called "Apophatic theology"). According to him, positive descriptions of God would be inaccurate, so the only true way to speak about God is to say what he is not—to ascribe negative properties to him. This way of understanding has come to be called the *via negativa*—the way of negation.

Chapter LVII

On attributes; remarks more recondite than the preceding. It is known that existence is an accident appertaining to all things, and therefore an element superadded to their essence. This must evidently be the case as regards everything the existence of which is due to some cause; its existence is an element superadded to its essence. But as regards a being whose existence is not due to any cause—God alone is that being, for His existence, as we have said, is absolute—existence and essence are perfectly identical; He is not a substance to which existence is joined as an accident, as an additional element. His existence is always absolute, and has never been a new element or an accident in Him. Consequently God exists without possessing the attribute of existence. Similarly He lives, without possessing the attribute of life; knows, without possessing the attribute of knowledge; is omnipotent without possessing the attribute of omnipotence; is wise, without possessing the attribute of wisdom; all this reduces itself to one and the same entity; there is no plurality in Him, as will be shown. It is further necessary to consider that unity and plurality are accidents supervening to an object according as it consists of many elements or of one. This is fully explained in the book called Metaphysics. In the same way as number is not the substance of the things numbered, so is unity not the substance of the thing which has the attribute of unity, for unity and plurality are accidents belonging to the category of discrete quantity, and supervening to such objects as are capable of receiving them.

To that being, however, which has truly simple, absolute existence, and in which composition is inconceivable, the accident of unity is as inadmissible as the accident of plurality; that is to say, God's unity is not an element superadded, but He is One without possessing the attribute of unity. The investigation of this subject, which is almost too subtle for our understanding, must not be based on current expressions employed in describing it, for these are the great source of error. It would be extremely difficult for us to find, in any language whatsoever, words adequate to this subject, and we can only employ inadequate language. In our endeavour to show that God does not include a plurality, we can only say "He is one," although "one" and "many" are both terms which serve to distinguish quantity. We therefore make the subject clearer, and show to the understanding the way of truth by saying He is one but does not possess the attribute of unity.

The same is the case when we say God is the First (*Kadmon*), to express that He has not been created; the term "First" is decidedly inaccurate, for it can in its true sense only be applied to a being that is subject to the relation of time; the latter, however, is an accident to motion which again is connected with a body. Besides the attribute "first" is a relative term, being in regard to time the same as the terms "long" and "short" are in regard to a line. Both expressions, "first" and "created," are equally inadmissible in reference to any being to which the attribute of time is not applicable, just as we do not say "crooked" or "straight" in reference to taste, "salted" or "insipid" in reference to the voice. These subjects are not unknown to those who have accustomed themselves to seek a true understanding of the things, and to establish their properties in accordance with the abstract notions which the mind has formed of them, and who are not misled by the inaccuracy of the words employed. All attributes, such as "the First," "the Last," occurring in the Scriptures in reference to God, are as metaphorical as the expressions "ear" and "eye." They simply signify that God is not subject to any change or innovation whatever; they do not imply that God can be described by time, or that there is any comparison between Him and any other being as regards time, and that He is called on that account "the first" and "the last." In short, all similar expressions are borrowed from the language commonly used among the people. In the same way we use "One" in reference to God, to express that there is nothing similar to Him, but we do not mean to say that an attribute of unity is added to His essence.

Chapter LVIII

This chapter is even more recondite than the preceding. Know that the negative attributes of God are the true attributes: they do not include any incorrect notions or any deficiency

whatever in reference to God, while positive attributes imply polytheism, and are inadequate, as we have already shown. It is now necessary to explain how negative expressions
can in a certain sense be employed as attributes, and how they are distinguished from
positive attributes. Then I shall show that we cannot describe the Creator by any means
except by negative attributes. An attribute does not exclusively belong to the one object
to which it is related; while qualifying one thing, it can also be employed to qualify other
things, and is in that case not peculiar to that one thing. E.g., if you see an object from a
distance, and on enquiring what it is, are told that it is a living being, you have certainly
learnt an attribute of the object seen, and although that attribute does not exclusively
belong to the object perceived, it expresses that the object is not a plant or a mineral.
Again, if a man is in a certain house, and you know that something is in the house, but
not exactly what, you ask what is in that house, and you are told, not a plant nor a mineral. You have thereby obtained some special knowledge of the thing; you have learnt
that it is a living being, although you do not yet know what kind of a living being it is.
The negative attributes have this in common with the positive, that they necessarily circumscribe the object to some extent, although such circumscription consists only in
the exclusion of what otherwise would not be excluded. In the following point, however, the negative attributes are distinguished from the positive. The positive attributes,
although not peculiar to one thing, describe a portion of what we desire to know, either
some part of its essence or some of its accidents; the negative attributes, on the other
hand, do not, as regards the essence of the thing which we desire to know, in any way
tell us what it is, except it be indirectly, as has been shown in the instance given by us.

After this introduction, I would observe that,—as has already been shown—God's
existence is absolute, that it includes no composition, as will be proved, and that we
comprehend only the fact that He exists, not His essence. Consequently it is a false
assumption to hold that He has any positive attribute; for He does not possess existence
in addition to His essence; it therefore cannot be said that the one may be described as
an attribute [of the other]; much less has He [in addition to His existence] a compound
essence, consisting of two constituent elements to which the attribute could refer; still
less has He accidents, which could be described by an attribute. Hence it is clear that He
has no positive attribute whatever. The negative attributes, however, are those which
are necessary to direct the mind to the truths which we must believe concerning God;
for, on the one hand, they do not imply any plurality, and, on the other, they convey to
man the highest possible knowledge of God; e.g., it has been established by proof that
some being must exist besides those things which can be perceived by the senses, or
apprehended by the mind; when we say of this being, that it exists, we mean that its
non-existence is impossible. We then perceive that such a being is not, for instance, like
the four elements, which are inanimate, and we therefore say that it is living, expressing
thereby that it is not dead. We call such a being incorporeal, because we notice that it is
unlike the heavens, which are living, but material. Seeing that it is also different from
the intellect, which, though incorporeal and living, owes its existence to some cause,
we say it is the first, expressing thereby that its existence is not due to any cause. We
further notice, that the existence, that is the essence, of this being is not limited to its
own existence; many existences emanate from it, and its influence is not like that of the
fire in producing heat, or that of the sun in sending forth light, but consists in constantly
giving them stability and order by well-established rule, as we shall show: we say, on
that account, it has power, wisdom, and will, i.e., it is not feeble or ignorant, or hasty,

and does not abandon its creatures; when we say that it is not feeble, we mean that its existence is capable of producing the existence of many other things; by saying that it is not ignorant, we mean "it perceives" or "it lives,"—for everything that perceives is living—by saying "it is not hasty, and does not abandon its creatures," we mean that all these creatures preserve a certain order and arrangement; they are not left to themselves; they are not produced aimlessly, but whatever condition they receive from that being is given with design and intention. We thus learn that there is no other being like unto God, and we say that He is One, i.e., there are not more Gods than one.

It has thus been shown that every attribute predicated of God either denotes the quality of an action, or—when the attribute is intended to convey some idea of the Divine Being itself, and not of His actions—the negation of the opposite. Even these negative attributes must not be formed and applied to God, except in the way in which, as you know, sometimes an attribute is negatived in reference to a thing, although that attribute can naturally never be applied to it in the same sense, as, e.g., we say, "This wall does not see." Those who read the present work are aware that, notwithstanding all the efforts of the mind, we can obtain no knowledge of the essence of the heavens— a revolving substance which has been measured by us in spans and cubits, and examined even as regards the proportions of the several spheres to each other and respecting most of their motions—although we know that they must consist of matter and form; but the matter not being the same as sublunary matter, we can only describe the heavens in terms expressing negative properties, but not in terms denoting positive qualities. Thus we say that the heavens are not light, not heavy, not passive and therefore not subject to impressions, and that they do not possess the sensations of taste and smell; or we use similar negative attributes. All this we do, because we do not know their substance. What, then, can be the result of our efforts, when we try to obtain a knowledge of a Being that is free from substance, that is most simple, whose existence is absolute, and not due to any cause, to whose perfect essence nothing can be superadded, and whose perfection consists, as we have shown, in the absence of all defects. All we understand is the fact that He exists, that He is a Being to whom none of His creatures is similar, who has nothing in common with them, who does not include plurality, who is never too feeble to produce other beings, and whose relation to the universe is that of a steersman to a boat; and even this is not a real relation, a real simile, but serves only to convey to us the idea that God rules the universe; that is, that He gives it duration, and preserves its necessary arrangement. This subject will be treated more fully. Praised be He! In the contemplation of His essence, our comprehension and knowledge prove insufficient; in the examination of His works, how they necessarily result from His will, our knowledge proves to be ignorance, and in the endeavour to extol Him in words, all our efforts in speech are mere weakness and failure!

Chapter LIX

The following question might perhaps be asked: Since there is no possibility of obtaining a knowledge of the true essence of God, and since it has also been proved that the only thing that man can apprehend of Him is the fact that He exists, and that all positive attributes are inadmissible, as has been shown; what is the difference among those who have obtained a knowledge of God? Must not the knowledge obtained by our teacher

Moses, and by Solomon, be the same as that obtained by anyone of the lowest class of philosophers, since there can be no addition to this knowledge? But, on the other hand, it is generally accepted among theologians and also among philosophers, that there can be a great difference between two persons as regards the knowledge of God obtained by them. Know that this is really the case, that those who have obtained a knowledge of God differ greatly from each other; for in the same way as by each additional attribute an object is more specified, and is brought nearer to the true apprehension of the observer, so by each additional negative attribute you advance toward the knowledge of God, and you are nearer to it than he who does not negative, in reference to God, those qualities which you are convinced by proof must be negatived. There may thus be a man who after having earnestly devoted many years to the pursuit of one science, and to the true understanding of its principles, till he is fully convinced of its truths, has obtained as the sole result of this study the conviction that a certain quality must be negatived in reference to God, and the capacity of demonstrating that it is impossible to apply it to Him. Superficial thinkers will have no proof for this, will doubtfully ask, Is that thing existing in the Creator, or not? And those who are deprived of sight will positively ascribe it to God, although it has been clearly shown that He does not possess it. E.g., while I show that God is incorporeal, another doubts and is not certain whether He is corporeal or incorporeal; others even positively declare that He is corporeal, and appear before the Lord with that belief. Now see how great the difference is between these three men; the first is undoubtedly nearest to the Almighty; the second is remote, and the third still more distant from Him. If there be a fourth person who holds himself convinced by proof that emotions arc impossible in God, while the first who rejects the corporeality, is not convinced of that impossibility, that fourth person is undoubtedly nearer the knowledge of God than the first, and so on, so that a person who, convinced by proof, negatives a number of things in reference to God, which according to our belief may possibly be in Him or emanate from Him, is undoubtedly a more perfect man than we are, and would surpass us still more if we positively believed these things to be properties of God. It will now be clear to you, that every time you establish by proof the negation of a thing in reference to God, you become more perfect, while with every additional positive assertion you follow your imagination and recede from the true knowledge of God. Only by such ways must we approach the knowledge of God, and by such researches and studies as would show us the inapplicability of what is inadmissible as regards the Creator, not by such methods as would prove the necessity of ascribing to Him anything extraneous to His essence, or asserting that He has a certain perfection, when we find it to be a perfection in relation to us. The perfections are all to some extent acquired properties, and a property which must be acquired does not exist in everything capable of making such acquisition.

You must bear in mind, that by affirming anything of God, you are removed from Him in two respects; first, whatever you affirm, is only a perfection in relation to us; secondly, He does not possess anything superadded to this essence; His essence includes all His perfections, as we have shown. Since it is a well-known fact that even that knowledge of God which is accessible to man cannot be attained except by negations, and that negations do not convey a true idea of the being to which they refer, all people, both of past and present generations, declared that God cannot be the object of human comprehension, that none but Himself comprehends what He is, and that our knowledge consists in knowing that we are unable truly to comprehend Him. All philosophers say,

"He has overpowered us by His grace, and is invisible to us through the intensity of His light," like the sun which cannot be perceived by eyes which are too weak to bear its rays. Much more has been said on this topic, but it is useless to repeat it here. The idea is best expressed in the book of Psalms, "Silence is praise to Thee" (lxv. 2). It is a very expressive remark on this subject; for whatever we utter with the intention of extolling and of praising Him, contains something that cannot be applied to God, and includes derogatory expressions; it is therefore more becoming to be silent, and to be content with intellectual reflection, as has been recommended by men of the highest culture, in the words "Commune with your own heart upon your bed, and be still" (Ps. iv. 4). You must surely know the following celebrated passage in the Talmud—would that all passages in the Talmud were like that!—although it is known to you, I quote it literally, as I wish to point out to you the ideas contained in it: "A certain person, reading prayers in the presence of Rabbi Haninah, said, 'God, the great, the valiant and the tremendous, the powerful, the strong, and the mighty.'—The rabbi said to him, Have you finished all the praises of your Master? The three epithets, 'God, the great, the valiant and the tremendous,' we should not have applied to God, had Moses not mentioned them in the Law, and had not the men of the Great Synagogue come forward subsequently and established their use in the prayer; and you say all this! Let this be illustrated by a parable. There was once an earthly king, possessing millions of gold coin; he was praised for owning millions of silver coin; was this not really dispraise to him?" Thus far the opinion of the pious rabbi. Consider, first, how repulsive and annoying the accumulation of all these positive attributes was to him; next, how he showed that, if we had only to follow our reason, we should never have composed these prayers, and we should not have uttered any of them. It has, however, become necessary to address men in words that should leave some idea in their minds, and, in accordance with the saying of our Sages, "The Torah speaks in the language of men," the Creator has been described to us in terms of our own perfections; but we should not on that account have uttered any other than the three above-mentioned attributes, and we should not have used them as names of God except when meeting with them in reading the Law. Subsequently, the men of the Great Synagogue, who were prophets, introduced these expressions also into the prayer, but we should not on that account use [in our prayers] any other attributes of God. The principal lesson to be derived from this passage is that there are two reasons for our employing those phrases in our prayers: first, they occur in the Pentateuch; secondly, the Prophets introduced them into the prayer. Were it not for the first reason, we should never have uttered them; and were it not for the second reason, we should not have copied them from the Pentateuch to recite them in our prayers; how then could we approve of the use of those numerous attributes! You also learn from this that we ought not to mention and employ in our prayers all the attributes we find applied to God in the books of the Prophets; for he does not say, "Were it not that Moses, our Teacher, said them, we should not have been able to use them"; but he adds another condition—"and had not the men of the Great Synagogue come forward and established their use in the prayer," because only for that reason are we allowed to use them in our prayers. We cannot approve of what those foolish persons do who are extravagant in praise, fluent and prolix in the prayers they compose, and in the hymns they make in the desire to approach the Creator. They describe God in attributes which would be an offence if applied to a human being; for those persons have no knowledge of these great and important principles, which are not accessible to the ordinary intelligence of man. Treating the Creator as a familiar object, they describe Him and speak of Him in any expressions they think proper; they eloquently continue to praise Him in that manner, and believe that they can thereby influence Him and produce an effect on Him. If they find some phrase suited to their object in the words of the Prophets they are still more inclined to consider that they are free to make use of such texts—which should at least be explained—to employ them in their literal sense, to derive new expressions from them, to form from them numerous variations, and to found whole compositions on them. This license is frequently met with in the compositions of the singers, preachers, and others who imagine themselves to be able to compose a poem. Such authors write things which partly are real heresy, partly contain such folly and absurdity that they naturally cause those who hear them to laugh, but also to feel grieved at the thought that such things can be uttered in reference to God. Were it not that I pitied the authors for their defects, and did not wish to injure them, I should have cited some passages to show you their mistakes; besides, the fault of their compositions is obvious to all intelligent persons. You must consider it, and think thus: If slander and libel is a great sin, how much greater is the sin of those who speak with looseness of tongue in reference to God, and describe Him by attributes which are far below Him; and I declare that they not only commit an ordinary sin, but unconsciously at least incur the guilt of profanity and blasphemy. This applies both to the multitude that listens to such prayers, and to the foolish man that recites them. Men, however, who understand the fault of such compositions, and, nevertheless, recite them, may be classed, according to my opinion, among those to whom the following words are applied: "And the children of Israel used words that were not right against the Lord their God" (2 Kings xvii. 9); and "utter error against the Lord" (Isa. xxxii. 6). If you are of those who regard the honour of their Creator, do not listen in any way to them, much less utter what they say, and still less compose such prayers, knowing how great is the offence of one who hurls aspersions against the Supreme Being. There is no necessity at all for you to use positive attributes of God with the view of magnifying Him in your thoughts, or to go beyond the limits which the men of the Great Synagogue have introduced in the prayers and in the blessings, for this is sufficient for all purposes, and even more than sufficient, as Rabbi Haninah said. Other attributes, such as occur in the books of the Prophets, may be uttered when we meet with them in reading those books; but we must bear in mind what has already been explained, that they are either attributes of God's actions, or expressions implying the negation of the opposite. This likewise should not be divulged to the multitude; but a reflection of this kind is fitted for the few only who believe that the glorification of God does not consist in *uttering* that which is not to be uttered, but in *reflecting* on that on which man should reflect.

We will now conclude our exposition of the wise words of R. Haninah. He does not employ any such simile as: "A king who possesses millions of gold denarii, and is praised as having hundreds"; for this would imply that God's perfections, although more perfect than those ascribed to man are still of the same kind; but this is not the case, as has been proved. The excellence of the simile consists in the words: "who possesses golden denarii, and is praised as having silver denarii"; this implies that these attributes, though perfections as regards ourselves, are not such as regards God; in reference to Him they would all be defects, as is distinctly suggested in the remark, "Is this not an offence to Him?"

I have already told you that all these attributes, whatever perfection they may denote according to your idea, imply defects in reference to God, if applied to Him in the same sense as they are used in reference to ourselves. Solomon has already given us sufficient instruction on this subject by saying, "For God is in heaven, and thou upon earth; therefore let thy words be few" (Eccles. v. 2).

Questions for reflection

1   How does Maimonides's understanding of divine simplicity lead him to the *via negativa*? What does it mean to say that God is simple?
2   If we can only apply negative ascriptions to God, can we have any real conception of God? Explain.
3   How could one hold to a view of scripture as being divinely inspired, as Maimonides did, while at the same time denying that the positive ascriptions made about God in scripture are really true? How did Maimonides resolve this tension?

Further reading

Marvin Fox (1990) *Interpreting Maimonides*. Chicago: University of Chicago Press. (A fairly comprehensive presentation.)

Moses Maimonides ([1190] 1903) *The Guide for the Perplexed*. Trans. M. Friedländer. (An online version of the book from which this selection was taken; found at http://www.sacred-texts.com/jud/gfp/index.htm.)

William Mann (1983) "Simplicity and Immutability in God," *International Philosophical Quarterly* 23 (3): 267–76. (Replies to objections to divine simplicity.)

Alvin Plantinga (1980) *Does God Have a Nature?* Milwaukee, WI: Marquette University Press. (Plantinga criticizes the doctrine of divine simplicity in the midst of an analysis of God's relation to necessary truth.)

Writings of Maimonides - Manuscripts and Early Print Edition. (Public digital copies of manuscripts from Maimonides provided by the Jewish National and University Library in commemoration of the 800th anniversary of his death; found at http://www.jnul.huji.ac.il/dl/mss/html/rambam_1.htm.)

_____

Chapter 8

Boethius

PROVIDENCE, FOREKNOWLEDGE, AND FREE WILL

Anicius Manlius Severinus Boethius (*c.* 480–524 CE) was a Roman philosopher, theologian, and statesman. This selection, written by Boethius while imprisoned and awaiting execution for a number of alleged charges against the Roman government, examines the possibility of human free will in a world governed by divine providence. It is written in dialectical style, using prose and verse, and includes Boethius himself and the Philosopher—an envisioned woman who is the personification of perfected human reason.

Boethius argues that divine foreknowledge—which includes the notion that whatever God's providence foresees must happen—and human free will are not incompatible concepts. On his view, God sees past, present, and future events as eternally present. In this way, he claims that future events are *necessary* with respect to God's knowledge of them, but they are *undetermined* with respect to their own natures. It is similar to the claim that if I know that a person is sitting, and she is indeed sitting, then she is necessarily sitting. It's not that my knowledge of her sitting necessitates her sitting, for she could have chosen not to sit. Similarly, Boethius maintains, God's knowledge of future human events is certain, but that does not negate the freedom of those actions.

_____

Prose 3

Boethius contends that divine foreknowledge and freedom of the human will are incompatible.

"Now I am confused by an even greater difficulty," I said.

"What is it?" Philosophy answered, "though I think I know what is bothering you."

"There seems to be a hopeless conflict between divine foreknowledge of all things and freedom of the human will. For if God sees everything in advance and cannot be deceived in any way, whatever his Providence foresees will happen, must happen. Therefore, if God foreknows eternally not only all the acts of men, but also their plans and wishes, there cannot be freedom of will; for nothing whatever can be done or even desired without its being known beforehand by the infallible Providence of God. If things could somehow be accomplished in some way other than that which God foresaw, his foreknowledge of the future would no longer be certain. Indeed, it would be merely uncertain opinion, and it would be wrong to think that of God.

"I cannot agree with the argument by which some people believe that they can solve this problem. They say that things do not happen because Providence foresees that they will happen, but, on the contrary, that Providence foresees what is to come because it will happen, and in this way they find the necessity to be in things, not in Providence. For, they say, it is not necessary that things should happen because they are foreseen, but only that things which will happen be foreseen—as though the problem were whether divine Providence is the cause of the necessity of future events, or the necessity of future events is the cause of divine Providence. But our concern is to prove that the fulfillment of things which God has foreseen is necessary, whatever the order of causes, even if the divine foreknowledge does not seem to make the occurrence of future events necessary. For example, if a man sits down, the opinion that he is sitting must be true; and conversely, if the opinion that someone is sitting be true, then that person must necessarily be sitting. Therefore, there is necessity in both cases: the man must be sitting and the opinion must be true. But the man is not sitting because the opinion is true; the opinion is true because the sitting came before the opinion about it. Therefore, even though the cause of truth came from one side, necessity is common to both.

"A similar line of reasoning applies to divine foreknowledge and future events. For even though the events are foreseen because they will happen, they do not happen because they are foreseen. Nevertheless, it is necessary either that things which are going to happen be foreseen by God, or that what God foresees will in fact happen; and either way the freedom of the human will is destroyed. But of course it is preposterous to say that the outcome of temporal things is the cause of eternal foreknowledge. Yet to suppose that God foresees future events because they are going to happen is the same as supposing that things which happened long ago are the cause of divine Providence. Furthermore, just as when I know that a thing is, that thing must necessarily be; so when I know that something will happen, it is necessary that it happen. It follows, then, that the outcome of something known in advance must necessarily take place.

"Finally, if anyone thinks that a thing is other than it actually is, he does not have knowledge but merely a fallible opinion, and that is quite different from the truth of knowledge. So, if the outcome of some future event is either uncertain or unnecessary, no one can know in advance whether or not it will happen. For just as true knowledge is not tainted by falsity, so that which is known by it cannot be otherwise than as it is known. And that is the reason why knowledge never deceives; things must necessarily be as true knowledge knows them to be. If this is so, how does God foreknow future possibilities whose existence is uncertain? If He thinks that things will inevitably happen which possibly will not happen, He is deceived. But it is wrong to say that, or even to think it. And if He merely knows that they may or may not happen, that is, if He knows only their contingent possibilities, what is such knowledge worth, since it does not know with certainty? Such knowledge is no better than that expressed by the ridiculous prophecy of Tiresias: 'Whatever I say will either be or not be.'[1] Divine Providence would be no better than human opinion if God judges as men do and knows only that uncertain events are doubtful. But if nothing can be uncertain to Him who is the most certain source of all things, the outcome is certain of all things which He knows with certainty shall be.

"Therefore, there can be no freedom in human decisions and actions, since the divine mind, foreseeing everything without possibility of error, determines and forces the outcome of everything that is to happen. Once this is granted, it is clear that the structure of all human affairs must collapse. For it is pointless to assign rewards and punishment to the good and wicked since neither are deserved if the actions of men are not free and voluntary. Punishment of the wicked and recognition of the good, which are now considered just, will seem quite unjust since neither the good nor the wicked are governed by their own will but are forced by the inevitability of predetermination. Vice and virtue will be without meaning, and in their place there will be utter confusion about what is deserved. Finally, and this is the most blasphemous thought of all, it follows that the Author of all good must be made responsible for all human vice since the entire order of human events depends on Providence and nothing on man's intention.

"There is no use in hoping or praying for anything, for what is the point in hope or prayer when everything that man desires is determined by unalterable process? Thus man's only bonds with God, hope and prayer, are destroyed. We believe that our just humility may earn the priceless reward of divine grace, for this is the only way in which men seem able to communicate with God; we are joined to that inaccessible light by supplication before receiving what we ask. But if we hold that all future events are governed by necessity, and therefore that prayer has no value, what will be left to unite us to the sovereign Lord of all things? And so mankind must, as you said earlier, be cut off from its source and dwindle into nothing.[2]

Poem 3

"What cause of discord breaks the ties which ought to bind this union of things? What God has set such conflict between these two truths? Separately each is certain, but put together they cannot be reconciled. Is there no discord between them? Can they exist side by side and be equally true?

"The human mind, overcome by the body's blindness, cannot discern by its dim light the delicate connections between things. But why does the mind burn with such desire to discover the hidden aspects of truth? Does it know what it is so eager to know? Then why does it go on laboriously trying to discover what it already knows? And if it does not know, why does it blindly continue the search? For who would want something of which he is unaware, or run after something he does not know? How can such a thing be found, or, if found, how would it be recognized by someone ignorant of its form?

"When the human mind knew the mind of God, did it know the whole and all its parts? Now the mind is shrouded in the clouds of the body, but it has not wholly forgotten itself; and, although it has lost its grasp of particulars, it still holds fast to the general truth. Therefore, whoever seeks the truth knows something: he is neither completely informed nor completely ignorant. He works with what he remembers of the highest truth, using what he saw on high in order to fill in the forgotten parts."

Prose 4

Philosophy begins her argument that divine Providence does not preclude freedom of the will by stressing the difference between divine and human knowledge.

"This is an old difficulty about Providence," Philosophy answered. "It was raised by Cicero in his book on divination,[3] and has for a long time been a subject of your own investigation, but so far none of you has treated it with enough care and conviction. The cause of the obscurity which still surrounds the problem is that the process of human reason cannot comprehend the simplicity of divine foreknowledge. If in any way we could understand that, no further doubt would remain. I shall try to make this clear after I have explained the things which trouble you.

"First, let me ask why you regard as inconclusive the reasoning of those who think that foreknowledge is no hindrance to free will because it is not the cause of the necessity of future things. For do you have any argument for the necessity of future events other than the principle that things which are known beforehand must happen? If, as you have just now conceded, foreknowledge does not impose necessity on future events, why must the voluntary outcome of things be bound to predetermined results? For the sake of argument, so that you may consider what follows from it, let us suppose that there is no foreknowledge. Then would the things which are done by free will be bound by necessity in this respect?"

"Not at all."

"Then, let us suppose that foreknowledge exists but imposes no necessity on things. The same independence and absolute freedom of will would remain.

"But you will say that even though foreknowledge does not impose necessity on future events, it is still a sign that they will necessarily happen. It must follow then that even if there were no foreknowledge the outcome of these future things would be necessary. For signs only show what is, they do not cause the things they point to. Therefore we must first prove that nothing happens other than by necessity, in order to demonstrate that foreknowledge is a sign of this necessity. Otherwise, if there is no necessity, then foreknowledge cannot be a sign of something that does not exist. Moreover, it is clear that firmly based proof does not rest on signs and extrinsic arguments but is deduced from suitable and necessary causes. But how can it be that things which are foreseen should not happen? We do not suppose that things will not happen, if Providence has foreknowledge that they will; rather we judge that, although they will happen, they have nothing in their natures which makes it necessary that they should happen. For we see many things in the process of happening before our eyes, just as the chariot driver sees the results of his actions as he guides his chariot; and this is true in many of our activities. Do you think that such things are compelled by necessity to happen as they do?"

"No. For the results of art would be vain if they were all brought about by compulsion."

"Then, since they come into being without necessity, these same things were not determined by necessity before they actually happened. Therefore, there are some things destined to happen in the future whose outcome is free of any necessity. For everyone, I think, would say that things which are now happening were going to happen before they actually came to pass. Thus, these things happen without necessity even though they were known in advance. For just as knowledge of things happening now does not imply necessity in their outcomes, so foreknowledge of future things imposes no necessity on their outcomes in the future.

"But, you will say, the point at issue is whether there can be any foreknowledge of things whose outcomes are not necessary. For these things seem opposed to each other, and you think that if things can be foreseen they must necessarily happen, and that if the necessity is absent they cannot be foreseen, and that nothing can be fully known unless it is certain. If uncertain things are foreseen as certain, that is the weakness of opinion, not the truth of knowledge. You believe that to judge that a thing is other than it is departs from the integrity of knowledge. Now the cause of this error lies in your assumption that whatever is known is known only by the force and nature of the things which are known; but the opposite is true. Everything which is known is known not according to its own power but rather according to the capacity of the knower.

"Let me illustrate with a brief example: the roundness of a body is known in one way by the sense of touch and in another by the sight. The sight, remaining at a distance, takes in the whole body at once by its reflected rays; but the touch makes direct contact with the sphere and comprehends it piecemeal by moving around its surface. A man himself is comprehended in different ways by the senses, imagination, reason, and intelligence. The senses grasp the figure of the thing as it is constituted in matter; the imagination, however, grasps the figure alone without the matter. Reason, on the other hand, goes beyond this and investigates by universal consideration the species itself which is in particular things. The vision of intelligence is higher yet, and it goes beyond the bounds of the universe and sees with the clear eye of the mind the pure form itself.

"In all this we chiefly observe that the higher power of knowing includes the lower, but the lower can in no way rise to the higher. For the senses achieve nothing beyond the material, the imagination cannot grasp universal species, reason cannot know simple forms; but the intelligence, as though looking down from on high, conceives the underlying forms and distinguishes among them all, but in the same way in which it comprehends the form itself which cannot be known to any other power. The intelligence knows the objects of the lower kinds of knowledge: the universals of the reason, the figures of the imagination, the matter of the senses, but not by using reason, or imagination, or senses. With a single glance of the mind it formally, as it were, sees all things. Similarly, when reason knows a universal nature, it comprehends all the objects of imagination and the senses without using either. For reason defines the general nature of her conception as follows: man is a biped, rational animal. This is a universal idea, but no one ignores the fact that man is also an imaginable and sensible object which reason knows by rational conception rather than by the imagination and senses. Similarly, although the imagination begins by seeing and forming figures with the senses, nevertheless it can, without the aid of the senses, behold sensible objects by an imaginative rather than a sensory mode of knowing.

"Do you see, then, how all these use their own power in knowing rather than the powers of the objects which are known? And this is proper, for since all judgment is in the act of the one judging, it is necessary that everyone should accomplish his own action by his own power, not by the power of something other than himself.

Poem 4

"Long ago the philosophers of the Porch at Athens,[4] old men who saw things dimly, believed that sense impressions and images were impressed on the mind by external objects, just as then they used to mark letters on a blank page of wax with their quick pens. But, if the active mind can discover nothing by its own powers, and merely remains passively subject to the impressions of external bodies, like a mirror reflecting the empty shapes of other things, where does that power come from which dwells in souls and sees all things? What is that power which perceives individual things and, by knowing them, can distinguish among them? What is the power which puts together again the parts it has separated and, pursuing its due course, lifts its gaze to the highest things, then descends again to the lowest, then returns to itself to refute false ideas with truth?

"This is a more effective, and a much more powerful cause than any which merely receives impressions from material things. Still, the sense impression comes first, arousing and moving the powers of the soul in the living body. When light strikes the eyes, or sound the ears, the aroused power of the mind calls into action the corresponding species which it holds within, joining them to the outward signs and mixing images with the forms it has hidden in itself.

Prose 5

To understand this mystery, human reason must contemplate the power of the divine intelligence.

"Thus, in the case of sentient bodies external stimuli affect the sense organs, and a physical sensation precedes the activity of the mind, calling the mind to act upon itself and in this way to activate the interior forms which before were inactive. Now if, as I say, in sentient bodies the soul is affected by external bodies but judges these stimuli presented to the body not passively, but by virtue of its own power, how much more do intelligences which are wholly free from all bodily affections use the power of the mind rather than objects extrinsic to themselves in arriving at judgments. According to this principle, various and different substances have different ways of knowing. There are certain immobile living things which are without any means of knowing other than by sense impressions. Shellfish and other forms of marine life which are nourished as they stick to rocks are creatures of this kind. Beasts which have the power of motion, on the other hand, have the impulse to seek and avoid certain things, and they have imagination. But reason is characteristic of the human race alone, just as pure intelligence belongs to God alone.

"It follows, then, that the most excellent knowledge is that which by its own nature knows not only its own proper object but also the objects of all lower kinds of knowledge. What, then, should we think if the senses and imagination were to oppose reason by arguing that the universal, which reason claims to know, is nothing? Suppose they were to argue that whatever can be sensed or imagined cannot be universal; and that therefore either the judgment of reason is true, and there are no objects of sense knowledge, or, since everyone knows that many things can be known by the senses and the imagination, that the conception of reason, which regards whatever is sensible and singular as if it were universal, is vain and empty. And suppose, further, that reason should answer that it conceives sensible and imaginable objects under the aspect of universality, but that the senses and imagination cannot aspire to the knowledge of universality because their knowledge cannot go beyond corporeal figures. Moreover, reason might continue, in matters of knowledge we ought to trust the stronger and more perfect judgment. In such a controversy we who possess the power of reason, as well as of imagination and sense perception, ought to take the side of reason.

"The situation is much the same when human reason supposes that the divine intelligence beholds future events only as reason herself sees them. For you argue that if some things seem not to have certain and necessary outcomes, they cannot be foreknown as certainly about to happen. Therefore, you say that there can be no fore-knowledge of these things, or, if we believe that there is such foreknowledge, that the outcome of all things is controlled by necessity. But if we, who are endowed with reason, could possess the intelligence of the divine mind, we would judge that just as the senses and imagination should accede to reason, so human reason ought justly to submit itself to the divine mind. Let us rise, if we can, to the summit of the highest intelligence; for there reason will see what in itself it cannot see: that a certain and def-inite foreknowledge can behold even those things which have no certain outcome. And this foreknowledge is not mere conjecture but the unrestricted simplicity of supreme knowledge.

Poem 5

"How varied are the shapes of living things on earth! Some there are with bodies stretched out, crawling through the dust, spending their strength in an unbroken furrow; some soar in the air, beating the wind with light wings, floating in easy flight along tracks of air. Some walk along the ground through woods and across green fields. All these, you observe, differ in their varied forms, but their faces look down and cause their senses to grow sluggish.

"The human race alone lifts its head to heaven and stands erect, despising the earth. Man's figure teaches, unless folly has bound you to the earth, that you who look upward with your head held high should also raise your soul to sublime things, lest while your body is raised above the earth, your mind should sink to the ground under its burden.

Prose 6

Philosophy solves the problem of Providence and free will by distinguishing between simple and con-ditional necessity.

"Since, as we have shown, whatever is known is known according to the nature of the knower, and not according to its own nature, let us now consider as far as is lawful the nature of the Divine Being, so that we may discover what its knowledge is. The common judgment of all rational creatures holds that God is eternal. Therefore let us consider what eternity is, for this will reveal both the divine nature and the divine knowledge.

"Eternity is the whole, perfect, and simultaneous possession of endless life. The

meaning of this can be made clearer by comparison with temporal things. For whatever lives in time lives in the present, proceeding from past to future, and nothing is so
constituted in time that it can embrace the whole span of its life at once. It has not yet
arrived at tomorrow, and it has already lost yesterday; even the life of this day is lived
only in each moving, passing moment. Therefore, whatever is subject to the condition
of time, even that which—as Aristotle conceived the world to be—has no beginning
and will have no end in a life coextensive with the infinity of time, is such that it cannot
rightly be thought eternal. For it does not comprehend and include the whole of infinite
life all at once, since it does not embrace the future which is yet to come. Therefore,
only that which comprehends and possesses the whole plenitude of endless life together,
from which no future thing nor any past thing is absent, can justly be called eternal.
Moreover, it is necessary that such a being be in full possession of itself, always present
to itself, and hold the infinity of moving time present before itself.

"Therefore, they are wrong who, having heard that Plato held that this world did
not have a beginning in time and would never come to an end,[5] suppose that the created world is coeternal with its Creator. For it is one thing to live an endless life, which
is what Plato ascribed to the world, and another for the whole of unending life to be
embraced all at once as present, which is clearly proper to the divine mind. Nor should
God be thought of as older than His creation in extent of time, but rather as prior to
it by virtue of the simplicity of His nature. For the infinite motion of temporal things
imitates the immediate present of His changeless life and, since it cannot reproduce or
equal life, it sinks from immobility to motion and declines from the simplicity of the
present into the infinite duration of future and past. And, since it cannot possess the
whole fullness of its life at once, it seems to imitate to some extent that which it cannot
completely express, and it does this by somehow never ceasing to be. It binds itself to a
kind of present in this short and transitory period which, because it has a certain likeness to that abiding, unchanging present, gives everything it touches a semblance of
existence. But, since this imitation cannot remain still, it hastens along the infinite road
of time, and so it extends by movement the life whose completeness it could not achieve
by standing still. Therefore, if we wish to call things by their proper names, we should
follow Plato in saying that God indeed is eternal, but the world is perpetual.[6]

"Since, then, every judgment comprehends the subjects presented to it according to
its own nature, and since God lives in the eternal present, His knowledge transcends all
movement of time and abides in the simplicity of its immediate present. It encompasses
the infinite sweep of past and future, and regards all things in its simple comprehension as if they were now taking place. Thus, if you will think about the foreknowledge
by which God distinguishes all things, you will rightly consider it to be not a foreknowledge of future events, but knowledge of a never changing present. For this reason,
divine knowledge is called providence, rather than prevision, because it resides above
all inferior things and looks out on all things from their summit.

"Why then do you imagine that things are necessary which are illuminated by this
divine light, since even men do not impose necessity on the things they see? Does your
vision impose any necessity upon things which you see present before you?"

"Not at all," I answered.

"Then," Philosophy went on, "if we may aptly compare God's present vision with
man's, He sees all things in his eternal present as you see some things in your temporal
present. Therefore, this divine foreknowledge does not change the nature and properties

of things; it simply sees things present before it as they will later turn out to be in what we regard as the future. His judgment is not confused; with a single intuition of his mind He knows all things that are to come, whether necessarily or not. Just as, when you happen to see simultaneously a man walking on the street and the sun shining in the sky, even though you see both at once, you can distinguish between them and realize that one action is voluntary, the other necessary; so the divine mind, looking down on all things, does not disturb the nature of the things which are present before it but are future with respect to time. Therefore, when God knows that something will happen in the future, and at the same time knows that it will not happen through necessity, this is not opinion but knowledge based on truth.

"If you should reply that whatever God foresees as happening cannot help but happen, and that whatever must happen is bound by necessity—if you pin me down to this word 'necessity'—I grant that you state a solid truth, but one which only a profound theologian can grasp. I would answer that the same future event is necessary with respect to God's knowledge of it, but free and undetermined if considered in its own nature. For there are two kinds of necessity: one is simple, as the necessity by which all men are mortals; the other is conditional, as is the case when, if you know that someone is walking, he must necessarily be walking. For whatever is known, must be as it is known to be; but this condition does not involve that other, simple necessity. It is not caused by the peculiar nature of the person in question, but by an added condition. No necessity forces the man who is voluntarily walking to move forward; but as long as he is walking, he is necessarily moving forward. In the same way, if Providence sees anything as present, that thing must necessarily be, even though it may have no necessity by its nature. But God sees as present those future things which result from free will. Therefore, from the standpoint of divine knowledge these things are necessary because of the condition of their being known by God; but, considered only in themselves, they lose nothing of the absolute freedom of their own natures.

"There is no doubt, then, that all things will happen which God knows will happen; but some of them happen as a result of free will. And, although they happen, they do not, by their existence, lose their proper natures by which, before they happened, they were able not to happen. But, you may ask, what does it mean to say that these events are not necessary, since by reason of the condition of divine knowledge they happen just as if they were necessary? The meaning is the same as in the example I used a while ago of the sun rising and the man walking. At the time they are happening, they must necessarily be happening; but the sun's rising is governed by necessity even before it happens, while the man's walking is not. Similarly, all the things God sees as present will undoubtedly come to pass; but some will happen by the necessity of their natures, others by the power of those who make them happen. Therefore, we quite properly said that these things are necessary if viewed from the standpoint of divine knowledge, but if they are considered in themselves, they are free of the bonds of necessity. In somewhat the same way, whatever is known by the senses is singular in itself, but universal as far as the reason is concerned.

"But, you may say, if I can change my mind about doing something, I can frustrate Providence, since by chance I may change something which Providence foresaw. My answer is this: you can indeed alter what you propose to do, but, because the present truth of Providence sees that you can, and whether or not you will, you cannot frustrate the divine knowledge any more than you can escape the eye of someone who is present and watching you, even though you may, by your free will, vary your actions. You may still wonder, however, whether God's knowledge is changed by your decisions, so that when you wish now one thing, now another, the divine knowledge undergoes corresponding changes. This is not the case. For divine Providence anticipates every future action and converts it to its own present knowledge. It does not change, as you imagine, foreknowing this or that in succession, but in a single instant, without being changed itself, anticipates and grasps your changes. God has this present comprehension and immediate vision of all things not from the outcome of future events, but from the simplicity of his own nature. In this way, the problem you raised a moment ago is settled. You observed that it would be unworthy of God if our future acts were said to be the cause of divine knowledge. Now you see that this power of divine knowledge, comprehending all things as present before it, itself constitutes the measure of all things and is in no way dependent on things that happen later.

"Since this is true, the freedom of the human will remains inviolate, and laws are just since they provide rewards and punishments to human wills which are not controlled by necessity. God looks down from above, knowing all things, and the eternal present of his vision concurs with the future character of our actions, distributing rewards to the good and punishments to the evil. Our hopes and prayers are not directed to God in vain, for if they are just they cannot fail. Therefore, stand firm against vice and cultivate virtue. Lift up your soul to worthy hopes, and offer humble prayers to heaven. If you will face it, the necessity of virtuous action imposed upon you is very great, since all your actions are done in the sight of a Judge who sees all things."

Notes

1   Horace, *Satires* II. 5. 59.
2   See Book IV, Poem 6.
3   *De divinatione* II. 8ff.
4   Zeno, founder of the Stoic school of philosophers, taught in the Stoa Poekile in Athens. For this reason Boethius calls his followers "philosophers of the Porch."
5   *Timaeus* 28ff.
6   *Timaeus* 37d ff.

Questions for reflection

1   What is Boethius's solution to the apparent contradiction between divine foreknowledge and human free will? Do you agree with him? In your answer, explain the difference between simple necessity and conditional necessity.
2   Consider the following scenario. Suppose that God knows today that tomorrow you will have a dinner choice involving two options: (1) steak and shrimp or (2) eggplant Parmesan. Suppose further that God knows which of the two you will choose. In an attempt to demonstrate divine foreknowledge to your friend who, suppose, doubts it, God creates a DVD which has a recording of your eating the eggplant Parmesan tomorrow evening (this would, it seems, certainly be possible for an omnipotent God). Your friend watches the DVD and thus knows what you will eat; he knows that you will choose #2. Now, do you really have the freedom to choose the steak and shrimp

for dinner tomorrow night? If you do, wouldn't this make God (and the DVD recording) wrong, and thus lacking in foreknowledge? If you cannot choose the steak and shrimp for dinner, then how can you have free will?

3   On Boethius's conception of divine providence (which includes God's seeing future events as present realities), how can God be *providentially* involved in the future? Isn't God basically just an observer on this account?

Further reading

Boethius ([480–524] 2002) *The Consolation of Philosophy*. Trans. Richard H. Green. Mineola, NY: Dover. (A classic work in philosophy dealing with some of the most difficult issues about human life and God; the selection above was taken from this work.)

William Lane Craig (2001) *Time and Eternity: Exploring God's Relationship to Time*. Wheaton, IL: Crossway. (An up-to-date philosophical analysis of time and eternity by a leading philosopher of religion and philosopher of time.)

John Martin Fisher, ed. (1989) *God, Foreknowledge, and Freedom*. Stanford, CA: Stanford University Press. (A collection of important essays addressing divine foreknowledge and human freedom; fairly technical.)

Paul Helm (1994) *The Providence of God*. Downers Grove, IL: InterVarsity Press. (Presents a sustained argument for theological determinism and responses to the Molinist and Open Theism views of providence.)

Luis de Molina ([1592] 1988) *On Divine Foreknowledge*. Trans. Alfred J. Freddoso. Ithaca, NY: Cornell University Press. (The classic presentation of Molinism—the view developed by Molina in which he attempts to affirm human free will and divine sovereignty and avoid theological fatalism.)

Chapter 9

Thomas Aquinas

OMNIPOTENCE

Thomas Aquinas (1225–74) was a Christian theologian and philosopher considered by many to be the Catholic Church's greatest theologian. He was a prolific writer on numerous topics, not the least of which has to do with the nature of God. In this selection taken from his *Summa Theologiae*—the work for which he is best known—he offers a brief explanation of divine omnipotence. While he admits the difficulty of attempting to define omnipotence, he notes that it cannot include things which are logically impossible or sinful.

   Aquinas wrote this work in dialogical fashion: (1) he begins with objections to the position he actually affirms; (2) he then states his own position; and (3) he concludes by replying to the objections that were raised. "The Philosopher" he refers to is the ancient Greek philosopher, Aristotle, by whom Aquinas was very much influenced.

Objection 1: It seems that God is not omnipotent. For movement and passiveness belong to everything. But this is impossible with God, for He is immovable, as was said above (Question [2], Article [3]). Therefore He is not omnipotent.

Objection 2: Further, sin is an act of some kind. But God cannot sin, nor "deny Himself" as it is said in 2 Tim. 2:13. Therefore He is not omnipotent.

Objection 3: Further, it is said of God that He manifests His omnipotence "especially by sparing and having mercy" [*Collect, 10th Sunday after Pentecost]. Therefore the greatest act possible to the divine power is to spare and have mercy. There are things much greater, however, than sparing and having mercy; for example, to create another world, and the like. Therefore God is not omnipotent.

Objection 4: Further, upon the text, "God hath made foolish the wisdom of this world" (1 Cor. 1:20), a gloss says: "God hath made the wisdom of this world foolish [*Vulg.:

'Hath not God', etc.] by showing those things to be possible which it judges to be impossible." Whence it would seem that nothing is to be judged possible or impossible in reference to inferior causes, as the wisdom of this world judges them; but in reference to the divine power. If God, then, were omnipotent, all things would be possible; nothing, therefore impossible. But if we take away the impossible, then we destroy also the necessary; for what necessarily exists is impossible not to exist. Therefore there would be nothing at all that is necessary in things if God were omnipotent. But this is an impossibility. Therefore God is not omnipotent.

On the contrary, It is said: "No word shall be impossible with God" (Lk. 1:37).

I answer that, All confess that God is omnipotent; but it seems difficult to explain in what His omnipotence precisely consists: for there may be doubt as to the precise meaning of the word 'all' when we say that God can do all things. If, however, we consider the matter aright, since power is said in reference to possible things, this phrase, "God can do all things," is rightly understood to mean that God can do all things that are possible; and for this reason He is said to be omnipotent. Now according to the Philosopher (Metaph. v, 17), a thing is said to be possible in two ways. First in relation to some power, thus whatever is subject to human power is said to be possible to man. Secondly absolutely, on account of the relation in which the very terms stand to each other. Now God cannot be said to be omnipotent through being able to do all things that are possible to created nature; for the divine power extends farther than that. If, however, we were to say that God is omnipotent because He can do all things that are possible to His power, there would be a vicious circle in explaining the nature of His power. For this would be saying nothing else but that God is omnipotent, because He can do all that He is able to do.

It remains therefore, that God is called omnipotent because He can do all things that are possible absolutely; which is the second way of saying a thing is possible. For a thing is said to be possible or impossible absolutely, according to the relation in which the very terms stand to one another, possible if the predicate is not incompatible with the subject, as that Socrates sits; and absolutely impossible when the predicate is altogether incompatible with the subject, as, for instance, that a man is a donkey.

It must, however, be remembered that since every agent produces an effect like itself, to each active power there corresponds a thing possible as its proper object according to the nature of that act on which its active power is founded; for instance, the power of giving warmth is related as to its proper object to the being capable of being warmed. The divine existence, however, upon which the nature of power in God is founded, is infinite, and is not limited to any genus of being; but possesses within itself the perfection of all being. Whence, whatsoever has or can have the nature of being, is numbered among the absolutely possible things, in respect of which God is called omnipotent. Now nothing is opposed to the idea of being except non-being. Therefore, that which implies being and non-being at the same time is repugnant to the idea of an absolutely possible thing, within the scope of the divine omnipotence. For such cannot come under the divine omnipotence, not because of any defect in the power of God, but because it has not the nature of a feasible or possible thing. Therefore, everything that does not imply a contradiction in terms, is numbered amongst those possible things, in respect of which God is called omnipotent: whereas whatever implies contradiction does not come within the scope of divine omnipotence, because it cannot have the aspect of possibility. Hence it is better to say that such things cannot be done, than that God cannot do them. Nor is this contrary to the word of the angel, saying: "No word shall be impossible with God." For whatever implies a contradiction cannot be a word, because no intellect can possibly conceive such a thing.

Reply to Objection 1: God is said to be omnipotent in respect to His active power, not to passive power, as was shown above (Article [1]). Whence the fact that He is immovable or impassible is not repugnant to His omnipotence.

Reply to Objection 2: To sin is to fall short of a perfect action; hence to be able to sin is to be able to fall short in action, which is repugnant to omnipotence. Therefore it is that God cannot sin, because of His omnipotence. Nevertheless, the Philosopher says (Topic. iv, 3) that God can deliberately do what is evil. But this must be understood either on a condition, the antecedent of which is impossible—as, for instance, if we were to say that God can do evil things if He will. For there is no reason why a conditional proposition should not be true, though both the antecedent and consequent are impossible: as if one were to say: "If man is a donkey, he has four feet." Or he may be understood to mean that God can do some things which now seem to be evil: which, however, if He did them, would then be good. Or he is, perhaps, speaking after the common manner of the heathen, who thought that men became gods, like Jupiter or Mercury.

Reply to Objection 3: God's omnipotence is particularly shown in sparing and having mercy, because in this is it made manifest that God has supreme power, that He freely forgives sins. For it is not for one who is bound by laws of a superior to forgive sins of his own free will. Or, because by sparing and having mercy upon men, He leads them on to the participation of an infinite good; which is the ultimate effect of the divine power. Or because, as was said above (Question [21], Article [4]), the effect of the divine mercy is the foundation of all the divine works. For nothing is due to anyone, except on account of something already given him gratuitously by God. In this way the divine omnipotence is particularly made manifest, because to it pertains the first foundation of all good things.

Reply to Objection 4: The absolute possible is not so called in reference either to higher causes, or to inferior causes, but in reference to itself. But the possible in reference to some power is named possible in reference to its proximate cause. Hence those things which it belongs to God alone to do immediately—as, for example, to create, to justify, and the like—are said to be possible in reference to a higher cause. Those things, however, which are of such kind as to be done by inferior causes are said to be possible in reference to those inferior causes. For it is according to the condition of the proximate cause that the effect has contingency or necessity, as was shown above (Question [14], Article [1], ad 2). Thus is it that the wisdom of the world is deemed foolish, because what is impossible to nature, it judges to be impossible to God. So it is clear that the omnipotence of God does not take away from things their impossibility and necessity.

Questions for reflection

1   What is the problem with defining divine omnipotence as "God's being able to do all things that are possible within his power"? How would you define omnipotence?
2   If God is omnipotent, can he perform *any* action, even contradictory ones? For example, can God draw a square circle? If not, does that mean he is not omnipotent?
3   What do you make of the paradoxical question that asks whether God can create a rock so large that he cannot lift it? Is this a philosophical trick question, or is it getting at a real metaphysical problem with the notion of omnipotence, or . . . ?

Further reading

Charles Hartshorne (1984) *Omnipotence and Other Theological Mistakes.* Albany, NY: State University of New York Press. (A process philosopher/theologian reexamines the concept of God and hones in on certain attributes such as omnipotence.)

Joshua Hoffman and Gary Rosenkrantz (1988) "Omnipotence Redux," *Philosophy and Phenomenological Research* 49 (2): 283–301. (A critical assessment of various recent views of omnipotence.)

Thomas V. Morris (1991) *Our Idea of God: An Introduction to Philosophical Theology.* Downers Grove, IL: InterVarsity Press. (A clear, accessible introduction to major issues in philosophical theology, including a chapter on the power of God.)

Nelson Pike (1969) "Omnipotence and God's Ability to Sin," *American Philosophical Quarterly* 6 (3): 208–16. (Argues that omnipotence and omnibenevolence are incompatible.)

Chapter 10

Ramanuja

GOD AS INFINITE, PERSONAL, AND GOOD

Ramanuja (c. 1017–1137 CE) was one of the most influential philosophers from the Indian subcontinent. He was born in South India, and his family was of the Brahmin caste (a priestly caste, and the highest of the four main Hindu castes). Historically within Hinduism, there have been different schools of thought regarding the nature of Brahman, or Ultimate Reality. One major school, *Advaita Vedānta* ("*Advaita*" means "non-duality" and "*Vedānta*" refers to the sacred Hindu scriptures, the Vedas), holds that Ultimate Reality is non-dual; that is, it affirms the oneness of God, the universe, and the self. Ramanuja was the chief proponent of a different view—a qualified non-dualist form of Vedānta Hinduism called *Vishishtadvaita* in which the individual soul is distinct from Brahman. He was also one of the main Hindu philosophers to systematically interpret the Vedas from a theistic perspective, and he argued for the soteriological (salvific) importance of *bhakti*, or devotion to a personal God. The following selection comes from several of Ramanuja's most significant philosophical works: *Śrībhāsya* (Commentary on the *Brahma Sūtras*), *Gītābhāsya* and *Vedārthasamgraha* (texts which examine the nature of Brahman).

Below are definitions of several Sanskrit terms for a clearer understanding of the following selection:

artha – success; one of the four central goals of Hinduism (along with dharma, kāma, and moksa).

Brahman – Ultimate Reality; the power underlying the cosmos. For Advaita Vedānta Hindus, Brahman is impersonal and identical with Atman; for others, such as Ramanuja, Brahman is a separate and personal God.

dharma – religious duty; the virtuous person willingly fulfills the duty of one's caste; one of the four central goals of Hinduism (along with artha, kāma, and moksa).

kāma – pleasure; one of the four central goals of Hinduism (along with artha, dharma, and moksa).

moksa – liberation from samsāra; one of the four central goals of Hinduism (along with artha, dharma, and kāma).

samsāra – the world of phenomenal experiences whereby the soul passes through a
   perpetual cycle of death and rebirth.
Upanisads – a revered portion of the Vedas.
Vedas – ancient scriptures of India.

The concept and nature of God*

By the word "Brahman" is denoted the Supreme Person, who is by inherent nature free
from all imperfections and possesses hosts of auspicious qualities which are countless
and of matchless excellence. In all contexts the term "Brahman" is applied to whatever
possesses the quality of greatness, but its primary and most significant meaning is that
Being whose greatness is of matchless excellence, both in His essential nature and in His
other qualities. It is only the Lord of all who is such a Being. Therefore the word "Brahman" is primarily used only to signify Him. . . .[1]

[Brahman is] that Supreme Person who is the Lord of all; whose essential nature is
opposed to everything defiling, whose will is ever accomplished; who possesses an infinite number of auspicious qualities, first among which are knowledge and bliss; who is
omniscient, omnipotent, and supremely merciful, from whom the creation, continued
existence and dissolution of the world proceed—He is Brahman. . . .[2]

That which is expressed with the term "Supreme Brahman" is the Lord, the Supreme
Person. . . . He is removed beyond any trace of evil. He possesses a host of auspicious
qualities such as knowledge and power, which are natural to Him and of matchless excellence. He is the one who is to be known through all the Vedas and Upanisads. He is
the sole cause of the entire universe and is its support. He causes all things to function. All duties enjoined by the Vedas constitute the worship of Him. Being worshiped
through these various duties He grants, according to the petition, the fruit of the nature
of dharma, artha, kāma and moksa.[3]

The Supreme Person, who is meant by the term "Supreme Brahman," has as His
sport the origination, maintenance, and dissolution of the entire universe. He is opposed
to all evil whatsoever, and His essential nature consists solely of what is auspicious. He
is a great ocean containing a host of all auspicious qualities, the first six of which are
knowledge, untiring strength, sovereignty, immutability, creative power, and splendor,
qualities which are natural to Him and of matchless excellence. . . .[4]

He is the cause of the origination, etc., of the universe; He is distinct in character
from all nonintelligent things such as Pradhāna [material nature] and from all intelligent
beings whether in a state of bondage or release; He is free from even the shadow of anything defiling; He is omniscient and omnipotent, and His will is ever accomplished; His
nature is comprised of all auspicious qualities; He is the inner Self of all, and He possesses unrestricted Lordship. . . .[5]

. . . He is the sole cause of the origination, continued existence, and dissolution of
the universe consisting of such varieties of intelligent beings and material things, and is
the sole cause of the cessation of samsāra. His essential nature is distinct from all entities
other than Himself by virtue of His opposition to all evil and His being wholly infinite
perfection. He has a host of such auspicious qualities, which are countless and of matchless excellence. He is known throughout the Upanisads by different terms such as "the

Self of all," "the Supreme Brahman," "the Supreme Light," "the Supreme Reality," "the Supreme Self" and "Being." He is the Lord, Nārāyana, the Supreme Person. . . ."[6]

Just as it is known from Scripture that there is a Supreme Person, whose name is the Supreme Brahman. . . even so is it known from Scripture that this Supreme Lord, when pleased by the faithful worship of His devotees . . . frees them from the influence of Ignorance which has the form of karma . . . allows them to obtain that bliss of matchless excellence which has the form of a direct intuition of His own true nature, and certainly does not turn them back [to samsāra]. . . .[7]

A message from Brahman

Focus your mind on Me. I am all-knowing; My will is ever accomplished; I am the sole cause of the entire universe, the Supreme Brahman, the Supreme Person.

Focus your mind on Me. My eye is long and immaculate like the petal of the white lotus; I have the magnificence of a dark rain cloud and such splendor as the brilliance of a thousand simultaneously rising suns.

Focus your mind on Me. I am an ocean filled with the immortal nectar of loveliness.

Focus your mind on Me. My four arms are broad and stout; My garment is a brilliant yellow, and I am adorned with immaculate diadems, fish-shaped earrings, pearl necklaces, golden bracelets, arm rings, and much more.

Focus your mind on Me. I am an unbounded ocean of mercy, gracious condescension, beauty, sweetness, profundity, generosity, and forgiving love; I am the refuge for all whomsoever without distinction.

Focus your mind on Me. I am the Master of all. . . .[8]

If you do not immediately succeed in achieving a state of steady concentration of your mind on Me, then try to attain Me by the discipline of practice. This consists in remembering Me with a supremely excellent love. I am inherently the antithesis of everything defiling and am a sea of infinite qualities of matchless excellence such as beauty, gracious condescension, benevolence, forgiving love, mercy, sweetness, profundity, generosity, courage, immutability [or valor], conquering might, omniscience, the possession of eternally realized objects of My desire, the power of ever accomplishing My will, being the Lord of all and the cause of every single thing. . . .[9]

Notes

*   [Quotations are taken from John Braisted Carman, *The Theology of Ramanuja: An Essay in Interreligious Understanding* (London: Yale University Press, 1974). Commentary and Sanskrit terms have been removed, and footnotes have been modified.]

1   *Śrībhāṣya* 1.1.1.
2   *Śrībhāṣya* 1.1.2.
3   *Gītābhāṣya* 18.42.
4   *Gītābhāṣya* 18.73.
5   *Śrībhāṣya* 1.4.1.
6   *Vedārthasamgraha*, para. 6.
7   *Śrībhāṣya* 4.4.21–22.
8   *Gītābhāṣya* 9.34.
9   *Gītābhāṣya* 12.9.

Questions for reflection

1   Describe Brahman as reflected in Ramanuja's words from this selection. Does Brahman, as portrayed here, differ from the God of Judaism? Christianity? Islam?
2   Ultimately, what is it Brahman is seeking from human beings?
3   Compare this selection with the one by Shankara in this volume (chapter 14). What are some differences between the way Brahman is depicted in the two selections? What are some similarities?

Further reading

C. J. Bartley (2002) *The Theology of Rāmānuja: Realism and Religion.* London: RoutledgeCurzon. (A study of Ramanuja's monotheistic theology along with his adherence to traditional Brahiminical orthodoxy.)

Gavin D. Flood (1996) *An Introduction to Hinduism.* Cambridge: Cambridge University Press. (A readable and very useful introduction to Hinduism.)

Arvind Sharma, ed. (2003) *The Study of Hinduism.* Columbia, SC: University of South Carolina Press. (Leading scholars from across the globe analyze various aspects of Hinduism from analytical, historical, and topical perspectives.)

George Thibaut (2004) *The Vedanta Sutras with the Commentary by Ramanuja.* Whitefish, MT: Kessinger Publishing. (Ramanuja's commentary on the important Vedānta Sutras.)

William J. Wainwright (1986), "Monotheism," in *Rationality, Religious Belief, and Moral Commitment.* Ed. Robert Audi and William J. Wainwright. Ithaca, NY: Cornell University Press. (A concise presentation of monotheism by a well-respected philosopher of religion.)

Chapter 11

Thomas V. Morris

GOD INCARNATE AND TRIUNE

Thomas V. Morris was formerly Professor of Philosophy at the University of Notre Dame and is currently Chairman of the Morris Institute for Human Values. In this essay, he explains and defends the classical Christian doctrines of the Incarnation of Christ and the Trinity. Morris notes that, on the surface, it appears that the Incarnation—the claim that Jesus was both *fully* God and *fully* man—seems metaphysically and logically impossible. However, his distinction between individual-essences and kind-essences opens the door for this possibility. Morris outlines two main views of the Incarnation, one commonly known as *kenotic Christology*, and one referred to as the *two-minds view*. In kenotic Christology, Christ freely chose to empty himself of his divinity for a time. Yet, according to Morris, this unsatisfactorily redefines what it means to be deity. On the two-minds view of the Incarnation, taking on a human body and mind did not require or involve relinquishing the proper resources of divinity. Rather, the Incarnation involved a duality of abstract natures, as well as a duality of consciousness or mentality.

In the second part of the essay, Morris focuses on the doctrine of the Trinity, the Christian understanding of God as existing in threefold form—three persons in the unity of one divine nature. He first contrasts this view with the heresies of modalism and polytheism and then argues for the doctrine of the Trinity, responding to *the problem of the lonely God* in his defense.

Morris concludes that neither the doctrine of the Trinity nor the doctrine of the Incarnation is an opaque mystery totally impenetrable to human thought. He claims that we can make important headway in our attempts to understand the most distinctive Christian claims about God.

. . . In this chapter we shall turn our attention to some claims about God made by Christians alone. In particular, we shall focus in on two theological doctrines that together define what is distinctive about the Christian idea of God: the doctrine of the Incarnation and the doctrine of the Trinity.

The doctrine of the Incarnation

By any reasonable account, the short life and ministry of Jesus of Nazareth had an extremely powerful impact on the people around him. Because of their experience of his life and teaching, and especially of the extraordinary events surrounding the end of his earthly career, his followers came to believe that creaturely categories were inadequate for conceptualizing who he is. Thus was born the distinctively Christian conviction that Jesus was, and is, both divine and human, God and man. The doctrine of the Incarnation is just the claim that in the case of Jesus the Christ, we are confronted by one person with two natures, human nature and the divine nature.

So the uniquely Christian proclamation was that Jesus is God Incarnate. Yet, he himself prayed to God and told his followers that when he left the earthly stage another comforter would come. This led to a threefold experience of divinity on the part of Christians, and a firm conviction that there is multiplicity within the unity of deity. It was this conviction that gave rise to the theologically precise doctrine of the Trinity, the belief that within the unity of the divine nature, God exists as three persons: God the Father, God the Son and God the Holy Spirit. With this development in the distinctively Christian view of deity, it was then possible to state the doctrine of the Incarnation with more precision. The claim is specifically that a properly divine person, God the Son, the second person of the divine Trinity, has taken on a human nature for us and our salvation. Before the time of the Incarnation, this person existed from all eternity as fully divine. Then, in the days of Herod the king, he took upon himself a fully human form of existence, yet never therein ceasing to be that which he eternally was. The early Christian experience of Christ thus finally led the Council of Chalcedon to decree in the year 451 that:

> Following therefore the holy Fathers, we confess one and the same our Lord Jesus Christ, and we all teach harmoniously [that he is] the same perfect in Godhead, the same perfect in manhood, truly God and truly man, the same of a reasonable soul and body; consubstantial with the Father in Godhead, and the same consubstantial with us in manhood, like us in all things except sin. . . one and the same Christ, Son, Lord, unique; acknowledged in two natures without confusion, without change, without division, without separation——the difference of the natures being by no means taken away because of the union, but rather the distinctive character of each nature being preserved, and (each) combining in one person. . . not divided or separated into two persons, but one and the same Son and only-begotten God, Word, Lord Jesus Christ; as the prophets of old and the Lord Jesus Christ himself taught us about him, and the symbol of the Fathers has handed down to us.[1]

By so speaking, the Council presented the Christian church with the definition of orthodoxy on the ontology of Christ.

But, of course, the central philosophical problem which quickly arises here is not difficult to discern. In the Judeo-Christian vision of reality, no beings could be more different from each other than God, the creator of all, and any kind of creature. And even granting the doctrine that human beings are created in the image of God, humanity and divinity can certainly seem to be so different as to render it metaphysically and even logically impossible for any single individual to be both human and divine, *truly* God and *truly* man. . . . God is omnipotent, omniscient, omnipresent, eternal, ontolog- ically independent, and absolutely perfect. We human beings, of course, have none of these properties. And this surely seems to be no accident. Could I possibly have been a greatest possible being? Could you have been uncreated, eternally existent, and omni- present in all of creation? Surely the logical complements, or opposites, of these divine properties are essential to you and to me. We could not exist without certain sorts of metaphysical limitations and dependencies—limitations and dependencies which are necessarily alien to the divine form of existence as it is conceived in Jewish and Chris- tian theology. From this, critics of Chalcedon have concluded that there are properties necessary for being divine that no human being could possibly have, and properties essential for being human that no divine being could possibly have. The dramatic story told by Chalcedon is then viewed as a metaphysical impossibility.

The tension inherent in the two-natures doctrine of Christ was felt from the very earliest days of reflective Christian theology, and led to the existence of many con- flicting opinions about Christ. The psilanthropists denied that Jesus was truly divine. The docetists concluded that he was not really human. The Arians denied that he was literally either. Apollinarians tried to whittle down the humanity to make room for the divinity. And Nestorians speculated on a composite Christ, one individual human person and one individual divine person, distinct from one another but acting in the closest possible relation of moral harmony. The church at large rejected all these strategies of partial or complete capitulation and insisted again and again on the Chalce- donian formula: one person, two natures—truly God and truly man.[2]

The philosophical question here is whether orthodoxy embraces a possibility. Can the doctrine even possibly be true? In recent years many critics of the doctrine have claimed that it is clearly incoherent. But I believe that a strategy of defense is available which, surprisingly, is fairly simple.[3] The initial operative assumption is that, in trying to understand the doctrine, we should indeed begin with the most exalted conception of divinity, a down-to-earth conception of humanity, and the metaphysical constraints passed on to us by the early ecumenical councils of the church. Given these starting points, the procedure is then to turn back the philosophical arguments against the Incarnation's possibility by the use of conceptual distinctions and metaphysical postu- lations that flout no strong, reflectively held intuitions, and that together succeed in providing a picture of the metaphysics of God Incarnate that will accord with the por- trayal of Christ in the documents of the New Testament.

In our attempt to understand and defend the doctrine of the Incarnation, we shall continue to use the most exalted conception of deity possible, that conception captured by perfect being theology. That is to say, we shall begin by thinking of any divine being as a greatest possible, or maximally perfect being. Divinity, or deity, we shall continue to construe as analogous to a natural kind, and thus as comprising a kind-essence, a clus- ter of properties individually necessary and jointly sufficient for belonging to the kind, or in this case, for being divine. We shall thus continue to think of omnipotence and omniscience, for example, as properties essential to deity. And, following the standard Anselmian intuitions . . . , we shall take the strongly modalized properties of *necessary* omnipotence (omnipotence in all possible worlds, and at all times in any such worlds) and *necessary* omniscience to be ingredient in deity as well. Thus, on this picture, . . . no individual could possibly be God without being omnipotent. And no being could count as literally divine without having that attribute necessarily. The picture of God we are assuming thus holds that such properties as omnipotence, omniscience, omnipresence, eternality, moral perfection and ontological independence must belong to any individual who is divine, and must be had with the strongest possible modal status. If such an exalted conception of divinity can be squared with the doctrine of the Incarnation, then presumably more modest conceptions could be as well.

All other things being equal, it would seem that the more extreme a conception we have of deity, the more trouble we are going to have mapping out a coherent account of a divine Incarnation. But I do not think critics of the Incarnation usually go wrong by having too exalted a conception of divinity. Rather, I think they most commonly come to judge the Incarnation an impossibility mainly on account of an incorrect, metaphysically flawed conception of humanity. Only if we assume that it is necessary for being human, or for having a human nature, that an individual lack *any* of those properties ingredient in deity, do we have an obvious logical and metaphysical obstacle to the orthodox two-natures view of Christ. And I believe that the critics of the doctrine have come to hold such a conception of human nature only by missing some fairly simple distinctions and by ignoring some intriguing metaphysical possibilities.

First, there is the fairly well-known distinction between an *individual-essence* and a *kind-essence*. An *individual-essence* is a cluster of properties essential for an individual's being the particular entity it is, properties without which it would not exist. A *kind-essence* is that cluster of properties without which . . . an individual would not belong to the particular natural kind it distinctively exemplifies. Of necessity, an individual can have no more than one individual-essence, or individual nature, but it does not follow from this, and is not, so far as I can tell, demonstrable from any other quarter, that an individual can have no more than one kind-essence. And this is surely a good thing, for if such an argument could be made out, it would block from the start the doctrine of the Incarnation, at least the orthodox two-natures view, without the need of turning to consider the specifics of divinity and humanity.

Once we have recognized a distinction like that between individual-essences and kind-essences, we can see that necessities intuitively thought to characterize individual human beings cannot automatically be deemed to be such in virtue of those beings' common human nature, as part of the kind-essence of humanity. You and I, and any of our neighbors, may be such that we necessarily are noneternal, created beings, and we may share that modal characterization with all of the human beings living on the surface of the earth today without its at all following that this necessity constitutes part of what it is to have a human nature. It may be the case that all of our individual essences incorporate these modal properties of limited metaphysical status without its being the case that these properties are metaphysical prerequisites for exemplifying the natural kind of being human. Of course, critics of the Incarnation have discerned such necessities while thinking about human beings, have identified them simply as ingredients in human nature, and, pointing out that quite contrary necessities form the divine nature, have gone on to conclude that it is impossible for a properly divine being to take on human nature.[4] But more caution is needed here than is customarily exercised. In drawing their conclusions about what is essential for being human, critics of the Incarnation have, I think, made some errors which can be highlighted and then avoided by the use of two more straightforward distinctions.

In trying to enumerate the properties essential for being human, some theologians have included the property of being sinful, but this is a property the decree of Chalcedon explicitly denies of Christ. Why would anyone ever think it is part of the kind-essence of humanity? Probably because they have employed a very simple and very inadequate method for determining the elements of human nature, a method that we can call the *look-around-town approach*: Look around town, and what do you see? Every human being you come across shares numerous properties with every other human in town, including, most likely, the property of being sinful. To conclude that being sinful is thus a part of human nature is, however, to miss a simple distinction. There are properties which happen to be *common* to members of a natural kind, and which may even be *universal* to all members of that kind, without being *essential* to membership in the kind. Mere observation alone can suffice to establish commonality. Thought experiments and modal intuitions must be drawn upon to determine necessity, or kind-essentiality. Once these distinctions are properly drawn, we can acknowledge the commonality of sinfulness among human beings while at the same time following Chalcedon in denying both its strict universality and its presence in the kind-essence which we call human nature.

Such properties as those of being contingent, created, noneternal, nonomnipotent, nonomniscient and nonomnipresent are certainly common to human beings. Apart from the case of Christ, they are even, presumably, universal human properties. But I submit that they are not kind-essential human properties. It is not true that an individual must be a contingent being, noneternal and nonomnipotent in order to exemplify human nature. It is possible for an individual to be human without being characterized by any of these limitation properties. And so it is possible for an individual who essentially lacks such properties, an individual who is properly divine, to take up at the same time a human nature.

The many properties of metaphysical limitation and dependence that characterize you and me do so, then, not because they are essential elements in our common human nature. They may characterize you and me necessarily. Presumably, they do. But it is not in virtue of our being human; rather, it is in virtue of our being the humans we are. Such properties may partially comprise our respective individual essences, or, more likely, may characterize us in virtue of the fact that we created human beings are *merely human*—we are no more than human. Humanity crowns our ontological status as the greatest foothold we have in the grand scheme of things. We are *fully human*: we have all the properties constituting the kind-essence of humanity. But we are merely human as well: we have certain limitation properties in virtue of being God's creatures. Those limitations need not be ingredient in our humanness, only in our creatureliness. Thus, God the Son, through whom all things are created, need not have taken on any of those limitation properties distinctive of our creatureliness in order to take on a human nature. He could have become fully human without being merely human.

Now, all these distinctions and defensive moves may be fine, each taken in itself, one by one. But the net result of applying them to a full defense of the Incarnation can appear problematic in the extreme. When we consult the pages of the New Testament, we see in the portrait of Jesus the workings of a mind which, extraordinarily wise and discerning as it may be, seems less than omniscient, and which appears, for all its strength, to lack the power of omnipotence in itself, having to turn heavenward for resources just as we do. We see a mind apparently conditioned by the first-century Palestinian worldview. We see a man who shared the anguish and joys of the human condition. Our metaphysical distinctions cannot be allowed to blind us to this. And it would be both foolish and heterodox to minimize it. We need a picture of the Incarnation that will account for all of these appearances.

Two pictures of God incarnate

We are completely clear on what it means to begin with an exalted conception of divinity. It may not be clear at all what I meant when I added above that we should also start with a down-to-earth conception of humanity. Now is the time to make it clear. Taking on a human nature involves taking on a human body and a human mind, no more and no less. What essentially constitutes a human body and a human mind we wait upon a perfected science, or a more complete revelation, to say. We have neither a very full-blown nor a very fine-grained understanding of either at this point. But we do know well enough what a human body is, and what a human mind is, for it to be informative to be told that taking on such a body and mind is taking on a human nature. It is both necessary and sufficient for being human. This is almost embarrassingly simple as metaphysics goes. No modal razzle-dazzle, no ontological arcana: If you have a human body and mind, you have a human nature—you exemplify the kind-essence of humanity. This is surely a down-to-earth conception of humanity if anything is.

For God the Son to become human, he thus had to take on a human body and a human mind, with all that entails. He did not have to become a created, contingent being. He just had to take on a created, contingent body and mind of the right sort. And so he was born of Mary the virgin and lived a human life.

But how did he manage this? Isn't it clear that taking on a human body and mind in order to live a human life involves taking on limitations of knowledge, power and presence? And aren't such limitations incompatible with divinity? As we have noted, the New Testament pictures an extraordinary individual living out a life among his fellows from limited human resources. How is this to be reconciled with his being divine? Some philosophers and theologians have believed that Jesus' limits force us to tone down a bit our conception of what deity consists in. They have come to think that facing up to what the New Testament shows us concerning Jesus' real limits requires us to conclude that in becoming incarnate he—that is, God the Son—gave up temporarily some of his unrestricted divine attributes, for example, his omniscience, his omnipotence and his omnipresence. This, they think, was required in order for him to take on the limitations involved in living a genuinely human life and sharing fully in our common human condition. This is the story told by *kenotic Christology* (from the Greek word *kenosis*, or "emptying"). If kenotic Christology is true, if God the Son temporarily empties himself, giving up his properly divine power, relinquishing his complete knowledge, and restricting his presence to the confines of his mortal shell while nonetheless remaining divine, it cannot be that divinity necessarily comprises or requires omnipotence, omniscience and omnipresence. For if during the early sojourn, the Second Person of the Trinity was divine but was without these exalted properties, they cannot be among those things required for true deity. As kenotic Christology is incompatible with seeing divinity as, at least in part, constituted by necessary omnipotence, necessary omniscience and necessary omnipresence, so it is also incompatible with holding all the simple, nonmodalized properties of omnipotence, omniscience and omnipresence to be requisites of divinity.

Well, then, on the kenotic view, what *are* the necessary truths about divinity? What is it to be God? The kenotic suggestion, perhaps, is something like this: In order to be literally divine, it is necessary for an individual to have in all possible worlds the property of *being omnipotent unless freely and temporarily choosing to be otherwise*, the property of *being omniscient unless freely and temporarily choosing to be otherwise*, and likewise for omnipresence. On this modally less extreme view of divinity, a divine being is not necessarily invulnerable to ignorance and weakness. He can render himself vulnerable to these deficiencies, he can take them on, while yet remaining truly divine.

Kenotic Christology began to be developed during the nineteenth century and continues to be refined today despite numerous critics—many of whom have just failed to grasp the subtlety with which the position can be deployed. And it must be said in behalf of the kenotic strategy that (1) what it seeks to accommodate in the biblical portrayal of Christ is indeed crucial to preserve, and (2) it is altogether legitimate and proper for a Christian to apply his convictions arising out of divine revelation and the events of salvation history to his philosophical theology, and in particular to his philosophical conception of God. There must be a dynamic interaction between what *a priori*, intuitive, or purely philosophical constraints there are on philosophical theology and the agreed data of revelation. The kenotic maneuver presents us with an intriguing possibility, yet I must admit that I have a hard time finding it satisfactory. It presents us with a far less exalted and less theoretically satisfying conception of Christ's deity. Its way of redefining the basic divine attributes seems extremely *ad hoc*, an exercise in metaphysical gerrymandering reflective of no more general philosophical distinctions. And my misgivings about such an account of Christ's deity are not without parallel in the weightiest theological treatises.

During the early years of the fifth century, Pope Leo wrote an essay on the Incarnation which the Council of Chalcedon embraced as properly capturing the two-natures view of Christ. Known as *The Tome of Leo*, it says of Christ that, among other things:

> He took on him "the form of a servant" without the defilement of sins, augmenting what was human, not diminishing what was divine; because that "emptying of himself," whereby the Invisible made himself visible, and the Creator and Lord of all things willed to be one among mortals, was a stooping down of compassion, not a failure of power. Accordingly, the same who, remaining in the form of God, made man, was made Man in the form of a servant, so the form of a servant does not impair the form of God.[5]

A sophisticated kenotic Christology can be argued to preserve the letter of Leo's claims, but I have difficulty seeing how it can be thought to be true to the spirit of those claims. But in case this is unclear, consider the great theologian Athanasius (*c*. A.D. 293–373), who wrote earlier concerning the incarnate Christ:

> He was not, as might be imagined, circumscribed in the body, nor, while present in the body, was he absent elsewhere; nor, while he moved the body, was the universe left void of his working and providence; but, thing most marvelous, Word as he was, so far from being contained by anything, he rather contained all things himself; and just as while present in the whole of creation, he is at once distinct in being from the universe, and present in all

things by his own power, . . . thus, even while present in a human body and himself quickening it, he was, without inconsistency, quickening the universe as well.[6]

So, for Athanasius, it seems that Christ was not limited in power, knowledge and effect to the workings of his human mind and body during the time of the Incarnation. There is no restricting of his being to the confines of the human alone. This is surely no kenotic, metaphysical emptying or relinquishing of the properly divine status or functioning. While having a human body and mind and living out a human life on this terrestrial globe, Christ nonetheless retained all of the resources and prerogatives of divinity in the most robust sense.

But can we make sense of such a view? Can we indeed have it all, the fullness of humanity and the fullness of divinity? I think so, for there is an alternative to the kenotic picture of Christ, an alternative which has been called the *two-minds view*.[7] On this account of the Incarnation, taking on a human body and mind did not require or involve relinquishing the proper resources of divinity. Just as we saw that God the Son's taking on of a created, contingent body and mind does not entail that he himself was a created, contingent being, so, on the two-minds view, his taking on of a body and mind limited in knowledge, power and presence does not entail that he himself, in his deepest continuing mode of existence, was limited in knowledge, power or presence. Rather, in the case of God Incarnate we must recognize something like two distinct minds or systems of mentality. There is first what we can call the eternal mind of God the Son, with its distinctively divine consciousness, whatever that might be like, encompassing the full scope of omniscience, empowered by the resources of omnipotence, and present in power and knowledge throughout the entirety of creation. And in addition to this divine mind, there is the distinctly earthly mind with its consciousness that came into existence and developed with the conception, human birth and growth of Christ's earthly form of existence. The human mind drew its visual imagery from what the eyes of Jesus saw, and its concepts from the languages he learned. This earthly mind, with its range of consciousness and self-consciousness, was thoroughly human, Jewish and first-century Palestinian in nature. By living out his earthly life from only the resources of his human body and mind, he took on the form of our existence and shared in the plight of our condition.

So, on the two-minds view, the Incarnation involved not just a duality of abstract natures, but a duality of consciousness or mentality, which was introduced into the divine life of God the Son. The two minds of Christ should be thought of as standing in something like an asymmetric accessing relation: The human mind was contained by, but did not itself contain, the divine mind; or, to portray it from the other side, the divine mind contained, but was not contained by, the human mind. Everything present to the human mind of Christ was thereby present to the divine mind as well, but not vice versa. There was immediate, direct access from the human mind to the divine mind, but no such converse immediacy of access. Insofar as Christ normally chose to live his earthly life out of his human resources alone, the words he spoke and the actions he performed by means of the body were words and actions arising out of his human mind. He had all the mental, intellectual, emotional and volitional resources we all have, lacking none. And it was these, not his divine resources, that he typically drew on for the personal history he enacted on this earth. But this living of a human life through human resources was, on the two-minds view, going on at the same time that he, in his properly divine form of existence, was continuing to exercise his omnipotence, with the wisdom of his omniscience, in his omnipresent activities throughout creation.

Can we, however, really hope to understand the two-minds view? Can we attain any firm grasp of what it might have been like for God Incarnate to have at one and the same time a limited human consciousness and an overarching divine mind? To some extent, I think we can. There are numerous earthly phenomena with which we are familiar that can be taken to provide very helpful, partial analogies to the two-minds view of Christ. There seem to exist, for example, cases of dreams in which the dreamer both plays a role within the environs of the dream story, operating with a consciousness formed from within the dream, and yet at the same time, *as* dreamer, retains an over-arching consciousness that the drama of the dream is just that—only a dream. Another sort of analogy can be provided by thought experiments dealing with artificial intelligence, in which two physical systems are each such as to be credited with mentality, and yet stand in such an asymmetric accessing relation that one can be considered a sub-system of the other, with its own distinctive origin and functions, but at the same time belonging to the unity of a larger system of mentality. And then there are numerous, powerful, partial analogies available in the literature dealing with human cases of multiple personality. In many such cases, there seem to be different centers or spheres of consciousness standing in an asymmetric accessing relation to an overarching or executive self, and ultimately belonging to one person. Of course, human cases of multiple personality involve severe dysfunction and undesirable traits starkly disanalogous to anything we want to acknowledge in the Incarnation. But this just helps us to see where the specific limits of this sort of analogy lie.

There are also certain phenomena having to do with hypnosis, brain commissurotomy, self-deception and *akrasia*, or weakness of will, in which there seem to be operative different levels or spheres of awareness, information retention and processing, or, in general, mentality which are, in important metaphysical ways, analogous to what the two-minds view recognizes in the case of the Incarnation. Again, it must be stressed that the negative aspects of these extraordinary, worldly cases of multiple mentality are not meant at all to characterize the Incarnation, and in fact can be argued decisively not to cloud Christ's case in the least. These are only partial analogies, which provide us with some imaginative grip on the two-minds picture.

One of the best analogies may be provided by the claim of twentieth-century psychologists that every normal human being partakes of a variety of levels of mentality. Consider for example the very simple distinction of the conscious human mind, the seat of occurrent awareness, from the unconscious mind. In most standard accounts of such a distinction, the unconscious mind stands to the conscious mind in much the same relation that the two-minds view sees between the divine and human minds in the case of Christ. God the Son, on this picture, took on every normal level or sphere of human mentality, but enjoyed the extra depth as well of his properly divine mindedness.

One interesting feature of all these analogies which have to do with human psychological phenomena is that they point toward what some theorists are calling a "multimind" view of persons in general.[8] On this sort of a view, a person is, or at least it is inevitable that a person potentially has, *a system of systems of mentality*, to use the broadest possible terminology. This systems view of the person is in close accord with the more generalized view of all of life as involving hierarchically stratified systems of organization and control, but is arrived at with evidence of its own, not as just the application of the more general view to the case of persons.

We can develop a systems view here in such a way that all finite mental systems are metaphysically open-ended for hierarchical subsumption by deeper, or higher, systems—use whichever vertical metaphor you prefer. Epistemologically, we typically come to recognize the existence of a multiplicity of mental systems in the case of a human being only when things go awry, as in multiple personality, commissurotomy, or what is called self-deception. But the systems view is that what we thus come to recognize, the multiplicity of systems of mentality, is always there in some form in normal cases as well, although functioning very differently, and thus being manifested very differently, if at all, to normal observation.

It is, of course, not my claim that a systems view of mentality proves the two-minds view of Christ, that it serves as any evidence for the truth of this theological view, or even that it establishes the possibility of this picture of the Incarnation. It only provides us with a general account of mentality that is thoroughly consonant with the main features of the metaphysical postulations distinctive of the two-minds view, and thus gives us a vantage point from which to come to better understand the view. It also helps to answer some questions that can otherwise seem to yield troubling problems for the view.

Did Christ have erroneous beliefs, such as would have been acquired through the natural functioning of his human mind in the social and intellectual environment in which he lived? Did he have a geocentric picture of the cosmos? Did he really not know who touched the hem of his garment? He had a limited human mind and a divine mind, so what is the answer, yes or no? Our ordinary practices and locutions for belief ascription can lead to puzzling questions concerning God Incarnate. But I think the two-minds view, rather than creating such puzzlement, actually helps us to see through it. First of all, we must be cautious about assuming that our ordinary linguistic practices are completely in order here, in such a way that they can act as altogether reliable touchstones of truth. If it is asked exactly what Christ believed, the two-minds view will direct us to ask what information was contained in his earthly mind, and then what information was contained in his divine mind. And this sort of response is to be expected on any multimind view of the person, or on any multisystems approach to mentality. Our ordinary, simple ways of posing and answering such questions in mundane contexts may provide less than absolutely reliable guidance where such metaphysical precision is required, as in the doctrine of the Incarnation.

But if the question is pressed concerning what the person God the Son himself believed on this or that issue, evading the question by appealing to the duality of minds can appear to threaten the unity of the person, and thus the coherence of the whole picture. The response of dividing the question does remind us of something important. God the Son Incarnate had two minds and chose to live out the life of the body on this earth normally through the resources of the human mind alone. That was the primary font of most of his earthly behavior and speech. Nevertheless, if the question is really pressed, if it is insisted that we be prepared, in principle, to say what he, the individual person, believed about this or that, we must appeal to the feature of hierarchical organization endemic to a systems view of mentality and, recognizing the priority of the divine, represent God the Son's ultimate belief state as captured in his divine omniscience. This feature of hierarchical organization thus does not leave us in puzzlement concerning the final story about the person.

This move seems to indicate a compatibility between metaphysical double-mindedness and personal unity. But what exactly does the personal unity of Christ consist in on the two-minds view? What makes the human mind of Jesus a mind of God the Son? A critic of this account of the Incarnation could point out, for example, that on the standard view of God as utterly omniscient, any divine person stands in a direct, immediate and complete asymmetric accessing relation to the mind of every human being. If standing in this relation is what makes Jesus' earthly mind a mind of God, all our minds are minds of God, and thus we are all divine incarnations. If this were a safe inference from the two-minds view, I think it is safe to say it would serve as an effective refutation of the view, demonstrating its unacceptability.

The accessing relation alone, however, is not intended by the two-minds view to count as a sufficient condition of Incarnation. Information flow by itself does not constitute mental, metaphysical ownership. So, what does? I must admit that I am no more sure about how to spell out what constitutes metaphysical ownership in the case of the Incarnation than I am about how to spell out exactly what it is for a range of mentality to be a part of my own mind, or to belong to me. There are mysteries here in any case, not just in the case of what the two-minds view claims about the Incarnation. But, fortunately, this is not all there is to be said.

What we can refer to as my human mental system was intended by God to define a person. If my human mental system is subsumed or overridden by any other causal system, my personal freedom is abrogated. The complete human mental system of Jesus was not intended alone to define a person. It was created to belong to a person with a divine mind as well as the ultimate, hierarchically maximal mental system. At any point during the metaphysical event of the Incarnation, it is thus possible that the human capacities of Christ, or the entirety of what we are calling his human mental system, be subsumed and overridden by the divine mind, without its being the case that any person's freedom is thereby abrogated. And this is a crucial difference between Jesus and any other human being, indeed, between Jesus and any free-willed *creature* of God. When our attention has been directed to this, it has been directed to the distinctiveness of the metaphysics of God Incarnate.

We are always in danger of misunderstanding the doctrine of the Incarnation, and the two-minds view of Christ in particular, if we forget that here, as in other properly metaphysical contexts, 'person' is an ultimate, ontological status term, not a composition term. The entirety of the human mental system of God the Son did not serve to compose a human person distinct from the person who was and is properly divine, because having the status of exemplifying a human body-mind composite was not the deepest truth about the ontological status of that individual. The personhood of Jesus was a matter of his ultimate ontological status and nothing less. This is the claim of the Christian tradition.

The two-minds view of Christ is extraordinarily interesting, philosophically and theologically, and, at least *prima facie*, it seems to me strongly preferable to the alternative of kenotic Christology. Something like one or the other of these pictures of the Incarnation is necessary, I think, if we are to make full sense of the manifest earthly career of Jesus from the perspective of a commitment to his divinity; or, to put it the other way around, if we are to make full sense of a belief in his divinity from the perspective of the manifest, earthly career of Jesus. From either point of view, we need some such account of the metaphysics of God Incarnate.

The doctrine of the Trinity

We already have indicated, in the briefest way possible, what the doctrine of the Trinity is. Now is the time to lay it out a bit more carefully. The threefold Christian experience of God, as recorded in the New Testament, has led to the Christian understanding of God as existing in threefold form—three persons in the unity of one divine nature. Jesus, as we have seen, is believed to be divine, God Incarnate. But he himself often indicated that he saw himself as standing in relation to a distinct divine person. He seems often to have prayed to God and to have said of himself that he had been sent by his heavenly father. So Christians have come to recognize, at the level of deity, both God the Father and God the Son, who have also come to be known, respectively, as the First Person and the Second Person of the divine Trinity. The special Comforter, whom Jesus promised his followers after his departure and who was believed to have come upon the church at Pentecost, endowing those early Christians with supernatural gifts, drawing others to Christ and working sanctification in the lives of all true believers, is identified in Christian theology as the Third Person of the divine Trinity, God the Holy Spirit. So we have as the object of Christian faith and worship three divine persons. But Christians have insisted from the earliest days that this is in no important way like pagan polytheism; it is not the worship of three independent gods.[9]

In any attempt to understand the doctrine of the Incarnation, the challenge is to secure the unity of the person of Christ while at the same time acknowledging the real distinctness of his two natures. In understanding the doctrine of the Trinity, the challenge is to balance the distinctness of the persons with the real unity of the divine nature, a unity sufficient to justify the Christian insistence that monotheism has not been utterly abandoned, that, in the words of Deuteronomy, "The LORD our God is one God" (Deut 6:4). But how is this to be done?

Throughout the centuries, many theologians and philosophers have tried to explain both the threeness and the oneness of the Trinity, while staying within the boundaries for an acceptable account laid down by the early church. In reaction against the views of the popular theologian Arius, who had claimed that at the deepest level of his being Jesus the Christ was a created being, brought into existence by God the Father at a particular time, the Council of Nicaea (A.D. 325) declared:

> We believe in one God, the Father almighty, maker of all things, visible and invisible;
>
> And in one Lord Jesus Christ, the Son of God, only-begotten, that is, from the substance of the Father, God from God, light from light, true God from true God, begotten not made, of one substance with the Father, through whom all things came into being, things in heaven and things on earth, who because of us men and because of our salvation came down and became incarnate, becoming man, suffered and rose again on the third day, ascended to the heavens, and will come to judge the living and the dead;
>
> And in the Holy Spirit.
>
> But as for those who say, there was when He was not and, before being born He was not, and that He came into existence out of nothing, or who assert that

the Son of God is from a different hypostasis or substance, or is created, or is subject to alteration or change—these the Catholic church anathematizes.[10]

The fully divine status of the Holy Spirit, who is no more than mentioned here (since the controversy addressed was over the Son), was made clear at the Council of Constantinople a few years later in 381. As the trinitarian language came to be developed in the Western church, the Son was said to have been eternally "begotten" by the Father, whereas the Spirit eternally "proceeded" from the Father and the Son. So, although the three persons were regarded as equally divine, there was believed to be a hierarchy of dependence relations within the exalted realm of divinity.

All the attempts to spell out the doctrine of the Trinity can be thought of as located along a spectrum, at one end of which is the error of *modalism*, and at the other end of which is *polytheism*. The heresy of modalism is the claim that the three "persons" are merely three appearances of God, or three roles God plays in salvation history. It is a view which holds that really there is only one divine individual, one ultimate bearer of the properties of divinity beneath these three "masks" or "modes of appearance." And, of course, polytheism is the belief in two or more distinct and independent deities. Modalism and polytheism are the Scylla and Charybdis between which all orthodox accounts of the Trinity must steer.

Within this range, we can distinguish between *singularity theories of the Trinity*, which attempt to stress the unity of the divine nature, without falling into modalism, and *social theories of the Trinity*, which attempt to highlight the diversity or distinctness of the three persons, without falling into polytheism. A social theory represents the Trinity as a community of three distinct persons, each with a distinct center of consciousness and will, yet all existing with the others in as close a relation of harmony and love as it is possible to stand in.

In a recent essay, "Could There Be More Than One God?" Richard Swinburne develops a fascinating version of a social theory.[11] Swinburne calls our attention to the fact that one important aspect of perfect goodness is perfect love. Now love must have an object, but, even more importantly, love must be shared. For in self-love one's love has an object, but surely, in order to be a fully loving person, any individual must extend his or her love beyond the bounds of self alone. Divine love is not only complete, it is eternal and necessary. So there must exist on the part of God some sharing of love which is both eternal and necessary. . . . [S]ome philosophers and theologians have argued that, because of the requirements of perfect love, God must of necessity create some contingent being or other, or some world of contingent beings, with whom to share his love. Otherwise, his love would not be complete. But this conclusion runs counter to the firmly held traditional claim that God was free not to create any contingent things at all. Let us refer to this problem as the *problem of the lonely God*.

Swinburne offers a solution to the problem of the lonely God which blocks this argument and avoids the conclusion that God needed to create something contingent like you or me. Suppose, he begins, that there is a primordial divine being with such attributes as omnipotence, omniscience, necessity and perfect goodness. Suppose this being eternally and necessarily exemplifies all the attributes constitutive of deity. He could not exemplify them all, however, without sharing love in the deepest and most complete way possible. But the deepest and most complete way of sharing love would be to share of oneself in giving being to another from one's own being. This divine individual thus eternally and necessarily begets, from his own being, a distinct person who, as so begotten, is a true Son of the Father, divine from divine being. We thus have a conception of a primordial divine being's giving existence, eternally and necessarily, to a second divine person with whom love can be perfectly shared. But there is another element of love, or form of love, yet to be attended to. Not only is it possible for one person to share love with a second person, it is possible for two people to join together in sharing mutual love with a third. Think of the way in which married couples naturally seek to express their love in the giving and nurturing of a distinct life. This seems to be a form of love, or a richness of love, distinct from the sharing which goes on only between one person and another. But the perfection of divine love must encompass every basic form, or level of richness, possible for love. So we must suppose that a third divine person proceeds from the Father and the Son, eternally and necessarily, as the object of the mutuality of their ultimate giving and sharing. This divine person, the Holy Spirit, both is loved by, and in turn loves, each of the other persons of the Trinity. And there is completeness in mutual love. The Father and Son love the Spirit. The Son and Spirit love the Father. The Father and Spirit love the Son. All the forms and depths of love are manifest within divinity, and there is no need of any other divine person to make possible the complete manifestation of love. On this view, there are necessarily three distinct persons within divinity, and just as necessarily, there are no others. Thus, there exists the divine Trinity worshiped by Christians.

Some philosophers have suggested that there could not possibly exist more than one omnipotent being, for if there were two or more, their wills could potentially conflict.[12] But there could not be any possible resolution of a conflict between omnipotent beings. So, these philosophers have thought, we must conclude that there cannot be more than one omnipotent individual. What exactly follows, however, is just that if there is more than one omnipotent being, they must be necessarily harmonious in will. But from where will that harmony come? What will be the principle of division of labor, or who will set the rules, so to speak, for the patterns of co-operation among equally omnipotent beings? Swinburne suggests that among omnipotent beings, there must be a hierarchy of responsibility or authority over such matters, and that this in itself indicates that there could not be a multiplicity of divine beings unless their ontology was much like what he argues to be the case in the Trinity. For Father, Son and Holy Spirit, the coordination responsibilities, or authority, will lie with the Father, as the primordial member of the Trinity. It would be a condition of the eternal and necessary existence of the other two persons that in some metaphysically prior way, the matters of coordination and harmonious function had already been settled. So they must eternally and necessarily derive from the Father. The New Testament itself contains reflections of this, as God the Son Incarnate seems clearly to defer to the Father and to the authority of the Father.[13]

On this view of the Trinity as consisting in a society of divine persons, we must therefore understand the possible exercise of the omnipotent power of each of the persons as constrained by the opportunities provided by whatever rules of coordination the Father lays down. Since such rules are necessary and come from a perfectly good person, Swinburne argues, each of the other members of the Trinity would necessarily welcome them and abide by them. And this is no unfortunate limitation on the freedom of each of the divine persons, as it is a necessary condition of the highest form of existence, encompassing the completeness of perfect goodness and love.

But a few final words of clarification are needed if we are to hope to attain a good grasp of this sort of social theory of the Trinity. The decree of Nicaea insisted that the Son was not made of previously existing created material, and that he was not created *ex nihilo* at some point in time, as presumably is the case with every contingent object. The *generation* of the Son and what has been called the *spiration* of the Spirit are viewed as sharings of the being or substance of God the Father, sufficient for the eternal and necessary coexistence of two divine persons distinct from the Father, himself a divine person. Each of them has all the attributes constitutive of deity. But it is obvious that our understanding of aseity, or ontological independence, must be qualified somewhat on this view. For the Son depends on the Father, and the Spirit depends on the Father and the Son. Only the Father's existence is primordial and underived. But as we have seen on this view, insofar as being perfectly good is a condition of his existence, and the existence of the Son and Spirit as objects and sharers in love is necessary for his goodness, he bears some sort of dependence relation to them. But neither the Trinity itself, nor any of the members of the Trinity, stands in any relation of ontological dependence on any source of being prior to, or independent of, either the Father or the community all three form. The divine Trinity itself is ontologically independent and thus self-sufficient.

On this view, each member of the Trinity can be viewed as a greatest possible being, such that no other being could possibly be greater. Or we could judge there to be an internal hierarchy of greatness within the Trinity, such that no being outside the Trinity can be as great as the Spirit or the Son, but God the Father is greater than all (as some readings of John 10:29 might be taken to suggest) in the interpretive context of trinitarian doctrine. But in order to avoid another heresy, that of *subordinationism*, this latter view would have to insist on the underlying divine unity, that each of the persons of the Trinity is indeed fully divine. Another distinct application of the Anselmian perspective could specify that it is the Trinity itself which is properly considered the greatest possible being. My point here is only that social trinitarians could make various moves at this point to square their theory with the perspective of perfect being theology.

To avoid polytheism of the sort rejected by the early church fathers, social trinitarians must insist on the unity of the divine essence (the persons all share the attributes of deity), the unity of the divine substance (they all share in the being of the Father), and the unity that exists on the level of divine activity: What one member of the Trinity performs, all are said to share in performing, each in his own way, so full and deep is their cooperation.

But social trinitarians are nonetheless often said to be polytheists, however strongly they protest and proclaim their monotheism. Many theologians and Christian philosophers are very uncomfortable with any social theory of the Trinity, and thus seek to develop instead some form of what I have called a singularity theory of God's tri-unity. The heresies associated with singularity theories involve holding that the threeness of God consists only in his manner of presentation of himself to us. Christian orthodoxy has insisted that the diversity of the divine be not just a matter of appearance, but a matter of eternal, ontological reality. Numerous biblical passages seem to suggest this (Jn 1:1–3; 8:58; 17:1–26), and the problem of the lonely God seems to demand it. But singularity theories have faced difficulties in attempting an account of the Trinity adequate for accommodating those New Testament passages and avoiding that problem.

Singularity theories stress the oneness of God as a single ultimate bearer of properties, a sole metaphysical individual. On this sort of view, the three persons of the Trinity are not to be conceived as any sort of society or community of severally divine individuals or entities. The threeness which we have come to talk of as "persons" is rather to be understood as some less distinct internal relatedness within the life of the one God. As the greatest of singularity theorists, Augustine (A.D. 354–430), put it, Father, Son and Holy Spirit are themselves somehow just existent relations within the Godhead. In so categorizing the members of the Trinity, Augustine was drawing upon an ancient understanding of the status, or metaphysics, of relations, which is nowadays quite difficult for us to find at all plausible or even intelligible.

But Augustine offered some analogies to help us to grasp this view of the Trinity.[14] It was his view that the nature of God is mirrored in the nature of his creation, to the extent that even the tri-unity of the divine will be found reflected in creatures. He reminds us that God is referred to in the plural in an important passage in Genesis and is represented as saying: "Let *us* make man in *our* image" (Gen 1:26). So it is primarily to the life of human beings that we should look for analogies to help us understand the Trinity. Ideally, we need to find a triad of elements, the first of which begets the second, and the third of which binds the other two together, suggests Augustine. He offers such varied examples as: (1) an external object perceived, (2) the mind's representation of it, (3) the act of concentrating or focusing the mind on it; (1) the self as lover, (2) the object loved (which can be within that same self), (3) the love that binds; (1) the mind's memory *knowledge* of itself, (2) the mind's *understanding* of itself, (3) the mind's *will*, or love, of itself; and (1) the mind as remembering God, (2) the mind as knowing God, and (3) the mind as loving God.

But the most obvious problem with all these analogies is that they involve some sort of process or internal relatedness within the life of one person, and the doctrine of the Trinity is that, in some remotely plausible sense of "person," there are three persons which exist as the one God over all. Augustine thought that this, however, was about the best we can do. The Trinity is ultimately a mystery which we cannot hope to fathom fully, at least in this life.

Are these sorts of psychological analogies the best a singularity theory of the Trinity can manage? Well, Augustine and the many medieval philosophers who endorsed some form of singularity theory were typically pressured away from any recognition of a deeper diversity within the divine by their acceptance of a doctrine of divine simplicity, according to which there is no real ontological complexity or composition within the life of God. . . . And it is difficult to see how anyone who endorses divine simplicity in the full-blown sense can accept even the analogies Augustine has given us as reflecting anything really to be found in the oneness of the divine. For these theorists, there can be no genuine ontological diversity, if strict simplicity really holds. Perhaps the best move for a singularity theorist who wants a plausible account of the Trinity, explicable by psychological analogies having to do with diversity within the sphere of individuality, is to jettison the constraints of the ancient doctrine of divine simplicity. When this is done, a new sort of analogy becomes available for the elaboration of a singularity theory.

Recall the two-minds view of God Incarnate developed in the previous section. Something like a multimind perspective could be used to explicate the doctrine of the Trinity as well. Suppose that there is only one ultimate divine bearer of properties, one fundamental individual who is God. If, as we argued in the previous section, it is compatible with the unity of the person of Christ that he have two minds, or two distinct spheres of mentality, then it should also be compatible with the unity of the one individual who is God that he have three divine minds, or three distinct spheres of perfect mentality, each capable of awareness and the initiation of action. And as the human mind of Christ was hierarchically answerable to the divine mind, imagine here a three-level hierarchy of answerability, with the mind designated as God the Father filling the role of overarching consciousness.

At this point the picture could be developed in different ways. Remembering that on any singularist theory, there is really only one divine individual, there is no conceptual pressure to assign each of the attributes constitutive of deity to each sphere of mentality within deity. Thus, it could be held that only the overarching consciousness of God the Father holds all the riches of omniscient knowledge. On this view, Christ need not have been speaking only of the limitations of his earthly mind when he talked of the passing away of heaven and earth and said: "But of that day or hour no one knows, not even the angels in heaven, nor the Son, but the Father alone" (Mk 13:32).

Likewise, it is possible for this sort of view to be developed in such a way that omnipotence is not assigned differentially to each sphere of mentality, thereby avoiding the coordination of activity problems of three omnipotent agents. The Son and the Spirit would then be divine, not in virtue of severally exemplifying all the attributes essential to deity, but rather through being centers of mentality belonging to the one true God as spheres of his own mindedness.

But there is nothing intrinsic to the multimind version of a singularity theory that would preclude our seeing each divine mind as enjoying the riches of omniscience and omnipotence. Each would be eternal, necessary components of the divine life. And each can be thought of as internally involved in contributing to the character and activities to be found in each of the others. The attribute of aseity, or ontological independence, could be reserved for the individual who exists with this multiminded richness of interior life, or could rather be attributed in qualified form to each of the spheres of mindedness. Neither Father, nor Son, nor Spirit depends for its existence on anything extratrinitarian, outside the life of divinity. But if there is ontologically only one ultimate divine entity, an individual God with these three spheres of mentality, it would be this single individual who most directly would answer to Anselm's concept of *the* greatest possible being and creation theology's concept of a single source of all.

Singularity theories seek to secure unambiguous monotheism, in line with the clear Judaic background of Christian theology. As such, there is much to be said for them. But it is difficult to render any confident judgment that any such theory can accommodate naturally the full data of biblical revelation and Christian experience. And it is a bit hard to see how any such theory will suffice to block what we have called the problem of the lonely God. Could I be said to experience the fullness of love just through my conscious mind's having a high regard for my unconscious mind, which in turn appreciated the conscious sphere? It is hard to see how even a richly differentiated self-love could suffice to capture all the facets that could possibly characterize the goodness of a full and perfect love. And if singularity theories are found inevitably wanting in this regard, it will be incumbent upon the Christian theist to find some form of a social theory to explicate the relation between threeness and oneness in the life of the triune God.

The main point that needs to be made here is that neither the doctrine of the Trinity nor the doctrine of the Incarnation is just an opaque mystery totally impenetrable to human thought. In each case we have seen that we can construct alternative, intelligible models or theories which offer quite interesting interpretations of initially paradoxical-looking ideas. As we have seen in the case of some of the attributes definitive of the divine, a fairly high degree of confidence concerning our conception of God at one level is compatible with having alternative explications, and thus with some degree of tentativeness, at a more fine-grained level of theological specificity. What is important to stress here, though, is that just as we can make progress in our efforts to think about the various basic attributes conceptually constitutive of our idea of deity, so, likewise, we can make important headway in our attempts to understand the most distinctive Christian claims about the greatest possible source of all.

Notes

1 Edward R. Hardy, ed., *Christology of the Later Fathers*, Library of Christian Classics (Philadelphia: Westminster Press, 1954), p. 373.
2 More on the ancient Christian heresies can be found in such standard texts as Charles Gore, *The Incarnation of the Son of God* (London: John Murray, 1891); H. M. Relton, *A Study in Christology* (London: SPCK, 1917); E. G. Jay, *Son of Man, Son of God* (Montreal: McGill University Press, 1965); and J. N. D. Kelly, *Early Christian Doctrines*, rev. ed. (New York: Harper and Row, 1978). The heresy of psilanthropism is pronounced "sill-AN-throw-pizm" and comes from two Greek words meaning "mere man." Docetism is pronounced "DOE-seh-tizm."
3 See Thomas V. Morris, *The Logic of God Incarnate* (Ithaca, N.Y.: Cornell University Press, 1986), for a full deployment of this strategy.
4 For an example, see A. D. Smith, "God' Death," *Theology* 80 (July 1979): 2 62–68.
5 Hardy, *Christology of the Later Fathers*, pp. 363–64.
6 Ibid., pp. 70–71.
7 See *The Logic of God Incarnate*, pp. 102–7 and 149–62.
8 For a popular presentation of this sort of view, see Robert Ornstein, *Multimind* (Boston: Houghton Mifflin, 1986).
9 For a clear presentation of the development of this doctrine, as well as the doctrine of the Incarnation, see J. N. D. Kelly, *Early Christian Doctrines*, rev. ed. (New York: Harper and Row, 1978). For the rejection of polytheism, see Cornelius Plantinga, Jr., "Social Trinity and Tritheism," in *Trinity, Incarnation and Atonement*, ed. Ronald J. Feenstra and Cornelius Plantinga, Jr. (Notre Dame: University of Notre Dame Press, 1989), pp. 21–47.
10 Kelly, *Early Christian Doctrines*, p. 232.
11 Richard Swinburne, "Could There Be More Than One God?" *Faith and Philosophy* 5 (July 1988): 225–41.
12 For an example of this sort of argument, and other related arguments, see William J. Wainwright, "Monotheism," in *Rationality, Religious Belief, and Moral Commitment*, ed. Robert Audi and William J. Wainwright (Ithaca, N. Y.: Cornell University Press, 1986), pp. 289–314.
13 See, for example, John 5:37, 45; 6:57; 14:10; 15:10, and many other such passages in the Gospels.
14 For a convenient summary and references, see Kelly, *Early Christian Doctrines*, pp. 271–79.

Questions for reflection

1   Which of the two views of the Incarnation—kenotic Christology or the two-minds view—do you find most reasonable? Why?

2   For the two-minds view, what makes Jesus one person rather than two persons? Is it a logical contradiction to believe that Jesus had an omniscient mind and a non-omniscient mind? Why or why not?

3   What is the problem of the lonely God? Why is it a problem? What role does the Trinity play in providing a solution to the problem?

4   Morris states that "Modalism and polytheism are the Scylla and Charybdis between which all orthodox accounts of the Trinity must steer." Can you explain what he means?

5   Does the doctrine of the Trinity dispel the heresies of modalism and polytheism? Explain.

Further reading

David Brown (1985) *The Divine Trinity*. London: Duckworth. (A widely discussed book on the Trinity.)

Stephen T. Davis, Daniel Kendall, and Gerald O'Collins, eds. (2002) *The Trinity: An Interdisciplinary Symposium on the Trinity*. Oxford: Oxford University Press. (A seminal collection of essays on the Trinity.)

Stephen T. Davis, Daniel Kendall, and Gerald O'Collins, eds. (2002) *The Incarnation: An Interdisciplinary Symposium on the Incarnation of the Son of God*. Oxford: Oxford University Press. (A seminal collection of essays on the Incarnation.)

Alister E. McGrath (1994) *Christian Theology: An Introduction*. Oxford: Blackwell. (Recommended for those with little or no background in theology or the history of Christian thought.)

Thomas V. Morris (1986) *The Logic of God Incarnate*. Ithaca, NY: Cornell University Press. (Considered by many to be one of the most important recent works on the Incarnation by a philosopher. Morris dives deeper into the topics presented here.)

Chapter 12

William Hasker

THE OPENNESS OF GOD

William Hasker is Emeritus Professor of Philosophy at Huntington University. He is a prominent voice in contemporary philosophical theology and has written widely on the issue of divine foreknowledge. He is a leading advocate of *open theism*—a view in which God lacks foreknowledge and takes risks with his free creatures. This selection provides a clear presentation of Hasker's openness position. It is divided into three parts: the first section focuses on the nature of divine foreknowledge; the second section examines divine providence and its relation to divine foreknowledge; and the third section explores the important question of whether God takes risks.

There are several terms used in this selection for which definitions may be beneficial:

counterfactuals of freedom – propositions about what a free creature would freely choose to do in any given situation (e.g., the proposition that you will drink a Starbucks Grande Latte tomorrow at 5:30 p.m. while discussing God's foreknowledge with your best friend).
middle knowledge – the view that God knows all counterfactuals of freedom and thus can direct the future according to his desires with this information in mind.
simple foreknowledge – the view that God has complete knowledge of the future in terms of what will happen, but he lacks hypothetical knowledge of the future—that is, he lacks knowledge of what would happen in any given future situation, when the situation in question never in fact arises.
theodicy – a way of justifying God given the evil in the world.

God's knowledge of the future

The central idea concerning God's knowledge of the future which emerges from our reflections can be simply stated: God knows everything about the future which it is logically possible for him to know. A slightly more formal definition of divine omniscience may be adapted from premise (C2) in chapter 4 [of *God, Time, and Knowledge*]:

(DO) God is omniscient = $_{df}$ It is impossible that God should at any time believe what is false, or fail to know any true proposition such that his knowing that proposition at that time is logically possible.

Earlier I argued that such a definition as (DO) ought to be uncontroversial, unless of course one wants to maintain that there are truths that are known by God even though it is logically impossible that he know them! Jonathan Kvanvig, however, has sharply criticized the notion that God could be called omniscient if there are truths he does not know. Kvanvig's criticisms are directed at Swinburne,[1] but they apply equally to the conception developed here. He says:

> There is . . . a quite severe paradox generated if this line of reasoning is allowed. Since human knowledge does not require infallibility, humans can know what some of the future free actions will be. God cannot, since his knowledge requires infallibility. Thus, an individual can be God and hence omniscient on Swinburne's view even if that individual knows less about a particular domain than mere humans. Such an implication is surely too adverse to sensibility to detain us even for a moment.[2]

I have no wish to further injure Kvanvig's sensibility, but if a few moments can be spared for consideration, the paradox can be made to disappear. God's knowledge concerning the future includes all of the future outcomes that are objectively possible, *as well as* knowledge of the objective likelihood that each outcome will occur, and in cases where one choice is overwhelmingly likely (though not as yet absolutely certain) to be made, God will know that also. So God's awareness of the future contains a great deal *more* than does what we call *our* "knowledge" of future free actions, though it is still not good enough to count as knowledge *for God*.

It is evident that this conception of omniscience as subject to logical limitations is influenced by the parallel considerations that have influenced many philosophers to accept logical limitations on divine omnipotence. Kvanvig, however, discounts the analogy:

> The analogy intended to support a limited doctrine of omniscience is between feasible tasks and knowable truths and between unfeasible tasks and unknowable truths; but the analogy is crucially defective. Whereas an unknowable truth is still a truth, an unfeasible task is not a task at all. . . . A good analogy here is the response one might make to a child who claimed to be drawing a square circle. We might say, "You may be drawing something, but it is not a square circle, for there aren't and can't be any such things."[3]

Now, Kvanvig's point works nicely as regards square circles, but there are other things that it is generally thought that God cannot do which cannot be thus dismissed. If, as Kvanvig agrees, God is essentially morally perfect, then presumably lying to the American people about their government's foreign policy is something God cannot do, but that is hardly because this is "not a task at all"! Will Kvanvig scoff at the claim that such a being could be omnipotent and yet be able to do "less about a particular domain than mere humans"?

It will no doubt have been noticed that the conclusions we have reached agree, on an important point, with the conception of God's knowledge developed in process theology. This is undeniably the case, but of course our arguments, in attesting the correctness of process theology's view on one point, by no means show that theology to be right on other points of contention. Nor, for that matter, do these arguments show process theology to be wrong. But on what I take to be the most central point of disagreement, namely, God's ontological self-sufficiency and independence from the world, I stand squarely with the classical theism of John Mason:

> Thou wast, O God, and thou wast blest,
>   Before the world began;
> Of thine eternity possessed
>   Before time's hour glass ran.
> Thou needest none thy praise to sing,
>   As if thy joy could fade;
> Could'st thou have needed anything,
>   Thou couldst have nothing made.[4]

Our concern in these pages, however, is with God's relationship to the future, both in knowing and in controlling it. (For God as for us, it is *only* the future that can be controlled—with regard to the present and the past, it is always already too late.) Here a difference emerges with Hartshorne, at least, in that we would affirm God's comprehensive and exact knowledge of the *possibilities* of the future[5]—and, as has already been said, of the gradually changing *likelihood* of each of those possibilities' being realized. And as the probability of a choice's being made in a certain way gradually increases toward certainty, God knows *that* also; often, no doubt, before the finite agent herself is aware of it. "Even before a word is on my tongue, lo, O LORD, thou knowest it altogether" (Psalm 139:4).

But we are concerned not only with God's *knowledge* of the future but with his *action* in the world based on that knowledge—and in that regard, the resources of the essentially classical theism here espoused differ radically from those available to process theism. To these matters we now turn.

Providence, prayer, and prophecy

As was pointed out as early as chapters 2 and 3 [of *God, Time, and Knowledge*], the greatest importance of foreknowledge is not foreknowledge itself but the implications it has for our understanding of God's activity in the world. This claim, I would maintain, is easily verified both from the writings of theologians and from the perceptions of ordinary, theologically unsophisticated believers. Drawing out the implications for the divine activity of the view here developed is not particularly difficult. What may prove difficult, or even impossible, is the task of convincing those who are attracted to another view of divine action that this view is adequate. Here, as elsewhere, I forbear trying to show in detail how the views espoused are implied by or consistent with the biblical text. For a general perspective on the problem, however, I will cite some words of Clark Pinnock:

> The Bible seems to be pretheoretical in its approach to the relationship between divine sovereignty and human freedom. Some passages can be read to support God's determining all things. Others, with equal strength, stress the significant freedom of human beings. A tension is allowed to stand in the biblical text; a definitive resolution is nowhere attempted.[6]

I believe there is wisdom in this statement. If anyone doubts that there are forceful texts on both sides, then probably she just has not read the Bible very much, or at any rate not the works of the Calvinist and Arminian theologians who take those texts as battle standards. If she acknowledges the tension but thinks there *is* a definitive resolution in the biblical text itself, then most likely she *has* read the theologians, on one side only of the controversy! But if Pinnock's statement is correct, as I believe it is, then it is *up to us* to construct a consistent position on the question, and to do it on the basis of biblical data without claiming that the text clearly or unambiguously supports the conclusion we have reached.

To be sure, the Christian tradition is closer to consensus in affirming comprehensive divine foreknowledge than it is with respect to predestination and human freedom. But again, it is not as though scriptural texts pointing in a different direction were lacking. Again I cite Pinnock:

> According to the Bible, God anticipates the future in a way analogous to our own experience. God tests Abraham to see what the patriarch will do, and then says through his messenger, "Now I know that you fear God" (Gen 22:12). God threatens Ninevah with destruction, and then calls it off when they repent (Jon 3:10). I do not receive the impression from the Bible that the future is all sewn up and foreknown. The future is envisaged as a realm in which significant decisions can still be made which can change the course of history.[7]

The difficulty is, of course, that "readers almost never. . . [read] the biblical story with this view in mind."[8] We have been strongly conditioned, most of us, to dismiss what was said to Abraham as "anthropomorphic" and to affirm texts that suggest a more comprehensive foreknowledge as the literal metaphysical truth. But why so? It is not because one thing is said *in the Bible* more clearly or emphatically than the other. But the "hermeneutical circle" within which we have encountered these texts constantly turns us around and tells us to face in a particular direction—a direction that may, when all is said and done, be more toward Athens than toward Jerusalem! What I am suggesting here is that the "dehellenization of Christian theology" that Wolterstorff celebrates in his own repudiation of divine timelessness may have just a small step further to take.[9]

But what *are* the implications for divine action of this view of God's knowledge? To begin with, God has complete, detailed, and utterly intimate knowledge of the entirety of the past and the present. He also, of course, knows the inward constitution, tendencies, and powers of each entity in the fullest measure. And, finally, he has full knowledge of his own purposes, and of how they may best be carried out. Everything God does is informed by the totality of this knowledge; the guidance he gives, if he chooses to give it, is wisdom pure and unalloyed. Knowing what he knows, God may sometimes know also that the uninterrupted course of natural action and human responses will best serve his deep purposes. He may, on the other hand, know that for his purpose to go forward there is need for his own direct touch and influence, whether recognized or unrecognized, on this or that human personality. Or finally, he may see that for his purpose best to be fulfilled what is called for is his immediate, purposeful intervention in the processes of nature—in other words, a miracle. Whatever God needs to do, he has the power to do; whatever he sees is best to do happens forthwith. And if we trust him, we can also trust his purposes, for they culminate in the Kingdom of God, which is our happiness and *shalom*.

And now I ask, is this not enough? If God is like this, is he not worthy of our most entire devotion? And if we hesitate to agree to this, is the hesitation because a God so described would truly be unworthy, or is it because of our attachment to a theory?

There is, I admit, one conceivable, or at least imaginable, resource that is lacking to God so described. God in this view cannot, as C. S. Lewis thought he did, know in advance by direct vision precisely what will occur and *prearrange* concomitant circumstances so as to meet the needs of the occasion. He cannot, for instance, know the sequence of free actions that led up to the encirclement at Dunkirk, and *on the basis of that knowledge* prearrange the weather patterns to allow for the successful evacuation of the Allied forces. It has already been argued that this conception of providential action is incoherent. But leaving that aside, why should it be thought that such a view of divine action is somehow *better* than the one put forward two paragraphs back? Just how is God disadvantaged, if he cannot act as Lewis describes? It is not as though his resources are strained to the limit, so that if he fails to anticipate exactly what will happen (like a commander who fails to reinforce the exact point at which the enemy will attack), he will fail to accomplish his ends. Such a finicky eking out of meager resources to attain the optimum results just is not appropriate to divine governance, so there is no reason to regret its being impossible.

Perhaps I can, after all, think of one reason that for some might suggest at least an imaginative preferability of this mode of divine providence. Suppose that, though not denying the miraculous in principle, one is sufficiently impressed by the modern prejudice against it to feel that, in a rationally respectable account of the faith, divine miraculous interventions ought to be kept as narrowly confined as possible. Then it may seem that Lewis's account of prearranged circumstances is better than either a direct claim about God's frequent miraculous interventions or the admission that God seldom, if ever, does anything *specific* about the problem situations that arise in everyday life.

It should be noted, however, that this really economizes on miracle only if the prearrangement takes place *right at the beginning of creation*. If God intervened, say, five months or five years in advance in order to get the sort of weather he wanted at Dunkirk, that would be just as much a miracle (though perhaps not as noticeable) as if he had quieted the waves instantly on the day of the evacuation. But the notion that all these prearrangements took place at the beginning of creation simply will not bear examination; other considerations aside, we now know with virtual certainty that physical processes are *not* strictly deterministic, and thus the quantum indeterminacy would preclude information's being carried forward with the required degree of exactitude.

What has been said about providence in general applies in particular to answers to prayer, and there is no reason to suppose that the lack of exact, fully detailed foreknowledge is more of a handicap in one case than in the other. It is worth noticing, by the way, that Christ said, "your Father knows what you *need* before you ask him" (Matthew 6:8;

emphasis added), and not that he knows what we *ask* before we ask him! There is certainly no clear biblical warrant for the notion that God answers specific prayers before they are offered, or for the idea that we should pray for what already lies in the past.[10]

Without doubt, many persons will see biblical prophecy as the most serious obstacle to acceptance of the view here set forth. Simply put, if God does not *know* what the future will be like, how can he *tell* us what it will be like? The difficulty is real but not insuperable. First, it should be noted that there is a very broad scholarly consensus that the main agenda for the biblical prophets was not prognosticating the future, but rather witnessing to the people concerning God's purposes and requirements and seeking to recall them to obedience. And this purpose clearly is often uppermost even when coming events are the explicit subject of the discourse. A striking text that bears this out, and also has important implications for our topic, is Jeremiah 18:7–10:

> If at any time I declare concerning a nation or a kingdom, that I will pluck up and break down and destroy it, and if that nation, concerning which I have spoken, turns from its evil, I will repent of the evil that I intended to do to it. And if at any time I declare concerning a nation or a kingdom that I will build and plant it, and if it does evil in my sight, not listening to my voice, then I will repent of the good which I had intended to do to it.

Here we are told that prophecies are to be interpreted as conditional *even when this is not explicitly stated*. But of course, a conditional prophecy requires no detailed foreknowledge of what will actually happen; the purpose, in many cases, is that what is foretold may *not* happen.

Clearly, not every biblical prophecy concerning the future is conditional, though a great many of them are. A second important category, however, must include *predictions based on foresight drawn from existing trends and tendencies*. Even with our own grossly inadequate knowledge of such trends and tendencies, we invest enormous amounts of energy trying to make forecasts in this way; evidently God with his perfect knowledge could do it much better. To take a simple example: Jesus was able to predict Peter's betrayal because he knew something about Peter which Peter himself did not know, namely, that Peter, though brave enough in a fight even against the odds (as in the Garden of Gethsemane), lacked the specific sort of courage as well as the faith needed to acknowledge his allegiance in a threatening situation where physical resistance was impossible.

Finally, however, there is a most important category of prophecies, namely, of *things that are foreknown because it is God's purpose to bring them about*. With regard to the major events of redemptive history this is evident: God did not *foresee* the death and resurrection of his Son; he declared them as going to happen, because he fully intended to bring them about. But the same interpretation may be given even to somewhat less momentous events. There is a striking passage on this in Geach's *Providence and Evil*:

> God is the supreme Grand Master who has everything under his control. Some of the players are consciously helping his plan, others are trying to hinder it; whatever the finite players do, God's plan will be executed; though various lines of God's play will answer to various moves of the finite players. God cannot be surprised or thwarted or cheated or disappointed. God, like some grand master of chess, can carry out his plan even if he has

announced it beforehand. "On that square," says the Grand Master, "I will
promote my pawn to Queen and deliver checkmate to my adversary": and
it is even so. No line of play that finite players may think of can force God to
improvise: his knowledge of the game already embraces all the possible variant lines of play, theirs does not.[11]

The rhetoric is strong; the example (at least) overstated. An amateur at chess playing
a grand master may have no choice about winning or losing, but he has a great deal
more choice about *how* he will lose than Geach allows.[12] Still, Geach is not claiming that
God's purpose and superior strategy enable him to foresee *everything* that will happen:
"Various lines of God's play will answer to various moves of the finite players." The central point is that God is able to carry out his overall plan despite whatever resistance
may be offered by human beings.

It should not be overlooked, furthermore, that God has at his disposal a great many
more different ways to influence the course of events than does a chess master. God
is perfectly capable of making someone an "offer he can't refuse"; many accounts of
conversion (for example) suggest that he has done just that. Some ways in which God
might control the course of events might strike us as manipulative, but this is not necessarily so, so long as a person is not influenced to act in a way inconsistent with his
own major intention and motivations. When God "hardened Pharaoh's heart" (whatever exactly that involved), he by no means gave to Pharaoh a temper and inclination
that were foreign to him; at most, he gave him a stronger disposition to do what he was
already inclined to do: defy God, and make things difficult for the Israelites. Here, as
elsewhere, the specifics are for us unknowable, but one thing is abundantly clear: *God's
capacity to control the detailed course of events is limited only by his self-restraint, not by any
inability to do so.* And as broad as is the scope of God's ability to control events, so also is
the possibility for prophecy based on God's intention so to do.

These, then, are the resources for understanding biblical prophecy consonant with
the understanding of omniscience here set forward. Some prophecies are conditional
on the actions of human beings; others are predictions based on existing trends and tendencies; still others are announcements of what God himself intends to bring about. Do
these categories enable one to deal with the phenomena of the biblical text? I believe
that they do, but the matter cannot be pursued further here. The reader is invited to
investigate the matter for herself, using the best commentaries and technical aids as
well as the Scriptures themselves.

Does God take risks?

It is evident that the view of God's governance of the world here proposed differs from
others that are commonly held. But wherein precisely does the difference lie? I believe
it can be formulated in a simple, yet crucial, question: *Does God take risks?* Or, to put the
matter more precisely, we may ask: *Does God make decisions that depend for their outcomes
on the responses of free creatures in which the decisions themselves are not informed by knowledge of
the outcomes?* If he does, then creating and governing a world is for God a risky business.
That this is so is evidently an implication of the views here adopted, and it is equally evident that it would be rejected by some Christian thinkers—those, for example, who

hold to a theory of predestination according to which everything that occurs is determined solely by God's sovereign decree.

But though the importance of the question about God's risk taking will be widely recognized, the bearing on this question of the positions discussed in this book is often misunderstood. Here the argument developed in chapter 3 [of *God, Time, and Knowledge*] is crucially important: *Simple foreknowledge and timeless knowledge have no bearing on the question whether or not God takes risks.* It is true that on these views God's knowledge of the future is complete and comprehensive, either before all time or outside of time in God's eternity. But on either of these views *God's knowledge of future events is derived from the actual occurrence of those events*, and thus in the order of explanation it is *subsequent* to the decisions on God's part which lead to the events' occurring. The reasoning for this conclusion is entirely clear and straightforward, and only inattention can have led to its being so widely overlooked.[13]

Short of absolute predestination, the only theory known to me that eliminates risk taking on God's part is the theory of middle knowledge. For on this theory God's knowledge of the future is *not* derived from the actual occurrence of the future events, but rather from the knowledge of the counterfactuals of freedom together with God's knowledge concerning which states of affairs he will actualize. But the knowledge of the counterfactuals is prior, in the order of explanation, to God's decisions about what to create, so that these decisions are indeed informed by full and complete knowledge of the respective outcomes of any possible choice God might make. The element of risk is eliminated entirely.

By this time the reader is well aware of my opinion that the philosophical prospects for middle knowledge are dim. To maintain the viability of this theory, one would have to defeat the arguments against middle knowledge in chapter 2 [of *God, Time, and Knowledge*], as well as the arguments for incompatibilism deployed in chapters 4 through 7 [of *God, Time, and Knowledge*]. Since I believe those arguments to be sound, I do not think that attempts to answer or evade them will be successful. But our purpose in this final chapter is not to rehearse these arguments from earlier in the book, but rather to address a quite different question: What sort of theory of divine providence should we *want* to have? Is it *better* if God takes risks with the world, or if he does not? Where do the interests of faith really lie in this matter?

From a certain standpoint it may seem evident that a risk-free world is preferable to one in which God takes risks. A world in which God's creative and providential action is guided by middle knowledge is a world in which nothing can ever turn out in the slightest respect differently than God intended. It is in a sense a world that provides absolute security for the believer, similar to that which is often felt to be the greatest benefit of the doctrine of predestination. It is not for nothing that William Craig states, "Given middle knowledge, the apparent contradiction between God's sovereignty, which seems to crush human freedom, and human freedom, which seems to break God's sovereignty, is resolved. In his infinite intelligence, God is able to plan a world in which his designs are achieved by creatures acting freely."[14]

Still, the need for this kind of theory is open to question. Might not the demand for a wholly risk-free divine plan be another example of a genuine religious need that has been, so to speak, subjected to metaphysical inflation and made to underwrite requirements that go beyond any legitimate need? Proponents of middle knowledge themselves would say this about the Calvinistic doctrine of sovereignty, and another example may well be the doctrines of absolute divine immutability and timelessness. Faith needs the assurance that God's character is absolutely reliable and that his purposes will hold true, but this need can be met without the excesses of the classical theory of absolute immutability. Similarly, we have argued above that the believer has every reason to trust God and to commit herself to him unreservedly, quite apart from theories that guarantee that God's plan is risk-free.

There are, on the other hand, reasons for questioning whether a risk-free providence is even desirable. Those who admire risk taking and experimentalism in human life may feel that the richness of God's life is diminished if we deny these attributes to him. And, on the other hand, the significance and value of human creativity may seem diminished if our most ennobling achievements are just the expected printouts from the divine programming. But perhaps the most serious difficulty here is one that also plagues Calvinistic doctrines of predestination: If we accentuate God's absolute control over everything that happens, we are forced to attribute to him the same control over evil events and actions as over good. On the theory of middle knowledge we can *never* say that some act of God's failed of its intended purpose, no matter how disastrous the outcome may be.[15] We cannot avoid saying, then, that God specifically chose for Hitler to become leader of the Third Reich and instigator of the Holocaust. To be sure, the proponent of middle knowledge, unlike the defender of absolute predestination, will say that it was through Hitler's *free will* that he became what he was—but the fact will remain that God, fully knowing Hitler's counterfactuals and the use he would make of his free will, chose that he should come into existence and should be confronted with precisely those situations that led to such incalculable evil.

These considerations can be brought into a clearer light if we consider the implications for our topic of two recent theodicies. Neither theodicist explicitly takes a position on the questions of foreknowledge and middle knowledge, but this will not hinder us from using their theories as exemplars and test cases for the understanding of divine providence.

The first of the two theodicies to be considered is found in Eleonore Stump's paper "The Problem of Evil."[16] Stump's theodicy in its entirety is quite complex, but her most striking claim is made in the context of a discussion of the suffering of children. She says:

> With considerable diffidence . . . I want to suggest that Christian doctrine is committed to the claim that a child's suffering is outweighed by the good for the child which can result from that suffering. . . . It seems to me that a perfectly good entity who was also omniscient and omnipotent must govern the evil resulting from the misuse of significant freedom in such a way that the sufferings of any particular person are outweighed by the good which the suffering produces *for that person*; otherwise, we might justifiably expect a good God somehow to prevent that *particular suffering*, either by intervening (in one way or another) to protect the victim, while still allowing the perpetrator his freedom, or by curtailing freedom in some select cases.[17]

It may occur to the reader that this claim is so strong as to be extremely implausible.[18] Rather than pursue this, however, let us consider the implications of Stump's theory for our understanding of divine providence. It is evident at once that for the theodicy to work there must be a very high degree of planning and coordination on God's part so as to insure that all of the apparently random events in the world's history work together to achieve his goal. (Remember that it is not a question of *some particular* evil having a good result for the sufferer; *every* instance of serious evil must be for the good of the sufferer.) And this, in turn, requires a high level of *control* over the course of events on God's part. Since Stump is a determined libertarian, this cannot come by way of absolute predestination, but one would think that for her scheme to work God must have *at least* as much control as would be afforded by middle knowledge. Yet middle knowledge, if it exists, would also create a serious problem for Stump,[19] for the following reason: In the majority of cases the principal benefit that flows from suffering is that of bringing the sufferer closer to God, of increasing the person's chances of union with God and ultimate salvation.[20] Yet it would appear that in many cases this is unavailing; in spite of the best God can do to persuade us to return to himself, we have it in our power, and some of us exercise that power, to resist to the end.[21] Now, what are we to say about the justification for the sufferings of those who are ultimately impenitent? What I think Stump clearly wants to say[22] is that God has done his best for them and that if even his best has failed to overcome their stubborn resistance, that is not his fault. But on the assumption of middle knowledge, it becomes extremely difficult to say this. For on that assumption, God chose to inflict the suffering *in the full light of the knowledge that it would be unavailing* and would bring the sufferer no spiritual benefit. The notion that one could then still say that the infliction of suffering is justified by the benefit to the sufferer is, to say the least, extremely puzzling.

We see, then, that Stump's theodicy is left in something of a quandary. For the theodicy to work, God must exercise a very close supervision over the affairs of the world—a supervision that, one might plausibly suppose, requires *at least* the degree of control which would be made possible by middle knowledge. But if God *does* possess middle knowledge, then he chooses in some cases to inflict suffering in the full knowledge that such suffering will be unavailing, and the central idea of the theodicy is in jeopardy.

The other theodicy to be considered is found in Michael Peterson's book *Evil and the Christian God.*[23] Peterson's theodicy, like Stump's, is rather complex; it incorporates elements of the freewill defense, of the natural-law defense for natural evil, and of the soul-making theodicy, along with still other ideas. But it contrasts most sharply with Stump's in its treatment of *gratuitous evil*, evil that is not a necessary condition of some greater good or of the prevention of some greater evil. Peterson's discussion of this topic is focused on the *principle of meticulous providence*, which is defined as follows:

(MP) An omnipotent, omniscient, wholly good God would prevent or eliminate the existence of really gratuitous or pointless evils.[24]

The term "meticulous providence" strikes me as a felicitous bit of terminology; though it is defined strictly in terms of the prevention or elimination of gratuitous evils, it suggests the very close, "meticulous" supervision of earthly affairs which would evidently be necessary if God is to insure that *no single instance of evil* is permitted to occur unless as a means to a greater good or the prevention of a greater evil.

Although Peterson does not discuss this point, I think it can readily be seen that there is a close connection between the ideas of meticulous providence and middle knowledge; so close, indeed, that meticulous providence *without* middle knowledge is difficult to conceive. Suppose, for instance, that some person is engaged in making a rather crucial decision, one that will result in great good if taken in a certain way, and great evil if taken in another way. If God lacks middle knowledge, then it would seem that God must simply take his chances and abide by the result. As we have already seen, simple foreknowledge of the outcome will do him no good, for the outcome can be fore-known only on the assumption that it does in fact occur, so that it is then "too late" for the wrong choice, however disastrous, to be prevented. Only middle knowledge would enable God to foresee the disastrous consequences that *would* ensue *if* the decision were allowed to be made, and thereby either to prevent the choice or to alter the circum-stances so that those consequences would be averted.

Now, Stump's theodicy, as we have seen, incorporates a principle even stronger than (MP); she requires, not just that each instance of suffering be the necessary means to a greater good, but that it be the means to such a good *for the sufferer himself*. Peterson, in contrast, argues forcefully that (MP) should be rejected. He says:

> As long as the theist understands his theological position to entail that there are no gratuitous evils, and as long as his efforts to show that there are none fall markedly shy of complete success, his conceptual commitments will always be in tension with ordinary experience of evil in the world. Theism will be forever plagued by a systematically insoluble problem. . . . Relinquishing the theological premise [viz., (MP)] . . . offers at least two important benefits to the theist who wrestles with the problem of gratu-itous evil. First, accepting the existence of some gratuitous evil is more consonant with our common experience than is the position which denies gratuitous evil *a priori*. Second, rejecting the principle of meticulous provi-dence opens the way for a deeper and more profound apprehension of God than that widely accepted principle allows.[25]

It should be noted that in denying that God prevents all gratuitous evils, Peterson is not claiming that God permits evils to occur *for no reason whatever*. The central idea, rather, is that God adopts certain *overall strategies* in his dealing with the world; these *strategies* are justified in that they enable the creation of great and significant goods, but they also permit the occurrence of *individual instances* of evil which are, as such, pure loss and *not* a means to any greater good.[26]

Peterson's case for his claim that the rejection of (MP) "opens the way for a deeper and more profound apprehension of God" is too rich and complex to summarize here. Some-thing of the spirit of his enterprise, however, is conveyed by the following quotation:

> If the conception of human free will is taken to involve the possibility of bringing about really gratuitous evil (specifically, moral evil), then God cannot completely prevent or eliminate gratuitous evil without severely diminishing free will. That would be logically impossible. At stake here is not merely the ability of humans to choose among options, but the ability to choose among significant kinds of options: between goods and evils, even the highest goods and most terrible evils. Thus, free will is most signifi-cant—and most fitting for the special sort of creature man is—if it includes the potential for utterly damnable choices and actions. This is part of the inherent risk in God's program for man.[27]

The reference to "risk" in the last sentence underscores my point about the relationship between this theodicy and middle knowledge: The theodicy that denies (MP) is a theodicy of divine risk taking, and risk taking is incompatible with middle knowledge.

At this point I wish to state some conclusions that are suggested (certainly they have not been rigorously established) by the foregoing reflections. Peterson's theodicy entails that God takes risks in governing the world; thus it entails that God does not have middle knowledge. This theodicy, and the understanding of divine providence which it involves, are clearly acceptable as judged by the canons of orthodox, mainstream Christian theology. It follows that the denial of middle knowledge, and the attribution of risk taking to God, are theologically acceptable. I believe, indeed, that a considerably stronger conclusion is warranted. The type of theodicy advocated by Peterson is not only *acceptable*; it is, in my view, clearly *preferable* to the type advocated by Stump, or indeed to any theodicy that accepts (MP). So the *best* Christian theodicy will deny middle knowledge and will affirm forcefully that *God the Creator and Redeemer is a risk taker!*

Conclusion

It is time to place the results of this chapter in perspective. I make no claim to have proved, through these reflections on divine action in the world, that the view of God's knowledge here advocated is the correct one and that other views are unsatisfactory. That burden of proof must be carried by the arguments in the previous chapters; it is by their success or failure that my work must be evaluated. Nor have I proved here that the conception of divine action encapsulated in the statement that God takes risks is the correct one, though some hints have been given as to how such a case could be made. Rather, my effort here has been to exhibit a conception of divine action which is consonant with the view of divine knowledge for which I have argued, and which satisfies the needs of Christian theology and Christian experience. To the extent to which that has been successfully done, it should help to relieve some of the religious and theological resistance to my arguments. And if this resistance can be alleviated, I am confident that the arguments will emerge victorious.

Notes

1   See Richard Swinburne, *The Coherence of Theism* (Oxford: Oxford University Press, 1977), pp. 171–72.
2   Jonathan L. Kvanvig, *The Possibility of an All-Knowing God* (New York: St. Martin's Press, 1986), p. 18.
3   Ibid., p. 22.
4   John Mason, "Thou wast, O God, and thou wast blest," in *Hymnal for Colleges and Schools*, ed. E. Harold Geer (New Haven, Conn.: Yale University Press, 1956), no. 110.
5   According to Harthshorne, possibilities are as such inherently vague and indeterminate, and can only be known as such. For an excellent discussion of Hartshorne's view as well as a defense of the classical view of God's comprehensive and exact knowledge of possibilities, see Richard A. Creel, *Divine Impassibility* (Cambridge: Cambridge University Press, 1986), chap. 3.

6   "God Limits His Knowledge," in *Predestination and Free Will: Four Views of Divine Sovereignty and Human Freedom*, ed. David Basinger and Randall Basinger (Downers Grove, Ill.: Inter-Varsity Press, 1986), p. 143.

7   Ibid., p. 157.

8   Ibid.

9   Nicholas Wolterstorff, "God Everlasting," in *God and the Good*, ed. Clifton J. Orlebeke and Lewis B. Smedes (Grand Rapids, Mich.: Eerdmans, 1975), p. 183.

10   This is admitted by William Lane Craig, *The Only Wise God* (Grand Rapids, Mich.: Baker, 1987), pp. 87–88; Craig, however, defends the philosophical coherence of such prayers. It should be noted that, on the view I am defending, God could know about a believer's *disposition* to pray concerning a certain matter and could respond on the basis of that disposition in advance of any specific prayer's being offered.

11   Peter Geach, *Providence and Evil* (Cambridge: Cambridge University Press, 1977), p. 58. Geach's book as a whole can be read as an exhibition of an understanding of divine providence which is consistent with the views adopted here.

12   Anthony Kenny makes this point: see *The God of the Philosophers* (Oxford: Oxford University Press, 1979), p. 59.

13   It has not been entirely overlooked; consider the following from William Lane Craig:

> Divine foreknowledge without prior middle knowledge would be exceedingly strange. Without middle knowledge, God would find himself, so to speak, with knowledge of the future but without any logically prior planning of that future. To see the point imagine that logically prior to the divine decision to create a world, God has only natural knowledge. If creatures are going to be genuinely free, then God's creation of the world is a blind act without any idea of how things will actually be. True, he knows at that prior moment all possible worlds, but he has virtually no idea which world he will in fact create, since he does not know how free creatures would act if he created them. All he knows are the possibilities, which are infinite in number. In a sense, what God knows in the logical moment after the decision to create must come as a total surprise to him. (*The Only Wise God*, pp. 134–35)

My reply to this would be that *whether or not* God has simple foreknowledge, we should conceive of his decisions about what to do as being made progressively, in stages, with the action at each point directed to the situation as it results from God's earlier decisions. The final result, then, would hardly be the "sudden shock" depicted by Craig! But his statement does nicely capture the uselessness of simple foreknowledge. Once again, I direct the reader's attention to the important article by David Basinger, "Middle Knowledge and Classical Christian Thought," *Religious Studies* 22 (1986): 407–22.

14   *The Only Wise God*, p. 135.

15   Freddoso objects to this; he says, "The theory of middle knowledge most emphatically does *not* entail that God *intends* whatever happens; it leaves ample room for God's *permitting* things to happen in a way that goes against his intentions" (personal communication). I question, however, whether the theory really does leave room for anything to happen that is not intended by God. To be sure, not everything that happens need be *desired* by God; in that sense we could perhaps say that God's *primary intention* embraces only the good that occurs and not the evil. But God has deliberately and with full knowledge chosen that *these good purposes shall be fulfilled through a plan that entails the actual occurrence (not just the possibility) of specific evils*, and once God has made this choice it is absolutely impossible that either God or anyone else will act so as to avert those evils. Must we not then say that he *intends* to achieve these goods by means of a process that involves those evils?

16   Eleonore Stump, "The Problem of Evil," *Faith and Philosophy* 2 (1985): 392–423.

17   Ibid., p. 411.
18   For discussion of this point, as well as other aspects of Stump's theodicy, see my "Suffering, Soul-Making, and Salvation," *International Philosophical Quarterly* 28 (1988): 3–19.
19   Eleonore Stump has acknowledged this point in discussion.
20   Stump, "The Problem of Evil," pp. 406–415.
21   It is worth noting, however, that middle knowledge lends itself rather readily to a belief in universal salvation: God may simply have chosen not to instantiate those essences concerning which he foresaw that, if instantiated, their instantiations would finally resist his grace.
22   Cf. Stump, "The Problem of Evil," pp. 411–12.
23   Michael Peterson, *Evil and the Christian God* (Grand Rapids, Mich.: Baker, 1982).
24   Ibid., p. 76.
25   Ibid., p. 89.
26   For more on this, see my "Suffering, Soul-Making, and Salvation."
27   Peterson, *Evil and the Christian God*, p. 104.

Questions for reflection

1   What is Professor Hasker's view of divine foreknowledge? Do you agree or disagree with him? Explain.
2   Do you believe that God has simple foreknowledge? Middle knowledge? What are your reasons for these beliefs?
3   Does God's omniscience entail that he knows the future? What if the future is not yet there to be known? Can God still be omniscient and lack knowledge of the future? Explain.
4   What does it mean to say that God takes risks? Do you believe that he does? If so, does that mean he is not in control of the universe? Why or why not?
5   Does one's view of God's knowledge affect how one prays? If so, how? If not, why not?

Further reading

James K. Beilby and Paul R. Eddy, eds. (2001) *Divine Foreknowledge: Four Views.* Downers Grove, IL: InterVarsity Press. (A very accessible work on divine foreknowledge including four different viewpoints by leading scholars.)

William Lane Craig (2000) *The Only Wise God: The Compatibility of Divine Foreknowledge and Human Freedom.* Eugene, OR: Wipf and Stock. (An argument for the middle knowledge view by a leading philosopher of religion.)

John Martin Fisher, ed. (1989) *God, Foreknowledge, and Freedom.* Stanford, CA: Stanford University Press. (A collection of important essays addressing divine foreknowledge and human freedom; fairly technical.)

William Hasker (1989) *God, Time, and Knowledge.* Ithaca, NY: Cornell University Press. (A clear, readable, and powerfully argued book addressing the issues of free will and divine foreknowledge; the selection above was taken from this book.)

Michael L. Peterson and Raymond J. VanArragon, eds. (2004) *Contemporary Debates in Philosophy of Religion.* Malden, MA: Blackwell. (Contains opposing positions defended by two leading philosophers of religion in William Hasker's "God Takes Risks" and Paul Helm's "God Does Not Take Risks.")

Clark Pinnock, Richard Rice, John Sanders, William Hasker, and David Basinger, eds. (1994) *The Openness of God*. Downers Grove, IL: InterVarsity Press. (Five well-respected philosophers and theologians present their case for open theism.)

Chapter 13

Nicholas Rescher

PROCESS THEOLOGY — GOD IN AND FOR NATURE

Nicholas Rescher is University Professor of Philosophy at the University of Pittsburgh where he also served as Chairman of the Center for Philosophy of Science. He offers the following synopsis of his essay:

(1) Process theology, with its abandonment of classical substantialism, puts our understanding of God onto a more straightened, less convoluted path. (2) It accomplishes this by viewing God as an active participant in the world's processual commerce—though, of course, without thereby endowing God with a physical nature. (3) God's active participation in the world involves processes of many sorts—productive, cognitive, and affective. This participative involvement of the divine in the world's affairs does not, however, preclude human free agency. (4) Process theology is not somehow rooted in science as a doctrine that functions in the explanation of nature's features. The service it renders to understanding does not lie in the order of explanation but rather in the order of appreciation—in enabling us to apprehend more correctly and clearly the grounds and implications of the fact that the world's arrangements can have worth and value.

1. God: substance or process?

We now turn to a very different theme, namely process theology.[1]

To be sure, not all process philosophers are theists—far from it. Process philosophizing has both a theist and a naturalistic wing. The theists see God as a major player in the realm of cosmic process, accounting for the world's order and intelligibility, its creative dynamism, and its teleological normativity. Naturalistic processists, by contrast, see such cosmic macroassets explicable in a nature-immanent way, and view the world as a self-sufficient and self-managing system.[2] The organismic and evolutionary tendencies of process thought offer useful resources to the latter position. But as this chapter will show, the process approach also provides theists with some potent conceptual and theoretical resources.

The neo-Platonic sympathies of the Church Fathers impelled Christian theology to adopt Greek philosophy's stance that in order to see God as existent we must conceive of him as a being, a *substance* of some sort. But, to the enthusiasm of philosophers and the vexation of theologians, this opened up a host of theoretical difficulties. Consider, for example, the following line of reflection: (1) On the traditional conception of the matter, a substance must always originate through the causality of substances. Q: So whence God? A: He is internally necessitated and free from any and all external causation. (2) Substances standardly have contingent properties. Q: Does God? A: No, he is in all respects (self-) necessitated. (3) Substances standardly have spatio-temporal emplacement within the world's causal order. Q: Does God? A: No, he, unlike standard substances, exists altogether outside space and time. And so on. No sooner had Western theology made God a substance in order to satisfy its ontological commitment to the predilections of Greek philosophy than it has to break all of the rules for substances and take away with one hand what it seemed to give with the other. If God is to be viewed as a substance, then this will clearly have to be a very nonstandard sort of substance that is at issue—so nonstandard that one begins to wonder about substantialism's relevancy.

Against this background, it is not surprising that process philosophy, with its characteristic abandonment of classical substantialism, comes to be in a position to put matters on a straighter, less convoluted path. The difficulties of a substance theology offer an open invitation to a process approach in this domain.

2. The process view of God

The God of scholastic Christian theology, like the deity of Aristotle on whose model this conception was in part based, is located outside of time—entirely external to the realm of change and process. By contrast, process theologians, however much they may disagree on other matters, take the radical (but surely not heretical) step of according God an active role also *within* the natural world's spatiotemporal frame. They envision a foothold for God also within the overall processual order of the reality that is supposed to be his creation. After all, active participation in the world's processual commerce need not make God into a physical or material object. (While the world indeed contains various physical processes such as the evolution of galaxies, it also contains immaterial processes such as the diffusion of knowledge or the emergence of order.)

For process theology, then, God does not constitute part of the world's matrix of physical processes but nevertheless, in some fashion or other, *participates* in it. Clearly, no ready analogy-model for this mode of participation (spectator, witness, judge, etc.) can begin to do full justice to the situation. But what matters first and foremost from the angle of process theology is *the fact that* God and his world are processually interconnected; the issue of *the manner how* is something secondary that can be left open for further reflection. So conceived, God is not exactly *of* the world of physical reality, but does indeed participate *in* it processually—everywhere touching, affecting, and informing its operations. Thus, while not emplaced in the world, the processists' God is nevertheless bound up with it in an experiential process of interaction with it. In general, process theists do not believe that God actually controls the world. The process God makes an impact persuasively, influencing but never unilaterally imposing the world's process.

Process theology accordingly invites us to think of God's relationship to the world in terms of a process of influence like "the spread of Greek learning in medieval Islam." Greek learning did not become literally *internal* to the Islamic world, but exerted a substantial and extensive influence upon and within it. Analogously, God is not of the world but exerts and extends an all-pervasive influence upon and within it. After all, processes need not themselves be spatial to have an impact upon things in space (think of a price inflation on the economy of a country.) The idea of process provides a category for conceptualizing God's relation to the world that averts many of the difficulties and perplexities of the traditional substance paradigm.

Even apart from process philosophy, various influential theologians have in recent years urged the necessity and desirability of seeing God not through the lens of unchanging stability but with reference to movement, change, development, and process.[3] But the process theorists among theologians want to go beyond this. For them, God is not only to be related to the world's processes in a productive manner, but must himself be regarded in terms of process—as encompassing processuality as a salient aspect of the divine nature.

To be sure, process theologians differ among themselves in various matters of emphasis. [Alfred North] Whitehead sees God in cosmological terms as an "actual occasion" functioning within nature, reflective of "the eternal urge of desire" that works "strongly and quietly by love," to guide the course of things within the world into "the creative advance into novelty." For [Charles] Hartshorne, by contrast, God is less an active force within the world's processual commerce than an intelligent being or mind that interacts with it. His God is less a force of some sort than a personal being who interacts with the other mind-endowed agents through personal contact and love. Hartshorne wants neither to separate God from the world too sharply nor yet to have him be pantheistically immanent in nature. He views God as an intelligent world-separated being who participates experientially in everything that occurs in nature and resonates with it in experiential participation.

Such differences of approach, however, are only of secondary importance. The crucial fact is that the stratagem of conceiving of God in terms of a *process* that is at work in and beyond the world makes it possible to overcome a whole host of substance-geared difficulties with one blow. For it now becomes far easier to understand how God can be and be operative. To be sure, the processual view of God involves a recourse to processes of a very special kind. But extraordinary (or even supranatural) *processes* pose far fewer difficulties than extraordinary (or let alone supranatural) *substances*, seeing that process is an inherently more flexible conception. After all, many sorts of processes are in their own way unique—or, at any rate, radically different from all others. Clearly, processes like the creation of a world or the inauguration of its lawful order are by their very nature bound to be unusual, but much the same can be said of any particular type of process. Moreover, through its recourse to the idea of a megaprocess that embraces and encompasses a variety of subordinate processes, process theology is able to provide a conceptual rationale for reconciling the idea of an all-pervasive and omnitemporal mode of reality with that of a manifold of finitely temporalized constituents.[4]

The processist view of nature as a spatiotemporal whole constituting one vast, all-embracing cosmic process unfolding under the directive aegis of a benign intelligence is, in various ways, in harmony with the Judeo-Christian view of things. For this tradition has always seen God as active within the historical process which, in consequence, represents not only a causal but also a purposive order. After all, the only sort of God who can have meaning and significance for us is one who stands in some active interrelationship with ourselves and our world. (Think here of the Nicene creed's phraseology: "the maker of all things . . . who for us men and for our salvation. . . .") But, of course, such an "active interrelationship" is a matter of the processes that constitute the participation and entry of the divine into the world's scheme of things—and conversely.

And, of course, not only is it feasible and potentially constructive for the relation of God to the world and its creatures to be conceived of in terms of processes, but it is so also with the relationship of people to God. Here, too, process theology sees such a relationship as thoroughly processual because it rests on a potentially interactive communion established in contemplation, worship, prayer, and the like.

In particular, for processists, there is little difficulty in conceiving God as a *person*. For once we have an account of personhood in general in process terms as a systemic complex of characteristic activities, it is no longer all that strange to see God in these terms as well. If we processify the human person, then we can more readily conceive of the divine person as the focal source of a creative intelligence that engenders and sustains the world and endows it with law, beauty (harmony and order), value, and meaning.

Then, too, there is the problem of the Trinity with its mystery of fitting three persons into one being or substance, which has always been a stumbling block for the substantialism of the Church Fathers. A process approach makes it possible to bypass this perplexity, for processes can conflate with and interpenetrate one another. With the laying of a single branch, a woodsman can be building a wall, erecting a house, and extending a village: one act, many processes; one mode of activity, many sorts of agency.

For process theology, then, God is active in relation to the world, and the world's people can and should be active in relation to God. People's relationship to the divine is a two-way street, providing for a benevolent God's care for the world's creatures and allowing those intelligent beings capable of realizing this to establish contact with God through prayer, worship, and spiritual communion. Process theology accordingly contemplates a wider realm of processes that embrace both the natural and the spiritual realms and interconnect God with the vast community of worshippers in one communal macroprocess that encompasses and gives embodiment to such a communion.

3. God in time and eternity: the problem of free will

The relation of God to time and its changes provides another focal theme for process theology. Proceeding under the aegis of the substance paradigm of Greek philosophy, the Church Fathers placed God outside time in a distinctive order of eternity. And here the question arises about how God can know—let alone comfort and commiserate with—the condition of beings existing in time. Saint Thomas here used the explanatory analogy of the spectator on a mountain watching the movement of travelers along the road in a valley below: The travelers cannot see around the twists and turns in the road to know what lies before them, but God, looking down from eternity, can see the whole in a single glance, all at once (*totum simul*). But, of course, any prospect of contingency or of innovation is blocked out on this picture, save as the misimpression of imperfect humans; as with the theologies of Calvin or Spinoza, all that ever happens is foreseeable and, indeed, foreseen—everything is provided for from the start, so to speak. The process theologian rejects any such radical separation of God and world in the interests of making what William James called ontological "elbow room" for contingency, innovation, and unpredictability. The processualists' deity is not the God of the great *omnis* (omnipotence, omniscience, omnibenevolence). To reemphasize: process theology envisions a God who, though not *of* the world, is nevertheless present *in* it in a way that renders him, too, subject to the temporality that pervades its domain.[5]

As theologians of this tendency see it, God's processual involvement in the world is of many sorts, preeminently productive, cognitive, and affective. Divine providence furnishes the reason for being of the world's intelligible order, and is God himself linked to created nature by cognitive processes of awareness and understanding. Moreover, God is linked to the world of created beings through a reciprocity of affective appreciation, and responds to the world's eventuation by way of approbation or disapproval. (But what sorts of things in "his" world can God possibly approve or disapprove of? This sphere would have to include the doings of autonymous agencies that "go their own way", including, most importantly, some of the free actions of intelligent creatures.)

Yet if—as most processists agree—divine intelligence can know about human free actions, then what becomes of our freedom of choice and will? Processists construe God's omniscience in terms of his knowing everything that *can* be known, and regard human free actions as involving—at least sometimes—matters that cannot be known in advance of the fact. About such matters God, like the rest of us, can only learn in the fullness of time. (For processists, time is so potent a factor that even God is not wholly its master.) Process theologians accordingly incline to look with favor on Faustus Socinus (Fausto Paolo Sozzini, 1539–1604) who maintained that human freedom is incompatible with divine foreknowledge of our free acts and that—since free action is an accomplished fact—there has to be room for a *change* in God (in particular, in respect to his knowledge) that is consequent upon the course of events. To be sure, God is omniscient and gets to know everything—but only in due course. On this basis, processists abandon the idea of God's immutability along with that of a total separation from the world's developments. From the angle of traditional Christian doctrines, the piety of process religiosity may be altogether orthodox, but its theology is not, the processists link between God and nature being somewhat too intimate.

4. God in and for nature

With [Pierre-Simon] Laplace, the processist can say regarding God as explainer of the observed world, "We have no need for that hypothesis" (*Nous n'avons pas besoin de cette hypothèse*). For him, the service that God renders us is not so much to make the world *explicable* as to provide an incentive for finding it *appreciable* and for endeavoring to make it more so.

Nature may well, in the end, prove to be explanatorily self-contained. Individually and seriatim, the world's particular phenomena can presumably all be accounted for in terms of nature's own processes, and no super- or supranatural agency need be invoked. But explaining the phenomena of nature and appreciating them in terms of an apprehension of their worth and value are very different things. To be sure, the fact that people make evaluations is itself a natural phenomenon that has natural explanations. But the normative fact that (often) they do so rightly—that the things people factually prize are (often) normatively worth prizing—is something of a different order.

While process philosophers grant God a productive role in the world's realm of things, they see this less in terms of the efficient causality at issue with the scientific explanation of things than in terms of the final causality that endows the world with an axiological dimension by making a place for values in its idea of things. As process theology sees it, God is rather the source of *inspiration* for the world's agents than a basis of *explanation* for what they do.

The presence of arrangements in the world *that we like and that please us* can be explained naturally with reference to biological evolutions: attunement of creatures to their environment. But the fact that the world's arrangements *have worth and value in and of themselves* cries out for reference to the divine. And here process theology takes its hold. The service it sees the divine as rendering to human understanding does not lie in the order of causal explanation but rather in the order of evaluative appreciation—in enabling us to apprehend more correctly and realistically the grounds and indications of the fact that the world's arrangements can have worth and value.

The presence of chance, chaos, and choice on the world scene means that the course of the world's development poses genuine alternatives—contingently open possibilities where the course of events can run in one channel rather than another. Things can evolve and eventuate for the better or for the worse. The course of physical, biological, and cultural evolution is strewn with endless contingencies. The restrictive necessities of physical process no more mean that things need go well than the restrictive necessities of chess rules mean that the game must be played well. The what and how of the world's course of happenings are some sort of (factual) thing, but their evaluative assessment is quite another (normative) one. The presence of value in a world of chance may not *demand* belief in a benign directive influence at work within the world's processual flux (it could all be "pure luck"), but it certainly *invites* it.

We live in a world where there is not only *change* but also *progress* (= change for the better)—which, as we have seen, is geared to the process of evolution in its various manifestations. And this higher-level normative fact may be explained in terms of a three-cornered relationship between God, the world, and the intelligently evaluative beings that exist within it. The workings of evolution—cosmic, biological, and social—are all natural processes that operate in and through the world's sphere of contingency and chance. But the (evaluative) fact that these processes function so as to yield something that has value is a circumstance which, as process theology sees it, profoundly manifests the presence of a benign intelligence at work in or through the phenomena of nature. As process theology sees it, it is in this relationship to the world as a locus of value, rather than to it as a manifold of phenomena, that the hand of God upon the world's processes manifests itself most strikingly.

To be sure, process philosophers differ from one another regarding the notion of God. Some take an immanentist line and view the divine as a force or factor at work within the cosmic processes to make for an ongoing enhancement of intelligible order and appreciable value. Others take a more transcendentist line and view the divinity as a processual being or entity—a superprocess of sorts that works upon, rather than within, the world's constitutive machine of processes. (Thus Whitehead admitted that while he called God a "principle of concretion," he did not really mean to call

God a principle but rather an actual entity that gives operative endowment to such a principle.[6])

Yet while processists differ regarding the nature of God, they generally agree that the proper appreciation of the natural sphere and its modus operandi involves recourse to a world-transcendent factor—that from an axiological point of view nature cannot be seen as a wholly self-contained and autonomous realm. A proper appreciation of the real accordingly involves reference to something extra- if not supranatural. So far, so good. But from a traditional Judeo-Christian standpoint, processists incline to the unorthodoxy of seeing God as a power rather than as a person—and, indeed, a power that, just like the world, incorporates real potentiality in its make-up.

It is not that process theology proposes to worship a different God or puts forward a different creed. In point of forms and formalities it is (or can be) perfectly orthodox. What is at issue is a matter of the interpretation or construction of the traditional formulas that the process approach makes available. No radical lapse from tradition need be envisioned here. Process theology can take a position that is not so much revisionist as explanatory; its line can be that of the question, "If a God along the traditional lines exists, then how can a being of this sort be most effectively (most intelligibly and least problematically) conceptualized?"

In the final reckoning, then, the process approach has some distinct advantages for theology over against a substance approach. Specifically, it makes it easier and less problematic to understand the nature of God as a person and this being's participating role in relation to the world. The process approach thus affords a framework for conceiving of God in a way that not only removes many of the difficulties inherent in the thing-oriented, substantial approach of traditional metaphysics but also makes it vastly easier to provide a philosophical rationale for many—though not all—of the leading conceptions of Judeo-Christian religiosity.

Notes

1   The major process theologians include Pierre Teilhard de Chardin (1881–1955) in France; Samuel Alexander (1859–1944), Conroy Loyd Morgan (1852–1936), William Temple (1882–1944), and Lionel Spencer Thornton (1884–1947) in Britain; and Alfred North Whitehead (1861–1967) and Charles Hartshorne (1897–[2000]) in the United States, together with their students and followers. For fuller information about process theology, which has been an increasingly active enterprise in recent years, the reader may consult Charles Birch, *A Purpose for Everything: Religion in a Postmodern Worldview* (Mystic, CT: Twenty-Third Publications, 1990); John B. Cobb and David R. Griffin, *Process Theology*; John B. Cobb, *Process Theology as Political Ecology* (Philadelphia: Westminster Press, 1982); Charles Hartshorne, *The Divine Relativity: A Social Conception of God* (New Haven: Yale University Press, 1948); idem, *A Natural Theology for Our Time* (La Salle, IL: Open Court, 1967); A. N. Whitehead, *Religion in the Making* (Cambridge: Cambridge University Press, 1930).

For useful anthologies on the topic, see Delwin Brown et al. (eds.), *Process Philosophy and Christian Thought* (Indianapolis: Bobbs-Merrill, 1971); Douglas Browning, *Philosophers of Process* (New York: Random House, 1965); Ewert H. Cousins (ed.), *Process Theology: Basic Writings*, which seeks to fuse the organismic tradition of Whitehead with the evolutionism of Teilhard de Chardin. Also, James R. Gray's *Modern Process Thought* (Lanham, MD: University Press of America, 1982) is an anthology focused largely on process theology.

2   Interesting deliberations by Donald W. Sherburne suggest for Whitehead himself the (declined) option of a naturalistic processism. See Sherburne, "Whitehead without God," *Christian Scholar* 60 (1907): 251–72.
3   See, for example, Michael J. Buckley, *Motion and Motion's God* (Princeton: Princeton University Press, 1971).
4   On this aspect of process theology see Josiah Royce, *The World and the Individual*, 2 vols. (New York: MacMillan, 1901–1902), Vol. I, chapter entitled "The Temporal and External"; E. S. Brightman, "A Temporalist View of God," in *The Journal of Religion*, vol. 2 (1932); A. O. Lovejoy, "The Obsolescence of the Eternal," in *The Philosophical Review*, vol. 18 (1909), pp. 479–502; and J. A. Leighton, "Time and the Logic of Monistic Idealism," in *Essays in Honor of J. E. Creighton* (New York: Macmillan, 1917), 151–161.
5   Compare Charles Valentine, "The Development of Process Philosophy," in *Process Theology: Basic Writings*, ed. Ewert H. Cousins.
6   Cf. *Process and Reality*, 374. See the report by A. H. Johnson in L. S. Ford and G. L. Kline (eds.), *Explorations in Whitehead's Philosophy* (New York: Fordham University Press, 1983), 4–10.

Questions for reflection

1   What is the process view of God?
2   How would you describe the difference between the process view of God and God as viewed pantheistically?
3   What are some ways in which the process view of God is similar to the Judeo-Christian view of God? Can someone within the Judeo-Christian tradition consistently hold to a process view of God?
4   Does the process conception of God offer a better understanding of God as a person than a traditional Judeo-Christian conception? Why or why not?

Further reading

John B. Cobb and David Ray Griffin (1977) *Process Theology: An Introductory Exposition.* Louisville, KY: Westminster John Knox Press. (An introduction to process theology by two leading process figures.)
James R. Gray, ed. (1982) *Modern Process Thought.* Lanham, MD: University Press of America. (An anthology which is largely focused on process theology.)
Charles Hartshorne (1948) *The Divine Relativity: A Social Conception of God.* New Haven, CT: Yale University Press. (Delineates a panentheistic conception of God whereby God is both absolute and relative.)
Nicholas Rescher (1996) *Process Metaphysics: An Introduction to Process Philosophy.* Albany, NY: State University of New York Press. (A solid, accessible introduction to process thought; the selection above is taken from this book.)
Alfred North Whitehead (1930) *Religion in the Making.* Cambridge: Cambridge University Press. (An elegant work on the nature of religion by the founder of process thought.)

Non-theistic perspectives of Ultimate Reality

Chapter 14

Shankara

BRAHMAN IS ALL

Shankara (eighth century CE) is the most renowned Indian philosopher to develop the
doctrine of Advaita Vedānta Hinduism. He wrote many works, including commentaries
on the Vedas (sacred Hindu texts). There are different schools of Vedānta, and the one he
expounded and defended includes metaphysical monism—the idea that Ultimate Reality
is one ("*Advaita*" means non-duality). Thus, Ultimate Reality (God, or Brahman) is undifferentiated unity; all is one. The multifaceted phenomenal world is an illusion (*maya*), and
hence there is the appearance that we are individual selves (*Atman*) when, in fact, we are
one with Brahman.

Brahman is the universe

Braham is the reality—the one existence, absolutely independent of human thought or
idea. Because of the ignorance of our human minds, the universe seems to be composed
of diverse forms. It is Brahman alone.

A jar made of clay is not other than clay. It is clay essentially. The form of the jar has
no independent existence. What, then, is the jar? Merely an invented name!

The form of the jar can never be perceived apart from the clay. What, then, is the
jar? An appearance! The reality is the clay itself.

This universe is an effect of Brahman. It can never be anything else but Brahman.
Apart from Brahman, it does not exist. There is nothing beside Him. He who says that
this universe has an independent existence is still suffering from delusion. He is like a
man talking in his sleep.

"The universe is Brahman"—so says the great seer of the Atharva Veda. The universe, therefore, is nothing but Brahman. It is superimposed upon Him. It has no
separate existence, apart from its ground.

If the universe, as we perceive it, were real, knowledge of the Atman would not put an end to our delusion. The scriptures would be untrue. The revelations of the Divine Incarnations would make no sense. These alternatives cannot be considered either desirable or beneficial by any thinking person.

Sri Krishna, the Incarnate Lord, who knows the secret of all truths, says in the [Bhagavad] Gita: "Although I am not within any creature, all creatures exist within me. I do not mean that they exist within me physically. That is my divine mystery. My Being sustains all creatures and brings them to birth, but has no physical contact with them."

If this universe were real, we should continue to perceive it in deep sleep. But we perceive nothing then. Therefore it is unreal, like our dreams.

The universe does not exist apart from the Atman. Our perception of it as having an independent existence is false, like our perception of blueness in the sky. How can a superimposed attribute have any existence, apart from its substratum? It is only our delusion which causes this misconception of the underlying reality.

No matter what a deluded man may think he is perceiving, he is really seeing Brahman and nothing else but Brahman. He sees mother-of-pearl and imagines that it is silver. He sees Brahman and imagines that it is the universe. But this universe, which is superimposed upon Brahman, is nothing but a name.

Brahman is supreme

Brahman is supreme. He is the reality—the one without a second. He is pure consciousness, free from any taint. He is tranquility itself. He has neither beginning nor end. He does not change. He is joy for ever.

He transcends the appearance of the manifold, created by Maya. He is eternal, for ever beyond reach of pain, not to be divided, not to be measured, without form, without name, undifferentiated, immutable. He shines with His own light. He is everything that can be experienced in this universe.

The illumined seers know Him as the uttermost reality, infinite, absolute, without parts—the pure consciousness. In Him they find that knower, knowledge and known have become one.

They know Him as the reality which can neither be cast aside (since He is ever-present within the human soul) nor grasped (since He is beyond the power of mind and speech). They know Him immeasurable, beginningless, endless, supreme in glory. They realize the truth: "I am Brahman".

Atman is Brahman

The scriptures establish the absolute identity of Atman and Brahman by declaring repeatedly: "That art Thou". The terms "Brahman" and "Atman", in their true meaning, refer to "That" and "Thou" respectively.

In their literal, superficial meaning, "Brahman" and "Atman" have opposite attributes, like the sun and the glow-worm, the king and his servant, the ocean and the well, or Mount Meru and the atom. Their identity is established only when they are understood in their true significance, and not in a superficial sense.

"Brahman" may refer to God, the ruler of Maya and creator of the universe. The

"Atman" may refer to the individual soul, associated with the five coverings which are effects of Maya. Thus regarded, they possess opposite attributes. But this apparent opposition is caused by Maya and her effects. It is not real, therefore, but superimposed.

These attributes caused by Maya and her effects are superimposed upon God and upon the individual soul. When they have been completely eliminated, neither soul nor God remains. If you take the kingdom from a king and the weapons from a soldier, there is neither soldier nor king.

The scriptures repudiate any idea of a duality in Brahman. Let a man seek illumination in the knowledge of Brahman, as the scriptures direct. Then those attributes, which our ignorance has superimposed upon Brahman, will disappear.

"Brahman is neither the gross nor the subtle universe. The apparent world is caused by our imagination, in its ignorance. It is not real. It is like seeing the snake in the rope. It is like a passing dream"—that is how a man should practice spiritual discrimination, and free himself from his consciousness of this objective world. Then let him meditate upon the identity of Brahman and Atman, and so realize the truth.

Through spiritual discrimination, let him understand the true inner meaning of the terms "Brahman" and "Atman", thus realizing their absolute identity. See the reality in both, and you will find that there is but one.

When we say: "This man is that same Devadatta whom I have previously met", we establish a person's identity by disregarding those attributes superimposed upon him by the circumstances of our former meeting. In just the same way, when we consider the scriptural teaching "That art Thou", we must disregard those attributes which have been superimposed upon "That" and "Thou".

The wise men of true discrimination understand that the essence of both Brahman and Atman is Pure Consciousness, and thus realize their absolute identity. The identity of Brahman and Atman is declared in hundreds of holy texts.

Give up the false notion that the Atman is this body, this phantom. Meditate upon the truth that the Atman is "neither gross nor subtle, neither short nor tall", that it is self-existent, free as the sky, beyond the grasp of thought. Purify the heart until you know that "I am Brahman". Realize your own Atman, the pure and infinite consciousness.

Just as a clay jar or vessel is understood to be nothing but clay, so this whole universe, born of Brahman, essentially Brahman, is Brahman only—for there is nothing else but Brahman, nothing beyond That. That is the reality. That is our Atman. Therefore, "That art Thou"—pure, blissful, supreme Brahman, the one without a second.

You may dream of place, time, objects, individuals, and so forth. But they are unreal. In your waking state, you experience this world, but that experience arises from your ignorance. It is a prolonged dream, and therefore unreal. Unreal also are this body, these organs, this life-breath, this sense of ego. Therefore, "That art Thou"— pure, blissful, supreme Brahman, the one without a second.

Because of delusion, you may mistake one thing for another. But, when you know its real nature, then that nature alone exists, there is nothing else but that. When the dream breaks, the dream-universe has vanished. Does it appear, when you wake, that you are other than yourself?

Caste, creed, family and lineage do not exist in Brahman. Brahman has neither name nor form; it transcends merit and demerit; it is beyond time, space and the objects of sense-experience. Such is Brahman, and "That art Thou". Meditate upon this truth.

It is supreme. It is beyond the expression of speech; but it is known by the eye of pure illumination. It is pure, absolute consciousness, the eternal reality. Such is Brahman, and "That art Thou". Meditate upon this truth.

It is untouched by those six waves—hunger, thirst, grief, delusion, decay and death—which sweep the ocean of worldliness. He who seeks union with it must meditate upon it within the shrine of the heart. It is beyond the grasp of the senses. The intellect cannot understand it. It is out of the reach of thought. Such is Brahman, and "That art Thou". Meditate upon this truth.

It is the ground upon which this manifold universe, the creation of ignorance, appears to rest. It is its own support. It is neither the gross nor the subtle universe. It is indivisible. It is beyond comparison. Such is Brahman, and "That art Thou". Meditate upon this truth.

It is free from birth, growth, change, decline, sickness and death. It is eternal. It is the cause of the evolution of the universe, its preservation and its dissolution. Such is Brahman, and "That art Thou". Meditate upon this truth.

It knows no differentiation or death. It is calm, like a vast, waveless expanse of water. It is eternally free and indivisible. Such is Brahman, and "That art Thou". Meditate upon this truth.

Though one, it is the cause of the many. It is the one and only cause, no other beside it. It has no cause but itself. It is independent, also, of the law of causation. It stands alone. Such is Brahman, and "That art Thou". Meditate upon this truth.

It is unchangeable, infinite, imperishable. It is beyond Maya and her effects. It is eternal, undying bliss. It is pure. Such is Brahman, and "That art Thou". Meditate upon this truth.

It is that one Reality which appears to our ignorance as a manifold universe of names and forms and changes. Like the gold of which many ornaments are made, it remains in itself unchanged. Such is Brahman, and "That art Thou". Meditate upon this truth.

There is nothing beyond it. It is greater than the greatest. It is the innermost self, the ceaseless joy within us. It is absolute existence, knowledge and bliss. It is endless, eternal. Such is Brahman, and "That art Thou". Meditate upon this truth.

Meditate upon this truth, following the arguments of the scriptures by the aid of reason and intellect. Thus you will be freed from doubt and confusion, and realize the truth of Brahman. This truth will become as plain to you as water held in the palm of your hand.

Questions for reflection

1   What does Shankara mean by saying "That are thou"? Why does it not seem so for most of us?

2   How could one who holds to Advaita Vedānta distinguish between virtues and vices? Are such distinctions even real? How does one's metaphysic affect one's moral understanding in this case?

3   How would you describe the difference between Shankara's conception of Brahman in this selection and Ramanuja's conception of Brahman in his selection (see chapter 10)? What are some differences? What are some similarities?

4   How would you compare Shankara's conception of Brahman with Lao Tzu's conception of the Tao (see chapter 15)?

Further reading

Anonymous ([c. 300–50 BCE] 2003) *The Bhagavad Gita*. New York: Penguin Classics. (A Hindu sacred text; this is the standard English translation.)

Anonymous ([eighth century BCE] 1965) *The Upanishads*. Trans. Juan Mascaro. New York: Penguin Classics. (The Upanishads are spiritual contemplations of the Vedas; this work contains the thirteen "Principal Upanishads" which explore such central doctrines as rebirth, karma, achieving detachment and spiritual bliss.)

Eliot Deutsch (1969) *Advaita Vedanta: A Philosophical Reconstruction*. Honolulu, HI: University of Hawaii Press. (A concise, clear exposition of Advaita Vedānta, especially as espoused by Shankara.)

Eliot Deutsch and Rohit Dalvi (2003) *The Essential Vedanta: A New Source Book of Advaita Vedanta*. Bloomington, IN: World Wisdom. (An excellent collection of significant Advaita texts.)

Hillary Rodrigues (2006) *Introducing Hinduism*. London: Routledge. (A lively, readable introduction to Hinduism; very helpful for those not familiar with the religion.)

Shankara ([eighth century] 1947) *Shankara's Crest-Jewel of Discrimination*. Trans. Swami Prabhavananda and Christopher Isherwood. Hollywood, CA: Vedanta Press. (The classic Advaita text about the path to true understanding of Brahman and Atman; the selection above was taken from this work.)

Arvind Sharma (1995) *The Philosophy of Religion and Advaita Vedanta: A Comparative Study in Religion and Reason*. University Park, PA: Pennsylvania State University Press. (A helpful examination of Advaita Vedānta in light of Western assumptions.)

Chapter 15

Lao Tzu

THE TAO

Lao Tzu (also "Laozi," flourished sixth century BCE) was a Chinese philosopher and, according to Chinese tradition, the founder of Taoism (also spelled "Daoism"). He wrote one of the seminal texts of Taoism, the *Tao Te Ching* (commonly translated as the *Classic of the Way and Virtue*), from which this selection is taken and which is widely understood to be a classic of religious writing and world literature. This selection focuses on the Tao — often translated as "the Way" — which in Taoism refers to the ineffable, fundamental reality and ground of all things, and the virtue of nature.

1 The Tao (Way) that can be told of is not the eternal Tao;
The name that can be named is not the eternal name.*
The Nameless is the origin of Heaven and Earth;
The Named is the mother of all things.
Therefore let there always be non-being so we may see their subtlety,
And let there always be being so we may see their outcome.
The two are the same,
But after they are produced, they have different names.
They both may be called deep and profound.
Deeper and more profound,
The door of all subtleties!

2 When the people of the world all know beauty as beauty,
There arises the recognition of ugliness.
When they all know the good as good,
There arises the recognition of evil.
Therefore:
Being and non-being produce each other;
Difficult and easy complete each other;
Long and short contrast each other;

High and low distinguish each other;
Sound and voice harmonize with each other;
Front and back follow each other.
Therefore the sage manages affairs without action
And spreads doctrines without words.
All things arise, and he does not turn away from them.
He produces them, but does not take possession of them.
He acts, but does not rely on his own ability.
He accomplishes his task, but does not claim credit for it.
It is precisely because he does not claim credit that his accomplishment remains
    with him.

4   Tao is empty (like a bowl).
It may be used but its capacity is never exhausted.
It is bottomless, perhaps the ancestor of all things.
It blunts its sharpness,
It unties its tangles.
It softens its light.
It becomes one with the dusty world.
Deep and still, it appears to exist forever.
I do not know whose son it is.
It seems to have existed before the Lord.

6   The spirit of the valley never dies.
        It is called the subtle and profound female.
The gate of the subtle and profound female
        Is the root of Heaven and Earth.
It is continuous, and seems to be always existing.
Use it and you will never wear it out.

7   Heaven is eternal and Earth everlasting.
They can be eternal and everlasting because they do not exist for themselves,
And for this reason can exist forever.
Therefore the sage places himself in the background, but finds himself in the
    foreground.
He puts himself away, and yet he always remains.
Is it not because he has no personal interests?
This is the reason why his personal interests are fulfilled.

8   The best (man) is like water.
Water is good; it benefits all things and does not compete with them.
It dwells in (lowly) places that all disdain.
This is why it is so near to Tao.
[The best man] in his dwelling loves the earth.
        In his heart, he loves what is profound.
        In his associations, he loves humanity.
        In his words, he loves faithfulness.
        In government, he loves order.
        In handling affairs, he loves competence.
        In his activities, he loves timeliness.
        It is because he does not compete that he is without reproach.

11 Thirty spokes are united around the hub to make a wheel,
     But it is on its non-being that the utility of the carriage depends.
Clay is molded to form a utensil,
     But it is on its non-being that the utility of the utensil depends.
Doors and windows are cut out to make a room,
     But it is on its non-being that the utility of the room depends.
Therefore turn being into advantage, and turn non-being into utility.

14 We look at it and do not see it;
     Its name is The Invisible.
We listen to it and do not hear it;
     Its name is The Inaudible.
We touch it and do not find it;
     Its name is The Subtle (formless).
These three cannot be further inquired into,
And hence merge into one.
Going up high, it is not bright, and coming down low, it is not dark.
Infinite and boundless, it cannot be given any name;
It reverts to nothingness.
This is called shape without shape,
Form without object.
It is The Vague and Elusive.
Meet it and you will not see its head.
Follow it and you will not see its back.
Hold on to the Tao of old in order to master the things of the present.
From this one may know the primeval beginning (of the universe).
This is called the bond of Tao.

21 The all-embracing quality of the great virtue follows alone from the Tao.
The thing that is called Tao is eluding and vague.
     Vague and eluding, there is in it the form.
     Eluding and vague, in it are things.
Deep and obscure, in it is the essence [spirit, life-force].
The essence is very real; in it are evidences.
From the time of old until now, its name (manifestations) ever remains,
By which we may see the beginning of all things.
How do I know that the beginnings of all things are so?
Through this (Tao).

25 There was something undifferentiated and yet complete,
Which existed before heaven and earth.
Soundless and formless, it depends on nothing and does not change.
It operates everywhere and is free from danger.
It may be considered the mother of the universe.
I do not know its name; I call it Tao.
If forced to give it a name, I shall call it Great.
Now being great means functioning everywhere.
Functioning everywhere means far-reaching.
Being far-reaching means returning to the original point.
Therefore Tao is great.

Heaven is great.

Earth is great.

And the king is also great.

There are four great things in the universe, and the king is one of them.

Man models himself after Earth.

Earth models itself after Heaven.

Heaven models itself after Tao.

And Tao models itself after Nature.

34 The Great Tao flows everywhere.

It may go left or right.

All things depend on it for life, and it does not turn away from them.

It accomplishes its task but does not claim credit for it.

It clothes and feeds all things but does not claim to be master over them.

Always without desires, it may be called The Small.

All things come to it and it does not master them; it may be called The Great.

Therefore (the sage) never strives himself for the great, and thereby the great is
   achieved.

37 Tao invariably takes no action, and yet there is nothing left undone.

If kings and barons can keep it, all things will transform spontaneously.

If, after transformation, they should desire to be active,

I would restrain them with simplicity, which has no name.

Simplicity, which has no name, is free of desires.

Being free of desires, it is tranquil.

And the world will be at peace of its own accord.

40 Reversion is the action of Tao.

Weakness is the function of Tao.

All things in the world come from being.

And being comes from non-being.

42 Tao produced the One.

The One produced the two.

The two produced the three.

And the three produced the ten thousand things.

The ten thousand things carry the yin and embrace the yang, and through the
   blending of the material force they achieve harmony.

People hate to be the orphaned, the lonely ones, and the unworthy.

And yet kings and lords call themselves by these names.

Therefore it is often the case that things gain by losing and lose by gaining.

What others have taught, I teach also:

"Violent and fierce people do not die a natural death."

I shall make this the father (basis or starting point) of my teaching.

Note

*   [All commentary, footnotes, and parenthetical terms from *A Source Book in Chinese Phil-
     osophy*, translated and compiled by Wing-tsit Chan, have been removed. The selections
     offered here generally follow the helpful flow provided by Gary E. Kessler in his *Philosophy*

of Religion: Toward a Global Perspective (New York: Wadsworth Publishing Company, 1999), 47–50.]

Questions for reflection

1   The *Tao Te Ching* opens with these words: "The Tao (Way) that can be told of is not the eternal Tao; The name that can be named is not the eternal name." Given what he goes on to say about the Tao, how do you interpret these words?

2   What are some characteristics of the Tao offered by Lao Tzu? Can one truly attain an understanding of the Tao or, as with Maimonides's *via negativa*, is it best to view the Tao in terms of what it is not? Explain.

3   The *yin* and the *yang* represent primal, complementary, opposite forces of the universe. How might such opposing forces be understood in terms of the harmony of the Tao?

4   How would you describe the Tao in your own words? How would you explain its relevance to someone unfamiliar with it?

Further reading

Wing-tsit Chan (1963) *A Source Book in Chinese Philosophy*. Princeton, NJ: Princeton University Press. (This book is a classic work in Chinese philosophy; the above selection is taken from it.)

D. C. Lau, trans. (1963) *Lao Tzu Tao Te Ching*. Baltimore, MD: Penguin. (A frequently used translation with a helpful introduction.)

James Miller (2003) *Daoism: A Short Introduction*. Oxford: Oneworld Publications. (A readable introduction to Taoism which emphasizes its role as a living tradition.)

Lao Tzu Page (A rich online source of materials on Lao Tzu and Taoism; found at http://www.taopage.org/laotzu/.)

Chapter 16

K. N. Jayatilleke

NIRVANA IS ULTIMATE
REALITY

K. N. Jayatilleke (1920–70) was a Buddhist scholar and Professor of Western and Eastern Philosophy at the University of Ceylon. In this selection, extracted from his book, *The Message of the Buddha*, he expounds on the doctrine of Nirvana as understood in Theravada Buddhism. He notes that the concept of Nirvana has occasionally been misunderstood by scholars and Buddhist practitioners—some have taken it to be annihilation; others have taken it to be identical with divinity; still others have thought that the Buddha was unconcerned about it. Jayatilleke argues that the concept of Nirvana as taught in early Buddhist texts is different from each of these.

Anuruddha – a first cousin of the Buddha and one of his disciples.
Arahats – the Buddha's most noble disciples.
Brahmā – in some forms of Buddhism "Brahmā" is the name given for a type of exalted and passionless deity.
Brahmajāla Sutta – the first sutta (word or sermon of the Buddha) of 34 suttas in the Long Discourses of Buddha.
Brāhmanimantanika Sutta – a sutta preached by the Buddha in which he discusses his visit to a place called Baka Brahmā.
Parinirvāna – the final Nirvana.
samsāra – the cycle of birth, death, and decay.
Suttanipāta – one of the earliest books of the Pali Canon, the standard scriptural collection of the Theravada tradition.

Nirvana

Nirvana or Nibbāna is considered to be "the reality" or "the ultimate reality" in Buddhism.* It is also a state of perfection or the highest good, which, at least, a few can attain in this life itself. It is the *summum bonum*, which not only all human beings but all beings in the universe should seek to attain. For unless and until they attain it, they are subject to the unsatisfactoriness and insecurity of conditioned existence, however pleasant it may be for a short or even a long period of time.

As with some of the other Buddhist concepts, the term Nirvana has sometimes been misunderstood by scholars. It is also by no means clear that all Buddhists understand the meaning and significance of the term in the way in which it was understood in the early Buddhist texts. Some have considered Nirvana to be a state of annihilation. Others deem it to be identical with Divinity and identify Nirvana with the Brahman of the Upanisads. Yet others who regarded Buddha as an Agnostic thought that he had no clear conception about the nature of Nirvana or was, in fact, unconcerned about it, since what was important was to find a solution to the problem of human anxiety and suffering rather than be concerned with the nature of ultimate reality. . . .

Finally, there are those who would assert that Nirvana is a transcendent state of reality, which the human mind, limited in its conceptions, cannot intellectually comprehend.

What then is the correct answer, if such an answer is possible? It is only a careful study of all the authentic texts, which can suggest an answer to this question.

The term Nirvana (Pali, Nibbāna) is claimed in the Buddhist texts to be pre-Buddhist in origin, although the term as such is not to be found in the extant preBuddhistic literature. The *Brahmajāla Sutta* refers to several schools of thought, which put forward different "theories about Nirvana that could be attained in this life." The thinkers who posited these theories resembled in some respects the modern Existentialist philosophers, who are concerned about the solutions to the problems of human anxiety and suffering and have found various theories concerning the nature of authentic living, which gives inner satisfaction to people and makes it possible for them to escape their boredom and anxiety. In other respects, these thinkers resemble the mystics of the different traditions, such as the Christian or Islamic (e.g. the Sūfīs), who claim to have found ultimate happiness in some contemplative mystic experience.

What concerns us here is the meaning of the term Nirvana. The first school of thought held that the soul experiences the highest Nirvana in this life when it is fully engrossed and immersed in the enjoyment of the pleasures of the five senses. Some of the other schools, however, held that sense-pleasures were not lasting and were a source of unhappiness and that the soul truly experiences the highest Nirvana in a contemplative state in which one is detached from sense-pleasures and aloof from morally evil states of mind. In these contexts we find that the term Nirvana is used to denote a state of positive happiness conceived as the most desirable in the light of their respective philosophies.

On the other hand, when we examine the pure etymology of the term, we find that the word is formed of the components, the prefix nis- and the root vā, meaning "to blow." The word would, therefore, mean "blowing out" or "extinction." On the occasion on which the Buddha finally passed away into Nirvana, Anuruddha described the Parinirvāna of the Buddha as, "The final liberation of mind was like the *extinction of a lamp*" (D. II. 157).

In the word Nirvana, therefore, we have a term which means both "extinction" as well as "the highest positive experience of happiness." Both these connotations are important for understanding the significance of the term as it is employed in the Buddhist texts.

Annihilation?

The meaning of "extinction" easily lent itself to the annihilationist interpretation of Nirvana. "The individual," according to Buddhism, is in fact a process or a "stream of becoming" continuing from life to life, which in the human state was conditioned by heredity, environment and the psychological past of the individual. This process of conditioning was due to causal factors such as the operation of desires fed by beliefs. When the desires and beliefs ceased to operate, so it was argued, with the extinction of greed, hatred and ignorance, the individual was extinguished and ceased to exist for good. If the Buddha did not openly state this (so they say), it was because individuals being self-centered have a longing for life and personal immortality and would be frightened to hear of the truth.

There are some Buddhist scholars who virtually give the same explanation. They only object to the use of the word "annihilation" to describe "the ceasing of 'the individual' for good." They argue that "annihilation" is possible only if there is a "being" to be annihilated. But there is no such "being." If there is no such "being" to be annihilated, there is no annihilation, for nothing or no one is annihilated. So what is wrong according to them is the use of the word "annihilation" to describe this state of affairs. They would not deny that the samsāric individual ceases to be for ever. This seems to be a merely verbal difference because, for all practical purposes, "the individual" is completely extinguished and if we are wrong (according to them) in saying so, it is because "the individual" did not exist in the first instance.

Such an interpretation leaves a lot of material unexplained in the early Buddhist texts. The Buddha certainly denied the persistence of an unchanging substratum or entity in the process of the individual but did not deny the phenomenal reality of the individual. The Buddha approves the use of the following language to describe the nature of individual existence on one occasion: "I did exist in the past, not that I did not, I will exist in the future, not that I will not and I do exist in the present, not that I do not" (D. I. 200). We must not forget that the Buddha held the view that "nothing exists" because everything passes away as one extreme point of view. The Buddhist criticism of the Materialist's position was that the Materialist posited without reason "the destruction of an existent individual."

When the Buddha himself was charged with being an Annihilationist with regard to his teaching about Nirvana, he counters it by saying that this was a gross misrepresentation of his teaching on the part of some of the other religious teachers (M. I. 140). In the same context, the Buddha gives his reasons for saying so. When a person's (i.e. monk's) mind becomes finally emancipated, even the most powerful and intelligent Gods of the cosmos are unable to trace where the consciousness of such a Transcendent One is located (ibid.). It is stated that this is so even while he is living. For, says the Buddha, such a Transcendent One cannot be probed even in this life.

When one's mind is emancipated, it does not become a dormant nonentity. If so the Buddha and the Arahats should have been apathetic individuals unconcerned about anything after attaining liberation. Instead, when the mind is purged of greed, hatred and ignorance it is transformed and shines with its natural lustre. It can then act spontaneously out of selflessness, compassion and understanding.

The Transcendent One or the Tathāgata (a word used both of the Buddha and the Arahats) cannot be measured by the conditioned constituents of his personality such as the body, the feelings, the ideas, the conative activities and the acts of cognition. Freed from reckoning in terms of these constituents of his personality, he is said to be "deep, immeasurable and unfathomable like the great ocean" (M. I. 487). Qualities like compassion and the other divine modes of behaviour, we may note, are called "the infinitudes."

Such an emancipated person, the depths of whose mind cannot be plumbed, it is said, cannot be considered to continue to exist after death as an individual (whose existence is invariably self-centered and conditioned), nor to cease to exist or be annihilated at death. Neither description was apt for these reasons as well as for others.

The question as to whether the liberated person continues to exist for ever in time as a distinct individual or is annihilated at death is clearly posed in the *Suttanipāta*, where the Buddha is asked the question: "The person who has attained the goal—does he not exist or does he exist eternally without defect; explain this to me well, O Lord, as you understand it?" (1075). If annihilation was a fact or the person ceased to exist altogether, the answer would have been quite clear; it would have been, "He does not exist," but this is expressly denied. The reason given is that, "The person who has attained the goal is *beyond measure*." Elsewhere, it is said that he does not come within time being beyond time or that he does not come within reckoning. In other words, we do not have the concepts or words to describe adequately the state of the emancipated person, who has attained the transcendent reality, whether it be when he lives with the body and the other constituents of personality or after death.

We may describe this situation in yet another way. Our minds function in this conditioned manner because they have become self-centered and corrupted by adventitious defilements and involvements in the course of our samsāric history. The mind, it is said, is naturally resplendent though it has been corrupted by adventitious defilements. It is often compared in this respect to gold ore, which has the defilements of iron, copper, tin, lead and silver, but when it is purified it becomes pliant, flexible, resplendent and not brittle.

So when the mind is cleansed of its defilements by meditative exercises and divested of its chief defilements, such as the obsessional attachment to sense-pleasures, aggressiveness, apathy, restlessness and scepticism about moral and spiritual values and their rationale, then it acquires a high degree of freedom, happiness, stability, serenity and awareness. Such a nature is in fact called "temporary Nirvana." When the mind is further purified, it acquires certain extra-sensory faculties such as telepathy, clairvoyance, etc., which are intrinsic to its nature. With the help of these faculties, it is possible to have an understanding of reality, which results in the mind being freed from the obsessions or inflowing impulses. Such a mind attains liberation. In the verses of the Brethren and Sisters we find the testimonies of several monks and nuns, who by these methods have gained emancipation.

Such a person is said to abide with his mind, having transcended its bounds. It is divested of personal strivings, being wholly dominated with the greatest freedom and spontaneity by selflessness, compassion and understanding.

However, despite his liberation, since he is still limited by his conditioned psychophysical individuality, it is called "the Nirvānic state with limitations still remaining." Although his roots of greed, hatred and ignorance have been destroyed, he is still subject to pleasant and unpleasant experiences associated with his senses but not originating from his mind (It. 38).

God or Brahman?

The question as to what happens to his psycho-physical personality at his final death is sometimes posed. "Where does the psycho-physical individuality cease to be without remainder?" The answer is given as follows: "Consciousness, without distinguishing mark, infinite and shining everywhere—here the material elements do not penetrate . . . but here it is that the conditioned consciousness ceases to be" (D. I. 223). Even the Commentary identifies the "infinite consciousness" with Nirvana, saying that "it is a term for Nirvāna" (D.A. II. 393), while the second occurrence of the term consciousness is described as "the last stages of consciousness or conditioned consciousness" (D.A. II. 393, 394).

The *Brāhmanimantanika Sutta* further corroborates the above interpretation. Here there is a dialogue between Buddha and Brahmā, and it is shown that the reality that the Buddha attains to is the ultimate and is beyond the ken even of Brahmā. The Buddha says: "Do not think that this is an empty or void state. There is this consciousness, without distinguishing mark, infinite and shining everywhere; it is untouched by the material elements and not subject to any power." The Buddha, it is said, can become invisible in it without being seen by any of the most powerful beings in the cosmos. In other words, it is the ultimate reality. . . .

However, all these phrases, "exists," "ceases to exist," etc. are misleading since they have a spatio-temporal connotation. Nirvana is not spatially located, nor located in time so that "one cannot say of Nirvana that it is past, present or future." It is also not causally conditioned. It is therefore not capable of conceptual formulation or literal description.

So the explanations given to us who have not attained it are compared to the attempt to explain the nature of light or colour to a man born blind. To tell him that light or colour is not a sound, nor a taste, nor smell, nor touch, is literally true, but since he is only acquainted with sounds, tastes, smells and touches he may think that colours are nothing or cannot exist. The problem with Nirvana is analogous. What we have to do with the blind man is to evolve a method of restoring his sight. When this is done, no explanation is necessary, but before that strictly no explanation was possible. So to explain Nirvana by some form of rational demonstration is impossible—it falls beyond the pale of logic. So all one can do is to show the person who is anxious to attain Nirvana the methods of doing so and then he is likely, if he carefully follows those methods, to have glimpses of it and perhaps eventually to attain it. At this stage no explanations would be necessary. This is precisely what the Buddha sets out to do and why he is averse to making detailed pronouncements about Nirvana. As a result of this, the questions pertaining to the existence of the Transcendent One after death are treated as "unanswered questions. . . ."

. . . Nirvana is . . . the Transcendent Reality, whose real nature we cannot grasp with our normal minds because of our self-imposed limitations. It is a state of freedom, power, perfection, knowledge and perfect happiness of a transcendent sort. It is also said to be a state of perfect mental health, which we should try to attain for our personal happiness as well as for harmonious living.

Note

*   [Most Sanskrit terms have been removed from the text.]

Questions for reflection

1   How would you describe Nirvana as presented here by Professor Jayatilleke? Can it be attained in this life?
2   According to Jayatilleke, what happens when one's mind is truly emancipated? How is this achieved?
3   After death, what happens to the emancipated person?
4   How is Nirvana the Ultimate Reality? Can it be explained to the one who has not attained it?

Further reading

Anonymous (2005) *The Dhammapada: A New Translation of the Buddhist Classic with Annotations.* Ed. and trans. Gil Fronsdal. Boston, MA: Shambhala Publications. (The Dhammapada—"path of righteousness"—is probably the best-known work of the Pali Canon (sacred texts in Buddhism) and the most widely read Buddhist scripture; it offers two central goals of the spiritual life: attaining happiness and achieving spiritual liberation and peace.)

K. N. Jayatilleke (1975) *The Message of the Buddha.* Ed. Ninian Smart. New York: The Free Press. (An exposition of central Buddhist teachings from a Theravada perspective; the selection above comes from this work.)

Anthony J. Tribe (2005) *Buddhist Thought.* London: Routledge. (A solid introduction to Buddhist thought from the Indian tradition; also includes a helpful bibliography.)

Paul Williams (1989) *Mahayana Buddhism: The Doctrinal Foundations.* London: Routledge. (An accessible overview of the Mahayana tradition in India but also includes discussions of Chinese and Tibetan developments.)

PART THREE

Arguments for and against the existence of God

A fundamental question in philosophy of religion is whether there are reasons and evidences for the belief that God/Ultimate Reality exists. Throughout the centuries there have been leading thinkers who have defended both sides of this issue. This section includes a number of essays, both classic and contemporary, arguing for and against God's existence.

The first argument type we shall look at is the cosmological argument. The word "cosmological" is derived from two Greek terms: *cosmos* = world or universe, and *logos* = rational account. There are different versions of the cosmological argument, but they all begin with the claim that the universe exists and, for one reason or another—depending on the argument form—it needs an explanation for its existence.

The first selection is by the medieval theologian and philosopher Thomas Aquinas. In very concise form, he offers five different proofs for the existence of God—what are now famously referred to as the "Five Ways." The first four proofs are different versions of the cosmological argument, and the final proof is a type of teleological argument. All four of the cosmological-type arguments have a common structure: they each begin with some kind of contingent or dependent beings and then argue to a non-contingent, uncaused Being—God.

The next selection, offered by William Lane Craig, is a different kind of cosmological argument referred to as the "*kalam* argument." This is a cutting-edge version of an argument which was developed in the Middle Ages by Islamic theologians. According to the argument, the universe began to exist at some point in the finite past. Since whatever begins to exist needs a cause, the universe itself must have a cause. Furthermore, the argument goes, this cause must be a personal God.

Of course not everyone is convinced by cosmological arguments. In the following selection, atheist philosopher J. L. Mackie offers critiques of several prominent versions of the argument, including those presented by Aquinas and Craig. Next, Quentin Smith provides a kind of cosmological argument for atheism. Through an examination of the nature of causation, he argues that God cannot logically be the cause of the universe. Since God is the cause of the universe according to the classical understanding, such a God cannot exist.

As with cosmological arguments, there are also different versions of the teleological, or design, argument. Rather than begin with the existence of the world as a foundational presupposition as the cosmological argument does, the design argument focuses on a specific aspect of the world—namely, the apparent order or design contained within it. In the eighteenth century, the design argument fell into disfavor by most philosophers due to the work of David Hume. In the nineteenth century, Charles Darwin's work seemed to sound the death knell for the argument. However, several decades ago, the design argument was resurrected and has returned with a vengeance. Recent developments in physics, cosmology, microbiology, and biochemistry, for example, have breathed new life into it—so much so that one of the leading atheist philosophers of the twentieth century has recently become a theist because of it.[1]

One of the most famous presentations of the design argument was given by William Paley in his early nineteenth-century book, *Natural Theology*. I have included his argument from that work in which he claims that, just as we find parts ordered to achieve a certain end in machines made by human beings, so in the natural world we find similar structures. Given the similarity between the ordered patterns in a machine, such as a watch, and the ordered patterns in the natural world, we can infer a designer of the world just as reasonably as we can the machine.

The subsequent two selections reflect new research in the sciences mentioned above. First, one of the major figures in the recent "Intelligent Design" movement—an intellectual movement which includes a scientific research program for investigating intelligent causes in the universe—is Michael Behe. Behe argues that evidence in biochemistry reveals a kind of complexity, what he calls "irreducible complexity," which reflects finely calibrated chemical "machines" in living organisms. These irreducibly complex systems, he argues, are better explained via an intelligent designer than they are through naturalistic Darwinian processes.

In the next selection, Robin Collins looks at recent discoveries in the realms of physics and cosmology. His focus is on the structure of the world in which living organisms are able to flourish, and he argues that the fine-tuning of the universe provides good evidence for preferring theism over naturalism.

Historically, as noted above, one of the central critics of the design argument was David Hume. His book, *Dialogues Concerning Natural Religion*, is one of the most important works written on the topic. The selection from it included here challenges the analogy between machines made by human beings and machine-like structures in the natural world. It also argues that even if one can infer an intelligent designer of the world, such a designer need not be anything like the God of the religions.

Each of the previous arguments mentioned is *a posteriori* in nature; that is, they include premises which are known through experience of the natural world. There is another kind of argument, however, which is *a priori* in nature; that is, it is based on premises which can be known independently of experience of the natural world. This argument type is called the ontological argument (from the Greek terms *ontos* = being, and *logos*).

In the eleventh century a Benedictine monk named Anselm desired an argument that would prove, beyond any doubt, that God exists. He discovered what he took to be such an argument in analyzing the very concept of God. Simply put, his argument goes something like this. God is the greatest conceivable being—"a being than which none greater can be conceived." Once a person understands the meaning of this concept, she sees that such a being must exist, for if it didn't exist it would not be a being than which none greater can be conceived; it would not be the *greatest* conceivable being. Thus, understanding the concept of God logically forces one to the conclusion that God exists. Many objections to Anselm's version of the ontological argument have been raised, not the least of which was offered by Anselm's fellow monk, Gaunilo of Marmoutier. Some of his criticisms are included in the following selection.

As with the cosmological and teleological arguments, there are various versions of the ontological argument as well as various criticisms of it. Probably the most widely discussed critique of the ontological argument was offered by Immanuel Kant in the eighteenth century. It centers around the issue of whether or not existence is a predicate—a property that a thing may either have or not have. In this selection, Kant argues that existence is not a predicate, and this conclusion, he maintains, undermines the ontological argument.

In the twentieth and now twenty-first centuries, with the rise of modal logic, new modal varieties of the argument have emerged. One important modal version is offered by the process theologian, Charles Hartshorne. Developed in the context of his neoclassical view of God, he argues in his version of the ontological argument that God's existence is logically necessary. He maintains that this version escapes Kant's criticism.

Besides the "big three" traditional arguments for God's existence (cosmological, teleological, and ontological) and the related counterarguments, there are also a number of recent arguments for and against belief in God. I have included three central ones in this volume. In the first essay, Paul Copan maintains that the supernatural is necessary to ground morality. Since objective moral values do exist, he argues, there must be a God. Next, Ludwig Feuerbach argues that God is a projection of the human mind. Freedom, he insists, involves realizing this truth. Finally, J. P. Moreland presents his noölogical argument ("noölogy" being the study of reason or the mind) in which he argues that consciousness is better explained given theism than given naturalism. All three of these arguments are fairly recent developments; nonetheless, much discussion has developed and probably will continue to develop with respect to them.

Many other important arguments for and against the existence of God could have been included here. But these selections are, no doubt, some of the most powerful and enduring of the lot. In the event that you would like to dive deeper into this material, I have listed classic and principal contemporary works on the subject at the end of each chapter.

Note

1   I am referring to Antony Flew. He acknowledges as much in his interview with Gary Habermas in an essay entitled "My Pilgrimage from Atheism to Theism: A Discussion between Antony Flew and Gary R. Habermas," *Philosophia Christi*, 6.2 (2004), 197–211.

The cosmological argument

Chapter 17

Thomas Aquinas

THE CLASSICAL COSMOLOGICAL ARGUMENT

Thomas Aquinas (1225–74) was a Dominican monk, theologian, and philosopher. He is considered by many to be the Catholic Church's greatest theologian. He wrote prolifically on numerous topics. In this selection, taken from his *Summa Theologiae*, he offers his celebrated "Five Ways"—five different proofs for the existence of God. The first four ways are understood to be forms of the cosmological argument, while the fifth way is taken to be a kind of teleological argument. Given their significance in the history of Western thought, I have preserved all five ways in this selection.

We proceed thus to the Third Article: It seems that God does not exist.

Objection 1. For if one of two contraries were infinite, the other would be altogether destroyed. But the word "God" means that He is infinite goodness. If, therefore, God existed, there would be no evil discoverable. But there is evil in the world. Therefore God does not exist.

Objection 2. Further, what can be accomplished by a few principles is not effected by many. But it seems that everything we see in the world can be accounted for by other principles, supposing God did not exist. For all natural things can be reduced to one principle, which is nature, and all voluntary things can be reduced to one principle, which is human reason, or will. Therefore there is no need to suppose God's existence.

On the contrary, It is said in the person of God: I am Who am (Exod. 3:14).

I answer that, The existence of God can be proved in five ways.

The first and more manifest way is the argument from motion. It is certain, and evident to our senses, that in this world some things are in motion. Now whatever is in motion is put in motion by another, for nothing can be in motion unless it is in potency to that towards which it is in motion. But a thing moves in so far as it is in act. For motion is nothing else than the reduction of something from potency to act. But nothing can be reduced from potency to act except by something in a state of act. Thus that which is actually hot, as fire, makes wood, which is potentially hot, to be actually hot, and thereby moves and changes it. Now it is not possible that the same thing should be at once in act and potency in the same respect, but only in different respects. For what is actually hot cannot simultaneously be potentially hot, though it is simultaneously potentially cold. It is therefore impossible that in the same respect and in the same way a thing should be both mover and moved, that is, that it should move itself. Therefore, whatever is moved must be moved by another. If that by which it is moved be itself moved, then this also must be moved by another, and that by another again. But this cannot go on to infinity, because then there would be no first mover, and, consequently, no other mover, seeing that subsequent movers move only because they are moved by the first mover, just as the staff moves only because it is moved by the hand. Therefore it is necessary to arrive at a first mover which is moved by no other. And this everyone understands to be God.

The second way is from the notion of efficient cause. In the world of sense we find there is an order of efficient causes. There is no case known (nor indeed, is it possible) in which a thing is found to be the efficient cause of itself, because in that case it would be prior to itself, which is impossible. Now in efficient causes it is not possible to go on to infinity, because in all efficient causes following in order, the first is the cause of the intermediate cause, and the intermediate is the cause of the ultimate cause, whether the intermediate cause be several, or one only. Now to take away the cause is to take away the effect. Therefore, if there be no first cause among efficient causes, there will be no ultimate, nor any intermediate cause. But if in efficient causes it is possible to go on to infinity, there will be no first efficient cause, neither will there be an ultimate effect, nor any intermediate efficient causes, all of which is plainly false. Therefore it is necessary to admit a first efficient cause, to which everyone gives the name of God.

The third way is taken from possibility and necessity, and runs thus. We find in nature things that are possible to be and not to be, since they are found to be generated, and to be corrupted, and consequently they are possible to be and not to be. But it is impossible for these always to exist, for that which is possible not to be at some time is not. Therefore, if everything is possible not to be, then at one time there could have been nothing in existence. Now if this were true, even now there would be nothing in existence, because that which does not exist only begins to exist by something already existing. Therefore, if at one time nothing was in existence, it would have been impossible for anything to have begun to exist; and thus even now nothing would be in existence—which is clearly false. Therefore, not all beings are merely possible, but there must exist something the existence of which is necessary. But every necessary thing either has its necessity caused by another, or not. Now it is impossible to go on to infinity in necessary things which have their necessity caused by another, as has been already proved in regard to efficient causes. Therefore we must admit the existence of some being having of itself its own necessity, and not receiving it from another, but rather causing in others their necessity. This all men speak of as God.

The fourth way is taken from the gradation to be found in things. Among beings there are some more and some less good, true, noble, and the like. But "more" and "less" are predicated of different things, according as they resemble in their different ways something which is the maximum, as a thing is said to be hotter according as it more nearly resembles that which is hottest. There is then, something which is truest, something best, something noblest, and, consequently, something which is most being; for those things that are greatest in truth are greatest in being, as it is written in the *Metaphysics*.[1] Now the maximum in any genus is the cause of all in that genus; as fire, which is the maximum of heat, is the cause of all hot things as is said in the same book.[2] Therefore there must also be something which is to all beings the cause of their being, goodness, and every other perfection. And this we call God.

The fifth way is taken from the governance of things. We see that things which lack knowledge, such as natural bodies, act for an end, and this is evident from their acting always, or nearly always, in the same way, so as to obtain the best result. Hence it is plain that they achieve their end not by chance, but by design. Now whatever lacks knowledge cannot move towards an end, unless it be directed by some being endowed with knowledge and intelligence, as the arrow is directed by the archer. Therefore some intelligent being exists by whom all natural things are ordered to their end; and this being we call God.

Reply to Objection 1. As Augustine says (*Enchiridion* xi):[3] "Since God is the highest good, He would not allow any evil to exist in His works, unless His omnipotence and good-ness were such as to bring good even out of evil." This is part of the infinite goodness of God, that He should allow evil to exist, and out of it produce good.

Reply to Objection 2. Since nature works for a determinate end under the direction of a higher agent, whatever is done by nature must be traced back to God, as to its first cause. So also whatever is done voluntarily must also be traced back to some higher cause other than human reason or will, since these can change and fail. For all things that are changeable and capable of defect must be traced back to an immovable and self-necessary first principle, as was shown in the body of the Article.

Notes

1   Aristotle, II, I (993^{b}30).
2   II, I (993^{b}25).
3   PL, 40, 236.

Questions for reflection

1   In the First Way argument, is Aquinas arguing that the universe could not be tempo-rally infinite and so must have a cause? Explain.
2   In the Second Way argument, how does Aquinas argue that efficient causes cannot go on to infinity? How is this argument different from the first?
3   Sketch the Third Way argument. What are its premises? Are they reasonable to believe? Why or why not?
4   There seems to be a common form among the first four ways. What is that form?
5   Which of the Five Ways do you find most persuasive? Why? Does it convince you? Explain.

Further reading

William Lane Craig (2001) *The Cosmological Argument from Plato to Leibniz.* Eugene, OR: Wipf and Stock. (Analyzes the cosmological arguments of thirteen major proponents, including significant Jewish and Islamic thinkers.)

Brian Davies (1992) *The Thought of Thomas Aquinas.* Oxford: Oxford University Press. (A helpful treatment of Aquinas's thought, including the Five Ways.)

Gottfried W. Leibniz ([1714] 1898/1951 reprint) "Monadology," in *The Monadology and Other Philosophical Writings.* Trans. Robert Latta. Oxford: Oxford University Press. (Contains Leibniz's "sufficient reasons" version of the cosmological argument.)

Plato ([c. 360 BC] 1988) *Laws.* Chicago, IL: University of Chicago Press. (Contains one of the earliest versions of the cosmological argument—see specifically Stephanus pagination numbers 893–6.)

William Rowe (1975) *The Cosmological Argument.* Princeton, NJ: Princeton University Press. (A critical study of versions of the cosmological argument.)

Chapter 18

William Lane Craig

THE *KALAM* COSMOLOGICAL ARGUMENT

William Lane Craig is Research Professor of Philosophy at Talbot School of Theology. He is a leading proponent of the *kalam* cosmological argument for the existence of God, which he defends in this selection. Professor Craig formulates the argument in three simple steps: (1) whatever begins to exist has a cause; (2) the universe began to exist; and (3) therefore, the universe has a cause. He examines each of these steps in turn.

Craig spends little time arguing for the first premise—that whatever begins to exist must have a cause—primarily since it is a seemingly obvious truth deeply rooted in human experience. While we may have the ability to imagine something coming into existence out of nothing, he notes that it is highly implausible that this should happen.

In order to defend the second premise of the argument, Craig utilizes arguments and evidences from physics and metaphysics. According to the first argument for this premise, it seems metaphysically impossible for an actually infinite number of things to exist. If the universe never had a beginning, however, there would be an actually infinite number of events in time. Since this is not possible, the universe must have had a beginning. Craig provides a second argument which, unlike the first, does not deny that an actually infinite number of things can exist. Rather, it denies that a collection of an actually infinite number of things can be formed by adding one thing after another. If the universe never had a beginning, however, the series of events in time would be such a collection. Since, he argues, this is metaphysically impossible, the universe must have a finite past and thus must have a beginning. The conclusion of these two arguments is also corroborated by modern physics, including the expansion and thermodynamic properties of the universe.

Further examination of the argument's conclusion—that the universe has a cause—leads Craig to conclude that this cause is an uncaused, personal agent—one who is immaterial, timeless, spaceless, and an enormously powerful creator. This is none other than God.

In my opinion the version of the cosmological argument which is most likely to be a sound and persuasive proof for the existence of God is the *kalam* cosmological argument based on the impossibility of an infinite temporal regress of events.* The argument may be formulated in three simple steps:

1. Whatever begins to exist has a cause.
2. The universe began to exist.
3. Therefore, the universe has a cause.

The point of the argument is to demonstrate the existence of a first cause which transcends and creates the entire realm of finite reality. Having reached that conclusion, one may then inquire into the nature of this first cause and assess its significance for theism.

Whatever begins to exist has a cause

The first premise is rooted in the metaphysical principle that 'something cannot come out of nothing' and is so intuitively obvious that I think scarcely anyone could sincerely believe it to be false. I therefore think it somewhat unwise to argue in favour of it, for any proof of the principle is likely to be less obvious than the principle itself, and, as Aristotle remarked, one ought not to try to prove the obvious via the less obvious. The proposition that 'Out of nothing, nothing comes' seems to me to be a sort of metaphysical first principle whose truth impresses itself upon us. In any case, the first premise, even if taken as a mere inductive generalization, seems as secure as any truth rooted in experience.

It is therefore not a little surprising to find atheists attempting to defeat the argument by attacking the first premise. For example, the late J. L. Mackie turned his main guns on this first premise, writing, 'there is *a priori* no good reason why a sheer origination of things, not determined by anything, should be unacceptable, whereas the existence of a god [*sic*] with the power to create something out of nothing is acceptable.'[1] Indeed, he believed that *creatio ex nihilo* raises problems: (1) if God began to exist at a point in time, then this is as great a puzzle as the beginning of the universe; (2) if God existed for infinite time, then the same arguments would apply to His existence as would apply to the infinite duration of the universe; and (3) if it be said that God is timeless, then this, says Mackie, is a complete mystery.

Now notice that Mackie never denies, much less refutes, the principle that whatever begins to exist has a cause. Rather, he simply demands what good reason there is *a priori* to accept it. He writes, 'As Hume pointed out, we can certainly conceive an uncaused beginning-to-be of an object; if what we can thus conceive is nevertheless in some way impossible, this still requires to be shown.'[2] But, as many philosophers have noted, imaginability is in no way a reliable guide to metaphysical possibility. Just because I can imagine in my mind's eye an object, say a horse, coming into existence from nothing, that in no way suggests that a horse really could come into existence that way. The fact that there is no formal contradiction in 'a horse's popping into being out of nothing' does not defeat the claim of the defender of the *kalam* argument that such a thing is metaphysically impossible. Does anyone in his right mind believe that, say, a raging tiger could suddenly come into existence uncaused, out of nothing, in this room right now? The same applies to the universe: if there were absolutely nothing prior to the existence of the universe—no God, no space, no time—how could the universe possibly have come to exist?

In fact, Mackie's appeal to Hume at this point is counter-productive. For Hume himself clearly believed the causal principle. In 1754 he wrote to John Stewart,

> But allow me to tell you that I never asserted so absurd a Proposition as *that anything might arise without a cause*: I only maintain'd, that our Certainty of the Falsehood of that Proposition proceeded neither from Intuition nor Demonstration, but from another source.[3]

Even Mackie, in response to the claim of atheist scientist Peter Atkins that the universe came into being out of nothing by sheer chance, demurred: 'I myself find it hard to accept the notion of self-creation *from nothing*, even *given* unrestricted chance. And how *can* this be given, if there really is nothing?'[4] Moreover, Mackie concedes, 'Still this [causal] principle has some plausibility, in that it is constantly confirmed in our experience (and also used, reasonably, in interpreting our experience).'[5] So, leaving *a priori* intuitions aside, why not at least accept the truth of the causal principle as plausible and reasonable—at the very least more so than its denial?

The answer is that in this particular case the theism implied by affirming the principle is, in Mackie's thinking, even more unintelligible than the denial of the principle. It makes more sense to believe that the universe came into being uncaused out of nothing than to believe that God created the universe out of nothing.

But is this really the case? Consider the three alternatives Mackie raises concerning *creatio ex nihilo*. Certainly, the proponent of the *kalam* argument would not hold (1) that God began to exist or (2) that God has existed for an infinite number of, say, hours, or any other unit of time. But what is wrong with (3), that God is, without creation, timeless? I would argue that God exists timelessly without creation and temporally since creation. This may be 'mysterious' in the sense of 'wonderful' or 'awe-inspiring,' but it is not, so far as I can see, unintelligible; and Mackie gives us no reason to think that it is. Moreover, there is also an alternative which Mackie failed to consider: (4) prior to creation God existed in an undifferentiated time in which hours, days and so forth simply do not exist. Because this time is undifferentiated, it is not incompatible with the *kalam* argument based on the impossibility of an infinite temporal regress of events. It seems to me, therefore, that Mackie is entirely unjustified in rejecting the first step of the argument as not being intuitively obvious, plausible and reasonable.

The universe began to exist

If we agree that whatever begins to exist has a cause, what evidence is there to support the crucial second premise, that 'the universe began to exist'? This premise may be supported by both deductive and inductive arguments from metaphysics and physics.

1. Argument from the impossibility of an actually infinite number of things

This argument can also be formulated in three steps:

1. An actually infinite number of things cannot exist.
2. A beginningless series of events in time entails an actually infinite number of things.
3. Therefore, a beginningless series of events in time cannot exist.

Since the universe is not distinct from the temporal series of past events, the demonstration that the series of temporal events had a beginning implies that the universe began to exist. Let us examine more closely each of the argument's two premises.

1. *An actually infinite number of things cannot exist.* In order to understand this first premise, we need to differentiate clearly between an actual infinite and a potential infinite. A potential infinite is a collection that is increasing toward infinity as a limit but never gets there. Such a collection is really indefinite, not infinite. For example, any finite distance can be subdivided into potentially infinitely many parts. One can keep on dividing parts in half forever, but one will never arrive at an actual 'infinitieth' division or come up with an actually infinite number of parts. By contrast, an actual infinite is not growing toward infinity; it is infinite, it is 'complete'. A collection is actually infinite just in case a proper part of the collection can be put into a one-to-one correspondence with the whole collection, so that the proper part has the same number of members as the whole (Principle of Correspondence). This notion of infinity is employed in set theory to designate sets that have an infinite number of members, such as $\{1, 2, 3, \ldots\}$. The argument, then, is not that a potentially infinite number of things cannot exist, but that an actually infinite number of things cannot exist. For if an actually infinite number of things could exist, this would spawn all sorts of absurdities.

Perhaps the best way to bring this home is by means of an illustration. Let me use one of my favorites, Hilbert's Hotel, a product of the mind of the great German mathematician David Hilbert.[6] Let us imagine a hotel with a finite number of rooms. Suppose, furthermore, that all the rooms are full. When a new guest arrives asking for a room, the proprietor apologizes, 'Sorry, all the rooms are full,' and the new guest is turned away. But now let us imagine a hotel with an infinite number of rooms and suppose once more that 'all the rooms are full.' There is not a single vacant room throughout the entire infinite hotel. Now suppose a new guest shows up, asking for a room. 'But of course!' says the proprietor, and he immediately shifts the person in room #1 into room #2, the person in room #2 into room #3, the person in room #3 into room #4, and so on, out to infinity. As a result of these room changes, room #1 now becomes vacant and the new guest gratefully checks in. But remember, before he arrived, all the rooms were full! Equally curious, according to the mathematicians, there are now no more persons in the hotel than there were before: the number is just infinite. But how can this be? The proprietor just added the new guest's name to the register and gave him his keys—how can there not be one more person in the hotel than before?

But the situation becomes even stranger. For suppose an infinity of new guests show up at the desk, each asking for a room. 'Of course, of course!' says the proprietor, and he proceeds to shift the person in room #1 into room #2, the person in room #2 into room #4, the person in room #3 into room #6, and so on out to infinity, always putting each former occupant into the room number twice his own. Because any natural number multiplied by two always equals an even number, all the guests wind up in even-numbered rooms. As a result, all the odd-numbered rooms become vacant, and the infinity of new guests is easily accommodated. And yet, before they came, all the rooms were full! And again, strangely enough, the number of guests in the hotel is the same after the infinity of new guests check in as before, even though there were as many new guests as old guests. In fact, the proprietor could repeat this process *infinitely many times*, and yet there would never be one single person more in the hotel than before.

But Hilbert's Hotel is even stranger than the German mathematician made it out to be. For suppose some of the guests start to check out. Suppose the guest in room #1 departs. Is there not now one less person in the hotel? Not according to the mathematicians—but just ask Housekeeping! Suppose the guests in rooms ##1, 3, 5 . . . check out. In this case an infinite number of people have left the hotel, but according to the mathematicians, there are no fewer people in the hotel—but don't talk to those people in Housekeeping! In fact, we could have every other guest check out of the hotel and repeat this process infinitely many times, and yet there would never be any fewer people in the hotel.

Now suppose the proprietor does not like having a half-empty hotel (it looks bad for business). No matter! By shifting occupants as before, but in reverse order, he transforms his half-vacant hotel into one that is jammed to the gills. One might think that by these maneuvers the proprietor could always keep this strange hotel fully occupied. But one would be wrong. For suppose that the persons in rooms ##4, 5, 6 . . . checked out. At a single stroke the hotel would be virtually emptied, the guest register reduced to but three names, and the infinite converted to finitude. And yet it would remain true that the *same* number of guests checked out this time as when the guests in rooms ##1, 3, 5 . . . checked out! Can anyone believe that such a hotel could exist in reality?

Hilbert's Hotel is absurd. Since nothing hangs on the illustration's involving a hotel, the above sorts of absurdities show in general that it is impossible for an actually infinite number of things to exist.[7] There is simply no way to avoid these absurdities once we admit the possibility of the existence of an actual infinite. Students sometimes react to such absurdities as Hilbert's Hotel by saying that we really do not understand the nature of infinity and, hence, these absurdities result. But this attitude is simply mistaken. Infinite set theory is a highly-developed and well-understood branch of mathematics, so that these absurdities can be seen to result precisely because we do understand the notion of a collection with an actually infinite number of members.

These considerations also show how superficial Mackie's response to this premise is.[8] He thinks that the absurdities are resolved by noting that for infinite groups the axiom that 'the whole is greater than its part' does not hold, as it does for finite groups. But far from being the solution, this is precisely the problem. Because in infinite set theory this axiom is denied, one gets all sorts of absurdities, like Hilbert's Hotel, when one tries to translate that theory into reality. Mackie's response does nothing to prove that the envisioned situations are not absurd, but only reiterates, in effect, that if an actual infinite were to exist and the Principle of Correspondence were valid with respect to it, then the relevant situations would result, which is not in dispute. Moreover, the contradictions that result when guests check out of the hotel are not even prima facie resolved by Mackie's analysis. (In trans-finite arithmetic, inverse operations of subtraction and division are prohibited because they lead to contradictions; but in reality, one cannot stop people from checking out of the hotel if they want to!) Hence, it is plausible that an actually infinite number of things cannot exist.[9]

2. *A beginningless series of events in time entails an actually infinite number of things.* This second premise seems pretty obvious. If the universe never began to exist, then prior to the present event there have existed an actually infinite number of previous events. Thus, a beginningless series of events in time entails an actually infinite number of things, namely, events.

3. *Therefore a beginningless series of events in time cannot exist.* If the above two premises are true, then the conclusion follows logically. The series of past events must be finite and have a beginning. Since, as I said, the universe is not distinct from the series of events, the universe therefore began to exist.

2. Argument from the impossibility of forming an actually infinite collection of things by successive addition

This argument is distinct from the foregoing argument, for it does not deny that an actually infinite number of things can exist. It denies that a collection containing an actually infinite number of things can be formed by adding one member after another. This argument, too, can be formulated in three steps:

1. The series of events in time is a collection formed by successive addition.
2. A collection formed by successive addition cannot be actually infinite.
3. Therefore, the series of events in time cannot be actually infinite.

Let us take a closer look at each of the three premises.

1. *The series of events in time is a collection formed by successive addition.* This seems rather obvious. The past did not spring into being whole and entire but was formed sequentially, one event occurring after another. Notice, too, that the direction of this formation is 'forward' in the sense that the collection of events grows with time. Although we sometimes speak of an 'infinite temporal regress' of events, in reality an infinite past would be an 'infinite temporal progress' of events with no beginning and its end in the present.

2. *A collection formed by successive addition cannot be actually infinite.* This is the crucial step. Sometimes this is called the impossibility of counting to infinity or the impossibility of traversing the infinite. This impossibility has nothing to do with the amount of time available: no matter how much time one has at one's disposal, an actual infinite cannot be so formed. For no matter how many numbers one counts or how many steps one takes, one can always add or take one more before arriving at infinity.

Now someone might say that while an infinite collection cannot be formed by beginning at a point and adding members, nevertheless an infinite collection could be formed by never beginning but ending at a point, that is to say, ending at a point after having added one member after another from eternity. But this method seems even more unbelievable than the first method. If one cannot count *to* infinity, how can one count down *from* infinity? If one cannot traverse the infinite by moving in one direction, how can one traverse it by moving in the opposite direction?

Indeed, the idea of a beginningless temporal series of events ending in the present seems absurd. To give just one illustration: consider Tristram Shandy, who, in the novel by Sterne, writes his autobiography so slowly that it takes him a whole year to record the events of a single day. According to Bertrand Russell, if Tristram Shandy were immortal, then the entire book could be completed, since by the Principle of Correspondence to each day there would correspond one year, and both are infinite.[10] Russell's assertion is wholly untenable, however, since the future is in reality a potential infinite only. Though he write for ever, Tristram Shandy would only get farther and farther behind, so that instead of finishing his autobiography he would progressively approach a state in which he would be infinitely far behind. But he would never reach such a state because the years and, hence, the days of his life would always be finite in number, though indefinitely increasing.

But let us turn the story about: suppose Tristram Shandy has been writing from eternity past at the rate of one day per year. Should not Tristram Shandy now be infinitely far behind? For if he has lived for an infinite number of years, Tristram Shandy has recorded an equally infinite number of past days. Given the thoroughness of his autobiography, these days are all consecutive days. At any point in the past or present, therefore, Tristram Shandy has recorded a beginningless, infinite series of consecutive days. But now the question inevitably arises: Which days are these? Where in the temporal series of events are the days recorded by Tristram Shandy at any given point? The answer can only be that *they are days infinitely distant from the present*. For there is no day on which Tristram Shandy is writing which is finitely distant from the last recorded day. This may be seen through an incisive analysis of the Tristram Shandy paradox given by Robin Small.[11] He points out that if Tristram Shandy has been writing for one year's time, then the most recent day he could have recorded is one year ago. But if he has been writing two years, then that same day could not have been recorded by him. For since his intention is to record consecutive days of his life, the most recent day he could have recorded is the day immediately after a day at least two years ago. This is because it takes a year to record a day, so that to record two days he must have two years. Similarly, if he has been writing three years, then the most recent day recorded could be no more recent than three years and two days ago. In other words, the longer he has written the further behind he has fallen. In fact, the recession into the past of the most recent recordable day can be plotted according to the formula (present date − n years of writing) + n − 1 days. But what happens if Tristram Shandy has, *ex hypothesi*, been writing for an infinite number of years? The most recent day of his autobiography recedes to infinity, that is to say, to a day infinitely distant from the present. Nowhere in the past at a finite distance from the present can we find a recorded day, for by now Tristram Shandy is infinitely far behind. The beginningless, infinite series of days which he has recorded are days which lie at an infinite temporal distance from the present. But there is no way to traverse the temporal interval from an infinitely distant event to the present, or, more technically, for an event which was once present to recede to an infinite temporal distance. Since the task of writing one's autobiography at the rate of one year per day seems obviously coherent, what follows from the Tristram Shandy story is that an infinite series of past events is absurd.

But now a deeper absurdity bursts into view. For even if every recorded past event lies at only a finite distance from the present, still, if the series of past events is actually infinite, we may ask, why did Tristram Shandy not finish his autobiography yesterday or the day before, since by then an infinite series of events had already elapsed? No matter how far along the series of past events one regresses, Tristram Shandy would have already completed his autobiography. Therefore, at no point in the infinite series of past events could he be finishing the book. We could never look over Tristram Shandy's shoulder to see if he were now writing the last page. For at any point an actually infinite sequence of events would have transpired and the book would have already been completed. Thus, at no time in eternity will we find Tristram Shandy writing, which is absurd, since we supposed him to be writing from eternity. And at no point will he finish the book, which is equally absurd, because for the book to be completed he must at some point have finished.

These illustrations reveal the absurdities involved in trying to form an actually infinite collection of things by successive addition. Hence, set theory has been purged of all temporal concepts; as Russell says, 'classes which are infinite are given all at once by the defining properties of their members, so that there is no question of "completion" or of "successive synthesis".'[12] The only way an actual infinite could come to exist in the real world would be by being created all at once, simply in a moment. It would be a hopeless undertaking to try to form it by adding one member after another.

Mackie's objections to this premise are off the target.[13] He thinks that the argument illicitly assumes an infinitely distant starting point in the past and then pronounces it impossible to travel from that point to today. If we take the notion of infinity 'seriously,' he says, we must say that in the infinite past there would be no starting point whatever, not even an infinitely distant one. Yet from any given point in the past, there is only a finite distance to the present.

Now I know of no proponent of the *kalam* argument who assumed that there was an infinitely distant starting point in the past. On the contrary, the beginningless character of the series of past events only serves to underscore the difficulty of its formation by successive addition. The fact that there is no beginning at all, not even an infinitely distant one, makes the problem worse, not better. It is thus not the proponent of the *kalam* argument who fails to take infinity seriously. To say the infinite past could have been formed by adding one member after another is like saying someone has just succeeded in writing down all the negative numbers, ending at −1. And, we may ask, how is Mackie's point that from any given moment in the past there is only a finite distance to the present even relevant to the issue? The defender of the *kalam* argument could agree to this without batting an eye. For the issue is how the whole series can be formed, not a finite portion of it. Does Mackie think that because every finite segment of the series can be formed by successive addition, the whole infinite series can be so formed? That is as logically fallacious as saying that because every part of an elephant is light in weight, the whole elephant is light in weight. Mackie's point is therefore irrelevant. It seems that this premise of the argument remains undefeated by his objections.

3. *Therefore, the series of events in time cannot be actually infinite.* Given the truth of the premises, the conclusion logically follows. If the universe did not begin to exist a finite

time ago, then the present moment would never arrive. But obviously it has arrived. Therefore, we know that the universe is finite in the past and began to exist.

3. *Argument based on the isotropic expansion of the universe*

In 1917, Albert Einstein made a cosmological application of his newly discovered gravitational theory, the General Theory of Relativity (GTR). In so doing he assumed that the universe is homogeneous and isotropic and that it exists in a steady state, with a constant mean mass density and a constant curvature of space. To his chagrin, however, he found that GTR would not permit such a model of the universe unless he introduced into his gravitational field equations a certain 'fudge factor' in order to counterbalance the gravitational effect of matter and so ensure a static universe. Unfortunately, Einstein's static universe was balanced on a razor's edge, and the least perturbation would cause the universe either to implode or to expand. By taking this feature of Einstein's model seriously, the Russian mathematician Alexander Friedman and the Belgian astronomer Georges Lemaître were able to formulate independently in the 1920s solutions to the field equations which predicted an expanding universe.

The monumental significance of the Friedman-Lemaître model lay in its historization of the universe. As one commentator has remarked, up to this time the idea of the expansion of the universe 'was absolutely beyond comprehension. Throughout all of human history the universe was regarded as fixed and immutable and the idea that it might actually be changing was inconceivable.'[14] But if the Friedman-Lemaître model were correct, the universe could no longer be adequately treated as a static entity existing, in effect, timelessly. Rather the universe has a history, and time will not be a matter of indifference for our investigation of the cosmos.

In 1929 the astronomer Edwin Hubble showed that the red shift in the optical spectra of light from distant galaxies was a common feature of all measured galaxies and was proportional to their distance from us. This red shift was taken to be a Doppler effect indicative of the recessional motion of the light source in the line of sight. Incredibly, what Hubble had discovered was the isotropic expansion of the universe predicted by Friedman and Lemaître on the basis of Einstein's GTR. It was a veritable turning point in the history of science. 'Of all the great predictions that science has ever made over the centuries,' exclaims John Wheeler, 'was there ever one greater than this, to predict, and predict correctly, and predict against all expectation a phenomenon so fantastic as the expansion of the universe?'[15]

According to the Friedman-Lemaître model, as time proceeds, the distances separating galactic masses become greater. It is important to understand that as a GTR-based theory, the model does not describe the expansion of the material content of the universe into a pre-existing, empty space, but rather the expansion of space itself. The ideal particles of the cosmological fluid constituted by the matter and energy of the universe are conceived to be at rest with respect to space but to recede progressively from one another as space itself expands or stretches, just as buttons glued to the surface of a balloon would recede from one another as the balloon inflates. As the universe expands, it becomes less and less dense. This has the astonishing implication that as one reverses the expansion and extrapolates back in time, the universe becomes progressively denser until one arrives at a state of infinite density at some point in the finite past.[16] This state represents a singularity at which space-time curvature, along with temperature, pressure, and density, becomes infinite. It therefore constitutes an edge or boundary to space-time itself. P. C. W. Davies comments,

> If we extrapolate this prediction to its extreme, we reach a point when all distances in the universe have shrunk to zero. An initial cosmological singularity therefore forms a past temporal extremity to the universe. We cannot continue physical reasoning, or even the concept of spacetime, through such an extremity. For this reason most cosmologists think of the initial singularity as the beginning of the universe. On this view the Big Bang represents the creation event; the creation not only of all the matter and energy in the universe, but also of spacetime itself.[17]

The term 'Big Bang,' originally a derisive expression coined by Fred Hoyle to characterize the beginning of the universe predicted by the Friedman-Lemaître model, is thus potentially misleading, since the expansion cannot be visualized from the outside (there being no 'outside,' just as there is no 'before' with respect to the Big Bang).

The standard Big Bang model, as the Friedman-Lemaître model came to be called, thus describes a universe which is not eternal in the past, but which came into being a finite time ago. Moreover—and this deserves underscoring—the origin it posits is an absolute origin out of nothing. For not only all matter and energy, but space and time themselves come into being at the initial cosmological singularity. As Barrow and Tipler emphasize, 'At this singularity, space and time came into existence; literally nothing existed before the singularity, so, if the Universe originated at such a singularity, we would truly have a creation *ex nihilo*.'[18] On such a model the universe originates *ex nihilo* in the sense that at the initial singularity it is true that 'There is no earlier space-time point' or it is false that 'Something existed prior to the singularity.'

Now such a conclusion is profoundly disturbing for anyone who ponders it. For, in the words of one astrophysical team, 'The problem of the origin [of the universe] involves a certain metaphysical aspect which may be either appealing or revolting.'[19] Revolted by the stark metaphysical alternatives presented to us by an absolute beginning of the universe, certain theorists have been understandably eager to subvert the Standard Model and restore an eternal universe. The history of twentieth-century cosmology has been the history of the repeated falsification of such non-standard theories and the corroboration of the Big Bang theory. It has been the overwhelming verdict of the scientific community that none of these alternative theories is superior to the Big Bang theory. Again and again models aimed at averting the prediction of the Standard Model of an absolute beginning of the universe have been shown either to be untenable or to fail to avert the beginning after all. For example, some theories, like the Oscillating Universe (which expands and re-contracts forever) or the Chaotic Inflationary Universe (which continually spawns new universes), do have a potentially infinite future but turn out to have only a finite past.[20] Vacuum Fluctuation Universe theories (which postulate an eternal vacuum out of which our universe is born) cannot explain why, if the vacuum was eternal, we do not observe an infinitely old universe.[21] The Quantum Gravity Universe theory propounded by James Hartle and Stephen Hawking, if interpreted realistically, still involves an absolute origin of the universe even if the universe does not begin in a so-called singularity, as it does in the Standard Big Bang theory.[22]

Hawking sums up the situation: 'Almost everyone now believes that the universe, and time itself, had a beginning at the Big Bang.'[23]

4. *Argument based on thermodynamic properties of the universe*

If this were not enough, there is a second inductive argument for the beginning of the universe based on the evidence of thermodynamics. According to the Second Law of Thermodynamics, processes taking place in a closed system always tend toward a state of equilibrium. For example, if we had a bottle containing a sealed vacuum, and we introduced into it some molecules of gas, the gas would spread itself out evenly throughout the bottle. It would be virtually impossible for the molecules to retreat, for example, into one corner of the bottle and remain. This is why, when we walk into a room, the air in the room never separates suddenly into oxygen at one end and nitrogen at the other. It is also why, when we step into the bath, we may be confident that it will be an even temperature instead of frozen solid at one end and boiling at the other. It is clear that life would not be possible in a world in which the Second Law of Thermodynamics did not operate.

Now our interest in the law is what happens when it is applied to the universe as a whole. The universe is, on a naturalistic view, a gigantic closed system, since it is everything there is and there is nothing outside it. What this seems to imply then is that, given enough time, the universe and all its processes will run down, and the entire universe will come to equilibrium. This is known as the heat death of the universe. Once the universe reaches this state, no further change is possible. The universe is dead.

There are two possible types of heat death for the universe. If the universe will eventually re-contract, it will die a 'hot' death. Beatrice Tinsley describes such a state:

> If the average density of matter in the universe is great enough, the mutual gravitational attraction between bodies will eventually slow the expansion to a halt. The universe will then contract and collapse into a hot fireball. There is no known physical mechanism that could reverse a catastrophic big crunch. Apparently, if the universe becomes dense enough, it is in for a hot death.[24]

If the universe is fated to re-contraction, then as it contracts the stars gain energy, causing them to burn more rapidly so that they finally explode or evaporate. As everything in the universe grows closer together, the black holes begin to gobble up everything around them, and eventually begin themselves to coalesce. In time, 'All the black holes finally coalesce into one large black hole that is coextensive with the universe,'[25] from which the universe will never re-emerge.

But suppose, as is more likely, that the universe will expand forever. Tinsley describes the fate of this universe:

> If the universe has a low density, its death will be cold. It will expand forever at a slower and slower rate. Galaxies will turn all of their gas into stars, and the stars will burn out. Our own sun will become a cold, dead remnant, floating among the corpses of other stars in an increasingly isolated Milky Way.[26]

At 10^{30} years the universe will consist of 90 percent dead stars, 9 percent supermassive black holes formed by the collapse of galaxies, and 1 percent atomic matter, mainly hydrogen. Elementary particle physics suggests that thereafter protons will decay into electrons and positrons, so that space will be filled with a rarefied gas so thin that the distance between an electron and a positron will be about the size of the present galaxy. At 10^{100} years, some scientists believe that the black holes themselves will dissipate by a strange effect predicted by quantum mechanics. The mass and energy associated with a black hole so warp space that they are said to create a 'tunnel' or 'worm-hole' through which the mass and energy are ejected in another region of space. As the mass of a black hole decreases, its energy loss accelerates, so that it is eventually dissipated into radiation and elementary particles. Eventually all black holes will completely evaporate and all the matter in the ever expanding universe will be reduced to a thin gas of elementary particles and radiation. The entire universe will be in its final state, from which no change will occur.

Very recent discoveries provide strong evidence that there is effectually a positive cosmological constant which causes the cosmic expansion to accelerate rather than decelerate. Paradoxically, since the volume of space increases exponentially, allowing greater room for more entropy production, the universe actually grows further and further from an equilibrium state as time proceeds. But the acceleration only hastens the cosmos's disintegration into increasingly isolated patches no longer causally connected with similarly marooned remnants of the expanding universe. Thus, the same pointed question raised by classical physics persists: why, if the universe has existed forever, are we not now in a cold, dark, dilute, and lifeless state?

Some theorists have tried to escape this conclusion by adopting an oscillating model of the universe which never reaches a final state of equilibrium. But wholly apart from the physical and observational difficulties confronting such a model, the thermodynamic properties of this model imply the very beginning of the universe that its proponents sought to avoid. For entropy increases from cycle to cycle in such a model, which has the effect of generating larger and longer oscillations with each successive cycle. As one scientific team explains,

> The effect of entropy production will be to enlarge the cosmic scale, from cycle to cycle . . . Thus, looking back in time, each cycle generated less entropy, had a smaller cycle time, and had a smaller cycle expansion factor than the cycle that followed it.[27]

Thus, as one traces the oscillations back in time, they become progressively smaller until one reaches a first and smallest oscillation. Zeldovich and Novikov therefore conclude, 'The multicycle model has an infinite future, but only a finite past.'[28] In fact, astronomer Joseph Silk estimates on the basis of current entropy levels that the universe cannot have gone through more than 100 previous oscillations.[29]

. . .

So whether one adopts a re-contracting model, an ever-expanding model, or an oscillating model, thermodynamics implies that the universe had a beginning. According to P. C. W. Davies, the universe must have been created a finite time ago and is in the process of winding down. Prior to the creation, says Davies, the universe simply did not exist. Therefore, he concludes, even though we may not like it, we must say that the universe's energy was somehow simply 'put in' at the creation as an initial condition.[30]

So we have two inductive arguments that the universe began to exist. First, the expansion of the universe implies that the universe had a beginning. Second, thermodynamics shows the universe began to exist. Therefore, on the basis of both philosophical argument and scientific evidence, I think we are justified in accepting our second premise, that the universe began to exist.

The universe has a cause

From the first premise—that 'whatever begins to exist has a cause'—and the second premise—that 'the universe began to exist'—it follows logically that 'the universe has a cause.' This conclusion ought to stagger us, to fill us with awe, for it means that the universe was brought into existence by something which is greater than and beyond it.

But what is the nature of this first cause of the universe? A conceptual analysis of what properties must be possessed by such an ultra-mundane cause enables us to recover a striking number of the traditional divine attributes. An analysis of what it is to be cause of the universe reveals that:

4. If the universe has a cause, then an uncaused, personal Creator of the universe exists, who *sans* the universe is beginningless, changeless, immaterial, timeless, spaceless, and enormously powerful.

From (3) and (4), it follows that

5. Therefore, an uncaused, personal Creator of the universe exists, who *sans* the universe is beginningless, changeless, immaterial, timeless, spaceless, and enormously powerful.

As the cause of space and time, this entity must transcend space and time and therefore exist atemporally and non-spatially, at least *sans* the universe. This transcendent cause must therefore be changeless and immaterial, since timelessness entails changelessness, and changelessness implies immateriality. Such a cause must be beginningless and uncaused, at least in the sense of lacking any antecedent causal conditions. Ockham's Razor will shave away further causes, since we should not multiply causes beyond necessity. This entity must be unimaginably powerful, since it created the universe out of nothing.

Finally, and most strikingly, such a transcendent cause is plausibly to be regarded as personal. As Swinburne points out, there are two types of causal explanation: scientific explanations in terms of laws and initial conditions and personal explanations in terms of agents and their volitions.[31] A first state of the universe cannot have a scientific explanation, since there is nothing before it, and therefore it can be accounted for only in terms of a personal explanation. Moreover, the personhood of the cause of the universe is implied by its timelessness and immateriality, since the only entities we know of which can possess such properties are either minds or abstract objects, and abstract objects do not stand in causal relations. Therefore the transcendent cause of the origin of the universe must be of the order of mind. This same conclusion is also implied by the origin of a temporal effect from a timeless cause. For if the cause of the universe were an impersonal set of necessary and sufficient conditions, it could not exist without its effect. The only way for the cause to be timeless and changeless but for its effect to originate *de novo* a finite time ago is for the cause to be a personal agent who freely chooses to bring about an effect without antecedent determining conditions. This type of causation is called 'agent causation,' and because the agent is free he can initiate new effects by freely bringing about conditions which were not previously present. A finite time ago a Creator endowed with free will could have acted to bring the world into being at that moment. In this way, God could exist changelessly and eternally but choose to create the world in time. By 'choose' one need not mean that the Creator changes His mind about the decision to create, but that He freely and eternally intends to create a world with a beginning. By exercising His causal power, He brings it about that a world with a beginning comes to exist. So the cause is eternal, but the effect is not. In this way, then, it is possible for the temporal universe to have come to exist from an eternal cause, through the free will of a personal Creator. Thus, we are brought, not merely to a transcendent cause of the universe, but to its personal Creator.

These purely philosophical arguments for the personhood of the cause of the origin of the universe receive powerful scientific confirmation from the observed fine-tuning of the universe, which bespeaks intelligent design. Without wanting to go into a discussion of the teleological argument, let me simply say that the incredibly complex and delicately balanced nexus of initial conditions necessary for intelligent life seems to be most plausibly explained if that nexus is the product of intelligent design, that is to say, if the cause of the beginning of the universe is a personal Creator. The scientific evidence thus serves to underscore the conclusion to which philosophical argument has led us. So we have both good philosophical and scientific reasons for regarding the cause of the universe as an uncaused, beginningless, timeless, spaceless, immaterial, changeless, powerful, personal Creator.

Now certain thinkers have objected to the intelligibility of this conclusion. For example, Adolf Grünbaum has marshalled a whole troop of objections against inferring a Creator of the universe.[32] As these are very typical, a brief review of his objections should be quite helpful. Grünbaum's objections fall into three groups. Group I seeks to cast doubt upon the concept of 'cause' in the argument for a cause of the universe.

1. When we say that everything has a cause, we use the word 'cause' to mean something that transforms previously existing materials from one state to another. But when we infer that the universe has a cause, we must mean by 'cause' something that creates its effect out of nothing. Since these two meanings of 'cause' are not the same, the argument is guilty of equivocation and is thus invalid.
2. It does not follow from the necessity of there being a cause that the cause of the universe is a conscious agent.
3. It is logically fallacious to infer that there is a single conscious agent who created the universe.

But these objections do not seem to present any insuperable difficulties:

1   The univocal concept of 'cause' employed throughout the argument is the concept of something which brings about or produces its effects. Whether this production involves transformation of already existing materials or creation out of nothing is an incidental question. Thus, the charge of equivocation is groundless.

2   The personhood of the cause does not follow from the cosmological argument proper, but from an analysis of the notion of a first cause of the beginning of the universe, confirmed by Anthropic considerations.

3   The inference to a single cause of the origin of the universe seems justified in the light of the principle, commonly accepted in science, that one should not multiply causes beyond necessity. One is justified in inferring only causes such as are necessary to explain the effect in question; positing any more would be gratuitous. Since the universe is a single effect originating in the Big Bang event, we have no grounds for inferring a plurality of causes.

The objections of Group II relate the notion of causality to the temporal series of events:

1   Causality is logically compatible with an infinite, beginningless series of events.

2   If everything has a cause of its existence, then the cause of the universe must also have a cause of its existence.

Both of these objections, however, seem to be based on misunderstandings.

1   It is not the concept of causality which is incompatible with an infinite series of past events. Rather the incompatibility, as we have seen, is between the notion of an actually infinite number of things and the series of past events. That causality has nothing to do with it may be seen by reflecting on the fact that the philosophical arguments for the beginning of the universe would work even if the events were all spontaneous, causally non-connected events.

2   The argument does not presuppose that everything has a cause. Rather the operative causal principle is that 'whatever begins to exist has a cause.' Something that exists eternally and, hence, without a beginning would not need to have a cause. This is not special pleading for God, since the atheist has always maintained the same thing about the universe: it is beginningless and uncaused. The difference between these two hypotheses is that the atheistic view has been shown to be untenable.

Group III objections are aimed at the alleged claim that creation from nothing surpasses all understanding:

1   If creation out of nothing is incomprehensible, then it is irrational to believe in such a doctrine.

2   An incomprehensible doctrine cannot explain anything.

But these objections are also unsuccessful:

1   Creation from nothing is not incomprehensible in Grünbaum's sense. By 'incomprehensible' Grünbaum appears to mean 'unintelligible' or 'meaningless'. But the statement that a finite time ago a transcendent cause brought the universe into being out of nothing is clearly a meaningful statement, not mere gibberish, as is evident from the very fact that we are debating it. We may not understand how the cause brought the universe into being out of nothing, but then it is even more incomprehensible, in this sense, how the universe could have popped into being out of nothing without any cause, material or productive. One cannot avert the necessity of cause by positing an absurdity.

2   The doctrine, being an intelligible statement, obviously does constitute a purported explanation of the origin of the universe. It may be a personal rather than a scientific explanation, but it is no less an explanation for that.

Grünbaum has one final objection against inferring a cause of the origin of the universe: the cause of the Big Bang can be neither after the Big Bang (since backward causation is impossible) nor before the Big Bang (since time begins at or after the Big Bang).[33] Therefore, the universe's beginning to exist cannot have a cause. But this argument pretty clearly confronts us with a false dilemma. For why could God's creating the universe not be simultaneous (or coincident) with the Big Bang? On the view I've defended, God may be conceived to be timeless or relatively timeless without creation and in time at and subsequent to the first moment of creation. None of Grünbaum's objections, therefore, seems to undermine the credibility of the *kalam* cosmological argument for a personal Creator of the universe.

Thus, we have been brought to the remarkable conclusion that an uncaused, personal Creator of the universe exists, who *sans* the universe is beginningless, changeless, immaterial, timeless, spaceless and enormously powerful. And this, as Thomas Aquinas laconically remarked, is what everyone means by 'God.'[34]

Notes

*   [This version of the essay has been slightly modified by William Lane Craig.]

1   J. L. Mackie, *The Miracle of Theism* (Oxford: Clarendon Press, 1982), p. 94.

2   Mackie, *Theism*, p. 89.

3   David Hume, *The Letters of David Hume*, 2 vols, ed. J. Y. T. Greig (Oxford: Clarendon Press, 1932), 1:187.

4   J. L. Mackie, critical notice of *The Creation*, by Peter Atkins, *Times Literary Supplement* (5 February 1982), p. 126.

5   Mackie, *Theism*, p. 89.

6   The story of Hilbert's Hotel is related in George Gamow, *One, Two, Three, Infinity* (London: Macmillan, 1946), p. 17.

7   What is the logical structure of the argument here? The proponent of the argument has two options open to him. On the one hand, he could argue that if an actual infinite were to exist, then the Principle of Correspondence would be valid with respect to it and that if an actual infinite were to exist and the Principle of Correspondence were to be valid with respect to it, then the various counter-intuitive situations would result. Therefore, if an actual infinite were to exist, the various counter-intuitive situations would result. ($A \rightarrow B$;

A & B → C; ∴ A → C). But because these are absurd and so really impossible, it follows that the existence of an actual infinite is impossible (¬◊C; ∴ ¬◊A).

On the other hand, the proponent of the argument might call into question the premise that if an actual infinite were to exist, then the Principle of Correspondence would be valid with respect to it. There is no reason to think that the principle is universally valid. It is merely a convention adopted in infinite set theory. Now, necessarily, if an actual infinite were to exist, then either the Principle of Correspondence or Euclid's maxim that 'The whole is greater than its part' would apply to it. ([A → B ∨ C]). But since the application of either of these two principles to an actual infinite results in counter-intuitive absurdities, it is plausible that if the existence of an actual infinite were possible, then if an actual infinite were to exist, neither of these two principles would be valid with respect to it. (◊A →¬[A → B ∨ C]). It therefore follows that the existence of an actual infinite is impossible, since the counterfactual that 'If an actual infinite were to exist, then neither principle would be valid with respect to it' is necessarily false (∴ ¬◊A).

8   Mackie, *Theism*, p. 93.

9   Students frequently ask if God, therefore, cannot be infinite. The question is based on a misunderstanding. When we speak of the infinity of God, we are not using the word in a mathematical sense to refer to an aggregate of an infinite number of finite parts. God's infinity is, as it were, qualitative, not quantitative. It means that God is metaphysically necessary, morally perfect, omnipotent, omniscient, eternal, etc.

10   Bertrand Russell, *The Principles of Mathematics*, 2nd edn (London: Allen & Unwin, 1937), pp. 358–9.

11   Robin Small, 'Tristram Shandy's Last Page,' *British Journal for the Philosophy of Science*, 37 (1986), pp. 214–15.

12   Bertrand Russell, *Our Knowledge of the External World*, 2nd edn (New York: W. W. Norton, 1929), p. 170.

13   Mackie, *Theism*, p. 93.

14   Gregory L. Naber, *Spacetime and Singularities: An Introduction* (Cambridge: Cambridge University Press, 1988), pp. 126–7.

15   John A. Wheeler, 'Beyond the Hole,' in *Some Strangeness in the Proportion*, ed. Harry Woolf (Reading, MA: Addison-Wesley, 1980), p. 354.

16   This is not to say that the density measurement takes on the value of a trans-finite cardinal number. Rather, the density is the mass divided by volume, and, since division by zero is impossible, the density of the universe at the initial cosmological singularity is said to be 'infinite' in this sense.

17   P. C. W. Davies, 'Spacetime Singularities in Cosmology,' in J. T. Fraser (ed.), *The Study of Time III* (New York: Springer Verlag, 1978), pp. 78–9.

18   John Barrow and Frank Tipler, *The Anthropic Cosmological Principle* (Oxford: Clarendon Press, 1986), p. 442.

19   Hubert Reeves, Jean Audouze, William A. Fowler and David N. Schramm, 'On the Origin of Light Elements,' *Astrophysical Journal*, 179 (1973), p. 912.

20   See I. D. Novikov and Ya. B. Zeldovich, 'Physical Processes near Cosmological Singularities', *Annual Review of Astronomy and Astrophysics*, 11 (1973), pp. 401–2; A. Borde and A. Vilenkin, 'Eternal Inflation and the Initial Singularity', *Physical Review Letters*, 72 (1994), pp. 3305, 3307.

21   Christopher Isham, 'Creation of the Universe as a Quantum Process' in R. J. Russell, W. R. Stoeger and G. V. Coyne (eds), *Physics, Philosophy and Theology: A Common Quest for Understanding* (Vatican City: Vatican Observatory, 1988), pp. 385–7.

22   See John D. Barrow, *Theories of Everything* (Oxford: Clarendon Press, 1991), pp. 67–8.

23   Stephen Hawking and Roger Penrose, *The Nature of Space and Time*, The Isaac Newton Institute Series of Lectures (Princeton, NJ: Princeton University Press, 1996), p. 20.

24   Beatrice Tinsley, 'From Big Bang to Eternity?' *Natural History Magazine* (October 1975), p. 103.
25   Duane Dicus et al., 'The Future of the Universe', *Scientific American* (March 1983), p. 99.
26   Tinsley, 'Big Bang', p. 105.
27   Duane Dicus et al., 'Effects of Proton Decay on the Cosmological Future', *Astrophysical Journal*, 252 (1982), pp. 1, 8.
28   Novikov and Zeldovich, 'Physical Processes near Cosmological Singularities,' pp. 401–2.
29   Joseph Silk, *The Big Bang*, 2nd edn (San Francisco: W. H. Freeman, 1989), pp. 311–12.
30   P. C. W. Davies, *The Physics of Time Asymmetry* (London: Surrey University Press, 1974), p. 104.
31   Richard Swinburne, *The Existence of God*, rev. edn (Oxford: Clarendon Press, 1991), pp. 32–48.
32   Adolf Grünbaum, 'The Pseudo-Problem of Creation in Physical Cosmology', in John Leslie (ed.), *Physical Cosmology and Philosophy*, Philosophical Topics (New York: Macmillan, 1990), pp. 92–112.
33   Adolf Grünbaum, 'Pseudo-Creation of the Big Bang', *Nature*, 344 (1990), p. 85.
34   Thomas Aquinas, *Summa Theologiae* 1a. 2.3.

Questions for reflection

1   Do you believe it is rational to hold the view that something could begin to exist without a cause? Explain.
2   Professor Craig uses two philosophical arguments to argue for the premise that the universe began to exist. Do you find either of them persuasive? Why or why not?
3   Is Craig being inconsistent in utilizing an argument against belief in the existence of an actual infinite to demonstrate God's existence? Isn't God infinite?
4   Why does Craig believe that the conclusion of the *kalam* argument leads one to a personal God rather than, say, an impersonal cause? Explain.
5   Explain why Craig claims that Hilbert's Hotel is metaphysically absurd, and how this absurdity supports his argument for the universe having a beginning. Do you agree with his conclusion? Why or why not?

Further reading

William Lane Craig (2000) *The Kalam Cosmological Argument*. Eugene, OR: Wipf and Stock. (A historical overview and defense of the *kalam* argument.)

William Lane Craig (2001) *The Cosmological Argument from Plato to Leibniz*. Eugene, OR: Wipf and Stock. (Analyzes the cosmological arguments of thirteen major proponents.)

William Lane Craig and Quentin Smith (1993) *Theism, Atheism, and Big Bang Cosmology*. Oxford: Clarendon Press. (A sustained debate on whether Big Bang cosmology supports theism or atheism.)

Nicholas Everitt (2004) *The Non-Existence of God*. London: Routledge. (Critically assesses traditional and recent arguments about God's existence.)

Leadership University. http://www.leaderu.com. (A website dedicated to theology and the integration of faith and learning; contains many academic papers on arguments for the existence of God.)

J. L. Mackie (1982) *The Miracle of Theism: Arguments for and against the Existence of God*. Oxford: Clarendon Press. (Atheist philosopher Mackie examines many of the arguments about God's existence; a contemporary classic.)

Chapter 19

J. L. Mackie

A CRITIQUE OF COSMOLOGICAL ARGUMENTS

J. L. Mackie (1917–81) was Reader in Philosophy at Oxford University and Fellow of University College, Oxford. He was one of the leading atheist philosophers of the twentieth century. In this selection, he criticizes various forms of the cosmological argument. First, he examines an argument commonly referred to as the "argument from sufficient reason," propounded by philosopher Gottfried Wilhelm Leibniz. The argument is based on the principle of sufficient reason in which nothing contingent occurs without a reason or explanation for why it occurs rather than not. Mackie focuses on two criticisms of the argument which are summed up in the following questions: "How do we know that everything must have a sufficient reason?" and "How can there be a necessary being, one that contains its own sufficient reason?" Unable to find sound answers for these questions, he rejects this form of the cosmological argument.

Mackie next examines arguments in which the claim is made that there cannot be an indefinite regress of causes—they must terminate in a first, uncaused cause (i.e., God). He notes especially Thomas Aquinas's Third Way argument and maintains that it includes the implicit assumption that anything whose essence does not involve existence must depend for its existence on something else; only God's essence involves existence, so everything owes its existence to him. Mackie sees no reason for accepting this assumption; it could just be that some kind of matter exists which does not depend on something else, even if its essence does not involve its existence.

The third form of the cosmological argument Mackie considers is the *kalam* cosmological argument, whose most ardent defender in recent decades is William Lane Craig. According to this argument, the universe (i.e., time, space, matter, and energy) must have a cause outside of itself; namely, a divine cause. One significant aspect of this argument is that the universe must have a cause since its history could not extend back into the infinite past. Mackie responds by claiming that it seems impossible to disprove, a priori, the possibility of an infinite past time. Furthermore, if time has a beginning, and God created it, then he must exist outside of it. This is sheer mystery, he argues, and neither a priori reasoning nor scientific evidence can provide a solution to it.

. . . [T]he cosmological argument, which is *par excellence* the philosophers' argument for theism . . . has been presented in many forms, but in one version or another it has been used by Greek, Arabic, Jewish, and Christian philosophers and theologians, including Plato, Aristotle, al Farabi, al Ghazali, Ibn Rushd (Averroes), Maimonides, Aquinas, Spinoza, and Leibniz.[2] What is common to the many versions of this argument is that they start from the very fact that there is a world or from such general features of it as change or motion or causation—not, like the argument from consciousness or the argument for design, from specific details of what the world includes or how it is ordered—and argue to God as the uncaused cause of the world or of those general features, or as its creator, or as the reason for its existence. I cannot examine all the variants of this argument that have been advanced, but I shall discuss three intendedly demonstrative approaches. . . . And although arguments to a first cause or a creator are more immediately attractive, and appeared earlier in history, than those which argue from the contingency of the world to a necessary being, the latter are in some respects simpler and perhaps more fundamental, so I shall begin with one of these.

Contingency and sufficient reason

Leibniz gives what is essentially the same proof in slightly different forms in different works; we can sum up his line of thought as follows.[3] He assumes the *principle of sufficient reason*, that nothing occurs without a sufficient reason why it is so and not otherwise. There must, then, be a sufficient reason for the world as a whole, a reason why something exists rather than nothing. Each thing in the world is contingent, being causally determined by other things: it would not occur if other things were otherwise. The world as a whole, being a collection of such things, is therefore itself contingent. The series of things and events, with their causes, with causes of those causes, and so on, may stretch back infinitely in time; but, if so, then however far back we go, or if we consider the series as a whole, what we have is still contingent and therefore requires a sufficient reason outside this series. That is, there must be a sufficient reason *for* the world which is *other than* the world. This will have to be a necessary being, which contains its own sufficient reason for existence. Briefly, things must have a sufficient reason for their existence, and this must be found ultimately in a necessary being. There must be something free from the disease of contingency, a disease which affects everything in the world and the world as a whole, even if it is infinite in past time.

This argument, however, is open to criticisms of two sorts, summed up in the questions 'How do we know that everything must have a sufficient reason?' and 'How can there be a necessary being, one that contains its own sufficient reason?' These challenges are related: if the second question cannot be answered satisfactorily, it will follow that things as a whole cannot have a sufficient reason, not merely that we do not know that they must have one.

Kant's criticism of the Leibnizian argument turns upon this second objection; he claims that the cosmological proof depends upon the already criticized ontological proof.[4] The latter starts from the concept of an absolutely necessary being, an *ens realissimum*, something whose essence includes existence, and tries to derive from that concept itself alone the fact that there is such a being. The cosmological proof 'retains the connection of absolute necessity with the highest reality, but instead of reasoning . . .

from the highest reality to necessity of existence, it reasons from the previously given unconditioned necessity of some being to the unlimited reality of that being'. However, Kant's claim that the cosmological proof 'rests' or 'depends' on the ontological one, that 'the so-called cosmological proof really owes any cogency which it may have to the ontological proof from mere concepts' is at least misleading. The truth is rather this. The cosmological argument purports to show, from the contingency of the world, in conjunction with the principle of sufficient reason, that there must be something else which is not contingent, which exists necessarily, which is or contains its own sufficient reason. When we ask how there could be such a thing, we are offered the notion of an *ens realissimum* whose essence includes existence. This is the notion which served as the starting-point of (in particular) Descartes's ontological proof. But the notion is being used quite differently in the two cases. Does this connection imply that successful criticism of the ontological proof undermines the cosmological one also? That depends on the nature of the successful criticism. If its outcome is that the very concept of something's essence including existence is illegitimate—which would perhaps have been shown by Kant's thesis that existence is not a predicate, or by the quantifier analysis of existence in general, if either of these had been correct and uncontroversial—then at least the final step in the cosmological proof is blocked, and Leibniz must either find some different explanation of how something might exist necessarily and contain its own sufficient reason, or else give up even the first step in his proof, abandoning the search for a sufficient reason of the world as a whole. But if the outcome of the successful criticism of the ontological proof were merely that we cannot validly start from a mere concept and thence derive actual existence—if we allowed that there was nothing illegitimate about the concept of a being whose essence includes existence, and insisted only that whatever a concept contains, it is always a further question whether there is something that instantiates it—then the cosmological proof would be unaffected by this criticism. For it does offer something that purports independently to answer this further question, namely the first step, the claim that the contingency of the world shows that a necessary being is required. Now our final criticisms [offered in chapter 3 of *The Miracle of Theism*], not only of Descartes's version of the ontological proof, but also of Anselm's and Plantinga's, were of this second sort. I said that the view that existence disappears wholly into the existential quantifier is controversial, and therefore did not press the first sort of criticism. Consequently the cosmological proof is not undermined by the so far established weakness of the ontological, though, since Kant thought he had carried through a criticism of the first sort, it would have been consistent for him to say that the cosmological proof was at least seriously threatened by it, that Leibniz would need to find some other account of how there could be a necessary being.

But perhaps we can still make something like Kant's point, even if we are relying only on a criticism of the second sort. Since it is always a further question whether a concept is instantiated or not, no matter how much it contains, the existence even of a being whose essence included existence would not be self-explanatory: there might have failed to be any such thing. This 'might' expresses at least a conceptual possibility; if it is alleged that this being none the less exists by a metaphysical necessity, we are still waiting for an explanation of this kind of necessity. The existence of this being is not logically necessary; it does not exist in all logically possible worlds; in what way, then, does it necessarily exist in this world and satisfy the demand for a sufficient reason?

It might be replied that we understand what it is for something to exist contingently, in that it would not have existed if something else had been otherwise: to exist necessarily is to exist but not contingently in this sense. But then the premiss that the natural world as a whole is contingent is not available: though we have some ground for thinking that each part, or each finite temporal stretch, of the world is contingent in this sense upon something else, we have initially no ground for thinking that the world as a whole would not have existed if something else had been otherwise; inference from the contingency of every part to the contingency *in this sense* of the whole is invalid. Alternatively, we might say that something exists contingently if and only if it might not have existed, and by contrast that something exists necessarily if and only if it exists, but it is not the case that it might not have existed. In this sense we could infer the contingency of the whole from the contingency of every part. But once it is conceded, for reasons just given, that it is not logically impossible that the alleged necessary being might not have existed, we have no understanding of how it could be true of this being that it is not the case that it might not have existed. We have as yet no ground for believing that it is even possible that something should exist necessarily in the sense required.

This criticism is reinforced by the other objection, 'How do we know that everything must have a sufficient reason?' I see no plausibility in the claim that the principle of sufficient reason is known *a priori* to be true. Leibniz thought that reliance on this principle is implicit in our reasoning both about physics and about human behaviour: for example, Archimedes argued that if, in a symmetrical balance, equal weights are placed on either side, neither will go down, because there is no reason why one side should go down rather than the other; and equally a rational being cannot act without a motive.[5] But what is being used by Archimedes is just the rule that like causes produce like effects. This, and in general the search for, and expectation of, causes and regularities and reasons, do indeed guide inquiry in many fields. But the principles used are not known *a priori*, and Samuel Clarke pointed out a difficulty in applying them even to human behaviour: someone who has a good reason for doing either A or B, but no reason for doing one of these rather than the other, will surely choose one arbitrarily rather than do neither.[6] Even if, as is possible, we have some innate tendency to look for and expect such symmetries and continuities and regularities, this does not give us an *a priori* guarantee that such can always be found. In so far as our reliance on such principles is epistemically justified, it is so *a posteriori*, by the degree of success we have had in interpreting the world with their help. And in any case these principles of causation, symmetry, and so on refer to how the world works; we are extrapolating far beyond their so far fruitful use when we postulate a principle of sufficient reason and apply it to the world as a whole. Even if, within the world, everything seemed to have a sufficient reason, that is, a cause in accordance with some regularity, with like causes producing like effects, this would give us little ground for expecting the world as a whole, or its basic causal laws themselves, to have a sufficient reason of some different sort.

The principle of sufficient reason expresses a demand that things should be intelligible *through and through*. The simple reply to the argument which relies on it is that there is nothing that justifies this demand, and nothing that supports the belief that it is satisfiable even in principle. As we have seen in considering the other main objection to Leibniz's argument, it is difficult to see how there even could be anything that would satisfy it. If we reject this demand, we are not thereby committed to saying that things are utterly unintelligible. The sort of intelligibility that is achieved by successful causal inquiry and scientific explanation is not undermined by its inability to make things intelligible through and through. Any particular explanation starts with premisses which state 'brute facts,' and although the brutally factual starting-points of one explanation may themselves be further explained by another, the latter in turn will have to start with something that it does not explain, *and so on however far we go*. But there is no need to see this as unsatisfactory.

A sufficient reason is also sometimes thought of as a final cause or purpose. Indeed, if we think of each event in the history of the world as having (in principle) been explained by its antecedent causes, but still want a further explanation of the whole sequence of events, we must turn to some other sort of explanation. The two candidates that then come to mind are two kinds of purposive or teleological explanation. Things are as they are, Plato suggested, because it is *better* that they should be so.[7] This can be construed either as implying that (objective) value is in itself creative . . . or as meaning that some intelligent being sees what would be better, chooses it, and brings it about. But why must we look for a sufficient reason of either of these sorts? The principle of sufficient reason, thus understood, expresses a demand for some kind of absolute purposiveness. But if we reject this demand, we are not thereby saying that 'man and the universe are ultimately meaningless'.[8] People will still have the purposes that they have, some of which they can fulfil, even if the question 'What is the purpose of the world as a whole?' has no positive answer.

The principle of sufficient reason, then, is more far-reaching than the principle that every occurrence has a preceding sufficient cause: the latter, but not the former, would be satisfied by a series of things or events running back infinitely in time, each determined by earlier ones, but with no further explanation of the series as a whole. Such a series would give us only what Leibniz called 'physical' or 'hypothetical' necessity, whereas the demand for a sufficient reason for the whole body of contingent things and events and laws calls for something with 'absolute' or 'metaphysical' necessity. But even the weaker, deterministic, principle is not an *a priori* truth, and indeed it may not be a truth at all; much less can this be claimed for the principle of sufficient reason. Perhaps it just expresses an arbitrary demand; it may be intellectually satisfying to believe that there is, objectively, an explanation for everything together, even if we can only guess at what the explanation might be. But we have no right to assume that the universe will comply with our intellectual preferences. Alternatively, the supposed principle may be an unwarranted extension of the determinist one, which, in so far as it is supported, is supported only empirically, by our success in actually finding causes, and can at most be accepted provisionally, not as an *a priori* truth. The form of the cosmological argument which relies on the principle of sufficient reason therefore fails completely as a demonstrative proof.

The regress of causes

There is a popular line of thought, which we may call the first cause argument, and which runs as follows: things must be caused, and their causes will be other things that must have causes, and so on; but this series of causes cannot go back indefinitely; it must terminate in a first cause, and this first cause will be God. This argument envisages a regress of causes in time, but says (as Leibniz, for one, did not) that this regress must stop somewhere. Though it has some initial plausibility, it also has obvious difficulties.

Why must the regress terminate at all? Why, if it terminates, must it lead to a single termination, to one first cause, rather than to a number—perhaps an indefinitely large number—of distinct uncaused causes? And even if there is just one first cause, why should we identify this with God? I shall come back to this argument and to possible replies to these objections, but first I want to look at a more elaborate philosophical argument that has some, though not much, resemblance to it.

Of Aquinas's 'five ways', the first three are recognizably variants of the cosmological proof, and all three involve some kind of terminated regress of causes.[9] But all of them are quite different from our first cause argument. The first way argues to a first mover, using the illustration of something's being moved by a stick only when the stick is moved by a hand; here the various movings are simultaneous; we do not have a regress of causes in time. Similarly the 'efficient causes' in the second way are contemporary agents. Both these arguments, as Kenny has shown, depend too much on antiquated physical theory to be of much interest now. The third way is much more significant. This argument is in two stages, and can be freely translated, with some condensation, as follows:

> First stage: If everything were able-not-to-be, then at some time there would have been nothing (because what is able-not-to-be, at some time is not); and then (since what does not exist cannot begin to be except through something which is) even now there would be nothing. It is plainly not true that there is nothing now; so it cannot be true that everything is able-not-to-be. That is, there must be at least one thing which is necessary.

> Second stage: Everything that is necessary either has a cause of its necessity outside itself, or it does not. But it is not possible to go to infinity in a series of necessary things each of which has a cause of its necessity outside itself; this is like what has been proved about efficient causes. Therefore we must assume something which is necessary through itself, which does not have a cause of its necessity outside itself, but which is the cause of the necessity of the other things; and this, men all call God.

This argument is quite different from our first cause argument and also from Leibniz's argument from contingency. Although it uses the contrast between things which are able-not-to-be (and therefore contingent) and those which are necessary, it is not satisfied with the conclusion that there is something necessary; it allows that there may be many necessary things, and reaches God only at the end of the second stage, as what has its necessity 'through itself' (*per se*). Clearly 'necessary' does not mean the same for Aquinas as for Leibniz. What it does mean will become clearer as we examine the reasoning.

In the first stage, the premiss 'what is able-not-to-be, at some time is not' seems dubious: why should not something which is *able* not to be nevertheless just happen to exist always? But perhaps Aquinas means by 'things that are able-not-to-be' (*possibilia non esse*) something like 'impermanent things', so that this premiss is analytic. Even so, the statement that if everything were such, at some time there would have been nothing, does not follow: some impermanent things might have lasted through all past time, and be going to display their impermanence by perishing only at some time in the future. But we may be able to understand Aquinas's thought by seeing what is said more explicitly by Maimonides, by whom Aquinas appears to have been influenced here.[10] His corresponding proof seems to assume that past time has been finite—and reasonably so, for if past time has been finite there would seem to be an easier argument for a divine creator, such as we shall consider below. The suggestion is that it would not have been possible for impermanent things to have lasted throughout an infinite time, and hence they would have perished already.

However, another objection is that there might be a series of things, each of which was impermanent and perished after a finite period, but whose periods of existence overlapped so that there never was a time when there was nothing. It would be a clear logical fallacy (of which some commentators have accused Aquinas) to infer 'at some time everything is not' from 'each thing at some time is not'. But we might defend Aquinas in either of two ways. First, if each thing were impermanent, it would be the most improbable good luck if the overlapping sequence kept up through infinite time. Secondly, even if this improbable luck holds, we might regard the series of overlapping things as itself a thing which had already lasted through infinite time, and so could not be impermanent. Indeed, if there were such a series which never failed, this might well indicate that there was some *permanent* stock of material of which the perishable things were composed and into which they disintegrated, thereby contributing to the composition of other things.

A third objection concerns the premiss that 'what does not exist cannot begin to be except through something that is'. This is, of course, a form of the principle that nothing can come from nothing; the idea then is that if our series of impermanent things had broken off, it could never have started again after a gap. But is this an *a priori* truth? As Hume pointed out, we can certainly conceive an uncaused beginning-to-be of an object; if what we can thus conceive is nevertheless in some way impossible, this still requires to be shown.[11] Still, this principle has some plausibility, in that it is constantly confirmed in our experience (and also used, reasonably, in interpreting our experience).

Altogether, then, the first stage of Aquinas's argument falls short of watertight demonstration, but it gives some lower degree of support to the conclusion that there is at least one thing that is necessary in the sense, which has now become clear, that it is permanent, that *for some reason* it is not able-not-to-be.

The second stage takes this conclusion as its starting-point. One permanent thing, it allows, may be caused to be permanent, sustained always in existence, by another. But, it holds, there cannot be an infinite regress of such things. Why not? Aquinas refers us to his earlier proof about efficient causes, in the second way. This runs:

> It is not possible to go to infinity in a series of efficient causes. For in all ordered efficient causes the first item is the cause of the intermediate one and the intermediate is the cause of the last (whether there is only one intermediate or more than one); now if the cause is removed, so is the effect. Therefore if there has not been a first item among efficient causes there will not be a last or an intermediate. But if one goes to infinity in a series of efficient causes, there will not be a first efficient cause, and so there will not be a last effect or intermediate efficient causes. . . .

Unfortunately this argument is unsound. Although in a *finite* ordered series of causes the intermediate (or the earliest intermediate) is caused by the first item, this would not be so if there were an infinite series. In an infinite series, every item is caused by an earlier item. The way in which the first item is 'removed' if we go from a finite to an infinite series does not entail the removal of the later items. In fact, Aquinas (both here and in the first way) has simply begged the question against an infinite regress of causes. But is this a sheer mistake, or is there some coherent thought behind it? Some examples (some of which would not themselves have been available to Aquinas, though analogues of them would have been) may suggest that there is. If we were told that there was a watch without a mainspring, we would hardly be reassured by the further information that it had, however, an infinite train of gear-wheels. Nor would we expect a railway train consisting of an infinite number of carriages, the last pulled along by the second last, the second last by the third last, and so on, to get along without an engine. Again, we see a chain, consisting of a series of links, hanging from a hook; we should be surprised to learn that there was a similar but infinite chain, with no hook, but links supported by links above them for ever. The point is that in these examples, and in the series of efficient causes or of necessary things, it is assumed that there is a relation of *dependence*—or, equivalently, one in the reverse direction of *support*—and, if the series were infinite, there would in the end be nothing for the effects to depend on, nothing to support them. And the same would be true if the regress were not infinite but circular.

There is here an implicit appeal to the following general principle: Where items are ordered by a relation of dependence, the regress must end somewhere; it cannot be either infinite or circular. Perhaps this principle was intended by al Farabi in the dictum that is translated 'But a series of contingent beings which would produce one another cannot proceed to infinity or move in a circle' (p. 83). As our examples show, this principle is at least highly plausible; the problem will be to decide when we have such a relation of dependence.

In the second stage of Aquinas's argument, therefore, the key notion is that any necessary—that is, permanent—thing either depends for its permanence on something else or is *per se necessarium* in a sense which can apply only to God. The actual text of the third way does not reveal Aquinas's thinking about this. But comparison of it with other passages in his writings and with Maimonides's proof suggests that the implicit assumption is that anything whose essence does not involve existence must, even if it is permanent, depend for its existence on something else.[12] This assumption would give the dependence which would call for an end to the regress and also ensure that nothing could end it but a being whose essence involved existence—which would explain the assertion that what is *per se necessarium* is what men all call God.

But the final objection to the argument is that we have no reason for accepting this implicit assumption. Why, for example, might there not be a permanent stock of matter whose essence did not involve existence but which did not derive its existence from anything else?

It is obvious that, as I said earlier, Aquinas's third way is very different from Leibniz's cosmological proof. Yet there has been a tendency to assimilate the former to the latter.[13] This is understandable, in that Aquinas would need something like the principle of sufficient reason to support what I have called the implicit assumption against our final objection: for example, there being a permanent stock of matter would be just a brute fact that had no sufficient reason, whereas something whose essence involved existence would seem to have, in itself, *per se*, a sufficient reason for its permanence. But in view of our criticisms of Leibniz's argument, no borrowing from it can rescue that of Aquinas.

But what about the popular first cause argument? Can we not now answer our ear-lier queries? Why must the regress of causes in time terminate? Because things, states of affairs, and occurrences *depend* on their antecedent causes. Why must the regress lead to one first cause rather than to many uncaused causes, and why must that one cause be God? Because anything other than God would need something else causally to depend upon. Moreover, the assumption needed for this argument is more plausible than that needed for Leibniz's proof, or for Aquinas's. The notion that everything must have a sufficient reason is a metaphysician's demand, as is the notion that anything permanent must depend for its permanence on something else unless its essence involves existence. But the notion that an effect *depends* on a temporally earlier cause is part of our ordinary understanding of causation: we all have some grasp of this asymmetry between cause and effect, however hard it may be to give an exact analysis of it.[14]

Nevertheless, this argument is not demonstratively cogent. Though we understand that where something has a temporally antecedent cause, it depends somehow upon it, it does not follow that everything (other than God) *needs* something else to depend on in this way. Also, what we can call al Farabi's principle, that where items are ordered by a relation of dependence, the regress must terminate somewhere, and cannot be either infinite or circular, though plausible, may not be really sound. But the great-est weakness of this otherwise attractive argument is that some reason is required for making God the one exception to the supposed need for something else to depend on: why should God, rather than anything else, be taken as the only satisfactory termina-tion of the regress? If we do not simply accept this as a sheer mystery (which would be to abandon rational theology and take refuge in faith), we shall have to defend it in something like the ways that the metaphysicians have suggested. But then this popular argument takes on board the burdens that have sunk its more elaborate philosophical counterparts.

Finite past time and creation

There is, as Craig explains, a distinctive kind of cosmological argument which, unlike those of Aquinas, Leibniz, and many others, assumes or argues that the past history of the world is finite.[15] This, which Craig calls, by its Arabic name, the *kalam* type of argu-ment, was favoured by Islamic thinkers who were suspicious of the subtleties of the philosophers and relied more on revelation than on reason. Nevertheless, they did pro-pound this as a rational proof of God's existence, and some of them used mathematical paradoxes that are descended from Zeno's, or that anticipate Cantor's, to show that there cannot be an actual infinite—in particular, an infinite past time. For example, if time past were infinite, an infinite stretch would have actually to have been traversed in order to reach the present, and this is thought to be impossible. Then there is an ingen-ious argument suggested by al Ghazali: the planet Jupiter revolves in its orbit once every twelve years, Saturn once every thirty years; so Jupiter must have completed more than twice as many revolutions as Saturn; yet if past time were infinite they would each have completed the same (infinite) number; which is a contradiction (pp. 101–2). The first of these (which Kant also uses in the thesis of his First Antinomy) just expresses a prejudice against an actual infinity. It assumes that, even if past time were infinite, there would still have been a starting-point of time, but one infinitely remote, so that an actual infinity would have had to be traversed to reach the present from there. But to take the hypothesis of infinity seriously would be to suppose that there was no starting-point, not even an infinitely remote one, and that from any specific point in past time there is only a finite stretch that needs to be traversed to reach the present. Al Ghazali's argument uses an instance of one of Cantor's paradoxes, that in an infinite class a part can indeed be equal to the whole: for example, there are just as many even numbers (2, 4, 6, etc.) as there are whole numbers (1, 2, 3, etc.), since these classes can be matched one-one with each other. But is this not a contradiction? Is not the class of even numbers both equal to that of the integers (because of this one-one correlation) and smaller than it (because it is a proper part of it, the part that leaves out the odd numbers)? But what this brings out is that we ordinarily have and use a criterion for one group's being smaller than another—that it is, or can be correlated one-one with, a proper part of the other—and a criterion for two groups' being equal in number—that they can be correlated one-one with each other—which together ensure that *smaller than* and *equal to* exclude one another for all pairs of finite groups, but not for pairs of infinite groups. Once we understand the relation between the two criteria, we see that there is no real contradiction.

In short, it seems impossible to disprove, *a priori*, the possibility of an infinite past time. Nevertheless, many people have shared, and many still do share, these doubts about an actual infinite in the real world, even if they are willing to leave mathematicians free to play their Cantorian games—which, of course, not all mathematicians, or all philosophers of mathematics, want to play. Also the view that, whatever we say about *time*, the *universe* has a finite past history, has in recent years received strong empirical support from the cosmology that is a branch of astronomy. So let us consider what the prospects would be for a proof of the existence of a god if we were supplied, from whatever source, with the premiss that the world has only a finite past history, and therefore a beginning in time, whether or not this is also the beginning of time. Here the crucial assumption is stated by al Ghazali: '[We] know by rational necessity that nothing which originates in time originates by itself, and that, therefore, it needs a creator' (p. 102). But *do* we know this by rational necessity? Surely the assumption required here is just the same as that which is used differently in the first cause argument, that anything other than a god needs a cause or a creator to depend on. But there is *a priori* no good reason why a sheer origination of things, not determined by anything, should be unacceptable, whereas the existence of a god with the power to create something out of nothing is acceptable.

When we look hard at the latter notion we find problems within it. Does God's existence have a sheer origination in time? But then this would be as great a puzzle as the sheer origination of a material world. Or has God existed for ever through an infinite time? But this would raise again the problem of the actual infinite. To avoid both of these, we should have to postulate that God's own existence is not in time at all; but this would be a complete mystery.

Alternatively, someone might not share al Ghazali's worries about the actual infinite, and might rely on an empirical argument—such as the modern cosmological evidence for the 'big bang'—to show that the material world had a beginning in time. For him, therefore, God's existence through an infinite time would be unproblematic. But he is still using the crucial assumptions that God's existence and creative power would be self-explanatory whereas the unexplained origination of a material world would be unintelligible and therefore unacceptable. But the first of these leads us back to the criticism stated in [the first section above]. . . . The notion, embedded in the ontological argument, of a being whose existence is self-explanatory because it is not the case that it might not have existed, is *not* defensible; so we cannot borrow that notion to complete any form of the cosmological argument. The second assumption is equally questionable. We have no good ground for an *a priori* certainty that there could not have been a sheer unexplained beginning of things. But in so far as we find this improbable, it should cast doubt on the interpretation of the big bang as an absolute beginning of the material universe; rather, we should infer that it must have had *some* physical antecedents, even if the big bang has to be taken as a discontinuity so radical that we cannot explain it, because we can find no laws which we can extrapolate backwards through this discontinuity.

In short, the notion of creation seems more acceptable than any other way out of the cosmological maze only because we do not look hard either at it or at the human experiences of making things on which it is modelled. It is vaguely explanatory, apparently satisfying; but these appearances fade away when we try to formulate the suggestion precisely. . . .

Notes

1   W. L. Craig, *The Cosmological Argument from Plato to Leibniz* (Macmillan, London, 1980). Quotations from al Farabi and al Ghazali are taken from this work.
2   The clearest account is in 'On the Ultimate Origination of Things', printed, e.g., in G. W. Leibniz, *Philosophical Writings* (Dent, London, 1934), pp. 32–41.
3   *Critique of Pure Reason*, Transcendental Dialectic, Book II, Chapter III, Section 5 (see n. 1 to Chapter 3 in *The Miracle of Theism* above).
4   *The Leibniz–Clarke Correspondence*, edited by H. G. Alexander (Manchester University Press, 1956 and 1976), Leibniz's Second Paper.
5   *The Leibniz–Clarke Correspondence*, Clarke's Third and Fifth Replies.
6   Plato, *Phaedo*, 97–9.
7   Craig, op. cit., p. 287.
8   A. Kenny, *The Five Ways* (Routledge & Kegan Paul, London, 1969).
9   Craig, op. cit., Chapter 4.
10 *Treatise*, Book I, Part iii, Section 3; contrast Kenny, op. cit., p. 67.
11 Craig, op. cit., pp. 142–3, 146–8.
12 Craig., op. cit., p. 283.
13 Cf. Chapter 7 of *The Cement of the Universe* (see n. 2 to Chapter 1 in *The Miracle of Theism* above).
14 Craig, op. cit., Chapter 3.

Questions for reflection

1   What do you make of the principle of sufficient reason? Is it reasonable to affirm it? To deny it? Can one plausibly use the principle in an argument for God's existence? Explain.
2   In reference to the argument based on a regress of causes, Professor Mackie makes the following point: "This argument envisages a regress of causes in time, but says . . . that this regress must stop somewhere. Though it has some initial plausibility, it

also has obvious difficulties. Why must the regress terminate at all? Why, if it terminates, must it lead to a single termination, to one first cause, rather than to a number—perhaps an indefinitely large number—of distinct uncaused causes?"

How might a defender of the regress of causes argument respond to Mackie? What would be a counter-response?

3   Compare W. L. Craig's selection on the *kalam* argument with Mackie's criticisms of it. What are the objections Mackie raises? Are they successful? Why or why not?

Further reading

Michael Martin (1990) *Atheism: A Philosophical Justification*. Philadelphia, PA: Temple University Press. (A philosophical defense of atheism; contains a chapter on the cosmological argument.)

Graham Oppy (A helpful internet website offering a number of articles criticizing the cosmological argument by philosopher Graham Oppy; found at http://www.infidels.org/library/modern/graham_oppy/index.html#ontological.)

William Rowe (1975) *The Cosmological Argument*. Princeton, NJ: Princeton University Press. (A critical study of versions of the cosmological argument.)

Bertrand Russell and Frederick Copleston (1964) "Debate on the Existence of God," in *The Existence of God*. Ed. John Hick. New York: Macmillan. (A famous debate on the existence of God; includes an interesting presentation of the cosmological argument by Fr. Copleston and a response by the well-known atheist philosopher Bertrand Russell.)

Richard Taylor (1992) *Metaphysics*. Englewood Cliffs, NJ: Prentice Hall. (Contains a very interesting and readable chapter on the cosmological argument.)

Chapter 20

Quentin Smith

A LOGICAL ARGUMENT AGAINST A DIVINE CAUSE

Quentin Smith is University Distinguished Faculty Scholar and Professor of Philosophy at Western Michigan University. In this essay he first notes that philosophers and theologians often take it for granted that the claim, "God is the cause of the universe," is a *logical* possibility. Furthermore, a number of them go on to argue that God's being the cause of the universe can be rationally demonstrated (such as Craig attempts to do in a previous chapter). Smith disagrees. He maintains that a divine cause of the beginning of the universe is a logical impossibility. Therefore, if the universe does have a cause for its existence, that cause is not God, and since an essential characteristic of God is being the Creator of all universes in existence, God must not exist.

Smith begins with a metaphysical examination of the nature of causation.

To set the stage for his main argument, Smith first reviews several different sample theories of causation with the end of showing that none of the existent definitions of causality are consistent with the notion that God caused the universe. The various philosophical definitions of causation generally contain notions of temporal priority (the cause must occur before the effect), spatiotemporal contiguity (the causal event must be spatially in contact with or spatially near the effect), and/or nomological relatedness (a law-like condition such as "every object like the cause produces always some object like the effect"). Smith argues that divine causation meets none of these three criteria. After arguing that this shows we have no clear and logically coherent philosophical theory of divine causation, Smith then undertakes to present his main argument, which is that there can be no possible definition or concept of causation that is consistent with the claim that God is the cause of the universe.

His main argument is that the very nature of God (as an omnipotent being) prohibits him/her from being the cause of the universe for the following reason. God's willing that the universe exist is a logically sufficient condition for its existence, and anything that is a logically sufficient condition for x cannot be the cause of x. For example, a table's being brown is a *logically sufficient condition* for the table's being colored, but it is not a *cause* of the table's being colored. Since God, by definition, is an omnipotent being, anything that God wills is always successful—i.e., God's willing an event to occur is a logically sufficient condition for that event's occurrence. But since a logically sufficient condition of x cannot be the cause of x, God's willing the universe to exist cannot be the cause of its existence. Smith examines criticisms of this argument and finds them inadequate. God simply and logically *cannot* have caused the universe to exist. Smith proceeds to argue that even the notion expressed by "willing" cannot be applied to God, since this notion is a causal notion.

Smith concludes the essay by noting that his arguments may seem to be only about the nature of causation and the nature of God. However, he suggests his arguments offer significant implications for the atheism/theism debate. He maintains that both the cosmological and teleological arguments actually turn out to be arguments for atheism rather than theism. These arguments, if successful, show that the universe has a cause; if it does have a cause, this cause cannot be God, which implies that God does not exist.

---

1. Introduction[1]

Some interesting light is thrown on the nature of causation, the origin of the universe, and arguments for atheism if we address the question: Is it *logically* possible that the universe has an originating divine cause?

I think that virtually all contemporary theists, agnostics, and atheists believe this is logically possible. Indeed, the main philosophical tradition from Plato to the present has assumed that the sentence "God is the originating cause of the universe" does not express a *logical* contradiction, even though many philosophers have argued that this sentence either is synthetic and meaningless (e.g., the logical positivists), or states a synthetic and a priori falsehood (e.g., Kant and Moore), or states a synthetic and a posteriori falsehood (e.g., contemporary defenders of the probabilistic argument from evil).

I believe the prevalence of this assumption is due to the fact that philosophers have not undertaken the requisite sort of metaphysical investigation into the nature of causation. This investigation is the purpose of this paper; specifically, I shall argue that the thesis that the universe has an originating divine cause is logically inconsistent with all extant definitions of causality and with a logical requirement upon these and all possible valid definitions or theories of causality. I will conclude that the cosmological and teleological arguments for a cause of the universe may have some force but that these arguments, traditionally understood as arguments for the existence of God, are in fact arguments for the nonexistence of God.

2. Causal definitions and the notion of an originating divine cause

Something is a *continuing cause* of the universe if and only if it causes each state of the universe. Something is an *originating cause* of the universe if and only if it causes the earliest state of the universe. If time is continuous, "the earliest state" may refer to an instantaneous state or (if the universe's history is half-open in the earlier direction) to a temporally extended state of some given length.

If big bang cosmology is true, the universe began to exist about fifteen billion years ago with the big bang. The big bang is the earliest state of the universe; "the big bang" may be taken to refer to a singularity that constitutes the first instantaneous state of the universe or (if one "cuts out" the singularity) to an explosion that constitutes the first half-open state of some brief length, e.g., the Planck length, 10^{-43} second. In my discussion, I shall treat the big bang as a logically possible example of an earliest state of the universe.

Considerations of agent causality are not germane to our discussion; our topic is the cause of the universe's beginning to exist, not the cause of God's *act of willing* that the universe begin to exist. We are not examining the relation between God (the agent) and his act of willing (the effect) but the relation between his act of willing (an event) and the beginning of the universe (another event). Thus, definitions of agent causality are irrelevant to our arguments; we are interested only in definitions of event causality, where the cause and the effect are both events.

Hume's definition of a cause

The most famous and influential definition of a cause is Hume's definition; indeed, most contemporary definitions include conditions that are similar in some respect to at least one of the three conditions included in Hume's definition:

> Contiguity in time and place is therefore a requisite circumstance to the operation of all causes. . . . Priority in time is . . . another requisite circumstance in every case. . . . [A] third circumstance [is] that of constant conjunction betwixt the cause and the effect. Every object like the cause produces always some object like the effect. Beyond these three circumstances of contiguity, priority, and constant conjunction I can discover nothing in this cause.[2]

Hume's definition includes three conditions for being a cause: temporal priority, spatiotemporal contiguity, and a nomological relation ("every object like the cause produces always some object like the effect").

(a) Temporal priority

If time began to exist with the universe, the "temporal priority" condition of Hume's definition implies that the universe cannot be caused to begin to exist, since there is no earlier time at which the cause could occur.

Even if there is time before the universe, the "temporal priority" condition rules out an originating divine cause if all divine acts are timeless.

However, the "temporal priority" condition only shows the universe cannot have an originating divine cause if time began to exist with the universe or if all divine acts are timeless. It is logically possible that time preceded the beginning of the universe, even if there are no known laws of physics according to which the physical variable t can take values earlier than the time at which space and mass-energy began to exist. Further, it is logically possible that God exists in time and that a pre-universe time is occupied by God's mental life, which includes his volitions. Thus, it is logically possible for a divine volition to meet the "temporal priority" condition of Hume's definition. The intractable problems begin with the other two conditions.

(b) Spatiotemporal contiguity

Hume's definition and many other definitions of causality require that the causal event is spatially in contact with, or is spatially near, the effect. God is said to be omnipresent, but this means that she is conscious of and stands in a volitional relation to each physical particular. It does not mean that divine volitions, which are nonphysical, touch or are in the spatial vicinity of the physical particulars that are the objects of these volitions.

God's act of willing that the big bang occur is not spatiotemporally contiguous with the big bang, since this act of willing does not have spatial coordinates. Two particulars c and e are spatiotemporally contiguous *only if* the spatial coordinates x, y, z that locate c on a manifold either are identical with the spatial coordinates x', y', z' of e or locate c in the neighborhood of e.

(c) Nomological relatedness

The third feature of Hume's definition, the nomological condition ("every object like the cause produces always some object like the effect"), is also common to many definitions of causality. Hume's definition belongs to the line of reductive definitions that define causes in terms of laws of nature and a set of noncausal relations (such as temporal priority and spatiotemporal contiguity) between two particulars c and e.[3] According to these definitions, c is a cause of e only if there is a law of nature L that enables a statement that e occurs to be deduced from the premises that c occurs and that the law L obtains. For example, Carl Hempel writes:

> [A] "cause" must be allowed to be a more or less complex set of circumstances or events, which might be described by a set of statements C_1, C_2, . . . , C_k.

> Thus the causal explanation implicitly claims that there are general laws— let us say, L_1, L_2, . . . , L_k—in virtue of which the occurrence of the causal antecedents mentioned in C_1, C_2, . . . , C_k is a sufficient condition for the occurrence of the explanadum event.[4]

A probabilistic law L may be permitted as well, in which case "to be deduced from" would be replaced by "to be inductively supported by."

However, the nomological condition for being a cause is logically inconsistent with a divine cause of the big bang, since God by definition is a supernatural being and his or her actions are not governed by laws of nature. Furthermore, the fact that God's willing is omnipotent makes "the big bang occurs" deducible from "God wills that the big bang occur" alone, without the need of any supplementary nomological premise, which violates the condition that a nomological premise is a logically necessary condition for the derivation of the conclusion that the effect exists from premises one of which is that the causal event occurs.

At this point, we have already ruled out virtually every extant definition of causality, since most every definition includes either the spatiotemporal contiguity condition or the nomological condition. We are left with noncontiguity and singularist definitions of causality.

A noncontiguity definition does not mention spatiotemporal contiguity and does not require the cause to be both temporally and spatially contiguous with the effect; variants of noncontiguity definitions may allow for timeless divine acts and/or temporal divine acts that are not spatially near or in contact with the effect. A singularist definition allows an event to cause an effect in a single case, without the cause and effect needing to instantiate some law. However, the extant formulations that are singularist and/or noncontiguity definitions are few and far between and prove problematic for a defender of the logical possibility of an originating divine cause.

Ducasse's singularist definition of a cause

The most famous singularist definition of a cause is C. J. Ducasse's. Ducasse's conception

> defines the cause of a particular event in terms of but a single occurrence of it, and thus in no way involves the supposition that it, or one like it, ever has occurred before or ever will again. The supposition of recurrence is thus wholly irrelevant to the meaning of cause; that supposition is relevant only to the meaning of law.[5]

Since the nomological condition is explicitly rejected, it seems this definition applies to God's willing that the big bang occurs.

However, further inspection of Ducasse's definition shows that it does not apply, since his definition requires spatiotemporal contiguity. Ducasse claims that the cause c is a sufficient condition of the effect e and that c is sufficient for e if (i) c is a change that occurred during a time and throughout a space terminating at an instant i at a surface s of an object; (ii) the change e occurred during a time and through a space beginning at the instant i at the surface s; (iii) no change other than c occurred during the time and through the space of c; and (iv) no change other than e occurred during the time and through the space of e.[6] Thus, Ducasse's account meets the singularist criterion but not the noncontiguity criterion. (Although Ducasse calls his account a "definition" of a cause, it is only a partial definition, since he begins his definition with "if," not "if and only if.")

The transference definition of a cause

Another possible candidate for a singularist and noncontiguity definition is based on the transference definition of causation, offered by Hector-Neri Castañeda, Galen Strawson, David Fair, Jerrold Aronson, and others.[7] Castañeda states that "the heart of production, or causation, seems, thus, to be transfer or transmission."[8] In the actual world, what is transferred is energy (according to Castañeda), but he uses the word "causity" as a generic term for whatever may be transferred. Can God's volition *transfer causity* to the big bang?

Castañeda's full theory implies a definition that includes the nomological condition: c is a cause of e if and only if *(i)* there is a transfer of causity from an object O_1 to an object O_2 in a circumstance x, with the event c being O_1's transmission of causity and the event e being O_2's acquisition of causity; *(ii)* every event of the same category as c that is in a circumstance of the same category as x is conjoined with an event of the same category as e.

Condition *(ii)* is intended as a nomological condition and thus rules out supernatural causes. But may we isolate *(i)*, "the heart of causation," and successfully argue that a singularist, noncontiguity, and transference condition is satisfied by a divine volition? It appears not, since there is a problem with causity. The causity cannot be identical with energy (Castañeda's claim about the actual identity of causity), since there is no energy in God (God being nonphysical). Indeed, the causity cannot be anything physical, since God is nonphysical. Nor can the causity be anything nonphysical, since the big bang is wholly physical. Thus, there appears to be no viable candidate for the causity transferred.

Counterfactual definitions of causation

David Lewis's definition imports counterfactual conditions into the definition of causation and seems to lend itself to a noncontiguity and singularist conception. According to Lewis, c causes e if and only if *(i)* c and e are events and both occur and it is the case that either *(ii)* if c had not occurred, e would not have occurred, or *(iii)* there is a causal chain linking c and e and each link d in the chain is such that if d had not occurred, then e would not have occurred. Since there is no causal chain between a divine volition and the big bang, condition *(iii)* is inapplicable and we may concentrate on *(i)* and *(ii)*.[9]

Are the divine volition and the big bang both events? According to Jaegwon Kim, an event is a substance exemplifying an n-adic property at a time.[10] Even if there is no pre-universe time, this need not rule out the applicability of Kim's definition to God's volition, since we may construe God's volition as simultaneous with the big bang. We may also follow Brian Leftow and allow that the logical position occupied by "at the time t" may be occupied by "at eternity" or "timelessly."[11] Alternately, we could follow Davidson and take an event as a particular that is not further definable, thus allowing that the divine volition is an event even if timeless.[12] Taking one of these routes, or, following Wolterstorff and others,[13] taking an event as something's exemplification of an n-adic property (without a time specification), would allow us to consider the divine volition as an event that is either timeless, simultaneous with, or earlier than the big bang. (In these various definitions, "event" and "state" may be taken to be synonyms.)

However, Lewis's counterfactual definition is not instantiated by a divine willing of the big bang. Let c be the divine willing of the big bang and let e be the big bang. If e had not occurred, then c would not have occurred. But this implies the false proposition that e is the cause of c, since c is counterfactually dependent on e. In this case (to use Lewis's words about a problem he generally notes), "we have a spurious reverse causal dependence of c on e, contradicting our supposition that e did not cause c."[14]

Lewis solves this problem by denying the counterfactual "if e had not occurred, c

would not have occurred." Lewis holds that it is instead true that "c would have occurred just as it did but would have failed to cause e."[15] But this entails that Lewis's definition cannot be instantiated by God's willing the big bang, since if c had occurred (if God had willed the big bang), then it would have necessarily caused e (the big bang); God is omnipotent and his willing is necessarily effective.

In summary, the above considerations suggest that there are no extant definitions of causality that are satisfied by God's willing the big bang to occur; I believe a survey of further extant definitions would show that most of them include at least one of the above-mentioned conditions (contiguity, a nomological condition, etc.), conditions that are violated by the divine volition. The definitions that do not include one of the above-mentioned conditions include some other condition that is violated by the divine volition; for example, John Mackie's definition of an INUS condition implies that a cause c is neither necessary nor sufficient for its effect e but is instead an insufficient and nonredundant part of an unnecessary but sufficient condition for e.[16] God's willing the big bang, however, is sufficient for the occurrence of the big bang and thus violates the condition "is neither necessary nor sufficient for its effect."

3. Causes and logically sufficient conditions

It may be responded at this juncture that the failure of God's creation of the big bang to satisfy any of the extant definitions of causality does not imply that God's volitional act is not a cause of the big bang. It may be that the correct definition of causality has not yet been discovered and that God's willing the big bang satisfies this correct, undiscovered definition. My argument that God cannot be a cause of the universe is at best a "weak inductive argument" based on the definitions that have been formulated up to the present point in time.

Further, the preceding considerations suggest a certain definition of causality that *is* satisfied by the originating divine volition, regardless of whether this definition has been defended by anybody. This definition reads: c is a cause of e if and only if c is a sufficient condition of e and c is earlier than e. This definition includes Hume's "temporal priority" condition but is both singularist and noncontiguous. (A definition is contiguous only if it includes both spatial and temporal contiguity.) This definition cannot be satisfied by an originating divine volition if all divine volitions are timeless or if there is no time before the beginning of the universe. But it is logically possible that there is time before the big bang and that a temporal deity performs a volition that both occurs before the big bang and is a sufficient condition of the big bang's occurrence.

It may also be said that we need not rely on the assumption that the divine volition must satisfy a *definition* of a cause in order to be a cause. It is arguable that causation is a simple relation, a conceptual primitive, and thus that there is no definition that could capture its nature.[17]

These three responses to my discussion in part 2 are perhaps not unreasonable; indeed, at least the first response (that part 2 presents an "inductive argument" based only on extant definitions) contains some truth.

However, all three responses are unavailing in face of the following crucial fact: there is an entailment relation between "c is a cause of e" and "c is not a *logically* sufficient condition of e." It is the case that:

(1) For any two particular events or states x and y, if x is a logically sufficient condition of y, then x is not a cause of y.

For example, a body's being in motion is a logically sufficient condition of the body's occupying space, but the body's being in motion is not the cause of the body's occupation of space. However, God's willing that the big bang occurs is a logically sufficient condition of the big bang, for the propositions expressed by "God wills that the big bang occur" and "the big bang does not occur" are logically incompatible. The reason for this is that God is omnipotent and thus his willing is always successful (of logical necessity); if an omnipotent being x wills e and e does not occur, then x is not omnipotent—which is a contradiction. (God can do everything that is logically possible; God cannot create a stone that is too heavy for him to lift, but creating such a stone is not a logical possibility. God would never will something to occur if the occurrence of that something were logically impossible—God is omniscient and omnibenevolent and would not knowingly engage in any futile effort.)

The variables in proposition (1) range over particular events or states; they do not range over particular events taken together with laws of nature or universal generalizations under which the particulars are subsumed. As we have seen, the nomological definitions of deterministic causation imply that a particular event c, in conjunction with a law of nature, logically necessitates the event e that is the effect. The sun's shining on a stone, in conjunction with the law that whatever is shined upon is warmed, logically necessitates that the stone is warmed. Proposition (1), however, implies only that *the sun's shining on the stone* does not logically necessitate *the stone's being warmed*. The sun's shining on the stone is a nonlogically sufficient condition of the stone's being warm (it is *nomologically sufficient*, in that it is logically sufficient for the stone's being warm only if it is conjoined with some law of nature).

Two objections may be made to my argument that divine volitions are logically sufficient conditions and therefore are not causes.

Objection 1. It may be objected that every cause can be described in a way that logically implies the occurrence of its effect and, therefore, that divine volitions are *not* dissimilar to causes. For example, the cause *the explosion that burned down the house* logically necessitates its effect *the burning down of the house*, since it is a logical contradiction to assert that "there is an explosion that burned down the house and yet there is no event of the house burning down."

But this objection is fallacious since "the explosion that burned down the house" does not refer merely to the cause but also refers to the effect. A definite description that refers merely to the causal event can be satisfied consistently with the non-occurrence of the effect; for example, the definite description "the explosion that occurred in the house" can be satisfied consistently with the nonsatisfaction of "the burning down of the house."

The fallaciousness of this objection can be explained more precisely in terms of referentially transparent and referentially opaque contexts. The definite description "the explosion that resulted in the burning down of the house" is a referentially transparent context; this implies that "the burning down of the house" occupies a position in "the explosion that resulted in the burning down of the house" that is open to substitution and quantification. A description of the form "the explosion that resulted in the F"

permits coreferring expressions to be substituted for "the F," and if a description of this form is satisfied, it follows that there is an F. Since the description of the effect, "the F," occurs in a referentially transparent context, "the explosion that resulted in the F" refers to both the cause and the effect.

By contrast, the definite description "the divine willing that the big bang occurs" is a referentially opaque context and refers merely to the divine volition. This description is referentially opaque since it is a propositional attitude construction, and positions within attitude constructions are not open to substitution and quantification.[18] Specifically, a definite description of the form "the willing by x that the F occurs" does not permit substitutions of coreferring expressions for "the F," and "the F" is not open to quantification. This implies that if a description of the form "the willing by x that the F occurs" is satisfied, it does not follow that there is an F. Since the description of the effect, "the F," occurs in an opaque context, "the willing by x that the F occurs" refers only to the cause.

Given this distinction, we may say that a definite description D of a cause also refers to the effect if and only if D includes a term for the effect that is open to substitution and quantification. A definite description D' of a cause does not refer to the effect if and only if D' either does not contain a term for the effect or contains a term for the effect in an opaque context.

This enables us to state our principle (1) about causes and logically sufficient conditions in semantic terms: The satisfaction of a definite description D of a cause logically implies the existence of the effect if and only if D includes a term for the effect in a referentially transparent context. Since the satisfaction of the definite description "the divine willing that the big bang occurs" logically implies that the big bang occurs, despite the fact that "the big bang" does not occur in a referentially transparent context, it follows that this description does not refer to a *cause*.

The reason that the satisfaction of the description "the divine willing that the big bang occurs" implies that there is a big bang is not due to the logical form of the description (the form is opaque) but is due to the content of the description. This content is distinctive in that it makes the relevant conditionals about the divine volition and the big bang *logical truths*. The expression "an omnipotent being" means, in part, a being whose acts of will necessarily actualize what is willed. Thus, the sentence "if an omnipotent being wills that the big bang is actualized, then the big bang is actualized" expresses the same proposition as the sentence "if an omnipotent being, whose acts of will necessarily actualize what is willed, wills that the big bang is actualized, then the big bang is actualized," which is a truth of logic.

Principle (1) about causes and logically sufficient conditions implies that *no causal conditional is a logical theorem*, where a causal conditional has the form "if c occurs, then e occurs" and substitutions for "c" are expressions that refer to the cause and do not include a term for the effect in a referentially transparent context.

These restatements of principle (1) in semantic and logical terms suffice to refute the first objection to my argument that the divine volition is not a cause, the objection that "for each cause c and effect e, there is some description of c that logically implies the existence of e."

Objection 2. The first objection to my argument about causes and logically sufficient conditions was that divine volitions are not unique, since every cause can be described in a way that logically implies the effect. A second objection is that there is some description of God's willing the big bang to occur that does *not* logically imply that the big bang occurs, and therefore (for this different reason) divine volitions are not dissimilar to causes. The description "the willing that has for its aim the actualization of the big bang" can be used as a definite description of the relevant divine volition and yet "there occurs the willing that has for its aim the actualization of the big bang, but the big bang is not actualized" is not a logical contradiction. It follows (the objection goes) that God's willing need not be regarded as a logically sufficient condition of the big bang. The objector may argue that the existence of such descriptions implies that whether or not a divine volition logically necessitates the existence of its volitional object is not a fact about the divine volition itself but is relative to how the volition is described.

But this objection is invalid, since the existence of a description of the divine volition that does not logically imply that the big bang occurs is consistent with the divine volition's necessarily possessing the relational property of being conjoined with the occurrence of the big bang. This consistency is an instance of the more general principle that "something that necessarily possesses a certain property F can be described by a definite description D that does not include F among its descriptive conditions, and D will not imply that whatever satisfies D necessarily possesses F." For example, the number 9 necessarily possesses oddness and is described by "the number of planets in our solar system"; but since "the number of planets in our solar system" does not include oddness among its descriptive conditions, it does not imply that whatever satisfies this description necessarily possesses oddness.

These responses to the two objections help to justify my claim that the proposition

(1) For any two particular events or states x and y, if x is a logically sufficient condition of y, then x is not a cause of y

both is true and precludes divine volitions from being causes.

Sosa's theory of causation

Does every philosopher accept that a particular event c that causes a particular event e cannot logically necessitate e? Ernest Sosa has suggested a theory of causality that might appear to be inconsistent with this thesis. Sosa distinguishes several types of causation: nomological causation, material causation, consequentialist causation, and inclusive causation. Of interest to us is Sosa's definition of consequentialist causation, since this definition is instantiated by God's willing the big bang to occur. In cases of consequentialist causation, "the cause does entail the result or consequence."[19]

Sosa lists several examples of consequentialist causation: *(i)* an apple's being red causes the apple to be colored; *(ii)* Tom's being in the room causes the general fact that there is someone in the room; *(iii)* Peter, Paul, and Mary are tall and the only people in the room, and this causes the general fact that everyone in the room is tall; *(iv)* an apple's being sweet, juicy, etc., causes the apple to have the value of goodness.

Sosa acknowledges that he has no analysis or definition of consequentialist causation, but he says it involves a consequence deriving necessarily from a cause "that is somehow more basic."[20]

The immediate rejoinder to Sosa's theory is that his cases of consequentialist causation are not cases of causation but cases of logical derivation or, more exactly, cases where the instantiation of one property F logically necessitates the instantiation of a second property G, or cases where the obtaining of one fact p logically necessitates the obtaining of a second fact q. When Sosa says that consequentialist causation does "seem to be a genuine form of causation,"[21] he seems to be mistaken. Indeed, the man or woman on the street, contemporary philosophers and scientists would all emphatically and correctly assert that these are not genuine cases of causation. But in fairness to Sosa, he acknowledges this very point and makes some plausible observations:

> It might be objected that much of the foregoing is a mere terminological maneuver, that it simply takes what philosophers have long called causation, relabels it 'nomological causation', and goes on to classify it with certain wholly other relations that philosophers have not heretofore called causal relations. And it might perhaps be that the word 'cause' and its cognates have been so closely and so persistently associated with nomological causation by philosophers that they must be surrendered. But even then the basic point would remain, for nomological causation is a relation between a source and a consequence or result, and so is material causation (e.g. generation), so is consequentialist causation (e.g. the apple is chromatically colored as a result of being red) and so is inclusive causation. . . . These are all source-consequence relations or result-yielding relations.[22]

Thus, we can agree with Sosa that causation can be classified with other result-yielding relations—such as the logical necessitation of a property F by another property G—as one type of result-yielding relation, but at the same time we can distinguish causation from these other noncausal result-yielding relations.

4. Analogical and literal descriptions

I suggest that the foregoing considerations give us good reason to believe that there is no actual or possible correct theory or definition of causality that is instantiated by God's willing the big bang.

How might the defender of divine causality answer these arguments? One answer might be to grant that God's willing is not a "cause" of the universe's beginning but instead is the "creator" or "producer" of the universe's beginning. But this change in terminology does not solve the problem: "c creates e" and "c produces e" each imply "c causes e," so the problem is not avoided. If we wish to stipulate that "c creates e" does not imply "c causes e," then we deprive the word "creates" of any apparent intelligibility. If "creates" no longer means what it normally means, then we are hard put to say what it means.

A similar problem affects an alternative solution, namely, that we say that God "wills" the universe to begin to exist but does not "cause" it to begin to exist. I provisionally used the terminology of "God's willing" and "divine volition" in the preceding discussion, but this usage calls for reevaluation. A statement of the form "x wills e and e occurs because of x's willing" logically implies "x's willing causes e." If God's act of willing is *not* an act of causation, it is difficult to say what the word "willing" means when applied to God. It does not mean what it means in such sentences as "John moved his broken limb by a sheer act of will."

Perhaps we can say that the words "willing" and "cause" are used in an analogical or metaphorical sense when applied to God. This means that God has some features that are analogous to the features we normally ascribe by "willing" and "cause" and also that God has some features that are different. The analogy for "willing" would be this: If a human wills something, this willing is a mental event that has for its aim bringing another event into existence. Likewise, we may say of God that he or she experiences a mental event and that this mental event has for its aim bringing another event into existence. This is the analogy. There is also a difference, in that God's willing is a logically sufficient condition for the existence of the event that is willed, whereas a human's willing is not logically sufficient for the event that is willed.

However, this resort to the "analogical" use of "willing" and "cause" threatens to break down the intelligibility of our talk about God's willing. The explanation of the analogical meaning of these words is in terms of other words that also have an analogical meaning. We said that God's willing is a mental event that "has for its aim bringing another event into existence." However, the literal meaning of the phrase about aiming for a goal implies that "it is logically possible that this goal is not achieved." When we say that Alice has the aim of writing a book, we mean, in part, that it is logically possible that she not succeed in achieving her aim. Given the literal meaning of "aims," a statement of the form "x aims to realize F and F is realized" is neither a logical nor an analytic truth. Consequently, the explanation of the analogical meaning of "divine willing" in terms of "aiming to do something" cannot involve a literal use of "aiming to do something." But if "aiming" is used analogically, then our problem of explaining what we mean by our words reappears. This problem does not appear to have a solution; we are embarked on a regress of explaining analogically used words in terms of other analogically used words, with no way to end this regress by an explanation that involves words in their normal and literal use. This regress is vicious; in order to understand phrase one, we need to understand phrase two, but in order to understand phrase two, we need to understand phrase three, and so on. This suggests that we cannot attach any definite meaning to the assertion that God causes, wills, or aims to bring the universe into existence.

A literal formulation of the divine relation to the big bang

But this is not to say that we cannot intelligibly talk about God and her relation to the big bang. It appears that we can at least say that there is some n-adic property F exemplified by God such that by virtue of exemplifying this property, God stands in relation to the big bang of being a logically sufficient condition of the big bang. Perhaps we can even be more precise and say that F is some mental property, where "mental" is understood in terms of intentionality (in the tradition of Brentano, Husserl, Chisholm, and Searle). Further, we can say this intentional act that is experienced by God has a certain property as its intentional object, the property *being the big bang*. The property *being the big bang* will thereby have a second-order property, viz., *being the intentional object of the divine intentional act A, such that being an intentional object of A is a logically sufficient condition of being exemplified.* Talk of "intentional act" may be literal here, since these are technical terms in the philosophical literature and "act" here has a different meaning than "act" in "Jane acted quickly to remedy the situation" or "the last act of the play was a disappointment."

If it is objected that "intentional act" does not have a univocal meaning between "humans perform (embodied, non-omniscient, and non-omnipotent) intentional acts" and "God performs (disembodied, omniscient, and omnipotent) intentional acts," then we can resort to a more general level of talk. We can say that there is a certain relation R in which God stands to the property *being the big bang* such that by virtue of God's standing in R to *being the big bang*, it is logically necessary that *being the big bang* is exemplified.

In summary, we are safe in saying that God does not cause the big bang but Rs the big bang, where "God Rs the big bang" means that God stands in a certain relation R to *being the big bang* such that by virtue of standing in this relation to this property, it is logically necessary that this property is exemplified. (For ease of expression, I will sometimes talk loosely in the following discussion of God's standing in R to the big bang, but such talk should be strictly analyzed in the way I analyzed "God Rs the big bang.")

5. Objections to the arguments that God cannot be a cause

First objection

It may be objected that the divine relation R cannot merely be that of being a logically sufficient condition of the big bang. God's standing in this logical relation to the big bang is not similar to the *sun's being orange* standing in relation to the *sun's being colored* as a logically sufficient condition. The sun's exemplification of being orange does not in any sense bring about or produce the sun's exemplification of being colored. But God's exemplification of R does bring about the big bang.

But this objection is overtly question begging. I have already argued that God's standing in relation to the big bang does not satisfy any extant definition of causation (part 2) and that it does not satisfy a logically necessary condition of being a cause (part 3). Thus, to introduce synonyms of "causes," such as "brings about" or "produces," etc., is simply to beg the question at issue.

It may be countered by the objector that there is an important disanalogy between the case of the relevant divine event and the case of other logically sufficient conditions, viz., that God's standing in relation to the big bang is an event, *a concrete particular*, and that the big bang is another concrete particular, whereas the other logical relations are between *abstract objects*.

This countering argument is inaccurate. According to one conception of events or states, an event or state is the exemplification of a property by something. God's exemplification of the polyadic property R is a state, and so is Jane's exemplification of running and her exemplification of being alive. The concrete state of Jane's exemplification of running is a logically sufficient condition of the concrete state of Jane's exemplification of being alive. Thus, there are two concrete states standing in the relation of one's being the logically sufficient condition of the other. This situation is similar in this respect to God's standing in the relevant relation to the big bang.

Nonetheless, the intuition may persist that there is an important ingredient in God's

relation to the big bang of logically necessitating it that is not present in the sun's orangeness logically necessitating the sun's being colored, or in Jane's running necessitating her
being alive, an ingredient that is metaphorically captured by causal language (e.g., "produces," "brings about," etc.). The objector may simply state that it is intuitively obvious
that there is this difference between the two cases, even if this difference cannot be
adequately expressed in words.

But this amounts to retreating to an ineffability theory. We now have the theory:
"God does not literally cause the big bang but in some metaphorical sense causes the
big bang, even though it is impossible to specify literally the analogy between causation
and God's relation to the big bang that justifies the metaphor." The ineffability theory
is that God's R-ing the big bang is a relation with two properties: one property of God's
R-ing the big bang is that the R-ing is a logically sufficient condition of the big bang, and
the second property is an indescribable property, which we may call an X-property,
such that the X-property is a property of God's R-ing that makes the R-ing analogous in
a relevant respect to a causal relation.

However, the ineffability theory fails for three reasons.

First, if the X-property makes the R-ing analogous to a causal relation, then the X-
property is some property shared in common by the causal relation and the R relation.
Since the X-property belongs to the causal relation, and we can literally describe the
causal relation, we should be able to literally specify the causal relation's X-property
and say that it is this property that the R relation has in common with the causal relation. But the ineffability theory fails to do this.

Second, the ineffability theory has no justification for asserting that there is this
X-property. The ineffability theory mentions no datum that the postulation of the X-
property is used to explain, and it introduces no premises from which the presence of
the X-property is deduced. The only apparent justification might be that one has had a
mystical experience and has directly "beheld" God's R-ing the big bang and "beheld"
the X-property of this R-ing, but that in reporting this intuition, one realized that there
are no adequate and literally used words that could describe this X-property. However,
if the theory that God metaphorically causes the universe to exist amounts to nothing
more than dark sayings about what is "beheld" in an ineffable mystical experience, then
this is not a theory based on natural reason but is a flight into mysticism and the deliverances of "supernatural reason." It would hold no interest for a philosopher intent on
constructing a worldview based on natural reason.

Third, the best explanation of the origins of the "intuition" that God metaphorically
causes the big bang, and is not merely a logically sufficient condition of the big bang,
does not imply that this intuition is true. The origin of this "intuition" is the long and
pervasive tradition (in philosophy, religion, and "ordinary language") of using causal
words—"causes," "creates," "wills," etc.—to describe God's relation to the beginning
of the universe. The psychological associations produced by the adoption of this linguistic tradition give rise to the "intuition" that there must be an X-property of God's
relation to the big bang that grounds the metaphorical usage of "causes."

There *are* differences between (for example) the orange-color relation and the R
relation of God to the big bang, but none are causal-like. Orange is a kind of color, but
God's relation to the big bang is not a kind of big bang. Further, the orangeness is a monadic property of the same thing of which being colored is a property, but the R property
is polyadic and interconnects different objects. Thirdly, being orange and being colored

are both physical properties, whereas the divine relation is a mental property and *being the big bang* is a physical property.

We can also specify formal features of the R relation: it is asymmetric, transitive, and irreflexive, but many noncausal relations also possess these formal features.

Second objection

The theist, agnostic, or atheist who believes it is logically intelligible to say that God is an originating cause of the universe may take the bull by the horns and arrogantly assert that God's being a logically sufficient condition of the big bang is a *counterexample* to the extant definitions of causation discussed in part 2, showing that these definitions are wrong, and that it is also a valid *counterexample* to my principle (1) which states that causes are not logically sufficient conditions. The objector proclaims: "All actual and possible contiguity or nomological definitions of causation are false. The correct definition is a noncontiguity and singularist definition that allows that some causal relations are logical relations."

The problem with this "arrogant objection" is that there is no apparent justification *apart from God's alleged acts of causation* for the belief that there is a correct definition of causation that is noncontiguous, singularist, and permits logical relations. But these acts of God are precisely the events whose causal nature is in dispute. To assume, in face of the arguments I have given, that these acts are causal relations is a question-begging response. In order to *demonstrate* that the relevant divine relation is a causal relation, we must have a logically independent reason to believe there is some correct definition of causation that the divine relation R satisfies. But there is no such reason. Consider the argument:

> (2) There is a sufficient reason *J* to believe that there is a correct definition of causation that is singularist, noncontiguous, and permits logical relations.

Therefore,

> (3) the divine relation R is a causal relation.

If the offered reason *J* is (3), then the argument that the divine relation R is a causal relation is question begging.

It may be objected that the defender of the "there cannot be a divine cause" thesis is in a similar question-begging situation and thus that there is a stand off. It may be said that the defender begs the question by assuming that (3) is false or cannot play the role of reason *J*.

This objection fails since the defender of the "there cannot be a divine cause" thesis has a non-question-begging argument for the falsity of (3). The argument is that all cases of causation not in dispute are inconsistent with the hypothesis that there is a correct definition of the sort mentioned in (2). Both parties to the dispute agree that physical events cause other physical events and that the mental events of intelligent organisms cause other events (assuming an appropriate philosophy of mind), and this agreement is the common ground between the opponent and defender of the "there cannot be a divine cause" thesis. But this common ground is inconsistent with the positive thesis—viz., that there can be a divine cause—if only for the reason that it is a logically necessary property of the agreed-upon cases of causation that the causal event *is not* a logically sufficient condition of the effect. Since these causal events are necessarily *not* logically sufficient conditions, a definition of *a cause* that encompassed both these causal events and God's relation to the big bang would include the contradiction "is not a logically sufficient condition and is a logically sufficient condition." The agreed-upon cases may also include nomological and contiguity conditions, and consequently there may be further contradictions—e.g., "instantiates some law of nature and does not instantiate any law of nature" and "is spatially contiguous with the effect and is not spatially contiguous with the effect."

Third objection

It may be argued that a disjunctive definition can solve the problem. Suppose we have this disjunctive definition of causation: *c* is a cause of *e* if and only if either *c* is a logically sufficient condition of *e* or *c* is not a logically sufficient condition of *e* and instead satisfies (say) the Humean conditions.

One problem with this disjunctive definition is that it classifies the sun's being orange as a cause of the sun's being colored. So it does not work for this reason, as well as for the other reasons mentioned in my discussion of Sosa's account of causation.

Even if we add a temporal priority condition, this disjunctive definition will not work. We may say: *c* is a cause of *e* if and only if *either c* is both a logically sufficient condition of *e* and temporally prior to *e* or *c* is not a logically sufficient condition of *e* and satisfies (say) the Humean conditions. However, the first disjunct is satisfied by many items that are not causes. John's being a living organism (or John's *being embodied in a mortal body at time t*) both is temporally prior to and is a logically sufficient condition of John's being dead, but John's being a living organism (or John's *being embodied in a mortal body at time t*) is not the cause of his death. His death is caused, say, by a car hitting him as he crosses the street. The concept expressed by "is a living organism" analytically includes the concept expressed by "is mortal," and the relevant logical truths (e.g., "if *x* is an organism that dies, then *x* dies") can be obtained by substituting synonyms for synonyms.

Suppose we become even more specific and say instead: *c* is a cause of *e* if and only if *either c* is God's standing in the *R* relation to *e* or *c* is not a logically sufficient condition of *e* and satisfies (say) the Humean conditions. But this attempt to produce a satisfactory definition fails for two interrelated reasons.

First, a logically necessary condition of a correct definition of a purely qualitative *universal*, be it a monadic property or a relation (such as causation or intentionality), is that it not include a disjunct mentioning one particular case that does not meet the general conditions described in the other disjunct. A purely qualitative universal does not include any particulars as constituents. An example of an impurely qualitative universal is *being taller than Mount Everest*. Definitions of purely qualitative universals mention general conditions and do not include any mention of a particular case, such as the particular case of God's standing in an *R* relation to something.

Second, if this logical condition of correct definitions of purely qualitative universals (viz., the condition of not mentioning a particular case in a disjunct) were allowed to be violated, then the procedure of testing definitions by the counterexampling method (the standard method of testing the correctness of definitions) would no longer be usable. Any counterexample to a definition could be made consistent with the definition by adding to it a disjunct that mentions the counterexample. To save the definition "*x* is a planet if and only if *x* is a large body that orbits a star and contains no life," we can expand it to "*x* is a planet if and only if *either* *x* is a large body that orbits a star and contains no life *or* *x* is the Earth." The distinction between correct definitions and ad hoc definitions would collapse.

Fourth objection

A final argument is that philosophers from Plato to Plantinga have described God's relevant mental state as a cause of the universe and, therefore, this is an acceptable notion. There is both an established philosophical usage for calling God's relation to the universe a "causal relation" and a long and venerable tradition that held it to be coherent to describe a divine mental state as a cause.

This argument, which is in effect an appeal to authority, is unsuccessful, since if this argument were admissible, it could be used to reject any new theory that is inconsistent with traditionally held theories. This appeal to authority at best motivates us to examine seriously the notion that God's mental states are causes, in deference to the fact that virtually all philosophers and laypersons have accepted this notion as logically unproblematic.

Perhaps to respond fully to this objection we also need an explanation of why this mistaken tradition has prevailed for so long and among so many philosophers. I think the main reason is that an investigation of the logical connection between what is expressed by "the universe's beginning to exist is the result of a divine act" and what is expressed by "the natural event *e* is the causal result of the natural event *c*" has not been systematically undertaken. (The main exception is the different but illuminating discussions of this connection in the recent writings of Adolf Grünbaum.)[23] Most philosophers have tacitly presupposed that the thesis that "divine causation is *logically* possible" is unproblematic; but once this thesis is examined, the presupposition is seen to be false.

6. Conclusion: cosmological and teleological arguments for God's nonexistence

The argument of this paper might seem at first glance to tell us more about the nature of causation and the nature of God than about atheism versus theism. "A divine state cannot cause the universe to begin to exist" does not entail that God does not exist or that the big bang is not a logical result of a divine state. It merely entails that we cannot describe a divine state as the originating cause of the universe.

Nonetheless, there are important and perhaps decisive implications for the debate between theism and atheism, namely, that arguments from the necessary truth, a priori truth, or empirical truth of some causal principle cannot be a relevant premise from which to deduce or induce that the big bang is the logical consequence of God's standing in the relation *R* to the property *being the big bang*. Consider the following argument:

(4) Whatever begins to exist has a cause.
(5) The universe begins to exist.

Therefore,

(6) the universe has a cause.

This argument fails to support the thesis that God exists or that there is a divine cause of the universe. Indeed, this argument entails that the universe's existence is the result of something other than a divine state, namely, a cause. Nor can any inductive argument that is based on the fact that every observed event has a cause be used to support the thesis that the big bang is the result of a divine state, since such an inductive argument instead would support the thesis that the big bang is the effect of some cause.

In fact, all the various cosmological and teleological arguments for the existence of God are really *arguments for God's nonexistence*. These arguments are arguments for the thesis that the universe has a cause and if the universe has a cause, God does not exist. This can be demonstrated as follows.

The traditional definition of God is: *x* is God if and only if *x* is omniscient, omnipotent, omnibenevolent, and is the cause of any universe that exists. We have seen that what is traditionally expressed by "God is the cause of the universe," if it is logically coherent, should be expressed instead by "God *Rs* the universe." Thus the correct definition of God reads: *x* is God if and only if *x* is omniscient, omnipotent, omnibenevolent, and *Rs* any universe that exists. It follows from this definition that it is an essential property of God that he *Rs* any universe that exists. Since this property is essential to God, there is no possible world in which it is true both that God exists and that there is a universe to which God does not have an *R* relation.

Our discussion of Sosa's theory of causation suggested that the causal relation and the divine *R* relation are two different types of *result-yielding* relations, to borrow Sosa's phrase. If the universe is the result of a *causal* result-yielding relation, it is not the result of an *R-type* result-yielding relation, and if the universe is the result of a divine act of *R*-ing, it is not the result of a cause. If there is a possible world in which some universe is the result of a cause, it follows that God does not exist in that possible world.

This shows how a cosmological argument for God's nonexistence may be explicitly constructed. The premises and inferences are set out in the following argument:

(4) Whatever begins to exist has a cause.
(5) The universe begins to exist.

Therefore,

(6) the universe has a cause.
(7) If the universe is the result of a cause, it is not the result of God's standing to the universe in an *R* relation.
(8) It is an essential property of God that he *Rs* any universe that exists.

Therefore [from (7) and (8)],

(9) there is no possible world in which it is true both that God exists and that there is a universe which is the result of a cause.

Therefore [from (6) and (9)],

(10) God does not exist.

If big bang cosmology is true [and thus (5) is true], it seems that the premise with the weakest or lowest epistemic status is the first premise, "Whatever begins to exist has a cause." But William Lane Craig says about this premise: "[T]he first premiss is so intuitively obvious, especially when applied to the universe, that probably no one in his right mind *really* believes it to be false."[24] If Craig is right and my argument is sound, it follows that probably no one in his right mind who believes that the universe has a beginning *really* believes that God exists.

The same considerations apply to the teleological argument, one version of which reads:

(11) Artifacts are caused to exist by some intelligent being(s) with some purpose in mind.
(12) The universe resembles an artifact.

Therefore, it is probable that:

(13) The universe is caused to exist by some intelligent being(s) with some purpose in mind.

If this is an adequate argument from analogy, then it is probably true that the result-yielding relation that is involved in the explanation of why the universe exists is a causal relation in which some intelligent being(s) stand(s) to the universe. It follows [given propositions (7) and (9)] that God probably does not exist..

Since the cosmological and teleological arguments have standardly been thought to be the strongest arguments for God's existence, and since they support atheism rather than theism, it now seems that the case for theism is very weak indeed. It is hard to imagine how one could ever inductively or deductively establish, or find it self-evident, that the big bang is the logical consequence of something's standing in an R relation to *being the big bang*. Perhaps there are some fairly plausible arguments that the big bang has a cause, but there are no extant or plausible arguments that the big bang has a logically sufficient condition in an acausal mental state. This suggests that belief in the existence of God is considerably less reasonable than even the most cautious natural theologians have standardly supposed.

Notes

1   Earlier versions of this paper were read at West Virginia University (February 1995) and
    at Southern Methodist University (March 1996). The philosophers at both universities
    offered helpful comments on these earlier versions. Mark Aronszajn and William Lane
    Craig wrote critical responses to earlier versions, which proved useful in writing the
    present draft. I am also grateful to Christopher Hill for several suggestions that enabled me
    to improve an earlier draft.
        Research for this paper was supported by an American Council of Learned Societies
    Fellowship for 1996 and by a National Endowment for the Humanities Summer Stipend
    for 1995.
2   David Hume, "An Abstract of a Treatise of Human Nature," in *An Enquiry Concerning Human
    Understanding* (New York: Bobbs-Merrill, 1955), 186–87.
3   It is worth noting that Michael Tooley's theory implies that a cause requires an underlying
    law of nature but that the cause is not specified solely by the law of nature and non-causal
    facts. Although Tooley's definition differs from the traditional *reductive* definitions, its
    inclusion of a nomological condition precludes it from being satisfied by a divine volition.
    See his *Causation: A Realist Approach* (Oxford: Clarendon Press, 1987).
4   Carl Hempel, *Aspects of Scientific Explanation* (New York: The Free Press, 1965), 348–49.
5   C. J. Ducasse, "On the Nature and the Observability of the Causal Relation," in *Causation*,
    ed. Ernest Sosa and Michael Tooley (Oxford: Oxford University Press, 1993), 129.
6   Ibid., 127.
7   Hector-Neri Castañeda, "Causes, Causity, and Energy," in *Midwest Studies in Philosophy IX*,
    ed. Peter A. French, Theodore E. Uehling, Jr., and Howard K. Wettstein (Minneapolis:
    University of Minnesota Press, 1984); Galen Strawson, "Realism and Causation," *Phil-
    osophical Quarterly* 37 (1987): 253–77; David Fair, "Causation and the Flow of Energy,"
    Erkenntnis 14 (1979): 219–50; Jerrold Aronson, "The Legacy of Hume's Analysis of Causa-
    tion," *Studies in the History and Philosophy of Science* 7 (1971): 135–36.
8   Castañeda, op cit., 22.
9   See David Lewis, "Causation," *Journal of Philosophy* 70 (1973): 556–67.
10 Jaegwon Kim, "Events As Property Exemplifications," in *Acton Theory*, ed. Myles Brand and
    Douglas Walton (Dordrecht: Reidel, 1976).
11 See Brian Leftow, *Time and Eternity* (Ithaca, N.Y.: Cornell University Press, 1993).
12 See Donald Davidson, "Causal Relations," in Sosa and Tooley, op. cit.
13 See Nicholas Wolterstorff, "God Everlasting," in *God and the Good*, ed. Clifton Orlebeke
    and Lewis Smedes (Grand Rapids, Mich.: Eerdmans, 1975); Quentin Smith, *Language and
    Time* (New York: Oxford University Press, 1993).
14 David Lewis, *Philosophical Papers*, vol. 2 (New York: Oxford University Press, 1983), 170.
15 Ibid.
16 See John Mackie, *The Cement of the Universe* (Oxford: Clarendon Press, 1974).
17 I argued for this approach in "The Concept of a Cause of the Universe," *Canadian Journal
    of Philosophy* 23 (1993): 1–24. In this earlier article, I claimed that cases of divine volitions
    are valid counterexamples to extant definitions of causality. However, I have since devel-
    oped a counterargument to this claim (see part 5, the second objection) that has led me to
    abandon the thesis that divine volitions are causes.
18 More exactly, a *notational occurrence* of a term in a position within attitude constructions
    is not open to substitution and quantification; a *relational occurrence* of a term in this posi-
    tion is open to substitution and quantification. "F" occurs relationally in "y desires that
    there is an F" if this is read as "$(\exists x) Fx.$ y desires that: $(\exists x) Fx.$" By contrast, "F" occurs nota-
    tionally if "y desires that there is an F" is read as "y desires that: $(\exists x) Fx.$" See David Kaplan,

"Opacity," in *The Philosophy of W. V. Quine*, ed. Lewis Edwin Hahn and Paul Arthur Schilpp (La Salle, Ill.: Open Court, 1986). When I talk about "positions within attitude construc-tions" I have in mind only positions within attitude constructions in which terms occur notationally.

19 Ernest Sosa, "Varieties of Causation," in Sosa and Tooley, op. cit., 240.
20 Ibid.
21 Ibid.
22 Ibid., 242.
23 Adolf Grünbaum, "The Pseudo-Problem of Creation in Physical Cosmology," in *Philosophy and Physical Cosmology*, ed. John Leslie (New York: Macmillan, 1990), 92–112; "Creation As a Pseudo-Explanation in Current Physical Cosmology," *Erkenntnis* 35 (1991): 233–54.
24 William Lane Craig and Quentin Smith, *Theism, Atheism, and Big Bang Cosmology* (Oxford: Clarendon Press, 1993), 57.

Questions for reflection

1   Why is God's causing the universe to exist a logical impossibility, according to Professor Smith?

2   How is God's willing for the universe to exist a problem for God's creating the universe?

3   Do you agree with Smith that there could not be a model of causation in which the claim "God caused the universe to exist" is a logical possibility? Why or why not?

4   How are the cosmological and teleological arguments actually arguments *against* the existence of God, according to Smith?

Further reading

William Lane Craig and Quentin Smith (1993) *Theism, Atheism, and Big Bang Cosmology*. Oxford: Clarendon Press. (A wonderful set of essays by Craig and Smith on whether big bang cosmology supports theism or atheism.)

Nicholas Everitt (2004) *The Non-existence of God*. London: Routledge. (An up-to-date, critical assessment of arguments for and against the existence of God; concludes that God's existence is in a way disprovable and that belief in God is in some senses irrational.)

J. L. Mackie (1982) *The Miracle of Theism: Arguments for and against the Existence of God*. Oxford: Clarendon Press. (A classic work by a prominent atheist philosopher of the twentieth century examining a variety of arguments for God's existence.)

Michael Martin and Ricki Monnier, eds. (2003) *The Impossibility of God*. Buffalo, NY: Prometheus Books. (A collection of essays, including some essays by Smith, which argue that there are logical problems with the notion of God.)

Michael Martin and Ricki Monnier, eds. (2006) *The Improbability of God*. Buffalo, NY: Prometheus Books. (A collection of essays, including some early essays by Smith, which argue that the evidence supports the view that God probably does not exist.)

The Website of Quentin Smith. http://www.qsmithwmu.com/ (Contains a number of Smith's published essays on a host of topics; also includes helpful links to other philosophers' websites.)

The teleological argument

Chapter 21

William Paley

THE CLASSICAL DESIGN ARGUMENT

William Paley (1743–1805) was a theologian, moral philosopher, and Christian apologist in eighteenth-century England. He is best-known for his design argument for God's existence which is contained in the following selection.

   He begins by noting that there is a significant difference between a stone and a watch. The latter, unlike the former, has a certain means-to-ends configuration by which we can infer an intelligent designer—a watchmaker. Analogously, in nature we also find means-to-ends configurations—even more grand than in a watch—and so we should also infer a Designer of the world.

State of the argument

In crossing a heath, suppose I pitched my foot against a *stone*, and were asked how the stone came to be there; I might possibly answer, that, for any thing I knew to the contrary, it had lain there for ever: nor would it perhaps be very easy to show the absurdity of this answer. But suppose I had found a *watch* upon the ground, and it should be inquired how the watch happened to be in that place; I should hardly think of the answer which I had before given, that, for any thing I knew, the watch might have always been there. Yet why should not this answer serve for the watch as well as for the stone? Why is it not as admissible in the second case, as in the first? For this reason, and for no other, viz. that, when we come to inspect the watch, we perceive (what we could not discover in the stone) that its several parts are framed and put together for a purpose, e. *g.* that they are so formed and adjusted as to produce motion, and that motion so regulated as to point out the hour of the day; that, if the different parts had been differently shaped from what they are, of a different size from what they are, or placed after any other manner, or in any other order, than that in which they are placed, either no motion at all would have been carried on in the machine, or none which would have answered the use that is now served by it. To reckon up a few of the plainest of these parts, and of their offices, all tending to one result: —We see a cylindrical box containing a coiled elastic spring, which, by its endeavour to relax itself, turns round the box. We next observe a flexible chain (artificially wrought for the sake of flexure), communicating the action of the spring from the box to the fusee. We then find a series of wheels, the teeth of which catch in, and apply to, each other, conducting the motion from the fusee to the balance, and from the balance to the pointer; and at the same time, by the size and shape of those wheels, so regulating that motion, as to terminate in causing an index, by an equable and measured progression, to pass over a given space in a given time. We take notice that the wheels are made of brass in order to keep them from rust; the springs of steel, no other metal being so elastic; that over the face of the watch there is placed a glass, a material employed in no other part of the work, but in the room of which, if there had been any other than a transparent substance, the hour could not be seen without opening the case. This mechanism being observed (it requires indeed an examination of the instrument, and perhaps some previous knowledge of the subject, to perceive and understand it; but being once, as we have said, observed and understood), the infer-ence, we think, is inevitable, that the watch must have had a maker: that there must have existed, at some time, and at some place or other, an artificer or artificers who formed it for the purpose which we find it actually to answer; who comprehended its construction, and designed its use.

I. Nor would it, I apprehend, weaken the conclusion, that we had never seen a watch made; that we had never known an artist capable of making one; that we were altogether incapable of executing such a piece of workmanship ourselves, or of understanding in what manner it was performed; all this being no more than what is true of some exqui-site remains of ancient art, of some lost arts, and, to the generality of mankind, of the more curious productions of modern manufacture. Does one man in a million know how oval frames are turned? Ignorance of this kind exalts our opinion of the unseen and unknown artist's skill, if he be unseen and unknown, but raises no doubt in our minds of the existence and agency of such an artist, at some former time, and in some place or other. Nor can I perceive that it varies at all the inference, whether the question arise concerning a human agent, or concerning an agent of a different species, or an agent possessing, in some respects, a different nature.

II. Neither, secondly, would it invalidate our conclusion, that the watch sometimes went wrong, or that it seldom went exactly right. The purpose of the machinery, the design, and the designer, might be evident, and in the case supposed would be evident, in what-ever way we accounted for the irregularity of the movement, or whether we could account for it or not. It is not necessary that a machine be perfect, in order to show with what design it was made: still less necessary, where the only question is, whether it were made with any design at all.

III. Nor, thirdly, would it bring any uncertainty into the argument, if there were a few parts of the watch, concerning which we could not discover, or had not yet discovered, in what manner they conduced to the general effect; or even some parts, concerning which we could not ascertain, whether they conduced to that effect in any manner what-ever. For, as to the first branch of the case; if by the loss, or disorder, or decay of the parts in question, the movement of the watch were found in fact to be stopped, or disturbed, or retarded, no doubt would remain in our minds as to the utility or intention of these parts, although we should be unable to investigate the manner according to which, or the connexion by which, the ultimate effect depended upon their action or assistance; and the more complex is the machine, the more likely is this obscurity to arise. Then, as to the second thing supposed, namely, that there were parts which might be spared, without prejudice to the movement of the watch, and that we had proved this by experiment, —these superfluous parts, even if we were completely assured that they were such, would not vacate the reasoning which we had instituted concerning other parts. The indication of contrivance remained, with respect to them, nearly as it was before.

IV. Nor, fourthly, would any man in his senses think the existence of the watch, with its various machinery, accounted for, by being told that it was one out of possible combinations of material forms; that whatever he had found in the place where he found the watch, must have contained some internal configuration or other; and that this configuration might be the structure now exhibited, viz. of the works of a watch, as well as a different structure.

V. Nor, fifthly, would it yield his inquiry more satisfaction to be answered, that there existed in things a principle of order, which had disposed the parts of the watch into their present form and situation. He never knew a watch made by the principle of order; nor can he even form to himself an idea of what is meant by a principle of order, distinct from the intelligence of the watch-maker.

VI. Sixthly, he would be surprised to hear that the mechanism of the watch was no proof of contrivance, only a motive to induce the mind to think so:

VII. And not less surprised to be informed, that the watch in his hand was nothing more than the result of the laws of *metallic* nature. It is a perversion of language to assign any law, as the efficient, operative cause of any thing. A law presupposes an agent; for it is only the mode, according to which an agent proceeds: it implies a power; for it is the order, according to which that power acts. Without this agent, without this power, which are both distinct from itself, the *law* does nothing; is nothing. The expression, "the law of metallic nature," may sound strange and harsh to a philosophic ear; but it seems quite as justifiable as some others which are more familiar to him, such as "the law of vegetable nature," "the law of animal nature," or indeed as "the law of nature" in general, when assigned as the cause of phænomena, in exclusion of agency and power; or when it is substituted into the place of these.

VIII. Neither, lastly, would our observer be driven out of his conclusion, or from his confidence in its truth, by being told that he knew nothing at all about the matter. He knows enough for his argument: he knows the utility of the end: he knows the subserviency and adaptation of the means to the end. These points being known, his ignorance of other points, his doubts concerning other points, affect not the certainty of his reasoning. The consciousness of knowing little, need not beget a distrust of that which he does know.

. . .

V. Our observer would further also reflect, that the maker of the watch before him, was, in truth and reality, the maker of every watch produced from it; there being no difference (except that the latter manifests a more exquisite skill) between the making of another watch with his own hands, by the mediation of files, lathes, chisels, &c. and the disposing, fixing, and inserting of these instruments, or of others equivalent to them, in the body of the watch already made in such a manner, as to form a new watch in the course of the movements which he had given to the old one. It is only working by one set of tools, instead of another.

The conclusion of which the *first* examination of the watch, of its works, construction, and movement, suggested, was, that it must have had, for the cause and author of that construction, an artificer, who understood its mechanism, and designed its use. This conclusion is invincible. A *second* examination presents us with a new discovery. The watch is found, in the course of its movement, to produce another watch, similar to itself; and not only so, but we perceive in it a system of organization, separately calculated for that purpose. What effect would this discovery have, or ought it to have, upon our former inference? What, as hath already been said, but to increase, beyond measure, our admiration of the skill, which had been employed in the formation of such a machine? Or shall it, instead of this, all at once turn us round to an opposite conclusion, viz. that no art or skill whatever has been concerned in the business, although all other evidences of art and skill remain as they were, and this last and supreme piece of art be now added to the rest? Can this be maintained without absurdity? Yet this is atheism.

Application of the argument

This is atheism: for every indication of contrivance, every manifestation of design, which existed in the watch, exists in the works of nature; with the difference, on the side of nature, of being greater and more, and that in a degree which exceeds all computation. I mean that the contrivances of nature surpass the contrivances of art, in the complexity, subtility, and curiosity of the mechanism; and still more, if possible, do they go beyond them in number and variety; yet, in a multitude of cases, are not less evidently mechanical, not less evidently contrivances, not less evidently accommodated to their end, or suited to their office, than are the most perfect productions of human ingenuity. . . .

Questions for reflection

1   Explain Paley's design argument. Is it a good argument? Why or why not?
2   Later in the essay (not included in this selection), Paley makes reference to the human eye as an example of a means-to-ends configuration in nature. What do you think of this example, especially given Darwin's theory of evolution?
3   How does Darwin's theory of evolution affect Paley's overall argument?
4   Does the fact that we already know that watches have watchmakers create a difficulty for Paley's analogy? Explain.
5   Compare this selection with David Hume's critique of the design argument. In your judgment, does he offer a devastating refutation of the argument? Explain.

Further reading

Access Research Network. http://www.arn.org/ (A website which includes many scholarly publications and other resources supporting intelligent design.)

William A. Dembski and Michael Ruse, eds. (2004) *Debating Design: From Darwin to DNA*. Cambridge: Cambridge University Press. (A collection of essays, pro and con, by leading scholars.)

D. L. LeMahieu (1976) *The Mind of William Paley*. Lincoln, NE: University of Nebraska Press. (An overview of Paley's theology and philosophy.)

J. P. Moreland (1994) *The Creation Hypothesis: Scientific Evidence for an Intelligent Designer*. Downers Grove, IL: InterVarsity Press. (A panel of scholars argues that there is solid scientific evidence for a Designer of the universe.)

William Paley (1802) *Natural Theology: Or, Evidences of the Existence and Attributes of the Deity Collected from the Appearances of Nature*. 12th edn. Charlottesville, VA: Ibis. (Paley's most famous work; the selection above is taken from it.)

Chapter 22

Michael J. Behe

A RECENT INTELLIGENT DESIGN ARGUMENT

Michael J. Behe is Professor of Biochemistry at Lehigh University and a Senior Fellow of the Discovery Institute's Center for Science and Culture. He is one of the leaders in the "intelligent design movement."

In his classic work, *The Origin of Species*, published in 1859, Charles Darwin offered an explanation for how the great variety of flora and fauna could have arisen through purely naturalistic means. His explanation centered around natural selection acting on random variation. However, there were apparent difficulties with the theory. One difficulty, which Darwin himself recognized, was the eye. It appeared not to be the kind of system which could have evolved through slow gradual processes since all, or at least most, of its components are necessary for its functioning as an eye. Darwin himself attempted to answer the question of how such a complex biological system could have evolved through gradual processes.

In this essay Professor Behe centers in on this same general question. He takes Darwin's own words and puts them to the test: "If it could be demonstrated that any complex organ existed which could not possibly have been formed by numerous, successive, slight modifications, my theory would absolutely break down." Behe argues that there are many such systems in biology—what he calls "irreducibly complex systems"—and he offers two examples. He then claims that a better explanation for them is some form of design by an intelligent agent rather than blind, natural selection and random mutation.

Urea and purpose

In the year 1828 the German chemist Friedrich Wöhler heated ammonium cyanate in his laboratory and was amazed to see that urea was produced. Why was he amazed? Because ammonium cyanate is an inorganic chemical—one that does not occur in living organisms. But urea was known to be a biological waste product. Wöhler was the first to demonstrate that a nonliving substance could give rise to a substance produced by living organisms. His experiment shattered the distinction between life and nonlife that was thought to exist up until that time. Moreover, it opened up all of life for scientific study. For if life is made of ordinary matter, the same as rocks and so on, then science can study it. And in the more than 170 years since Wöhler's experiment, science has learned a lot about life. We have discovered the structure of DNA, cracked the genetic code, learned to clone genes, and cells, and even whole organisms.

What has the progress of science told us about the ultimate nature of the universe and life? Well, of course, there are a lot of opinions on the subject, but I think we can break them down into two opposite sides. The first side can perhaps be represented by Richard Dawkins, professor of the public understanding of science at Oxford University. Professor Dawkins has stated that: "The universe we observe has precisely the properties we should expect if there is at bottom no design, no purpose, no evil and no good, nothing but pointless indifference."[1] Certainly a dreary view, but a seriously proposed one.

The second point of view can be represented by Joseph Cardinal Ratzinger, an advisor to Pope John Paul II. About ten years ago Cardinal Ratzinger wrote a little book entitled *In the Beginning: A Catholic Understanding of the Story of Creation and the Fall*. In the book Cardinal Ratzinger wrote:

> Let us go directly to the question of evolution and its mechanisms. Microbiology and biochemistry have brought revolutionary insights here. . . . . It is the affair of the natural sciences to explain how the tree of life in particular continues to grow and how new branches shoot out from it. This is not a matter for faith. But we must have the audacity to say that the great projects of the living creation are not the products of chance and error. . . . [They] point to a creating Reason and show us a creating Intelligence, and they do so more luminously and radiantly today than ever before. Thus we can say today with a new certitude and joyousness that the human being is indeed a divine project, which only the creating Intelligence was strong and great and audacious enough to conceive of. Human beings are not a mistake but something willed.[2]

I would like to make three points about the Cardinal's argument. First, unlike Professor Dawkins, Ratzinger says that nature does appear to exhibit purpose and design. Secondly, to support the argument he points to *physical evidence*—the "great products of the living creation", which "point to a creating Reason". Not to philosophical, or theological, or scriptural arguments, but to tangible structures. Thirdly, Ratzinger cites the science of biochemistry—the study of the molecular foundation of life—as having particular relevance to his conclusion. It is my purpose in this essay to show why I think Cardinal Ratzinger has the stronger position, and why Professor Dawkins need not despair.

Explaining the eye

Of course much of this discussion about the nature of life began in 1859, when Charles Darwin published *The Origin of Species*. In his book Darwin proposed to do what no one had been able to do before him—explain how the great variety and complexity of life might have arisen solely through unguided natural processes. His proposed mechanism was, of course, natural selection acting on random variation. In a nutshell, Darwin recognized that there is variety in all species. Some members of a species are larger than others, some faster, some darker in color. Darwin knew that not all members of a species that are born will survive to reproduce, simply because there is not enough food to sustain them all. And so he reasoned that the ones whose chance variation gave them an edge in the struggle to survive would tend to survive and leave offspring. If the variation could be inherited, then over time the characteristics of the species might change. And over great periods of time, great changes might occur.

Darwin's theory was a very elegant idea. Nonetheless, even in the mid-nineteenth century biologists knew of a number of biological systems that did not appear to be able to be built in the gradual way that Darwin envisioned. One in particular was the eye. Biologists of the time knew that the eye was a very complex structure, containing many components, such as a lens, retina, tear ducts, ocular muscles, and so forth. They knew that if an animal were so unfortunate as to be born without one of the components, the result would be a severe loss of vision or outright blindness. So they doubted that such a system could be put together in the many steps required by natural selection.

Charles Darwin, however, knew about the eye too. And he wrote about it in a section of the *Origin of Species* appropriately entitled "Organs of Extreme Perfection and Complication", in which he said that he did not really know how the eye might have evolved. Nonetheless, he wrote that if you look at the eyes of modern organisms, you see considerable variety. In some organisms there really is not an "eye", but rather just a patch of light-sensitive cells. Now, that arrangement is sufficient for enabling an organism to know if it is in light or darkness, but it does not enable an organism to determine which direction the light is coming from, because light coming from virtually any angle will stimulate the light-sensitive cells. However, Darwin continued, if you take that patch of light-sensitive cells and place it in a small depression, as is seen in some modern animals, light coming from one side will cast a shadow over part of the light-sensitive spot, while the rest is illuminated. In theory such an arrangement could allow the creature to determine which direction the light is coming from. And that would be an improvement. If the cup were deepened, the direction-finding ability would be increased. And if the cup were filled with a gelatinous material, that could be the beginning of a crude lens, a further improvement. Using arguments like these, Darwin was able to convince many of his contemporaries that a gradual evolutionary pathway led from something as simple as a light-sensitive spot to something as complicated as the modern vertebrate eye. And if evolution could explain the eye . . . well, what could it not explain?

But there was a question left unaddressed by Darwin's scheme—where did the light-sensitive spot come from? It seems an odd starting point, since most objects are not light sensitive. Nonetheless, Darwin decided not even to attempt to address the question. He wrote that: "How a nerve comes to be sensitive to light hardly concerns us more than how life itself originated."[3]

Well, in the past half-century science has become interested in both those questions: the mechanism of vision and the origin of life. Nonetheless, Darwin was correct, I think, to refuse to address the question, because the science of his day did not have the physical or conceptual tools to begin to investigate it. Just to get a flavor of the science of the mid-nineteenth century, remember that atoms—the basis of all chemistry—were then considered to be theoretical entities. No one was sure if they really existed. The cell, which we now know to be the basis of life, was thought to be a simple glob of proto-plasm, not much more than a microscopic piece of Jell-O. So Darwin refused to address the question and left it as a black box in the hope that future discoveries would vindicate his theory.

"Black box" is a phrase used in science to indicate some machine or system that does something interesting, but no one knows how it works. Its mechanism is unknown because we cannot see inside the box to observe it, or if we can see the workings, they are so complicated that we still do not understand what is going on. For most of us (and certainly for me) a good example of a black box is a computer. I use a computer to process words or play games, but I do not have the foggiest idea how it works. And even if I were to remove the cover and see the inside circuitry, I still could not say how it worked. Well, to scientists of Darwin's day, the cell was a black box. It did very interesting things, but no one knew how.

When people see a black box in action, they have a psychological tendency to assume that it must be operating by some simple mechanism—the insides of the box must be uncomplicated and working on some easily understood principle. A good example of this tendency was the belief in the spontaneous generation of cellular life from sea mud. In the nineteenth century two prominent scientists and admirers of Darwin—Ernst Haeckel and Thomas Huxley—thought that some mud scraped up by an exploring vessel might be living cells. They could believe this because they thought a cell was, in Haeckel's words, a "simple little lump of albuminous combination of carbon".[4] With the tremendous progress biology has made in this century, of course, we know differently. Now that modern science has opened the black box of the cell, we need to readdress the question that stumped Darwin. What is needed to make a light-sensitive spot? What happens when a photon of light impinges upon a retina?

When a photon first hits the retina, it interacts with a small organic molecule called II-cis-retinal.[5] The shape of retinal is rather bent, but when retinal interacts with the photon, it straightens out, isomerizing into trans-retinal. This is the signal that sets in motion a whole cascade of events resulting in vision. When retinal changes shape, it forces a change in the shape of the protein rhodopsin, which is bound to it. The change in rhodopsin's shape exposes a binding site that allows the protein transducin to stick to it. Now part of the transducin complex dissociates and interacts with a protein called phosphodiesterase. When that happens, the phosphodiesterase acquires the ability chemically to cut a small organic molecule called cyclic-GMP, turning it into 5'-GMP. There is a lot of cyclic-GMP in the cell, and some of it sticks to another protein called an ion channel. Normally the ion channel allows sodium ions into the cell. When the concentration of cyclic-GMP decreases because of the action of the phosphodiesterase, however, the cyclic-GMP bound to the ion channel eventually falls off, causing a change in shape that shuts the channel. As a result, sodium ions can no longer enter the cell, the concentration of sodium in the cell decreases, and the voltage across the cell membrane changes. That in turn causes a wave of electrical polarization to be sent down the optic nerve to the brain. And, when interpreted by the brain, that is vision. So, this is what modern science has discovered about how Darwin's "simple" light-sensitive spot functions.

Darwin's criterion

Although most people will surely think the above description of the visual cascade is complicated, it is really just a little sketch of the chemistry of vision that ignores a number of things that a functioning visual system actually requires. For instance, I have not discussed the regeneration of the system—how it gets back to the starting point in preparation for the next incoming photon. Nonetheless, I think that the discussion above is sufficient to show that what Darwin and his contemporaries took as simple starting points have turned out to be enormously complex—much more complex than Darwin ever envisioned.

But how can we tell if the eye and other organisms are too complex to be explained by Darwin's theory? It turns out that Darwin himself gave us a criterion by which to judge his theory. He wrote in the *Origin of Species* that: "If it could be demonstrated that any complex organ existed which could not possibly have been formed by numerous, successive, slight modifications, my theory would absolutely break down."[6] But what sort of organ or system could not be formed by "numerous, successive, slight modifications"? Well, to begin with, one that is *irreducibly complex*. "Irreducibly complex" is a fancy phrase, but it stands for a very simple concept. As I wrote in *Darwin's Black Box: The Biochemical Challenge to Evolution*, an irreducibly complex system is: "a single system which is composed of several well-matched, interacting parts that contribute to the basic function, and where the removal of any one of the parts causes the system to effectively cease functioning."[7] Less formally, the phrase "irreducibly complex" just means that a system has a number of components that interact with each other, and if any are taken away the system no longer works. A good illustration of an irreducibly complex system from our everyday world is a simple mechanical mousetrap. The mousetraps that one buys at the hardware store generally have a wooden platform to which all the other parts are attached. It also has a spring with extended ends, one of which presses against the platform, the other against a metal part called the hammer, which actually does the job of squashing the mouse. When one presses the hammer down, it has to be stabilized in that position until the mouse comes along, and that is the job of the holding bar. The end of the holding bar itself has to be stabilized, so it is placed into a metal piece called the catch. All of these pieces are held together by assorted staples.

Now, if the mousetrap is missing the spring, or hammer, or platform, it does not catch mice half as well as it used to, or even a quarter as well. It does not catch mice at all. Therefore it is irreducibly complex. It turns out that irreducibly complex systems are headaches for Darwinian theory, because they are resistant to being produced in the gradual, step-by-step manner that Darwin envisioned. For example, if we wanted to evolve a mousetrap, where would we start? Could we start with just the platform and hope to catch a few mice rather inefficiently? Then add the holding bar, and improve the efficiency a bit? Then add the other pieces one at a time, steadily improving the whole apparatus? No, of course we cannot do that, because the mousetrap does not work at all until it is essentially completely assembled.

Biochemical challenges to Darwinism

Mousetraps are one thing, biological systems another. What we really want to know is whether there are any irreducibly complex biological systems, or cellular systems, or biochemical systems. And it turns out that there are many such irreducibly complex systems. Let us consider two examples. The first is called the cilium. A cilium is a little hairlike organelle on the surface of many types of cells. It has the intriguing ability to beat back and forth, moving liquid over the surface of a cell. In some tissue in the lungs, each cell contains hundreds of cilia that beat in synchrony. Interspersed among the ciliated cells are larger ones called goblet cells. The goblet cells secrete mucus into the lining of the lungs, which is swept by the ciliary beating up to the throat where it can be coughed out, along with any dust particles or other foreign objects that might have made their way into the lungs. But what makes a little hairlike organelle beat back and forth? Work in the past several decades has shown that cilia are actually very complicated molecular machines.

The basic structure of a cilium consists of nine double microtubules.[8] [See cross-section of a cilium illustration.] Each of the double microtubules contains two rings made up of ten and thirteen strands respectively of the protein tubulin. In the middle of the cilium are two single microtubules. All of the microtubules are connected to each other by various types of connectors. Neighboring double microtubules are connected by a protein called nexin. The outer double microtubules are connected to the inner single microtubules by radial spokes. And the two inner microtubules are attached by a small connecting bridge. Additionally, on each double microtubule there are two appendages: an outer dynein bridge and an inner dynein bridge. Although this all sounds complicated, such a brief description cannot do justice to the full complexity of the cilium, which, thorough biochemical studies have shown, contains about two hundred different kinds of protein parts.

But how does the cilium work? Studies have shown that it works by a "sliding-fiber mechanism". Neighboring microtubules are the fibers; dynein is a "motor protein". When the cilium is working, the dynein, bound to one strand, reaches over, attaches to a neighboring microtubule, and pushes down. When that happens, the microtubules start to slide with respect to each other. They would continue to slide until they fell apart, except that they are held together by the linker protein nexin. Initially rather loose, as the fibers slide, the nexin becomes more and more taut. As the tension on the nexin and microtubules increases beyond a certain point, the microtubules bend. Thus the sliding motion is converted into a bending motion.

If one thinks about it, it is easy to see that the cilium is irreducibly complex. If it were not for the microtubules, there would be nothing to slide. If the dynein were missing, the whole apparatus would lie stiff and motionless. And if the nexin linkers were missing, the whole apparatus would fall apart when the dynein started to push the microtubules, as it does in experiments when the nexin linkers are removed. Much like a mousetrap, a cilium needs a number of parts to function. And, again like a mousetrap, its gradual production in a step-by-step Darwinian fashion is quite difficult to envision.

Another example of an irreducibly complex biochemical system is in some ways like the cilium in that it is an organelle for motion. But in other ways it is completely different. The bacterial flagellum is quite literally an outboard motor that enables some bacteria to swim.[9] [See figure above.] Like the machines that power our motorboats, the flagellum is a rotary device, in which the rotating surface pushes against the liquid medium, propelling the bacterium along. The part of the flagellum that acts as the propeller is a long whip-like structure made of a protein called flagellin. The propeller is attached to the drive shaft by hook protein, which acts as a universal joint, allowing freedom of rotation

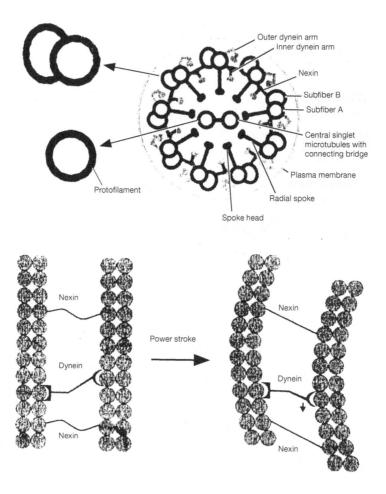

(Top) Cross-section of a cilium showing the fused double-ring structure of the outer microtubules, the single-ring structure of the central microtubules, connecting proteins, and dynein motor. (Bottom) The sliding motion induced by dynein "walking" up a neighboring microtubule is converted to a bending motion by the flexible linker protein nexin. From Voet and Voet, *Biochemistry*, 2nd edn. © 1995 John Wiley and Sons, Inc. Reprinted by permission of John Wiley and Sons, Inc.

for the propeller and drive shaft. The drive shaft is attached to the rotary motor, which uses a flow of acid from outside of the bacterium to the inside in order to power its turning. The drive shaft has to poke through the bacterial membrane, and several types of proteins act as bushing material to allow that to happen. Although this description makes the flagellum sound complicated, it really does not do justice to its full complexity. Thorough genetic studies have shown that about forty different proteins are required for a functional flagellum, either as parts of the flagellum itself or as parts of the system that builds this machine in the cell. And in the absence of most of those proteins, one does not get a flagellum that spins half as fast as it used to, or a quarter as fast. Either no flagellum gets produced at all, or one that does not work at all. Much like a cilium or mousetrap, the flagellum requires a number of parts to work. Therefore it is irreducibly complex, and its origin presents quite a stumbling block to Darwinian theory.

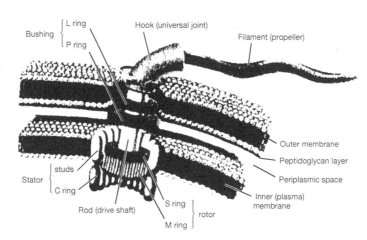

Drawing of a bacterial flagellum showing the filament, hook, and the motor imbedded in the inner and outer cell membranes and the cell wall. From Voet and Voet, *Biochemistry*, 2nd edn. © 1995 John Wiley and Sons, Inc. Reprinted by permission of John Wiley and Sons, Inc.

Darwinian imagination

I did not discover the cilium or flagellum. It was not I who worked out their mechanisms of action. That work was done by dozens and dozens of laboratories around the world over the course of decades. But if these structures cannot be explained by Darwinian theory, as I contend, then what have other scientists been saying about the origin of molecular machines? One place to look for an answer to that question is in the *Journal of Molecular Evolution*. As its name implies, *JME* was set up specifically to investigate how life might have arisen and then diversified at the molecular level. It is a good journal, which publishes interesting, rigorous material. Of the approximately forty scientists on its editorial board, about fifteen or so are members of the National Academy of Sciences. However, if you pick up a recent copy, you will find that the great majority of papers concern something called "sequence analysis". Briefly, proteins—the components of molecular machines—are made up of "sequences" of amino acids stitched together. Now, if one knows the sequence of amino acids in a protein (or in its gene) then one can compare the sequence to a similar protein from another species and see where the two sequences are the same, similar, or different. For example, suppose one compared the sequence of the oxygen-carrying protein hemoglobin from a dog to that from a horse. One could then ask, are the amino acid residues in the first position of the two proteins the same or different? How about the second position? the third? the fortieth? And so on. Knowing the answer to that question would be interesting and could indicate how closely related the two species are, and that would be an interesting thing to know.

For our purposes, however, the important point to keep in mind is that comparing sequences does not allow one to conclude how complex molecular machines, such as the cilium or flagellum, could have arisen step by Darwinian step. Perhaps an example would help to show why. Suppose that you compared the bones in the forelimb of a dog to those in the forelimb of a horse. And you observed that there were the same number of bones, and they were arranged in a similar pattern. Knowing that would be interesting, and that might allow you to conclude how closely related the animals are, which again would be an interesting thing to know. However, comparing the bones in the forelimb of a dog to those of a horse will not tell you where bones came from in the first place. In order to do that, you have to build models, do experiments, and so forth. It turns out that virtually none of the papers in the *Journal of Molecular Evolution* over the past decade has done such experimental work or model building.[10] The overwhelming percentage of papers are concerned with sequence analysis. Again, I hasten to say that sequence analysis is interesting and can tell one many things, but sequence analysis alone cannot say how complex molecular machines could have been produced in a Darwinian fashion.

If one looks at other journals, at the *Proceedings of the National Academy of Sciences*, *Cell*, the *Journal of Molecular Biology*, and so on, the story is the same. There are many, many studies comparing sequences, but very few concerning the Darwinian production of complex molecular machines. The few that do consider the problems of Darwinian evolution are invariably too broad to test rigorously. But if the scientific literature—the journals—do not contain answers to the question of how Darwinian processes could produce such intricate molecular machines, then why do many scientists believe that they can produce them? Well, it is difficult to say in detail, but certainly a part of the answer to that question is that scientists are taught, as part of their scientific training, that Darwinism is true. A good illustration can be found in the excellent textbook *Biochemistry*, by Voet and Voet. In the first chapter, where the textbook is introducing students to the biochemical view of the world, there is a marvelous, full-color drawing depicting the orthodox view of how life arose and diversified. In the top third of the drawing there are illustrated a volcano, lightning flashes, little rays of sunlight, and some gases floating around—and that, students are meant to infer, is how life started. The middle third of the picture shows a stylized drawing of a DNA molecule leading out from the origin-of-life ocean and into a bacterial cell—showing us how life developed. (The bacterium is depicted with a flagellum that, in the far-off view, looks as simple as a hair.) The bottom third of the picture shows the Garden of Eden, with a number of animals produced by evolution milling about. In their midst are a man and woman in the buff (which will no doubt attract student interest). If you look closely you see that the woman is offering the man an apple. And that, students are implicitly led to believe, is how life diversified.

But if you look through the text for serious scientific answers to how any of those processes could have occurred, you will not find them. In the *Origin of Species* at a number of points Darwin appealed to the imagination of his readers. But imagination is a two-edged sword. An imaginative person might see things that other people miss. Or he might see things that are not there. An examination of the science literature seems to show that Darwinism has become stuck in the world of imagination.

Apprehending design

My criticisms of Darwinian theory are not really new. A number of other scientists have previously noted that the biochemistry of life is really quite complex and does not seem to fit the gradualistic mechanism that Darwin proposed. Further, it has been pointed out by others that the scientific literature contains few real explanations of the molecular

foundations of life. Scientists like Stuart Kauffman of the Santa Fe Institute, James Sha-
piro of the University of Chicago, and Lynn Margulis of the University of Massachusetts
have all stated that natural selection is not a good explanation for some aspects of life.

Where I differ from those other critics is in the alternative I propose. I have written that if you look at molecular machines, such as the cilium, the flagellum, and others,
they look like they were designed—purposely designed by an intelligent agent. That
proposal has attracted a bit of attention. Some of my critics have pointed out that I am a
Roman Catholic and imply therefore that the proposal of intelligent design is a religious
idea, not a scientific one. I disagree. I think the conclusion of intelligent design in these
cases is completely empirical. That is, it is based entirely on the physical evidence, along
with an understanding of how we come to conclude that an object was designed. Every
day of our lives we decide, consciously or not, that some things were designed, others
not. How do we do that? How do we reach those conclusions?

To begin to see how we conclude that an object or system was designed, imagine
that you are walking with a friend in the woods. Suddenly your friend is pulled up by
the ankle by a vine and left dangling in the air. After you cut him down, you reconstruct
the situation. You see that the vine was tied to a tree limb that was bent down and held
by a stake in the ground. The vine was covered by leaves so that you would not notice it,
and so on. From the way the parts were arranged, you would quickly conclude that this
was no accident—this was a designed trap. Your conclusion is not based on religious
beliefs; it is one based firmly in the physical evidence.

Let us ask a few more questions about the vine-trap. First, who designed it? After
reflecting for a minute we see that we do not have enough information to answer that
question. Maybe it was an enemy of yours or your friend's; maybe it was a prankster.
Without more information we cannot decide who designed the trap. Nonetheless, from
the interaction of the parts of the trap, we can conclude that it was indeed designed. A
second question is, when was the trap designed? Again, after a minute's thought, we see
that we do not yet have enough information to answer the question. Without more data,
we cannot decide if the trap was designed an hour ago, a day ago, a week ago, or longer.
But again, we apprehend from the interaction of the parts of the trap the fact of design
itself. The bottom line is that we need additional information to answer questions such
as who, what, where, when, why, and how the trap was designed. But the fact that the
trap was designed is apprehended directly from observing the system.

Although we apprehend design easily and intuitively, it can also be treated in an
academically rigorous manner. An excellent start has been made in treating the design
problem in a philosophically and scientifically rigorous way by the philosopher and
mathematician William Dembski in his monograph *The Design Inference: Eliminating
Chance through Small Probabilities*.[11]

In conclusion, I would like to hearken back to the quotations with which I began
this essay. In my view there is every reason, based on hard empirical observation, to
conclude with Joseph Cardinal Ratzinger that "the great projects of the living creation
are not the products of chance and error. . . . [They] point to a creating Reason and
show us a creating Intelligence, and they do so more luminously and radiantly today
than ever before."

Notes

1   G. Easterbrook, "Science and God: A Warming Trend?" *Science* 277 (1997): 890–93.
2   J. Ratzinger, *In the Beginning: A Catholic Understanding of the Story of Creation and the Fall* (Grand Rapids, Mich.: Eerdmans, 1986), pp. 54–56.
3   C. Darwin, *On the Origin of Species* (1876; reprint, New York: New York University Press, 1988), p. 151.
4   J. Farley, *The Spontaneous Generation Controversy from Descartes to Oparin* (Baltimore: Johns Hopkins University Press, 1977), p. 73.
5   T. M. Devlin, *Textbook of Biochemistry* (New York: Wiley-Liss, 1997), chap. 22.3.
6   Darwin, *Origin*, p. 154.
7   M. J. Behe, *Darwin's Black Box: The Biochemical Challenge to Evolution* (New York: Free Press, 1996), p. 39.
8   D. Voet and J. G. Voet, *Biochemistry* (New York: J. Wiley and Sons, 1995), pp. 1252–59.
9   Ibid., pp. 1259–60.
10 Behe, *Darwin's*, chap. 8.
11 W. Dembski, *The Design Inference: Eliminating Chance through Small Probabilities* (Cambridge: Cambridge University Press, 1998).

Questions for reflection

1   Explain Professor Behe's general argument for an intelligent designer. Do you find it persuasive? Why or why not?
2   What are some similarities between the mousetrap example and the flagellar motor? What are some differences? Are the differences significant enough to cause the analogy to be ineffective? Why or why not?
3   Is there the danger of invoking a "god-of-the-gaps" problem by using Behe's irreducible complexity argument? If so, what is the danger? If not, why not?
4   Do you think scientific theory can include positing intelligent design at some level? Or must natural science presuppose a purely naturalistic view of the origin and development of living organisms? Explain your answer.

Further reading

Michael J. Behe (1996) *Darwin's Black Box: The Biochemical Challenge to Evolution.* New York: Free Press. (Presents a scientific argument that natural selection and random mutation fail as a mechanism for explaining certain complex, biomolecular systems.)
William A. Dembski (1998) *The Design Inference: Eliminating Chance Through Small Probabilities.* Cambridge: Cambridge University Press. (A philosopher and mathematician examines the notion of distinguishing events due to intelligent causes from events due to undirected natural causes.)
William A. Dembski and Michael Ruse, eds. (2004) *Debating Design: From Darwin to DNA.* Cambridge: Cambridge University Press. (Includes a number of essays from both sides of the biological origins debate.)
Phillip E. Johnson (1993) *Darwin on Trial.* Downers Grove, IL: InterVarsity Press. (The forerunner of the intelligent design movement; argues that aspects of Darwinian evolution are based on faith in philosophical naturalism rather than scientific fact.)
Robert T. Pennock, ed. (2001) *Intelligent Design Creationism and Its Critics: Philosophical, Theological, and Scientific Perspectives.* Cambridge, MA: MIT Press. (Contains influential essays by both creationists and their critics.)

Chapter 23

Robin Collins

A RECENT FINE-TUNING ARGUMENT

Robin Collins is Professor of Philosophy at Messiah College specializing in science and religion. In this essay, he argues that the fine-tuning of the cosmos for conscious embodied life (CEL) offers significant evidence for preferring theism over two forms of naturalism—the naturalistic single-universe hypothesis (NSU) and the naturalistic multiverse hypothesis. He also examines three major objections to the argument and proposes that other features of the universe, such as the beauty and elegance of the laws of nature, suggest design as well. While he concedes that the argument does not offer proof for the existence of the theistic God, he notes that a cumulative case for theism can be made by considering other arguments as well, such as those provided by Richard Swinburne.

Introduction*

Design arguments have a long history, probably being the most commonly-cited argument for believing in a deity. In ancient India, for instance, the argument from design was advanced by the so-called Nyāya (or logical-atomist) school (100–1000 CE), which argued for the existence of a deity based on the order of the world, which they compared both to human artifacts and to the human body (Smart 1964: 153–4). In the West, the design argument goes back to at least Heraclitus (500 BCE). It reached its highpoint with the publication of Paley's *Natural Theology* (1802), which primarily appealed to the intricate structure of plants and animals as evidence for design. With the advent of Darwin's theory of evolution, this version of the argument underwent an almost fatal blow, though it has gained a small following recently among advocates of the so-called intelligent design movement. By far the most widely cited evidence for design, however, is that from findings in physics and cosmology during the twentieth century. In this essay we will mainly focus on the evidence from the so-called fine-tuning of the cosmos for conscious, embodied life (CEL), though we will briefly look at other evidence from the beauty and elegance of the laws of nature.

The evidence of fine-tuning

Many examples of this fine-tuning can be given, a few of which we will briefly recount here. One particularly important category of fine-tuning is that of the *constants* of physics. The constants of physics are a set of fundamental numbers that, when plugged into the laws of physics, determine the basic structure of the universe. An example of such a constant is the gravitational constant G that is part of Newton's law of gravity, $F = GM_1M_2/r^2$, where F is the force between two masses, M_1 and M_2, and r is the distance between them. G essentially determines the strength of gravity between two masses. If one were to double the value of G, for instance, then the force of gravity between any two masses would double.

So far, physicists have discovered four forces in nature: gravity, the weak force, electromagnetism, and the strong nuclear force that binds protons and neutrons together in an atom. As measured in a certain set of standard dimensionless units (Barrow and Tipler 1986: 292–5), gravity is the weakest of the forces, and the strong nuclear force is the strongest, being a factor of 10^{40}—or ten thousand billion, billion, billion, billion—times stronger than gravity.

Various calculations show that the strength of each of the forces of nature must fall into a very small CEL-permitting region for CEL to exist. As just one example, consider gravity. Compared to the total range of forces, the strength of gravity must fall in a relatively narrow range in order for CEL to exist. If we increased the strength of gravity a billion-fold, for instance, the force of gravity on a planet with the mass and size of the earth would be so great that organisms anywhere near the size of human beings, whether land-based or aquatic, would be crushed. (The strength of materials depends on the electromagnetic force via the fine-structure constant, which would not be affected by a change in gravity.) Even a much smaller planet of only 40 feet in diameter—which is not large enough to sustain organisms of our size—would have a gravitational pull of one thousand times that of earth, still too strong for organisms of our brain size, and hence level of intelligence, to exist. As astrophysicist Martin Rees notes, "In an imaginary strong gravity world, even insects would need thick legs to support them, and no animals could get much larger" (Rees 2000: 30). Other calculations show that if the gravitational force were increased by more than a factor of 3000, the maximum life-time of a star would be a billion years, thus severely inhibiting the probability of CEL evolving (Collins 2003). Of course, a three-thousand-fold increase in the strength of gravity is a lot, but compared to the total range of the strengths of the forces in nature (which span a range of 10^{40}, as we saw above), it is very small, being one part in a billion, billion, billion, billion.

There are other cases of the fine-tuning of the constants of physics besides the strength of the forces, however. Probably the most widely discussed (and esoteric) among physicists and cosmologists is the fine-tuning of what is known as the *cosmological constant*. This is a number in Einstein's theory of general relativity that influences the expansion rate of the universe. If the cosmological constant were not fine-tuned to within an extremely narrow range—one part in 10^{53} or even 10^{120} of its "theoretically natural" range of values—the universe would expand so rapidly that all matter would quickly disperse, and thus galaxies, stars, and even small aggregates of matter could never form (e.g., Rees 2000: 95–102, 154–5; Collins 2003).[1]

Besides the constants of physics, however, there is also the fine-tuning of the laws.

If the laws of nature were not just right, CEL would probably be impossible. For example, consider again the four forces of nature. If gravity (or a force like it) did not exist, masses would not clump together to form stars or planets and hence the existence of complex CEL would be seriously inhibited, if not rendered impossible; if the electromagnetic force didn't exist, there would be no chemistry; if the strong nuclear force didn't exist, protons and neutrons could not bind together and hence no atoms with atomic numbers greater than hydrogen would exist; and if the strong nuclear force were a long-range force (like gravity and electromagnetism) instead of a short-range force that only acts between protons and neutrons in the nucleus, all matter would either almost instantaneously undergo nuclear fusion and explode or be sucked together forming a black hole.

Similarly, other laws and principles are necessary for CEL. As prominent Princeton physicist Freeman Dyson points out (Dyson 1979: 251), if the Pauli-exclusion principle did not exist, which dictates that no two fermions can occupy the same quantum state, all electrons would occupy the lowest atomic orbit, eliminating complex chemistry; and if there were no quantization principle, which dictates that particles can only occupy certain discrete allowed quantum states, there would be no atomic orbits and hence no chemistry since all electrons would be sucked into the nucleus.

If the above is not enough, there are two other major types of fine-tuning. First, the initial distribution of mass-energy at the beginning of the universe (as measured by its entropy) must be just right for CEL. Roger Penrose, former Oxford University professor of mathematical physics, has calculated the necessary precision to be unimaginably precise – on the order of one part in one followed by 10^{120} zeros (Penrose, 1989, p. 343). Second, in his book *Nature's Destiny*, biochemist Michael Denton extensively discusses various higher-level features of the natural world, such as the many unique properties of carbon, oxygen, water, and the electromagnetic spectrum, that are conducive to the existence of complex biochemical systems. As one of many examples Denton presents, both the atmosphere and water are transparent to electromagnetic radiation in a thin band in the visible region, but nowhere else except radio waves. If, instead, either of them absorbed electromagnetic radiation in the visible region, the existence of terrestrial CEL would be seriously inhibited, if not rendered impossible (Denton 1998: 56–7). These higher-level coincidences indicate a deeper level fine-tuning of the fundamental laws and constants of physics.

As the above examples indicate, the evidence for fine-tuning is both extensive and varied, even if one has doubts about some individual cases. As philosopher John Leslie has pointed out, "clues heaped upon clues can constitute weighty evidence despite doubts about each element in the pile" (Leslie 1988: 300). At the very least, these cases of fine-tuning show the truth of Freeman Dyson's observation that there are many "lucky accidents in physics" (1979: 251) without which CEL would be impossible.

The argument formulated

Now it is time to consider the way in which the existence of a fine-tuned universe supports theism. In this section, I will argue that the evidence of fine-tuning primarily gives us a reason for preferring theism over what could be called the naturalistic single-universe hypothesis (NSU)—that is, the hypothesis that there is only one universe, and it exists as an inexplicable fact. (We will examine the typical alternative explanation of the fine-tuning offered by many naturalists—what has come to be called the *multiverse* hypothesis—in a section below.) We will present our argument for the case of the fine-tuning of the constants, but with some modifications it applies to the other types of fine-tuning for CEL mentioned above.

Although the fine-tuning argument against the NSU can be cast in several different forms—such as inference to the best explanation—I believe the most rigorous way of formulating the argument is in terms of what is often called the *likelihood principle*, a standard principle of confirmation theory (e.g., see Sober 2002). *Simply put, the principle says that whenever we are considering two competing non-ad-hoc hypotheses, an observation counts as evidence in favor of the hypothesis under which the observation has the highest probability (or is the least improbable).*[2] Since the type of probability in the likelihood principle is what is known as *epistemic probability* (see below), the likelihood principle can be reworded more intuitively in terms of what could be called the *surprise principle*: namely, whenever we are considering two competing hypotheses, an observation counts as evidence in favor of the hypothesis under which it is least surprising. Moreover, the degree to which the observation counts in favor of one hypothesis over another is proportional to the degree to which the observation is more probable (or less surprising) under the one hypothesis than the other.

Using this principle, we can develop the fine-tuning argument in a two-step form as follows:

> Premise (1) The existence of a universe with CEL is not highly improbable (or surprising) under theism.
> Premise (2) Because of the fine-tuning, the existence of a universe with CEL is very improbable (surprising) under the NSU.
> Conclusion: From premises (1) and (2) and the likelihood principle, it follows that the fine-tuning data provides significant evidence to favor of theism over the NSU.

At this point, we should pause to note two features of this argument. First, the argument does not say that the fine-tuning evidence proves theism, or even that it is likely that theism is true. Indeed, of itself it does not even show that we are epistemically warranted in believing in theism over the NSU. In order to justify these sorts of claims, we would have to look at the full range of evidence both for and against the theistic hypothesis—something I am *not* doing in this essay. Rather, the argument merely concludes that the fine-tuning significantly *supports* theism *over* the NSU. (I say "significantly supports" because presumably the ratio of probabilities for the existence of a CEL-permitting universe under theism versus the NSU is quite large.)

In this way, the evidence of the fine-tuning argument is much like DNA found on the gun. By the "likelihood" or "surprise principle," the DNA on the gun provide significant evidence that the defendant is guilty because their existence would be much more surprising if the defendant were innocent than if he were guilty. Yet, one could not conclude merely from them alone that the defendant is likely to be guilty, for there could be other countervailing evidence, such as the testimony of reliable witnesses that he was not at the scene of the crime. The DNA would still count as significant evidence of guilt, but this evidence would be counterbalanced by the testimony of the witnesses. Similarly the evidence of fine-tuning significantly supports theism over the NSU, though it does not itself show that, everything considered, theism is the most plausible explanation of the existence of a universe with CEL.

Support for the premises

Support for Premise (1): Premise (1) is easy to support and somewhat less controversial than premise (2). The argument in support of it can be simply stated as follows: *since God is an all-good being, and in and of itself it is good for embodied, intelligent, conscious beings to exist, it not highly surprising or highly improbable that God would create a world that could support CEL.* Thus, the fine-tuning is not highly improbable under theism.[3]

Support for Premise (2): Upon looking at the data, many people find it very obvious that the fine-tuning is highly improbable under the NSU. And it is easy to see why when we think of the fine-tuning in terms of various analogies. In the "dart-board analogy," for example, the range of theoretically possible values for fundamental constants of physics can be represented as a dart-board that fills the whole galaxy, and the conditions necessary for CEL to exist as a small inch-wide target. From analogies such as this it seems intuitively obvious to many people that it would be highly improbable for the fine-tuning to occur under the NSU—that is, for the dart to hit the target by chance.

Now some philosophers, such as Keith Parsons (1990: 182), object to the claim that the fine-tuning is highly improbable under the NSU by arguing that since we only have one universe, the notion of the fine-tuning of the universe being probable or improbable is meaningless. Further, apart from this objection, many would like to see a more philosophically sophisticated reason than offered by analogies such as the one above for why a CEL-permitting universe would be less probable under the NSU than theism.

Although I do not have space to provide a full-scale response to these challenges, I will briefly sketch an answer. The first is to note that, as mentioned above, the relevant notion of probability occurring in the fine-tuning argument is a widely recognized type of probability called *epistemic probability* (e.g., see Hacking 1975; Plantinga 1993: chs. 8 and 9). Roughly, the epistemic probability of a proposition can be thought of as the degree of confidence or belief we rationally should have in the proposition. Further, for our purposes, the conditional epistemic probability of a proposition R on another proposition S—written as $P(R/S)$— could be defined roughly as the degree to which the proposition S *of itself* should rationally lead us to expect that R is true, although there is yet no accepted precise definition of this idea. Under our proposed definition of epistemic probability, therefore, the statement that *the existence of a CEL-permitting cosmos is very improbable under the NSU* is to be understood as making a statement about the degree to which the NSU would or should, *of itself*, rationally lead us to expect a CEL-permitting cosmos, given the narrowness of the CEL-permitting range.

The notion *of itself* is important here. The rational degree of expectation should not be confused with the degree to which one should expect the constants of physics to fall within the CEL range if one believed the NSU. For even those who believe in this hypothesis should expect the constants of physics to be CEL-permitting since this follows from the fact that we are alive. Rather, the conditional epistemic probability in this case is the degree to which the NSU *of itself* should lead us to expect constants of physics to be CEL-permitting. This means that in assessing the conditional epistemic

probability in this and other similar cases, one must exclude contributions to our expectations arising from other information we have, such as that we are alive. In the case at
hand, one way of doing this is by means of the following sort of thought experiment.
Imagine a disembodied being with mental capacities and a knowledge of physics comparable to that of the most intelligent physicists alive today, except that the being does
not know whether the values of the constants of physics allow for CEL to arise. Further,
suppose that this disembodied being believed in the NSU. Then, the degree that being
should rationally expect the constants of physics to be CEL-permitting will be equal to
our conditional epistemic probability, since its expectation is solely a result of its belief
in the NSU, not other factors such as its awareness of its own existence.

Given this understanding of the notion of conditional epistemic probability, it is not
difficult to see that the conditional epistemic probability of a constant of physics having
a CEL-permitting value under the NSU will be much smaller than under theism. The
reason is simple when we think about our imaginary disembodied being. If such a being
were a theist, it would have some reason to believe that the values of constants would
fall into the CEL-permitting region (see the argument in support of premise (1) above).
On the other hand, if the being were a subscriber to the NSU, it would have no reason
to think the value would be in the CEL-permitting region instead of any other part of
the range of "theoretically possible" values it could have had. Thus, the being has more
reason to believe the constants would fall into the CEL-permitting region under theism
than the NSU; that is, the epistemic probability under theism is larger than under the
NSU, or put differently, the existence of a CEL-permitting universe is more surprising
under the NSU than theism. How much more surprising? That depends on the degree
of fine-tuning. Here, I will simply note that it seems obvious that in general the higher
the degree of fine-tuning—that is, the smaller the width of the CEL-permitting range
is to the "theoretically possible" range—the greater the surprise under the NSU, and
hence the greater the ratio of the two probabilities. To go beyond these statements and
to assign actual epistemic probabilities (or degrees of surprise) under the NSU—or to
further justify these claims of improbability—would require defending a version of the
probabilistic principle of indifference, which is beyond the scope of this essay.

Objections to the argument

As powerful as the fine-tuning argument against the NSU might seem to be, several major
objections have been raised against it. In this section, we will consider some of these
objections in turn.

Objection 1: More fundamental law objection

One criticism of the fine-tuning argument is that, as far as we know, there could be a
more fundamental law under which the constants of physics *must* have the values they
do. Thus, given such a law, it is not improbable that the known constants of physics fall
within the CEL-permitting range. Besides being entirely speculative, the problem with
postulating such a law is that it simply moves the improbability of the fine-tuning up
one level, to that of the postulated physical law itself. As astrophysicists Bernard Carr

and Martin Rees note, "even if all apparently anthropic coincidences could be explained [in terms of some grand unified theory], it would still be remarkable that the relationships dictated by physical theory happened also to be those propitious for life" (Carr and Rees 1979: 612).

For the theist, then, the development of a grand unified theory would not undercut the case for theism, but would only serve to deepen our appreciation of the ingenuity of the creator: Instead of separately fine-tuning each individual parameter, in this view God simply carefully chose those laws that would yield CEL-permitting values for each parameter.

Objection 2: Other forms of life objection

Another objection commonly raised against the fine-tuning argument is that as far as we know, other forms of CEL could exist even if the constants of physics were different. So, it is claimed, the fine-tuning argument ends up presupposing that all forms of CEL must be like us. One answer to this objection is that many cases of fine-tuning do not make this presupposition. If, for example, the cosmological constant were much larger than it is, matter would disperse so rapidly that no planets, and indeed no stars, could exist. Without stars, however, there would exist no stable energy sources for complex material systems of any sort to evolve. So, all the fine-tuning argument presupposes in this case is that the evolution of CEL requires some stable energy source. This is certainly a very reasonable assumption.

Objection 3: The "who designed God?" objection

Perhaps the most common objection that atheists raise to the argument from design, of which the fine-tuning argument is one instance, is that postulating the existence of God does not solve the problem of design but merely transfers it up one level, to the question of who designed God. One response to the fine-tuning argument is that it only relies on comparison of the epistemic probabilities of fine-tuning under the two different hypotheses, not on whether the new hypothesis reduces the overall complexity of one's worldview. As an analogy, if complex, intricate structures (such as aqueducts and buildings) existed on Mars, one could conclude that their existence would support the hypothesis that intelligent, extraterrestrial beings existed on Mars in the past, even if such beings are much more complex than the structures to be explained.

Second, however, for reasons entirely independent of the argument from design, God has been thought to have little, if any internal complexity. Indeed, medieval philosophers and theologians often went as far as advocating the doctrine of divine simplicity, according to which God is claimed to be absolutely simple, without any internal complexity, and hence not in need of design So, atheists who push this objection have a lot of arguing to do to make it stick. (For a more detailed treatment of the "Who Designed God? Objection," see Collins 2005.)

The multiverse hypothesis

Another objection to considering fine-tuning as evidence for design is the proposal that there are a very large number of universes, each with different values for the fundamental parameters of physics. If such multiple universes exist, it would be no surprise that the parameters in one of them would have just the right values for the existence of CEL—just as in the case where if enough lottery tickets were generated, it would be no surprise that one of them would turn out to be the winning number.

How did these universes come into existence? Typically, the answer is to postulate some kind of physical process, what I will call a "universe generator." Against the naturalistic version of the universe-generator hypothesis, one could argue that the universe generator itself must be "well designed" to produce even one CEL-sustaining universe. After all, even a mundane item such as a bread-making machine, which only produces loaves of bread instead of universes, must be well-designed as an appliance *and* have just the right ingredients (flour, yeast, gluten, and so on) in just the right amounts to produce decent loaves of bread. Indeed, as I have shown in detail elsewhere (Collins forthcoming), if one carefully examines the most popular, and most well-developed universe-generator hypothesis—that arising out of inflationary cosmology—one finds that it contains just the right fields and laws to generate CEL-permitting universes. Eliminate one of the fields or laws and no CEL-sustaining universes would be produced. If this is right, then invoking some sort of universe generator as an explanation of fine-tuning only pushes the issue of design up one level to the question of who or what designed it. However, it does eliminate the quantitative aspects of fine-tuning based on the constants of physics, and therefore arguably weakens the case for design.

Besides the universe-generator hypothesis, a very small minority of scientists and philosophers have proposed what could be called a *metaphysical* multiverse hypothesis, according to which universes are thought to exist on their own without being generated by any physical process. Typically, advocates of this view—such as the late Princeton University philosopher David Lewis (1986) and MIT astrophysicist Max Tegmark (1998)—propose that every possible set of laws is instantiated in some universe or another. One problem with this hypothesis is that it cannot explain why we inhabit a universe that is so orderly and has such low initial entropy: it is much more likely for there to exist local islands with the sort of order necessary for CEL than for the entire universe to have such an ordered arrangement. Thus, their hypothesis cannot explain the highly ordered character of the universe as a whole. Among others, George Schlesinger (1984) has raised this objection against Lewis's hypothesis. This sort of objection was raised against a similar explanation of the high degree of order in our universe offered by the famous physicist Ludwig Boltzmann, and has generally been considered fatal to Boltzmann's explanation (Davies 1974: 103).

Despite these objections and the fact that the multiverse hypothesis typically has been advanced by naturalists as an alternative explanation to design, I am not objecting to the notion of many universes itself. I actually believe that theists should be open to the idea that God created our universe by means of a universe generator. It makes some sense that an infinitely creative deity would create other universes, not just our own.

Other evidences for design

Besides the fine-tuning for CEL, there are other significant evidences for design based on the findings of physics and cosmology, such as the extraordinary degree of beauty, elegance, harmony, and ingenuity exhibited by the fundamental mathematical structure of the universe. For instance, Nobel Prize-winning physicist Steven Weinberg, himself an atheist, devotes a whole chapter of his book, *Dreams of a Final Theory* (Chapter 6, "Beautiful Theories"), to explaining how the criteria of beauty and elegance are commonly used to guide physicists in formulating the right laws. Because this beauty and elegance has been so successful in guiding physicists in developing highly successful theories, it is difficult to claim that this beauty and elegance is merely in the eye of the beholder. Today, this use of beauty and elegance as a guide is particularly evident in the popularity of superstring theory, which is widely considered the most feasible candidate for a truly fundamental theory in physics. Yet, it is almost entirely motivated by considerations of elegance, having no direct experimental support in its favor (Greene 1999: 214).

Now such beauty, elegance, and ingenuity make sense if the universe was created by God. I would contend, however, that apart from some sort of design hypothesis, there is no reason to expect the fundamental laws to be elegant or beautiful. The metaphysical multiverse hypothesis, for example, cannot in any obvious way explain why we observe a universe with such an elegant and beautiful fundamental structure, since under this hypothesis there would be many, many universes that contained observers in which the underlying mathematical structure would not be beautiful. Thus theism makes more sense of this aspect of the world than naturalism, whether that naturalism is of the single-universe or multiverse variety (see Collins forthcoming). Similar things could be said about the fact that the world is arranged in just the right way so that we can understand its underlying structure, something which could be called the "discoverability" of the laws of physics, as for example discussed by Eugene Wigner (1960) and Mark Steiner (1998).

Conclusion

In this essay, I have argued that the fine-tuning of the cosmos for CEL provides significant evidence for preferring theism over the NSU. I then argued that although one can partially explain the fine-tuning of the constants of physics by invoking some sort of multiverse generator, we have good reasons to believe that the multiverse generator itself would need to be well designed, and hence that hypothesizing some sort of multiverse generator only pushes the case for design up one level. I further argued that other features of the structure of the universe, such as the beauty and elegance of the laws of nature, also suggest design. When all the evidence is considered, I believe, one has a good cumulative case argument for an intelligent cause of the universe—that is, an argument in which many lines of evidence point to the same conclusion. Of course, one would need additional arguments, such as those offered by Richard Swinburne (2004: ch. 5), to conclude that this intelligent cause is the theistic God. Finally, even with this cumulative case argument, to conclude that it is likely that the theistic God exists, one would need to examine all the arguments for and against the existence of God, something that is obviously beyond the scope of this essay.

Notes

*   [This is a slightly revised version of an earlier essay published in *The Routledge Companion to Philosophy of Religion*. Ed. Chad Meister and Paul Copan, London: Routledge, 2007.]

1   Collins (2003) has re-examined and updated the evidence for the fine-tuning of the constants of physics, presenting six fairly solid cases of fine-tuning and pointing out some major flaws in the literature.

2   The qualification that the hypotheses be non-ad-hoc is one way of dealing with certain potential counterexamples to this principle in which one merely constructs a hypothesis after the fact to account for some unlikely event. A sufficient condition for a hypothesis being non-ad-hoc is that it was widely believed or proposed prior to the evidence, which is the case with both theism and atheism.

3   One might object to this argument by claiming that because of the existence of evil, we do not know that the existence of embodied, conscious, intelligent beings is a good thing as the argument seems to assume. To address this objection, let E represent the claim that embodied, conscious beings exist and let E= represent the claim that embodied conscious beings exist in the universe *and* that their embodied existence is a positive good (that is, something that increases the overall value of reality). Then, it follows from the above argument that claim E= is not highly improbable under theism. But, E= entails E, and we know that for all types of probability, if one claim R entails another claim S, then the probability of S is greater than or equal to that of R. Hence, if E= is not highly improbable under theism, then it follows that E isn't either.

References

Barrow, J. and F. Tipler (1986) *The Anthropic Cosmological Principle*, Oxford: Oxford University Press.

Carr, B. J. and M. J. Rees (1979) "The Anthropic Cosmological Principle and the Structure of the Physical World," *Nature* 278 (12 April): 605–612.

Collins, R. (2003) "The Evidence for Fine-Tuning," in N. Manson (ed.), *God and Design*, London: Routledge.

—— (2005) "Hume, Fine-Tuning and the Who Designed God? Objection," in J. Sennett and D. Groothius (eds.), *In Defense of Natural Theology: A Post-Humean Assessment*, Downers Grove, IL: InterVarsity Press.

—— (forthcoming) "A Theistic Perspective on the Multiverse Hypothesis," in B. Carr (ed.), *Universe or Multiverse?* Cambridge: Cambridge University Press.

Davies, P. (1974) *The Physics of Time Asymmetry*, Berkeley, CA: University of California Press.

Denton, M. (1998) *Nature's Destiny: How the Laws of Biology Reveal Purpose in the Universe*, New York: The Free Press.

Dyson, F. (1979) *Disturbing the Universe*, New York: Harper and Row.

Greene, B. (1999) *The Elegant Universe: Superstrings, Hidden Dimensions, and the Quest for the Ultimate Theory*, New York: W.W. Norton and Company.

Hacking, I. (1975) *The Emergence of Probability: A Philosophical Study of Early Ideas about Probability, Induction and Statistical Inference*, Cambridge: Cambridge University Press.

Leslie, J. (1988) "How to Draw Conclusions from a Fine-Tuned Cosmos," in R. Russell, et al. (eds.), *Physics, Philosophy and Theology: A Common Quest for Understanding*, Vatican City State: Vatican Observatory Press.

Lewis, D. (1986) *On the Plurality of Worlds*, New York: Basil Blackwell.

Parsons, K. (1990) "Is There a Case for Christian Theism?" in J.P. Moreland and K. Nielsen (eds.), *Does God Exist? The Great Debate*, Nashville, TN: Thomas Nelson.

Penrose, Roger (1989). *The Emperor's New Mind: Concerning Computers, Minds, and the Laws of Physics*, New York: Oxford University Press.

Plantinga, A. (1993) *Warrant and Proper Function*, Oxford: Oxford University Press.

Rees, M. (2000) *Just Six Numbers: The Deep Forces that Shape the Universe*, New York: Basic.

Schlesinger, G. (1984) "Possible Worlds and the Mystery of Existence," *Ratio* 26: 1–18.

Smart, N. (1964) *Doctrine and Argument in Indian Philosophy*, London: Allen and Unwin.

Sober, E. (2002) "Bayesianism—Its Scope and Limits," in R. Swinburne (ed.), *Bayes's Theorem*, Oxford: Oxford University Press.

Steiner, M. (1998) *The Applicability of Mathematics as a Philosophical Problem*, Cambridge, MA: Harvard University Press.

Swinburne, R. (2004) *The Existence of God*, 2nd edn, Oxford: Clarendon Press.

Tegmark, M. (1998) "Is 'the theory of everything' merely the ultimate ensemble theory?" *Annals of Physics* 270: 1–51. Preprint at http://arxiv.org/abs/gr-qc/9704009.

Weinberg, S. (1992) *Dreams of a Final Theory*, New York: Vintage Books.

Wigner, E. (1960) "The Unreasonable Effectiveness of Mathematics in the Natural Sciences," *Communications on Pure and Applied Mathematics* 13: 1–14. Available at http://www.dartmouth.edu/~matc/MathDrama/reading/Wigner.html.

Questions for reflection

1   Explain the fine-tuning argument as explicated by Professor Collins. What do you take to be the strongest objection to it? Which is more plausible for you—the argument or the objection? Why?

2   What do you make of the analogy, used as a response to the "Who created God?" objection, of the aqueducts and buildings on Mars? Is it a fair analogy? Why or why not?

3   How does Collins's argument against the multiverse generator work? Do you agree with his conclusion? Explain.

4   What do you make of the position, offered by Keith Parsons, that since we only have one universe, the claim that its fine-tuning is probable or improbable is a meaningless one? What do you make of Collins's response to the claim?

5   Are beauty and elegance purely subjective notions? If so, how does this affect the evidence for design? Also, if so, how is it that beauty and elegance are being used to guide physicists in formulating the right laws? Does the answer to this latter question demonstrate their objectivity? Explain.

Further reading

Paul Davies (1982) *The Accidental Universe*. Cambridge: Cambridge University Press. (One of the first books by a leading theoretical physicist that presents the evidence for the fine-tuning of the universe.)

Rodney D. Holder (2004) *God, the Multiverse, and Everything: Modern Cosmology and the Argument from Design*. Aldershot: Ashgate. (Argues that the evidence of fine-tuning supports theism.)

John Leslie (1989) *Universes*. London: Routledge. (Explores the question of multiple universes as an alternative to a design explanation of fine-tuning.)

Neil Manson, ed. (2003) *God and Design: The Teleological Argument and Modern Science*. New

York: Routledge. (Twenty-one authors vigorously debate the merits of divine teleology, from the realm of biology to cosmology.)

Neil Manson and Jay W. Richards, eds. (2005) *Philosophical Issues in Intelligent Design.* Special Issue of *Philosophia Christi* n.s. 7/2 (December). (Contains a debate regarding whether fine-tuning can be considered improbable.)

Leonard Susskind (2005) *The Cosmic Landscape: String Theory and the Illusion of Intelligent Design.* New York: Little, Brown and Company. (A leading physicist presents the multiverse alternative to design based on superstring theory.)

Chapter 24

David Hume

A CRITIQUE OF THE DESIGN ARGUMENT

David Hume (1711–76) was a philosopher, historian, essayist, and skeptic. He is widely taken to be one of the most important philosophers to write in the English language. In the following selection, he presents his classic critique of the design argument. It is written in the form of a dialogue and includes three interlocutors: Cleanthes, who represents the natural theologian; Demea, who represents the orthodox believer; and Philo, who represents the skeptic.

First, Cleanthes provides an argument by analogy in which he notes that throughout the natural world we find an "adapting of means to ends" which is very much like what we find in designed machines. Since there is such a close resemblance between these natural entities and such machines, it is reasonable to infer that the natural entities are designed as well.

Philo then responds by arguing that the analogy between the world and a machine is flawed since there are not the kinds of similarities necessary for a strong analogy. Philo then argues, following Cleanthes' principle that "like effects prove like causes," that even if the analogy was strong enough to be successful, it would not necessarily provide us with the God of the theistic religions—a God who is infinite, perfect, incorporeal, and one.

Cleanthes: Not to lose any time in circumlocutions, said *Cleanthes*, addressing himself to *Demea*, much less in replying to the pious declamations of *Philo*, I shall briefly explain how I conceive this matter. Look round the world: Contemplate the whole and every part of it: You will find it to be nothing but one great machine, subdivided into an infinite number of lesser machines, which again admit of subdivisions to a degree beyond what human senses and faculties can trace and explain. All these various machines, and even their most minute parts, are adjusted to each other with an accuracy which ravishes into admiration all men who have ever contemplated them. The curious adapting of means to ends, throughout all nature, resembles exactly, though it much exceeds, the productions of human contrivance; of human design, thought, wisdom, and intelligence. Since therefore the effects resemble each other, we are led to infer, by all the rules of analogy, that the causes also resemble, and that the Author of Nature is somewhat similar to the mind of man, though possessed of much larger faculties, proportioned to the grandeur of the work which he has executed. By this argument *a posteriori*, and by this argument alone, do we prove at once the existence of a Deity and his similarity to human mind and intelligence.

Demea: I shall be so free, *Cleanthes*, said *Demea*, as to tell you that from the beginning I could not approve of your conclusion concerning the similarity of the Deity to men; still less can I approve of the mediums by which you endeavor to establish it. What! No demonstration of the Being of God! No abstract arguments! No proofs *a priori*! Are these which have hitherto been so much insisted on by philosophers all fallacy, all sophism? Can we reach no farther in this subject than experience and probability? I will say not that this is betraying the cause of a Deity; but surely, by this affected candor, you give advantages to atheists which they never could obtain by the mere dint of argument and reasoning.

Philo: What I chiefly scruple in this subject, said *Philo*, is not so much that all religious arguments are by *Cleanthes* reduced to experience, as that they appear not be even the most certain and irrefragable of that inferior kind. That a stone will fall, that fire will burn, that the earth has solidity, we have observed a thousand and a thousand times; and when any new instance of this nature is presented, we draw without hesitation the accustomed inference. The exact similarity of the cases gives us a perfect assurance of a similar event, and a stronger evidence is never desired nor sought after. But wherever you depart, in the least, from the similarity of the cases, you diminish proportionably the evidence; and may at last bring it to a very weak *analogy*, which is confessedly liable to error and uncertainty. After having experienced the circulation of the blood in human creatures, we make no doubt that it takes place in *Titius* and *Maevius*; but from its circulation in frogs and fishes it is only a presumption, though a strong one, from analogy that it takes place in men and other animals. The analogical reasoning is much weaker when we infer the circulation of the sap in vegetables from our experience that the blood circulates in animals; and those who hastily followed that imperfect analogy are found, by more accurate experiments, to have been mistaken.

If we see a house, *Cleanthes*, we conclude, with the greatest certainty, that it had an architect or builder because this is precisely that species of effect which we have experienced to proceed from that species of cause. But surely you will not affirm that the universe bears such a resemblance to a house that we can with the same certainty infer a similar cause, or that the analogy is here entire and perfect. The dissimilitude is so striking that the utmost you can here pretend to is a guess, a conjecture, a presumption concerning a similar cause; and how that pretension will be received in the world, I leave you to consider.

Cleanthes: It would surely be very ill received, replied *Cleanthes*; and I should be deservedly blamed and detested did I allow that the proofs of a Deity amounted to no more than a guess or conjecture. But is the whole adjustment of means to ends in a house and in the universe so slight a resemblance? The economy of final causes? The order, proportion, and arrangement of every part? Steps of a stair are plainly contrived that human legs may use them in mounting; and this inference is certain and infallible. Human legs are also contrived for walking and mounting; and this inference, I allow, is not altogether so certain because of the dissimilarity which you remark; but does it, therefore, deserve the name only of presumption or conjecture?

Demea: Good God! cried *Demea*, interrupting him, where are we? Zealous defenders of religion allow that the proofs of a Deity fall short of perfect evidence! And you, *Philo*, on whose assistance I depended in proving the adorable mysteriousness of the Divine Nature, do you assent to all these extravagant opinions of *Cleanthes*? For what other name can I give them? or, why spare my censure when such principles are advanced, supported by such an authority, before so young a man as *Pamphilus*?

Philo: You seem not to apprehend, replied *Philo*, that I argue with *Cleanthes* in his own way, and, by showing him the dangerous consequences of his tenets, hope at last to reduce him to our opinion. But what sticks most with you, I observe, is the representation which *Cleanthes* has made of the argument *a posteriori*; and, finding that that argument is likely to escape your hold and vanish into air, you think it so disguised that you can scarcely believe it to be set in its true light. Now, however much I may dissent, in other respects, from the dangerous principle of *Cleanthes*, I must allow that he has fairly represented that argument, and I shall endeavor so to state the matter to you that you will entertain no further scruples with regard to it.

    Were a man to abstract from everything which he knows or has seen, he would be altogether incapable, merely from his own ideas, to determine what kind of scene the universe must be, or to give the preference to one state or situation of things above another. For as nothing which he clearly conceives could be esteemed impossible or implying a contradiction, every chimera of his fancy would be upon an equal footing; nor could he assign any just reason why he adheres to one idea or system, and rejects the others which are equally possible.

    Again, after he opens his eyes and contemplates the world as it really is, it would be impossible for him at first to assign the cause of any one event, much less of the whole of things, or of the universe. He might set his fancy a rambling, and she might bring him in an infinite variety of reports and representations. These would all be possible; but, being all equally possible, he would never of himself give a satisfactory account for his preferring one of them to the rest. Experience alone can point out to him the true cause of any phenomenon.

    Now, according to this method of reasoning, *Demea*, it follows (and is, indeed, tacitly allowed by *Cleanthes* himself) that order, arrangement, or the adjustment of final causes, is not of itself any proof of design, but only so far as it has been experienced to proceed from that principle. For aught we can know *a priori*, matter may contain the source or spring of order originally within itself, as well as mind does; and there is no more difficulty in conceiving that the several elements, from an internal unknown cause, may fall into the most exquisite arrangement, than to conceive that their ideas, in the great universal mind, from a like internal unknown cause, fall into that arrangement. The equal possibility of both these suppositions is allowed. But, by experience, we find, according to *Cleanthes*, that there is a difference between them. Throw several pieces of steel together, without shape or form; they will never arrange themselves so as to compose a watch. Stone and mortar and wood, without an architect, never erect a house. But the ideas in a human mind, we see, by an unknown, inexplicable economy, arrange themselves so as to form the plan of a watch or house. Experience, therefore, proves that there is an original principle of order in mind, not in matter. From similar effects we infer similar causes. The adjustment of means to ends is alike in the universe, as in a machine of human contrivance. The causes, therefore, must be resembling.

I was from the beginning scandalized, I must own, with this resemblance which is asserted between the Deity and human creatures, and must conceive it to imply such a degradation of the Supreme Being as no sound theist could endure. With your assistance, therefore, *Demea*, I shall endeavor to defend what you justly call the adorable mysteriousness of the Divine Nature, and shall refute this reasoning of *Cleanthes*, provided he allows that I have made a fair representation of it.

When *Cleanthes* had assented, *Philo*, after a short pause, proceeded in the following manner.

That all inferences, *Cleanthes*, concerning fact are founded on experience, and that all experimental reasonings are founded on the supposition that similar causes prove similar effects, and similar effects similar causes, I shall not at present much dispute with you. But observe, I entreat you, with what extreme caution all just reasoners proceed in the transferring of experiments to similar cases. Unless the cases be exactly similar, they repose no perfect confidence in applying their past observation to any particular phenomenon. Every alteration of circumstances occasions a doubt concerning the event; and it requires new experiments to prove certainly that the new circumstances are of no moment or importance. A change in bulk, situation, arrangement, age, disposition of the air, or surrounding bodies; any of these particulars may be attended with the most unexpected consequences. And unless the objects be quite familiar to us, it is the highest temerity to expect with assurance, after any of these changes, an event similar to that which before fell under our observation. The slow and deliberate steps of philosophers here, if anywhere, are distinguished from the precipitate march of the vulgar, who, hurried on by the smallest similitude, are incapable of all discernment or consideration.

But can you think, *Cleanthes*, that your usual phlegm and philosophy have been preserved in so wide a step as you have taken when you compared to the universe houses, ships, furniture, machines; and, from their similarity in some circumstances, inferred a similarity in their causes? Thought, design, intelligence, such as we discover in men and other animals, is no more than one of the springs and principles of the universe, as well as heat or cold, attraction or repulsion, and a hundred others which fall under daily observation. It is an active cause by which some particular parts of nature, we find, produce alterations on other parts. But can a conclusion, with any propriety, be transferred from parts to the whole? Does not the great disproportion bar all comparison and inference? From observing the growth of a hair, can we learn anything concerning the generation of a man? Would the manner of a leaf's blowing, even though perfectly known, afford us any instruction concerning the vegetation of a tree?

But allowing that we were to take the *operations* of one part of nature upon another for the foundation of our judgment concerning the *origin* of the whole (which never can be admitted), yet why select so minute, so weak, so bounded a principle as the reason and design of animals is found to be upon this planet? What peculiar privilege has this little agitation of the brain which we call "thought", that we must thus make it the model of the whole universe? Our partiality in our own favor does indeed present it on all occasions, but sound philosophy ought carefully to guard against so natural an illusion.

So far from admitting, continued *Philo*, that the operations of a part can afford us any just conclusion concerning the origin of the whole, I will not allow any one part to form a rule for another part if the latter be very remote from the former. Is there any reasonable ground to conclude that the inhabitants of other planets possess thought, intelligence, reason, or anything similar to these faculties in men? When nature has so extremely diversified her manner of operation in this small globe, can we imagine that she incessantly copies herself throughout so immense a universe? And if thought, as we may well suppose, be confined merely to this narrow corner, and has even there so limited a sphere of action, with what propriety can we assign it for the original cause of all things? The narrow views of a peasant who makes his domestic economy the rule for the government of kingdoms is in comparison a pardonable sophism.

But were we ever so much assured that a thought and reason resembling the human were to be found throughout the whole universe, and were its activity elsewhere vastly greater and more commanding than it appears in this globe; yet I cannot see why the operations of a world constituted, arranged, adjusted, can with any propriety be extended to a world which is in its embryo-state, and is advancing towards that constitution and arrangement. By observation we know somewhat of the economy, action, and nourishment of a finished animal; but we must transfer with great caution that observation to the growth of a foetus in the womb, and still more to the formation of an animalcule in the loins of its male parent. Nature, we find, even from our limited experience, possesses an infinite number of springs and principles which incessantly discover themselves on every change of her position and situation. And what new and unknown principles would actuate her in so new and unknown a situation as that of the formation of a universe, we cannot, without the utmost temerity, pretend to determine.

A very small part of this great system, during a very short time, is very imperfectly discovered to us; and do we thence pronounce decisively concerning the origin of the whole?

Admirable conclusion! Stone, wood, brick, iron, brass, have not, at this time, in this minute globe of earth, an order or arrangement without human art and contrivance; therefore, the universe could not originally attain its order and arrangement without something similar to human art. But is a part of nature a rule for another part very wide of the former? Is it a rule for the whole? Is a very small part a rule for the universe? Is nature in one situation a certain rule for nature in another situation vastly different from the former?

And can you blame me, *Cleanthes*, if I here imitate the prudent reserve of *Simonides*, who, according to the noted story, being asked by *Hiero*, *What God was?* desired a day to think of it, and then two days more; and after that manner continually prolonged the term, without ever bringing in his definition or description? Could you even blame me if I had answered, at first, *that I did not know*, and was sensible that this subject lay vastly beyond the reach of my faculties? You might cry out skeptic and raillier, as much as you pleased; but, having found in so many other subjects much more familiar the imperfections and even contradictions of human reason, I never should expect any success from its feeble conjectures in a subject so sublime and so remote from the sphere of our observation. When two *species* of objects have always been observed to be conjoined together, I can *infer*, by custom, the existence of one wherever I *see* the existence of the other; and this I call an argument from experience. But how this argument can have place where the objects, as in the present case, are single, individual, without parallel or specific resemblance, may be difficult to explain. And will any man tell me with a serious countenance that an orderly universe must arise from some thought and art like the human because we have experience of it? To ascertain this reasoning it were requisite that we had experience of the origin of worlds; and it is not sufficient, surely, that we have seen ships and cities arise from human art and contrivance. . .

. . .

Philo: But to show you still more inconveniences, continued *Philo*, in your anthropomorphism, please to take a new survey of your principles. *Like effects prove like causes.* This is the experimental argument; and this, you say too, is the sole theological argument. Now it is certain that the liker the effects are which are seen and the liker the causes which are inferred, the stronger is the argument. Every departure on either side diminishes the probability and renders the experiment less conclusive. You cannot doubt of the principle; neither ought you to reject its consequences.

All the new discoveries in astronomy which prove the immense grandeur and magnificence of the works of nature are so many additional arguments for a Deity, according to the true system of theism; but, according to your hypothesis of experimental theism, they become so many objections, by removing the effect still farther from all resemblance to the effects of human art and contrivance. For if *Lucretius*, even following the old system of the world, could exclaim:

Who is strong enough to rule the sum, who to hold in hand and control the mighty bridle of the unfathomable deep? who to turn about all the heavens at one time, and warm the fruitful worlds with ethereal fires, or to be present in all places and at all times.[1]

If Tully[2] esteemed this reasoning so natural as to put it into the mouth of his Epicurean:

What power of mental vision enabled your master Plato to descry the vast and elaborate architectural process which, as he makes out, the deity adopted in building the structure of the universe? What method of engineering was employed? What tools and levers and derricks? What agents carried out so vast an understanding? And how were air, fire, water, and earth enabled to obey and execute the will of the architect?[3]

If this argument, I say, had any force in former ages, how much greater must it have at present when the bounds of nature are so infinitely enlarged and such a magnificent scene is opened to us? It is still more unreasonable to form our idea of so unlimited a cause from our experience of the narrow productions of human design and invention.

The discoveries by microscopes, as they open a new universe in miniature, are still objections, according to you; arguments, according to me. The farther we push our researches of this kind, we are still led to infer the universal cause of all to be vastly different from mankind, or from any object of human experience and observation.

And what say you to the discoveries in anatomy, chemistry, botany? . . . **Cleanthes:** These surely are no objections, replied *Cleanthes*; they only discover new instances of art and contrivance. It is still the image of mind reflected on us from innumerable objects. **Philo:** Add a mind *like the human*, said *Philo*. **Cleanthes:** I know of no other, replied *Cleanthes*. **Philo:** And the liker, the better, insisted *Philo*. **Cleanthes:** To be sure, said *Cleanthes*.

Philo: Now, *Cleanthes*, said *Philo*, with an air of alacrity and triumph, mark the consequences. *First*, by this method of reasoning you renounce all claim to infinity in any of the attributes of the Deity. For, as the cause ought only to be proportioned to the effect, and the effect, so far as it falls under our cognizance, is not infinite: What pretensions have we, upon your suppositions, to ascribe that attribute to the Divine Being? You will still insist that, by removing him so much from all similarity to human creatures, we give in to the most arbitrary hypothesis, and at the same time weaken all proofs of his existence.

Secondly, you have no reason, on your theory, for ascribing perfection to the Deity, even in his finite capacity; or for supposing him free from every error, mistake, or incoherence, in his undertakings. There are many inexplicable difficulties in the works of Nature which, if we allow a perfect author to be proved *a priori*, are easily solved, and become only seeming difficulties from the narrow capacity of man, who cannot trace infinite relations. But according to your method of reasoning, these difficulties become all real; and, perhaps, will be insisted on as new instances of likeness to human art and contrivance. At least, you must acknowledge that it is impossible for us to tell, from our limited views, whether this system contains any great faults or deserves any considerable praise if compared to other possible and even real systems. Could a peasant, if the *Aeneid* were read to him, pronounce that poem to be absolutely faultless, or even assign to it its proper rank among the productions of human wit, he who had never seen any other production?

But were this world ever so perfect a production, it must still remain uncertain whether all the excellences of the work can justly be ascribed to the workman. If we survey a ship, what an exalted idea must we form of the ingenuity of the carpenter who framed so complicated, useful, and beautiful a machine? And what surprise must we feel when we find him a stupid mechanic who imitated others, and copied an art which, through a long succession of ages, after multiplied trials, mistakes, corrections, deliberations, and controversies, had been gradually improving? Many worlds might have been botched and bungled, throughout an eternity, ere this system was struck out; much labor lost; many fruitless trials made; and a slow but continued improvement carried on during infinite ages in the art of world-making. In such subjects, who can determine where the truth, nay, who can conjecture where the probability lies, amidst a great number of hypotheses which may be proposed, and a still greater which may be imagined?

And what shadow of an argument, continued *Philo*, can you produce from your hypothesis to prove the unity of the Deity? A great number of men join in building a house or ship, in rearing a city, in framing a commonwealth; why may not several deities combine in contriving and framing a world? This is only so much greater similarity to human affairs. By sharing the work among several, we may so much further limit the attributes of each, and get rid of that extensive power and knowledge which must be supposed in one deity, and which, according to you, can only serve to weaken the proof of his existence. And if such foolish, such vicious creatures as man can yet often unite in framing and executing one plan, how much more those deities or demons, whom we may suppose several degrees more perfect?

To multiply causes without necessity is indeed contrary to true philosophy, but this principle applies not to the present case. Were one deity antecedently proved by your theory who were possessed of every attribute requisite to the production of the universe, it would be needless, I own (though not absurd), to suppose any other deity existent. But while it is still a question whether all these attributes are united in one subject or dispersed among several independent beings; by what phenomena in nature can we pretend to decide the controversy? Where we see a body raised in a scale, we are sure that there is in the opposite scale, however concealed from sight, some counterpoising weight equal to it; but it is still allowed to doubt whether that weight be an aggregate of several distinct bodies or one uniform united mass. And if the weight requisite very much exceeds anything which we have ever seen conjoined in any single body, the former supposition becomes still more probable and natural. An intelligent being of such vast power and capacity as is necessary to produce the universe, or, to speak in the language of ancient philosophy, so prodigious an animal, exceeds all analogy and even comprehension.

But further, *Cleanthes*, men are mortal, and renew their species by generation; and this is common to all living creatures. The two great sexes of male and female, says *Milton*, animate the world. Why must this circumstance, so universal, so essential, be excluded from those numerous and limited deities? Behold, then, the theogeny of ancient times brought back upon us.

And why not become a perfect anthropomorphite? Why not assert the deity or deities to be corporeal, and to have eyes, a nose, mouth, ears, etc.? *Epicurus* maintained that no man had ever seen reason but in a human figure; therefore, the gods must have a human figure. And this argument, which is deservedly so much ridiculed by *Cicero*, becomes, according to you, solid and philosophical.

In a word, *Cleanthes*, a man who follows your hypothesis is able, perhaps, to assert or conjecture that the universe sometime arose from something like design: But beyond that position he cannot ascertain one single circumstance, and is left afterwards to fix every point of his theology by the utmost license of fancy and hypothesis. This world, for aught he knows, is very faulty and imperfect, compared to a superior standard; and was only the first rude essay of some infant deity who afterwards abandoned it, ashamed of his lame performance: It is the work only of some dependent, inferior deity, and is the object of derision to his superiors: It is the production of old age and dotage in some superannuated deity; and ever since his death has run on at adventures, from the first impulse and active force which it received from him. . . . You justly give signs of horror, *Demea*, at these strange suppositions; but these, and a thousand more of the same kind, are *Cleanthes'* suppositions, not mine. From the moment the attributes of the Deity are supposed finite, all these have place. And I cannot, for my part, think that so wild and unsettled a system of theology is, in any respect, preferable to none at all.

Cleanthes: These suppositions I absolutely disown, cried *Cleanthes*: They strike me, however, with no horror, especially when proposed in that rambling way in which they drop from you. On the contrary, they give me pleasure when I see that, by the utmost indulgence of your imagination, you never get rid of the hypothesis of design in the universe, but are obliged at every turn to have recourse to it. To this concession I adhere steadily; and this I regard as a sufficient foundation for religion.

Notes

1   [*On the Nature of Things*, II, 1096–1099 (trans. by W. D. Rouse).]
2   [Tully was a common name for the Roman lawyer and philosopher, Marcus Tullius Cicero, 106–43 B.C.]
3   [Cicero, *The Nature of the Gods*, I, viii, 19 (trans. by H. Rackham).]

Questions for reflection

1   What is the design argument which Cleanthes presents in this selection? Is it a good argument, in your opinion? Why or why not?
2   Does Philo destroy the argument? If so, how?
3   Explain Demea's role in this dialogue. What is his general position regarding the design argument?
4   Do you think the criticisms offered in this selection undermine recent versions of the design argument, such as those offered in this reader? Explain.
5   How does Darwin's theory of evolution affect an argument from design?

Further reading

Richard Dawkins (1987) *The Blind Watchmaker*. New York: W. W. Norton & Company. (A very influential book defending a naturalistic explanation of the apparent design in the world.)
David Hume ([1779] 1998) *Dialogues Concerning Natural Religion*. 2nd edn. Indianapolis, IN: Hackett. (A formidable critique of the argument from design; the selection above is taken from Parts II and V of this work.)
Neil A. Manson, ed. (2003) *God and Design: The Teleological Argument and Modern Science*. London: Routledge. (Includes essays for and against the design argument.)
Michael Ruse (1982) *Darwinism Defended*. Reading, MA: Addison-Wesley. (A solid defense of Darwinism by a leading philosopher of biology.)
Victor J. Stenger (2003) *Has Science Found God? The Latest Results in the Search for Purpose in the Universe*. Amherst, NY: Prometheus Books. (A critique of fine-tuning and other alleged design evidences.)

The ontological argument

Chapter 25

Anselm of Canterbury

THE CLASSICAL ONTOLOGICAL ARGUMENT

Anselm of Canterbury (1033–1109) was a Christian philosopher and theologian and Archbishop of Canterbury from 1093–1109. He wrote on a number of issues in philosophical theology, but he is best known for his *ontological argument* presented in his book, the *Proslogium* (which is the selection offered below). He notes in the preface to this book that he wanted to know if there existed "a single argument which would require no other for its proof than itself alone; and alone would suffice to demonstrate that God truly exists, and that there is a supreme good requiring nothing else, which all other things require for their existence and well-being . . .". He developed what he took to be such an argument — one that was later dubbed by Immanuel Kant the "ontological argument" (from the Greek terms "*ontos*" = being and "*logos*" = rational account).

Anselm's argument is based on the idea of God as a perfect Being. It begins by realizing that I can get into my understanding (in my mind, as it were) the notion of a being than which none greater can be conceived. However, if a being than which none greater can be conceived exists in my mind only, then it is not the greatest possible being. For a being that exists in reality is greater than one that exists only in one's mind. So, once we understand the very nature of the concept itself (i.e., the concept of a being than which no greater can be conceived), then it brings us to realize that such a being must exist in reality as well as in our mind. In other words, it can be proved that God exists merely from an analysis of the concept of a being than which none greater can be conceived.

Chapter II

Truly there is a God, although the fool hath said in his heart, There is no God.

And so, Lord, do thou, who dost give understanding to faith, give me, so far as thou knowest it to be profitable, to understand that thou art as we believe; and that thou art that which we believe. And, indeed, we believe that thou art a being than which nothing greater can be conceived. Or is there no such nature, since the fool hath said in his heart, there is no God? (Psalms xiv. I). But, at any rate, this very fool, when he hears of this being of which I speak—a being than which nothing greater can be conceived—understands what he hears, and what he understands is in his understanding; although he does not understand it to exist.

For, it is one thing for an object to be in the understanding, and another to understand that the object exists. When a painter first conceives of what he will afterwards perform, he has it in his understanding, but he does not yet understand it to be, because he has not yet performed it. But after he has made the painting, he both has it in his understanding, and he understands that it exists, because he has made it.

Hence, even the fool is convinced that something exists in the understanding, at least, than which nothing greater can be conceived. For, when he hears of this, he understands it. And whatever is understood, exists in the understanding. And assuredly that, than which nothing greater can be conceived, cannot exist in the understanding alone. For, suppose it exists in the understanding alone: then it can be conceived to exist in reality; which is greater.

Therefore, if that, than which nothing greater can be conceived, exists in the understanding alone, the very being, than which nothing greater can be conceived, is one, than which a greater can be conceived. But obviously this is impossible. Hence, there is no doubt that there exists a being, than which nothing greater can be conceived, and it exists both in the understanding and in reality.

Chapter III

God cannot be conceived not to exist. —God is that, than which nothing greater can be conceived. —That which can be conceived not to exist is not God.

And it assuredly exists so truly, that it cannot be conceived not to exist. For, it is possible to conceive of a being which cannot be conceived not to exist; and this is greater than one which can be conceived not to exist. Hence, if that, than which nothing greater can be conceived, can be conceived not to exist, it is not that, than which nothing greater can be conceived. But this is an irreconcilable contradiction. There is, then, so truly a being than which nothing greater can be conceived to exist, that it cannot even be conceived not to exist; and this being thou art, O Lord, our God.

So truly, therefore, dost thou exist, O Lord, my God, that thou canst not be conceived not to exist; and rightly. For, if a mind could conceive of a being better than thee, the creature would rise above the Creator; and this is most absurd. And, indeed, whatever else there is, except thee alone, can be conceived not to exist. To thee alone, therefore, it belongs to exist more truly than all other beings, and hence in a higher degree than all others. For, whatever else exists does not exist so truly, and hence in a less degree it belongs to it to exist. Why, then, has the fool said in his heart, there is no God (Psalms xiv. I), since it is so evident, to a rational mind, that thou dost exist in the highest degree of all? Why, except that he is dull and a fool?

Chapter IV

> How the fool has said in his heart what cannot be conceived.—A thing may be conceived in two ways: (1) when the word signifying it is conceived: (2) when the thing itself is understood. As far as the word goes, God can be conceived not to exist; in reality he cannot.

But how has the fool said in his heart what he could not conceive; or how is it that he could not conceive what he said in his heart? since it is the same to say in the heart, and to conceive.

But, if really, nay, since really, he both conceived, because he said in his heart; and did not say in his heart, because he could not conceive; there is more than one way in which a thing is said in the heart or conceived. For, in one sense, an object is conceived, when the word signifying it is conceived; and in another, when the very entity, which the object is, is understood.

In the former sense, then, God can be conceived not to exist; but in the latter, not at all. For no one who understands what fire and water are can conceive fire to be water, in accordance with the nature of the facts themselves, although this is possible according to the words. So, then, no one who understands what God is can conceive that God does not exist; although he says these words in his heart, either without any, or with some foreign, signification. For, God is that than which a greater cannot be conceived. And he who thoroughly understands this, assuredly understands that this being so truly exists, that not even in concept can it be non-existent. Therefore, he who understands that God so exists, cannot conceive that he does not exist.

I thank thee, gracious Lord, I thank thee; because what I formerly believed by thy bounty, I now so understand by thine illumination, that if I were unwilling to believe that thou dost exist, I should not be able not to understand this to be true.

Chapter V

> God is whatever it is better to be than not to be; and he, as the only self-existent being, creates all things from nothing.

What art thou, then, Lord God, than whom nothing greater can be conceived? But what art thou, except that which, as the highest of all beings, alone exists through itself, and creates all other things from nothing? For, whatever is not this is less than a thing which can be conceived of. But this cannot be conceived of thee. What good, therefore, does the supreme Good lack, through which every good is? Therefore, thou art just, truthful, blessed, and whatever it is better to be than not to be. For it is better to be just than not just; better to be blessed than not blessed.

Questions for reflection

1   How would you paraphrase Anselm's ontological argument for God's existence?
2   If this argument demonstrates that God exists, does it prove that a particular deity exists (e.g., the Christian, Islamic, Jewish, or Hindu God)?

3   If the argument does work (and, of course, this it hotly contested), what does it prove about God? Does it prove all that Anselm thinks it does?
4   If it can be demonstrated that God exists because the concept of a perfect being entails its existence, then does the concept of a perfect airplane prove that it exists? Explain the difference, if there is one.
5   Do you believe the argument works? Why or why not?

Further reading

Anselm of Canterbury ([1077–8] 1962) *St. Anselm: Basic Writings*. LaSalle, IL: Open Court Publishing. (It is now widely understood that Anselm offered two versions of the ontological argument. His first argument was presented above. In the next chapter, a response to Anselm is offered by a monk named Gaunilo. Anselm's second version of the ontological argument (found in the Appendix of *St. Anselm: Basic Writings*) is contained in his reply to Gaunilo's critique. It is based on the idea of necessary existence—not only does God exist, he exists necessarily.)

Brian Davies and Brian Leftow, eds. (2004) *The Cambridge Companion to Anselm*. Cambridge: Cambridge University Press. (A helpful collection of readable essays on a variety of topics by leading scholars.)

René Descartes ([1641] 1955) *Meditations*. New York: Dover. (Contains Descartes's version of the ontological argument.)

Graham Oppy (1996) *Ontological Arguments and Belief in God*. Cambridge: Cambridge University Press. (A comprehensive overview of versions of the ontological argument.)

Alvin Plantinga (1974) *The Nature of Necessity*. Oxford: Clarendon Press. (A modal version of the ontological argument utilizing the metaphysics of possible worlds that is invulnerable to Kant's critique.)

Chapter 26

Gaunilo of Marmoutier

GAUNILO'S RESPONSE TO ANSELM

Gaunilo (eleventh century) was a Benedictine monk of Marmoutier. In this selection he responds to Anselm's ontological argument. His response, entitled "In Behalf of the Fool," is derived from the biblical fools mentioned in the book of Psalms (Psalm 14:1; Psalm 53:1), and while Gaunilo no doubt believes that God exists, he nevertheless offers several significant criticisms of Anselm's alleged proof. One objection Gaunilo raises is that the argument is built on the faulty premise that if something exists in the mind, we can reason to its extra-mental existence. Clearly, there are many unreal objects which exist in one's mind, so why should the concept of the greatest possible being be any different than these unreal, mental objects? Another objection is based on the analogy of the greatest possible island. Even if one can get the concept of such an island in mind, it does not follow that it exists in reality. Given this, why should it follow that, if one has the concept of the greatest possible Being in mind, it must exist in reality?

In behalf of the fool: an answer to the argument of Anselm in the proslogium

1. If one doubts or denies the existence of a being of such a nature that nothing greater than it can be conceived, he receives this answer:

The existence of this being is proved, in the first place, by the fact that he himself, in his doubt or denial regarding this being, already has it in his understanding; for in hearing it spoken of he understands what is spoken of. It is proved, therefore, by the fact that what he understands must exist not only in his understanding, but in reality also.

And the proof of this is as follows.—It is a greater thing to exist both in the understanding and in reality than to be in the understanding alone. And if this being is in the understanding alone, whatever has even in the past existed in reality will be greater than this being. And so that which was greater than all beings will be less than some being, and will not be greater than all: which is a manifest contradiction.

And hence, that which is greater than all, already proved to be in the understanding, must exist not only in the understanding, but also in reality: for otherwise it will not be greater than all other beings.

2. The fool might make this reply:

This being is said to be in my understanding already, only because I understand what is said. Now could it not with equal justice be said that I have in my understanding all manner of unreal objects, having absolutely no existence in themselves, because I understand these things if one speaks of them, whatever they may be?

Unless indeed it is shown that this being is of such a character that it cannot be held in concept like all unreal objects, or objects whose existence is uncertain: and hence I am not able to conceive of it when I hear of it, or to hold it in concept; but I must understand it and have it in my understanding; because, it seems, I cannot conceive of it in any other way than by understanding it, that is, by comprehending in my knowledge its existence in reality.

But if this is the case, in the first place there will be no distinction between what has precedence in time—namely, the having of an object in the understanding—and what is subsequent in time—namely, the understanding that an object exists; as in the example of the picture, which exists first in the mind of the painter, and afterwards in his work.

Moreover, the following assertion can hardly be accepted: that this being, when it is spoken of and heard of, cannot be conceived not to exist in the way in which even God can be conceived not to exist. For if this is impossible, what was the object of this argument against one who doubts or denies the existence of such a being?

Finally, that this being so exists that it cannot be perceived by an understanding convinced of its own indubitable existence, unless this being is afterwards conceived of—this should be proved to me by an indisputable argument, but not by that which you have advanced: namely, that what I understand, when I hear it, already is in my understanding. For thus in my understanding, as I still think, could be all sorts of things whose existence is uncertain, or which do not exist at all, if some one whose words I should understand mentioned them. And so much the more if I should be deceived, as often happens, and believe in them: though I do not yet believe in the being whose existence you would prove.

3. Hence, your example of the painter who already has in his understanding what he is to paint cannot agree with this argument. For the picture, before it is made, is contained in the artificer's art itself; and any such thing, existing in the art of an artificer, is nothing but a part of his understanding itself. A joiner, St. Augustine says, when he is about to make a box in fact, first has it in his art. The box which is made in fact is not life; but the box which exists in his art is life. For the artificer's soul lives, in which all these things are, before they are produced. Why, then, are these things life in the living soul of the artificer, unless because they are nothing else than the knowledge or understanding of the soul itself?

With the exception, however, of those facts which are known to pertain to the mental nature, whatever, on being heard and thought out by the understanding, is perceived to be real, undoubtedly that real object is one thing, and the understanding itself, by which the object is grasped, is another. Hence, even if it were true that there is a being than which a greater is inconceivable: yet to this being, when heard of and understood, the not yet created picture in the mind of the painter is not analogous.

4. Let us notice also the point touched on above, with regard to this being which is greater than all which can be conceived, and which, it is said, can be none other than God himself. I, so far as actual knowledge of the object, either from its specific or general character, is concerned, am as little able to conceive of this being when I hear of it, or to have it in my understanding, as I am to conceive of or understand God himself: whom, indeed, for this very reason I can conceive not to exist. For I do not know that reality itself which God is, nor can I form a conjecture of that reality from some other like reality. For you yourself assert that that reality is such that there can be nothing else like it.

For, suppose that I should hear something said of a man absolutely unknown to me, of whose very existence I was unaware. Through that special or general knowledge by which I know what man is, or what men are, I could conceive of him also, according to the reality itself, which man is. And yet it would be possible, if the person who told me of him deceived me, that the man himself, of whom I conceived, did not exist; since that reality according to which I conceived of him, though a no less indisputable fact, was not that man, but any man.

Hence, I am not able, in the way in which I should have this unreal being in concept or in understanding, to have that being of which you speak in concept or in understanding, when I hear the word *God* or the words, *a being greater than all other beings*. For I can conceive of the man according to a fact that is real and familiar to me: but of God, or a being greater than all others, I could not conceive at all, except merely according to the word. And an object can hardly or never be conceived according to the word alone.

For when it is so conceived, it is not so much the word itself (which is, indeed, a real thing—that is, the sound of the letters and syllables) as the signification of the word, when heard, that is conceived. But it is not conceived as by one who knows what is generally signified by the word; by whom, that is, it is conceived according to a reality and in true conception alone. It is conceived as by a man who does not know the object, and conceives of it only in accordance with the movement of his mind produced by hearing the word, the mind attempting to image for itself the signification of the word that is heard. And it would be surprising if in the reality of fact it could ever attain to this.

Thus, it appears, and in no other way, this being is also in my understanding, when I hear and understand a person who says that there is a being greater than all conceivable beings. So much for the assertion that this supreme nature already is in my understanding.

5. But that this being must exist, not only in the understanding but also in reality, is thus proved to me:

If it did not so exist, whatever exists in reality would be greater than it. And so the being which has been already proved to exist in my understanding, will not be greater than all other beings.

I still answer: if it should be said that a being which cannot be even conceived in terms of any fact, is in the understanding, I do not deny that this being is, accordingly, in my understanding. But since through this fact it can in no wise attain to real existence also, I do not yet concede to it that existence at all, until some certain proof of it shall be given.

For he who says that this being exists, because otherwise the being which is greater than all will not be greater than all, does not attend strictly enough to what he is saying. For I do not yet say, no, I even deny or doubt that this being is greater than any real object. Nor do I concede to it any other existence than this (if it should be called existence) which it has when the mind, according to a word merely heard, tries to form the image of an object absolutely unknown to it.

How, then, is the veritable existence of that being proved to me from the assumption, by hypothesis, that it is greater than all other beings? For I should still deny this, or doubt your demonstration of it, to this extent, that I should not admit that this being is in my understanding and concept even in the way in which many objects whose real existence is uncertain and doubtful, are in my understanding and concept. For it should be proved first that this being itself really exists somewhere; and then, from the fact that it is greater than all, we shall not hesitate to infer that it also subsists in itself.

6. For example: it is said that somewhere in the ocean is an island, which, because of the difficulty, or rather the impossibility, of discovering what does not exist, is called the lost island. And they say that this island has an inestimable wealth of all manner of riches and delicacies in greater abundance than is told of the Islands of the Blest; and that having no owner or inhabitant, it is more excellent than all other countries, which are inhabited by mankind, in the abundance with which it is stored.

Now if some one should tell me that there is such an island, I should easily understand his words, in which there is no difficulty. But suppose that he went on to say, as if by a logical inference: "You can no longer doubt that this island which is more excellent than all lands exists somewhere, since you have no doubt that it is in your understanding. And since it is more excellent not to be in the understanding alone, but to exist both in the understanding and in reality, for this reason it must exist. For if it does not exist, any land which really exists will be more excellent than it; and so the island already understood by you to be more excellent will not be more excellent."

If a man should try to prove to me by such reasoning that this island truly exists, and that its existence should no longer be doubted, either I should believe that he was jesting, or I know not which I ought to regard as the greater fool: myself, supposing that I should allow this proof; or him, if he should suppose that he had established with any certainty the existence of this island. For he ought to show first that the hypothetical excellence of this island exists as a real and indubitable fact, and in no wise as any unreal object, or one whose existence is uncertain, in my understanding.

7. This, in the mean time, is the answer the fool could make to the arguments urged against him. When he is assured in the first place that this being is so great that its non-existence is not even conceivable, and that this in turn is proved on no other ground than the fact that otherwise it will not be greater than all things, the fool may make the same answer, and say:

When did I say that any such being exists in reality, that is, a being greater than all others?—that on this ground it should be proved to me that it also exists in reality to such a degree that it cannot even be conceived not to exist? Whereas in the first place it should be in some way proved that a nature which is higher, that is, greater and better, than all other natures, exists; in order that from this we may then be able to prove all attributes which necessarily the being that is greater and better than all possesses.

Moreover, it is said that the non-existence of this being is inconceivable. It might better be said, perhaps, that its non-existence, or the possibility of its non-existence, is unintelligible. For according to the true meaning of the word, unreal objects are unintelligible. Yet their existence is conceivable in the way in which the fool conceived of the non-existence of God. I am most certainly aware of my own existence; but I know, nevertheless, that my non-existence is possible. As to that supreme being, moreover, which God is, I understand without any doubt both his existence, and the impossibility of his non-existence. Whether, however, so long as I am most positively aware of my existence, I can conceive of my non-existence, I am not sure. But if I can, why can I not conceive of the non-existence of whatever else I know with the same certainty? If, however, I cannot, God will not be the only being of which it can be said, it is impossible to conceive of his non-existence.

8. The other parts of this book are argued with such truth, such brilliancy, such grandeur; and are so replete with usefulness, so fragrant with a certain perfume of devout and holy feeling, that though there are matters in the beginning which, however rightly sensed, are weakly presented, the rest of the work should not be rejected on this account. The rather ought these earlier matters to be reasoned more cogently, and the whole to be received with great respect and honor.

Questions for reflection

1   What are the different objections to the ontological argument contained in this selection by Gaunilo? Briefly describe each of them.
2   Can you conceive of God's non-existence? If so, what follows from this regarding the ontological argument?
3   Anselm offers replies to each of these objections. Search out his replies (see internet reference below). Are they solid answers to Gaunilo's objections? Why or why not?

Further reading

Daniel A. Dombrowski (2006) *Rethinking the Ontological Argument: A Neoclassical Theistic Response.* Cambridge: Cambridge University Press. (A defense of the ontological argument against contemporary critics based on a process concept of God.)

Internet Medieval Sourcebook: Anselm on God's Existence. http://www.fordham.edu/halsall/source/anselm.html (An online version of Anselm's argument, along with Gaunilo's responses and Anselm's replies.)

Internet Medieval Sourcebook: Philosophers' Criticisms of Anselm's Ontological Argument for the Being of God. http://www.fordham.edu/halsall/basis/anselm-critics.html (A helpful internet resource from a collection of public domain texts related to medieval history.)

Graham Oppy (1996) *Ontological Arguments and Belief in God.* Cambridge: Cambridge University Press. (A comprehensive overview of versions of the ontological argument.)

Chapter 27

Immanuel Kant

A CRITIQUE OF THE
ONTOLOGICAL ARGUMENT

Immanuel Kant (1724–1804) was a German philosopher — the last great philosopher of the Enlightenment period. In this selection, taken from his celebrated work, *Critique of Pure Reason*, he presents an important and influential critique of the ontological argument. Put succinctly, the objection he raises is that "existence is not a predicate." For the ontological argument to work, it must assume that existence *is* a predicate. Consider the following example. If I were to describe the five dollar bill in my pocket, I could offer a number of attributes, or properties, of the bill. I could note that it is made of high quality paper, that it is colored green, that it weighs so much, and so on. Each of these descriptions adds to our knowledge of what it is. But when I say that the five dollar bill in my pocket not only has all of these properties, but that it also *exists*, I'm not adding anything new to the concept. I'm merely noting that the various properties of the bill are exemplified. Existence, then, is not a property or predicate. This conclusion has significant ramifications for the ontological argument.

(In the essay, Kant mentions Descartes in reference to the ontological argument, but the essence of this critique applies to Anselm's as well as Descartes's version of the argument.)

thaler – silver coins issued by different German states from the fifteenth to the nineteenth centuries.

The impossibility of an ontological proof of the existence of God*

It is evident, from what has been said, that the concept of an absolutely necessary being is a concept of pure reason, that is, a mere idea the objective reality of which is very far from being proved by the fact that reason requires it. For the idea instructs us only in regard to a certain unattainable completeness, and so serves rather to limit the understanding than to extend it to new objects. But we are here faced by what is indeed strange and perplexing, namely, that while the inference from a given existence in general to some absolutely necessary being seems to be both imperative and legitimate, all those conditions under which alone the understanding can form a concept of such a necessity are so many obstacles in the way of our doing so.

In all ages men have spoken of an *absolutely necessary* being, and in so doing have endeavoured, not so much to understand whether and how a thing of this kind allows even of being thought, but rather to prove its existence. There is, of course, no difficulty in giving a verbal definition of the concept, namely, that it is something the non-existence of which is impossible. But this yields no insight into the conditions which make it necessary to regard the non-existence of a thing as absolutely unthinkable. It is precisely these conditions that we desire to know, in order that we may determine whether or not, in resorting to this concept, we are thinking anything at all. The expedient of removing all those conditions which the understanding indispensably requires in order to regard something as necessary, simply through the introduction of the word *unconditioned*, is very far from sufficing to show whether I am still thinking anything in the concept of the unconditionally necessary, or perhaps rather nothing at all.

Nay more, this concept, at first ventured upon blindly, and now become so completely familiar, has been supposed to have its meaning exhibited in a number of examples; and on this account all further enquiry into its intelligibility has seemed to be quite needless. Thus the fact that every geometrical proposition, as, for instance, that a triangle has three angles, is absolutely necessary, has been taken as justifying us in speaking of an object which lies entirely outside the sphere of our understanding as if we understood perfectly what it is that we intend to convey by the concept of that object.

All the alleged examples are, without exception, taken from *judgments*, not from *things* and their existence. But the unconditioned necessity of judgments is not the same as an absolute necessity of things. The absolute necessity of the judgment is only a conditioned necessity of the thing, or of the predicate in the judgment. The above proposition does not declare that three angles are absolutely necessary, but that, under the condition that there is a triangle (that is, that a triangle is given), three angles will necessarily be found in it. So great, indeed, is the deluding influence exercised by this logical necessity that, by the simple device of forming an *a priori* concept of a thing in such a manner as to include existence within the scope of its meaning, we have supposed ourselves to have justified the conclusion that because existence necessarily belongs to the object of this concept— always under the condition that we posit the thing as given (as existing)— we are also of necessity, in accordance with the law of identity, required to posit the existence of its object, and that this being is therefore itself absolutely necessary—and this, to repeat, for the reason that the existence of this being has already been thought in a concept which is assumed arbitrarily and on condition that we posit its object.

If, in an identical proposition, I reject the predicate while retaining the subject, contradiction results; and I therefore say that the former belongs necessarily to the latter. But if we reject subject and predicate alike, there is no contradiction; for nothing is then left that can be contradicted. To posit a triangle, and yet to reject its three angles, is self-contradictory; but there is no contradiction in rejecting the triangle together with its three angles. The same holds true of the concept of an absolutely necessary being. If its existence is rejected, we reject the thing itself with all its predicates;

and no question of contradiction can then arise. There is nothing outside it that would then be contradicted, since the necessity of the thing is not supposed to be derived from anything external; nor is there anything internal that would be contradicted, since in rejecting the thing itself we have at the same time rejected all its internal properties. 'God is omnipotent' is a necessary judgment. The omnipotence cannot be rejected if we posit a Deity, that is, an infinite being; for the two concepts are identical. But if we say, 'There is no God', neither the omnipotence nor any other of its predicates is given; they are one and all rejected together with the subject, and there is therefore not the least contradiction in such a judgment.

We have thus seen that if the predicate of a judgment is rejected together with the subject, no internal contradiction can result, and that this holds no matter what the predicate may be. The only way of evading this conclusion is to argue that there are subjects which cannot be removed, and must always remain. That, however, would only be another way of saying that there are absolutely necessary subjects; and that is the very assumption which I have called in question, and the possibility of which the above argument professes to establish. For I cannot form the least concept of a thing which, should it be rejected with all its predicates, leaves behind a contradiction; and in the absence of contradiction I have, through pure *a priori* concepts alone, no criterion of impossibility.

Notwithstanding all these general considerations, in which everyone must concur, we may be challenged with a case which is brought forward as proof that in actual fact the contrary holds, namely, that there is one concept, and indeed only one, in reference to which the not-being or rejection of its object is in itself contradictory, namely, the concept of the *ens realissimum*. It is declared that it possesses all reality, and that we are justified in assuming that such a being is possible (the fact that a concept does not contradict itself by no means proves the possibility of its object: but the contrary assertion I am for the moment willing to allow).[1] Now [the argument proceeds] 'all reality' includes existence; existence is therefore contained in the concept of a thing that is possible. If, then, this thing is rejected, the internal possibility of the thing is rejected— which is self-contradictory.

My answer is as follows. There is already a contradiction in introducing the concept of existence—no matter under what title it may be disguised—into the concept of a thing which we profess to be thinking solely in reference to its possibility. If that be allowed as legitimate, a seeming victory has been won; but in actual fact nothing at all is said: the assertion is a mere tautology. We must ask: Is the proposition that *this or that thing* (which, whatever it may be, is allowed as possible) *exists*, an analytic or a synthetic proposition? If it is analytic, the assertion of the existence of the thing adds nothing to the thought of the thing; but in that case either the thought, which is in us, is the thing itself, or we have presupposed an existence as belonging to the realm of the possible, and have then, on that pretext, inferred its existence from its internal possibility— which is nothing but a miserable tautology. The word 'reality', which in the concept of the thing sounds other than the word 'existence' in the concept of the predicate, is of no avail in meeting this objection. For if all positing (no matter what it may be that is posited) is entitled reality, the thing with all its predicates is already posited in the concept of the subject, and is assumed as actual; and in the predicate this is merely repeated. But if, on the other hand, we admit, as every reasonable person must, that all existential propositions are synthetic, how can we profess to maintain that the predicate of existence cannot be rejected without contradiction? This is a feature which is found only in analytic propositions, and is indeed precisely what constitutes their analytic character.

I should have hoped to put an end to these idle and fruitless disputations in a direct manner, by an accurate determination of the concept of existence, had I not found that the illusion which is caused by the confusion of a logical with a real predicate (that is, with a predicate which determines a thing) is almost beyond correction. Anything we please can be made to serve as a logical predicate; the subject can even be predicated of itself; for logic abstracts from all content. But a *determining* predicate is a predicate which is added to the concept of the subject and enlarges it. Consequently, it must not be already contained in the concept.

'Being' is obviously not a real predicate; that is, it is not a concept of something which could be added to the concept of a thing. It is merely the positing of a thing, or of certain determinations, as existing in themselves. Logically, it is merely the copula of a judgment. The proposition, 'God is omnipotent', contains two concepts, each of which has its object—God and omnipotence. The small word 'is' adds no new predicate, but only serves to posit the predicate *in its relation* to the subject. If, now, we take the subject (God) with all its predicates (among which is omnipotence), and say 'God is', or 'There is a God', we attach no new predicate to the concept of God, but only posit the subject in itself with all its predicates, and indeed posit it as being an *object* that stands in relation to my *concept*. The content of both must be one and the same; nothing can have been added to the concept, which expresses merely what is possible, by my thinking its object (through the expression 'it is') as given absolutely. Otherwise stated, the real contains no more than the merely possible. A hundred real thalers do not contain the least coin more than a hundred possible thalers. For as the latter signify the concept, and the former the object and the positing of the object, should the former contain more than the latter, my concept would not, in that case, express the whole object, and would not therefore be an adequate concept of it. My financial position is, however, affected very differently by a hundred real thalers than it is by the mere concept of them (that is, of their possibility). For the object, as it actually exists, is not analytically contained in my concept, but is added to my concept (which is a determination of my state) synthetically; and yet the conceived hundred thalers are not themselves in the least increased through thus acquiring existence outside my concept.

By whatever and by however many predicates we may think a thing—even if we completely determine it—we do not make the least addition to the thing when we further declare that this thing *is*. Otherwise, it would not be exactly the same thing that exists, but something more than we had thought in the concept; and we could not, therefore, say that the exact object of my concept exists. If we think in a thing every feature of reality except one, the missing reality is not added by my saying that this defective thing exists. On the contrary, it exists with the same defect with which I have thought it, since otherwise what exists would be something different from what I thought. When, therefore, I think a being as the supreme reality, without any defect, the question still remains whether it exists or not. For though, in my concept, nothing may be lacking of the possible real content of a thing in general, something is still lacking in its relation to my whole state of thought, namely, [in so far as I am unable to assert] that knowledge of this object is also possible *a posteriori*. And here we find the source of our present difficulty. Were we dealing with an object of the senses, we could not confound the existence of the thing with the mere concept of it. For through the concept

the object is thought only as conforming to the *universal conditions* of possible empirical knowledge in general, whereas through its existence it is thought as belonging to the
context of experience as a whole. In being thus connected with the *content* of experience
as a whole, the concept of the object is not, however, in the least enlarged; all that has
happened is that our thought has thereby obtained an additional possible perception. It
is not, therefore, surprising that, if we attempt to think existence through the pure category alone, we cannot specify a single mark distinguishing it from mere possibility.

Whatever, therefore, and however much, our concept of an object may contain, we
must go outside it, if we are to ascribe existence to the object. In the case of objects of
the senses, this takes place through their connection with some one of our perceptions,
in accordance with empirical laws. But in dealing with objects of pure thought, we have
no means whatsoever of knowing their existence, since it would have to be known in a
completely *a priori* manner. Our consciousness of all existence (whether immediately
through perception, or mediately through inferences which connect something with
perception) belongs exclusively to the unity of experience; any [alleged] existence outside this field, while not indeed such as we can declare to be absolutely impossible, is of
the nature of an assumption which we can never be in a position to justify.

The concept of a supreme being is in many respects a very useful idea; but just
because it is a mere idea, it is altogether incapable, by itself alone, of enlarging our
knowledge in regard to what exists. It is not even competent to enlighten us as to the
possibility of any existence beyond that which is known in and through experience. The
analytic criterion of possibility, as consisting in the principle that bare positives (realities) give rise to no contradiction, cannot be denied to it. But since the realities are not
given to us in their specific characters; since even if they were, we should still not be
in a position to pass judgment; since the criterion of the possibility of synthetic knowledge is never to be looked for save in experience, to which the object of an idea cannot
belong, the connection of all real properties in a thing is a synthesis, the possibility of
which we are unable to determine *a priori*. And thus the celebrated Leibniz is far from
having succeeded in what he plumed himself on achieving—the comprehension *a priori*
of the possibility of this sublime ideal being.

The attempt to establish the existence of a supreme being by means of the famous
ontological argument of Descartes is therefore merely so much labour and effort lost;
we can no more extend our stock of [theoretical] insight by mere ideas, than a merchant
can better his position by adding a few noughts to his cash account.

Notes

* [All bracketed translator's footnotes have been removed.]

1 A concept is always possible if it is not self-contradictory. This is the logical criterion of
possibility, and by it the object of the concept is distinguishable from the *nihil negativum.*
But it may none the less be an empty concept, unless the objective reality of the synthesis through which the concept is generated has been specifically proved; and such proof, as
we have shown above, rests on principles of possible experience, and not on the principle
of analysis (the law of contradiction). This is a warning against arguing directly from the
logical possibility of concepts to the real possibility of things.

Questions for reflection

1   Explain what the claim "existence is not a predicate" means. Do you agree that it is not a predicate? Why or why not?

2   How does Kant use the above claim to demonstrate the faultiness of the ontological argument?

3   While it is possible to give a *verbal definition* of the concept of a necessary being, Kant argues that this provides "no insight into the conditions which make it necessary to regard the non-existence of a thing as absolutely unthinkable." Do you agree? How does this affect the ontological argument?

4   Kant makes the following claim: "There is already a contradiction in introducing the concept of existence—no matter under what title it may be disguised—into the concept of a thing which we profess to be thinking solely in reference to its possibility." Do you agree with his claim? Explain.

Further reading

Immanuel Kant ([1781] 1965) *Critique of Pure Reason*. Trans. Norman Kemp Smith. New York: St. Martin's Press. (Kant offers criticisms of the teleological, cosmological, and ontological arguments; the selection above is taken from this work.)

Gordon E. Michalson, Jr. (1999) *Kant and the Problem of God*. Oxford: Blackwell. (An unorthodox reading of Kant which sees him as a precursor to nineteenth-century atheism rather than a forerunner to liberal Protestant theology.)

Graham Oppy (1996) *Ontological Arguments and Belief in God*. Cambridge: Cambridge University Press. (A comprehensive discussion and critique of various versions of the ontological argment.)

Alvin Plantinga, ed. (1968) *The Ontological Argument, from St. Anselm to Contemporary Philosophers*. London: Macmillan. (A good selection of essays on the argument, pro and con.)

Ralph C. S. Walker (1978) *Kant*. New York: Routledge. (An informative biographical summary of Kant's thought.)

Chapter 28

Charles Hartshorne

A RECENT ONTOLOGICAL ARGUMENT

Charles Hartshorne (pronounced "harts-horn"; 1897–2000) was a leading process phil-osopher, theologian, and metaphysician. He defended a neoclassical, process view of God in which God is understood not to be pure "being" but rather eternal "becoming."

Hartshorne also provided an ontological proof for God's existence, and he is often cred-ited for bringing the ontological argument back to the fore after its calamitous defeat by Immanuel Kant in the eighteenth century. Hartshorne claimed to have detected two differ-ent versions of the ontological argument in Anselm's writings and it is the second version, he argued, that is the more persuasive. He maintained that the argument leads us to the disjunction that either "God exists" is true necessarily or "God exists" is false necessar-ily since the notion of God cannot contain contingency with respect to his existence. In this selection he then develops a ten-step modal argument from Anselm's second version which is logically valid and which, he claims, both is immune to Kant's criticism and demonstrates that a perfect being exists.

Becker's Postulate—developed by Oskar Becker, it is the claim that all modal status is necessary; for instance, that the possibility of *P* implies the necessity of the possibility of P.
modal—pertaining to the modes of propositions (*de dicto*) or of existence (*de re*) as necessary or possible.
valid argument—an argument in which if the premises are true, the conclusion necessarily follows.

The irreducibly modal structure of the argument

. . . Had the [Ontological Argument] been known as the Modal Argument, the chances of genuine inquiry would have been greater. Critics have generally discussed the problem as though it concerned a mere question of fact, of contingent existence versus contingent non-existence. This is not a modal distinction in an unambiguous sense, inasmuch as the mode of contingency is the neutrality of a predicate as between existence and non-existence, and the denial of such neutrality is the disjunction: necessarily existent or necessarily non-existent (i.e., impossible). To squeeze this modal complexity into the mere dichotomy, "existent versus non-existent," is to fail to discuss what Anselm was talking about. He repeatedly expressed the principle that "contingently-existing perfect thing" is contradictory in the same way as "non-existing perfect thing." However, since what is not exemplified in truth is certainly not necessarily exemplified ($\sim p \sim N p$), and since what is not necessary could not be necessary ($\sim N p \ N \sim N p$), to exclude contingency (this exclusion being the main point of the Argument) is to exclude factual non-existence as well as merely factual existence, leaving, as the only status which the idea of perfection can have (supposing it not meaningless or contradictory), that of necessary exemplification in reality; and it then, by the principle $N p \ p$, "the necessarily true is true," becomes contradictory to deny that perfection is exemplified. (Here, and throughout, we use the arrow sign for strict, not material, implication.)

Is it this subtle, beautifully logical reasoning that we meet in the numerous refutations? Rather we find a gross simplification which amounts to the straw-man procedure.

The logical structure of the Anselmian argument, in its mature or "Second" form, may be partially formalized as follows:

'q' for '$(\exists x)Px$' There is a perfect being, or perfection exists
'N' for 'it is necessary (logically true) that'
'$\sim$' for 'it is not true that'
'v' for 'or'
'$p{\rightarrow}q$' for 'p strictly implies q' or '$N \sim (p \& \sim q)$'

1. $q{\rightarrow}Nq$	"Anselm's Principle": perfection could not exist contingently [hence, the assertion that it exists could not be contingently but only necessarily true.*]
2. $Nq \ v \sim Nq$	Excluded Middle
3. $\sim Nq{\rightarrow}N \sim Nq$	Form of Becker's Postulate: modal status is always necessary
4. $NqvN \sim Nq$	Inference from (2, 3)
5. $N \sim Nq{\rightarrow}N \sim q$	Inference from (1): the necessary falsity of the consequent implies that of the antecedent (Modal form of modus tollens)
6. $NqvN \sim q$	Inference from (4, 5)
7. $\sim N \sim q$	Intuitive postulate (or conclusion from other theistic arguments): perfection is not impossible
8. Nq	Inference from (6, 7)
9. $Nq{\rightarrow}q$	Modal axiom
10. q	Inference from (8, 9)

Those who challenge the Argument should decide which of these 10 items or inferential steps to question. Of course one may reject one or more of the assumptions (1, 3, 7); but reject is one thing, refute or show to be a mere sophistry is another. To me at

least, the assumptions are intuitively convincing, provided perfection is properly construed, a condition Anselm did not fulfill. Moreover, no absurd consequence seems
derivable from them by valid reasoning.

Concerning (1). Note that we do not take as initial assumption that $\sim q$ is directly
contradictory, or that a nonexistent being must therefore be imperfect. Nonexistent
subjects cannot be said to have predicates, even inconsistent ones. Rather we reason
that by virtue of (1) and certain principles of modal logic,

$$((\exists x)\, Px\, \&\sim N\, (\exists x) Px) \rightarrow\, \sim Px$$

and thus the antecedent is necessarily false, since it both asserts and by implication denies
perfection, not of a supposed non-existent but of a supposed contingently-existent subject. Such a subject can very well have predicates, and indeed all ordinary subjects are
precisely of this kind. Thus we make contingency and its negation, not existence or non-
existence, the predicates with which the argument is concerned, in connection with the
predicate perfection.

The postulate of logical possibility (7) is in my view the hardest to justify. One way
of doing this is to employ one or more of the other theistic proofs, some forms of which
demonstrate that perfection must be at least conceivable. Here, however, we encounter
Kant's contention that the other proofs themselves need support from the ontological
[argument]. Yet Kant's own analysis showed that what the other proofs need from the
ontological [argument] is not really its conclusion (8 or 10), but only the exclusion of
contingency from perfection (6), and this is a mere logical transformation of Anselm's
Principle (1). Thus there need be no vicious circle in employing all the proofs in mutual
support. They are all complex, involving a number of assumptions and steps, and where
one is weakest another may be strongest. There need be no simple linear order, and
indeed there is none, among them. Here too we must do our own thinking, and not
expect Kant or Hume to have done it for us.

That modality with respect to existence is a predicate is assumed by the critics
of the Argument themselves. For they hold, in effect, that to every predicate there is
attached the status of contingency, i.e., its existence and non-existence must alike be
conceivable. Obviously, if "contingent" is a predicate, so is "non-contingent"; just as,
if "perfect" is a predicate, so is "imperfect." This is then, so far as it goes, an answer to
the crucial Logical-type Counterargument: modality is (at least) as high in the type-
sequence as property! We shall see presently, however, that only neoclassical theism
can consistently avail itself of this rebuttal.

It is to be noted that Anselm's Principle does not say that perfection would be imperfect if it were unexemplified, but that anything exemplifying it merely contingently (so that
it could have been unexemplified) would be imperfect, and so would not exemplify it after
all. Thus the "homological mistake" is not committed (12th Counter-argument). Moreover (and here too Anselm is subtler than most of his critics), "is necessarily exemplified"
follows by Becker's Postulate from "could be necessarily exemplified," since $\sim N \sim Np$ Np.
This disposes of the 5th Counter-argument, "Hypothetical Necessity Only."

Something should be said about the meaning of "necessity," symbolized by 'N'. As
every logician knows, there are many interpretations of this symbol. In general it means
analytic or L-true, true by necessity of the meanings of the terms employed. This is the
sense intended in the present essay. However, what is analytic in one language may, as

Quine and others have sufficiently emphasized, not be so in another.[1] (Here, too, we see how absurd it is to suppose that the Ontological question is a simple one.) I cannot exhaust the modal subject here and now. But I must make clear the difference between merely conditional necessity and absolute necessity. As von Wright has it, this last is the same as "necessity upon tautological conditions": not necessity assuming p, or necessity assuming not-p, but necessity, p or not-p. Since "p or not-p" must be true, it is meaningless to say, "q might be necessary but is not," when "necessary" is taken in the sense of "upon tautological conditions." This is the only sense at issue in connection with the ontological argument. The divine existence is by definition unconditioned, and its necessity can only be absolute, valid no matter what, or "given p or not-p." Thus if God logically could be necessary He must be, since no contingent condition can be relevant.

The technical difficulty with regard to the Argument is that the idea of God is apparently not a conception of formal logic. Hence even if the idea implies the necessity of a corresponding object, so that the denial of such an object is contradictory, still the whole question seems to fall outside the basic rules of any language. However, the matter is not so simple. There ought to be a formal rule concerning the division between necessary and contingent statements, and as we shall see, by some reasonable criteria for this division, the statement "Divine Perfection exists" falls on the side of necessity. Moreover, there may well be an aspect of the idea of God which is formal in the logical sense. If for instance, "deity" connotes, among other things, "the sole individual definable a priori" (distinguished a priori from all others, actual or possible), is this not a formal characterization? Or suppose it follows from the meaning of "God" that it can only refer to an individual "such that, given any statement about any other individual whatever, this statement can be translated without loss of meaning or truth into a statement about God." (Thus for S is P we can always say God knows that S is P.) Of no other individual than God, I believe, could the quoted stipulation hold; yet it is a formal or logical stipulation. No special fact is mentioned, but only the ideas of individual, statement, and translatability or equivalence. No doubt some problems arise here, but I shall not attempt to deal with them now.

Carnap has proposed the notion of "meaning postulates," as a device for introducing analytic judgments, other than the merely logical, into a language.[2] The objection has been that apparently any scientific law could be turned into an a priori necessity by suitable meaning postulates, thus trivializing the procedure. However, as Bowman Clarke, in an unpublished thesis, has proposed, the trivialization may be avoided if we limit meaning postulates to ideas of metaphysical generality, ideas of unlimited range in space-time, and applicable to all grades of existence, low or high.[3] I think also that metaphysical universality is the same thing as the absence of exclusiveness to be discussed in § IX [of The Logic of Perfection], and that God (in His necessary essence only) is universal or non-exclusive, involved in all possible things. It may be that Carnap's proposal, qualified and developed in some such way, will solve the technical problem of reconciling the logical meaning of "necessary" with the ontological in the unique divine case.

One way to put the argument is this: any language adequate to formulate the meaning of "perfect" in the theistic sense will make "perfection exists" analytic or L-true. Moreover, a language which does this will not thereby become inconsistent. This is more than can be said for a language making "perfect island exists" L-true (using "island" in anything like the dictionary sense). Since modal status is always necessary, mistakes in assigning such status can only lead to contradiction. Suppose, for instance, we should speak of a "necessarily-existent" island. Since the necessarily so is of course so, said island must exist. What is wrong? Simply that the notion of island is that of a contingent thing, resulting from causes whose operation is not infallible and everlasting. If an island could be necessary, anything could be so, and since the possibly necessary must be necessary ($\sim N \sim Np\ Np$), there would be no contingency or necessary in a significant sense. Thus a language which required one to admit as a genuine concept "necessarily-existing island" would be self-inconsistent. The "necessarily-existing island" must exist, but also it must not and cannot exist. We can only start over again, by dismissing the alleged definition as ill-formed. If then the notion of "necessarily-existing perfection" were likewise illegitimate, a contradiction would result from its use. If the contradiction can be exhibited, there is an end of the matter. But can it? If not, then the notion may be legitimate. And since religion seems to require the idea, there is some burden of proof on the negative. (In the foregoing I assume that we are not limited to classical theism as explication of "perfect," for if we were, then I would grant the charge of inconsistency without further ado.) To reason, "If the metaphysically perfect could be necessary, anything could be so," would be silly. . . . The metaphysically perfect is a radically exceptional case, on any analysis. "Perfect island" never did mean metaphysically perfect island, to any honest and careful thinker; for the phrase is too glaringly absurd. It never meant, *either* (classical theism) the exhaustion, through an island, of all possibility so far as positive or valuable, *or* (neoclassical theism) coincidence of actuality with the island's actuality and of possibility with the island's possibility. And if it did mean either of these things, then it meant nonsense. To be thus is not to be an island, but to be God.

The Cosmological Argument, not to be dealt with here, would perhaps show that any language adequate to formulate the universal categories, or to discuss the most general cosmological questions, would also make "perfection exists" L-true.

The foregoing meaning of 'N' justifies the axioms that all modalities reduce to three: $Np, N \sim p, (\sim N\ p\ \&\ \sim N \sim p)$; and that $\sim N \sim Np\ Np$, and $\sim Np\ N \sim Np$ (*what could be necessary is so, and what is not necessary could not be so*). It must be understood that propositions are here identified by their meaning, not in some extrinsic way. As Church remarks, "the proposition occurring first on a certain page" may happen to be, in a certain language, a necessary proposition, but "it" might also have been a contingent proposition.[4] Clearly one is not in such cases dealing with the same proposition, so far as meaning is concerned. Some modal systems, at least, recognize the above axioms (Lewis, Prior, Carnap).

In systems of "strict implication," it has been termed a paradox that a necessary proposition is strictly implied by any proposition whatever. I agree with Lewis in not finding this paradoxical, at least if we consider only those cases which are free from empirical concepts. That "blue cheese contains micro-organisms" (if this is part of what we mean by cheese) is only trivially a priori or necessary; for there might have been no such thing as cheese, or even any idea of such a thing. What is strictly a priori and purely necessary here is only some such principle as that the consequences of a defined term must be accepted if the term is accepted. This much more abstract proposition, or something like it, is, I believe, in a genuine sense implied by any proposition and any thought at all. I hold similarly that the validity of the Argument, if it be valid, can only mean that the existence of perfection is non-trivially necessary, an implicit or more or less hidden ingredient of any concept or any belief whatever. It follows that it must be highly abstract, highly general; and this consequence I accept and emphasize. We shall see that while this is no threat to neoclassical, it is to classical, theism.

Is existence a predicate?

Logicians, including some who would rather be seen in beggars' rags than in the company of the Ontological Argument, have held that existence is, after all, a sort of predicate, even of ordinary things.[5] But for our purpose this is unimportant, since the Argument does not depend upon the treatment of ordinary existence. The status which Anselm and Descartes . . . deduce from "conceived as perfect" is not "conceived as existent," but rather "conceived as existentially non-contingent," i.e., conceived as that which "cannot be conceived not to exist." It is the existential modality which is taken as part of the meaning of the conceived property perfection. But whereas, in the ordinary or contingent case, neither "existent" nor "non-existent" can be inferred from the modal status, from "non-contingent" one may infer "necessarily existent unless impossible." (To exclude impossibility, the Argument as it stands does not suffice, except for one who grants that "the fool's" or non-theist's idea of God is self-consistent. But here the other theistic arguments may help.)

Notes

*   [Later editions of this essay included this clarification at Professor Hartshorne's request.]

1   Quine's conclusion that all truth is synthetic is fairly but powerfully criticized by A. Hofstadter in "The Myth of the Whole, a Consideration of Quine's View of Knowledge." *J. of Phil.,* LI (1954), 397–417.
2   See R. Carnap, *Meaning and Necessity,* Second Ed. (Chicago: The University of Chicago Press, 1956), pp. 222–229; and R. M. Martin, *The Notion of Analytic Truth* (Philadelphia: University of Pennsylvania Press, 1959), pp. 87–90.
3   See Carnap's somewhat analogous proposal in *Meaning and Necessity,* Sec. 21. Also my paper, "Existential Propositions and the Law of Categories." *Proceedings of the Tenth International Congress of Philosophy,* Amsterdam, August 11–18, 1948, edited by E. W. Beth, H. J. Pos and J. H. A. Hollak, Fascicule I, pp. 342–344.
4   A. Church, in his article in *Structure, Method and Meaning: Essays in Honor of Henry M. Sheffer,* edited by P. Henle (New York: The Liberal Arts Press, 1951), pp. 22–23, footnote.
5   See H. Reichenbach, *Elements of Symbolic Logic* (New York: The Macmillan Company, 1947), pp. 333–334.

Questions for reflection

1   What are your initial impressions of Hartshorne's ontological argument? Can you explain how the premises of the argument should be understood?
2   This argument is in a valid form. Whether or not you agree with the conclusion, where might a reasonable person who does not accept the conclusion dissent from one or more of the premises?
3   Premise seven is sometimes taken to be a crucial premise: that perfection is not impossible. Hartshorne takes it to be an intuitive postulate that it is possible that God exists. If so, given the disjunction that either "God exists" is true necessarily or "God exists" is false necessarily, it would seem to follow that "God exists" is true necessarily. What do you make of this line of reasoning?

4   Does the argument escape the "Perfect Island" criticism? Explain.
5   Does this version of the argument escape Kant's criticism? If so, how? If not, why not?

Further reading

Daniel A. Dombrowski (2006) *Rethinking the Ontological Argument: A Neoclassical Theistic Response.* Cambridge: Cambridge University Press. (Building on Hartshorne's work, he defends the ontological argument against contemporary critics using a process concept of God.)

Charles Hartshorne (1962) *The Logic of Perfection.* LaSalle, IL: Open Court. (Contains his modal argument given above and further reflections on the process view of God.)

Graham Oppy (1995) *Ontological Arguments and Belief in God.* Cambridge: Cambridge University Press. (Provides a comprehensive discussion of the ontological argument including a taxonomy and analysis of both historical and recent versions of the argument.)

Alvin Plantinga (1974) *The Nature of Necessity.* Oxford: Clarendon Press. (Develops a version of the ontological argument in terms of possible worlds.)

Alvin Plantinga, ed. (1965) *The Ontological Argument: From St. Anselm to Contemporary Philosophers.* London: Macmillan. (Another important collection of essays on the ontological argument from leading historical and contemporary thinkers including Thomas Aquinas, René Descartes, Benedict de Spinoza, Gottfried Wilhelm Leibniz, Arthur Schopenhauer, G. E. Moore, William P. Alston, and J. N. Findley.)

Religious Studies on the Web: Ontological Argument. http://www.rsweb.org.uk/phil/ontological.html (A website with numerous articles on the ontological argument, both pro and con.)

Non-traditional arguments

Chapter 29

Paul Copan

THE MORAL ARGUMENT

Paul Copan is Pledger Family Chair of Philosophy and Ethics at Palm Beach Atlantic University. In the following selection, he argues that objective moral values are properly basic and make sense in a theistic, but not in a non-theistic, universe. The central argument of the essay can be put simply in the following syllogism: (1) If objective moral values exist, then God exists; (2) objective moral values do exist; (3) therefore, God exists. Copan offers evidence for the premises and other supporting claims for the argument and replies to various objections to them. He also responds to the notorious Euthyphro dilemma in which it is argued that either God's moral commands are arbitrary or there is an autonomous moral standard which God must consult.

Introduction

Civil rights leader Martin Luther King Jr. wrote from a Birmingham, AL, jail: "One may well ask: How can you advocate breaking some laws and obeying others?" The answer, he noted, "lies in the fact that there are two kinds of laws: just and unjust."[1] King spoke of an "eternal law" or "natural law" to which we are subject.

Do objective moral values exist? If so, do they make sense in a non-theistic world? And if so, what metaphysical grounds do we have for affirming their existence? I shall contend that

1   objective moral values do exist and are properly basic;
2   they do not make sense in a non-theistic world (most time will be spent in this area, focusing primarily on naturalism, although my argument would apply to other non-theistic alternatives), but are properly grounded in a theistic worldview in which human beings have been uniquely created in God's image and thus reflect certain divine properties in important—even if limited—ways; and

3   the Euthyphro argument does not undermine the connection between God and objective moral values.

The argument undergirding my chapter is thus:

> If objective moral values exist, then God exists.
> Objective moral values do exist.
> Therefore, God exists.

Such values are inexplicable non-theistically—or, more specifically, naturalistically. This "natural law," which transcends human history and cultures, is rooted in the very nature or character of a good God. Because we humans are uniquely made in the divine image, we are capable of *recognizing* or *discovering* moral principles; we do not *invent* them.

Even if we cannot move inferentially from objective moral values to the omniscient and omnipotent God of Abraham, Isaac, and Jacob, at least we can say that we live in an "ontologically haunted universe."[2] Moral values serve as one of the *signals of transcendence*.[3] We humans, who have been made in God's image, are endowed with moral capacities (e.g. conscience, moral responsibility and freedom, the recognition of our need for grace and mercy in the face of moral failure) so that, at a minimum, we may infer a personal Being to whom each of us is accountable (Romans 1:19–20; 2:14–15) and with whom we must be in right relationship—even if the moral argument does not logically bring us to an all-powerful, all-knowing Being.

Moral values as properly basic

Rather than being the product of culture, individual preference, or socio-biological evolution, objective moral values do indeed exist: *kindness is a virtue and not a vice; torturing babies for fun is immoral; rape is morally reprehensible.* Most of us find such truths obvious—just as we find $2 + 2 = 4$ and *modus ponens* perspicuously true. Basic moral truths exist regardless of

- the *plurality of moral beliefs* over time and across cultures (i.e. even if cultures throughout history have carried out morally reprehensible activities, this fact does *not* entail that objective moral values are non-existent); and
- the *alleged evolutionary benefit from believing certain moral tenets* (certain beliefs and actions may be right—such as self-sacrifice for others—even if such practices do not necessarily prolong my or my species' existence).

As with basic logical truths, so it is with moral truths. To deny them is to reject something fundamental about our humanness. Atheist philosopher Kai Nielsen comments on the vileness of child abuse and wife-beating:

> It is more reasonable to believe such elemental things to be evil than to believe any skeptical theory that tells us we cannot know or reasonably believe any of these things to be evil. . . . I firmly believe that this is bedrock and right and that anyone who does not believe it cannot have probed deeply enough into the grounds of his moral beliefs.[4]

Nicholas Rescher rightly notes: "If [members of a particular tribe] think that it is acceptable to engage in practices like the sacrifice of first-born children, then their grasp on the conception of morality is somewhere between inadequate and non-existent."[5] When the murderous intentions of Stalin, Hitler, or Pol Pot are applauded or deemed justifiable because "it seemed good from *their* perspective," right-thinking persons will denounce such twisted approbations.

Although culture may *influence* one's moral perceptions, it need not *dictate* them. Throughout history, civilizations have produced moral reformers such as William Wilberforce or Martin Luther King Jr., who withstood the cultural tide against them and recognized the dignity and rights of *all* human beings, who are made in the image of God. (According to the Jewish-Christian tradition, sin has brought damage to our God-given nature but has not eradicated or eclipsed its intrinsic goodness.)[6]

As Robert Audi has eloquently argued, we ought to take seriously fundamental or pre-theoretical moral intuitions that arise as we confront particular moral situations.[7] As Romans 1:20 and 2:14 indicate, we are responsible humans who are equipped with the capacity to recognize right and wrong—even if partially distorted by culture and hardening of heart. While such directly apprehended intuitions are not necessarily infallible or indefeasible (e.g. further clarification and refining may be required—just as with objects of sense perception), they can serve as a partial guide for detecting the world's moral framework.

Many of our moral beliefs are *properly basic*. That is, they are properly grounded in certain appropriate circumstances. For example, we are properly *appalled* at a man's adultery with his personal assistant and his abandoning his wife and children; there is no need to explain away our shock and horror at such actions. Even if it is impossible to prove in some scientific/positivistic fashion (a position which itself cannot be proven scientifically) that moral values exist, we probably find ourselves far more certain of the wrongness of such actions than we may be of the truth of Einstein's relativity theories or of the universe's expansion.

As with particular *epistemic* beliefs (my belief that I had chocolate-chip pancakes for breakfast last Saturday), so it is with my *moral* beliefs (the terrorist attacks on September 11, 2001, were morally reprehensible). Holding to such beliefs is properly basic, and thus rational and justifiable. That is, I am violating no epistemic norm in holding these beliefs, and, as Alvin Plantinga puts it, I am doing my epistemic duty *in excelsis*.[8] Although these prima facie beliefs may be defeasible,[9] in the absence of any decent defeaters for holding them there is just no good reason to reject them. For instance, I may be taking prescribed drugs with hallucinogenic side-effects such that I see pancakes when no pancakes are present. Similarly, many of our *moral* perceptions are so inescapable that we would do serious damage to our noetic structure in rejecting their validity.

Of course, there are relativists or social constructionists, who would have us believe that morality is relative to personal preferences or particular cultures. Of course, one wonders why moral relativists generally uphold the cardinal and universally binding standard of "tolerance"[10] and get upset when their own "rights" are violated or their property is stolen. Moral relativists are usually *selectively* relativistic—until *their* rights are violated or *their* property is stolen. That is, they tend to be armchair relativists—not practical relativists.

For the perspectivalist or social constructionist, she finds herself in the awkward position of either saying nothing at all ("this is just my perspective that it is all a matter of perspective") or contradicting herself ("it is all a matter of perspective—*except mine, which is universally true*").[11] Perspectivalism ends up being either trivial or incoherent.

It seems that the *credulity principle* is appropriate with regard to both our *sense* perceptions and our *moral* intuitions/perceptions: both are innocent until proven guilty. I am wise to accept their testimony *unless* I have an overriding reason to doubt them. Moreover, given the *logical* possibility of being morally or epistemically misguided does not entail comprehensive skepticism regarding such perceptions. There is no need to take such epistemic and moral skepticism with radical seriousness.[12] Furthermore, talk of human equality, rights, value, or worth by political philosophers (e.g. Ronald Dworkin, John Rawls) reflects a common commitment to ideals we generally take seriously. (Of course, such thinkers tend to *posit* such ideals; their refusal to offer a coherent metaphysical grounding for such rights is a glaring deficiency, as we shall see below.)

Thus there are no overriding reasons—including relativism's denial of moral values or (as we shall see below) socio-biological evolution as the basis for moral values—to deny their objectivity or applicability to all human beings.

An unnatural fit: non-theism and objective moral values

The United Nations Universal Declaration of Human Rights of 1948 declares: "All human beings are born free and equal in dignity and rights. They are endowed with reason and conscience and should act towards one another in a spirit of brotherhood." Notice how the dignity and rights of human beings are simply *posited*. What is noticeably lacking are any *grounds* or *basis* for believing this to be the case. By contrast, America's Declaration of Independence connects the "self-evident" value and "unalienable rights" of human beings to God their Creator. The Jewish-Christian Scriptures declare that human beings—both male and female—have been made "in the image of God" (Genesis 1:26–7). We have been uniquely made by God as personal, relational, volitional, moral, rational, self-aware, and spiritual beings—attributes that God has to a maximal degree. Even atheists, who deny God's existence, can hold to the same objective moral values as theists, and this is no surprise—because they have been made in the selfsame divine image and are therefore capable of moral reflection and action just as theists are. So while they, being morally sensitive human beings, believe that moral realism (i.e. *mind-independent moral truths exist*)[13] is *logically* justified, the more fundamental question of *metaphysical* justification remains.

Naturalistic moral realists (NMRs) claim such justification. David Brink puts it this way: "Ethical naturalism claims that moral facts are nothing more than familiar facts about the natural, including social, world."[14] He expands on this summary: "moral facts *are* natural and social scientific (e.g. social, psychological, economic, and biological facts)."[15] Michael Smith claims that in all respects (including the moral), we are "constrained" by the truth of naturalism, "the view that the world is amenable to study through empirical science."[16] What makes moral claims true are naturalistic features, which are themselves "posits, or composites of posits, of empirical science."[17] Moral features *are* natural features.[18]

Peter Railton claims that any charge that morality is "odd" is eliminated when we take the view that moral facts are *constituted by* natural facts.[19] (Brink claims that moral properties are *constituted by* and not *identical to*, natural properties.)[20] Railton prefers to see emergent moral properties as supervening upon—but not reducible to—physical ones.[21] This would be similar to wetness supervening on H_2O, whereas hydrogen and oxygen by themselves do not have the property of wetness. Railton does not believe that moral facts are bizarre or *sui generis*: "there need be nothing odd about causal mechanisms for learning moral facts if these facts are constituted by natural facts."[22] If moral properties supervene on one set of conditions (e.g. when a brain and nervous system are sufficiently and complexly developed—or when a certain level of social interconnectedness arises), then it is necessarily true that moral properties supervene on an identical set of conditions elsewhere or at another time. Moral properties are in the *effect* but not in the *cause*. Thus *nature*, Brink claims, is the only place we can look in an attempt to find the moral realm: "We are natural and social creatures, and I know of nowhere else to look for ethics than this rich conjunction of facts."[23]

Noted ethical theorist William Frankena claims that the theist cannot appeal to the naturalistic fallacy (the allegedly illicit shift from *is* to *ought*) without question-begging.[24] He criticizes "religionist" ethics,[25] maintaining that there is no *logical* reason that we *must* conceive ethics as a part of religion (moving from the *is* of "God loves us" to the *ought* of "we must love one another").[26] And even though ethical principles are not all logically dependent upon theology, "it does not follow that they cannot be justified in any objective and rational sense."[27]

But is this really the case?[28] Is morality as natural as granola? Did human dignity and moral obligation just emerge through the course of naturalistic evolution? I suggest that the answer is no. Rather, it is *theism* that furnishes the metaphysical resources to make sense of the instantiation of moral properties in the form of objective moral values, human dignity, human rights, and obligations. Theism actually offers us a more suitable environment and thus a more plausible explanation for the existence of objective moral values (i.e. the instantiation of moral properties).

Three considerations for a theory's explanatory superiority

Thesis: In deciding between two competing hypotheses, we should look for (a) the more natural (less ad hoc) transition from the overall theory to the entity in question, (b) the more unified theory, and (c) the more basic theory.[29]

First, the *natural fit* criterion: take hypotheses X and Y. If explanations for particular entities are repeatedly ad hoc under X but flow naturally from Y, then Y is a superior explanation. When we look at naturalism vs. theism, we must ask: is there a naturalness in flow from theory to the particular entity in question, or is the transition disjointed?

To illustrate, take the feature of *libertarian freedom*: if theism and scientific naturalism are the only games in town, the balances would be tipped in the favor of theism. After all, in contrast to naturalism's mechanistic universe in which efficient causality (under some covering law model of explanation) predominates, theism has ample room for a personal cause or agency, which involves final (and not merely efficient) causation.[30] The buck stops with the agent—not certain prior conditions and states. The agent chooses/acts with a certain goal in mind, not simply because certain impulses, motivations, and conditions direct him—even if they play an influential role.

We could similarly speak of theism's preferable explanatory power over naturalism with regard to the emergence of first life or consciousness or the existence of rationality and the correspondence of our minds to the external world. The *worldview context* is clearly an important feature in adjudicating between competing hypotheses.

The same applies to objective moral values, which flow readily from a supremely valuable Being to us as his valuable creatures. Such a smooth transition does not appear in the move from mindless, valueless, naturalistic evolutionary processes to—*voilà*—objective moral values and human dignity.

Second, the *unification* criterion: another factor worth considering is whether a worldview has some kind of *grand unifying factor for all its features* or not. Are explanations within a theory *unified* and inter-connected, or are they disparate and unrelated? Again, it seems that God's role as the unifier of the variety of features of the world—the universe's origin and fine-tuning, the emergence of life and of consciousness, the existence of rationality and of morally significant beings—is the superior explanation or grounding when contrasted with a naturalistic alternative (in which numerous, unconnected series of causes and effects bring about these features). God as the background factor serves as the natural unifier (e.g. through primary or, usually, secondary causation).

The framework of naturalistic moral realism lacks any kind of unification of the brute facts that the naturalist takes for granted. The naturalist must deal with the following hurdles—accounting for the origin of the universe, the fine-tuned nature of the universe making it fit for life, the actual emergence of first life, the emergence of consciousness, the emergence of moral and intrinsically valuable beings, etc.—in a kind of "that's just the way things worked out" perspective. We have a hodge-podge of disparate brute necessary conditions which somehow led to the existence of moral persons, yet nothing unifies them. Again, *the theist has no such problem*, with God as the unifier of these "hurdles." If one is open to the supernatural, a Grand Unified Theory or Theory of Everything is on the horizon! As Del Ratzsch notes: "When a value is produced by a long, tricky, precarious process, when it is generated and preserved by some breathtaking complexity, when it is realized against all odds, then intent—even design—suddenly becomes a live and reasonable question."[31]

To the naturalist, we put the question: would moral properties be instantiated even if humans did *not* exist? If *not*, why think that the alleged supervening moral properties have any objectivity at all or are non-arbitrary, since we could have developed differently (e.g. most humans might come to think rape is acceptable, and arguments could easily be made showing how this could be conducive to human survival)?[32] If, however, moral properties exist in a *Platonic* sense, then it is strange *in excelsis* and staggeringly coincidental that (a) these moral properties should "just exist" *and* that (b) they should correspond to beings who "just evolved" to such a point that they have emerged as intrinsically valuable. It is as though these moral properties were *just waiting* for us to evolve. In a theistic universe, these two unconnected features come together unproblematically.

The third criterion is *basicality*: if important relevant features are more basic in hypothesis Y than in Z, then Y is the preferable one.[33] Does a worldview leave us with certain brute facts and conundrums that we must simply take for granted, or does the worldview more ably furnish ontological foundations or more ultimate explanations for their existence? Take the phenomenon of consciousness. The materialist philosopher of mind Colin McGinn writes:

> How is it possible for conscious states to depend upon brain states? How can technicolour phenomenology arise from soggy grey matter? . . . How

could the aggregation of millions of individually insentient neurons generate subjective awareness? We know that brains are the *de facto* causal basis of consciousness, but we have, it seems, no understanding of how this can be so. It strikes us as miraculous, eerie, even faintly comic.[34]

Is consciousness merely a surd (as with the naturalist worldview), or is there some deeper, more basic explanation to account for its existence?

Ironically, NMRs such as David Brink will commonly appeal to the emergence of the mental as a springboard for their claim justifying the supervenience of the moral. Says Brink: "Assuming materialism is true, mental states supervene on physical states, yet few think that mental states are metaphysically queer."[35] A quick reality check turns out that this naturalistic position is truly question-begging. The emergence of consciousness is deeply problematic, and to base the emergence of moral properties on an appeal to the emergence of consciousness from matter is grossly ill conceived. Again, we cite McGinn:

> Consider the universe before conscious beings came along: the odds did not look good that such beings could come to exist. The world was all just physical objects and physical forces, devoid of life. . . . We have a good idea of how the Big Bang led to the creation of stars and galaxies, principally by force of gravity. But we know of no comparable force that might explain how ever-expanding lumps of matter might have developed into conscious life.[36]

As with consciousness, so it is with instantiated moral properties. Do moral properties *just happen to be instantiated*, or do human beings *just have* intrinsic value, or is there a more fundamental explanation for these instantiated properties? It would seem that with regard to consciousness and moral values—and other phenomena listed above—theism "offers suggestions for answers to a wide range of otherwise intractable questions."[37] As though by osmosis, naturalists readily borrow metaphysical capital from the theistic worldview.[38] Naturalism experiences a great logical difficulty of moving from *is* to *ought*. For the theist, humans are made in the divine image and thus have value by virtue of their nature. And naturalism has no *predictive value* when it comes to the instantiation of moral properties, which is not the case with theism.

A common naturalistic rejection of objective moral values

Thesis: The greater plausibility of theism with regard to the instantiation of moral properties/the existence of objective moral values is reinforced by the fact that many naturalists themselves find it difficult to account for the instantiation of moral properties such as moral values, obligations, personal dignity/rights, whereas this has not been a problem for theists.

Frankena's claim that theistic use of the naturalistic fallacy to argue for a supernatural basis as question-begging is further undermined by the claims of various naturalists of all stripes who believe the rejection of objective moral values to be the ineluctable entailment of their naturalism. In the florilegium below, note how a number of them deem objective moral values to be utterly at odds with an atheistic world.

- Jonathan Glover claims morality may survive "when seen to be a human creation."[39] We must "re-create ethics."[40]
- Bertrand Russell stood on the "firm foundation of unyielding despair."[41] He claimed that "the whole subject of ethics arises from the pressure of the community on the individual."[42]
- J. L. Mackie found moral properties "queer" in a naturalistic universe: "If . . . there are . . . objective values, they make the existence of a god more probable than it would have been without them. Thus we have . . . a defensible argument from morality to the existence of a god."[43]
- Jean-Paul Sartre believed that "man exists, turns up, appears on the scene, and, only afterwards, defines himself."[44] The human being "at first . . . is nothing."[45]
- Steven Weinberg asserts that "The more the universe seems comprehensible, the more it also seems pointless," and trying to understand the universe is "one of the very few things that lifts human life a little above the level of farce."[46]
- E. O. Wilson maintains that "precepts and religious faith are entirely material products of the mind."[47] Moral feeling rooted in the hypothalamus and the limbic system is a "device of survival in social organisms."[48]
- James Rachels insists that "Man is a moral (altruistic) being, not because he intuits the rightness of loving his neighbor, or because he responds to some noble ideal, but because his behavior is comprised of tendencies which natural selection has favoured."[49]
- Michael Ruse declares that we have developed an "awareness of morality—a sense of right and wrong and a feeling of obligation to be thus governed—because such an awareness is of biological worth."[50]
- Richard Dawkins declares, "The universe we observe has precisely the properties we should expect if there is, at bottom, no design, no purpose, no evil and no good, nothing but blind pitiless indifference."[51]
- Paul Draper agrees with Mackie: "A moral world is . . . very probable on theism."[52]

You get the picture. The truth of moral realism is far from clear, given naturalism. Theists, on the other hand, face no such difficulty. Theists maintain that moral realism and God's existence are ontologically connected. The reason they are connected is rooted in the concept of *personhood*.

The intrinsic connection between morality and personhood

Thesis: The reason human persons exist is because a personal God exists, in whose image we have been made. The instantiation of moral properties is internally related to (or bound up with) personhood, and if no persons existed, then no moral properties would be instantiated.

Philosopher Wes Morriston asks a Euthyphro-like question about God's goodness: "is God good because he has these [moral] properties? Or are they good because God has them?"[53] Even if Morriston showed that there is a theological problem in God's just "happening to have" certain moral properties over which he exerted no control,[54] he *still* has not shown that there could be an instantiation of moral properties *apart from*

God. God's character *may still* be the source of goodness and objective moral values, even though his being good is not something God brought about. If the instantiation of moral properties is inextricably bound up with personhood, then it would follow that a personal God, in whose image we have been made as morally valuable, is the source of moral values (more on this below).

Take the parallel phenomenon of (self-)consciousness: to use Morriston's language, God just "happens to have" the property of (self-)consciousness over which he has no control. However, one could readily argue that if God did not exist [and thus no (self-)conscious creatures], then no property of (self-)consciousness would be instantiated either.

In addition to the instanced properties of (self-)consciousness and value, we could say the same about those of free agency, dignity, rationality, or deep relationality that human beings experience. The instantiation of these properties is necessarily bound up with personhood, and without persons, these distinctive properties would not become instantiated.

How do some naturalists ground morality metaphysically? Boyd speaks of certain "homeostatic property clusters," which he claims offer an "extremely deep insight" into the possibility of natural definitions of morality.[55] Thus even if moral properties such as goodness are *natural* properties, they are not strictly *physical* ones.[56] It should be noted, however, that this "homeostatic cluster" which defines moral goodness is *social* rather than *individual*:

> The properties in homeostasis are to be thought of as instances of the sat-
> isfaction of particular human needs among people generally, rather than
> within the life of a single individual . . . [the homeostatic consequential-
> ist claims that] the satisfaction of those needs for one individual tends to be
> conducive to their satisfaction for others, and it is to the homeostatic unity
> of human needs satisfaction in the society generally that she or he appeals in
> proposing a definition of the good.[57]

According to Brink, moral facts are realized (or constituted) by "organized combina-tions of natural and social scientific facts and properties."[58]

Boyd asserts that there could be a parallel type of supervenience at a *social* level when an appropriate equilibrium or balance of conditions is reached. There are, first, many *human needs*—whether physical/medical, psychological, or social (e.g. love and friendship). Now, under a "wide variety" of circumstances, these human goods are "homeostatically clustered"—that is, they are mutually supportive of one another. And when this balance is supported by psychological or social mechanisms they contribute to the homeostasis.

Thus, the cluster of goods and homeostatic mechanisms which unify them *defines* moral goodness. Actions, policies, and character traits are morally good "to the extent that they foster the realization of these goods or to develop and sustain the homeostatic mechanisms upon which their unity depends."[59] Correct moral choices contribute to and even strengthen this balance.[60]

In response, why does moral goodness only emerge in the context of the *social* rather than at the *individual* level? Boyd answers: "The properties in homeostasis are to be thought of as instances of the satisfaction of particular human needs among people generally, rather than within the life of a single individual."[61] Although he does not specify, one wonders what is the ontological status of the individual *apart from* the needs and well-being of society—namely, in terms of inherent moral worth. Boyd's own utilitarian consequentialism actually undermines intrinsic dignity and views individual humans as of instrumental worth alone, bringing the greatest good to the greatest number.[62]

However, do human persons have *no* intrinsic value *until* they are part of a community in which various needs and circumstances are "balanced"? Do individual human rights develop solely in this context of equilibrium, balance, or unity? If humans are merely *instrumental* in achieving such a unity, then we deny a bedrock principle of the intrinsic dignity and rights of the human individual—a denial worthy of rejection.

If, on the other hand, the naturalist claims that intrinsic dignity somehow emerges when an organism is sufficiently neurologically complex, the same problem remains (i.e. accounting for the emergence of value or dignity). As Kant argued regarding the actual infinite, *dignity cannot be formed by successive addition*. Intrinsic value must be given at the outset; otherwise, it does not matter how many nonpersonal and nonvaluable components we happen to stack up. From valuelessness, valuelessness comes.

I would argue that a *personal* Creator, who made human *persons* in his image, serves as the ontological basis for the existence of objective moral values, moral obligation, human dignity and rights. Without the existence of a personal God, there would be no persons at all; and if no persons existed, then no moral properties would be instantiated in our world. The syllogism would look something like this:

> If persons (whether human or divine) exist, moral properties are instanced.
> A divine, supremely valuable personal Creator is necessary for the existence of personal—and thus intrinsically valuable—human beings.
> Therefore, if God did not exist (and thus no human persons would either), no moral properties would be instantiated either.[63]

Without *personhood*, there would be no moral properties instantiated. Thus God is necessary to ground the instantiation of moral properties. Moral categories (right/wrong, good/bad, praiseworthy/blameworthy) get to the essence of who we fundamentally are. They apply to us *as persons* (e.g. a good architect may be good *as an architect*, but not *as a human being/person*).[64] Moral values and personhood are intertwined.

The trustworthiness of our moral faculties

Thesis: One's worldview context is critical regarding the trustworthiness of our moral (and rational) faculties: given naturalistic evolution, why should we trust these faculties if they have been shaped by processes that direct us merely toward survival and reproduction? They just are, but fail to inform us about what ought to be.

The geneticist and Nobel Prize winner, Francis Crick, writes in his book, *The Astonishing Hypothesis*:

> The Astonishing Hypothesis is that "You," your joys and your sorrows, your memories and your ambitions, your sense of personal identity and free will, are in fact no more than the behavior of a vast assembly of nerve cells and

their associated molecules. . . . This hypothesis is so alien to the ideas of most people today that it can truly be called "astonishing."[65]

But if Crick is right, then his book is "no more than the behavior of a vast assembly of nerve cells and their associated molecules"! Falling prey to the self-excepting fallacy, Crick gives the impression that he, unlike the rest of us, has somehow been able to evade the physiological forces that determine what the rest of us think. He gives the impression that the behavior of *his* particular nerve cells and their associated molecules had absolutely *nothing* to do with his conclusions!

Here we look at a significant objection to objective moral values—namely, the socio-biological evolutionary development of human beings. If the evolutionary process has blindly shaped and hard-wired us toward survival and reproduction, then this can lead to serious doubts about the reliability of our rational and moral faculties. The evolutionary process is interested in fitness and survival, not in true belief.[66] Darwin was deeply troubled by this:

> With me the horrid doubt always arises whether the convictions of man's mind, which has been developed from the mind of the lower animals, are of any value or at all trustworthy. Would anyone trust in the convictions of a monkey's mind, if there are any convictions in such a mind?[67]

Can we trust our minds if we are nothing more than the products of naturalistic evolution trying to fight, feed, flee, and reproduce? Perhaps we have come to believe certain ideas—moral and non-moral—simply because they help us *survive* and not by virtue of their being *true*. Naturalistic moral realism suffers from the same defects found within the naturalistic philosophy of mind: although naturalism may offer some basis for *holding moral beliefs*, it furnishes no basis for claiming they are *true*. George Mavrodes writes of the naturalist position: "morality has a survival value for a species such as ours because it makes possible continued cooperation. . . . "[68] Thus, "the existence of moral feelings" is not absurd in a naturalistic world. Rather it is "the existence of moral *obligations* that is absurd." Mavrodes continues: "It is quite possible . . . for one to feel (or to believe) that he has a certain obligation without actually having it, and also vice versa."[69]

So we may *believe* that human beings are intrinsically valuable, and this helps the *homo sapiens* species survive, but it may be *false*. We may *believe* with full conviction that we have moral obligations—but be completely wrong. We may have the belief that our wills are free and that our choices do make a difference, but, again, we may be in serious error. If we accept a "scientific" account of epistemology, then we do not have access to the *truth-status* of these beliefs. They may help us to survive, but we may be completely wrong. Daniel Dennett calls our moral bent a *mistake*. But this widespread compliance with the mistaken—but common—"rule worship" (following the voice of conscience) has the happy consequence when we tend to comply—namely, societal cohesion and flourishing.[70] If the naturalist is right, then maybe we are being *systematically deceived* in order to survive and get along in society.

Which worldview furnishes us with more solid grounding for believing that our beliefs about moral obligations and human dignity are not reducible to our being hardwired to survive and reproduce? If naturalism is true, why think we have moral *obligations*? Rather, our moral beliefs just *are* and *could have been different* (e.g. *rape* could have contributed to survival). To help us beyond brute facts and naturalistic "just so" stories, a theistic world, in which a good, rational Being has made us in his image such that we can have confidence that our belief-producing mechanism is not unreliable, so a theistic worldview inspires confidence that we can *know* moral truths—even if they do not contribute one whit to our survival. Theism gives us no reason to be skeptical about our general capacity to think rationally, about the reliability of our sense perceptions, and about a general capacity to move towards the truth. Naturalism, on the other hand, does not inspire confidence in our belief-forming mechanisms. Naturalistic morality may still be true, but there seems to be no way that we can confidently know it.

Philosopher of religion Alvin Plantinga makes this case as follows:

> From a theistic point of view, human beings, like cathedrals and Boeing 747s, have been designed; we might say they are divine artifacts. . . . furthermore, God has created us human beings "in his own image"; in certain crucial and important respects, we resemble him. God is an actor, a creator, one who chooses certain ends and takes action to accomplish them. He is therefore a *practical* being. But God is also, crucially, an *intellectual* or *intellecting* being. He apprehends concepts, believes truths, has knowledge. In setting out to create human beings in his image, then, God set out to create *rational* creatures: creatures with reason or *ratio*; creatures that reflect his capacity to grasp concepts, entertain propositions, hold beliefs, envision ends, and act to accomplish them. Furthermore, he proposed to create creatures who reflect his ability to hold *true* beliefs. He therefore created us with that astonishingly subtle and articulate battery of cognitive faculties and powers. . . . From this perspective it is easy enough to say what it is for our faculties to be working properly: they are working properly when they are working in the way they were intended to work by the being who designed and created both them and us.[71]

Theism offers us a better hope for firmly grounding morality. It seems that naturalism has the potential to undermine our conviction that objective moral values exist. If our moral *beliefs* are by-products of Darwinistic evolution, why think that we actually *have* dignity, rights, and obligations?

The facts that (a) naturalistic evolutionists such as Crick, Wilson, Dennett, Dawkins, and their ilk, can make pronouncements they believe to be true (as distinct from simply helping them to survive) and (b) they believe they have drawn rational and objective conclusions from data they have observed actually indicate that they are living as practical theists. They demonstrate what theists have always maintained—that we live in a rational and knowable universe because God is its designer and we have been made in God's likeness.

The undermining of morality by its very own "scientific basis"

Thesis: What appears to be the greatest strength of current naturalistic moral realism—its "scientific" basis—ends up being undercut by the naturalistic worldview itself. Physicalism seems to undergird naturalism, but physical properties are radically different from moral ones. And to be consistent, it may be simpler for the naturalist to reject the existence of moral values rather than unnecessarily bloat his ontology.

Thomas Nagel rightly speaks of "the scientism and reductionism of our time. One of the tendencies it supports is the ludicrous overuse of evolutionary biology to explain everything about life, including everything about the human mind."[72] Science, despite its accomplishments, is highly overrated. Science may *enhance* aesthetic and moral perceptions (e.g. beauty in music has been linked to certain mathematical and logical qualities),[73] but it does not speak to the *whole* of it.

For instance, the materialist Colin McGinn wonders how consciousness, which is so *unlike* matter, could have emerged from matter:

> The property of consciousness itself (or specific conscious states) is not an observable or perceptible property of the brain. You can stare into a living conscious brain, your own or someone else's, and see there a wide variety of instantiated properties—its shape, colour, texture, etc.—but you will not thereby see what the subject is experiencing, the conscious state itself.[74]

In appealing to the alleged supervenience of the mental/conscious upon non-conscious matter to justify supervenience of the moral upon the non-moral, the NMR rightly doubts that his (quasi-) physicalism (rooted in the Big Bang and the universe's evolution) is sufficient to account for the emergence of subjective awareness, which has no physical properties (color, shape, size, spatial location, and the like). There is a metaphysical canyon that one finds difficult to bridge.

Similarly, one must deny that instantiated moral properties—unlike gray matter—are, say, orange, approximately 2 inches across, of an oblong shape, rough to the touch, and somewhat elastic. But how do we move from a universe, which inexplicably originates and produces matter and energy, to objective moral values or human dignity (which have no color, shape, size, spatial location, and the like)? Again, the gap is significant for the naturalist, but there is none for the theist. For the naturalist, it seems difficult to insist that from one set of (subvening) properties emerges another set of (supervening) properties even though each set does not come close to approximating the other.

An irony supervenes upon our discussion! Physicalists chide substance dualists for not having any way of showing that soul and body could interact. Jaegwon Kim, for instance, doubts that "an immaterial substance, with no material characteristics and totally outside physical space, could causally influence, and be influenced by, the motions of material bodies that are strictly governed by physical law."[75] Allegedly, the problem of "mental causation" (i.e. the mental's effects on the physical body) doomed Cartesian dualism.[76] But what do we make of the *physical* causes and processes producing the instancing of *mental* or *moral* properties? There seems to be something of naturalistic bias at work here: *why is there a problem with a mental-to-physical causation (for the theist—or substance dualist) but not—or at least not much of—a problem with physical-to-mental causation (for the naturalistic property dualist)?* It seems that the criticism must cut both ways, and if the naturalist can have her way, why cannot the theist (or, more specifically, the substance dualist) have his? And if God—a powerful, non-corporeal Being—exists and created the universe, then we have a precedent for a non-material agent interacting with the physical world.[77]

Another problem with the scientific account is this: *in the name of simplicity and scientism, it may have to do away with instantiated moral properties altogether.* The naturalistic philosopher or scientist typically claims that if natural processes can account for the origin of the universe, the fine-tuning of the universe, the emergence of first life, the emergence of consciousness, the emergence of rationality, and the emergence of moral, intrinsically valuable beings (an exceedingly tall order!), then, in the name of simplicity, we do not need to invoke God as an explanation.

But what if the shoe is on the other foot? What if we can use non-moral, natural terms to explain certain events that NMRs typically take as morally weighted? *Why not eliminate objective morality in the name of simplicity?* NMRs claim that moral facts help explain certain actions performed by individuals (e.g. "Hitler killed millions of Jews because he was morally depraved"). But it is questionable whether NMRs have adequately made their case for the explanatory *necessity* of moral facts. A non-realist could proffer this explanation:

> Hitler was a very bitter and angry person. Because of various false beliefs about Jews (most importantly his belief that Jews were responsible for Germany's defeat in World War I), he found hatred for the Jews to be a satisfying way of releasing his pent-up hostility and anger. His moral beliefs did not place any bounds or restraints on his expression of that hatred.[78]

While NMRs may argue that moral facts are *relevant* to explain Hitler's behavior, they generally fail to show that moral facts are *necessary* to explain Hitler's behavior. That is, "moral properties seem to be dispensable for explanatory purposes. Natural properties seem to be doing all of the work in the explanations in question."[79]

Further, *nothing is explained* by assuming that moral facts are constituted by natural facts: "The best explanations of human behavior available to us at the present time do not make use of claims to the effect that moral facts are constituted by natural facts . . . and it is a mystery how those properties cause or explain observable phenomena."[80] Simply to *posit* that moral properties have been instantiated is a far cry from *explaining* how this is so. One can respond to the NMR (who typically chides the theist for "unnecessarily" adding an extra entity—God—to his ontology in order to explain the instantiation of moral properties) by turning the tables: you have made your bed of parsimony; now sleep in it!

In the end, the scientific account of moral realism is primarily an *epistemological methodology*—not an *ontological basis* for morality. Many moral realists justify their claims simply by appealing to scientific—i.e. *epistemological*—categories (e.g. recognizing moral values, refining moral judgments) without offering substantial reasons for any *actual* basis of humans' intrinsic value or moral obligation. And even at the epistemological level, the scientific methodology is inadequate. In the words of Thomas Carson: "[naturalistic] moral realists have not yet proffered theories developed in sufficient detail to be very useful in explaining or predicting the relevant (moral) phenomena";[81] to date, "no [naturalistic] moralist-realist theory has anything like the explanatory or predictive power of atomic theory."[82] Robert Audi would agree:

> There is much reason to think . . . that the issue of moral realism should not be cast wholly in terms of the comparison with scientific models. It simply

may not be assumed that only causal or nomic properties are real, or that moral knowledge is possible only if it is causally or nomically grounded in the natural world. Our moral beliefs often concern particular persons or acts; they are responsive to observations; and, together with our wants, they explain our behavior. But this does not require that moral properties are natural, and it allows that general moral knowledge is a priori.[83]

The Euthyphro argument: dilemma or red herring?

Our discussion of the moral argument would be incomplete without addressing the oft-raised Euthyphro question. In Plato's *Euthyphro* dialogue, Socrates asks: "Is what is holy holy because the gods approve it, or do they approve it because it is holy?"[84] This raises the dilemma: are God's commands *arbitrary* (i.e. is something good *because* God commands it—and he could have commanded an opposite imperative)? Or is there some *autonomous moral standard* (which God consults in order to command)?[85] In other words, is the ground of morality, as Bertrand Russell put it, rooted in "no reason except [divine] caprice"?[86] Or is the problem, as Robin Le Poidevin puts it, that "we can, apparently, only make sense of these doctrines [that God is good and wills us to do what is good] if we think of goodness as being defined independently of God"?[87]

I believe that the ultimate resolution to this dilemma is that *God's good character/ nature* sufficiently grounds objective morality; thus we need to look nowhere else for such a standard. We have been made in the divine image, without which we would neither (a) be moral beings nor (b) have the capacity to recognize objective moral values.[88] The ultimate solution to the Euthyphro dilemma focuses on the *nature* or *character* of God as the source of objective moral values. Thus, we (who have been made to resemble God in certain ways) have the capacity to recognize them, and thus his commands—far from being arbitrary—are in accordance with that nature.[89]

The atheist may push the Euthyphro dilemma further by questioning whether the very *character* of God is good because it is God's character or it is God's character because it is good. Several responses are in order.

First, *if a good God does not exist, why think that morally responsible, intrinsically valuable, rights-bearing beings would exist at all?* Without God, moral properties would never be instantiated. Personhood is the locus of objective moral values, and without God, no persons would exist. Contextually, theism favors such moral obligations and human dignity, not naturalism.

Second, *if the naturalist is correct, then she herself cannot escape a similar dilemma; her argument offers her no actual advantage*: We can ask the NMR: "Are these moral values good simply because they are good, or is there some independent standard of good to which they conform?" She faces the same alleged dilemma of *arbitrariness* or some *autonomous standard*. So it is difficult to see why the theist's stopping point—God—is arbitrary and the naturalist's is not. The sword cuts both ways. Le Poidevin's comment that we must think of goodness as defined independently of God is merely *posited*. But two entities are sufficient to establish relations—namely, God's character and objective moral values; the third (some standard independent of God) becomes superfluous.

Third, *the naturalist's query is pointless since we must eventually arrive at some self-sufficient and self-explanatory stopping point beyond which the discussion can go no further*. Imagine that

God does not exist and that we have a Platonic form of the Good from which all values derive. At this point, it would appear silly to ask, "Why is the Good good?" Rather, we have an ultimate ground for morality, and everything is good in approximation to this. Again, why is atheism any less arbitrary a stopping-point than theism?[90]

Fourth, *God, who is essentially perfect, does not have obligations to some external moral standard; God simply acts, and it is good as he naturally does what is good.*[91] The revised Euthyphro dilemma wrongly assumes God has moral *obligations.* If such an external standard existed, God would be obligated to it. But God's actions and will operate according to the divine nature. So God's goodness should not be viewed as his *fulfilling* moral obligations but as *expressing the way he is*: "No preliminary stage of checking the relevant principles is required."[92]

Fifth, *the idea that God could be evil or command evil is utterly contrary to the very definition of God; otherwise, such a being would not be God and would not be worthy of worship.* Worshiping God because of his great power or knowledge is inadequate. A being worthy of worship must also be essentially good. As Robert Adams states: "Belief in the existence of an evil or amoral God would be morally intolerable."[93]

Sixth, *the acceptance of objective values assumes a kind of ultimate goal or cosmic design plan for human beings, which would make no sense given naturalism, but makes much sense given theism (which presumes a design plan).* Objective moral values presuppose (1) a fixed human nature (all human beings have a moral nature and possess dignity/rights) and (2) that a certain kind of life is better than another and thus ought to be pursued by every human being (i.e. teleology). It is exceedingly difficult to make sense of a brute cosmic purpose for all human beings apart from a transcendental purposive Creator. The brute fact of the value of human beings and a corresponding overarching purpose for their eudaimonistic living (another brute fact) are for naturalism nothing more than, as John Rist suggests, an "ethical hangover from a more homogeneous Christian past."[94]

In light of these reasons, there seems to be no good reason to take the Euthyphro dilemma seriously.

Conclusion

Truly, the *supernatural* is necessary to ground morality.[95] While objective morality appears *logical* and obvious to some naturalists, the more fundamental question is *metaphysical*: *can there be persons possessing inherent rights and dignity apart from a good God, in whose image they have been made?* NMRs such as Frankena wrongly frame the theological basis for moral obligation,[96] and others have simply failed to grasp the proper grounding for morality.[97]

Which hypothesis proves most resourceful when it comes to providing grounds for such an affirmation—a naturalistic one or a theistic (or supernaturalistic) one? NMRs persistently *fail to proffer any substantive metaphysic or ontology of personhood from a naturalistic vantage point to account for the intrinsic value of persons adequately—a necessary starting point for moral realism.* To my mind, it is the theistic one that does the more adequate job. The naturalistic worldview presents an inherent clash of ideals or stories. On the one hand, there is no cosmic purpose (but an unguided evolutionary process), no intelligent design, no guarantee of justice and moral rectification in the afterlife. But on the other hand, the NMR makes pronouncements about how objective moral values have emerged despite the universe's purposelessness and impersonal nature, how we *ought* to treat one another, how we *ought* to live up to moral principles even while death—yea, non-existence—stares us in the face.[98] The metaphysical chasm between the NMR's cosmic context and objective moral values is huge.

Not so with theism! It furnishes us with a grand ontological match between "our deepest moral values" and "the fundamental structures of reality."[99] Even the naturalist Richard B. Brandt concludes that there has been no significant recent advance to show how "moral/value properties are identical to (or even coextensive with) natural properties;" such attempts appear to "break down at every point."[100] Carson argues that despite the prominent versions of naturalistic moral realism available, "none is worthy of our acceptance."[101]

Ontologically, then, objective moral values would not exist if God did not. But if they exist, then we have very good reason to think God exists.

Notes

1   "Letter from Birmingham Jail" (16 April 1963) (www.stanford.edu/group/King). King added "One has not only a legal but a moral responsibility to obey just laws, but conversely, one has a moral responsibility to disobey unjust laws."

2   Dallas Willard, "Language, Being, God, and the Three Stages of Theistic Evidence," in J. P. Moreland and Kai Nielsen (eds) *Does God Exist? The Great Debate* (Nashville: Thomas Nelson, 1990), 207 (reprinted by Prometheus Press: Buffalo, NY).

3   Peter Berger, *A Rumor of Angels,* 2nd edn, New York: Doubleday, 1990), 59.

4   Kai Nielsen, *Ethics Without God*, revised edn, (Buffalo, NY: Prometheus Books, 1990), 10–11.

5   Nicholas Rescher, *Moral Absolutes: An Essay on the Nature and Rationale of Morality,* Vol. 2 (New York: Peter Lang, 1989), 43.

6   One does not need to be a theist to acknowledge this admixture. Atheist Michael Martin admits humans (1) "seem so ungod-like" and are "morally flawed," *and* (2) have "mathematical, scientific, and technological knowledge which enables them to construct elegant mathematical systems, and to build huge skyscrapers, dams, and bridges" [A Response to Paul Copan's Critique of Atheistic Objective Morality," *Philosophia Christi* 2 (Series 2), (2000), 88]. Also, see my reply to Martin's essay in the same issue of *Philosophia Christi*, "Atheistic Goodness Revisited," 91–104.

7   Robert Audi, *Moral Knowledge and Ethical Character* (New York: Oxford University Press, 1997), 32–65. According to Audi, moral intuitions are (1) *non-inferential* or *directly apprehended*; (2) *firm* (they must be believed as propositions); (3) *comprehensible* (intuitions are formed in the light of an adequate understanding of their propositional objects; (4) *pre-theoretical* (not dependent on theories nor are they themselves theoretical hypotheses). Audi rejects that prima facie intuitions are indefeasible; he argues for a particularist approach to intuitions (i.e. moral knowledge does not emerge from reflection on abstract principles, but it is derived from reflection on particular cases). He argues that duty still exists even if overridden in certain instances (e.g. keeping a promise is overridden by circumstances preventing me from keeping it, but I still have a duty to explain to the person why I could not keep the promise). For another defense of intuitionism, see David McNaughton, "Intuitionism" in *The Blackwell Guide to Ethical Theory*, Hugh LaFollette (ed.) (Malden, MA: Blackwell Publishers, 2000), 268–87.

8   Alvin Plantinga, "Reason and Belief in God," in *Faith and Rationality,* Alvin Plantinga and Nicholas Wolterstorff (eds) (Notre Dame, IN: University of Notre Dame Press, 1983),

16–93; idem, "Self-Profile," in *Alvin Plantinga,* Profiles 5, James Tomberlin and Peter van Inwagen, (eds) (Dordrecht: D. Reidel, 1985), 55–64.

9   Such properly basic beliefs are not ultima facie (or all-things-considered) justified, only prima facie.

10 Historically, *tolerance* has not been understood as "accepting all views as true or worthy of belief"; if this were so, then the relativist would violate his standard by rejecting moral realism. In truth, we do not tolerate chocolate or the music of Johann Sebastian Bach. Tolerance has to do with putting up with what we find false, disagreeable, or erroneous.

11 On the deep problems of perspectivalism, see Thomas Nagel, *The Last Word* (New York: Oxford University Press, 1997), 3–76. See also Curtis L. Hancock, "Social Construct Theory: Relativism's Latest Fashion," in *The Failure of Modernism: The Cartesian Legacy and Contemporary Pluralism,* Brendan Sweetman (ed.) (Mishawaka, IN: American Maritain Association, 1999), 242–58.

12 See Brendan Sweetman, "The Pseudo-Problem of Skepticism," in *The Failure of Modernism: The Cartesian Legacy and Contemporary Pluralism,* Brendan Sweetman (ed.) (Mishawaka, IN: American Maritain Association, 1999), 228–41.

13 David Brink, *Moral Realism and the Foundations of Ethics* (New York: Cambridge University Press, 1980), 17. Richard Boyd adds as a component another feature (epistemic condition) to moral realism: "Ordinary canons of moral reasoning – together with ordinary canons of scientific and everyday factual reasoning – constitute, under many circumstances at least, a reliable method for obtaining and improving (approximate) moral knowledge" ["How To Be a Moral Realist," in *Moral Discourse and Practice: Some Philosophical Approaches,* Stephen Darwall, Allan Gibbard, and Peter Railton (eds) (New York: Oxford University Press, 1997)], 105.

14 Brink, *Moral Realism and the Foundations of Ethics,* 156.

15 Ibid., 156–7.

16 Michael Smith, "Moral Realism," in *The Blackwell Guide to Ethical Theory,* Hugh LaFollette (ed.) (Malden, MA: Blackwell Publishers, 2000), 23.

17 Ibid.

18 Michael Smith, "Moral Realism," 24.

19 Railton, "Moral Realism," *The Philosophical Review* 95 (April 1986), 171.

20 According to Brink, "If G actually composes or realizes F, but F can be, or could have been, realized differently, then G constitutes, but is not identical with, F", *Moral Realism,* 157. Brink calls such a constitution a "synthetic moral necessity" (166).

21 Railton urges: "moral properties supervene upon natural properties, and may be reducible to them", "Moral Realism," 165.

22 Ibid. Also, Railton urges: "moral properties supervene upon natural properties, and may be reducible to them" (171).

23 Brink, *Moral Realism,* 207.

24 William Frankena, "The Naturalistic Fallacy," in *Readings in Ethical Theory,* 2nd edn, Wilfrid Sellars and John Hospers (eds) (New York: Appleton-Century-Crofts, 1970), 54–62; see also William K. Frankena, "Obligation and Motivation in Recent Moral Philosophy," in *Perspectives on Morality: Essays by William K. Frankena,* K. E. Goodpaster (ed.) (Notre Dame, IN: Univerisity of Notre Dame Press, 1976), 49–73.

25 William K. Frankena, "Is Morality Logically Dependent Upon Religion?", in Paul Helm (ed.), *Divine Commands and Morality* (Oxford: Oxford University Press, 1981), 14–33.

26 Ibid., 16. According to the ordinary canons of logic, "a conclusion containing the term 'ought' or 'right' cannot be logically derived from premises which do not contain this term" (ibid., 18).

27 Ibid., 31.

28 Perhaps certain naturalistic moral realists are confident in their position because they

have grossly misunderstood the theistic basis for ethics. One such culprit is Peter Railton: "Some Questions About the Justification of Morality," *Philosophical Perspectives* 6 (1992), 27–53. He construes the connection between God and morality in terms of: "the policing and punishing functions of God." Thus we can dispense with such a "suprahuman grader" who would "mark us down" for our failings. With the "death of God," the "universal policeman" is gone (29). Railton then proceeds to offer a comparison between this basis for morality with "divine bases" (45). We have no need for such "middlemen" between the justificatory impulse and norms of behavior. I think that rumors of God's death have been greatly exaggerated, and Railton confuses matters by bifurcating divine power and divine goodness, as though God's moral character has nothing to do with the exertion of his power.

Another failure in Railton is his utilization of the genetic fallacy (45), resorting to the Freudian canard of psycho-analyzing religious believers (as though naturalists are immune to psychoanalysis for their atheism!).

Brink believes that the theist is stuck on the two horns of the Euthyphro dilemma, *Moral Realism,* 158. However, the theist can reject the horns of the dilemma in favor of rooting moral properties in the character or nature of God.

29 I refer to such an approach in Paul Copan, "Can Michael Martin Be a Moral Realist? *Sic et Non*," *Philosophia Christi* 1, 2 (Series 2) (1999), 45–72, and "Atheistic Goodness Revisited," *Philosophia Christi* 2, 1 (Series 2) (2000), 91–104.

30 See Vance G. Morgan, "The Metaphysics of Naturalism," *American Catholic Philosophical Quarterly* 75:3 (Summer 2001), 409–31.

31 *Nature, Design, and Science* (Albany, NY: State University of New York Press, 2001), 68.

32 Randy Thornhill and Craig T. Palmer, *A Natural History of Rape: Biological Bases of Sexual Coercion* (Cambridge, MA: MIT Press, 2000).

33 See Chapter 10 by J. P. Moreland [in *The Rationality of Theism*, Paul Copan and Paul K. Moser (eds) (London and New York: Routledge, 2003).]

34 Colin McGinn, *The Problem of Consciousness* (Oxford: Basil Blackwell, 1990), 10–11.

35 Brink, "Moral Realism and the Skeptical Arguments from Disagreement and Queerness," 120. Brink offers a more detailed argument in his *Moral Realism and the Foundation for Ethics,* 156–67.

36 Colin McGinn, *The Mysterious Flame: Consciousness Minds in a Material World* (New York: Basic Books, 1999).

37 Alvin Plantinga, "Natural Theology," in *Companion to Metaphysics,* Jaegwon Kim and Ernest Sosa (eds) (Cambridge: Blackwell, 1995), 347.

38 Louis P. Pojman, "A Critique of Contemporary Egalitarianism: A Christian Perspective," *Faith and Philosophy* 8 (October 1991), 501.

39 Jonathan Glover, *Humanity: A Moral History of the Twentieth Century* (London: Jonathan Cape, 1999), 41. He speaks of the need to "start to establish a tradition" that will help us find previous atrocities "intolerable" (42).

40 Ibid., 42.

41 Bertrand Russell, "A Free Man's Worship," in *Why I Am Not a Christian* (New York: Simon and Schuster, 1957), 107.

42 Bertrand Russell, *Human Society in Ethics and Politics* (London: Allen & Unwin, 1954), 124.

43 J. L. Mackie, *The Miracle of Theism* (Oxford: Clarendon Press, 1982), 115–16.

44 Jean-Paul Sartre, *Existentialism and Human Emotions* (New York: Philosophical Library, 1957), 15.

45 Ibid.

46 Stephen Weinberg, *The First Three Minutes: A Modern View of the Origin of the Universe* (New York: HarperCollins), 154–55.

47 Edward O. Wilson, *Consilience* (New York: Random House, 1998), 269.

48   Ibid., 268.
49   James Rachels, *Created From Animals: The Moral Implications of Darwinism* (Oxford: Oxford University Press, 1990), 77.
50   Michael Ruse, *The Darwinian Paradigm* (London: Routledge, 1989), 262.
51   Richard Dawkins, *River Out of Eden: A Darwinian View of Life* (New York: Basic Books/ Harper Collins, 1995), 132–3.
52   Cited in Greg Ganssle, "Necessary Moral Truths and the Need for Explanation," *Philosophia Christi* 2, 1 (Series 2) (2000), 111.
53   "Must There Be a Standard of Moral Goodness Apart from God?", *Philosophia Christi* 3, 1 (Series 2) (2001), 129.
54   Various suggestions are still under discussion in this area. Alvin Plantinga raises this issue in *Does God Have a Nature?* (Milwaukee: Marquette University Press, 1980). Plantinga suggests elsewhere: "God is a necessary being who has essentially the property of thinking just the thoughts he does think; these thoughts, then, are conceived or thought by God in every possible world and thus exist necessarily" [Plantinga, "How To Be an Anti-Realist," *Proceedings and Addresses of the American Philosophical Association* 56 (1982), 70]. Thomas Morris and Christopher Menzel have expanded upon Plantinga's thoughts: "Absolute Creation," in *Anselmian Explorations,* Thomas V. Morris (ed.) (Notre Dame, IN: University of Notre Dame Press, 1987), 161–78. See also Charles Taliaferro, *Contemporary Philosophy of Religion* (Oxford: Blackwell, 1998), 65–72.
55   Boyd, "How To Be a Moral Realist," 116.
56   Ibid., 199.
57   Ibid., 133n.
58   Brink, *Moral Realism,* 159; this is similar to "tableness" suvervening on properly arranged microphysical particles.
59   Boyd, "How To Be a Moral Realist," 122.
60   Ibid.
61   Ibid., 133n.
62   See Tom Regan's criticism of utilitarianism, in which individuals are like cups or receptacles, which have no value in themselves, nor are they equally valuable: "What has value is what goes into us, what we serve as receptacles for; our feelings of satisfaction have positive value, our feelings of frustration have negative value" ["The Case for Animal Rights," in *People, Penguins and Plastic Trees,* 2nd edn, Christine Pierce and Donald Van DeVeer (eds) (Belmont, CA: Wadsworth Publishing Company, 1995), 75].
63   Some theists claim that moral properties exist independently of God – for example, C. Stephen Layman, *The Shape of the Good: Christian Reflections and the Foundation of Ethics* (Notre Dame, IN: University of Notre Dame Press), 44–52; Richard Swinburne, *The Coherence of Theism* (Oxford: Oxford University Press, 1977), 204. For reasons spelled out here and elsewhere, this position has its problems. Paul Copan, "Can Michael Martin Be a Moral Realist? *Sic et Non,*" *Philosophia Christi* 1, 2 (Series 2) (1999), 45–72, and "Atheistic Goodness Revisited," *Philosophia Christi* 2, 1 (Series 2) (2000), 105–12.
64   David S. Oderberg, *Moral Theory: A Non-Consequentialist Approach* (Malden, MA: Blackwell, 2000), 1.
65   Francis Crick, *The Astonishing Hypothesis: The Scientific Search for the Soul* (New York: Charles Scribner's Sons, 1994), 3.
66   Alvin Plantinga, *Warrant and Proper Function* (New York: Oxford University Press, 1993), 219.
67   Letter to William Graham Down, 3 July 1881, in *The Life and Letters of Charles Darwin,* Francis Darwin (ed.) (London: John Murray, 1887), 315–16 (includes an autobiographical chapter).
68   George I. Mavrodes, "Religion and the Queerness of Morality," in *Rationality, Religious*

Belief, and Moral Commitment, Robert Audi and William Wainwright (eds) (Ithaca, NY: Cornell University Press, 1986), 219.

69 Ibid.

70 Daniel Dennett, *Darwin's Dangerous Idea* (New York: Simon and Schuster, 1995), 507.

71 Plantinga, *Warrant and Proper Function,* 197.

72 Thomas Nagel, *The Last Word* (New York: Oxford University Press, 1997), 131.

73 See Douglas R. Hofstadter, *Gödel, Escher, Bach: An Eternal Golden Braid* (New York: Vintage, 1980).

74 Ibid., 1.

75 Jaegwon Kim, *Philosophy of Mind* (Boulder, CO: Westview Press, 1996), 4.

76 I am not claiming here to hold to a Cartesian dualism. For an alternative, more organic substance dualism, see J. P. Moreland and Scott Rae, *Body and Soul* (Downers Grove, IL: InterVarsity Press, 2000).

77 For a defense of such a mind-body interaction, see Charles Taliaferro, *Consciousness and the Mind of God* (Cambridge: Cambridge University Press, 1994).

78 This point is taken from Thomas Carson, *Value and the Good Life* (Notre Dame, IN: University of Notre Dame Press, 2000), 194. He is utilizing an argument made by Gilbert Harman.

79 Ibid., 198.

80 Ibid., 198–9.

81 Ibid., 199.

82 Ibid.

83 Robert Audi, "Ethical Naturalism and the Explanatory Power of Moral Concepts," in *Naturalism: A Critical Appraisal,* Steve J. Wagner and Richard Warner (eds) (Notre Dame, IN: University of Notre Dame Press, 1993), 111.

84 Plato, *Euthyphro* 10a, in *Plato, The Collected Dialogues of Plato,* Edith Hamilton and Huntington Cairns (eds) Lane Cooper (trans.) (Princeton: Princeton University Press, 1961), 178.

85 These terms are taken from Mark D. Linville, "On Goodness: Human and Divine," *American Philosophical Quarterly* 27 (April 1990), 143–52.

86 Bertrand Russell, *Human Society in Ethics and Politics* (New York: Simon & Schuster, 1962), 38.

87 Robin Le Poidevin, *Arguing for Atheism* (London: Routledge, 1996), 85.

88 Thus, while there is a strong version of the divine command theory (in which God could just as easily have commanded, "Thou *shalt* murder"), the more moderate versions root divine commands in God's character: "Theists of all stripes will insist that God is perfectly just" [Philip Quinn, *Divine Commands and Moral Requirements* (Oxford: Clarendon Press, 1978), 136]. Robert Merrihew Adams asserts: "It matters what God's attributes are. God is supremely knowledgeable and wise – he is omniscient, after all; and that is very important motivationally. It makes a difference if you think of commands as coming from someone who completely understands both us and our situation. It matters not only that God is loving but also that he is just." ["Divine Commands and Obligation" *Faith and Philosophy* 4 (July 1988), 272].

89 See Thomas V. Morris essays, "Duty and Divine Goodness" and "The Necessity of God's Goodness" in *Anselmian Explorations* (Notre Dame, IN: University of Notre Dame Press, 1987), 26–41 and 42–69; William P. Alston, "Some Suggestions for Divine Command Theorists," in *Christian Theism and the Problems of Philosophy,* Michael D. Beaty (ed.) (Notre Dame, IN: University of Notre Dame Press, 1990); Mark D. Linville, "Euthyphro and His Kin," in *The Logic of Rational Theism,* Vol. 24, William Lane Craig and Mark McLeod (eds) (Lewiston, NY: Edwin Mellen, 1990), 187–210.

90 William Alston asks this question in "Some Suggestions for Divine Command Theorists,"

in Michael D. Beaty (ed.) *Christian Theism and the Problems of Philosophy* (Notre Dame, IN: University of Notre Dame Press, 1990), 303–26.

91   The question is raised: why praise God for doing the good *naturally?* But as Thomas Morris rightly claims, "praise is never strictly appropriate for duty satisfactions." Rather, we rightly praise God – as we do any person – for moral acts of *supererogation* (i.e. going beyond the requirements of duty). *Why* then should God be praised? According to the Judeo-Christian tradition, God's *condescension* and *grace* – undeserved kindness – offer justifiable reasons to praise him. God was not obligated to create at all. Nor was God, having freely willed to create, obliged to make the best possible world – only a good one, but not a less-than-good one. God is also not obligated to communicate with and enter into covenant relations with his creatures. He is not morally compelled to forgive human transgression nor to give second chances to those who have defied his authority. Such actions are not the fulfillment of duty but acts of supererogation. See Thomas V. Morris, "Duty and Divine Goodness," in *Anselmian Explorations* (Notre Dame, IN: University Press, 1987), 35, 38.

92   Alston, "Some Suggestions for Divine Command Theorists," 320.

93   "Moral Arguments for Theistic Belief," in *Rationality and Religious Belief,* C. F. Delaney (ed.) (Notre Dame, IN: University of Notre Dame Press, 1979), 135.

94   John M. Rist, *Real Ethics* (Cambridge, Cambridge University Press, 2002), 2.

95   G. E. Moore did not go far enough by saying that morality is *non*-natural. H. P. Owen suggests: "although 'ought' can never be derived, or at least never wholly, from 'is' where 'is' lacks moral evaluation, any over-all moral theory of life is bound to involve a correspondingly over-all view of man and his destiny." H. P. Owen, "Morality and Christian Theism," *Religious Studies* 20 (1984), 16.

96   Surprisingly, Frankena's claim that theists, in attempting to establish a religious basis for morality, move illegitimately from "God is love" to "We ought to love others" is wrongly construed. A more adequate formulation would be:

> Human *persons* have been made in the image of a good, necessarily valuable, *personal* Being (God).
> Human *persons* are thus inherently constituted with intrinsic value, rights, and moral obligations.
> Therefore, we *ought* to treat human beings (persons) as worthy of respect, as ends in themselves (rather than means to ends), as morally responsible agents, etc.

97   For example, God as a divine policeman, whom we merely obey out of fear of punishment rather than out of love; or God as commanding arbitrarily, who could command just the opposite.

98   Thanks to Ronald Tacelli on this point.

99   Peter Byrne, *The Moral Interpretation of Religion* (Edinburgh: University of Edinburgh Press, 1998), 168.

100   Richard B. Brandt, *Facts, Values, and Morality* (Cambridge: Cambridge University Press, 1996), 183.

101   *Value and the Good Life*, 187.

Questions for reflection

1   Do you agree with Professor Copan that moral values are properly basic? Explain your answer.
2   Why is it that objective moral values appear, prima facie, to be an unnatural fit in a non-theistic universe?
3   Consider the frightening words of murderer Ted Bundy to his victim:

Then I learned that all moral judgments are "value judgments," that all value judgments are subjective, and that none can be proved to be either "right" or "wrong" . . . I discovered that to become truly free, truly unfettered, I had to become truly uninhibited. And I quickly discovered that the greatest obstacle to my freedom, the greatest block and limitation to it, consists in the insupportable "value judgment" that I was bound to respect the rights of others. I asked myself, who were these "others"? Other human beings, with human rights? Why is it more wrong to kill a human animal than any other animal, a pig or a sheep or a steer? Is your life more to you than a hog's life to a hog? Why should I be willing to sacrifice my pleasure more for the one than for the other? Surely, you would not, in this age of scientific enlightenment, declare that God or nature has marked some pleasures as "moral" or "good" and others as "immoral" or "bad"? In any case, let me assure you, my dear young lady, that there is absolutely no comparison between the pleasure I might take in eating ham and the pleasure I anticipate in raping and murdering you. That is the honest conclusion to which my education has led me—after the most conscientious examination of my spontaneous and uninhibited self.*

How might one respond to these chilling remarks if she denies the existence of objective moral values?

4   Explain the Euthyphro argument and Copan's response. Does the latter solve the dilemma? Why or why not?

*   A statement by Ted Bundy, paraphrased and rewritten by Harry V. Jaffa, *Homosexuality and the National Law* (Claremont Institute of the Study of Statesmanship and Political Philosophy, 1990), 3–4.

Further reading

Robert Merrihew Adams (1999) *Finite and Infinite Goods: A Framework for Ethics.* New York: Oxford University Press. (Provides a philosophical account of the theistic basis for ethics.)

Gordon Graham (2001) *Evil and Christian Ethics.* Cambridge: Cambridge University Press. (Discusses moral philosophy and evil in the context of recent New Testament scholarship, suggesting the biblical framework offers the most plausible context for grappling with evil.)

David Hume ([1739/40] 1978) *A Treatise of Human Nature.* Ed. L. A. Selby-Bigge, revised by P. H. Nidditch. 2nd edn. Oxford: Clarendon Press. (Contains a skeptical argument about ethics; note especially pages 455–76.)

J. L. Mackie (1977) *Ethics: Inventing Right and Wrong.* Harmondsworth: Penguin. (Argues for error theory—that people generally, and falsely, tend to understand moral values as being objectively true.)

John Rist (2001) *Real Ethics: Rethinking the Foundations of Morality.* Cambridge: Cambridge University Press. (Surveys the history of ethics and offers a defense of a realist ethical theory.)

Chapter 30

Ludwig Feuerbach

RELIGION AS PROJECTION

Ludwig Feuerbach (1804–72) was a German atheist philosopher who is best known for his criticisms of Idealism and religion, most notably Christianity. In the following selection, taken from *The Essence of Christianity*, he argues that the basis of religion is consciousness, but consciousness of a special sort. Human consciousness involves the awareness of one's own nature, and the nature of others, as objects of thought. Religion involves the self-consciousness which a person has of his or her own nature. Unlike other animals, however, this nature is not finite and limited, but infinite and unlimited. For human beings, there is an alienation between what we are (consisting of the bad qualities of imperfection and sinfulness) and what we ought to be (consisting of the good qualities of absolute perfection and sinlessness). We project the "ought" onto another—an idealized self—whom we refer to as "God." It is only as we realize this truth, and begin attributing the good qualities to ourselves rather than to a projected other, that we can experience freedom and escape self-alienation.

The essential nature of man

Religion has its basis in the essential difference between man and the brute—the brutes have no religion. It is true that the old uncritical writers on natural history attributed to the elephant, among other laudable qualities, the virtue of religiousness; but the religion of elephants belongs to the realm of fable. Cuvier, one of the greatest authorities on the animal kingdom, assigns, on the strength of his personal observations, no higher grade of intelligence to the elephant than to the dog.

But what is this essential difference between man and the brute? The most simple, general, and also the most popular answer to this question is—consciousness:—but consciousness in the strict sense; for the consciousness implied in the feeling of self as an individual, in discrimination by the senses, in the perception and even judgment of outward things according to definite sensible signs, cannot be denied to the brutes. Consciousness in the strictest sense is present only in a being to whom his species, his essential nature, is an object of thought. The brute is indeed conscious of himself as an individual—and he has accordingly the feeling of self as the common centre of successive sensations—but not as a species: hence, he is without that consciousness which in its nature, as in its name, is akin to science. Where there is this higher consciousness there is a capability of science. Science is the cognizance of species. In practical life we have to do with individuals; in science, with species. But only a being to whom his own species, his own nature, is an object of thought, can make the essential nature of other things or beings an object of thought.

Hence the brute has only a simple, man a twofold life: in the brute, the inner life is one with the outer; man has both an inner and an outer life. The inner life of man is the life which has relation to his species, to his general, as distinguished from his individual, nature. Man thinks—that is, he converses with himself. The brute can exercise no function which has relation to its species without another individual external to itself; but man can perform the functions of thought and speech, which strictly imply such a relation, apart from another individual. Man is himself at once I and thou; he can put himself in the place of another, for this reason, that to him his species, his essential nature, and not merely his individuality, is an object of thought.

Religion being identical with the distinctive characteristic of man, is then identical with self-consciousness—with the consciousness which man has of his nature. But religion, expressed generally, is consciousness of the infinite; thus it is and can be nothing else than the consciousness which man has of his own—not finite and limited, but infinite nature. A really finite being has not even the faintest adumbration, still less consciousness, of an infinite being, for the limit of the nature is also the limit of the consciousness. The consciousness of the caterpillar, whose life is confined to a particular species of plant, does not extend itself beyond this narrow domain. It does, indeed, discriminate between this plant and other plants, but more it knows not. A consciousness so limited, but on account of that very limitation so infallible, we do not call consciousness, but instinct. Consciousness, in the strict or proper sense, is identical with consciousness of the infinite; a limited consciousness is no consciousness; consciousness is essentially infinite in its nature.[1] The consciousness of the infinite is nothing else than the consciousness of the infinity of the consciousness; or, in the consciousness of the infinite, the conscious subject has for his object the infinity of his own nature.

What, then, *is* the nature of man, of which he is conscious, or what constitutes the specific distinction, the proper humanity of man?[2] Reason, Will, Affection. To a complete man belong the power of thought, the power of will, the power of affection. The power of thought is the light of the intellect, the power of will is energy of character, the power of affection is love. Reason, love, force of will, are perfections—the perfections of the human being—nay, more, they are absolute perfections of being. To will, to love, to think, are the highest powers, are the absolute nature of man as man, and the basis of his existence. Man exists to think, to love, to will. Now that which is the end, the ultimate aim, is also the true basis and principle of a being. But what is the end of reason? Reason. Of love? Love. Of will? Freedom of the will. We think for the sake of thinking; love for the sake of loving; will for the sake of willing—*i.e.*, that we may be free. True existence is thinking, loving, willing existence. That alone is true, perfect, divine, which exists for its own sake. But such is love, such is reason, such is will.

The divine trinity in man, above the individual man, is the unity of reason, love, will. Reason, Will, Love, are not powers which man possesses, for he is nothing without them, he is what he is only by them; they are the constituent elements of his nature, which he neither has nor makes, the animating, determining, governing powers—divine, absolute powers—to which he can oppose no resistance.[3]

How can the feeling man resist feeling, the loving one love, the rational one reason? Who has not experienced the overwhelming power of melody? And what else is the power of melody but the power of feeling? Music is the language of feeling; melody is audible feeling—feeling communicating itself. Who has not experienced the power of love, or at least heard of it? Which is the stronger—love or the individual man? Is it man that possesses love, or is it not much rather love that possesses man? When love impels a man to suffer death even joyfully for the beloved one, is this death-conquering power his own individual power, or is it not rather the power of love? And who that ever truly thought has not experienced that quiet, subtle power—the power of thought? When thou sinkest into deep reflection, forgetting thyself and what is around thee, dost thou govern reason, or is it not reason which governs and absorbs thee? Scientific enthusiasm—is it not the most glorious triumph of intellect over thee? The desire of knowledge—is it not a simply irresistible, and all-conquering power? And when thou suppressest a passion, renouncest a habit, in short, achievest a victory over thyself, is this victorious power thy own personal power, or is it not rather the energy of will, the force of morality, which seizes the mastery of thee, and fills thee with indignation against thyself and thy individual weaknesses?

. . .

The essence of religion considered generally

Wherever, therefore, the denial of the sensual delights is made a special offering, a sacrifice well-pleasing to God, there the highest value is attached to the senses, and the sensuality which has been renounced is unconsciously restored, in the fact that God takes the place of the material delights which have been renounced. The nun weds herself to God; she has a heavenly bridegroom, the monk a heavenly bride. But the heavenly virgin is only a sensible presentation of a general truth, having relation to the essence of religion. Man denies as to himself only what he attributes to God. Religion abstracts from man, from the world; but it can only abstract from the limitations, from the phenomena; in short, from the negative, not from the essence, the positive, of the world and humanity: hence, in the very abstraction and negation it must recover that from which it abstracts, or believes itself to abstract. And thus, in reality, whatever religion consciously denies—always supposing that what is denied by it is something essential, true, and consequently incapable of being ultimately denied—it unconsciously restores in God. Thus, in religion man denies his reason; of himself he knows nothing of God, his thoughts are only worldly, earthly; he can only believe what God reveals to him. But on this account the thoughts of God are human, earthly thoughts: like man, he has plans in his mind, he accommodates himself to circumstances and grades of intelligence, like a tutor with his pupils; he calculates closely the effect of his gifts and revelations; he observes man in all his doings; he knows all things, even the most earthly, the commonest, the most trivial. In brief, man in relation to God denies his own knowledge, his own thoughts, that he may place them in God. Man gives up his personality; but in return, God, the Almighty, infinite, unlimited being, is a person; he denies human dignity, the human *ego*; but in return God is to him a selfish, egoistical being, who in all things seeks only himself, his own honour, his own ends; he represents God as simply seeking the satisfaction of his own selfishness, while yet he frowns on that of every other being; his God is the very luxury of egoism.[4] Religion further denies goodness as a quality of human nature; man is wicked, corrupt, incapable of good; but on the other hand, God is only good—the Good Being. Man's nature demands as an object goodness, personified as God; but is it not hereby declared that goodness is an essential tendency of man? If my heart is wicked, my understanding perverted, how can I perceive and feel the holy to be holy, the good to be good? Could I perceive the beauty of a fine picture if my mind were æsthetically an absolute piece of perversion? Though I may not be a painter, though I may not have the power of producing what is beautiful myself, I must yet have æsthetic feeling, æsthetic comprehension, since I perceive the beauty that is presented to me externally. Either goodness does not exist at all for man, or, if it does exist, therein is revealed to the individual man the holiness and goodness of human nature. That which is absolutely opposed to my nature, to which I am united by no bond of sympathy, is not even conceivable or perceptible by me. The holy is in opposition to me only as regards the modifications of my personality, but as regards my fundamental nature it is in unity with me. The holy is a reproach to my sinfulness; in it I recognise myself as a sinner; but in so doing, while I blame myself, I acknowledge what I am not, but ought to be, and what, for that very reason, I, according to my destination, can be; for an "ought" which has no corresponding capability does not affect me, is a ludicrous chimæra without any true relation to my mental constitution. But when I acknowledge goodness as my destination, as my law, I acknowledge it, whether consciously or unconsciously, as my own nature. Another nature than my own, one different in quality, cannot touch me. I can perceive sin as sin, only when I perceive it to be a contradiction of myself with myself—that is, of my personality with my fundamental nature. As a contradiction of the absolute, considered as another being, the feeling of sin is inexplicable, unmeaning. . . .

As with the doctrine of the radical corruption of human nature, so is it with the identical doctrine, that man can do nothing good, *i.e.*, in truth, nothing of himself—by his own strength. For the denial of human strength and spontaneous moral activity to be true, the moral activity of God must also be denied; and we must say, with the Oriental nihilist or pantheist: the Divine being is absolutely without will or action, indifferent, knowing nothing of the discrimination between evil and good. But he who defines God as an active being, and not only so, but as morally active and morally critical,—as a being who loves, works, and rewards good, punishes, rejects, and condemns evil,—he who thus defines God only in appearance denies human activity, in fact, making it the highest, the most real activity. He who makes God act humanly, declares human activity to be divine; he says: A god who is not active, and not morally or humanly active, is no god; and thus he makes the idea of the Godhead dependent on the idea of activity, that is, of human activity, for a higher he knows not.

Man—this is the mystery of religion—projects his being into objectivity,[5] and then again makes himself an object to this projected image of himself thus converted into a subject; he thinks of himself not as an object to himself, but as the object of an object, of another being than himself. Thus here. Man is an object to God. That man is good or evil is not indifferent to God; no! He has a lively, profound interest in man's being good; he wills that man should be good, happy—for without goodness there is no happiness. Thus the religious man virtually retracts the nothingness of human activity, by making his dispositions and actions an object to God, by making man the end of God—for that which is an object to the mind is an end in action; by making the divine activity a means of human salvation. God acts, that man may be good and happy. Thus man, while he is apparently humiliated to the lowest degree, is in truth exalted to the highest. Thus, in and through God, man has in view himself alone. It is true that man places the aim of his action in God, but God has no other aim of action than the moral and eternal salvation of man: thus man has in fact no other aim than himself. The divine activity is not distinct from the human.

How could the divine activity work on me as its object, nay, work in me, if it were essentially different from me; how could it have a human aim, the aim of ameliorating and blessing man, if it were not itself human? Does not the purpose determine the nature of the act? When man makes his moral improvement an aim to himself, he has divine resolutions, divine projects; but also, when God seeks the salvation of man, he has human ends and a human mode of activity corresponding to these ends. Thus in God man has only his own activity as an object. But for the very reason that he regards his own activity as objective, goodness only as an object, he necessarily receives the impulse, the motive not from himself, but from this object. He contemplates his nature as external to himself, and this nature as goodness; thus it is self-evident, it is mere tautology to say that the impulse to good comes only from thence where he places the good.

God is the highest subjectivity of man abstracted from himself; hence man can do nothing of himself, all goodness comes from God. The more subjective God is, the more completely does man divest himself of his subjectivity, because God is, *per se*, his relinquished self, the possession of which he however again vindicates to himself. As the action of the arteries drives the blood into the extremities, and the action of the veins brings it back again, as life in general consists in a perpetual systole and diastole; so is it in religion. In the religious systole man propels his own nature from himself, he throws himself outward; in the religious diastole he receives the rejected nature into his heart again. God alone is the being who acts of himself, —this is the force of repulsion in religion; God is the being who acts in me, with me, through me, upon me, for me, is the principle of my salvation, of my good dispositions and actions, consequently my own good principle and nature, —this is the force of attraction in religion.

The course of religious development which has been generally indicated consists specifically in this, that man abstracts more and more from God, and attributes more and more to himself. This is especially apparent in the belief in revelation. That which to a later age or a cultured people is given by nature or reason, is to an earlier age, or to a yet uncultured people, given by God. Every tendency of man, however natural—even the impulse to cleanliness, was conceived by the Israelites as a positive divine ordinance. From this example we again see that God is lowered, is conceived more entirely on the type of ordinary humanity, in proportion as man detracts from himself. How can the self-humiliation of man go further than when he disclaims the capability of fulfilling spontaneously the requirements of common decency?[6] The Christian religion, on the other hand, distinguished the impulses and passions of man according to their quality, their character; it represented only good emotions, good dispositions, good thoughts, as revelations, operations—that is, as dispositions, feelings, thoughts, —of God; for what God reveals is a quality of God himself: that of which the heart is full overflows the lips; as is the effect such is the cause; as the revelation, such the being who reveals himself. A God who reveals himself in good dispositions is a God whose essential attribute is only moral perfection. The Christian religion distinguishes inward moral purity from external physical purity; the Israelites identified the two.[7] In relation to the Israelitish religion, the Christian religion is one of criticism and freedom. The Israelite trusted himself to do nothing except what was commanded by God; he was without will even in external things; the authority of religion extended itself even to his food. The Christian religion, on the other hand, in all these external things made man dependent on himself, *i.e.*, placed in man what the Israelite placed out of himself in God. Israel is the most complete presentation of Positivism in religion. In relation to the Israelite, the Christian is an *esprit fort*, a free-thinker. Thus do things change. What yesterday was still religion is no longer such today; and what today is atheism, tomorrow will be religion. . . .

   That is dependent the possibility of whose existence lies out of itself; that is independent which has the possibility of its existence in itself. Life therefore involves the contradiction of an existence at once dependent and independent,—the contradiction that its possibility lies both in itself and out of itself. The understanding alone is free from this and other contradictions of life; it is the essence perfectly self-subsistent, perfectly at one with itself. . . Thinking is existence in self; life, as differenced from thought, existence out of self: life is to give from oneself; thought is to take into oneself. Existence out of self is the world; existence in self is God. To think is to be God. The act of thought, as such, is the freedom of the immortal gods from all external limitations and necessities of life. . . .

Appendix

Man has his highest being, his God, in himself; not in himself as an individual, but in his essential nature, his species. No individual is an adequate representation of his species, but only the human individual is conscious of the distinction between the species and the individual; in the sense of this distinction lies the root of religion. The yearning of man after something above himself is nothing else than the longing after the perfect type of his nature, the yearning to be free from himself, *i.e.*, from the limits and defects of his individuality. Individuality is the self-conditionating, the self-limitation of the species. Thus man has cognizance of nothing above himself, of nothing beyond the nature of humanity; but to the individual man this nature presents itself under the form of an individual man. Thus, for example, the child sees the nature of man *above itself* in the form of its parents, the pupil in the form of his tutor. But all feelings which man experiences towards a superior man, nay, in general, all moral feelings which man has towards man, are of a religious nature.[8] *Man feels nothing towards God which he does not also feel towards man. Homo homini deus est.* Want teaches prayer; but in misfortune, in sorrow, man kneels to entreat help of man also. Feeling makes God a man, but for the same reason it makes man a God. How often in deep emotion, which alone speaks genuine truth, man exclaims to man: Thou art, thou hast been my redeemer, my saviour, my protecting spirit, my God! We feel awe, reverence, humility, devout admiration, in thinking of a truly great, noble man; we feel ourselves worthless, we sink into nothing, even in the presence of human greatness. The purely, truly human emotions are religious; but for that reason the religious emotions are purely human: the only difference is, that the religious emotions are vague, indefinite; but even this is only the case when the object of them is indefinite. Where God is positively defined, is the object of positive religion, there God is also the object of positive, definite human feelings, the object of fear and love, and therefore he is a positively human being; for there is nothing more in God than what lies in feeling. . . .

The certainty of God is here nothing else than the self-certainty of human feeling, the yearning after God is the yearning after unlimited, uninterrupted, pure feeling. In life the feelings are interrupted; they collapse; they are followed by a state of void, of insensibility. The religious problem, therefore, is to give fixity to feeling in spite of the vicissitudes of life, and to separate it from repugnant disturbances and limitations: God himself is nothing else than undisturbed, uninterrupted feeling, feeling for which there exists no limits, no opposite. If God were a being distinct from thy feeling, he would be known to thee in some other way than simply in feeling; but just because thou perceivest him only by feeling, he exists only in feeling—he is himself only feeling.

Notes

1   "Objectum intellectus esse illimitatum sive omne verum ac, ut loquuntur, omne ens ut ens, ex eo constat, quod ad nullum non genus rerum extenditur, nullumque est, cujus cognoscendi capax non sit, licet ob varia obstacula multa sint, quæ re ipsa non norit."—Gassendi (Opp. Omn. Phys.).

2   The obtuse Materialist says: "Man is distinguished from the brute *only* by consciousness—he is an animal with consciousness superadded;" not reflecting, that in a being which awakes to consciousness, there takes place a qualitative change, a differentiation of the entire nature. For the rest, our words are by no means intended to depreciate the nature of the lower animals. This is not the place to enter further into that question.

3   "Toute opinion est assez forte pour se faire exposer au prix de la vie."—Montaigne.

4   Gloriam suam plus amat Deus quam omnes creaturas. "God can only love himself, can only think of himself, can only work for himself. In creating man, God seeks his own ends, his own glory," &c.—Vide P. Bayle, *Ein Beitrag zur Geschichte der Philos. u. Menschh.*, pp. 104–107.

5   The religious, the original mode in which man becomes objective to himself, is (as is clearly enough explained in this work) to be distinguished from the mode in which this occurs in reflection and speculation; the latter is voluntary, the former involuntary, necessary—as necessary as art, as speech. With the progress of time, it is true, theology coincides with religion.

6   Deut. xxiii. 12, 13.

7   See, for example, Gen. xxxv. 2; Levit. xi. 44; xx. 26; and the Commentary of Le Clerc on these passages.

8   "Manifestum igitur est tantum religionis sanguini et affinitati, quantum ipsis Diis immortalibus tributum: quia inter ista tam sancta vincula non magis, quam in aliquo loco sacrato nudare se, nefas esse credebatur."—Valer. Max. (l. ii. c. i.)

Questions for reflection

1   Describe how, for Feuerbach, God is the outward projection of a person's human nature. How is human nature infinite and unlimited on Feuerbach's view? What are the three aspects of this nature?
2   Feuerbach grants that both human beings and other animals have consciousness. So why do humans have religion but the other animals do not—what do the former have that the latter lack?
3   What does Feuerbach mean when he says "To think is to be God?"
4   Explain what you think Feuerbach means when he says that God is only a feeling. Do you agree with him? Why or why not?

Further reading

Van A. Harvey (1997) *Feuerbach and the Interpretation of Religion*. Cambridge: Cambridge University Press. (Harvey argues that Feuerbach's work is important to the study of religion and that his significance has been widely overlooked.)

Van A. Harvey (2003) "Ludwig Andreas Feuerbach" in the *Stanford Encyclopedia of Philosophy*. http://plato.stanford.edu/entries/ludwig-feuerbach/. (A concise overview of Feuerbach's life and thought by a leading scholar.)

Michael Martin (1991) *The Case Against Christianity*. Philadelphia, PA: Temple University Press. (An atheist philosopher provides a rational analysis of the central Christian doctrines.)

Charles Alan Wilson (1990) *Feuerbach and the Search for Otherness*. New York: Peter Lang. (Wilson argues that Feuerbach was fixated on the problem of subjectivism, and thus throughout his works attempted to liberate philosophy from the ego—the search for otherness.)

Chapter 31

J. P. Moreland

THE NOÖLOGICAL ARGUMENT

J. P. Moreland is Distinguished Professor of Philosophy at Talbot School of Theology. In this essay he argues that consciousness provides evidence for belief in God. He notes that there are both inductive and deductive versions of the argument, and he explicates one version of the latter. His argument (AC) includes seven premises, and the one most generally criticized is number five—that the explanation for the existence of mental states is not a natural scientific one. In defending premise number five, he offers four reasons why many hold that naturalism requires the rejection of consciousness, at least consciousness understood dualistically. He then briefly examines the nature of naturalism and explains why, given certain naturalist ontological commitments, consciousness poses a problem for those affirming this position. In the rest of the essay, he examines and critiques three representative naturalist options: (1) John Searle's biological naturalism, (2) Colin McGinn's agnostic naturalism, and (3) panpsychism.

Consciousness is among the most mystifying features of the cosmos. Colin McGinn claims that its arrival borders on sheer magic because there seems to be no naturalistic explanation for it: "How can mere matter originate consciousness? How did evolution convert the water of biological tissue into the wine of consciousness? Consciousness seems like a radical novelty in the universe, not prefigured by the after-effects of the Big Bang; so how did it contrive to spring into being from what preceded it?" (McGinn 1999: 13–14). Accordingly some argue that, while finite mental entities may be inexplicable on a naturalist worldview, they may be best explained by theism, thereby furnishing evidence for God's existence. This chapter will attempt to clarify the argument for God's existence from finite consciousness (hereafter, AC) and evaluate three alternatives to it.

Two preliminaries

Two preliminary assumptions should be made explicit. First, premise 1 of AC (below) posits a commonsense understanding of mental states such as sensations, thoughts, beliefs, desires, and volitions. So understood, mental states are in no sense physical since they possess features—e.g., an intrinsic feel such as the hurtfulness of pain, and intentionality (ofness or aboutness directed towards an object; for example, a particular thought is of or about the moon)—not owned by physical states. One way to reject AC is to reject this assumption. Since most rivals to AC assume with its advocates a dualist construal of consciousness, we shall grant this dualist assumption in what follows.

Second, causal explanations in the natural sciences should exhibit a kind of causal necessity—physical causal explanations must show why an effect must follow given the relevant causal conditions. At least five reasons have been proffered for this assumption:

(a)   Causal necessitation unpacks the deepest, core realist notion of causation—namely, causal production according to which a cause "brings about" or "produces" its effect.

(b)   Causal necessitation fits the paradigm cases of causal explanation (e.g., macro-solidity/impenetrability in terms of micro-lattice structures, repulsive forces; mass proportions in chemical reactions in terms of atomic models of atoms/molecules, bonding orbitals, energy stability, charge distribution) central to the core theories (e.g., the atomic theory of matter) that constitute a naturalist world-view and in terms of which it is purported to have explanatory superiority to rival worldviews.

(c)   Causal necessitation provides a way of distinguishing accidental generalizations (e.g., plants grow when exposed to the sun's heat) from true causal laws (plants grow when exposed to the sun's light).

(d)   Causal necessitation supports the derivation of counterfactuals (e.g., if that chunk of gold had been placed in aqua regia, then it would have dissolved) from causal laws (gold dissolves in aqua regia).

(e)   Causal necessitation clarifies the direction of causality and rules out the attempt to explain a cause by its effect.

The argument from consciousness

AC may be expressed in inductive or deductive form. As an inductive argument, AC may be construed as claiming that given theism and naturalism as the live options fixed by our background beliefs, theism provides a better explanation of consciousness than naturalism and, thus, receives some confirmation from the existence of consciousness.

AC may also be expressed in deductive form. Here is one deductive version of AC:

1   Genuinely non-physical mental states exist.
2   There is an explanation for the existence of mental states.
3   Personal explanation is different from natural scientific explanation.
4   The explanation for the existence of mental states is either a personal or natural scientific explanation.

5   The explanation is not a natural scientific one.
6   Therefore, the explanation is a personal one.
7   If the explanation is personal, then it is theistic.
8   Therefore, the explanation is theistic.

Theists such as Robert Adams (Adams 1992) and Richard Swinburne (Swinburne 1997: 174–199; 2004: 192–212) have advanced a slightly different version of AC which focuses on mental/physical correlations and not merely on the existence of mental states. Either way, AC may be construed as a deductive argument.

Premises 2, 4, and 5 are the ones most likely to come under attack. We are granting 1 for the sake of argument. Premise 3 turns on the fact that personal explanation differs from event causal covering law explanations employed in natural science. Associated with *event* causation is a covering law model of explanation according to which some event (the *explanandum*) is explained by giving a correct deductive or inductive argument for that event. Such an argument contains two features in its *explanans*: a (universal or statistical) law of nature *and* initial causal conditions.

By contrast, a *personal* explanation (divine or otherwise) of some state of affairs brought about intentionally by a person will employ notions such as the intention of the agent, the relevant power of the agent that was exercised in causing the state of affairs, and the means used to accomplish the intention.

Advocates of AC employ the difference between these two modes of explanation to justify premise 2. Briefly, the argument is that given a defense of premises 4 and 5, there is no natural scientific explanation of mental entities. Thus, the phenomena cited in 1 may not be taken as unique facts that can be explained naturalistically. Moreover, the appearance of mental entities and their regular correlation with physical entities are puzzling phenomena that cry out for explanation. Since personal explanation is something people use all the time, this distinctive form of explanation is available, and its employment regarding the phenomena cited in 1 removes our legitimate puzzlement regarding them.

Premise 7 seems fairly uncontroversial. To be sure, Humean style arguments about the type and number of deities involved could be raised at this point, but these issues would be intramural theistic problems of small comfort to naturalists. That is, if the explanation for finite conscious minds is supernatural, then naturalism is false.

Premise 4 will be examined in conjunction with two alternatives to AC that reject it: Colin McGinn's position and panpsychism.

That leaves 5. At least four reasons have been offered for why there is no natural scientific explanation for the existence of mental states (or their regular correlation with physical states):

(a) *The uniformity of nature.* Prior to the emergence of consciousness, the universe contained nothing but aggregates of particles/waves standing in fields of forces relative to each other. The story of the development of the cosmos is told in terms of the rearrangement of micro-parts into increasingly more complex structures according to natural law. On a naturalist depiction of matter, it is brute mechanical, physical stuff. The emergence of consciousness seems to be a case of getting something from nothing. In general, physico-chemical reactions do not generate consciousness, but they do in the brain. Yet brains seem similar to other parts of organisms' bodies (e.g., both are

collections of cells completely describable in physical terms). How can like causes produce radically different effects? The appearance of mind is utterly unpredictable and
inexplicable. This radical discontinuity seems like an inhomogeneous rupture in the
natural world. Similarly, physical states have spatial extension and location but mental
states seem to lack spatial features. Space and consciousness sit oddly together. How did
spatially-arranged matter conspire to produce non-spatial mental states? From a naturalist point of view, this seems utterly inexplicable.

(b) *Contingency of the mind/body correlation.* The regular correlation between types of
mental states and physical states seems radically contingent. Why do pains instead of
itches, and thoughts or feelings of love, get correlated with specific brain states? Based
on strong conceivability, zombie worlds (worlds physically like ours in which creatures' bodies move like ours do but in which there is no consciousness) and inverted
qualia worlds (worlds where people discriminate red objects from other objects and use
the word "red" while pointing to them, but do so on the basis of having a sensation of
blue while looking at red objects and who have a sensation of red while looking at blue
objects) are possible. No amount of knowledge of the brain state will help to answer
this question. Given the requirement of causal necessitation for naturalistic causal
explanations, there is *in principle* no naturalistic explanation for either the existence of
mental states or their regular correlation with physical states. For the naturalist, the
regularity of mind/body correlations must be taken as contingent brute facts. But these
facts are inexplicable from a naturalistic standpoint, and they are radically unique compared to all other entities in the naturalist ontology. Thus, it begs the question simply to
announce that mental states and their regular correlations with certain brain states is a
natural fact.

(c) *Epiphenomenalism and causal closure.* Most naturalists believe that their worldview
requires that all entities whatever are either physical or depend on the physical for their
existence and behavior. One implication of this belief is commitment to the causal closure of the physical. On this principle, when one is tracing the causal antecedents of any
physical event, one will never have to leave the level of the physical. Physical effects have
only physical causes. Rejection of the causal closure principle would imply a rejection
of the possibility of a complete and comprehensive physical theory of all physical phenomena—something that no naturalist should reject. Thus, if mental phenomena are
genuinely non-physical, then they must be epiphenomena—effects caused by the physical that do not themselves have causal powers. But epiphenomenalism is false. Mental
causation seems undeniable. The admission of epiphenomenal non-physical mental entities may be taken as a refutation of naturalism. Why? Because if a form of naturalism
implies epiphenomenalism and epiphenomenalism is false, then that form of naturalism
is false.

(d) *The inadequacy of evolutionary explanations.* Naturalists are committed to the view that,
in principle, evolutionary explanations can be offered for the appearance of all organisms and their parts. It is not hard to see how an evolutionary account could be given
for new and increasingly complex physical structures that constitute different organisms. However, organisms are black boxes as far as evolution is concerned. As long as an
organism, when receiving certain inputs, generates the correct behavioral outputs under

the demands of fighting, fleeing, reproducing and feeding, the organism will survive. What goes on inside the organism is irrelevant and only becomes significant for the processes of evolution when an output is produced. Strictly speaking, it is the output, not what caused it, which bears on the struggle for reproductive advantage. Moreover, the functions organisms carry out consciously *could just as well have been done unconsciously*. Thus, both the sheer existence of conscious states, the precise mental content that constitutes them, and their regular correlation with types of physical states is outside the pale of evolutionary explanation.

We have looked at four reasons why many scholars, including many naturalists, hold that naturalism requires the rejection of consciousness construed along dualist lines.

The naturalistic worldview

At this point, it may be wise to look briefly at the nature of naturalism as a worldview to gain further insight into why consciousness is such a problem for naturalists. Naturalism usually includes the following:

*   different aspects of a naturalist epistemic attitude (e.g., a rejection of so-called "first philosophy" in which there is no philosophical knowledge or justified beliefs that are independent of and more basic than scientific knowledge), along with an acceptance of either strong or weak scientism (either science provides justified beliefs or science is vastly better than other disciplines in providing justified beliefs);
*   a Grand Story which amounts to a causal account of how all entities whatsoever have come to be, told in terms of an event causal story described in natural scientific terms with a central role given to the atomic theory of matter and evolutionary biology;
*   a general ontology in which the only entities allowed are those that either (i) bear a relevant similarity to those thought to characterize a completed form of physics or (ii) can be explained according to the causal necessitation requirement in terms of the Grand Story and the naturalist epistemic attitude.

For our purposes, it is important to say a bit more about naturalist ontological commitments. A good place to start is with what Frank Jackson calls the location problem (Jackson 1998: 1–5). According to Jackson, given that naturalists are committed to a fairly widely-accepted physical story about how things came to be and what they are, the location problem is the task of locating or finding a place for some entity (e.g., semantic contents, mind, agency) in that story. As an illustration, Jackson shows how the solidity of macro-objects can be located within a naturalist worldview. If solidity is taken as impenetrability, then given the lattice structure of atoms composing, say, a table and chair, it becomes obvious why they cannot penetrate each other. Given the naturalist micro-story, the macro-world could not have been different: the table could not penetrate the chair. Location requires showing how the troublesome entity had to arise given the Grand Story.

There are three constraints for developing a naturalist ontology and locating entities within it:

(i)   entities should be knowable by empirical, scientific means;
(ii)   the origin of those entities should be necessitated by physical entities and pro-
       cesses according to the Grand Story;
(iii) entities should bear a relevant similarity to those found in chemistry and physics
       or be shown to depend necessarily on entities in chemistry and physics.

Given theism and naturalism as rivals, theists who employ the argument from consciousness seek to capitalize on the naturalistic failure to come to terms with consciousness by
offering a rival explanation for its appearance. That failure is why most prominent naturalists (e.g., David Papineau 1993) reject premise 1 of AC ("Genuinely non-physical
mental states exist") and either eliminate or, in one way or another, identify conscious
states with physical ones.

    Unfortunately for naturalists, consciousness has stubbornly resisted treatment in
physical terms. Consciousness has been recalcitrant for naturalists, and premise 1 is
hard to dismiss. Aware of this problem, various naturalists who accept premise 1 have
proposed certain alternatives to theism and AC. In the next section, we shall look at
three representative options.

Alternatives to AC

#1: John Searle's biological naturalism

John Searle has developed a naturalistic account of consciousness which would, if successful, provide justification for rejecting premise 5 of AC (Searle 1992). According
to Searle, for fifty years philosophy of mind has been dominated by strict physicalism
because it was seen as a crucial implication of taking the naturalistic turn. For these
naturalists, if one abandons strict physicalism, one has rejected a scientific naturalist
approach to the mind/body problem and opened oneself up to the intrusion of religious
concepts and arguments about the mental.

    By contrast, Searle's own solution to the mind/body problem is biological natural-
ism: while mental states are exactly what dualists describe them to be, nevertheless,
they are merely emergent biological states and processes that causally supervene upon a
suitably structured, functioning brain. Brain processes cause mental processes, which
are not ontologically reducible to the former. Consciousness is just an ordinary (i.e.,
physical) feature of the brain and, as such, is merely an ordinary feature of the natural
world.

    Given that he characterizes consciousness as dualists do, why does Searle claim that
biological naturalism does not represent a rejection of scientific naturalism which, in
turn, opens the door for religious concepts about and explanations for the mental? Searle's answer to this question is developed in three steps.

    In step one, he cites several examples of emergence (liquidity, solidity, features of
digestion) that he takes to be unproblematic for naturalists and claims that emergent
consciousness is analogous to the unproblematic cases.

    In step two, he formulates two reasons why consciousness is not a problem for natu-
ralists: (i) The emergence of consciousness is not a problem if we stop trying to picture
or image consciousness. (ii) In standard cases (heat, color), an ontological reduction

352 J. P. MORELAND

(e.g., identifying a specific color with a wavelength) is based on a causal reduction (e.g., claiming that a specific color is caused by a wavelength) because our pragmatic interests are in reality, not appearance.

In these cases we can distinguish the *appearance* of heat and color from the *reality*, place the former in consciousness, leave the latter in the objective world, and go on to define the phenomenon itself in terms of its causes. We can do this because our interests are in the reality and not the appearance. The ontological reduction of heat to its causes leaves the appearance of heat the same. Regarding consciousness, we are interested in the appearances, and thus the irreducibility of consciousness is merely due to pragmatic considerations, not to some deep metaphysical problem.

In step three, Searle claims that an adequate scientific explanation of the emergence of consciousness consists in a detailed, lawlike set of correlations between mental and physical state tokens.

Several things may be said in response to Searle's position. Regarding steps one and two, his cases of emergence (rigidity, fluidity) are not good analogies to consciousness since the former are *easy* to locate in the naturalist epistemology and ontology, but consciousness is *not*. Given a widely accepted physicalist description of atoms, molecules, lattice structure, and the like, the rigidity or fluidity of macro-objects follows necessarily. But there is no clear necessary connection between any physical state and any mental state. For example, given a specific brain state normally "associated" with the mental state of being appeared to redly, inverted qualia worlds (worlds with that physical state but radically different mental states "associated" with it), zombie worlds (worlds with that physical state and no mental states at all) and disembodied worlds (worlds with beings possessing mental states with no physical entities at all) are still metaphysically possible. It is easy to locate solidity in a naturalist framework but the same cannot be said for consciousness.

Further, the emergence of genuinely new properties in macro-objects that are not part of the micro-world (e.g., heat construed as warmth, color construed commonsensically as a quality) presents problems for naturalists in the same way consciousness does and, historically, that is why they were placed in consciousness. Contrary to Searle, they were not so placed because of the pragmatics of our interests. For example, historically, the problem was that if so-called secondary qualities (tastes, smells, colors, sounds, textures) were kept in the mind-independent world, there was no naturalistic explanation for why they emerged on the occasion of a mere rearrangement in micro-parts exhaustively characterized in terms of primary qualities (primary qualities are those features taken to exhaust the nature of matter, e.g., mass, size, shape, location, being in motion or at rest, having such and such forces of attraction or repulsion, vibrating at a certain frequency). Secondary qualities construed along commonsense lines are not among the primary qualities employed to characterize the micro-world and, indeed, seem contingently linked to the micro-world. It is this straightforward ontological problem, not the pragmatics of reduction or the attempt to image consciousness, that presents difficulties for naturalism.

In fact, the emergence of mental properties is more like the emergence of normative (e.g., moral) properties than the properties of solidity or digestion. Even the atheist J. L. Mackie admitted that the emergence of moral properties provided evidence for a moral argument for God's existence analogous to AC: "Moral properties constitute so odd a cluster of properties and relations that they are most unlikely to have arisen in the ordinary course of events without an all-powerful god to create them" (Mackie 1982: 115). Mackie is right on this point. Given theism, if a naturalist were simply to claim that the emergence of moral properties was a basic naturalistic fact, this would be an ad hoc, question-begging ploy of assuming a point not congruent with a naturalistic worldview. Searle's "explanation" of consciousness is guilty of the same charge.

Regarding step three, "explanations" in science that do not express the sort of necessity we have been discussing are better taken as *descriptions*, not *explanations*. For example, the ideal gas equation is a description of the behavior of gases. An explanation of that behavior is provided by the atomic theory of gas. Further, given theism and AC, it is question-begging and *ad hoc* for Searle to assert that mental entities and mental/physical correlations are basic, since such entities are natural in light of theism but unnatural given philosophical naturalism. As naturalist Jaegwon Kim notes, the correlations are not explanations (Kim 1996: 8). They are the very things that need explaining and, given a proper understanding of the real questions, no naturalistic explanation seems to be forthcoming. By misconstruing the problem, Searle fails to address the real issue and, weighed against AC, his position is inadequate.

#2: Colin McGinn's agnostic naturalism

Naturalist Colin McGinn has offered a different solution (McGinn 1999). Given the radical difference between mind and matter as it is depicted by current or even an ideal future physics, there is no naturalistic solution that stays within the widely accepted naturalist epistemology and ontology. Darwinian explanations fail as well because they cannot account for why consciousness appeared in the first place. What is needed is a radically different kind of solution to the origin of mind, one that must meet two conditions: (i) it must be a naturalistic solution, and (ii) it must depict the emergence of consciousness and its regular correlation with matter as necessary and not contingent facts.

McGinn claims that there must be two kinds of unknowable natural properties that solve the problem. There must be some general properties of matter that enter into the production of consciousness when assembled into a brain. Thus, all matter has the potentiality to underlie consciousness. Further, there must be some natural property of the brain he calls C* that unleashes these general properties.

The temptation to take the origin of consciousness as a mystery, indeed, a mystery that is best explained theistically, is due to our ignorance of these properties. However, given C* and the general properties of matter, the unknowable link between mind and matter is ordinary, commonplace and necessitates the emergence of consciousness. Unfortunately, evolution did not give humans the faculties needed to know these properties and, thus, they are in principle beyond our grasp. We will forever be agnostic about their nature. However, they must be there since there must be some naturalistic explanation of mind as all other solutions have failed.

McGinn offers two further descriptions of these unknowable yet ordinary properties that link matter and mind: (i) they are not sense perceptible, and (ii) since matter is spatial and mind non-spatial, they are either in some sense pre-spatial or are spatial in a way that is itself unknowable to our faculties. In this way, these unknowable properties contain at least the potentiality for both ordinary spatial features of matter and the non-spatial features of consciousness as judged by our usual concept of space.

In sum, the mind/matter link is an unknowable mystery due to our cognitive limitations resulting from our evolution. And since the link is quite ordinary, we should not be puzzled by the origin of mind, and no theistic explanation is required.

Critics have offered at least three criticisms of McGinn's position. First, given McGinn's agnosticism about the properties that link mind and matter, how can he confidently assert some of their features? How does he know they are non-sensory, pre-spatial or spatial in an unknowable way? How does he know some of these properties underlie all matter? Indeed, what possible justification can he give for their reality? The only one he suggests is that we must provide a naturalistic solution and all ordinary naturalistic ones either deny consciousness or fail to solve the problem. But given the presence of AC, McGinn's claims are simply question-begging. Indeed, his agnosticism seems to be a convenient way of hiding behind naturalism and avoiding a theistic explanation. Given that theism enjoys a positive degree of justification prior to the problem of consciousness, he should avail himself of the explanatory resources of theism.

Second, it is not clear that his solution is a version of naturalism, except in name only. In contrast to other entities in the naturalist ontology, McGinn's linking properties cannot be known scientifically, nor are they relevantly similar to the rest of the naturalist ontology. Thus, it becomes vacuous to call these properties "naturalistic." McGinn's own speculations strike one as *ad hoc* in light of the inadequacies of naturalistic explanations. In fact, McGinn's solution is actually closer to an agnostic form of panpsychism (see below) than to naturalism. Given AC, McGinn's solution is an ad hoc readjustment of naturalism.

Third, McGinn does not solve the problem of consciousness; he merely relocates it. Rather than having two radically different entities (unlocated mind and located matter, that seem to be contingently connected), he offers us unknowable properties with two radically different aspects (e.g., his links contain the potentiality for ordinary spatiality and non-spatiality, for ordinary materiality and mentality). Moreover, these radically different aspects of the linking properties are just as contingently related (the capacity for spatiality and non-spatiality do not require each other to exist and, indeed, seem to contingently connected; the same may be said for the capacities for materiality and mentality). And they seem to be without a linking intermediary to connect these contingently related features every bit as much as non-spatial mental and spatial physical properties fail to have an intermediary connecting link on a dualist perspective. The contingency comes from the nature of mind and matter as naturalists conceive it. It does not solve the problem of the contingency of a connecting link to remove it from mind and matter directly and to relocate the contingent connection by characterizing it as two aspects (potential for spatiality and for non-spatiality; potential for materiality and for non-materiality) of some unknowable entity.

#3: Panpsychism

Currently, there are few serious advocates of panpsychism, though it has been suggested by Thomas Nagel (Nagel 1986) and David Chalmers (Chalmers 1996). The main exception to this rule is panpsychist David Skrbina (Skrbina 2005). Roughly, panpsychism is the view that all matter has consciousness within it. Since each parcel of matter has its own consciousness, the brain is conscious since it is just a collection of those parcels. Consciousness is pervasive in nature; so its apparent emergence in particular cases is not something that requires special explanation. One can distinguish two forms of panpsychism. According to the strong version, all matter has conscious states in it in the same sense that organisms such as dogs and humans do. According to the weak form, regular matter has consciousness in a degraded, attenuated way in the form of proto-mental states that, under the right circumstances, yield conscious mental states without themselves being conscious.

The strong form is quite implausible. For one thing, regular matter gives no evidence whatever of possessing consciousness. Further, if all matter has consciousness, why does it emerge in special ways only when certain configurations of matter are present? And if conscious human beings are in some sense merely combinations of little bits of consciousness, how are we to account for the unity of consciousness and why do people have no memory of the conscious careers of the bits of matter prior to their combination to form humans? There is no answer to these questions and few, if any, hold to strong panpsychism.

What about the weak version? Given the current intellectual climate, a personal theistic or a naturalistic explanation would exhaust at least the live—if not the logical—options. It is widely thought that weak panpsychism has serious problems in its own right (e.g., explaining what an incipient or proto-mental entity is; how the type of unity that appears to characterize the self could emerge from a mere system of parts standing together in various causal and spatio-temporal relations; and why certain physical conditions are regularly correlated with the actualization of consciousness when the connection between consciousness and those conditions seems to be utterly contingent).

Moreover, panpsychism is arguably less reasonable than theism on other grounds. Given justification for this claim, theism enjoys greater positive epistemic justification than does panpsychism prior to consideration of the issue of consciousness, and all things being equal, the appeal to panpsychism to explain consciousness is undermotivated.

Finally, panpsychism is merely a label for and not an explanation of the phenomena to be explained. As Geoffrey Madell notes, "the sense that the mental and the physical are just inexplicably and gratuitously slapped together is hardly allayed by adopting . . . a panpsychist . . . view of the mind, for [it does not] have any explanation to offer as to why or how mental properties cohere with physical" (Madell 1988: 3).

Conclusion

Prominent naturalist Jaegwon Kim has observed that "if a whole system of phenomena that are prima facie not among basic physical phenomena resists physical explanation, and especially if we don't even know where or how to begin, it would be time to reexamine one's physicalist commitments" (Kim 1998: 96). For Kim, genuinely non-physical mental entities are the paradigm case of such a system of phenomena. Kim's advice to fellow naturalists is that they must simply admit the irreality of the mental and recognize that naturalism exacts a steep price and cannot be had on the cheap. However, if feigning anesthesia—denying that consciousness construed along commonsense lines is real—is the price to be paid to retain naturalism, then the price is too high. Fortunately, the theistic argument from consciousness reminds us that it is a price that does not need to be paid.

References

Adams, Robert (1992) "Flavors, Colors and God," reprinted in *Contemporary Perspectives in Religious Epistemology*, R. Douglas Geivett, Brendan Sweetman (eds), New York: Oxford University Press.
Chalmers, David (1996) *The Conscious Mind*, New York: Oxford University Press.
Kim, Jaegwon (1998) *Mind in a Physical World*, Cambridge, MA: MIT Press.
———. (1996) *Philosophy of Mind*, Boulder, CO: Westview Press.
Jackson, Frank (1998) *From Metaphysics to Ethics*, Oxford: Clarendon Press.
Mackie, J. L. (1982) *The Miracle of Theism*, Oxford: Clarendon Press.
Madell, Geoffrey (1988) *Mind and Materialism*, Edinburgh: Edinburgh University Press.
McGinn, Colin (1999) *The Mysterious Flame*, New York: Basic Books.
Nagel, Thomas (1986) *The View from Nowhere*, New York: Oxford University Press.
Papineau, David (1993) *Philosophical Naturalism*, Oxford: Blackwell.
Searle, John (1992) *The Rediscovery of the Mind*, Cambridge, MA: MIT Press.
Skrbina, David (2005) *Panpsychism in the West*, Notre Dame, IN: University of Notre Dame Press.
Swinburne, Richard (1997) *The Evolution of the Soul*, Oxford: Clarendon Press.
———. (2004) *The Existence of God*, Oxford: Clarendon Press.

Questions for reflection

1   Briefly explain the deductive argument from consciousness (AC). What do you take to be a significant objection to it? Why?
2   Professor Moreland grants premise 1 of AC: "Genuinely non-physical mental states exist." What might be some reasons for granting it? What might be some reasons for not granting it?
3   What are some reasons why consciousness poses difficulties for naturalists? Can you think of problems it poses for theists?
4   How might AC be developed as an inductive argument?
5   Do you find any of the three alternatives to AC reasonable? Do you find either of the alternatives more persuasive than AC? Explain.

Further reading

William Hasker (1999) *The Emergent Self*. Ithaca, NY: Cornell University Press. (Contains a rigorous defense of property and substance dualism.)
Jaegwon Kim (2005) *Physicalism or Something Near Enough*. Princeton, NJ: Princeton University Press. (Updates the debate about physicalism and presents Kim's version of epiphenomenal property dualism.)
J. P. Moreland (1998) "Searle's Biological Naturalism and the Argument from Consciousness," *Faith and Philosophy* 15: 1–24. (Offers a critique of Searle's position and defends the argument from consciousness.)
John Searle (1992) *The Rediscovery of the Mind*. Cambridge, MA: MIT Press. (Defends a common sense view of consciousness and argues that all a naturalist needs to do to explain it is to correlate it with various brain states.)
Richard Swinburne (1997) *The Evolution of the Soul*. Oxford: Clarendon Press. (Presents a careful case for property and substance dualism, and defends the argument from consciousness.)

PART FOUR

Faith, reason, and evidence

Throughout the centuries, many religious believers have held that arguments and evidences can and should be used in support of religious belief. Many atheists also agree that evidence and reason are important factors in religious belief. One major difference between these believers and atheists, of course, is that the former assert that there are arguments and evidences strong enough to justify belief in God while the latter deny this. Furthermore, there are also religious believers who maintain that religion is primarily a matter of *faith* and that arguments and evidences should play no role in religious belief, and there are other believers who hold that reasoning is important in religion even though arguments and evidences are unnecessary. Actually, this variety of relations between faith and reason does not exhaust the possibilities; there are myriad ways of understanding it. So, you might wonder, what is an appropriate relationship between them? That is the central question of this section.

For several centuries a number of Western thinkers have agreed with William Clifford, author of the next essay, that we are somehow epistemically or morally obligated to have reasons or evidences for our beliefs—religious or otherwise. If we don't have such reasons or evidences, then we are not justified in holding the beliefs in question. We can call this view *evidentialism*. Clifford begins his essay with a powerful example of a shipowner who chooses to believe that his ship is seaworthy despite his lack of evidence for this belief. In fact, the evidence points to the contrary. The ship sinks, and Clifford argues that the owner is morally guilty because his beliefs were not based on good evidence. He then develops a principle whereby it is always wrong to believe anything based on insufficient evidence.

One recognized response to this form of evidentialism was offered by William James in the nineteenth century. In the next selection, James attempts to offer a philosophical justification for religious faith. He raises the question of whether one is ever justified in allowing the passions to influence belief. He maintains that there are such occasions, namely those where we are faced with a genuine option which simply cannot be decided on rational grounds. In these situations, a person legitimately makes a choice by the "passional nature" rather than by rational intellect.

More recently, Alvin Plantinga objects to evidentialism on the grounds that it is rooted in a faulty epistemology—classical foundationalism—which ends up being self-defeating. For Plantinga and other proponents of what is called "Reformed Epistemology," one does not need evidence to warrant belief in God, for the belief that God exists can be taken as a "properly basic" belief. In order to understand his point, consider this: You no doubt believe that your best friend exists as a real human being. But did you come to this conclusion through advanced philosophical reasoning? Most likely not; you just believe it. So too, argues Plantinga, can we have such a reasonable belief about God. To argue that we must have some further justification for this belief is to buy into faulty epistemology.

Another approach altogether about religious faith, in particular about belief in God, was offered by Blaise Pascal. In his classic Wager Argument, Pascal provides a pragmatic reason for believing in God: it is a better bet. He argues that the possible benefits of believing in God are much greater than the benefits of non-belief. Even if the evidence for God is scant or non-existent, the rational person will wager on God since she has the possibility of eternal gain by believing and the possibility of eternal loss by choosing not to believe.

Chapter 32

W. K. Clifford

THE ETHICS OF BELIEF

William Kingdon (W. K.) Clifford (1845–79) was a British mathematician and philosopher. In this essay, he argues for the position typically referred to as "evidentialism"—the view that we shouldn't accept a particular claim as being true unless we have good evidence for that claim. The title of Clifford's paper is appropriately given: "The Ethics of Belief." He begins with an example in which the relationship between ethics and belief is a close one. A shipowner realizes that his ship might need some repair before setting sail. However, he convinces himself otherwise. He remembers that the ship has had many successful voyages; he notes to himself that he believes in Providence; and he removes any distrust he might have about the shipbuilders who constructed the vessel. Sadly, the ship sinks.

Clifford then makes the point that the shipowner is morally responsible for this catastrophe, and the reason he is culpable is that his beliefs were not based on evidence. Clifford then offers, and provides reasons for, his famous principle: "it is wrong always, everywhere, and for anyone, to believe anything upon insufficient evidence." This principle has significant ramifications for all variety of beliefs, including religious ones.

A shipowner was about to send to sea an emigrant ship. He knew that she was old, and not over-well built at the first; that she had seen many seas and climes, and often had needed repairs. Doubts had been suggested to him that possibly she was not seaworthy. These doubts preyed upon his mind and made him unhappy; he thought that perhaps he ought to have her thoroughly overhauled and refitted, even though this should put him to great expense. Before the ship sailed, however, he succeeded in overcoming these melancholy reflections. He said to himself that she had gone safely through so many voyages and weathered so many storms that it was idle to suppose she would not come safely home from this trip also. He would put his trust in Providence, which could hardly fail to protect all these unhappy families that were leaving their fatherland to seek for better times elsewhere. He would dismiss from his mind all ungenerous suspicions about the honesty of builders and contractors. In such ways he acquired a sincere and comfortable conviction that his vessel was thoroughly safe and seaworthy; he watched her departure with a light heart, and benevolent wishes for the success of the exiles in their strange new home that was to be; and he got his insurance-money when she went down in mid-ocean and told no tales.

What shall we say of him? Surely this, that he was verily guilty of the death of those men. It is admitted that he did sincerely believe in the soundness of his ship; but the sincerity of his conviction can in no wise help him, because *he had no right to believe on such evidence as was before him*. He had acquired his belief not by honestly earning it in patient investigation, but by stifling his doubts. And although in the end he may have felt so sure about it that he could not think otherwise, yet inasmuch as he had knowingly and willingly worked himself into that frame of mind, he must be held responsible for it.

Let us alter the case a little, and suppose that the ship was not unsound after all; that she made her voyage safely, and many others after it. Will that diminish the guilt of her owner? Not one jot. When an action is once done, it is right or wrong for ever; no accidental failure of its good or evil fruits can possibly alter that. The man would not have been innocent, he would only have been not found out. The question of right or wrong has to do with the origin of his belief, not the matter of it; not what it was, but how he got it; not whether it turned out to be true or false, but whether he had a right to believe on such evidence as was before him.

There was once an island in which some of the inhabitants professed a religion teaching neither the doctrine of original sin nor that of eternal punishment. A suspicion got abroad that the professors of this religion had made use of unfair means to get their doctrines taught to children. They were accused of wresting the laws of their country in such a way as to remove children from the care of their natural and legal guardians; and even of stealing them away and keeping them concealed from their friends and relations. A certain number of men formed themselves into a society for the purpose of agitating the public about this matter. They published grave accusations against individual citizens of the highest position and character, and did all in their power to injure these citizens in the exercise of their professions. So great was the noise they made, that a Commission was appointed to investigate the facts; but after the Commission had carefully inquired into all the evidence that could be got, it appeared that the accused were innocent. Not only had they been accused on insufficient evidence, but the evidence of their innocence was such as the agitators might easily have obtained, if they had attempted a fair inquiry. After these disclosures the inhabitants of that country looked upon the members of the agitating society, not only as persons whose judgment was to be distrusted, but also as no longer to be counted honourable men. For although they had sincerely and conscientiously believed in the charges they had made, *yet they had no right to believe on such evidence as was before them*. Their sincere convictions, instead of being honestly earned by patient inquiring, were stolen by listening to the voice of prejudice and passion.

Let us vary this case also, and suppose, other things remaining as before, that a still more accurate investigation proved the accused to have been really guilty. Would this make any difference in the guilt of the accusers? Clearly not; the question is not whether their belief was true or false, but whether they entertained it on wrong grounds. They would no doubt say: "Now you see that we were right after all; next time perhaps you will believe us." And they might be believed, but they would not thereby become honourable men. They would not be innocent, they would only be not found out. Every one of them, if he chose to examine himself *in foro conscientiæ*, would know that he had acquired and nourished a belief, when he had no right to believe on such evidence as was before him; and therein he would know that he had done a wrong thing.

It may be said, however, that in both of these supposed cases it is not the belief which is judged to be wrong, but the action following upon it. The shipowner might say: "I am perfectly certain that my ship is sound, but still I feel it my duty to have her examined, before trusting the lives of so many people to her." And it might be said to the agitator: "However convinced you were of the justice of your cause and the truth of your convictions, you ought not to have made a public attack upon any man's character until you had examined the evidence on both sides with the utmost patience and care."

In the first place, let us admit that, so far as it goes, this view of the case is right and necessary; right, because even when a man's belief is so fixed that he cannot think otherwise, he still has a choice in regard to the action suggested by it and so cannot escape the duty of investigating on the ground of the strength of his convictions; and necessary, because those who are not yet capable of controlling their feelings and thoughts must have a plain rule dealing with overt acts.

But this being premised as necessary, it becomes clear that it is not sufficient, and that our previous judgment is required to supplement it. For it is not possible so to sever the belief from the action it suggests as to condemn the one without condemning the other. No man holding a strong belief on one side of a question, or even wishing to hold a belief on one side, can investigate it with such fairness and completeness as if he were really in doubt and unbiased; so that the existence of a belief not founded on fair inquiry unfits a man for the performance of this necessary duty.

Nor is that truly a belief at all which has not some influence upon the actions of him who holds it. He who truly believes that which prompts him to an action has looked upon the action to lust after it, he has committed it already in his heart. If a belief is not realised immediately in open deeds, it is stored up for the guidance of the future. It goes to make a part of that aggregate of beliefs which is the link between sensation and action at every moment of all our lives, and which is so organised and compacted together that no part of it can be isolated from the rest, but every new addition modifies the structure of the whole. No real belief, however trifling and fragmentary it may seem, is ever truly insignificant; it prepares us to receive more of its like, confirms those which resembled it before, and weakens others; and so gradually it lays a stealthy train in our inmost thoughts, which may some day explode into overt action, and leave its stamp upon our character for ever.

And no one man's belief is in any case a private matter which concerns himself alone. Our lives are guided by that general conception of the course of things which has been created by society for social purposes. Our words, our phrases, our forms and processes and modes of thought, are common property, fashioned and perfected from age to age; an heirloom which every succeeding generation inherits as a precious deposit and a sacred trust to be handed on to the next one, not unchanged but enlarged and purified, with some clear marks of its proper handiwork. Into this, for good or ill, is woven every belief of every man who has speech of his fellows. An awful privilege, and an awful responsibility, that we should help to create the world in which posterity will live.

In the two supposed cases which have been considered, it has been judged wrong to believe on insufficient evidence, or to nourish belief by suppressing doubts and avoiding investigation. The reason of this judgment is not far to seek: it is that in both these cases the belief held by one man was of great importance to other men. But forasmuch as no belief held by one man, however seemingly trivial the belief, and however obscure the believer, is ever actually insignificant or without its effect on the fate of mankind, we have no choice but to extend our judgment to all cases of belief whatever. Belief, that sacred faculty which prompts the decisions of our will, and knits into harmonious working all the compacted energies of our being, is ours not for ourselves, but for humanity. It is rightly used on truths which have been established by long experience and waiting toil, and which have stood in the fierce light of free and fearless questioning. Then it helps to bind men together, and to strengthen and direct their common action. It is desecrated when given to unproved and unquestioned statements, for the solace and private pleasure of the believer; to add a tinsel splendour to the plain straight road of our life and display a bright mirage beyond it; or even to drown the common sorrows of our kind by a self-deception which allows them not only to cast down, but also to degrade us. Whoso would deserve well of his fellows in this matter will guard the purity of his belief with a very fanaticism of jealous care, lest at any time it should rest on an unworthy object, and catch a stain which can never be wiped away.

It is not only the leader of men, statesman, philosopher, or poet, that owes this bounden duty to mankind. Every rustic who delivers in the village alehouse his slow, infrequent sentences, may help to kill or keep alive the fatal superstitions which clog his race. Every hard-worked wife of an artisan may transmit to her children beliefs which shall knit society together, or rend it in pieces. No simplicity of mind, no obscurity of station, can escape the universal duty of questioning all that we believe.

It is true that this duty is a hard one, and the doubt which comes out of it is often a very bitter thing. It leaves us bare and powerless where we thought that we were safe and strong. To know all about anything is to know how to deal with it under all circumstances. We feel much happier and more secure when we think we know precisely what to do, no matter what happens, than when we have lost our way and do not know where to turn. And if we have supposed ourselves to know all about anything, and to be capable of doing what is fit in regard to it, we naturally do not like to find that we are really ignorant and powerless, that we have to begin again at the beginning, and try to learn what the thing is and how it is to be dealt with—if indeed anything can be learnt about it. It is the sense of power attached to a sense of knowledge that makes men desirous of believing, and afraid of doubting.

This sense of power is the highest and best of pleasures when the belief on which it is founded is a true belief, and has been fairly earned by investigation. For then we may justly feel that it is common property, and holds good for others as well as for ourselves. Then we may be glad, not that *I* have learned secrets by which I am safer and stronger, but that *we men* have got mastery over more of the world; and we shall be strong, not for ourselves, but in the name of Man and in his strength. But if the belief has been accepted on insufficient evidence, the pleasure is a stolen one. Not only does it deceive ourselves by giving us a sense of power which we do not really possess, but it is sinful, because it is stolen in defiance of our duty to mankind. That duty is to guard ourselves from such beliefs as from a pestilence, which may shortly master our own body and then spread to the rest of the town. What would be thought of one who, for the sake of a sweet fruit, should deliberately run the risk of bringing a plague upon his family and his neighbours?

And, as in other such cases, it is not the risk only which has to be considered; for a bad action is always bad at the time when it is done, no matter what happens afterwards. Every time we let ourselves believe for unworthy reasons, we weaken our powers of self-control, of doubting, of judicially and fairly weighing evidence. We all suffer severely enough from the maintenance and support of false beliefs and the fatally wrong actions which they lead to, and the evil born when one such belief is entertained is great and wide. But a greater and wider evil arises when the credulous character is maintained and supported, when a habit of believing for unworthy reasons is fostered and made permanent. If I steal money from any person, there may be no harm done by the mere transfer of possession; he may not feel the loss, or it may prevent him from using the money badly. But I cannot help doing this great wrong towards Man, that I make myself dishonest. What hurts society is not that it should lose its property, but that it should become a den of thieves; for then it must cease to be society. This is why we ought not to do evil that good may come; for at any rate this great evil has come, that we have done evil and are made wicked thereby. In like manner, if I let myself believe anything on insufficient evidence, there may be no great harm done by the mere belief; it may be true after all, or I may never have occasion to exhibit it in outward acts. But I cannot help doing this great wrong towards Man, that I make myself credulous. The danger to society is not merely that it should believe wrong things, though that is great enough; but that it should become credulous, and lose the habit of testing things and inquiring into them; for then it must sink back into savagery.

The harm which is done by credulity in a man is not confined to the fostering of a credulous character in others, and consequent support of false beliefs. Habitual want of care about what I believe leads to habitual want of care in others about the truth of what is told to me. Men speak the truth to one another when each reveres the truth in his own mind and in the other's mind; but how shall my friend revere the truth in my mind when I myself am careless about it, when I believe things because I want to believe them, and because they are comforting and pleasant? Will he not learn to cry, "Peace," to me, when there is no peace? By such a course I shall surround myself with a thick atmosphere of falsehood and fraud, and in that I must live. It may matter little to me, in my cloud-castle of sweet illusions and darling lies; but it matters much to Man that I have made my neighbours ready to deceive. The credulous man is father to the liar and the cheat; he lives in the bosom of this his family, and it is no marvel if he should become even as they are. So closely are our duties knit together, that whoso shall keep the whole law, and yet offend in one point, he is guilty of all.

To sum up; it is wrong always, everywhere, and for anyone, to believe anything upon insufficient evidence.

If a man, holding a belief which he was taught in childhood or persuaded of afterwards, keeps down and pushes away any doubts which arise about it in his mind, purposely avoids the reading of books and the company of men that call in question or discuss it, and regards as impious those questions which cannot easily be asked without disturbing it— the life of that man is one long sin against mankind.

If this judgment seems harsh when applied to those simple souls who have never known better, who have been brought up from the cradle with a horror of doubt, and taught that their eternal welfare depends on *what* they believe, then it leads to the very serious question, *Who hath made Israel to sin?*

It may be permitted me to fortify this judgment with the sentence of Milton[1]—

> "A man may be a heretic in the truth; and if he believe things only because his pastor says so, or the assembly so determine, without knowing other reason, though his belief be true, yet the very truth he holds becomes his heresy."

And with this famous aphorism of Coleridge[2]:—

> "He who begins by loving Christianity better than Truth, will proceed by loving his own sect or Church better than Christianity, and end in loving himself better than all."

Inquiry into the evidence of a doctrine is not to be made once for all, and then taken as finally settled. It is never lawful to stifle a doubt; for either it can be honestly answered by means of the inquiry already made, or else it proves that the inquiry was not complete.

"But," says one, "I am a busy man; I have no time for the long course of study which would be necessary to make me in any degree a competent judge of certain questions, or even able to understand the nature of the arguments." Then he should have no time to believe.

Notes

1   *Areopagitica.*
2   *Aids to Reflection.*

Questions for reflection

1   What is the point of the shipowner analogy? Is it a good analogy? Explain.
2   Do you agree with Clifford's famous principle: ". . . it is wrong always, everywhere, and for anyone, to believe anything upon insufficient evidence"? What are his reasons for this claim? Do you agree with them?
3   On Clifford's view, how much evidence, and what kind of evidence, would be necessary for appropriate belief in God? Is such evidence attainable?
4   Do faith and reason conflict? Are they contradictory notions? Elucidate.
5   Should we ever believe anything without evidence? Are there different kinds of evidences for different kinds of beliefs?

Further reading

W. K. Clifford (1999) *The Ethics of Belief and Other Essays.* Amherst, NY: Prometheus Books. (Important essays by Clifford, including the one in this selection.)

Earl Conee and Richard Feldman (2004) *Evidentialism: Essays in Epistemology.* Oxford: Clarendon Press. (A defense of the traditional position in epistemology—that justified attitudes towards any given proposition are determined completely by the person's evidence.)

Nancy Frankenberry (1987) *Religion and Radical Empiricism.* Albany, NY: State University of New York Press. (Examines such important questions as "How are religious claims justified?" and "What evidence could count for or against such claims?")

R. Douglas Geivett and Brendan Sweetman, eds. (1992) *Contemporary Perspectives on Religious Epistemology.* Oxford: Oxford University Press. (A superb collection of essays on religious epistemology from a wide variety of perspectives.)

D. Z. Phillips (2001) *Religion and the Hermeneutics of Contemplation.* Cambridge: Cambridge University Press. (Argues that intellectuals can appropriately understand religion without being for or against it.)

Chapter 33

William James

THE WILL TO BELIEVE

William James (1842–1910) was a philosopher and psychologist who advanced a philosophical view known in America as pragmatism. In this selection he argues, contrary to Clifford's position in "The Ethics of Belief," that there are occasions when having beliefs in the absence of evidence is warranted.

In life we sometimes need to make choices even when there is little, if any, evidence available on which to base our decisions. James calls this deciding between hypotheses an "option," and he delineates several such kinds of decisions: (1) living or dead, (2) forced or avoidable, and (3) momentous or trivial. A *genuine option* is one that is living, forced, and momentous. Religion, he maintains, is such an option for some people. So, in these cases, even given a lack of evidence, faith may be the best choice. In making this choice, he maintains, we must use our non-intellectual or "passional" nature. He thus defends the following thesis: "Our passional nature not only lawfully may, but must, decide an option between propositions, whenever it is a genuine option that cannot by its nature be decided on intellectual grounds; for to say, under such circumstance, 'Do not decide, but leave the question open,' is itself a passional decision—just like deciding yes or no—and is attended with the same risk of losing the truth."

I[1]

Let us give the name of *hypothesis* to anything that may be proposed to our belief; and just as the electricians speak of live and dead wires, let us speak of any hypothesis as either *live* or *dead*. A live hypothesis is one which appeals as a real possibility to him to whom it is proposed. If I ask you to believe in the Mahdi, the notion makes no electric connection with your nature—it refuses to scintillate with any credibility at all. As an hypothesis it is completely dead. To an Arab, however (even if he be not one of the Mahdi's followers), the hypothesis is among the mind's possibilities: it is alive. This shows that deadness and liveness in an hypothesis are not intrinsic properties, but relations to the individual thinker. They are measured by his willingness to act. The maximum of liveness in an hypothesis means willingness to act irrevocably. Practically, that means belief, but there is some believing tendency wherever there is willingness to act at all.

Next, let us call the decision between two hypotheses an *option*. Options may be of several kinds. They may be—first, *living* or *dead*; secondly, *forced* or *avoidable*; thirdly, *momentous* or *trivial*; and for our purposes we may call an option a *genuine* option when it is of the forced, living, and momentous kind.

1. A living option is one in which both hypotheses are live ones. If I say to you: "Be a theosophist or be a Mohammedan," it is probably a dead option, because for you neither hypothesis is likely to be alive. But if I say: "Be an agnostic or be a Christian," it is otherwise: trained as you are, each hypothesis makes some appeal, however small, to your belief.

2. Next, if I say to you: "Choose between going out with your umbrella or without it," I do not offer you a genuine option, for it is not forced. You can easily avoid it by not going out at all. Similarly, if I say, "Either love me or hate me," "Either call my theory true or call it false," your option is avoidable. You may remain indifferent to me, neither loving nor hating, and you may decline to offer any judgment as to my theory. But if I say, "Either accept this truth or go without it," I put on you a forced option, for there is no standing place outside of the alternative. Every dilemma based on a complete logical disjunction, with no possibility of not choosing, is an option of this forced kind.

3. Finally, if I were Dr. Nansen and proposed to you to join my North Pole expedition, your option would be momentous; for this would probably be your only similar opportunity, and your choice now would either exclude you from the North Pole sort of immortality altogether or put at least the chance of it into your hands. He who refuses to embrace a unique opportunity loses the prize as surely as if he tried and failed. *Per contra*, the option is trivial when the opportunity is not unique, when the stake is insignificant, or when the decision is reversible if it later prove unwise. Such trivial options abound in the scientific life. A chemist finds an hypothesis live enough to spend a year in its verification: he believes in it to that extent. But if his experiments prove inconclusive either way, he is quit for his loss of time, no vital harm being done.

It will facilitate our discussion if we keep all these distinctions well in mind.

II

The next matter to consider is the actual psychology of human opinion. When we look at certain facts, it seems as if our passional and volitional nature lay at the root of all our convictions. When we look at others, it seems as if they could do nothing when the intellect had once said its say. Let us take the latter facts up first.

Does it not seem preposterous on the very face of it to talk of our opinions being modifiable at will? Can our will either help or hinder our intellect in its perceptions of truth? Can we, by just willing it, believe that Abraham Lincoln's existence is a myth, and that the portraits of him in *McClure's Magazine* are all of some one else? Can we, by any effort of our will, or by any strength of wish that it were true, believe ourselves well and about when we are roaring with rheumatism in bed, or feel certain that the sum of the two one-dollar bills in our pocket must be a hundred dollars? We can *say* any of these things, but we are absolutely impotent to believe them; and of just such things is the whole fabric of the truths that we do believe in made up—matters of fact, immediate or remote, as Hume said, and relations between ideas, which are either there or not there for us if we see them so, and which if not there cannot be put there by any action of our own.

In Pascal's *Thoughts* [*Pensées*] there is a celebrated passage known in literature as Pascal's wager. In it he tries to force us into Christianity by reasoning as if our concern with truth resembled our concern with the stakes in a game of chance. Translated freely his words are these: You must either believe or not believe that God is—which will you do? Your human reason cannot say. A game is going on between you and the nature of things which at the day of judgment will bring out either heads or tails. Weigh what your gains and your losses would be if you should stake all you have on heads, or God's existence: if you win in such case, you gain eternal beatitude; if you lose, you lose nothing at all. If there were an infinity of chances, and only one for God in this wager, still you ought to stake your all on God; for though you surely risk a finite loss by this procedure, any finite loss is reasonable, even a certain one is reasonable, if there is but the possibility of infinite gain. Go, then, and take holy water, and have masses said; belief will come and stupefy your scruples. . . . Why should you not? At bottom, what have you to lose?

You probably feel that when religious faith expresses itself thus, in the language of the gaming-table, it is put to its last trumps. Surely Pascal's own personal belief in masses and holy water had far other springs; and this celebrated page of his is but an argument for others, a last desperate snatch at a weapon against the hardness of the unbelieving heart. We feel that a faith in masses and holy water adopted wilfully after such a mechanical calculation would lack the inner soul of faith's reality; and if we were ourselves in the place of the Deity, we should probably take particular pleasure in cutting off believers of this pattern from their infinite reward. It is evident that unless there be some pre-existing tendency to believe in masses and holy water, the option offered to the will by Pascal is not a living option. Certainly no Turk ever took to masses and holy water on its account; and even to us Protestants these means of salvation seem such foregone impossibilities that Pascal's logic, invoked for them specifically, leaves us unmoved. As well might the Mahdi write to us, saying, "I am the Expected One whom God has created in his effulgence. You shall be infinitely happy if you confess me; otherwise you shall be cut off from the light of the sun. Weigh, then, your infinite gain if I am genuine against your finite sacrifice if I am not!" His logic would be that of Pascal; but he would vainly use it on us, for the hypothesis he offers us is dead. No tendency to act on it exists in us to any degree.

The talk of believing by our volition seems, then, from one point of view, simply silly. From another point of view it is worse than silly, it is vile. When one turns to the magnificent edifice of the physical sciences, and sees how it was reared; what thousands of disinterested moral lives of men lie buried in its mere foundations; what patience and postponement, what choking down of preference, what submission to the icy laws of outer fact are wrought into its very stones and mortar; how absolutely impersonal it stands in its vast augustness—then how besotted and contemptible seems every little sentimentalist who comes blowing his voluntary smoke-wreaths, and pretending to decide things from out of his private dream! Can we wonder if those bred in the rugged and manly school of science should feel like spewing such subjectivism out of their mouths? The whole system of loyalties which grow up in the schools of science go dead against its toleration; so that it is only natural that those who have caught the scientific fever should pass over to the opposite extreme, and write sometimes as if the incorruptibly truthful intellect ought positively to prefer bitterness and unacceptableness to the heart in its cup.

> It fortifies my soul to know
> That though I perish, Truth is so—

sings Clough, while Huxley exclaims: "My only consolation lies in the reflection that, however bad our posterity may become, so far as they hold by the plain rule of not pretending to believe what they have no reason to believe, because it may be to their advantage so to pretend [the word 'pretend' is surely here redundant], they will not have reached the lowest depth of immorality." And that delicious *enfant terrible* Clifford writes: "Belief is desecrated when given to unproved and unquestioned statements for the solace and private pleasure of the believer. . . . Whoso would deserve well of his fellows in this matter will guard the purity of his belief with a very fanaticism of jealous care, lest at any time it should rest on an unworthy object, and catch a stain which can never be wiped away. . . . If [a] belief has been accepted on insufficient evidence [even though the belief be true, as Clifford on the same page explains] the pleasure is a stolen one. . . . It is sinful because it is stolen in defiance of our duty to mankind. That duty is to guard ourselves from such beliefs as from a pestilence which may shortly master our own body and then spread to the rest of the town. . . . It is wrong always, everywhere, and for every one, to believe anything upon insufficient evidence."

III

All this strikes one as healthy, even when expressed, as by Clifford, with somewhat too much of robustious pathos in the voice. Free will and simple wishing do seem, in the matter of our credences, to be only fifth wheels to the coach. Yet if anyone should thereupon assume that intellectual insight is what remains after wish and will and sentimental preference have taken wing, or that pure reason is what then settles our opinions, he would fly quite as directly in the teeth of the facts.

It is only our already dead hypotheses that our willing nature is unable to bring to life again. But what has made them dead for us is for the most part a previous action of our willing nature of an antagonistic kind. When I say "willing nature," I do not mean only such deliberate volitions as may have set up habits of belief that we cannot now escape from—I mean all such factors of belief as fear and hope, prejudice and passion, imitation and partisanship, the circumpressure of our caste and set. As a matter of fact we find ourselves believing, we hardly know how or why. Mr. Balfour gives the name of "authority" to all those influences, born of the intellectual climate, that make hypotheses possible or impossible for us, alive or dead. Here in this room, we all of us believe in molecules and the conservation of energy, in democracy and necessary progress, in Protestant Christianity and the duty of fighting for "the doctrine of the immortal Monroe," all for no reasons worthy of the name. We see into these matters with no more inner clearness, and probably with much less, than any disbeliever in them might possess. His unconventionality would probably have some grounds to show for its conclusions; but for us, not insight, but the *prestige* of the opinions, is what makes the spark shoot from them and light up our sleeping magazines of faith. Our reason is quite satisfied, in nine hundred and ninety-nine cases out of every thousand of us, if it can find a few arguments that will do to recite in case our credulity is criticized by some one else. Our faith is faith in some one else's faith, and in the greatest matters this is most the case. Our belief in truth itself, for instance, that there is a truth, and that our minds and it are made for each other—what is it but a passionate affirmation of desire, in which our social system backs us up? We want to have a truth; we want to believe that our experiments and studies and discussions must put us in a continually better and better position towards it; and on this line we agree to fight out our thinking lives. But if a Pyrrhonistic sceptic asks us *how we know* all this, can our logic find a reply? No! certainly it cannot. It is just one volition against another—we willing to go in for life upon a trust or assumption which he, for his part, does not care to make.[2]

As a rule we disbelieve all facts and theories for which we have no use. Clifford's cosmic emotions find no use for Christian feelings. Huxley belabors the bishops because there is no use for sacerdotalism in his scheme of life. Newman, on the contrary, goes over to Romanism, and finds all sorts of reasons good for staying there, because a priestly system is for him an organic need and delight. Why do so few "scientists" even look at the evidence for telepathy, so called? Because they think, as a leading biologist, now dead, once said to me, that even if such a thing were true, scientists ought to band together to keep it suppressed and concealed. It would undo the uniformity of Nature and all sorts of other things without which scientists cannot carry on their pursuits. But if this very man had been shown something which as a scientist he might *do* with telepathy, he might not only have examined the evidence, but even have found it good enough. This very law which the logicians would impose upon us—if I may give the name of logicians to those who would rule out our willing nature here—is based on nothing but their own natural wish to exclude all elements for which they, in their professional quality of logicians, can find no use.

Evidently, then, our non-intellectual nature does influence our convictions. There are passional tendencies and volitions which run before and others which come after belief, and it is only the latter that are too late for the fair; and they are not too late when the previous passional work has been already in their own direction. Pascal's argument, instead of being powerless, then seems a regular clincher, and is the last stroke needed to make our faith in masses and holy water complete. The state of things is evidently far from simple; and pure insight and logic, whatever they might do ideally, are not the only things that really do produce our creeds.

IV

Our next duty, having recognized this mixed-up state of affairs, is to ask whether it be simply reprehensible and pathological, or whether, on the contrary, we must treat it as a normal element in making up our minds. The thesis I defend is, briefly stated, this: *Our passional nature not only lawfully may, but must, decide an option between propositions, whenever it is a genuine option that cannot by its nature be decided on intellectual grounds; for to say, under such circumstances, "Do not decide, but leave the question open," is itself a passional decision—just like deciding yes or no—and is attended with the same risk of losing the truth. . . .*

VII

One more point, small but important, and our preliminaries are done. There are two ways of looking at our duty in the matter of opinion—ways entirely different, and yet ways about whose difference the theory of knowledge seems hitherto to have shown very little concern. *We must know the truth;* and *we must avoid error*—these are our first and great commandments as would-be knowers; but they are not two ways of stating an identical commandment, they are two separable laws. Although it may indeed happen that when we believe the truth *A*, we escape as an incidental consequence from believing the falsehood *B*, it hardly ever happens that by merely disbelieving *B* we necessarily believe *A*. We may in escaping *B* fall into believing other falsehoods, *C* or *D*, just as bad as *B*; or we may escape *B* by not believing anything at all, not even *A*.

Believe truth! Shun error!—these, we see, are two materially different laws; and by choosing between them we may end by coloring differently our whole intellectual life. We may regard the chase for truth as paramount, and the avoidance of error as secondary; or we may, on the other hand, treat the avoidance of error as more imperative, and let truth take its chance. Clifford, in the instructive passage which I have quoted, exhorts us to the latter course. Believe nothing, he tells us, keep your mind in suspense forever, rather than by closing it on insufficient evidence incur the awful risk of believing lies. You, on the other hand, may think that the risk of being in error is a very small matter when compared with the blessings of real knowledge, and be ready to be duped many times in your investigation rather than postpone indefinitely the chance of guessing true. I myself find it impossible to go with Clifford. We must remember that these feelings of our duty about either truth or error are in any case only expressions of our passional life. Biologically considered, our minds are as ready to grind out falsehood as veracity, and he who says, "Better go without belief forever than believe a lie!" merely shows his own preponderant private horror of becoming a dupe. He may be critical of many of his desires and fears, but this fear he slavishly obeys. He cannot imagine anyone questioning its binding force. For my own part, I have also a horror of being duped; but I can believe that worse things than being duped may happen to a man in this world: so Clifford's exhortation has to my ears a thoroughly fantastic sound. It is like a general informing his soldiers that it is better to keep out of battle forever than to risk a single wound. Not so are victories either over enemies or over nature gained. Our errors are surely not such awfully solemn things. In a world where we are so certain to incur them in spite of all our caution, a certain lightness of heart seems healthier than this excessive nervousness on their behalf. At any rate, it seems the fittest thing for the empiricist philosopher.

VIII

And now, after all this introduction, let us go straight at our question. I have said, and now repeat it, that not only as a matter of fact do we find our passional nature influencing us in our opinions, but that there are some options between opinions in which this influence must be regarded both as an inevitable and as a lawful determinant of our choice.

I fear here that some of you my hearers will begin to scent danger, and lend an inhospitable ear. Two first steps of passion you have indeed had to admit as necessary—

we must think so as to avoid dupery, and we must think so as to gain truth; but the surest path to those ideal consummations, you will probably consider, is from now onwards to take no further passional step.

Well, of course, I agree as far as the facts will allow. Wherever the option between losing truth and gaining it is not momentous, we can throw the chance of *gaining truth* away, and at any rate save ourselves from any chance of *believing falsehood*, by not making up our minds at all till objective evidence has come. In scientific questions, this is almost always the case; and even in human affairs in general, the need of acting is seldom so urgent that a false belief to act on is better than no belief at all. Law courts, indeed, have to decide on the best evidence attainable for the moment, because a judge's duty is to make law as well as to ascertain it, and (as a learned judge once said to me) few cases are worth spending much time over: the great thing is to have them decided on *any* acceptable principle, and got out of the way. But in our dealings with objective nature we obviously are recorders, not makers, of the truth; and decisions for the mere sake of deciding promptly and getting on to the next business would be wholly out of place. Throughout the breadth of physical nature facts are what they are quite independently of us, and seldom is there any such hurry about them that the risks of being duped by believing a premature theory need be faced. The questions here are always trivial options, the hypotheses are hardly living (at any rate not living for us spectators), the choice between believing truth or falsehood is seldom forced. The attitude of sceptical balance is therefore the absolutely wise one if we would escape mistakes. What difference, indeed, does it make to most of us whether we have or have not a theory of the Rontgen rays, whether we believe or not in mind-stuff, or have a conviction about the causality of conscious states? It makes no difference. Such options are not forced on us. On every account it is better not to make them, but still keep weighing reasons *pro et contra* with an indifferent hand.

I speak, of course, here of the purely judging mind. For purposes of discovery such indifference is to be less highly recommended, and science would be far less advanced than she is if the passionate desires of individuals to get their own faiths confirmed had been kept out of the game. See for example the sagacity which Spencer and Weismann now display. On the other hand, if you want an absolute duffer in an investigation, you must, after all, take the man who has no interest whatever in its results: he is the warranted incapable, the positive fool. The most useful investigator, because the most sensitive observer, is always he whose eager interest in one side of the question is balanced by an equally keen nervousness lest he become deceived.[3] Science has organized this nervousness into a regular *technique*, her so-called method of verification; and she has fallen so deeply in love with the method that one may even say she has ceased to care for truth by itself at all. It is only truth as technically verified that interests her. The truth of truths might come in merely affirmative form, and she would decline to touch it. Such truth as that, she might repeat with Clifford, would be stolen in defiance of her duty to mankind. Human passions, however, are stronger than technical rules. "*Le cœur a ses raisons*," as Pascal says, "*que la raison ne connaît pas*"; and however indifferent to all but the bare rules of the game the umpire, the abstract intellect, may be, the concrete players who furnish him the materials to judge of are usually, each one of them, in love with some pet "live hypothesis" of his own. Let us agree, however, that wherever there is no forced option, the dispassionately judicial intellect with no pet hypothesis, saving us, as it does, from dupery at any rate, ought to be our ideal.

The question next arises: Are there not somewhere forced options in our speculative questions, and can we (as men who may be interested at least as much in positively gaining truth as in merely escaping dupery) always wait with impunity till the coercive evidence shall have arrived? It seems *a priori* improbable that the truth should be so nicely adjusted to our needs and powers as that. In the great boarding-house of nature, the cakes and the butter and the syrup seldom come out so even and leave the plates so clean. Indeed, we should view them with scientific suspicion if they did.

IX

Moral questions immediately present themselves as questions whose solution cannot wait for sensible proof. A moral question is a question not of what sensibly exists, but of what is good, or would be good if it did exist. Science can tell us what exists; but to compare the *worths*, both of what exists and of what does not exist, we must consult not science, but what Pascal calls our heart. Science herself consults her heart when she lays it down that the infinite ascertainment of fact and correction of false belief are the supreme goods for man. Challenge the statement, and science can only repeat it oracularly, or else prove it by showing that such ascertainment and correction bring man all sorts of other goods which man's heart in turn declares. The question of having moral beliefs at all or not having them is decided by our will. Are our moral preferences true or false, or are they only odd biological phenomena, making things good or bad for *us*, but in themselves indifferent? How can your pure intellect decide? If your heart does not *want* a world of moral reality, your head will assuredly never make you believe in one. Mephistophelian scepticism, indeed, will satisfy the head's play-instincts much better than any rigorous idealism can. Some men (even at the student age) are so naturally cool-hearted that the moralistic hypothesis never has for them any pungent life, and in their supercilious presence the hot young moralist always feels strangely ill at ease. The appearance of knowingness is on their side, of *na veté* and gullibility on his. Yet, in the inarticulate heart of him, he clings to it that he is not a dupe, and that there is a realm in which (as Emerson says) all their wit and intellectual superiority is no better than the cunning of a fox. Moral scepticism can no more be refuted or proved by logic than intellectual scepticism can. When we stick to it that there *is* truth (be it of either kind), we do so with our whole nature, and resolve to stand or fall by the results. The sceptic with his whole nature adopts the doubting attitude; but which of us is the wiser, Omniscience only knows.

Turn now from these wide questions of good to a certain class of questions of fact, questions concerning personal relations, states of mind between one man and another. *Do you like me or not?*—for example. Whether you do or not depends, in countless instances, on whether I meet you half-way, am willing to assume that you must like me, and show you trust and expectation. The previous faith on my part in your liking's existence is in such cases what makes your liking come. But if I stand aloof, and refuse to budge an inch until I have objective evidence, until you shall have done something apt, as the absolutists say, *ad extorquendum assensum meum*, ten to one your liking never comes. How many women's hearts are vanquished by the mere sanguine insistence of some man that they *must* love him! he will not consent to the hypothesis that they cannot. The desire for a certain kind of truth here brings about that special truth's existence; and so it is in innumerable cases of other sorts. Who gains promotions, boons, appointments, but the man in whose life they are seen to play the part of live hypotheses, who discounts them, sacrifices other things for their sake before they have come, and takes risks for them in advance? His faith acts on the powers above him as a claim, and creates its own verification.

A social organism of any sort whatever, large or small, is what it is because each member proceeds to his own duty with a trust that the other members will simultaneously do theirs. Wherever a desired result is achieved by the co-operation of many independent persons, its existence as a fact is a pure consequence of the precursive faith in one another of those immediately concerned. A government, an army, a commercial system, a ship, a college, an athletic team, all exist on this condition, without which not only is nothing achieved, but nothing is even attempted. A whole train of passengers (individually brave enough) will be looted by a few highwaymen, simply because the latter can count on one another, while each passenger fears that if he makes a movement of resistance, he will be shot before any one else backs him up. If we believed that the whole car-full would rise at once with us, we should each severally rise, and train-robbing would never even be attempted. There are, then, cases where a fact cannot come at all unless a preliminary faith exists in its coming. *And where faith in a fact can help create the fact*, that would be an insane logic which should say that faith running ahead of scientific evidence is the "lowest kind of immorality" into which a thinking being can fall. Yet such is the logic by which our scientific absolutists pretend to regulate our lives!

X

In truths dependent on our personal action, then, faith based on desire is certainly a lawful and possibly an indispensable thing.

But now, it will be said, these are all childish human cases, and have nothing to do with great cosmical matters, like the question of religious faith. Let us then pass on to that. Religions differ so much in their accidents that in discussing the religious question we must make it very generic and broad. What then do we now mean by the religious hypothesis? Science says things are; morality says some things are better than other things; and religion says essentially two things.

First, she says that the best things are the more eternal things, the overlapping things, the things in the universe that throw the last stone, so to speak, and say the final word. "Perfection is eternal"—this phrase of Charles Secrétan seems a good way of putting this first affirmation of religion, an affirmation which obviously cannot yet be verified scientifically at all.

The second affirmation of religion is that we are better off even now if we believe her first affirmation to be true.

Now, let us consider what the logical elements of this situation are *in case the religious hypothesis in both its branches be really true*. (Of course, we must admit that possibility at the outset. If we are to discuss the question at all, it must involve a living option. If for any of you religion be a hypothesis that cannot, by any living possibility, be true, then you need go no farther. I speak to the "saving remnant" alone.) So proceeding, we see, first, that religion offers itself as a *momentous* option. We are supposed to gain, even now, by our belief, and to lose by our non-belief, a certain vital good. Secondly, religion is a *forced* option, so far as that good goes. We cannot escape the issue by remaining scepti- cal and waiting for more light, because, although we do avoid error in that way *if religion be untrue*, we lose the good, *if it be true*, just as certainly as if we positively chose to dis- believe. It is as if a man should hesitate indefinitely to ask a certain woman to marry him because he was not perfectly sure that she would prove an angel after he brought her home. Would he not cut himself off from that particular angel-possibility as decisively as if he went and married some one else? Scepticism, then, is not avoidance of option; it is option of a certain particular kind of risk. *Better risk loss of truth than chance of error—* that is your faith-vetoer's exact position. He is actively playing his stake as much as the believer is; he is backing the field against the religious hypothesis, just as the believer is backing the religious hypothesis against the field. To preach scepticism to us as a duty until "sufficient evidence" for religion be found, is tantamount therefore to telling us, when in presence of the religious hypothesis, that to yield to our fear of its being error is wiser and better than to yield to our hope that it may be true. It is not intellect against all passions, then; it is only intellect with one passion laying down its law. And by what, forsooth, is the supreme wisdom of this passion warranted? Dupery for dupery, what proof is there that dupery through hope is so much worse than dupery through fear? I, for one, can see no proof; and I simply refuse obedience to the scientist's command to imitate his kind of option, in a case where my own stake is important enough to give me the right to choose my own form of risk. If religion be true and the evidence for it be still insufficient, I do not wish, by putting your extinguisher upon my nature (which feels to me as if it had after all some business in this matter), to forfeit my sole chance in life of getting upon the winning side—that chance depending, of course, on my will- ingness to run the risk of acting as if my passional need of taking the world religiously might be prophetic and right.

All this is on the supposition that it really may be prophetic and right, and that, even to us who are discussing the matter, religion is a live hypothesis which may be true. Now, to most of us religion comes in a still further way that makes a veto on our active faith even more illogical. The more perfect and more eternal aspect of the universe is repre- sented in our religions as having personal form. The universe is no longer a mere *It* to us, but a *Thou*, if we are religious; and any relation that may be possible from person to person might be possible here. For instance, although in one sense we are passive por- tions of the universe, in another we show a curious autonomy, as if we were small active centres on our own account. We feel, too, as if the appeal of religion to us were made to our own active good-will, as if evidence might be forever withheld from us unless we met the hypothesis half-way. To take a trivial illustration: just as a man who in a company of gentlemen made no advances, asked a warrant for every concession, and believed no one's word without proof, would cut himself off by such churlishness from all the social rewards that a more trusting spirit would earn—so here, one who should shut himself up in snarling logicality and try to make the gods extort his recognition willy-nilly, or not get it at all, might cut himself off forever from his only opportu- nity of making the gods' acquaintance. This feeling, forced on us we know not whence, that by obstinately believing that there are gods (although not to do so would be so easy both for our logic and our life) we are doing the universe the deepest service we can, seems part of the living essence of the religious hypothesis. If the hypothesis *were* true in all its parts, including this one, then pure intellectualism, with its veto on our making willing advances, would be an absurdity; and some participation of our sympathetic nature would be logically required. I, therefore, for one, cannot see my way to accepting the agnostic rules for truth-seeking, or wilfully agree to keep my willing nature out of the game. I cannot do so for this plain reason, that *a rule of thinking which would absolutely prevent me from acknowledging certain kinds of truth if those kinds of truth were really there, would be an irrational rule.* That for me is the long and short of the formal logic of the situation, no matter what the kinds of truth might materially be.

I confess I do not see how this logic can be escaped. But sad experience makes me fear that some of you may still shrink from radically saying with me, *in abstracto*, that we have the right to believe at our own risk any hypothesis that is live enough to tempt our will. I suspect, however, that if this is so, it is because you have got away from the abstract logical point of view altogether, and are thinking (perhaps without realizing it) of some particular religious hypothesis which for you is dead. The freedom to "believe what we will" you apply to the case of some patent superstition; and the faith you think of is the faith defined by the schoolboy when he said, "Faith is when you believe something that you know ain't true." I can only repeat that this is misapprehension. *In concreto*, the freedom to believe can only cover living options which the intellect of the individual cannot by itself resolve; and living options never seem absurdities to him who has them to consider. When I look at the religious question as it really puts itself to concrete men, and when I think of all the possibilities which both practically and theoretically it involves, then this command that we shall put a stopper on our heart, instincts, and courage, and *wait*—acting of course meanwhile more or less as if religion were *not* true[4]—till doomsday, or till such time as our intellect and senses working together may have raked in evidence enough—this command, I say, seems to me the queerest idol ever manufactured in the philosophic cave. Were we scholastic absolutists, there might be more excuse. If we had an infallible intellect with its objective certitudes, we might feel ourselves disloyal to such a perfect organ of knowledge in not trusting to it exclusively, in not waiting for its releasing word. But if we are empiricists, if we believe that no bell in us tolls to let us know for certain when truth is in our grasp, then it seems a piece of idle fantasticality to preach so solemnly our duty of waiting for the bell. Indeed we *may* wait if we will—I hope you do not think that I am denying that—but if we do so, we do so at our peril as much as if we believed. In either case we *act*, taking our life in our hands. No one of us ought to issue vetoes to the other, nor should we bandy words of abuse. We ought, on the contrary, delicately and profoundly to respect one another's mental freedom: then only shall we bring about the intellectual republic; then only shall we have that spirit of inner tolerance without which all our outer tolerance is soulless, and which is empiricism's glory; then only shall we live and let live, in speculative as well as in practical things.

. . .[L]et me end by a quotation from [Fitz-James Stephen]. "What do you think of yourself? What do you think of the world? . . . These are questions with which all must deal as it seems good to them. They are riddles of the Sphinx, and in some way or other we must deal with them. . . . In all important transactions of life we have to take a leap in the dark. . . . If we decide to leave the riddles unanswered, that is a choice; if we waver in our answer, that, too, is a choice: but whatever choice we make, we make it at our peril. If a man chooses to turn his back altogether on God and the future, no one can prevent him; no one can show beyond reasonable doubt that he is mistaken. If a man thinks otherwise and acts as he thinks, I do not see that anyone can prove that *he* is mistaken. Each must act as he thinks best; and if he is wrong, so much the worse for him. We stand on a mountain pass in the midst of whirling snow and blinding mist, through which we get glimpses now and then of paths which may be deceptive. If we stand still we shall be frozen to death. If we take the wrong road we shall be dashed to pieces. We do not certainly know whether there is any right one. What must we do? 'Be strong and of a good courage.' Act for the best, hope for the best, and take what comes. . . . If death ends all, we cannot meet death better."[5]

Notes

1   An address to the Philosophical Clubs of Yale and Brown Universities. Published in the *New World*, June, 1896.
2   Compare the admirable page 310 in S. H. Hodgson's *Time and Space*, London, 1865.
3   Compare Wilfrid Ward's Essay, "The Wish to Believe," in his *Witnesses to the Unseen*, Macmillan & Co., 1893.
4   Since belief is measured by action, he who forbids us to believe religion to be true, necessarily also forbids us to act as we should if we did believe it to be true. The whole defence of religious faith hinges upon action. If the action required or inspired by the religious hypothesis is in no way different from that dictated by the naturalistic hypothesis, then religious faith is a pure superfluity, better pruned away, and controversy about its legitimacy is a piece of idle trifling, unworthy of serious minds. I myself believe, of course, that the religious hypothesis gives to the world an expression which specifically determines our reactions, and makes them in a large part unlike what they might be on a purely naturalistic scheme of belief.
5   *Liberty, Equality, Fraternity,* p. 353, 2d edition. London, 1874.

Questions for reflection

1   What is a genuine option, and how is it an important element of James's argument?
2   Why is it sometimes rational, or justified, according to James, to hold religious beliefs even given a lack of evidence? Is this a legitimate move? Explain.
3   How is James's position not merely wishful thinking? Or is it?
4   Do you think James is denying a role for reason and evidence in religious belief? Why or why not?
5   Compare and contrast James's position with Clifford's position. Which one do you find most reasonable? Why?

Further reading

Graham Bird (1987) *William James*. London: Routledge & Kegan Paul. (An accessible introduction to James's thought; this work is in the Arguments of the Philosophers series.)
William James ([1879–1907] 1948) *Essays in Pragmatism*. Ed. Alburey Castell. New York: Hafner Press. (Important essays by James as well as a helpful introduction to his work; the selection above was taken from this book.)
William James (1902/1961) *The Varieties of Religious Experience*. New York: Collier Books; repr. London: Collier Macmillan Publishers. (An analysis of various types of religious experience, primarily Christian.)

Ruth Anna Putnam, ed. (1997) *The Cambridge Companion to William James*. Cambridge: Cambridge University Press. (Cutting-edge essays on various aspects of James's thought by leading scholars; includes an extensive bibliography.)

Richard Swinburne (1984) *Faith and Reason*. Oxford: Oxford University Press. (In this third volume of his trilogy on philosophical theology, Swinburne argues that religious faith requires total commitment but does not require fully convinced belief.)

Chapter 34

Alvin Plantinga

BELIEF IN GOD AS PROPERLY BASIC

Alvin Plantinga is John A. O'Brien Professor of Philosophy at the University of Notre Dame. He is one of the leading proponents of a fairly recent movement in philosophy of religion referred to as "Reformed" epistemology (so-named because of its adherents' sympathies with certain religious ideas of the Reformed branch of Protestant Christianity). According to Reformed epistemologists, (propositional) evidence or argument isn't needed for rational or justified belief in God.

    In this essay, Professor Plantinga challenges the "evidentialist objection" that belief in God is unreasonable since there is insufficient evidence for it. He argues that the objection is rooted in a faulty epistemology—one which demands that properly basic beliefs are self-evident, or incorrigible (i.e., beliefs which cannot be corrected by evidence), or evident to the senses. This "classical foundationalist" position cannot satisfy its *own* criterion since *it* is not self-evident, or incorrigible, or evident to the senses. So, the evidentialist criticism that belief in God is not properly basic, based on these conditions, is fundamentally flawed. Contrary to the classical foundationalist, none of these conditions is necessary for proper basicality. Furthermore, belief in God *is* properly basic, Plantinga argues; it need not be based on further beliefs.

Many philosophers have urged the *evidentialist* objection to theistic belief; they have argued that belief in God is irrational or unreasonable or not rationally acceptable or intellectually irresponsible or noetically substandard, because, as they say, there is insufficient evidence for it.[1] Many other philosophers and theologians—in particular, those in the great tradition of natural theology—have claimed that belief in God is intellectually acceptable, but only because the fact is there is sufficient evidence for it. These two groups unite in holding that theistic belief is rationally acceptable only if there is sufficient evidence for it. More exactly, they hold that a person is rational or reasonable in accepting theistic belief only if she has sufficient evidence for it—only if, that is, she knows or rationally believes some *other* propositions which support the one in question, and believes the latter on the basis of the former. In [4] I argued that the evidentialist objection is rooted in *classical foundationalism*, an enormously popular picture or total way of looking at faith, knowledge, justified belief, rationality and allied topics. This picture has been widely accepted ever since the days of Plato and Aristotle; its near relatives, perhaps, remain the dominant ways of thinking about these topics. We may think of the classical foundationalist as beginning with the observation that some of one's beliefs may be *based upon* others; it may be that there are a pair of propositions A and B such that I believe A *on the basis of B*. Although this relation isn't easy to characterize in a revealing and non-trivial fashion, it is nonetheless familiar. I believe that the word 'umbrageous' is spelled u-m-b-r-a-g-e-o-u-s: this belief is based on another belief of mine: the belief that that's how the dictionary says it's spelled. I believe that $72 \times 71 = 5112$. This belief is based upon several other beliefs I hold: that $1 \times 72 = 72$; $7 \times 2 = 14$; $7 \times 7 = 49$; $49 + 1 = 50$; and others. Some of my beliefs, however, I accept but don't accept on the basis of any other beliefs. Call these beliefs *basic*. I believe that $2 + 1 = 3$, for example, and don't believe it on the basis of other propositions. I also believe that I am seated at my desk, and that there is a mild pain in my right knee. These too are basic to me; I don't believe them on the basis of any other propositions. According to the classical foundationalist, some propositions are *properly* or *rightly* basic for a person and some are not. Those that are not, are rationally accepted only on the basis of *evidence*, where the evidence must trace back, ultimately, to what is properly basic. The existence of God, furthermore, is not among the propositions that are properly basic; hence a person is rational in accepting theistic belief only if he has evidence for it.

Now many Reformed thinkers and theologians[2] have rejected *natural theology* (thought of as the attempt to provide proofs or arguments for the existence of God). They have held not merely that the proffered arguments are unsuccessful, but that the whole enterprise is in some way radically misguided. In [5], I argue that the reformed rejection of natural theology is best construed as an inchoate and unfocused rejection of classical foundationalism. What these Reformed thinkers really mean to hold, I think, is that belief in God need not be based on argument or evidence from other propositions at all. They mean to hold that the believer is entirely within his intellectual rights in believing as he does even if he doesn't know of any good theistic argument (deductive or inductive), even if he doesn't believe that there is any such argument, and even if in fact no such argument exists. They hold that it is perfectly rational to accept belief in God without accepting it on the basis of any other beliefs or propositions at all. In a word, they hold that *belief in God is properly basic*. In this paper I shall try to develop and defend this position.

But first we must achieve a deeper understanding of the evidentialist objection. It is important to see that this contention is a *normative* contention. The evidentialist objector holds that one who accepts theistic belief is in some way irrational or noetically substandard. Here 'rational' and 'irrational' are to be taken as normative or evaluative terms; according to the objector, the theist fails to measure up to a standard he ought to conform to. There is a right way and a wrong way with respect to belief as with respect to actions; we have duties, responsibilities, obligations with respect to the former just as with respect to the latter. So Professor Blanshard:

> . . . everywhere and always belief has an ethical aspect. There is such a thing
> as a general ethics of the intellect. The main principle of that ethic I hold to

be the same inside and outside religion. This principle is simple and sweeping: Equate your assent to the evidence. [1] p. 401.

This "ethics of the intellect" can be construed variously; many fascinating issues—issues we must here forebear to enter—arise when we try to state more exactly the various options the evidentialist may mean to adopt. Initially it looks as if he holds that there is a duty or obligation of some sort not to accept without evidence such propositions as that God exists—a duty flouted by the theist who has no evidence. If he has no evidence, then it is his duty to cease believing. But there is an oft remarked difficulty: one's beliefs, for the most part, are not directly under one's control. Most of those who believe in God could not divest themselves of that belief just by trying to do so, just as they could not in that way rid themselves of the belief that the world has existed for a very long time. So perhaps the relevant obligation is not that of divesting myself of theistic belief if I have no evidence, (that is beyond my power) but to try to cultivate the sorts of intellectual habits that will tend (we hope) to issue in my accepting as basic only propositions that are properly basic.

Perhaps this obligation is to be thought of *teleologically*: it is a moral obligation arising out of a connection between certain intrinsic goods and evils and the way in which our beliefs are formed and held. (This seems to be W. K. Clifford's way of construing the matter.) Perhaps it is to be thought of *aretetically*: there are valuable noetic or intellectual states (whether intrinsically or extrinsically valuable); there are also corresponding intellectual virtues, habits of acting so as to promote and enhance those valuable states. Among one's obligations, then, is the duty to try to foster and cultivate these virtues in oneself or others. Or perhaps it is to be thought of *deontologically*: this obligation attaches to us just by virtue of our having the sort of noetic equipment human beings do in fact display; it does not arise out of a connection with valuable states of affairs. Such an obligation, furthermore, could be a special sort of moral obligation; on the other hand, perhaps it is a *sui generis* non-moral obligation.

Still further, perhaps the evidentialist need not speak of duty or obligation here at all. Consider someone who believes that Venus is smaller than Mercury, not because he has evidence of any sort, but because he finds it amusing to hold a belief no one else does—or consider someone who holds this belief on the basis of some outrageously bad argument. Perhaps there isn't any obligation he has failed to meet. Nevertheless his intellectual condition is deficient in some way; or perhaps alternatively there is a commonly achieved excellence he fails to display. And the evidentialist objection to theistic belief, then, might be understood, as the claim, not that the theist without evidence has failed to meet an obligation, but that he suffers from a certain sort of intellectual deficiency (so that the proper attitude toward him would be sympathy rather than censure).

These are some of the ways, then, in which the evidentialist objection could be developed; and of course there are still other possibilities. For ease of exposition, let us take the claim deontologically; what I shall say will apply *mutatis mutandis* if we take it one of the other ways. The evidentialist objection, therefore, presupposes some view as to what sorts of propositions are correctly, or rightly, or justifiably taken as basic; it presupposes a view as to what is *properly* basic. And the minimally relevant claim for the evidentialist objector is that belief in God is *not* properly basic. Typically this objection has been rooted in some form of *classical foundationalism*, according to which a proposition p is properly basic for a person S if and only if p is either self-evident or incorrigible for S (modern foundationalism) or either self-evident or 'evident to the senses' for S (ancient and medieval foundationalism). In [4] I argued that both forms of foundationalism are self referentially incoherent and must therefore be rejected.

Insofar as the evidentialist objection is rooted in classical foundationalism, it is poorly rooted indeed: and so far as I know, no one has developed and articulated any other reason for supposing that belief in God is not properly basic. Of course it doesn't follow that it *is* properly basic; perhaps the class of properly basic propositions is broader than classical foundationalists think, but still not broad enough to admit belief in God. But why think so? What might be the objections to the Reformed view that belief in God is properly basic?

I've heard it argued that if I have no evidence for the existence of God, then if I accept that proposition, my belief will be groundless, or gratuitous, or arbitrary. I think this is an error; let me explain.

Suppose we consider perceptual beliefs, memory beliefs, and beliefs which ascribe mental states to other persons: such beliefs as

(1) I see a tree,
(2) I had breakfast this morning,

and

(3) That person is angry.

Although beliefs of this sort are typically and properly taken as basic, it would be a mistake to describe them as *groundless*. Upon having experience of a certain sort, I believe that I am perceiving a tree. In the typical case I do not hold this belief on the basis of other beliefs; it is nonetheless not groundless. My having that characteristic sort of experience—to use Professor Chisholm's language, my being appeared treely to—plays a crucial role in the formation and justification of that belief. We might say this experience, together, perhaps, with other circumstances, is what *justifies* me in holding it; this is the *ground* of my justification, and, by extension, the ground of the belief itself.

If I see someone displaying typical pain behavior, I take it that he or she is in pain. Again, I don't take the displayed behavior as *evidence* for that belief; I don't infer that belief from others I hold; I don't accept it on the basis of other beliefs. Still, my perceiving the pain behavior plays a unique role in the formation and justification of that belief; as in the previous case, it forms the ground of my justification for the belief in question. The same holds for memory beliefs. I seem to remember having breakfast this morning; that is, I have an inclination to believe the proposition that I had breakfast, along with a certain past-tinged experience that is familiar to all but hard to describe. Perhaps we should say that I am appeared to pastly; but perhaps this insufficiently distinguishes the experience in question from that accompanying beliefs about the past not grounded in my own memory. The phenomenology of memory is a rich and unexplored realm; here I have no time to explore it. In this case as in the others, however, there is a justifying circumstance present, a condition that forms the ground of my justification for accepting the memory belief in question.

In each of these cases, a belief is taken as basic, and in each case properly taken as basic. In each case there is some circumstance or condition that confers justification; there is a circumstance that serves as the *ground* of justification. So in each case there will be some true proposition of the sort

(4) In condition *C*, *S* is justified in taking *p* as basic.

Of course *C* will vary with *p*. For a perceptual judgment such as

(5) I see a rose colored wall before me,

C will include my being appeared to in a certain fashion. No doubt *C* will include more. If I'm appeared to in the familiar fashion but know that I'm wearing rose colored glasses, or that I am suffering from a disease that causes me to be thus appeared to, no matter what the color of the nearby objects, then I'm not justified in taking (5) as basic. Similarly for memory. Suppose I know that my memory is unreliable; it often plays me tricks. In particular, when I seem to remember having breakfast, then, more often than not, I *haven't* had breakfast. Under these conditions I am not justified in taking it as basic that I had breakfast, even though I seem to remember that I did.

So being appropriately appeared to, in the perceptual case, is not sufficient for justification; some further condition—a condition hard to state in detail—is clearly necessary. The central point, here, however, is that a belief is properly basic only in certain conditions; these conditions are, we might say, the ground of its justification and, by extension, the ground of the belief itself. In this sense, basic beliefs are not, or are not necessarily, *groundless* beliefs.

Now similar things may be said about belief in God. When the Reformers claim that this belief is properly basic, they do not mean to say, of course, that there are no justifying circumstances for it, or that it is in that sense groundless or gratuitous. Quite the contrary. Calvin holds that God "reveals and daily discloses himself to the whole workmanship of the universe," and the divine art "reveals itself in the innumerable and yet distinct and well ordered variety of the heavenly host." God has so created us that we have a tendency or disposition to see his hand in the world about us. More precisely, there is in us a disposition to believe propositions of the sort *this flower was created by God* or *this vast and intricate universe was created by God* when we contemplate the flower or behold the starry heavens or think about the vast reaches of the universe.

Calvin recognizes, at least implicitly, that other sorts of conditions may trigger this disposition. Upon reading the Bible, one may be impressed with a deep sense that God is speaking to him. Upon having done what I know is cheap, or wrong, or wicked I may feel guilty in God's sight and form the belief *God disapproves of what I've done*. Upon confession and repentance, I may feel forgiven, forming the belief *God forgives me for what I've done*. A person in grave danger may turn to God, asking for his protection and help; and of course he or she then forms the belief that God is indeed able to hear and help if he sees fit. When life is sweet and satisfying, a spontaneous sense of gratitude may well up within the soul; someone in this condition may thank and praise the Lord for his goodness, and will of course form the accompanying belief that indeed the Lord is to be thanked and praised.

There are therefore many conditions and circumstances that call forth belief in God: guilt, gratitude, danger, a sense of God's presence, a sense that he speaks, perception of various parts of the universe. A complete job would explore the phenomenology of all these conditions and of more besides. This is a large and important topic; but here I can only point to the existence of these conditions.

Of course none of the beliefs I mentioned a moment ago is the simple belief that God exists. What we have instead are such beliefs as

(6) God is speaking to me,
(7) God has created all this,
(8) God disapproves of what I have done,
(9) God forgives me,

and

(10) God is to be thanked and praised.

These propositions are properly basic in the right circumstances. But it is quite consistent with this to suppose that the proposition *there is such a person as God* is neither properly basic nor taken as basic by those who believe in God. Perhaps what they take as basic are such propositions as (6)-(10), believing in the existence of God on the basis of propositions such as those. From this point of view, it isn't exactly right to say that it is belief in God that is properly basic; more exactly, what are properly basic are such propositions as (6)-(10), each of which self-evidently entails that God exists. It isn't the relatively high level and general proposition *God exists* that is properly basic, but instead propositions detailing some of his attributes or actions.

Suppose we return to the analogy between belief in God and belief in the existence of perceptual objects, other persons, and the past. Here too it is relatively specific and concrete propositions rather than their more general and abstract colleagues that are properly basic. Perhaps such items are

(11) There are trees,
(12) There are other persons,

and

(13) The world has existed for more than 5 minutes,

are not in fact properly basic; it is instead such propositions as

(14) I see a tree,
(15) That person is pleased,

and

(16) I had breakfast more than an hour ago,

that deserve that accolade. Of course propositions of the latter sort immediately and self-evidently entail propositions of the former sort; and perhaps there is thus no harm in speaking of the former as properly basic, even though so to speak is to speak a bit loosely.

The same must be said about belief in God. We may say, speaking loosely, that belief in God is properly basic; strictly speaking, however, it is probably not that proposition but such propositions as (6)-(10) that enjoy that status. But the main point, here, is that belief in God or (6)-(10), are properly basic; to say so, however, is not to deny that there are justifying conditions for these beliefs, or conditions that confer justification on one who accepts them as basic. They are therefore not groundless or gratuitous.

A second objection I've often heard: if belief in God is properly basic, why can't *just any* belief be properly basic? Couldn't we say the same for any bizarre aberration we can think of? What about voodoo or astrology? What about the belief that the Great Pumpkin returns every Halloween? Could I properly take *that* as basic? And if I can't, why can I properly take belief in God as basic? Suppose I believe that if I flap my arms with sufficient vigor, I can take off and fly about the room; could I defend myself against the charge of irrationality by claiming this belief is basic? If we say that belief in God is properly basic, won't we be committed to holding that just anything, or nearly anything, can properly be taken as basic, thus throwing wide the gates to irrationalism and superstition?

Certainly not. What might lead one to think the Reformed epistemologist is in this kind of trouble? The fact that he rejects the criteria for proper basicality purveyed by classical foundationalism? But why should *that* be thought to commit him to such tolerance of irrationality? Consider an analogy. In the palmy days of positivism, the positivists went about confidently wielding their verifiability criterion and declaring meaningless much that was obviously meaningful. Now suppose someone rejected a formulation of that criterion—the one to be found in the second edition of A. J. Ayer's *Language, Truth and Logic*, for example. Would that mean she was committed to holding that

(17) Twas brillig; and the slithy toves did gyre and gymble in the wabe

contrary to appearances, makes good sense? Of course not. But then the same goes for the Reformed epistemologist; the fact that he rejects the Classical Foundationalist's criterion of proper basicality does not mean that he is committed to supposing just anything is properly basic.

But what then is the problem? Is it that the Reformed epistemologist not only rejects those criteria for proper basicality, but seems in no hurry to produce what he takes to be a better substitute? If he has no such criterion, how can he fairly reject belief in the Great Pumpkin as properly basic?

This objection betrays an important misconception. How do we rightly arrive at or develop criteria for meaningfulness, or justified belief, or proper basicality? Where do they come from? Must one have such a criterion before one can sensibly make any judgments—positive or negative—about proper basicality? Surely not. Suppose I don't know of a satisfactory substitute for the criteria proposed by classical foundationalism; I am nevertheless entirely within my rights in holding that certain propositions are not properly basic in certain conditions. Some propositions seem self-evident when in fact they are not; that is the lesson of some of the Russell paradoxes. Nevertheless it would be irrational to take as basic the denial of a proposition that seems self-evident to you. Similarly, suppose it seems to you that you see a tree; you would then be irrational in taking as basic the proposition that you don't see a tree, or that there aren't any trees.

In the same way, even if I don't know of some illuminating criterion of meaning, I can quite properly declare (17) meaningless.

And this raises an important question—one Roderick Chisholm has taught us to ask. What is the status of criteria for knowledge, or proper basicality, or justified belief? Typically, these are universal statements. The modern foundationalist's criterion for proper basicality, for example, is doubly universal:

(18) For any proposition A and person S, A is properly basic for S if and only if A is incorrigible for S or self-evident to S.

But how could one know a thing like that? What are its credentials? Clearly enough, (18) isn't self-evident or just obviously true. But if it isn't, how does one arrive at it? What sorts of arguments would be appropriate? Of course a foundationalist might find (18) so appealing, he simply takes it to be true, neither offering argument for it, nor accepting it on the basis of other things he believes. If he does so, however, his noetic structure will be self-referentially incoherent. (18) itself is neither self-evident nor incorrigible; hence in accepting (18) as basic, the modern foundationalist violates the condition of proper basicality he himself lays down in accepting it. On the other hand, perhaps the foundationalist will try to produce some argument for it from premises that are self-evident or incorrigible: it is exceedingly hard to see, however, what such an argument might be like. And until he has produced such arguments, what shall the rest of us do—we who do not find (18) at all obvious or compelling? How could he use (18) to show us that belief in God, for example, is not properly basic? Why should we believe (18), or pay it any attention?

The fact is, I think, that neither (18) nor any other revealing necessary and sufficient condition for proper basicality follows from clearly self-evident premises by clearly acceptable arguments. And hence the proper way to arrive at such a criterion is, broadly speaking, *inductive*. We must assemble examples of beliefs and conditions such that the former are obviously properly basic in the latter, and examples of beliefs and conditions such that the former are obviously *not* properly basic in the latter. We must then frame hypotheses as to the necessary and sufficient conditions of proper basicality and test these hypotheses by reference to those examples. Under the right conditions, for example, it is clearly rational to believe that you see a human person before you: a being who has thoughts and feelings, who knows and believes things, who makes decisions and acts. It is clear, furthermore, that you are under no obligation to reason to this belief from others you hold; under those conditions that belief is properly basic for you. But then (18) must be mistaken; the belief in question, under those circumstances, is properly basic, though neither self-evident nor incorrigible for you. Similarly, you may seem to remember that you had breakfast this morning, and perhaps you know of no reason to suppose your memory is playing you tricks. If so, you are entirely justified in taking that belief as basic. Of course it isn't properly basic on the criteria offered by classical foundationalists; but that fact counts not against you but against those criteria.

Accordingly, criteria for proper basicality must be reached from below rather than above; they should not be presented as *ex Cathedra*, but argued to and tested by a relevant set of examples. But there is no reason to assume, in advance, that everyone will agree on the examples. The Christian will of course suppose that belief in God is entirely proper and rational; if he doesn't accept this belief on the basis of other propositions, he will conclude that it is basic for him and quite properly so. Followers of Bertrand Russell and Madelyn Murray O'Hare may disagree, but how is that relevant? Must my criteria, or those of the Christian community, conform to their examples? Surely not. The Christian community is responsible to *its* set of examples, not to theirs.

Accordingly, the Reformed epistemologist can properly hold that belief in the Great Pumpkin is not properly basic, even though he holds that belief in God is properly basic and even if he has no full fledged criterion of proper basicality. Of course he is committed to supposing that there is a relevant *difference* between belief in God and belief in the Great Pumpkin, if he holds that the former but not the latter is properly basic. But this should prove no great embarrassment; there are plenty of candidates. These candidates are to be found in the neighborhood of the conditions I mentioned in the last section that justify and ground belief in God. Thus, for example, the Reformed epistemologist may concur with Calvin in holding that God has implanted in us a natural tendency to see his hand in the world around us; the same cannot be said for the Great Pumpkin, there being no Great Pumpkin and no natural tendency to accept beliefs about the Great Pumpkin.

By way of conclusion then: being self-evident, or incorrigible, or evident to the senses is not a necessary condition of proper basicality. Furthermore, one who holds that belief in God *is* properly basic is not thereby committed to the idea that belief in God is groundless or gratuitous or without justifying circumstances. And even if he lacks a general criterion of proper basicality, he is not obliged to suppose that just any or nearly any belief—belief in the Great Pumpkin, for example—is properly basic. Like everyone should, he begins with examples; and he may take belief in the Great Pumpkin as a paradigm of irrational basic belief.

Notes

1   See, for example [1], pp. 400ff, [2], pp. 345 ff, [3], p. 22, [6], pp. 3ff. and [7], pp. 87 ff. In [4] I consider and reject the evidentialist objection to theistic belief.
2   A Reformed thinker or theologian is one whose intellectual sympathies lie with the Protestant tradition going back to John Calvin (not someone who was formerly a theologian and has since seen the light).

References

[1]   Blanshard, Brand, *Reason and Belief* (London: Allen & Unwin, 1974).
[2]   Clifford, W. K., "The Ethics of Belief" in *Lectures and Essays* (London: Macmillan, 1879).
[3]   Flew, A. G. N., *The Presumption of Atheism* (London: Pemberton Publishing Co., 1976).
[4]   Plantinga, A., "Is Belief in God Rational?" in *Rationality and Religious Belief*, ed. C. Delaney (Notre Dame: University of Notre Dame Press, 1979).
[5]   ——, "The Reformed Objection to Natural Theology," *Proceedings of the American Catholic Philosophical Association*, 1980.
[6]   Russell, Bertrand, "Why I am not a Christian," in *Why I am Not a Christian* (New York: Simon & Schuster, 1957).
[7]   Scrivin, Michael, *Primary Philosophy* (New York: McGraw-Hill, 1966).

Questions for reflection

1   What is Professor Plantinga's main objection to classical foundationalism? Do you agree with it? Why or why not?
2   Plantinga argues that even if there is no evidence for the existence of God, the belief that God exists need not be groundless, or gratuitous, or arbitrary. What are his reasons for saying this?
3   Do you think belief in God is properly basic? State your reasons for your position.
4   What are some intellectual habits that might cultivate one's accepting as basic only propositions that are, in fact, properly basic?
5   Is there a place for natural theology (i.e., the attempt to give reasons for the existence of God based on knowledge of the natural world) in Reformed epistemology? What role might arguments and evidence play here, if any?

Further reading

R. Douglas Geivett and Brendan Sweetman, eds. (1992) *Contemporary Perspectives on Religious Epistemology*. Oxford: Oxford University Press. (A superb collection of essays on religious epistemology from a wide variety of perspectives.)

Dewey Hoitenga (1991) *From Plato to Plantinga: An Introduction to Reformed Epistemology*. Albany, NY: State University of New York Press. (An accessible introduction to the topic; attempts to show that certain Reformed intuitions run throughout intellectual history.)

Alvin Plantinga and Nicholas Wolterstorff, eds. (1984) *Faith & Rationality: Reason & Belief in God*. Notre Dame, IN: University of Notre Dame Press. (A collection of important essays in Reformed epistemology by several prominent philosophers.)

Alvin Plantinga (1993) *Warrant: The Current Debate*. Oxford: Oxford University Press. (The first of Plantinga's "Warrant" trilogy in which he examines the nature of epistemic warrant; here he offers a survey of the various positions.)

Alvin Plantinga (1993) *Warrant and Proper Function*. Oxford: Oxford University Press. (The second of Plantinga's "Warrant" trilogy; in this work he argues that fundamental to epistemic warrant is the proper functioning of one's cognitive faculties in the appropriate environment.)

Alvin Plantinga (2000) *Warranted Christian Belief*. Oxford: Oxford University Press. (The third volume in Plantinga's "Warrant" trilogy; this one examines the role of warrant in theistic belief.)

Chapter 35

Blaise Pascal

THE WAGER

Blaise Pascal (1623–62) was a renowned French mathematician, physicist, and philoso-pher. After a mystical experience in 1654, he devoted his time and energy to philosophy and theology. While Pascal did not believe that God's existence could be proven through rational argument, he did maintain that belief in God can be a prudential move. Based on a type of early decision theory and probability theory, Pascal argues in the following famous selection that believing in the Christian God is a better bet than not believing. The wager can be put simply as follows. There are a limited number of options concerning belief in God: (1) Belief in God and he does exist; (2) Belief in God and he does not exist; (3) Disbelief in God and he does exist; (4) Disbelief in God and he does not exist. If we choose to believe in God and he does exist, we have an infinite gain. If we choose to believe in God and he does not exist, we have not lost much (if anything). If we choose to disbelieve in God and he does exist, we have an infinite loss. If we choose to disbelieve in God and he does not exist, we neither gain nor lose much (if anything). So, Pascal maintains, the best gamble is for belief in God.

Infinity – nothing. Our soul is cast into the body where it finds number, time, dimensions; it reasons about these things and calls them natural, or necessary, and can believe nothing else.

Unity added to infinity does not increase it at all, any more than a foot added to an infinite measurement: the finite is annihilated in the presence of the infinite and becomes pure nothingness. So it is with our mind before God, with our justice before divine jus-tice. There is not so great a disproportion between our justice and God's as between unity and infinity.

God's justice must be as vast as his mercy. Now his justice towards the damned is less vast and ought to be less startling to us than his mercy towards the elect.

We know that the infinite exists without knowing its nature, just as we know that it is untrue that numbers are finite. Thus it is true that there is an infinite number, but we do not know what it is. It is untrue that it is even, untrue that it is odd, for by adding a unit it does not change its nature. Yet it is a number, and every number is even or odd. (It is true that this applies to every finite number.)

Therefore we may well know that God exists without knowing what he is.

Is there no substantial truth, seeing that there are so many true things which are not truth itself?

Thus we know the existence and nature of the finite because we too are finite and extended in space.

We know the existence of the infinite without knowing its nature, because it too has extension but unlike us no limits.

But we do not know either the existence or the nature of God, because he has neither extension nor limits.

But by faith we know his existence, through glory we shall know his nature.

Now I have already proved that it is quite possible to know that something exists without knowing its nature.

Let us now speak according to our natural lights.

If there is a God, he is infinitely beyond our comprehension, since, being indivisible and without limits, he bears no relation to us. We are therefore incapable of knowing either what he is or whether he is. That being so, who would dare to attempt an answer to the question? Certainly not we, who bear no relation to him.

Who then will condemn Christians for being unable to give rational grounds for their belief, professing as they do a religion for which they cannot give rational grounds? They declare that it is a folly, *stultitiam*,[1] in expounding it to the world, and then you complain that they do not prove it. If they did prove it they would not be keeping their word. It is by being without proof that they show they are not without sense. 'Yes, but although that excuses those who offer their religion as such, and absolves them from the criticism of producing it without rational grounds, it does not absolve those who accept it.' Let us then examine this point, and let us say: 'Either God is or he is not.' But to which view shall we be inclined? Reason cannot decide this question. Infinite chaos separates us. At the far end of this infinite distance a coin is being spun which will come down heads or tails. How will you wager? Reason cannot make you choose either, reason cannot prove either wrong.

Do not then condemn as wrong those who have made a choice, for you know nothing about it. 'No, but I will condemn them not for having made this particular choice, but any choice, for, although the one who calls heads and the other one are equally at fault, the fact is that they are both at fault: the right thing is not to wager at all.'[2]

Yes, but you must wager. There is no choice, you are already committed. Which will you choose then? Let us see: since a choice must be made, let us see which offers you the least interest. You have two things to lose: the true and the good; and two things to stake: your reason and your will, your knowledge and your happiness; and your nature has two things to avoid: error and wretchedness. Since you must necessarily choose, your reason is no more affronted by choosing one rather than the other. That is one point cleared up. But your happiness? Let us weigh up the gain and the loss involved in calling heads that God exists. Let us assess the two cases: if you win you win everything, if you lose you lose nothing. Do not hesitate then; wager that he does exist. 'That is wonderful. Yes, I must wager, but perhaps I am wagering too much.' Let us see: since there is an equal chance of gain and loss, if you stood to win only two lives for one you could still wager, but supposing you stood to win three?

You would have to play (since you must necessarily play) and it would be unwise of you, once you are obliged to play, not to risk your life in order to win three lives at a game in which there is an equal chance of losing and winning. But there is an eternity of life and happiness. That being so, even though there were an infinite number of chances, of which only one were in your favour, you would still be right to wager one in order to win two; and you would be acting wrongly, being obliged to play, in refusing to stake one life against three in a game, where out of an infinite number of chances there is one in your favour, if there were an infinity of infinitely happy life to be won. But here there is an infinity of infinitely happy life to be won, one chance of winning against a finite number of chances of losing, and what you are staking is finite. That leaves no choice; wherever there is infinity, and where there are not infinite chances of losing against that of winning, there is no room for hesitation, you must give everything. And thus, since you are obliged to play, you must be renouncing reason if you hoard your life rather than risk it for an infinite gain, just as likely to occur as a loss amounting to nothing.

For it is no good saying that it is uncertain whether you will win, that it is certain that you are taking a risk, and that the infinite distance between the certainty of what you are risking and the uncertainty of what you may gain makes the finite good you are certainly risking equal to the infinite good that you are not certain to gain. This is not the case. Every gambler takes a certain risk for an uncertain gain, and yet he is taking a certain finite risk for an uncertain finite gain without sinning against reason. Here there is no infinite distance between the certain risk and the uncertain gain: that is not true. There is, indeed, an infinite distance between the certainty of winning and the certainty of losing, but the proportion between the uncertainty of winning and the certainty of what is being risked is in proportion to the chances of winning or losing. And hence if there are as many chances on one side as on the other you are playing for even odds. And in that case the certainty of what you are risking is equal to the uncertainty of what you may win; it is by no means infinitely distant from it. Thus our argument carries infinite weight, when the stakes are finite in a game where there are even chances of winning and losing and an infinite prize to be won.

This is conclusive and if men are capable of any truth this is it.

'I confess, I admit it, but is there really no way of seeing what the cards are?' — 'Yes. Scripture and the rest, etc.' — 'Yes, but my hands are tied and my lips are sealed; I am being forced to wager and I am not free; I am being held fast and I am so made that I cannot believe. What do you want me to do then?' — 'That is true, but at least get it into your head that, if you are unable to believe, it is because of your passions, since reason impels you to believe and yet you cannot do so. Concentrate then not on convincing yourself by multiplying proofs of God's existence but by diminishing your passions. You want to find faith and you do not know the road. You want to be cured of unbelief and you ask for the remedy: learn from those who were once bound like you and who now wager all they have. These are people who know the road you wish to follow, who have been cured of the affliction of which you wish to be cured: follow the way by which they began. They behaved just as if they did believe, taking holy water, having masses said, and so on. That will make you believe quite naturally, and will make you more docile.'[3] — 'But that is what I am afraid of.' — 'But why? What have you to lose? But to show you that this is the way, the fact is that this diminishes the passions which are your great obstacles. . .'

End of this address

'Now what harm will come to you from choosing this course? You will be faithful, honest, humble, grateful, full of good works, a sincere, true friend. . . It is true you will not enjoy noxious pleasures, glory and good living, but will you not have others?

'I tell you that you will gain even in this life, and that at every step you take along this road you will see that your gain is so certain and your risk so negligible that in the end you will realize that you have wagered on something certain and infinite for which you have paid nothing.'

'How these words fill me with rapture and delight! —'

'If my words please you and seem cogent, you must know that they come from a man who went down upon his knees before and after to pray this infinite and indivisible being, to whom he submits his own, that he might bring your being also to submit to him for your own good and for his glory: and that strength might thus be reconciled with lowliness.'

Notes

1   Cf. I. Cor. 1. 18.
2   The word Pascal uses for 'heads' is '*croix*' (nowadays '*face*'), thus relating the gambler's call to the folly of the Cross just quoted.
3   *abêtira.* That is, the unbeliever will act unthinkingly and mechanically, and in this become more like the beasts, from whom man was differentiated, according to contemporary philosophy, by his faculty of reason.

Questions for reflection

1   What is Pascal's wager, in your own words? Do you find it convincing?
2   Do you think it is possible for a person to choose to believe or disbelieve in God at will? Explain your answer.
3   Do you think coming to believe in God through a gamble of this sort is an appropriate way to attain such belief? Why or why not?
4   Given the different world religions, which God/Ultimate Reality should one bet on based on Pascal's wager? Why?
5   What is faith? Is it important?

Further reading

Blaise Pascal ([1670] 1995) *Pensées.* Revised edition. Trans. A. J. Krailsheimer. New York: Penguin. (Pascal's pensées, or "thoughts," on Christianity; the selection above was taken from this classic book.)

Jeff Jordan, ed. (1994) *Gambling on God: Essays on Pascal's Wager.* Lanham, MD: Rowman & Littlefield. (A superb collection of essays on the Wager.)

Alban Krailsheimer (1980) *Pascal.* Oxford: Past Masters. (A helpful introduction to Pascal and his thought.)

Michael Martin (1983) "Pascal's Wager as an Argument for Not Believing in God," *Religious Studies* 19: 57–64. (An interesting twist on the argument by an atheist philosopher.)

Nicholas Rescher (1985) *Pascal's Wager: A Study of Practical Reasoning in Philosophical Theology.* Notre Dame, IN: University of Notre Dame Press. (A careful analysis and defense of Pascal's Wager.)

Stephen R. Welch. *Pascal's Wager.* http://www.infidels.org/library/modern/theism/wager.html (A website containing many resources on Pascal's wager.)

PART FIVE

Science, religion, and miracles

In one way or another, science and religion have been at odds for centuries. Whether referring to the ancient Ionian philosophers who were seeking rational explanations of change in
the physical world, or to Copernicus and Galileo who appealed to astronomical evidence for
understanding the movements of the starry heavens, or to Charles Darwin who sought natural explanations for the origin and advancement of living organisms, there have been those
thinkers who sought for a *logos* (rational account) rather than a *mythos* (religious or mythi-
cal account) for explaining phenomena in the natural world. Of course, there have also been
those who were not happy with explaining natural phenomena in purely naturalistic terms.
Both historically and in recent times, many religious adherents have thought it necessary to
posit non-natural (supernatural) reasons and explanations for events in the natural world.
This kind of disagreement has affected the academy as well as the culture at large.

One prime example is that of miracles. A religious person, for example, may claim to
have been "miraculously" healed by God of some disease or ailment. On a grander scale,
Christian faith has historically been based on belief in the miracle of the resurrection of
Jesus of Nazareth. A non-religious person may claim that the suggestion of a miracle,
whether small or large, is based on unwarranted bias, and a naturalistic (i.e., scientific)
explanation—even if that explanation is not yet known—is always a more reasonable
choice in our scientific age and should be sought accordingly.

Who is right in these matters, and how could one know? These are the kinds of questions tackled in this section.

First, David Hume argues that the wise person always proportions his belief to the evidence. He goes on to contend that there has never been enough evidence offered to provide
proof that a miracle has occurred. After all, he maintains, a miracle is a violation of the
laws of nature—laws which have been firmly established through the accumulation of much
empirical evidence. In order to believe in a miracle—an event which is based on the testimony of another—the evidence for it would need to be greater than the evidence that was
utilized in establishing the law of which it is an alleged violation. Since we never have evidence of this sort, we should not believe that a miracle has occurred.

Not surprisingly, Hume's position has been met with rigorous responses since its publication in the eighteenth century. In recent times, Richard Swinburne has been a forceful critic. A number of his works address a fundamental issue relevant to belief in miracles: whether miracles are even possible given the world in which we live. If naturalism is true (naturalism taken here to be the view that there are no supernatural entities or events), then miracles are ruled out *a priori*. On the other hand, if theism is true, then the existence of miracles—especially those that are of the kind God would perform—should not be all that surprising. The next selection, then, offered by Swinburne, is taken from a larger work in which he first provides arguments for belief in God. After offering what he takes to be solid evidence for God, he argues that the evidence for some miracle claims (he defines a miracle as a suspension or violation of a natural law by God) is strong enough to warrant belief in them.

Another example of the tension between science and religion is the creation/evolution controversy. This issue is often addressed by contrasting two positions: Darwinian evolution versus special creationism as spelled out in the book of Genesis in the Bible. Both sides cite "scientific" evidence for their positions. Recently, however, the debate has taken a turn as analytic philosophers have moved into the fray and raised new questions and challenges. In the next selection, Alvin Plantinga argues that if naturalistic evolution is operative in the world, then we are not warranted in believing in it. Put simply, if both naturalism and Darwinian evolution are true, our cognitive faculties have developed for purposes of survival, not for finding truth. Given this, we should not believe that our cognitive faculties are reliable. Hence, any beliefs formed by our cognitive faculties, including the combined beliefs of naturalism and evolution, should be rejected.

Religious belief is tremendously important for many people across the globe, and it is, by anyone's lights, a very influential force in the world. In the final essay of this section, Daniel Dennett argues that religion is a natural, human phenomenon. As such, it conforms to the natural laws of physics and biology and should therefore be studied scientifically. Furthermore, through careful scientific investigation and analysis, we can perhaps further its evolution in positive directions, for there is much to gain or lose depending on how it evolves globally.

Chapter 36

David Hume

THE UNREASONABILITY OF BELIEF IN MIRACLES

David Hume (1711–76) was a philosopher, historian, essayist, and skeptic. He is widely taken to be one of the most important philosophers to write in the English language. In the following selection, Hume develops his classic argument on miracles. "A wise man," he claims, "proportions his belief to the evidence." What kind of evidence would warrant believing in a miracle? A miracle is, after all, "a violation of the laws of nature" and thus a highly improbable event. The laws of nature have been established by uniform and unalterable experience—that's why they are referred to as "laws" of nature. This fact alone, Hume maintains, provides an argument against belief in miracles. For it would take at least as much evidence to establish the validity of an alleged miracle as it does to establish the laws of which the miracle is an apparent violation. But this we never find. In cases of miraculous claims, the burden of proof lies solely in the testimony of human witnesses. Yet human testimony, no matter how convincing, has never provided more solid evidence for the occurrence of such violations of the laws of nature than the evidence which establishes the laws themselves.

Hume gives four reasons why the testimony on which a miracle is founded has never provided a full proof: (1) in all of history, there has never been a miracle attested to by an adequate number of intelligent, trusted, and reputable individuals as to prove its validity; (2) the surprise and wonder of miraculous and extraordinary claims inclines the generality of humankind toward a passionate tendency to believe them, even if they are clearly false; (3) supernatural and miraculous claims primarily thrive among, or at least originate from, ignorant and barbarous peoples and nations, thus adding to their uncertainty; and (4) there is no testimony for any miracle that has not been opposed by many witnesses, and thus the testimonial evidence for such events is unreliable.

Hume's argument against miracles has profound implications for religious believers. Because the origins of so many of the world's religions abound in, and are often even grounded upon, the miraculous, Hume undermines the reasonability of belief in them. His primary example is Christianity, and he argues that the miracles found in the Bible, although attributed to God, are no more probable than any other miraculous claims given the reasons noted above. Thus, he argues that one cannot hold to the religion (as typically understood) based on reason. It takes faith. However, he jests, the faith that would be required to believe in the miraculous claims of a religion such as this would take a miracle of its own, as one would have to abandon all understanding and deny custom and experience to believe them.

———————————

Part I[1]

There is, in Dr. Tillotson's writings,[2] an argument against the *real presence*,[3] which is as concise, and elegant, and strong as any argument can possibly be supposed against a doctrine, so little worthy of a serious refutation. It is acknowledged on all hands, says that learned prelate, that the authority, either of the scripture or of tradition, is founded merely in the testimony of the apostles, who were eye-witnesses to those miracles of our Saviour, by which he proved his divine mission. Our evidence, then, for the truth of the *Christian* religion is less than the evidence for the truth of our senses; because, even in the first authors of our religion, it was no greater; and it is evident it must diminish in passing from them to their disciples; nor can any one rest such confidence in their testimony, as in the immediate object of his senses. But a weaker evidence can never destroy a stronger; and therefore, were the doctrine of the real presence ever so clearly revealed in scripture, it were directly contrary to the rules of just reasoning to give our assent to it. It contradicts sense, though both the scripture and tradition, on which it is supposed to be built, carry not such evidence with them as sense; when they are considered merely as external evidences, and are not brought home to every one's breast, by the immediate operation of the Holy Spirit.

Nothing is so convenient as a decisive argument of this kind, which must at least *silence* the most arrogant bigotry and superstition, and free us from their impertinent solicitations. I flatter myself, that I have discovered an argument of a like nature, which, if just, will, with the wise and learned, be an everlasting check to all kinds of superstitious delusion, and consequently, will be useful as long as the world endures. For so long, I presume, will the accounts of miracles and prodigies be found in all history, sacred and profane.

Though experience be our only guide in reasoning concerning matters of fact; it must be acknowledged, that this guide is not altogether infallible, but in some cases is apt to lead us into errors. One, who in our climate, should expect better weather in any week of June than in one of December, would reason justly, and conformably to experience; but it is certain, that he may happen, in the event, to find himself mistaken. However, we may observe, that, in such a case, he would have no cause to complain of experience; because it commonly informs us beforehand of the uncertainty, by that contrariety of events, which we may learn from a diligent observation. All effects follow not with like certainty from their supposed causes. Some events are found, in all countries and all ages, to have been constantly conjoined together: Others are found to have been more variable, and sometimes to disappoint our expectations; so that, in our reasonings concerning matter of fact, there are all imaginable degrees of assurance, from the highest certainty to the lowest species of moral evidence.

A wise man, therefore, proportions his belief to the evidence. In such conclusions as are founded on an infallible experience, he expects the event with the last degree of assurance, and regards his past experience as a full *proof* of the future existence of that event. In other cases, he proceeds with more caution: He weighs the opposite experiments: He considers which side is supported by the greater number of experiments: To that side he inclines, with doubt and hesitation; and when at last he fixes his judgment, the evidence exceeds not what we properly call *probability*. All probability, then, supposes an opposition of experiments and observations, where the one side is found to overbalance the other, and to produce a degree of evidence, proportioned to the superiority. A hundred instances or experiments on one side, and fifty on another, afford a doubtful expectation of any event; though a hundred uniform experiments, with only one that is contradictory, reasonably beget a pretty strong degree of assurance. In all cases, we must balance the opposite experiments, where they are opposite, and deduct the smaller number from the greater, in order to know the exact force of the superior evidence.

To apply these principles to a particular instance; we may observe, that there is no species of reasoning more common, more useful, and even necessary to human life, than that which is derived from the testimony of men, and the reports of eye-witnesses and spectators. This species of reasoning, perhaps, one may deny to be founded on the relation of cause and effect. I shall not dispute about a word. It will be sufficient to observe, that our assurance in any argument of this kind is derived from no other principle than our observation of the veracity of human testimony, and of the usual conformity of facts to the reports of witnesses. It being a general maxim, that no objects have any discoverable connexion together, and that all the inferences, which we can draw from one to another, are founded merely on our experience of their constant and regular conjunction; it is evident, that we ought not to make an exception to this maxim in favour of human testimony, whose connexion with any event seems, in itself, as little necessary as any other. Were not the memory tenacious to a certain degree; had not men commonly an inclination to truth and a principle of probity; were they not sensible to shame, when detected in a falsehood: Were not these, I say, discovered by *experience* to be qualities, inherent in human nature, we should never repose the least confidence in human testimony. A man delirious, or noted for falsehood and villainy, has no manner of authority with us.

And as the evidence, derived from witnesses and human testimony, is founded on past experience, so it varies with the experience, and is regarded either as a *proof* or a *probability*, according as the conjunction between any particular kind of report and any kind of object has been found to be constant or variable. There are a number of circumstances to be taken into consideration in all judgments of this kind; and the ultimate standard, by which we determine all disputes, that may arise concerning them, is always derived from experience and observation. Where this experience is not entirely uniform on any side, it is attended with an unavoidable contrariety in our judgments, and with the same opposition and mutual destruction of argument as in every other kind of evidence. We frequently hesitate concerning the reports of others. We balance the opposite circumstances, which cause any doubt or uncertainty; and when we discover a superiority on any side, we incline to it; but still with a diminution of assurance, in proportion to the force of its antagonist.

This contrariety of evidence, in the present case, may be derived from several different causes; from the opposition of contrary testimony; from the character or number of the witnesses; from the manner of their delivering their testimony; or from the union of all these circumstances. We entertain a suspicion concerning any matter of fact, when the witnesses contradict each other; when they are but few, or of a doubtful character; when they have an interest in what they affirm; when they deliver their testimony with hesitation, or on the contrary, with too violent asseverations. There are many other particulars of the same kind, which may diminish or destroy the force of any argument, derived from human testimony.

Suppose, for instance, that the fact, which the testimony endeavours to establish, partakes of the extraordinary and the marvellous; in that case, the evidence, resulting from the testimony, admits of a diminution, greater or less, in proportion as the fact is more or less unusual. The reason, why we place any credit in witnesses and historians, is not derived from any *connexion*, which we perceive *a priori*, between testimony and reality, but because we are accustomed to find a conformity between them. But when the fact attested is such a one as has seldom fallen under our observation, here is a contest of two opposite experiences; of which the one destroys the other, as far as its force goes, and the superior can only operate on the mind by the force, which remains. The very same principle of experience, which gives us a certain degree of assurance in the testimony of witnesses, gives us also, in this case, another degree of assurance against the fact, which they endeavour to establish; from which contradiction there necessarily arises a counterpoise, and mutual destruction of belief and authority.

I should not believe such a story were it told me by Cato; was a proverbial saying in Rome, even during the lifetime of that philosophical patriot.[4] The incredibility of a fact, it was allowed, might invalidate so great an authority.

The Indian prince,[5] who refused to believe the first relations concerning the effects of frost, reasoned justly; and it naturally required very strong testimony to engage his assent to facts, that arose from a state of nature, with which he was unacquainted, and which bore so little analogy to those events, of which he had had constant and uniform experience. Though they were not contrary to his experience, they were not conformable to it.[6]

But in order to increase the probability against the testimony of witnesses, let us suppose, that the fact, which they affirm, instead of being only marvellous, is really miraculous; and suppose also, that the testimony, considered apart and in itself, amounts to an entire proof; in that case, there is proof against proof, of which the strongest must prevail, but still with a diminution of its force, in proportion to that of its antagonist.

A miracle is a violation of the laws of nature; and as a firm and unalterable experience has established these laws, the proof against a miracle, from the very nature of the fact, is as entire as any argument from experience can possibly be imagined. Why is it more than probable, that all men must die; that lead cannot, of itself, remain suspended in the air; that fire consumes wood, and is extinguished by water; unless it be, that these events are found agreeable to the laws of nature, and there is required a violation of these laws, or in other words, a miracle to prevent them? Nothing is esteemed a miracle, if it ever happen in the common course of nature. It is no miracle that a man, seemingly in good health, should die on a sudden: because such a kind of death, though more unusual than any other, has yet been frequently observed to happen. But it is a miracle, that a dead man should come to life; because that has never been observed, in any age or country. There must, therefore, be a uniform experience against every miraculous event, otherwise the event would not merit that appellation. And as a uniform experience amounts to a proof, there is here a direct and full *proof*, from the nature of the fact, against the existence of any miracle; nor can such a proof be destroyed, or the miracle rendered credible, but by an opposite proof, which is superior.[7]

The plain consequence is (and it is a general maxim worthy of our attention), 'That no testimony is sufficient to establish a miracle, unless the testimony be of such a kind, that its falsehood would be more miraculous, than the fact, which it endeavours to establish: And even in that case there is a mutual destruction of arguments, and the superior only gives us an assurance suitable to that degree of force, which remains, after deducting the inferior.' When anyone tells me, that he saw a dead man restored to life, I immediately consider with myself, whether it be more probable, that this person should either deceive or be deceived, or that the fact, which he relates, should really have happened. I weigh the one miracle against the other; and according to the superiority, which I discover, I pronounce my decision, and always reject the greater miracle. If the falsehood of his testimony would be more miraculous, than the event which he relates; then, and not till then, can he pretend to command my belief or opinion.

Part II

In the foregoing reasoning we have supposed, that the testimony, upon which a miracle is founded, may possibly amount to an entire proof, and that the falsehood of that testimony would be a real prodigy: But it is easy to show, that we have been a great deal too liberal in our concession, and that there never was a miraculous event established on so full an evidence.

For *first*, there is not to be found, in all history, any miracle attested by a sufficient number of men, of such unquestioned good-sense, education, and learning, as to secure us against all delusion in themselves; of such undoubted integrity, as to place them beyond all suspicion of any design to deceive others; of such credit and reputation in the eyes of mankind, as to have a great deal to lose in case of their being detected in any falsehood; and at the same time, attesting facts, performed in such a public manner, and in so celebrated a part of the world, as to render the detection unavoidable: All which circumstances are requisite to give us a full assurance in the testimony of men.

Secondly. We may observe in human nature a principle, which, if strictly examined, will be found to diminish extremely the assurance, which we might, from human testimony, have, in any kind of prodigy. The maxim, by which we commonly conduct ourselves in our reasonings, is, that the objects, of which we have no experience, resemble those, of which we have; that what we have found to be most usual is always most probable; and that where there is an opposition of arguments, we ought to give the preference to such as are founded on the greatest number of past observations. But though, in proceeding by this rule, we readily reject any fact which is unusual and incredible in an ordinary degree; yet in advancing farther, the mind observes not always the same rule; but when anything is affirmed utterly absurd and miraculous, it rather the more readily admits of such a fact, upon account of that very circumstance, which ought to destroy all its authority. The passion of *surprise* and *wonder*, arising from miracles, being an agreeable emotion, gives a sensible tendency towards the belief of those events, from which it is derived. And this goes so far, that even those who cannot enjoy this pleasure immediately, nor can believe those miraculous events, of which they are informed, yet love to partake of the satisfaction at second-hand or by rebound, and place a pride and delight in exciting the admiration of others.

With what greediness are the miraculous accounts of travellers received, their descriptions of sea and land monsters, their relations of wonderful adventures, strange men, and uncouth manners? But if the spirit of religion join itself to the love of wonder, there is an end of common sense; and human testimony, in these circumstances, loses all pretensions to authority. A religionist may be an enthusiast, and imagine he sees what has no reality: he may know his narrative to be false, and yet persevere in it, with the best intentions in the world, for the sake of promoting so holy a cause: or even where this delusion has not place, vanity, excited by so strong a temptation, operates on him more powerfully than on the rest of mankind in any other circumstances; and self-interest with equal force. His auditors may not have, and commonly have not, sufficient judgment to canvass his evidence: what judgment they have, they renounce by principle, in these sublime and mysterious subjects: or if they were ever so willing to employ it, passion and a heated imagination disturb the regularity of its operations. Their credulity increases his impudence: and his impudence overpowers their credulity.

Eloquence, when at its highest pitch, leaves little room for reason or reflection; but addressing itself entirely to the fancy or the affections, captivates the willing hearers, and subdues their understanding. Happily, this pitch it seldom attains. . . .

The many instances of forged miracles, and prophecies, and supernatural events, which, in all ages, have either been detected by contrary evidence, or which detect themselves by their absurdity, prove sufficiently the strong propensity of mankind to the extraordinary and the marvellous, and ought reasonably to beget a suspicion against all relations of this kind. This is our natural way of thinking, even with regard to the most common and most credible events. For instance: there is no kind of report, which rises so easily, and spreads so quickly, especially in country places and provincial towns, as those concerning marriages . . .. The pleasure of telling a piece of news so interesting, of propagating it, and of being the first reporters of it, spreads the intelligence. And this is so well known, that no man of sense gives attention to these reports, till he find them confirmed by some greater evidence. Do not the same passions, and others still stronger, incline the generality of mankind to believe and report, with the greatest vehemence and assurance, all religious miracles?

Thirdly. It forms a strong presumption against all supernatural and miraculous relations, that they are observed chiefly to abound among ignorant and barbarous nations; or if a civilized people has ever given admission to any of them, that people will be found to have received them from ignorant and barbarous ancestors, who transmitted them with that inviolable sanction and authority, which always attend received opinions. When we peruse the first histories of all nations, we are apt to imagine ourselves transported into some new world; where the whole frame of nature is disjointed, and every element performs its operations in a different manner, from what it does at present. Battles, revolutions, pestilence, famine, and death, are never the effect of those natural causes, which we experience. Prodigies, omens, oracles, judgments, quite obscure the few natural events, that are intermingled with them. But as the former grow thinner every page, in proportion as we advance nearer the enlightened ages, we soon learn, that there is nothing mysterious or supernatural in the case, but that all proceeds from the usual propensity of mankind towards the marvellous, and that, though this inclination may at intervals receive a check from sense and learning, it can never be thoroughly extirpated from human nature.

It is strange, a judicious reader is apt to say, upon the perusal of these wonderful historians, *that such prodigious events never happen in our days*. But it is nothing strange, I hope, that men should lie in all ages. You must surely have seen instances enough of that frailty. You have yourself heard many such marvellous relations started, which, being treated with scorn by all the wise and judicious, have at last been abandoned even by the vulgar. Be assured, that those renowned lies, which have spread and flourished to such a monstrous height, arose from like beginnings; but being sown in a more proper soil, shot up at last into prodigies almost equal to those which they relate. . . .

The advantages are so great, of starting an imposture among an ignorant people, that, even though the delusion should be too gross to impose on the generality of them (*which, though seldom, is sometimes the case*) it has a much better chance for succeeding in remote countries, than if the first scene had been laid in a city renowned for arts and knowledge. The most ignorant and barbarous of these barbarians carry the report abroad. None of their countrymen have a large correspondence, or sufficient credit and authority to contradict and beat down the delusion. Men's inclination to the marvellous has full opportunity to display itself. And thus a story, which is universally exploded in the place where it was first started, shall pass for certain at a thousand miles distance. . . .

I may add as a *fourth* reason, which diminishes the authority of prodigies, that there is no testimony for any, even those which have not been expressly detected, that is not opposed by an infinite number of witnesses; so that not only the miracle destroys the credit of testimony, but the testimony destroys itself. To make this the better understood, let us consider, that, in matters of religion, whatever is different is contrary; and that it is impossible the religions of ancient Rome, of Turkey, of Siam, and of China should, all of them, be established on any solid foundation. Every miracle, therefore, pretended to have been wrought in any of these religions (and all of them abound in miracles), as its direct scope is to establish the particular system to which it is attributed; so has it the same force, though more indirectly, to overthrow every other system. In destroying a rival system, it likewise destroys the credit of those miracles, on which that system was established; so that all the prodigies of different religions are to be regarded as contrary facts, and the evidences of these prodigies, whether weak or strong, as opposite to each other. According to this method of reasoning, when we believe any miracle of Mahomet or his successors, we have for our warrant the testimony of a few barbarous Arabians: And on the other hand, we are to regard the authority of Titus Livius, Plutarch, Tacitus, and, in short, of all the authors and witnesses, Grecian, Chinese, and Roman Catholic, who have related any miracle in their particular religion; I say, we are to regard their testimony in the same light as if they had mentioned that Mahometan miracle, and had in express terms contradicted it, with the same certainty as they have for the miracle they relate. This argument may appear over subtile and refined; but is not in reality different from the reasoning of a judge, who supposes, that the credit of two witnesses, maintaining a crime against any one, is destroyed by the testimony of two others, who affirm him to have been two hundred leagues distant, at the same instant when the crime is said to have been committed. . . .

There surely never was a greater number of miracles ascribed to one person, than those, which were lately said to have been wrought in France upon the tomb of Abbé

Paris, the famous Jansenist, with whose sanctity the people were so long deluded. The curing of the sick, giving hearing to the deaf, and sight to the blind, were every where talked of as the usual effects of that holy sepulchre. But what is more extraordinary; many of the miracles were immediately proved upon the spot, before judges of unquestioned integrity, attested by witnesses of credit and distinction, in a learned age, and on the most eminent theatre that is now in the world. Nor is this all: a relation of them was published and dispersed every where; nor were the *Jesuits*, though a learned body, supported by the civil magistrate, and determined enemies to those opinions, in whose favour the miracles were said to have been wrought, ever able distinctly to refute or detect them.[8] Where shall we find such a number of circumstances, agreeing to the corroboration of one fact? And what have we to oppose to such a cloud of witnesses, but the absolute impossibility or miraculous nature of the events, which they relate? And this surely, in the eyes of all reasonable people, will alone be regarded as a sufficient refutation. . . .

The wise lend a very academic faith to every report which favours the passion of the reporter; whether it magnifies his country, his family, or himself, or in any other way strikes in with his natural inclinations and propensities. But what greater temptation than to appear a missionary, a prophet, an ambassador from heaven? Who would not encounter many dangers and difficulties, in order to attain so sublime a character? Or if, by the help of vanity and a heated imagination, a man has first made a convert of himself, and entered seriously into the delusion; who ever scruples to make use of pious frauds, in support of so holy and meritorious a cause?

The smallest spark may here kindle into the greatest flame; because the materials are always prepared for it. The *avidum genus auricularum*,[9] the gazing populace, receive greedily, without examination, whatever soothes superstition, and promotes wonder.

How many stories of this nature have, in all ages, been detected and exploded in their infancy? How many more have been celebrated for a time, and have afterwards sunk into neglect and oblivion? Where such reports, therefore, fly about, the solution of the phenomenon is obvious; and we judge in conformity to regular experience and observation, when we account for it by the known and natural principles of credulity and delusion. And shall we, rather than have a recourse to so natural a solution, allow of a miraculous violation of the most established laws of nature? . . .

In the infancy of new religions, the wise and learned commonly esteem the matter too inconsiderable to deserve their attention or regard. And when afterwards they would willingly detect the cheat, in order to undeceive the deluded multitude, the season is now past, and the records and witnesses, which might clear up the matter, have perished beyond recovery.

No means of detection remain, but those which must be drawn from the very testimony itself of the reporters: and these, though always sufficient with the judicious and knowing, are commonly too fine to fall under the comprehension of the vulgar.

Upon the whole, then, it appears, that no testimony for any kind of miracle has ever amounted to a probability, much less to a proof; and that, even supposing it amounted to a proof, it would be opposed by another proof; derived from the very nature of the fact, which it would endeavour to establish. It is experience only, which gives authority to human testimony; and it is the same experience, which assures us of the laws of nature. When, therefore, these two kinds of experience are contrary, we have nothing to do but subtract the one from the other, and embrace an opinion, either on one side or the other, with that assurance which arises from the remainder. But according to the principle here explained, this subtraction, with regard to all popular religions, amounts to an entire annihilation; and therefore we may establish it as a maxim, that no human testimony can have such force as to prove a miracle, and make it a just foundation for any such system of religion.

I beg the limitations here made may be remarked, when I say, that a miracle can never be proved, so as to be the foundation of a system of religion. For I own, that otherwise, there may possibly be miracles, or violations of the usual course of nature, of such a kind as to admit of proof from human testimony; though, perhaps, it will be impossible to find any such in all the records of history. Thus, suppose, all authors, in all languages, agree, that, from the first of January 1600, there was a total darkness over the whole earth for eight days: suppose that the tradition of this extraordinary event is still strong and lively among the people: that all travellers, who return from foreign countries, bring us accounts of the same tradition, without the least variation or contradiction: it is evident, that our present philosophers, instead of doubting the fact, ought to receive it as certain, and ought to search for the causes whence it might be derived. The decay, corruption, and dissolution of nature, is an event rendered probable by so many analogies, that any phenomenon, which seems to have a tendency towards that catastrophe, comes within the reach of human testimony, if that testimony be very extensive and uniform.

But suppose, that all the historians who treat of England, should agree, that, on the first of January 1600, Queen Elizabeth died; that both before and after her death she was seen by her physicians and the whole court, as is usual with persons of her rank; that her successor was acknowledged and proclaimed by the parliament; and that, after being interred a month, she again appeared, resumed the throne, and governed England for three years: I must confess that I should be surprised at the concurrence of so many odd circumstances, but should not have the least inclination to believe so miraculous an event. I should not doubt of her pretended death, and of those other public circumstances that followed it: I should only assert it to have been pretended, and that it neither was, nor possibly could be real. You would in vain object to me the difficulty, and almost impossibility of deceiving the world in an affair of such consequence; the wisdom and solid judgment of that renowned queen; with the little or no advantage which she could reap from so poor an artifice: all this might astonish me; but I would still reply, that the knavery and folly of men are such common phenomena, that I should rather believe the most extraordinary events to arise from their concurrence, than admit of so signal a violation of the laws of nature.

But should this miracle be ascribed to any new system of religion; men, in all ages, have been so much imposed on by ridiculous stories of that kind, that this very circumstance would be a full proof of a cheat, and sufficient, with all men of sense, not only to make them reject the fact, but even reject it without farther examination. Though the Being to whom the miracle is ascribed, be, in this case, Almighty, it does not, upon that account, become a whit more probable; since it is impossible for us to know the attributes or actions of such a Being, otherwise than from the experience which we have of his productions, in the usual course of nature. This still reduces us to past observation, and obliges us to compare the instances of the violation of truth in the testimony of men, with those of the violation of the laws of nature by miracles, in order to judge which of them is most likely and probable. As the violations of truth are more common in the testimony concerning religious miracles, than in that concerning any other matter of fact; this must diminish very much the authority of the former testimony, and make us form a general resolution, never to lend any attention to it, with whatever specious pretence it may be covered. . . .

I am the better pleased with the method of reasoning here delivered, as I think it may serve to confound those dangerous friends or disguised enemies to the *Christian Religion*, who have undertaken to defend it by the principles of human reason. Our most holy religion is founded on *Faith*, not on reason; and it is a sure method of exposing it to put it to such a trial as it is, by no means, fitted to endure. To make this more evident, let us examine those miracles, related in scripture; and not to lose ourselves in too wide a field, let us confine ourselves to such as we find in the *Pentateuch*, which we shall examine, according to the principles of these pretended Christians, not as the word or testimony of God himself, but as the production of a mere human writer and historian. Here then we are first to consider a book, presented to us by a barbarous and ignorant people, written in an age when they were still more barbarous, and in all probability long after the facts which it relates, corroborated by no concurring testimony, and resembling those fabulous accounts, which every nation gives of its origin. Upon reading this book, we find it full of prodigies and miracles. It gives an account of a state of the world and of human nature entirely different from the present: Of our fall from that state: Of the age of man, extended to near a thousand years: Of the destruction of the world by a deluge: Of the arbitrary choice of one people, as the favourites of heaven; and that people the countrymen of the author: Of their deliverance from bondage by prodigies the most astonishing imaginable: I desire anyone to lay his hand upon his heart, and after a serious consideration declare, whether he thinks that the falsehood of such a book, supported by such a testimony, would be more extraordinary and miraculous than all the miracles it relates; which is, however, necessary to make it be received, according to the measures of probability above established.

What we have said of miracles may be applied, without any variation, to prophecies; and indeed, all prophecies are real miracles, and as such only, can be admitted as proofs of any revelation. If it did not exceed the capacity of human nature to foretell future events, it would be absurd to employ any prophecy as an argument for a divine mission or authority from heaven. So that, upon the whole, we may conclude, that the *Christian Religion* not only was at first attended with miracles, but even at this day cannot be believed by any reasonable person without one. Mere reason is insufficient to convince us of its veracity: And whoever is moved by *Faith* to assent to it, is conscious of a continued miracle in his own person, which subverts all the principles of his understanding, and gives him a determination to believe what is most contrary to custom and experience.

Notes

1   [A draft of this section was extant as early as 1737; although Hume had apparently entertained the idea of including it in the *Treatise*, evidence suggests that he withheld it for fear of displeasing Joseph Butler, whose approval of the work he sought. The essay was first published as part of the *Enquiry* and is thought by many to be a direct reply to two influential works, one by Thomas Sherlock (1678–1761), Bishop of London, *Tryal of* the *Witnesses*

of the *Resurrection of Jesus* (1729); the other was Zachary Pearce's (1690–1774) *Miracles of Jesus Vindicated* (1729).]

2   [John Tillotson (1630–1694), a Presbyterian theologian who became Archbishop of Canterbury in 1691, argued in *Rule of Faith* (1676) and *A Doctrine Against Transubstantiation* (1684) that transubstantiation could never be established as part of Christian doctrine.]

3   [The presence of the body and blood of Christ in the bread and wine of the Eucharist.]

4   Plutarch, in vita Catonis Min. 19 [*Life of Cato* (the Younger)].

5   [A variation of this story appears in Locke's *Essay Concerning Human Understanding* IV. 15., as a story about the King of Siam and a Dutch ambassador. An account closer to Hume's is mentioned by Butler in the Introduction to his *Analogy of Religion, Natural and Revealed, to the Constitution and Course of Nature* (1736).]

6   No Indian, it is evident, could have experience that water did not freeze in cold climates. This is placing nature in a situation quite unknown to him; and it is impossible for him to tell *a priori* what will result from it. It is making a new experiment, the consequence of which is always uncertain. One may sometimes conjecture from analogy what will follow; but still this is but conjecture. And it must be confessed, that, in the present case of freezing, the event follows contrary to the rules of analogy, and is such as a rational Indian would not look for. The operations of cold upon water are not gradual, according to the degrees of cold; but whenever it comes to the freezing point, the water passes in a moment, from the utmost liquidity to perfect hardness. Such an event, therefore, may be denominated *extraordinary*, and requires a pretty strong testimony, to render it credible to people in a warm climate: But still it is not *miraculous*, nor contrary to uniform experience of the course of nature in cases where all the circumstances are the same. The inhabitants of Sumatra have always seen water fluid in their own climate, and the freezing of their rivers ought to be deemed a prodigy: But they never saw water in Muscovy during the winter; and therefore they cannot reasonably be positive what would there be the consequence.

7   Sometimes an event may not, *in itself*, *seem* to be contrary to the laws of nature, and yet, if it were real, it might, by reason of some circumstances, be denominated a miracle; because, in *fact*, it is contrary to these laws. Thus if a person, claiming a divine authority, should command a sick person to be well, a healthful man to fall down dead, the clouds to pour rain, the winds to blow, in short, should order many natural events, which immediately follow upon his command; these might justly be esteemed miracles, because they are really, in this case, contrary to the laws of nature. For if any suspicion remain, that the event and command concurred by accident, there is no miracle and no transgression of the laws of nature. If this suspicion be removed, there is evidently a miracle, and a transgression of these laws; because nothing can be more contrary to nature than that the voice or command of a man should have such an influence. A miracle may be accurately defined, *a transgression of a law of nature by a particular volition of the Deity, or by the interposition of some invisible agent.* A miracle may either be discoverable by men or not. This alters not its nature and essence. The raising of a house or ship into the air is a visible miracle. The raising of a feather, when the wind wants ever so little of a force requisite for that purpose, is as real a miracle, though not so sensible with regard to us.

8   This book was writ by Mons. Montgeron, counsellor or judge of the parliament of Paris, a man of figure and character, who was also a martyr to the cause, and is now said to be somewhere in a dungeon on account of his book. . . .

9   [Literally, "a gossip hungry race"; this is an adaptation or misquotation of *Humanum genus est avidum nimus auricularum* "the human race is too gossip-hungry" (Lucretius, *De Rerum Natura*, iv. 594).]

Questions for reflection

1   Explain Hume's understanding/definition of a miracle. Is it a legitimate one, in your view? Are there problems with it? Explain.
2   Is it only uneducated and barbarous people who claim to have experienced miracles in religion? What conclusions can be drawn from your answer to this question?
3   If one has good reason for holding to atheism, should he require more evidence for believing in a particular alleged miracle than, say, a theist who has good reason for believing in God? Should one's worldview affect her belief in miracles? If so, how? If not, why not?
4   Does Hume's understanding of a miracle rule out the possibility of ever knowing that one has occurred? Or does it just rule out the reasonability of believing in one based on the testimony of others? Or neither?

Further reading

Antony Flew (1961) *Hume's Philosophy of Belief*. New York: Humanities Press. (A restatement of Hume's argument, perhaps even more forcefully presented.)
Robert J. Fogelin (2006) *A Defense of Hume on Miracles*. Princeton, NJ: Princeton University Press. (A recent, well-argued defense of Hume's case against miracles.)
R. Douglas Geivett and Gary R. Habermas (1997) *In Defense of Miracles: A Comprehensive Case for God's Action in History*. Downers Grove, IL: InterVarsity Press. (A team of scholars provides a case for God's acting in history and offers responses to objections.)
J. Houston (1994) *Reported Miracles: A Critique of Hume*. Cambridge: Cambridge University Press. (A sophisticated assessment of Hume's argument.)
Alastair McKinnon (1967) "'Miracle' and 'Paradox,'" *American Philosophical Quarterly* 4 (4): 308–14. (Challenges the coherence of miracles.)

Chapter 37

Richard Swinburne

A CASE FOR MIRACLES

Richard Swinburne is Emeritus Nolloth Professor of the Philosophy of the Christian Religion, University of Oxford, and Fellow of the British Academy. He is one of the leading Christian apologists of our time. In the book from which the following selection was extracted, entitled *Is There a God?*, Professor Swinburne spends the first six chapters using arguments from natural theology to demonstrate that God provides the best explanation of the existence and orderliness of the universe and the evolution of human beings and their being conscious. He then argues, in this selection, that in so far as one has reasons for believing that God exists, there is reason to believe that God intervenes in human history—that is, performs miracles. It would be odd, he notes, to suppose that God would *not* do so.

He first defines a miracle as a violation or suspension of natural laws, brought about by God. He then briefly describes criteria—including background knowledge and historical evidence—for assessing a particular miracle claim. He argues that we do have enough evidence of events occurring contrary to natural laws such that some of them at least—most especially the kind that God would have reason to perform—are probably genuine miracles. Furthermore, if the total evidence for such events is strong enough, it could even provide direct evidence for God's existence.

I have argued so far that the claim that God created and sustains our universe is the hypothesis that best accounts for its general structure—its very existence, its conformity to natural laws, its being fine tuned to evolve animals and humans, and these latter being conscious beings with sensations, thoughts, beliefs, desires, and purposes who can make great differences to themselves and the world in deeply significant ways. I have argued too that the existence of evil of the kind we find on earth does not count against that claim. The evidence considered so far, therefore, gives a significant degree of probability to that claim—that there is a God. However, if there is a God, who, being perfectly good, will love his creatures, one would expect him to interact with us occasionally more directly on a personal basis, rather than merely through the natural order of the world which he constantly sustains—to answer our prayers and to meet our needs. He will not, however, intervene in the natural order at all often, for, if he did, we would not be able to predict the consequences of our actions and so we would lose control over the world and ourselves. If God answered most prayers for a relative to recover from cancer, then cancer would no longer be a problem for humans to solve. Humans would no longer see cancer as a problem to be solved by scientific research—prayer would be the obvious method of curing cancer. God would then have deprived us of the serious choice of whether to put money and energy into finding a cure for cancer or not to bother; and of whether to take trouble to avoid cancer (e.g. by not smoking) or not to bother. Natural laws determining that certain events will cause good effects and other ones cause bad effects enable us to discover which produce which and to use them for ourselves. Natural laws are like rules, instituted by parents, schools, or governments, stating that these actions will be punished and those ones rewarded. Once we discover the rules, we acquire control over the consequences of our actions—we can then choose whether to be rewarded or to risk being punished. But loving parents will rightly occasionally break their own rules in answer to special pleading—it means that they are persons in interaction, not just systems of rules. And for a similar reason one might expect God occasionally to break his own rules, and intervene in history.

Miracles and natural laws

One might expect God occasionally to answer prayer when it is for a good cause—such as the relief of suffering and restoration to health of mind or body, and for awareness of himself and of important spiritual truths. And one might also expect him to intervene occasionally without waiting for our prayer—to help us to make the world better in various ways when we have misused our freedom. A divine intervention will consist either in God acting in areas where natural laws do not determine what happens (perhaps our mental life is not fully determined by natural laws), or in God temporarily suspending natural laws. Let us call interventions of the latter kind miracles and interventions of the former kind non-miraculous interventions. A miracle is a violation or suspension of natural laws, brought about by God. Does human history contain events of a kind which God, if he exists, would be expected to bring about and yet which do not occur as a result of the operation of natural laws? It certainly contains large numbers of events of the kind which God would be expected to bring about, but about which we have no idea whether they occurred as a result of the operation of natural laws or not. I pray for my friend to get better from cancer and he does. Since we do not normally know in any detail the exact state of his body when he had cancer, nor do we know in any detail the natural laws which govern the development of cancer, we cannot say whether the recovery occurs as a result of natural laws or not. The pious believer believes that God intervened, and the hard-headed atheist believes that only natural laws were at work. Human history also contains *reports* of many events which, *if* they occurred as reported, clearly would not have occurred as a result of natural laws, and which are also events of a kind that God might be expected to bring about. The Second Book of Kings records that a sick and doubting King Hezekiah sought a sign of encouragement from God that he, Hezekiah, would recover and that God would save

Jerusalem from the Assyrians. In response to the prayer of the prophet Isaiah that God would give Hezekiah a sign, the shadow cast by the sun reportedly went 'backwards ten steps' (2 Kgs. 20:11). The latter can only have happened if the laws of mechanics (governing the rotation of the earth on its axis, and so the direction of the sun from Jerusalem), or the laws of light (governing how light from the sun forms shadows in the region of Hezekiah's palace), had been suspended.

I suggest that, in so far as we have other reason to believe that there is a God, we have reason to believe that God intervenes in history in some such cases (we may not know which) and so that some of the events happened as described, although not necessitated to do so by natural laws. It would be odd to suppose that God, concerned for our total well-being, confined his interventions to those areas (if any) where natural laws leave it undetermined what will happen—for example, confined his interventions to influencing the mental lives of human beings. If he has reason to interact with us, he has reason very occasionally to intervene to suspend those natural laws by which our life is controlled; and in particular, since the bodily processes which determine our health are fairly evidently subject to largely deterministic natural laws, he has reason very occasionally to intervene in those. Conversely, in so far as we have other reason to believe that there is no God, we have reason to believe that natural processes are the highest-level determinants of what happens and so that no events happen contrary to laws of nature. In other words, background knowledge (our other reasons for general belief about how the world works—e.g. reasons for believing that there is a God, or that there is no God) is rightly a very important factor in assessing what happened on particular occasions (more so here than in assessing the worth of large scientific or religious theories. . .).

Background knowledge and historical evidence

But, while background knowledge must be a powerful factor in determining what is reasonable to believe about what happened on particular occasions, it is not, of course, the only factor. We have the detailed historical evidence of what observers seem to recall having happened, what witnesses claim to have observed, and any physical traces of past events (documents, archaeological remains, and so on).

That background knowledge must weigh heavily in comparison with the detailed historical evidence in assessing particular claims about the past can be seen from innumerable non-religious examples. If a well-established scientific theory leads you to expect that stars will sometimes explode, then some debris in the sky of a kind which could have been caused by an exploding star but which (though improbably) just might have some other cause may be reasonably interpreted as debris left by an exploding star. But, if a well-established theory says that stars cannot explode, you will need very strong evidence that the debris could not have had another cause before interpreting it as debris of an exploding star. However, in the case of purported miraculous interventions, the background knowledge will be of two kinds. It will include the scientific knowledge of what are the relevant laws of nature—for example, the laws of light and the laws governing the rotation of the earth, which (since laws of nature operate almost all the time) lead us to expect that on that particular occasion Hezekiah's shadow did not move backwards. But it will also include the other evidence that there is a God able and having reason sometimes (but not necessarily on any one particular occasion) to intervene to suspend the operation of natural laws. In view of these conflicting bodies of background knowledge, we would need quite a bit of particular historical evidence to show that, on any particular occasion, God intervened in a miraculous way. The historical evidence could be backed up by argument that that particular purported miracle was one which God had strong reason for bringing about.

To balance detailed historical evidence against background evidence of both kinds to establish what happened on any particular occasion is a difficult matter on which we are seldom going to be able to reach a clear verdict. But detailed historical evidence about what happened could in principle be substantial. To take a simple, imaginary, and not especially religiously significant example, we ourselves might have apparently seen someone levitate (that is, rise in the air, not as a result of strings or magnets or any other known force for which we have checked). Many witnesses, proved totally trustworthy on other occasions where they would have had no reason to lie, might report having observed such a thing. There might even be traces in the form of physical effects which such an event would have caused—for example, marks on the ceiling which would have been caused by a levitating body hitting it. But against all this there will still be the background knowledge of what are the laws of nature, in this case the laws of gravity; and all the evidence in favour of these being the laws of nature will be evidence that they operated at the time in question, and so that no levitation occurred.

Note that any detailed historical evidence that the levitation occurred will, as such, be evidence against the laws of gravity being the laws of nature—just as evidence that some piece of metal did not expand when heated would be evidence that it is not a law of nature that all metals expand when heated. But if, much though we may try, we fail to find further exceptions to our purported law—if, for example, we cannot produce another levitation by recreating the circumstances in which the former one purportedly occurred—that will be grounds for believing that, if the former occurred, it was not an event in accord with some hitherto undiscovered law of nature, but rather a violation or suspension of a law.

In such cases, we would, I think, be most unlikely to have enough detailed historical evidence that the event occurred to outweigh the scientific background knowledge that such events cannot occur, unless we also had substantial religious background knowledge showing not merely that there is a God but that he had very good reason on this particular occasion to work this particular miracle. In the case of a purported levitation, I doubt that we would ever have such evidence. That is not, of course, to say that levitations do not occur, only that we are most unlikely to have enough reason to believe that one did occur on any particular occasion. Note that in all such cases what we are doing is to seek the simplest theory of what happened in the past which leads us to account for the data (what I have here called the detailed historical evidence), and which fits in best with our background knowledge . . . .

I am, however, inclined to think that we do have enough historical evidence of events occurring contrary to natural laws of a kind which God would have reason to bring out to show that probably some of them (we do not know which) are genuine miracles. There are many reports of purported miracles, ancient and modern, some of them quite well documented. (See for example, the cure of the Glasgow man from cancer described in D. Hickey and G. Smith, *Miracle* (1978), or some of the cases discussed in Rex Gardiner, *Healing Miracles* (1986). For a more sceptical account of some purported Lourdes miracles, see, for contrast, D. J. West, *Eleven Lourdes Miracles* (1957).) Or, rather, we have enough detailed historical evidence in some such cases given that we have a certain amount of background evidence to support the claim that there is a God, able and willing to intervene in history. But, of course, the reader must consider the evidence in such cases for himself or herself. The occurrence of such detailed historical evidence is itself further evidence of the existence of God . . . because one would expect to have it if there is a God but not otherwise—for if natural laws are the highest-level determinants of what happens, there is every reason to expect that they will not be suspended.

Evidence and the existence of God

It is so often said in such cases that we 'may be mistaken'. New scientific evidence may show that the event as reported was not contrary to natural laws—we simply misunderstood what were the natural laws. Maybe we have just misunderstood how cancer develops; a patient sometimes 'spontaneously' recovers by purely natural processes. Or, if many people claim to have observed someone levitate, maybe they have all been subject to hallucination. Maybe. But the rational enquirer in these matters, as in all matters, must go on the evidence available. If that evidence shows that the laws of nature are such and such, that if the event happened as described it was contrary to them, that the new evidence had no tendency to show that the supposed laws are not the true laws (because in all other similar cases they are followed), that there is very strong historical evidence (witnesses, and so on) that the event occurred, then it is rational to believe that a miracle occurred. We are rational to believe, while allowing the possibility that evidence might turn up later to show that we are mistaken. 'We may be mistaken' is a knife which cuts both ways—we may be mistaken in believing that an event is not a divine intervention when really it is, as well as the other way round.

Historians often affirm that, when they are investigating particular claims about past events important to religious traditions—for example, about what Jesus did and what happened to him—they do so without making any religious or anti-religious assumptions. In practice most of them do not live up to such affirmations. Either they heavily discount such biblical claims as that Jesus cured the blind on the grounds that such things do not happen; or (more commonly in past centuries) they automatically accept the testimony of witnesses to what Jesus did, on the grounds that biblical witnesses are especially reliable. But what needs to be appreciated is that background evidence ought to influence the investigator—as it does in all other areas of enquiry. Not to allow it to do so is irrational.

The existence of detailed historical evidence for the occurrence of violations of natural laws of a kind which God, if there is a God, would have had reason to bring about is itself evidence for the existence of God. Though not nearly enough on its own, it makes its contribution; and with other evidence . . . it could be enough to establish the existence of God, if the other evidence is not enough on its own. Consider, by analogy, a detective investigating a crime and considering the hypothesis that Jones committed the crime. Some of his clues will be evidence for the occurrence of some event, an event which, if it occurred, would provide evidence in its turn for the hypothesis that Jones committed the crime. The former might, for example, be the evidence of witnesses who claim to have seen Jones near the scene of the crime. Even if Jones was near the scene of the crime, that is in its turn on its own fairly weak evidence that he committed the crime. Much more evidence is needed. But because the testimony of witnesses is evidence for Jones having been near the scene of the crime, and Jones having been near the scene is some evidence that he committed it, the testimony of the witnesses is nevertheless some (indirect) evidence for his having committed the crime. Likewise, evidence of witnesses who claim to observe a violation of natural laws is indirect evidence for the existence of God, because the occurrence of such violations would be itself more direct evidence for the existence of God. If the total evidence becomes strong enough, then it will justify asserting that God exists, and hence that the event in question was not merely a violation, but brought about by God and thus a miracle.

Questions for reflection

1   Describe the difference between a miracle and a non-miraculous intervention. Might there be reason to believe in one and not the other? Why or why not?
2   What are some relevant factors to consider in determining what is reasonable to believe about a particular alleged miracle?
3   Suppose that some event occurred which, at first blush, you and a number of others took to be a miracle. How can you be justified in believing that it was a miracle as opposed to, say, an event which occurred based on a natural law of which we are currently unaware (or based on a misunderstanding of current natural laws)? How should the rational enquirer approach such matters?
4   What reason could God possibly have for violating the laws of nature, especially given that he is an all-good and all-powerful God and therefore would have arranged for things to happen in a good way?
5   How does one's worldview affect belief in miracles? How should it affect such belief?

Further reading

David Basinger and Randall Basinger (1986) *Philosophy and Miracle: The Contemporary Debate.* Lewiston, NY: Edwin Mellen Press. (An overview and assessment of various issues on the topic.)
David Hume ([1777] 1977) "On Miracles," in *An Enquiry Concerning Human Understanding.* Ed. Eric Steinberg. Indianapolis, IN: Hackett. (The classic critique of miracles.)
C. S. Lewis (2001) *Miracles.* New York: HarperCollins. (A defense of belief in miracles; responds to Hume's arguments.)
Richard Swinburne (1996) *Is There a God?* Oxford: Oxford University Press. (An accessible defense of theism; the selection above was taken from this book.)
Richard Swinburne, ed. (1989) *Miracles.* New York: Macmillan. (A helpful collection of essays on miracles.)

Chapter 38

Alvin Plantinga

NATURALISM AND SCIENCE

Alvin Plantinga is John A. O'Brien Professor of Philosophy at the University of Notre Dame. In several works he has defended his evolutionary argument against naturalism (EAAN). According to this argument, the conjunction of naturalism N—the view that there are no supernatural entities or beings, including God—with the belief in evolution E is self referentially incoherent. The argument unfolds this way: the combination of N&E provides an undefeated defeater for the belief in R—the proposition that our cognitive faculties are reliable. But it also provides a defeater for *any* belief produced by these faculties, including the belief in N&E. In this selection he provides a concise formulation of EAAN.

. . . Take *philosophical naturalism* to be the belief that there aren't any supernatural beings— no such person as God, for example, but also no other supernatural entities, and nothing at all like God.[1] My claim was that naturalism and contemporary evolutionary theory are at serious odds with one another—and this despite the fact that the latter is ordinarily thought to be one of the main pillars supporting the edifice of the former. (Of course I am *not* attacking the theory of evolution, or the claim that human beings have evolved from simian ancestors, or anything in that neighborhood; I am instead attacking the conjunction of *naturalism* with the view that human beings have evolved in that way. I see no similar problems with the conjunction of *theism* and the idea that human beings have evolved in the way contemporary evolutionary science suggests.) More particularly, I argued that the conjunction of naturalism with the belief that we human beings have evolved in conformity with current evolutionary doctrine—'evolution' for short—is in a certain interesting way self-defeating or self-referentially incoherent. Still more particularly, I argued that naturalism and evolution—'N&E' for short—furnishes one who accepts it with a *defeater* for the belief that our cognitive faculties are reliable—a defeater that can't be defeated. But then this conjunction also furnishes a defeater for any belief produced by our cognitive faculties, including, in the case of one who accepts it, N&E itself: hence its self-defeating character.

The argument

So much for a quick overview of the argument. More specifically, EAAN [the evolutionary argument against naturalism] begins from certain doubts about the *reliability* of our cognitive faculties, where, roughly, a cognitive faculty—memory, perception, reason—is reliable if the great bulk of its deliverances are true.[2] These doubts are connected with the *origin* of our cognitive faculties. According to current evolutionary theory, we human beings, like other forms of life, have developed from aboriginal unicellular life by way of such mechanisms as natural selection and genetic drift working on sources of genetic variation: the most popular is random genetic mutation. Natural selection discards most of these mutations (they prove deleterious to the organisms in which they appear), but some of the remainder turn out to have adaptive value and to enhance fitness; they spread through the population and thus persist. According to this story, it is by way of these mechanisms, or mechanisms very much like them, that all the vast variety of contemporary organic life has developed; and it is by way of these same mechanisms that our cognitive faculties have arisen.

Now according to traditional Christian (and Jewish and Muslim) thought, we human beings have been created in the image of God. This means, among other things, that God created us with the capacity for achieving *knowledge*—knowledge of our environment by way of perception, of other people by way of something like what Thomas Reid calls *sympathy*, of the past by memory and testimony, of mathematics and logic by reason, of morality, of our own mental life, of God himself, and much more.[3] And the above evolutionary account of our origins is compatible with the theistic view that God has created us in his image.[4] So evolutionary theory taken by itself (without the patina of philosophical naturalism that often accompanies expositions of it) is not as such in tension with the idea that God has created us and our cognitive faculties in such a way that the latter are reliable, that (as the medievals liked to say) there is an adequation of intellect to reality.

But if *naturalism* is true, there is no God, and hence no God (or anyone else) overseeing our development and orchestrating the course of our evolution. And this leads directly to the question whether it is at all likely that our cognitive faculties, given naturalism and given their evolutionary origin, would have developed in such a way as to be reliable, to furnish us with mostly true beliefs. Darwin himself expressed this doubt: "With me," he said,

> the horrid doubt always arises whether the convictions of man's mind, which has been developed from the mind of the lower animals, are of any value or at all trustworthy. Would anyone trust in the convictions of a monkey's mind, if there are any convictions in such a mind?[5]

The same thought is put more explicitly by Patricia Churchland. She insists that the most important thing about the human brain is that it has evolved; this means, she says, that its principal function is to enable the organism to *move* appropriately:

> Boiled down to essentials, a nervous system enables the organism to succeed in the four F's: feeding, fleeing, fighting and reproducing. The principle chore of nervous systems is to get the body parts where they should be in

order that the organism may survive. . . . Improvements in sensorimotor control confer an evolutionary advantage: a fancier style of representing is advantageous *so long as it is geared to the organism's way of life and enhances the organism's chances of survival* [Churchland's emphasis]. Truth, whatever that is, definitely takes the hindmost.[6]

What Churchland means, I think, is that evolution is directly interested (so to speak) only in *adaptive behavior* (in a broad sense including physical functioning), not in true belief. Natural selection doesn't care what you *believe;* it is interested only in how you *behave.* It selects for certain kinds of behavior: those that enhance fitness, which is a measure of the chances that one's genes will be widely represented in the next and subsequent generations. It doesn't select for belief, except insofar as the latter is appropriately related to behavior. But then the fact that we have evolved guarantees at most that we *behave* in certain ways—ways that contribute to our (or our ancestors') surviving and reproducing in the environment in which we have developed. Perhaps Churchland's claim can be understood as the suggestion that the objective probability[7] that our cognitive faculties are reliable, given naturalism and given that we have been cobbled together by the processes to which contemporary evolutionary theory calls our attention, is low. Of course she doesn't explicitly mention naturalism, but it certainly seems that she is taking it for granted. For if theism were true, God might be directing and orchestrating the variation in such a way as to produce, in the long run, beings created in his image and thus capable of knowledge; but then it wouldn't be the case that truth takes the hindmost.

We can put Churchland's claim as

P(R/N&E) is low,

where 'R' is the proposition that our cognitive faculties are reliable, 'N' the proposition that naturalism is true, and 'E' the proposition that we have evolved according to the suggestions of contemporary evolutionary theory.[8] I believe this thought—the thought that P(R/N&E) is low—is also what worries Darwin in the above quotation: I shall therefore call it 'Darwin's Doubt'.

Are Darwin and Churchland right? Well, they are certainly right in thinking that natural selection is directly interested only in behavior, not belief, and that it is interested in belief, if at all, only indirectly, by virtue of the relation between behavior and belief. If adaptive behavior guarantees or makes probable reliable faculties, then perhaps P(R/N&E) will be fairly high: we or rather our ancestors engaged in at least reasonably adaptive behavior, so it must be that our cognitive faculties are at least reasonably reliable, in which case it is likely that most of our beliefs are true. On the other hand, if our having reliable faculties *isn't* guaranteed by or even particularly probable with respect to adaptive behavior, then presumably P(R/N&E) will be rather low. If, for example, behavior isn't caused or governed by belief, the latter would be, so to speak, invisible to natural selection; in that case it would be unlikely that the great preponderance of true belief over false required by reliability would be forthcoming.[9] So the question of the value of P(R/N&E) really turns on the relationship between belief and behavior. Our having evolved and survived makes it likely that our cognitive faculties are reliable and our beliefs are for the most part true, only if it would be impossible or unlikely that creatures more or less like us should behave in fitness-enhancing ways but nonetheless hold mostly false beliefs.[10]

Is this impossible or unlikely? That depends upon the relation between belief and behavior. What would or could that relation be? To try to guard against interspecific chauvinism, I suggested that we think, not about ourselves and our behavior, but about a population of creatures a lot like us on a planet a lot like earth (Darwin suggested we think about monkeys in this connection). These creatures are *rational:* that is, they form beliefs, reason, change beliefs, and the like. We imagine furthermore that they and their cognitive systems have evolved by way of the mechanisms to which contemporary evolutionary theory directs our attention, unguided by the hand of God or anyone else. Now what is P(R/N&E), specified, not to us, but to them? To answer, we must think about the relationship between their beliefs and their behavior. There are four mutually exclusive and jointly exhaustive possibilities.[11]

(1) One possibility is *epiphenomenalism*:[12] their behavior is not caused by their beliefs. On this possibility, their movement and behavior would be caused by something or other—perhaps neural impulses—which would be caused by other organic conditions including sensory stimulation: but belief would not have a place in this causal chain leading to behavior. This view of the relation between behavior and belief (and other mental phenomena such as feeling, sensation, and desire) is currently rather popular, especially among those strongly influenced by biological science. The December 1992 issue of *Time* magazine reports that J. M. Smith, a well-known biologist, wrote "that he had never understood why organisms have feelings. After all, orthodox biologists believe that behavior, however complex, is governed entirely by biochemistry and that the attendant sensations—fear, pain, wonder, love—are just shadows cast by that bio-chemistry, not themselves vital to the organism's behavior." Smith could have added that (according to biological orthodoxy) the same goes for beliefs—at least if beliefs are not themselves just biochemical phenomena. If this way of thinking is right with respect to our hypothetical creatures, their beliefs would be *invisible* to evolution; and then the fact that their belief-forming mechanisms arose during their evolutionary history would confer little or no probability on the idea that their beliefs are mostly true, or mostly nearly true. Indeed, the probability of those beliefs' being for the most part true would have to be rated fairly low (or inscrutable). On N&E and this first possibility, therefore, the probability of R will be rather low.

(2) A second possibility is *semantic* epiphenomenalism: it could be that their beliefs do indeed have causal efficacy with respect to behavior, but not by virtue of their *content*. Put in currently fashionable jargon, this would be the suggestion that beliefs are indeed causally efficacious, but by virtue of their *syntax*, not by virtue of their *semantics*. On a naturalist or at least a materialist way of thinking, a belief could perhaps be some-thing like a long-term pattern of neural activity, a long-term neuronal event. This event will have properties of at least two different kinds. On the one hand, there are its neu-rophysiological or electrochemical properties: the number of neurons involved in the belief, the connections between them, their firing thresholds, the rate and strength at which they fire, the way in which these change over time and in response to other neural activity, and so on. Call these *syntactical* properties of the belief. On the other hand, however, if the belief is really a *belief*, it will be the belief that *p* for some propo-

sition *p*. Perhaps it is the belief that there once was a brewery where the Metropolitan Opera House now stands. This proposition, we might say, is the *content* of the belief in question. So in addition to its syntactical properties, a belief will also have *semantical* properties[13]—for example, the property of being the belief that there once was a brewery where the Metropolitan Opera House now stands. (Other semantical properties: *being true or false, entailing that there has been at least one brewery, being consistent with the proposition that all men are mortal*, and so on.) And this second possibility is that belief is indeed causally efficacious with respect to behavior, but by virtue of the *syntactic* properties of a belief, not its semantic properties. If the first possibility is widely popular among those influenced by biological science, this possibility is widely popular among contemporary philosophers of mind; indeed, Robert Cummins goes so far as to call it the "received view."[14]

On this view, as on the last, P(R/N&E) (specified to those creatures) will be low. The reason is that truth or falsehood are, of course, among the *semantic* properties of a belief, not its syntactic properties. But if the former aren't involved in the causal chain leading to behavior, then once again beliefs—or rather, their semantic properties, including truth and falsehood—will be invisible to natural selection.[15] But then it will be unlikely that their beliefs are mostly true, and hence unlikely that their cognitive faculties are reliable. The probability of R on N&E together with this possibility (as with the last), therefore, will be relatively low.

(3) It could be that beliefs are causally efficacious—'semantically' as well as 'syntactically'—with respect to behavior, but *maladaptive*: from the point of view of fitness these creatures would be better off without them. The probability of R on N&E together with this possibility, as with the last two, would also seem to be relatively low.

(4) Finally, it could be that the beliefs of our hypothetical creatures are indeed both causally connected with their behavior and also adaptive. (I suppose this is the commonsense view of the connection between behavior and belief in our own case.) What is the probability (on this assumption together with N&E) that their cognitive faculties are reliable; and what is the probability that a belief produced by those faculties will be true? I argued that this probability isn't nearly as high as one is initially inclined to think. For one thing, if behavior is caused by *belief*, it is also caused by *desire* (and other factors—suspicion, doubt, approval and disapproval, fear—that we can here ignore). For any given adaptive action, there will be many belief–desire combinations that could produce that action; and very many of those belief–desire combinations will be such that the belief involved is false.

So suppose Paul is a prehistoric hominid; a hungry tiger approaches. Fleeing is perhaps the most appropriate behavior: I pointed out that this behavior could be produced by a large number of different belief–desire pairs. To quote myself:

> Perhaps Paul very much *likes* the idea of being eaten, but when he sees a tiger, always runs off looking for a better prospect, because he thinks it unlikely that the tiger he sees will eat him. This will get his body parts in the right place so far as survival is concerned, without involving much by way of true belief. . . . Or perhaps he thinks the tiger is a large, friendly,

cuddly pussycat and wants to pet it; but he also believes that the best way to pet it is to run away from it. . . . or perhaps he thinks the tiger is a regularly recurring illusion, and, hoping to keep his weight down, has formed the resolution to run a mile at top speed whenever presented with such an illusion; or perhaps he thinks he is about to take part in a sixteen-hundred-meter race, wants to win, and believes the appearance of the tiger is the starting signal; or perhaps. . . . Clearly there are any number of belief-cum-desire systems that equally fit a given bit of behavior.[16]

Accordingly, there are many belief–desire combinations that will lead to the adaptive action; in many of these combinations, the beliefs are false. Without further knowledge of these creatures, therefore, we could hardly estimate the probability of R on N&E and this final possibility as high.

A problem with the argument as thus presented is this. It is easy to see, for just *one* of Paul's actions, that there are many different belief–desire combinations that yield it; it is less easy to see how it could be that most or all of his beliefs could be false but nonetheless adaptive or fitness enhancing. Could Paul's beliefs really be mainly false, but still lead to adaptive action? Yes indeed; perhaps the simplest way to see how is by thinking of systematic ways in which his beliefs could be false but still adaptive. Perhaps Paul is a sort of early Leibnizian and thinks everything is conscious (and suppose that is false); furthermore, his ways of referring to things all involve definite descriptions that entail consciousness, so that all of his beliefs are of the form *That so-and-so conscious being is such-and-such.* Perhaps he is an animist and thinks everything is alive. Perhaps he thinks all the plants and animals in his vicinity are witches, and his ways of referring to them all involve definite descriptions entailing witchhood. But this would be entirely compatible with his belief's being adaptive; so it is clear, I think, that there would be many ways in which Paul's beliefs could be for the most part false, but adaptive nonetheless. From a naturalistic point of view, furthermore, we need not restrict ourselves to merely possible examples. Most of mankind has endorsed supernatural beliefs of one kind or another; according to the naturalist, such beliefs are adaptive though false.

What we have seen so far is that there are four mutually exclusive and jointly exhaustive possibilities with respect to that hypothetical population: epiphenomenalism simpliciter, semantic epiphenomenalism, the possibility that their beliefs are causally efficacious with respect to their behavior but maladaptive, and the possibility that their beliefs are both causally efficacious with respect to behavior and also adaptive. $P(R/N\&E)$ will be the weighted average of $P(R/N\&E\&P_i)$ for each of the four possibilities P_i—weighted by the probabilities, on N&E, of those possibilities. The probability calculus gives us a formula here:

$$P(R/N\&E) = (P(R/N\&E\&P_1) \times P(P_1/N\&E)) + (P(R/N\&E\&P_2) \times P(P_2/N\&E)) + (P(R/N\&E\&P_3) \times P(P_3/N\&E)) + (P(R/N\&E\&P_4) \times P(P_4/N\&E)).$$

Of course the very idea of a calculation (suggesting, as it does, the assignment of specific real numbers to these various probabilities) is laughable: the best we can do are vague estimates. Still, that will suffice for the argument. Now let's agree that P_3— the proposition that belief enters the causal chain leading to behavior both by virtue of neurophysiological properties and by virtue of semantic properties, but is nevertheless maladaptive—is very unlikely; it is then clear from the formula that its contribution to P(R/N&E) can safely be ignored. Note further that epiphenomenalism simpliciter and semantic epiphenomenalism unite in declaring or implying that the *content* of belief lacks causal efficacy with respect to behavior; the content of belief does not get involved in the causal chain leading to behavior. So we can reduce these two possibilities to one: the possibility that the content of belief has no causal efficacy. Call this possibility '–C'. What we have so far seen is that the probability of R on N&E&–C is low or inscrutable, and that the probability of R on N&E&C is also inscrutable or at best moderately high. We can therefore simplify (1) to

(2) $P(R/N\&E) = P(R/N\&E\&C) \times P(C/N\&E) + P(R/N\&E\&\text{-}C) \times P(-C/N\&E)$,

i.e., the probability of R on N&E is the weighted average of the probabilities of R on N&E&C and N&E&–C (weighted by the probabilities of C and –C on N&E).

We have already noted that the left-hand term of the first of the two products on the right side of the equality is either moderately high or inscrutable; the left-hand term of the second product is either low or inscrutable. What remains is to evaluate the weights, the right-hand terms of the two products. So what is the probability of –C, given N&E: what is the probability that one or the other of the two epiphenomenalistic scenarios is true? Note that according to Robert Cummins, semantic epiphenomenalism is in fact the received view as to the relation between belief and behavior.[17] That is because it is extremely hard, given materialism, to envisage a way in which the content of a belief could get causally involved in behavior. If a belief just is a neural structure of some kind—a structure that somehow possesses content—then it is exceedingly hard to see how content can get involved in the causal chain leading to behavior. For if a given such structure had had a different content but the same neurophysiological properties, its causal contribution to behavior, one thinks, would be the same. What causes the muscular contractions involved in behavior are physiological states of the nervous system, including physiological properties of those structures that constitute beliefs; the content of those beliefs appears to be causally irrelevant. So it is exceedingly hard to see, given N&E, how the content of a belief can have causal efficacy.

It is exceedingly hard to see, that is, how epiphenomenalism—semantic or simpliciter—can be avoided, given N&E. (There have been some valiant efforts but things don't look hopeful.) So it looks as if P(–C/N&E) will have to be estimated as relatively high; let's say (for definiteness) .7, in which case P(C/N&E) will be .3. Let's also estimate that P(R/N&E&–C) is, say, .2. Then P(R/N&E) will be at most .45, less than ½. Of course we could easily be wrong; the argument for a low estimate of P(R/N&E) is by no means irresistible; our estimates of the various probabilities involved in estimating P(R/N&E) with respect to that hypothetical population were (naturally enough) both imprecise and poorly grounded. You might reasonably hold, therefore, that the right course here is simple agnosticism: one just doesn't know what P(R/N&E) is. You doubt that it is very high; but you aren't prepared to say that it is low: you have no definite opinion at all as to what that probability might be. Then this probability is *inscrutable* for you. This too seems a sensible attitude to take. The sensible thing to think, then, is that P(R/N&E) is either low or inscrutable.

Now return to Darwin's Doubt, and observe that if this is the sensible attitude to take to P(R/N&E) specified to that hypothetical population, then it will also be the sensible attitude toward P(R/N&E) specified to us. If N&E is true with respect to us, then we are relevantly like them in that our cognitive faculties have the same kind of origin and provenance as theirs are hypothesized to have. And the next step in the argument was to point out that each of these attitudes—the view that P(R/N&E) is low and the view that this probability is inscrutable—gives the naturalist-evolutionist a defeater for R. It gives him a reason to doubt it, a reason not to affirm it. I argued this by analogy. Among the crucially important facts, with respect to the question of the reliability of a group of cognitive faculties, are facts about their origin. Suppose I believe that I have been created by an evil Cartesian demon who takes delight in fashioning creatures who have mainly false beliefs (but think of themselves as paradigms of cognitive excellence): then I have a defeater for my natural belief that my faculties are reliable. Turn instead to the contemporary version of this scenario, and suppose I come to believe that I have been captured by Alpha-Centaurian superscientists who have made me the subject of a cognitive experiment in which I have been given mostly false beliefs: then, again, I have a defeater for R. But to have a defeater for R it isn't necessary that I believe that in fact I have been created by a Cartesian demon or been captured by those Alpha-Centaurian superscientists. It suffices for me to have such a defeater if I have considered those scenarios, and the probability that one of those scenarios is true, is inscrutable for me. It suffices if I have considered those scenarios, and for all I know or believe one of them is true. In these cases too I have a reason for doubting, a reason for withholding[18] my natural belief that my cognitive faculties are in fact reliable.

Now of course defeaters can be themselves defeated. For example, I know that you are a lifeguard and believe on that ground that you are an excellent swimmer. Then I learn that 45 percent of Frisian lifeguards are poor swimmers, and I know that you are Frisian: this gives me a defeater for the belief that you are a fine swimmer. Then I learn still further that you have graduated from the Department of Lifeguarding at the University of Leeuwarden and that one of the requirements for graduation is being an excellent swimmer: that gives me a defeater for the defeater of my original belief: a defeater-defeater as we might put it.[19] But (to return to our argument) can the defeater the naturalist has for R be in turn defeated? I argued that it can't.[20] It could be defeated only by something—an argument, for example—that involves some other belief (perhaps as a premise). Any such belief, however, will be subject to the very same defeater as R is. So this defeater can't be defeated. But if I have an undefeated defeater for R, then by the same token I have an undefeated defeater for any other belief B that my cognitive faculties produce, a reason to be doubtful of that belief, a reason to withhold it. For any such belief will be produced by cognitive faculties that I cannot rationally believe to be reliable. Clearly the same will be true for any belief they produce: if I can't rationally believe that the faculties that produce that belief are reliable, I have a reason for rejecting the belief. So the devotee of N&E has a defeater for just any belief he holds— a defeater, as I put it, that is ultimately undefeated. This means, then, that he has an ultimately undefeated defeater for N&E itself. And that means that the conjunction of naturalism with evolution is self-defeating, such that one can't rationally accept it. I went on to add that anyone who accepts naturalism ought also to accept evolution; evolution is the only game in town, for the naturalist, with respect to the question of how all this variety of flora and fauna has arisen. If that is so, finally, then naturalism simpliciter is self-defeating and cannot rationally be accepted—at any rate by someone who is apprised of this argument and sees the connections between N&E and R.

Notes

1   If my project were giving an analysis of philosophical naturalism, much more would have to be said (for example, if we don't know what naturalism is, will it help to explain it in terms of supernaturalism?); for present purposes we can ignore the niceties.

2   *Very* roughly: a thermometer stuck on seventy-two degrees isn't reliable even if it is located somewhere (San Diego?) where it is seventy-two degrees nearly all of the time. What the thermometer (and our cognitive faculties) would do if things were different in certain (hard to specify) respects is also relevant. Again, if our aim were to analyze *reliability* much more would have to be said. Note that for reliability thus construed, it is not enough that the beliefs produced be fitness enhancing.

3   Thus Thomas Aquinas: "Since human beings are said to be in the image of God in virtue of their having a nature that includes an intellect, such a nature is most in the image of God in virtue of being most able to imitate God" (*Summa Theologica* Ia q. 93 a.4); and 'Only in rational creatures is there found a likeness of God which counts as an image. . . . As far as a likeness of the divine nature is concerned, rational creatures seem somehow to attain a representation of [that] type in virtue of imitating God not only in this, that he is and lives, but especially in this, that he understands" (*Summa Theologica* Ia q.93 a.6).

4   You might think not: if our origin involves *random* genetic variation, then we and our cognitive faculties would have developed by way of *chance* rather than by way of design, as would be required by our having been created by God in his image. But this is to import far too much into the biologist's term 'random'. Those random variations are random in the sense that they don't arise out of the organism's design plan and don't ordinarily play a role in its viability; perhaps they are also random in the sense that they are not predictable. But of course it doesn't follow that they are random in the much stronger sense of not being caused, orchestrated, and arranged by God. And suppose the biologists, or others, *did* intend this stronger sense of 'random': then their theory (call it 'T') would indeed entail that human beings have not been designed by God. But T would not be more probable than not with respect to the evidence. For there would be an empirically equivalent theory (the theory that results from T by taking the weaker sense of 'random' and adding that God has orchestrated the mutations) that is inconsistent with T but as well supported by the evidence; if so, T is not more probable than not with respect to the relevant evidence.

5   Letter to William Graham, Down, July 3, 1881, in *The Life and Letters of Charles Darwin Including an Autobiographical Chapter*, ed. Francis Darwin (London: John Murray, Albemarle Street, 1887), 1:315–316. Evan Fales and Omar Mirza have pointed out that Darwin probably had in mind, here, not everyday beliefs such as that the teapot is in the cupboard, but something more like religious and philosophical convictions.

6   Churchland, "Epistemology in the Age of Neuroscience," *Journal of Philosophy* 84 (October 1987): 548.

7   For an account of objective probability, see my *Warrant and Proper Function* (hereafter *WPF*), (New York: Oxford University Press, 1993), 161ff.

8   In *WPF* the probability at issue was the slightly more complex P(R/N&E&C), where C was a proposition setting out some of the main features of our cognitive system (see *WPF*, 220). I now think the additional complexity unnecessary.

9   Alternatively, we might say that the probability here is inscrutable, such that we can't make an estimate of it. Granted: it is unlikely that a large set of beliefs (comparable in size to the

number of beliefs a human being has) should contain mainly truths; that gives us a reason for regarding the probability in question as low. On the other hand, we know something further about the relevant set of propositions, namely, that it is a set each member of which is believed by someone. How does this affect the probability? Perhaps we don't know what to say, and should conclude that the probability in question is inscrutable. (Here I am indebted to John Hare.)

10   Must we concur with Donald Davidson, who thinks it is "impossible correctly to hold that anyone could be mostly wrong about how things are?" (See his "A Coherence Theory of Truth and Knowledge," in *Kant oder Hegel?* ed. Dieter Henrich [Stuttgart: Klett-Cotta Buchhandlung, 1983], 535.) No; what Davidson shows (if anything) is that it isn't possible for me to *understand* another creature unless I suppose that she holds mainly true beliefs. That may (or more likely, may not) be so; but it doesn't follow that there couldn't be creatures with mainly false beliefs, and a fortiori it doesn't follow that my own beliefs are mainly true. Davidson went on to argue that an *omniscient* interpreter would have to use the same methods we have to use and would therefore have to suppose her interlocutor held mostly true beliefs; given the omniscient interpreter's omniscience, he concluded that her interlocutor would in fact have mostly true beliefs. In so concluding, however, he apparently employs the premise that any proposition that would be believed by any omniscient being is true; this premise directly yields the conclusion that there is an omniscient being (since any omniscient being worth its salt will believe that there *is* an omniscient being), a conclusion to which Davidson may not wish to commit himself quite so directly. See *WPF*, 80–81.

11   In *WPF* the argument involves five mutually exclusive and jointly exhaustive possibilities; here I telescope the first two.

12   So called first by T. H. Huxley ("Darwin's bull dog"): "It may be assumed . . . that molecular changes in the brain are the causes of all the states of consciousness. . . . [But is] there any evidence that these states of consciousness may, conversely, cause . . . molecular changes [in the brain] which give rise to muscular motion? I see no such evidence. . . . [Consciousness appears] to be . . . completely without any power of modifying [the] working of the body, just as the steam whistle . . . of a locomotive engine is without influence upon its machinery." T. H. Huxley, "On the Hypothesis that Animals are Automata and its History" (1874), in *Method and Results* (London: Macmillan, 1893), 239–240. Later in the essay: "To the best of my judgment, the argumentation which applies to brutes holds equally good of men; and therefore, . . . all states of consciousness in us, as in them, are immediately caused by molecular changes of the brain-substance. It seems to me that in men, as in brutes, there is no proof that any state of consciousness is the cause of change in the motion of the matter of the organism. . . . We are conscious automata." (243–244). (Note the occurrence here of that widely endorsed form of argument, 'I know of no proof that not-p; therefore there is no proof that not-p; therefore p'.) However, I am here using the term to denote *any* view according to which belief isn't involved in the causal chain leading to behavior, whether or not that view involves the dualism that is apparently part of Huxley's version.

13   Granted: the analogies between these properties and syntax and semantics is a bit distant and strained; here I am just following current custom.

14   *Meaning and Mental Representation* (Cambridge: MIT Press, 1989), 130. In *Explaining Behavior* (Cambridge: MIT Press, 1988) Fred Dretske makes a valiant (but in my opinion unsuccessful) effort to explain how, given materialism about human beings, it could be that beliefs (and other representations) play a causal role in the production of behavior by virtue of their content or semantics. Part of the problem is that Dretske's account implies that there are no distinct but logically equivalent beliefs, and indeed no distinct but causally equivalent beliefs.

15   We must also consider here the possibility that the syntax and semantics of belief are the effects of a common cause: perhaps there is a cause of a belief's having certain adaptive syntactic properties, which also causes the belief to have the semantic properties it does (it brings it about that the event in question is the belief that *p* for some proposition *p*); and perhaps this cause brings it about that a *true* proposition is associated with the belief (the neuronal event) in question. (Here I was instructed by William Ramsey and Patrick Kain.) What would be the likelihood, given N&E, that there is such a common cause at work? I suppose it would be relatively low; why should this common cause associate *true* propositions with these neuronal events? But perhaps the right answer is not that the probability in question is low, but that it is inscrutable.

16   *WPF*, 225–226.

17   *Meaning and Mental Representation*, 130.

18   I shall use this term to mean *failing to believe*, so that I withhold *p* if either I believe its denial or I believe neither it nor its denial.

19   As in fact John Pollock *does* put it; see his *Contemporary Theories of Knowledge* (Totowa, N.J.: 1986), 38–39.

20   *WPF*, 233–234.

Questions for reflection

1   Explain, in summary form, Professor Plantinga's evolutionary argument against naturalism (EAAN). Do you find it plausible? If so, explain why. If not, what problems do you find with it?

2   What do you take to be the relationship between belief and behavior? How is it relevant to EAAN?

3   Do you agree that the probability of R is conditional on N&E? Why or why not?

4   Does our having evolved and survived make it more likely than not that our cognitive faculties are reliable and our beliefs true? Could belief–desire systems which do not reflect the way things are provide as much beneficial adaptive action as one which does reflect the way things are? Is one more probable than the other? Explain.

5   If a naturalist believes that false beliefs are not adaptive, what could she say about the widespread human belief in the supernatural?

Further reading

James Beilby, ed. (2002) *Naturalism Defeated: Essays on Plantinga's Evolutionary Argument Against Naturalism*. Ithaca, NY: Cornell University Press. (Includes the essay above as well as eleven critiques by distinguished philosophers and Plantinga's responses to them.)

William Lane Craig and J. P. Moreland, eds. (2000) *Naturalism: A Critical Analysis*. London: Routledge. (A critique of the major varieties of contemporary naturalism.)

Alvin Plantinga (2000) *Warranted Christian Belief*. Oxford: Oxford University Press. (The third volume in Plantinga's "Warrant" trilogy; this one examines the role of warrant in theistic belief and also includes some responses to criticisms of the EAAN argument.)

Michael Rea (2002) *World Without Design: The Ontological Consequences of Naturalism*. Oxford: Clarendon Press (Argues that philosophical naturalism is without rational foundation.)

Chapter 39

Daniel C. Dennett

SCIENCE AND RELIGION

Daniel C. Dennett is Professor of Philosophy and Co-Director of the Center for Cognitive Studies at Tufts University. In this essay he first notes that religion is a natural phenomenon—a human phenomenon which consists of such things as events, organisms, structures, and the like, all of which conform to the laws of physics and biology. He then proposes a wide, concentrated effort whereby religion becomes an object of scientific study. He points out that a good science of religion is not only possible, but that it *should* be explored, most especially since few forces in the world are as influential as religion, and whatever happens with religion in the future will no doubt have incredible significance to planet earth. Thus, we should carefully examine religion and work together to revise and reform it as necessary.

I. Religion as a natural phenomenon

> As every enquiry which regards religion is of the utmost importance, there are two questions in particular which challenge our attention, to wit, that concerning its foundation in reason, and that concerning its origin in human nature.
>
> —David Hume, *The Natural History of Religion*

What do I mean when I speak of religion as a natural phenomenon?

I might mean that it's like natural food—not just tasty but healthy, unadulterated, "organic." (That, at any rate, is the myth.) So do I mean: "Religion is *healthy*; it's good for you!"? This might be true, but it is not what I mean.

I might mean that religion is not an artifact, not a product of human intellectual activity. Sneezing and belching are natural, reciting sonnets is not; going naked—*au naturel*—is natural; wearing clothes is not. But it is obviously false that religion is natural in this sense.

Religions are transmitted culturally, through language and symbolism, not through the genes. You may get your father's nose and your mother's musical ability through your genes, but if you get your religion from your parents, you get it the way you get your language, through upbringing. So of course that is not what I mean by *natural*.

With a slightly different emphasis, I might mean that religion is *doing what comes naturally*, not an acquired taste, or an artificially groomed or educated taste. In this sense, speaking is natural but writing is not; drinking milk is natural but drinking a dry martini is not; listening to tonal music is natural but listening to atonal music is not; gazing at sunsets is natural but gazing at late Picasso paintings is not. There is some truth to this: religion is not an unnatural act . . . . But it is not what I mean.

I might mean that religion is natural as opposed to *supernatural*, that it is a human phenomenon composed of events, organisms, objects, structures, patterns, and the like that all obey the laws of physics or biology, and hence do not involve miracles. And that *is* what I mean. Notice that it could be true that God exists, that God is indeed the intelligent, conscious, loving creator of us all, and yet *still* religion itself, as a complex set of phenomena, is a perfectly natural phenomenon. Nobody would think it was presupposing atheism to write a book subtitled *Sports as a Natural Phenomenon* or *Cancer as a Natural Phenomenon*. Both sports and cancer are widely recognized as natural phenomena, not supernatural, in spite of the well-known exaggerations of various promoters. (I'm thinking, for instance, of two famous touchdown passes known respectively as the Hail Mary and the Immaculate Reception, to say nothing of the weekly trumpetings by researchers and clinics around the world of one "miraculous" cancer cure or another.)

Sports and cancer are the subject of intense scientific scrutiny by researchers working in many disciplines and holding many different religious views. They all assume, tentatively and for the sake of science, that the phenomena they are studying are natural phenomena. This doesn't prejudge the verdict that they are. Perhaps there *are* sports miracles that actually defy the laws of nature; perhaps some cancer cures *are* miracles. If so, the only hope of ever demonstrating this to a doubting world would be by adopting the scientific method, with its assumption of no miracles, and showing that science was utterly unable to account for the phenomena. Miracle-hunters must be scrupulous scientists or else they are wasting their time—a point long recognized by the Roman Catholic Church, which at least goes through the motions of subjecting the claims of miracles made on behalf of candidates for sainthood to objective scientific investigation. So no deeply religious person should object to the scientific study of religion with the presumption that it is an entirely natural phenomenon. If it isn't entirely natural, if there really are miracles involved, the best way—indeed, the only way—to show that to doubters would be to demonstrate it scientifically. Refusing to play by these rules only creates the suspicion that one doesn't really believe that religion is supernatural after all.

In assuming that religion is a natural phenomenon, I am not prejudging its value to human life, one way or the other. Religion, like love and music, is natural. But so are smoking, war, and death. In this sense of *natural*, everything artificial is natural! The Aswan Dam is no less natural than a beaver's dam, and the beauty of a skyscraper is no less natural than the beauty of a sunset. The natural sciences take everything in Nature as their topic, and that includes both jungles and cities, both birds and airplanes, the good, the bad, the ugly, the insignificant, and the all-important as well.

Over two hundred years ago, David Hume wrote two books on religion. One was about religion as a natural phenomenon, and its opening sentence is the epigraph of this section. The other was about the "foundation in reason" of religion, his famous *Dialogues Concerning Natural Religion* (1779). Hume wanted to consider whether there was any good reason—any *scientific* reason, we might say—for believing in God. *Natural* religion, for Hume, would be a creed that was as well supported by evidence and argument as Newton's theory of gravitation, or plane geometry. He contrasted it with *revealed* religion, which depended on the revelations of mystical experience or other extra-scientific paths to conviction. I gave Hume's *Dialogues* a place of honor in my 1995 book, *Darwin's Dangerous Idea*—Hume is yet another of my heroes—so you might think that I intend to pursue this issue still further . . . but that is not in fact my intention. This time I am pursuing Hume's other path. Philosophers have spent two millennia and more concocting and criticizing arguments for the existence of God, such as the Argument from Design and the Ontological Argument, and arguments against the existence of God, such as the Argument from Evil. Many of us brights have devoted considerable time and energy at some point in our lives to looking at the arguments for and against the existence of God, and many brights continue to pursue these issues, hacking away vigorously at the arguments of the believers as if they were trying to refute a rival scientific theory. But not I. I decided some time ago that diminishing returns had set in on the arguments about God's existence, and I doubt that any breakthroughs are in the offing, from either side. Besides, many deeply religious people insist that all those arguments—on both sides—simply miss the whole point of religion, and their demonstrated lack of interest in the arguments persuades me of their sincerity. Fine. So what, then, *is* the point of religion?

What is this phenomenon or set of phenomena that means so much to so many people, and why—and how—does it command allegiance and shape so many lives so strongly? That is the main question I will address here. . . .

II. Some questions about science

Can *science study religion?*

> To be sure, man is, zoologically speaking, an animal. Yet, he *is* a unique animal, differing from all others in *so* many fundamental ways that a separate science for man *is* well-justified.
> —Ernst Mayr, *The Growth of Biological Thought*

There has been some confusion about whether the earthly manifestations of religion should count as a part of Nature. Is religion out-of-bounds to science? It all depends on what you mean. If you mean the religious experiences, beliefs, practices, texts, artifacts, institutions, conflicts, and history of *H. sapiens*, then this is a voluminous catalogue of unquestionably natural phenomena. Considered as psychological states, drug-induced hallucination and religious ecstasy are both amenable to study by neuroscientists and psychologists. Considered as the exercise of cognitive competence, memorizing the periodic table of elements is the same sort of phenomenon as memorizing the Lord's Prayer. Considered as examples of engineering, suspension bridges and cathedrals both obey the law of gravity and are subject to the same sorts of forces and stresses. Considered as salable manufactured goods, both mystery novels and Bibles fall under the regularities of economics. The logistics of holy wars do not differ from the logistics of entirely secular conflicts. "Praise the Lord and pass the ammunition!" as the World War II song said. A *crusade* or a *jihad* can be investigated by researchers in many disciplines, from anthropology and military history to nutrition and metallurgy.

In his book *Rocks of Ages* (1999), the late Stephen Jay Gould defended the political hypothesis that science and religion are two "non-overlapping *magisteria*"—two domains of concern and inquiry that can coexist peacefully as long as neither poaches on the other's special province. The *magisterium* of science is factual truth on all matters, and the *magisterium* of religion, he claimed, is the realm of morality and the meaning of life. Although Gould's desire for peace between these often warring perspectives was laudable, his proposal found little favor on either side, since in the minds of the religious it proposed abandoning all religious claims to factual truth and understanding of the natural world (including the claims that God created the universe, or performs miracles, or listens to prayers), whereas in the minds of the secularists it granted too much authority to religion in matters of ethics and meaning. Gould exposed some clear instances of immodest folly on both sides, but the claim that *all* conflict between the two perspectives is due to overreaching by one side or the other is implausible, and few readers were persuaded. But whether or not the case can be made for Gould's proposal, my proposal is different. There may be some domain that is religion's alone to command, some realm of human activity that science can't properly address and religion can, but that does not mean that science cannot or should not study this very fact. Gould's own book was presumably a product of just such a scientific investigation, albeit a rather informal one. He looked at religion with the eyes of a scientist and thought he could see a boundary that revealed two domains of human activity. Was he right? That is presumably a scientific, factual question, not a religious question. I am not suggesting that science should *try to do* what religion does, but that it should *study*, scientifically, what religion does.

One of the surprising discoveries of modern psychology is how easy it is to be ignorant of your own ignorance. You are normally oblivious of your own blind spot, and people are typically amazed to discover that we don't see colors in our peripheral vision. It *seems* as if we do, but we don't, as you can prove to yourself by wiggling colored cards at the edge of your vision—you'll see motion just fine but not be able to identify the color of the moving thing. It takes special provoking like that to get the *absence* of information to reveal itself to us. And the absence of information about religion is what I want to draw to everyone's attention. We have neglected to gather a wealth of information about something of great import to us.

This may come as a surprise. Haven't we been looking carefully at religion for a long time? Yes, of course. There have been centuries of insightful and respectful scholarship about the history and variety of religious phenomena. This work, like the bounty gathered by dedicated bird-watchers and other nature lovers before Darwin's time, is proving to be a hugely valuable resource to those pioneers who are now beginning, for the first time really, to study the natural phenomena of religion through the eyes of contemporary science. Darwin's breakthrough in biology was enabled by his deep knowledge of the wealth of empirical details scrupulously garnered by hundreds of pre-Darwinian, non-Darwinian natural historians. Their theoretical innocence was itself an important check on his enthusiasm; they had not gathered their facts with an eye to proving Darwinian theory correct, and we can be equally grateful that almost all the "natural history of religion" that has been accumulated to date is, if not theoretically innocent, at least oblivious to the sorts of theories that now may be supported or under-cut by it.

The research to date has hardly been neutral, however. We don't just walk up to religious phenomena and study them point-blank, as if they were fossils or soybeans in a field. Researchers tend to be either respectful, deferential, diplomatic, tentative—or hostile, invasive, and contemptuous. It is just about impossible to be neutral in your approach to religion, because many people view neutrality in itself as hostile. If you're not for us, you're against us. And so, since religion so clearly matters so much to so many people, researchers have almost never even attempted to be neutral; they have tended to err on the side of deference, putting on the kid gloves. It is either that or open hostility. For this reason, there has been an unfortunate pattern in the work that has been done. People who want to study religion usually have an ax to grind. They either want to defend their favorite religion from its critics or want to demonstrate the irra-tionality and futility of religion, and this tends to infect their methods with bias. Such distortion is not inevitable. Scientists in every field have pet theories they hope to con-firm, or target hypotheses they yearn to demolish, but, knowing this, they take a variety of tried-and-true steps to prevent their bias from polluting their evidence-gathering: double-blind experiments, peer review, statistical tests, and many other standard con-straints of good scientific method. But in the study of religion, the stakes have often been seen to be higher. If you think that the disconfirmation of a hypothesis about one religious phenomenon or another would not be just an undesirable crack in the founda-tion of some theory but a moral calamity, you tend not to run all the controls. Or so, at least, it has often seemed to observers.

That impression, true or false, has created a positive feedback loop: scientists don't want to deal with second-rate colleagues, so they tend to shun topics where they see what they take to be mediocre work being done. This self-selection is a frustrating pat-tern that begins when students think about "choosing a major" in college. The best students typically shop around, and if they are unimpressed by the work they are intro-duced to in the first course in a field, they cross that field off their list for good. When I was an undergraduate, physics was still the glamour field, and then the race to the moon drew more than its share of talent. (A fossil trace is the phrase "Hey, it's not rocket science.") This was followed by computer science for a while, and all along—for half a century and more—biology, especially molecular biology, has attracted many of the smartest. Today, cognitive science and the various strands of evolutionary biol-ogy—bio-informatics, genetics, developmental biology—are on the rise. But through all this period, sociology and anthropology, social psychology, and my own home field, philosophy, have struggled along, attracting those whose interests match the field well, including some brilliant people, but having to combat somewhat unenviable reputa-tions. As my old friend and former colleague, Nelson Pike, a respected philosopher of religion, once ruefully put it:

> If you are in a company of people of mixed occupations, and somebody asks what you do, and you say you are a college professor, a glazed look comes into his eye. If you are in a company of professors from various departments, and somebody asks what is your field, and you say philosophy, a glazed look comes into his eye. If you are at a conference of philosophers, and somebody asks you what you are working on, and you say philosophy of religion. . .[1]

This is not just a problem for philosophers of religion. It is equally a problem for sociologists of religion, psychologists of religion, and other social scientists—economists, political scientists—and for those few brave neuroscientists and other biologists who have decided to look at religious phenomena with the tools of their trade. One of the factors is that people think they already know everything they need to know about religion, and this received wisdom is pretty bland, not provocative enough to inspire either refutation or extension. In fact, if you set out to design an impermeable barrier between scientists and an underexplored phenomenon, you could hardly do better than to fabricate the dreary aura of low prestige, backbiting, and dubious results that currently envelops the topic of religion. And since we know from the outset that many people think such research violates a taboo, or at least meddles impertinently in matters best left private, it is not so surprising that few good researchers, in any discipline, want to touch the topic. I myself certainly felt that way until recently.

These obstacles can be overcome. In the twentieth century, a lot was learned about how to study human phenomena, social phenomena. Wave after wave of research and criticism has sharpened our appreciation of the particular pitfalls, such as biases in data-gathering, investigator-interference effects, and the interpretation of data. Statistical and analytical techniques have become much more sophisticated, and we have begun setting aside the old oversimplified models of human perception, emotion, motivation, and control of action and replacing them with more physiologically and psychologically realistic models. The yawning chasm that was seen to separate the sciences of the mind (*Geisteswissenschaften*) from the natural sciences (*Naturwissenschaften*) has not yet been bridged securely, but many lines have been flung across the divide. Mutual suspicion and professional jealousy as well as genuine theoretical controversy continue to shake almost all efforts to carry insights back and forth on these connecting routes, but every day the traffic grows. The question is not whether good science of religion as a natural phenomenon is possible: it is. The question is whether we should do it.

Should *science study religion?*

Look before you leap.

—Aesop, "The Fox and the Goat"

Research is expensive and sometimes has harmful side effects. One of the lessons of the twentieth century is that scientists are not above confabulating justifications for the work they want to do, driven by insatiable curiosity. Are there in fact good reasons, aside from sheer curiosity, to try to develop the natural science of religion? Do we need this for anything? Would it help us choose policies, respond to problems, improve our world? What do we know about the future of religion? Consider five wildly different hypotheses:

1. *The Enlightenment is long gone; the creeping "secularization" of modern societies that has been anticipated for two centuries is evaporating before our eyes.* The tide is turning and religion is becoming more important than ever. In this scenario, religion soon resumes something like the dominant social and moral role it had before the rise of modern science in the seventeenth century. As people recover from their infatuation with technology and material comforts, spiritual identity becomes a person's most valued attribute, and

populations come to be ever more sharply divided among Christianity, Islam, Judaism, Hinduism, and a few other major multinational religious organizations. Eventually—it might take another millennium, or it might be hastened by catastrophe—one major faith sweeps the planet.

2. *Religion is in its death throes; today's outbursts of fervor and fanaticism are but a brief and awkward transition to a truly modern society in which religion plays at most a ceremonial role.* In this scenario, although there may be some local and temporary revivals and even some violent catastrophes, the major religions of the world soon go just as extinct as the hundreds of minor religions that are vanishing faster than anthropologists can record them. Within the lifetimes of our grandchildren, Vatican City becomes the European Museum of Roman Catholicism, and Mecca is turned into Disney's Magic Kingdom of Allah.

3. *Religions transform themselves into institutions unlike anything seen before on the planet: basically creedless associations selling self-help and enabling moral teamwork, using ceremony and tradition to cement relationships and build "long-term fan loyalty."* In this scenario, being a member of a religion becomes more and more like being a Boston Red Sox fan, or a Dallas Cowboys fan. Different colors, different songs and cheers, different symbols, and vigorous competition—would you want your daughter to marry a Yankees fan?—but aside from a rabid few, everybody appreciates the importance of peaceful coexistence in a Global League of Religions. Religious art and music flourish, and friendly rivalry leads to a degree of specialization, with one religion priding itself on its environmental stewardship, providing clean water for the world's billions, while another becomes duly famous for its concerted defense of social justice and economic equality.

4. *Religion diminishes in prestige and visibility, rather like smoking; it is tolerated, since there are those who say they can't live without it, but it is discouraged, and teaching religion to impressionable young children is frowned upon in most societies and actually outlawed in others.* In this scenario, politicians who still practice religion can be elected if they prove themselves worthy in other regards, but few would advertise their religious affiliation—or affliction, as the politically incorrect insist on calling it. It is considered as rude to draw attention to the religion of somebody as it is to comment in public about his sexuality or whether she has been divorced.

5. *Judgment Day arrives. The blessed ascend bodily into heaven, and the rest are left behind to suffer the agonies of the damned, as the Antichrist is vanquished.* As the Bible prophecies foretold, the rebirth of the nation of Israel in 1948 and the ongoing conflict over Palestine are clear signs of the End Times, when the Second Coming of Christ sweeps all the other hypotheses into oblivion.

Other possibilities are describable, of course, but these five hypotheses highlight the extremes that are taken seriously. What is remarkable about the set is that just about anybody would find at least one of them preposterous, or troubling, or even deeply offensive, but every one of them is not just anticipated but yearned for. People act on what they yearn for. We are at cross-purposes about religion, to say the least, so we can anticipate problems, ranging from wasted effort and counterproductive campaigns if we are lucky to all-out war and genocidal catastrophe if we are not.

Only one of these hypotheses (at most) will turn out to be true; the rest are not just wrong but wildly wrong. Many people think they know which is true, but nobody does. Isn't that fact, all by itself, enough reason to study religion scientifically? Whether you want religion to flourish or perish, whether you think it should transform itself or stay just as it is, you can hardly deny that whatever happens will be of tremendous significance to the planet. It would be useful to your hopes, whatever they are, to know more about what is likely to happen and why. In this regard, it is worth noting how assiduously those who firmly believe in number 5 scan the world news for evidence of prophecies fulfilled. They sort and evaluate their sources, debating the pros and cons of various interpretations of those prophecies. They think there is a reason to investigate the future of religion, and they don't even think the course of future events lies within human power to determine. The rest of us have all the more reason to investigate the phenomena, since it is quite obvious that complacency and ignorance could lead us to squander our opportunities to steer the phenomena in what we take to be the benign directions.

Looking ahead, anticipating the future, is the crowning achievement of our species. We have managed in a few short millennia of human culture to multiply the planet's supply of look-ahead by many orders of magnitude. We know when eclipses will occur centuries in advance; we can predict the effects on the atmosphere of adjustments in how we generate electricity; we can anticipate in broad outline what will happen as our petroleum reserves dwindle in the next decades. We do this not with miraculous prophecy but with basic perception. We gather information from the environment, using our senses, and then we use science to cobble together anticipations based on that information. We mine the ore, and then refine it, again and again, and it lets us see into the future—dimly, with lots of uncertainty, but much better than a coin toss. In every area of human concern, we have learned how to anticipate and then avoid catastrophes that used to blindside us.[2] We have recently forestalled a global disaster due to a growing hole in the ozone layer because some far-seeing chemists were able to prove that some of our manufactured compounds were causing the problem. We have avoided economic collapses in recent years because our economic models have shown us impending problems.

A catastrophe averted is an anticlimax, obviously, so we tend not to appreciate how valuable our powers of look-ahead are. "See?" we complain. "It wasn't going to happen after all." The flu season in the winter of 2003–2004 was predicted to be severe, since it arrived earlier than usual, but the broadcast recommendations for inoculation were so widely heeded that the epidemic collapsed as rapidly as it began. Ho-hum. It has become something of a tradition in recent years for the meteorologists on television to hype an oncoming hurricane or other storm, and then for the public to be underwhelmed by the actual storm. But sober evaluations show that many lives are saved, destruction is minimized. We accept the value of intensely studying El Niño and the other cycles in ocean currents so that we can do better meteorological forecasting. We keep exhaustive records of many economic events so that we can do better economic forecasting. We should extend the same intense scrutiny, for the same reasons, to religious phenomena. Few forces in the world are as potent, as influential, as religion. As we struggle to resolve the terrible economic and social inequities that currently disfigure our planet, and minimize the violence and degradation we see, we have to recognize that if we have a blind spot about religion our efforts will almost certainly fail, and may make matters much worse. We wouldn't permit the world's food-producing interests to deflect us from studying human agriculture and nutrition, and we have learned not to exempt the banking-and-insurance world from intense and continuous scrutiny. Their effects are too important to take on faith. So what I am calling for is a concerted effort to achieve a mutual agreement under which religion—all religion—becomes a proper object of scientific study.

Here I find that opinion is divided among those who are already convinced that this would be a good idea, those who are dubious and inclined to doubt that it would be of much value, and those who find the proposal evil—offensive, dangerous, and stupid. Not wanting to preach to the converted, I am particularly concerned to address those who hate this idea, in hopes of persuading them that their repugnance is misplaced. This is a daunting task, like trying to persuade your friend with the cancer symptoms that she really ought to see a doctor *now*, since her anxiety may be misplaced and the sooner she learns that the sooner she can get on with her life, and if she does have cancer, timely intervention may make all the difference. Friends can get quite annoyed when you interfere with their denial at times like that, but perseverance is called for. Yes, I want to put religion on the examination table. If it is fundamentally benign, as many of its devotees insist, it should emerge just fine; suspicions will be put to rest and we can then concentrate on the few peripheral pathologies that religion, like every other natural phenomenon, falls prey to. If it is not, the sooner we identify the problems clearly the better. Will the inquiry itself generate some discomfort and embarrassment? Almost certainly, but that is a small price to pay. Is there a risk that such an invasive examination will make a healthy religion ill, or even disable it? Of course. There are always risks. Are they worth taking? Perhaps not, but I haven't yet seen an argument that persuades me of this. . . . The only arguments worth attending to will have to demonstrate that (1) religion provides net benefits to humankind, and (2) these benefits would be unlikely to survive such an investigation. I, for one, fear that if we don't subject religion to such scrutiny now, and work out together whatever revisions and reforms are called for, we will pass on a legacy of ever more toxic forms of religion to our descendants. I can't prove that, and those who are dead sure that this will not happen are encouraged to say what supports their conviction, aside from loyalty to their tradition, which goes without saying and doesn't count for anything here.

In general, knowing more improves your chances of getting what you value. That's not quite a truth of logic, since uncertainty is not the only factor that can lower the probability of achieving one's goals. The costs of knowing (such as the cost of *coming to know*) must be factored in, and these costs may be high, which is why "Wing it!" is sometimes good advice. Suppose there is a limit on how much knowledge about some topic is good for us. If so, then, whenever that limit is reached (if that is possible— the limit may be unreachable for one reason or another), we should prohibit or at least strongly discourage any further seeking of knowledge on that topic, as antisocial activity. This may be a principle that never comes into play, but we don't know that, and we should certainly accept the principle. It may be, then, that some of our major disagreements in the world today are about whether we've reached such a limit. This reflection puts the Islamist[3] conviction that Western science is a bad thing in a different light: it may not be an ignorant mistake so much as a profoundly different view of where the threshold is. Sometimes ignorance is bliss. We need to consider such possibilities carefully.

Might music be bad for you?

> Music, the greatest good that mortals know,
>   And all of heaven we have below.

—Joseph Addison

> Is it not strange that sheep's guts should hale souls out of men's bodies?

—William Shakespeare

It is not that I don't sympathize with the distaste of those who resist my proposal. Trying to imagine what their emotional response to my proposal would be, I have come up with an unsettling thought experiment that seems to me to do the trick. (I am speaking now to those who, like me, are *not* appalled by the idea of this examination.) Imagine how you would feel if you were to read in the science section of the *New York Times* that new research conducted at Cambridge University and Caltech showed that music, long viewed as one of the unalloyed treasures of human culture, is actually bad for your health, a major risk factor for Alzheimer's and heart disease, a mood-distorter that impairs judgment in subtle but clearly deleterious ways, a significant contributor to aggressive tendencies, xenophobia, and weakness of will. Early and habitual exposure to music, both performing and listening, makes you 40 percent more likely to suffer serious depression, knocks an average of ten points off your IQ, and nearly doubles the probability that you will commit an act of violence at some time in your life. A panel of researchers recommends that people restrict their music intake to no more than an hour a day (including everything from elevator music and background music on television to symphony concerts) and that the widespread practice of music lessons for children be curtailed immediately.

A side from the utter disbelief with which I would greet a report of such "findings," I can detect in my imagined reactions a visceral defensive surge, along the lines of "So much the worse for Cambridge and Caltech! What do *they* know about music?" and "I don't care if it is true! Anybody who tries to take away my music had better be prepared for a fight, because a life without music isn't worth living. I don't care if it 'hurts' me, and I don't even care if it 'hurts' others—we're going to have music, and that's all there is to it." That is how I would be tempted to respond. I would rather not live in a world without music. "But why?" someone might ask. "It's just some silly sawing away and making noise together. It doesn't feed the hungry or cure cancer or . . ." I answer: "But it brings great comfort and joy to hundreds of millions of people. Sure, there are excesses and controversies, but, still, can anybody doubt that music is by and large a good thing?" "Well, yes," comes the reply. There are religious sects—the Taliban, for instance, but also Puritan sects of yore in Christianity and no doubt others—that have held that music is an evil pastime, a sort of drug to be forbidden. The idea is not clearly insane, so we should accept the intellectual burden of showing that it is an error.

I recognize that many people feel about religion the way I feel about music. They may be right. Let's find out. That is, let's subject religion to the same sort of scientific inquiry that we have done with tobacco and alcohol and, for that matter, music. Let's find out why people love their religion, and what it's good for. And we should no more take the existing research to settle the issue than we took the tobacco companies' campaigns about the safety of cigarette smoking at face value. Sure, religion saves lives. So does tobacco—ask those GIs for whom tobacco was an even greater comfort than religion during World War II, the Korean War, and Vietnam.

I'm prepared to look hard at the pros and cons of music, and if it turns out that music causes cancer, ethnic hatred, and war, then I'll have to think seriously about how to live without music. It is only because I am so supremely confident that music *doesn't* do much harm that I can enjoy it with such a clear conscience. If I were told by credible people that music might be harmful to the world, all things considered, I would feel morally bound to examine the evidence as dispassionately as I could. In fact, I would feel guilty about my allegiance to music if I didn't check it out.

But isn't the hypothesis that the costs of religion outweigh the benefits even more ludicrous than the fantastic claim about music? I don't think so. Music may be what Marx said religion is: the opiate of the masses, keeping working people in tranquilized subjugation, but it may also be the rallying song of revolution, closing up the ranks and giving heart to all. On this point, music and religion have quite similar profiles. In other regards, music looks far less problematic than religion. Over the millennia, music has started a few riots, and charismatic musicians may have sexually abused a shocking number of susceptible young fans, and seduced many others to leave their families (and their wits) behind, but no crusades or jihads have been waged over differences in musical tradition, no pogroms have been instituted against the lovers of waltzes or ragas or tangos. Whole populations haven't been subjected to obligatory scale-playing or kept in penury in order to furnish concert halls with the finest acoustics and instruments. No musicians have had fatwas pronounced against them by musical organizations, not even accordionists.

The comparison of religion to music is particularly useful here, since music is another natural phenomenon that has been ably studied by scholars for hundreds of years but is only just beginning to be an object of the sort of scientific study I am recommending. There has been no dearth of professional research on music theory—harmony, counterpoint, rhythm—or the techniques of musicianship, or the history of every genre and instrument. Ethnomusicologists have studied the evolution of musical styles and practices in relation to social, economic, and other cultural factors, and neuroscientists and psychologists have rather recently begun studying the perception and creation of music, using all the latest technology to uncover the patterns of brain activity associated with musical experience, musical memory, and related topics. But most of this research still takes music for granted. It seldom asks: Why does music exist? There is a short answer, and it is true, so far as it goes: it exists because we love it, and hence we keep bringing more of it into existence. But why do we love it? Because we find that it is beautiful. But why is it beautiful to us? This is a perfectly good biological question, but it does not yet have a good answer. Compare it, for instance, with the question: Why do we love sweets? Here we know the evolutionary answer, in some detail, and it has some curious twists. It is no accident that we find sweet things to our liking, and if we want to adjust our policies regarding sweet things in the future, we had better understand the evolutionary basis of their appeal. We mustn't make the mistake of the man in the old joke who complained that, just when he'd finally succeeded in training his donkey not to eat, the stupid animal up and died on him.

Some things are necessary to life, and some things are at least so life-enhancing or life-enabling that we tamper with them at our peril, and we need to figure out these roles and needs. Ever since the Enlightenment in the eighteenth century, many quite well informed and brilliant people have confidently thought that religion would soon vanish, the object of a human taste that could be satisfied by other means. Many are still waiting, somewhat less confidently. Whatever religion provides for us, it is something that many *think* they cannot live without. Let's take them seriously this time, for they might be right. But there is only one way to take them seriously: we need to study them scientifically.

Notes

1   [Renford Bambrough, "Editorial: Subject and Epithet," *Philosophy*, vol. 55 (1980), 289–90.]
2   For more on the role of science in avoidance, and the explosion of "evitability" that human civilization has achieved, see my *Freedom Evolves* (New York: Viking, 2003).
3   Following recent practice, I use the term "Islamist" to refer to those radical or fundamentalist strains of Islamic thought that in general condemn democracy, women's rights, and the freedom of inquiry in which science and technology can flourish. Many, probably most, Islamic thinkers and leaders are deeply opposed to the Islamist position.

Questions for reflection

1   Professor Dennett describes religion as a "natural phenomenon." Do you think most religious adherents would agree that it is a *natural* phenomenon? Can a theist consistently believe both that religion is given by, and primarily about, God, and also that it is a natural phenomenon?
2   Should religion be studied scientifically? What are some benefits of a natural science of religion? What are some risks or concerns?
3   What are some obstacles to the scientific study of religion?
4   Which of the five futuristic hypotheses do you believe is more realistic? Why?
5   Why does Dennett compare religion to music?

Further reading

Richard Dawkins (1987) *The Blind Watchmaker*. New York: W. W. Norton. (Argues that science demonstrates that the only creator is the blind forces of physics; a readable, international bestseller.)
Daniel C. Dennett (1996) *Darwin's Dangerous Idea: Evolution and the Meanings of Life*. Reprint edn. New York: Simon & Schuster. (Presents Dennett's philosophical argument for Darwinism.)
Daniel C. Dennett (2006) *Breaking the Spell: Religion as a Natural Phenomenon*. New York: Viking. (Explores the evolution of religion and argues for a scientific examination of religion; the essay above is taken from this book.)
Michael Ruse (2000) *Can a Darwinian Be a Christian?: The Relationship Between Science and Religion*. Cambridge: Cambridge University Press. (A Darwinian philosopher of science argues that one can be a Christian and a Darwinian, but it is no easy task.)

PART SIX

The self and
the human condition

Recently in an undergraduate course I was teaching we were examining the question "Who am I?" One of my students noted that since he looks nothing like he did when he was a child, he's really not the same person after all. Another student noted that he is not the same person he used to be either, but not because of physical changes. He's not the same person, he said, because he had a spiritual change—a religious conversion of sorts in which he used to focus on selfish gain whereas now he's primarily interested in helping the needs of the poor and oppressed.

The "Who am I?" question conjures up many related questions: "What am I?" "What is my nature?" "Do I have a nature?" "Why do I behave the way I do?" "What is my station in life, and why?" and so on. These kinds of questions have been asked by people of all stripes throughout the ages, and radically different answers have been given by religious and non-religious thinkers alike.

One salient answer to the "Who am I?" question is that I am a free person, body and soul, created in the image of God. This is a typical Judeo-Christian answer. But within the traditions of Judaism and Christianity, there is also a recognition that something is awry with the human condition; something is wrong with us as individuals. We sometimes act in ways discordant with what we take to be right and good. But why?

In the first reading of this section, taken from the classic autobiography of a fifth-century Christian bishop, the author—St. Augustine—describes in detail a mischievous activity that he and his friends engaged in during their youth: they stole some pears from a neighbor. Augustine's anguish about his actions strikes most readers as misplaced. Who frets over such a minor indiscretion done as a youngster? But his lament is more deeply rooted, for he came to the realization that he did the deed for no reason other than his love for the evil of doing it. This was his state of being; he oftentimes desired evil for its own sake. For Augustine, as for most Christians historically, this reflects the fallen state of human beings. We are all "sinners" in need of redemption, and it is only by the grace of God that we can be freed from the clutches of sin.

Contrary to Augustine's view that human nature is fallen and naturally bent toward evil, the Confucian philosopher Mencius argues in the next selection that human nature is naturally good. The reason human beings tend to act in evil ways is not because of their nature, but because of the various cultural influences affecting their thoughts, words, and deeds. It's not that people need to be redeemed from sin; rather, they need to be educated into the virtues that are latent within them.

Also contrary to Augustine's view of the self as a fallen human being stands the work of Friedrich Nietzsche. He construes "good" and "bad" differently than either Augustine or Mencius. In a superior type of morality—what he calls "master morality"—"good" and "bad" mean roughly "noble" and "contemptible." It is the noble person who is to be valued, the one who "experiences *itself* as determining values;" the one who seeks the will to power. In contrast to noble persons are contemptible persons, those who adhere to (Christian) slave morality. In another often-quoted passage, he describes it this way:

> What is good? All that enhances the feeling of power, the Will to Power, and the power itself in man. What is bad?—All that proceeds from weakness. What is happiness?—The feeling that power is increasing—that resistance has been overcome.
>
> Not contentment, but more power; not peace at any price, but war; not virtue, but competence (virtue in the Renaissance sense, *virtu*, free from moralistic acid). The first principle of our humanism: The weak and the failures shall perish. They ought even to be helped to perish.
>
> What is more harmful than any vice?—Practical sympathy and pity for all the failures and all the weak: Christianity.[1]

This, concisely put, is Nietzsche's humanistic understanding of the good, the noble human being, and the will to power.

The next reading is by Nagarjuna, a Mahayana Buddhist philosopher from roughly the second century CE—a time of rigorous debate among various Buddhist schools. He is primarily known for his view of sunyata, or emptiness, and for a dialectical method in which he reduces opposing philosophical positions to a set of mutually exclusive contradictions. For Nagarjuna, there are no substantial entities in nature; nothing is fixed and continuous; everything is sunyata. In this selection he applies his teaching to the (empty) self. When one finally understands the impermanence of all things and ceases to believe in either the existence of or the non-existence of substantial realities, one has achieved nirvana.

Another view of the self and the human condition is offered by Zen Buddhist scholar D. T. Suzuki. His emphasis in this reading is on karma—a view intertwined in and fundamental to both Buddhist and Hindu thought—and the self. Unlike the theistic traditions which ground morality in God and in which God plays a significant role in the human condition, Suzuki notes that karma emphasizes individual freedom and moral responsibility, but it does so without the necessity of postulating a God. Furthermore, he argues, true individuality is a fiction; the individual self is an illusion. What we are, and how we act, is inextricably linked to "others," and there are no clear bounds of demarcation between "I" and "they."

Note

1   Friedrich Nietzsche, *The Antichrist*, trans. Walter Kaufmann (New York: Random House, 1968).

Chapter 40

Augustine

THE FALLEN SELF

Aurelius Augustine (also referred to as "St. Augustine of Hippo" or, more commonly, "Augustine;" 354–430 CE) was a Christian bishop in North Africa, a Neoplatonist philosopher, and an influential theologian. Next to Jesus of Nazareth and the Apostle Paul, he has probably had more influence on Christian thought than anyone in history. The following work is taken from Augustine's autobiographical work entitled *The Confessions*, which is both a literary classic and a profound work of philosophical insight and self-reflection. This selection begins with a confession of youth—he and his friends had stolen some pears. At first glance, such proclivities seem little more than childish pranks that virtually all children engage in at some point in their lives. So why does Augustine anguish over this event, considering himself a wretch, a thief, and a criminal who has done considerable evil? It is because, in his fallen state, he loved evil for its own sake. It's not that stealing pears is such a great evil in and of itself, but the fact that he stole them for the very purpose of stealing is abominable. Augustine uses the incident as a parable for the self in its fallen condition.

But there is hope, Augustine maintains, for the grace of God can untangle him from this "twisted and tangled knot" and bring him to a life of goodness, justice, peace, and joy.

iv (9) Theft receives certain punishment by your law (Exod. 20:15), Lord, and by the law written in the hearts of men (Rom. 2:14) which not even iniquity itself destroys. For what thief can with equanimity endure being robbed by another thief? He cannot tolerate it even if he is rich and the other is destitute. I wanted to carry out an act of theft and did so, driven by no kind of need other than my inner lack of any sense of, or feeling for, justice. Wickedness filled me. I stole something which I had in plenty and of much better quality. My desire was to enjoy not what I sought by stealing but merely the excitement of thieving and the doing of what was wrong. There was a pear tree near our vineyard laden with fruit, though attractive in neither colour nor taste. To shake the fruit off the tree and carry off the pears, I and a gang of naughty adolescents set off late at night after (in our usual pestilential way) we had continued our game in the streets. We carried off a huge load of pears. But they were not for our feasts but merely to throw to the pigs. Even if we ate a few, nevertheless our pleasure lay in doing what was not allowed.

Such was my heart, O God, such was my heart. You had pity on it when it was at the bottom of the abyss. Now let my heart tell you what it was seeking there in that I became evil for no reason.[1] I had no motive for my wickedness except wickedness itself. It was foul, and I loved it. I loved the self-destruction, I loved my fall, not the object for which I had fallen but my fall itself. My depraved soul leaped down from your firmament to ruin.[2] I was seeking not to gain anything by shameful means, but shame for its own sake.

v (10) There is beauty in lovely physical objects, as in gold and silver and all other such things. When the body touches such things, much significance attaches to the rapport of the object with the touch. Each of the other senses has its own appropriate mode of response to physical things. Temporal honour and the power of giving orders and of being in command have their own kind of dignity, though this is also the origin of the urge to self-assertion. Yet in the acquisition of all these sources of social status, one must not depart from you, Lord, nor deviate from your law. The life which we live in this world has its attractiveness because of a certain measure in its beauty and its harmony with all these inferior objects that are beautiful. Human friendship is also a nest of love and gentleness because of the unity it brings about between many souls. Yet sin is committed for the sake of all these things and others of this kind when, in consequence of an immoderate urge towards those things which are at the bottom end of the scale of good,[3] we abandon the higher and supreme goods, that is you, Lord God, and your truth and your law (Ps. 118:142). These inferior goods have their delights, but not comparable to my God who has made them all. It is in him that the just person takes delight; he is the joy of those who are true of heart (Ps. 63:11).

(11) When a crime is under investigation to discover the motive for which it was done, the accusation is not usually believed except in cases where the appetite to obtain (or the fear of losing) one of those goods which we have called inferior appears a plausible possibility. They are beautiful and attractive even if, in comparison with the higher goods which give true happiness, they are mean and base. A man committed murder. Why? Because he loved another's wife or his property; or he wanted to acquire money to live on by plundering his goods; or he was afraid of losing his own property by the action of his victim; or he had suffered injury and burned with desire for revenge. No one would commit murder without a motive, merely because he took pleasure in killing. Who would believe that? It was said of one brutal and cruel man [Catiline] that he was evil and savage without reason.[4] Yet the preceding passage gave the motive: 'lest disuse might make his hand or mind slow to react'. Why did he wish for that? Why so? His objective was to capture the city by violent crimes to obtain honours, government, and wealth; to live without fear of the laws and without the difficulty of attaining his ambitions because of the poverty of his family estate and his known criminal record. No, not even Catiline himself loved his crimes; something else motivated him to commit them.

vi (12) Wretch that I was, what did I love in you, my act of theft, that crime which I did at night in the sixteenth year of my life? There was nothing beautiful about you, my thieving. Indeed do you exist at all for me to be addressing you?

The fruit which we stole was beautiful because it was your creation, most beautiful of all Beings, maker of all things, the good God, God the highest good and my true good. The fruit was beautiful, but was not that which my miserable soul coveted. I had a quantity of better pears. But those I picked solely with the motive of stealing. I threw away what I had picked. My feasting was only on the wickedness which I took pleasure in enjoying. If any of those pears entered my mouth, my criminality was the piquant sauce. And now, Lord my God, I inquire what was the nature of my pleasure in the theft. The act has nothing lovely about it, none of the loveliness found in equity and prudence, or in the human mind whether in the memory or in the senses or in physical vitality. Nor was it beautiful in the way the stars are, noble in their courses, or earth and sea full of newborn creatures which, as they are born, take the place of those which die;[5] not even in the way that specious vices have a flawed reflection of beauty.

(13) Pride imitates what is lofty; but you alone are God most high above all things. What does ambition seek but honour and glory? Yet you alone are worthy of honour and are glorious for eternity. The cruelty of powerful people aims to arouse fear. Who is to be feared but God alone? What can be seized or stolen from his power? When or where or how or by whom? Soft endearments are intended to arouse love. But there are no caresses tenderer than your charity, and no object of love is more healthy than your truth, beautiful and luminous beyond all things. Curiosity appears to be a zeal for knowledge; yet you supremely know all. Ignorance and stupidity are given the names of simplicity and innocence; but there is no greater simplicity than in you. And what greater innocence than yours, whereas to evil men their own works are damaging? Idleness appears as desire for a quiet life; yet can rest be assured apart from the Lord? Luxury wants to be called abundance and satiety; but you are fullness and the inexhaustible treasure of incorruptible pleasure. Prodigality presents itself under the shadow of generosity; but you are the rich bestower of all good things. Avarice wishes to have large possessions; you possess everything. Envy contends about excellence; but what is more excellent than you? Anger seeks revenge; who avenges with greater justice than you? Fear quails before sudden and unexpected events attacking things which are loved, and takes precautions for their safety; to you is anything unexpected or sudden? Or who can take away from you what you love? There is no reliable security except with you. Regret wastes away for the loss of things which cupidity delighted in. Its wish would be that nothing be taken away, just as nothing can be taken from you.

(14) So the soul fornicates (Ps. 72:27) when it is turned away from you and seeks outside you the pure and clear intentions which are not to be found except by returning to you. In their perverted way all humanity imitates you. Yet they put themselves at a distance from you and exalt themselves against you. But even by thus imitating you they acknowledge that you are the creator of all nature and so concede that there is no place where one can entirely escape from you. Therefore in that act of theft what was the object of my love, and in what way did I viciously and perversely imitate my Lord? Was my pleasure to break your law, but by deceit since I had not the power to do that by force? Was I acting like a prisoner with restricted liberty who does without punishment what is not

permitted, thereby making an assertion of possessing a dim resemblance to omnipotence? Here is a runaway slave fleeing his master and pursuing a shadow (Job 7:2). What rottenness! What a monstrous life and what an abyss of death! Was it possible to take pleasure in what was illicit for no reason other than that it was not allowed?

vii (15) 'What shall I render to the Lord?' (Ps. 115:2) who recalls these things to my memory, but my soul feels no fear from the recollection. I will love you, Lord, and I will give thanks and confession to your name because you have forgiven me such great evils and my nefarious deeds. I attribute to your grace and mercy that you have melted my sins away like ice (Ecclus. 3:17). I also attribute to your grace whatever evil acts I have not done. What could I not have done when I loved gratuitous crime? I confess that everything has been forgiven, both the evil things I did of my own accord, and those which I did not do because of your guidance.

No one who considers his frailty would dare to attribute to his own strength his chastity and innocence, so that he has less cause to love you—as if he had less need of your mercy by which you forgive the sins of those converted to you. If man is called by you, follows your voice, and has avoided doing those acts which I am recalling and avowing in my own life, he should not mock the healing of a sick man by the Physician, whose help has kept him from falling sick, or at least enabled him to be less gravely ill. He should love you no less, indeed even more; for he sees that the one who delivered me from the great sicknesses of my sins is also he through whom he may see that he himself has not been a victim of the same great sicknesses.

viii (16) 'What fruit had I', wretched boy, in these things (Rom. 6:21) which I now blush to recall, above all in that theft in which I loved nothing but the theft itself? The theft itself was a nothing, and for that reason I was the more miserable. Yet had I been alone I would not have done it—I remember my state of mind to be thus at the time—alone I would never have done it. Therefore my love in that act was to be associated with the gang in whose company I did it. Does it follow that I loved something other than the theft? No, nothing else in reality because association with the gang is also a nothing. What is it in reality? Who can teach me that, but he who 'illuminates my heart' (Ecclus. 2:10) and disperses the shadows in it? What else has stirred my mind to ask and discuss and consider this question? If I had liked the pears which I stole and actually desired to enjoy them, I could by myself have committed that wicked act, had it been enough to attain the pleasure which I sought. I would not have needed to inflame the itch of my cupidity through the excitement generated by sharing the guilt with others. But my pleasure was not in the pears; it was in the crime itself, done in association with a sinful group.

ix (17) What was my state of mind? It is quite certain that it was utterly shameful and a disgrace to me that I had it. Yet what was it? 'Who understands his sins?' (Job 10:15). It was all done for a giggle, as if our hearts were tickled to think we were deceiving those who would not think us capable of such behaviour and would have profoundly disapproved. Why then did I derive pleasure from an act I would not have done on my own? Is it that nobody can easily laugh when alone? Certainly no one readily laughs when alone; yet sometimes laughter overcomes individuals when no one else is present if their senses or their mind perceive something utterly absurd. But alone I would not have done it, could not conceivably have done it by myself. See, before you, my God, the living memory of my soul. Alone I would not have committed that crime, in which my pleasure lay not in what I was stealing but in the act of theft. But had I been alone, it would have given me absolutely no pleasure, nor would I have committed it. Friendship can be a dangerous enemy, a seduction of the mind lying beyond the reach of investigation.[6] Out of a game and a jest came an avid desire to do injury and an appetite to inflict loss on someone else without any motive on my part of personal gain, and no pleasure in settling a score. As soon as the words are spoken 'Let us go and do it', one is ashamed not to be shameless.

x (18) Who can untie this extremely twisted and tangled knot? It is a foul affair, I have no wish to give attention to it; I have no desire to contemplate it. My desire is for you, justice and innocence, you are lovely and splendid to honest eyes; the satiety of your love is insatiable. With you is utter peace and a life immune from disturbance. The person who enters into you 'enters into the joy of the Lord' (Matt. 25:21), and will not be afraid; he will find himself in the supreme Good where it is supremely good to be. As an adolescent I went astray from you (Ps. 118:76), my God, far from your unmoved stability. I became to myself a region of destitution.[7]

Notes

1   Echo of Sallust's language about Catiline. Augustine presents himself as a new Catiline.
2   Like Lucifer.
3   Throughout his writings Augustine holds to a doctrine of gradations of goodness. The good of the body is inferior to that of the soul; the will, in itself midway, may turn to higher or to lower things, and may err by preferring inferior goods to superior.
4   Sallust, *Catiline* 16 (also cited by Augustine, *Sermon on Ps. 108*, 3).
5   Augustine regarded the cycle of birth and death as 'beautiful'; i.e. death is evil to the individual, not to the race.
6   Similarly ix.ii. (2).
7   The Prodigal Son is fused with a Neoplatonic theme of the soul's destitution without God, which is taken up at the beginning of book III and again in vii. x (16). Destitution in the soul distant from God is a theme in Porphyry (*De abstinentia* 3. 27 and *Sententiae* 40), based on Plato's *Symposium*.

Questions for reflection

1   Describe Augustine's depiction of the self. Is it accurate, in your estimation? Do we practice evil for no reason except the evil itself? Are there (also) other reasons why people do evil? Explain.
2   Do you agree with Augustine that individuals tend to do more evil when in a group than when alone? If so, why might this be?
3   What role does God play in Augustine's analysis of the human condition?

Further reading

Augustine ([397–401] 1998) *Confessions*. Trans. Henry Chadwick. Oxford: Oxford University Press. (Augustine's autobiography; the above selection was taken from this book.)

Peter Brown (1967) *Augustine of Hippo*. Berkeley, CA: University of California Press. (Probably the best biography in print; a modern classic in its own right.)

Etienne Gilson (1960) *The Christian Philosophy of Saint Augustine*. New York: Random House. (A well-known Thomist's presentation of Augustine's philosophy.)

Christopher Kirwan (1989) *Augustine*. London: Routledge. (An analysis of Augustine's philosophy from a contemporary analytic perspective.)

James Wetzel (1992) *Augustine and the Limits of Virtue*. Cambridge: Cambridge University Press. (Focuses on Augustine's moral psychology.)

_____

Chapter 41

Mencius

HUMAN NATURE IS
NATURALLY GOOD

Mencius (fourth century BCE) was a Chinese philosopher/sage who articulated and defended what many Confucians understand to be orthodox Confucianism. He is recognized as one of the foremost Chinese thinkers of antiquity, and he is best known for his view that human nature is naturally good (some Confucian thinkers held that human nature is evil), although it becomes bent toward evil through cultural influences. Mencius taught that through the proper cultivation of the heart and mind, four significant moral virtues emerge from within: humanity, righteousness, propriety, and wisdom.

Kao Tzu – lived from c. 420–c. 350 BCE; nothing more is known about him.

_____

Kao Tzu said, "Human nature is like the willow tree, and righteousness is like a cup or a bowl.* To turn human nature into humanity and righteousness is like turning the willow into cups and bowls." Mencius said, "Sir, can you follow the nature of the willow tree and make the cups and bowls, or must you violate the nature of the willow tree before you can make the cups and bowls? If you are going to violate the nature of the willow tree in order to make cups and bowls, then must you also violate human nature in order to make it into humanity and righteousness? Your words, alas! would lead all people in the world to consider humanity and righteousness as calamity [because they required the violation of human nature]!"

Kao Tzu said, "Man's nature is like whirling water. If a breach in the pool is made to the east it will flow to the east. If a breach is made to the west it will flow to the west. Man's nature is indifferent to good and evil, just as water is indifferent to east and west." Mencius said, "Water, indeed, is indifferent to the east and west, but is it indifferent to high and low? Man's nature is naturally good just as water naturally flows downward. There is no man without this good nature; neither is there water that does not flow downward. Now you can strike water and cause it to splash upward over your forehead, and by damming and leading it, you can force it uphill. Is this the nature of water? It is the forced circumstance that makes it do so. Man can be made to do evil, for his nature can be treated in the same way.". . .

Mencius said, "If you let people follow their feelings (original nature), they will be able to do good. This is what is meant by saying that human nature is good. If man does evil, it is not the fault of his natural endowment. The feeling of commiseration is found in all men; the feeling of shame and dislike is found in all men; the feeling of respect and reverence is found in all men; and the feeling of right and wrong is found in all men. The feeling of commiseration is what we call humanity; the feeling of shame and dislike is what we called righteousness; the feeling of respect and reverence is what we called propriety (*li*); and the feeling of right and wrong is what we called wisdom. Humanity, righteousness, propriety, and wisdom are not drilled into us from outside. We originally have them with us. Only we do not think [to find them]. Therefore it is said, 'Seek and you will find it, neglect and you will lose it.' . . .

Mencius said, "In good years most of the young people behave well. In bad years most of them abandon themselves to evil. This is not due to any difference in the natural capacity endowed by Heaven. The abandonment is due to the fact that the mind is allowed to fall into evil. Take for instance the growing of wheat. You sow the seeds and cover them with soil. The land is the same and the time of sowing is also the same. In time they all grow up luxuriantly. When the time of harvest comes, they are all ripe. Although there may be a difference between the different stalks of wheat, it is due to differences in the soil, as rich or poor, to the unequal nourishment obtained from the rain and the dew, and to differences in human effort. Therefore all things of the same kind are similar to one another. Why should there be any doubt about men? The sage and I are the same in kind. . . ."

. . . I like life and I also like righteousness. If I cannot have both of them, I shall give up life and choose righteousness. I love life, but there is something I love more than life, and therefore I will not do anything improper to have it. I also hate death, but there is something I hate more than death, and therefore there are occasions when I will not avoid danger. If there is nothing that man loves more than life, then why should he not employ every means to preserve it? And if there is nothing that man hates more than death, then why does he not do anything to avoid danger? There are cases when a man does not take the course even if by taking it he can preserve his life, and he does not do anything even if by doing it he can avoid danger. Therefore there is something men love more than life and there is something men hate more than death. It is not only the worthies alone who have this moral sense. All men have it, but only the worthies have been able to preserve it. . . .

Kung-tu Tzu asked, "We are all human beings. Why is it that some men become great and others become small?" Mencius said, "Those who follow the greater qualities in their nature become great men and those who follow the smaller qualities in their nature become small men." "But we are all human beings. Why is it that some follow their greater qualities and others follow their smaller qualities?" Mencius replied, "When our senses of sight and hearing are used without thought and are thereby obscured by material things, the material things act on the material senses and lead them astray. That is all. The function of the mind is to think. If we think, we will get them (the principles of things). If we do not think, we will not get them. This is what Heaven has given to us. If we first build up the nobler part of our nature, then the inferior part cannot overcome it. It is simply this that makes a man great." . . .

Mencius said, "There is nobility of Heaven and there is nobility of man. Humanity, righteousness, loyalty, faithfulness, and the love of the good without getting tired of it constitute the nobility of Heaven, and to be a grand official, a great official, and a high official—this constitutes the nobility of man. The ancient people cultivated the nobility of Heaven, and the nobility of man naturally came to them. People today cultivate the nobility of Heaven in order to seek for the nobility of man, and once they have obtained the nobility of man, they forsake the nobility of Heaven. Therefore their delusion is extreme. At the end they will surely lose [the nobility of man] also." . . .

Mencius said, "All men have the mind which cannot bear [to see the suffering of] others. The ancient kings had this mind and therefore they had a government that could not bear to see the suffering of the people. When a government that cannot bear to see the suffering of the people is conducted from a mind that cannot bear to see the suffering of others, the government of the empire will be as easy as making something go round in the palm."

"When I say that all men have the mind which cannot bear to see the suffering of others, my meaning may be illustrated thus: Now, when men suddenly see a child about to fall into a well, they all have a feeling of alarm and distress, not to gain friendship with the child's parents, nor to seek the praise of their neighbors and friends, nor because they dislike the reputation [of lack of humanity if they did not rescue the child]. From such a case, we see that a man without the feeling of commiseration is not a man; a man without the feeling of shame and dislike is not a man; a man without the feeling of deference and compliance is not a man; and a man without the feeling of right and wrong is not a man. The feeling of commiseration is the beginning of humanity; the feeling of shame and dislike is the beginning of righteousness; the feeling of deference and compliance is the beginning of propriety; and the feeling of right and wrong is the beginning of wisdom. Men have these Four Beginnings just as they have their four limbs. Having these Four Beginnings, but saying that they cannot develop them is to destroy themselves. When they say that their ruler cannot develop them, they are destroying their ruler. If anyone with these Four Beginnings in him knows how to give them the fullest extension and development, the result will be like fire beginning to burn or a spring beginning to shoot forth. When they are fully developed, they will be sufficient to protect all people within the four seas (the world). If they are not developed, they will not be sufficient even to serve one's parents." . . .

Mencius said, "When Heaven is about to confer a great responsibility on any man, it will exercise his mind with suffering, subject his sinews and bones to hard work, expose his body to hunger, put him to poverty, place obstacles in the paths of his deeds, so as to stimulate his mind, harden his nature, and improve wherever he is incompetent."

Mencius said, "He who exerts his mind to the utmost knows his nature. He who knows his nature knows Heaven. To preserve one's mind and to nourish one's nature is the way to serve Heaven. Not to allow any double-mindedness regardless of longevity or brevity of life, but to cultivate one's person and wait for [destiny (*ming*, fate, Heaven's decree or mandate) to take its own course] is the way to fulfill one's destiny." . . .

Mencius said, "All things are already complete in oneself. There is no greater joy than to examine oneself and be sincere. When in one's conduct one vigorously exercises altruism, humanity is not far to seek, but right by him." . . .

Note

* [All translator's footnotes have been removed. With some exceptions, this selection generally follows the helpful flow provided by Eliot Deutsch in his *Introduction to World Philosophies* (Upper Saddle River, NJ: Prentice Hall, 1997), 85–86.]

Questions for reflection

1 Do you agree with Mencius when he says that human nature is naturally good? Do young children generally reflect his views about human nature and societal influences? Explain.

2 Mencius states that there is something we should love more than life. What is it, and why do you think he makes this claim? Do you agree with him on this?

3 What are the Four Beginnings that Mencius mentions? In terms of the Four Beginnings, how do people destroy themselves?

Further reading

Anonymous (2005) *Mencius.* Reprint edn. Trans. D. C. Lau. New York: Penguin Classics. (A very good translation of the primary source of Mencius's thought; contains a collection of his sayings and discussions.)

Confucius ([551–479 BCE] 1998) *The Analects.* Trans. D. C. Lau. New York: Penguin Classics. (The standard English translation of this Confucian masterpiece.)

Kwong-loi Shun (1997) *Mencius and Early Chinese Thought.* Stanford, CA: Stanford University Press. (A scholarly study of the thought of Mencius; fairly technical.)

L. H. Yearley (1990) *Mencius and Aquinas: Theories of Virtue and Conceptions of Courage.* Albany, NY: State University of New York Press. (A comparative study of the virtues as taught by Mencius and Thomas Aquinas.)

_____

Chapter 42

Friedrich Nietzsche

THE NOBLE HUMAN BEING

Friedrich Nietzsche (1844–1900) was a German philologist and existentialist philosopher. He was raised in a pious Lutheran home and went on to study theology at the University of Bonn and philology at Leipzig. Somewhere along the way he became an atheist, and he is known today primarily for his challenges to traditional Christian morality.

   A central teaching of Nietzsche's, included here, is the idea of the fundamental force that drives living beings, including human beings: the will to power. The will to power is an affirmation of life and a will to live, to grow, and to dominate. Not all beings are equal in ability, however, and the noble human being is a person who advances the will to power, who "honors himself as one who is powerful, also as one who has power over himself, who knows how to speak and be silent, who delights in being severe and hard with himself and respects all severity and hardness." One's development into a noble human being is hindered by "slave morality"—the Judeo-Christian view of morality invented by impotent, hateful, and cowardly priests to deceive individuals into believing that one should denounce the will to power and value meekness and weakness. The noble person, however, affirms "master morality" and separates herself from those who buy into slave morality.

_____

[Section] 257

Every enhancement of the type "man" has so far been the work of an aristocratic society—and it will be so again and again—a society that believes in the long ladder of an order of rank and differences in value between man and man, and that needs slavery in some sense or other. Without that *pathos of distance* which grows out of the ingrained difference between strata—when the ruling caste constantly looks afar and looks down upon subjects and instruments and just as constantly practices obedience and command, keeping down and keeping at a distance—that other, more mysterious pathos could not have grown up either—the craving for an ever new widening of distances within the soul itself, the development of ever higher, rarer, more remote, further-stretching, more comprehensive states—in brief, simply the enhancement of the type "man," the continual "self-overcoming of man," to use a moral formula in a supra-moral sense.

To be sure, one should not yield to humanitarian illusions about the origins of an aristocratic society (and thus of the presupposition of this enhancement of the type "man"): truth is hard. Let us admit to ourselves, without trying to be considerate, how every higher culture on earth so far has *begun*. Human beings whose nature was still natural, barbarians in every terrible sense of the word, men of prey who were still in possession of unbroken strength of will and lust for power, hurled themselves upon weaker, more civilized, more peaceful races, perhaps traders or cattle raisers, or upon mellow old cultures whose last vitality was even then flaring up in splendid fireworks of spirit and corruption. In the beginning, the noble caste was always the barbarian caste: their predominance did not lie mainly in physical strength but in strength of the soul— they were more *whole* human beings (which also means, at every level, "more whole beasts").

[Section] 258

Corruption as the expression of a threatening anarchy among the instincts and of the fact that the foundation of the affects, which is called "life," has been shaken: corruption is something totally different depending on the organism in which it appears. When, for example, an aristocracy, like that of France at the beginning of the Revolution, throws away its privileges with a sublime disgust and sacrifices itself to an extravagance of its own moral feelings, that is corruption; it was really only the last act of that centuries-old corruption which had led them to surrender, step by step, their governmental prerogatives, demoting themselves to a mere *function* of the monarchy (finally even to a mere ornament and showpiece). The essential characteristic of a good and healthy aristocracy, however, is that it experiences itself *not* as a function (whether of the monarchy or the commonwealth) but as their *meaning* and highest justification—that it therefore accepts with a good conscience the sacrifice of untold human beings who, *for its sake*, must be reduced and lowered to incomplete human beings, to slaves, to instruments. Their fundamental faith simply has to be that society must *not* exist for society's sake but only as the foundation and scaffolding on which a choice type of being is able to raise itself to its higher task and to a higher state of *being*[1]—comparable to those sun-seeking vines of Java—that are called *Sipo Matador*—that so long and so often enclasp an oak tree with their tendrils until eventually, high above it but supported by it, they can unfold their crowns in the open light and display their happiness.

[Section] 259

Refraining mutually from injury, violence, and exploitation and placing one's will on a par with that of someone else—this may become, in a certain rough sense, good manners among individuals if the appropriate conditions are present (namely, if these men are actually similar in strength and value standards and belong together in *one* body). But as soon as this principle is extended, and possibly even accepted as the *fundamen-*

tal principle of society, it immediately proves to be what it really is—a will to the *denial* of life, a principle of disintegration and decay.

Here we must beware of superficiality and get to the bottom of the matter, resisting all sentimental weakness: life itself is *essentially* appropriation, injury, overpowering of what is alien and weaker; suppression, hardness, imposition of one's own forms, incorporation and at least, at its mildest, exploitation—but why should one always use those words in which a slanderous intent has been imprinted for ages?

Even the body within which individuals treat each other as equals, as suggested before—and this happens in every healthy aristocracy—if it is a living and not a dying body, has to do to other bodies what the individuals within it refrain from doing to each other: it will have to be an incarnate will to power, it will strive to grow, spread, seize, become predominant—not from any morality or immorality but because it is *living* and because life simply *is* will to power. But there is no point on which the ordinary consciousness of Europeans resists instruction as on this: everywhere people are now raving, even under scientific disguises, about coming conditions of society in which "the exploitative aspect" will be removed—which sounds to me as if they promised to invent a way of life that would dispense with all organic functions. "Exploitation" does not belong to a corrupt or imperfect and primitive society: it belongs to the *essence* of what lives, as a basic organic function; it is a consequence of the will to power, which is after all the will of life.

If this should be an innovation as a theory—as a reality it is the *primordial fact* of all history: people ought to be honest with themselves at least that far.

[Section] 260

Wandering through the many subtler and coarser moralities which have so far been prevalent on earth, or still are prevalent, I found that certain features recurred regularly together and were closely associated—until I finally discovered two basic types and one basic difference.

There are *master morality* and *slave morality*[2]—I add immediately that in all the higher and more mixed cultures there also appear attempts at mediation between these two moralities, and yet more often the interpenetration and mutual misunderstanding of both, and at times they occur directly alongside each other—even in the same human being, within a *single* soul.[3] The moral discrimination of values has originated either among a ruling group whose consciousness of its difference from the ruled group was accompanied by delight—or among the ruled, the slaves and dependents of every degree.

In the first case, when the ruling group determines what is "good," the exalted, proud states of the soul are experienced as conferring distinction and determining the order of rank. The noble human being separates from himself those in whom the opposite of such exalted, proud states finds expression: he despises them. It should be noted immediately that in this first type of morality the opposition of "good" and "bad" means approximately the same as "noble" and "contemptible." (The opposition of "good" and "*evil*" has a different origin.) One feels contempt for the cowardly, the anxious, the petty, those intent on narrow utility; also for the suspicious with their unfree glances, those who humble themselves, the doglike people who allow themselves to be maltreated, the begging flatterers, above all the liars: it is part of the fundamental faith of all aristocrats that the common people lie. "We truthful ones"—thus the nobility of ancient Greece referred to itself.

It is obvious that moral designations were everywhere first applied to *human beings* and only later, derivatively, to actions. Therefore it is a gross mistake when historians of morality start from such questions as: why was the compassionate act praised? The noble type of man experiences *itself* as determining values; it does not need approval; it judges, "what is harmful to me is harmful in itself"; it knows itself to be that which first accords honor to things; it is *value-creating*. Everything it knows as part of itself it honors: such a morality is self-glorification. In the foreground there is the feeling of full-ness, of power that seeks to overflow, the happiness of high tension, the consciousness of wealth that would give and bestow: the noble human being, too, helps the unfor-tunate, but not, or almost not, from pity, but prompted more by an urge begotten by excess of power. The noble human being honors himself as one who is powerful, also as one who has power over himself, who knows how to speak and be silent, who delights in being severe and hard with himself and respects all severity and hardness. "A hard heart Wotan put into my breast," says an old Scandinavian saga: a fitting poetic expres-sion, seeing that it comes from the soul of a proud Viking. Such a type of man is actually proud of the fact that he is *not* made for pity, and the hero of the saga therefore adds as a warning: "If the heart is not hard in youth it will never harden." Noble and courageous human beings who think that way are furthest removed from that morality which finds the distinction of morality precisely in pity, or in acting for others, or in *désintéressement*; faith in oneself, pride in oneself, a fundamental hostility and irony against "selflessness" belong just as definitely to noble morality as does a slight disdain and caution regarding compassionate feelings and a "warm heart."

It is the powerful who *understand* how to honor; this is their art, their realm of invention. The profound reverence for age and tradition—all law rests on this double reverence—the faith and prejudice in favor of ancestors and disfavor of those yet to come are typical of the morality of the powerful; and when the men of "modern ideas," conversely, believe almost instinctively in "progress" and "the future" and more and more lack respect for age, this in itself would sufficiently betray the ignoble origin of these "ideas."

A morality of the ruling group, however, is most alien and embarrassing to the present taste in the severity of its principle that one has duties only to one's peers; that against beings of a lower rank, against everything alien, one may behave as one pleases or "as the heart desires," and in any case "beyond good and evil"—here pity and like feelings may find their place.[4] The capacity for, and the duty of, long gratitude and long revenge—both only among one's peers—refinement in repaying, the sophisticated concept of friendship, a certain necessity for having enemies (as it were, as drainage ditches for the affects of envy, quarrelsomeness, exuberance—at bottom, in order to be capable of being good *friends*): all these are typical characteristics of noble moral-ity which, as suggested, is not the morality of "modern ideas" and therefore is hard to empathize with today, also hard to dig up and uncover.[5]

It is different with the second type of morality, *slave morality*. Suppose the violated, oppressed, suffering, unfree, who are uncertain of themselves and weary, moralize: what will their moral valuations have in common? Probably, a pessimistic suspicion about the whole condition of man will find expression, perhaps a condemnation of man along with his condition. The slave's eye is not favorable to the virtues of the powerful:

he is skeptical and suspicious, *subtly* suspicious, of all the "good" that is honored there—he would like to persuade himself that even their happiness is not genuine. Conversely, those qualities are brought out and flooded with light which serve to ease existence for those who suffer: here pity, the complaisant and obliging hand, the warm heart, patience, industry, humility, and friendliness are honored—for here these are the most useful qualities and almost the only means for enduring the pressure of existence. Slave morality is essentially a morality of utility.

Here is the place for the origin of that famous opposition of "good" and "evil": into evil one's feelings project power and dangerousness, a certain terribleness, subtlety, and strength that does not permit contempt to develop. According to slave morality, those who are "evil" thus inspire fear; according to master morality it is precisely those who are "good" that inspire, and wish to inspire, fear, while the "bad" are felt to be contemptible.

The opposition reaches its climax when, as a logical consequence of slave morality, a touch of disdain is associated also with the "good" of this morality—this may be slight and benevolent—because the good human being has to be *undangerous* in the slaves' way of thinking: he is good-natured, easy to deceive, a little stupid perhaps, *un bonhomme*.[6] Wherever slave morality becomes preponderant, language tends to bring the words "good" and "stupid" closer together.

One last fundamental difference: the longing for *freedom*, the instinct for happiness and the subtleties of the feeling of freedom belong just as necessarily to slave morality and morals as artful and enthusiastic reverence and devotion are the regular symptom of an aristocratic way of thinking and evaluating.

This makes plain why love *as passion*—which is our European specialty—simply must be of noble origin: as is well known, its invention must be credited to the Provençal knight-poets, those magnificent and inventive human beings of the "*gai saber*"[7] to whom Europe owes so many things and almost owes itself.——

[Section] 261

Among the things that may be hardest to understand for a noble human being is vanity: he will be tempted to deny it, where another type of human being could not find it more palpable. The problem for him is to imagine people who seek to create a good opinion of themselves which they do not have of themselves—and thus also do not "deserve"—and who nevertheless end up *believing* this good opinion themselves. This strikes him half as such bad taste and lack of self-respect, and half as so baroquely irrational, that he would like to consider vanity as exceptional, and in most cases when it is spoken of he doubts it.

He will say, for example: "I may be mistaken about my value and nevertheless demand that my value, exactly as I define it, should be acknowledged by others as well—but this is no vanity (but conceit or, more frequently, what is called 'humility' or 'modesty')." Or: "For many reasons I may take pleasure in the good opinion of others: perhaps because I honor and love them and all their pleasures give me pleasure; perhaps also because their good opinion confirms and strengthens my faith in my own good opinion; perhaps because the good opinion of others, even in cases where I do not share it, is still useful to me or promises to become so—but all that is not vanity."

The noble human being must force himself, with the aid of history, to recognize that, since time immemorial, in all somehow dependent social strata the common man *was* only what he was *considered*: not at all used to positing values himself, he also attached no other value to himself than his masters attached to him (it is the characteristic *right of masters* to create values).

It may be understood as the consequence of an immense atavism that even now the ordinary man still always *waits* for an opinion about himself and then instinctively submits to that—but by no means only a "good" opinion; also a bad and unfair one (consider, for example, the great majority of the self-estimates and self-underestimates that believing women accept from their father-confessors, and believing Christians quite generally from their church).

In accordance with the slowly arising democratic order of things (and its cause, the intermarriage of masters and slaves), the originally noble and rare urge to ascribe value to oneself on one's own and to "think well" of oneself will actually be encouraged and spread more and more now; but it is always opposed by an older, ampler, and more deeply ingrained propensity—and in the phenomenon of "vanity" this older propensity masters the younger one. The vain person is delighted by *every* good opinion he hears of himself (quite apart from all considerations of its utility, and also apart from truth or falsehood), just as every bad opinion of him pains him: for he submits to both, he *feels* subjected to them in accordance with that oldest instinct of submission that breaks out in him.

It is "the slave" in the blood of the vain person, a residue of the slave's craftiness—and how much "slave" is still residual in woman, for example!—that seeks to *seduce* him to good opinions about himself; it is also the slave who afterwards immediately prostrates himself before these opinions as if he had not called them forth.

And to say it once more: vanity is an atavism.

Notes

1   Cf. the outlook of the heroes of the *Iliad*.
2   While the ideas developed here, and explicated at greater length a year later in the first part of the *Genealogy of Morals,* had been expressed by Nietzsche in 1878 in section 45 of *Human, All-Too-Human*, this is the passage in which his famous terms "master morality" and "slave morality" are introduced.
3   These crucial qualifications, though added immediately have often been overlooked. "Modern" moralities are clearly mixtures; hence their manifold tensions, hypocrisies, and contradictions.
4   The final clause that follows the dash, omitted in the Cowan translation, is crucial and qualifies the first part of the sentence: a noble person has no *duties* to animals but treats them in accordance with his feelings, which means, if he is noble, with pity.
     The ruling masters, of course, are not always noble in this sense, and this is recognized by Nietzsche in *Twilight of the Idols*, in the chapter "The 'Improvers' of Mankind," in which he gives strong expression to his distaste for Manu's laws concerning outcastes (*Portable Nietzsche*, pp. 503–05); also in *The Will to Power* (ed. W. Kaufmann, New York, Random House, 1967), section 142. Indeed, in *The Antichrist*, section 57, Nietzsche contradicts outright his formulation above: "When the exceptional human being treats the mediocre more tenderly than himself and his peers, this is not mere courtesy of the heart—it is simply his *duty*."

More important: Nietzsche's obvious distaste for slave morality and the fact that he makes a point of liking master morality better does not imply that he endorses master morality. Cf. the text for note 3 above.

5   Clearly, master morality cannot be discovered by introspection nor by the observation of individuals who are "masters" rather than "slaves." Both of these misunderstandings are widespread. What is called for is rather a rereading of, say, the *Iliad* and, to illustrate "slave morality," the New Testament.

6   Literally "a good human being," the term is used for precisely the type described here.

7   "Gay science": in the early fourteenth century the term was used to designate the art of the troubadours, codified in *Leys d'amors*. Nietzsche subtitled his own *Fröhliche Wissenschaft* (1882) "*la gaya scienza*," placed a quatrain on the title page, began the book with a fifteen-page "Prelude in German Rhymes," and in the second edition (1887) added, besides a Preface and Book V, an "Appendix" of further verses.

Questions for reflection

1   Describe Nietzsche's noble human being. Do you agree with his view? Why or why not?

2   What is "slave morality?" What is "master morality?"

3   Nietzsche states, "Slave morality is essentially a morality of utility." What do you think he means by this? Do you agree? Explain.

4   Why is it difficult for the noble human being to understand vanity? What does Nietzsche think such a person *should* understand about it?

5   How might the noble human being respond to the claim that if there is no God, everything is morally permissible?

Further reading

Maudemarie Clark (1990) *Nietzsche on Truth and Philosophy*. Cambridge: Cambridge University Press. (Examines Nietzsche's philosophy with rigorous philosophical analysis, most notably regarding his notion of truth; also includes a chapter on the will to power.)

Martin Heidegger (1991) *Nietzsche*. Trans. David Farrell Krell. New York: Harper Collins. (This interpretation influenced later Continental readings of Nietzsche.)

Brian Leiter (2002) *Routledge Philosophy Guidebook to Nietzsche on Morality*. London: Routledge. (A comprehensive interpretation of Nietzsche's critique of traditional morality.)

Friedrich Nietzsche ([1906] 1968) *The Will to Power*. New York: Vintage. (An important collection of outlines and notes written by Nietzsche.)

Friedrich Nietzsche ([1886] 1989) *Beyond Good and Evil: Prelude to a Philosophy of the Future*. Trans. Walter Kaufmann. New York: Vintage Books. (A work on philosophy, religion, morality, and politics; the selection above was taken from this central work.)

Chapter 43

Nagarjuna

THE EMPTY SELF

Nagarjuna (*c.* 150–250 CE) was a Mahayana Buddhist philosopher who lived roughly five hundred years after the time of the Buddha. He is primarily known for developing a position called *sunyata*, or emptiness, and for utilizing a dialectical method of contradictions. He engaged in philosophical discussions with those from various rival Buddhist schools and demonstrated that not only do each of their views have within themselves inherent contradictions, but that *every* standpoint can be reduced to absurdity. Every concept must be contrasted with its opposite in order for it to be understood, and thus every concept entails its own negation. Thus, one cannot rationally argue that the nature or essence of a concept or thing exists, for in doing so one lands in contradictions. This applies even to the concepts of death and rebirth (samsâra) and desireless freedom (nirvana). Furthermore, since it cannot be logically maintained that entities have substantial natures, it is best to think of them as "empty" — as having no fixed essences. This is Nagarjuna's "middle way" — a view midway between the metaphysical claim that something either exists or does not exist.

In the following selection Nagarjuna applies this teaching to the self, or perhaps more aptly, to the "no-self" or "empty self." It is important to note that he did not believe that human beings are nothing, but rather that considering oneself an enduring substantial entity is absurd. For Nagarjuna, nirvana turns out to be the cessation of belief in both real substantial entities and in the complete denial of the self.

Examination of self and entities

1 If the self were the aggregates,
It would have arising and ceasing (as properties).
If it were different from the aggregates,
It would not have the characteristics of the aggregates.

2 If there were no self,
   Where would the self's (properties) be?
   From the pacification of the self and what belongs to it,
   One abstains from grasping onto "I" and "mine."

3 One who does not grasp onto "I" and "mine,"
   That one does not exist.
   One who does not grasp onto "I" and "mine,"
   He does not perceive.

4 When views of "I" and "mine" are extinguished,
   Whether with respect to the internal or external,
   The appropriator ceases.
   This having ceased, birth ceases.

5 Action and misery having ceased, there is nirvāna.
   Action and misery come from conceptual thought.
   This comes from mental fabrication.
   Fabrication ceases through emptiness.

6 That there is a self has been taught,
   And the doctrine of no-self,
   By the buddhas, as well as the
   Doctrine of neither self nor nonself.

7 What language expresses is nonexistent.
   The sphere of thought is nonexistent.
   Unarisen and unceased, like nirvāna
   Is the nature of things.

8 Everything is real and is not real,
   Both real and not real,
   Neither real nor not real.
   This is Lord Buddha's teaching.

9 Not dependent on another, peaceful and
   Not fabricated by mental fabrication,
   Not thought, without distinctions,
   That is the character of reality (that-ness).

10 Whatever comes into being dependent on another
    Is not identical to that thing.
    Nor is it different from it.
    Therefore it is neither nonexistent in time nor permanent.

11 By the buddhas, patrons of the world,
    This immortal truth is taught:
    Without identity, without distinction;
    Not nonexistent in time, not permanent.

12 When the fully enlightened ones do not appear,
    And when the disciples have disappeared,
    The wisdom of the self-enlightened ones
    Will arise completely without a teacher.

Examination of views

1 The views "in the past I was" or "I was not"
   And the view that the world is permanent, etc.,
   All of these views
   Depend on a prior limit.

2 The view "in the future I will become other" or "I will not do so"
   And that the world is limited, etc.,
   All of these views
   Depend on a final limit.

3 To say "I was in the past"
   Is not tenable.
   What existed in the past
   Is not identical to this one.

4 According to you, this self is that,
   But the appropriator is different.
   If it is not the appropriator,
   What is your self?

5 Having shown that there is no self
   Other than the appropriator,
   The appropriator should be the self.
   But it is not your self.

6 Appropriating is not the self.
   It arises and ceases.
   How can one accept that
   Future appropriating is the appropriator?

7 A self that is different
   From the appropriating is not tenable.
   If it were different, then in a nonappropriator
   There should be appropriation. But there isn't.

8 So it is neither different from the appropriating
   Nor identical to the appropriating.
   There is no self without appropriation.
   But it is not true that it does not exist.

9 To say "in the past I wasn't"
   Would not be tenable.
   This person is not different
   From whoever existed in previous times.

10 If this one were different,
   Then if that one did not exist, I would still exist.
   If this were so,
   Without death, one would be born.

11 Annihilation and the exhaustion of action would follow;
   Different agents' actions
   Would be experienced by each other.
   That and other such things would follow.

12 Nothing comes to exist from something that did not exist.

From this errors would arise.
The self would be produced
Or, existing, would be without a cause.

13 So, the views "I existed," "I didn't exist,"
Both or neither,
In the past
Are untenable.

14 To say "in the future I will exist or
Will not exist,"
Such a view is like
Those involving the past.

15 If a human were a god,
On such a view there would be permanence.
The god would be unborn.
For any permanent thing is unborn.

16 If a human were different from a god,
On such a view there would be impermanence.
If the human were different from the god,
A continuum would not be tenable.

17 If one part were divine and
One part were human,
It would be both permanent and impermanent.
That would be irrational.

18 If it could be established that
And the view that the world is permanent, etc.,
All of these views
Depend on a prior limit permanent nor impermanent.

19 If anyone had come from anyplace
And were then to go someplace,
It would follow that cyclic existence was beginningless.
This is not the case.

20 If nothing is permanent,
What will be impermanent,
Permanent and impermanent,
Or neither?

21 If the world were limited,
How could there be another world?
If the world were unlimited,
How could there be another world?

22 Since the continuum of the aggregates
Is like the flame of a butterlamp,
It follows that neither its finitude
Nor its infinitude makes sense.

23 If the previous were disintegrating
And these aggregates, which depend
Upon those aggregates, did not arise,
Then the world would be finite.

24 If the previous were not disintegrating
    And these aggregates, which depend
    Upon those aggregates, did not arise,
    Then the world would be infinite.
25 If one part were finite and
    One part were infinite,
    Then the world would be finite and infinite.
    This would make no sense.
26 How could one think that
    One part of the appropriator is destroyed
    And one part is not destroyed?
    This position makes no sense.
27 How could one think that
    One part of the appropriation is destroyed
    And one part is not destroyed?
    This position makes no sense.
28 If it could be established that
    It is both finite and infinite,
    Then it could be established that
    It is neither finite nor infinite.
29 So, because all entities are empty,
    Which views of permanence, etc., would occur,
    And to whom, when, why, and about what
    Would they occur at all?
30 I prostrate to Gautama
    Who through compassion
    Taught the true doctrine,
    Which leads to the relinquishing of all views.

Questions for reflection

1   What do you think Nagarjuna is saying in stanzas one through twelve?
2   What does he claim the Buddha was teaching about the nature of entities?
3   What do you think Nagarjuna is getting at in the section above entitled "Examination of views?"
4   How might Nagarjuna respond to the argument that his own view of the empty self is a contradictory notion since there seems to be a self making the claim? Or that there seems to be a self (namely you) who is apparently understanding the claim about the empty self?
5   How might the realization that the self is not an enduring substance lead one to nirvana?

Further reading

David Kalupahana (1986) *The Philosophy of the Middle Way*. Albany, NY: State University of New York Press. (A recent translation of Nagarjuna's work, the *Mulamadhyamakakarika*; the introduction by Kalupahana presents a new hypothesis about the work.)

Nancy McCagney (1997) *Nagarjuna and the Philosophy of Openness*. Lanham, MD: Rowman & Littlefield. (Argues that the concept of space in Mahayana Buddhism plays a significant role in
Nagarjuna's understanding of sunyata.)

Nagarjuna ([c. 200 CE] 1995) *The Fundamental Wisdom of the Middle Way: Nagarjuna's Mulamadhyamakakarika*. Trans. Jay L. Garfield. Oxford: Oxford University Press. (Nagarjuna's
greatest work; the selection above was taken from this book.)

Frederick J. Streng (1967) *Emptiness: A Study in Religious Meaning*. Nashville, TN: Abingdon
Press. (A study of Nagarjuna and his interpretation of Ultimate Reality.)

Chapter 44

D. T. Suzuki

KARMA AND THE SELF IN ZEN BUDDHISM

Daisetz Teitaro (D. T.) Suzuki (1870–1966) was Professor of Buddhist philosophy at Otani University, Kyoto, and he also taught at American universities, including Columbia and Harvard. He was a leading proponent of Zen Buddhism in the West. Zen Buddhism is in one sense a branch of Mahāyāna Buddhism (the "Greater Vehicle"—one of the two major branches of Buddhist belief), and in another sense it is a merging of Mahayana Buddhism and Taoism. Like other Buddhist sects, Zen includes the Buddhist doctrines of the Four Noble Truths and the Noble Eightfold Path. In the following piece, Suzuki expounds on the notions of karma and the self. He summarizes them this way: "The principle of Karma is 'Whatever a man sows that will he also reap', and this governs the whole life of the Buddhist; for in fact what makes up one's individuality is nothing else than his own Karma."

Four Noble Truths – central Buddhist teachings: suffering, the cause of suffering, cessation of suffering, and the way leading to the cessation of suffering—the Noble Eightfold Path.
Hīnayāna Buddhism – the "Lesser Vehicle;" the other major branch of Buddhism along with Mahāyāna; also referred to as "Theravada" Buddhism.
Nagarjuna – an influential Buddhist philosopher from India.
(Noble) Eightfold Path – the Buddhist path to the cessation of suffering: right understanding, right intention, right speech, right action, right livelihood, right effort, right mindfulness, right concentration.

The doctrine of Karma

Superficially, passivity does not seem to be compatible with the intellectual tendency of Buddhism, especially of Zen, which strongly emphasizes the spirit of self-reliance as is seen in such passages as 'The Bhodisattva-mahāsattva retiring into a solitude all by himself, should reflect within himself, by means of his own inner intelligence, and not depend upon anybody else;'[1] or as we read in the *Dhammapada* [sacred Buddhist writings]:

> 'By self alone is evil done,
> By self is one disgraced;
> By self is evil undone,
> By self alone is he purified;
> Purity and impurity belong to one;
> No one can purify another.'[2]

Besides the four Noble Truths, the Twelvefold Chain of Origination, the Eightfold Path of Righteousness, etc.—all tend towards enlightenment and emancipation, and not towards absolute dependence or receptivity. 'To see with one's own eyes and be liberated' is the Buddhist motto, and there is apparently no room for passivity. For the latter can take place only when one makes oneself a receptacle for an outside power.

The attainment of passivity in Buddhism is especially obstructed by the doctrine of Karma. The doctrine of Karma runs like warp and weft through all the Indian fabrics of thought, and Buddhism as a product of the Indian imagination could not escape taking it into its own texture. The Jātaka Tales, making up the history of the Buddha while he was yet at the stage of Bodhisattvahood and training himself for final supreme enlightenment, are no more than the idea of Karma concretely applied and illustrated in the career of a morally perfected personage. Sakyamuni could not become a Buddha unless he had accumulated his stock of merit (*kuśalamūla*) throughout his varied lives in the past.

The principle of Karma is 'Whatever a man sows that will he also reap', and this governs the whole life of the Buddhist; for in fact what makes up one's individuality is nothing else than his own Karma. So we read in the *Milindapañha*, 'All beings have their Karma as their portion; they are heirs of their Karma; they are sprung from their Karma; their Karma is their refuge; Karma allots beings to meanness or greatness.'[3] This is confirmed in the *Samyutka-nikāya*:

> 'His good deeds and his wickedness,
> Whate'er a mortal does while here;
> 'Tis this that he can call his own,
> This with him take as he goes hence,
> This is what follows after him,
> And like a shadow ne'er departs.'[4]

According to the *Visuddhimagga*, Chapter XIX, Karma is divisible into several groups as regards the time and order of fruition and its quality: (1) that which bears fruit in the present existence, that which bears fruit in rebirth, that which bears fruit at no fixed time, and bygone Karma; (2) the weighty Karma, the abundant, the close-at-hand, and the habitual; (3) the productive Karma, the supportive, the counteractive, and the destructive.[5] There is thus a round of Karma and a round of fruit going on all the time. And who is the bearer of Karma and its fruit?

'No doer is there does the deed,
Nor is there one who feels the fruit;
Constituent parts alone roll on;
This view alone is orthodox.

And thus the deed, and thus the fruit
Roll on and on, each from its cause;
As of the round of tree and seed,
No one can tell when they began.

Not in its fruit is found the deed,
Nor in the deed finds one the fruit;
Of each the other is devoid,
Yet there's no fruit without the deed,

Just as no store of fire is found
In jewel, cow-dung, or the sun,
Nor separate from these exists,
Yet short of fuel no fire is known;

Even so we ne'er within the deed
Can retribution's fruit descry.
Not yet in any place without;
Nor can in fruit the deed be found.

Deeds separate from their fruits exist,
And fruits are separate from the deeds;
But consequent upon the deed
Fruit doth into being come.

No god of heaven or Brahma-world
Doth cause the endless round of birth;
Constituent parts alone roll on,
From cause and from material sprung.'[6]

The working of Karma is apparently quite impersonal, as is explained in these quotations, and it may seem altogether indifferent for anybody whether he did something good or bad. There is no doer of deeds, nor is there any sufferer of their fruit. The five Aggregates or constituent parts (*skandhas*) are combined and dissolved in accordance with the inevitable law of Karma, but as long as there is no personal agent at the back of all this, who really feels the value of Karma, it does not seem to matter what kind of deed is committed and what kind of fruit is brought forth. Still the Buddhists are advised not to practise wickedness:

'If a man do wrong,
Let him not do it repeatedly,
Let him not take pleasure therein;
Painful is wrong's accumulation.'[7]

Why painful? Why pleasurable? The Hīnayānist reasoning is logically thoroughgoing, but when it comes to the question of practical psychology, mere reasoning does not avail. Is the feeling no more real than the mere bundling together of the five Aggregates? The combination—that is, unity—seems to be more than the fact of combination. Whatever this is, as I am not going to discuss the doctrine of Karma here in detail, let it suffice to give another quotation from Nāgārjuna's *Mūlamadhyamakakārikās*, Chapter XVII, where the doctrine of Karma appears in a new garment.[8]

'All sentient beings are born according to their Karma: good people are born in the heavens, the wicked in the hells, and those who practise the paths of righteousness realize Nirvāna. By disciplining himself in the six virtues of perfection, a man is able to benefit his fellow-beings in various ways, and this is sure in turn to bring blessings upon him, not only in this but also in the next life. Karma may be of two sorts: inner or mental, which is called *cetana* and physical, expressing itself in speech and bodily movement. This is technically known as Karma "after having intended".[9]

'Karma may also be regarded as with or without "intimation".[10] An act with intimation is one the purpose of which is perceptible by others, while an act without intimation is not at all expressed in physical movements; it follows that when a strong act with intimation is performed it awakens the tendency in the mind of the actor to perform again deeds, either good or bad, of a similar nature.

'It is like a seed from which a young plant shoots out and bears fruit by the principle of continuity; apart from the seed there is no continuity; and because of this continuity there is fruition. The seed comes first and then the fruit; between them there is neither discontinuity nor constancy. Since the awakening of a first motive, there follows an uninterrupted series of mental activities, and from this there is fruition. Apart from the first stirring of the mind, there will be no stream of thoughts expressing themselves in action. Thus there is a continuity of Karma and its fruit. Therefore, when the ten deeds of goodness and purity are performed, the agent is sure to enjoy happiness in this life and be born after death among celestial beings.

'There is something in Karma that is never lost even after its performance; this something called *avipranāśa*[11] is like a deed of contract, and Karma, an act, is comparable to debt. A man may use up what he has borrowed, but owing to the document he has some day to pay the debt back to the creditor. This "unlosable" is always left behind even after Karma and is not destroyed by philosophical intuition.[12] If it is thus destructible, Karma will never come to fruition. The only power that counteracts this "unlosable" is moral discipline.[13] Every Karma once committed continues to work out its consequence by means of the "unlosable" until its course is thwarted by the attainment of Arhatship [achieving Nirvāna] or by death, or when it has finally borne its fruit. This law of Karma applies equally to good and bad deeds.'

While Nāgārjuna's idea is to wipe out all such notions as doer, deed, and sufferer, in other words, the entire structure of Karma-theory, this introduction of the idea 'unlosable' is instructive and full of suggestions..

Taking all in all, however, there is much obscurity in the doctrine of Karmaic continuity, especially when its practical working is to be precisely described; and, theoretically too, we are not quite sure of its absolute tenability. But this we can state of it in a most general way that Karma tends to emphasize individual freedom, moral responsibility, and feeling of independence; and further, from the religious point of view, it does not necessitate the postulate of a God, or a creator, or a moral judge, who passes judgments upon human behaviour, good or bad.

This being the case, the Buddhist conviction that life is pain will inevitably lead to a systematic teaching of self-discipline, self-purification, and self-enlightenment, the moral centre of gravity being always placed on the self, and not on any outside agent. This is the principle of Karma applied to the realization of Nirvāna. But, we may ask, What is this 'self'? And again, What is that something that is never 'lost' in a Karma committed either mentally or physically? What is the connection between 'self' and the 'unlosable'? Where does this 'unlosable' lodge itself?

Between the Buddhist doctrine of no-ego-substance and the postulate that there should be something 'not to be lost' in the continuation of Karma-force, which makes the latter safely bear fruit, there is a gap which must be bridged somehow if Buddhist philosophy is to make further development. To my mind, the conception of the Ālayavijñāna ('All-conserving soul') where all the Karma-seeds are deposited was an inevitable consequence. But in the meantime let us see what 'self' really stands for.

The conception of self

'Self' is a very complex and elusive idea, and when we say that one is to be responsible for what one does by oneself, we do not exactly know how far this 'self' goes and how much it includes in itself. For individuals are so intimately related to one another not only in one communal life but in the totality of existence—so intimately indeed that there are really no individuals, so to speak, in the absolute sense of the word.

Individuality is merely an aspect of existence; in thought we separate one individual from another and in reality too we all seem to be distinct and separable. But when we reflect on the question more closely we find that individuality is a fiction, for we cannot fix its limits, we cannot ascertain its extents and boundaries, they become mutually merged without leaving any indelible marks between the so-called individuals. A most penetrating state of interrelationship prevails here, and it seems to be more exact to say that individuals do not exist, they are merely so many points of reference, the meaning of which is not at all realizable when each of them is considered by itself and in itself apart from the rest.

Individuals are recognizable only when they are thought of in relation to something not individual; though paradoxical, they are individuals so long as they are not individuals. For when an individual being is singled out as such, it at once ceases to be an individual. The 'individual self' is an illusion.

Thus, the self has no absolute, independent existence. Moral responsibility seems to be a kind of intellectual makeshift. Can the robber be really considered responsible for his deeds? Can this individual be really singled out as the one who has to suffer all the consequences of his anti-social habits? Can he be held really responsible for all that made him such as he is? Is his *svabhāva* [nature] all his own make? This is where lies the main crux of the question, 'How far is an individual to be answerable for his action?' In other words, 'How far is this "he" separable from the community of which he is a component part?' Is not society reflected in him? Is he not one of the products created by society?

There are no criminals, no sinful souls in the Pure Land, not necessarily because no such are born there but mainly because all that are born there become pure by virtue of the general atmosphere into which they are brought up. Although environment is not everything, it, especially social environment, has a great deal to do with the shaping of individual characters. If this is the case, where shall we look for the real signification of the doctrine of Karma?

The intellect wants to have a clear-cut, well-delineated figure to which a deed or its 'unlosable' something has to be attached, and Karma becomes mathematically describable as having its originator, perpetrator, sufferer, etc. But when there are really no individuals and Karma is to be conceived as nowhere originated by any specifically definable agent, what would become of the doctrine of Karma as advocated by Buddhists? Evidently there is an act, either good or bad or indifferent; there is one who actually thrusts a dagger, and there is one who actually lies dead thus stabbed; and yet shall we have to declare that there is no killer, no killing, and none killed? What will then become of moral responsibility? How can there be such a thing as accumulation of merit or attainment of enlightenment? Who is after all a Buddha, and who is an ignorant, confused mortal?

Can we say that society, nay, the whole universe, is responsible for the act of killing if this fact is once established? And that all the causes and conditions leading to it and all the results that are to be connected with it are to be traced to the universe itself? Or is it that the individual is an ultimate absolute fact and what goes out from him comes back to him without any relation to his fellow-beings and to his environment, social and physical?

In the first case, moral responsibility evaporates into an intangible universality; in the second case, the intangible whole gets crystallized in one individual, and there is indeed moral responsibility, but one stands altogether in isolation as if each of us were like a grain of sand in no relation to its neighbours. Which of these positions is more exactly in conformity with facts of human experience? When this is applied to the Buddhist doctrine of Karma, the question comes to this: Is Buddhist Karma to be understood individualistically or cosmologically?

Mahāyāna Buddhism on the theory of Karma

As far as history goes, Buddhism started with the individualistic interpretation of Karma, and when it reached its culminating point of development in the rise of Mahāyāna, the doctrine came to be cosmically understood. But not in the vague, abstract, philosophical way as was before referred to but concretely and spiritually in this wise: the net of the universe spreads out both in time and space from the centre known as 'my self', where it is felt that all the sins of the world are resting on his own shoulders. To atone for them he is determined to subject himself to a system of moral and spiritual training which he considers would cleanse him of all impurities, and by cleansing him cleanse also the whole world of all its demerits.

This is the Mahāyāna position. Indeed, the distinction between the Mahāyāna and the Hīnayāna forms of Buddhism may be said to be due to this difference in the treatment of Karma-conception. The Mahāyāna thus came to emphasize the 'other' or 'whole' aspect of Karma, and, therefore, of universal salvation, while the Hīnayāna adhered to the 'self' aspect. As Karma worked, according to the Hīnayānists, apparently impersonally but in point of fact individualistically, this life of pain and suffering was to be got rid of by self-discipline, by moral asceticism, and self-knowledge. Nobody outside could help the sufferer out of his afflictions; all that the Buddha could do for him was to teach him the way to escape; but if he did not walk this way by himself, he could not be made to go straight ahead even by the power and virtue of the Buddha. 'Be ye a lamp and a refuge to yourselves' (*attadīpa-attasarana*) was the injunction left by the Buddha to his Hīnayāna followers, for the Buddha could not extend his spiritual virtue and attainment over to his devotees or to his fellow-beings. From the general position of the Hīnayānists, this was inevitable:

'Not in the sky,
Not in the midst of the sea,
Nor entering a cleft of the mountains,
Is found that realm on earth
Where one may stand and be
From an evil deed absolved.'[14]

But the Mahāyāna was not satisfied with this narrowness of spiritual outlook; the Mahāyāna wanted to extend the function of Karunā (love) to the furthest end it could reach. If one's Prajñā (wisdom) could include in itself the widest possible system of universes, why could not Karunā too take them all under its protective wings? Why could not the Buddha's wish (*pranidhāna*) for the spiritual welfare of all beings also efficiently work towards its realization? The Buddha attained his enlightenment after accumulating so much stock of merit for ever so many countless kalpas (eons). Should we conceive this stock of merit to be available only for his own benefit?

Karma must have its cosmological meaning. In fact, individuals are such in so far as they are thought of in connection with one another and also with the whole system which they compose. One wave good or bad, once stirred, could not help affecting the entire body of water. So with the moral discipline and the spiritual attainment of the Buddha, they could not remain with him as an isolated event in the communal life to which he belonged. Therefore, it is said that when he was enlightened the whole universe shared in his wisdom and virtue. The Mahāyāna stands on this fundamental idea of enlightenment . . .

Notes

1   *The Lankāvatāra*, the author's English translation, p. 115. . . .
2   The *Dhammapada*, p. 165. The translation is by A. J. Edmunds. . . .
3   Quoted from Warren's *Buddhism in Translations,* p. 255.
4   Loc. cit., p. 214.
5   Loc. cit., pp. 245*ff.*
6   Warren, pp. 248–9.
7   The *Dhammapada*, p. 117, translated by A. J. Edmunds.
8   Edited by Louis de la Vallée Poussin. Pp. 302 *ff.* For a detailed exposition of the theory of Karma, see the *abhidharmakośa* (translated by the same author), Chapter IV. What follows is an abstract.
9   *Cetayitvā.*
10   'Indication', *vijñapti.*
11   'Not lost', or 'unlosable', or 'indestructible'.

12   *Darśanamārga.*
13   *Bhāvanamārga.*
14   *The Dhammapada*, p. 127. Translated by Albert J. Edmunds.

Questions for reflection

1   How would you describe karma as it is presented here by Suzuki?
2   How does karma emphasize individual freedom, moral responsibility, and a feeling of independence?
3   What is the self, according to Suzuki? What does he mean when he says that "individuality is a fiction"?
4   What does it mean to achieve Nirvāna if there is no individuality?
5   What is the Mahāyāna Buddhist idea of enlightenment, as expressed in this selection?

Further reading

Heinrich Dumoulin (2005) *Zen Buddhism: A History.* Volume 1: *India and China.* Bloomington, IN: World Wisdom. (A history of Zen from its beginnings in India up through the Sung period in China.)

Heinrich Dumoulin (2005) *Zen Buddhism: A History.* Volume 2: *Japan.* Bloomington, IN: World Wisdom. (A history of Zen as it developed in Japan.)

D. T. Suzuki (1991) *An Introduction to Zen Buddhism.* New York: Grove/Atlantic. (A very accessible introduction and guide to Zen Buddhism.)

Alan W. Watts (1999) *The Way of Zen.* New York: Vintage. (A contemporary classic; designed especially with Western readers in mind.)

PART SEVEN

Religious experience

There are abundant varieties of experiences in human life, but one type especially stands out as unique: religious experience. What is religious experience, you might wonder? While it is difficult to offer a concise definition, it is basically any experience one has that is related to his or her religious life. However, the really interesting and distinctive experiences commonly associated with the concept are more esoteric in nature. We can no doubt point to countless examples. The history of religion is filled with individuals who claim to have had visions of God, or to have experienced the oneness of Brahman, or to have seen an angel, or to have spoken in tongues, or to have feared the presence of Satan, or to have had a conversion from spiritual death to life. Countless persons from every creed and culture have claimed to have had these sorts of esoteric or numinous experiences. Here, as an example, is a description of a Christian religious experience:

> God is more real to me than any thought or thing or person. I feel his presence positively, and the more as I live in closer harmony with his laws as written in my body and mind. I feel him in the sunshine or rain; and awe mingled with a delicious restfulness most nearly describes my feelings. I talk to him as a companion in prayer and praise, and our communion is delightful. He answers me again and again, often in words so clearly spoken that it seems my outer ear must have carried the tone, but generally in strong mental impressions. Usually a text of Scripture, unfolding some new view of him and his love for me, and care for my safety. I could give hundreds of instances, in school matters, social problems, financial difficulties, etc. That he is mine and I am his never leaves me, it is an abiding joy. Without it life would be a blank, a desert, a shoreless, trackless waste.[1]

Philosophical reflection on these kinds of experiences raises a host of questions. For example, are they veridical? What causes a religious experience? How do we distinguish religious experience from other types of experience? Can such experiences provide evidence for God/Ultimate Reality? These and other questions are addressed in the essays in this section.

A special kind of religious experience is called a "mystical experience" and often refers to a state of being in which all distinctions seem to disappear, even the distinction between the individual as subject and all other objects. A sense of union with the divine commonly follows, making this a kind of pantheistic experience. In such cases, the mystic begins to realize the following words from sacred Hindu texts: "That art Thou . . . Not a part, not a mode of That, but identically That, that Absolute Spirit of the World."[2] In the first selection, William James offers four characteristics of mystical experience, what he considers the deepest type of religious experience. He also provides examples from several religious traditions.

One of the most famous mystics is Julian of Norwich, a Christian from the fourteenth century. It is debated whether her experiences should be considered pantheistic or theistic. She has what she calls visions, or "showings," and describes them in some intense detail. I have included a well-known selection by Julian to give you a sense of how a classic mystic expresses such experiences.

Not all religious experiences involve an awareness of a *divine* reality, however. Many experiences in Eastern religion include no such awareness whatever. For example, in the next essay, D. T. Suzuki describes Zen Buddhist satori, or a state of enlightenment. He defines it as "an intuitive looking into the nature of things in contradistinction to the analytical or logical understanding of it" and offers the central characteristics of satori. It is the heart of Zen, he contends, an awakening that takes place in an individual. This is a religious experience that involves not a moment, or an extended time, but rather is concerned with the whole of life. As he notes, "For what Zen proposes to do is the revolution, and the revaluation as well, of oneself as a spiritual unity."

Another important issue related to religious experiences is their origin. There have been a number of explanations offered for how such experiences, and religion in general, originated. Sigmund Freud provided one explanation in the subsequent essay which still affects the way many people view these matters. For Freud, religion arises from a desire for a father figure. When we were children, many of us had a father to look after us and protect us. As we moved into adulthood, however, we realized that our earthly fathers are finite and limited—unable to meet our continually growing needs. At a subconscious level, he maintained, we then reified a Fatherly Being who could take care of all our needs. In other words, we literally wished God into existence. One could, of course, take Freud's general thesis on religion and apply it, with some modifications, to religious experience as well.

Others take religious experience to be a source of knowledge about, or to provide justified belief for, God or Ultimate Reality. In the last essay of this section, Douglas Geivett examines the evidential value of religious experience. Two issues of importance here are (1) whether those who have had a religious experience can legitimately take that experience to be non-inferential grounds for their own religious beliefs, and (2) whether the religious experiences of another can offer any evidential weight to one who has not had them. Geivett examines issues and delineates a general pattern in recent arguments from religious experience. He also considers objections to these arguments and explores naturalistic explanations for religious experience.

Notes

1   A quote from a twenty-seven-year-old Christian man; William James ([1902] 1992) *The Varieties of Religious Experience: A Study in Human Nature* (New York: Longmans, Green, and Co.), 70–71.

2   Ibid., 419. These selections are taken from the Upanishads and the Vedas.

Chapter 45

William James

MYSTICISM

William James (1842–1910) was a philosopher and psychologist who advanced a philo-sophical view known in America as pragmatism. The following selection is taken from his classic work entitled *The Varieties of Religious Experience*—arguably one of the most important works ever written on the psychology of religion. According to James, mystical experiences are real and worthy of investigation. In this selection he first offers four distinct characteristics of such experiences: ineffability, noetic quality, transiency, and passivity. He then provides examples of such experiences from the religious traditions of Hindus, Bud-dhists, Muslims, and Christians.

Over and over again in these lectures I have raised points and left them open and unfin-ished until we should have come to the subject of mysticism.* Some of you, I fear, may have smiled as you noted my reiterated postponements. But now the hour has come when mysticism must be faced in good earnest, and those broken threads wound up together. One may say truly, I think, that personal religious experience has its root and centre in mystical states of consciousness; so for us, who in these lectures are treating personal experience as the exclusive subject of our study, such states of consciousness ought to form the vital chapter from which the other chapters get their light. Whether my treatment of mystical states will shed more light or darkness, I do not know, for my own constitution shuts me out from their enjoyment almost entirely, and I can speak of them only at second hand. But though forced to look upon the subject so externally, I will be as objective and receptive as I can; and I think I shall at least succeed in convinc-ing you of the reality of the states in question, and of the paramount importance of their function.

First of all, then, I ask, What does the expression 'mystical states of consciousness' mean? How do we part off mystical states from other states?

The words 'mysticism' and 'mystical' are often used as terms of mere reproach, to throw at any opinion which we regard as vague and vast and sentimental, and without a base in either facts or logic. For some writers a 'mystic' is any person who believes in thought-transference, or spirit-return. Employed in this way the word has little value: there are too many less ambiguous synonyms. So, to keep it useful by restricting it, I will do what I did in the case of the word 'religion,' and simply propose to you four marks which, when an experience has them, may justify us in calling it mystical for the purpose of the present lectures. In this way we shall save verbal disputation, and the recriminations that generally go therewith.

1. *Ineffability.*——The handiest of the marks by which I classify a state of mind as mystical is negative. The subject of it immediately says that it defies expression, that no adequate report of its contents can be given in words. It follows from this that its quality must be directly experienced; it cannot be imparted or transferred to others. In this peculiarity mystical states are more like states of feeling than like states of intellect. No one can make clear to another who has never had a certain feeling, in what the quality or worth of it consists. One must have musical ears to know the value of a symphony; one must have been in love one's self to understand a lover's state of mind. Lacking the heart or ear, we cannot interpret the musician or the lover justly, and are even likely to consider him weak-minded or absurd. The mystic finds that most of us accord to his experiences an equally incompetent treatment.

2. *Noetic quality.*——Although so similar to states of feeling, mystical states seem to those who experience them to be also states of knowledge. They are states of insight into depths of truth unplumbed by the discursive intellect. They are illuminations, revelations, full of significance and importance, all inarticulate though they remain; and as a rule they carry with them a curious sense of authority for after-time.

These two characters will entitle any state to be called mystical, in the sense in which I use the word. Two other qualities are less sharply marked, but are usually found. These are:——

3. *Transiency.*——Mystical states cannot be sustained for long. Except in rare instances, half an hour, or at most an hour or two, seems to be the limit beyond which they fade into the light of common day. Often, when faded, their quality can but imperfectly be reproduced in memory; but when they recur it is recognized; and from one recurrence to another it is susceptible of continuous development in what is felt as inner richness and importance.

4. *Passivity.*——Although the oncoming of mystical states may be facilitated by preliminary voluntary operations, as by fixing the attention, or going through certain bodily performances, or in other ways which manuals of mysticism prescribe; yet when the characteristic sort of consciousness once has set in, the mystic feels as if his own will were in abeyance, and indeed sometimes as if he were grasped and held by a superior power. This latter peculiarity connects mystical states with certain definite phenomena of secondary or alternative personality, such as prophetic speech, automatic writing, or the mediumistic trance. When these latter conditions are well pronounced, however, there may be no recollection whatever of the phenomenon, and it may have no significance for the subject's usual inner life, to which, as it were, it makes a mere interruption. Mystical states, strictly so called, are never merely interruptive. Some memory of their content always remains, and a profound sense of their importance. They modify the inner life of the subject between the times of their recurrence. Sharp divisions in this region are, however, difficult to make, and we find all sorts of gradations and mixtures.

These four characteristics are sufficient to mark out a group of states of consciousness peculiar enough to deserve a special name and to call for careful study. Let it then be called the mystical group.

Our next step should be to gain acquaintance with some typical examples. Professional mystics at the height of their development have often elaborately organized experiences and a philosophy based thereupon. But . . . phenomena are best understood when placed within their series, studied in their germ and in their over-ripe decay, and compared with their exaggerated and degenerated kindred. The range of mystical experience is very wide, much too wide for us to cover in the time at our disposal. Yet the method of serial study is so essential for interpretation that if we really wish to reach conclusions we must use it. I will begin, therefore, with phenomena which claim no special religious significance, and end with those of which the religious pretensions are extreme.

The simplest rudiment of mystical experience would seem to be that deepened sense of the significance of a maxim or formula which occasionally sweeps over one. "I've heard that said all my life," we exclaim, "but I never realized its full meaning until now." "When a fellow-monk," said Luther, "one day repeated the words of the Creed: 'I believe in the forgiveness of sins,' I saw the Scripture in an entirely new light; and straightway I felt as if I were born anew. It was as if I had found the door of paradise thrown wide open." This sense of deeper significance is not confined to rational propositions. Single words and conjunctions of words; effects of light on land and sea, odors and musical sounds, all bring it when the mind is tuned aright. Most of us can remember the strangely moving power of passages in certain poems read when we were young, irrational doorways as they were through which the mystery of fact, the wildness and the pang of life, stole into our hearts and thrilled them. The words have now perhaps become mere polished surfaces for us; but lyric poetry and music are alive and significant only in proportion as they fetch these vague vistas of a life continuous with our own, beckoning and inviting, yet ever eluding our pursuit. We are alive or dead to the eternal inner message of the arts according as we have kept or lost this mystical susceptibility. . . .

Somewhat deeper plunges into mystical consciousness are met with in yet other dreamy states. Such feelings as these which Charles Kingsley describes are surely far from being uncommon, especially in youth:—

> "When I walk the fields, I am oppressed now and then with an innate feeling that everything I see has a meaning, if I could but understand it. And this feeling of being surrounded with truths which I cannot grasp amounts to indescribable awe sometimes. . . . Have you not felt that your real soul was imperceptible to your mental vision, except in a few hallowed moments?"

A much more extreme state of mystical consciousness is described by J. A. Symonds; and probably more persons than we suspect could give parallels to it from their own experience.

"Suddenly," writes Symonds, "at church, or in company, or when I was reading, and always, I think, when my muscles were at rest, I felt the approach of the mood. Irresistibly it took possession of my mind and will, lasted what seemed an eternity, and disappeared in a series of rapid sensations which resembled the awakening from anæsthetic influence. One reason why I disliked this kind of trance was that I could not describe it to myself. I cannot even now find words to render it intelligible. It consisted in a gradual but swiftly progressive obliteration of space, time, sensation, and the multitudinous factors of experience which seem to qualify what we are pleased to call our Self. In proportion as these conditions of ordinary consciousness were subtracted, the sense of an underlying or essential consciousness acquired intensity. At last nothing remained but a pure, absolute, abstract Self. The universe became without form and void of content. But Self persisted, formidable in its vivid keenness, feeling the most poignant doubt about reality, ready, as it seemed, to find existence break as breaks a bubble round about it. And what then? The apprehension of a coming dissolution, the grim conviction that this state was the last state of the conscious Self, the sense that I had followed the last thread of being to the verge of the abyss, and had arrived at demonstration of eternal Maya or illusion, stirred or seemed to stir me up again. The return to ordinary conditions of sentient existence began by my first recovering the power of touch, and then by the gradual though rapid influx of familiar impressions and diurnal interests. At last I felt myself once more a human being; and though the riddle of what is meant by life remained unsolved, I was thankful for this return from the abyss—this deliverance from so awful an initiation into the mysteries of skepticism.

"This trance recurred with diminishing frequency until I reached the age of twenty-eight. It served to impress upon my growing nature the phantasmal unreality of all the circumstances which contribute to a merely phenomenal consciousness. Often have I asked myself with anguish, on waking from that formless state of denuded, keenly sentient being, Which is the unreality?—the trance of fiery, vacant, apprehensive, skeptical Self from which I issue, or these surrounding phenomena and habits which veil that inner Self and build a self of flesh-and-blood conventionality? Again, are men the factors of some dream, the dream-like unsubstantiality of which they comprehend at such eventful moments? What would happen if the final stage of the trance were reached?"

In a recital like this there is certainly something suggestive of pathology. The next step into mystical states carries us into a realm that public opinion and ethical philosophy have long since branded as pathological, though private practice and certain lyric strains of poetry seem still to bear witness to its ideality. I refer to the consciousness produced by intoxicants and anæsthetics, especially by alcohol. The sway of alcohol over mankind is unquestionably due to its power to stimulate the mystical faculties of human nature, usually crushed to earth by the cold facts and dry criticisms of the sober hour. Sobriety diminishes, discriminates, and says no; drunkenness expands, unites, and says yes. It is in fact the great exciter of the *Yes* function in man. It brings its votary from the chill periphery of things to the radiant core. It makes him for the moment one with truth. Not through mere perversity do men run after it. To the poor and the unlettered it stands in the place of symphony concerts and of literature; and it is part of the deeper mystery and tragedy of life that whiffs and gleams of something that we immediately recognize as excellent should be vouchsafed to so many of us only in the fleeting earlier phases of what in its totality is so degrading a poisoning. The drunken consciousness is one bit of the mystic consciousness, and our total opinion of it must find its place in our opinion of that larger whole.

Nitrous oxide and ether, especially nitrous oxide, when sufficiently diluted with air, stimulate the mystical consciousness in an extraordinary degree. Depth beyond depth of truth seems revealed to the inhaler. This truth fades out, however, or escapes, at the moment of coming to; and if any words remain over in which it seemed to clothe itself, they prove to be the veriest nonsense. Nevertheless, the sense of a profound meaning having been there persists; and I know more than one person who is persuaded that in the nitrous oxide trance we have a genuine metaphysical revelation.

Some years ago I myself made some observations on this aspect of nitrous oxide intoxication, and reported them in print. One conclusion was forced upon my mind at that time, and my impression of its truth has ever since remained unshaken. It is that our normal waking consciousness, rational consciousness as we call it, is but one special type of consciousness, whilst all about it, parted from it by the filmiest of screens, there lie potential forms of consciousness entirely different. We may go through life without suspecting their existence; but apply the requisite stimulus, and at a touch they are there in all their completeness, definite types of mentality which probably somewhere have their field of application and adaptation. No account of the universe in its totality can be final which leaves these other forms of consciousness quite disregarded. How to regard them is the question,—for they are so discontinuous with ordinary consciousness. Yet they may determine attitudes though they cannot furnish formulas, and open a region though they fail to give a map. At any rate, they forbid a premature closing of our accounts with reality. Looking back on my own experiences, they all converge towards a kind of insight to which I cannot help ascribing some metaphysical significance. The keynote of it is invariably a reconciliation. It is as if the opposites of the world, whose contradictoriness and conflict make all our difficulties and troubles, were melted into unity. Not only do they, as contrasted species, belong to one and the same genus, but *one of the species*, the nobler and better one, *is itself the genus, and so soaks up and absorbs its opposite into itself.* This is a dark saying, I know, when thus expressed in terms of common logic, but I cannot wholly escape from its authority. I feel as if it must mean something, something like what the hegelian philosophy means, if one could only lay hold of it more clearly. Those who have ears to hear, let them hear; to me the living sense of its reality only comes in the artificial mystic state of mind. . . .

We have now seen enough of this cosmic or mystic consciousness, as it comes sporadically. We must next pass to its methodical cultivation as an element of the religious life. Hindus, Buddhists, Mohammedans, and Christians all have cultivated it methodically.

In India, training in mystical insight has been known from time immemorial under the name of yoga. Yoga means the experimental union of the individual with the divine. It is based on persevering exercise; and the diet, posture, breathing, intellectual concentration, and moral discipline vary slightly in the different systems which teach it. The yogi, or disciple, who has by these means overcome the obscurations of his lower nature sufficiently, enters into the condition termed *samâdhi*, "and comes face to face with facts which no instinct or reason can ever know." He learns—

> That the mind itself has a higher state of existence, beyond reason, a superconscious state, and that when the mind gets to that higher state, then this knowledge beyond reasoning comes. . . . All the different steps in yoga are intended to bring us scientifically to the superconscious state or samâdhi. . . . Just as unconscious work is beneath consciousness, so there is another work which is above consciousness, and which, also, is not accompanied with the feeling of egoism. . . . There is no feeling of *I*, and yet the mind works, desireless, free from restlessness, objectless, bodiless. Then the Truth shines in its full effulgence, and we know ourselves—for Samâdhi

lies potential in us all—for what we truly are, free, immortal, omnipotent, loosed from the finite, and its contrasts of good and evil altogether, and identical with the Atman or Universal Soul.

The Vedantists say that one may stumble into superconsciousness sporadically, without the previous discipline, but it is then impure. Their test of its purity, like our test of religion's value, is empirical: its fruits must be good for life. When a man comes out of Samâdhi, they assure us that he remains "enlightened, a sage, a prophet, a saint, his whole character changed, his life changed, illumined."

The Buddhists use the word 'samâdhi' as well as the Hindus; but 'dhyâna' is their special word for higher states of contemplation. There seem to be four stages recognized in dhyâna. The first stage comes through concentration of the mind upon one point. It excludes desire, but not discernment or judgment: it is still intellectual. In the second state the intellectual functions drop off, and the satisfied sense of unity remains. In the third stage the satisfaction departs, and indifference begins, along with memory and self-consciousness. In the fourth stage the indifference, memory, and self-consciousness are perfected. [Just what 'memory' and 'self-consciousness' mean in this connection is doubtful. They cannot be the faculties familiar to us in the lower life.] Higher stages still of contemplation are mentioned—a region where there exists nothing, and where the meditator says: "There exists absolutely nothing," and stops. Then he reaches another region where he says: "There are neither ideas nor absence of ideas," and stops again. Then another region where, "having reached the end of both idea and perception, he stops finally." This would seem to be, not yet Nirvâna, but as close an approach to it as this life affords.

In the Mohammedan world the Sufi sect and various dervish bodies are the possessors of the mystical tradition. The Sufis have existed in Persia from the earliest times, and as their pantheism is so at variance with the hot and rigid monotheism of the Arab mind, it has been suggested that Sufism must have been inoculated into Islam by Hindu influences. We Christians know little of Sufism, for its secrets are disclosed only to those initiated. To give its existence a certain liveliness in your minds, I will quote a Moslem document, and pass away from the subject.

Al-Ghazzali, a Persian philosopher and theologian, who flourished in the eleventh century, and ranks as one of the greatest doctors of the Moslem church, has left us one of the few autobiographies to be found outside of Christian literature. Strange that a species of book so abundant among ourselves should be so little represented elsewhere—the absence of strictly personal confessions is the chief difficulty to the purely literary student who would like to become acquainted with the inwardness of religions other than the Christian.

M. Schmölders has translated a part of Al-Ghazzali's autobiography into French: —

. . . The first condition for a Sufi is to purge his heart entirely of all that is not God. The next key of the contemplative life consists in the humble prayers which escape from the fervent soul, and in the meditations on God in which the heart is swallowed up entirely. But in reality this is only the beginning of the Sufi life, the end of Sufism being total absorption in God. The intuitions and all that precede are, so to speak, only the threshold for those who enter. From the beginning, revelations take place in so flagrant a shape that the Sufis see before them, whilst wide awake, the angels and the souls of the prophets. They hear their voices and obtain their favors. Then the transport rises from the perception of forms and figures to a degree which escapes all expression, and which no man may seek to give an account of without his words involving sin.

Whoever has had no experience of the transport knows of the true nature of prophetism nothing but the name. He may meanwhile be sure of its existence, both by experience and by what he hears the Sufis say. As there are men endowed only with the sensitive faculty who reject what is offered them in the way of objects of the pure understanding, so there are intellectual men who reject and avoid the things perceived by the prophetic faculty. A blind man can understand nothing of colors save what he has learned by narration and hearsay. Yet God has brought prophetism near to men in giving them all a state analogous to it in its principal characters. This state is sleep. If you were to tell a man who was himself without experience of such a phenomenon that there are people who at times swoon away so as to resemble dead men, and who [in dreams] yet perceive things that are hidden, he would deny it [and give his reasons]. Nevertheless, his arguments would be refuted by actual experience. Wherefore, just as the understanding is a stage of human life in which an eye opens to discern various intellectual objects uncomprehended by sensation; just so in the prophetic the sight is illumined by a light which uncovers hidden things and objects which the intellect fails to reach. The chief properties of prophetism are perceptible only during the transport, by those who embrace the Sufi life. The prophet is endowed with qualities to which you possess nothing analogous, and which consequently you cannot possibly understand. How should you know their true nature, since one knows only what one can comprehend? But the transport which one attains by the method of the Sufis is like an immediate perception, as if one touched the objects with one's hand.

This incommunicableness of the transport is the keynote of all mysticism. Mystical truth exists for the individual who has the transport, but for no one else. In this, as I have said, it resembles the knowledge given to us in sensations more than that given by conceptual thought. Thought, with its remoteness and abstractness, has often enough in the history of philosophy been contrasted unfavorably with sensation. It is a commonplace of metaphysics that God's knowledge cannot be discursive but must be intuitive, that is, must be constructed more after the pattern of what in ourselves is called immediate feeling, than after that of proposition and judgment. But *our* immediate feelings have no content but what the five senses supply; and we have seen and shall see again that mystics may emphatically deny that the senses play any part in the very highest type of knowledge which their transports yield.

In the Christian church there have always been mystics. Although many of them have been viewed with suspicion, some have gained favor in the eyes of the authorities. The experiences of these have been treated as precedents, and a codified system of mystical theology has been based upon them, in which everything legitimate finds its place. The basis of the system is 'orison' or meditation, the methodical elevation of the soul towards God. Through the practice of orison the higher levels of mystical experience may be attained. It is odd that Protestantism, especially evangelical Protestantism, should seemingly have abandoned everything methodical in this line. Apart from what prayer may lead to, Protestant mystical experience appears to have been almost exclusively sporadic. It has been left to our mind-curers to reintroduce methodical meditation into our religious life.

The first thing to be aimed at in orison is the mind's detachment from outer sensations, for these interfere with its concentration upon ideal things. Such manuals as Saint Ignatius's Spiritual Exercises recommend the disciple to expel sensation by a graduated series of efforts to imagine holy scenes. The acme of this kind of discipline would be a semi-hallucinatory mono-ideism—an imaginary figure of Christ, for example, coming fully to occupy the mind. Sensorial images of this sort, whether literal or symbolic, play an enormous part in mysticism. But in certain cases imagery may fall away entirely, and in the very highest raptures it tends to do so. The state of consciousness becomes then insusceptible of any verbal description. Mystical teachers are unanimous as to this. Saint John of the Cross, for instance, one of the best of them, thus describes the condition called the 'union of love,' which, he says, is reached by 'dark contemplation.' In this the Deity compenetrates the soul, but in such a hidden way that the soul—

> finds no terms, no means, no comparison whereby to render the sublimity of the wisdom and the delicacy of the spiritual feeling with which she is filled. . . . We receive this mystical knowledge of God clothed in none of the kinds of images, in none of the sensible representations, which our mind makes use of in other circumstances. Accordingly in this knowledge, since the senses and the imagination are not employed, we get neither form nor impression, nor can we give any account or furnish any likeness, although the mysterious and sweet-tasting wisdom comes home so clearly to the inmost parts of our soul. Fancy a man seeing a certain kind of thing for the first time in his life. He can understand it, use and enjoy it, but he cannot apply a name to it, nor communicate any idea of it, even though all the while it be a mere thing of sense. How much greater will be his powerlessness when it goes beyond the senses! This is the peculiarity of the divine language. . . .

I cannot pretend to detail to you the sundry stages of the Christian mystical life. Our time would not suffice, for one thing; and moreover, I confess that the subdivisions and names which we find in the Catholic books seem to me to represent nothing objectively distinct. So many men, so many minds: I imagine that these experiences can be as infinitely varied as are the idiosyncrasies of individuals. . . .

I have now sketched with extreme brevity and insufficiency, but as fairly as I am able in the time allowed, the general traits of the mystic range of consciousness. *It is on the whole pantheistic and optimistic, or at least the opposite of pessimistic. It is anti-naturalistic, and harmonizes best with twice-bornness and so-called other-worldly states of mind. . . .*

Note

* [All footnotes from original essay have been omitted.]

Questions for reflection

1   What are mystical states of consciousness, according to William James?
2   Has James convinced you of the reality of mystical states of consciousness? Explain.
3   In your own words, what are his four characteristics which indicate a mystical experience?
4   What do you make of James's point that certain intoxicants, such as alcohol, can induce another kind of ''consciousness''? If mystical states can be induced in this manner, what does this imply about *religious* mystical states, if anything?
5   Do some research on a person who has had a mystical experience and offers a description of it. How does this person describe the experience? Does it match James's characteristics above?

Further reading

Louis Dupré (1976) *Transcendent Selfhood: The Rediscovery of the Inner Life*. New York: Seabury. (Chapter eight offers an important discussion of the nature of the self as informed by mysticism.)

William James ([1902] 2002) *The Varieties of Religious Experience*. London: Routledge. (James's influential work on religious experience; the selection above was taken from this book.)

Steven T. Katz, ed. (1978) *Mysticism and Philosophical Analysis*. New York: Oxford University Press. (An important collection of articles by Steven Katz, Ninian Smart, Peter Moore, George Mavrodes, and others.)

Joseph Maréchal (1964) *Psychology of the Mystics*. Albany, NY: Magi Books. (An excellent psychological study.)

Rudolf Otto (1958) *The Idea of the Holy*. New York: Oxford University Press. (A classic on religious thought and experience which includes a discussion on mysticism.)

Chapter 46

Julian of Norwich

EXPERIENCING GOD

Julian of Norwich (1342–c. 1416) is considered to be one of the great Christian mystics. Not much is known about her life, but she was probably a Benedictine nun living as a recluse in the English city of Norwich. She was born in England during the time of the "Black Death," one of the most calamitous plagues in human history in which tens of millions died worldwide. Familiar with pain and suffering, she desired a greater understanding of Christ's Passion. When she was thirty years old, her prayers were fulfilled: she suffered from a serious illness which almost cost her life. During this period she experienced a series of visions or "showings"—intense religious experiences which she later wrote about in her *Revelations of Divine Love*. Several of her experiences revealed in this book are included in the following selection.

Of the time of these revelations, and how she begged for three things.
These revelations were shown to a simple, uneducated[1] creature in the year of our Lord 1373, on the eighth day of May; she had already asked God for three gifts: the first was vivid perception of his Passion, the second was bodily sickness in youth at thirty years of age, the third was for God to give her three wounds.

As for the first, it seemed to me that I could feel the Passion of Christ to some extent, but yet I longed by God's grace to feel it more strongly. I thought how I wished I had been there at the crucifixion with Mary Magdalene and with others who were Christ's dear friends, and therefore I longed to be shown him in the flesh so that I might have more knowledge of our Saviour's bodily suffering and of our Lady's fellow-suffering and that of all his true friends who then saw his pain; I wanted to be one of them and suffer with him. I never wished for any other sight or showing of God until my soul left my body. I begged for this so that after the showing I would have a truer perception of Christ's Passion.

The second gift came to me with contrition: I longed eagerly to be on my deathbed, so that I might in that sickness receive all the rites of Holy Church, that I might myself believe I was dying and that everyone who saw me might believe the same, for I wanted no hopes of earthly life. I longed to have in this sickness every kind of suffering both of body and soul that I would experience if I died, with all the terror and turmoil of the fiends,[2] except for actually giving up the ghost. And I thought of this because I wished to be purged by the mercy of God and afterwards to live more to God's glory because of that sickness; and that I should die more quickly, for I longed to be soon with my God. I longed for these two things—the Passion and the sickness—with one reservation, saying, "Lord, you know what I would have, if it is your will that I should have it; and if it is not your will, good Lord, do not be displeased, for I only want what you want."

As for the third gift, by the grace of God and the teaching of Holy Church, I conceived a great longing to receive three wounds[3] in my life: that is to say, the wound of true contrition, the wound of kind compassion and the wound of an earnest longing for God. And this last petition was with no reservation.

The first two of the longings just mentioned passed from my mind, and the third stayed with me continually.

Of the sickness obtained from God by petition.
And when I was thirty and a half years old, God sent me a bodily sickness in which I lay for three days and three nights; and on the fourth night I received all the rites of Holy Church and did not believe that I would live until morning. And after this I lingered on for two days and two nights. And on the third night I often thought that I was dying, and so did those who were with me. And I thought it was a great pity to die while still young; but this was not because there was anything on earth that I wanted to live for, nor because I feared any suffering, for I trusted God's mercy. I wanted to live so as to love God better and for longer, and therefore know and love him better in the bliss of heaven. For it seemed to me that all the short time I had lived here was as nothing compared with that heavenly bliss. So I thought, "Good Lord, may my ceasing to live be to your glory!" And I understood, both with my reason and by the bodily pains I felt, that I was dying. And I fully accepted the will of God with all the will of my heart. Thus I endured till day, and by then my body was dead to all sensation from the waist down. Then I felt I wanted to be supported in a sitting position, so that my heart could be more freely at God's disposition, and so that I could think of God while I was still alive.

My parish priest was sent for to be present at my death, and by the time he came my eyes were fixed and I could not speak. He set the cross before my face and said, "I have brought you the image of your Maker and Saviour. Look upon it and be comforted." It seemed to me that I was well as I was, for my eyes were looking fixedly upwards into heaven, where I trusted that I was going with God's mercy. But nevertheless I consented to fix my eyes on the face of the crucifix if I could, and so I did, because I thought that I might be able to bear looking straight ahead for longer than I could manage to look upwards. After this my sight began to fail and the room was dark all around me as though it had been night, except for the image of the cross, in which I saw an ordinary, household light—I could not understand how. Everything except the cross was ugly to me, as if crowded with fiends. After this the upper part of my body began to die to such an extent that I had almost no feeling and was short of breath. And then I truly believed that I had died. And at this moment, all my suffering was suddenly taken from me, and I seemed to be as well, especially in the upper part of my body, as ever I was before. I marvelled at this sudden change, for it seemed to me a mysterious work of God, not a natural one. And yet, although I felt comfortable, I still did not expect to live, nor did feeling more comfortable comfort me entirely, for I felt that I would rather have been released from this world.

Then it suddenly occurred to me that I should entreat our Lord graciously to give me the second wound, so that my whole body should be filled with remembrance and feeling of his blessed Passion; for I wanted his pains to be my pains, with compassion, and then longing for God. Yet in this I never asked for a bodily sight or showing of God, but for fellow-suffering, such as a naturally kind soul might feel for our Lord Jesus; he was willing to become a mortal man for love, so I wanted to suffer with him.

Here begins the first revelation of the precious crowning of Christ, as listed in the first chapter; and how God fills the heart with the greatest joy; and of his great meekness; and how the sight of Christ's Passion gives sufficient strength against all the temptations of the fiends; and of the great excellency and meekness of the blessed Virgin Mary.

Then I suddenly saw the red blood trickling down from under the crown of thorns, hot and fresh and very plentiful, as though it were the moment of his Passion when the crown of thorns was thrust on to his blessed head, he who was both God and man, the same who suffered for me like that. I believed truly and strongly that it was he himself who showed me this, without any intermediary. And as part of the same showing the Trinity suddenly filled my heart with the greatest joy. And I understood that in heaven it will be like that for ever for those who come there. For the Trinity is God, God is the Trinity; the Trinity is our maker and protector, the Trinity is our dear friend for ever, our everlasting joy and bliss, through our Lord Jesus Christ. And this was shown in the first revelation, and in all of them; for it seems to me that where Jesus is spoken of, the Holy Trinity is to be understood. And I said, "Benedicite domine!"[4] Because I meant this with such deep veneration, I said it in a very loud voice; and I was astounded with wonder and admiration that he who is so holy and awe-inspiring was willing to be so familiar with a sinful being living in wretched flesh. I supposed that the time of my temptation had now come, for I thought that God would allow me to be tempted by fiends before I died. With this sight of the blessed Passion, along with the Godhead that I saw in my mind, I knew that I, yes, and every creature living, could have strength to resist all the fiends of hell and all spiritual temptation.

Then he brought our blessed Lady into my mind. I saw her spiritually in bodily likeness, a meek and simple maid, young—little more than a child, of the same bodily form as when she conceived. God also showed me part of the wisdom and truth of her soul, so that I understood with what reverence she beheld her God and Maker, and how reverently she marvelled that he chose to be born of her, a simple creature of his own making. And this wisdom and faithfulness, knowing as she did the greatness of her Maker and the littleness of her who was made, moved her to say very humbly to Gabriel, "Behold, the handmaid of the Lord."[5] With this sight I really understood that she is greater in worthiness and grace than all that God made below her; for, as I see it, nothing that is made is above her, except the blessed Manhood of Christ.

How God is everything that is good to us, tenderly enfolding us; and everything that is made is as nothing compared to almighty God; and how there is no rest for man until he sets himself and every-thing else at nought for the love of God.

At the same time, our Lord showed me a spiritual vision of his familiar love. I saw that for us he is everything that we find good and comforting. He is our clothing, wrapping us for love, embracing and enclosing us for tender love, so that he can never leave us, being himself everything that is good for us, as I understand it.

In this vision he also showed a little thing, the size of a hazel-nut in the palm of my hand, and it was as round as a ball. I looked at it with my mind's eye and thought, "What can this be?" And the answer came to me, "It is all that is made." I wondered how it could last, for it was so small I thought it might suddenly have disappeared. And the answer in my mind was, "It lasts and will last for ever because God loves it; and everything exists in the same way by the love of God." In this little thing I saw three properties: the first is that God made it, the second is that God loves it, the third is that God cares for it. But what the maker, the carer and the lover really is to me, I cannot tell; for until I become one substance with him, I can never have complete rest or true happiness; that is to say, until I am so bound to him that there is no created thing between my God and me.

We need to know the littleness of all created beings and to set at nothing everything that is made in order to love and possess God who is unmade. This is the reason why we do not feel complete ease in our hearts and souls: we look here for satisfaction in things which are so trivial, where there is no rest to be found, and do not know our God who is almighty, all wise, all good; he is rest itself. God wishes to be known, and is pleased that we should rest in him; for all that is below him does nothing to satisfy us; and this is why, until all that is made seems as nothing, no soul can be at rest. When a soul sets all at nothing for love, to have him who is everything, then he is able to receive spiritual rest.

Our Lord God also showed that it gives him very great pleasure when a simple soul comes to him in a bare, plain and familiar way. For, as I understand this showing, it is the natural yearning of the soul touched by the Holy Ghost to say, "God, of your goodness, give me yourself; you are enough for me, and anything less that I could ask for would not do you full honour. And if I ask anything that is less, I shall always lack something, but in you alone I have everything." And such words are very dear to the soul and come very close to the will of God and his goodness; for his goodness includes all his creatures and all his blessed works, and surpasses everything endlessly, for he is what has no end. And he has made us only for himself and restored us by his blessed Passion and cares for us with his blessed love. And all this is out of his goodness.

How we should pray; of the great and tender love that our Lord has for man's soul; and how he wants us to devote ourselves to knowing and loving him.
This showing was made to teach our souls to be wise and cling to the goodness of God. And at that point our usual way of praying came into my thoughts; how usually, because we do not understand or know about love, we pray indirectly. Then I saw that it really honours God more, and gives more joy, if we ask him to answer our prayers through his own goodness, and cling to it by his grace, with true understanding and loving steadfastness, than if we approach him through all the intermediaries[6] that heart can devise. For all these intermediaries are diminishing, we are not giving God full honour; but his own goodness is everything, there is nothing lacking.

And this is what came into my thoughts at that time: we pray to God by his holy flesh and by his precious blood, his holy Passion, his glorious death and wounds; and all the blessed kindness, the unending life that we have from these is from his goodness. And we pray to him by the love of the sweet Mother who bore him, and all the help we have from her is from his goodness. And we pray by the holy cross upon which he died, and all the strength and help we gain from the cross is from his goodness. And in the same way, all the help that is given to us by special saints and by all the blessed company of heaven, the precious love and unending friendship that we receive from them, we receive from his goodness. For in his goodness, God has ordained a great many excellent means to help us, of which the chief and principal one is the blessed Humanity which he took from the Virgin, with all the means which went before and come afterwards which belong to our redemption and our eternal salvation. Therefore it pleases him that we should seek and worship him in these intermediate ways while understanding and knowing that he is the goodness of all; for the goodness of God is the highest object of prayer and it reaches down to our lowest need. It quickens our soul and gives it life, and makes it grow in grace and virtue. It is nearest in nature and readiest in grace; for it is the same grace which the soul seeks and always will seek until we truly know him who has enclosed us in himself; for he does not despise what he has made, nor does he disdain to serve us in the simplest task that belongs by nature to our bodies, through love of the soul which he has made in his own likeness; for as the body is clad in the cloth, and the flesh in the skin, and the bones in the flesh, and the heart in the chest, so are we, soul and body, clad in the goodness of God and enclosed in it; yes, and more inwardly, because all these may waste and wear away, but God's goodness is always strong, and incomparably near to us; for truly our loving God wants our souls to cling to him with all their might, and wants us to cling to his goodness for ever. For of everything the heart could devise, this is what most pleases God and most readily benefits us; for our soul is so specially loved by him that is highest that it surpasses the knowledge of all beings—that is to say that there is no being made that can know how much and how sweetly and how tenderly our Maker loves us.

And therefore with his grace and his help we may stand and gaze at him in the spirit, with unending amazement at this high, surpassing, inestimable love that almighty God has for us in his goodness. And therefore we may reverently ask our loving friend whatever we wish; for our natural wish is to have God, and God's good wish is to have us. And we can never stop wishing or longing until we fully and joyfully possess him, and then we shall wish for nothing more; for he wants us to be absorbed in knowing and loving him until the time when we reach fulfilment in heaven.

And that is why this lesson of love was shown, with all that follows, as you will see; for the strength and the foundation of everything was shown in the first vision; for of all else, beholding and loving our Maker makes the soul see itself as most puny, and most fills it with reverent awe and true meekness, with abundance of love for its fellow Christians.

Notes

1   *uneducated*: See Introduction [Julian of Norwich, *Revelations of Divine Love*, New York: Penguin Books, 1998], pp. viii-ix.
2   *terror and turmoil of the fiends*: See ST n. I.
3   *three wounds*: Cf. ST chapter I, where Julian explains that she was influenced by the legend that Saint Cecilia had received three literal wounds in her neck.

4   *Benedicite domine*: 'Blessed be thou, Lord!'
5   *Behold, the handmaid of the Lord*: Luke 1:38.
6   *intermediaries*: For 'intermediaries' Julian's word is *menys*. She urges that God is more hon-
    oured by being prayed to directly, as God; at the same time, she is careful to add that he is
    not displeased by prayers directed to his Humanity, to the saints, etc.—a necessary addi-
    tion at a time when the Church was persecuting Lollards.

Questions for reflection

1   Describe Julian's experiences. What general themes emerge from them?
2   In reference to Jesus, Julian says the following: "he was willing to become a mortal
    man for love, so I wanted to suffer with him." Many of the early Christians desired
    such suffering in order to be like Jesus in dying as well as in living. Do you believe this
    to be an appropriate desire? Explain your answer.
3   According to Julian, her experiences were a "lesson of love." What does she believe
    was the reason for this lesson?
4   How might one having religious experiences differentiate between real experiences
    of the divine on the one hand and delusion or hallucination on the other?
5   Many men and women, throughout the centuries and from differing religions, have
    had intense religious experiences. Given that many of the different religious tradi-
    tions are contradictory in their views of the divine/Ultimate Reality, does this affect
    the veracity of the religious experiences? Explain.

Further reading

Timothy Beardsworth (1977) *A Sense of Presence*. Oxford: Religious Experience Research Unit.
    (An interesting compilation of reports on experiences of God.)
Julian of Norwich ([*c.* 1393] 1998) *Revelations of Divine Love*. Trans. Elizabeth Spearing. New
    York: Penguin Books. (An excellent translation of this classic work; the selection above was
    taken from it.)
Julian of Norwich. http://www.luminarium.org/medlit/julian.htm (A helpful website which includes
    many resources on Julian.)
C. B. Martin (1959) *Religious Belief*. Ithaca, NY: Cornell University Press. (Examines religious
    belief, including mystical experience, and offers an unsympathetic appraisal.)
R. P. Aug. Poulain (1978) *The Graces of Interior Prayer*. Whitefish, MT: Kessinger Publishing. (A
    reprint of the 1910 classic of Catholic mystical theology; offers insightful and practical rules
    for discerning apparitions and revelations.)

Chapter 47

D. T. Suzuki

SATORI/ENLIGHTENMENT

Daisetz Teitaro (D. T.) Suzuki (1870–1966) was Professor of Buddhist philosophy at Otani University, Kyoto, and he taught at American universities, including Columbia and Harvard. He was a leading proponent of Zen Buddhism in the West. In this selection he describes the essence of Zen as involving satori, or enlightenment—a way of "looking into the nature of things" and understanding reality ("satori" literally means "to understand")—which provides a "fresher, deeper, more satisfying aspect" of life. It is not easily attained, however, and it cannot be attained through logical, dualistic reasoning or cognitive explanation; it must be directly experienced. In the second half of this selection he describes eight chief characteristics of satori.

I

The essence of Zen Buddhism consists in acquiring a new viewpoint on life and things generally. By this I mean that if we want to get into the inmost life of Zen, we must forgo all our ordinary habits of thinking which control our everyday life, we must try to see if there is any other way of judging things, or rather if our ordinary way is always sufficient to give us the ultimate satisfaction of our spiritual needs. If we feel dissatisfied somehow with this life, if there is something in our ordinary way of living that deprives us of freedom in its most sanctified sense, we must endeavour to find a way somewhere which gives us a sense of finality and contentment. Zen proposes to do this for us and assures us of the acquirement of a new point of view in which life assumes a fresher, deeper, and more satisfying aspect. This acquirement, however, is really and naturally the greatest mental cataclysm one can go through with in life. It is no easy task, it is a kind of fiery baptism, and one has to go through the storm, the earthquake, the overthrowing of the mountains, and the breaking in pieces of the rocks.

   This acquiring of a new point of view in our dealings with life and the world is popularly called by Japanese Zen students "satori" (*wu* in Chinese). It is really another name for Enlightenment (*anuttara-samyak-sambodhi*), which is the word used by the Buddha and his Indian followers ever since his realization under the Bodhi-tree by the River Nairanjana. There are several other phrases in Chinese designating this spiritual experience, each of which has a special connotation, showing tentatively how this phenomenon is interpreted. At all events there is no Zen without satori, which is indeed the Alpha and Omega of Zen Buddhism. Zen devoid of satori is like a sun without its light and heat. Zen may lose all its literature, all its monasteries, and all its paraphernalia; but as long as there is satori in it it will survive to eternity. I want to emphasize this most fundamental fact concerning the very life of Zen; for there are some even among the students of Zen themselves who are blind to this central fact and are apt to think when Zen has been explained away logically or psychologically, or as one of the Buddhist philosophies which can be summed up by using highly technical and conceptual Buddhist phrases, Zen is exhausted, and there remains nothing in it that makes it what it is. But my contention is, the life of Zen begins with the opening of satori (*kai wu* in Chinese).

   Satori may be defined as an intuitive looking into the nature of things in contradistinction to the analytical or logical understanding of it. Practically, it means the unfolding of a new world hitherto unperceived in the confusion of a dualistically-trained mind. Or we may say that with satori our entire surroundings are viewed from quite an unexpected angle of perception. Whatever this is, the world for those who have gained a satori is no more the old world as it used to be; even with all its flowing streams and burning fires, it is never the same one again. Logically stated, all its opposites and contradictions are united and harmonized into a consistent organic whole. This is a mystery and a miracle, but according to the Zen masters such is being performed every day. Satori can thus be had only through our once personally experiencing it.

   Its semblance or analogy in a more or less feeble and fragmentary way is gained when a difficult mathematical problem is solved, or when a great discovery is made, or when a sudden means of escape is realized in the midst of most desperate complications; in short, when one exclaims "Eureka! Eureka!" But this refers only to the intellectual aspect of satori, which is therefore necessarily partial and incomplete and does not touch the very foundations of life considered one indivisible whole. Satori as the Zen experience must be concerned with the entirety of life. For what Zen proposes to do is the revolution, and the revaluation as well, of oneself as a spiritual unity. The solving of a mathematical problem ends with the solution, it does not affect one's whole life. So with all other particular questions, practical or scientific, they do not enter the basic life-tone of the individual concerned. But the opening of satori is the remaking of life itself. When it is genuine—for there are many simulacra of it—its effects on one's moral and spiritual life are revolutionary, and they are so enhancing, purifying, as well as exacting. When a master was asked what constituted Buddhahood, he answered, "The bottom of a pail is broken through." From this we can see what a complete revolution is produced by this spiritual experience. The birth of a new man is really cataclysmic.

   In the psychology of religion this spiritual enhancement of one's whole life is called "conversion". But as the term is generally used by Christian converts, it cannot be applied in its strict sense to the Buddhist experience, especially to that of the Zen followers; the term has too affective or emotional a shade to take the place of satori, which is above all noetic. The general tendency of Buddhism is, as we know, more intellectual than emotional, and its doctrine of Enlightenment distinguishes it sharply from the Christian view of salvation; Zen as one of the Mahayana schools naturally shares a large amount of what we may call transcendental intellectualism, which does not issue in logical dualism. When poetically or figuratively expressed, satori is "the opening of the mind-flower," or "the removing of the bar," or "the brightening up of the mind-works."

. . .

IV

. . . As to the opening of satori, all that Zen can do is to indicate the way and leave the rest all to one's own experience; that is to say, following up the indication and arriving at the goal—this is to be done by oneself and without another's help. With all that the master can do, he is helpless to make the disciple take hold of the thing unless the latter is inwardly fully prepared for it. Just as we cannot make a horse drink against his will, the taking hold of the ultimate reality is to be done by oneself. Just as the flower blooms out of its inner necessity, the looking into one's own nature must be the outcome of one's own inner overflowing. This is where Zen is so personal and subjective, in the sense of being inner and creative.

Zen does not give us any intellectual assistance, nor does it waste time in arguing the point with us; but it merely suggests or indicates, not because it wants to be indefinite, but because that is really the only thing it can do for us. If it could, it would do anything to help us come to an understanding. In fact Zen is exhausting every possible means to do that, as we can see in all the great masters' attitudes towards their disciples.[1] When they are actually knocking them down, their kindheartedness is never to be doubted. They are just waiting for the time when their pupils' minds get all ripened for the final moment. When this is come, the opportunity of opening an eye to the truth of Zen lies everywhere. One can pick it up in the hearing of an inarticulate sound, or listening to an unintelligible remark, or in the observation of a flower blooming, or in the encountering of any trivial everyday incident such as stumbling, rolling up a screen, using a fan, etc. These are all sufficient conditions that will awaken one's inner sense. Evidently a most insignificant happening, and yet its effect on the mind infinitely surpasses all that one could expect of it. A light touch of an ignited wire, and an explosion shaking the very foundations of the earth. In fact, all the causes of satori are in the mind. That is why when the clock clicks, all that has been lying there bursts up like a volcanic eruption or flashes out like a bolt of lightning.[2] Zen calls this "returning to one's own home"; for its followers will declare: "You have now found yourself; from the very beginning nothing has been kept away from you. It was yourself that closed the eye to the fact. In Zen there is nothing to explain, nothing to teach, that will add to your knowledge. Unless it grows out of yourself, no knowledge is really of value to you, a borrowed plumage never grows."

As Satori strikes at the primary fact of existence, its attainment marks a turning-point in one's life. The attainment, however, must be thorough-going and clear-cut in order to produce a satisfactory result. To deserve the name "satori" the mental revolution must be so complete as to make one really and sincerely feel that there took place a fiery baptism of the spirit. The intensity of this feeling is proportional to the amount of effort the opener of satori has put into the achievement. For there is a gradation in satori as to its intensity, as in all our mental activity. The possessor of a lukewarm satori may suffer no such spiritual revolution as Rinzai . . . whose case is quoted below. Zen is a matter of character and not of the intellect, which means that Zen grows out of the will as the first principle of life. A brilliant intellect may fail to unravel all the mysteries of Zen, but a strong soul will drink deep of the inexhaustible fountain. I do not know if the intellect is superficial and touches only the fringe of one's personality, but the fact is that the will is the man himself, and Zen appeals to it. When one becomes penetratingly conscious of the working of this agency, there is the opening of satori and the understanding of Zen. As they say, the snake has now grown into the dragon; or, more graphically, a common cur—a most miserable creature wagging its tail for food and sympathy, and kicked about by the street boys so mercilessly—has now turned into a golden-haired lion whose roar frightens to death all the feeble-minded.

Therefore, when Rinzai was meekly submitting to the "thirty blows" of Obaku, he was a pitiable sight; as soon as he attained satori he was quite a different personage, and his first exclamation was, "There is not much after all in the Buddhism of Obaku." And when he saw the reproachful Obaku again, he returned his favour by giving him a slap on the face. "What an arrogance, what an impudence!" Obaku exclaimed; but there was reason in Rinzai's rudeness, and the old master could not but be pleased with this treatment from his former tearful Rinzai.

When Tokusan gained an insight into the truth of Zen he immediately took up all his commentaries on the *Diamond Sutra*, once so valued and considered indispensable that he had to carry them wherever he went; he now set fire to them, reducing all the manuscripts to nothingness. He exclaimed, "However deep your knowledge of abstruse philosophy, it is like a piece of hair placed in the vastness of space; and however important your experience in things worldly, it is like a drop of water thrown into an unfathomable abyss."

On the day following the incident of the flying geese, to which reference is made elsewhere, Baso appeared in the preaching-hall, and was about to speak before a congregation, when Hyakujo came forward and began to roll up the matting.[3] Baso without protesting came down from his seat and returned to his own room. He then called Hyakujo and asked him why he rolled up the matting before he had uttered a word.

"Yesterday you twisted my nose," replied Hyakujo, "and it was quite painful."

"Where," said Baso, "was your thought wandering then?"

"It is not painful any more today, master."

How differently he behaves now! When his nose was pinched, he was quite an ignoramus in the secrets of Zen. He is now a golden-haired lion, he is master of himself, and acts as freely as if he owned the world, pushing away even his own master far into the background.

There is no doubt that satori goes deep into the very root of individuality. The change achieved thereby is quite remarkable, as we see in the examples above cited.

When our consideration is limited to the objective side of satori as illustrated so far, it does not appear to be a very extraordinary thing—this opening an eye to the truth of Zen. The master makes some remarks, and if they happen to be opportune enough, the disciple will come at once to a realization and see into a mystery hitherto undreamed of. It seems all to depend upon what kind of mood or what state of mental preparedness one is in at the moment. Zen is after all a haphazard affair, one may be tempted to think; but when we know that it took Nangaku (Nanyueh) eight long years to answer the question "Who is he that thus cometh towards me?" we shall realize the fact that there was in him a great deal of mental anguish and tribulation which he had to go through before he could come to the final solution and declare, "Even when one asserts that it is a somewhat, one misses it altogether." We must try to look into the psychological aspect of satori, where is revealed the inner mechanism of opening the door to the eternal secrets of the human soul. This is done best by quoting some of the masters themselves whose introspective statements are on record.

Koho (Kao-feng, 1238–1285) was one of the great masters in the latter part of the Sung dynasty. When his master first let him attend to the "Joshu's Mu,"[4] he exerted himself hard on the problem. One day his master, Setsugan (Hsueh-yen), suddenly asked him, "Who is it that carries for you this lifeless corpse of yours?" The poor fellow did not know what to make of the question, for the master was merciless and it was usually followed by a hard knocking down. Later, in the midst of his sleep one night, he recalled the fact that once when he was under another master he was told to find out the ultimate signification of the statement "All things return to one,"[5] and this kept him up the rest of that night and through the several days and nights that succeeded. While in this state of an extreme mental tension he found himself one day looking at Goso Hoyen's verse on his own portrait, which partly read:

> One hundred years—thirty-six thousand morns,
> This same old fellow moveth on for ever!

This at once made him dissolve his eternal doubt as to "Who's carrying around this lifeless body of yours?" He was baptized and became an altogether new man.

He leaves us in his *Goroku* ("Sayings Recorded") an account of those days of the mental strain in the following narrative: "In olden days when I was at Sokei (Shuangching), and before one month was over after my return to the Meditation Hall there, one night while deep in sleep I suddenly found myself fixing my attention on the question 'All things return to the One, but where does this One return?' My attention was so rigidly fixed on this that I neglected sleeping, forgot to eat, and did not distinguish east from west, nor morning from night. While spreading the napkin, producing the bowls, or attending to my natural wants, whether I moved or rested, whether I talked or kept silent, my whole existence was wrapped up with the question 'Where does this one return?' No other thoughts ever disturbed my consciousness; no, even if I wanted to stir up the least bit of thought irrelevant to the central one, I could not do so. It was like being screwed up or glued; however much I tried to shake myself off, it refused to move. Though I was in the midst of a crowd or congregation, I felt as if I were all by myself. From morning till evening, from evening till morning, so transparent, so tranquil, so majestically above all things were my feelings! Absolutely pure and not a particle of dust! My one thought covered eternity; so calm was the outside world, so oblivious of the existence of other people I was. Like an idiot, like an imbecile, six days and nights thus elapsed when I entered the Shrine with the rest, reciting the Sutras, and happened to raise my head and looked at the verse by Goso. This made me all of a sudden awake from the spell, and the meaning of 'Who carries this lifeless corpse of yours?' burst upon me—the question once given by my old master. I felt as if this boundless space itself were broken up into pieces, and the great earth were altogether levelled away. I forgot myself, I forgot the world, it was like one mirror reflecting another. I tried several ko-an in my mind and found them so transparently clear! I was no more deceived as to the wonderful working of Prajna (transcendental wisdom)." When Koho saw his old master later, the latter lost no time in asking him, "Who is it that carries this lifeless corpse of yours?" Koho burst out a "Kwats!" Thereupon the master took up a stick ready to give him a blow, but the disciple held it back, saying, "You cannot give me a blow today." "Why can't I?" was the master's demand. Instead of replying to him, however, Koho left the room briskly. The following day the master asked him, "All things return to the One, and where does the One return to?" "The dog is lapping the boiling water in the cauldron." "Where did you get this nonsense?" reprimanded the master. "You had better ask yourself," promptly came the response. The master rested well satisfied.

These cases show what mental process one has to go through before the opening of satori takes place. Of course these are prominent examples and highly accentuated, and every satori is not preceded by such an extraordinary degree of concentration. But an experience more or less like these must be the necessary antecedent to all satori, especially to that which is to be gone through at the outset of the study. The mirror of mind or the field of consciousness then seems to be so thoroughly swept clean as not to leave a particle of dust on it.

When thus all mentation is temporarily suspended, even the consciousness of an effort to keep an idea focused at the centre of attention is gone—that is, when, as the Zen followers say, the mind is so completely possessed or identified with its object of thought that even the consciousness of identity is lost as when one mirror reflects another, the subject feels as if living in a crystal palace, all transparent, refreshing, buoyant, and royal. But the end has not yet been reached, this being merely the preliminary condition leading to the consummation called satori. If the mind remains in this state of fixation, there will be no occasion for its being awakened to the truth of Zen. The state of "Great Doubt" (tai-gi), as it is technically known, is the antecedent. It must be broken up and exploded into the next stage, which is looking into one's nature or the opening of satori.

The explosion, as it is nothing else, generally takes place when this finely balanced equilibrium tilts for one reason or another. A stone is thrown into a sheet of water in perfect stillness, and the disturbance at once spreads all over the surface. It is somewhat like this. A sound knocks at the gate of consciousness so tightly closed, and it at once reverberates through the entire being of the individual. He is awakened in the most vivid sense of the word. He comes out baptized in the fire of creation. He has seen the work of God in his very workshop. The occasion may not necessarily be the hearing of a temple bell, it may be reading a stanza, or seeing something moving, or the sense of touch irritated, when a most highly accentuated state of concentration bursts out into a satori.

V. Chief characteristics of Satori

1. *Irrationality.* By this I mean that satori is not a conclusion to be reached by reasoning, and defies all intellectual determination. Those who have experienced it are always at a loss to explain it coherently or logically. When it is explained at all, either in words or gestures, its content more or less undergoes a mutilation. The uninitiated are thus unable to grasp it by what is outwardly visible, while those who have had the experience discern

what is genuine from what is not. The satori experience is thus always characterized by irrationality, inexplicability, and incommunicability.

Listen to Tai-hui once more: "This matter [i.e. Zen] is like a great mass of fire; when you approach it your face is sure to be scorched. It is again like a sword about to be drawn; when it is once out of the scabbard, someone is sure to lose his life. But if you neither fling away the scabbard nor approach the fire, you are no better than a piece of rock or of wood. Coming to this pass, one has to be quite a resolute character full of spirit."[6] There is nothing here suggestive of cool reasoning and quiet metaphysical or epistemological analysis, but of a certain desperate will to break through an insurmountable barrier, of the will impelled by some irrational or unconscious power behind it. Therefore, the outcome also defies intellection or conceptualization.

2. *Intuitive insight*. That there is noetic quality in mystic experiences has been pointed out by James in his *Varieties of Religious Experience*, and this applies also to the Zen experience known as satori. Another name for satori is "ken-sho" (*chien-hsing* in Chinese) meaning "to see essence or nature," which apparently proves that there is "seeing" or "perceiving" in satori. That this seeing is of quite a different quality from what is ordinarily designated as knowledge need not be specifically noticed. Hui-k'e is reported to have made this statement concerning his satori which was confirmed by Bodhidharma himself: "[As to my satori], it is not a total annihilation; it is knowledge of the most adequate kind; only it cannot be expressed in words." In this respect Shen-hui was more explicit, for he says that "the one character *chih* (knowledge) is the source of all mysteries."[7]

Without this noetic quality satori will lose all its pungency, for it is really the reason of satori itself. It is noteworthy that the knowledge contained in satori is concerned with something universal and at the same time with the individual aspect of existence. When a finger is lifted, the lifting means, from the viewpoint of satori, far more than the act of lifting. Some may call it symbolic, but satori does not point to anything beyond itself, being final as it is. Satori is the knowledge of an individual object and also that of Reality which is, if I may say so, at the back of it.

3. *Authoritativeness*. By this I mean that the knowledge realized by satori is final, that no amount of logical argument can refute it. Being direct and personal it is sufficient unto itself. All that logic can do here is to explain it, to interpret it in connection with other kinds of knowledge with which our minds are filled. Satori is thus a form of perception, an inner perception, which takes place in the most interior part of consciousness. Hence the sense of authoritativeness, which means finality. So, it is generally said that Zen is like drinking water, for it is by one's self that one knows whether it is warm or cold. The Zen perception being the last term of experience, it cannot be denied by outsiders who have no such experience.

4. *Affirmation*. What is authoritative and final can never be negative. For negation has no value for our life, it leads us nowhere; it is not a power that urges, nor does it give one a place to rest. Though the satori experience is sometimes expressed in negative terms, it is essentially an affirmative attitude towards all things that exist; it accepts them as they come along regardless of their moral values. Buddhists call this *kshanti*, "patience," or more properly "acceptance," that is, acceptance of things in their suprarelative or transcendental aspect where no dualism of whatever sort avails.

Some may say that this is pantheistic. The term, however, has a definite philosophic meaning and I would not see it used in this connection. When so interpreted the Zen experience exposes itself to endless misunderstandings and "defilements." Tai-hui says in his letter to Miao-tsung: "An ancient sage says that the Tao itself does not require special disciplining, only let it not be defiled. I would say: To talk about mind or nature is defiling; to talk about the unfathomable or the mysterious is defiling; to practise meditation or tranquillization is defiling; to direct one's attention to it, to think about it is defiling; to be writing about it thus on paper with a brush is especially defiling. What then shall we have to do in order to get ourselves oriented, and properly apply ourselves to it? The precious vajra sword is right here and its purpose is to cut off the head. Do not be concerned with human questions of right and wrong. All is Zen just as it is, and right here you are to apply yourself." Zen is Suchness—a grand affirmation.

5. *Sense of the Beyond.* Terminology may differ in different religions, and in satori there is always what we may call a sense of the Beyond; the experience indeed is my own but I feel it to be rooted elsewhere. The individual shell in which my personality is so solidly encased explodes at the moment of satori. Not, necessarily, that I get unified with a being greater than myself or absorbed in it, but that my individuality, which I found rigidly held together and definitely kept separate from other individual existences, becomes loosened somehow from its tightening grip and melts away into something indescribable, something which is of quite a different order from what I am accustomed to. The feeling that follows is that of a complete release or a complete rest—the feeling that one has arrived finally at the destination. "Coming home and quietly resting" is the expression generally used by Zen followers. The story of the prodigal son in the *Saddharmapundarika*, in the *Vajra-samadhi*, and also in the New Testament points to the same feeling one has at the moment of a satori experience.

As far as the psychology of satori is considered, a sense of the Beyond is all we can say about it; to call this the Beyond, the Absolute, or God, or a Person is to go further than the experience itself and to plunge into a theology or metaphysics. Even the "Beyond" is saying a little too much. When a Zen master says, "There is not a fragment of a tile above my head, there is not an inch of earth beneath my feet," the expression seems to be an appropriate one. I have called it elsewhere the Unconscious, though this has a psychological taint.

6. *Impersonal Tone.* Perhaps the most remarkable aspect of the Zen experience is that it has no personal note in it as is observable in Christian mystic experiences. There is no reference whatever in Buddhist satori to such personal and frequently sexual feelings and relationships as are to be gleaned from these terms: flame of love, a wonderful love shed in the heart, embrace, the beloved, bride, bridegroom, spiritual matrimony, Father, God, the Son of God, God's child, etc. We may say that all these terms are interpretations based on a definite system of thought and really have nothing to do with the experience itself. At any rate, alike in India, China, and Japan, satori has remained thoroughly impersonal, or rather highly intellectual.

Is this owing to the peculiar character of Buddhist philosophy? Does the experience itself take its colours from the philosophy or theology? Whatever this is, there is no doubt that in spite of its having some points of similitude to the Christian mystic experience, the Zen experience is singularly devoid of personal or human colour-ings. Chao-pien, a great government officer of the Sung dynasty, was a lay-disciple of Fachʻuan of Chiang-shan. One day after his official duties were over, he found himself leisurely sitting in his office, when all of a sudden a clash of thunder burst on his ear, and he realized a state of satori. The poem he then composed depicts one aspect of the Zen experience:

> Devoid of thought, I sat quietly by the desk in my official room,
> With my fountain-mind undisturbed, as serene as water;
> A sudden clash of thunder, the mind-doors burst open,
> And lo, there sitteth the old man in all his homeliness.

This is perhaps all the personal tone one can find in the Zen experience, and what a distance between "the old man in his homeliness" and "God in all his glory," not to say anything about such feelings as "the heavenly sweetness of Christ's excellent love," etc.! How barren, how unromantic satori is when compared with the Christian mystic experiences!

Not only satori itself is such a prosaic and non-glorious event, but the occasion that inspires it also seems to be unromantic and altogether lacking in supersensuality. Satori is experienced in connection with any ordinary occurrence in one's daily life. It does not appear to be an extraordinary phenomenon as is recorded in Christian books of mysticism. Someone takes hold of you, or slaps you, or brings you a cup of tea, or makes some most commonplace remark, or recites some passage from a sutra or from a book of poetry, and when your mind is ripe for its outburst, you come at once to satori. There is no romance of love-making, no voice of the Holy Ghost, no plenitude of Divine Grace, no glorification of any sort. Here is nothing painted in high colours, all is grey and extremely unobtrusive and unattractive.

7. *Feeling of Exaltation.* That this feeling inevitably accompanies satori is due to the fact that it is the breaking-up of the restriction imposed on one as an individual being, and this breaking up is not a mere negative incident but quite a positive one fraught with signification because it means an infinite expansion of the individual. The general feeling, though we are not always conscious of it, which characterizes all our functions of consciousness, is that of restriction and dependence, because consciousness itself is the outcome of two forces conditioning or restricting each other. Satori, on the contrary, essentially consists in doing away with the opposition of two terms in whatsoever sense—and this opposition is the principle of consciousness . . . while satori is to realize the Unconscious which goes beyond the opposition.

To be released of this, therefore, must make one feel above all things intensely exalted. A wandering outcast maltreated everywhere not only by others but by himself finds that he is the possessor of all the wealth and power that is ever attainable in this world by a mortal being—if this does not give him a high feeling of self-glorification, what could? Says a Zen master, "When you have satori you are able to reveal a palatial mansion made of precious stones on a single blade of grass; but when you have no satori, a palatial mansion itself is concealed behind a simple blade of grass."

Another Zen master, evidently alluding to the *Avatamsaka*, declares: "O monks, lo and behold! A most auspicious light is shining with the utmost brilliancy all over the great chiliocosm, simultaneously revealing all the countries, all the oceans, all the

Sumerus, all the suns and moons, all the heavens, all the lands—each of which number as many as hundreds of thousands of kotis. O monks, do you not see the light?" But the Zen feeling of exaltation is rather a quiet feeling of self-contentment; it is not at all demonstrative, when the first glow of it passes away. The Unconscious does not proclaim itself so boisterously in the Zen consciousness.

8. *Momentariness.* Satori comes upon one abruptly and is a momentary experience. In fact, if it is not abrupt and momentary, it is not satori. This abruptness (*tun*) is what characterizes the Hui-neng school of Zen ever since its proclamation late in the seventh century. His opponent Shen-hsiu was insistent on a gradual unfoldment of Zen consciousness. Hui-neng's followers were thus distinguished as strong upholders of the doctrine of abruptness. This abrupt experience of satori, then, opens up in one moment (*ekamuhurtena*) an altogether new vista, and the whole existence is appraised from quite a new angle of observation.

Notes

1   See Chapter 5, "Practical Methods of Zen Instruction," [in D. T. Suzuki, *Zen Buddhism: Selected Writings of D. T. Suzuki*, ed. William Barrett, Garden City, NY: Doubleday Anchor, 1956] p. 111.
2   The lightning simile in the *Kena-Upanishad* (IV, 30), as is supposed by some scholars, is not to depict the feeling of inexpressive awe as regards the nature of Brahman, but it illustrates the bursting out of enlightenment upon consciousness. "A-a-ah" is most significant here.
3   This is spread before the Buddha and on it the master performs his bowing ceremony, and its rolling up naturally means the end of a sermon.
4   This is one of the most noted ko-an and generally given to the uninitiated as an eye-opener. When Joshu was asked by a monk whether there was Buddha-Nature in the dog, the master answered "Mu!" (*wu* in Chinese), which literally means "no." But as it is nowadays understood by the followers of Rinzai, it does not mean anything negative as the term may suggest to us ordinarily, it refers to something most assuredly positive, and the novice is told to find it out by himself, not depending upon others (*aparapaccaya*), as no explanation will be given nor is any possible. This ko-an is popularly known as "Joshu's Mu or Muji." A ko-an is a theme or statement or question given to the Zen student for solution, which will lead him to a spiritual insight. The subject will be fully treated in the Second Series of the *Essays in Zen Buddhism.*
5   Another ko-an for beginners. A monk once asked Joshu, "All things return to the One, but where does the One return?" To which the master answered, "When I was in the province of Seiju (Ts'ing-chou) I had a monkish garment made which weighed seven kin (*chin*).
6   Tai-hui's sermon at the request of Li Hsuan-chiao.
7   *Miao* is a difficult term to translate; it often means "exquisiteness," "indefinable subtlety." In this case *miao* is the mysterious way in which things are presented to this ultimate knowledge. Tsung-mi on *Zen Masters and Disciples.*

Questions for reflection

1   After reading this essay, how would you define satori?
2   Briefly describe each of the chief characteristics of satori.

3   What are some similarities between satori and Christian mystical experiences? What are some differences?

4   What do you think the Zen master meant when he said the following: "When you have satori you are able to reveal a palatial mansion made of precious stones on a single blade of grass; but when you have no satori, a palatial mansion itself is concealed behind a simple blade of grass."

5   Suzuki describes satori as a "transcendental intellectualism," but he also makes the point that it cannot be grasped through "analytic or logical understanding" and that it defies "intellection or conceptualization." Given its "irrationality," how can one grasp satori?

Further reading

Masao Abe (1989) *Zen and the Western Thought*. Honolulu, HI: The University of Hawaii Press. (A collection of articles by a leading contemporary Zen scholar.)

Steven Heine and Dale S. Wright, eds. (2005) *Zen Classics: Formative Texts in the History of Zen Buddhism*. (A collection of important texts which developed the Buddhist movement in Japan.)

Joseph Mitsuo Kitagawa (1987) *On Understanding Japanese Religion*. Princeton, NJ: Princeton University Press. (Essays on Japanese religion by a historian of religions.)

D. T. Suzuki (1956) *Zen Buddhism: Selected Writings of D. T. Suzuki*. Ed. William Barrett. Garden City, NY: Doubleday Anchor Books. (A helpful collection of essays on a variety of topics; the selection above was taken from this work.)

D. T. Suzuki (1991) *An Introduction to Zen Buddhism*. New York: Grove Press. (A very accessible introduction and guide to Zen Buddhism.)

Chapter 48

Sigmund Freud

RELIGIOUS IDEAS AS WISH FULFILLMENTS

Sigmund Freud (1856–1939) was an Austrian neurologist and psychologist, and the father of psychoanalysis. He is often considered one of the most influential thinkers of the twentieth century. He offers in this selection the argument that feelings of helplessness and fear in childhood foster a desire for fatherly, loving protection. This desire, or wish, for a protective figure carries on into adulthood and demands a greater, more powerful being than a human father. Two further desires are prominent: the substantiation of universal justice and a continuation of our own existence after death. These wishes are satisfied through the "illusion" of divine Providence. This religious idea also provides answers for other curiosities of human beings, such as how the universe began and how the mind and body are related.

In maintaining that religion is an illusion, Freud is not claiming that it is necessarily false. Rather, he is offering a psychological perspective of religion as being a human wish fulfillment.

tabes dorsalis – a medical condition caused by an untreated syphilis infection in which sensory information to the brain is affected by the degeneration of nerve cells and fibers.

. . . These [religious ideas], which are given out as teachings, are not precipitates of experience or end-results of thinking: they are illusions, fulfilments of the oldest, strongest and most urgent wishes of mankind. The secret of their strength lies in the strength of those wishes. As we already know, the terrifying impression of helplessness in childhood aroused the need for protection—for protection through love—which was provided by the father; and the recognition that this helplessness lasts throughout life made it necessary to cling to the existence of a father, but this time a more powerful one. Thus the benevolent rule of a divine Providence allays our fear of the dangers of life; the establishment of a moral world-order ensures the fulfilment of the demands of justice, which have so often remained unfulfilled in human civilization; and the prolongation of earthly existence in a future life provides the local and temporal framework in which these wish-fulfilments shall take place. Answers to the riddles that tempt the curiosity of man, such as how the universe began or what the relation is between body and mind, are developed in conformity with the underlying assumptions of this system. It is an enormous relief to the individual psyche if the conflicts of its childhood arising from the father-complex—conflicts which it has never wholly overcome—are removed from it and brought to a solution which is universally accepted.

When I say that these things are all illusions, I must define the meaning of the word. An illusion is not the same thing as an error; nor is it necessarily an error. Aristotle's belief that vermin are developed out of dung (a belief to which ignorant people still cling) was an error; so was the belief of a former generation of doctors that *tabes dorsalis* is the result of sexual excess. It would be incorrect to call these errors illusions. On the other hand, it was an illusion of Columbus's that he had discovered a new sea-route to the Indies. The part played by his wish in this error is very clear. One may describe as an illusion the assertion made by certain nationalists that the Indo-Germanic race is the only one capable of civilization; or the belief, which was only destroyed by psychoanalysis, that children are creatures without sexuality. What is characteristic of illusions is that they are derived from human wishes. In this respect they come near to psychiatric delusions. But they differ from them, too, apart from the more complicated structure of delusions. In the case of delusions, we emphasize as essential their being in contradiction with reality. Illusions need not necessarily be false—that is to say, unrealizable or in contradiction to reality. For instance, a middle-class girl may have the illusion that a prince will come and marry her. This is possible; and a few such cases have occurred. That the Messiah will come and found a golden age is much less likely. Whether one classifies this belief as an illusion or as something analogous to a delusion will depend on one's personal attitude. Examples of illusions which have proved true are not easy to find, but the illusion of the alchemists that all metals can be turned into gold might be one of them. The wish to have a great deal of gold, as much gold as possible, has, it is true, been a good deal damped by our present-day knowledge of the determinants of wealth, but chemistry no longer regards the transmutation of metals into gold as impossible. Thus we call a belief an illusion when a wish-fulfillment is a prominent factor in its motivation, and in doing so we disregard its relations to reality, just as the illusion itself sets no store by verification.

Having thus taken our bearings, let us return once more to the question of religious doctrines. We can now repeat that all of them are illusions and insusceptible of proof. No one can be compelled to think them true, to believe in them. Some of them are so improbable, so incompatible with everything we have laboriously discovered about the reality of the world, that we may compare them—if we pay proper regard to the psychological differences—to delusions. Of the reality value of most of them we cannot judge; just as they cannot be proved, so they cannot be refuted. We still know too little to make a critical approach to them. The riddles of the universe reveal themselves only slowly to our investigation; there are many questions to which science to-day can give no answer. But scientific work is the only road which can lead us to a knowledge of reality outside ourselves. It is once again merely an illusion to expect anything from intuition and introspection; they can give us nothing but particulars about our own mental life, which are hard to interpret, never any information about the questions which religious doctrine finds it so easy to answer. It would be insolent to let one's own arbitrary will step into the breach and, according to one's personal estimate, declare this or that part of the religious system to be less or more acceptable. Such questions are too momentous for that; they might be called too sacred.

At this point one must expect to meet with an objection. 'Well then, if even obdurate sceptics admit that the assertions of religion cannot be refuted by reason, why should I not believe in them, since they have so much on their side—tradition, the agreement of mankind, and all the consolations they offer?' Why not, indeed? Just as no one can be forced to believe, so no one can be forced to disbelieve. But do not let us be satisfied with deceiving ourselves that arguments like these take us along the road of correct thinking. If ever there was a case of a lame excuse we have it here. Ignorance is ignorance; no right to believe anything can be derived from it. In other matters no sensible person will behave so irresponsibly or rest content with such feeble grounds for his opinions and for the line he takes. It is only in the highest and most sacred things that he allows himself to do so. In reality these are only attempts at pretending to oneself or to other people that one is still firmly attached to religion, when one has long since cut oneself loose from it. Where questions of religion are concerned, people are guilty of every possible sort of dishonesty and intellectual misdemeanour. Philosophers stretch the meaning of words until they retain scarcely anything of their original sense. They give the name of 'God' to some vague abstraction which they have created for themselves; having done so they can pose before all the world as deists, as believers in God, and they can even boast that they have recognized a higher, purer concept of God, notwithstanding that their God is now nothing more than an insubstantial shadow and no longer the mighty personality of religious doctrines. Critics persist in describing as 'deeply religious' anyone who admits to a sense of man's insignificance or impotence in face of the universe, although what constitutes the essence of the religious attitude is not this feeling but only the next step after it, the reaction to it which seeks a remedy for it. The man who goes no further, but humbly acquiesces in the small part which human beings play in the great world—such a man is, on the contrary, irreligious in the truest sense of the word.

To assess the truth-value of religious doctrines does not lie within the scope of the present enquiry. It is enough for us that we have recognized them as being, in their psychological nature, illusions. But we do not have to conceal the fact that this discovery also strongly influences our attitude to the question which must appear to many to be the most important of all. We know approximately at what periods and by what kind of men religious doctrines were created. If in addition we discover the motives which led to this, our attitude to the problem of religion will undergo a marked displacement. We shall tell ourselves that it would be very nice if there were a God who created the world and was a benevolent Providence, and if there were a moral order in the universe and an after-life; but it is a very striking fact that all this is exactly as we are bound to wish it to be. And it would be more remarkable still if our wretched, ignorant and downtrodden ancestors had succeeded in solving all these difficult riddles of the universe.

Questions for reflection

1   What does Freud mean by the term "illusion"? In what instances does he consider a belief to be an illusion?

2   What is characteristic of illusions, as depicted by Freud, and how do they differ from delusions?
3   Do you believe that all religious doctrines are illusions and insusceptible of proof? Do you believe that all religious experiences are illusions? Why or why not?
4   Are the Gods of Christianity, or Judaism, or Islam, or Hinduism, the kind of Gods one would wish for, especially given the moral demands which are required of their followers? Explain.
5   From this reading, what do you think was Freud's own view about the truth of religious beliefs and experiences? Do you agree with this view? Why do you believe what you do about these things?

Further reading

Mircea Eliade (1968) *The Sacred and the Profane: The Nature of Religion*. Fort Washington, PA: Harvest Books. (Examines the nature of religion by tracing through history various manifestations of the sacred in nature and human society and contrasts the religious point of view with that of the non-religious, or "profane," person.)

Sigmund Freud ([1927] 1961) *The Future of an Illusion*. Trans. James Strachey. New York: Norton and Norton. (A classic work on religion; the selection above was taken from this work.)

Michael Martin (1990) *Atheism: A Philosophical Justification*. Philadelphia, PA: Temple University Press. (Chapter six critiques religious experience as being evidence for belief in God.)

Rudolph Otto (1958) *The Idea of the Holy*. Oxford: Oxford University Press. (A religious classic; Otto explores the idea of God as transcendent and "wholly other.")

Chapter 49

R. Douglas Geivett

THE EVIDENTIAL VALUE OF RELIGIOUS EXPERIENCE

R. Douglas Geivett is Professor of Philosophy in the Talbot Department of Philosophy, Biola University. In this essay he first notes that oftentimes those with firsthand religious experiences take them to be non-inferential grounds for their own religious beliefs. But what evidential weight do religious experiences truly provide, if any, to those who have had them? What about to those who have not had such experiences but know of others who have? He explores these questions and notes the general pattern in recent arguments from religious experience which include these experiences as non-inferential evidence for God's existence. He dubs this pattern "the *standard argument* from religious experience." He then culls from the argument three major components upon which it hinges and examines a variety of objections to these three components. He also explores more general objections, including naturalistic explanations for religious experience, and concludes by sketching his own conception of the evidential value of religious experience.

. . .

I begin with the obvious fact that many individuals across a wide spectrum of religious traditions have had experiences of a religious nature. Without settling the question of their veridicality,[1] these experiences may be called "religious experiences." That religious experiences occur, then, is not usually contested. What is contested is that religious experiences are sometimes veridical, or that it is reasonable to believe that some religious experiences are veridical, and hence that it is reasonable, for example, to believe on the basis of some such experiences that God exists.

I say *some* such experiences because some—not all—religious experiences are "of-God experiences." I use the term "of-God experiences" for alleged experiences of God, which again *may* or *may not* be veridical. And I use "experiences of God" more narrowly, as a label for *of-God experiences* that *are* veridical, that is experiences where God is either directly or indirectly present to the subject, in a thoroughgoing realist sense of "present."[2] . . .

. . . The real question is whether *of-God experiences* are *experiences of God*. The usual way of treating this question is as an explanation-seeking question. Here is a phenomenon—namely, of-God experiences—whose reality is not to be denied. But what explains its occurrence? Not surprisingly, a standard objection to the evidential value of religious experience is that religious experiences can be explained as well, or better, in terms acceptable to a metaphysical naturalist. . . .

The standard argument for the existence of God

The most typical conception of the positive evidential value of religious experience emphasizes the *non-inferential* grounding of religious belief by religious experience. Most proponents of this general conception endorse three claims that largely determine the pattern of the main variety of B-type argument from religious experience for the existence of God.[3] The first claim is that the principle of credulity is a fundamental principle of rationality that applies to cases of perceptual experience (e.g. sense perception). The second is that religious experience is a species of perceptual experience that relevantly resembles sense perception. A third claim concerns the possibility of converting the non-inferential grounding of religious experience for a subject into grounds for recipients of a subject's testimony, on the basis of a principle of testimony. These three claims are central to what I call "the *standard argument* from religious experience."

The principle of credulity

. . . Consider the following three propositions:

1   It seems to subject S that God is present to S in S's experience.
2   God is present to S in S's experience.
3   God exists.

Let us suppose that most skeptics about experiences of God accept proposition 1 on the basis of S's testimony. . . .

The way is now clear to consider two questions. First, can the truth of proposition 1 count as adequate grounds for S's acceptance of proposition 2, and hence of S's acceptance of proposition 3? Second, can the truth of proposition 1 count as adequate grounds for another's acceptance of proposition 2, and hence of his/her acceptance of proposition 3? . . .

Let us first explore why someone might think that the truth of proposition 1 provides grounds for S to accept proposition 2, and hence proposition 3. Here is where the principle of credulity comes into play. As Richard Swinburne writes, "How things seem to be is good grounds for a belief about how things are."[4] For example, the experience of it seeming to me that my keys are locked inside my car is good evidence in support of my supposing that my keys are locked inside my car. Swinburne claims that "it is a principle of rationality that (in the absence of special considerations), if it seems (epistemically) to a subject that x is present, then probably x is present; what one seems to perceive is probably so."[5] He then says that "it would seem to follow that, in the absence of special considerations, all religious experiences ought to be taken by their subjects as genuine, and hence as substantial grounds for belief in the existence of their apparent object."[6] Thus, if the religious experience in question is an of-God experience, the subject ought to take this experience as grounds for belief in the existence of God. . . .

The analogy with sense perception: the parity thesis

. . .

It does seem, however, that some discernible and appropriately strong analogy between sense experience and religious experience is needed in order to assert the transferability of the principle of credulity from the one experiential context (i.e. sense experience) to the other (i.e. religious experience). Swinburne does not develop the analogy at length; arguably, he does not develop it at all. . . .

In contrast to Swinburne, William Alston takes great pains to establish a relevantly strong analogy between sense perception and what he calls "mystical perception" (which comes close enough to what we are here calling "of-God experiences").[7] Alston argues at length that "mystical experience can be construed as *perception* in the same generic sense of the term as sense perception."[8] Of-God experiences, then, are experiences of *perceiving God* (hence, the title of Alston's book).

. . . The strong analogy between sense perception and perception of God ensures strong epistemological parity between the evidence of sense perception in grounding beliefs about the physical world and the perception of God in grounding beliefs about God. . . . Or, to put it the way that Alston does in one passage, perception of God "has basically the same epistemic status" as sense perception, such that "no one who subscribes to the former is in any position to cavil at the latter."[9] . . .

This is not the place to rehearse all of the technical details in Alston's account. . . . Alston's argument for parity is subtle and sophisticated. Failure to attend to the details of his position has led to numerous and frequent misunderstandings of the significance of important differences between sense perception and perception of God. I revisit this matter in the sections "Objections to the standard argument" and "A revised conception" below.

The principle of testimony

It's time to return to a question that we set aside earlier: . . . Can the truth of proposition 1, allowed by a recipient of testimony concerning S's experience, count as adequate grounds for the recipient's acceptance of proposition 2, and hence for his acceptance of proposition 3?

Richard Swinburne thinks so. In support of his conviction, he invokes the principle of testimony: "(in the absence of special considerations) the experiences of others are (probably) as they report them."[10] This principle, combined with the principle of credulity, yields the following result: "things are (probably) as others claim to have perceived them."[11] In short, if things probably are as others have perceived them, then acceptance of their testimony about having of-God experiences should lead one to accept that these of-God experiences are experiences of God and therefore that God exists. . . .

Naturally, this line of argument has been subjected to considerable close examination by others who remain unconvinced. It is to their protests that we turn in the next two sections.

Objections to the standard argument

The objections considered in this section all have to do with the machinery of the standard argument from religious experience to the existence of God. These can be conveniently sorted into challenges confronting the key components of the standard argument: the parity thesis, the application of the principle of credulity to of-God experiences, and the possibility of grounding belief in God on the testimony of subjects concerning their of-God experiences.

Challenges to the parity thesis

The main challenges to the parity thesis have to do with differences, or disanalogies, between sense experience and experience of God. For example, C. B. Martin observes that there are standard ways of testing for veridicality when it comes to sense experience. But "when it comes to such a case as knowing God . . . the society of tests and checkup procedures, which surround other instances of knowing, completely vanishes."[12] . . . Martin does not insist that experiences of God be subject to precisely the same tests that we use when checking up on sense experience. But he does insist that there must be some *standard* procedures for testing the veridicality of experiences of God.[13]

As it happens, Alston acknowledges that the perception of God differs from the perception of physical objects in just the respect that Martin alleges.[14] It is not that there are no procedures at all for testing of-God experiences.[15] It is, rather, that the available procedures cannot be applied to of-God experiences with the rigor and reliability that we are accustomed to when it comes to sense experience. But there is an explanation for this: the object presented in an of-God experience is a *personal* being, whose behavior is not as predictable as the behavior of physical objects. . . .

Does this answer the objection? Not completely. For one might say that it matters not why standard checking procedures are not available; it only matters that they are not available. But then we must ask: "Matters to what?" The answer, presumably, is that this matters to the justification of beliefs based on of-God experiences. And that may be true. But the precise bearing of this on epistemic justification needs to be spelled out. For even if it should be desirable to have an independent means of testing for the veridicality of religious experiences, and even if such means are widely available for testing sense perception, it does not follow that the availability of an independent testing procedure is *necessary* for justified belief. In the absence of standardized tests, experientially based belief will still normally be prima facie justified. What *is* critical is that there be no defeaters for the justification of experience-based belief that God exists.

There are other differences as well. Here are some that Alston explicitly recognizes:

> Sense perception is insistently and unavoidably present in all our waking hours, and the experiential awareness of God is a rare phenomenon except for a very few souls. Sense perception, especially vision, is vivid and richly detailed, bursting with information, whereas the experience of God is dim, meager, and obscure. Sense perception is shared by all human beings, whereas the experience of God, though more widely dispersed than is often supposed, is still by no means universal.[16]

Clearly, these are all differences that make an epistemological difference. Many of Alston's critics have stressed these and other differences in their attack on the parity thesis.[17]

So why aren't these differences defeaters for Alston's claim regarding epistemic parity between of-God experience and sense experience? Answer: because these differences have no bearing on the "generic identity of structure" between the two modes of experience, for they do not defeat the crucial evidence-making feature of all perceptual experience. That feature is the presentational character of perceptual experience. Since this feature is the most epistemically distinguishing structural component in generic perceptual experience, it is the most epistemically relevant feature of individual species of perceptual experience, including both sense perception and perception of God. . . .

. . . [S]trong epistemic parity of this sort forces a painful choice on anyone who would prefer to deny the evidential value of religious experience:

1   allow that of-God experience is a legitimate non-inferential ground for belief that God exists;
2   acquiesce to skepticism about sense perception; or
3   repudiate both skepticism about sense perception and the reliability of experience of God, on pain of inconsistency.

Despite the attractions of the epistemic parity thesis, it is possible that it has been overdrawn.

Challenges to the principle of credulity

As I argue [below] in 'A revised conception', the manifest differences between sense experience and experience of God do nothing to undermine the application of the principle of credulity to of-God experiences. But the application of this principle to religious experience has been challenged. Most challenges materialize as restrictions precluding application of the principle to religious experience. Let us consider three distinct attempts at restricting application of the principle.

First, William Rowe recommends the following gloss on the principle of credulity: it "presupposes that we have some understanding of what reasons there might be for questioning our experiences and some way of telling whether or not these reasons are present."[18] He reasons that "it is quite difficult to discover reasons for thinking that someone's [of-God experience] is delusive," for "it is entirely up to God whether to reveal his presence to some human being."[19]

This objection will already be familiar from our consideration of C. B. Martin's objection to thinking of experience of God as perceptual. There are additional problems with this suggestion.

1   . . . The principle of credulity enshrines the notion that belief grounded non-inferentially in perceptual experience is innocent until proven guilty. But Rowe's restriction effectively counsels the reverse attitude of guilty until proven innocent. One and the same experience cannot be both innocent until proven guilty and guilty until proven innocent.

2   Rowe's restriction, if generalized, has two deleterious effects. It launches an infinite regress and it undermines the evidence of sense experience. For any belief-forming practice, there will always be additional checks and tests that one could conduct; an interminable regress of testing protocols is unavoidable. And what is a restriction for one modality of belief formation that is governed by the principle of credulity is a restriction for any other modality that is governed by the principle of credulity, including sense perception. But sense perception is considered by many (rightly, I think) to be a basic source of justified belief and knowledge.[20] On the other hand, if the restriction is not generalized, it is arbitrary to require it only in the context of religious experience.

Second, Michael Martin has argued for a "negative principle of credulity" as the complement to the principle of credulity. He reasons that if "experiences of God are good grounds for the existence of God," then "experiences of the absence of God [may as well be] good grounds for the nonexistence of God."[21]

In his original statement of the argument from religious experience, Richard Swinburne decries the significance of "negative seemings." These are, he reasons, no evidence of how things are. He adds that "there are no good grounds for supposing that if there is a God, the atheist would have experienced him."[22]

The problem is that even if it is true that an atheist might not experience a God that does exist and is experienced by others, it does not follow that negative seemings have no evidential value. For even though they are negative, they are seemings about the way things are, and often enough it seeming to be that something is not the case is quite good evidence that it is not the case. For example, it now seems to me that there is no elephant in the room with me as I write. That particular negative seeming impresses me as very good evidence that things *are not* the way they *seem not* to be; I am right to believe that there is no elephant in the room with me.

Furthermore, negative seemings are all the more telling when the very thing that ought to be present under certain conditions seems not to be present under those conditions. So, sticking to the existence of God to illustrate, if we were right to think that God's presence would be irresistibly evident to everyone, or to everyone who cared to notice him, then God's seeming not to exist would really count for something. Or, if God's presence should be particularly manifest to those suffering horrific pain, and it seems to the one who suffers that God is not present, then again the negative seeming has force.

So Michael Martin must be given his due. But that means that we must also be careful not to let him get away with too much. And he does claim too much by asserting that negative seemings are on a par, epistemically, with positive seemings, especially with respect to God's existence.

Sometimes even the obvious must be said, and even repeated: God is not an elephant, nor is he much like an elephant. I wonder what Martin thinks he knows about how God's presence would have to be manifest, if, contrary to fact (according to Martin), God did exist? Size is not really at issue. But perhaps it's the alleged omnipresence of God that has got Martin thinking this way. However, divine omnipresence is more a matter of the scope of God's consciousness of things than it is a matter of our consciousness of God. Furthermore, God is a personal being with a will and intentions and capacities. How and whether, or when, he chooses to disclose himself is up to him. And the criteria he uses may have to do with choices we make. After all, even experience of human persons as persons and not solely as bodies in a physical world depends on relational dynamics that include openness towards one another and a host of other attitudinal states. . . .

A third restriction on the principle of credulity has been suggested by Paul Draper, who allows that the principle is a fundamental principle of rationality, but denies that it is a universal principle of rationality. It does not apply to "all persons in all epistemic situations"; rather, it applies only to "'epistemically immature' persons," such as "children first learning about the world." The principle of credulity comes to be "modified as we mature intellectually," so that, "as we grow older, we learn to treat different sorts of perceptual claims differently."[23] Some are met with a greater degree of initial credulity; others with a greater degree of initial skepticism.

According to Draper, four factors influence the degree of initial credulity we are prepared to allow. Perceptual experience provides relatively weak evidence if the claim purportedly supported by that evidence is (a) highly specific, (b) very significant (as opposed to trivial), (c) about extraordinary objects not otherwise known to exist and be perceivable, or (d) dependent upon an extraordinary mode of perception.[24] Draper's thesis is that "all four of these factors diminish the amount of direct evidence that theistic experiences provide for basic perceptual claims about God."[25]

How are these four factors that influence the degree of initial credulity identified? They are identified on the basis of observing actual belief-forming practices within contexts of perceptual experience. But notice, it is more precisely an examination of our habits in *sense* perception that yields this list of factors governing levels of initial credulity. But perceiving God, in the sense that we are considering, is not a form of sense perception. It is likely that differences between sense perception and the perception of God correlate with differences in initial credulity factors. Following Draper's example of observing belief-forming habits in sense perception for the purposes of specifying initial credulity factors, we should examine the actual practices of subjects having of-God experiences if we want to know what factors govern their levels of initial credulity. An examination of actual practice will reveal that not all of-God experiences are treated equally by the subjects who have them. An array of degrees of credulity will be found within this context, even if this array differs from that specified for sense perception. In the domain of religious experience, differences in *spiritual* maturity, for example, will specially account for differences in degree of initial credulity.

Even *epistemic* maturity is context-relative and not just a matter of general attainment. One who is relatively epistemically mature in contexts of ordinary sense perception may not be so mature in contexts of mystical perception. Thus, Draper's restriction on the principle of credulity relative to religious experience may not be warranted; it may be too restrictive.

Challenges to the principle of testimony

For subjects of religious experience, belief that God exists may be non-inferentially grounded in their of-God experiences. The only access others have to a subject's experiential grounds is the testimony of the subjects. For this reason, the *standard argument* from religious experience requires a principle of testimony. In general, the experiences of others are probably as they report them.

There is an initial difficulty to overcome, however. Typically, the strength of justification afforded by testimony is lower than that afforded by direct experiential evidence. . . .

. . . First, whether or not a person is prepared to accept the testimony of others about a matter depends greatly on what is personally at stake. In matters of great human concern, standards for the acceptance of testimonial evidence will be fairly high. How high they should be relative to religious experience is to some extent a matter of personal decision. But I can imagine that for many the standards will be much higher when the question of God's existence is in the balance than it is in most other situations.

Second, one may well wonder why a question of such moment should be decided on the basis of experiences others have had. Why should some have to rely heavily on the testimony of others, rather than enjoy immediate, non-inferential justification of their own, especially when it would seem that God is perfectly capable of presenting himself to anyone? . . .

Third, of-God experiences may be numerous indeed. But the problem here is that while there is an impressive plurality of such experiences, there is an equally impressive variety of conceptual contents associated with these types of experiences as their justified outputs. This generates a two-fold problem: some of this variety betrays the presence of conflicting conceptions of God arising out of experiences of God; and, where no conflict is discernable, it is nevertheless difficult to ascertain the degree to which the entity experienced in of-God experiences is the same being across experiences.[26] Furthermore, of-God experiences do not exhaust the class of religious experiences whose possible veridicality is of interest. Perhaps the strength of testimonial evidence regarding of-God experiences is vitiated by equally numerous reports of nontheistic religious experiences.

In the final section I make a few suggestions in response to the difficulties that have been raised in this section. But first we must consider briefly three more general challenges to the evidential value of religious experience.

Three additional objections

The objections we have so far considered concern the basic structure and machinery of the *standard argument* for the existence of God based on religious experience. They concern the elements of the argument itself. In this section I discuss three objections that pose challenges to any positive construal of the evidence of religious experience relative to the existence of God.

The problem of religious diversity

A particularly thorny issue for our topic has to do with the reality of religious diversity and the way conflicting beliefs are tethered to religious experience.

First, as we shall see, background beliefs may very well contribute to the way particular subjects understand and interpret their religious experiences. If these background beliefs explain much of the disparity of perspective that we find in the world, it cannot be the singular fault of religious experience. While background beliefs do not necessarily distort an understanding of religious experience, they certainly could.

Second, religious experience may sometimes be given a richer interpretation than the phenomenology of the experience by itself would support, because of the role played by background beliefs and expectations. On the other hand, an experience rich in conceptualizeable content may not be understood by the subject in the full sense of which it is capable. This, too, may be a consequence of the operation of beliefs and attitudes in the background. This invites a distinction between of-God experiences where the subject perceives God and of-God experiences where the subject does not perceive God, but not because the experiences are not veridical. Assuming veridicality, we should perhaps speak instead of *experiences of God*, and distinguish between those where God is recognized by the subject and those where God is not recognized. The point of making this distinction is that many religious experiences may be experiences of God in the second sense. . . .

Finally, among conflicting claims rooted to a significant degree in experience is the tradition of metaphysical naturalism. This places pretty much everyone in the same boat. The fact that religious traditions vary conceptually and doctrinally despite their respective appeals to religious experience cannot by itself be taken to vitiate the value of religious experience in favor of some amorphous naturalism. Naturalism as a commitment on the part of individuals is very seldom amorphous. It varies in form and perspective. Phenomena and explanations that seem perfectly innocuous from the perspective of some naturalists are utterly scandalous from the perspective of other naturalists.[27] This relatively rich diversity parallels the diversity of religious traditions, not only in richness of diversity, but also for the role that experience plays in the formation of naturalistic beliefs about particular matters of controversy among naturalists.

In any case, if the experiences (including the lack of of-God experiences) of naturalists are added to the mix of perspectives embraced by people, and the question is posed, "What are we to make of reality, given the diverse perspectives of people rooted in their respective experiences?", why should we privilege a non-religious perspective over a particular religious perspective?[28]

The availability of naturalistic explanations

As I noted at the outset, a B-type argument for the existence of God does take seriously an explanation-seeking question: are *of-God experiences* bona fide *experiences of God*, or do they have some other explanation? I pointed out that a metaphysical naturalist may well acknowledge the reality of of-God experiences, but he will most assuredly cavil at the suggestion that many such experiences are veridical. One standard objection to the evidential value of religious experience is that religious experiences can be explained as well or better in terms acceptable to a metaphysical naturalist. . . .

The modern world is acquainted with a profusion of psychological pathologies. These pathologies have been accorded splendiferous power to explain away religious experience. Recognized pathologies that have been credited with this vaunted explanatory power include, for starters: hypersuggestibility (from self-induced hypnotic suggestion to brainwashing); deprivation; sexual frustration; anxiety, panic, and amorphous foreboding that tend to trigger defense mechanisms; regression; mental illness (from hysteria to delusions to manic depression); and, abnormal physiological states induced by drugs.[29] With a list like that, it is easy to imagine that for every yet-to-be catalogued pathology, there is a new naturalistic explanation for religious experience waiting to be commandeered for deployment against experience-of-God claims. Come to think of it, it is a wonder more naturalists do not simply invent from scratch a pathology specific to of-God experiences.

I invite naturalists with the appropriate disposition (whatever the psychological explanation for *that* might be) to sift the data pertaining to of-God experiences using "pathological personality variables" to eliminate all the demonstrably wacky cases of alleged experience of God. Let them even perform a further reduction by setting aside all cases where there is a strong presumption in favor of pathological explanation. What remains following this exercise will still be a substantial body of testimonial evidence that resists assimilation to pathological causes. With regard to this substantial residue, all the naturalist can do is suggest that the remaining cases may well be pathological as well.

Now the evidence for this more modest claim about what is possible just is the evidence of pathology in the easy cases. But what makes them easy cases is that they bear the marks of pathology on their sleeves, as it were. The remaining cases do not. So what possible bearing could identifiable pathologies passing for of-God experiences have on those of-God experiences that show no indication, in their own right, of being pathological? The best explanation for this difference may well be that experiences in the first group are artificial and experiences in the second group are veridical. There must, after all, be *some* explanation for this difference.

As a matter of fact, another sort of explanation has been proposed. This brings us to our final objection.[30]

The role of background beliefs

Some skeptics about religious experience have thought to explain the character of religious experience by emphasizing the role of background beliefs in religious experience . . . so that their having of-God experiences can be completely chalked up to their having these background beliefs going into the experience.[31]

The first thing to notice here is that background beliefs are just as likely to illuminate an experience as they are to distort. To the extent that background beliefs do condition one's understanding of an of-God experience, it will matter whether those background beliefs enjoy an appropriate degree of justification by independent means. This means that in such cases belief in God must already have some positive epistemic standing. It would be a mistake to think that of-God experiences contribute nothing at all to the epistemic status of a belief already held and independently justified. No amount of external, public evidence for the existence of God can substitute for relationship with God, however much it may justify belief in God. If the evidence of natural theology (cosmological and design arguments for the existence of God, for example) implies (as I believe it does) that God is a personal being with a keen interest in the human condition and a desire for relationship between Himself and human persons, then of-God experiences will not only be the vehicle of such relationship but also tend to confirm the hypothesis supported by natural theology.

Second, quite often subjects having of-God experiences report that their experiences were the occasion of acquiring religious beliefs that they did not already have. Indeed, reluctant naturalists have sometimes converted to belief in God on the basis of what they describe as religious experience of one kind or another. Not only are these cases impressive counter-examples to the generalization embodied in the explanation under consideration, but some appropriate explanation is needed to account for the conversion of a person out of commitment to a strong naturalist package of beliefs. Others have converted from some variety of generic theism to a more robust theism like Christianity, again with experience of God playing a key role.[32]

Third, the role of background beliefs among those who do not experience God must also be taken into consideration as a factor explaining their not experiencing God. First, there is the obvious role that confident belief that God does not exist will almost certainly play in this regard. I confess, I have sometimes suspected that, however ambiguous the evidence for theism may seem to some people, anyone with a confident belief that God does not exist just is not paying attention. (And let us not forget, committed metaphysical naturalists, are, for all intents and purposes, confident of the non-existence of God.) But even if one is not an atheist, one may have in the background to one's own experiences beliefs that limit the prospects of having of-God experiences, even if God does exist and desires to be known in experience. There is the real danger that the supposed "hiddenness of God" is actually due to background beliefs and attitudes that people have about how God must be prepared to manifest himself if he exists. There is the real possibility that the chief barrier to experiencing the presence of God lies within our own noetic and attitudinal structures.[33]

A revised conception

Where does the critical discussion of the sections "Objections to the standard argument" and "Three additional objections" leave the argument from religious experience for the existence of God? What are we to make of the evidential value of religious experience in light of the difficulties treated in those sections?

First, the chief lesson to be learned from the discussion in "Three additional objections" is that the evidence of religious experience should not be quarantined from whatever evidence is available from other sources. All available evidence should be assimilated into a cumulative case for personal theism that is sensitive to the complex logical relations that hold among the various categories of evidence. The evidence of religious experience should be respected enough to foster serious inquiry into the availability of other evidences for theism. Alternatively, the evidences of cosmology, anthropic design, and human consciousness . . . may be seen to support a reasonable expectation that the personal God responsible for creating and ordering our universe, thereby arranging for our physical flourishing, and for creating us with faculties associated with immaterial minds (including aspirations for spiritual flourishing and the potential for relationship with God), also desires relationship with us. This expectation may be tested in human experience and confirmed by of-God experiences we have independent reason to believe are veridical.

The religious experiences of others may further elicit sympathy for the possibility of experience of God among those who have not yet had such experiences. The attitudes and dispositions that accompany this sort of sympathy may put nonbelievers in a better position to appraise all of the data for personal theism, and even to encounter God in their own experience. At the very least, if they are agnostics who appreciate the momentous nature of the religious quest and recognize the role that attitudes play in guiding appropriate pursuit of God as a possibly real being personally interested in a relationship, then they may be encouraged to engage in a devotional experiment that would lead to a personal awareness of God in their own experience.[34]

All of this suggests that there is yet a third way to incorporate the data of religious experience into an argument for personal theism. As it is best regarded as a cumulative case argument, let us call it a C-type argument. How might this argument relate to the strengths and weaknesses of the standard B-type argument explored earlier in this chapter? Here I wish to make several suggestions.

My first recommendation is that we relax the strong claim on behalf of epistemic parity that figures so prominently in the standard argument. There are disanalogies between sense perception and of-God experience; some have substantial epistemological consequences. (This is not to be lamented. Some disanalogies are religiously quite significant.) It does not serve the purposes of an argument from religious experience to the existence of God to emphasize the similarities and then have to explain repeatedly why notable dissimilarities do not undermine the basic argument. Abandoning ambitious claims on behalf of epistemic parity will help to forestall confusion about the significance of the very real similarities that do exist.

Of-God experiences are irreducibly *sui generis*. This does not mean that there are no analogies between of-God experiences and other modes of experience. Sense perception is one domain where we meet with significant analogies. All salient analogies between sense perception and "perception" of God are due to the subject-object presentational structure that they have in common. In both modes of experience, a subject is directly acquainted with an object that is presented to the subject's consciousness as existing, having some set of properties, and standing in certain relations to other objects in experience, where the object that is presented is taken to be in some way the cause of the experience.

I have no objection to characterizing perception in some generic sense in terms of this basic structure. But then other experiences will count as perceptual as well. (In fact, on some accounts, even the intuitional grasp of mathematical or logical truths may be regarded as similarly perceptual.[35]) Among perceptual experiences understood in this generic sense, of-God experiences bear the strongest resemblance to experiences of, or "encounters" with, other *persons*. If the sensory imagery subjects often use to describe of-God experiences suggests close comparison with sense perception, other elements in their descriptions for of-God experiences point to a different comparison. The object presented in of-God experiences is presented as a personal being, and the resulting acquaintance with the object presented is personal in nature. It is typical of Christian believers, for example, to speak of having a personal relationship with God, where they mean this quite literally. The much ballyhooed "ineffability" of so much religious experience may, in of-God experiences at least, be due to the I-Thou character of the experiences. Little wonder that language may fail a subject attempting to articulate the details of her experience of a personal deity and the knowledge that she acquires through such direct acquaintance.[36]

My second recommendation concerns the principle of credulity. If there are differences between sense perception and perception of God that undercut an ambitious claim for epistemic parity between the two modes of experience, these differences do not affect the applicability of the principle of credulity to experiences of God. This principle is far more generalizable than is acknowledged in most discussions of it. Its application ranges over a host of epistemic contexts. In fact, it is difficult to think of a context where it does not apply. Consider Swinburne's "principle of testimony." Is it anything more than a special case of a principle of credulity applied to belief based on testimony? Although Swinburne does defend the principle of credulity by drawing an analogy with sense perception, its actual defense may be more successful if it is derived from our habits across the whole range of doxastic practices.

In any event, the undeniable similarity between sense perception and experience of God *as modes of experience that have a presentational aspect*, permits an extension of the use of the principle of credulity in sense experience to its use in of-God experiences. For it is with respect to the presentational character of sense perception that the principle of credulity is germane. The "seemings" that occur in sense perception are to be taken at face value, barring the existence of contraindications. Analogous "seemings" also occur in of-God experiences. And for that reason there is cause for endorsing a principle of credulity in the rational appraisal of such experiences.

This affords a mitigated (scaled-down) claim to epistemic parity between sense perception and the "perception" of God. Both modes of experience are governed by similar principles of rationality. Approval of the use of fundamental principles of rationality in the domain of sense perception and disapproval of their use in the domain of religious experience suggests that the decision about proper domains of application is arbitrary. But it is not. On the other hand, consistent disapproval in all cases will land one in the "skeptical bog", warned about by Swinburne and Alston. A modest epistemic parity thesis survives acknowledgement of epistemologically significant disanalogies between sense perception and experience of God.

Turning, finally, to the principle of testimony, I recommend a more expansive construal of the nature and significance of testimony. Testimonial evidence must be weighed relative to the credibility of the witness. Credibility of the witness is a function of the witness's perceived character and expertise. With regard to character, various virtues are relevant, but basic honesty is especially important. With regard to expertise, there must be confidence that a witness has a certain minimal ability to grasp whatever it is that her testimony pertains to and can talk about it intelligently and accurately. The moral fruits of religious experience in the lives of their subjects concern both dimensions of credibility. All of these conditions of credible testimony have been discussed in the literature on religious experience.

But there is an additional component that deserves more attention. It is arguably the most important. Transcending the particular virtues and competencies of an expert witness is the overall impression the witness creates in others. Some individuals enjoy a stature that far outstrips the reputation of others. These individuals are without peers. Their testimony has eminently greater weight. They are the paragons.

In the realm of religious experience, there are few who would regard themselves as paragons of religious practice. Those who do advertise themselves in this way had better have impeccable credentials. Genuine models of spirituality are in short supply. Amateurs and hoaksters abound. Even the most admirable figures confess their neophyte status. So far as I can tell, there is one shining exception. Those in search of a model of spiritual perceptiveness can do no better than attend respectfully to the life and teachings of Jesus Christ. He had an authoritative bearing that led a multitude to remark about it and inspired many to make it the pattern of their own highest aspirations. Among the many figures whom we admire for their spiritual devotion, whom we would be most prepared to trust for reliable testimony about of-God experiences, I dare say the preponderance of them are figures who have made Jesus their own model.

The centuries-long tradition of religious experience traceable to the effect of Jesus Christ in the lives of people across cultures should provoke a measure of curiosity about the possible veridicality of alleged experiences of God. A certain feeling of exposure by acquaintance with the person and teaching of Jesus is a commonly reported religious experience that may be shared by believers and nonbelievers alike.

I conclude, then, with the testimony of a band of men who knew Jesus most intimately. His presence in their lives was so transformational that they invoked the most exalted language they could find to give expression to it, language that linked their own personal destinies to the power of his presence. Their words are especially arresting for being a direct response to Jesus himself: "Lord, to whom shall we go? You have the words of eternal life."[37]

Notes

1   An experience is veridical, in the sense I have in mind, only if what seems to be presented in the experience actually exists and has the properties that it seems to have, given the experience.

2   It is admittedly arbitrary to employ the terms "of-God experiences" and "experiences of God" the way I do; but it is convenient to have some way of referring to the contrasting notions, and this seems to me to be as good a way as any.

3   Earlier, in the unabridged version of Geivett's essay "The Evidential Value of Religious Experience," he writes: "What is *non-inferential evidence* for the believing subject of a religious experience is, for the nonbelieving outside observer, data for a potential *inference* to the existence of God." Arguments of this sort he calls "*B-type* arguments from religious experience." See R. Douglas Geivett, "The Evidential Value of Religious Experience," in *The Rationality of Theism*, Paul Copan and Paul K. Moser (eds) (New York: Routledge, 2003), 177, where he also states what he means by an *A-type* argument.

4   Richard Swinburne, *The Existence of God* (Oxford: Clarendon Press, 1979), 254.

5   Ibid., 254.

6   Ibid., 254.

7   For his reasons for resisting the term "religious experience," see William P. Alston, *Perceiving God: The Epistemology of Religious Experience* (Ithaca, NY: Cornell University Press, 1991), 34–5. The basic problem is that the term is "obfuscating," which, if true, would sure enough be a reason to avoid it. For present purposes, I take no position on the matter.

8   Ibid., 66. The details are spelled out in Chapter one of Alston's book (i.e. pp. 9–67).

9   William P. Alston, "Religious Experience and Religious Belief," in *Contemporary Perspectives*

on Religious Epistemology, R. Douglas Geivett and Brendan Sweetman (eds) (New York: Oxford University Press, 1992), 302.

10   See Swinburne, *The Existence of God*, 272.

11   Ibid., 272.

12   C. B. Martin, *Religious Belief* (Ithaca, NY: Cornell University Press, 1959), 70.

13   Others who insist both that certifiability by independent checks is necessary and that they are not sufficiently available in the case of religious experience include Antony Flew, *God and Philosophy* (London: Hutchinson, 1966); Paul Schmidt, *Religious Knowledge* (Glencoe, IL: The Free Press, 1961); and, Ronald Hepburn, *Christianity and Paradox: Critical Studies in Twentieth-Century Theology* (London: C.A. Watts & Co., Ltd, 1958), 37.

14   Alston, "Religious Experience and Religious Belief," 299.

15   See Alston, *Perceiving God*, 209–22. See also William J. Wainwright, *Mysticism: A Study of Its Nature, Cognitive Value, and Moral Implications* (Madison, WI: University of Wisconsin Press, 1981), 82–102, for a list of six tests employed by Christian theists seeking to distinguish between veridical and nonveridical of-God experiences; and Caroline Franks Davis, *The Evidential Force of Religious Experience* (Oxford: Clarendon Press, 1989), 71–7.

16   Alston, *Perceiving God*, 36, 49, and Alston, "Religious Experience and Religious Belief," 299.

17   For a recent example, see Peter Byrne, "Perceiving God and Realism," *Philo* 3.2, available on the internet as of 12 April 2002, at http://www.philoonline.org/library/byrne_3_2.htm.

18   William L. Rowe, *Philosophy of Religion: An Introduction*, 3rd edn (Belmont, CA: Wadsworth, 2001), 61.

19   Rowe, *Philosophy of Religion*, 61.

20   See George I. Mavrodes, *Belief in God: A Study in the Epistemology of Religion* (New York: Random House, 1970), 76.

21   Michael Martin, "The Principle of Credulity and Religious Experience," *Religious Studies* 22 (1986): 79–93; and Michael Martin, *Atheism: A Philosphical Justification* (Philadelphia, PA: Temple University Press, 1990).

22   See Swinburne, *The Existence of God*, 254–55.

23   Paul Draper, "God and Perceptual Evidence," *International Journal for Philosophy of Religion* 32 (1992), 157–58.

24   Ibid., 158–9.

25   Ibid., 159.

26   Some of these difficulties arise quite apart from the context of testimonial evidence we are considering. But it is here, perhaps, that difficulties of this sort are most disconcerting.

27   I think, for example, of the various naturalist accounts of mind-body phenomena.

28   For a fuller treatment of the challenge of religious diversity, see Davis, *The Evidential Force of Religious Experience*, Ch. 7, and Wainwright, *Mysticism*, 107–10.

29   These examples are culled from a catalogue of pathologies discussed in Davis, *The Evidential Force of Religious Experience*, 195–223.

30   For detailed discussions of reductionist strategies for dealing with religious experience, see Davis, *The Evidential Force of Religious Experience*, Ch. 8; Jerome Gellman, *Experience of God and the Rationality of Theistic Belief* (Ithaca, NY: Cornell University Press, 1997), Ch. 5; Jerome Gellman, *Mystical Experience of God: A Philosophical Inquiry* (Aldershot, UK: Ashgate, 2001), Chs 4 and 5; and Keith E. Yandell, *The Epistemology of Religious Experience* (Cambridge, UK: Cambridge University Press, 1993), Chs 6 and 7. For a helpful general discussion of the proper way to study the phenomenon of religion, see Roger Trigg, *Rationality and Religion* (Oxford: Basil Blackwell, 1998), Ch. 2.

31   Perhaps the most notable proponent of this strategy is Wayne Proudfoot. See his "Explaining Religious Experience" in Geivett and Sweetman, *Contemporary Perspectives on Religious Epistemology*.

32   For examples of Christian philosophers for whom experience of God was an important contribution to their conversion to belief in God, see several autobiographical essays in Kelly Clark, (ed.) *Philosophers Who Believe: The Spiritual Journeys of 11 Leading Thinkers* (Downers Grove, IL: InterVarsity Press, 1993); and Thomas V. Morris, *God and the Philosophers: The Reconciliation of Faith and Reason* (New York, NY: Oxford University Press, 1994). Examples of converts among intellectuals throughout history and across the disciplines further support the point being made.

33   . . . For more discussion of the role of background beliefs in the interpretation of religious experience, see Davis, *The Evidential Force of Religious Experience*, Ch. 6, and Wainwright, *Mysticism*, 1981, 18–33.

34   For more on these matters, see R. Douglas Geivett, "A Pascalian Rejoinder to the Presumption of Atheism," in *God Matters: An Anthology*, Christopher Bernard and Raymond Martin (eds) (Longman, 2002); Caroline Franks Davis, "The Devotional Experiment," *Religious Studies* 22 (1986), 15–28; and, H. H. Price, *Belief* (London: George Allen & Unwin, 1969), lectures 9 and 10.

35   See Laurence BonJour, *In Defense of Pure Reason* (Cambridge: Cambridge University Press, 1998).

36   See C. E. Raven, *Natural Religion and Christian Theology*, Vol. 2 (Cambridge, UK: Cambridge University Press, 1953), 47; St Teresa of Avila, *The Complete Works of Saint Teresa of Jesus*, Vol. 1, *Life*, E. Allison Peers (trans. and ed.) (London: Sheed & Ward, 1946), 326; and, Davis, *The Evidential Force of Religious Experience*, 77–82. For a valiant and compelling attempt to articulate the nature of the I-Thou encounter, see Martin Buber, *I and Thou*, Walter Kaufmann (trans. and ed.) (New York, NY: Charles Scribner's, 1970).

37   *The Gospel of John* (6.68).

Questions for reflection

1   What is the *standard argument* from religious experience? Explain its three major components.

2   Do you agree with the principle of credulity that "How things seem to be is good grounds for a belief about how things are"? Why or why not? Do you think this principle offers good reason for those who have had religious experiences to believe them to be veridical?

3   What do you make of atheist philosopher Michael Martin's claim that if "experiences of God are good grounds for the existence of God," then "experiences of the absence of God [may as well be] good grounds for the nonexistence of God"?

4   Have you had religious experiences, or do you know others who claim to have had them? Can you describe them?

5   Do you believe that one's own religious experiences could provide epistemic support for his or her belief in God? Do you believe someone else's religious experiences could provide epistemic support for another's belief in God? Explain.

Further reading

William P. Alston (1991) *Perceiving God: The Epistemology of Religious Experience*. Ithaca, NY: Cornell University Press. (Argues that religious experience provides a solid basis for theistic belief; a contemporary classic.)

Caroline Franks Davis (1989) *The Evidential Force of Religious Experience*. Oxford: Oxford University

Press. (A thoroughly argued assessment of the value of religious experiences as evidence for religious belief. She analyzes classical and contemporary sources from different world religions and offers an account of various types of religious experiences.)

Jerome I. Gellman (1997) *Experience of God and the Rationality of Theistic Belief*. Ithaca, NY: Cornell University Press. (Gellman argues that mystical experiences can provide a rational basis for belief in God's existence. He also examines reductionist explanations of apparent experiences of God and finds them insufficient.)

Jerome I. Gellman (2001) *Mystical Experience of God, a Philosophical Enquiry*. London: Ashgate. (This is a sequel to *Experience of God and the Rationality of Theistic Belief*. It revises the argument of the earlier book and considers and turns back several new philosophical objections.)

Gwen Griffith-Dickson (2000) *Human and Divine: An Introduction to the Philosophy of Religious Experience*. London: Gerald Duckworth. (Analyzes religious experiences among the world's religions and philosophical traditions, noting especially Continental European and Eastern philosophy without ignoring Anglo-American perspectives.)

William James ([1901–2] 1985) *The Varieties of Religious Experience*. Cambridge, MA: Harvard University Press. (A classic work on religious experience from a foremost American pragmatic philosopher. Originally delivered by James as the Gifford Lectures.)

Keith Yandell (2004) *The Epistemology of Religious Experience*. Cambridge: Cambridge University Press. (An analytic philosopher argues against the view that religious experience is ineffable and for the view that strong numinous experience provides evidence that God exists; a rather technical treatment of the topic, but well worth a careful read.)

PART EIGHT

The problem of evil

There is one apparent reality that every human being is confronted with: evil. Whether rich or poor, young or old, Oriental or Occidental, every conscious person who has ever lived has had to deal with some form of evil (including suffering) in his or her life. Given its ubiquitous nature, all of the major worldviews and religions have responded to evil in one way or another. But one worldview in particular is challenged by it more than the others, at least at first glance.

Theists generally affirm that the qualities of God include being omniscient, omnipotent, and omnibenevolent. But the coexistence of God (understood as having these qualities) and evil raises some glaring problems. One problem is referred to as the *logical* problem of evil, and it can be put simply as follows: The following two propositions are logically contradictory:

God—an omnipotent, omniscient, and omnibenevolent being—exists.

and

Evil—in its many manifestations—exists.

One way of spelling out the logical inconsistency is as follows:

1   If God exists, then God is an omnipotent (all-powerful), omniscient (all-knowing), and omnibenevolent (wholly-good) being.
2   An omnibenevolent being would have the desire to eliminate evil.
3   An omnipotent being would have the power to eliminate evil.
4   An omniscient being would have the knowledge to eliminate evil.
5   Evil exists.
6   Therefore, God (an omnipotent, omniscient, and omnibenevolent being) does not exist.

A second problem is referred to as the *evidential* problem of evil. According to this problem, the kind and amount of evil in the world provides reasonable evidence for the belief that God, as an omniscient, omnipotent, and omnibenevolent being, does not exist.

In a classic essay on the evidential problem of evil (the first essay in this section), William Rowe offers an argument in which he maintains that given the intense suffering that exists in the world, it is reasonable not to believe in God. He uses the story of a fawn trapped in a forest fire. The fawn is horribly burned and lies in agony for days before it finally dies. Such suffering appears to be gratuitous; that is, there seems to be no reason an omnipotent, omniscient, omnibenevolent God would allow it, especially since it was preventable without losing some greater good or permitting some evil equally bad or worse in the process.

How might a theist respond to these problems of evil? Two types of strategies have been offered. One type is called a *defense*, which is an attempt to demonstrate that it is not unreasonable, or illogical, to believe in the coexistence of God and evil; in other words, there is no formal contradiction in affirming propositions (1) and (2) above. This generally involves an attempt to show that either premise 2 or premise 4 is not necessarily true. A second type of response is called a *theodicy*, which is an attempt to justify God given the evil in the world. Unlike a defense, a theodicy is not a rebuttal of the claim of logical inconsistency, but rather a positive claim that there are good reasons for why God allows evil in the world.

Another important point to keep in mind in this discussion is that philosophers often make a distinction between *natural* evil and *moral* evil. Natural evils are events that occur in nature such as tornadoes, earthquakes, disease, and so on which cause harm or suffering to people or animals. The causes of natural evils are impersonal forces. Moral evils are events which are brought about by human agents intentionally acting for the purpose of causing harm or suffering to people or animals. Examples would include raping, torturing, and murdering innocent individuals.

In the second reading, John Hick offers a soul-making theodicy. He first contrasts two different kinds of theodicies: Augustinian and Irenaean. According to the Augustinian theodicy, human beings were created by God as sinless beings in a perfect, Edenic paradise. However, through their free will, they chose to sin and thus brought about the evil in the world. God is gracious, however, and sent his Son into the world to redeem the elect. They will, one day in the hereafter, be glorified in heaven and will spend a blissful eternity there with God. The wicked, on the other hand, will be separated from God in eternal punishment and damnation.

The Irenaean theodicy — what Hick also calls the "soul-making" theodicy — however, is quite different. Developed from ideas of Irenaeus, a Greek bishop in the ancient Christian church, Adam (the alleged first human being) is not seen as falling into sin but as an infant developing into a mature and virtuous human being. Human history involves the unfolding story of *homo sapiens* being perfected in soul as they make choices in the challenging environments in which they are placed. God is thus working through the evolution of humanity to create perfected souls. Unlike the Augustinian theodicy, which focuses primarily on moral evil, this soul-making theodicy offers a way of accounting for both the moral and the natural evil in the world.

In the next essay Alvin Plantinga provides a response to the logical problem of evil. His defense is similar to Augustine's theodicy, most notably its inclusion of the free will of human beings as a central component. However, Plantinga is not attempting to justify God-given evil—he is not offering a theodicy. Rather, he is simply rebutting the atheologian's (the one who argues against belief in God) claims that there is a contradiction between the two propositions that God exists and evil exists.

Besides free will, Plantinga also utilizes the notion of *transworld depravity*—that in every possible world, human beings freely choose to do evil. Given these two possibilities (free will and transworld depravity), it is logically possible that God could not create a world with free creatures (which is a better world than one not having such creatures) without that world having evil. So, there is no contradiction between (1) and (2). This argument is now widely taken by theists and atheists to be a solid rebuttal to the logical problem of evil.

But some theists and others believe that showing the coexistence of God and evil is not enough since what most people worry about is the coexistence of *certain kinds of evil* and God. In the next essay, Marilyn McCord Adams makes this very point. What's needed by the theist is a response to the existence of *horrendous* evils—evils which are so terrible that when a person experiences them she doubts that her life overall can be taken as a great good. Adams attempts to offer such a response.

The essays so far in this section have focused on debates relevant to the theistic view of God. However, all of the major worldviews and religions have responded to evil in one way or another. The next reading is a Buddhist response to one form of evil: suffering. Contrary to Western caricatures of the Buddhist position on suffering which sees life as a tragedy of misery, taking the standpoint of the Buddha, argues David Kalupahana, leads one to a different conclusion. A proper (Buddhist) understanding of the self as a non-enduring substance and the renunciation of craving eliminates the problem of suffering and leads one to experience human life with optimism and sanguinity.

Chapter 50

William L. Rowe

THE PROBLEM OF EVIL

William L. Rowe was Professor of Philosophy at Purdue University for many years and he is a leading proponent of the *evidential* argument from evil. In this selection—a contemporary classic—he first argues that given the existence of intense suffering in the world, it is rational to disbelieve in an omnipotent and omniscient God. He uses the example of the apparently pointless suffering of a fawn burned by lightning. He notes that there appear to be countless examples of such events, and while it cannot be proven that they are, indeed, pointless, the atheist is nonetheless rational in holding that they are, and thus is rational in rejecting belief in God.

He next examines a possible theistic response to the argument; namely, that since there are (some theists maintain) rational grounds for believing in an omnipotent, omniscient, God, there does not exist pointless suffering (even if we don't know the reasons for it). Professor Rowe notes several responses an atheist could make to this rebuttal and defends one of them, what he calls "friendly atheism." This is the view that a theist could have reasons for belief in God such that she is being rational in holding them even though they are not, on the informed atheist's account, rational to hold.

This paper is concerned with three interrelated questions. The first is: Is there an argument for atheism based on the existence of evil that may rationally justify someone in being an atheist? To this first question I give an affirmative answer and try to support that answer by setting forth a strong argument for atheism based on the existence of evil.[1] The second question is: How can the theist best defend his position against the argument for atheism based on the existence of evil? In response to this question I try to describe what may be an adequate rational defense for theism against any argument for atheism based on the existence of evil. The final question is: What position should the informed atheist take concerning the rationality of theistic belief? Three different answers an atheist may give to this question serve to distinguish three varieties of atheism: unfriendly atheism, indifferent atheism, and friendly atheism. In the final part of the paper I discuss and defend the position of friendly atheism.

Before we consider the argument from evil, we need to distinguish a narrow and a broad sense of the terms "theist," "atheist," and "agnostic." By a "theist" in the narrow sense I mean someone who believes in the existence of an omnipotent, omniscient, eternal, supremely good being who created the world. By a "theist" in the broad sense I mean someone who believes in the existence of some sort of divine being or divine reality. To be a theist in the narrow sense is also to be a theist in the broad sense, but one may be a theist in the broad sense—as was Paul Tillich—without believing that there is a supremely good, omnipotent, omniscient, eternal being who created the world. Similar distinctions must be made between a narrow and a broad sense of the terms "atheist" and "agnostic." To be an atheist in the broad sense is to deny the existence of any sort of divine being or divine reality. Tillich was not an atheist in the broad sense. But he was an atheist in the narrow sense, for he denied that there exists a divine being that is all-knowing, all-powerful and perfectly good. In this paper I will be using the terms "theism," "theist," "atheism," "atheist," "agnosticism," and "agnostic" in the narrow sense, not in the broad sense.

I

In developing the argument for atheism based on the existence of evil, it will be useful to focus on some particular evil that our world contains in considerable abundance. Intense human and animal suffering, for example, occurs daily and in great plenitude in our world. Such intense suffering is a clear case of evil. Of course, if the intense suffering leads to some greater good, a good we could not have obtained without undergoing the suffering in question, we might conclude that the suffering is justified, but it remains an evil nevertheless. For we must not confuse the intense suffering in and of itself with the good things to which it sometimes leads or of which it may be a necessary part. Intense human or animal suffering is in itself bad, an evil, even though it may sometimes be justified by virtue of being a part of, or leading to, some good which is unobtainable without it. What is evil in itself may sometimes be good as a means because it leads to something that is good in itself. In such a case, while remaining an evil in itself, the intense human or animal suffering is, nevertheless, an evil which someone might be morally justified in permitting.

Taking human and animal suffering as a clear instance of evil which occurs with great frequency in our world, the argument for atheism based on evil can be stated as follows:

1. There exist instances of intense suffering which an omnipotent, omniscient being could have prevented without thereby losing some greater good or permitting some evil equally bad or worse.[2]
2. An omniscient, wholly good being would prevent the occurrence of any intense suffering it could, unless it could not do so without thereby losing some greater good or permitting some evil equally bad or worse.
3. There does not exist an omnipotent, omniscient, wholly good being.

What are we to say about this argument for atheism, an argument based on the profusion of one sort of evil in our world? The argument is valid; therefore, if we have rational grounds for accepting its premises, to that extent we have rational grounds for accepting atheism. Do we, however, have rational grounds for accepting the premises of this argument?

Let's begin with the second premise. Let s_1 be an instance of intense human or animal suffering which an omniscient, wholly good being could prevent. We will also suppose that things are such that s_1 will occur unless prevented by the omniscient, wholly good (OG) being. We might be interested in determining what would be a *sufficient* condition of OG failing to prevent s_1. But, for our purpose here, we need only try to state a *necessary* condition for OG failing to prevent s_1. That condition, so it seems to me, is this:

> *Either* (i) there is some greater good, G, such that G is obtainable by OG only if OG permits s_1,[3]
> *or* (ii) there is some greater good, G, such that G is obtainable by OG only if OG permits either s_1 or some evil equally bad or worse,
> *or* (iii) s_1 is such that it is preventable by OG only if OG permits some evil equally bad or worse.

It is important to recognize that (iii) is not included in (i). For losing a good greater than s_1 is not the same as permitting an evil greater than s_1. And this because the *absence* of a good state of affairs need not itself be an evil state of affairs. It is also important to recognize that s_1 might be such that it is preventable by OG *without* losing G (so condition (i) is not satisfied) but also such that if OG did prevent it, G would be loss *unless* OG permitted some evil equal to or worse than s_1. If this were so, it does not seem correct to require that OG prevent s_1. Thus, condition (ii) takes into account an important possibility not encompassed in condition (i).

Is it true that if an omniscient, wholly good being permits the occurrence of some intense suffering it could have prevented, then either (i) or (ii) or (iii) obtains? It seems to me that it is true. But if it is true then so is premise (2) of the argument for atheism. For that premise merely states in more compact form what we have suggested must be true if an omniscient, wholly good being fails to prevent some intense suffering it could prevent. Premise (2) says that an omniscient, wholly good being would prevent the occurrence of any intense suffering it could, unless it could not do so without thereby losing some greater good or permitting some evil equally bad or worse. This premise (or something not too distant from it) is, I think, held in common by many atheists and nontheists. Of course, there may be disagreement about whether something is good, and whether, if it is good, one would be morally justified in permitting some intense suffering to occur in order to obtain it. Someone might hold, for example, that no good is great enough to justify permitting an innocent child to suffer terribly.[4] Again, someone might hold that the mere fact that a given good outweighs some suffering and would be loss if the suffering were prevented, is not a morally sufficient reason for permitting the suffering. But to hold either of these views is not to deny (2). For (2) claims only that *if* an omniscient, wholly good being permits intense suffering *then* either there is some greater good that would have been loss, or some equally bad or worse evil that would have occurred, had the intense suffering been prevented. (2) does not purport to describe what might be a *sufficient* condition for an omniscient, wholly good being to permit intense suffering, only what is a *necessary* condition. So stated, (2) seems to express a belief that accords with our basic moral principles, principles shared by both theists and nontheists. If we are to fault the argument for atheism, therefore, it seems we must find some fault with its first premise.

Suppose in some distant forest lightning strikes a dead tree, resulting in a forest fire. In the fire a fawn is trapped, horribly burned, and lies in terrible agony for several days before death relieves its suffering. So far as we can see, the fawn's intense suffering is pointless. For there does not appear to be any greater good such that the prevention of the fawn's suffering would require either the loss of that good or the occurrence of an evil equally bad or worse. Nor does there seem to be any equally bad or worse evil so connected to the fawn's suffering that it would have had to occur had the fawn's suffering been prevented. Could an omnipotent, omniscient being have prevented the fawn's apparently pointless suffering? The answer is obvious, as even the theist will insist. An omnipotent, omniscient being could have easily prevented the fawn from being horribly burned, or, given the burning, could have spared the fawn the intense suffering by quickly ending its life, rather than allowing the fawn to lie in terrible agony for several days. Since the fawn's intense suffering was preventable and, so far as we can see, pointless, doesn't it appear that premise (1) of the argument is true, that there do exist instances of intense suffering which an omnipotent, omniscient being could have prevented without thereby losing some greater good or permitting some evil equally bad or worse.

It must be acknowledged that the case of the fawn's apparently pointless suffering does not *prove* that (1) is true. For even though we cannot see how the fawn's suffering is required to obtain some greater good (or to prevent some equally bad or worse evil), it hardly follows that it is not so required. After all, we are often surprised by how things we thought to be unconnected turn out to be intimately connected. Perhaps, for all we know, there is some familiar good outweighing the fawn's suffering to which that suffering is connected in a way we do not see. Furthermore, there may well be unfamiliar goods, goods we haven't dreamed of, to which the fawn's suffering is inextricably connected. Indeed, it would seem to require something like omniscience on our part before we could lay claim to *knowing* that there is no greater good connected to the fawn's suffering in such a manner than an omnipotent, omniscient being could not have achieved that good without permitting that suffering or some evil equally bad or worse. So the case of the fawn's suffering surely does not enable us to *establish* the truth of (1).

The truth is that we are not in a position to prove that (1) is true. We cannot know with certainty that instances of suffering of the sort described in (1) do occur in our world. But it is one thing to *know* or *prove* that (1) is true and quite another thing to have *rational grounds* for believing (1) to be true. We are often in the position where in the light of our experience and knowledge it is rational to believe that a certain statement is true, even though we are not in a position to prove or to know with certainty that the statement is true. In the light of our past experience and knowledge it is, for example, very reasonable to believe that neither Goldwater nor McGovern will ever be elected President, but we are scarcely in the position of knowing with certainty that neither will ever be elected President. So, too, with (1), although we cannot know with certainty that it is true, it perhaps can be rationally supported, shown to be a rational belief.

Consider again the case of the fawn's suffering. Is it reasonable to believe that there is some greater good so intimately connected to that suffering that even an omnipotent, omniscient being could not have obtained that good without permitting that suffering or some evil at least as bad? It certainly does not appear reasonable to believe this. Nor does it seem reasonable to believe that there is some evil at least as bad as the fawn's suffering such that an omnipotent being simply could not have prevented it without permitting the fawn's suffering. But even if it should somehow be reasonable to believe either of these things of the fawn's suffering, we must then ask whether it is reasonable to believe either of these things of *all* the instances of seemingly pointless human and animal suffering that occur daily in our world. And surely the answer to this more general question must be no. It seems quite unlikely that *all* the instances of intense suffering occurring daily in our world are intimately related to the occurrence of greater goods or the prevention of evils at least as bad; and even more unlikely, should they somehow all be so related, that an omnipotent, omniscient being could not have achieved at least some of those goods (or prevented some of those evils) without permitting the instances of intense suffering that are supposedly related to them. In the light of our experience and knowledge of the variety and scale of human and animal suffering in our world, the idea that none of this suffering could have been prevented by an omnipotent being without thereby losing a greater good or permitting an evil at least as bad seems an extraordinary absurd idea, quite beyond our belief. It seems then that although we cannot *prove* that (1) is true, it is, nevertheless, altogether *reasonable* to believe that (1) is true, that (1) is a *rational* belief.[5]

Returning now to our argument for atheism, we've seen that the second premise expresses a basic belief common to many theists and nontheists. We've also seen that our experience and knowledge of the variety and profusion of suffering in our world provides *rational support* for the first premise. Seeing that the conclusion, "There does not exist an omnipotent, omniscient, wholly good being" follows from these two premises, it does seem that we have *rational support* for atheism, that it is reasonable for us to believe that the theistic God does not exist.

II

Can theism be rationally defended against the argument for atheism we have just examined? If it can, how might the theist best respond to that argument? Since the argument from (1) and (2) to (3) is valid, and since the theist, no less than the nontheist, is more than likely committed to (2), it's clear that the theist can reject this atheistic argument only by rejecting its first premise, the premise that states that there are instances of intense suffering which an omnipotent, omniscient being could have prevented without thereby losing some greater good or permitting some evil equally bad or worse. How, then, can the theist best respond to this premise and the considerations advanced in its support?

There are basically three responses a theist can make. First, he might argue not that (1) is false or probably false, but only that the reasoning given in support of it is in some way *defective*. He may do this either by arguing that the reasons given in support of (1) are *in themselves* insufficient to justify accepting (1), or by arguing that there are other things we know which, when taken in conjunction with these reasons, do not justify us in accepting (1). I suppose some theists would be content with this rather modest response to the basic argument for atheism. But given the validity of the basic argument and the theist's likely acceptance of (2), he is thereby committed to the view that (1) is false, not just that we have no good reasons for accepting (1) as true. The second two responses are aimed at showing that it is reasonable to believe that (1) is false. Since the theist is committed to this view I shall focus the discussion on these two attempts, attempts which we can distinguish as "the direct attack" and "the indirect attack."

By a direct attack, I mean an attempt to reject (1) by pointing out goods, for example, to which suffering may well be connected, goods which an omnipotent, omniscient being could not achieve without permitting suffering. It is doubtful, however, that the direct attack can succeed. The theist may point out that some suffering leads to moral and spiritual development impossible without suffering. But it's reasonably clear that suffering often occurs in a degree far beyond what is required for character development. The theist may say that some suffering results from free choices of human beings and might be preventable only by preventing some measure of human freedom. But, again, it's clear that much intense suffering occurs not as a result of human free choices. The general difficulty with this direct attack on premise (1) is twofold. First, it cannot succeed, for the theist does not know what greater goods might be served, or evils prevented, by each instance of intense human or animal suffering. Second, the theist's own religious tradition usually maintains that in this life it is not given to us to know God's purpose in allowing particular instances of suffering. Hence, the direct attack against premise (1) cannot succeed and violates basic beliefs associated with theism.

The best procedure for the theist to follow in rejecting premise (1) is the indirect procedure. This procedure I shall call "the G. E. Moore shift," so-called in honor of the twentieth century philosopher, G. E. Moore, who used it to great effect in dealing with the arguments of the skeptics. Skeptical philosophers such as David Hume have advanced ingenious arguments to prove that no one can know of the existence of any material object. The premises of their arguments employ plausible principles, principles which many philosophers have tried to reject directly, but only with questionable success. Moore's procedure was altogether different. Instead of arguing directly against the premises of the skeptic's arguments, he simply noted that the premises implied, for example, that he (Moore) did not know of the existence of a pencil. Moore then proceeded indirectly against the skeptic's premises by arguing:

I do know that this pencil exists.
If the skeptic's principles are correct I cannot know of the existence of this pencil.

∴ The skeptic's principles (at least one) must be incorrect.

Moore then noted that his argument is just as valid as the skeptic's, that both of their arguments contain the premise "If the skeptic's principles are correct Moore cannot know of the existence of this pencil," and concluded that the only way to choose between the two arguments (Moore's and the skeptic's) is by deciding which of the first premises it is more rational to believe—Moore's premise "I do know that this pencil exists" or the skeptic's premise asserting that his skeptical principles are correct. Moore concluded that his own first premise was the more rational of the two.[6]

Before we see how the theist may apply the G. E. Moore shift to the basic argument for atheism, we should note the general strategy of the shift. We're given an argument: *p, q*, therefore, *r*. Instead of arguing directly against *p*, another argument is constructed— not-*r, q*, therefore, not-*p*—which begins with the denial of the conclusion of the first argument, keeps its second premise, and ends with the denial of the first premise as its conclusion. Compare, for example, these two:

I.	II.
p	not-*r*
q	*q*
———	———
r	not-*p*

It is a truth of logic that If I is valid II must be valid as well. Since the arguments are the same so far as the second premise is concerned, any choice between them must concern their respective first premises. To argue against the first premise (*p*) by constructing the counter argument II is to employ the G. E. Moore shift.

Applying the G. E. Moore shift against the first premise of the basic argument for atheism, the theist can argue as follows:

not-3. There exists an omnipotent, omniscient, wholly good being.
2. An omniscient, wholly good being would prevent the occurrence of any intense suffering it could, unless it could not do so without thereby losing some greater good or permitting some evil equally bad or worse.

therefore,

not-1. It is not the case that there exist instances of intense suffering which an omnipotent, omniscient being could have prevented without thereby losing some greater good or permitting some evil equally bad or worse.

We now have two arguments: the basic argument for atheism from (1) and (2) to (3), and the theist's best response, the argument from (not-3) and (2) to (not-1). What the theist then says about (1) is that he has rational grounds for believing in the existence of the theistic God (not-3), accepts (2) as true, and sees that (not-1) follows from (not-3) and (2). He concludes, therefore, that he has rational grounds for rejecting (1). Having rational grounds for rejecting (1), the theist concludes that the basic argument for atheism is mistaken.

III

We've had a look at a forceful argument for atheism and what seems to be the theist's best response to that argument. If one is persuaded by the argument for atheism, as I find myself to be, how might one best view the position of the theist? Of course, he will view the theist as having a false belief, just as the theist will view the atheist as having a false belief. But what position should the atheist take concerning the *rationality* of the theist's belief? There are three major positions an atheist might take, positions which we may think of as some varieties of atheism. First, the atheist may believe that no one is rationally justified in believing that the theistic God exists. Let us call this position "unfriendly atheism." Second, the atheist may hold no belief concerning whether any theist is or isn't rationally justified in believing that the theistic God exists. Let us call this view "indifferent atheism." Finally, the atheist may believe that some theists are rationally justified in believing that the theistic God exists. This view we shall call "friendly atheism." In this final part of the paper I propose to discuss and defend the position of friendly atheism.

If no one can be rationally justified in believing a false proposition then friendly atheism is a paradoxical, if not incoherent position. But surely the truth of a belief is not a necessary condition of someone's being rationally justified in having that belief. So in holding that someone is rationally justified in believing that the theistic God exists, the friendly atheist is not committed to thinking that the theist has a true belief. What he is committed to is that the theist has rational grounds for his belief, a belief the atheist rejects and is convinced he is rationally justified in rejecting. But is this possible? Can someone, like our friendly atheist, hold a belief, be convinced that he is rationally justified in holding that belief, and yet believe that someone else is equally justified in believing the opposite? Surely this is possible. Suppose your friends see you off on a flight to Hawaii. Hours after take-off they learn that your plane has gone down at sea. After a twenty-four hour search, no survivors have been found. Under these circumstances they are rationally justified in believing that you have perished. But it is hardly rational for you to believe this, as you bob up and down in your life vest, wondering why the search planes have failed to spot you. Indeed, to amuse yourself while awaiting your fate, you might very well reflect on the fact that your friends are rationally justified in believing that you are now dead, a proposition you disbelieve and are rationally justified in disbelieving. So, too, perhaps an atheist may be rationally justified in his atheistic belief and yet hold that some theists are rationally justified in believing just the opposite of what he believes.

What sort of grounds might a theist have for believing that God exists? Well, he might endeavor to justify his belief by appealing to one or more of the traditional arguments: Ontological, Cosmological, Teleological, Moral, etc. Second, he might appeal to certain aspects of religious experience, perhaps even his own religious experience. Third, he might try to justify theism as a plausible theory in terms of which we can account for a variety of phenomena. Although an atheist must hold that the theistic God does not exist, can he not also believe, and be justified in so believing, that some of these "justifications of theism" do actually rationally justify some theists in their belief that there exists a supremely good, omnipotent, omniscient being? It seems to me that he can.

If we think of the long history of theistic belief and the special situations in which people are sometimes placed, it is perhaps as absurd to think that no one was ever rationally justified in believing that the theistic God exists as it is to think that no one was ever justified in believing that human beings would never walk on the moon. But in suggesting that friendly atheism is preferable to unfriendly atheism, I don't mean to rest the case on what some human beings might reasonably have believed in the eleventh or thirteenth century. The more interesting question is whether some people in modern society, people who are aware of the usual grounds for belief and disbelief and are acquainted to some degree with modern science, are yet rationally justified in accepting theism. Friendly atheism is a significant position only if it answers this question in the affirmative.

It is not difficult for an atheist to be friendly when he has reason to believe that the theist could not reasonably be expected to be acquainted with the grounds for disbelief that he (the atheist) possesses. For then the atheist may take the view that some theists are rationally justified in holding to theism, but would not be so were they to be acquainted with the grounds for disbelief—those grounds being sufficient to tip the scale in favor of atheism when balanced against the reasons the theist has in support of his belief.

Friendly atheism becomes paradoxical, however, when the atheist contemplates believing that the theist has all the grounds for atheism that he, the atheist, has, and yet is rationally justified in maintaining his theistic belief. But even so excessively friendly a view as this perhaps can be held by the atheist if he also has some reason to think that the grounds for theism are not as telling as the theist is justified in taking them to be.[7]

In this paper I've presented what I take to be a strong argument for atheism, pointed out what I think is the theist's best response to that argument, distinguished three positions an atheist might take concerning the rationality of theistic belief, and made some remarks in defense of the position called "friendly atheism." I'm aware that the central points of the paper are not likely to be warmly received by many philosophers. Philosophers who are atheists tend to be tough minded—holding that there are no good reasons for supposing that theism is true. And theists tend either to reject the view that the existence of evil provides rational grounds for atheism or to hold that religious belief has nothing to do with reason and evidence at all. But such is the way of philosophy.[8]

Notes

1   Some philosophers have contended that the existence of evil is *logically inconsistent* with the existence of the theistic God. No one, I think, has succeeded in establishing such an extravagant claim. Indeed, granted incompatibilism, there is a fairly compelling argument for the view that the existence of evil is logically consistent with the existence of the theistic God. (For a lucid statement of this argument see Alvin Plantinga, *God, Freedom, and Evil* (New York, 1974), pp. 29–59). There remains, however, what we may call the *evidential* form—as opposed to the *logical* form—of the problem of evil: the view that the variety and profusion of evil in our world, although perhaps not logically inconsistent with the existence of the theistic God, provides, nevertheless, *rational support* for atheism. In this paper I shall be concerned solely with the evidential form of the problem, the form of the problem which, I think, presents a rather severe difficulty for theism.

2   If there is some good, *G*, greater than an evil, (1) will be false for the trivial reason that no matter what evil, *E*, we pick the conjunctive good state of affairs consisting of *G* and *E* will outweigh *E* and be such that an omnipotent being could not obtain it without permitting *E*. (See Alvin Plantinga, *God and Other Minds* [Ithaca, 1967], p. 167.) To avoid this objection we may insert "unreplaceable" into our premises (1) and (2) between "some" and "greater." If *E* isn't required for *G*, and *G* is better than *G* plus *E*, then the good conjunctive state of affairs composed of *G* and *E* would be *replaceable* by the greater good of *G* alone. For the sake of simplicity, however, I will ignore this complication both in the formulation and discussion of premises (1) and (2).

3   Three clarifying points need to be made in connection with (i). First, by "good" I don't

mean to exclude the fulfillment of certain moral principles. Perhaps preventing s_1 would preclude certain actions prescribed by the principles of justice. I shall allow that the satisfaction of certain principles of justice may be a good that outweighs the evil of s_1. Second, even though (i) may suggest it, I don't mean to limit the good in question to something that would *follow in time* the occurrence of s_1. And, finally, we should perhaps not fault *OG* if the good *G*, that would be loss were s_1 prevented, is not actually greater than s_1, but merely such that allowing s_1 and *G*, as opposed to preventing s_1 and thereby losing *G*, would not alter the balance between good and evil. For reasons of simplicity, I have left this point out in stating (i), with the result that (i) is perhaps a bit stronger than it should be.

4   See Ivan's speech in Book V, Chapter IV of *The Brothers Karamazov.*

5   One might object that the conclusion of this paragraph is stronger than the reasons given warrant. For it is one thing to argue that it is unreasonable to think that (1) is false and another thing to conclude that we are therefore justified in accepting (1) as true. There are propositions such that believing them is much more reasonable than disbelieving them, and yet are such that *withholding judgment* about them is more reasonable than believing them. To take an example of Chisholm's: it is more reasonable to believe that the Pope will be in Rome (on some arbitrarily picked future date) than to believe that he won't; but it is perhaps more reasonable to suspend judgment on the question of the Pope's whereabouts on that particular date, than to believe that he will be in Rome. Thus, it might be objected, that while we've shown that believing (1) is more reasonable than disbelieving (1), we haven't shown that believing (1) is more reasonable than withholding belief. My answer to this objection is that there are things we know which render (1) probable to the degree that it is more reasonable to believe (1) than to suspend judgment on (1). What are these things we know? First, I think, is the fact that there is an enormous variety and profusion of intense human and animal suffering in our world. Second, is the fact that much of this suffering seems quite unrelated to any greater goods (or the absence of equal or greater evils) that might justify it. And, finally, there is the fact that such suffering as is related to greater goods (or the absence of equal or greater evils) does not, in many cases, seem so intimately related as to require its permission by an omnipotent being bent on securing those goods (the absence of those evils). These facts, I am claiming, make it more reasonable to accept (1) than to withhold judgment on (1).

6   See, for example, the two chapters on Hume in G. E. Moore, *Some Main Problems of Philosophy* (London, 1953).

7   Suppose that I add a long sum of numbers three times and get result *x*. I inform you of this so that you have pretty much the same evidence I have for the claim that the sum of the numbers is *x*. You then use your calculator twice over and arrive at result *y*. You, then, are justified in believing that the sum of the numbers is *not x*. However, knowing that your calculator has been damaged and is therefore unreliable, and that you have no reason to think that it is damaged, *I* may reasonably believe not only that the sum of the numbers is *x*, but also that you are justified in believing that the sum is not *x*. Here is a case, then, where you have all of my evidence for *p*, and yet I can reasonably believe that you are justified in believing not-*p*—for I have reason to believe that your grounds for not-*p* are not as telling as you are justified in taking them to be.

8   I am indebted to my colleagues at Purdue University, particularly to Ted Ulrich and Lilly Russow, and to philosophers at The University of Nebraska, Indiana State University, and the University of Wisconsin at Milwaukee for helpful criticisms of earlier versions of this paper.

Questions for reflection

1   Describe in your own words Professor Rowe's evidential argument from evil. Do you accept the premises as stated? Do you agree with the conclusion? Explain.
2   Regarding the case of the fawn's suffering, Professor Rowe raises the following question: "Is it reasonable to believe that there is some greater good so intimately connected to that suffering that even an omnipotent, omniscient being could not have obtained that good without permitting that suffering or some evil at least as bad?" What is your response? What ramifications regarding theism/atheism follow from your response?
3   What is "friendly atheism"? Do you think both atheists and theists can each be rationally justified in their beliefs about God given the existence of evil in the world? If so, what does this imply about beliefs?
4   How would you define evil? Does your definition affect the evidential argument as presented in this essay? If so, how?
5   Compare and contrast this argument from evil with Professor Hick's soul-making theodicy. Does the theodicy adequately address examples of intense pain and suffering such as presented in the fawn case? Explain.

Further reading

Evidential Argument from Evil. http://www.infidels.org/library/modern/nontheism/atheism/evil.html (A webpage with links to a number of essays on the topic.)

Daniel Howard-Snyder, ed. (1996) *The Evidential Argument from Evil*. Indianapolis, IN: Indiana University Press. (A scholarly collection of essays from a variety of perspectives.)

J. L. Mackie (1955) "Evil and Omnipotence," *Mind* 64: 200–12. (A very influential formulation of an argument for atheism given evil; consists of a logical rather than an evidential type of argument.)

Michael Martin (1990) *Atheism*. Philadelphia, PA: Temple University Press. (Includes a wide-ranging critique of theistic responses to the problem of evil; note especially chapters 14–17.)

Michael L. Peterson (1998) *God and Evil: An Introduction to the Issues*. Boulder, CO: Westview Press. (A very lucid general introduction to the topic.)

William L. Rowe (1991) "Ruminations about Evil," *Philosophical Perspectives* 5, 69–88. (More reflections on the evidential argument presented above.)

Chapter 51

John Hick

A SOUL-MAKING THEODICY

John Hick is Danforth Professor of the Philosophy of Religion, Emeritus, at Claremont Graduate University. His book, *Evil and the God of Love*, is generally considered to be one of the most important books written in the past century on the problem of evil. In the following selection he argues for what is often referred to as the "soul-making theodicy." Unlike a *defense* against the problem of evil (such as the free will defense offered in the following chapter), which is a response to an argument against God's allowing evil, a *theodicy* is an attempt to justify God's allowing evil in the world. Professor Hick contrasts an "Augustinian type" theodicy—one which sees evil as the result of a cosmic moral fall by beings with free will—with what he calls an "Irenaean type" theodicy, developed from ideas of the early Christian bishop Ireneaus (120–202 CE). He briefly explains why he finds an Augustinian theodicy unsatisfactory, then expounds upon and defends his soul-making theodicy in which humans begin as imperfect and immature beings who can, through their own free responses within a challenging environment, gradually grow towards what God seeks for them.

Can a world in which sadistic cruelty often has its way, in which selfish lovelessness is so rife, in which there are debilitating diseases, crippling accidents, bodily and mental decay, insanity, and all manner of natural disasters be regarded as the expression of infinite creative goodness? Certainly all this could never by itself lead anyone to believe in the existence of a limitlessly powerful God. And yet even in a world which contains these things innumerable men and women have believed and do believe in the reality of an infinite creative goodness, which they call God. The theodicy project starts at this point, with an already operating belief in God, embodied in human living, and attempts to show that this belief is not rendered irrational by the fact of evil. It attempts to explain how it is that the universe, assumed to be created and ultimately ruled by a limitlessly good and limitlessly powerful Being, is as it is, including all the pain and suffering and all the wickedness and folly that we find around us and within us. The theodicy project is thus an exercise in metaphysical construction, in the sense that it consists in the formation and criticism of large-scale hypotheses concerning the nature and process of the universe.

Since a theodicy both starts from and tests belief in the reality of God, it naturally takes different forms in relation to different concepts of God. In this essay I shall be discussing the project of a specifically Christian theodicy; I shall not be attempting the further and even more difficult work of comparative theodicy, leading in turn to the question of a global theodicy.

The two main demands upon a theodicy hypothesis are (1) that it be internally coherent, and (2) that it be consistent with the data both of the religious tradition on which it is based, and of the world, in respect both of the latter's general character as revealed by scientific enquiry and of the specific facts of moral and natural evil. These two criteria demand, respectively, possibility and plausibility.

Traditionally, Christian theology has centered upon the concept of God as both limitlessly powerful and limitlessly good and loving; and it is this concept of deity that gives rise to the problem of evil as a threat to theistic faith. The threat was definitively expressed in Stendhal's bombshell, "The only excuse for God is that he does not exist!" The theodicy project is the attempt to offer a different view of the universe which is both possible and plausible and which does not ignite Stendhal's bombshell.

Christian thought has always included a certain range of variety, and in the area of theodicy it offers two broad types of approach. The Augustinian approach, representing until fairly recently the majority report of the Christian mind, hinges upon the idea of the fall, which has in turn brought about the disharmony of nature. This type of theodicy is developed today as "the free will defense." The Irenaean approach, representing in the past a minority report, hinges upon the creation of humankind through the evolutionary process as an immature creature living in a challenging and therefore person-making world. I shall indicate very briefly why I do not find the first type of theodicy satisfactory, and then spend the remainder of this essay in exploring the second type.

In recent years the philosophical discussion of the problem of evil has been dominated by the free-will defense. A major effort has been made by Alvin Plantinga and a number of other Christian philosophers to show that it is logically possible that a limitlessly powerful and limitlessly good God is responsible for the existence of this world. For all evil may ultimately be due to misuses of creaturely freedom. But it may nevertheless be better for God to have created free than unfree beings; and it is logically possible that any and all free beings whom God might create would, as a matter of contingent fact, misuse their freedom by falling into sin. In that case it would be logically impossible for God to have created a world containing free beings and yet not containing sin and the suffering which sin brings with it. Thus it is logically possible, despite the fact of evil, that the existing universe is the work of a limitlessly good creator.

These writers are in effect arguing that the traditional Augustinian type of theodicy, based upon the fall from grace of free finite creatures—first angels and then human beings—and a consequent going wrong of the physical world, is not logically impossible. I am in fact doubtful whether their argument is sound, and will return to the question later. But even if it should be sound, I suggest that their argument wins only a Pyrrhic victory, since the logical possibility that it would establish is one which, for very many people today, is fatally lacking in plausibility. For most educated inhabitants of the modern world regard the biblical story of Adam and Eve, and their temptation by the devil, as myth rather than as history; and they believe that so far from having been created finitely perfect and then falling, humanity evolved out of lower forms of life, emerging in a morally, spiritually, and culturally primitive state. Further, they reject as incredible the idea that earthquake and flood, disease, decay, and death are consequences either of a human fall, or of a prior fall of angelic beings who are now exerting an evil influence upon the earth. They see all this as part of a pre-scientific world view, along with the stories of the world having been created in six days and of the sun standing still for twenty-four hours at Joshua's command. One cannot, strictly speaking, disprove any of these ancient biblical myths and sagas, or refute their confident elaboration in the medieval Christian picture of the universe. But those of us for whom the resulting theodicy, even if logically possible, is radically implausible, must look elsewhere for light on the problem of evil.

I believe that we find the light that we need in the main alternative strand of Christian thinking, which goes back to important constructive suggestions by the early Hellenistic Fathers of the Church, particularly St. Irenaeus (A.D. 120–202). Irenaeus himself did not develop a theodicy, but he did—together with other Greek-speaking Christian writers of that period, such as Clement of Alexandria—build a framework of thought within which a theodicy became possible which does not depend upon the idea of the fall, and which is consonant with modern knowledge concerning the origins of the human race. This theodicy cannot, as such, be attributed to Irenaeus. We should rather speak of a type of theodicy, presented in varying ways by different subsequent thinkers (the greatest of whom has been Friedrich Schleiermacher), of which Irenaeus can properly be regarded as the patron saint.

The central theme out of which this Irenaean type of theodicy has arisen is the two-stage conception of the creation of humankind, first in the "image" and then in the "likeness" of God. Re-expressing this in modern terms, the first stage was the gradual production of *homo sapiens*, through the long evolutionary process, as intelligent ethical and religious animals. The human being is an animal, one of the varied forms of earthly life and continuous as such with the whole realm of animal existence. But the human being is uniquely intelligent, having evolved a large and immensely complex brain. Further, the human being is ethical—that is, a gregarious as well as an intelligent animal, able to realize and respond to the complex demands of social life. And the human being is a religious animal, with an innate tendency to experience the world in terms of the presence and activity of supernatural beings and powers. This then is early *homo sapiens*, the intelligent social animal capable of awareness of the divine. But early *homo sapiens* is not the Adam and Eve of Augustinian theology, living in perfect harmony with self, with nature, and with God. On the contrary, the life of this being must have been a constant struggle against a hostile environment, and capable of savage violence against one's fellow human beings, particularly outside one's own immediate group; and this being's concepts of the divine were primitive and often blood-thirsty. Thus existence "in the image of God" was a potentiality for knowledge of and relationship with one's Maker rather than such knowledge and relationship as a fully realized state. In other words, people were created as spiritually and morally immature creatures, at the beginning of a long process of further growth and development, which constitutes the second stage of God's creative work. In this second stage, of which we are a part, the intelligent, ethical, and religious animal is being brought through one's own free responses into what Irenaeus

called the divine "likeness." The human animal is being created into a child of God. Irenaeus' own terminology (*eikon, homoiosis; imago, similitudo*) has no particular merit, based
as it is on a misunderstanding of the Hebrew parallelism in Genesis 1:26; but his conception of a two-stage creation of the human, with perfection lying in the future rather
than in the past, is of fundamental importance. The notion of the fall was not basic to
this picture, although it was to become basic to the great drama of salvation depicted by
St. Augustine and accepted within western Christendom, including the churches stem-
ming from the Reformation, until well into the nineteenth century. Irenaeus himself
however could not, in the historical knowledge of his time, question the fact of the fall;
though he treated it as a relatively minor lapse, a youthful error, rather than as the infinite crime and cosmic disaster which has ruined the whole creation. But today we can
acknowledge that there is no evidence at all of a period in the distant past when humankind was in the ideal state of a fully realized "child of God." We can accept that, so far as
actual events in time are concerned, there never was a fall from an original righteousness and grace. If we want to continue to use the term fall, because of its hallowed place
in the Christian tradition, we must use it to refer to the immense gap between what we
actually are and what in the divine intention is eventually to be. But we must not blur our
awareness that the ideal state is not something already enjoyed and lost, but is a future
and as yet unrealized goal. The reality is not a perfect creation which has gone tragically
wrong, but a still continuing creative process whose completion lies in the eschaton.

Let us now try to formulate a contemporary version of the Irenaean type of theodicy, based on this suggestion of the initial creation of humankind, not as a finitely
perfect, but as an immature creature at the beginning of a long process of further
growth and development. We may begin by asking why one should have been created as
an imperfect and developing creature rather than as the perfect being whom God is presumably intending to create? The answer, I think, consists in two considerations which
converge in their practical implications, one concerned with the human's relationship to
God and the other with the relationship to other human beings. As to the first, we could
have the picture of God creating finite beings, whether angels or persons, directly in his
own presence, so that in being conscious of that which is other than one's self the creature is automatically conscious of God, the limitless divine reality and power, goodness
and love, knowledge and wisdom, towering above one's self. In such a situation the disproportion between Creator and creatures would be so great that the latter would have
no freedom in relation to God; they would indeed not exist as independent autonomous
persons. For what freedom could finite beings have in an immediate consciousness of
the presence of the one who has created them, who knows them through and through,
who is limitlessly powerful as well as limitlessly loving and good, and who claims their
total obedience? In order to be a person, exercising some measure of genuine freedom,
the creature must be brought into existence, not in the immediate divine presence, but
at a "distance" from God. This "distance" cannot of course be spatial; for God is omnipresent. It must be an epistemic distance, a distance in the cognitive dimension. And
the Irenaean hypothesis is that this "distance" consists, in the case of humans, in their
existence within and as part of a world which functions as an autonomous system and
from within which God is not overwhelmingly evident. It is a world, in Bonhoeffer's
phrase, *etsi deus non daretur*, as if there were no God. Or rather, it is religiously ambiguous, capable both of being seen as a purely natural phenomenon and of being seen as
God's creation and experienced as mediating his presence. In such a world one can exist

as a person over against the Creator. One has space to exist as a finite being, a space created by the epistemic distance from God and protected by one's basic cognitive freedom, one's freedom to open or close oneself to the dawning awareness of God which is experienced naturally by a religious animal. This Irenaean picture corresponds, I suggest, to our actual human situation. Emerging within the evolutionary process as part of the continuum of animal life, in a universe which functions in accordance with its own laws and whose workings can be investigated and described without reference to a creator, the human being has a genuine, even awesome, freedom in relation to one's Maker. The human being is free to acknowledge and worship God; and is free—particularly since the emergence of human individuality and the beginnings of critical consciousness during the first millennium B.C.—to doubt the reality of God.

Within such a situation there is the possibility of the human being coming freely to know and love one's Maker. Indeed, if the end-state which God is seeking to bring about is one in which finite persons have come in their own freedom to know and love him, this requires creating them initially in a state which is not that of their already knowing and loving him. For it is logically impossible to create beings already in a state of having come into that state by their own free choices.

The other consideration, which converges with this in pointing to something like the human situation as we experience it, concerns our human moral nature. We can approach it by asking why humans should not have been created at this epistemic distance from God, and yet at the same time as morally perfect beings? That persons could have been created morally perfect and yet free, so that they would always in fact choose rightly, has been argued by such critics of the free-will defense in theodicy as Antony Flew and J. L. Mackie, and argued against by Alvin Plantinga and other upholders of that form of theodicy. On the specific issue defined in the debate between them, it appears to me that the criticism of the freewill defense stands. It appears to me that a perfectly good being, although formally free to sin, would in fact never do so. If we imagine such a being in a morally frictionless environment, involving no stresses or temptation, then we must assume that one would exemplify the ethical equivalent of Newton's first law of motion, which states that a moving body will continue in uniform motion until interfered with by some outside force. By analogy, a perfectly good being would continue in the same moral course forever, there being nothing in the environment to throw one off it. But even if we suppose the morally perfect being to exist in an imperfect world, in which one is subject to temptations, it still follows that, in virtue of moral perfection, one will always overcome those temptations—as in the case, according to orthodox Christian belief, of Jesus Christ. It is, to be sure, logically possible, as Plantinga and others argue, that a free being, simply as such, may at any time contingently decide to sin. However, a responsible free being does not act randomly, but on the basis of moral nature. And a free being whose nature is wholly and unqualifiedly good will accordingly never in fact sin.

But if God could, without logical contradiction, have created humans as wholly good free beings, why did he not do so? Why was humanity not initially created in possession of all the virtues, instead of having to acquire them through the long hard struggle of life as we know it? The answer, I suggest, appeals to the principle that virtues which have been formed within the agent as a hard won deposit of his own right decisions in situations of challenge and temptation, are intrinsically more valuable than virtues created within him ready made and without any effort on his own part. This principle expresses a basic value-judgment, which cannot be established by argument but which one can only present, in the hope that it will be as morally plausible, and indeed compelling, to others as to oneself. It is, to repeat, the judgement that a moral goodness which exists as the agent's initial given nature, without ever having been chosen by him in the face of temptations to the contrary, is intrinsically less valuable than a moral goodness which has been built up through the agent's own responsible choices through time in the face of alternative possibilities.

If, then, God's purpose was to create finite persons embodying the most valuable kind of moral goodness, he would have to create them, not as already perfect beings but rather as imperfect creatures who can then attain to the more valuable kind of goodness through their own free choices as in the course of their personal and social history new responses prompt new insights, opening up new moral possibilities, and providing a milieu in which the most valuable kind of moral nature can be developed.

We have thus far, then, the hypothesis that one is created at an epistemic distance from God in order to come freely to know and love the Maker; and that one is at the same time created as a morally immature and imperfect being in order to attain through freedom the most valuable quality of goodness. The end sought, according to this hypothesis, is the full realization of the human potentialities in a unitary spiritual and moral perfection in the divine kingdom. And the question we have to ask is whether humans as we know them, and the world as we know it, are compatible with this hypothesis.

Clearly we cannot expect to be able to deduce our actual world in its concrete character, and our actual human nature as part of it, from the general concept of spiritually and morally immature creatures developing ethically in an appropriate environment. No doubt there is an immense range of possible worlds, any one of which, if actualized, would exemplify this concept. All that we can hope to do is to show that our actual world is one of these. And when we look at our human situation as part of the evolving life on this planet we can, I think, see that it fits this specification. As animal organisms, integral to the whole ecology of life, we are programmed for survival. In pursuit of survival, primitives not only killed other animals for food but fought other human beings when their vital interests conflicted. The life of prehistoric persons must indeed have been a constant struggle to stay alive, prolonging an existence which was, in Hobbes' phrase, "poor, nasty, brutish and short." And in his basic animal self-regardingness humankind was, and is, morally imperfect. In saying this I am assuming that the essence of moral evil is selfishness, the sacrificing of others to one's own interests. It consists, in Kantian terminology, in treating others, not as ends in themselves, but as means to one's own ends. This is what the survival instinct demands. And yet we are also capable of love, of self-giving in a common cause, of a conscience which responds to others in their needs and dangers. And with the development of civilization we see the growth of moral insight, the glimpsing and gradual assimilation of higher ideals, and tension between our animality and our ethical values. But that the human being has a lower as well as a higher nature, that one is an animal as well as a potential child of God, and that one's moral goodness is won from a struggle with one's own innate selfishness, is inevitable given one's continuity with the other forms of animal life. Further, the human animal is not responsible for having come into existence as an animal. The ultimate responsibility for humankind's existence, as a morally imperfect creature, can only rest with the Creator. The human does not, in one's own degree of freedom and responsibility, choose one's origin, but rather one's destiny.

This then, in brief outline, is the answer of the Irenaean type of theodicy to the question of the origin of moral evil: the general fact of humankind's basic self-regarding animality is an aspect of creation as part of the realm of organic life; and this basic self-regardingness has been expressed over the centuries both in sins of individual selfishness and in the much more massive sins of corporate selfishness, institutionalized in slavery and exploitation and all the many and complex forms of social injustice.

But nevertheless our sinful nature in a sinful world is the matrix within which God is gradually creating children of God out of human animals. For it is as men and women freely respond to the claim of God upon their lives, transmuting their animality into the structure of divine worship, that the creation of humanity is taking place. And in its concrete character this response consists in every form of moral goodness, from unselfish love in individual personal relationships to the dedicated and selfless striving to end exploitation and to create justice within and between societies.

But one cannot discuss moral evil without at the same time discussing the non-moral evil of pain and suffering. (I propose to mean by "pain" physical pain, including the pains of hunger and thirst; and by "suffering" the mental and emotional pain of loneliness, anxiety, remorse, lack of love, fear, grief, envy, etc.). For what constitutes moral evil as evil is the fact that it causes pain and suffering. It is impossible to conceive of an instance of moral evil, or sin, which is not productive of pain or suffering to anyone at any time. But in addition to moral evil there is another source of pain and suffering in the structure of the physical world, which produces storms, earthquakes, and floods and which afflicts the human body with diseases—cholera, epilepsy, cancer, malaria, arthritis, rickets, meningitis, etc.—as well as with broken bones and other outcomes of physical accident. It is true that a great deal both of pain and of suffering is humanly caused, not only by the inhumanity of man to man but also by the stresses of our individual and corporate lifestyles, causing many disorders—not only lung cancer and cirrhosis of the liver but many cases of heart disease, stomach and other ulcers, strokes, etc.—as well as accidents. But there remain nevertheless, in the natural world itself, permanent causes of human pain and suffering. And we have to ask why an unlimitedly good and unlimitedly powerful God should have created so dangerous a world, both as regards its purely natural hazards of earthquake and flood, etc., and as regards the liability of the human body to so many ills, both psychosomatic and purely somatic.

The answer offered by the Irenaean type of theodicy follows from and is indeed integrally bound up with its account of the origin of moral evil. We have the hypothesis of humankind being brought into being within the evolutionary process as a spiritually and morally immature creature, and then growing and developing through the exercise of freedom in this religiously ambiguous world. We can now ask what sort of a world would constitute an appropriate environment for this second stage of creation? The development of human personality—moral, spiritual, and intellectual—is a product of challenge and response. It does not occur in a static situation demanding no exertion and no choices. So far as intellectual development is concerned, this is a well-established principle which underlies the whole modern educational process, from preschool nurseries designed to provide a rich and stimulating environment, to all forms of higher education designed to challenge the intellect. At a basic level the essential part played in learning by the learner's own active response to environment was strikingly demonstrated by the Held and Hein experiment with kittens.[1] Of two litter-mate kittens in the same artificial environment one was free to exercise its own freedom and intelligence in exploring the environment, whilst the other was suspended in a kind of "gondola" which moved whenever and wherever the free kitten moved. Thus the second kitten had a similar succession of visual experiences as the first, but did not exert itself or make any choices in obtaining them. And whereas the first kitten learned in the normal way to conduct itself safely within its environment, the second did not. With no interaction with a challenging environment there was no development in its behavioral patterns. And I think we can safely say that the intellectual development of humanity has been due to interaction with an objective environment functioning in accordance with its own laws, an environment which we have had actively to explore and to co-operate with in order to escape its perils and exploit its benefits. In a world devoid both of dangers to be avoided and rewards to be won we may assume that there would have been virtually no development of the human intellect and imagination, and hence of either the sciences or the arts, and hence of human civilization or culture.

The fact of an objective world within which one has to learn to live, on penalty of pain or death, is also basic to the development of one's moral nature. For it is because the world is one in which men and women can suffer harm—by violence, disease, accident, starvation, etc.—that our actions affecting one another have moral significance. A morally wrong act is, basically, one which harms some part of the human community; whilst a morally right action is, on the contrary, one which prevents or neutralizes harm or which preserves or increases human well being. Now we can imagine a paradise in which no one can ever come to any harm. It could be a world which, instead of having its own fixed structure, would be plastic to human wishes. Or it could be a world with a fixed structure, and hence the possibility of damage and pain, but whose structure is suspended or adjusted by special divine action whenever necessary to avoid human pain. Thus, for example, in such a miraculously pain-free world one who falls accidentally off a high building would presumably float unharmed to the ground; bullets would become insubstantial when fired at a human body; poisons would cease to poison; water to drown, and so on. We can at least begin to imagine such a world. And a good deal of the older discussion of the problem of evil—for example in Part xi of Hume's *Dialogues Concerning Natural Religion*—assumed that it must be the intention of a limitlessly good and powerful Creator to make for human creatures a pain-free environment; so that the very existence of pain is evidence against the existence of God. But such an assumption overlooks the fact that a world in which there can be no pain or suffering would also be one in which there can be no moral choices and hence no possibility of moral growth and development. For in a situation in which no one can ever suffer injury or be liable to pain or suffering there would be no distinction between right and wrong action. No action would be morally wrong, because no action could have harmful consequences; and likewise no action would be morally right in contrast to wrong. Whatever the values of such a world, it clearly could not serve a purpose of the development of its inhabitants from self-regarding animality to self-giving love.

Thus the hypothesis of a divine purpose in which finite persons are created at an epistemic distance from God, in order that they may gradually become children of God through their own moral and spiritual choices, requires that their environment, instead of being a pain-free and stress-free paradise, be broadly the kind of world of which we find ourselves to be a part. It requires that it be such as to provoke the theological problem of evil. For it requires that it be an environment which offers challenges to be met, problems to be solved, dangers to be faced, and which accordingly involves real possibilities of hardship, disaster, failure, defeat, and misery as well as of delight and happiness, success, triumph and achievement. For it is by grappling with the real problems of a real environment, in which a person is one form of life among many, and which is not designed to minister exclusively to one's well-being, that one can develop in intelligence and in such qualities as courage and determination. And it is in the relationships of human beings with one another, in the context of this struggle to survive and flourish, that they can develop the higher values of mutual love and care, of self-sacrifice for others, and of commitment to a common good.

To summarize thus far:

(1)   The divine intention in relation to humankind, according to our hypothesis, is to create perfect finite personal beings in filial relationship with their Maker.

(2)   It is logically impossible for humans to be created already in this perfect state, because in its spiritual aspect it involves coming freely to an uncoerced consciousness of God from a situation of epistemic distance, and in its moral aspect, freely choosing the good in preference to evil.

(3)   Accordingly the human being was initially created through the evolutionary process, as a spiritually and morally immature creature, and as part of a world which is both religiously ambiguous and ethically demanding.

(4)   Thus that one is morally imperfect (i.e., that there is moral evil), and that the world is a challenging and even dangerous environment (i.e., that there is natural evil), are necessary aspects of the present stage of the process through which God is gradually creating perfected finite persons.

In terms of this hypothesis, as we have developed it thus far, then, both the basic moral evil in the human heart and the natural evils of the world are compatible with the existence of a Creator who is unlimited in both goodness and power. But is the hypothesis plausible as well as possible? The principal threat to its plausibility comes, I think, from the sheer amount and intensity of both moral and natural evil. One can accept the principle that in order to arrive at a freely chosen goodness one must start out in a state of moral immaturity and imperfection. But is it necessary that there should be the depths of demonic malice and cruelty which each generation has experienced, and which we have seen above all in recent history in the Nazi attempt to exterminate the Jewish population of Europe? Can any future fulfillment be worth such horrors? This was Dostoyevsky's haunting question: "Imagine that you are creating a fabric of human destiny with the object of making men happy in the end, giving them peace and rest at last, but that it was essential and inevitable to torture to death only one tiny creature—that baby beating its breast with its fist, for instance—and to found that edifice on its unavenged tears, would you consent to be the architect on those conditions?"[2] The theistic answer is one which may be true but which takes so large a view that it baffles the imagination. Intellectually one may be able to see, but emotionally one cannot be expected to feel, its truth; and in that sense it cannot satisfy us. For the theistic answer is that if we take with full seriousness the value of human freedom and responsibility, as essential to the eventual creation of perfected children of God, then we cannot consistently want God to revoke that freedom when its wrong exercise becomes intolerable to us. From our vantage point within the historical process we may indeed cry out to God to revoke his gift of freedom, or to overrule it by some secret or open intervention. Such a cry must have come from millions caught in the Jewish Holocaust, or in the yet more recent laying waste of Korea and Vietnam, or from the victims of racism in many parts of the world. And the thought that humankind's moral freedom is indivisible, and can lead eventually to a consummation of limitless value which could never be attained without that freedom, and which is worth any finite suffering in the course of its creation, can be of no comfort to those who are now in the midst of that suffering. But whilst fully acknowledging this, I nevertheless want to insist that this eschatological answer may well be true. Expressed in religious language it tells us to trust in God even in the midst of deep suffering, for in the end we shall participate in his glorious kingdom.

Again, we may grant that a world which is to be a person-making environment cannot be a pain-free paradise but must contain challenges and dangers, with real possibilities of many kinds of accident and disaster, and the pain and suffering which they bring. But need it contain the worst forms of disease and catastrophe? And need misfortune fall upon us with such heartbreaking indiscriminateness? Once again there are answers, which may well be true, and yet once again the truth in this area may offer little in the way of pastoral balm. Concerning the intensity of natural evil, the truth is probably that our judgments of intensity are relative. We might identify some form of natural evil as the worst that there is—say the agony that can be caused by death from cancer—and claim that a loving God would not have allowed this to exist. But in a world in which there was no cancer, something else would then rank as the worst form of natural evil. If we then eliminate this, something else; and so on. And the process would continue until the world was free of all natural evil. For whatever form of evil for the time being remained would be intolerable to the inhabitants of that world. But in removing all occasions of pain and suffering, and hence all challenge and all need for mutual care, we should have converted the world from a person-making into a static environment, which could not elicit moral growth. In short, having accepted that a person-making world must have its dangers and therefore also its tragedies, we must accept that whatever form these take will be intolerable to the inhabitants of that world. There could not be a person-making world devoid of what we call evil; and evils are never tolerable— except for the sake of greater goods which may come out of them.

But accepting that a person-making environment must contain causes of pain and suffering, and that no pain or suffering is going to be acceptable, one of the most daunting and even terrifying features of the world is that calamity strikes indiscriminately. There is no justice in the incidence of disease, accident, disaster and tragedy. The righteous as well as the unrighteous are struck down by illness and afflicted by misfortune. There is no security in goodness, but the good are as likely as the wicked to suffer "the slings and arrows of outrageous fortune." From the time of Job this fact has set a glaring question mark against the goodness of God. But let us suppose that things were otherwise. Let us suppose that misfortune came upon humankind, not haphazardly and therefore unjustly, but justly and therefore not haphazardly. Let us suppose that instead of coming without regard to moral considerations, it was proportioned to desert, so that the sinner was punished and the virtuous rewarded. Would such a dispensation serve a person-making purpose? Surely not. For it would be evident that wrong deeds bring disaster upon the agent whilst good deeds bring health and prosperity; and in such a world truly moral action, action done because it is right, would be impossible. The fact that natural evil is not morally directed, but is a hazard which comes by chance, is thus an intrinsic feature of a person-making world.

In other words, the very mystery of natural evil, the very fact that disasters afflict human beings in contingent, undirected and haphazard ways, is itself a necessary feature of a world that calls forth mutual aid and builds up mutual caring and love. Thus on the one hand it would be completely wrong to say that God sends misfortune upon individuals, so that their death, maiming, starvation or ruin is God's will for them. But on the other hand God has set us in a world containing unpredictable contingencies and dangers, in which unexpected and undeserved calamities may occur to anyone; because only in such a world can mutual caring and love be elicited. As an abstract philosophical hypothesis this may offer little comfort. But translated into religious language it tells us that God's good purpose enfolds the entire process of this world, with all its good and bad contingencies, and that even amidst tragic calamity and suffering we are still within the sphere of his love and are moving towards his kingdom.

But there is one further all-important aspect of the Irenaean type of theodicy, without which all the foregoing would lose its plausibility. This is the eschatological aspect. Our hypothesis depicts persons as still in course of creation towards an end-state of perfected personal community in the divine kingdom. This end-state is conceived of as one in which individual egoity has been transcended in communal unity before God. And in the present phase of that creative process the naturally self-centered human animal has the opportunity freely to respond to God's non-coercive self-disclosures, through the work of prophets and saints, through the resulting religious traditions, and through the individual's religious experience. Such response always has an ethical aspect; for the growing awareness of God is at the same time a growing awareness of the moral claim which God's presence makes upon the way in which we live.

But it is very evident that this person-making process, leading eventually to perfect human community, is not completed on this earth. It is not completed in the life of the individual—or at best only in the few who have attained to sanctification, or moksha, or nirvana on this earth. Clearly the enormous majority of men and women die without having attained to this. As Eric Fromm has said, "The tragedy in the life of most of us is that we die before we are fully born."[3] And therefore if we are ever to reach the full realization of the potentialities of our human nature, this can only be in a continuation of our lives in another sphere of existence after bodily death. And it is equally evident that the perfect all-embracing human community, in which self-regarding concern has been transcended in mutual love, not only has not been realized in this world, but never can be, since hundreds of generations of human beings have already lived and died and accordingly could not be part of any ideal community established at some future moment of earthly history. Thus if the unity of humankind in God's presence is ever to be realized it will have to be in some sphere of existence other than our earth. In short, the fulfillment of the divine purpose, as it is postulated in the Irenaean type of theodicy, presupposes each person's survival, in some form of bodily death, and further living and growing towards that end state. Without such an eschatological fulfillment, this theodicy would collapse.

A theodicy which presupposes and requires an eschatology will thereby be rendered implausible in the minds of many today. I nevertheless do not see how any coherent theodicy can avoid dependence upon an eschatology. Indeed I would go further and say that the belief in the reality of a limitlessly loving and powerful deity must incorporate some kind of eschatology according to which God holds in being the creatures whom he has made for fellowship with himself, beyond bodily death, and brings them into the eternal fellowship which he has intended for them. I have tried elsewhere to argue that such an eschatology is a necessary corollary of ethical monotheism; to argue for the realistic possibility of an after-life or lives, despite the philosophical and empirical arguments against this; and even to spell out some of the general features which human life after death may possibly have.[4] Since all this is a very large task, which would far exceed the bounds of this [essay], I shall not attempt to repeat it here but must refer the reader to my existing discussion of it. It is that extended discussion that constitutes my answer to the question whether an Irenaean theodicy, with its eschatology, may not be as implausible as an Augustinian theodicy, with its human or angelic fall. (If it is, then the latter is doubly implausible; for it also involves an eschatology!)

There is however one particular aspect of eschatology which must receive some treatment here, however brief and inadequate. This is the issue of "universal salvation" versus "heaven and hell" (or perhaps annihilation instead of hell). If the justification of evil within the creative process lies in the limitless and eternal good of the end state to which it leads, then the completeness of the justification must depend upon the completeness, or universality, of the salvation achieved. Only if it includes the entire human race can it justify the sins and sufferings of the entire human race throughout all history. But, having given human beings cognitive freedom, which in turn makes possible moral freedom, can the Creator bring it about that in the end all his human creatures freely turn to God in love and trust? The issue is a very difficult one; but I believe that it is in fact possible to reconcile a full affirmation of human freedom with a belief in the ultimate universal success of God's creative work. We have to accept that creaturely freedom always occurs within the limits of a basic nature that we did not ourselves choose; for this is entailed by the fact of having been created. If then a real though limited freedom does not preclude our being endowed with a certain nature, it does not preclude our being endowed with a basic Godward bias, so that, quoting from another side of St. Augustine's thought, "our hearts are restless until they find their rest in Thee."[5] If this is so, it can be predicted that sooner or later, in our own time and in our own way, we shall all freely come to God; and universal salvation can be affirmed, not as a logical necessity but as the contingent but predictable outcome of the process of the universe, interpreted theistically. Once again, I have tried to present this argument more fully elsewhere, and to consider various objections to it.[6]

On this view the human, endowed with a real though limited freedom, is basically formed for relationship with God and destined ultimately to find the fulfillment of his or her nature in that relationship. This does not seem to me excessively paradoxical. On the contrary, given the theistic postulate, it seems to me to offer a very probable account of our human situation. If so, it is a situation in which we can rejoice; for it gives meaning to our temporal existence as the long process through which we are being created, by our own free responses to life's mixture of good and evil, into "children of God" who "inherit eternal life."

Notes

1   R. Held and A. Hein, "Movement-produced stimulation in the development of visually guided behaviour", *Journal of Comparative and Physiological Psychology*, Vol. 56 (1963), pp. 872–876.

2   Fyodor Dostoyevsky, *The Brothers Karamazov*, trans. by Constance Garnett (New York: Modern Library, n.d.), Bk. V, chap. 4, p. 254.

3   Erich Fromm, "Values, Psychology, and Human Existence," in *New Knowledge of Human Values*, ed. A. H. Maslow (New York: Harper, 1959), p. 156.

4   John Hick, *Death and Eternal Life* (New York: Harper & Row, and London: Collins, 1976).

5   *The Confessions of St. Augustine*, trans. by F. J. Sheed (New York: Sheed and Ward, 1942), Bk. I, chap. 1, p. 3.

6   Hick, *Death and Eternal Life,* chap. 13.

Questions for reflection

1   Explain the soul-making theodicy as explicated above. What are some of its strengths? What are some of its weaknesses?

2   Is the soul-making theodicy generally congruent with orthodox Christian doctrine? Are there tensions between them? Explain.

3   Could an Augustinian theodicy and an Irenaean theodicy be combined, or are they mutually exclusive? Explain.

4   Explain the difference between moral evil and natural evil. Does Professor Hick's theodicy adequately address both kinds of evil?

5   How does Hick's eschatological view of the universal salvation of humankind relate to his soul-making theodicy?

Further reading

Stephen T. Davis, ed. (1981) *Encountering Evil: Live Options in Theodicy.* Atlanta, GA: John Knox Press. (Six Christian philosophers and theologians respond to intellectual and moral questions raised by the reality of evil; the selection above is taken from this volume.)

R. Douglas Geivett (1993) *Evil and the Evidence for God: The Challenge of John Hick's Theodicy.* Philadelphia, PA: Temple University Press. (Compares the Irenaean and Augustinian traditions in theodicy and offers a critique of Professor Hick's soul-making theodicy.)

John Hick (2007) *Evil and the God of Love.* 3rd edn. New York: HarperSanFrancisco. (A modern classic on the problem of evil.)

Michael L. Peterson (1998) *God and Evil: An Introduction to the Issues.* Boulder, CO: Westview Press. (An accessible introduction to the problem of evil; includes a chapter on theodicy.)

Chapter 52

Alvin Plantinga

A FREE WILL DEFENSE

Alvin Plantinga is John A. O'Brien Professor of Philosophy at the University of Notre Dame. He has written widely in metaphysics, epistemology, and philosophy of religion. In this selection, he offers his free will defense—a demonstration that there is no logical inconsistency in believing the following two propositions: (1) God is omniscient, omnipotent, and wholly good, and (2) evil exists.

Central to the argument is the idea of one's being *significantly free*—that is, having within one's power the ability to perform or refrain from some morally significant action. The essence of the defense is that, although God is omnipotent, there are some "possible worlds" that God could not have actualized; given free will, it is *possible* that God could not have created a morally good universe without that universe containing moral evil. It follows that it is possible that God has a good reason for creating a world, like ours, which contains evil. There is no *logical* inconsistency, then, in affirming the two propositions noted above.

This free will defense is widely accepted as providing the theistic solution to the logical problem of evil.

The Free Will Defense

In what follows I shall focus attention upon the Free Will Defense. I shall examine it more closely, state it more exactly, and consider objections to it; and I shall argue that in the end it is successful. Earlier [in *God, Freedom, and Evil*] we saw that among good states of affairs there are some that not even God can bring about without bringing about evil: those goods, namely, that *entail* or *include* evil states of affairs. The Free Will Defense can be looked upon as an effort to show that there may be a very different kind of good that God can't bring about without permitting evil. These are good states of affairs that don't include evil; they do not entail the existence of any evil whatever; nonetheless God Himself can't bring them about without permitting evil.

So how does the Free Will Defense work? And what does the Free Will Defender mean when he says that people are or may be free? What is relevant to the Free Will Defense is the idea of *being free with respect to an action*. If a person is free with respect to a given action, then he is free to perform that action and free to refrain from performing it; no antecedent conditions and/or causal laws determine that he will perform the action, or that he won't. It is within his power, at the time in question, to take or perform the action and within his power to refrain from it. Freedom so conceived is not to be confused with unpredictability. You might be able to predict what you will do in a given situation even if you are free, in that situation, to do something else. If I know you well, I may be able to predict what action you will take in response to a certain set of conditions; it does not follow that you are not free with respect to that action. Secondly, I shall say that an action is *morally significant*, for a given person, if it would be wrong for him to perform the action but right to refrain or *vice versa*. Keeping a promise, for example, would ordinarily be morally significant for a person, as would refusing induction into the army. On the other hand, having Cheerios for breakfast (instead of Wheaties) would not normally be morally significant. Further, suppose we say that a person is *significantly free*, on a given occasion, if he is then free with respect to a morally significant action. And finally we must distinguish between *moral evil* and *natural evil*. The former is evil that results from free human activity; natural evil is any other kind of evil.[1]

Given these definitions and distinctions, we can make a preliminary statement of the Free Will Defense as follows. A world containing creatures who are significantly free (and freely perform more good than evil actions) is more valuable, all else being equal, than a world containing no free creatures at all. Now God can create free creatures, but He can't *cause* or *determine* them to do only what is right. For if He does so, then they aren't significantly free after all; they do not do what is right *freely*. To create creatures capable of *moral good*, therefore, He must create creatures capable of moral evil; and He can't give these creatures the freedom to perform evil and at the same time prevent them from doing so. As it turned out, sadly enough, some of the free creatures God created went wrong in the exercise of their freedom; this is the source of moral evil. The fact that free creatures sometimes go wrong, however, counts neither against God's omnipotence nor against His goodness; for He could have forestalled the occurrence of moral evil only by removing the possibility of moral good.

I said earlier [in *God, Freedom, and Evil*] that the Free Will Defender tries to find a proposition that is consistent with

(1) God is omniscient, omnipotent, and wholly good

and together with (1) entails that there is evil. According to the Free Will Defense, we must find this proposition somewhere in the above story. The heart of the Free Will Defense is the claim that it is *possible* that God could not have created a universe containing moral good (or as much moral good as this world contains) without creating one that also contained moral evil. And if so, then it is possible that God has a good reason for creating a world containing evil.

Now this defense has met with several kinds of objections. For example, some philosophers say that *causal determinism* and *freedom*, contrary to what we might have thought, are not really incompatible.[2] But if so, then God could have created free creatures who were free, and free to do what is wrong, but nevertheless were causally determined to do only what is right. Thus He could have created creatures who were free to do what was wrong, while nevertheless preventing them from ever performing any wrong actions—simply by seeing to it that they were causally determined to do only what is right. Of course this contradicts the Free Will Defense, according to which there is inconsistency in supposing that God determines free creatures to do only what is right. But is it really possible that all of a person's actions are causally determined while some of them are free? How could that be so? According to one version of the doctrine in question, to say that George acts freely on a given occasion is to say only this: *if George had chosen to do otherwise, he would have done otherwise.* Now George's action *A* is causally determined if some event *E*—some event beyond his control—has already occurred, where the state of affairs consisting in *E's* occurrence conjoined with George's *refraining* from performing *A*, is a causally impossible state of affairs. Then one can consistently hold both that all of a man's actions are causally determined and that some of them are free in the above sense. For suppose that all of a man's actions are causally determined and that he *couldn't*, on any occasion, have made any choice or performed any action different from the ones he did make and perform. It could still be true that if he *had* chosen to do otherwise, he would have done otherwise. Granted, he couldn't have chosen to do otherwise; but this is consistent with saying that *if* he had, things would have gone differently.

This objection to the Free Will Defense seems utterly implausible. One might as well claim that being in jail doesn't really limit one's freedom on the grounds that if one were *not* in jail, he'd be free to come and go as he pleased. So I shall say no more about this objection here.[3]

A second objection is more formidable. In essence it goes like this. Surely it is possible to do only what is right, even if one is free to do wrong. It is *possible*, in that broadly logical sense, that there be a world containing free creatures who always do what is right. There is certainly no *contradiction* or *inconsistency* in this idea. But God is omnipotent; his power has no nonlogical limitations. So if it's possible that there be a world containing creatures who are free to do what is wrong but never in fact do so, then it follows that an omnipotent God could create such a world. If so, however, the Free Will Defense must be mistaken in its insistence upon the possibility that God is omnipotent but unable to create a world containing moral good without permitting moral evil. J. L. Mackie . . . states this objection:

> If God has made men such that in their free choices they sometimes prefer what is good and sometimes what is evil, why could he not have made men such that they always freely choose the good? If there is no logical impossibility in a man's freely choosing the good on one, or on several occasions, there cannot be a logical impossibility in his freely choosing the good on every occasion. God was not, then, faced with a choice between making innocent automata and making beings who, in acting freely, would sometimes go wrong; there was open to him the obviously better possibility of making beings who would act freely but always go right. Clearly, his failure to avail himself of this possibility is inconsistent with his being both omnipotent and wholly good.[4]

Now what, exactly, is Mackie's point here? This. According to the Free Will Defense, it is possible both that God is omnipotent and that He was unable to create a world containing moral good without creating one containing moral evil. But, replies Mackie, this limitation on His power to create is inconsistent with God's omnipotence. For surely it's *possible* that there be a world containing perfectly virtuous persons—persons who are significantly free but always do what is right. Surely there are *possible worlds* that contain moral good but no moral evil. But God, if He is omnipotent, can create any possible world He chooses. So it is *not* possible, contrary to the Free Will Defense, both that God is omnipotent and that He could create a world containing moral good only by creating one containing moral evil. If He is omnipotent, the only limitations of His power are *logical* limitations; in which case there are no possible worlds He could not have created.

This is a subtle and important point. According to the great German philosopher G.W. Leibniz, *this* world, the actual world, must be the best of all possible worlds. His reasoning goes as follows. Before God created anything at all, He was confronted with an enormous range of choices; He could create or bring into actuality any of the myriads of different possible worlds. Being perfectly good, He must have chosen to create the best world He could; being omnipotent, He was able to create any possible world He pleased. He must, therefore, have chosen the best of all possible worlds; and hence *this* world, the one He did create, must be the best possible. Now Mackie, of course, agrees with Leibniz that God, if omnipotent, could have created any world He pleased and would have created the best world he could. But while Leibniz draws the conclusion that this world, despite appearances, must be the best possible, Mackie concludes instead that there is no omnipotent, wholly good God. For, he says, it is obvious enough that this present world is not the best of all possible worlds.

The Free Will Defender disagrees with both Leibniz and Mackie. In the first place, he might say, what is the reason for supposing that *there is* such a thing as the best of all possible worlds? No matter how marvelous a world is—containing no matter how many persons enjoying unalloyed bliss—isn't it possible that there be an even better world containing even more persons enjoying even more unalloyed bliss? But what is really characteristic and central to the Free Will Defense is the claim that God, though omnipotent, could not have actualized just any possible world He pleased.

Was it within God's power to create any possible world He pleased?

This is indeed the crucial question for the Free Will Defense. If we wish to discuss it with insight and authority, we shall have to look into the idea of *possible worlds*. And a sensible first question is this: what sort of thing is a possible world? The basic idea is that a possible world is a *way things could have been*; it is a *state of affairs* of some kind. Earlier we spoke of states of affairs, in particular of good and evil states of affairs. Suppose we look at this idea in more detail. What sort of thing is a state of affairs? The following would be examples:

> Nixon's having won the 1972 election
> 7 + 5's being equal to 12
> All men's being mortal

and

> Gary, Indiana's, having a really nasty pollution problem.

These are *actual* states of affairs: states of affairs that do in fact *obtain*. And corresponding to each such actual state of affairs there is a true proposition—in the above cases, the corresponding propositions would be *Nixon won the 1972 presidential election, 7 + 5 is equal to 12, all men are mortal,* and *Gary, Indiana, has a really nasty pollution problem.* A proposition *p corresponds* to a state of affairs *s*, in this sense, if it is impossible that *p* be true and *s* fail to obtain and impossible that *s* obtain and *p* fail to be true.

But just as there are false propositions, so there are states of affairs that do *not* obtain or are *not* actual. *Kissinger's having swum the Atlantic* and *Hubert Horatio Humphrey's having run a mile in four minutes* would be examples. Some states of affairs that do not obtain are *impossible*: e.g., *Hubert's having drawn a square circle, 7 + 5's being equal to 75,* and *Agnew's having a brother who was an only child.* The propositions corresponding to these states of affairs, of course, are necessarily false. So there are states of affairs that *obtain* or *are actual* and also states of affairs that don't obtain. Among the latter some are *impossible* and others are *possible.* And a possible world is a possible state of affairs. Of course not every possible state of affairs is a possible world; *Hubert's having run a mile in four minutes* is a possible state of affairs but not a possible world. No doubt it is an *element* of many possible worlds, but it isn't itself inclusive enough to be one. To be a possible world, a state of affairs must be very large—so large as to be *complete* or *maximal.*

To get at this idea of completeness we need a couple of definitions. . . . [A] state of affairs *A includes* a state of affairs *B* if it is not possible that *A* obtain and *B* not obtain or if the conjunctive state of affairs *A but not B*—the state of affairs that obtains if and only if *A* obtains and *B* does not—is not possible. For example, *Jim Whittaker's being the first American to climb Mt. Everest* includes *Jim Whittaker's being an American.* It also includes *Mt. Everest's being climbed, something's being climbed, no American's having climbed Everest before Whittaker did,* and the like. *Inclusion* among states of affairs is like *entailment* among propositions; and where a state of affairs *A* includes a state of affairs *B*, the proposition corresponding to *A* entails the one corresponding to *B*. Accordingly, *Jim Whittaker is the first American to climb Everest* entails *Mt. Everest has been climbed, something has been climbed,* and *no American climbed Everest before Whittaker did.* Now suppose we say further that a state of affairs *A precludes* a state of affairs *B* if it is not possible that *both* obtain, or if the conjunctive state of affairs *A and B* is impossible. Thus *Whittaker's being the first American to climb Mt. Everest* precludes *Luther Jerstad's being the first American to climb Everest,* as well as *Whittaker's never having climbed any mountains.* If *A* precludes *B*, then *A's* corresponding proposition entails the denial of the one corresponding to *B*. Still further, let's say that the *complement* of a state of affairs is the state of affairs that obtains just in case *A* does not obtain. [Or we might say that the complement (call it *A**) of *A* is the state of affairs corresponding to the *denial* or *negation* of the proposition corresponding to *A*.] Given these definitions, we can say what it is for a state of affairs to be *complete*: *A* is a complete state of affairs if and only if for every state of affairs *B*, either *A includes B* or *A precludes B*. (We could express the same thing by saying that if *A* is a complete state of affairs, then for every state of affairs *B*, either *A* includes *B* or *A* includes *B**, the complement of *B*.) And now we are able to say what a possible world is: a possible world is any possible state of affairs that is complete. If *A* is a possible world, then it says something about everything; every state of affairs *S* is either included in or precluded by it.

Corresponding to each possible world *W*, furthermore, there is a set of propositions that I'll call *the book on W*. A proposition is in the book on *W* just in case the state of affairs to which it corresponds is included in *W*. Or we might express it like this. Suppose we say that a proposition *P* is *true in a world W* if and only if *P would have been true if W had been actual*—if and only if, that is, it is not possible that *W* be actual and *P* be false. Then the book on *W* is the set of propositions true in *W*. Like possible worlds, books are *complete*; if *B* is a book, then for any proposition *P*, either *P* or the denial of *P* will be a member of *B*. A book is a *maximal consistent set* of propositions; it is so large that the addition of another proposition to it always yields an explicitly inconsistent set.

Of course, for each possible world there is exactly one book corresponding to it (that is, for a given world *W* there is just one book *B* such that each member of *B* is true in *W*); and for each book there is just one world to which it corresponds. So every world has its book.

It should be obvious that exactly one possible world is actual. At *least* one must be, since the set of true propositions is a maximal consistent set and hence a book. But then it corresponds to a possible world, and the possible world corresponding to this set of propositions (since it's the set of *true* propositions) will be actual. On the other hand there is at *most* one actual world. For suppose there were two: W and *W'*. These worlds cannot include all the very same states of affairs; if they did, they would be the very same world. So there must be at least one state of affairs *S* such that *W* includes *S* and *W'* does not. But a possible world is maximal; *W'*, therefore, includes the complement *S** of *S*. So if both W and *W'* were actual, as we have supposed, then both *S* and *S** would be actual— which is impossible. So there can't be more than one possible world that is actual.

Leibniz pointed out that a proposition *p* is necessary if it is true in every possible world. We may add that *p* is possible if it is true in one world and impossible if true in none. Furthermore, *p entails q* if there is no possible world in which *p* is true and *q* is false; and *p is consistent with q* if there is at least one world in which both *p* and *q* are true.

A further feature of possible worlds is that people (and other things) *exist* in them. Each of us exists in the actual world, obviously; but a person also exists in many worlds distinct from the actual world. It would be a mistake, of course, to think of all of these worlds as somehow "going on" at the same time, with the same person reduplicated through these worlds and actually existing in a lot of different ways. This is not what is meant by saying that the same person exists in different possible worlds. What is meant, instead, is this: a person Paul exists in each of those possible worlds *W* which is such that, if *W had been actual*, Paul would have existed—actually existed. Suppose Paul had been an inch taller than he is, or a better tennis player. Then the world that does in fact obtain would not have been actual; some other world—*W'*, let's say—would have obtained instead. If *W'* had been actual, Paul would have existed; so Paul exists in *W'*. (Of course there are still other possible worlds in which Paul does not exist—worlds, for example, in which there are no people at all.) Accordingly, when we say that Paul exists in a world *W*, what we mean is that Paul *would have* existed had W been actual. Or we could put it like this: Paul exists in each world *W* that includes the state of affairs consisting in Paul's existence. We can put this still more simply by saying that Paul exists in those worlds whose books contain the proposition *Paul exists*.

But isn't there a problem here? *Many* people are named "Paul": Paul the apostle, Paul J. Zwier, John Paul Jones, and many other famous Pauls. So who *goes* with "Paul exists"? Which Paul? The answer has to do with the fact that books contain *propositions*—not sentences. They contain the sort of thing sentences are used to express and assert. And the same sentence—"Aristotle is wise," for example—can be used to express many different propositions. When Plato used it, he asserted a proposition predicating wisdom of his famous pupil; when Jackie Onassis uses it, she asserts a proposition predicating wisdom of her wealthy husband. These are distinct propositions (we might even think they differ in truth value); but they are expressed by the same sentence. Normally (but not always) we don't have much trouble determining which of the several propositions expressed by a given sentence is relevant in the context at hand. So in this case a given person, Paul, exists in a world *W* if and only if *W*'s book contains the proposition that says that *he*—that particular person—exists. The fact that the sentence we use to express this proposition can also be used to express *other* propositions is not relevant.

After this excursion into the nature of books and worlds we can return to our question. Could God have created just any world He chose? Before addressing the question, however, we must note that God does not, strictly speaking, *create* any possible worlds or states of affairs at all. What He creates are the heavens and the earth and all that they contain. But He has not created states of affairs. There are, for example, the state of affairs consisting in God's existence and the state of affairs consisting in His nonexistence. That is, there is such a thing as the state of affairs consisting in the existence of God, and there is also such a thing as the state of affairs consisting in the nonexistence of God, just as there are the two propositions *God exists* and *God does not exist*. The theist believes that the first state of affairs is actual and the first proposition true; the atheist believes that the second state of affairs is actual and the second proposition true. But, of course, both propositions *exist*, even though just one is true. Similarly, there are two states of affairs here, just one of which is actual. So both states of affairs *exist*, but only one *obtains*. And God has not created either one of them since there never was a time at which either did not exist. Nor has He created the state of affairs consisting in the earth's existence; there was a time when *the earth* did not exist, but none when the state of affairs consisting in the earth's existence didn't exist. Indeed, God did not bring into existence any states of affairs at all. What He did was to perform actions of a certain sort—creating the heavens and the earth, for example—which resulted in the *actuality* of certain states of affairs. God *actualizes* states of affairs. He actualizes the possible world that does in fact obtain; He does not create it. And while He has created Socrates, He did not create the state of affairs consisting in Socrates' existence.[5]

Bearing this in mind, let's finally return to our question. Is the atheologian right in holding that if God is omnipotent, then He could have actualized or created any possible world He pleased? Not obviously. First, we must ask ourselves whether God is a *necessary* or a *contingent* being. A *necessary* being is one that exists in every possible world—one that would have existed no matter which possible world had been actual; a contingent being exists only in some possible worlds. Now if God is not a necessary being (and many, perhaps most, theists think that He is not), then clearly enough there will be many possible worlds He could not have actualized—all those, for example, in which He does not exist. Clearly, God could not have created a world in which He doesn't even exist.

So, if God is a contingent being then there are many possible worlds beyond His power to create. But this is really irrelevant to our present concerns. For perhaps the atheologian can maintain his case if he revises his claim to avoid this difficulty; perhaps he will say something like this: if God is omnipotent, then He could have actualized any of those possible worlds *in which He exists*. So if He exists and is omnipotent, He could have actualized (contrary to the Free Will Defense) any of those possible worlds in which He exists and in which there exist free creatures who do no wrong. He could have actualized worlds containing moral good but no moral evil. Is this correct?

Let's begin with a trivial example. You and Paul have just returned from an Australian hunting expedition: your quarry was the elusive double-wattled cassowary. Paul captured an aardvark, mistaking it for a cassowary. The creature's disarming ways have won it a place in Paul's heart; he is deeply attached to it. Upon your return to the States you offer Paul $500 for his aardvark, only to be rudely turned down. Later you ask yourself, "What would he have done if I'd offered him $700?" Now what is it, exactly, that you are asking? What you're really asking in a way is whether, under a *specific set of conditions*, Paul would have sold it. These conditions include your having offered him $700 rather than $500 for the aardvark, everything else being as much as possible like the conditions that did in fact obtain. Let S' be this set of conditions or state of affairs. S' includes the state of affairs consisting in your offering Paul $700 (instead of the $500 you did offer him); of course it does not include his *accepting* your offer, and it does not include his *rejecting* it; for the rest, the conditions it includes are just like the ones that did obtain in the actual world. So, for example, S' includes Paul's being free to accept the offer and free to refrain; and if in fact the going rate for an aardvark was $650, then S' includes the state of affairs consisting in the going rate's being $650. So we might put your question by asking which of the following conditionals is true:

(23) If the state of affairs S' had obtained, Paul would have accepted the offer
(24) If the state of affairs S' had obtained, Paul would not have accepted the offer.

It seems clear that at least one of these conditionals is true, but naturally they can't both be; so exactly one is.

Now since S' includes neither Paul's accepting the offer nor his rejecting it, the antecedent of (23) and (24) does not entail the consequent of either. That is,

(25) S' obtains

does not entail either

(26) Paul accepts the offer

or

(27) Paul does not accept the offer.

So there are possible worlds in which both (25) and (26) are true, and other possible worlds in which both (25) and (27) are true.

We are now in a position to grasp an important fact. Either (23) or (24) is in fact true; and either way there are possible worlds God could not have actualized. Suppose, first of all, that (23) is true. Then it was beyond the power of God to create a world in which (1) Paul is free to sell his aardvark and free to refrain, and in which the other states of affairs included in S' obtain, and (2) Paul does not sell. That is, it was beyond His power to create a world in which (25) and (27) are both true. There is at least one possible world like this, but God, despite His omnipotence, could not have brought about its actuality. For let W be such a world. To actualize W, God must bring it about that Paul is free with respect to this action, and that the other states of affairs included in S' obtain. But (23), as we are supposing, is true; so if God had actualized S' and left Paul *free* with respect to this action, he would have sold: in which case W would not have been actual. If, on the other hand, God had *brought it about* that Paul didn't sell or had *caused him* to refrain from selling, then Paul would not have been free with respect to this action; then S' would not have been actual (since S' includes Paul's being free with respect to it), and W would not have been actual since W includes S'.

Of course if it is (24) rather than (23) that is true, then another class of worlds was beyond God's power to actualize—those, namely, in which S' obtains and Paul *sells* his aardvark. These are the worlds in which both (25) and (26) are true. But either (23) or (24) is true. Therefore, there are possible worlds God could not have actualized. If we consider whether or not God could have created a world in which, let's say, both (25) and (26) are true, we see that the answer depends upon a peculiar kind of fact; it depends upon what Paul would have freely chosen to do in a certain situation. So there are any number of possible worlds such that it is partly up to Paul whether God can create them.[6]

That was a past tense example. Perhaps it would be useful to consider a future tense case, since this might seem to correspond more closely to God's situation in choosing a possible world to actualize. At some time t in the near future Maurice will be free with respect to some insignificant action—having freeze-dried oatmeal for breakfast, let's say. That is, at time t Maurice will be free to have oatmeal but also free to take something else—shredded wheat, perhaps. Next, suppose we consider S', a state of affairs that is included in the actual world and includes Maurice's being free with respect to taking oatmeal at time t. That is, S' includes Maurice's being free at time t to take oatmeal and free to reject it. S' does not include Maurice's taking oatmeal, however; nor does it include his rejecting it. For the rest S' is as much as possible like the actual world. In particular there are many conditions that do in fact hold at time t and are *relevant* to his choice—such conditions, for example, as the fact that he hasn't had oatmeal lately, that his wife will be annoyed if he rejects it, and the like; and S' includes each of these conditions. Now God no doubt knows what Maurice will do at time t, if S obtains; He knows which action Maurice would freely perform if S were to be actual. That is, God knows that one of the following conditionals is true:

(28) If S' were to obtain, Maurice will freely take the oatmeal

or

(29) If S' were to obtain, Maurice will freely reject it.

We may not know which of these is true, and Maurice himself may not know; but presumably God does.

So either God knows that (28) is true, or else He knows that (29) is. Let's suppose it is (28). Then there is a possible world that God, though omnipotent, cannot create. For consider a possible world W' that shares S' with the actual world (which for ease of reference I'll name "Kronos") and in which Maurice does *not* take oatmeal. (We know there *is* such a world, since S' does not include Maurice's taking the oatmeal.) S' obtains in W' just as it does in Kronos. Indeed, everything in W' is just as it is in Kronos up to time t. But whereas in Kronos Maurice takes oatmeal at time t, in W' he does not. Now W' is a perfectly possible world; but it is not within God's power to create it or bring about its actuality. For to do so He must actualize S'. But (28) is in fact true. So if God actualizes S' (as He must to create W') and leaves Maurice free with respect to the action in question, then he will take the oatmeal; and then, of course, W' will not be actual. If, on the other hand, God causes Maurice to *refrain* from taking the oatmeal, then he is not *free* to take it. That means, once again, that W' is not actual; for in W' Maurice is free to take the oatmeal (even if he doesn't do so). So if (28) is true, then this world W' is one that God can't actualize; it is not within His power to actualize it even though He is omnipotent and it is a possible world.

Of course, if it is (29) that is true, we get a similar result; then too there are possible worlds that God can't actualize. These would be worlds which share S' with Kronos and in which Maurice *does* take oatmeal. But either (28) or (29) *is* true; so either way there is a possible world that God can't create. If we consider a world in which S' obtains and in which Maurice freely chooses oatmeal at time t, we see that whether or not it is within God's power to actualize it depends upon what Maurice would do if he were free in a certain situation. Accordingly, there are any number of possible worlds such that it is partly up to Maurice whether or not God can actualize them. It is, of course, up to God whether or not to create Maurice and also up to God whether or not to make him free with respect to the action of taking oatmeal at time t. (God could, if He chose, cause him to succumb to the dreaded *equine obsession*, a condition shared by some people and most horses, whose victims find it *psychologically impossible* to refuse oats or oat products.) But if He creates Maurice and creates him free with respect to this action, then whether or not he actually performs the action is up to Maurice—not God.[7]

Now we can return to the Free Will Defense and the problem of evil. The Free Will Defender, you recall, insists on the possibility that it is not within God's power to create a world containing moral good without creating one containing moral evil. His atheological opponent—Mackie, for example—agrees with Leibniz in insisting that *if* (as the theist holds) God is omnipotent, then it *follows* that He could have created any possible world He pleased. We now see that this contention—call it "Leibniz' Lapse"—is a mistake. The atheologian is right in holding that there are many possible worlds containing moral good but no moral evil; his mistake lies in endorsing Leibniz' Lapse. So one of his premises— that God, if omnipotent, could have actualized just any world He pleased—is false.

Could God have created a world containing moral good but no moral evil?

Now suppose we recapitulate the logic of the situation. The Free Will Defender claims that the following is possible:

> (30) God is omnipotent, and it was not within His power to create a world containing moral good but no moral evil.

By way of retort the atheologian insists that there are possible worlds containing moral good but no moral evil. He adds that an omnipotent being could have actualized any possible world he chose. So if God is omnipotent, it follows that He could have actualized a world containing moral good but no moral evil; hence (30), contrary to the Free Will Defender's claim, is not possible. What we have seen so far is that his second premiss—Leibniz' Lapse—is false.

Of course, this does not settle the issue in the Free Will Defender's favor. Leibniz' Lapse (appropriately enough for a lapse) is false; but this doesn't show that (30) is possible. To show this latter we must demonstrate the possibility that among the worlds God could not have actualized are all the worlds containing moral good but no moral evil. How can we approach this question?

Instead of choosing oatmeal for breakfast or selling an aardvark, suppose we think about a morally significant action such as taking a bribe. Curley Smith, the mayor of Boston, is opposed to the proposed freeway route; it would require destruction of the Old North Church along with some other antiquated and structurally unsound buildings. L. B. Smedes, the director of highways, asks him whether he'd drop his opposition for $1 million. "Of course," he replies. "Would you do it for $2?" asks Smedes. "What do you take me for?" comes the indignant reply. "That's already established," smirks Smedes; "all that remains is to nail down your price." Smedes then offers him a bribe of $35,000; unwilling to break with the fine old traditions of Bay State politics, Curley accepts. Smedes then spends a sleepless night wondering whether he could have bought Curley for $20,000.

Now suppose we assume that Curley was free with respect to the action of taking the bribe—free to take it and free to refuse. And suppose, furthermore, that he would have taken it. That is, let us suppose that

(31) If Smedes had offered Curley a bribe of $20,000, he would have accepted it.

If (31) is true, then there is a state of affairs S' that (1) includes Curley's being offered a bribe of $20,000; (2) does not include either his accepting the bribe or his rejecting it; and (3) is otherwise as much as possible like the actual world. Just to make sure S' includes every relevant circumstance, let us suppose that it is a *maximal world segment*. That is, add to S' any state of affairs compatible with but not included in it, and the result will be an entire possible world. We could think of it roughly like this: S' is included in at least one world W in which Curley takes the bribe and in at least one world W' in which he rejects it. If S' is a maximal world segment, then S' is what remains of W when *Curley's taking the bribe* is deleted; it is also what remains of W' when *Curley's rejecting the bribe* is deleted. More exactly, if S' is a maximal world segment, then every possible state of affairs that includes S', but isn't included by S', is a possible world. So if (31) is true, then there is a maximal world segment S' that (1) includes Curley's being offered a bribe of $20,000; (2) does not include either his accepting the bribe or his rejecting it; (3) is otherwise as much as possible like the actual world—in particular, it includes Curley's being free with respect to the bribe; and (4) is such that if it were actual then Curley would have taken the bribe. That is,

(32) If S' were actual, Curley would have accepted the bribe

is true.

Now, of course, there is at least one possible world W' in which S' is actual and Curley does not take the bribe. But God could not have created W'; to do so, He would have been obliged to actualize S', leaving Curley free with respect to the action of taking the bribe. But under these conditions Curley, as (32) assures us, would have accepted the bribe, so that the world thus created would not have been S'.

Curley, as we see, is not above a bit of Watergating. But there may be worse to come. Of course, there are possible worlds in which he is significantly free (i.e., free with respect to a morally significant action) and never does what is wrong. But the sad truth about Curley may be this. Consider W', any of these worlds: in W' Curley is significantly free, so in W' there are some actions that are morally significant for him and with respect to which he is free. But at least one of these actions—call it A—has the following peculiar property. There is a maximal world segment S' that obtains in W' and is such that (1) S' includes Curley's being free *re* A but neither his performing A nor his refraining from A; (2) S' is otherwise as much as possible like W'; and (3) if S' had been actual, Curley would have gone wrong with respect to A.[8] (Notice that this third condition holds in fact, in the actual world; it does not hold in that world W'.)

This means, of course, that God could not have actualized W'. For to do so He'd have been obliged to bring it about that S' is actual; but then Curley would go wrong with respect to A. Since in W' he always does what is right, the world thus actualized would not be W'. On the other hand, if God *causes* Curley to go right with respect to A or *brings it about that* he does so, then Curley isn't free with respect to A; and so once more it isn't W' that is actual. Accordingly God cannot create W'. But W' was just any of the worlds in which Curley is significantly free but always does only what is right. It therefore follows that it was not within God's power to create a world in which Curley produces moral good but no moral evil. Every world God can actualize is such that if Curley is significantly free in it, he takes at least one wrong action.

Obviously Curley is in serious trouble. I shall call the malady from which he suffers *transworld depravity*. (I leave as homework the problem of comparing transworld depravity with what Calvinists call "total depravity.") By way of explicit definition:

> (33) A person P suffers from transworld depravity if and only if the following holds: for every world W such that P is significantly free in W and P does only what is right in W, there is an action A and a maximal world segment S' such that
> > (1) S' includes A's being morally significant for P
> > (2) S' includes P's being free with respect to A
> > (3) S' is included in W and includes neither P's performing A nor P's refraining from performing A

and

> > (4) If S' were actual, P would go wrong with respect to A.

(In thinking about this definition, remember that (4) is to be true in fact, in the actual world—not in that world W.)

What is important about the idea of transworld depravity is that if a person suffers from it, then it wasn't within God's power to actualize any world in which that person is significantly free but does no wrong—that is, a world in which he produces moral good but no moral evil.

We have been considering a crucial contention of the Free Will Defender: the contention, namely, that

(30) God is omnipotent, and it was not within His power to create a world containing moral good but no moral evil.

How is transworld depravity relevant to this? As follows. Obviously it is possible that there be persons who suffer from transworld depravity. More generally, it is possible that *everybody* suffers from it. And if this possibility were actual, then God, though omnipotent, could not have created any of the possible worlds containing just the persons who do in fact exist, and containing moral good but no moral evil. For to do so He'd have to create persons who were significantly free (otherwise there would be no moral good) but suffered from transworld depravity. Such persons go wrong with respect to at least one action in any world God could have actualized and in which they are free with respect to morally significant actions; so the price for creating a world in which they produce moral good is creating one in which they also produce moral evil.

Notes

1   This distinction is not very precise (how, exactly, are we to construe "results from"?); but perhaps it will serve our present purposes.
2   See, for example, A. Flew, "Divine Omnipotence and Human Freedom," in *New Essays in Philosophical Theology*, eds. A. Flew and A. MacIntyre (London: SCM, 1955), pp. 150–153.
3   For further discussion of it see Plantinga, *God and Other Minds*, pp. 132–135.
4   Mackie, in *The Philosophy of Religion*, pp. 100–101.
5   Strict accuracy demands, therefore, that we speak of God as *actualizing* rather than creating possible worlds. I shall continue to use both locutions, thus sacrificing accuracy to familiarity. For more about possible worlds see my book *The Nature of Necessity* (Oxford: The Clarendon Press, 1974), chaps. 4–8.
6   For a fuller statement of this argument see Plantinga, *The Nature of Necessity*, chap. 9, secs. 4–6.
7   For a more complete and more exact statement of this argument see Plantinga, *The Nature of Necessity*, chap. 9, secs. 4–6.
8   A person goes wrong with respect to an action if he either wrongfully performs it or wrongfully fails to perform it.

Questions for reflection

1   How is a theodicy, such as the one presented in chapter 1 by Professor Hick, different from the free will defense presented here?
2   The concept of free will is, of course, central to the free will defense. For the defense to be successful in the way Professor Plantinga intends, must it include a *libertarian* notion of free will? Why? How might a theistic compatibilist respond to evil?
3   According to the free will defense it is possible that it is not within God's power to create a world containing moral good without creating one containing moral evil. Does it follow from this that God is not omnipotent? Why or why not?
4   What is Leibniz' Lapse? Why does Professor Plantinga claim that it is a mistake for the atheologian to endorse it?

5   What do you take to be the most significant objection to the free will defense? All things considered, which is more plausible: the defense or this objection to it? Explain your answer.

Further reading

John Hick (2007) *Evil and the God of Love*. 3rd edn. San Francisco: Harper & Row. (Develops a soul-making theodicy in opposition to "Augustinian-type" theodicies which rely on the doctrine of the Fall.)

J. L. Mackie (1955) "Evil and Omnipotence," *Mind* 64: 200–12. (Probably the most widely influential formulation of the atheological argument from evil.)

Alvin Plantinga (1977) *God, Freedom, and Evil*. Grand Rapids, MI: Eerdmans. (A classic work on the problem of evil as well as an interesting formulation of the ontological argument; the selection above was taken from this book.)

William L. Rowe (1979) "The Problem of Evil and Some Varieties of Atheism," *American Philosophical Quarterly* 16: 335–41. (Presents a widely discussed version of the evidential problem of evil; it is contained in Chapter 50 of this volume.)

Peter van Inwagen (1991) "The Problem of Evil, the Problem of Air, and the Problem of Silence," *Philosophical Perspectives* 5: 135–65. (Provides a response to the evidential problem of evil.)

Chapter 53

Marilyn McCord Adams

HORRENDOUS EVIL

Marilyn McCord Adams is Regius Professor of Divinity at the University of Oxford. In this essay she responds to what she and many others consider the deepest of religious problems—the problem of evil. There are various versions of the problem, but a common one concerns itself with the apparent contradiction in holding that God is omniscient, omnipotent, and omnibenevolent on the one hand, and that evil exists on the other.

One standard reply is to show that there is no *logical* contradiction in affirming the existence of both God and evil. However, Professor Adams doesn't think that showing the logical compossibility (i.e., the co-existence of things in the same possible world) of God with some evil or other will do much good because what we are worried about is the logical compossibility of God with evils in the amounts and kinds found in the actual world, which include what she labels "horrendous evils." Horrendous evils are those which, when experienced by a particular person, give that person reason to doubt whether her life could, considered in totality, be taken to be a great good to her. Some examples of horrendous evils include the rape of a woman and axing off of her arms, slow death by starvation, and having to choose which of one's children shall live and which will be killed by terrorists. Taking a "general reasons-why" approach whereby some general reason is offered to cover all forms of evil (e.g., God's desire to make a world exhibiting a perfect balance of retributive justice constitutes a reason why a perfectly good God would make a world with the kinds and amounts of evil we have in this world) doesn't seem to provide much help. For example, is the following really an acceptable reply to the evil of a truck-driver accidentally running over his young son: "This was the price God was willing to pay for the world in which we live—one which has the best balance of moral good over evil"? Adams doesn't think so.

However, as a *Christian* philosopher, she believes a more adequate response can be provided. Rather than focusing on the possible reasons *why* God might allow evils of this sort, she maintains that it is enough to show *how* God can be good and yet permit their existence. She argues that all evils, even those of the horrendous sort, are redeemable. She notes that there is good reason for Christians to believe that God will, in the end, engulf and defeat all personal horrors through integrating participation in the evils into their relationship with God. She offers three possible dimensions of integration: (1) identifying with the sufferings of Christ, (2) experiencing divine gratitude, and (3) identifying temporal suffering with a vision of the inner life of God. Given such integrations, all human beings—even those who have experienced the most horrendous evils—will, in the eschaton, be able to find ultimate meaning and goodness in the lives they lived.

1. Introduction

Over the past thirty years, analytic philosophers of religion have defined 'the problem of evil' in terms of the prima-facie difficulty in consistently maintaining

(1) God exists, and is omnipotent, omniscient, and perfectly good

and

(2) Evil exists.

In a crisp and classic article, 'Evil and Omnipotence',[1] J. L. Mackie emphasized that the problem is not that (1) and (2) are logically inconsistent by themselves, but that they together with quasi-logical rules formulating attribute-analyses—such as

(P1) A perfectly good being would always eliminate evil so far as it could,

and

(P2) There are *no limits* to what an omnipotent being can do—constitute an inconsistent premiss-set. He added, of course, that the inconsistency might be removed by substituting alternative and perhaps more subtle analyses, but cautioned that such replacements of (P1) and (P2) would save 'ordinary theism' from his charge of positive irrationality, only if true to its 'essential requirements'.[2]

In an earlier paper, 'Problems of Evil: More Advice to Christian Philosophers',[3] I underscored Mackie's point and took it a step further. In debates about whether the argument from evil can establish the irrationality of religious belief, care must be taken, both by the atheologians who deploy it and by the believers who defend against it, to ensure that the operative attribute-analyses accurately reflect that religion's understanding of divine power and goodness. It does the atheologian no good to argue for the falsity of Christianity on the ground that the existence of an omnipotent, omniscient, pleasure-maximizer is incompossible with a world such as ours, because Christians never believed God was a pleasure-maximizer anyway. But equally, the truth of Christianity would be inadequately defended by the observation that an omnipotent, omniscient egoist could have created a world with suffering creatures, because Christians insist that God loves other (created) persons than Himself. The extension of 'evil' in (2) is likewise important. Since Mackie and his successors are out to show that 'the several parts of the essential theological doctrine are inconsistent with *one another*',[4] they can accomplish their aim only if they circumscribe the extension of 'evil' as their religious opponents do. By the same token, it is not enough for Christian philosophers to explain how the power, knowledge, and goodness of God could coexist with some evils or other; a full account must exhibit the compossibility of divine perfection with evils in the amounts and of the kinds found in the actual world (and evaluated as such by Christian standards).

The moral of my earlier story might be summarized thus: where the internal coherence of a system of religious beliefs is at stake, successful arguments for its inconsistency must draw on premises (explicitly or implicitly) internal to that system or obviously acceptable to its adherents; likewise for successful rebuttals or explanations of consistency. The thrust of my argument is to push both sides of the debate towards more detailed attention to and subtle understanding of the religious system in question.

As a Christian philosopher, I want to focus in this paper on the problem for the truth of Christianity raised by what I shall call 'horrendous' evils. Although our world is riddled with them, the biblical record punctuated by them, and one of them—namely, the passion of Christ; according to Christian belief, the judicial murder of God by the people of God—is memorialized by the Church on its most solemn holiday (Good Friday) and in its central sacrament (the Eucharist), the problem of horrendous evils is largely skirted by standard treatments for the good reason that they are intractable by them. After showing why, I will draw on other Christian materials to sketch ways of meeting this, the deepest of religious problems.

2. Defining the category

For present purposes, I define 'horrendous evils' as 'evils the participation in (the doing or suffering of) which gives one reason prima facie to doubt whether one's life could (given their inclusion in it) be a great good to one on the whole'.[5] Such reasonable doubt arises because it is so difficult humanly to conceive how such evils could be overcome. Borrowing Chisholm's contrast between *balancing off* (which occurs when the opposing values of *mutually exclusive* parts of a whole partially or totally cancel each other out) and *defeat* (which cannot occur by the mere addition to the whole of a new part of opposing value, but involves some 'organic unity' among the values of parts and wholes, as when the positive aesthetic value of a whole painting defeats the ugliness of a small colour patch),[6] horrendous evils seem prima facie, not only to balance off but to engulf the positive value of a participant's life. Nevertheless, that very horrendous proportion, by which they threaten to rob a person's life of positive meaning, cries out not only to be engulfed, but to be made meaningful through positive and decisive defeat.

I understand this criterion to be objective, but relative to individuals. The example of habitual complainers, who know how to make the worst of a good situation, shows individuals not to be incorrigible experts on what ills would defeat the positive value of their lives. Nevertheless, nature and experience endow people with different strengths; one bears easily what crushes another. And a major consideration in determining whether an individual's life is/has been a great good to him/her on the whole, is invariably and appropriately how it has seemed to him/her.[7]

I offer the following list of paradigmatic horrors: the rape of a woman and axing off of her arms, psychophysical torture whose ultimate goal is the disintegration of personality, betrayal of one's deepest loyalties, cannibalizing one's own offspring, child abuse of the sort described by Ivan Karamazov, child pornography, parental incest, slow death by starvation, participation in the Nazi death camps, the explosion of nuclear bombs over populated areas, having to choose which of one's children shall live and which be executed by terrorists, being the accidental and/or unwitting agent of the disfigurement or death of those one loves best. I regard these as *paradigmatic*, because I believe most people would find in the doing or suffering of them prima-facie reason to doubt the positive meaning of their lives.[8] Christian belief counts the crucifixion of Christ another: on the one hand, death by crucifixion seemed to defeat Jesus' Messianic vocation; for according to Jewish law, death by hanging from a tree made its victim ritually accursed, definitively excluded from the compass of God's people, *a fortiori* disqualified from being the Messiah. On the other hand, it represented the defeat of its perpetrators' leadership vocations, as those who were to prepare the people of God for the Messiah's coming, killed and ritually accursed the true Messiah, according to later theological understanding, God Himself.

3. The impotence of standard solutions

For better and worse, the by now standard strategies for 'solving' the problem of evil are powerless in the face of horrendous evils.

3.1. Seeking the reason-why

In his model article 'Hume on Evil',[9] Pike takes up Mackie's challenge, arguing that (P1) fails to reflect ordinary moral intuitions (more to the point, I would add, Christian beliefs), and traces the abiding sense of trouble to the hunch that an omnipotent, omniscient being could have no reason compatible with perfect goodness for permitting (bringing about) evils, because all legitimate excuses arise from ignorance or weakness. Solutions to the problem of evil have thus been sought in the form of counter-examples to this latter claim, i.e. logically possible reasons-why that would excuse even an omnipotent, omniscient God! The putative logically possible reasons offered have tended to be *generic* and *global*: generic in so far as some *general* reason is sought to cover all sorts of evils; global in so far as they seize upon some feature of the world as a whole. For example, philosophers have alleged that the desire to make a world with one of the following properties—'the best of all possible worlds',[10] 'a world a more perfect than which is impossible', 'a world exhibiting a perfect balance of retributive justice',[11] 'a world with as favorable a balance of (created) moral good over moral evil as God can weakly actualize'[12]—would constitute a reason compatible with perfect goodness for God's creating a world with evils in the amounts and of the kinds found in the actual world. Moreover, such general reasons are presented as so powerful as to do away with any need to catalogue types of evils one by one, and examine God's reason for permitting each in particular. Plantinga explicitly hopes that the problem of horrendous evils can thus be solved without being squarely confronted.[13]

3.2. The insufficiency of global defeat

A pair of distinctions is in order here: (i) between two dimensions of divine goodness in relation to creation—namely, 'producer of global goods' and 'goodness to' or 'love of individual created persons'; and (ii) between the overbalance/defeat of evil by good on the global scale, and the overbalance/defeat of evil by good within the context of an individual person's life.[14] Correspondingly, we may separate two problems of evil parallel to the two sorts of goodness mentioned in (i).

In effect, generic and global approaches are directed to the first problem: they defend divine goodness along the first (global) dimension by suggesting logically possible strategies for the global defeat of evils. But establishing God's excellence as a producer of global goods does not automatically solve the second problem, especially in a world containing horrendous evils. For God cannot be said to be good or loving to any created persons the positive meaning of whose lives He allows to be engulfed in and/or defeated by evils—that is, individuals within whose lives horrendous evils remain undefeated. Yet, the only way unsupplemented global and generic approaches could have to explain the latter, would be by applying their general reasons-why to particular cases of horrendous suffering.

Unfortunately, such an exercise fails to give satisfaction. Suppose for the sake of argument that horrendous evil could be included in maximally perfect world orders; its being partially constitutive of such an order would assign it that generic and global positive meaning. But would knowledge of such a fact defeat for a mother the prima-facie reason provided by her cannibalism of her own infant to wish that she had never been born? Again, the aim of perfect retributive balance confers meaning on evils imposed. But would knowledge that the torturer was being tortured give the victim who broke down and turned traitor under pressure any more reason to think his/her life worth while? Would it not merely multiply reasons for the torturer to doubt that his/her life could turn out to be a good to him/her on the whole? Could the truck-driver who accidentally runs over his beloved child find consolation in the idea that this middle-known[15] but unintended side-effect was part of the price God accepted for a world with the best balance of moral good over moral evil he could get?

Not only does the application to horrors of such generic and global reasons for divine permission of evils fail to solve the second problem of evil; it makes it worse by adding *generic prima-facie* reasons to doubt whether human life would be a great good to individual human beings in possible worlds where such divine motives were operative. For, taken in isolation and made to bear the weight of the whole explanation, such reasons-why draw a picture of divine indifference or even hostility to the human plight. Would the fact that God permitted horrors because they were constitutive means to His end of global perfection, or that He tolerated them because He could obtain that global end anyway, make the participant's life more tolerable, more worth living for him/her? Given radical human vulnerability to horrendous evils, the ease with which humans participate in them, whether as victim or perpetrator, would not the thought that God visits horrors on anyone who caused them, simply because he/she deserves it, provide one more reason to expect human life to be a nightmare?

Those willing to split the two problems of evil apart might adopt a divide-and-conquer strategy, by simply denying divine goodness along the second dimension. For example, many Christians do not believe that God will ensure an overwhelmingly good life to each and every person He creates. Some say the decisive defeat of evil with good is promised only within the lives of the obedient, who enter by the narrow gate. Some speculate that the elect may be few. Many recognize that the sufferings of this present life are as nothing compared to the hell of eternal torment, designed to defeat goodness with horrors within the lives of the damned.

Such a road can be consistently travelled only at the heavy toll of admitting that human life in worlds such as ours is a bad bet. Imagine (adapting Rawls's device) persons in a pre-original position, considering possible worlds containing managers of differing power, wisdom, and character, and subjects of varying fates. The question they are to answer about each world is whether they would willingly enter it as a human being, from behind a veil of ignorance as to which position they would occupy. Reason would, I submit, dictate a negative verdict for worlds whose omniscient and omnipotent manager permits ante-mortem horrors that remain undefeated within the context of the human participant's life; *a fortiori*, for worlds in which some or most humans suffer eternal torment.

3.3. Inaccessible reasons

So far, I have argued that generic and global solutions are at best incomplete: however well their account of divine motivating reasons deals with the first problem of evil, the attempt to extend it to the second fails by making it worse. This verdict might seem prima facie tolerable to standard generic and global approaches and indicative of only a minor modification in their strategy: let the above-mentioned generic and global reasons cover divine permission of non-horrendous evils, and find other *reasons* compatible with perfect goodness *why* even an omnipotent, omniscient God would permit horrors.

In my judgement, such an approach is hopeless. As Plantinga[16] points out, where horrendous evils are concerned, not only do we not know God's *actual* reason for permitting them; we cannot even *conceive* of any plausible candidate sort of reason consistent with worthwhile lives for human participants in them.

4. The how of God's victory

Up to now, my discussion has given the reader cause to wonder whose side I am on anyway. For I have insisted, with rebels like Ivan Karamazov and John Stuart Mill, on spotlighting the problem horrendous evils pose. Yet, I have signaled my preference for a version of Christianity that insists on both dimensions of divine goodness, and maintains not only (a) that God will be good enough to created persons to make human life a good bet, but also (b) that each created person will have a life that is a great good to him/her on the whole. My critique of standard approaches to the problem of evil thus seems to reinforce atheologian Mackie's verdict of 'positive irrationality' for such a religious position.

4.1. Whys versus hows

The inaccessibility of reasons-why seems especially decisive. For surely an all-wise and all-powerful God, who loved each created person enough (a) to defeat any experienced horrors within the context of the participant's life, and (b) to give each created person a life that is a great good to him/her on the whole, would not permit such persons to suffer horrors for no reason.[17] Does not our inability even to conceive of plausible candidate reasons suffice to make belief in such a God positively irrational in a world containing horrors? In my judgement, it does not.

To be sure, motivating reasons come in several varieties relative to our conceptual grasp: There are (i) reasons of the sort we can readily understand when we are informed of them (e.g. the mother who permits her child to undergo painful heart surgery because it is the only humanly possible way to save its life). Moreover, there are (ii) reasons we would be cognitively, emotionally, and spiritually equipped to grasp if only we had a larger memory or wider attention span (analogy: I may be able to memorize small town street plans; memorizing the road networks of the entire country is a task requiring more of the same, in the way that proving Gödel's theorem is not). Some generic and global approaches insinuate that divine permission of evils has motivating reasons of this sort. Finally, there are (iii) reasons that we are cognitively, emotionally, and/or spiritually too immature to fathom (the way a two-year-old child is incapable of understanding its mother's reasons for permitting the surgery). I agree with Plantinga that our ignorance of divine reasons for permitting horrendous evils is not of types (i) or (ii), but of type (iii).

Nevertheless, if there are varieties of ignorance, there are also varieties of reassurance.[18] The two-year-old heart patient is convinced of its mother's love, not by her cognitively inaccessible reasons, but by her intimate care and presence through its painful experience. The story of Job suggests something similar is true with human participation in horrendous suffering: God does not give Job His reasons-why, and implies that Job isn't smart enough to grasp them; rather Job is lectured on the extent of divine power, and sees God's goodness face to face! Likewise, I suggest, to exhibit the logical compossibility of both dimensions of divine goodness with horrendous suffering, it is not necessary to find logically possible reasons *why* God might permit them. It is enough to show *how* God can be good enough to created persons despite their participation in horrors—by defeating them within the context of the individual's life and by giving that individual a life that is a great good to him/her on the whole.

4.2. What sort of valuables?

In my opinion, the reasonableness of Christianity can be maintained in the face of horrendous evils only by drawing on resources of religious value theory. For one way for God to be *good to* created persons is by relating them appropriately to relevant and great goods. But philosophical and religious theories differ importantly on what valuables they admit into their ontology. Some maintain that 'what you see is what you get', but nevertheless admit a wide range of valuables, from sensory pleasures, the beauty of nature and cultural artefacts, the joys of creativity, to loving personal intimacy. Others posit a transcendent good (e.g. the Form of the Good in Platonism, or God, the Supremely Valuable Object, in Christianity). In the spirit of Ivan Karamazov, I am convinced that the depth of horrific evil cannot be accurately estimated without recognizing it to be incommensurate with any package of merely non-transcendent goods and so unable to be balanced off, much less defeated, thereby.

Where the internal coherence of Christianity is the issue, however, it is fair to appeal to its own store of valuables. From a Christian point of view, God is a being a greater than which cannot be conceived, a good incommensurate with both created goods and temporal evils. Likewise, the good of beatific, face-to-face intimacy with God is simply incommensurate with any merely non-transcendent goods or ills a person might experience. Thus, the good of beatific face-to-face intimacy with God would *engulf* (in a sense analogous to Chisholmian balancing off) even the horrendous evils humans experience in this present life here below, and overcome any prima-facie reasons the individual had to doubt whether his/her life would or could be worth living.

4.3. Personal meaning, horrors defeated

Engulfing personal horrors within the context of the participant's life would vouchsafe to that individual a life that was a great good to him/her on the whole. I am still inclined to think it would guarantee that immeasurable divine goodness to any person thus benefited. But there is good theological reason for Christians to believe that God would go further, beyond engulfment to defeat. For it is the nature of persons to look for meaning, both in their lives and in the world. Divine respect for and commitment to created personhood would drive God to make all those sufferings which threaten to destroy the positive meaning of a person's life meaningful through positive defeat.[19]

How could God do it? So far as I can see, only by integrating participation in horrendous evils into a person's relationship with God. Possible dimensions of integration are charted by Christian soteriology. I pause here to sketch three:[20] (i) First, because God in Christ participated in horrendous evil through His passion and death, human experience of horrors can be a means of *identifying* with Christ, either through *sympathetic* identification (in which each person suffers his/her own pains, but their similarity enables each to know what it is like for the other) or through *mystical* identification (in which the created person is supposed literally to experience a share of Christ's pain[21]). (ii) Julian of Norwich's description of heavenly welcome suggests the possible defeat of horrendous evil through divine gratitude. According to Julian, before the elect have a chance to thank God for all He has done for them, God will say, 'Thank you for all your suffering, the suffering of your youth.' She says that the creature's experience of divine gratitude will bring such full and unending joy as could not be merited by the whole sea of human pain and suffering throughout the ages.[22] (iii) A third idea identifies temporal suffering itself with a vision into the inner life of God, and can be developed several ways. Perhaps, contrary to medieval theology, God is not impassible, but rather has matched capacities for joy and for suffering. Perhaps, as the Heidelberg catechism suggests, God responds to human sin and the sufferings of Christ with an agony beyond human conception.[23] Alternatively, the inner life of God may be, strictly speaking and in and of itself, beyond both joy and sorrow. But, just as (according to Rudolf Otto) humans experience divine presence now as *tremendum* (with deep dread and anxiety), now as *fascinans* (with ineffable attraction), so perhaps our deepest suffering as much as our highest joys may themselves be direct visions into the inner life of God, imperfect but somehow less obscure in proportion to their intensity. And if a face-to-face vision of God is a good for humans incommensurate with any non-transcendent goods or ills, so any vision of God (including horrendous suffering) would have a good aspect in so far

572   MARILYN McCORD ADAMS

as it is a vision of God (even if it has an evil aspect in so far as it is horrendous suffering). For the most part, horrors are not recognized as experiences of God (any more than the city slicker recognizes his visual image of a brown patch as a vision of Beulah the cow in the distance). But, Christian mysticism might claim, at least from the post-mortem perspective of the beatific vision, such sufferings will be seen for what they were, and retrospectively no one will wish away any intimate encounters with God from his/her life-history in this world. The created person's experience of the beatific vision together with his/her knowledge that intimate divine presence stretched back over his/her ante-mortem life and reached down into the depths of his/her worst suffering, would provide retrospective comfort independent of comprehension of the reasons-why akin to the two-year-old's assurance of its mother's love. Taking this third approach, Christians would not need to commit themselves about what in any event we do not know: namely, whether we will (like the two-year-old) ever grow up enough to understand the reasons why God permits our participation in horrendous evils. For by contrast with the best of earthly mothers, such divine intimacy is an incommensurate good and would cancel out for the creature any need to know why.

5. Conclusion

The worst evils demand to be defeated by the best goods. Horrendous evils can be overcome only by the goodness of God. Relative to human nature, participation in hor-rendous evils and loving intimacy with God are alike disproportionate: for the former threatens to engulf the good in an individual human life with evil, while the latter guar-antees the reverse engulfment of evil by good. Relative to one another, there is also disproportion, because the good that God *is*, and intimate relationship with Him, is incommensurate with created goods and evils alike. Because intimacy with God so out-scales relations (good or bad) with any creatures, integration into the human person's relationship with God confers significant meaning and positive value even on horren-dous suffering. This result coheres with basic Christian intuition: that the powers of darkness are stronger than humans, but they are no match for God!

Standard generic and global solutions have for the most part tried to operate within the territory common to believer and unbeliever, within the confines of religion-neutral value theory. Many discussions reflect the hope that substitute attribute-analyses, can-didate reasons-why, and/or defeaters could issue out of values shared by believers and unbelievers alike. And some virtually make this a requirement on an adequate solution. Mackie knew better how to distinguish the many charges that may be levelled against religion. Just as philosophers may or may not find the existence of God plausible, so they may be variously attracted or repelled by Christian values of grace and redemp-tive sacrifice. But agreement on truth-value is not necessary to consensus on internal consistency. My contention has been that it is not only legitimate, but, given horren-dous evils, necessary for Christians to dip into their richer store of valuables to exhibit the consistency of (1) and (2).[24] I would go one step further: assuming the pragmatic and/or moral (I would prefer to say, broadly speaking, religious) importance of believ-ing that (one's own) human life is worth living, the ability of Christianity to exhibit how this could be so despite human vulnerability to horrendous evil, constitutes a prag-matic/moral/religious consideration in its favour, relative to value schemes that do not.

To me, the most troublesome weakness in what I have said lies in the area of conceptual under-development. The contention that God suffered in Christ or that one person can experience another's pain requires detailed analysis and articulation in metaphysics and philosophy of mind. I have shouldered some of this burden elsewhere,[25] but its full discharge is well beyond the scope of this paper.

Notes

1 J. L. Mackie, 'Evil and Omnipotence', *Mind*, 64 (1955) . . . ; repr. in Nelson Pike (ed.), *God and Evil* (Englewood Cliffs, NJ: Prentice-Hall, 1964), 46–60.

2 Ibid. 47.

3 Marilyn McCord Adams, 'Problems of Evil: More Advice to Christian Philosophers', *Faith and Philosophy* (Apr. 1988), 121–43.

4 Mackie, 'Evil and Omnipotence', pp. 46–7. (emphasis mine).

5 Stewart Sutherland (in his comment 'Horrendous Evils and the Goodness of God—II', *Proceedings of the Aristotelian Society*, suppl. vol. 63 (1989), 311–23; esp. 311) takes my criterion to be somehow 'first-person'. This was not my intention. My definition may be made more explicit as follows: an evil *e* is horrendous if and only if participation in *e* by person *p* gives everyone prima-facie reason to doubt whether *p*'s life can, given *p*'s participation in *e*, be a great good to *p* on the whole.

6 Roderick Chisholm, 'The Defeat of Good and Evil' . . . .

7 Cf. Malcolm's astonishment at Wittgenstein's dying exclamation that he had had a wonderful life, *Ludwig Wittgenstein: A Memoir* (London: Oxford University Press, 1962), 100.

8 Once again, more explicitly, most people would agree that a person *p*'s doing or suffering of them constitutes prima-facie reason to doubt whether *p*'s life can be, given such participation, a great good to *p* on the whole.

9 'Hume on Evil', *Philosophical Review*, 72 (1963), 180–97 . . . ; reprinted in Pike (ed.), *God and Evil,* p. 88.

10 Following Leibniz, Pike draws on this feature as part of what I have called his Epistemic Defence ('Problems of Evil: More Advice to Christian Philosophers', pp. 124–5).

11 Augustine, *On Free Choice of Will,* iii. 93–102, implies that there is a maximum value for created worlds, and a plurality of worlds that meet it. All of these contain rational free creatures; evils are foreseen but unintended side-effects of their creation. No matter what they choose, however, God can order their choices into a maximally perfect universe by establishing an order of retributive justice.

12 Plantinga takes this line in numerous discussions, in the course of answering Mackie's objection to the Free Will Defence, that God should have made sinless free creatures. Plantinga insists that, given incompatibilist freedom in creatures, God cannot strongly actualize any world He wants. It is logically possible that a world with evils in the amounts and of the kinds found in this world is the best that He could do, Plantinga argues, given His aim of getting some moral goodness in the world.

13 Alvin Plantinga, 'Self-Profile', in James E. Tomberlin and Peter van Inwagen (eds.), *Profiles: Alvin Plantinga* (Dordrecht, Boston, Mass., and Lancaster, Pa.: Reidel, 1985), 38.

14 I owe the second of these distinctions to a remark by Keith De Rose in our Fall 1987 seminar on the problem of evil at UCLA.

15 Middle knowledge, or knowledge of what is 'in between' the actual and the possible, is the sort of knowledge of what a free creature *would do* in every situation in which that creature could possibly find himself. Following Luis de Molina and Francisco Suarez, Alvin Plantinga ascribes such knowledge to God, prior in the order of explanation to God's decision

about which free creatures to actualize (in *The Nature of Necessity* (Oxford: Clarendon Press, 1974), pp. 164–93) . . . . Robert Merrihew Adams challenges this idea in his article 'Middle Knowledge and the Problem of Evil', *American Philosophical Quarterly,* 14 (1977) . . . ; repr. in *The Virtue of Faith* (New York: Oxford University Press, 1987), 77–93.

16   Alvin Plantinga, 'Self-Profile', pp. 34–5.

17   This point was made by William Fitzpatrick in our Fall 1987 seminar on the problem of evil at UCLA.

18   Contrary to what Sutherland suggests ('Horrendous Evils', pp. 314–15), so far as the compossibility problem is concerned, I intend no illicit shift from reason to emotion. My point is that intimacy with a loving other is a good, participation in which can defeat evils, and so provide everyone with reason to think a person's life can be a great good to him/her on the whole, despite his/her participation in evils.

19   Note, once again, contrary to what Sutherland suggests ('Horrendous Evils', pp. 321–3) 'horrendous evil *e* is defeated' entails *none* of the following propositions: '*e* was not horrendous', '*e* was not unjust', '*e* was not so bad after all'. Nor does my suggestion that even horrendous evils can be defeated by a great enough (because incommensurate and uncreated) good, in any way impugn the reliability of our moral intuitions about injustice, cold-bloodedness, or horror. The judgement that participation in *e* constitutes prima-facie reason to believe that *p*'s life is ruined, stands and remains a daunting measure of *e*'s horror.

20   In my paper 'Redemptive Suffering: A Christian Solution to the Problem of Evil', in Robert Audi and William J. Wainwright (eds.), *Rationality, Religious Belief, and Moral Commitment: New Essays in Philosophy of Religion* (Cornell University Press, 1986), 248–67, I sketch how horrendous suffering can be meaningful by being made a vehicle of divine redemption for victim, perpetrator, and onlooker, and thus an occasion of the victim's collaboration with God. In 'Separation and Reversal in Luke-Acts', in Thomas Morris (ed.), *Philosophy and the Christian Faith* (Notre Dame, Ind.: Notre Dame University Press, 1988), 92–117, I attempted to chart the redemptive plot-line whereby horrendous sufferings are made meaningful by being woven into the divine redemptive plot. My considered opinion is that such collaboration would be too strenuous for the human condition were it not to be supplemented by a more explicit and beatific divine intimacy.

21   For example, Julian of Norwich tells us that she prayed for and received the latter (*Revelations of Divine Love,* ch. 17). Mother Theresa of Calcutta seems to construe Matthew 25:31–46 to mean that the poorest and the least are Christ, and that their sufferings are Christ's (Malcolm Muggeridge, *Something Beautiful for God* (New York: Harper & Row, 1960), 72–5).

22   *Revelations of Divine Love*, ch. 14. I am grateful to Houston Smit for recognizing this scenario of Julian's as a case of Chisholmian defeat.

23   Cf. Plantinga, 'Self-Profile', p. 36.

24   I develop this point at some length in 'Problems of Evil: More Advice to Christian Philosophers', pp. 127–35.

25   For example in 'The Metaphysics of the Incarnation in Some Fourteenth Century Franciscans', in William A. Frank and Girard J. Etzkorn (eds.), *Essays Honoring Allan B. Wolter* (St. Bonaventure, NY: The Franciscan Institute, 1985), 21–57.

In the development of these ideas, I am indebted to the members of our Fall 1987 seminar on the problem of evil at UCLA—especially to Robert Merrihew Adams (its co-leader) and to Keith De Rose, William Fitzpatrick, and Houston Smit. I am also grateful to the Very Revd. Jon Hart Olson for many conversations in mystical theology.

Questions for reflection

1   How does Professor Adams's approach to the problem of evil differ from other the-
     istic approaches, such as the one offered by Alvin Plantinga in this section? Can the
     various approaches be integrated? Explain.
2   What are horrendous evils, and how do they differ from non-horrendous evils? What
     makes horrendous evils more problematic, in terms of a response to the problem of
     evil?
3   Consider the following scenario. Suppose that a child, we'll call her Suzanne, has the
     horrible disease referred to as Rhizomelic Chondrodysplasia Punctata, or RCDP. Its
     symptoms include cataracts, shortened arms and legs, and mental retardation. Fur-
     thermore, over half of the children who have the disease die before the age of two.
     Suzanne is now eight, severely mentally handicapped, and she has suffered terribly
     with the disease and its many complications all her life. She is now dying and will not
     see her ninth birthday. Is it reasonable to believe that her life is one in which, in eter-
     nity, she would be able to find ultimate meaning and goodness given Adams's three
     dimensions of integration? Explain.
4   Compare and contrast Adams's response to evil/suffering with the Buddhist perspec-
     tive offered by Professor Kalupahana in the following chapter. Which do you find
     most satisfying? Why?

Further reading

Marilyn McCord Adams (1999) *Horrendous Evils and the Goodness of God*. Ithaca, NY: Cornell Uni-
     versity Press. (Elaborates on the position defended in the essay above.)
Marilyn McCord Adams (2006) *Christ and Horrors: The Coherence of Christology*. Cambridge: Cam-
     bridge University Press. (Develops her position further from a theological point of view.)
Marilyn McCord Adams and Robert Merrihew Adams, eds. (1990) *The Problem of Evil*. Oxford:
     Oxford University Press. (A scholarly collection of essays from a variety of perspectives; the
     essay above was taken from this book.)
Richard Swinburne (1998) *Providence and the Problem of Evil*. Oxford: Oxford University Press.
     (Argues that God allows evil because God desires more for us than pleasure or escape from
     pain; God wants us to learn, to love, and to develop the right kind of character.)
Peter van Inwagen (2006) *The Problem of Evil*. Oxford: Oxford University Press. (The Gifford Lec-
     tures delivered at the University of St. Andrews in 2003; argues that the vast amount of
     suffering in the world does not show that God does not exist.)

Chapter 54

David J. Kalupahana

SUFFERING—A BUDDHIST PERSPECTIVE

David J. Kalupahana is Emeritus Professor of Philosophy at the University of Hawaii and a leading authority on Buddhist thought. In this essay, he first notes that certain Western philosophers, including Arthur Schopenhauer, Friedrich Nietzsche and Karl Jaspers, have interpreted the Buddhist notion of suffering from a Western/Greek perspective. This has led them to view Buddhism as a pessimistic religion in which "all is suffering." However, understanding it in light of its proper non-substantialist (or non-absolutist) and pragmatic origins leads one to a different conclusion. Noting that understanding the epistemological standpoint of the Buddha is paramount, and drawing on helpful concepts from philosopher/psychologist William James, Kalupahana argues that, in the Buddhist conception of suffering, one's dispositions play a central role; it is "the greed for the pleasant and the aversion or hatred toward the unpleasant [which] constitute suffering." The renunciation of craving and the realization of impermanence are central beliefs for a true follower of the teachings of the Buddha. As such, human life is not a tragedy, but an opportunity.

Sarvāstivādins (probably derived from the phrase sarva asti—"everything exists") – a group of Buddhists who emerged in the third century BCE; they were realists who believed that the dharmas—the most basic elements of existence—exist in the past, the present and the future. As with other sects of Buddhism, they rejected the belief in the individual self as a substantial being.

Vasubandhu (c. fourth century CE) – a foremost Buddhist teacher and a leading figure in the development of Mahāyāna Buddhism in India.

. . . [A] genuine realization that there is suffering in the world dawns upon the enlightened one with the development of wisdom.* What is genuine about this realization?

The Buddha's statement that there is suffering in the world . . . has been the subject of much discussion among some of the leading philosophers in the modern world like Schopenhauer, Nietzsche and Jaspers. Unfortunately, most of these philosophers have attempted to understand the concept of suffering in Buddhism in terms of the conception of tragedy familiar to them in the Western philosophical and literary traditions reaching back to the early Greeks. As a result, we are left with the impression that Buddhism is a pessimistic religion. Whether such an interpretation of the Buddhist tradition is valid or not can be decided only after a careful study of the problem of suffering placed in the context of the non-substantialist and pragmatic teachings of the Buddha . . . .

Pessimism and optimism are two contradicting attitudes adopted mostly by those who are prone to substantialist or absolutist ways of thinking. If the Buddha was a genuine non-substantialist or a non-absolutist, then there is no justification for applying such exclusive categories as pessimism or optimism to describe his teachings. Before proceeding to explain the psychology of suffering in Buddhism, it would be necessary to indicate how and when this unacceptable interpretation of Buddhism emerged.

In spite of the Buddha's emphasis on the idea that all experienced phenomena are non-substantial, substantialist thinking gradually infiltrated Buddhism, crystalizing itself in the doctrines of the Sarvāstivādins. The following discussion of happiness and suffering couched in extremely substantialist language is reported by Vasubandhu:

> When [the Buddha] declared: "One should perceive happy feeling as suffering," both [happiness and suffering] are available therein. Happiness is *inherently* so, because there is pleasantness. However, eventually there is suffering, because of its changing and impermanent nature. When that [feeling] is perceived as happiness, it contributes to enlightenment, through its enjoyment. When it is perceived as suffering, it leads to release, by being non-attached to it.[1]

This discussion was generated as a result of the Sarvāstivāda attempt to recognize both happiness and suffering existing as substances. Indeed, the Buddhist metaphysician seems to have been trapped by the substantialist Brahmanical opponents who continued to misquote the Buddha's statement regarding suffering. The Buddha's statement is sometimes couched in the language of universals. Thus we have the phrase: "All dispositions are suffering" (*sabbe sankhārā dukkhā*). He consistently, and it seems consciously, avoided considering all phenomena to be suffering. Nowhere in the discourses attributed to him do we come across the statement: "All phenomena are suffering" (*sabbe dhammā dukkhā*). However, the use of the term *sabbam* ("all, everything") in the above context misled most interpreters, especially the Brahmanical thinkers and the later Buddhist metaphysicians, to assuming that the Buddha was making unqualified universal statements. They took the Buddha to be saying:

> All is impermanent (*sabbam aniccam*).
> All is suffering (*sabbam dukkham*).
> All is non-substantial (*sabbam anattam*).

They failed to realize the absolutist implication of the above statements in contrast to the universal statements that are identified, concretized or embodied in the following manner:

All this is impermanent (sabbam idam aniccam).
All this is suffering (sabbam idam dukkham).
All *this* is non-substantial (*sabbam idam anattam*).

It is the failure to distinguish these two types of universal statements, the absolute and the limited, that led not only to the dilemma of the Sarvāstivādins (referred to in the passage quoted above) with their conceptions of happiness and suffering as two substantial entities that need reconciliation, but also to the interpretation of Buddhism as a doctrine of "universal suffering" by modern European scholars.

The Brahmanical and Buddhist ideological conflict continued until the disappearance of the latter from the Indian soil. Later Brahmanical philosophers like Udayana Acārya continued to attribute distorted statements like *sarvam duhkham* ("all is suffering") to the Buddha, and revelled at their success in demolishing Buddhism,[2] hardly realizing that they were exposing the contradiction in their own substantialist thinking.

Nineteenth century Western philosophers like Schopenhauer, who pioneered the study of Asian thought in the West before careful editing and translating of Buddhist texts were carried out in Western languages, were most probably led by the Brahmanical interpreters of Buddhism. Schopenhauer was one of the first to characterize Buddhism as a pessimistic religion propounding a theory of "universal suffering," a characterization that seems to have appealed to his own inclinations and temperament. William James, quoting J. Misland (*Luther et le Serf-Arbitre*, 1884), notes that "Germanic races have tended rather to think of Sin in the singular, and with a capital S, as of something ineradicably ingrained in our natural subjectivity, and never to be removed by any superficial piecemeal operations," and that "undoubtedly the northern tone in religion has inclined to the more intimately pessimistic persuasion, . . ."[3]

Such being the manner in which Buddhism came to be looked upon as a pessimistic religion, it would now be possible to examine the implications of pessimism and optimism, and evaluate the Buddha's conception of suffering. In this connection James' two chapters in *The Varieties of Religious Experience* on "The Religion of the Healthy-mindedness," and "The Sick Soul" will be of great assistance. These two chapters are elaboration of two types of human beings referred to by Francis W. Newman as "the once-born and the twice-born."[4] James takes the "once-born" as an example of the "healthy-minded." A quotation from Newman illustrates the character of such a person:

They see God, not as a Strict Judge, not as a Glorious Potentate; but as the animating Spirit of a beautiful harmonious world, Beneficient and Kind, Merciful as well as Pure. The same characters generally have no metaphysical tendencies: they do not look back into themselves. Hence they are not distressed by their own imperfections; yet it would be absurd to call them self-righteous; for they hardly think of themselves *at all*. This childlike quality of their nature makes the opening of religion very happy to them: for they no more shrink from God, than a child from an emperor, before whom the parent trembles: in fact, they have no vivid conception of any of the qualities in which the severer Majesty of God consists. He is to them the impersonation of Kindness and Beauty. They read his character not in the disordered world of man, but in romantic and harmonious nature.[5]

In the pre-Buddhist background, such an attitude seems to emerge in the substantialist tradition of the *Upaniṣads* where the individual empirical self is negated in favor of a more permanent and eternal self (*ātman*) which came to be looked upon as possessing the characteristics of "the real" (*sat*), "consciousness" (*cit*) and "bliss" (*ānanda*). The emphasis is on the blissful and harmonious self pervading the universe, including man, and suffering being confined to the individual empirical self which should not be the object of thought at all. This could not be considered the shallower version of the healthy-mindedness, sometimes depicted in the attitude of the materialists in India, but represents what James calls the "profounder" level of healthy-mindedness. The contrary of this is the "sick soul" which "cannot so swiftly throw off the burden of the consciousness of evil, but are *congenitally fated to suffer from its presence.*"[6]

The one school of thought in the Indian context that comes anywhere close to this way of thinking is Jainism. The Jaina view of life, in spite of its relationship to Buddhism in certain aspects, was criticized by the Buddha. Their view of karma is often referred to in the Buddhist texts as *pubbe-kata-hetu* which implies that all present experiences are the inevitable results of the inexhorable past actions. The Buddha initiates the criticism of this theory by raising questions regarding its epistemological foundations.

> From what you say, reverent Jains, you do not know whether you yourselves were in the past, or whether you were not; you do not know whether in the past you yourselves did this evil deed like this or like that; you do not know that so much suffering is worn away, or that so much suffering is to be worn away, or that when so much suffering is worn away, all suffering will become worn away; you do not know the getting rid of the bad states of mind here and now, or the arising of the good states.[7]

Having rejected the substantialist implications of the Jaina theory of karma,[8] the Buddha concludes:

> If, monks, the pleasure and pain which creatures undergo are due to what was previously done, certainly, monks, the Jainas were formerly doers of deeds that were badly done in that they now experience such painful, severe, sharp feelings. If, monks, the pleasure and pain which creatures undergo are due to creation by an overlord, certainly, monks, the Jainas were created by an evil overlord in that they now experience such painful, severe, sharp feelings. If, monks, the pleasure and pain which creatures undergo are due to destiny, certainly, monks, the Jainas are of evil destiny in that they now experience such painful, severe, sharp feelings. If, monks, the pleasure and pain which creatures undergo are due to their species, certainly, monks, the Jainas are of evil species in that they experience such painful, severe, sharp feelings. If, monks, the pleasure and pain creatures undergo are due to effort here and now, certainly, monks, the Jainas are of evil effort here and now in that they now experience such painful, severe and sharp feelings.[9]

The point made clear is that none of these causes, *taken in itself,* can be presented as *the* cause or condition of human experience to the neglect of everything else. Human experience is complex; so are the conditions that give rise to such experience. It is possible that James came to realize the difference between the Jaina and Buddhist theories of karma after he completed writing his Gifford Lectures, and in the postscript . . . opted for the more non-substantialist Buddhist theory of karma.

In criticizing the Jaina thinkers for presenting a very deterministic theory of karma that leads to a pessimistic view of life, the Buddha raised questions regarding the epistemological means by which they reached their conclusions. To understand what these epistemological puzzles are it would be appropriate to return to James' examination of pessimism in the Western world. James quotes two interesting passages in order to explain the type of questions that eventually lead to a tragic or pessimistic view of life. The first is from the Greek classics.

> Naked came I upon the earth, naked I go below the ground—why then do I vainly toil when I see the end naked before me? How did I come to be? Whence am I? Whereof did I come? To pass away. How can I learn ought when naught I know? Being nought I came to life: once more shall I be what I was. Nothing and nothingness is the whole race of mortals.[10]

Next is a quotation from Tolstoy, a pessimist from the modern world of science and technology.

> This is no fable, but the literal incontestable truth which every one may understand. What will be the outcome of what I do today? Of what I shall do tomorrow? What will be the outcome of all my life? Why should I live? Why should I do anything? Is there in life any purpose which the inevitable death awaits me does not undo and destroy?
>
> These questions are the simplest in the world. From the stupid child to the wisest old man, they are in the soul of every human being. Without an answer to them, it is impossible, as I experienced, for life to go on.[11]

The former quotation refers to the uncertainties regarding the past and the latter regarding the future. In both instances, the anxieties about the past and the future have become obstacles against dealing with the present. While the optimist's response to this anxiety may appear to be "childlike," the pessimist has lost all hope. The Buddha did realize, as did the Greeks and Tolstoy, that these are genuine questions raised by human beings. "Did I exist in the past or not? Will I exist in the future or not? Do I exist in the present or do I not exist in the present?"[12] are questions for which human beings have sought answers from the dawn of history. However, the Buddha also realized that human beings have often transgressed the limits of reflection and investigation in attempting to answer these questions. . . . There is no need to list the variety of answers that one can find in the different traditions. Most of them fall under the broad categories of eternalism and annihilationism, and as far as the Buddha is concerned they are dispositional answers,[13] which can neither be confirmed nor denied. Abandoning such speculations and without carrying on the reflections and investigations to their extremes, the Buddha concentrated upon what is given in the historical past and the present in order to understand the nature of human life. As such, Tolstoy cannot quote the Buddha in support of his tragic or pessimistic view of life.[14]

The Buddha's explanation of suffering is presented in the following statement, regarding the first of the four truths he had realized through wisdom.

> Birth is suffering; old age is suffering; sickness is suffering; death is suffering. Sorrow, lamentation and dejection are suffering. Association with the unpleasant is suffering; separation from the pleasant is suffering; not getting what one wishes for is suffering. In brief, the five aggregates of grasping are suffering.[15]

Any attempt to understand the nature of this truth, and for that matter, any of the four truths, independent of the epistemological source, namely, wisdom and the conditions that prevent the development of such wisdom . . . would be utterly futile. It is, indeed, for this reason that an enlightened disciple like Nāgārjuna devoted an entire chapter to the examination of the four perversions (*Kārikā* XXIII) before undertaking an explanation of the four truths (*Kārikā* XXIV).

To repeat the four confusions or perversions listed earlier, they consist of the identification of

A.   the impermanent with the permanent,
B.   the not unsatisfactory with the unsatisfactory,
C.   the non-substantial with the substantial, and
D.   the unpleasant with the pleasant.

Here again, one needs to keep in mind the epistemological standpoint of the Buddha before proceeding to analyse the perversions. For example, perversions A and C are not on the same epistemological standing as perversions B and D. The Buddha recognized the impermanent and the non-substantial on the basis of experience. Yet he did not admit any experience that can provide us with knowledge of the permanent and the substantial. The rationalist method of assuming knowledge of the impermanent strictly on the basis of the knowledge of the permanent, and the knowledge of the non-substantial strictly on the basis of the knowledge of the substantial was not acceptable to the Buddha. Empirically, neither the permanent nor the substantial are *known*. However, this is not the case with the perversions B and D. Experience of pleasant and unpleasant sensations does occur even in the enlightened ones. . . . Yet this does not indicate a sharp or absolute dichotomy between cognition and emotion. As pointed out earlier, it is indeed the excessive emotive element, namely, anxiety, that gives rise to the belief in the permanent and the substantial. Thus the difference between perversions A and C, on the one hand, and perversions B and D, on the other, is that in the former the cognition is stretched beyond its legitimate limit to assume the existence of permanent and substantial events, whereas in the latter what is given in experience is mixed up, that is wrongly identified.

Keeping these four perversions in mind, one can proceed to examine the Buddha's definition of suffering. For the annihilationist materialists (as it is for some of the modern scientists), who seem to know almost with certainty that birth is the beginning of human existence and death is the ultimate end, the adoption of an optimistic view of life is easy. If birth is not a new phenomenon but the re-appearance of a permanent and eternal self, and death is not a real death but merely a temporary phase in the same permanent and eternal self that will eventually reach its source, as the eternal-ists of the Upanisadic tradition believed, optimism could again reign supreme. On the contrary, if one is extremely skeptical as to how birth has come to be, and what possibly could happen after death, the tragic sense can be heightened and there is reason for being pessimistic.

However, for the Buddha who was willing to recognize retrocognition as a valid source of knowledge, and for whom the beginning of the stream of consciousness need not be strictly confined to a definite point in the present life of a human being, birth is the result of a process of dependent arising involving physical as well as psychological factors. While excessive craving for survival constitutes one of the psychological conditions for the birth of a human being, birth will not occur unless the necessary physical conditions provided by the parents are also available.[16] Furthermore, birth could be a source of suffering in the present life only if this craving for survival continues to dominate a person's life; not if he, after being born, adopts an attitude of renunciation or dispassion for such continuation. Birth is thus the result of excessive craving or passion for survival and the availability of other necessary physical conditions. Birth becomes a source of suffering only in this conditional, but not in an absolute, sense. In other words, there is no intrinsic relationship between birth and suffering. If they were to be so related, there could not be any freedom from suffering for one who is born, at least in the present life.

The same holds true of decay or old age. It is the unwillingness to accept decay as a fact of life that causes frustration and unhappiness.

Death turns out to be the most intolerable cause of suffering. Eternal life after death, or sometimes eternal life uninterrupted by death have been sought for as ways of overcoming this hazard of existence. For the Buddha, the only way to overcome suffering associated with death is through the realization of the impermanence of life and the renunciation of craving for its continuance beyond its possible limits. In this particular case, the nature of one's dispositions plays a dominant role. While the dispositional tendencies involving excessive craving for life can lead to re-birth (and a repetition of the process of suffering), the complete annihilation of such dispositional tendencies can result in premature death (i.e. suicide). Hence the Buddha's emphasis is on the appeasement of dispositions . . . as a means of avoiding suffering. The appeasement of dispositions enables a person to enjoy the satisfactions of life without being a slave to them and having to face either constant frustrations or fear and fret. In other words, it allows for the recognition of what is called the "life instinct" yet not making it an obsession.

Underscoring the condition that renders birth, old age, decay and death intolerable sources of suffering, thereby eliminating the joys of human life, the Buddha points out that "association with the unpleasant and not getting what one wishes for are suffering." In other words, it is one's excessive craving or yearning or obsession that makes the unpleasant intolerable and the pleasant excessively satisfying. Pleasant and unpleasant experiences are, in a sense, not suffering. Only the greed for the pleasant and the aversion or hatred toward the unpleasant constitute suffering.

For this very reason, the Buddha summarizes his exposition of suffering by saying that the five aggregates of grasping are suffering. This is sometimes taken to mean that the Buddha condemned the psychophysical personality as a putrid, despicable phenomenon to be gotten rid of or sacrificed without the least hesitation in favor of a more exalted and eternal personality after death. This is too hasty a conclusion. It is hard to find the statement in the discourses of the Buddha which reads: "The five aggregates are suffering". What the Buddha considered to be suffering is not the psychophysical per-sonality consisting of the five aggregates, but grasping for it.

The abandoning or relinquishing of grasping does not mean the immediate disin-tegration of the human personality. Grasping is not like a plaster that holds the pieces of the mosaic together. It is what causes suffering once the personality has come to be, even though its elimination can prevent the recurrence or the rebirth of a new person-ality after death. . . .

The Buddha's perception of life is therefore neither pessimistic nor optimistic. To use a term from James, it is rather melioristic.[17] Commenting upon Schopenhauer's attempt to see similarity between Buddhism and his own philosophical outlook, Walter Kaufmann has made the following remark:

> One might have expected Schopenhauer to realize all this, since he stressed the universality of suffering more than any previous philosopher. But at this point he felt a kinship to Buddhism—the universality of suffering is the first of the Buddha's "four noble truths"—and Buddhism and tragedy represent two utterly different responses to suffering.[18]

To this may be added in conclusion that the Buddha did not advocate a notion of "univer-sal suffering" (see above) and, therefore, without looking upon human life as a *tragedy*, perceived it as an *opportunity*.

Notes

* [Most parenthetical Sanskrit and Pali terms, as well as accompanying references to the source texts, noted in the original essay have been removed.]

1 *Abhidharmakośa-bhāsya*, ed. Pralhad Pradhan (Patna: K. P. Jayaswal Research Institute, 1967), 331.
2 *Atmatattvaviveka*, p. 3, *sarvam janasamvedanasiddham duhkham*, meaning "all human experi-ences are suffering."
3 *The Varieties of Religious Experience*, ed. Frederick Burkhardt (Cambridge, MA: Harvard University Press, 1985), 114–115.
4 *The Soul; its Sorrows and its Aspirations*, 1852, pp. 89, 92, quoted by James, *The Varieties of Religious Experience*, 73.
5 *The Varieties of Religious Experience*, 73.
6 ibid., p. 114, emphasis mine.
7 *Majjhima-nikāya*, ed. V. Trenckner and R. Chalmers, 3 volumes (London: PTS, 1887–1901), 2.215.
8 ibid., 2.219–222.
9 ibid., 2.222.
10 Quoted from *Oedipus in Colonus*, 1225; see *The Varieties of Religious Experience*, 120, note 9.
11 *The Varieties of Religious Experience*, 130.
12 *Majjhima-nikāya*, 3.94–99.
13 *Samyutta-nikāya*, ed. L. Feer, 5 volumes (London: PTS, 1884–1904), 3.94–99.
14 *The Varieties of Religious Experience*, 130.
15 *Samyutta-nikāya*, 5.421.

16   *Majjhima-nikāya*, 1.265.
17   *Pragmatism,* ed. Frederick Burkhardt (Cambridge, MA: Harvard University Press, 1968), 136.
18   *Tragedy and Philosophy* (Princeton: Princeton University Press, 1968), 339.

Questions for reflection

1   What, exactly, did the Buddha consider to be suffering, according to Professor Kalupahana?

2   Does the "abandoning of grasping" involve the elimination of human personality? Why or why not?

3   Kalupahana states that it is "one's excessive craving or yearning or obsession that makes the unpleasant intolerable and the pleasant excessively satisfying." And that "the greed for the pleasant and the aversion or hatred toward the unpleasant constitute suffering." Do you agree? Would the complete absence of craving lead to a complete absence of suffering? Explain.

4   What is evil according to the Buddhist conception? Is evil synonymous with suffering? If not, how are they different?

Further reading

BuddhaNet. http://www.buddhanet.net/ (A web link whose vision is to link together people from around the globe who are committed to the Buddha's teachings and lifestyle.)

Michael Carrithers (2001) *The Buddha: A Very Short Introduction.* Oxford: Oxford University Press. (A concise and informative account of the Buddha.)

Rupert Gethin (1998) *The Foundations of Buddhism.* Oxford: Oxford University Press. (Focuses on the ideas and practices which make up the common heritage of the various Buddhist traditions.)

David J. Kalupahana (1987) *The Principles of Buddhist Psychology.* Albany, NY: State University of New York Press. (Includes explications of Buddhist concepts as well as reflections on them in various Buddhist traditions; the selection above was taken from this book.)

PART NINE

Death and the afterlife

One of the most significant issues pondered in life is what happens to us when we die. Since the Axial Period[1] at least, whether we live on after death, and what "living on" after death might mean, have been fundamental human questions in which philosophers and religious thinkers have expended much intellectual energy. *Who* and *what* we think we are, of course, has a significant bearing on what we think happens to us when we die. Part Six explored various answers to the first questions from a variety of thinkers. In this section the focus is specifically on immortality.

Alfred North Whitehead made the claim that philosophical thinking in the West is but a series of footnotes to Plato. No doubt this exaggerated line contains some truth, and perhaps nowhere is this more so the case than in the way we in the West think about the afterlife. For Plato, human beings have an incorporeal aspect — a soul — which survives the death and decay of the body, and he offers in the first reading philosophical reasons for why the soul lives on after death. This topic becomes of central concern when one is directly confronted with one's own mortality or the death of a loved one and it was, no doubt, close to Plato's heart, if for no other reason than that his comrade and philosophical mentor, Socrates, was executed while Plato was in the prime of life. What Plato would desire from us, I suspect, is not merely an analysis of the plausibility of his own arguments; rather, in addition to this endeavor, he would also want us to engage in the broader dialectic on the question and meaning of immortality.

In the next selection, Stephen Davis agrees with Plato that there is a substantial self that lives on after the death of the body, but he argues that there is more to a fully realized self than one's soul. He argues, in accordance with the early Church Fathers, that after the death of the body one is in an incomplete state of human existence. Since being human entails both body and soul, a resurrection of the body is a necessary eventuality for one to be fully human in the afterlife.

It is one thing to affirm life after death and to believe that God will usher us into eternal paradise once we exit the physical world. But why would a benevolent God allow death at all? Furthermore, if the God of the resurrection exists, why is he so hidden in this life?

Paul Moser tackles these and other fundamental questions of death and dying. He agrees with Plato that "philosophy done right prepares us for dying and death," and he argues that there is a purpose in divine hiddenness and that God is inviting us to trust in him in this life. Death, he insists, is a dramatic reminder that our well-being and even our rationality are doomed if we fail in this endeavor of trusting in God, for otherwise our lives turn out to be an empty tragedy.

Not everyone is convinced that survival after death can be inferred from belief in a benevolent God. Charles Taliaferro responds to the view that God need not grant us immortality. He argues that immortality perhaps includes a variety of "non-time-enclosed goods" — goods whose value is not lost if they are temporally unlimited. He also maintains that an afterlife is relevant to events in this life, including evil ones. If God loves us, he insists, we have good reason to believe that he will sustain our existence indefinitely.

While the traditional theistic traditions of Christianity, Islam, and Judaism posit an enduring substantial and individuated soul, there is another view of the afterlife that sees things quite differently. In the next reading, Sri Aurobindo describes the self in both individual and pantheistic terms based on his interpretation of the Hindu Vedas. He believes that, while they refer to the various gods of the Hindu pantheon, they ultimately teach that there is one divine and unchanging Absolute — a divine Reality behind the veil of the physical world. This has weighty import on how one understands life and death, for this Absolute is both divine and Self — an unindividuated Consciousness which underlies the individuated self of the physical universe. The true Self does not reincarnate, and an understanding of this central truth leads one to moksha — eternal bliss.

It seems that the believer in God/Ultimate Reality can reasonably take hope in affirming some form of immortality. But what about the non-believer? Should an atheist fear death? This is the central question addressed by Robin Le Poidevin in the final reading of this section. He presents a case for the view that an atheist can have hope even though life comes to an end. By adhering to a particular view of time referred to as the "B-theory" (a view in which there is no passage of time whereby temporal moments literally come to be and cease to exist), all temporal states are equally real, and so in this way our "temporal" lives will always be.

Note

1   "Axial Period" is a phrase so dubbed by philosopher Karl Jaspers to denote the period from roughly 800 BCE to 200 BCE — a time of widespread revolution in religious and philosophical thought which occurred in both the Orient and the Occident. It includes such important figures as Homer, Socrates, Isaiah, Zoroaster, Siddhartha Gautama, Confucius, and the authors of the Hindu Vedas. During this time new "axes" were created which influenced philosophical and religious thought for the next two millennia.

Chapter 55

Plato

IMMORTALITY OF THE SOUL

Plato (*c.* 427–347 BCE) was a Greek philosopher and one of the most important thinkers in the history of Western culture. He held the view that the body and the soul are two
distinct substances, and one of them—the soul—is the true self which lives on after death,
while the other one—the body—simply decays at death. Plato wrote in dialogue form, and
he typically spoke through the character of his beloved teacher, Socrates. In this selection
(taken from the *Phaedo*), he argues that if we practice philosophy in the right way we can
be cheerful in the face of death, for the soul of the one who rightly practices philosophy is
immortal (since it is pure and divine-like) and thus cannot be scattered or destroyed.

Let him be, he said. I want to make my argument before you, my judges, as to why I think
that a man who has truly spent his life in philosophy is probably right to be of good cheer in
the face of death and to be very hopeful that after death he will attain the greatest blessings yonder. I will try to tell you, Simmias and Cebes, how this may be so. I am afraid
that other people do not realize that the one aim of those who practise philosophy in the
proper manner is to practise for dying and death. Now if this is true, it would be strange
indeed if they were eager for this all their lives and then resent it when what they have
wanted and practised for a long time comes upon them.

Simmias laughed and said: "By Zeus, Socrates, you made me laugh, though I was in
no laughing mood just now. I think that the majority, on hearing this, will think that it
describes the philosophers very well, and our people in Thebes would thoroughly agree
that philosophers are nearly dead and that the majority of men is well aware that they
deserve to be."

And they would be telling the truth, Simmias, except for their being aware. They are
not aware of the way true philosophers are nearly dead, nor of the way they deserve to
be, nor of the sort of death they deserve. But never mind them, he said, let us talk among
ourselves. Do we believe that there is such a thing as death?

Certainly, said Simmias.

Is it anything else than the separation of the soul from the body? Do we believe that death is this, namely, that the body comes to be separated by itself apart from the soul, and the soul comes to be separated by itself apart from the body? Is death anything else than that?

No, that is what it is, he said.

Consider then, my good sir, whether you share my opinion, for this will lead us to a better knowledge of what we are investigating. Do you think it is the part of a philosopher to be concerned with such so-called pleasures as those of food and drink?

By no means.

What about the pleasures of sex?

Not at all.

What of the other pleasures concerned with the service of the body? Do you think such a man prizes them greatly, the acquisition of distinguished clothes and shoes and the other bodily ornaments? Do you think he values these or despises them, except in so far as one cannot do without them?

I think the true philosopher despises them.

Do you not think, he said, that in general such a man's concern is not with the body but that, as far as he can, he turns away from the body towards the soul?

I do.

So in the first place, such things show clearly that the philosopher more than other men frees the soul from association with the body as much as possible?

Apparently.

A man who finds no pleasure in such things and has no part in them is thought by the majority not to deserve to live and to be close to death; the man, that is, who does not care for the pleasures of the body.

What you say is certainly true.

Then what about the actual acquiring of knowledge? Is the body an obstacle when one associates with it in the search for knowledge? I mean, for example, do men find any truth in sight or hearing, or are not even the poets[1] forever telling us that we do not see or hear anything accurately, and surely if those two physical senses are not clear or precise, our other senses can hardly be accurate, as they are all inferior to these. Do you not think so?

I certainly do, he said.

When then, he asked, does the soul grasp the truth? For whenever it attempts to examine anything with the body, it is clearly deceived by it.

True.

Is it not in reasoning if anywhere that any reality becomes clear to the soul?

Yes.

And indeed the soul reasons best when none of these senses troubles it, neither hearing nor sight, nor pain nor pleasure, but when it is most by itself, taking leave of the body and as far as possible having no contact or association with it in its search for reality.

That is so.

And it is then that the soul of the philosopher most disdains the body, flees from it and seeks to be by itself?

It appears so.

What about the following, Simmias? Do we say that there is such a thing as the Just itself, or not?

We do say so, by Zeus.

And the Beautiful, and the Good?

Of course.

And have you ever seen any of these things with your eyes?

In no way, he said.

Or have you ever grasped them with any of your bodily senses? I am speaking of all things such as Size, Health, Strength and, in a word, the reality of all other things, that which each of them essentially is. Is what is most true in them contemplated through the body, or is this the position: whoever of us prepares himself best and most accurately to grasp that thing itself which he is investigating will come closest to the knowledge of it?

Obviously.

Then he will do this most perfectly who approaches the object with thought alone, without associating any sight with his thought, or dragging in any sense perception with his reasoning, but who, using pure thought alone, tries to track down each reality pure and by itself, freeing himself as far as possible from eyes and ears, and in a word, from the whole body, because the body confuses the soul and does not allow it to acquire truth and wisdom whenever it is associated with it. Will not that man reach reality, Simmias, if anyone does?

What you say, said Simmias, is indeed true.

All these things will necessarily make the true philosophers believe and say to each other something like this: "There is likely to be something such as a path to guide us out of our confusion, because as long as we have a body and our soul is fused with such an evil we shall never adequately attain what we desire, which we affirm to be the truth. The body keeps us busy in a thousand ways because of its need for nurture. Moreover, if certain diseases befall it, they impede our search for the truth. It fills us with wants, desires, fears, all sorts of illusions and much nonsense, so that, as it is said, in truth and in fact no thought of any kind ever comes to us from the body. Only the body and its desires cause war, civil discord and battles, for all wars are due to the desire to acquire wealth, and it is the body and the care of it, to which we are enslaved, which compel us to acquire wealth, and all this makes us too busy to practice philosophy. Worst of all, if we do get some respite from it and turn to some investigation, everywhere in our investigations the body is present and makes for confusion and fear, so that it prevents us from seeing the truth.

It really has been shown to us that, if we are ever to have pure knowledge, we must escape from the body and observe matters in themselves with the soul by itself. It seems likely that we shall, only then, when we are dead, attain that which we desire and of which we claim to be lovers, namely, wisdom, as our argument shows, not while we live; for if it is impossible to attain any pure knowledge with the body, then one of two things is true: either we can never attain knowledge or we can do so after death. Then and not before, the soul is by itself apart from the body. While we live, we shall be closest to knowledge if we refrain as much as possible from association with the body or join with it more than we must, if we are not infected with its nature but purify ourselves from it until the god himself frees us. In this way we shall escape the contamination of the body's folly; we shall be likely to be in the company of people of the same kind, and by our own efforts we shall know all that is pure, which is presumably the truth, for it is not permitted to the impure to attain the pure."

Such are the things, Simmias, that all those who love learning in the proper manner must say to one another and believe. Or do you not think so?

I certainly do, Socrates.

And if this is true, my friend, said Socrates, there is good hope that on arriving where I am going, if anywhere, I shall acquire what has been our chief preoccupation in our past life, so that the journey that is now ordered for me is full of good hope, as it is also for any other man who believes that his mind has been prepared and, as it were, purified.

It certainly is, said Simmias.

And does purification not turn out to be what we mentioned in our argument some time ago, namely, to separate the soul as far as possible from the body and accustom it to gather itself and collect itself out of every part of the body and to dwell by itself as far as it can both now and in the future, freed, as it were, from the bonds of the body?

Certainly, he said.

And that freedom and separation of the soul from the body is called death?

That is altogether so.

It is only those who practise philosophy in the right way, we say, who always most want to free the soul; and this release and separation of the soul from the body is the preoccupation of the philosophers?

So it appears.

Therefore, as I said at the beginning, it would be ridiculous for a man to train himself in life to live in a state as close to death as possible, and then to resent it when it comes?

Ridiculous, of course.

In fact, Simmias, he said, those who practise philosophy in the right way are in training for dying and they fear death least of all men. Consider it from this point of view: if they are altogether estranged from the body and desire to have their soul by itself, would it not be quite absurd for them to be afraid and resentful when this happens? If they did not gladly set out for a place, where, on arrival, they may hope to attain that for which they had yearned during their lifetime, that is, wisdom, and where they would be rid of the presence of that from which they are estranged?

Many men, at the death of their lovers, wives or sons, were willing to go to the underworld, driven by the hope of seeing there those for whose company they longed, and being with them. Will then a true lover of wisdom, who has a similar hope and knows that he will never find it to any extent except in Hades, be resentful of dying and not gladly undertake the journey thither? One must surely think so, my friend, if he is a true philosopher, for he is firmly convinced that he will not find pure knowledge anywhere except there. And if this is so, then, as I said just now, would it not be highly unreasonable for such a man to fear death?

It certainly would, by Zeus, he said.

Then you have sufficient indication, he said, that any man whom you see resenting death was not a lover of wisdom but a lover of the body, and also a lover of wealth or of honours, either or both.

It is certainly as you say.

And, Simmias, he said, does not what is called courage belong especially to men of this disposition?

Most certainly.

And the quality of moderation which even the majority call by that name, that is, not to get swept off one's feet by one's passions, but to treat them with disdain and orderliness, is this not suited only to those who most of all despise the body and live the life of philosophy?

Necessarily so, he said.

If you are willing to reflect on the courage and moderation of other people, you will find them strange.

In what way, Socrates?

You know that they all consider death a great evil?

Definitely, he said.

And the brave among them face death, when they do, for fear of greater evils?

That is so.

Therefore, it is fear and terror that make all men brave, except the philosophers. Yet it is illogical to be brave through fear and cowardice.

It certainly is.

. . .

So the soul is more like the invisible than the body, and the body more like the visible?—Without any doubt, Socrates.

Haven't we also said some time ago that when the soul makes use of the body to investigate something, be it through hearing or seeing or some other sense—for to investigate something through the senses is to do it through the body—it is dragged by the body to the things that are never the same, and the soul itself strays and is confused and dizzy, as if it were drunk, in so far as it is in contact with that kind of thing?

Certainly.

But when the soul investigates by itself it passes into the realm of what is pure, ever existing, immortal and unchanging, and being akin to this, it always stays with it whenever it is by itself and can do so; it ceases to stray and remains in the same state as it is in touch with things of the same kind, and its experience then is what is called wisdom?

Altogether well said and very true, Socrates, he said.

Judging from what we have said before and what we are saying now, to which of these two kinds do you think that the soul is more   alike and more akin?

I think, Socrates, he said, that on this line of argument any man, even the dullest, would agree that the soul is altogether more like that which always exists in the same state rather than like that which does not.

What of the body?

That is like the other.

Look at it also this way: when the soul and the body are together, nature orders the one to be subject and to be ruled, and the other to rule and be master. Then again, which do you think is like the divine and which like the mortal? Do you not think that the nature of the divine is to rule and to lead, whereas it is that of the mortal to be ruled and be subject?

I do.

Which does the soul resemble?

Obviously, Socrates, the soul resembles the divine, and the body resembles the mortal.

Consider then, Cebes, whether it follows from all that has been said that the soul is most like the divine, deathless, intelligible, uniform, indissoluble, always the same as itself, whereas the body is most like that which is human, mortal, multiform, unintelligible, soluble and never consistently the same. Have we anything else to say to show, my dear Cebes, that this is not the case?

We have not.

Well then, that being so, is it not natural for the body to dissolve easily, and for the soul to be altogether indissoluble, or nearly so?

Of course.

You realize, he said, that when a man dies, the visible part, the body, which exists in the visible world, and which we call the corpse, whose natural lot it would be to dissolve, fall apart and be blown away, does not immediately suffer any of these things but remains for a fair time, in fact, quite a long time if the man dies with his body in a suitable condition and at a favourable season? If the body is emaciated or embalmed, as in Egypt, it remains almost whole for a remarkable length of time, and even if the body decays, some parts of it, namely bones and sinews and the like, are nevertheless, one might say, deathless. Is that not so?

Yes.

Will the soul, the invisible part which makes its way to a region of the same kind, noble and pure and invisible, to Hades in fact, to the good and wise god whither, god willing, my soul must soon be going—will the soul, being of this kind and nature, be scattered and destroyed on leaving the body, as the majority of men say? Far from it, my dear Cebes and Simmias, but what happens is much more like this: if it is pure when it leaves the body and drags nothing bodily with it, as it had no willing association with the body in life, but avoided it and gathered itself together by itself and always practised this, which is no other than practising philosophy in the right way, in fact, training to die easily. Or is this not training for death?

It surely is.

A soul in this state makes its way to the invisible, which is like itself, the divine and immortal and wise, and arriving there it can be happy, having rid itself of confusion, ignorance, fear, violent desires and the other human ills and, as is said of the initiates, truly spend the rest of time with the gods. Shall we say this, Cebes, or something different?

This, by Zeus, said Cebes.

But I think that if the soul is polluted and impure when it leaves the body, having always been associated with it and served it, bewitched by physical desires and pleasures to the point at which nothing seems to exist for it but the physical, which one can touch and see or eat and drink or make use of for sexual enjoyment, and if that soul is accustomed to hate and fear and avoid that which is dim and invisible to the eyes but intelligible and to be grasped by philosophy—do you think such a soul will escape pure and by itself?

Impossible, he said.

It is no doubt permeated by the physical, which constant intercourse and association with the body, as well as considerable practice, has caused to become ingrained in it?

Quite so.

We must believe, my friend, that this bodily element is heavy, ponderous, earthy and visible. Through it, such a soul has become heavy and is dragged back to the visible region in fear of the unseen and of Hades. It wanders, as we are told, around graves and monuments, where shadowy phantoms, images that such souls produce, have been seen, souls that have not been freed and purified but share in the visible, and are therefore seen.

That is likely, Socrates. . . .

Note

1   "Even the poets" because poetry concerns itself with the world of sense and appeals to the passions and emotions of the lowest part of the soul in the *Republic* (595a ff.), whereas in the *Phaedo* passions and emotions are attributed to the body.

Questions for reflection

1   How is the practice of philosophy a practice in dying and death, according to Plato?
2   How does the philosopher, more than other people, free the soul from association with the body?
3   What does the existence of the Just, the Good, and the Beautiful have to do with immortality?
4   Why does Plato argue that we should refrain as much as possible from association with the body? How is the body harmful to the soul?
5   Describe Plato's argument for why the soul of the one who rightly practices philosophy is immortal. How is the argument structured? Is it reasonable? Defend your position.

Further reading

Paul M. Churchland (1984) *Matter and Consciousness.* Cambridge, MA: MIT Press. (A readable presentation of the mind–body problem by a materialist.)

René Descartes ([1641] 1972) *Meditations on First Philosophy,* in *The Philosophical Works of Descartes,* Vol. 1. Ed. E. S. Haldane and G. R. T. Ross. Cambridge: Cambridge University Press. (Descartes offers his argument for substance dualism; note especially meditations 2 and 6.)

Paul Edwards, ed. (1992) *Immortality,* New York: Macmillan. (A helpful collection of excerpts on immortality from different thinkers from Plato to today.)

John Perry (1978) *A Dialogue on Personal Identity and Immortality.* Indianapolis, IN: Hackett. (A fun-to-read conversation/dialogue which fairly presents different sides of the immortality debate.)

Richard Swinburne (1997) *The Evolution of the Soul.* Oxford: Clarendon Press. (A contemporary philosopher from Oxford University defends a dualist position.)

Chapter 56

Stephen T. Davis

RESURRECTION OF THE BODY

Stephen T. Davis is Russell K. Pitzer Professor of Philosophy at Claremont McKenna College. In this selection he explains and defends the traditional Christian view of the resurrection of the body after death. In his defense he also argues for what he calls the theory of "temporary disembodiment"—the idea that human beings are essentially material bodies *and* immaterial souls and that, while they can temporarily exist apart, they do so in an incomplete form of human existence. He then notes three claims which are central to the theory: 1) after death, the soul exists for a time in an intermediate state without the body, 2) at a certain time (the general resurrection) the body will be raised by God and reunited with the soul, and 3) the body will then be transformed by God into a "glorified body"—one with new kinds of properties.

As Professor Davis notes, the general view of the Church Fathers was that the glorified body must consist of the same material as the earthly body; otherwise, the resurrected person will not be the same person as the one in the previous body. Many contemporary Christian thinkers do not hold to this "Patristic theory" but rather believe that the glorified body will be an entirely new body. He responds to this "modern" view, and replies to philosophical objections to disembodied existence based on alleged problems of personal identity. He concludes by affirming that both views of the resurrected body are plausible. In either case, while death disassembles us for a time, we have the hope that we will continue to exist nonetheless, and eventually God will give us a body once again—this time a glorified one.

I

One traditional Christian view of survival of death runs, in outline form, something like this: On some future day all the dead will be bodily raised, both the righteous and the unrighteous alike, to be judged by God; and the guarantee and model of the general resurrection (i.e., the raising of the dead in the last days) is the already accomplished resurrection of Jesus Christ from the dead.

My aim in this chapter is to explain and defend this basic view of resurrection. There are many ways in which it might be understood, of course, and perhaps more than one is coherent and even plausible from a Christian point of view. I shall defend one particular interpretation of the theory—an interpretation advocated by many of the Church Fathers, especially second-century Fathers, as well as by Augustine and Aquinas.

After a brief introduction to the issues, I will discuss in turn what I take to be the three most important claims made in the version of the theory that I wish to defend. Then I will consider one typical aspect of the traditional theory that has important philosophical as well as theological ramifications—namely, the notion that our resurrection bodies will consist of the same matter as do our present earthly bodies. Finally, since the version of the theory that I wish to defend envisions a period of existence in a disembodied state, I will defend the theory against some of the arguments of contemporary philosophers who find the very notion of disembodied existence incoherent.

II

There are several ways in which the basic concept of resurrection sketched in the opening paragraph can be fleshed out. One option is to understand the nature of the human person, and hence the nature of resurrection, in a basically materialist or physicalist way. Perhaps human beings are essentially material objects; perhaps some version of identity theory or functionalism is true. This option is not without its attractions; indeed, there was a time when I would have accepted it. But since it is no longer my preferred way of defending the notion of resurrection, I am going to defer discussion of it to another context . . .

Another option is to collapse talk of resurrection into talk of the immortality of the soul. A closely related strategy (and . . . a popular one in recent theology) is to interpret resurrection in a spiritual rather than bodily sense (if this in the end differs significantly from immortality). Such a view will doubtless be based on some version of mind-body (or soul-body) dualism. (People who endorse "spiritual" views of the resurrection often insist that they are talking about the resurrection of *the whole person*, but somehow the body seems typically to be left out.) Let us define dualism as the doctrine which says (1) that human beings consist of both material bodies and immaterial souls and (2) that the soul is the essence of the person (the real you is your soul, not your body). It then can be added that the body corrupts at death and eventually ceases to exist, but the soul is essentially immortal.

It is surprising (to me at least) that so many twentieth-century Christian thinkers are tempted toward some such notion as this. For it is quite clear, in both Scripture and tradition, that classical dualism is not the Christian position. For one thing, the biblical view is not that the soul is the essence of the person and is only temporarily housed or even imprisoned in a body; human beings seem rather to be understood in Scripture as psycho-physical entities, as unities of body and soul. For another, the notion that the body is essentially evil and must be escaped from (an idea often associated with versions of classical dualism) was condemned by virtually every orthodox Christian thinker who discussed death and resurrection in the first two hundred years after the apostolic age.

The Christian idea is rather that the body was created by God and is good; the whole person, body and soul alike, is what needs to be saved. Finally, as I have already suggested, the biblical notion is not that we survive death because immortality is simply a natural property of souls; if we survive death, it is because God miraculously gives us life. Apart from God's intervention, death would mean annihilation for us. Thus Irenaeus says, "Our survival forever comes from his greatness, not from our nature" (*Against Heresies*) 5.3.2).

It would be interesting to explore this option further, and especially to consider why so many recent and contemporary Christian theologians are drawn to it, how they might distinguish "spiritual resurrection" from immortality of the soul, and how they might defend the theory against criticisms such as those just noted, but this would take us too far afield. As I have suggested, my aim here is to explore and defend a third way of understanding the traditional Christian notion of resurrection, a theory held in one form or another by virtually all (but not quite all) of the Church Fathers who discussed resurrection.[1] I will call this theory "temporary disembodiment."

This theory of resurrection is based on a view of human nature which says that human beings are essentially material bodies *and* immaterial souls; the soul is separable from the body, but neither body nor soul alone (i.e., without the other) constitutes a complete human being. Thus Pseudo-Justin asks,

> Is the soul by itself man? No; but the soul of man. Would the body be called man? No, but it is called the body of man. If, then, neither of these is by itself man, but that which is made up of the two together is called man, and God has called *man* to life and resurrection, He has called not a part, but the whole, which is the soul and the body. (*On the Resurrection*, chap. 8)

What this theory says, then, is that human beings are typically and normally psycho-physical beings, that the soul can exist for a time apart from the body and retain personal identity, but that this disembodied existence is only temporary and constitutes a radically attenuated and incomplete form of human existence.

I call the theory temporary disembodiment because it envisions the following scenario: We human beings are born, live for a time as psycho-physical beings, and then die. After death we exist in an incomplete state as immaterial souls. Some time later in the eschaton, God miraculously raises our bodies from the ground, transforms them into "glorified bodies," and reunites them with our souls, thus making us complete and whole again.

Belief in temporary disembodiment has several theological and philosophical advantages. For one thing, many Christian thinkers have seen a comfortable fit between it and the view of human nature expressed in the Bible, the Pauline writings particularly. The apostle seems to hold that human beings consist of both material bodies and immaterial souls, that the body is not merely an adornment or drape for the soul but that it is indeed good, since it can be the temple of the Holy Spirit (1 Cor. 3:16–17; 6:19–20), and that the soul is in some sense separable from the body (2 Cor. 5:6–8; 12:2–3). What the body does is provide the soul with a vehicle for action in the world, for the expression of intentions and desires; and the soul provides the body with animation and direction.[2]

For another thing, the theory seems to offer a tidy way to reconcile the traditional view that the general resurrection does not occur until the eschaton with Jesus' statement to the good thief on the cross, "*Today* you will be with me in Paradise" (Luke 23:43). The explanation (which naturally goes far beyond Jesus' simple statement) is as follows: the thief would be with Jesus in paradise that very day in the form of a disembodied soul, only to be raised bodily much later. The theory may also help resolve a similar tension that is sometimes said to exist in Pauline thought, with texts such as 1 Corinthians 15 and 1 Thessalonians 4 pointing toward the idea of a future, eschatological resurrection (with those who die beforehand existing until then in a kind of bodiless sleep) and texts such as 2 Corinthians 5:8 and Philippians 1:23 suggesting the idea that death for the Christian is an immediate gain since one is immediately at home with the Lord. Of course, this would leave unresolved the issue of how one could simultaneously be both "at home with the Lord" and "in an incomplete state."

Finally, this theory would seem to be more helpful than others with regard to resolving the problem of personal identity after death. At least this theory does not introduce the difficulty of a temporal gap in the existence of persons—although it does assume a gap in their existence as complete, unified persons. . . . In temporary disembodiment there is no moment subsequent to our births in which you and I simply do not exist: we exist either as whole persons (soul-bodies) or as mere souls at every moment until eternity.

III

There are three main aspects of temporary disembodiment that require discussion both from a philosophical and from a theological perspective. Let me now consider them in turn. The first is the notion that after death the soul exists for a time (i.e., until the resurrection) in an intermediate state without the body. The second is the notion that at the time of the parousia the body will be raised from the ground and reunited with the soul. And the third is the notion that the body will then be transformed into what is called a "glorified body."

The first main claim of temporary disembodiment, then, is that after death the soul temporarily exists without the body. This differs from physicalist concepts of resurrection . . . , which hold that the person does not exist at all in the period between death and resurrection. Temporary disembodiment need not be based on classical dualism as defined earlier, but it is based on one tenet of classical dualism—namely, the claim that human beings consist (or in this case at least normally consist) of both material bodies and immaterial souls. (The soul is not said to be the essence of the person, however, and is said to survive death not because immortality is one of its natural properties but because God causes it to survive death.)[3]

Almost all Christians believe that people exist in some kind of interim state between death and resurrection, but beyond this point there are many theological differences. Some, for example, think of the interim state as purgatorial in nature, and others do not. Some hold that spiritual change (e.g., repentance) is possible during the interim period, and others do not. Some think the soul rests or sleeps, that it is not active or conscious during the interim period, and others do not. It is not part of my purpose to express an opinion on either of the first two items of disagreement. However, on the third I will argue that the soul is conscious in the interim state. The biblical metaphor of sleep (Luke 8:52; 1 Cor. 15:20) is not to be taken as a literal description. If that were the case, it would be difficult to make sense of the notion of a disembodied thing being in the presence of God ("Today you will be with me in Paradise"). If a soul is neither physically present nor in any sense aware of the presence of God, in what sense can it be said to be in his presence?[4]

Furthermore, since sleeping seems essentially to be a bodily activity, the claim that a soul sleeps at the very least needs considerable explanation.

The state of being without a body is an abnormal state of the human person. This points to one of the clear differences between temporary disembodiment and immortality of the soul, for the second doctrine (at least in versions of it influenced by Plato) entails that disembodiment is the true or proper or ideal state of the human person. On the theory we are considering, however, the claim is that a disembodied soul lacks many of the properties and abilities that are normal for and proper to human persons. Disembodied existence is a kind of minimal existence.

Which properties typical of embodied human persons will disembodied souls have and which will they lack? Clearly they will lack those properties that essentially involve corporeality. They will not be able to experience bodily pains and pleasures. They will not be able to perceive their surroundings (using the spatial word "surroundings" in a stretched sense)—at least not in the ways in which we perceive our surroundings (i.e., through the eyes, ears, etc.). They will not be able to engage in bodily activities. Taking a walk, getting dressed, playing catch—these sorts of activities will be impossible.

But if by the word "soul" we mean in part the constellation of those human activities that would typically be classified as "mental," then the claim that our souls survive death entails the claim that our mental abilities and properties survive death. This means that human persons in the interim state can be said to have experiences, beliefs, wishes, knowledge, memory, inner (rather than bodily) feelings, thoughts, language (assuming memory of earthly existence)—in short, much of what makes up what we call personality. H. H. Price, in his classic article "Survival and the Idea of 'Another World,'" argues convincingly that disembodied souls can also be aware of each other's existence, can communicate with each other telepathically, and can have dreamlike (rather than bodily) perceptions of their world.[5]

But Aquinas argues that the disembodied existence of the person in the interim state is so deficient that attainment of ultimate happiness is impossible. No one in whom some perfection is lacking is ultimately happy, for in such a state there will always be unfulfilled desires. It is contrary to the nature of the soul to be without the body, Aquinas says, and he takes this to mean both that the disembodied state must only be temporary and that the true bliss of the human person is only attained after reembodiment (i.e., in the general resurrection). "Man cannot achieve his ultimate happiness," he says, "unless the soul be once again united to the body."[6]

IV

The second main claim of the theory that I am calling temporary disembodiment is that at the general resurrection the body will be raised from the ground and reunited with the soul. As the second-century writer Athenagoras says, "There must certainly be a resurrection of bodies whether dead or even quite corrupted, and the same men as before must come to be again. The law of nature appoints an end . . . for those very same men who lived in a previous existence, and it is impossible for the same men to come together again if the same bodies are not given back to the same souls. Now the same soul cannot recover the same body in any other way than by resurrection."[7]

As Athenagoras stresses, the idea is that each person's selfsame body will be raised; it will not be a different and brand-new body but the old body. Echoing the argument of very many of the Fathers, Aquinas notes the reason for this: "If the body of the man who rises is not to be composed of the flesh and bones which now compose it, the man who rises will not be numerically the same man."[8] Furthermore, in the resurrection there will be only one soul per body and only one body per soul. As Augustine puts it, "Each single soul shall possess its own body."[9] Were this not the case—that is, if souls were to split and animate more than one body or if one body were to be animated by more than one soul—the problem of personal identity would be unsolvable, and the Christian hope that we will live after death would be incoherent.

The Fathers and Scholastics insisted, then, that both body and soul must be present or else the person does not exist, or at least does not exist fully or completely or in a state capable of ultimate happiness. "A man cannot be said to exist as such when the body is dissolved or completely scattered," says Athenagoras, "even though the soul remain by itself."[10] And Aquinas agrees: "My soul is not I, and if only souls are saved *I* am not saved, nor is any man."[11] Thus the Christian hope of survival is not merely the hope that our souls will survive death (although it is significant that they will do so in a temporarily disembodied form) but rather the hope that one day God will miraculously raise our bodies and reunite them with our souls.

What is it, then, that guarantees personal identity in the resurrection? What is it that ensures that it will really be *us* in the kingdom of God and not, say, clever replicas of us? Aquinas argues as follows: since human beings consist of bodies and souls, and since both souls and the matter of which our bodies consist survive death, personal identity is secured when God collects the scattered matter, miraculously reconstitutes it as a human body, and reunites it with the soul.[12] This seems to me to be a powerful argument. If God one day succeeds in doing these very things, personal identity will be secure. It will be us and not our replicas who will be the denizens of the kingdom of God.

V

The third main claim of temporary disembodiment is that in the resurrection the old body will be transformed into a "glorified body" with certain quite new properties. . . . The notion that resurrected persons will have glorified bodies is based primarily on Paul's discussion of the resurrection in 1 Corinthians 15, and secondarily on the unusual properties that the risen Jesus is depicted as having in some of the accounts of the resurrection appearances (e.g., the apparent ability of the risen Jesus in John 20 to enter a room despite the fact that the doors were locked). In 1 Corinthians 15, Paul notes that some ask how the dead are raised and what kind of body they will have. He answers that their new "glorified" or "spiritual" bodies (*soma pneumatikon*) will be a transformation of the old bodies rather than a *de novo* creation (much as a stalk of grain is a transformation of a seed of grain—it exists because of changes that have occurred in the seed and can be considered a new state of the grain). Further, Paul argues, while the old or natural body is physical, perishable, mortal, and sown in weakness and dishonor, the glorified body is spiritual, imperishable, immortal, and sown in strength and honor. The first body is in the image of the man of dust; the second body is in the image of the man of heaven.

. . . [T]he term "spiritual body" might be misleading; it should not be taken as a denial of corporeality or as a last-minute capitulation to some version of the immortality of the soul as opposed to bodily resurrection. By this term, Paul means not a body whose stuff or matter is spiritual (whatever that might mean) or an immaterial existence of some sort; rather, he means a body that is fully obedient to and dominated by the Holy Spirit. "Flesh and blood cannot inherit the kingdom of God," says Paul (1 Cor. 15:50). What enters the kingdom of heaven, then, is not this present weak and mortal body of flesh and blood but the new glorified body. This new body is a physical body (Paul's use of the word *soma* implies as much),[13] and it is materially related to the old body (taking seriously Paul's simile of the seed), but is a body transformed in such ways as make it fit to live in God's presence. If by the term "physical object" we mean an entity that has spatio-temporal location and is capable of being empirically measured, tested, or observed in some sense, then my argument is that the new body of which Paul speaks is a physical object.

Temporary disembodiment, then, entails that human souls can animate both normal earthly bodies and glorified resurrection bodies. Continuity between the two bodies is provided by the presence of both the same soul and the same matter in both bodies. "Nor does the earthly material out of which men's mortal bodies are created ever perish," says Augustine; "but though it may crumble into dust and ashes, or be dissolved into vapors and exhalations, though it may be transformed into the substance of other bodies, or dispersed into the elements, though it should become food for beasts or men, and be changed into their flesh, it returns in a moment of time to that human soul which animated it at the first and which caused it to become man, and to live and grow."[14] The matter of our present bodies may be arranged differently in the resurrection, he says, but the matter will be restored.

Many of the theologians of the early church and of the medieval period also stressed the perfection of the glorified body. They maintained that it will be free of every bodily defect. It will be fully controlled by the spirit of God and thus immune to evil. It will not suffer. It will not grow old or die. It will have "agility" which, as noted above, is an ability like that of the risen Jesus to come and go at will, unimpeded by things like walls and doors. It will exist in a state of fulfilled desire. It will need no material food or drink but will be nourished by the elements of the eucharist.[15]

VI

Is the picture of resurrection just presented coherent? Is it plausible? The main objections that have been raised against it in recent philosophy revolve around the problem of personal identity. Some philosophers argue that, so far as disembodied existence is concerned, this problem cannot be solved. They contend that if it is some immaterial aspect of me that survives death, it will not be me that survives death. Since the view of survival of death that I am defending essentially involves a period of disembodied existence, I will try to defend the view against these sorts of objections. But a prior problem must be considered first—whether the Fathers and Scholastics were correct in their strong claim (I will call this claim "the Patristic theory") that if it is to be me in the kingdom of

God, the very matter of my original earthly body must be raised. After discussing this point, I proceed to consider the arguments of those philosophers who oppose the notion of disembodied existence because of the problem of personal identity.

Why did Aquinas and the Fathers who influenced him insist that the same matter that constituted my old body must be raised? Let us see if we can construct an argument on their behalf. Like many arguments in the area of personal identity, it involves a puzzle case. Suppose that I own a defective personal computer which I rashly decide to try to repair myself. Having taken it apart (there are now, say, sixty separate computer components scattered on my workbench), I find that I am unable to repair it. I call the outlet that sold me the computer, and the manager suggests I simply bring all sixty components to the store for repair. I do so, but through a horrible series of misunderstandings and errors, the sixty pieces of the computer are then sent to sixty different addresses around the country. That constitutes the heart of my story, but there are two separate endings to it. *Ending number one*: It takes three years for everything to be sorted out, for the pieces to be located and collected in one place, for the repairs to be made, and for the parts to be reassembled and restored, in full working order, to my desk. *Ending number two:* After three years of trying in vain to locate and collect the scattered pieces, the manager gives up, collects sixty similar parts, assembles them, and the resulting computer ends up on my desk.

I do not wish to raise the interesting question of whether my computer *existed* during the three-year period. I am concerned only with the related question of whether the computer now located on my desk is *the same* computer as the one that was there three years ago. So far as ending number one is concerned, it seems most natural to affirm that the computer I now possess is indeed the same computer as the one that I possessed before. The computer may or may not have had a gap in its existence (i.e., a period when it did not exist), but it seems clear that identity has been preserved here. So far as ending number two is concerned, it seems most natural to deny that the computer I now possess is the same computer as the one that I possessed before. Furthermore, we would doubtless insist on this denial even if all of the sixty components the manager used to construct the computer I now possess were qualitatively indistinguishable from the sixty old components. What I now have is a qualitatively similar but numerically different computer.

Now I doubt that the Church Fathers often pondered personal identity test cases involving computers, and it is obvious that personal computers are different from human beings in many striking ways. But it was perhaps *the sort* of insight arrived at above that led them to take the strong stand that they took on the resurrection. It was their belief that only if God reassembles the very particles of which my body once consisted will it be me who is raised. If other particles are used, the result will be what we would call a replica of me rather than me.

But despite the above argument, does it still not seem that Aquinas and the Fathers in their strong stand have made the solution to the problem of personal identity more difficult than it need be? Even granting the point that some of the particles of the matter of which our bodies consist will endure for the requisite number of years, why insist that God must re-collect it—that very matter—in the resurrection? For surely in the interim state it will be us (and not soul-like replicas of us) who will exist without any body at all; surely the Fathers and Scholastics insist on this much. Thus the presence of the soul alone must suffice for personal identity; what philosophers call the memory criterion (which is typically taken to include not just memory but all one's "mental" characteristics and properties) must suffice by itself. Identity of memory, personality, and other "mental" aspects of the person are sufficient conditions of personal identity. To admit this much is not necessarily to abandon the traditional notion that the soul is not the whole person and that the whole person must be raised; it is merely to insist that the existence of my soul entails *my* existence. Otherwise talk of my existence in the interim state is meaningless.

I do not claim that the Patristic theory is logically inconsistent. It is possible coherently to hold that when I die my soul will be me during the interim period but that it will no longer be me if my soul in the eschaton animates a body consisting of totally new matter, even if the new body is qualitatively indistinguishable from the old one. Perhaps an essential property of my soul is that it can animate only *this* body—where "this body" means in part a body consisting of *these* particles. So if *per impossible* my soul were to animate a different body, the result would not be me. Or perhaps every configuration of particles that can possibly constitute a human body has as one of its essential properties that it can be animated by one and only one particular soul. But while logically consistent, this view seems to me exceedingly difficult to defend.

So far as the problem of personal identity is concerned, it is accordingly not easy to see why a defender of temporary disembodiment could not dispense with all talk of God one day re-collecting the molecules, atoms, quarks, or whatever of our bodies. Perhaps human beings in this regard are unlike computers. Why not say that God can award us brand-new bodies materially quite unrelated to (although qualitatively similar to) the old ones? If the existence of the soul is sufficient for personal identity, and if the human soul never at any moment subsequent to its creation fails to exist, it will be us who exist after the resurrection in the kingdom of God whether or not our old bodies are reconstituted.

Furthermore, it needs to be noted here that identity of particles of bodily matter does not seem necessary to preserve the identity of an ordinary human person even during the course of a lifetime. As Frank Dilley notes, "We constantly replace our atoms over time and there is no reason to think that an eighty year old person has even a single atom in common with the newborn babe. If a person maintains personal identity over a process of total atom-by-atom replacement, it is difficult to see why such identity would not be preserved through a sudden replacement of all the atoms at once."[16]

Dilley's argument seems plausible, but we should notice that it does not necessarily follow. Perhaps gradual replacement of all the individual atoms of a human body is consistent with personal identity while all-at-once replacement of them is not. Perhaps some strong sort of material continuity is needed. One of the difficulties encountered by philosophers who discuss personal identity is that different persons' intuitions run in different directions. For example, in a slightly different connection, Peter van Inwagen argues that sameness of person requires both (1) sameness of atoms and (2) regular and natural causal relationships between those atoms, and so if God were now to try to raise Napoleon Bonaparte from the dead by omnisciently locating the atoms of which his body once consisted and miraculously reassembling them, the result would not be Napoleon.[17] I do not agree with van Inwagen here; I see no convincing reason for his second stipulation. I raise the point merely to show that van Inwagen's intuitions run in a different direction than Dilley's. Since Dilley's case of sudden-replacement-of-all-the-atoms-at-once seems to constitute something *unnatural* and *irregular*, van Inwagen would doubtless deny that in such cases personal identity would be preserved.

What if there were, so to speak, some natural way of reassembling persons out of totally new matter? Derek Parfit considers in detail a series of test cases involving an imagined teletransporter, a machine that is designed to send a person to distant places like Mars by (1) recording the exact state of all the body's cells (including those of the brain), (2) destroying the body and brain, and (3) transmitting the information at the speed of light to Mars, where (4) a replicator creates out of new matter a body and brain exactly like the old one.[18] Suppose Parfit enters the machine and is "teletransported to Mars." Would the resulting Parfit-like person on Mars *be* Parfit? Here again our intuitions might differ, even in this relatively simple case (i.e., apart from considerations of such complications as the original Parfit somehow surviving on earth or fifteen Parfit-like persons somehow appearing on Mars). Those who, like the Church Fathers and Aquinas, hold to some strong requirement about material continuity will deny that it is Parfit. Those who stress the memory criterion are free to affirm that Parfit is now on Mars, as are those (e.g., John Hick) who believe that identity is exact similarity plus uniqueness. Those who think that identity is exact similarity plus the right kind of causal origin or causal ancestry might go either way, depending on whether they think the operation of a teletransporter constitutes an appropriate sort of causal origin for the Parfit-like person on Mars.

The moral of the story thus far is that the Fathers and Aquinas may be right in what they say about resurrection, but it is not clear that they are right. Their position may be consistent, but it does seem implausible to hold both (1) that it will be me in the interim period without any body at all (i.e., the presence of my soul is sufficient for personal identity) and (2) that it will not be me in the eschaton, despite the presence of my soul, if the body that my soul then animates consists of new matter. There may be other (perhaps theological) reasons why we should hold that it must be the very matter of our old bodies that is to be raised, but so far as the problem of personal identity is concerned, a strong case can be made that it will not matter.

Recent and contemporary Christian theologians who discuss resurrection seem for the most part to have departed from the Patristic theory. The more common thesis is that our glorified bodies will be wholly different bodies, not necessarily consisting of any of the old matter at all. As John Hick, an articulate spokesperson for this new point of view, says, "What has become a widely accepted view in modern times holds that the resurrection body is a new and different body given by God, but expressing the personality within its new environment as the physical body expressed it in the earthly environment. The physical frame decays or is burned, disintegrating and being dispersed into the ground or the air, but God re-embodies the personality elsewhere."[19] Frequently connected with this view is an exegetical claim—namely, that by the term "the body" St. Paul meant not the physical organism but rather something akin to "the whole personality." What will be raised from the dead, then, is not the old body but rather the *person*, and in being raised the person will be given a brand-new body by God.

It is not hard to see why such a view has come to be widely adopted. (1) As noted above, personal identity does not seem to require the resurrection of the same matter of which the old body consisted. (2) The Patristic theory seems to many contemporary Christians to be scientifically outmoded and difficult to believe; the idea that in order to raise me God must one day cast about, locate, and collect the atoms of which my earthly body once consisted seems to many people absurd. (3) Many such theologians want to hold in any case that the kingdom of God is not spatially related to our present world, that it exists in a space all its own, and so it can contain no material from this spatio-temporal manifold.

I am unable to locate any philosophical or logical difficulties in the "modern" theory. It seems to me a possible Christian view of resurrection, and it can fit smoothly with the other aspects of the traditional notion that I am calling temporary disembodiment. Are there any theological reasons, then, for a Christian to retain the old theory and believe that the matter of our old bodies will be raised? Two points should be made here. The first is that the most natural reading of 1 Corinthians 15 is along the lines of the Patristic theory. Paul seems to be suggesting there that the old body *becomes* or *changes into* (rather than *is replaced by*) the new body, just as a seed becomes or changes into a plant. Thus, just as there is material continuity between the seed and the plant, so there will be material continuity between the old body and the new; the plant is *a new form of* the seed. Note also Paul's use in verses 42 and 43 of the expression "*It* is sown . . . *it* is raised . . .," as if the one thing (a human body) is at one time in a certain state and at a later time in another state (see also vv. 53, 54).[20] Furthermore, as noted already, Paul's use of the term *soma* reveals that what he had in mind was a body; it is simply a lexical mistake to say that he merely meant "the whole personality" or some such thing.[21]

The second point has to do with the difficulty that God will face in collecting the atoms, quarks, or whatever fundamental particles human bodies consist of. This may well be the oldest philosophical objection ever raised against the Christian notion of resurrection. Virtually every one of the Fathers who discussed resurrection tried to answer it, as did Aquinas. Such scenarios as this were suggested: What if a Christian dies at sea and his body is eaten by various fishes who then scatter to the seven seas? How can God later resurrect that body? Or what if another Christian is eaten by cannibals, so that some of the material of her body becomes the material of their bodies? And suppose God later wants to raise all of them from the dead, cannibals and Christian alike. Who gets what particles? How does God decide?

The move made by virtually all of the Fathers in response to this objection is to appeal to omnipotence. You and I might not be able to locate and reconstitute the relevant atoms of someone's body, especially after many years or even centuries have passed, but God can do this very thing. And as long as (1) the basic constituents of matter (e.g., atoms) endure through time (as contemporary physical theory says they normally do) and (2) it is merely a matter of God locating and collecting the relevant constituents, I believe the Fathers were right. An omnipotent being could do that.

But with the cannibalism case and other imaginable cases in which God must decide which constituent parts shared at different times by two (or even two thousand) separate persons go where, the matter is more serious. The problem does not seem insoluble, but much more needs to be said. Perhaps some constituent parts of human bodies are essential to those bodies and some are not. That is, perhaps God will only need to collect the essential parts of our bodies and use them, so to speak, as building blocks around which to reconstruct our new bodies. And perhaps omnipotence must accordingly guarantee that no essential part of one person's earthly body is ever a constituent part, or an essential constituent part, of someone else's body. If these stipulations or ones like them are followed (e.g., Augustine's idea that atoms will be raised in that human body in which they *first* appeared),[22] it still seems that the Fathers were correct—an omnipotent being will be able to raise us from the ground.

Reacting against these and similar patristic appeals to omnipotence in order to rationalize resurrection, Paul Badham argues as follows:

> Given belief in a once-for-all act of creation on the pattern of Genesis 1, then the act of resurrection cannot be difficult for an all-powerful God. Given that God made the first man by direct action, the restoration of a decomposed man becomes an easy task. Given that man consists of particles, it is easy to believe that omnipotence could reassemble these particles. But today each of these premises has lost its validity, and hence the conclusions drawn from them cannot stand. That man as a species is part of a slowly evolving process of life and in every respect continuous with the processes of nature from which he has emerged does not provide a congenial background for the idea of resurrection. Further, our increasing knowledge of the incredible complexity and constant changing of our physical components makes it difficult to see the resurrection as simply involving the re-collection of our physical particles. We are not composed of building bricks but of constantly changing living matter.[23]

It is not easy to see exactly what Badham is getting at with these arguments. Of course he is right that human bodies are incredibly complex and that they consist of constantly changing living matter. But does this deny—or indeed does contemporary physics deny—the idea that our bodies consist of particles? I think not. Furthermore, it is hard to see how a commitment to evolutionary theory (a commitment I make) undercuts the ability of an omnipotent being to raise human beings from the dead. Perhaps it does undercut the sort of simplistic argument that we occasionally find in the Fathers to the effect that since God already did the difficult job of creating human beings *de novo* by assembling the particles of their bodies, God can also do the far easier job of reassembling them in the eschaton.[24] But surely claims about what is easy and what is hard for an omnipotent being to do are suspect anyway. The point that the Fathers were making is that whatever difficulties resurrection presents can be overcome by an omnipotent being. I believe that point still stands and is not rendered improbable or implausible by evolution.

VII

Several philosophers have argued in recent years that the concept of disembodied existence is incoherent or at least that no disembodied thing can be identified with some previously existing human person. Antony Flew, Bernard Williams, D. Z. Phillips, Terence Penelhum, and John Perry, among others, have jointly presented what might be called the standard arguments against survival of death in disembodied form.[25] P. T. Geach has similarly argued against the notion of *permanent* disembodied existence, though he supports something like the theory that I am calling temporary disembodiment.[26] Now, I am inclined to hold that the standard arguments have been successfully answered by defenders of disembodied existence;[27] that is to say, I believe the notion of survival of death (and even permanent survival of death) in disembodied form is intelligible and logically possible. Furthermore, one result of recent discussion of the puzzle cases in the area of personal identity is that many philosophers are now prepared to defend the notion that we can imagine cases in which the memory criterion will suffice by itself. But since the arguments of Flew, Williams, Phillips, and Penelhum have been discussed thoroughly in the journals, let me instead focus on the case John Perry makes in his excellent little book *A Dialogue on Personal Identity and Immortality*.

Perry seems, in this dialogue, to speak primarily through the character of Gretchen Weirob, a mortally injured but still lucid philosopher who does not believe in life after death. Weirob seems to present three main arguments against the conceivability or possibility of survival of death. All are versions of arguments that we find elsewhere in the literature, but the virtue of Perry's work is that they are presented with great clarity and vividness. Perry's first argument has to do with the soul and personal identity, the second concerns memory and personality identity, and the third is an argument about the possibility of duplication of persons.

The first argument says that immaterial and thus unobservable souls can have nothing to do with establishing personal identity. Personal identity does not consist in sameness of soul, for if it did, we would never know who we are or who others are. Since souls are not observable, no thesis having to do with souls is testable (not even the thesis, "My soul is I"). So I cannot know whether other human beings have souls, or even whether I have a soul; I have no idea whether I have one soul or several, or whether I have one soul for a time and then later a different soul. Thus there are no criteria for determining what constitutes "the same soul" and hence no way to make informed judgments about it. We might simply on faith assume criteria such as "Same body, same soul" or "Same mental traits, same soul," but since we never independently observe souls, there is no way to test these principles and thus no reason to think that they apply. But since we evidently are able to make correct personal identity judgments about persons, it follows that personal identity has nothing to do with souls. Personal identity must instead be based on bodily criteria. Thus, concludes Perry, no thesis about my survival of death via the survival of my soul is coherent.

Perry's second argument is that the memory criterion of personal identity, which those who believe in immortality must rely on, is never sufficient to establish personal identity. This is because of the obvious fact that memory is fallible. Without some further criterion, we will never be able to distinguish between apparent memories and genuine memories. In fact, believers in immortality are committed to a kind of circularity—they claim that genuine memory explains personal identity (i.e., a purported Jones in the afterlife really is Jones only if the purported Jones genuinely remembers from Jones's point of view events in Jones's past), and they claim that identity marks the difference between apparent and genuine memories (the purported Jones can have genuine memories of events in Jones's past only if the purported Jones *is* Jones; otherwise the memories are merely *apparent* memories). Thus, again, the thesis that our souls survive death, which must rely on the memory criterion of personal identity, is incoherent.

Finally, Perry argues that the thesis of survival of death through immortality is rendered incoherent by the possibility of multiple qualitatively identical persons in the afterlife. As Weirob puts it,

> either God, by creating a Heavenly person with a brain modeled after mine,
> does not really create someone identical with me but merely someone sim-

ilar to me, or God is somehow limited to making only one such being. I can see no reason why, if there were a God, He should be so limited. So I take the first option. He would create someone similar to me, but not someone who would *be* me. Either your analysis of memory is wrong, and such a being does not, after all, remember what I am doing or saying, or memory is not sufficient for personal identity. Your theory has gone wrong somewhere, for it leads to absurdity.[28]

When told by one of the discussants that God may well refrain from creating multiple qualitatively identical persons in the afterlife and that if God does so refrain, the immortality thesis is coherent, Weirob replies that a new criterion has now been added. What suffices for personal identity (i.e., what makes it such that the purported Jones in the afterlife *is* Jones) is not just memory but rather memory plus lack of competition. This opens an odd way for someone to be killed in the afterlife, she remarks: God need only create, so to speak, an identical twin to Jones, and then *neither* would be Jones—Jones would then not have survived death. This would rather oddly make identity depend on something entirely extrinsic to the person involved. And if memory does not secure personal identity where there are two or more Joneses in the afterlife, it does not secure personal identity at all. Weirob concludes that it is best simply to abandon any thought of survival of death—when my body dies, I die.

Perry's first argument in favor of the notion that survival of death is incoherent is based on an element of truth, but he uses it in an erroneous way. Throughout his book he seems illicitly to jump back and forth between talk about criteria of personal identity and talk about evidence for personal identity. It is surely true that the soul is not observable, except in the sense that observation of a person's behavior is usually evidence of personality or of the state of the soul.[29] So the presence or absence of a soul or of a certain soul is not something for which we can successfully test, at least not directly. What this shows, I believe, is that the soul does not provide *evidence for* personal identity. We cannot, for example, prove that a given person really is our long-lost friend by proving that this person really has our long-lost friend's soul. But it still might be true that the soul provides *a criterion of* personal identity. That is, it still might be the case that the person really is our long-lost friend if this person and our long-lost friend have the same soul. It might even be true to say that a purported Jones in the afterlife is the same person as the Jones who once lived on earth if the purported Jones has Jones's soul. How we might test for or come to know this is another matter. Perhaps only God can know for sure who has what soul. Perhaps the rest of us will never know—at least apart from divine revelation—whether the purported Jones has Jones's soul. But it can still be true that if they have the same soul, they are two different temporal episodes of the same person.

And the claim that personal identity consists in or amounts to the presence of the soul does not rule out the possibility of our making reliable personal identity judgments on other grounds, as Weirob seems to claim it does. Those who believe in the possibility of disembodied existence need not deny that there are other criteria of personal identity (e.g., if a person has the same body as my long-lost friend, this person *is* my long-lost friend) and other ways of producing evidence in favor of or against personal identity claims.

Perry's second argument is also based on an element of truth—memory certainly is fallible; we do have to distinguish between apparent memories and genuine memories. So unless I have access to some infallible way of making this distinction, the mere fact that the purported Jones seems to remember events in Jones's life from Jones's point of view will not establish beyond conceivable doubt that the purported Jones is Jones (although it might count as evidence for it). As above, however, this does not rule out the possibility that memory is a criterion of personal identity. If the purported Jones does indeed remember events in Jones's life from Jones's point of view, then the purported Jones is Jones.

It is sometimes claimed that the memory criterion is parasitic on the bodily criterion and that use of the memory criterion never suffices by itself to establish identity. But such claims are surely false. We sometimes do make secure identity claims based on the memory criterion alone—e.g., when we receive a typed or printed letter from a friend. We hold that it is our friend who wrote the letter solely on the basis of memories and personality traits apparently possessed by the author of the letter that seem to be memories and personality traits that our friend has or ought to have. Of course if doubts were to arise, we would try to verify or falsify the claim that our friend wrote the letter by the use of any evidence or criterion that might seem promising. We might check the letter for fingerprints; we might try to see if it was written on our friend's typewriter; we might even telephone our friend and ask whether she wrote the letter. This is not to suggest that we must always rely on the bodily criterion; there may well be cases in which we try to verify an identity claim originally based on the bodily criterion by means of memories. It is simply to suggest that in cases of doubt we will be inclined to look at both sorts of criteria.

But in cases where the bodily criterion cannot be used (e.g., during the interim period postulated in temporary disembodiment), can identity claims rationally be made? Can we ever be sure that a disembodied putative Stephen Davis *is* Stephen Davis? The problem is especially acute since memory is notoriously fallible. Without recourse to the bodily criterion, how can we distinguish between actual memories and purported memories? Of course, so far as a *criterion* of personal identity is concerned, the quick response to this objection is the assertion that God will ensure that our apparent memories are genuine memories. And that will suffice. So far as *evidence* of personal identity is concerned, I would argue that secure identity claims can be made without resort to the bodily criterion in cases in which there are very many memories from very many different people that cohere together well. The context makes all the difference. If there are, say, one hundred disembodied souls all wondering whether everyone else is in fact who he or she claims to be, it would be irrational to deny that their memories are genuine if those memories all fit together, confirm each other, and form a coherent picture. Doubt would still be conceivable but not rational. And something like this is precisely what defenders of temporary disembodiment claim will occur during the interim period.[30]

The third or duplication argument is one that critics of disembodied existence frequently appeal to, but I will not discuss it here. . . . Let me then close this section with one further point.

Although the view I am defending in this chapter—temporary disembodiment—does not require the coherence of any notion of permanent disembodiment (such as the doctrine of the immortality of the soul), I nevertheless hold both temporary and permanent disembodiment to be coherent. As we have already noted, Geach argues strongly that only temporary disembodiment is coherent, that the problem of the personal identity of a disembodied person is manageable only on the basis of an assumption of its capacity or potential to be reunited with a given body at some point. Otherwise, he says, disembodied minds cannot be differentiated.[31] If Geach is right, only temporary disembodiment is coherent; immortality of the soul is not. Or at least those who believe in immortality of the soul must add an item to their theory—perhaps something about a permanently disembodied soul permanently retaining the (forever unrealized) *capacity* to be reunited with a given body.

VIII

It should be evident by this point that I do not consider what I have been calling the Patristic theory to be normative for Christians today. The "modern" theory seems to me an acceptable interpretation of resurrection. God's ability to raise us from the dead in the eschaton does not seem to depend on God's ability to locate and reunite the very particles of which our bodies once consisted. Nevertheless, the Patristic theory also constitutes an acceptable understanding of resurrection for Christians. The standard objections to it are answerable, and the most natural exegesis of 1 Corinthians 15:35–50 supports it. Furthermore, I would argue that respect for Christian tradition must grant great weight to views held by virtually all the Church Fathers unless there is serious reason to depart from what they say. It seems to me quite possible that God will one day raise us from the dead in the very way that the Fathers and Aquinas suggest.

My overall conclusion is that the theory of resurrection that I have been considering (which can be interpreted in either the Patristic or the "modern" way) is a viable notion for Christians. Temporary disembodiment seems eminently defensible, both philosophically and theologically. I do not claim that it is the only viable option for Christian belief about life after death; I do claim that it is an acceptable way for Christians to understand those words from the Apostles' Creed that say, "I believe in . . . the resurrection of the body."

Much contemporary philosophy tends, in its understanding of human nature, in a behaviorist or even materialist direction. No one who believes in temporary disembodiment can embrace philosophical materialism, but such believers can have great sympathy with any view that says that a disembodied person would hardly be a human person in the full sense of the term. Both philosophical materialists and those who believe in temporary disembodiment can accept the notion that a disembodied person is only a minimal person, a mere shadow of a true human person.

Christians can accordingly embrace the notion that full and true and complete human life is bodily life. That is why they look forward to "the resurrection of the body." The central idea here is that death disassembles us for a while, and then God (either in the Patristic or the "modern" way) puts us back together again. In a sense, then, we human beings are God's artifacts.[32] The unity over time of an artifact (e.g., my computer) is a function in part of natural processes of behavior and change *and* of the intentions of its creators and users. . . . In any case, the idea is that at some time after death, God will reconstitute us in a new and perfected way. As Pseudo-Justin says, "In the resurrection the flesh shall rise entire. For if on earth He healed the sickness of the flesh, and made the body whole, much more will He do this in the resurrection, so that the flesh shall rise perfect and entire" (*On the Resurrection*, chap. 4).

Notes

1   See Harry A. Wolfson, "Immortality and Resurrection in the Philosophy of the Church Fathers," in *Immortality and Resurrection*, ed. Krister Stendahl (New York: Macmillan, 1965), pp. 64–72. See also Lynn Boliek, *The Resurrection of the Flesh* (Grand Rapids: William B. Eerdmans, 1962).

2   See Robert H. Gundry, *Soma in Biblical Theology: With Emphasis on Pauline Anthropology* (Cambridge: Cambridge University Press, 1976), p. 159.

3   See Wolfson, "Immortality and Resurrection in the Philosophy of the Church Fathers," pp. 56–60, 63–64.

4   It does not seem to make sense to speak of some disembodied thing x being "in the presence of" some other thing y, where "in the presence of" means "in the spatial vicinity of." The notion could be coherently understood, however, as something like "being acutely aware of and sensitive to." But since this sense, too, is ruled out by the concept of spiritual sleep, I am unable to provide a sensible construal of the notion of a disembodied and unconscious person being in the presence of God.

5   Price, "Survival and the Idea of 'Another World,'" in *Language, Metaphysics, and Death*, ed. John Donnelly (New York: Fordham University Press, 1978), pp. 176–95. I do not wish to commit myself entirely to Price's theory; among others, John Hick has detected difficulties in it (see *Death and Eternal Life* [New York: Harper & Row, 1976], pp. 265–77). But Price's main point—that disembodied survival of death is possible—seems to me correct.

6   Aquinas, *Summa Contra Gentiles*, 4.79.11.

7   Athenagoras, *Embassy for Christians and the Resurrection of the Dead*, trans. Joseph H. Crehan (London: Longmans, Green, 1956), pp. 115–16.

8   Aquinas, *Summa Contra Gentiles*, 4.84.7.

9   Augustine, *The Enchiridion on Faith, Hope, and Love*, ed. Henry Paolucci (Chicago: Henry Regnery, 1961), 87.

10 Athenagoras, *Embassy for Christians and the Resurrection of the Dead*, p. 115.

11 Aquinas, quoted by P. T. Geach in *God and the Soul* (London: Routledge & Kegan Paul, 1969), p. 22.

12 Aquinas, *Summa Contra Gentiles*, 4.81.

13 See Gundry, *Soma in Biblical Theology*, pp. 164ff. For more on this and other points made in this paragraph, see also C. F. D. Moule, "St. Paul and Dualism: The Pauline Concept of Resurrection," *New Testament Studies* 12 (January 1966): 106–23; and Ronald J. Sider, "The Pauline Conception of the Resurrection Body in I Corinthians XV, 35–54," *New Testament Studies* 21 (April 1975): 428–39.

14 Augustine, *The Enchiridion on Faith, Hope, and Love*, 88.

15 See Irenaeus, *Against Heresies*, 5.2.3; Augustine, *The Enchiridion on Faith, Hope, and Love*, 91; Aquinas, *Summa Contra Gentiles*, 4.83–87.

16 Dilley, "Resurrection and the 'Replica Objection,'" *Religious Studies* 19 (December 1983): 462.

17 Van Inwagen, "The Possibility of Resurrection," *International Journal for Philosophy of Religion* 9 (1978): 119.

18 Parfit, *Reasons and Persons* (Oxford: Oxford University Press, 1986), pp. 199–200. I mention here only the most simple of the test cases involving teletransportation that Parfit discusses. Nor will I consider in this chapter what I take to be the central theses of Part 3 of his book.

19 Hick, *Death and Eternal Life*, p. 186.

20 Commenting on Paul's argument in 1 Corinthians 15:53, Tertullian says, "when he says '*this* corruptible' and '*this* mortal,' he utters the words while touching the surface of his own body" (*On the Resurrection of the Flesh*, 51).

21   Gundry makes this point convincingly; see *Soma in Biblical Theology,* p. 186. See also Sider, "The Pauline Conception of the Resurrection Body in I Corinthians XV, 35–54," pp. 429–38; and Bruce Reichenbach, "On Disembodied Resurrection Persons: A Reply," *Religious Studies* 18 (June 1982): 227.

22   Augustine, *The Enchiridion on Faith, Hope, and Love*, 88. See also *The City of God*, 22.20.

23   Badham, *Christian Beliefs about Life after Death* (London: Macmillan Press, 1976), p. 50. Despite my disagreement with him on this point, I must admit that Badham does successfully rebut several unconvincing patristic arguments about bodily resurrection.

24   See, e.g., Irenaeus, *Against Heresies*, 5.3.2; and Tertullian, *On the Resurrection of the Flesh*, 11.

25   For Flew's argument, see "Immortality," in *The Encyclopedia of Philosophy*, ed. Paul Edwards (New York: Macmillan, 1967); the articles collected in Part III of *The Presumption of Atheism and Other Essays* (London: Elek/Pemberton, 1976); and *The Logic of Mortality* (Oxford: Basil Blackwell, 1987). For Williams's argument, see *Problems of the Self* (Cambridge: Cambridge University Press, 1973). For Phillips's argument, see *Death and Immortality* (New York: St. Martin's Press, 1970). For Penelhum's argument, see *Survival and Disembodied Existence* (New York: Humanities Press, 1970). For Perry's argument, see *A Dialogue on Personal Identity and Immortality* (Indianapolis: Hackett, 1978).

26   See Geach, *God and the Soul*, pp. 17–29.

27   For examples of this defense, see Richard L. Purtill, "The Intelligibility of Disembodied Survival," *Christian Scholar's Review* 5 (1975): 15–26; and Paul Helm, "A Theory of Disembodied Survival and Re-embodied Existence," *Religious Studies* 14 (March 1978). See also Bruce Reichenbach, *Is Man the Phoenix? A Study of Immortality* (Washington: University Press of America, 1983).

28   Perry, *A Dialogue on Personal Identity and Immortality*, p. 3.

29   I owe this point to W. S. Anglin.

30   I will not try to answer Perry's charge of circularity, because I believe Parfit has decisively done so with the notion that he calls quasi-memories. See *Reasons and Persons*, pp. 220ff.

31   Geach, *God and the Soul*, pp. 23–28.

32   This idea was suggested to me by Richard Warner.

Questions for reflection

1   According to Professor Davis, what are some theological and philosophical advantages to holding to the theory of temporary disembodiment? What do you make of them?

2   What is the difference between classical dualism and the kind of dualism defended by Davis? Why is the distinction important?

3   One of the difficulties with believing that our current bodies can be resurrected is the troubling problem of cannibals eating a person, and thus taking another person's atoms into their bodies. One main solution is that while *we* might not be in a position to locate and reconstitute the relevant atoms of someone's body, since God is omnipotent, he will be able to do so. Is this answer simply an appeal to mystery? What do you think of Davis's reflections on this problem?

4   Do you believe in bodily resurrection? State your reasons for your answer.

Further reading

John W. Cooper (1989) *Body, Soul, and Life Everlasting: Biblical Anthropology and the Monism–Dualism Debate*. Grand Rapids, MI: Eerdmans. (A study of biblical anthropology which includes theological, philosophical, and scientific discussions on the nature and destiny of human persons.)

Stephen T. Davis (1993) *Risen Indeed: Making Sense of the Resurrection*. Grand Rapids, MI: Eerdmans. (Provides a defense of the Christian view of the resurrection utilizing arguments and evidences from history, philosophy, and theology; the essay above was taken from this book.)

Paul Edwards, ed. (1992) *Immortality*. New York: Macmillan. (A helpful collection of essays, including passages from Plato's *Phaedo* and Thomas Aquinas's *Summa Theologiae*.)

John Perry (1978) *A Dialogue on Personal Identity and Immortality*. Indianapolis, IN: Hackett. (A very accessible and lively conversation on the issues of personal identity and immortality.)

Krister Stendahl, ed. (1965) *Immortality and Resurrection*. New York: Macmillan. (Includes an excellent collection of essays by scholars investigating whether the New Testament affirms belief in immortality and resurrection.)

Chapter 57

Paul K. Moser

DEATH, DYING, AND THE HIDDENNESS OF GOD

Paul K. Moser is Professor and Chairperson of Philosophy at Loyola University of Chicago. In this selection he focuses on the issues of death, dying, and divine hiddenness. Theists believe that death happens: we are born at some point, we live for a time, and then we die. But this raises all manner of questions. What is death? What does death have to do with us as persons? What can we learn from the fact that we die? Can there be hope in the face of death? Theists affirm hope, but if the God of theism exists, where is he in the midst of our daily lives and struggles? Why isn't God's presence more evident to us? Why would God allow death? Moser responds to such questions—contrasting Christian theism with materialism (the view that the physical universe is all there is)—and lays out the alternatives each has to offer.

In the *Phaedo*, Plato claims that "those who really apply themselves in the right way to philosophy are directly and of their own accord preparing themselves for dying and death" (64A). This claim sounds very strange to us today. If Plato is right, contemporary philosophers have failed to "apply themselves in the right way to philosophy." So, maybe contemporary philosophers aren't true footnotes to Plato after all. Maybe they have missed his main point about the point of philosophy. Even so, the important questions regarding death are not about Plato.

What has death to do with philosophy? Or, more immediately, what has death to do with *us*, with us *as persons*, regardless of whether we are philosophers? Does death have an important lesson for us, even if we are inclined to ignore its lesson? Let's begin with the obvious: death happens.

The reality of death

Death is the cessation of *bodily* life. Some mind-body dualists, under Plato's influence, deny that death is the cessation of *mental* life. It is, however, the end of embodied life, at least as we know it. So, when we die, others will bury or cremate our bodies, even if they don't do the same to *us*, to our souls. Mind-body dualists and materialists agree on this much: bodily death happens. They disagree, however, on whether our bodily death allows for our mental survival.

We might deny that death happens. Still, we will die. We can run but we cannot hide from death. The reality of death marks the human predicament, wherever we go in space and/or time. Death is universal for humans. The reality of death is the reality of a pervasive destructive *power*. It destroys us at least physically, if not mentally and socially too. It sometimes is delayable, given the powers of modern medicine. Still, death seems unavoidable if we are left to our own resources. Its power seems immune to our best medicine and science. Death inevitably triumphs over humans and our powers.

What, if anything, is the significance of death? The answer depends on what exactly death is. One question is whether it is an *irreversible* destructive power. Is death forever? Given materialism about reality, it is: there is no coming back. If reality is uniformly material, entropy meets no lasting counterbalance, and death doesn't either. Our best physics tells us that in the long term the physical universe is destined to break down. The energy of the physical universe will naturally disperse if it is not counterbalanced. Consider, for instance, how a cube of ice will naturally melt in a heated room. The same ice cube does not ever return from its dispersion. The material world thus does not offer us, as the persons we are, a lasting alternative to death. It leaves us with dying and death, with the dispersing of bodily life. If we depend for our existence on bodily life, we too will be dispersed forever, given materialism.

Loss in death

Given materialism, we will no longer be persons after our death. So, there is no lasting hope for *us*, regarding our future as persons. We have no lasting future; so, we have no lastingly good future. Our destiny is just the abyss of dispersed physical energy. We will then have, in the abyss, no value in ourselves because we will have ceased to exist. People who were once valuable will then no longer be valuable. We will no longer be important, or worthwhile. Our existence and value will have ceased, never to be recovered. Some people may remember us, but mere memories are not the persons we are. We ourselves will not survive in memories. We will be gone forever, dispersed and done for, given materialism.

The loss of us will be a real loss. Why? Because we now are valuable—that is, worthwhile and good—in many ways. We exemplify goodness in many respects, even though we exemplify evil too. So, our funerals will be a sad occasion for many people—not for *us*, of course, but for many others. Their sadness will correspond to the loss of us with regard to what *was* valuable about us, including our being alive. People who pretend that death is no loss at all are misguided, perhaps even self-deceived. They need a reality check from the spontaneous responses of people at funerals. One might spin the reality of death to fit a far-fetched theory, but the responses of the uninitiate at funerals are telling indeed.

Materialists might take an extreme position here. If our value as persons ceases at death, as it will given materialism, then our death is not important after all, because we aren't truly valuable. We are just insignificant energy centers waiting entropically (so to speak) to be dispersed. Such extremism is confused. The fact that we have no *lasting*, or ultimate, value, given materialism, doesn't entail that we have no value at all. We can still have *temporary* value, and we do, even though materialism makes our ultimate future bleak. Correspondingly, we can reasonably have *short-term* hope for our temporary well-being. Hope for our lasting, or ultimate, well-being would be misplaced. Materialism offers no basis for such hope. Entropy will leave us all without hope. The final hopelessness of materialism is palpable. Lasting meaning, or purpose, is likewise excluded. Camus (1955), for example, paints a powerful portrait of life without lasting meaning.

Our ultimately hopeless destiny, given materialism, is a reality beyond our power to change. We can't save ourselves or anyone else from the abyss of final dispersion and destruction. Our intelligence, however sophisticated, can't save us. Our philosophy, however profound, can't save us. Our willful drive, however resolute, can't save us. Nor can our families, friends, colleagues, or community save us, however well-intentioned they are. Death will leave us in its cold wake, regardless of our cleverness, drive, or acquaintances. Materialism, then, is less than cheery about death. Materialists should be too, at least as long as they embrace materialism. The grave is their destiny.

Outside help

In the face of death, we can reasonably be hopeful only if we have outside help from a power that can overcome death. This would be *outside* help, because its power would be beyond us. We lack the power of our own to overcome death. The needed help would be actual help, not merely possible help. It would offer us the actual opportunity to overcome death, to survive the destruction brought by death.

Could an *impersonal* power save us from death? This would be a power without plans, intentions, or goals. It would enable us to survive destruction by death, but it would not do so intentionally, or purposively. It would happen blindly, in the way the wind, for instance, could blindly form a three-dimensional portrait of Mother Teresa's face on the sandy shoreline of Lake Michigan. The wind *could* do this, but we cannot count on it to do so. If it happens, it is unpredictable for all practical purposes and thus beyond what we can reasonably hope for. If it were to happen for Mother Teresa (against all odds), we could not reasonably assume that it will happen for another person too. We thus wouldn't wait on the shoreline for someone's portrait to emerge from the sand. If we did, our sanity would be questioned.

Our *grounded* hope in surviving death, *if* we have such hope, requires a ground for supposing that death will be overcome by us. This ground cannot be the unpredictable vicissitudes of local wind movements. It requires a ground predictable and trustworthy by us, that is, predictable and trustworthy in practice. The announced intentions of a reliable, trustworthy personal agent would offer such a ground. We know this from everyday experience, as we often form a grounded hope on the basis of the announced intentions of other persons. For example, I reasonably hope that my return home from the campus will be timely, given that a trustworthy friend has promised to give me a ride home. This hope has a basis different in kind from the basis for my wish that the wind inscribe a human portrait on the shoreline of Lake Michigan. My hope is grounded in a good reason; my wish is not.

Let's consider the kind of outside help that would come from a trustworthy personal agent who has the power to overcome death. I have said "would come," rather than "does come," to avoid begging a likely question: namely, "*Is* there actually such help?" Another likely question is: "If there's outside help from a personal agent, why would that agent allow death to occur in the first place?" Some people hold that such an agent, if genuinely helpful, would block death from the start. Here we have the beginnings of an analogue to the so-called problem of evil for theism.

Would a superhuman personal agent allow us to undergo death even though that agent seeks to help us to overcome death? If so, why? A noteworthy answer comes from Paul's epistle to the Romans: "The creation was subjected to futility, not by its own will, but by the will of the One who subjected it, in [the One's] hope that the creation will be freed from its slavery to decay and brought into the glorious freedom of the children of God" (8:20–21). Let's unpack this.

Paul's reference to futility echoes the writer of Ecclesiastes: "Futility of futilities! All is futility" (Eccl. 1:2, 12:8). They have in mind what is ultimately pointless, in vain, when left to its own ways. Paul thus suggests that God introduced death to show that the ways of creation on its own are ultimately futile, pointless, meaningless. In particular, as a part of creation, we humans ultimately come to naught on our own. Death leaves us with a hopeless destiny if we are left to our own resources. All of our own projects and achievements, even our philosophical labors, will meet the same fate: futility. They are all destined for the abyss, never to be revived. This seems to be nothing but bad news, but is it really?

Paul suggests that a certain hope lies behind the futility of death: God's hope of freeing people from futility to enter the family of God. Death is portrayed as a means to bring about this hope. How can death, our death, lead to life, our life? How can such loss yield such good?

Dying to live

Death can enable a needed learning curriculum for us if it serves the teaching purposes of an agent who can overcome death for us. What might such an agent have to teach us with death, our death? We all need instruction about our desperate situation when left to our own resources. We need to learn that all of our best intentions, efforts, and achievements will ultimately be futile, meaningless, if we are on our own. Death is the intended wake-up call to this humbling lesson. It shows that we cannot think, will, or work ourselves into lasting satisfaction by our own resources. It shows that we are fragile and even ultimately hopeless on our own. Death announces that we need outside help for lasting satisfaction and meaning. It solemnly warns us who remain: if we stay to ourselves, without outside power, we are done for, forever.

The reality of death fits perfectly with the view that we are creatures intended to depend on One greater than ourselves, on One who can overcome death for us. Such depending is just trust. It is faith, *not* as guesswork or a leap beyond evidence, but as willing reliance on One whom we need to overcome death, to live lastingly. What exactly is this reliance, and how does death bear on it?

For shorthand, let's introduce talk of "God" for the One in question. The slippery word "God" is a title, not a proper name. It signifies One who not only can overcome death but also is worthy of worship, i.e., unconditional commitment and adoration as our morally impeccable Maker and Sustainer. We can use a title intelligibly, even the title "God," without begging the question whether God exists. A title can have semantic significance owing to its connotation, even if it lacks denotation. So, our use of the term "God" as a title does not automatically ignore the qualms of atheists and agnostics.

Our trusting, depending, or relying on God appropriately is just willingly counting on God as our Savior and Lord, that is, as our Redeemer and Master. In counting on God thus, I commit to God as *my* God. I thereby commit to putting God's will over my will, just as Jesus did in the Garden of Gethsemane as he prayed to God: "Not what I will, but what You will" (Mark 14:36). In trusting God, I commit to dying to my own selfish ways to live to God's ways. In short, I resolve to die to my selfishness to live to God. This entails a commitment to reject selfishness, in particular, any selfishness that involves exalting my will above God's. In selfishness, I fail to honor God as God. I put myself and my ways first. The call to faith in God is, in contrast, a call to die to selfishness in order to live to One who can overcome death for us. Whatever else it is, it is *not* a call to leap beyond evidence, as if faith in God were necessarily defective from a cognitive viewpoint. Trust in God can, in principle, be at least as cognitively good as your trusting in your best friend.

Why assume, however, that I must die to my ways to live to God? Isn't this a perversely harsh understanding of what faith in God involves? Not if my own case is at all representative of the human condition. My problem is the human problem: deep-seated selfishness, the antithesis to the unselfish love integral to God's morally impeccable character. I'm also very good at hiding my selfish ways from myself and others. I tell myself stories of how they are reasonable and even good. Our inveterate selfishness qualifies us as morally deficient and thus disqualifies us immediately as God. The title "God," requiring a morally impeccable character of its holder, does not apply to ourselves. Even so, we have the persistent tendency to play God in at least some area of our lives. We pose as Lord over at least part of our lives, particularly in areas we deem vital to our well-being. One such area concerns how we treat our enemies, that is, our acquaintances who are a clear threat to our well-being. At best, we ignore them; at worst, we seek to destroy them. Rarely do we show them unselfish forgiving love, the kind of merciful love found in the true God (see Matt. 5:43–48). The risk is, we suppose, too great, too threatening to our comfort and well-being. We thereby choose against the ways of an all-loving God. We presume to know better. We thus play God. Trust in God is the refusal to play God.

Another area where we play God concerns what is to count as suitable evidence of God's reality. We presume to be in a position, on our own, to say what kind of evidence God *must* supply regarding God's reality. We reason, in agreement with Bertrand Russell and many other philosophers: If God is real, God would be revealed in way *W*. For instance, God would show up with considerable fireworks or at least Pomp and Circumstance. God, however, is not revealed in way *W*. Hence, God is not real. Russell (1970) thus anticipated his preferred response if after death he met God: "God, you gave us insufficient evidence." We thereby exalt ourselves as cognitive judge, jury, and executioner over God. God, we suppose, must be revealed on *our* cognitive terms. In such cognitive idolatry (see Moser 2002), we set up our cognitive standards in ways that preclude so-called "reasonable" acknowledgment of God's reality. Our cognitive pride thus becomes suicidal. We play God to our own demise. The reality of our impending death exhibits that without the true God, we are ultimately hopeless. We are then impostors in playing God.

We must die to our playing God, if we are to live lastingly. Death is our final notice. It calls us to the stark realization that our playing God will not last but will instead lead to the grave, once and for all. In shattering us, death ultimately ruins all of our projects too. The needed power for lasting life, then, is not from us or our projects. Only pride gone blind would lead one to deny this. Even in the face of death, our selfish pride endures. In the absence of the humbling effects of death, our pride would run wild indeed. Death reveals that what is lastingly important is not from us. It exposes our core insecurity (and impotence) about life itself, that is, our insecurity about the future of our lives. We know *that* our lives will end, but we have no idea of *when* they will end. Our end could come in twenty years or it could come in twenty minutes. This indefiniteness makes for insecurity and anxiety, at least when we honestly attend to the matter. As a result, we typically divert attention in ways that lead to indifference about death and related realities.

How not to approach death

Avoidance and indifference toward death threaten all of us at times, in our fear, insecurity, and weakness. Blaise Pascal writes:

> the fact that there are men indifferent to the loss of their being . . . is not natural. They are quite different with regard to everything else: they fear even the most insignificant things, they foresee them, feel them, and the same man who spends so many days and nights in rage over the loss of some office or over some imaginary affront to his honour is the very one who, without anxiety or emotion, knows he is going to lose everything through death. It is a monstrous thing to see in the same heart and at the same time both this sensitivity to the slightest things and this strange insensitivity to the greatest (1660 [1995]: sec. 681).

We ignore and become indifferent to death, because we know that our own resources cannot overcome it. We know that death will triumph over us. So, we conclude, let's just resign ourselves to it. We then fail to seek the needed solution (the One who is the solution) in the right way.

Russell acknowledges the inadequacy of our own resources in the face of death, but still recommends intentional and courageous "contemplation" of our fate in death. He claims: "it remains only to cherish . . . the lofty thoughts that ennoble [our] little day; . . . to worship at the shrine that [our] own hands have built." He means the shrine that our *minds* have built. Russell also recommends that we approach the dying "to give them the pure joy of a never-tiring affection, to strengthen failing courage, to instill faith in hours of despair" (1903 [1957]: 18). Faith? In what? Russell is silent, because he has no hope-conferring object of faith to offer.

Russell's rhetoric may sound good, but he cannot deliver on it. The eternal truths he loves passionately offer no hope to the dying. How could they? They cannot overcome death for the dying. So, they are no basis for us to "instill faith in hours of despair." Russell deserves credit for facing death as an immediate problem even for philosophers. He has, however, no basis for his courage, his joy, or his faith. His faith does not yield living through dying, because his faith has no *object* of faith that can overcome death. The mere *attitude* of faith, being a psychological human state, does nothing to overcome death. Russell, then, is not helpful in solving the human plight. He offers no genuine help. He has no good news for us, the dying.

Do we want outside help? Some of us don't. Thomas Nagel claims that the existence of God poses a serious "cosmic authority problem" for us, so much so that he hopes that God does not exist. Nagel writes: "I want atheism to be true . . .. I hope there is no God! I don't want there to be a God; I don't want the universe to be like that" (1997: 130). Contrast this bold attitude with the tempered attitude of the Yale surgeon, Dr. Richard Selzer (2000), who likewise is not a theist: "Probably the biggest, saddest thing about my own life is that I never had faith in God. I envy people who do. Life without faith is rather a hard proposition." An undeniable hardship of life without God is that ultimately it all comes to naught, and we have indications of this futility of life. Selzer rightly feels the pain of life without God. Somehow, Nagel doesn't. He evidently misses the tragedy of a bypassed opportunity of a lastingly good life. Something has gone wrong.

It would be a strange, defective God who didn't pose a serious cosmic authority problem for humans. Part of the status of being *God*, after all, is that God has unique authority, or lordship, over humans. Since we humans aren't God, the true God would have authority over us and would seek to correct our profoundly selfish ways. Nagel confesses to having a fear of any religion involving God. Such fear seems widespread among humans, and all humans may share it at least at times. It stems from human fear of losing our supposed lordship over our decisions and lives. We want to be able to say, as the blindly arrogant song goes: "I did it my way." Willful children are very good at exhibiting this attitude, and adults can be too. Our attitude is: "It's my way, or no way." Human willfulness runs deeper than the reach of reason. One's willfulness, tragically, can be *consistently* suicidal. Reason is no panacea, after all. If it were, we wouldn't need God.

Our supposedly self-protective fear, confessed by Nagel, may *seem* to be for our own good. It blocks, however, our receiving a lastingly good life. Consider the existence of an all-loving God who sustains, and who alone can sustain, lastingly good life for humans. The existence of such a God is a good thing, all things considered, for us humans. Nagel hopes that there is no such God. In doing so, he hopes that something good, all things considered, for all of us does not exist. Such a hope against the reality of something good for us arises from Nagel's desire to have moral independence and authority. At least, I can't find a better diagnosis.

Nagel's desire is willful in a way that flouts good judgment. It rests on this attitude: "If I can't have my moral independence of God, even though God is all-loving and good for me, then I hope that God doesn't exist. I don't want to exist in a universe where God is the moral authority over me and others. I just won't stand for that kind of moral non-independence. If I can't be morally independent of God, then I just won't be at all." Nagel is willing to sacrifice something good for himself and others (namely, lastingly good life) for the sake of a willful desire to be morally independent of God. If, however, God is all-loving (as God is by title), this willful attitude is dangerously misguided. Its willfulness invites the needless destruction of suicide in a world blessed by the presence of an all-loving God. We thus have a case where willfulness blocks good judgment. This is a trademark of the human condition of *supposedly* self-protective fear.

Our attitudes toward God's existence are not purely cognitive in their origin and sustenance. Our *willfulness* looms large. Let's turn, then, to the role of *evidence* regarding God as the One who can overcome death for us.

Hidden help

If God exists, God is hidden. Pascal was dead right: ". . . any religion which does not say that God is hidden is not true" (1660 [1995]: sec. 275). Jesus himself thanks God for hiding. After giving his disciples instructions regarding their preaching of the kingdom of God, Jesus prays as follows:

> I thank you, Father, Lord of heaven and earth, because you have hidden these things from the wise and the learned, and you have revealed them to infants. Yes, Father, this seemed good in your sight (Luke 10:21; cf. Matt. 11:25–26; Isa. 45:15).

If an all-loving God aims to help us to overcome death, shouldn't we all receive an explicit revelation of God's reality that is beyond reasonable doubt? Wouldn't an all-loving God appear clearly to dispel doubts about God's reality and the significance of human death?

We think we know what we *should* expect of an all-loving God. As a result, we confidently set the parameters for God's reality as if they were decisive regarding God's reality. We seldom ask, however, what *God* would expect of *us*. We'll do so here. An all-loving God would promote unselfish love, and thus would not settle for our simply knowing that God exists. I could know that God exists but hate God. Indeed, my hate toward God could increase as my evidence of God's reality increases. As I get more evidence of God as a genuine moral authority over me, I could easily deepen my hate toward God. This could come from willful insistence that I be my own moral authority at least in certain areas of my life.

Hate toward God is not good for anyone, including the one who hates God. It blocks a congenial relationship between a person and the only One who can overcome death and supply lastingly good life for that person. So, an all-loving God would not promote hate toward God. For the person resolutely opposed to God, more evidence of God's reality would typically be harmful. It would intensify and solidify opposition to God. Jesus thus advises his messengers not to cast his sacred message before resolute opponents, lest they trample it under foot (Matt. 7:6). Such a mean-spirited response by Jesus' opponents would be good for no one, not even the opponents. An all-loving God seeks to break willful opposition but not typically by means of a counterproductive direct assault on it. Instead, God typically invites us in various ways to come to our senses, and then waits. Since people aren't pawns, we should not expect universal success on God's part. Because people can freely reject God's invitation, some people might not ever come around to acknowledge God, despite God's best efforts.

What of "agnostics"? They withhold judgment regarding God's existence on the basis of allegedly counterbalanced evidence. They reportedly endorse agnosticism "for reasons of evidence." Typically, however, agnostics overlook the most important evidence of God's reality: namely, the reality of God's genuinely unselfish love in Jesus and thereby in the life of a person who yields to him as Lord and thus receives God's Spirit. This kind of love prompts the apostle Paul to make the following *cognitively* relevant point: "[Christian] hope does not disappoint, because the love of God has been poured out within our hearts through the Holy Spirit who was given to us" (Romans 5:6). Paul thus identifies a kind of evidence that saves one from disappointment in hoping in God: the presence of God's Spirit accompanied by God's unselfish love. Followers of Jesus often fail to live up to the high calling toward God's holy love, but this does not challenge the distinctive evidence just noted.

Evidence from the presence of God's Spirit is akin to the evidence from conscience regarding, for instance, the goodness of a case of self-giving kindness and the evil of a case of needless torture. Such evidence from conscience, although genuine, does not yield a non-question-begging argument against skeptics, but this is no defect in the evidence. In addition, such evidence can be suppressed by us, and we will dismiss it if we *will* to do something in conflict with it. Still, the evidence from conscience is genuine and salient. Likewise for the evidence of God's Spirit, which comes typically with the conviction in conscience that we have fallen short of God's unselfish holy ways.

Volitional factors loom large in acquiring evidence of God's reality. An all-loving God would seek to be known *as God*, for the good of humans. So, God would seek to be known as *our* God. God sent Jesus as living proof that God is for us, not against us. The self-giving sacrifice of Jesus aims to alert us to God's intervention on our behalf. In his journey from Gethsemane to Calvary, Jesus resists ("dies to") selfishness in order to live to God. He subjects his will to the unselfish will of his Father. This subjection of the will is cognitively as well as morally significant. It highlights autobiographical factors in receiving evidence of God's reality as God. As I yield to God's call to obey, as Jesus did, God emerges as *my* God, and I thereby become God's servant and child. Only in such volitional yielding on my part does God become *my* God. My firm knowledge of God as my God thus depends on volitional factors concerning me, concerning my exercise of my will in relation to God. I must yield my will in response to the convicting and redirecting intervention of God's Spirit in my conscience. I can have no firm knowledge of God as my God in a will-free manner. We tell ourselves that *if* God appeared to us in an astonishing manner, *then* we would yield to God as God. This, however, is doubtful, because we then have already set ourselves up as cognitive judge over God.

The evidence from the presence of God's Spirit does not yield a non-question-begging argument for God's reality. This is no problem, because the reality of evidence does not depend on a non-question-begging argument. For example, I do not have a non-question-begging argument for my belief that I am awake now (at least relative to an extreme skeptic's questions), but I still have good evidence that I am awake now. Whether an argument is non-question-begging varies with the questions actually raised in an exchange. Evidence itself is not exchange-relative in this way. Our *having* evidence does not entail *giving* an answer of any kind. So, we should not be troubled by our lacking a non-question-begging argument relative to an agnostic's questions. We should rather identify the evidence suited to an all-loving God who seeks volitional transformation rather than mere reasonable belief.

Commitment to the true God can yield unsurpassed explanatory value, at least in certain areas of inquiry. Such a commitment, we might argue, makes the best sense of who we are and of why we have come into existence. The reasonableness of theistic belief is thus sometimes recommended as underwritten by an inference to a best explanation.

Still, the foundational evidence of God's reality is irreducibly a matter of experiencing the presence of God's personal Spirit. This presence is not an argument of any kind. It is rather God's authoritative call on a person's life. If a call promotes hate, it is not from an all-loving God. False gods compete with the true God, and they are known by the standard of unselfish love.

Some agnostics will demand that we begin with mere "existence-arguments" concerning God. This is misguided. In the case of the true God, essence, character, and value must not be bracketed for the sake of mere existence-arguments. The present approach holds these together, thereby maintaining the explanatory, psychological, and existential distinctiveness of the evidence supplied by the Jewish-Christian God. Genuine existence-evidence regarding the true God comes not as a needed preliminary to, but instead *through*, the Good News of what God has done for us in Jesus, in concert with the convicting and drawing power of God's Spirit. Proper conviction of God's reality comes through the transforming working of God's personal Spirit in conjunction with the Good News of what God has done for us. So, we should begin not with mere existence-evidence but rather with evidence of what God has done and is doing in terms of His gracious personal calling through the Good News of Jesus. We will thus avoid the risk of being diverted to deism, mere theism, or something else less robust than the reality of the true God and Father of Jesus. We will then highlight God's gracious offer of reconciliation to all people, even unsophisticated people, via the Good News of Jesus. A person doesn't have to be able to follow intricate arguments to receive evidence of God's reality. This is good news indeed.

Arguments aside, the Good News of Jesus need not be lost on people raised within non-theistic traditions. The convicting and drawing power of God's Spirit can begin to transform receptive people from any tradition, even receptive people who do not yet acknowledge this Spirit as the Spirit of the risen Jesus. When the Good News of Jesus actually comes to the latter people, it will, in due course, bring them to acknowledge the work of God's Spirit within them as the work of the Spirit of the risen Jesus. The Good News of Jesus has its base in a power that cuts much deeper than arguments and religious traditions: the transforming power of the Spirit of the living God.

Conclusion

For the person eager to follow God's ways, the available evidence is subtle but adequate. It is subtle in order to keep people humble, free of prideful triumphalism of the kind that destroys community. In our pride, we would readily turn a conveniently available God into a self-serving commodity. This tendency prompted Jesus to say that "it's an evil generation that seeks for a sign" (Matt. 16:4). The evidence available to us fits with the curriculum of death: the aim is to teach us to trust the One who alone can save us from death and corruption.

The lesson is that we must turn from our ways to get in line with the true God. This is difficult news, because we have a hard time trusting a God we cannot see. We fear that our well-being and rationality will be at risk if we trust this invisible God. The truth of the matter is that our well-being and rationality are at risk and even doomed if we fail to trust God. Death serves as a vivid reminder. Without God as our trusted Savior, only death awaits us. As we die to our ways in order to live to God, we receive

God as our Savior from death and corruption. Nothing can then extinguish us, not even death. Death leaves us, then, either with lives that are ultimately an empty tragedy or with a God subjecting this world to futility in order to save it. In sincerely hoping for the latter, we become open to a kind of evidence that will change us forever, even from death to life. If we have the courage to hope in God, we'll see that Plato was right: Philosophy done right prepares us for dying and death. It also leads to the One we need.

References

Camus, A. (1955) *The Myth of Sisyphus*, trans. J. O'Brien. New York: Knopf.

Moser, P. K. (2002) "Cognitive Idolatry and Divine Hiding." In D. Howard-Snyder and P. K. Moser (eds.), *Divine Hiddenness*. New York: Cambridge University Press.

Nagel, T. (1997) *The Last Word*. New York: Oxford University Press.

Pascal, B. (1660 [1995]) *Pensées*, trans. H. Levi. New York: Oxford University Press.

Plato (1969) *Phaedo*. In *The Last Days of Socrates*, trans. H. Tredennick. London: Penguin.

Russell, B. (1903 [1957]) "A Free Man's Worship." In *Mysticism and Logic*. Garden City, NY: Doubleday.

———. (1970) "The Talk of the Town." *New Yorker* (February 21), 29. Cited in A. Seckel (ed.) (1986) *Bertrand Russell on God and Religion*. Buffalo: Prometheus, 11.

Selzer, R. (2000) "Interview." *Teen Ink* (December).

Questions for reflection

1   What purpose, if any, could an all-loving God have in allowing human death? Could death be intended to be a wake-up call of some sort? If so, to what end?

2   If there is no personal God, what is the best story we could tell about the meaning, or purpose, of human life? Will this story recommend for or against ultimate despair, or hopelessness? Will it recommend against suicide?

3   Is it logically coherent to suppose that the existence of an all-loving God would be elusive, or hidden, to some extent? If so, what could God's purpose be in divine elusiveness? Might we be the problem here? If so, how?

4   How should we expect to be able to know the reality of an all-loving God? Are we already in a good position, given our selfish tendencies, to come to know God's reality? Or, might we need to undergo significant change as we come to know divine reality?

5   Barring coercion, could an all-loving God come to know us, given our selfish and dishonest ways? If not, should we expect to be able on our own to come to know God's reality? Do we have due cognitive modesty in this connection?

Further reading

Paul K. Moser (2002) "Cognitive Idolatry and Divine Hiding," in *Divine Hiddenness*. Ed. D. Howard-Snyder and P. Moser. New York: Cambridge University Press. (Identifies purposes of divine hiding.)

Blaise Pascal ([1660] 1995) *Pensées*. Trans. H. Levi. New York: Oxford University Press. (Acknowledges the relevance of human will to divine hiding.)

Bertrand Russell ([1903] 1957) *Mysticism and Logic*. Garden City, NY: Doubleday. (See the chapter entitled "A Free Man's Worship" for a statement of life in an accidental universe.)

J. L. Schellenberg (1993) *Divine Hiddenness and Human Reason*. Ithaca, NY: Cornell University Press. (Argues that given the moral character of God to which theists are committed, divine hiddenness is problematic—so much so that an argument for atheism can be generated from it.)

Nicholas Wolterstorff (1987) *Lament for a Son*. Grand Rapids, MI: Eerdmans. (A philosopher reflects on the death of his own son and discovers new meaning in the notion of a suffering God.)

Chapter 58

Charles Taliaferro

WHY WE NEED IMMORTALITY

Charles Taliaferro is Professor of Philosophy at St. Olaf College. In this essay he responds to Grace Jantzen's contention that survival after death cannot be inferred from the fact that God is loving. In his response he makes a distinction between a *time-enclosed good*, which he defines as "any good project, thing, event, state or process which is good but its good value is not preserved if it is temporally unlimited in extent" (e.g., eating a tasty meal), and a *non-time-enclosed good*, which he defines as "any good project, event, state or process which is good and its good value is not lost if it is temporally unlimited in extent." He notes that for an afterlife to be truly good, it cannot consist of a singular time-enclosed good. But there is no reason to suspect that an afterlife cannot include an indefinite variety of time-enclosed and non-time-enclosed goods. He argues that if we have reason to believe God deeply loves us, then we have reason to believe that God will preserve our lives, especially since as persons we possess a value which is not exhausted over time.

He also responds to Jantzen's claim that an afterlife does not alter the problem of evil which confronts theists. He agrees that positing an afterlife does not make the occurrences of evil in this life good. However, he argues that (1) an afterlife does have a bearing on the extent of evil in this life, and (2) evil may well give rise to some good.

In defending the belief in an afterlife, he also responds to three objections to it: (1) that such a belief introduces an undesirable dichotomy between persons and nonpersons, humans and nature, (2) that the notion of an afterlife is logically or metaphysically impossible, and (3) that there is something pretentious or presumptuous about belief in an afterlife.

He concludes by agreeing with Jantzen that Christians should not think that "life after death is a matter of course" and notes that he has not shown her to be incorrect in claiming that Christian faith can be profound and meaningful without an afterlife. However, he hopes to have shown some of the motives for why believing in an afterlife is a central issue in classical Christianity and why there is meaning and profundity in such belief.

> There is no such thing as a natural death: nothing that happens to a man is ever natural, since his presence calls the world into question. All men must die: but for every man his death is an accident and, even if he knows it and consents to it, an unjustifiable violation.
>
> Simone de Beauvoir[1]

In an early volume of *Modern Theology* Grace Jantzen raises doubts about whether we should give an affirmative answer to the question in her article title "Do We Need Immortality?"[2] She does not argue that there is no life after death, nor that it is irrational for anyone to hope for immortality. But she does contend that certain portraits of the afterlife are religiously and morally suspect, that the existence of an afterlife does not substantially alter the theistic problem of evil, and that our survival of death cannot be inferred from the fact that God is loving. I am in agreement with Professor Jantzen's characteristically stimulating and astute paper at many points, especially with her stance that "Christian faith and Christian commitment bases itself not first and foremost on a hope of survival of death, but on the intrinsic value of a relationship with God." (p. 43) Nonetheless, I believe she does not sufficiently appreciate the nature and desirability of life after death as it is envisioned in classical Christianity.

The value of life after death

Jantzen correctly points out that bare survival of death may not be at all desirable, but could be horrifying. Moreover, few would argue with her that certain forms of the afterlife may also be undesirable owing to their boring or tedious character. Jantzen underscores some of the drawbacks of dining with neanderthals (p. 34) and the rich but limited value to endless feasting.

> A paradise of sensuous delights would become boring, it would in the long run be pointless and utterly unfulfilling. We can perhaps imagine ways of making a very long feast meaningful; we do, after all, cope with lengthy terrestrial social occasions by choosing interesting conversational partners, and making the dinner occasions not merely for food and drink but also for stimulating discussion and for giving and receiving friendship the value of which extends beyond the termination of the dinner. But if the feasting literally never came to an end, if there were no progress possible from the sensuous enjoyment of paradise to anything more meaningful, then we might well wish, like Elina Macropolis, to terminate the whole business and destroy the elixir of youth. (p. 34, 35)

Even an eternal life of intellectually stimulating projects would become wearisome. She paints the outcome of pursuing everlasting projects in terms which may please the procrastinator.

> If we could go on pursuing an endless series of projects, it might not matter very much which ones we chose first: we could always do others later. Nor would it matter how vigorously we pursued them—for there would always

be more time—nor how challenging they were or how well they developed us and brought out the best in us—for there would always be other opportunities. But if fulfillment is something which must be reached in this life if it is to be reached at all, we will be far less cavalier about the choices we make affecting our own fulfillment, and also, very importantly, in our relationships with others for whose fulfillment we are partly responsible. (p. 36)

If there is no life after death, the projects of this life as well as the feasts, friendships, and sensuous delights assume a great importance and value. If there is an afterlife we face the problem of being cavalier with this one.

In assessing Jantzen's position let us distinguish two general sorts of goods, what we may call time-enclosed goods and non-time-enclosed goods. A time-enclosed good is any good project, thing, event, state or process which is good but its good value is not preserved if it is temporally unlimited in extent. Thus, your eating a tasty meal is good, but a time-enclosed good, for surely your meal would lose its good value if it were to continue uninterrupted for a year or a thousand years or be everlasting in temporal extent. It is not necessarily bad or evil for a time-enclosed good to cease to be. A non-time-enclosed good is any good project, event, state or process which is good and its good value is not lost if it is temporally unlimited in extent.

If everlasting life after death for you and me is something good and, thus, something to be desired, this continued life must be imagined to consist in more than pursual of a singular time-enclosed good. Perhaps there could be one exception to this which I mention only to set to one side. Imagine you endlessly pursue some singular time-enclosed good, but owing, say, to a continuous lapse of memory you fail to realize your ongoing activity. The meal before you is the same you have had for several millennia but not being aware of your endless dining, the meal surprises you and seems as fresh and unusual as ever. This strategy could also be deployed against the problem of being cavalier noted above. Perhaps we would only treat some projects in a cavalier fashion if we *knew* there would be endless opportunity to pursue them. The problem could be avoided if we posit a world in which there are endless opportunities for us to act upon but we do not realize it. Imagine we will live forever but we think our lives could end at any point. Such a defense of the afterlife is too desperate. The resulting portrait of God's hampering our memory and forever keeping secret our immortality so that we may not be bored with life after death seems pitiful at best. Let us also put to one side what may be called biological skepticism. A critic may allow that there could, in principle, be a non-time-enclosed good for you and me, but owing to our biological makeup, our need for sleep and so on, it is not possible for us to partake in. If the God who preserves us in existence after death is omnipotent, presumably none of these biological obstacles need keep us from partaking in the good. I know of no reason why you and I might not enjoy a life after death in a profoundly different embodiment.[3]

In my view Jantzen fails to give sufficient attention to the possibility of there being some singular non-time-enclosed good. In this life we may not be able to appreciably grasp the character of this great good, but then it might be odd if we could conceptually grasp it now. Orthodox and Catholic theology has identified this non-time-bound good as the beatific vision in which our beatitude is achieved in an experience of God's glory. It would be useful to explore the historical development of this understanding of final grace from philosophical and religious sources (scriptural references Mt. 5:8 and I Jn 3:2 have figured prominently in its early theological development). However, as even the proponents of this understanding of 'last things' insist on our present inability to imaginatively grasp this great good, appeal to a beatific vision will carry little weight with the skeptic, and I shall therefore pursue an alternative stance in what follows.

I do not think Jantzen gives sufficient weight to the possibility of an afterlife with a great, perhaps indefinite variety or alteration of time-enclosed goods. Many ethicists have recognized the good of variety, *bonum variationis*.[4] We may well imagine an afterlife replete with an ever altering mixture of goods including the sensuous, aesthetic, moral, intellectual, and religious. Such a portrait of the afterlife makes no appeal to experiences altogether dissimilar to those we are capable of having now, albeit in a piecemeal sometimes marred form. I believe that being a person is itself a non-time-enclosed good precisely because it is possible for a person to engage in a rich, perhaps endless variety of time-enclosed goods. In other words, it is good and desirable for you to forever partake of goods in an ever altering pattern despite the fact that only partaking of a single one of these goods without interruption would become undesirable. Some time-enclosed goods may involve enterprises which lose their value after being performed only once. But it is difficult to believe all our time-enclosed goods have this character. Of course, there may come a point when an individual person, Miriam, loses the desire to live and whose life becomes so engulfed in pain that we think her death would be merciful. But if we are to make any sense out of the sorrow we feel over her death, surely we must see her death as the ending of something valuable. I submit that Miriam's good or value cannot be exhausted or fulfilled in any absolute final sense in this life. She is dying and death under current physical conditions may be the least worst alternative, but surely (if we love her) her continued life under healthier, perhaps we should say glorious, conditions is what we should prefer, if such an alternative were available. I argue later that if we have reason to believe God loves her fully and deeply, we have reason to believe God will preserve the life of Miriam who as a person possesses a good or value which is not exhausted over time.

Jantzen makes no suggestion that God is bored with either Godself or the world. If Jantzen is correct in her view of the limited goods of an endless life, why should not God desire 'to terminate the whole business'? Perhaps God has no desire to do so because God is a non-time-enclosed good or because of the endless created order of ever-changing time-enclosed goods God delights in. If God has reason not to be bored or weary of a deathless life, why could not you and I find everlasting life of value in virtue of even a minute participation in the goods that God delights in?[5]

If there are goods worthy of pursuit and interest the problem of procrastination and being cavalier about one's projects seems to be a case of the problem of evil.

The problem of evil and immortality

Jantzen holds that the existence of an afterlife does not substantially alter the problem of evil facing the theist. She puts her point succinctly:

> One might argue that only if it (the afterlife) is, is God just: the sufferings of this present world can only be justified by the compensation of eternal life.

> But this, in the first place, is shocking theodicy: it is like saying that I may
> beat my dog at will provided that I later give him a dish of his favourite liver
> chowder. What happens after death—no matter how welcome—does not
> make present evil good. (p. 40)

I agree that what occurs after death does not make what evil that occurs in this life
good. But there are two important points that are overlooked.

First, whether or not there is an afterlife and what its character consists in has a bearing upon the extent of evil that exists in this life. Erik murdered Miriam out of deep
malice. Imagine there is no afterlife. He is responsible for annihilating a person. Miriam
has ceased to exist due to Erik's hateful act. Imagine there is an afterlife. Erik is still profoundly guilty for endeavoring to annihilate Miriam. Miriam has lost a great good, her
present life and relations; perhaps the murder itself involved profound suffering. But
Erik did not extinguish her life altogether. Belief in an afterlife need in no way reduce
our moral convictions about the moral outrage and obscenity of murder. Still, if there
is no afterlife, I judge the murder to have resulted in a far greater evil (Miriam's perishing altogether) than if there is an afterlife (Miriam still exists and some companionship
and exchange with her is possible after death). I believe this to be the case with respect
to the world's great evils as well. Consider the holocaust under two conditions: one in
which millions were annihilated in an absolute sense, the other one in which the millions died but are not annihilated. Under either condition, Nazism remains a moral
outrage and horror, but the evil perpetrated by the Nazis is worse if their victims ceased
to be altogether and God allowed the millions who suffered to perish everlastingly.

Second, there are respects in which an evil may give rise to some good. Thus, many
ethicists have argued that sorrowing over some past evil one has committed constitutes
a good. It would be better if the evil Erik performed had never occurred. Given that it
has occurred, his taking pleasure in his deed tends to enhance or aggravate the evil. In
a converse fashion, there is a respect in which a sorrowful regret for a past act can be
good.[6] You have grown to have a right relation to values, values you yourself imperiled.
Giving a dog a nice meal after beating him does not make your having beaten him good.
But just as the act could give rise to an additional evil (your later relishing the act and
pleasure in the memory) it could also give rise to a good (perhaps you will embrace your
dog with Franciscan tenderness). And if there is some afterlife for Erik and Miriam,
perhaps too there is the opportunity for forgiveness and an altered profoundly good relationship. A world in which there is no such afterlife is one in which this greater good is
unrealizable after death. Does it not seem that a loving Creator would want to provide
occasion for this greater good?

What about the problem of the procrastinator who is given an opportunity to pursue
the great goods of an afterlife and elects to reject them? Arguably, the mere fact that
someone is confronted with something of great value and he is apprised of its goodness
does not entail that he will love it. Grace Jantzen herself raises doubts about the depiction of an afterlife in works by John Hick in which all creatures come to embrace the
love of God. On her view, Mr. Hick's portrait of the afterlife involves an inadequate
appreciation of the value of free will.

> Part of what it means to be free is that our choices have consequences. It is
> playing too lightly with the responsibility of freedom to suggest that these

consequences, at least in their effects upon ourselves, are always reversible, even if only in the endless life to come. (p. 40)

While I hope that the lives of all created persons here are followed by renewed opportunities for turning to God and overturning some of the evils we perpetrate in this life (through sorrowing over past evils and achieving some reconciliation with those we harm and have harmed us), I share Jantzen's insistence upon the value of freedom. I therefore believe that the afterlife will not be forced on persons who continuously and relentlessly freely elect to perish everlastingly. But voluntary choices like this are only fully voluntary when made under certain conditions. Ignorance and connative impairment tend to vitiate freedom. For the choice of extinction to be fully voluntary I think it needs to be made under conditions different from the ones that now prevail, conditions which can profoundly distort our exercise of free will. If someone elects to voluntarily perish then I think the person voluntarily wills an evil end, the destruction of a person. But if possession of freedom is good and it is good that persons have this power to elect a Godward life or Godless death, then this perishing must be seen as a real possibility. The good of an afterlife and the good of this life is in no way lessened by supposing that a person may lose her life absolutely only under condition of fully voluntarily choosing to do so.[7]

The love of God

I believe one of the most weighty motives for thinking there is an afterlife rests in the conviction that God is loving.[8] Jantzen questions whether the appeal to Divine love provides a foundation for belief in an individual's survival of death.

> Christian theology does hold that there are other things which are precious to God and which, in spite of that, perish forever. Christian theologians increasingly recognize that it is not the case that the whole earth, every primrose, every songbird, all the galaxies of all the heavens, exist for the benefit of humanity alone. Yet it is true that God brought about the existence of all these things and delights in them; then it is also true that some of the things he delights in perish forever. (p. 41, 42)

She goes on to point out that the limited, temporally finite character of many of our valued relationships is not to be valued less for their limitation.

> Just as that which is morally valuable is valuable for its own sake and not for the reward it can bring, so also trust in God, if it is worthwhile at all, is worthwhile even if it cannot go on forever. A relationship with another human being does not become pointless just because at some point it will end with the death of one of the partners; why should it be thought that a relationship with God would be pointless if one day it too should end. (p. 42, 43)

I do not think this is altogether wrong. The commonplace dictum 'A friendship that ends is no friendship' may not hold in all cases.

My reservations about Jantzen's stance here rest upon her neglecting an important correlation between love and preferring the existence of the beloved to her nonexistence. There may be different forms of love; some theologians distinguish love in terms of *philia, eros, amor, agape* and *caritas*. Whatever its form, I believe there is what may be termed a vivifying feature of love. Consider Thomas Carson's characterization of love in *The Status of Morality*.

> Whether someone loves or hates something on the whole is ultimately a function of how he is disposed to act. A person who loves something will choose or prefer its existence or occurrence to its non-existence or non-occurrence, all other things being equal, a person who hates something will choose or prefer its non-existence or non-occurrence to its existence or occurrence, all other things being equal.[9]

In his lively masterpiece *On Love* Ortega y Gasset expresses an analogous position in more poetic terms.

> Love itself is, by nature, a transitive act in which we exert ourselves on behalf of what we love. Although we are quiescent, when we are a hundred leagues from the object and not even thinking about it, if we love the object an indefinable flow of a warm and affirmative nature will emanate from us. This is clearly observable if we compare love with hate. To hate something or someone is not "being" passive, like being sad, but, in some way, it is a terribly negative action, ideally destructive of the hated object.[10]

While hatred aims at crippling the one hated and is often expressed in a pleasure in an enemy's misfortune, love delights in the fulfillment of the beloved and is expressed in a desire that the beloved find such fulfillment.

The Ortega-Carson account seems to me to be fundamentally correct, though I do not think their characterization of love succeeds as an *analysis* of what it is to love and hate. It is instead plausible to think that loving and the requisite preferring are two distinct acts or undergoings rather than a single state or thing. If the Ortega-Carson account were an analysis, love would be understood as not simply leading to the requisite preferences; love would be the preference designated. But as an analysis this faces the problem of accounting for the fact that I may prefer your existence to non-existence *because* I love you. My loving you may be the reason for my preference and thus my loving you does not consist solely in the preference itself. (Consider an analogy, Eric's being an unmarried male is not what explains his being a bachelor. Being a bachelor simply is being an unmarried male. Loving you and preferring your existence seem different from this case, however, as the former can be employed to explain the latter.)

While Ortega's and Carson's depiction of love does not count as an analysis of what love is in itself, they are on the right track in their insistence upon the correlation of love and preference. Cases that appear to belie their thesis can be accounted for by specifying the many respects in which we love and hate others. Erik may claim to hate his parents and yet prefer their existence to their non-existence. But what precisely does Erik hate about his parents? He may hate their smugness, pretension, and abusiveness. According to our understanding of love and hatred, Erik's hatred of his parents' faults involves his preferring the non-existence of these faults rather than their existence. This is consistent with his preferring, all things considered, that his parents exist rather than not exist.[11]

Fundamental to Christianity is the belief that the cosmos is the result of God's creative loving activity. Insofar as God loves something God prefers its existence to its non-existence. Insofar as God loves you and me, and loves us absolutely, God prefers our existence to non-existence and we may have confidence that God will uphold us in existence to the degree that we are confident that God loves us.

Let us return to Jantzen's objections to this form of argument. Is it not true that God loves many things including many animals who pass out of existence? I am not sure how many things pass out of existence, nor am I sure whether (or how many) nonhuman animals enjoy some afterlife. However, I suggest that our theological reflection in this area be guided by our consideration of what constitutes the fulfillment or good of the thing loved. Earlier I contended that persons are themselves non-time-enclosed goods. That is, the complete fulfillment of a person is not exhausted by the fulfillment of some singular time-enclosed personal good activity (feasting). There is a transcendental character to persons such that our good or value is greater than the good or value of such undertakings. As such, to love a person deeply and profoundly is to prefer her rich and endless fulfillment rather than her non-existence or her existence under dire, unfulfilled conditions. Consider Jantzen's case of a friendship between persons which is valuable despite the fact that it "cannot go on forever". Her stance seems plausible when the friends are both human and it is not within the power of either friend to preserve the other from annihilation. But I would seriously doubt the "love" of a partner who had it within her power to sustain me in existence, an existence in which I can flourish and yet she either actively brought about my extinction or passively allowed me to perish irretrievably.

Perhaps God loves many things which do perish. My own conviction is that insofar as any creature has the kind of non-time-enclosed good which characterizes being a person, God will preserve it in being. If the case for treating dolphins and chimpanzees as persons is plausible, the case for their having an afterlife is plausible.

I defend this view further in the course of considering three objections:

1 Belief in an afterlife for persons introduces an undesirable dichotomy between persons and nonpersons, humans and nature. Even if we believe that not all nonhuman animals will perish, our attitude to much of the "lower" animals is bound to be cavalier.

I do not think this follows at all. To love a person must be distinguishable from loving a non-person because persons have features non-persons do not. But the natural world of songbirds, plants, rocks and planets may still be loved and cherished as real, *bona fide* goods. That there is a natural world is good and we must be careful to respect our kinship to fellow creatures who do not possess the transcendental powers of personhood.[12] I do not think my doubting that there is an afterlife for elephants compromises my concern for their preservation nor my convictions about the evils over our present cruel treatment of those and other nonhuman animals. As some proponents of animal rights have argued, the fact (if it is a fact) that nonhuman animals will not enjoy an afterlife may constitute an important case for vegetarianism and legal sanctions against killing nonhuman animals on the grounds that we should ensure that their lives are no shorter than they would be naturally.[13]

2 Belief in an afterlife is belief in something logically or metaphysically impossible. Created persons simply cannot survive death.

If this objection holds then to desire to survive death is to desire something unrealizable. Insofar as love is rational and it is irrational to desire or prefer something impossible, then the argument from Divine love falters indeed. But it is by no means obvious that an afterlife for humans is impossible. I have argued for its conceivability elsewhere and note that many philosophers who do not think we will survive death concede that such survival is at least possible.[14]

3 Isn't there something pretentious or presumptuous for us to believe in an afterlife? Such belief seems to be more of an expression of vain self-regard than disinterested love.

A true belief can be held for morally suspect reasons and undoubtedly some persons believe in an afterlife out of some colossal self-inflation. But surely it need not be vain or pompous of me to desire and hope for your survival of death out of my love for you. If our critic finds this impossible, I suspect he would "discover" egotism and pretentiousness behind all acts of love and compassion whatever.

I believe Jantzen has ably brought to light the fact that Christians should not think "life after death is a matter of course" and "guaranteed", though our reasons for thinking this diverge somewhat. I think we should not do so because God's love of us and the created order has the character of a gracious, free gift and is not itself a matter of course. That God should have lovingly created us to begin with was not guaranteed. Thus, I do not think persons as such have a moral right to an afterlife. But I do think that if we have reason to believe God loves us deeply, we have reason to expect an afterlife and even to feel that our perishing absolutely would be a violation (to use Simone de Beauvoir's strong language). It would be a violation because it would violate a fundamental feature of love.[15]

In the course of my arguments I have not shown Jantzen to be incorrect that "*a* rich Christian faith does not require a doctrine of life after death in order to be profound and meaningful." (p. 33, emphasis mine) There can be a variety of forms of Christianity and various levels of profundity and meaning. But I do hope to have drawn fuller attention to the motives behind why classical Christianity has found belief in the afterlife to have its peculiar centrality, meaning and profundity.

Notes

1 Simone de Beauvoir, *A Very Easy Death*, translated by Patrick O'Brien, N.Y.: G. P. Putnam's Sons, 1966, p. 106.
2 Grace M. Jantzen, "Do We Need Immortality?", *Modern Theology*, volume 1, number 1, October 1984. All references to Jantzen's paper are noted in the text.
3 I have defended the coherence of Divine omnipotence in "The Magnitude of Omnipotence", *International Journal for Philosophy of Religion*, 1983, vol. 14, pp. 99–106, and discussed ways in which God might enhance our powers in "Nagel's Vista or Taking Subjectivity Seriously", *The Southern Journal of Philosophy*, 1988, Vol. XXVI, No. 3, p. 395, 396. See references in footnote 13 below.
4 The good of variety itself is underscored by various ethicists, including F. Brentano, G. E. Moore, and George Kratkov. See R. M. Chisholm's *Brentano and Intrinsic Value* (Cambridge:

Cambridge University Press, 1986) for a defense of the *bonum variationis* as a distinctive category of values.

5   Thomas Morris makes a related point in his criticism of the process theological treatment of life after death, "God and the World", *Process Theology*, edited by Ronald Nash (Grand Rapids: Baker Book House, 1987).

6   See Chisholm, cited above. This has also been argued vigorously by Robert Nozick in *Philosophical Explanations* (Cambridge: Harvard University Press, 1981).

7   I address this issue in "Does God Violate Your Right to Privacy?", *Theology*, forthcoming.

8   Traditional Christian apologetics has emphasized the evidence of the historical resurrection of Jesus Christ as a principal reason for believing in life after death. In this paper I lay stress on an argument from the love of God as the early Christian portrayal of Christ's resurrection is itself supposed to be evidence of God's special loving activity.

9   Thomas Carson, *The Status of Morality* (Boston: Reidel, 1984), p. 3.

10   Ortega y Gasset, *On Love* (New York: Meridian, 1957), p. 47.

11   For an illuminating account of love and attendant notions of preferring the existence to the non-existence of the beloved, see "On Regretting the Evils of this World" by William Hasker, *Southern Journal of Philosophy*, Volume XIX, number 4, pp. 425–437.

12   The existence of a rock may be good, even a non-time-enclosed good and worthy of our taking pleasure in. But the language of love in which we desire not just the existence but the fulfillment of the beloved makes little sense when used of a rock. There is a large difference between being a fulfilled person and an unfulfilled person, but I have no idea of what it would mean for there to be an unfulfilled rock. I follow Joel Feinberg's view of rocks, plants and nonhuman animals in "The Rights of Animals and Unborn Generations", *Rights, Justice and the Bounds of Liberty* (Princeton: Princeton University Press, 1980).

13   See Tom Regan's *The Case for Animal Rights* (Berkeley: University of California Press, 1983).

14   See "Pollock's Body Switching," *The Philosophical Quarterly*, vol. 36, no. 4, October, 1985, pp. 57–61; "Dualism and the Problem of Individuation". *Religious Studies*, 22, 1986, pp. 263–276; "A Modal Argument for Dualism", *Southern Journal of Philosophy*, Vol. XXIV, no. 1, Spring 1986, pp. 95–108. In the last article I critically assess works by John Pollock, D. M. Armstrong, Richard Boyd, and David Lewis, all of whom think a kind of bodiless, post-mortem personal life is possible but will not occur. My own work has aimed at establishing the coherence of an afterlife on the basis of a plausible dualist understanding of persons. Jantzen's own philosophical anthropology and theistic world view is non-dualist in character. See her fascinating *God's World, God's Body* (Philadelphia: The Westminster Press, 1984) and our debate about Divine incorporeality in *Modern Theology*, Volume 3, no. 2, January 1987. Even if a dualist understanding of created persons is rejected, I believe that a plausible alternative physicalist account of individual afterlife can be constructed. See Bruce Reichenbach's *Is Man the Phoenix? A Study of Immortality* (Grand Rapids: Wm. B. Eerdmans, 1978).

15   It would be obviously fallacious to argue that there is an afterlife simply on the grounds that we would find it desirable. A more sophisticated argument from desire can be developed and I refer the reader to Robert Holyer's "The Argument from Desire", *Faith and Philosophy*, Volume 5, no. 1, January 1988, pp. 61–71.

Questions for reflection

1   What are some of Professor Jantzen's reasons for maintaining that survival after death cannot be inferred from the fact that God is loving?

2   How is it that, on Professor Taliaferro's view, a time-enclosed good in eternity could
     actually be *good*?
3   Explain Taliaferro's response to Jantzen's claim that the existence of an afterlife
     does not alter the problem of evil which confronts theists. Do you agree with him?
     Why or why not?
4   If God does love things which perish (a sparrow, say, or my friend's cat, Jack), why
     could it not be that God deeply loves us even if we perish? How does Taliaferro
     respond to this question? What is your own view, and why?

Further reading

Kevin Corcoran, ed. (2001) *Soul, Body and Survival*. Ithaca, NY: Cornell University Press. (Includes
     constructive contributions on the possibility of an afterlife.)
Grace M. Jantzen (1984) "Do We Need Immortality?," *Modern Theology* 1 (1): 33–44. (The essay
     to which Taliaferro responds in this selection.)
D. Z. Phillips (2004) *The Problem of Evil and The Problem of God*. Minneapolis, MN: Fortress
     Press. (Argues for the sufficiency of this life in terms of human potential.)
Charles Taliaferro (1994/2005) *Consciousness and the Mind of God*. Cambridge: Cambridge Univer-
     sity Press. (Develops a concept of persons which allows for an afterlife.)
Charles Taliaferro (2006) *Love, Love, Love, and Other Essays*. Cambridge: Cowley Publications.
     (Develops the thesis that the sufficiency of this life in terms of human potential leads to a tragic
     view of the human condition.)
Evelyn Underhill ([1910] 2001) *Mysticism*. Oxford: Oneworld. (A classic which underscores the
     transcendent, non-time-enclosed goodness of persons and experience; also documents the
     abundant testimony in Jewish, Christian, and Islamic literature about the never-ending good-
     ness of the redeemed in union with the divine.)

Chapter 59

Sri Aurobindo

REBIRTH AND THE SELF

Sri Aurobindo (1872–1950) was an Indian nationalist, poet, philosopher, guru, and prolific author. In this selection, he first responds to common and crude notions of rebirth and reincarnation. He then notes that for both Buddhists and Vedantins (i.e., a stream of Hinduism), rebirth is not a survival of personality, for personality is a constantly changing composite. As such, survival of an identical personality after death is a contradiction in terms. "To view ourselves as such and such a personality getting into a new case of flesh is to stumble about in the ignorance, to confirm the error of the material mind and the senses." Unlike the Buddhists, however, who deny a real self, the Vedantists grant an unchanging and imperishable self. Aurobindo differentiates between this true Self (Purusha) and the changing self of personality which is rooted in Prakriti (the basic matter of which the universe is made). While the changing self of personality—a complex composite of material and mental stuffs and experiences—reincarnates, the true Self does not; rather, it is unborn, undying, and that in which all bodies exist.

The following poem, written by Aurobindo, captures the essence of his message on the eternal Self as one evolves from ignorance to understanding:

> Only the illimitable Permanent
> Is here. A Peace stupendous, featureless, still.
> Replaces all,—what once was I, in It
> A silent unnamed emptiness content
> Either to fade in the Unknowable
> Or thrill with the luminous seas of the Infinite.

(Last verse of his *Nirvana*)

Human thought in the generality of men is no more than a rough and crude acceptance of unexamined ideas. Our mind is a sleepy or careless sentry and allows anything to pass the gates which seems to it decently garbed or wears a plausible appearance or can mumble anything that resembles some familiar password. Especially is this so in subtle matters, those remote from the concrete facts of our physical life and environment. Even men who will reason carefully and acutely in ordinary matters and there consider vigilance against error an intellectual or a practical duty, are yet content with the most careless stumbling when they get upon higher and more difficult ground. Where precision and subtle thinking are most needed, there they are most impatient of it and averse to the labour demanded of them. Men can manage fine thought about palpable things, but to think subtly about the subtle is too great a strain on the grossness of our intellects; so we are content with making a dab at the truth, like the painter who threw his brush at his picture when he could not get the effect that he desired.

We mistake the smudge that results for the perfect form of a verity.

It is not surprising then that men should be content to think crudely about such a matter as rebirth. Those who accept it, take it usually ready-made, either as a cut-and-dried theory or a crude dogma. The soul is reborn in a new body,—that vague and almost meaningless assertion is for them sufficient. But what is the soul and what can possibly be meant by the rebirth of a soul? Well, it means reincarnation; the soul, whatever that may be, had got out of one case of flesh and is now getting into another case of flesh. It sounds simple,—let us say, like the Djinn of the Arabian tale expanding out of and again compressing himself into his bottle or perhaps as a pillow is lugged out of one pillow-case and thrust into another. Or the soul fashions for itself a body in the mother's womb and then occupies it, or else, let us say, puts off one robe of flesh and then puts on another.

But what is it that thus "leaves" one body and "enters" into another? Is it another, a psychic body and subtle form, that enters into the gross corporeal form,—the Purusha perhaps of the ancient image, no bigger than a man's thumb, or is it something in itself formless and impalpable that incarnates in the sense of becoming or assuming to the senses a palpable shape of bone and flesh? In the ordinary, the vulgar conception there is no birth of a soul at all, but only the birth of a new body into the world occupied by an old personality unchanged from that which once left some now discarded physical frame. It is John Robinson who has gone out of the form of flesh he once occupied; it is John Robinson who tomorrow or some centuries hence will re-incarnate in another form of flesh and resume the course of his terrestrial experiences with another name and in another environment. Achilles, let us say, is reborn as Alexander, the son of Philip, a Macedonian, conqueror not of Hector but of Darius, with a wider scope, with larger destinies; but it is still Achilles, it is the same personality that is reborn, only the bodily circumstances are different. It is this survival of the identical personality that attracts the European mind today in the theory of reincarnation. For it is the extinction or dissolution of the personality, of this mental, nervous and physical composite which I call myself that is hard to bear for the man enamoured of life, and it is the promise of its survival and physical reappearance that is the great lure. The one objection that really stands in the way of its acceptance is the obvious non-survival of memory. Memory is the man, says the modern psychologist, and what is the use of the survival of my personality, if I do not remember my past, if I am not aware of being the same person still and always? What is the utility? Where is the enjoyment? The old Indian thinkers,—I am not speaking of the popular belief which was crude enough and thought not at all about the matter,—the old Buddhistic and Vedantist thinkers surveyed the whole field from a very different standpoint.

They were not attached to the survival of the personality; they did not give to that survival the high name of immortality; they saw that personality being what it is, a constantly changing composite, the survival of an identical personality was a non-sense, a contradiction in terms. They perceived indeed that there is a continuity and they sought to discover what determines this continuity and whether the sense of identity which enters into it is an illusion or the representation of a fact, of a real truth, and, if the latter, then what that truth may be. The Buddhist denied any real identity. There is, he said, no self, no person; there is simply a continuous stream of energy in action like the continuous flowing of a river or the continuous burning of a flame. It is this continuity which creates in the mind the false sense of identity. I am not now the same person that I was a year ago, not even the same person that I was a moment ago, any more than the water flowing past yonder ghaut is the same water that flowed past it a few seconds ago; it is the persistence of the flow in the same channel that preserves the false appearance of identity. Obviously, then, there is no soul that reincarnates, but only Karma that persists in flowing continuously down an apparently uninterrupted channel. It is Karma that incarnates; Karma creates the form of a constantly changing mentality and physical bodies that are, we may presume, the result of that changing composite of ideas and sensations which I call myself. The identical "I" is not, never was, never will be. Practically, so long as the error of personality persists, this does not make much difference and I can say in the language of ignorance that I am reborn in a new body; practically, I have to proceed on the basis of that error. But there is this important point gained that it is all an error and an error which can cease; the composite can be broken up for good without any fresh formation, the flame can be extinguished, the channel which called itself a river destroyed. And then there is non-being, there is cessation, there is the release of the error from itself.

The Vedantist comes to a different conclusion; he admits an identical, a self, a persistent immutable reality,—but other than my personality, other than this composite which I call myself. In the Katha Upanishad the question is raised in a very instructive fashion quite apposite to the subject we have in hand. Nachiketas, sent by his father to the world of Death, thus questions Yama, the lord of that world: Of the man who has gone forward, who has passed away from us, some say that he is and others "this he is not"; which then is right? what is the truth of the great passage? Such is the form of the question and at first sight it seems simply to raise the problem of immortality in the European sense of the word, the survival of the identical personality. But that is not what Nachiketas asks. He has already taken as the second of three boons offered to him by Yama the knowledge of the sacred Flame by which man crosses over hunger and thirst, leaves sorrow and fear far behind him and dwells in heaven securely rejoicing.

Immortality in that sense he takes for granted as, already standing in that farther world, he must surely do. The knowledge he asks for involves the deeper, finer problem, of which Yama affirms that even the gods debated this of old and it is not easy to know, for subtle is the law of it; something survives that appears to be the same person, that descends into hell, that ascends into heaven, that returns upon the earth with a new body, but is it really the same person that thus survives? Can we really say of the man "He still is," or must we not rather say "This he no longer is"? Yama too in his answer speaks not at all of the survival of death, and he only gives a verse or two to a bare description of that constant rebirth which all serious thinkers admitted as a universally acknowledged truth.

What he speaks of is the Self, the real Man, the Lord of all these changing appearances; without the knowledge of that Self the survival of the personality is not immortal life but a constant passing from death to death; he only who goes beyond personality to the real Person becomes the Immortal. Till then a man seems indeed to be born again and again by the force of his knowledge and works, name succeeds to name, form gives place to form, but there is no immortality.

Such then is the real question put and answered so divergently by the Buddhist and the Vedantin. There is a constant reforming of personality in new bodies, but this personality is a mutable creation of force at its work streaming forward in Time and never for a moment the same, and the ego-sense that makes us cling to the life of the body and believe readily that it is the same idea and form, that it is John Robinson who is reborn as Sidi Hossain, is a creation of the mentality. Achilles was not reborn as Alexander, but the stream of force in its works which created the momentarily changing mind and body of Achilles flowed on and created the momentarily changing mind and body of Alexander. Still, said the ancient Vedanta, there is yet something beyond this force in action, Master of it, one who makes it create for him new names and forms, and that is the Self, the Purusha, the Man, the Real Person. The ego-sense is only its distorted image reflected in the flowing stream of embodied mentality.

Is it then the Self that incarnates and reincarnates? But the Self is imperishable, immutable, unborn, undying. The Self is not born and does not exist in the body; rather the body is born and exists in the Self. For the Self is one everywhere,—in all bodies, we say, but really it is not confined and parcelled out in different bodies except as the all-constituting ether seems to be formed into different objects and is in a sense in them. Rather all these bodies are in the Self; but that also is a figment of space-conception, and rather these bodies are only symbols and figures of itself created by it in its own consciousness. Even what we call the individual soul is greater than its body and not less, more subtle than it and therefore not confined by its grossness. At death it does not leave its form, but casts it off, so that a great departing Soul can say of this death in vigorous phrase, "I have spat out the body." What then is it that we feel to inhabit the physical frame? What is it that the Soul draws out from the body when it casts off this partial physical robe which enveloped not it, but part of its members? What is it whose issuing out gives this wrench, this swift struggle and pain of parting, creates this sense of violent divorce? The answer does not help us much. It is the subtle or psychical frame which is tied to the physical by the heart-strings, by the cords of life-force, of nervous energy which have been woven into every physical fibre. This the Lord of the body draws out and the violent snapping or the rapid or tardy loosening of the life-cords, the exit of the connecting force constitutes the pain of death and its difficulty.

Let us then change the form of the question and ask rather what it is that reflects and accepts the mutable personality, since the Self is immutable? We have in fact an immutable Self, a real Person, lord of this ever-changing personality which, again, assumes ever-changing bodies, but the real Self knows itself always as above the mutation, watches and enjoys it, but is not involved in it.

Through what does it enjoy the changes and feel them to be its own, even while knowing itself to be unaffected by them? The mind and ego-sense are only inferior instruments; there must be some more essential form of itself which the Real Man puts forth, puts in front of itself, as it were, and at the back of the changings to support and mirror them without being actually changed by them. This more essential form is or seems to be in man the mental being or mental person which the Upanishads speak of as the mental leader of the life and body, *manomayah prana-sharira-neta*. It is that which maintains the ego-sense as a function in the mind and enables us to have the firm conception of continuous identity in Time as opposed to the timeless identity of the Self.

The changing personality is not this mental person; it is a composite of various stuff of Nature, a formation of Prakriti and is not at all the Purusha. And it is a very complex composite with many layers; there is a layer of physical, a layer of nervous, a layer of mental, even a final stratum of supramental personality; and within these layers themselves there are strata within each stratum. The analysis of the successive couches of the earth is a simple matter compared with the analysis of this wonderful creation we call the personality. The mental being in resuming bodily life forms a new personality for its new terrestrial existence; it takes material from the common matter-stuff, life-stuff, mind-stuff of the physical world and during earthly life it is constantly absorbing fresh material, throwing out what is used up, changing its bodily, nervous and mental tissues. But this is all surface work; behind is the foundation of past experience held back from the physical memory so that the superficial consciousness may not be troubled or interfered with by the conscious burden of the past but may concentrate on the work immediately in hand. Still that foundation of past experience is the bedrock of personality; and it is more than that. It is our real fund on which we can always draw even apart from our present superficial commerce with our surroundings. That commerce adds to our gains, modifies the foundation for a subsequent existence.

Moreover, all this is, again, on the surface. It is only a small part of ourselves which lives and acts in the energies of our earthly existence. As behind the physical universe there are worlds of which ours is only a last result, so also within us there are worlds of our self-existence which throw out this external form of our being. The subconscient, the superconscient are oceans from which and to which this river flows. Therefore to speak of ourselves as a soul reincarnating is to give altogether too simple an appearance to the miracle of our existence; it puts into too ready and too gross a formula the magic of the supreme Magician. There is not a definite psychic entity getting into a new case of flesh; there is a metempsychosis, a reinsouling, a rebirth of new psychic personality as well as a birth of a new body. And behind is the Person, the unchanging entity, the Master who manipulates this complex material, the Artificer of this wondrous artifice.

This is the starting-point from which we have to proceed in considering the problem of rebirth. To view ourselves as such and such a personality getting into a new case of flesh is to stumble about in the ignorance, to confirm the error of the material mind and the senses. The body is a convenience, the personality is a constant formation for whose development action and experience are the instruments; but the Self by whose will and for whose delight all this is, is other than the body, other than the action and experience, other than the personality which they develop. To ignore it is to ignore the whole secret of our being.

Questions for reflection

1   Aurobindo makes the following claim: ". . . he only who goes beyond personality to the real Person becomes the Immortal." What does he mean?

2   What does Aurobindo make of the obvious difficulty that memory of previous lives does not continue on to the present life?

3   Who is the real Self behind the self? Describe differences between the Self and the self.

4   What are some reasons for belief in reincarnation? What are some reasons for disbelief?

Further reading

Sri Aurobindo Ashram. http://www.sriaurobindoashram.org/index.php (Website of the Ashram—an intentional community focused on spiritual encouragement and development.)

Sri Aurobindo (1991) *Rebirth and Karma*. Twin Lakes, WI: Lotus Press. (An in-depth study on rebirth and karma.)

Paul Edwards (2001) *Reincarnation: A Critical Examination*. Amherst, NY: Prometheus Books. (An unsympathetic, philosophical analysis of many aspects of reincarnation from a leading religious skeptic.)

Joseph Head and Sylvia Cranston, eds. (1968) *Reincarnation: An East–West Anthology*. Wheaton, IL: Theosophical Publishing House. (A helpful anthology which includes a variety of views on the subject.)

Wendy Doniger O'Flaherty, ed. (1985) *Karma and Rebirth in Classical Indian Traditions*. Berkeley, CA: University of California Press. (A collection of works on the meaning and implications of karma and rebirth; includes a helpful and extensive bibliography.)

Chapter 60

Robin Le Poidevin

SHOULD THE ATHEIST FEAR DEATH?

Robin Le Poidevin is Professor of Metaphysics at the University of Leeds. In this selection he examines some of the reasons one might fear death and whether such reasons are good. At first glance, it seems that the theist's view of death is one in which she can take hope and comfort, given her belief in an eternal, unchanging, omnibenevolent God, whereas for the atheist, the thought of death may lead to fear and consternation since all of life is transitory and short-lived. However, given a certain theory of time, the atheist need not fear all the features we represent death as having, for on this view death is not a passing into the void; rather, it is just a temporal aspect of our lives.

First, he notes that many of the puzzling questions raised by the thought of death are informed by a particular view of time. He then examines two very different views of time: (1) the A-theory in which time passes and consists of past, present, and future, and (2) the B-theory in which time does not pass; it is more akin to space. For the A-theorist—and the ordinary conception of time—time flows along like a river; for the B-theorist, time is like a frozen sea—there is no passage, for the notions of past, present, and future represent our own perspective of time, not the actual nature of time. On the B-theory, the existence of time is simply the way things stand in the relations of earlier than, simultaneous with, and later than, other things. On this view, then, the "future" is just as real as the "past" and "present." So, as an atheist, one can still have hope. For even though it appears that transience pervades all we value, if there is no real passage of time, nothing is transitory; everything—including the entire span of our lives—is eternally real.

If you were to destroy in mankind the belief in immortality, not only love but every living force maintaining the life of the world would at once be dried up.

Fyodor Dostoyevsky, *The Brothers Karamazov*

Riddles of mortality

We come, finally, to the topic of death. It is here that the contrast between theism and atheism seems at its sharpest. For when we contemplate death, theism can comfort us in both personal and impersonal terms. In personal terms, theism can offer us the hope of eternal life, a better existence beyond death. In impersonal terms, it offers an antidote to our dismay at the transience of all natural things. Everything that we see passes away, but God is eternal and unchanging. And, in so far as those things which are valuable, such as love and goodness, reside in him, these too are eternal. For the atheist, it seems, there is nothing but change and decay.

Not all theists, however, believe in life after death. And some nontheistic religions involve the idea of the immortality of the soul. So the contrast between theism and atheism need not always be quite as sharp as it was presented above. Nevertheless, theists often have a distinctive view of death and transience, a view from which they draw comfort and strength. What resources has the atheist at his disposal when he contemplates the end of all things? In this . . . chapter, we shall look at some of the reasons why death is dreaded, and consider whether these reasons are good ones.

Death is a temporal phenomenon, in that it is a kind of change, and so takes place in time. Further, many of the puzzles it raises involve aspects of time. Here are some of the most prominent questions:

1   Why do we care more about future non-existence after our death than about *past* non-existence before our birth?
2   Why are we appalled by the attenuation of the effects of our life after we die? Why, for example, do we fear being forgotten and our various projects crumbling to nothing?
3   Why are we repelled by the thought of endless stretches of future time in which the universe is, as the Second Law of Thermodynamics seems to predict, frozen and lifeless?
4   Why, if we are appalled by death, are some of us also (perhaps even more) appalled by its opposite: the infinite extension of our life? Is this not paradoxical, to want to be neither mortal nor immortal?

In what follows, we shall see how these puzzles are informed by a certain picture of time, and what happens when we shift to a different picture.

The river of time and the sea of ice

In some respects, time seems utterly unlike space, and their dissimilarity goes deeper than the mere fact that time has only one dimension whereas space has three. On the first theory of time we shall present, which I will call the *A-theory*, time consists intrinsically of a past, present and future. Space, in contrast, does *not* consist intrinsically of a 'here' and a 'there'. 'Here' is wherever I happen to be, but that need not be the same place as the place which is 'here' to you. Whatever 'here' denotes depends simply on the location of the speaker. We can put this by saying that the distinction between here and there is relative to a particular position in space. What is remarkable about the present moment, however, is that it seems to be the same for all of us. This is so, for the A-theorist, because when we distinguish between what is present and what is not present, the distinction corresponds to an objective division in time and is not relative to the position in time of the speaker. Even if there were no observers, there would still be a present moment, distinct from past and future moments. But there would be no unique place which was 'here', since the hereness of a place just reflects an observer's perspective. We may, of course, talk of the perspective of an inanimate object and say that its location is 'here' with respect to that object, but we must still admit that 'hereness' is not an intrinsic feature of any place.

There are two variants of the A-theory which take a stance on the reality of past and future. On the first of these, which we might call the *closed past, open future* view, the past is real, the future is not. What this metaphysical statement means is that there are *past* facts, whether or not those facts are in principle accessible to us, but no *future* facts. For example, there is a fact of the matter as to whether or not the last dinosaur (or dinosaurs) suffered from indigestion, whether or not there is any evidence one way or the other. There is, however, as yet no fact of the matter as to whether human beings will colonise Pluto. It may be that some statements we can make about the future are now true, but if they are, they are so only because there are some present facts which guarantee that the statements in question are true. For example, because the Sun can only produce a finite amount of energy before it is finally extinguished, it is inevitable that the Sun will not exist for an infinite amount of time. Conditions being as they are, things cannot turn out otherwise. So that is one truth about the future. But those statements whose truth (or falsity) is not guaranteed by the present state of things are neither true nor false. What will happen is, to a large extent, open.

A more extreme variant of the A-theory is the *open past, open future* view. On this view, neither the future *nor the past* is real: only the present is real. Suppose we ask a question like, 'Did Ethelred the Unready visit (the place we now call) Brighton?' If there is now no trace of such a visit, nor any evidence to show that he never visited Brighton, then it is, on this view, neither true nor false that Ethelred the Unready visited Brighton.

These are the two most familiar versions of the A-theory. It is true that the A-theorist may want to accept the reality of both the past and the future, but since one of the most influential sources of motivation for the A-theory is the belief that the future is not real, we can, I think, ignore this third variant. As for the other two, I suspect that our intuitions oscillate between them. It is quite hard to accept that many statements about the past are neither true nor false. We are much more likely to suppose that there is a fact of the matter with respect to every statement we could make about the past, and that the lack of evidence in certain cases demonstrates no more than our ignorance of those facts. On the other hand, we are drawn to the view that the present is a privileged position and are uncomfortable with the notion that the past is as real as the present. Augustine neatly caught this discomfort when he asked whether there was a 'secret place' to which the past went when it was over. His conclusion was that the past exists only in our memories.

The A-theory is an attempt to capture in precise terms our sense of the passage, or transience, of time. It is, for some, the truth behind the metaphorical picture of the river of time. In striking contrast to this view is the *B-theory*, which altogether denies that time passes and holds that time is much more like space than we generally suppose. For the B-theorist, the division between past, present and future is closely analogous to the division between the spatially local and the distant. A given time is present only with respect to some particular event or observation. Without observers, it would make no sense to talk of a present moment except in the entirely ordinary sense that every time is present with respect to itself, just as every place is local with respect to itself. Past, present and future therefore simply represent our perspective on time, not the intrinsic nature of time itself. What we call the past is simply that series of events which are earlier than the time at which we happen to be talking. The future is simply that series of events which are later than the time at which we are talking. There is no reason to pick out the earlier series of events as more real than the later series of events, any more than we have good reason to think of distant places as unreal, simply because we do not happen to be at them. Consequently, what we call the future is just as real as what we call the present.

If the A-theory can be represented in the picturesque metaphor of the river of time, a suitable metaphor for the B-theory would be the sea of ice, the ninth and last circle of hell as presented in Dante's *Inferno*. In this circle are those who have merited eternal punishment through betraying their benefactors, and all but their heads are submerged in the frozen sea. They provide an image of the world as presented by the B-theory if we think of them as the events which constitute the history of the world. Just as, on the B-theory, events do not move through time by first being future then becoming present and finally receding into the past, so the heads of the damned are fixed in the sea of ice.

This image, however, encourages the thought, often expressed by those hostile to the B-theory, that the B-theorist makes time an illusion. Supporters of the A-theory take time's passage as its essential characteristic and would regard a world without the passage of time as a world without time and change at all. The B-theorist, however, contends that what it is for time to exist is for things to stand in the relations of earlier than, simultaneous with, and later than, other things. My birth, for example, occurred during Harold Macmillan's premiership, was earlier than the assassination of John F. Kennedy and was later than the construction of the Berlin Wall. All that is required for change, according to the B-theory, is that objects have different properties at different times. Suppose we describe this kind of change as a *first-order change*: change in objects. An event is simply a change in the properties of one or more objects. Then to insist that events themselves must change in respect of their pastness, presentness or futurity is to invoke the idea of *second-order change*: changes themselves changing. A-theorists, in effect, hold that without second-order change there can be no first-order change. The B-theorist will simply deny this connection: there is first-order change, but no second-order change.

A further challenge faced by the B-theorist is to explain the arrow, or direction, of time. An important disanalogy between time and space is that, whereas we can, within limits, travel in any direction in space, we cannot, it seems, travel in any direction in time. We cannot visit the past, and we cannot visit the future. It may be said that the future visits us, but then of course it is no longer future, but present. I cannot, at least given the current state of our technology, decide that tomorrow I shall visit the year 2062. Even defenders of the possibility of time-travel concede that there is in ordinary life an arrow of time, and that it is something for builders of time-machines to overcome. Now the A-theorist takes the arrow of time to be of a piece with the passage of time. Where we are in time is something which time itself imposes on us: it is not a matter for our choosing. Since the B-theorist denies the passage of time, this might be thought to be equivalent to the denial that time has a direction. But it is not equivalent. B-theorists think of time as analogous to space in certain crucial respects, but they do not have to think of them as being analogous in *all* respects. Precisely what constitutes the direction of time is not something agreed upon by all B-theorists, but an influential answer is that the direction of time is nothing more than the direction of *causation*. It is a necessary truth, on this account, that causes always precede their effects. We cannot causally affect what happens at times earlier than our actions; we can only affect what happens at times later than our actions. This is why we cannot visit the past, for to do so would be to affect earlier events. Thus we do not need the passage of time to explain the arrow of time.

We can summarise the two theories as follows:

The A-theory

Time passes, and the division between past, present and future is an objective feature of time itself: it does not merely reflect our perspective on time (i.e. where in time we happen to be located). There are two variants:

(a) The closed past, open future view: the past is real, the future not.
(b) The open past, open future view: neither past nor future is real.

The B-theory

Time does not pass, and the division between past, present and future merely reflects our perspective. All times are equally real.

So much, then, for our two theories of time. The A-theory is the one we intuitively adopt, but I hope I have said enough about the B-theory to show that it is at least a viable alternative to our intuitive view. It is time now to return to our first question about death, namely, why we care more about future non-existence after our death than about past non-existence before our birth.

Death in the mirror

In an often-cited passage, Lucretius makes a point which is sometimes taken to imply that the fear of death is irrational:

> Again, look back and see how the ancient past of everlasting time before we are born has been nothing to us. Nature then shows us this as a mirror of future time after our final death. Does anything appear horrible there, does anything seem sad? (*de Rerum Natura*, Book 3, quoted in [Richard] Sorabji [*Time, Creation and the Continuum*, London] 1983, p. 176)

Whether or not Lucretius wanted, by this, to show the irrationality of our fears, it does provoke the thought that, since we are not appalled by the mirror-image of death, namely the fact that we did not exist before our birth (or conception), we should not be

SHOULD THE ATHEIST FEAR DEATH?   647

appalled when we look at death itself. Let us call this *the mirror-image argument*. It is, at best, incomplete. The fact is that we do, in general, care more about the future than about the past. What is about to happen to us is a more immediate source of concern than what has happened to us. And when we do brood over what has happened to us, it is often in virtue of its implications for what will happen in the future. Now, given this asymmetry of our concerns, it is simply not true that future non-existence will appear to us as nothing more than the mirror-image of past non-existence. But perhaps it ought to appear to us as nothing more than that. So there are two questions. First, what *explains* the asymmetry in our attitudes? Second, is it *rational* to hold on to this asymmetry?

Let us turn first to the A-theory of time for answers to these questions. For the A-theorist, there is an objective difference between past and future, and this is a view of the world reflected by our emotional reactions to events. When an unpleasant, or unfortunate, event is still future, we dread it. When it is past, we feel relief. Death is an unfortunate event, and so, being future, it is something we dread. This goes some way to explaining why we dread future non-existence, but it does not, by itself, rationalise that fear. Perhaps it is only when the event is an unpleasant *experience* that we dread it when it is future and feel relief when it is past. Now non-existence is certainly not an experience. So perhaps it is not to be dreaded?

There is, however, another explanation of why future non-existence is objectively worse than past non-existence, and it has a connection, though rather a subtle one, with the A-theory of time. Let us begin with the consideration that death is bad to the extent that it deprives us of pleasures that we would otherwise have enjoyed. Of course, this implies that death is good to the extent that it saves us from pains that we would otherwise have suffered, but for simplicity let us consider the case where the pleasures that would have been enjoyed outweigh the pains that would have been suffered. Now this does not, by itself, undermine the mirror-image argument, since we can reason as follows: a premature death may be bad, for the reasons given above, but it is no more bad than a late birth. Given that I was born in 1962, the fact (if it is one) that I shall die in 1998 is bad because I am thereby deprived of pleasures that I value. But the reverse of this is equally true: given that I shall die in 1998, the fact that I was not born until 1962 is bad, because had I been born earlier (i.e. had all the events which led up my conception and birth been earlier) I could have had more of the pleasures that I value. A late birth is just as much a depriver of pleasures as a premature death.

Now, of course, we do not ordinarily reason like this. We take our own, or anyone else's, birth date to be fixed, and so see the premature death as the bad thing, not the fact that the birth was as late as it was. Why we do this has, I suggest, to do with the variant of the A-theory that has the greatest hold on our intuitions, namely the closed past, open future view. When I contemplate my birth, I see it as something fixed. It is a fact that I was born in 1962. But when I contemplate my death, I seem to contemplate something not yet fixed. It is not just that I do not know when I shall die but, on the open future view, there is as yet no fact of the matter as to when I shall die. A number of possibilities present themselves, and I naturally prefer those possible futures where I die in old age to those where I die in early middle age. Those possibilities are of more interest to me than the rather abstract possibility that I should have been born in 1952, or 1922. Consequently it does not occur to me to bemoan the fact that I was born when I was, and not earlier. In addition, an early death seems to be objectively bad because it closes off what were genuine possibilities of extended existence, whereas my birth did not close off any genuine possibilities of my having been born earlier.

But now, see what happens when we switch to the B-theory of time. On this view, all times are equally real. What will happen is just as determinate as what has happened. So the date of my death is just as fixed as the date of my birth. I do not mean by this that, by virtue of the present state of things, it is *inevitable* that I shall die in, say, 1998. I may not yet be suffering from any terminal illness. All I mean is that the statement 'I shall die in 1998' is already either true or false. Suppose it is true. Then it is still possible that I should have died in 2038, but only in the rather abstract sense in which it is possible that I should have been born in 1922. A premature death is no more of an evil than a delayed birth. What is bad is simply that my life span is only 36 years rather than 76 years.

So the B-theory undermines one reason to think that future non-existence is more of an evil than past non-existence. It does not, however, undermine the reasonableness of adopting different attitudes to past and future in general. The B-theorist can, in fact, give a very natural explanation of why we are more concerned with the future, by appealing to the account of the direction of time presented in the previous section. The direction of time, it was suggested, consists in the fact that we can only causally affect later events, not earlier ones. We can, therefore, only act to bring about something in the future, not to bring about something in the past. If we are to be effective agents, therefore, we must turn our attention more to the future than to the past. If we spend too much time brooding on the past, rather than planning for the future, we are less likely to be effective agents, since most of our thoughts will be concerned with what, as it turns out, we cannot affect. Natural selection will therefore favour predominantly forward-looking individuals. Our bias towards the future thus has a biological basis.

But is it legitimate to extend this bias to future times after our death? It is rational to be concerned about the future if we can affect it, but if it is rational to care *only* about what we can directly affect, then it is not rational to care about times after our death, since, being dead, we cannot directly affect them. However, we can still *indirectly* affect what happens after our death, by, for example, initiating projects that are carried on by others. Whether it is rational to care about times after our death, therefore, depends largely on what motivates our actions. If we are simply interested in the experienced quality of our lives, and have reason to act only in so far as our actions will improve that quality, then it is not rational to care about those future times when we can have absolutely no experiences whatsoever. Arguably, however, we are interested in rather more than simply the experienced quality of our lives. We are also motivated to do entirely altruistic things, which will improve the quality of *other* people's lives. This is certainly something we can indirectly affect even when we are dead.

It is often suggested, of course, that even apparently purely altruistic behaviour has an element of self-interest in it. We may imagine a prominent benefactor being concerned, not only for the continued welfare of the beneficiaries, but also that he or she should continue to be recognised as the benefactor. No doubt it is a great comfort to think that one's good works will continue after death, but it would remove a considerable layer of icing from the cake to be told that, after death, we would become entirely *incognito*. This takes us to our second question: why are we appalled by the idea that the effects of our life will, after our death, be rapidly attenuated?

Immortality: real and vicarious

In the poem *Ozymandias*, Shelley conjures up the image of a ruined monument to a once great ruler, consisting of little more than 'Two vast and trunkless legs of stone' and a 'shattered visage' lying alone in the desert. We are given no more than a hint of the extent of his dominion:

> And on the pedestal these words appear:
> "My name is Ozymandias, king of kings:
> Look on my works, ye Mighty, and despair!"
> Nothing beside remains. Round the decay
> Of that colossal wreck, boundless and bare
> The lone and level sands stretch far away.

In the context of such complete obliteration, the inscription seems merely pathetic. The fact that there was once a great empire is made less significant, it seems, by its eventual destruction, and the pretensions of its ruler in consequence seem absurd.

The fate of Ozymandias is a reminder of our own: 'Remember thou art dust, and to dust thou shalt return'. It shows that our attempt to achieve a kind of vicarious immortality through our children, books, charitable works, or whatever, may ultimately be frustrated. Why does it matter to us to have such memorials? Why is the thought of being utterly forgotten and reduced to nothing so appalling? Again, it is, I suggest, a particular view of time which is informing our desires and fears, but this time it is the *second* variant of the A-theory, the open past, open future view, which is doing so. On this view, the past is unreal, and what is true about the past is so only by virtue of the traces that now remain of it. The consequence of such a view is that, if there are no traces of a given event which is conjectured to have taken place, then there is simply no fact of the matter as to whether the event took place or not. Thus, the significance of the past is determined entirely from our present perspective. This is not just the trivial truth that what is significant to us now can only be determined from our present perspective, but the more substantial thesis that what is actually true about the past is constituted by present fact. This provides further significance to the activities of those historical revisionists who deny the existence of the Holocaust. If history is rewritten and decisive evidence destroyed, then, on the open past view, it would at some future date *no longer be determinately true* that the Holocaust occurred. This, then, is why we are concerned to live on in the guise of our various productions and projects: to prevent the truth about the past from being obliterated. If all traces of our lives are lost, then we become, in a literal sense, non-persons.

This also provides an answer to our third question. If, at some future time, nothing at all exists, then the truth, not just about us, but about our history and everything we care about, is also lost.

If we are influenced by the open past, open future view, however, then we are not consistent in our application of it. On this view, only the present is real, so what matters is what is the case *now*. My significance should be assessed from my present perspective, not some imagined future one. In laying down our own memorials, we project ourselves in imagination into some future time when we no longer exist (this feat of imagination itself involves some conflict, at least if it involves the image of *ourselves* witnessing our non-existence) and consider our significance from that perspective. But at present, that future time is unreal, and we should accord that future perspective not more significance than our present one, but less significance.

The shift to the B-theory removes all talk of a privileged perspective. If all times are equally real, then, regardless of whether all traces of my life will be destroyed, it will always be the case that I once lived and did various deeds. These truths can never be obliterated, even if the evidence for them is. I have nothing to fear, at least in this respect, from the ravages of time.

But, it might be said, even if we recognise that the past is as real as the present, we may still wish the effects of our life to continue beyond our deaths. This may show how difficult it is to rid ourselves of the A-theory of time, but there is another source of this desire: we measure our significance by the extent of the causal consequences of our actions. The more temporally extended these effects are, the more significant we consider ourselves to be. But, equally, the more *spatially* extended those effects are, the more significant we consider ourselves to be. Hence the desire to affect the lives of many individuals, the desire to have our books read widely, the desire to extend our empires. So our craving for vicarious immortality need not imply any disanalogy between time and space.

We now turn to our final question: why, if we are appalled by death, are we also (perhaps even more) appalled by its opposite: the infinite extension of our life? The answer to this is surely very simple. Most of our pleasures are transient and, though we may often regret their passing, they would cease to be pleasures if they went on and on. We would simply become bored with them. Most of the things we strive for in life are valuable precisely because we only have a limited amount of time to acquire and enjoy them.

It does not follow from this, however, that an infinite life would necessarily be unpleasant. Suppose there are immortal beings who see the world as it really is, and not merely from a limited perspective. Now, if the B-theory of time is the true one, then our ordinary experience of time as a series of transient moments, on which experience the feeling of tedium depends, reflects only our perspective on reality. So, since the immortal beings have no perspective, their experience of time would not be as a series of transient moments. We can barely imagine what experience would be like for them, but it would surely be sufficiently different for eternal life to be for them nothing like the horror it would be for us.

Summary

If we do not believe that we continue to exist in some disembodied form after death, then the prospect of death may seem appalling. However, our attitude towards death is, to some extent, conditioned by our view of time. According to our ordinary conception of things, based on everyday experience, time flows in the sense that events are for ever receding into the past. Future events assume a greater significance than past ones, and future misfortune seems far worse than past misfortune. Part of this ordinary conception is a view of past and future as less real than the present: the past has gone, and the future has not yet arrived. This implies that, when we are dead, we cease to be part of reality, and our significance is thereby diminished.

In this chapter, we explored the possibility that the ordinary conception of time might be false, that time does not in fact flow, and that all times are equally real. Past, present and future, according to this different view of things, are closely analogous to the distinction between here and there. This view of time lends some support to the suggestion that our future non-existence after our deaths should be nothing more to us than our past non-existence before our births.

There are certain metaphysical conceptions of the world which affect the way we look at things, and the way we see ourselves. I believe that the theory of time, according to which all times are real, is one such conception. For some people, the psychological effects of such an idea are wholly negative ones. If future times are real, it has been argued, then what is to be is already in some sense fixed, and so we are in the grip of fate. But, as I have tried to show in these last pages, this view of time can affect us in positive ways. We need not be dismayed by the apparent transience of everything we value, for, if the passage of time is an illusion, such things are eternally real. And death is no longer the passage into oblivion: it is simply one of the temporal limits of our lives . . . .

Questions for reflection

1 How would you explain the difference between the A-theory of time and the B-theory of time?
2 Explain how the A-theory, in one or other of its two variants, leads us (1) to suppose that future non-existence is objectively worse than past non-existence, and (2) to desire a kind of immortality through the traces we leave behind.
3 How is it that, according to the B-theory, one need not fear death?
4 Which theory of time do you believe is most plausible, and why? How does your view of time affect your view of life and death?

Further reading

Paul Edwards, ed. (1992) *Immortality*. New York: Macmillan. (Thirty-four essays on immortality from Plato, Lucretius, Descartes, Hume, and others.)

Epicurus ([c. 300 BC] 1940) *The Stoic and Epicurean Philosophers*. Ed. Whitney J. Oates. New York: The Modern Library. (In "Letter to Menoeceus" in this volume, Epicurus argues that the fear of death is irrational.)

Robin Le Poidevin and Murray MacBeath, eds. (1993) *The Philosophy of Time*. Oxford: Oxford University Press. (An important collection of essays on central topics in the philosophy of time.)

Hugh Mellor (1998) *Real Time II*. London: Routledge. (A reworking and extended defense of his B-theory argument.)

Thomas Nagel (1979) *Mortal Questions*. Cambridge: Cambridge University Press. (The chapter entitled "Death" explores the meaning and value of human life and includes a discussion of the relationship between time and death.)

PART TEN

Recent trends

Philosophy of religion is a bourgeoning field of study which has experienced incredible transformation over the past half-century. Since the 1960s, much of this discussion has focused on theistic issues; in particular, topics related to Christian theism have been at the fore. Many of these discussions are still blooming, and I suspect that new and interesting developments related to them will continue to emerge in the coming decades. But there are also non-theistic currents and themes in this transitional field which are important and often overlooked—currents and themes which take into consideration the wide diversity of religious beliefs, both theistic and non-theistic. I have attempted to include a number of such currents in this volume. In addition, however, there are also recent trends emerging which are providing rich, fruitful, and culturally relevant resources in the field. A number of important works come to mind, and I have included in this section three that I believe deserve special attention.

First, while the literature on feminist philosophy of religion is still fairly scant, it is quickly gaining ascendancy due to such important publications as Pamela Anderson's *A Feminist Philosophy of Religion: The Rationality of Myths and Religious Beliefs* (1998) and Grace Jantzen's *Becoming Divine: Towards a Feminist Philosophy of Religion* (1999). Feminist philosophers of religion have demonstrated that gender bias and ethnocentrism have, to some extent, shaped the discussions and problems in the field. From the viewpoint of feminist thinkers, analytic philosophy—while addressing significant themes of traditional theism, rational justification of religious belief and so on—has not engaged relevant questions posed by feminist concerns. In the next essay, then, Pamela Anderson raises some of these questions and notes how social location and personal commitment form our beliefs, and how gender affects our understanding of the divine.

Another important trend in philosophy of religion is the recognition of universal moral principles or ideals among the major religious systems and an attending desire to work out a global ethic commensurate with them—one which supports international human rights, encourages positive interreligious relations, and fosters widespread public ethics education, among other things. Sallie King introduces two proposals for just such an ethic. While she grants that these ideas are only a start, and that religious leaders among the various traditions need to draft similar plans before consensus is offered on a final draft, this is most certainly a move in the right direction.

A final essay focuses on the growing interest among philosophers of religion in environmental concerns. It is no doubt true that religious groups are becoming increasingly more aware of and involved in environmental issues. For example, religious leaders and adherents worldwide are entering into the fray of the environmental movement, and new ecotheologies are developing across the globe. There is also a growing awareness among environmentalists of the significance of certain spiritual values for the care of the environment. Roger Gottlieb brings these issues to light and describes their significance for the future of our planet.

I suspect that these new trends, among others, will be significant factors in shaping philosophy of religion in the twenty-first century. I take this to be a positive move, for what we have here are not merely abstract reflections on religious dogma and doctrine (as profitable as they are in and of themselves), but fertile insights for personal, social, and global engagement.

Chapter 61

Pamela Sue Anderson

FEMINISM IN
PHILOSOPHY OF RELIGION

Pamela Sue Anderson is Reader in Philosophy of Religion, University of Oxford, and Fellow in Philosophy at Regent's Park College, Oxford. She has published widely on issues in feminism and philosophy of religion. In this essay, she points out that the last century has demonstrated noteworthy advances in Western philosophy and, more specifically, in philosophy of religion. One significant development includes a recognition of the way social location and personal commitment shape our various beliefs, attitudes, and actions—notably the ways gender as an aspect of our locatedness has shaped our understanding of the divine, as well as how our commitment to a certain conception of the divine shapes gender. While the past reflects a failure to recognize this locatedness and the gendered norms of the various religious traditions—it objectified women and created self-fulfilling beliefs about the divine—feminist voices have spawned a developing awareness of the reciprocally related aspects of philosophical method, historical positioning, and political commitment in philosophy of religion, creating "new horizons" for feminism, philosophy, and religion. Yet ethical and epistemological scrutiny of these horizons remain tasks for maintaining philosophy's self-reflexivity.

Reflecting back on the previous century, we can assert with confidence that the dawn of the twenty-first century has ushered in significant changes in western philosophy.* In particular, philosophy's self-definition is being transformed by an increasing awareness of its own history and locatedness. Philosophers who seek to remain true to the original reflexive nature of philosophy in ancient Greece have had to recognize the relevant and reciprocally related aspects of western philosophy's material and social locatedness; notably, this has meant the recognition of gender. Feminism has been characterized by its political commitment to change, to critical thought and action; consistent with this characterization, feminism in philosophy constitutes a vehicle for transformation. Yet progress in philosophy is never easy; and feminism in philosophy was strongly resisted in the twentieth century by Anglo-American philosophers who defined themselves in terms of a certain norm of neutrality. Furthermore, "feminism" is not one thing; this label covers a whole range of different feminist voices and views. And yet in the context of any particular philosophical text, the discourses of feminism have gained a critical focus in elucidating the gendered nature of philosophy.

My concern in this chapter is feminism in philosophy of religion. The philosophy of religion as a branch of philosophy increasingly overlaps other branches of philosophy, including ethics, epistemology, metaphysics, philosophy of science, linguistic philosophy and history of philosophy. Feminism in philosophy of religion faces similar problems, issues and struggles as does feminism in (almost) any of the other branches of contemporary philosophy. It challenges in a fundamental manner philosophy's ideals as these have *both* objectified women and led to self-fulfilling beliefs about the divine (i.e. men have been propped up by their ideal of the divine). For example, Augustine's account of relations between women and men, and men and the divine: women and men are equal in terms of their capacity to reason, but men are propped up by the male-gendered ideal (God) toward which they also move (Augustine, 1961, p. 344; cf. Deutscher, 1997, pp. 154–68).

However, feminism in philosophy of religion has not been part of the concern generally of philosophers or of feminists. This is true of each of the latter for equally fundamental reasons; and these reasons have to do with assuming philosophy's ideals as norms for our critical thought and action. Precisely because of its commitment to a distinctive norm of neutrality, philosophy has strongly resisted political and religious commitments; and in supporting the norms of critical thinking and concrete action for change, feminism has resisted religious commitments because of the tendency of the latter to support patriarchal tradition. Nevertheless, a growing awareness of how social location and personal commitments inevitably shape our philosophical perspectives creates one of the significant new horizons for feminism and philosophy. This means looking at—and challenging— the horizon that has been shaped by certain central and fundamental ideals; in particular, the divine as the ideal moral agent and the ideal observer. These ideals have, in turn, fixed our gendered norms of thought and action (cf. Jaggar, 2000, pp. 227–8, 239–41).

Feminism in philosophy of religion seeks the transformation of the most traditional aspects of philosophy's self-definition, transforming those norms most resistant to change. Commitments to certain norms reinforced by religious ideals should not go unnoticed by philosophers or feminists in that they contain a potentially powerful force for legitimating *either* change *or* the status quo. There is a gap, if not *aporia*, between the truth of what is in reality possible and the actual present situation. In this case, feminists and philosophers generally have failed to give attention to their locatedness in the past and present, but especially to the religious norms of the particular traditions to which they are related wittingly or unwittingly.

Consider the impressive collection of philosophy essays in *The Cambridge Companion to Feminism in Philosophy* which is supposed to "encompass . . . at least all of the core subject areas commonly taught in Anglophone undergraduate philosophy courses" (Fricker and Hornsby, eds. 2000, p. 5). Yet it contains no essay on, or even a mention of, feminism in philosophy of religion. Perhaps philosophy of religion is not commonly taught as a "core" subject area in analytic philosophy; without a survey of philosophy courses in the Anglophone world it is difficult to know for certain. Yet philosophy of religion remains on the syllabus of undergraduate and A-level philosophy, so not including philosophy of religion in *The Cambridge Companion* seems deliberate. To be honest, this branch of "philosophy" remains a problem for feminist and non-feminist philosophers.

For one thing, analytic philosophy of religion as practiced in the Anglophone world can be unwittingly marginalized, or treated as non-core, because it is practiced most vocally by conservative, at times aggressively apologetic, theologians. Such dogmatism is a problem for philosophers; it is not obviously compatible with the critical spirit of philosophy, or feminism! For another thing, at least in this context, it is possible that feminists have not been able to imagine that either feminism or philosophy could exist in the subject area . . . of *religion*. On the one hand, there is the political commitment of feminism that seems to clash, if it is not inconsistent, with a personal religious (or "private") commitment; and on the other hand, there is once more the supposed neutrality of philosophy, especially of analytic philosophy.

Today it is still relevant to quote Margaret Whitford's claim that "the feminist philosopher" who may be "a theoretical impossibility . . . obstinately insists on existing" (Whitford, 1992, p. 112). The feminist philosopher does actually exist, and seeks to thrive, *in* philosophy of religion. Furthermore, religion responds to a human need to try to understand ourselves, the world around us, and to form theories about the place of human beings in the universe, creating pictures of our relations to others, the world and what might be conceived to be the divine. Ignoring philosophy of religion would, then, imply a failure to recognize how men and women have located themselves, and how this locatedness has objectified women (and some men) in materially and socially specific ways, while creating self-fulfilling beliefs about the divine. This failure has hurt both women and relations between men, women and the divine.

Core topics for feminism in philosophy of religion

Much evidence exists to support a common core of topics for feminism in philosophy of religion and in other branches of philosophy. On this count, several things are initially striking to me about the points of view on feminism in philosophy appearing in *The Cambridge Companion*. First of all, the imagery of Neurath's boat expresses the reformist nature of the project of feminism in philosophy. Yet the same imagery introduces a reformist project in the Preface to *A Feminist Philosophy of Religion* where a feminist reform seeks to rebuild philosophy at the level of fundamental presuppositions, and Quine's idea of rebuilding philosophy is assumed: "We can change [the conceptual scheme that we grew up in] bit by bit, plank by plank, though meanwhile there is nothing to carry us along but the evolving conceptual scheme itself" (Quine, 1953, pp. 78–9, as quoted in Anderson, 1998, pp. x–xi). The point is that philosophers cannot detach themselves completely from their conceptual scheme to achieve an absolutely correct representation of reality. However, this does not imply that philosophers have to give up the search for objectivity or for true belief. Truth and objectivity are topics debated by feminist philosophers of religion, too.

Second, *The Companion* recalls the importance of the philosophical imaginary brought to light by French feminist philosopher Michèle Le Doeuff (1989). The imagery of a boat, or ship on the open sea, is also recalled a number of times in *A Feminist Philosophy of Religion* (Anderson, 1998, pp. x–xi, 11–12 and 215–16), in order to illustrate the evolving role of this very imagery in the history of philosophy. As part of the philosophical imaginary (that which, although often ignored, necessarily accompanies philosophical thought), the imagery's significance changes as we move from ancient Greece, to Francis Bacon in sixteenth-century England, to Kant in eighteenth-century Germany, to Neurath and Quine in the last century—and finally, to Luce Irigaray. Anderson's overall debt also remains to Le Doeuff who offers an original account of the philosophical imaginary. Le Doeuff encourages women in philosophy to read the texts in the history of western philosophy according to the impact of the text on its social context in the past, including the 'upshot' for the culture(s) influenced by the text, but also to read texts fully aware of our present situation so that we allow for the possibilities in new readings of past texts (Le Doeuff, 1991, pp. 166–70). In this way, feminism in philosophy supports change for a very different future in philosophy (Lloyd, 2000, pp. 256–8).

Therefore, in addition to reading Quine's imagery in terms of its significance for conceptions of objectivity in the history of modern philosophy, we employ the figure of the lone mariner to suggest the ways in which we might transform "him", that is, he who serves as a gendered ideal with "his" own philosophical history. Neurath and Quine create a picture of a mariner, but a lone mariner also appears prior to modern philosophy in the ancient text of Homer's *Odyssey* and later appears in the mid-twentieth-century text of Horkheimer and Adorno, *Dialectic of Enlightenment* (1947). The cultural upshot of these philosophical texts culminates with the question of the subject in the postmodern debates. However, these past texts not only tell us something about philosophy's past, they offer us material for transforming the subjects of philosophy's future. For instance, we find Irigaray miming the possible roles of future female subjects in her *Marine Lover of Friedrich Nietzsche* (1991). Her mime demonstrates that in modern philosophy the subject increasingly dissociates himself from "marine waters," which represent the disorderly turbulent nature of desire, the mysterious forces of embodiment and of material nature; her marine waters symbolize nature as threatening to reason in particular. The result is a paradoxical—or an unsustainable—account of the embodied male philosophical subject who has denied his own relations to nature, to his body and desire. The "marine lover" offers (us) imagery for exploring new conceptions of relations between male and female subjects for feminism in philosophy. The textual and historical exploration of imagery forces reflection upon our beliefs about the subjects of philosophy and the actual shape of our gendered self-images: we recognize ourselves as materially and socially located, whether women or men in philosophy.

Philosophical method, historical locatedness and political commitment

Take a step back to see the larger picture of feminism in philosophy. Feminist philosophers unravel a whole web of fundamental issues that are common to philosophy of religion and other branches of philosophy. At least three reciprocally related issues become the focus of feminism. Three sets of issues related to philosophical method, to the historical locatedness of philosophy and to the inevitability of political commitment, which were first faced by feminism in philosophy of science, resonate with issues being confronted by positivist and post-postivist, foundationalist and anti-foundationalist philosophers of religion.

First, a strong methodological similarity exists between feminism in philosophy of science and feminism in philosophy of religion. Without changing the truth of Alison

Wylie's "Feminism in Philosophy of Science: Making Sense of Contingency and Constraint", we can reread her central claims in terms of philosophy of religion. Where Wylie writes "science(s)" and "philosophy of science" I can read, without confusion, "religion(s)" and "philosophy of religion" as follows:

> . . . feminists see [religion] as an important locus of gender inequality and as a key source of legitimation for this inequality; feminists both within and outside [religion] have developed close critical analyses of the androcentrism they find inherent in the institutions, practices and content of [religion]. (Wylie, 2000, p. 166)

Ignorance of feminist critical analyses of androcentrism in western philosophy exhibits a serious failure of western philosophy to remain reflexive about fundamental dimensions of their deeply embedded self-image. A curious failure to be reflexive about the gendered nature of this self-image has shaped epistemic practices and ethical reflection in terms of an ideal observer (Anderson, 2005; and Taliaferro, 2005). This leads to the next set of issues concerning both philosophy of science and philosophy of religion.

Second, feminist critiques and reconstructions of philosophy of religion, like those in philosophy of science, have begun to face issues related to the locatedness of the epistemic practices and institutions of religions, as well as their contextual values. In particular, ". . . feminist engagement[s] with [philosophy of religion]—constructive and critical— raise epistemological questions about ideals of objectivity, the status of evidence and the role of orienting (often unacknowledged) contextual values" (cf. Wylie, 2000, p. 166). Early in the twentieth century, philosophy of religion was to a large extent modeled on the positivist methods and values of science. The internal critiques of positivism in the 1960s and 1970s eventually forced scientists and at least some philosophers of religion, and notably certain feminist philosophers, to consider post-positivist research which turned to fine-grained, discipline- and practice-specific studies of belief, acquisition of religious knowledge, knowledge-making practices and methodologies.

Third, feminism in philosophy of religion, like in science, has faced issues raised by certain sorts of philosophical critics, most notably positivist(-like) critics. Echoing the words of Wylie concerning philosophy of science, we easily find that, "Despite substantial overlap between philosophical and feminist interests in [religion], a number of outspoken critics argue that the very idea of feminist philosophy of [religion] (or, more generally, feminist epistemology) is a contradiction in terms" (Wylie, 2000, p. 166). For example, a definite sense of contradiction—between the political and the (supposedly) neutral—is implicit in a recent disagreement where an analytic philosopher of religion brackets the feminism in the text of a feminist philosopher of religion, in order to critically assess her methodology. The implicit objection would be that philosophy of religion must stand up methodologically to criticism without relying upon the political commitment of feminism. "In response to objections of this sort, feminist philosophers of [religion can] argue [following philosophers of science] that their critics make a number of highly problematic assumptions about" philosophy of religion, or more specifically, the justification of religious belief. Arguments that were well established by the late 1970s—"arguments from the theory-ladenness of evidence, the under-determination of theory by evidence, and various forms of holism. . ."—make it clear that the empirical basis of any knowledge-based discipline, whether science or religion, cannot be treated as, in Wylie's words, "a foundational given in any straight-forward sense, and that objectivity cannot be identified with strict value neutrality and the context of independence of epistemic standards" (Wylie, 2000, pp. 166–7; Potter, 2006, pp. 8–11 and 153–76).

A similar response can be given to Paul Helm, who is a prominent philosopher of religion apparently in the grip of the assumption of the strict value-neutrality that derives originally from positivist philosophy of science (Cf. Anderson, 2004a, pp. 94–6). Helm's manner of criticism of feminist philosophy of religion also exhibits a strong resist-ance to the reflexive nature of philosophy which would allow for recognition and critique of both its androcentrism and ethnocentrism. He not only brackets feminism, appar-ently to remain philosophically neutral about a methodological issue, in his article, "The Indispensability of Belief to Religion," but he refuses to try to understand the terms of continental philosophy (Helm, 2001). Both of these refusals seem to go together, and could be explained by residual positivist assumptions, which allow "the philosopher" to be unaware of his own sexism and social location.

Nevertheless, Miranda Fricker and Jennifer Hornsby seem correct in their "Intro-duction" to *The Cambridge Companion to Feminism in Philosophy*, that:

> analytic philosophy creates an intellectual climate in which it is especially problematic to acknowledge locatedness. This is surely an important part of the explanation why continental philosophy can seem more hospitable to feminist projects . . . [yet] the [feminist] imperative of *social* criticism will ensure that feminist philosophy of any kind is likely to share an affinity with work in the continental tradition . . . We believe it is philosophically valuable that work written in the Anglo-American paradigm can produce genuine engagement with questions typically raised in the continental tradi-tion. (Fricker and Hornsby, 2000, p. 8; emphasis added)

Although a significant set of philosophical questions are raised by continental philoso-phers fascinated with religion (especially with mystical experience), analytic philosophers of religion continue to resist a continental approach to philosophy, including its approach to philosophy's locatedness.

The clash between science-derived method and post-positivist thinking

With the above in mind, note a few lines from Helm's criticism of Grace Jantzen's femi-nist philosophy of religion. First, Helm states

> In *Becoming Divine* Grace Jantzen turns her back on Anglo-American phil-osophy of religion and the way of doing philosophy which it embodies in favour of certain continental European ways. Jantzen thinks that these ways offer a better prospect for developing a feminist philosophy of religion. [My] paper is not at all concerned with the issue of feminism, but only with the methodological turn that Jantzen makes. . . . I argue that for her, belief is as indispensable in religion and in the philosophy of religion as it is for the

Anglo-American philosophy of religion which she rejects. Further, the only argument she offers for her position is a genetic argument for the origins of religious beliefs. . . . (Helm, 2001, p. 75)

Second, Jantzen replies as follows:

[Helm's] article, in fact, is as neat an illustration as I could have wished of exactly my point: the preoccupation of philosophers of religion with beliefs to the exclusion of consideration of issues of gender and justice, while refusing to consider how rationality as they perceive it is constructed upon masculinist desire. Helm briefly acknowledges that there is much more to religion than beliefs . . . But in practice his article, like the discipline of which it is a part, proceeds as though that were not so. . . . (Jantzen, 2001, p. 88)

This narrowness in the conception of religion and religious practices adds to the lack of interest in philosophy of religion shown by philosophers and feminists working in other branches of philosophy. Jantzen's alternative conception of religion depends upon her qualified use of a psychoanalytic model derived from the continental tradition, but especially from her particular readings of Luce Irigaray and Adriana Cavarero. If sympathetic with a post-positivist epistemology, a philosopher might agree with criticizing the blindness of the analytic philosopher of religion to his own sexism and ethnocentrism. Jantzen explains,

. . . In my book I use (with qualifications) a psychoanalytic model to show . . . either that specific [Christian] beliefs, or indeed the emphasis upon the centrality of beliefs in general, arise out of projections, fears, or desire for mastery . . . while technically this does not confirm or deny the truth of the beliefs themselves, it does put the insistence upon their preservation and justification in a different light . . . What is being silenced, what positions of dominance are being reinscribed . . .?

[Further she asserts] . . . what I am after is a scrutiny of the projections, desires, and fears that underlie beliefs and subject positions. This scrutiny must, to be sure, also be applied to a feminist position . . . (Jantzen, 2001, p. 89)

Admittedly, serious scrutiny of Jantzen's philosophical position from the point of view of feminism in post-positivist epistemology finds both significance and danger in her particular gendered ideal of the divine for women (cf. Anderson 2006). Yet assessment of these dangers will not be pursued here. Instead, to grasp the critical relation between science-derived method and post-postivist thinking about religion, consider Marilyn McCord Adams who, as an Anglican theologian, writes in the field of analytic philosophy of religion. Adams reflects insightfully upon the modeling of religion on scientific methods of inquiry, scientific values and standards of epistemic practice. She recognizes some of the aforementioned methodological issues, as well as the different respective responses of science and religion to the human need to make sense of ourselves, the world and the reality of our social-material locatedness as philosophers. Adams sees different patterns of the cosmos being drawn by religion and science:

Intelligence gives us an advantage relative to other animals . . . We can
study ourselves, try to discover what patterns of character and forms of
social organizations frustrate human life and what make it flourish. Religion and science respond to this need to get our bearings, albeit in different
ways. Both draw pictures of the cosmos, offer estimates of human being and
its prospects. Both are fruitful with corollary recommendations as to better
and worse ways to negotiate life. (Adams, 1999, pp. 1–2)

British philosopher Mary Midgley shares this concern about the patterns underlying our thought about human beings. But Midgley introduces a working definition of
myth to articulate a relation between the symbolic stories which inform our thought
and science. She defends the existence of myth as "symbolic stories which play a crucial
role in our imaginative and intellectual life by expressing the patterns that underlie our
thought." (Midgley 1994, p. 109) Here Midgley recognizes a philosophical problem in
"the lure of simplicity" deriving from modern science. In her words,

[the] clash is sharpened today by the notion we now hold of ourselves as thoroughly scientific beings, individuals too clear-headed and well-organized to
use blurred or ambivalent concepts. The concepts that we need to use for
everyday life are, however, often in some ways blurred or ambivalent because
life itself is too complex for simple descriptions. For instance, notions such
as love, care, trust and consent are incredibly complicated. The concept of a
friend is not a simple one, and people who insist on oversimplifying it cannot
keep their friends, nor indeed be friends themselves, because they do not
properly understand what a friend is. (Midgley, 2004, p. 137; also see pp. 5–
6, 128–9, 137 and 142–5)

Adams herself admits that the answers we give as philosophers run the danger of
oversimplification:

. . . in relation to what it would be helpful to know, human cognitive powers
are *limited*. Whether individually or collectively, we are inveterate *over-
simplifiers*, marginalizing some data in order to come up with tractable
systematizations, over time striving for more complexity without sacrificing
too much simplicity, only eventually to face such massive misfits as to have to
begin again. Idealized scientific method takes the successive approximations
approach for granted; its program of testing hypotheses even goes looking
for falsifying evidence . . . [Religions] too face crises, especially when their
accounts are inadequate to handle the very features of life for which they are
most needed. (Adams, 1999, pp. 1–2, emphasis added)

Thus Adams recognizes the often debilitating tension between, on the one hand, unity and
simplicity as epistemological values (of science) and, on the other hand, complexity which
allows an openness to truth and its opposite, falsehood, in our philosophical theories about
reality.
For a central example of the problem of simplicity in philosophy of religion, consider the philosophical assessments of evil: "its nature, source and consequences: how

and to what extent it takes root in human beings, whether and how it can be eradicated, how in the midst of it we should conduct ourselves through life" (Adams, 1999, p. 2). In the twentieth century a restrictive employment of the epistemological principles of unity and simplicity by philosophers of religion results in some inadequate "solutions" to the problem of evil. In Adams' words,

> . . . our philosophical propensity for generic solutions—our search for a single explanation that would cover all evils at once—has permitted us to ignore the worst evils in particular (what I shall call horrendous evils) and so to avoid confronting the problems they pose. (Adams, 1999, p. 3; see also pp. 26–8, 33, 36f, 195–6, 197–8)

We might agree with Adams' account of the analytic philosopher of religion William Rowe whose debates concerning the logical and evidential problem of evil are ". . . carried on at too high a level of abstraction. By agreeing to a focus on what Rowe came to label 'restricted standard theism,' both sides avoided responsibility to a particular tradition" (Adams, 1999, pp. 3, 15; cf. Anderson, 1998, pp. 40–1). Nevertheless, a particular understanding of the tradition of Christian theology is still implied even in this restricted standard theism.

In *Horrendous Evils and the Goodness of God*, Adams steers a middle road through issues of theory and practice, between theories in philosophy of religion which have been modeled on the scientific virtues of unity, simplicity, empirical adequacy, internal coherence, etc, and praxis-orientating solutions to actual suffering. She also steers a difficult path between concern for individual participants in horrendous evil (i.e. horrors in which all integrity is destroyed) and concern for making this lived experience meaningful at a more abstract level of philosophy, or what she calls "the symbolic level" (Adams, 1999, pp. 106–51, 196). In particular, she defends herself against the feminist or social criticism—that her approach would only satisfy the worries of bourgeois individuals. She admits that social systems and economic structures cause massive evils. Yet she poses a serious challenge to an exclusively practical response. She argues that proposals for a global transformation of social structures in order to eradicate evil in the world are likely to fail to respond adequately to individuals who seek to understand real pain and to render meaningful (their own) suffering; a theoretical account of individual participants in horrors is necessary for the meaning-making potential, or integrity, of that person.

It seems to follow that Adams would challenge *both* Jantzen's total rejection of the social structure, which Jantzen contends reflects the necrophilia of a masculinist imaginary, *and* Jantzen's proposal for a new social imaginary, or "feminist religious symbolic," which would be life-enhancing and not preoccupied with death like the masculinist symbolic. Yet, would this feminist alternative be able to address the particularity of horrendous evils, which evacuate life of any positive meaning? Even a post-christian, non-realist feminist would concur with the Christian realist Adams, and not with the feminist Jantzen, on the need to render meaningful the individual experiences of bodily life which are in fact negative, and possibly, horrendous. Real life involves all degrees of distress, decay and death; the reality of our social and personal lives is not always life-enhancing; and individual participants in evil cannot make their particular experiences meaningful—or regain integrity—by trying to sweep them away as a mere construction, or residue, of the masculinist symbolic.

Is the influence of feminism in philosophy reflected in the sensitivity to both the actual lived experiences of participants in horrendous evil and the sources of evil in social structures? Or, in this case, is Adams merely defensive of her individualist predisposition in the face of more radical criticism? It is hoped that philosophy of religion, however gradually, accommodates the insights of feminism in philosophy more generally.

Feminist epistemology and its significance for philosophy of religion

The insights of feminism in epistemology are significant for feminism in philosophy of religion. In "Feminism in Epistemology: Pluralism without Postmodernism," Miranda Fricker addresses the philosophical question of "pluralism," as raised by postmodernism's rejection of unity, especially any unifying perspective on the world. Fricker confronts the competing values of plurality and unity, of resistance to authoritarian uses of reason and acceptance of rational authority. In the end, she concludes that the "first-order" level of our disagreements and of plurality in practice—where social differences give rise to differences in our everyday perspectives—must remain distinct from the levels of (our) epistemological, ontological and metaphysical claims to unity or agreement (Fricker, 2000, pp. 159–61). The correct level for plurality is the ground level, while reason seeks unity at an epistemological level where rational authority is not mere authoritarianism. Critical scrutiny of what is given (rational) authority implies an epistemological level of discourse on which there is the possibility of agreement, as well as judgment of what is in fact a terrorist use of reason.

Next, we can apply Fricker's distinction in levels—with the correct, ground level for pluralism—to postmodernism in feminist philosophy of religion. For this I return to Jantzen whose feminist position has raised valuable concerns about claims to neutrality in philosophy of religion. Jantzen questions an exclusive preoccupation with the justification of religious belief which tends to reinforce the androcentrism of analytic philosophy of religion as traditionally practised in the Anglophone world. Jantzen also celebrates the "postmodern" play of plurality and difference. But then, unlike Fricker, she stops with the assumption that the postmodern rejection of authoritarian uses of reason is correct and goes no further with the question of rational authority. The danger which, I think, Fricker correctly points out, is that the postmodern celebration of plurality implies the loss of any rational authority. This means the loss of any rational authority—or credibility—for judging good and bad beliefs, or inclusive, exclusive and hurtful practices. Yet the realism and the rational authority which enable recognition of actual injustices are lost at the peril of women and marginalized others. The valuable lesson to be learnt by philosophers of religion from feminism in epistemology is, then, not to lose the ability to scrutinize beliefs rationally, even feminist belief. As mentioned earlier in her response to Helm, Jantzen encourages a particular sort of scrutiny of belief but resists an epistemology of religious belief.

The ways in which philosophy's constitutive virtues and standards of epistemic practice are interpreted and employed with or against each other should be considered in the light of the changing awareness of gender and related historical, material and social factors. This implies the (feminist) view that knowledge, including justified true belief, cannot be claimed without bringing in ethics—or ethical evaluation and, often unwittingly, a host of ethical assumptions. These include certain constitutive values or virtues: notably, principles of unity, simplicity, empirical adequacy, internal coherence, external consistency and explanatory power (Anderson, 2001; cf. Longino, 1987; Wylie, 2000). Ethical terms are also implicit in references to the epistemic *duties* of truth (including self-reflexivity), as well as the fundamental *value* assigned to rational authority and credibility. In turn, scrutiny of the ethical terms which constitute epistemic practices has revealed injustice in the multiple exclusions of knowers by gender which is differentiated by multiple material and social factors such as sexual orientation, race, ethnicity and religion (Williams, 1991; Fricker, 1999, 2000). These exclusions of subjects of knowledge result in the failure to treat women and non-privileged persons as credible knowers, as well as failing to recognize certain forms of knowledge; for example, "know how" and non-standard forms of practical knowledge as in the "tales" of illiterate women remain generally unacknowledged by traditional epistemologists (Dalmiya and Alcoff, 1993; Anderson, 2004b).

In the telling terms of Rae Langton's "Feminism in Epistemology: Exclusion and Objectification," when it comes to knowledge "women get left out" and "women get hurt." There are sins of both omission and commission. Examples of the former include being left out as subjects of knowledge:

> whether because they lack the knowledge men have, or because they lack knowledge of themselves as women, or because they lack credibility, or because their perspectives on the world are omitted, or because they are excluded by a mistaken traditional conception of knowledge [—women get left out] (Langton, 2000, p. 134)

This account of the sin of commission is especially insightful for debates about the nature of belief in philosophy of religion. It enables assessing whether religious beliefs have (deceptively) shaped the way the world is, resulting in the anomalous condition of making the world fit the belief. For example, women who are submissive may confirm the powerful patriarch's belief that women should be left to be submissive, but this is in fact a distortion of the potential of real women by their inferior social position and/or their lack of political and material power.

Langton's account explains how it is that women are actively hurt by objectification. This (latter) is a sin of commission: it cannot be remedied simply by letting women in. Appropriating Langton's account of objectification, we can give the particular wrong of objectification sustained scrutiny with regard to ethical ideals and religious beliefs (as well as projections) of contemporary philosophers (for example, Jantzen 2001, p. 89). Bearing in mind Jantzen's caution against an obsessive preoccupation with the justification of belief, feminism could constructively focus upon the construction of belief and belief's relation to the world. Elizabeth Anscombe's original—what Jantzen might call "masculinist"—account of "direction of fit" (Anscombe, 1957) serves as a useful yardstick; that is, *belief aims to fit the world, while desire aims for the world to fit it*. Langton builds upon Anscombe's account to develop an incisive argument concerning objectification as distinct from objective belief that is true, if it actually fits the world:

> If objectivity is about how mind conforms to world, objectification is about the opposite: objectification is, roughly, about some of the ways in which

world conforms to mind. Objectification is a process in which the social world comes to be shaped by perception, desire and belief: a process in which women, for example, are made objects because of men's perceptions and desires and beliefs. To say that women are made objects is to speak in metaphors, albeit familiar ones; but, to make a start, it has something to do with how some men see women. (Langton, 2000, p. 138)

The ethical problem for feminism is not with the direction of fit for belief or for desire, but it is with the anomalies (1) where belief takes the direction of fit of desire, resulting in (the self-deception of) wishful thinking; (2) when such thinking begins to shape the world, then objects come to confirm the wish as self-fulfilling belief.

My last example is the ideal observer theory which has been employed to support a divine ethic by Charles Taliaferro. This, first, links ethical discourse about ideal agency and religious (i.e. theistic) discourse about a God's eye point of view; and, second, it assumes an ideal vantage in any ethical debate (Taliaferro 2005; Anderson 2005). A question of circularity is immediately raised: if the theory assumes the existence of the very ideal it wishes to justify, then it appears to beg the question of its existence. In fact, no man can achieve the ideal observer position and be omniscient, omnipercipient and impartial (O'Neill, 2000, pp. 150–6). Second, a question of a sin of commission is posed: does the ideal observer theory hurt women by failing to understand the partiality premise of women's ethical thinking? It does not see that a feminist rejection of impartial ethical thought is decisive for the ideal observer standpoint. This means a failure to recognize feminist ethics as a serious challenge both to the ideal observer's omnipercipience and to the very theory which is supposed to endorse it.

The belief that the ideal agent is omniscient, omnipercipient and impartial cannot fit the world. Instead this belief is aimed to fit the direction of the agent's desire for a God's eye view. If the latter is assumed, then desire could gain the power to actively shape the agent's perceptions; if powerful enough this overall conception would shape the social world so that the ideal agent (who, by definition, cannot be an actual individual man, let alone a woman) will shape reality to fit his belief as an ideal observer whose perception determines an idealized, theistic picture of reality. Thus we face the problem of a self-fulfilling belief.

For her part, Jantzen avoids the harm done by this traditional idealization, or self-fulfilling belief, of the male theist who assumes the reality of an omniscient, omnipercipient and impartial, divine agent as model for the ideal observer; the latter not only confidently claims to ensure the truth of religious belief but serves as the ideal vantage point for moral judgment (for example, of our epistemic and discursive practices). Instead Jantzen proposes a *projection* of the divine as a gendered ideal for women who seek to become fully themselves, and so divine as "natals" who are born, finite, but flourish in this life.

However, Jantzen's feminist proposal is not completely safe either; a projection of the divine for women is only a step away from objectification. That is, as long as projection is like wishful thinking, belief arranges itself to desire's direction of fit; projection/wishing wants the world to conform to one's belief. Wishful thinking is more obviously characterized by self-deception insofar as the thought does not become true. For example, belief that "evil" is only part of the masculinist symbolic remains a wish. This is a self-deception for the one who projects the ideal of a feminist religious symbolic which sees reality as life-enhancing only, but also for those who follow and accept it, while excluding those whose lives fail to fit the desired ideal. Nevertheless, the next step to objectification is dangerously easy: given enough social power from those subjects who follow, the privileged female subjects make their wish a self-fulfilling belief whereby it becomes true at least for those feminists whose life is flourishing. Yet this is precisely the sort of exclusion and objectification which feminism in epistemology aims to eradicate!

Concluding reflections

To conclude, let us see how far we have come in reflecting upon the ideals and self-images of philosophy, and in particular, in considering the ethical and epistemological scrutiny of the ideals in philosophy of religion as relevant to feminism in philosophy more generally. Perhaps it has become clearer why feminism in philosophy of religion has not immediately come to mind when philosophers think of feminism in philosophy. That is, its (religious) ideals are rejected by feminism's critical thought and norms for change. Yet self-reflexivity as an epistemic virtue, and an ethical value, should compel philosophers—and feminists—to scrutinize the nature of the most fundamental beliefs about themselves, their place in the universe, and their relations with others, especially insofar as they are supported (or propped up) by divine ideals. We may have the grounds to argue that *feminism in philosophy as well as feminism in theology* lack a dimension of self-awareness because both philosophy and theology (for opposite reasons) have ignored the ideals which are shaped by *philosophy of religion*. Are there seriously important issues, problems and assumptions confronted by feminism in philosophy of religion that are common to the other branches of philosophy in which feminism has had a crucial role to play? Can these branches of philosophy be both helped by and mutually informative of feminism as a critical impetus for change, i.e. critical thought and action? It is hoped that the answer is "yes" to both questions. At least a positive answer to these questions would maintain a common horizon for both feminism and philosophy.

Works cited

Adams, Marilyn McCord. (1999) *Horrendous Evils and the Goodness of God*. Ithaca, NY: Cornell University Press.

Anderson, Pamela Sue. (1998) *A Feminist Philosophy of Religion: The Rationality and Myths of Religious Belief*. Oxford: Blackwell.

———. (2002) "Gender and the Infinite: On the Aspiration to be All There Is," *International Journal for Philosophy of Religion*, 50, pp. 1–18.

———. (2004a) "An Epistemological-Ethical Approach: Learning to Listen," In *Feminist Philosophy of Religion: Critical Readings*, edited by Pamela Sue Anderson and Beverley Clack. London/New York: Routledge, pp. 87–102.

———. (2004b) "Des contes dits au féminin: pour une éthique de nouveaux espaces." In *Espace(s) public(s), espace(s) privée(s): Enjeux et partages*, edited by Alban Cain. Université de Cergy-Pontoise, CICC. Paris, France: L'Harmattan, pp. 43–52.

———. (2005) "What's Wrong With the God's Eye Point of View: A Constructive Feminist Critique of the Ideal Observer Theory." In *Faith and Philosophical Analysis: The Impact of*

Analytical Philosophy on the Philosophy of Religion, edited by Harriet A. Harris and Christopher J. Insole. Aldershot, Hants: Ashgate, pp. 85–99.

———. (2006) "Life, Death and (Inter)subjectivity: Realism and Recognition in Continental Philosophy," *International Journal of Philosophy of Religion*, Special edition – Issues in Continental Philosophy of Religion: DOI 10.1007/s11153-006-0013-6.

Anscombe, Elizabeth. (1957) *Intention*. Oxford: Blackwell.

Augustine. (1961) *Confessions*. Translated by R. S. Pine-Coffin. Harmondsworth: Penguin Classics.

Dalmiya, Vrinda and Linda Alcoff. (1993) "Are 'Old Wives' Tales' Justified?" In *Feminist Epistemologies*, edited by Linda Alcoff and Elizabeth Potter. London: Routledge, pp. 217–41.

Deutscher, Penelope. (1997) *Yielding Gender: Feminism, Deconstruction and the History of Philosophy*. London: Routledge.

Fricker, Miranda. (1999) "Epistemic Oppression and Epistemic Practice," *Civilization and Oppression: Canadian Journal of Philosophy*, supplementary volume, ed. Catherine Wilson, pp. 191–210.

———. (2000) "Feminism in Epistemology: Pluralism without Postmodernism." In *The Cambridge Companion to Feminism in Philosophy*, ed. Miranda Fricker and Jennifer Hornsby, Cambridge: Cambridge University Press, pp. 146–65.

Fricker, Miranda and Jennifer Hornsby, ed. (2000) *The Cambridge Companion to Feminism in Philosophy*. Cambridge: Cambridge University Press.

Gatens, Moira. (1996) *Imaginary Bodies: Ethics, Power and Corporeality*. London: Routledge.

Grimshaw, Jean. (1986) "Autonomy and Identity in Feminist Thinking," in *Feminist Perspectives in Philosophy*, ed. Morwenna Griffiths and Margaret Whitford. Bloomington: Indiana University Press, pp. 90–108.

Helm, Paul. (2001) "The Indispensability of Belief to Religion," *Religious Studies*, 37, pp. 75–86.

Irigaray, Luce. (1991) *Marine Lover of Friedrich Nietzsche*, trans. Gillian C. Gill. New York: Columbia University Press.

Jaggar, Alison. (2000) "Feminism in Ethics: Moral Justification." In *The Cambridge Companion to Feminism in Philosophy*, ed. Miranda Fricker and Jennifer Hornsby, Cambridge: Cambridge University Press, pp. 225–44.

Jantzen, Grace. (1996) "What's the Difference: Knowledge and Gender in (Post) Modern Philosophy of Religion," *Religious Studies*, 32, pp. 431–48.

———. (1998) *Becoming Divine: Towards A Feminist Philosophy of Religion*. Manchester: Manchester University Press.

———. (2001) "What Price Neutrality? A Reply to Paul Helm," *Religious Studies*, 37, pp. 87–91.

Langton, Rae. (2000) "Feminism in Epistemology: Exclusion and Objectification." In *The Cambridge Companion to Feminism in Philosophy*, ed. Miranda Fricker and Jennifer Hornsby, Cambridge: Cambridge University Press, pp. 127–45.

Le Doeuff, Michèle. (1989) *The Philosophical Imaginary*, trans. Colin Gordon. London: The Athlone Press.

———. (1991) *Hipparchia's Choice: An Essay Concerning Women, Philosophy, etc.* trans. Trista Selous. Oxford: Blackwell; (forthcoming) republication with a slightly revised translation by the author. New York: Columbia University Press.

Lloyd, Genevieve. (1984; 1993) *The Man of Reason: "Male" and "Female" in Western Philosophy*. London: Routledge.

———. (2000) "Feminism in History of Philosophy: Appropriating the Past." In *The Cambridge Companion to Feminism in Philosophy*, ed. Miranda Fricker and Jennifer Hornsby, Cambridge: Cambridge University Press, pp. 245–63.

Longino, Helen. (1990) *Science as Social Knowledge: Values and Objectivity in Scientific Inquiry*. Princeton, NJ: Princeton University Press.

Midgley, Mary. (1994) *The Ethical Primate: Humans, Freedom and Morality*. London: Routledge.

———. (2004) *The Myths We Live By*. London: Routledge.

Murdoch, Iris. (1970) *The Sovereignty of Good*. London: Routledge & Kegan Paul.

O'Neill, Onora. (2000) *Bounds of Justice*. Cambridge: Cambridge University Press.

Potter, Elizabeth. (2006) *Feminism and Philosophy of Science: An Introduction*. London and New York: Routledge.

Quine, Willard van Orman. (1953) *From a Logical Point of View: Logico-Philosophical Essays*. New York: Harper & Row.

Soskice, Janet. (1992) "Love and Attention." In *Philosophy, Religion and the Spiritual Life*, ed. Michael McGee. Cambridge: Cambridge University Press, pp. 59–72; reprinted in *Feminist Philosophy of Religion: Critical Readings*, ed. Pamela Sue Anderson and Beverley Clack. London/New York: Routledge (2004), pp. 199–209.

Taliaferro, Charles. (2005) "The God's Eye Point of View: A Divine Ethic." In *Faith and Philosophical Analysis: The Impact of Analytical Philosophy on the Philosophy of Religion*, edited by Harriet A. Harris and Christopher J. Insole. Aldershot, Hants: Ashgate, pp. 76–84.

Whitford, Margaret. (1992) "The Feminist Philosopher: A Contradiction in Terms?," *Women: A Cultural Review*, 3:2, Autumn, pp. 111–20.

Williams, Patricia. (1991) *The Alchemy of Race and Rights*. Cambridge, MA: Harvard University Press.

Wylie, Alison. (2000) "Feminism in Philosophy of Science: Making Sense of Contingency and Constraint." In *The Cambridge Companion to Feminism in Philosophy*, ed. Miranda Fricker and Jennifer Hornsby, Cambridge: Cambridge University Press, pp. 166–84.

Note

*   [This essay, originally published as "Feminism in Philosophy of Religion," in *Explorations in Contemporary Continental Philosophy of Religion*, ed. Deane-Peter Baker and Patrick Maxwell, Amsterdam: Rodopi, 2003, 189–206, has been modified by Professor Anderson for this volume.]

Questions for reflection

1   How do social location and personal commitment shape gender and our ideals of gender? How do they shape beliefs about the divine?

2   Describe ways in which religion (or a particular religion) has provided legitimation for gender inequality. What are positive steps that can be taken to help remedy this problem?

3   How can critical reflection upon the epistemic injustices in philosophy of religion actually change it, especially its practices?

4   What can the feminist interventions into philosophy of science tell philosophers of religion about their own epistemic practices?

5   What points might be made by feminist philosophers with Quine's imagery about a boat at sea? For example, what is the point about objectivity?

Further reading

Pamela Sue Anderson (1998) *A Feminist Philosophy of Religion: The Rationality and Myths of Religious Belief*. Oxford: Blackwell. (This is the first monograph published explicitly as a prolegomenon to feminist philosophy of religion in the Anglo-American context. The author engages critically from a feminist standpoint, on the one hand, with theism and the traditional epistemological method for its justification modeled on philosophy of science and, on the other hand, with contemporary continental approaches to questions of rationality, religious desire, and divinity informed by psycholinguist and hermeneutical readings of myth and symbol. A distinctive focus on the philosophical imaginary of Western philosophy of religion is uniquely informed by Michèle Le Doeuff.)

Pamela Sue Anderson and Beverly Clack, eds. (2004) *Feminist Philosophy of Religion: Critical Readings*. London: Routledge. (This collection of critical readings offers a range of voices in response to the two monographs on feminist philosophy of religion published in 1998. Characterized by open debate and fundamental disagreements, it generates rich material for engaging critically with philosophy of religion. While the first part presents different approaches, the second part of the collection focuses on the core topics emerging in this field of lively philosophical debate.)

Lorraine Code (2006) *Ecological Thinking: The Politics of Epistemic Location*. New York and Oxford: Oxford University Press. (This recent work on feminist thinking addresses timely questions about the politics involved in our epistemic locations, shedding new light on how philosophers of religion might revise their practices to avoid perverse and oppressive assumptions, notably about their ideals and idealized situations. Code returns epistemological questions to the messier circumstances in which beliefs are typically formed and contested; our beliefs about God should not be excluded from the issues Code is raising in epistemology.)

Grace M. Jantzen (1998) *Becoming Divine; Towards a Feminist Philosophy of Religion*. Manchester: Manchester University Press, 1998. (A strongly argued and richly referenced case for the creation of new tasks in philosophy of religion on feminist grounds, this monograph, published in the same year as Anderson's, established Jantzen as a formidable figure in the transformation of the field. Jantzen insists on nothing less than becoming divine as the way to subvert the past preoccupation with death and a masculinist method of rigour and binary logic, replacing the latter with natality and a feminist concern for flourishing in this life.)

Elizabeth Potter (2006) *Feminism and Philosophy of Science: An Introduction*. New York and London: Routledge. (This clear, up-to-date introduction to feminist philosophy of science asks the question, "Can gender values influence scientific research and the research still be rational?" Potter demonstrates that "the mark of a feminist philosophy of science" is to give a positive reply to this question, distinguishing the points at which values can influence science. Potter's cogent work offers to feminist philosophers of religion, following or revising a scientific method, the framework to demonstrate both how religious values can and have influenced philosophy, and which of these values can be good for women.)

Mark Wynn (2005) *Emotional Experience and Religious Understanding: Integrating Perception, Conception and Feeling*. Cambridge: Cambridge University Press. (Although not directly influenced by feminists in philosophy of religion, Wynn's account of the role of emotion, properly reconceived, in matters of religion offers a significant argument against the separation of objective content and emotion or "inwardness." Having too often been associated with confusion due to feelings, women in particular should find Wynn's defense of an approach to philosophy of religion which incorporates the latter into both perception and conception a welcome alternative.)

Chapter 62

Sallie King

RELIGION AND A GLOBAL ETHIC

Sallie King is Professor of Religion at James Madison University. In this essay she introduces proposals for a Global Ethic—a "consensus statement on ethics from the world's
religions." The proposals are built upon the ethical common ground that exists among
the world's religions, including, among other things, the rights of humans to be treated
humanely and the "Golden Rule." While she sees these proposals as a start, she believes
that similar drafts by other religions should be submitted before a final draft is agreed
upon. In this way, those of all religions will take ownership in the process.

The central goal of the Global Ethic is to point to the common ethical ground that
already exists between people of all religions. Furthermore, it offers the following possibilities: (1) advancing the discussion on the issue of universality and relativism in ethics;
(2) lending support to international human rights; (3) providing a tool for healing interreligious relations; and (4) moving forward in establishing public school ethics education.
Professor King believes that such a Global Ethic is within reach.

The "Global Ethic" is a proposed consensus statement on ethics from the world's religions
that is emerging from the community of persons engaged in interreligious dialogue, most
prominently from the Parliament of the World's Religions held in 1993. Although it has
engendered considerable interest among those engaged in dialogue, heretofore it has
received little attention from comparative ethicists.

In this [essay] I will briefly describe the Global Ethic and then introduce themes in
comparative ethics that are inherent to a discussion of this Ethic. I will devote the greatest part of the [essay] to an examination of specific concerns about and potential uses of
the Global Ethic.

Proposals for a global ethic

There are two main proposals before the international community for instituting a global ethic. The better-known and more important proposal was initially elaborated by theologian Hans Küng of Tübingen, Germany, and then amended and subsequently issued by the Parliament of the World's Religions.[1] The second was composed by Leonard Swidler of the Department of Religion at Temple University in Philadelphia; it is discussed at conferences and on the Internet by way of Swidler's Center for Global Ethics. I shall briefly describe each proposal in turn.

Parliament of the World's Religions

> By a global ethic we do not mean a global ideology or a single unified religion beyond all existing religions, and certainly not the domination of one religion over all others. By a global ethic we mean a fundamental consensus on binding values, irrevocable standards, and personal attitudes (Küng and Kuschel 1993, 21; emphasis in original removed).

> We know that our various religious and ethical traditions often offer very different bases of what is helpful and what is unhelpful for men and women, what is right and what is wrong, what is good and what is evil. We do not wish to gloss over or ignore the serious differences among the individual religions. However, they should not hinder us from proclaiming publicly *those things which we already hold in common* and which we jointly affirm, each on the basis of our own religious or ethical grounds (Küng and Kuschel 1993, 22).

. . . The Global Ethic is intended as a consensus statement of the world's religions of that core area of their various ethical affirmations that they all hold in common. At the same time, it should not exclude the ethical values of the nonreligious. The Ethic declares: "We confirm that there is already a consensus among the religions which can be the basis for a global ethic—a minimal fundamental consensus concerning binding values, irrevocable standards, and fundamental moral attitudes" (Küng and Kuschel 1993, 18; emphasis removed). Thus, while claiming to represent absolute norms, the Ethic attempts to be no more than "minimal," allowing individual religions to express their own full ethical visions, as has always been the case.

What, then, does the Ethic affirm? It is based upon "a fundamental demand: Every human being must be treated humanely." Human rights are expressly affirmed ("Every human being without distinction . . . possesses an inalienable and untouchable dignity. And everyone, the individual as well as the state, is therefore obliged to honour this dignity and protect it. Humans must always be the subjects of rights.") The Ethic also affirms beneficence ("Possessed of reason and conscience, every human is obliged to behave in a genuinely human fashion, to do good and avoid evil!"), as well as positive and negative forms of the Golden Rule, of which, in his commentary, Küng cites versions from many religions:

There is a principle which is found and has persisted in many religious and ethical traditions of humankind for thousands of years: What you do not wish done to yourself, do not do to others! Or in positive terms: What you wish done to yourself, do to others! This should be the irrevocable, unconditional norm for all areas of life (Küng and Kuschel 1993, 23–24, 71–72; emphasis removed).

These fundamental principles then issue in the affirmation of "four irrevocable directives" that serve as "broad . . . guidelines for human behaviour." An obvious effort has been made to ground the four directives in the ancient ethical codes found in the world's religions. They are presented as follows.

1. "Commitment to a culture of non-violence and respect for life." Based upon ethical traditions found in the ancient codes of many religions that declare: "You shall not kill!" (or, in positive terms: "Have respect for life!"), this directive enjoins behavior that respects the human rights to "life, safety, and the free development of personality," declaring that conflicts "should be resolved without violence within a framework of justice" and that we should work "within an international order of peace which itself has need of protection and defence against perpetrators of violence." It further declares: "Armament is a mistaken path. . . . There is no survival for humanity without global peace!" and commends the development of a "culture of non-violence," extending to the protection of animals, plants, and the Earth.
2. "Commitment to a culture of solidarity and a just economic order." Based upon ancient religious codes that state: "You shall not steal!" (or, in positive terms: "Deal honestly and fairly!"), this directive states: "No one has the right to rob or dispossess in any way whatsoever any other person or the commonweal. Further, no one has the right to use her or his possessions without concern for the needs of society and Earth." Emphasizing that there will never be peace without a just economic order, it declares: "Wherever might oppresses right, we have an obligation to resist—whenever possible, non-violently." It advocates "a sense of moderation and modesty" instead of unbridled consumption.
3. "Commitment to a culture of tolerance and a life of truthfulness." Based upon ancient religious codes that declare: "You shall not lie!" (or, in positive terms: "Speak and act truthfully!"), this directive applies to everyone, but it singles out as bearing especially great responsibility for truthfulness persons who work for the mass media; artists, writers, and scientists; the leaders of countries; politicians and political parties; and representatives of religion.
4. "Commitment to a culture of equal rights and partnership between men and women." Although this directive seems to point in another direction, it is based upon the ancient religious codes' insistence: "You shall not commit sexual immorality!" (or, in positive terms: "Respect and love one another!"). The directive condemns all forms of sexual exploitation and sexual discrimination, including "patriarchal domination and degradation, which are

expressions of violence." It endorses both celibacy and marriage; the latter "should guarantee security and mutual support to husband, wife, and child. It should secure the rights of all family members" (Küng and Kuschel 1993, 24–34; emphasis removed).

Finally, the Ethic put forth by the parliament concludes with an appeal for a "transformation of consciousness" and a "conversion of the heart" to change life on Earth for the better (Küng and Kuschel 1993, 35–36; emphasis removed). It is followed by a list of signatories from religious leaders at the parliament, who included Baha'is, Brahma Kumaris, Buddhists, Christians, practitioners of native religions, Hindus, Jains, Jews, Muslims, neopagans, Sikhs, Taoists, Theosophists, Zoroastrians, and members of inter-religious organizations (Küng and Kuschel 1993, 37–39).

Swidler's proposal

Leonard Swidler's "Universal Declaration of a Global Ethic" grew out of his long commitment to ecumenism. In 1991, he and Hans Küng jointly published "Editorial: Toward a 'Universal Declaration of Global Ethos'" in the *Journal of Ecumenical Studies*, calling for the composition of a global ethic. The draft that resulted is especially well known in ecumenical circles.

Swidler's Universal Declaration is conceived as the same sort of document as that issued by the parliament: a consensus statement of the world's religions and a declaration of the shared core area of ethical commitment, conceived as "the fundamental attitude toward good and evil, and the basic and middle principles needed to put it into action." It finds in each religious tradition, "grounds in support of universal human rights, . . . a call to work for justice and peace, and . . . concern for conservation of the earth" (Swidler 1996b, 1). Like the parliament's Ethic, Swidler's declaration cites the Golden Rule as a fundamental principle that "has been affirmed in many religious and ethical traditions" (Swidler 1996b, 2).

The Universal Declaration affirms eight basic principles:

> (1) Because freedom is of the essence of being human, every person is free to exercise and develop every capacity, so long as it does not infringe on the rights of other persons. . . . (2) Because of their inherent equal dignity, all humans should always be treated as ends, never as mere means. . . . (3) Although humans have greater intrinsic value than non-humans, all such things, living and non-living, do possess intrinsic value simply because of their existence and, as such, are to be treated with due respect. . . . (4) Humans . . . seek to unite themselves, that is, their "selves," with what they perceive as the good: in brief, they love. . . . This loving/loved "self" needs to continue its natural expansion/transcendence to embrace the community, nation, world, and cosmos. (5) This expansive and inclusive nature of love should be recognized as an active principle in personal and global interaction. (6) Those who hold responsibility for others are obliged to help those for whom they hold responsibility. (7) Every human's religion or belief should be granted its due freedom and respect. (8) Dialogue . . . is a necessary means

. . . whereby men and women can live together on this globe in an authentically human manner. (Swidler 1996b, 2–3) . . .

Comments and preliminary remarks

. . . If I do not specify otherwise, in the following discussion the word "Ethic" and the
phrase "Global Ethic" refer to the parliament's version. With the endorsement of the
Parliament of the World's Religions, this version must be regarded as preeminent. Swidler's proposal will be referred to as the "Universal Declaration."

Themes in comparative religious ethics

Relativism versus absolutism

The Global Ethic is one chapter, now in the forefront, of the larger discussion in comparative ethics on the possibility of a common morality. Robert Merrihew Adams
defines "common morality" as "the large area of overlap of the diverse moralities of different people and groups of people" (Adams 1993, 99). This is precisely how the Global
Ethic is conceived, with the focus in its case upon the morality shared by the different
religions of the world. As the common morality discussion immediately raises all the
issues associated with the debate between relativism and absolutism, so does the Global
Ethic discussion.

There is no question that the Global Ethic supports a version of absolutism. The document's introduction states, "We affirm that there is an irrevocable, unconditional norm
for all areas of life" (Küng and Kuschel 1993, 15). The question, then, is: Does the Ethic
affirm absolutism in a way that is acceptable or unacceptable?

The Global Ethic seems to be uniquely constructed to address this challenge. On
the one hand, it claims to be the common ground that *already exists* among the world's
religions—the overlapping, shared area among the various particular ethical systems of
the religions. It "represents the minimum of what the religions of the world already have
in common now in the ethical sphere" (Küng and Kuschel 1993, 8). Thus, if this is correct, the Ethic does not impose anything on anyone but merely points to what is already
there; it is "not a new invention but only a new discovery" (Küng and Kuschel 1993, 71;
emphasis removed). On the other hand, its framers insist that while the Global Ethic is
necessary, it is not sufficient; it serves as a minimal base that the various particular ethical systems must elaborate and supplement. As Küng writes in his commentary:

> I should make it clear that even in the future, the global ethic cannot replace,
> say, the Torah of the Jews, the Christian Sermon on the Mount, the Muslim
> Qur'an, the Hindu Bhagavadgita, the Discourses of Buddha or the Sayings
> of Confucius. How could anyone come to think that the different religions
> wanted to avoid the foundation for their faith and life, thought and actions?
> These sacred scriptures offer as it were a maximal ethic, compared with
> which the Declaration Toward a Global Ethic can offer only a minimal ethic.
> (Küng and Kuschel 1993, 73)

Thus, the Global Ethic claims not to be in a *position* to displace any religion's ethical system. It is supplemental, not alternative. Each particular religion's ethical system is preserved inviolate. The only thing the Global Ethic aspires to negate and displace is ethical relativism.

In its negation of relativism, does the Global Ethic constitute a pernicious form of absolutism? There are three parts to the answer. First, if (and only if) the world's various religions are able to freely embrace the Ethic as representing a view consonant with their own can accusations of imperialism be avoided. Second, to the extent that the Global Ethic permits genuine diversity in those areas beyond the minimal common ground of shared ethical commitment that it declares inviolate, it again avoids imperialism. We will return to these two issues below.

The third issue involves whether it can be considered "pernicious absolutism" to declare inviolate the core area of commitment to nonviolence, justice, truthfulness, and the avoidance of sexual immorality. David Little provides a framework for discussing this issue by arguing in favor of an intuitionism in which human beings immediately know that certain things (his example is gratuitous torture) are "simply and transparently wrong in themselves." For Little, the recognition of such intuitions is a measure of both the mental and spiritual health of individuals and the viability of moral theories (1993, 80, 81). (Persons who violate them may be regarded, following Ronald Dworkin, as "criminals against humanity.") If we follow this approach, the question of whether the Ethic's declaration that nonviolence, justice, truthfulness, and sexual morality are absolute moral norms constitutes a pernicious form of absolutism hinges upon whether these values represent the fundamental ethical intuitions of humankind. Such a way of considering the issue seems to be very much in harmony with the thinking of the framers of both versions of the Ethic . . . .

Concerns regarding a global ethic

Process

Concerns about the process by which the Global Ethic has been composed and affirmed have been well explored by Paul Knitter and June O'Connor; these concerns generally amount to worries about control. O'Connor eloquently sums up the issue with the simple question, "Whose consensus?" (O'Connor 1994, 161).

Knitter, for his part, worries that neither the parliament nor Swidler are paying attention to the fact that "our language and our truth claims are not only *culturally* conditioned, but they are also *economically* and *politically* conditioned. . . . Our interpretations and our language . . . can . . . *oppress* the ability of others to assert and live their own truths" (Knitter 1995, 222). This is not a problem particular to the parliament and Swidler but a "systemic distortion," a pervasive tendency "within all use of language." However, the parliament and Swidler do need to take particular note, because:

> Whenever the language of civil discourse and religious dialogue comes forth
> from those who are in political or economic power, such language can all too
> easily be a ploy to maintain the structures of power. The discourse becomes
> "managerial"—it manages what will be discussed, the method for discus-

sion, and the goals of the discussion; what does not fit these determinations is judged, in the political discourse, as a disruptive "interest group"; in the religious dialogue it might be called a *closed* or *primitive* or *fundamentalist* or *polytheistic* or *feminist* perspective (Knitter 1995, 222–225).

This raises three important issues.

First, are the Parliament of the World's Religions and/or Swidler guilty of employing a "managerial" process in composing and revising their documents? . . . Of course, the key fact is that the document was already the product of extensive discussions among representatives of world religions before it ever reached the parliament. Moreover, anyone who has ever served on a committee can understand the impossibility of working in a milieu such as the parliament, with hundreds of participants attempting to revise a single document. Nevertheless, this process of consultation was not widely understood at the parliament, and the proceedings appeared to some to be quite "managerial" indeed (the drafting of the Ethic is discussed at length in Gómez-Ibáñez 1996 and Küng 1993). . . .

Fear that the powerful will use a Global Ethic against the less powerful follows directly from the above concern about managerial process. Margaret Farley expresses this concern succinctly:

> Feminists resist theories of common morality primarily because they have been harmful to women (and to some men). In the name of universality, of a total view of human nature and society, such theories have in fact been exclusive, oppressive, and repressive of women and of men who do not belong to a dominant group. Whether consciously or unconsciously, the formulators of such theories have inaccurately universalized a particular perspective; as a result, the needs and moral claims of some groups and individuals have been left out, their roles and duties distorted, and their full voices silenced. (Farley 1993, 171)

In short, history gives ample evidence that when a powerful group manages a discussion in such a way that they declare their perspective to be the universally correct one, the less powerful may well suffer the consequences: Women and minorities may be forced to "be" what hegemonic men think they are. . . .

Finally, in response to the "Whose consensus?" question, it must be said that the Global Ethic is clearly at best a consensus of the mainstream and the liberal or progressive wings of the various world religions. As Karl-Josef Kuschel reports: "Even at the planning stage, evangelical and fundamentalist church groups refused to collaborate in the Parliament" (Küng and Kuschel 1993, 95). Participants in interreligious dialogue know how difficult it can be to get evangelicals and fundamentalists to participate. We should be mindful of this and nuance Knitter's concern about managerial discourse that marginalizes groups including, as he specifies, "fundamentalists." For surely it is one thing to be pushed to the margins by a powerful group and another to refuse to participate in discussions when repeatedly invited. . . .

In sum, the Global Ethic is a liberal document, another piece of evidence that there is probably more unity among liberal adherents of a variety of the world's religions than there is between liberals and conservatives of the same religion. One might hope that fundamentalists in the many religions might be spurred on by the prospect of the Global Ethic to participate more readily in intrareligious dialogue. It is at least as likely, however, that this prospect will only further fortify resistance to such dialogue. Perhaps the Ethic is just one more stark reminder of the urgency and difficulty of intrareligious dialogue between liberals and conservatives. In the end, the identification of common ground between the latter seems a much more difficult task than the establishment of a Global Ethic that mainstream and liberal strands of the world's religions can endorse.

Content

1. Have the framers of the Global Ethic moved too quickly and facilely to pronouncements of moral similarity among the world's religions? O'Connor raises this issue in a way that will elicit sympathy from many scholars.

> The accent on similarity is likely to trouble scholars and teachers of the world's religions. For professors rightly resist easy generalizations from students who exude enthusiastic claims that "all the religions are really saying the same thing, deep down" or that "the world's religions are simply different paths to the same reality." On the contrary, scholars and teachers invite students to enter the complexity of the religions, to explore the contradictions of the religions, and to study the cultural and historical specificity of religions. They tend to discourage the discovery of similarity as too easy for the new student, as premature in effort, and thus as superficial and inaccurate in conclusion. (O'Connor 1994, 161)

Although this statement is certainly true in itself, I doubt that it applies to the Global Ethic. The latter does not express a claim that "all the religions are really saying the same thing, deep down" or that "the world's religions are simply different paths to the same reality." Indeed, the strength of the Global Ethic is its ability to point to a small but important area of claimed overlap in the area of ethics only, while stressing the uniqueness of the various religions in other respects. It says nothing whatsoever about soteriology, to which the above claims probably refer. So while it is true that scholars of world religions are allergic to the kind of statement that O'Connor mentions, the appropriate scholarly response to the Global Ethic, it seems to me, is a more careful scrutiny of the particular claim that the Ethic *does* make.

   2. *Is* there a consensus? The claim that the Ethic makes, of course, is that there is a particular area of unity among the world's religions constituted by a small set of normative ethical statements that they all affirm. The real issue, and one quite interesting and important for scholars to consider, is whether this claim is true. This, indeed, is the key to the entire Ethic.

   Consider, for example, nonviolence, the first of the four "irrevocable directives" of the Global Ethic. Is it the case that Buddhism and Islam have the same view on nonviolence? How could it be said that they do? Nonharmfulness (*ahimsa*) is the first of the Buddhist lay precepts, regarded as essential behavior for all Buddhists. The paradigm behavioral examples are the Buddha, who spoke against war and intervened to stop a war; and King Aśoka, who gave up war when he converted to Buddhism. In the case of Islam, although peace is a central value, war is still regarded as acceptable and even a duty under certain circumstances. The paradigm example is Muhammad, who led the fighting in many battles. How can it be said that the views of these two religions on the use of violence are the same? They certainly are not the same in their fully developed forms.

However, this is not the entire issue. The framers of the Global Ethic are attempting to determine whether language on the subject of nonviolence can be found that both Buddhists and Muslims (as well as others) could jointly affirm. This is another matter. For example, the parliament's version of the Ethic calls us to affirm a "commitment to a culture of non-violence and respect for life." This will satisfy Buddhists. On the other hand, the discussion of the directive states: "Persons who hold political power must . . . commit themselves to the most non-violent, peaceful solutions possible" (Küng and Kuschel 1993, 25). This allows considerably more maneuvering space and might make the Ethic acceptable to those who are not absolute pacifists but note that the use of violence is never directly condoned—this allows the Ethic to remain acceptable to pacifists. . . .

We know what it means if language cannot be found that all will affirm: it means there is no unity on this point of moral behavior. What, however, does it mean if the language can be carefully adjusted and nuanced until all major religions can affirm it? Does it mean that we have found the point of shared moral vision? Or does it mean only that we are benefiting from the abilities of some very skilled wordsmiths, or possibly very skilled scholars of comparative religious ethics? I think we need not be so cynical. The evidence of the Global Ethic seems to confirm Robert Merrihew Adams's assertion that there is a core of common morality (lying, stealing, and killing are generally held to be wrong) that shades off into areas that are morally less clear (white lies, property rights, and euthanasia are debated) (1993, 95). Assuming that this is the case, it would indeed require skilled wordsmiths and ethicists to carefully formulate just the right language, even given a true area of common morality.

3. The parliament's Global Ethic seems to have some difficulty with coherence. On the one hand, the Ethic fundamentally intends to represent "the minimum of what the religions of the world already have in common now in the ethical sphere" (Küng and Kuschel 1993, 8; emphasis removed). On the other hand, Gómez-Ibáñez relates that he and Küng agreed that "we must challenge the world with the ethic"; "the ethic should raise the level of ethical standards and expectations" (Gómez-Ibáñez 1996, 4, 5). In other words, there is an is/ought struggle being waged within the pages of the Ethic, an attempt to reflect what "already" is hand in hand with an attempt to raise standards beyond where they presently are. These are two quite different tasks! . . .

Potential uses of a global ethic

One of the reasons comparative religious ethicists look with interest toward interreligious dialogue is that such dialogue constitutes an arena of conversation, which may result in practical efforts to address concrete human needs.

Indeed, the framers of the Global Ethic intend very consciously to make a real difference in the world. After sketching the all-too-familiar ills—economic, political, ecological, and social—that beset us, the text of the Ethic reads:

On the basis of personal experiences and the burdensome history of our planet we have learned

> that a better global order cannot be created or enforced by laws, pre-scriptions, and conventions alone;
> that the realization of peace, justice, and the protection of earth depends on the insight and readiness of men and women to act justly;
> that action in favour of rights and freedoms presumes a consciousness of responsibility and duty, and that therefore both the minds and hearts of women and men must be addressed;
> that rights without morality cannot long endure, and that there will be *no better global order without a global ethic*. (Küng and Kuschel 1993, 20–21)

Thus, a global ethic, if it fulfills the intention of its creators, should contribute toward the development of a better global order.

Of what practical use could a global ethic be? I will discuss six such uses, which fall into the three categories of theoretical-educational-cultural, political, and religious.

Theoretical-educational-cultural

1. In direct proportion to the breadth of dissemination it receives, the Global Ethic will inevitably stimulate thought and discussion regarding the possibility of a common ethic and the similarity or uniqueness of ethical systems cross-culturally. Indeed, the Ethic may be the only document directed at a broad, popular audience to directly address this theme from the point of view of an affirmation of a common ethic. Given the pervasiveness in modern Western culture of both subliminal and overt messages espousing cultural and ethical relativism, this document has the potential to level the playing field somewhat, to give those wishing to resist relativism some materials to draw upon in the debate.

2. Marcus Braybrooke suggests that the Global Ethic "could play an important part in Values Education, perhaps particularly in Britain where there is widespread concern about moral standards" (1994, 101). The same could be said of the United States! Indeed, if broadly affirmed by groups representative of a diverse society, the Global Ethic could be used as the basis of ethical instruction in public schools within pluralistic societies such as the United States and Great Britain. . . .

3. As O'Connor points out, the Global Ethic helps "to highlight the important distinction between the ethical and the political-legal arenas of life." She elaborates upon the usefulness of this distinction:

> People who are not in touch with the moral and ethical heritages of human life and those who ignore, dismiss, or repudiate those heritages tend to rely on individual rights, contractual agreements, political arrangements, and cultural conventions for a sense of what is good. Yet history documents an enduring tension between the ethical and the legal, a tension that makes visible a difference between them. Resistance movements of diverse sorts (democratic, socialist, anarchic), civil rights and other human rights movements, ethnic pride movements, and women's liberation movements, for example, illustrate

> in multiple and various ways a single point: social and civil laws and cultural customs can be morally unjustifiable, ethically intolerable. (1994, 159)

Public schools, in the United States and other countries, have not been known for their readiness to teach materials potentially challenging to the political status quo. Nonetheless, given some of the values that American society publicly embraces, the schools need to be continually pressed on this point. Consideration of the Global Ethic with respect to the ethical-legal distinction would make a very appropriate activity for public school celebration of Martin Luther King Jr. Day, for example.

Thinking along the same lines as O'Connor, Khalid Duran states that in the Muslim world the Global Ethic could become a focal point for the "age-old conflict between the scholars of the law and the teachers of ethics who feel that stagnation of the law has led to what are, from an ethical point of view, absurdities. . . . Muslims who put ethics above and the law beneath will be thrilled to hear of this project. Those who take the shari'a [law] as their shield without understanding the difference between shari'a and akhl q [ethics] will be apprehensive" (1996, 3). It is clear that from Duran's perspective, the influence of the Global Ethic will be beneficial to this debate.

4. If (and only if) the Global Ethic were to be broadly embraced and affirmed, it would succeed in negating the specter of relativism without thereby establishing a pernicious absolutism. Indeed, the Global Ethic's primary usefulness comes from its ability to rein in both extreme reactions to pluralism. To relativists it says: "There is an absolute"; to exclusive absolutists it says: "The truth that you treasure is also found elsewhere, it is not your exclusive possession."

Political

5. The Global Ethic has an important affinity with the UN Universal Declaration of Human Rights. In places, the Ethic uses explicit "rights" language:

> All people have a right to life, safety, and the free development of personality in so far as they do not injure the rights of others. No one has the right physically or psychically to torture, injure, much less kill, any other human being. And no people, no state, no race, no religion has the right to hate, to discriminate against, to "cleanse," to exile, much less to liquidate a "foreign" minority which is different in behaviour or holds different beliefs (Küng and Kuschel 1993, 25).

Indeed, the Global Ethic is in part conceived as supporting the Universal Declaration of Human Rights; as Küng comments, "a declaration on a global ethic should provide ethical support for the UN Declaration on Human Rights, which is so often ignored, violated and evaded. Treaties, laws, agreements are observed only if there is an underlying ethical will really to observe them" (Küng and Kuschel 1993, 56).

The UN declaration on human rights, and associated international covenants, have already faced considerable scrutiny on the question of universality versus cultural relativism. Do international human rights covenants simply impose a particular, Western set of ethical and political views upon the world? The Consultation Group on Universality vs. Relativism in Human Rights, sponsored by the Project on Religion and Human Rights, studied this question and found the following:

> In analyzing the positions of speakers in the international debate about universality vs. relativism in human rights, it found that state actors often use the language of cultural particularity and relativism as a screen to perpetuate and defend human rights violations for self-interested political ends. It also found, by contrast, that nongovernmental organizations and individuals tend to use elements of local culture to translate human rights into cultural idioms so that they might be more effectively recognized and respected. . . . Moreover, the Group found that many oppressed people(s)—regardless of their cultural imbeddedness and differences—have little or no difficulty with the notion of universal human rights: the Group regarded this fact as one of the most decisive in the debate. (Twiss and Grelle 1995, 26–27)

These observations readily apply to the human rights aspects of the Global Ethic as well. . . .

Simply put, no one wants to be tortured, injured, killed, hated, discriminated against, "cleansed," exiled, or liquidated, and they do not want these things done to others they care about. Whether, on this basis, they follow a subliminal principle of universalization, or whether they are simply looking at the situation pragmatically, the result is the same: People all over the world recognize that if they don't want their own basic human rights violated, their best bet is to try to prevent all human rights violations. Hence, the nearly universal acceptance of the principles and language of human rights. . . .

Religious

The Global Ethic could be useful for overcoming interreligious suspicion and divisiveness, as follows.

6. On October 25, 1993, the Harrisonburg, Virginia, *Daily News Record* carried a story on its (lower) front page under the headline "Girl Scouts Vote to Allow Members to Drop God from Pledge." Part of the text read: "Promising to serve Allah instead of God, or simply to serve, is now OK for Girl Scouts, but the decision to allow the choice was not universally cheered Sunday by people outside the scouts. 'This is one more organization that has become morally relativistic and that's deeply disappointing,' said Tom Minnery, a spokesman for Focus on the Family, an evangelical Christian organization based in Colorado Springs, Colo." (cited in King 1995b, 214).

This conservative Christian clearly believes that to serve Allah or "simply to serve" is less moral, in some sense, than to serve the Christian God. Thus, to him, and to those he represents, non-Christian morals are inferior to Christian morals. Indeed, the notion that those whose lives are based on other values and religions are moral at all seems alien to his way of thinking. This identifies a real problem: the inability of conservatives within every religion to recognize the morality of the other *as* morality.

The Global Ethic strikes directly at this point. If the more conservative followers of the world's religions came to see that the morality of the "other" shares significant moral ground with "my" or "our" morality, their automatic impulse to reject and often vilify what is different from "me" and what "we" believe would be undercut at the base. Thus, the Global Ethic could be a powerful teaching tool to convey the message that "my" morality overlaps in important ways with the morality of that "other" religion of which I am suspicious and mistrustful; my conclusion can only be that the "other" is not so entirely "other" as I had thought. Given the deep human tendency to fear and reject the "other," a foundational area of unity, publicly acknowledged by the world's major religious leaders and reiterated frequently in each religion's teachings, could be powerful medicine indeed.

Conclusion

We have seen throughout this chapter that the Global Ethic has the potential to constitute a breakthrough on the question of universality and relativism in ethics. In addition, it provides important support for international human rights; it is a highly useful tool for healing interreligious relations; and it may offer a way forward for establishing public school ethics education. However, none of this potential can be realized unless the Ethic is genuinely embraced by a great and diverse array of representatives of the world's religions after a period of careful scrutiny and consideration. On the contrary, if the Ethic is pushed forward by any of its composers, endorsers, or supporters without proper scrutiny and voluntary affirmation by the world's religions, its fundamental nature will be transformed, it will lose every shred of its efficacy, and it will become nothing but an expression of imperialism.

It is to be hoped that those now responsible for the Ethic will ensure that it receives the most open and transparent scrutiny possible, that both positive and negative responses receive wide circulation, and that alternative drafts from other religions be circulated as well; in short, that no one could have cause to complain of being railroaded into approving a document that might be difficult for them to accept on the basis of their own religious values. The Global Ethic is worthless if it is not genuinely embraced by all faiths. In the end, a rush to agreement that is not based upon the identification of true common ground could only lead to disappointments and feelings of betrayal. We would be much better off with no Global Ethic than with a false one. But we would also, I believe, be better off with a true Global Ethic than with none at all. And, indeed, a true Global Ethic does seem to be within reach.

Note

1.   The author wishes to express her very great appreciation to Jim Kenney and Daniel Gómez-Ibáñez for their separate and very helpful comments to her on the topic of the parliament and the resulting global ethic.

References

Adams, Robert Merrihew. 1993. "Religious Ethics in a Pluralistic Society." In *Prospects for a Common Morality*, edited by Gene Outka and John P. Reeder Jr., 93–113. Princeton: Princeton University Press.

Braybrooke, Marcus. 1994. "Report on the Chicago Parliament of the World's Religions: Declaration Toward a Global Ethic." *Faith and Freedom* 47 (Autumn and Winter):91–102.

Duran, Khalid. 1996. "Leonard Swidler's Draft of a Global Ethic: A Muslim Perspective." On-line posting, http://rain.org/~origin/gethic/geth004.

Farley, Margaret A. 1993. "Feminism and Universal Morality." In *Prospects for a Common Morality*, edited by Gene Outka and John P. Reeder Jr., 170–190. Princeton: Princeton University Press.

Gómez-Ibáñez, Daniel. 1996. "Moving Towards a Global Ethic." On-line posting, http://www.silcom.com/~origin/sbcr/sbcr231.

Hick, John. 1996. "Towards a Universal Declaration of a Global Ethic: A Christian Comment." On line posting, http://rain.org/~origin/gethic/geth003.

King, Sallie B. 1995a. "A Buddhist Perspective on a Global Ethic and Human Rights." *Journal of Dharma* 20, 2 (April-June):122–136.

———. 1995b. "It's a Long Way to a Global Ethic: A Response to Leonard Swidler." *Buddhist-Christian Studies* 15:213–219.

Knitter, Paul F. 1995. "Pitfalls and Promises for a Global Ethics." *Buddhist-Christian Studies* 15:222–229.

Kung, Hans. 1993. "The History, Significance, and Method of the Declaration Toward a Global Ethic." In *A Global Ethic: The Declaration of the Parliament of the World's Religions*, edited by Hans Küng and Karl-Josef Kuschel, 43–76. New York: Continuum.

Küng, Hans, ed. 1996. *Yes to a Global Ethic*. New York: Continuum.

Küng, Hans, and Karl-Josef Kuschel, eds. 1993. *A Global Ethic: The Declaration of the Parliament of the World's Religions*. New York: Continuum.

Little, David. 1993. "The Nature and Basis of Human Rights." In *Prospects for a Common Morality*, edited by Gene Outka and John P. Reeder Jr., 73–92. Princeton: Princeton University Press.

Mutombo, Nkulu. 1996. "The African Charter on Human and Peoples' Rights: An African Contribution to the Project of Global Ethic." On-line posting, http://astro.temple.edu/~dialogue/Center/mutombo.html.

O'Connor, June. 1994. "Does a Global Village Warrant a Global Ethic?" *Religion* 24:155–164.

Outka, Gene, and John P. Reeder Jr., eds. 1993. *Prospects for a Common Morality*. Princeton: Princeton University Press.

Suu Kyi, Aung San. 1996. "Towards a Culture of Peace and Development." In *Yes to a Global Ethic*, edited by Hans Küng, 222–236. New York: Continuum.

Swidler, Leonard. 1996a. "Center for Global Ethics." On-line posting, http://rain.org/origin/gethic/geth-022.

———. 1996b. "Universal Declaration of a Global Ethic." On-line posting, http://astro.temple.edu/~di-alogue/Center/declarel.html.

Swidler, Leonard, and Hans Küng. 1991. "Editorial: Toward a 'Universal Declaration of Global Ethos.'" *Journal of Ecumenical Studies* 28, 1 (Winter):123–125.

Twiss, Sumner B., and Bruce Grelle. 1995. "Human Rights and Comparative Religious Ethics: A New Venue." *The Annual of the Society of Christian Ethics*: 21–48.

Questions for reflection

1   What is a Global Ethic? What are some of its features?

2   Why do you think a Global Ethic has received so little attention from comparative ethicists?

3   What concerns might be raised concerning the institution of a Global Ethic? Can they be overcome? Why or why not?

4   Must a version of moral absolutism be held in order for a Global Ethic to be realized? Explain.

5   Do you believe that a Global Ethic can be genuinely embraced by leading representatives of the world's religions? Why or why not?

Further reading

Hans Küng and Karl-Josef Kuschel, eds. (1993) *A Global Ethic: The Declaration of the Parliament of the World's Religions*. New York: Continuum. (Includes the Declaration of a Global Ethic produced at the Parliament of the World's Religions.)

Hans Küng, ed. (1996) *Yes to a Global Ethic*. New York: Continuum. (Includes a "Yes!" to the Declaration of a Global Ethic produced at the Parliament of the World's Religions as well as a variety of voices on the meaning of a Global Ethic from leaders of the world's religions.)

Gene Outka and John P. Reeder Jr., eds. (1993) *Prospects for a Common Morality*. Princeton, NJ: Princeton University Press. (Includes a variety of positions on how far moral judgments are binding across cultures and traditions.)

Chapter 63

Roger S. Gottlieb

RELIGION AND THE
ENVIRONMENT

Roger S. Gottlieb is Professor of Philosophy at Worcester Polytechnic Institute. In this selection he notes how religious groups are becoming more environmentally conscious, while environmental politics are becoming more religious. First, the environmental movement "has challenged and changed religion throughout the world," and many religious leaders across the globe are taking action, realizing the plight of the earth and its inhabitants. Religious organizations have become a part of the environmental movement, and new theologies of nature have emerged whose adherents get involved in political life. Confronted with an environmental crisis, many religious groups are not only advocating an "ecotheology" but an "ecojustice" as well.

But just as religions have, to some extent, "turned Green," so too "Green politics" have, in significant ways, become religious. Whether connected with a particular religious group or not, "when environmental politics are motivated by a concern for life as a whole or ecosystems above and beyond the human," they are, argues Gottlieb, "profoundly spiritual and, in a deep and general sense, *religious*." Furthermore there is, he maintains, a growing awareness among environmentalists of the role of spiritual values—values which foster a sense of self that "acknowledges dependence, mutuality, and happiness *without* requiring endless 'development,' soulless gadgetry, and the elimination of other life forms."

Religion and environmental politics are now authentic partners. As a result they can, like never before in history, bring about beneficial environmental changes.

I

. . . [I]n the environmental movement there is a dramatic confirmation of the major ideas of this book [*Joining Hands*]. World-making politics and emancipatory religion have joined in environmental politics and ecological spirituality. Theology has been transformed by political awareness and action. And political ideology has transcended the constraints of individual rights and group self-interest. If the civil rights struggle shows religion transforming the world of politics and feminist theology demonstrates the political transformation of religion, then the environmental movement reveals the two working together in critically important ways, at times virtually fusing to form a historically unprecedented phenomenon.

II

Modern environmentalism has challenged and changed religion throughout the world. Awakened by environmental activists, religious institutions have been moved by the seriousness of pollution, climate change, endangered species issues, resource depletion, and overpopulation. Religious leaders, theologians, and local clergy have signed on to the recognition that the earth as a whole is in an unprecedented predicament. Even if this response is not uniform and absolute, it is still extremely widespread.

Using language that would not be out of place in a Greenpeace broadside, Rabbi Arthur Hertzberg, vice president of the World Jewish Congress, has warned: "Now when the whole world is in peril, when the environment is in danger of being poisoned, and various species, both plant and animal, are becoming extinct, it is our Jewish responsibility to put the defense of the whole of nature at the very center of our concern."[1] In 1990, Pope John Paul II spoke of the worldwide threat caused by "*a lack of due respect for nature . . . the plundering of natural resources and . . . the widespread destruction of the environment.*"[2] The Dalai Lama, in his foreword to the first major anthology of writings on Buddhism and ecology, wrote: "The Earth, our Mother, is telling us to behave. All around, signs of nature's limitations abound. Moreover, the environmental crisis currently underway involves all of humanity, making national boundaries of secondary importance."[3]

Yet claims that we are in ecological hot water do not, in themselves, make for a particularly religious contribution to environmentalism. Part of what is so important about that contribution is that it brings to the context a new language, expressing a distinct point of view. For instance, Bartholomew I, ecumenical patriarch of the Eastern Orthodox Church's more than 100 million members, wrote in 1997:

> To commit a crime against the natural world is a sin. For humans to cause species to become extinct and to destroy the biological diversity of God's creation . . . to degrade the integrity of Earth by causing changes in its climate, by stripping the Earth of its natural forests . . . to contaminate the Earth's waters, its land, its air, and its life, with poisonous substances: these are sins.[4]

Conversely, as a Protestant theologian and environmental activist puts it: "The specter of ecocide raises the risk of deicide: to wreak environmental havoc on the earth is to run the risk that we will do irreparable, even fatal harm to the mystery we call God."[5]

A religious perspective applied to the earth, to a "nature" that because of human action has become the "environment," offers insights and prompts emotions that a purely secular story cannot. Spiritual language offers the environmental movement a means to express its passion, hope, and love, regardless of whether activists accept the explicit details of one theology or another. Instead of a large rock with vegetation growing on it, the world becomes "creation" or "the goddess." We experience the world as "holy"—and mean we believe in a God who created it, or that it is of "ultimate concern," or simply that it is heartbreakingly beautiful and infinitely worth cherishing and preserving. Commonplace processes—the co-evolution of a rain-forest plant with its pollinating insect partners, how wetlands clean water, the murmur of whale songs—become "daily miracles."

When religion engages in environmental concerns, the customary boundaries of "religious issues" in political life are decisively broken. Asserting that environmental degradation is not only a health danger, an economic catastrophe, or an aesthetic blight but also *sacrilegious*, *sinful*, and an *offense against God* catapults religions directly into questions of political power, social policy, and the overall direction of secular society. Religious organizations now take it as given that their voices deserve to be heard on issues such as energy, economic development, population, transportation, industrial production, and agriculture. These topics are, to put it mildly, a far cry from the usual public religious concern with abortion, school prayer, tax exemptions for churches, Holocaust memorials, national Christmas trees, or even pornography in the media.

. . .

The secular left, too, has begun to realize that religious organizations are part of the environmental movement. In the May 2001 issue of *The Nation*, environmentalist David Helvarg has listed actions by the National Council of Churches, the Evangelical Environmental Network, and the Jewish Council of Public Affairs in an article titled, "Bush Unites the Enviros."[6] Over the past several years, all of the major environmental magazines—including *Sierra*, *Audubon*, *Amicus Journal*, and *E Magazine*—have run features on the rise of religious environmentalism.[7] They have recognized that from the National Religious Partnership for the Environment, with constituent groups numbering 100 million Americans, to the New England Friends' recent collective commitment to "speak truth to power" in protecting human health and the environment, self-defined religious groups are now major players on the environmental stage.

On the religious side, the environmental crisis is seen by some thinkers as the critical test of their faith's contemporary relevance. As Catholic priest and cultural historian Thomas Berry, whose own attempt to offer a new understanding of humanity's place in the cosmos has been enormously influential, says: "The future of the Catholic church in America, in my view, will depend above all on its capacity to assume a religious responsibility for the fate of the earth."[8] Bearing this out, the web site of the Lutheran Church offers study material on "health and the environment." One situation offered for reflection asks what a "Christian response" would be to a family whose children are suffering from environmentally caused asthma and who cannot move because no one will buy their house, which is surrounded by polluting industries.[9] For Lutherans, in other words, the interlocking contexts of health, the economy, and pollution are now part of their ministry—as much as sexual ethics or the discipline of prayer.

These few instances of the extremely numerous meetings between religion and environmentalism further exemplify modern religion's political transformation. Historically, the dominant attitudes of religious leaders toward modern industrialism—that is, to the immediate source of the environmental crisis—was positive. Once it was clear that capitalism and democracy were here to stay, most churches saw increases in scientific knowledge and technical expertise as promising a better life. Provided that industrial workers achieved a reasonable standard of living, technology meant progress. Challenges to the modern economy came from poets like Blake and Wordsworth, anti-Communist Western Marxists like Max Horkheimer and Herbert Marcuse, philosophers like Martin Heidegger, and imaginative nature lovers like Thoreau and John Muir. As in the case of feminism, it was only after a political movement brought global ecological crisis to the fore of public discussion that religion jumped on board.[10] Yet jump on board it did, and with an energy and acumen that has, so far, outpaced corporations, organized labor, the academic community, and such professionals as doctors or lawyers.

Besides an acknowledgment of the severity of the crisis, new theologies have been devised in which the earth, or nature, or our fellow creatures are recognized as carrying a divine and sacred meaning. Such theologies are in stark contrast to what has been the dominant position of world religions, especially those of the West. Despite the presence of occasional dissenting voices, Western religions long stressed the gap between humans and the rest of creation, espousing ethical systems in which concern for the nonhuman was peripheral at best. Just as feminism has required a new valuation of women, so the ecological crisis has led to a new—or at least a revised—sense of our proper relationship to nature.

These new theologies sometimes originate in attempts to recover the few nature-respecting elements that can be found in tradition. Thus, Lynn White, whose 1967 essay criticizing the "anthropocentrism" (human-centeredness) of Western religions helped initiate a dialogue on the subject that continues to this day, did not suggest a total rejection of Christianity. Rather, he proposed St. Francis's love of animals and the whole of physical creation as an alternative to the reigning Christian attitudes.[11] Similarly, essayist and farmer Wendell Berry challenged dominant interpretations of the biblical passage often cited as divine justification for human dominion, God's command to Adam: "Go forth, subdue the earth, and master it" (Genesis 1:28). By stressing the importance of other passages of the Torah, especially Deuteronomy 8:10 ("Thou shalt bless the lord thy God for the good land which He has given you"), Berry teaches that biblical ethics requires us to live "knowingly, lovingly, skillfully, reverently" rather than "ignorantly, greedily, clumsily, destructively." In the first case, our use of Creation will be a "sacrament," in the latter, a "desecration."[12] Jewish writers have recovered biblical and Talmudic doctrines stressing the sinfulness of squandering resources (*bal tashchit* ["do not waste"]), holidays celebrating the birthday of the trees, and biblical restrictions on the exploitation of animals (if your ox is threshing your grain, you can't muzzle him, even if he ends up eating some of it!). These traditions are then applied to a host of contemporary ecological issues, such as recycling, carpooling, the disposal of toxics, the waste of food, factory farming, and the protection of old-growth forests.[13]

Buddhist teacher Thich Nhat Hanh has adapted the mindfulness practice of Buddhist *gathas* (short prayers or poems used to focus attention) to include ecological awareness. For instance, while planting trees, one may recite: "I entrust myself to Buddha;/Buddha entrusts himself to me./I entrust myself to Earth;/Earth entrusts herself to me."[14] The National Council of Churches offers the following prayer to be included in First Sunday after Easter as part of a service called "Witnessing to the Resurrection: Caring for God's Creation":

> We pursue profits and pleasures that harm the land and pollute the waters.
> We have squandered the earth's gifts on technologies of destruction.

> The land mourns, and all who live in it languish; together with the wild
> animals and the birds of the air, even the fish of the sea are perishing.[15]

Or in the words of the general secretary of the United Methodist Church: "Our
biblical tradition affirms that God calls people of faith to defend and protect all of God's
creation, both human and non-human."[16]

III

Feminist versions of Christianity and Judaism may, in good conscience, focus their efforts
on creating inclusive God language, getting women into positions of power in religious
organizations, and criticizing the sexism of past doctrine. By contrast, the new theologies of nature necessarily involve their adherents in political life. Once religions assert
that "ecology and justice, stewardship of creation and redemption are interdependent"[17]
or that "[w]here human life and health are at stake, economic gain must not take precedence,"[18] they are—like it or not—headed for a confrontation with the dominant
powers of economics and politics.

In this confrontation, religious discourse has and will continue to play a significant
role. If this is not a universal religious response, it is an extremely widespread one. As
one journalist puts it: "More and more it appears religion and ecology are walking hand-
in-hand. The sermon titles are the Kyoto treaty on global warming and endangered
species protection."[19] . . .

Buddhists in both the United States and Japan have actively resisted the storage and
transportation of dangerous nuclear material, while in Germany, Buddhists have challenged both the ethics and the environmental consequences of factory farming.[20] Christian
groups have formed coalitions to reduce global warming, have held religious services to
celebrate lakes, and have authorized study groups to reduce the environmental impact
of church buildings. National and international organizations have formed to radically
transform theological education to take account of the environmental crisis.[21]

In these and thousands more examples, it is clear that to be ethical in relation to
environmental issues is also to be political. The economy, the government, the military, health care, transportation, and just about everything else are called into question.
Believers may still pray for a pure heart and train their awareness mindfully, but environmental problems simply cannot be solved through individual action. . . .

As they confront the environmental crisis, many religious groups throughout the
world advocate not only the values of "ecotheology" but the pursuit of "ecojustice," i.e.,
the seamless blending of concern for earth's creation and human beings, the biotically
marginalized and the socially powerless, endangered species and endangered human
communities. This blending includes issues of class, race, gender, and indigenous rights,
alongside more familiar concern with "nature." It requires—and is achieving—a comprehensive understanding of political life that joins religious visionaries with the most
sophisticated and principled of secular political movements.

Consider the comprehensive notions of environmental racism and environmental
justice, phrases that refer to the fact that racial minorities and the poor in the United
States, just like indigenous peoples worldwide, are exposed to a great deal more pollution than are the racially and economically dominant groups. Lacking social power, their

lives are held as less valuable; the environmental crisis is written on—and in—their bodies.[22] During the last thirty years, a comprehensive concern with environmental justice developed with the constant input of black religious social activists.[23] The historic 1987 report *Toxic Wastes and Race*, the first comprehensive account of environmental racism, was researched and written by the commission for racial justice of the United Church of Christ.[24] This report detailed the fundamental racial and class inequality in the siting and cleanup of hazardous wastes in the United States. Its lead investigator, Reverend Benjamin Chavis, was instrumental in connecting the civil rights, religious, and environmental communities of the South. Four years later, in 1991, the very first principle of the historic National People of Color Environmental Leadership Summit proclaimed that "environmental justice affirms the sacredness of mother Earth, ecological unity and the interdependence of all species, and the right to be free from ecological destruction."[25] A few years later, President Clinton ordered government agencies to take environmental justice issues into account in their programs.

Alongside racial and class issues, an ecojustice perspective focuses on the ways in which Western thought has historically equated women and nature and devalued both. The initial justification for this dual subordination was found in the claim that both lacked the holiness or closeness to God of men. Later, it was men's (self-proclaimed) rationality that was thought to justify masculine social privileges. In terms of concrete social policy, contemporary Western schemes of economic development for poor countries often have disastrous effects on Third World women, whose lives and livelihood are tied to their immediate surroundings. For example, in poorer countries men plant cash crops, but women plant subsistence crops. When export agriculture promoting a single agricultural commodity takes over, women in the local community are hurt more than men. Awareness of the combination of the cultural devaluation of women with their economic subordination helps create an "ecofeminism" that has powerful religious and political implications.[26]

The religious presence in environmental politics, like a good deal of the entire environmental movement, not only breaks barriers between religion and politics, theology, and social activism but also helps develop a world-making *political* agenda that may avoid being limited to one or another particular social group. Religions have a powerful contribution to make here. Insofar as they have a mandate, it is, after all, from God: a God who is not tied, one hopes, to the valid but inevitably partial concerns of one political group or another. Of course, in the past much of traditional religion was rabidly sectarian, racist, colonialist, or just downright nasty. But religions that have been deeply affected by the liberal and radical politics of the last two centuries have moved beyond those moral failings, or at least are trying to.

. . .

It is simply no longer true of religions, as political radicals have been claiming for nearly two centuries: "They concentrate on the individual and not social institutions; they are unwilling to envision radical social changes; they cannot see the links among different moral and political concerns; they seek changes in attitudes or values rather than in basic social institutions; they are unwilling to learn from the insights of world-making political theory." Such criticisms may well continue to apply to some groups, but they have become completely inapplicable to others. The great divide between religion and progressive politics, weakened by Protestant abolitionism, the social teachings of the Catholic Church, and the social gospel of the late nineteenth century, cracked by Gandhi and [Martin Luther] King and the religious presence in the peace and anti-apartheid movements, has in the global environment movement finally been decisively overcome.

IV

If religions have to some extent turned Green, Green politics are in some important ways religious. In the contemporary environmental movement, even those groups totally unconnected to religiously identified organizations are often practicing a new kind of politics, one in which a religious or spiritual sensibility is present. It is this simultaneous transformation of both religion and political activism that helps make environmental politics dramatically new and historically important.

The politics I have in mind here include but are not limited to government programs and laws. Politics, as political scientist Paul Wapner says, also "takes place in the home, office, and marketplace."[27] At one end of the spectrum of activities and concerns that make up Green politics, we find direct actions aimed at stopping some particular instance of "development" or some concrete industrial practice. When the women of India's Chipko movement physically encircle the trees of their beloved forest (which provides herbs, fodder for animals, and firewood) to prevent them from being chopped down, when Greenpeace plugs the outflow pipe of a chemical factory, when thousands protest "free trade" agreements that would cripple communities' rights to limit ecological degradation, environmental politics means putting your body on the line to protect both other species and human beings. At the other end of the spectrum, we find attempts to influence world culture through teaching, writing, films, Internet sites, poetry, and art. In between these two poles are a host of governmental and non-governmental policies, institutions, and activities: from government regulation of pesticide use to the creation of wildlife refuges, from lobbying to protect wetlands to resisting environmental racism, from researching the duplicity of the chemical industry to organizing neighbors to clean up a local river. In this light, non-governmental organizations like transnational environmental groups "contribute to addressing global environmental problems by heightening world-wide concern for the environment. They persuade vast numbers of people to care about and take actions to protect the earth's ecosystems."[28]

What gives this wide spectrum of Green politics a religious or spiritual dimension? Well, in some cases this dimension will not be present. If we seek to preserve a forest so that we can hunt big game in it (one of the original motivations for wildlife preservation efforts)[29] or if our sole concern with pesticides is their effect on human health, then our approach to environmental issues is purely "instrumental." It is, we might say, simply a continuation of the "anthropocentric" attitudes that have marked Western culture for at least 3,000 years, attitudes resting on the belief that only human beings are morally valuable. In this form, caring for a river or an endangered species is little different from concern over auto safety or tennis elbow—valuable and important, to be sure, but not historically new or spiritually significant.

If however, we are at least partly motivated by "ecocentric" or biocentric values, if there is an element of "deep ecology" in our passion, if we see nature as a mother, a lover, or a partner, then the situation is different[30]—for then we are expressing a distinct vision of the value of our surroundings and a new and powerful sense of the meaning of human identity itself.[31] When environmental politics are motivated by a concern for life as a whole or ecosystems above and beyond the human, I believe, they are profoundly spiritual and, in a deep and general sense, *religious*.

Whether known as deep ecology, ecofeminism, bioregionalism, the land ethic, or simply the special place that some beach, forest, or mountain has in our hearts, this sensibility involves a passionate communion with the earth. What is "deep" about this perspective is the experience—and the conviction—that our surroundings are essential to who we are. And this is not just because they are useful, but because we are tied to them by invisible threads of inspiration, memory, esthetic delight, emotional connection, and simple wonder. Sky and earth, bird and fish, each leaf on each tree—without them, we could not be ourselves. As one of the architects of modern environmental politics, David Brower, wrote: "To me, God and Nature are synonymous."[32] Poisoning nature thus not only leads to the concrete suffering of soaring cancer rates and our children's asthma but creates the emotional and spiritual crisis comparable to what would happen if our families were murdered, our cathedrals bombed, or our holy books burned. . . .

This spiritual vision of environmental politics also provides a crucial alternative to the destructive values of the global marketplace, values that privilege economic growth, rising exports, and individual autonomy above all else. The "religion" of modernity demands control over nature and a model of development that turns every meadow and village into the same old mall. Nature is thought of as a thing, an element to be used. Selfhood is defined by consumption, and there is a widespread attempt to broadcast excessive styles of consumption throughout the world.

Sulak Sivaraksa, Buddhist environmental activist from Thailand, writes that "Western consumerism is the dominant ethic in the world today . . . The new 'spiritual advisors' are from Harvard Business School, Fletcher School of Law and Diplomacy, and London School of Economics. . . . The department stores have become our shrines, and they are constantly filled with people. For the young people, these stores have replaced the Buddhist temples."[33] The drive toward globalization, says a Third World Christian theologian, is often seen as a sort of new religion: "it has its God: profit and money. It has its high priests: GATT [General Agreement on Tariffs and Trade], WTO [World Trade Organization], IMF-WB. It has its doctrines and dogmas: import liberalization, deregulation . . . It has its temples: the super megamalls. It has its victims on the altar of sacrifice: the majority of the world—the excluded and marginalized poor."[34]

Referring to the conflict between native peoples and economic development over the proposed building of a massive, ecosystem-destroying and native-people-uprooting hydroelectric dam in James Bay, Ontario, David Kinsley argues:

> If hunting animals is a sacred occupation among the Mistassini Cree, building dams to harness power for electricity is equally sacred for many members of modern industrial society. . . . the conflict between the Cree and [Ontario political leader] Bourassa, then, is not so much a conflict between a religious view and a secular view as it is a conflict between two contrasting visions of the nature of human beings and human destiny, that is, two conflicting myths about the place of human beings in the natural order, two contrasting ecological visions.[35]

Charlene Spretnak describes the difference between these two visions: "Modern culture . . . is based on mechanistic analysis and control of human systems as well as Nature . . . nationalistic chauvinism, sterile secularism, and monoculture shaped by mass media. . . . Green values, by contrast, seek a path of 'ecological wisdom' and attempt to integrate freedom *and* tradition, the individual *and* the community, science *and* Nature, men *and* women."[36] To accomplish that goal, said leader of the German Green Party Petra Kelly, "We must learn to . . . recognize the interconnectedness of all living creatures, and to respect the value of each thread in the vast web of life. This is a spiritual perspective, and it is the foundation of all Green politics."[37] Or as Earth First! activist Mark Davis said, in explaining why he broke the law in trying to prevent the further expansion of a ski resort into mountains revered by the Hopi and Navajo, "[T]he bottom line is that those mountains are sacred, and that what has occurred there, despite our feeble efforts, is a terrible spiritual mistake."[38]

In fact, spiritual values in general and the value(s) of nature in particular give us a way out of the ecocidal cul-de-sac of the endless mall. They help us to develop an alternative sense of self that acknowledges dependence, mutuality, and happiness *without* requiring endless "development," soulless gadgetry, and the elimination of other life forms. This alternative allows the withdrawal of psychic energy from a cultural and economic system that threatens the earth and people alike. In the same vein, a spiritual relationship with the natural world allows us to orient political struggle in a direction not tied (or at least less tied) by psychic addiction to the very social system that destroys us. Greens have, some observers believe, "moved beyond materialist values while at the same time embracing some preindustrial values derived from indigenous non-European cultures. These value shifts have been tied to specific issues that are crucial for the Greens but often ignored by the Democratic Left."[39] The interface of spiritual and Green values has helped create the emerging discipline of "ecopsychology," which is oriented to understanding the psychic costs of our alienation from the rest of the earth, and the psychologically and spiritually healing experiences that come from lessening that alienation.[40] . . .

Environmentalists can be dramatically different from each other. They include those who long nostalgically for a hunter-gatherer lifestyle, those who support Aldo Leopold's call for "an individual responsibility for the health of the land,"[41] as well as hard-headed city planners eager to replace cars with bikes, integrate communities with an ecofriendly Internet, and design apartment complexes with organic rooftop gardens. Yet the comprehensive values referred to by Spretnak [and] Kelly . . . resonate throughout much of the movement. These include a distrust of uncontrolled economic growth and thoughtless technological innovation, in combination with the belief that both the market and technology should serve collective rather than narrowly human interests. There is a corresponding belief that has clear spiritual overtones: the idea that human life has other purposes than the acquisition of power and wealth. It is stressed, rather, that we live for the development of wisdom, peacefulness, harmonious coexistence with the earth, and the quiet (itself a radical demand in these deafening times) enjoyment of life. Journalist Mark Dowie suggests that despite the enormous diversity of the environmental movement, a number of common principles can be found. Along with familiar political goals, these include an ethical and spiritual redefinition of human beings as part of nature and not its master or the only part that really matters.[42]

What applying these values would mean is often far from clear. Since the ecological crisis is a product of our entire civilization, broader in scope and more universally threatening than any other form of political injustice or collective irrationality, the transformation called for is correspondingly large. We might take as a hopeful example the enormous social success of Kerala, India's southernmost state, which has dramatically increased literacy and education, reduced infant mortality, raised life expectancy to nearly Western levels, improved women's social position, and cultivated a culture of intellectual and artistic engagement *without* high levels of industrialization or the raising of per capita income. We might consider Colombia's village of Gaviotas, where appropriate technology has led to a sustainable life in the midst of a formerly barren wasteland, sustainable crops help regenerate a rain forest, and children's swings power the water pumps.[43] We might notice how the citizens of Maine, who suffer each year through several weeks of highly annoying and virtually impossible-to-stop black flies, reject the use of potentially dangerous chemical pesticides, even if it will cost them tourist income. "If people can't live with the flies," some say, "they just shouldn't come here."[44]

We can see the new sensibility expressed in political campaigns aimed at inclusive goals of protecting endangered species, preserving the culture and ecosystems of indigenous peoples, and preventing industrial pollution. In one powerful example, international activity mobilized in response to the Narmada River Valley Project in India.[45] Called by critics the "world's greatest planned environmental disaster," the project envisaged thirty major, 135 medium, and 3,000 minor dams throughout Central India. If completed as planned, it would have displaced close to 400,000 people, destroyed wildlife habitat, and flooded some of the last remaining tropical forests in India. As early as 1977, local opposition formed when people realized that there was in fact no land available for the residents who were to be displaced—that they would simply join the tens of millions of other "refugees from development." During the next decade and a half, opposition grew and took a variety of forms: road blockades, hunger fasts, demonstrations at state capitals, and massive gatherings at sites that were to be flooded. A ring of international solidarity formed. Japanese environmentalists persuaded their government not to advance money to it, while American activists pressured the World Bank. The San Francisco-based International Rivers Project organized financial and technical aid. In 1992, facing reports that the entire project was marked by fraud and incompetence, legislators in Finland, Sweden, and the United States asked the World Bank not to lend any more money. In this heartening case, the more familiar dimension of human rights mixed with concern for other species; citizens of different countries and continents gave time, energy, and money to support those of another. A vital mix of personal and group self-interest, abstract political principle, and transpersonal celebration of the earth took shape. . . .

In all these struggles, environmentalism is not simply interest-group politics applied to forests and toxic incinerators. Rather, it is informed by a comprehensive vision of human identity and of how that identity is interrelated with the universe as a whole. This vision deserves to be considered, in the broadest sense, religious.

V

When the United Church of Christ talks about racism in citing toxic waste sites, when religious organizations instruct the president of the United States on global warming, when Buddhist monks protest globalization, they show how contemporary religious and spiritual voices have adopted some of the conceptual tools of progressive political theory. Broad orientations toward human identity (we are kin to the rain forest); or to moral values (we have obligations to other species and to humans injured by our industrial practices); or to the meaning of life or the cosmos (our task is to be part of life, we are to be loving stewards to the earth) have always been part of religion. However, when the critique of dams, the diagnosis of racism in the placing of Superfund sites, and analysis of the economic and human costs of globalization are added in, something new is afoot.

For example, consider the Dalai Lama's suggestion that "[w]hen we talk about preservation of the environment, it is related to many other things. Ultimately, the decision must come from the human heart. The key point is to have a genuine sense of universal responsibility, based on love and compassion, and clear awareness."[46] This statement correctly points out that each person who opposes the juggernaut of industrialism must make a personal commitment, with no guarantee of "success," to a daunting task. However, the statement ignores the fact that *personal* awareness, love, and compassion are extremely limited if they are not joined by an understanding of—and an attempt to change—our collective institutions. The Dalai Lama—exactly like the author of this [essay] and, in all probability, the reader as well—plugs into the same electronic grid as everyone else, burns fossil fuels to fly from place to place, and employs the resources of our environmentally unsustainable society in his struggle to save some vestige of his people's national identity. His personal love and compassion, in short, do not keep him from contributing to the mess! Understanding the problems, criticizing them fully, and offering alternatives requires a "social" ecology whose nuts-and-bolts account of the economic and political sources of ecocrisis take its place alongside appeals to personal love, compassion, and awareness. . . .

Whether those who use such language to describe social problems needing religious attention are ministers, professors of political science, or paid organizers, the language itself is the stuff of progressive political theory and originates in secular political movements. Without these perspectives, the new values of environmental theology simply cannot comprehend the real world.

. . .

VI

We can now return to the question of religious pluralism, of how politically oriented religious groups can function in modern society without undermining the enlightenment values of religious freedom, free speech, and a reasonable separation of church and state.

Religious participation in environmental politics, it seems to me, has solved this problem: if not by addressing it theoretically then—more important—in practice. The common bond of love of the earth and the use of the vocabulary of divinity, sacredness, and ultimate concern far outweighs the names of gods, the holidays celebrated, or the precise form of prayer. In interfaith partnerships for environmental reform and programmatic statements, religious environmentalists have realized the goal . . . : to hold fast to ethics while allowing for a pluralism of metaphysics. . . .

Religions now enter the modern world as legitimate and authentic partners in the political drama of making—and remaking—the world. Further, their values now color the world's most important political movement. Surprisingly, as time progresses it is getting harder and harder to tell the two of them apart.

Notes

1   In Libby Bassett, ed., *Earth and Faith: A Book of Reflection for Action* (New York: United Nations Environmental Programme, 2000), p. 11.

2   Pope John Paul II, "The Ecological Crisis: A Common Responsibility," in Roger S. Gottlieb, ed., *This Sacred Earth* (New York: Routledge, 1995), p. 230. Emphasis in original.

3   Foreword to Allan Hunt Badiner, ed., *Dharma Gaia: A Harvest of Essays in Buddhism and Ecology* (Berkeley, CA: Parallax Press, 1990).

4   Bassett, *Earth and Faith*, p. 52.

5   Mark Wallace, *Fragments of the Spirit* (New York: Continuum, 1996), p. 141.

6   *Nation*, May 7, 2001.

7   For example, *Sierra* (November-December 1998).

8   Thomas Berry, "Ecology and the Future of Catholicism," in Albert P. LaChance and John E. Carroll, eds., *Embracing Earth: Catholic Approaches to Ecology* (Maryknoll, NY: Orbis Books, 1994), p. xi.

9   See www.elca.org.

10 A range of information and sources can be found in Gottlieb, *This Sacred Earth.*

11 Lynn White, "The Historical Roots of Our Ecological Crisis," *Science* 155 (3767), March 12, 1967.

12 Wendell Berry, *The Gift of Good Land* (San Francisco: North Point Press, 1981), pp. 317–318.

13 Ellen Bernstein and Dan Fink, *Let the Earth Teach You Torah* (Philadelphia: Shomrei Adama, 1992).

14 Quoted in Gottlieb, *This Sacred Earth*, p. 449.

15 National Council of Churches web site, www.nccusa.org.

16 See www.umc.org.

17 American Baptist Churches, "Creation and the Covenant of Caring," in Gottlieb, *This Sacred Earth*, p. 239.

18 "Safety and Health in Workplace and Community," United Methodist Book of Resolutions, 1996, www.umc.org.

19 Justin Torres, "Religion and Environmentalism: Match Made in Heaven?" January 19, 2000, www.cns.com.

20 For a range of political activities of Buddhists see Christopher S. Queen, ed., *Engaged Buddhism in the West* (Boston: Wisdom, 2000).

21 For example, Theological Education to Meet the Environmental Challenge, www.webofcreation.org, has organized dozens of major conferences and offers resources to seminaries, divinity schools, and so on.

22 Of the now enormous literature on environmental racism and environmental justice, one might start with Robert D. Bullard, *Unequal Protection: Environmental Protection and Communities of Color* (San Francisco: Sierra Club Books, 1994); and James Lester, David Allen, and Kelly Hill, *Environmental Injustice in the United States: Myths and Realities* (Boulder: Westview Press, 2001).

23 Deeohn Ferris and David Hahn-Baker, "Environmentalists and Environmental Justice Policy," in Bunyan Bryant, ed., *Environmental Justice: Issues, Policies, and Solutions* (Washington, DC: Island Press, 1995).

24   Commission for Racial Justice, *Toxic Wastes and Race in the United States* (New York: United Church of Christ, 1987).

25   Reprinted in Gottlieb, *This Sacred Earth*, p. 634.

26   See discussion in Peter Wenz, *Environmental Ethics Today* (New York: Oxford University Press, 2001), pp. 200–208. Also, Vandana Shiva, *The Violence of the Green Revolution* (Atlantic Highlands, NJ: Zed Books, 1991). For a useful overview of the by now large ecofeminist literature, see Victoria Dayton, "Ecofeminism," in Dale Jamieson, ed., *A Companion to Environmental Philosophy* (London: Blackwell, 2001).

27   Paul Wapner, *Environmental Activism and World Civic Politics* (Albany: State University of New York Press, 1996), p. 41.

28   Ibid., p. 42.

29   Raymond Bonner, *At the Hand of Man: Peril and Hope for Africa's Wildlife* (New York: Knopf, 1993).

30   Macy, *World as Lover, World as Self*; Carolyn Merchant, *Earthcare: Women and the Environment* (New York: Routledge, 1999); Riane Eisler, *The Chalice and the Blade: Our History, Our Future* (San Francisco: Harper and Row, 1988).

31   Of many sources, see George Sessions, ed., *Deep Ecology for the Twenty-First Century* (Boston: Shambala, 1994). For connections with traditional religions, see David Barnhill and Roger S. Gottlieb, eds., *Deep Ecology and World Religions: New Essays on Common Ground* (Albany: State University of New York Press, 2001).

32   David Brower, *Let the Mountains Talk, Let the Rivers Run* (New York: HarperCollins, 1995), p. 176.

33   Sulak Sivaraksa, "The Religion of Consumerism," in Kenneth Kraft and Stephanie Kaza, eds., *Dharma Rain: Sources of Buddhist Environmentalism* (Boston: Shambala, 2000), pp. 178–179.

34   Mary John Mananzan, "Globalization and the Perennial Question of Justice," in Mary Hembrow Snyder, ed., *Spiritual Question for the Twenty-First Century* (Maryknoll, NY: Orbis Books, 2001), p. 157.

35   David Kinsley, *Ecology and Religion: Ecological Spirituality in Cross-Cultural Perspective* (Englewood Cliffs, NJ: Prentice-Hall, 1995).

36   Charlene Spretnak, "The Spiritual Dimension of Green Politics," in Gottlieb, *This Sacred Earth*, pp. 532–535.

37   Kelly, *Thinking Green*, p. 37.

38   Bron Taylor, "Earth First! From Primal Spirituality to Ecological Resistance," in Gottlieb, *This Sacred Earth*, pp. 545–546.

39   Daniel Neal Graham, "The Theory of a Transformational Political Movement: Green Political Theory," in Stephen Wolpert, Christ Slaton, and E. W. Schwerin, eds., *Transformational Politics: Theory, Study, and Practice* (Albany: State University of New York Press, 1998), p. 75.

40   Theodore Roszak, Mary E. Gomes, and Allen D. Kanner, eds., *Ecopsychology: Restoring the Earth, Healing the Mind* (San Francisco: Sierra Club Books, 1995).

41   Aldo Leopold, *A Sand County Almanac* (New York: Oxford University Press, 1949), p. 258.

42   Mark Dowie, *Losing Ground: American Environmentalism at the Close of the Twentieth Century* (Cambridge: MIT Press, 1996), p. 226.

43   See McKibben, *Hope, Human and Wild*; Alan Wiesman, *Gaviotas: A Village to Reinvent the World* (Chelsea, VT: Chelsea Green Publishing, 1998).

44   Sue Hubbell, *Broadsides from the Other Orders: A Book of Bugs* (New York: Random House, 1993), pp. 74–89.

45   See accounts of this in Bruce Rich, *Mortgaging the Earth*, pp. 251–253; and Madhava Gadgil and Ramachandra Guha, "Ecological Conflicts and the Environmental Movement in India," in Dharam Gahi, ed., *Development and Environment: Sustaining People and Nature* (Oxford and Cambridge: Blackwell, 1994).

46   Bassett, *Earth and Faith*, p. 144.

Questions for reflection

1   What are some ways religious adherents and environmentalists have joined forces, as described by Professor Gottlieb? In your opinion, is this a positive move? Why or why not?

2   List some ways in which Green politics have become religious as described by Gottlieb. Do you think these "advances" are beneficial to the movement?

3   Gottlieb maintains that "environmentalism is not simply interest-group politics applied to forests and toxic incinerators. Rather, it is informed by a comprehensive vision of human identity and of how that identity is interrelated with the universe as a whole. This vision deserves to be considered, in the broadest sense, religious." In what sense is the vision religious?

4   What are some practical ways, not mentioned in this essay, that a local religious group can work together with local environmentalists in your area? What are some real and lasting benefits of these particular groups joining forces in your community?

Further reading

Forum on Religion and Ecology: www.environment.harvard.edu/religion (An excellent web source and the largest multireligious project attempting to produce comprehensive resolutions to our environmental problems.)

Roger S. Gottlieb, ed. (2003) *This Sacred Earth: Religion, Nature, Environment.* 2nd edn. London: Routledge. (A compilation of scripture, institutional statements, and essays on religious environmentalism drawing from a wide variety of religious traditions and perspectives.)

Roger S. Gottlieb (2004) *Joining Hands: Politics and Religion Together for Social Change.* Boulder, CO: Westview Press. (Examines the union of religion and politics in tackling social issues and advancing social change; the essay above was taken from this book.)

Roger S. Gottlieb, ed. (2006) *The Oxford Handbook of Religion and Ecology.* New York: Oxford University Press. (Leading scholars provide the definitive overview of recent developments in the interaction between religion and ecology.)

Roger S. Gottlieb (2006) *A Greener Faith: Religious Environmentalism and Our Planet's Future.* New York: Oxford University Press. (A clearly articulated examination of environmental theology, ethics, and activism among the major religious traditions and religion's role in the future of global environmental stewardship.)

Bron Taylor, ed. (2005) *Encyclopedia of Religion and Nature.* New York: Continuum International Publishers. (Through various movements, persons, and ideas, this two-volume work provides an exploration of religion and nature in light of the ecological crisis.)

GLOSSARY

Absolute 1. Not relative; 2. Ultimate Reality ("The Absolute").

Actual infinite A completed whole whose members cannot increase or decrease in number.

Advaita Vedānta (Sanskrit terms) A monistic (non-dual) school of Hindu thought which includes the view that only Brahman exists ("Advaita" means "non-duality" and "Vedānta" refers to the sacred Hindu scriptures, the Vedas).

Agnosticism The view that one cannot be certain whether God exists; it is often contrasted with theism—belief in God—and atheism—disbelief in God.

Allah "God" in Arabic—the exclusive God of Islam.

Analects The collected sayings of Confucius, dating to *c.* 500 BCE.

Anthropic principle The term is used differently by atheists and theists. For theists, it is the view that the initial conditions and constants of the universe are finely tuned for human life—a view which suggests an intelligent designer of the universe. For atheists, it is the view that we should not be surprised that the initial conditions and constants of the universe are such that life is possible; for if they were otherwise, we would not be here to observe them.

Anthropomorphism Refers to the tendency to understand God, or the divine, in human categories or as having human properties. Derived from two Greek words: anthropos ("human being") and morphe ("form").

Apophatic theology A theology which attempts to describe God in terms of what God is not rather than in terms of what God is (also referred to as *via negativa*—Latin for "negative way"); it is common among the mystics.

A posteriori Known or knowable on the basis of experience; knowledge that is based entirely on sense experience.

A priori Known or knowable independent of, or prior to, experience; knowledge that is not based on sense experience.

Argument A claim and the attending premise(s) which support the claim.

Artha (Sanskrit term) Success; one of the four central goals of Hinduism, along with dharma, kāma, and moksa.

Atheological Reflecting the atheistic viewpoint.

Atman (Sanskrit term) The ultimate Self, which is held to be identical to all "selves" and to Brahman.

Avatar (Sanskrit term) An incarnation of God.

Axiom A self-evident proposition or principle to which an inference may be deduced.

Basic belief A belief which is not based on other beliefs (non-inferential knowledge); for example, the belief that there are other minds besides one's own.

Beatific vision The immediate awareness and knowledge of God one will enjoy, as perfect happiness, seeing God face to face in heaven.

Big Bang theory A scientific theory attempting to explain the beginning of the universe; according to the current standard account, the universe (time, space, matter, and energy) exploded into existence as a singularity roughly 13 billion years ago and has continued to expand ever since.

Bodhisattva One who has reached enlightenment but forfeits nirvana in order to help others reach enlightenment.

Brahma The creator God of Hinduism. Brahma, Shiva (sustainer God), and Vishnu (destroyer God) comprise the Hindi triad of central cosmic deities.

Brahman (Sanskrit term) In Hinduism, Ultimate Reality; the power underlying the cosmos; absolute divine reality. For Advaita Vedānta Hindus, Brahman is impersonal and identical with Atman; for others, such as Ramanuja, Brahman is a separate and personal God.

Buddha The "enlightened" or "awakened" one; the term is sometimes used to refer to the founder of Buddhism—Siddhartha Guatama (563–483 BCE)—and sometimes refers to other persons who have achieved a state of enlightenment.

Contingent An event is contingent if it might not have occurred; a proposition is contingent if its denial is logically possible; a being is contingent if it could have not existed—if it is not logically necessary (the opposite of a Necessary Being).

Cosmological argument An argument for the existence of God in which it is maintained that since there is a cosmos which exists, rather than just nothing, it must have been caused by something beyond it, namely God.

Counterfactuals of freedom Propositions about what a free creature would freely choose to do in any given situation.

Creationism In Judaism, Christianity, and Islam, the belief that the universe was miraculously created by God. The term is also used to refer to the special acts of God in creating specific kinds of living organisms in contrast to standard evolutionary theory (when used this way, it is sometimes called "scientific creationism").

Dao (or Tao) (Chinese term) "Way"; it has different meanings for different traditions: for the Confucians it refers to the life of virtue; for the Daoists it refers to the fundamental reality governing the universe.

Deductive argument An argument in which if the premises are true, the conclusion must follow (put differently, to affirm the premises and deny the conclusion leads to a contradiction). Here is a standard example: All people are mortal; Socrates is a person; therefore, Socrates is mortal.

Deism The belief that God exists, but such belief is based on reason rather than revelation or faith and also includes the view that the deity does not interfere with the creation.

Design argument (or teleological argument) An argument for the existence of God based on the observation of (apparent) design, order, or purpose exhibited in the world.

Dharma (Sanskrit term) In Hinduism, it means religious duty (the virtuous person willingly fulfills the duty of one's caste); one of the four central goals of Hinduism, along with artha, kāma, and moksa. In Buddhism, it is a central term that has many meanings, including the Buddha's teaching, law, conduct, duty, morality, and nature.

Epistemology The domain of philosophy that is primarily concerned with knowledge—its origins, nature, extent, and justification.

Evolution The theory that all living things have evolved from pre-existing forms through purely natural processes, most notably through the mechanism of natural selection.

Fideism The view that religious belief should be based on faith rather than reason.

Foundationalism The view in epistemology that knowledge and belief rest on the foundation of basic beliefs.

Free will defense A response to the atheist's charge that the following two propositions entail a contradiction: (1) God exists and (2) evil exists.

Free will theodicy Unlike the free will defense, a free will theodicy is an attempt to justify God's ways to human beings (from the Greek terms theos = god and dike = justice) whereby evil is a genuine possibility given free will.

Henotheism A view in which one affirms or gives allegiance to one deity but does not deny the existence of other deities.

Incarnation The enfleshment of God in human form; for Christians, Jesus Christ is the incarnation of God.

Irreducible complexity A system which consists of multiple interacting parts that contribute to the basic function of the system whereby the removal of any of its parts would cause the system to quit functioning; Michael Behe argues that such systems exist in living organisms, and that they could not have been produced gradually via minor, successive modifications of previous systems since any precursor would be by definition nonfunctional.

Isotropy Being independent of direction; having the same value when measured in different directions.

***Kalam* cosmological argument** A version of the cosmological argument for God's existence in which it is claimed this since whatever begins to exist needs a cause, and since the universe began to exist, the universe must need a cause; it is further argued that this cause must be a personal creator.

Kāma (Sanskrit term) Pleasure; one of the four central goals of Hinduism, along with artha, dharma, and moksa.

Many-worlds hypothesis The view that there are a large number of universes, perhaps an infinite number of them, and the fundamental parameters of physics vary from universe to universe (also called the "many universes hypothesis," the "multi-universe hypothesis," and the "world-ensemble hypothesis").

Master morality Nietzsche's concept of a morality developed by the ruling class based on strength and power; it is a morality of the noble human being who understands the "good" as the strong and powerful and the "bad" as the impotent and cowardly. It is the opposite of slave morality.

Middle knowledge The view that God knows all counterfactuals of freedom and thus can direct the future according to his desires with this information in mind.

Moksa (Sanskrit term) Liberation from samsāra; one of the four central goals of Hinduism, along with artha, dharma, and kāma.

Moral argument for God An argument for God's existence in which it is claimed that, since the existence of objective moral values requires an objective grounding and since objective moral values exist, there must also exist an objective grounding which we call God.

Natural theology The view that the existence of God can be demonstrated through the use of reason unaided by special revelation (e.g., the design argument, the *kalam* argument, etc.).

Necessary Being A being which, if it exists, exists necessarily; that is, it cannot not exist.

Nirvana (Sanskrit term which literally means extinction) In Buddhism, it is the complete extinction of suffering and the causes of suffering; it is the highest form of happiness.

Noetic (from the Greek word nous = mind/intellect) Relating to the mind or its contents (e.g., beliefs, desires, etc.).

Ontological argument An a priori argument in which it is claimed that understanding the concept of God demonstrates the existence of God.

Open theism A fairly recent view in which God is understood to be omniscient, but that omniscience does not entail having exhaustive knowledge of the future since the future does not yet exist such that it could be known (even by an omniscient being); God lacks foreknowledge.

Oscillating universe A model of the universe in which it goes through periods of expansion and contraction in which gravity causes the universe to contract, and some mechanism (yet unknown) causes it to expand; this cycle continues indefinitely.

Panentheism The view that God permeates the world but, unlike pantheism, God is not identical with the world.

Pantheism The view that everything is God and God is everything; usually includes the notion that the "all" is ultimately impersonal. Derived from two Greek terms: pan ("all") and theos ("God").

Possible world Used in conjunction with the modal notions of possibility, necessity, and contingency; the way the world might have been, whereby each of an infinite number of logically possible states of affairs is taken to be a "world" (the actual world is understood to be one of the many ways the world might have been). Also relates to the modal status of propositions: a possible proposition is one that is true in at least one possible world, a necessary proposition is one that is true in all possible worlds, and a contingent proposition is one that is true in some possible worlds and false in other possible worlds.

Potential infinite A finite number which can continue to increase over time by adding yet another number, but which has no end.

Problem of evil Includes a variety of arguments against belief in God given the existence of evil in the world; typical categories include logical, evidential, and existential arguments.

Process theism A form of theism (originated by Alfred North Whitehead and further developed by Charles Hartshorne) in which God is interdependent with the world and is also affected by those in the world; God and the world evolve together.

Properly basic belief A basic belief which one is warranted in holding.

Reincarnation The view that a person is reborn after death in a different body, perhaps many times and in many different forms (also used as a synonym for transmigration, although the latter often includes rebirth of one's soul occurring in animals as well).

Resurrection The view that an individual, after dying, is fully and completely brought back to life; the same body is involved in the process.

Samsāra (Sanskrit term) The world of phenomenal experiences whereby the soul passes through a perpetual cycle of death and rebirth.

Second law of thermodynamics Processes occurring in a closed system tend to move toward a state of thermodynamic equilibrium—a state of maximum disorder and minimum usable energy (i.e., entropy—a measure of the amount of energy in disordered form in a system—increases over time).

Simple foreknowledge The view that God has complete knowledge of the future in terms of what will happen, but he lacks hypothetical knowledge of the future—that is, he lacks knowledge of what would happen in any given future situation, when the situation in question never in fact arises.

Singularity The initial instant of time; on one model of the universe, this was a state of infinite density and infinite temperature.

Slave morality Nietzsche's concept of a morality developed by the weak and powerless which is based on utility—the "good" is what is most useful for the group; this is the opposite of master morality.

Specified complexity A feature of an event in which the following characteristics are exhibited: it is complex and not easily repeatable through chance (i.e., highly improbable), and it is specified in that it matches an independently identifiable pattern. Proponents of Intelligent Design theory maintain that specified complexity is a reliable indicator of design by an intelligent agent.

Teleological argument (See design argument)

Theodicy An argument aimed at justifying the goodness of God given the existence of evil in the world.

Trinity The view in historic Christianity that within the nature of the one God there are three eternal and coequal persons: Father, Son, and Holy Spirit.

Upanisads A revered portion of the Vedas.

Vedas Ancient sacred scriptures of India; the oldest scriptures of Hinduism.

Via negativa (See apophatic theology)

Will to power Nietzsche's view that all existence (most notably living things, such as human beings) is striving for advancement and domination.

Worldview A collection of beliefs and ideas centered around the fundamental issues of life; the conceptual grid through which one views reality.

INDEX

Lightning Source UK Ltd.
Milton Keynes UK
UKHW051335270620
365673UK00004B/97

9 780415 408912